ISBN 978-0-265-26407-2
PIBN 10981163

1 MONTH OF
FREE
READING

at

www.ForgottenBooks.com

By purchasing this book you are eligible for one month membership to ForgottenBooks.com, giving you unlimited access to our entire collection of over 1,000,000 titles via our web site and mobile apps.

To claim your free month visit:

www.forgottenbooks.com/free981163

English
Français
Deutsche
Italiano
Español
Português

www.forgottenbooks.com

Mythology Photography **Fiction**
Fishing Christianity **Art** Cooking
Essays Buddhism Freemasonry
Medicine **Biology** Music **Ancient
Egypt** Evolution Carpentry Physics
Dance Geology **Mathematics** Fitness
Shakespeare **Folklore** Yoga Marketing
Confidence Immortality Biographies
Poetry **Psychology** Witchcraft
Electronics Chemistry History **Law**
Accounting **Philosophy** Anthropology
Alchemy Drama Quantum Mechanics
Atheism Sexual Health **Ancient History**
Entrepreneurship Languages Sport
Paleontology Needlework Islam
Metaphysics Investment Archaeology
Parenting Statistics Criminology
Motivational

SESSIONAL PAPERS

VOLUME 9

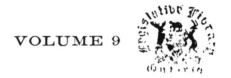

SIXTH SESSION OF THE TWELFTH PARLIAMENT

OF THE

DOMINION OF CANADA

SESSION 1916

VOLUME LI.

ALPHABETICAL INDEX

TO THE

SESSIONAL PAPERS

OF THE

PARLIAMENT OF CANADA

SIXTH SESSION, TWELFTH PARLIAMENT, 1916.

3060—1

See also Alphabetical List, Page 1.

LIST OF SESSIONAL PAPERS

Arranged in Numerical Order, with their titles at full length; the dates when Ordered and when presented to the House of Parliament; the name of the Senator or Member who moved for each Sessional Paper, and whether it is ordered to be Printed or Not Printed.

CONTENTS OF VOLUME E.

Fifth Census of Canada, 1911—Volume V—Forest. Fishery, Fur and Mineral Production.
Fifth Census of Canada, 1911—Volume VI—Occupations of the people.

CONTENTS OF VOLUME 1.

(This volume is bound in three parts.)

1. Report of the Auditor General for the year ended 31st March, 1915, Volume 1, Parts a b and A to L; Volume III, Parts V to Z. Presented by Sir Thomas White, February 7 1916.
Printed for distribution and sessional papers.

1. Report of the Auditor General for the year ended 31st March, 1915, Volume II, Parts M to U. Presented by Sir Thomas White, February 10, 1916.
Printed for distribution and sessional papers.

1. Report of the Auditor General for the year ended 31st March, 1915, Volume IV, part ZZ. Presented by Sir Thomas White, February 14, 1916.
Printed for distribution and sessional papers.

CONTENTS OF VOLUME 2.

2. The Public Accounts of Canada for the fiscal year ending March 31, 1915. Presented by Sir Thomas White, February 1, 1916.. ...*Printed for distribution and sessional papers.*

3. Estimates of sums required for the service of the Dominion for the year ending March 31, 1917. Presented by Sir Thomas White, 1916.
Printed for distribution and sessional papers.

4. Supplementary Estimates of sums required for the service of the Dominion for the year ending March 31, 1916. Presented by Sir Thomas White, 1916.
Printed for distribution and sessional papers.

5. Supplementary Estimates of sums . required for the service of the Dominion for the year ending March 31, 1917. Presented by Sir Thomas White, 1916.
Printed for distribution and sessional papers.

5a. Further Supplementary Estimates for the service of the Dominion for the year ending March 31, 1917. Presented by Sir Thomas White, 1916.
Printed for distribution and sessional papers.

5b. Further Supplementary Estimates for the fiscal year ending March 31, 1917. Presented by Sir Thomas White, May. 1916.. .. .. ..*Printed for distribution and sessional papers.*

CONTENTS OF VOLUME 3.

6. List of Shareholders in the Chartered Banks of the Dominion of Canada as on December 31, 1915. Presented by Sir Thomas White, February 1, 1916.
Printed for distribution and sessional papers.

CONTENTS OF VOLUME 4.

7. Report on certified cheques, drafts or bills of.exchange, dividends, remaining unpaid and unclaimed balances in Chartered Banks of the Dominion of Canada, for five years and upwards prior to December 31, 1915.   Presented by Sir Thomas White, February 1, 1916. *Printed for distribution and sessional papers.*

CONTENTS OF VOLUME 5.

(This volume is bound in two parts.)

8. Report of the Superintendent of Insurance for the year 1915.   Presented by Sir Thomas White, 1916.. .. ..*Printed for distribution and sessional papers.*

9. Abstract of Statements of Insurance Companies in Canada for the year ended December 31 1915.   Presented by Sir Thomas White, April 10, 1916. *Printed for distribution and sessional papers.*

CONTENTS OF VOLUME 6.

10. Report of the Department of Trade and Commerce for the fiscal year ended March 31, 1915: Part I.—Canadian Trade (Imports in and Exports from Canada).   Presented by Sir George Foster, January 13, 1916.. ..*Printed for distribution and sessional papers.*

CONTENTS OF VOLUME 7.

10a. Report of the Department of Trade and Commerce for the fiscal year ended March 31, 1915: Part II.—Canadian Trade with ·(1) France, (2) Germany, (3) United Kingdom, (4) United States.   Presented by Sir George Foster, 1916. *Printed for distribution and sessional papers.*

10b. Report of the Department of Trade and Commerce for the fiscal year ended March 31, 1915: Part III.—Canadian Trade with foreign countries (except France, Germany, the United Kingdom and United States).   Presented by Sir George Foster, 1916. *Printed for distribution and sessional papers.*

10c. Report of the Department of Trade and Commerce for the fiscal year ended March 31, 1916: (Part IV.—Miscellaneous Information.)   Presented by Sir George Foster, 1916. *Printed for distribution and sessional papers.*

10d. Report of the Grain Commissioners for Canada. (Part V.)   Presented by Sir George Foster, 1916.. .. ..*Printed for distribution and sessional papers.*

CONTENTS OF VOLUME 8.

10e. Report of the Department of Trade and Commerce for the fiscal year .ended March 31, 1915: Part VI.—Subsidized Steamship Services, with statistics showing steamship traffic to December 31, 1915, and Estimates for the fiscal year 1916-17.   Presented by Sir George Foster, 1916.. .. ..*Printed for distribution and sessional papers.*

10f. Report of Trade and Commerce for the fiscal year ended March 31, 1915: Part VII.—Trade of Foreign Countries, Treaties and Conventions.   Presented by Sir George Foster, 1916. *Printed for distribution and sessional papers.*

CONTENTS OF VOLUME 9.

11. Report of the Department of Customs for the year ended March 31, 1915.   Presented by Hon. Mr. Reid, January 18, 1916.. .. ..*Printed for distribution and sessional papers.*

CONTENTS OF VOLUME 10.

12, 13, 14. Reports, Returns and Statistics of the Inland Revenue of the Dominion of Canada, for the year ended March 31, 1915.   Part I.—Excise.   Part II.—Inspection of Weights and Measures, Gas and Electricity.   Part III.—Adulteration of Food.   Presented by Hon. Mr. Patenaude, February 18, 1916..*Printed for distribution and sessional papers.*

CONTENTS OF VOLUME 11.

15. Report of the Minister of Agriculture for the Dominion of Canada, for the year ended March 31, 1915. Presented by Hon. Mr. Burrell, January 20, 1916.
Printed for distribution and sessional papers.

15a. Report of the Dairy and Cold Storage Commissioner for the fiscal year ending March 31, 1915. (Dairying, Fruit, Extension of Markets and Cold Storage.) Presented by Hon. Mr. Burrell, February 1, 1916.. .. ..*Printed for distribution and sessional papers.*

15b. Report of the Veterinary Director General for the year ending March 31, 1915. Presented by Hon. Mr. Burrell, 1916.. .. ..*Printed for distribution and sessional papers.*

15c. Report on "The Agricultural Instruction Act," 1914-15, pursuant to Section 8, Chapter 5 of 3-4 George V. Presented by Hon. Mr. Burrell January 24, 1916.
Printed for distribution and sessional papers.

CONTENTS OF VOLUME 12.

16. Report of the Director and Officers of the Experimental Farms for the year ending March 31, 1915. Presented by Hon. Mr. Burrell, January 31, 1916.
Printed for distribution and sessional papers.

CONTENTS OF VOLUME 13.

17. Criminal Statistics for the year ended September 30, 1914. (Appendix to the Report of the Minister of Trade and Commerce for the year 1914.) Presented by Sir George Foster, 1916.. .. ..*Printed for distribution and sessional papers.*

18. Return of By-elections for the House of Commons of Canada held during the year 1915. Presented by Hon. Mr. Speaker, 1916.. ..*Printed for distribution and sessional papers.*

CONTENTS OF VOLUME 14.

(This volume is bound in two parts.)

19. Report of the Minister of Public Works on the works under his control for the fiscal year ended March 31, 1915. Presented by Hon. Mr. Rogers, January 13, 1916.
Printed for distribution and sessional papers.

19a. Ottawa River Storage for year 1915.. .. .. ..*Printed for distribution and sessional papers.*

19b. Interim Report of the Commission appointed to examine into certain general conditions of Transportation bearing on the economic problem of the proposed Georgian Bay Canal. Presented by Hon. Mr. Rogers, April 14, 1916.
Printed for distribution and sessional papers.

CONTENTS OF VOLUME 15.

20. Annual Report of the Department of Railways and Canals, for the fiscal year from April 1, 1914, to March 31, 1915. Presented by Hon. Mr. Cochrane, February 2, 1916.
Printed for distribution and sessional papers.

20a. Canal Statistics for the season of navigation, 1915. Presented by Hon. Mr. Reid, May 17, 1916.. .. ..*Printed for distribution and sessional papers.*

20b. Railway Statistics of the Dominion of Canada, for the year ended June 30, 1915. Presented by Hon. Mr. Cochrane, April 4, 1916.. ..*Printed for distribution and sessional papers.*

CONTENTS OF VOLUME 16.

20c. Tenth Report of the Board of Railway Commissioners for Canada, for the year ending March 31, 1915. Presented by Hon. Mr. Cochrane, February 2, 1916.
Printed for distribution and sessional papers.

20d. Telephone Statistics of the Dominion of Canada, for the year ended June 30, 1915. Presented by Hon. Mr. Cochrane, April 13, 1915.
Printed for distribution and sessional papers.

20e. Express Statistics of the Dominion of Canada, for the year ended June 30, 1915. Presented by Hon. Mr. Cochrane, April 13, 1916.. ..*Printed for distribution and sessional papers.*

20f. Telegraph Statistics of the Dominion of Canada, for the year ended June 30, 1915. Presented by Hon. Mr. Cochrane, May 16, 1916.
Printed for distribution and sessional papers.

CONTENTS OF VOLUME 17.

21. Forty-eighth Annual Report of the Department of Marine and Fisheries, for the year 1914-1915.—Marine. Presented by Hon. Mr. Hazen, January 13, 1916.
Printed for distribution and sessional papers.

22. List of Shipping issued by the Department of Marine and Fisheries, being a list of vessels on the registry books of the Dominion of Canada on December 31, 1915. Presented by Hon. Mr. Hazen, 1916.. .. ..*Printed for distribution and sessional papers.*

23. Supplement to the Forty-eighth Annual Report of the Department of Marine and Fisheries for the fiscal year 1914-15. Marine.—Steamboat Inspection Report.
Printed for distribution and sessional papers.

CONTENTS OF VOLUME 18.

24. Report of the Postmaster General for the year ended March 31, 1915. Presented by Hon. Mr. Casgrain, January 13, 1916.. .. ..*Printed for distribution and sessional papers.*

CONTENTS OF VOLUME 19.

25. Annual Report of the Department of the Interior for the fiscal year ending March 31, 1915. Presented by Hon. Mr. Roche, January 13, 1916.
Printed for distribution and sessional papers.

25b. Annual Report of the Topographical Surveys Branch of the Department of the Interior, 1914-15. Presented by Hon. Mr. Roche, May 1, 1916.
Printed for distribution and sessional papers.

CONTENTS OF VOLUME 20.

25c. Report of progress of stream measurements for the calendar year 1915. Presented by Hon. Mr. Roche, 1916.. .. ..*Printed for distribution and sessional papers.*

25d. Fourteenth Report of the Geographic Board of Canada for year ended March 31, 1915.
Printed for distribution and sessional papers.

CONTENTS OF VOLUME 21.

25e. British Columbia Hydrographic Surveys .. ..*Printed for distribution and sessional papers.*

25f. Manitoba Hydrographic Surveys, 1912-14.. ..*Printed for distribution and sessional papers.*

25g Report of the Chief Medical Officer Department of the Interior, for 1915.
Printed for distribution and sessional papers.

CONTENTS OF VOLUME 22.

26. Summary Report of the Geological Survey Department of Mines, for the calendar year 1914. Presented by Hon. Mr. Roche, 1916.
Printed for distribution and sessional papers.

26a. Summary Report of the Mines Branch for the calendar year 1914. Presented by Hon. Mr. Roche, 1916.. .. ..*Printed for distribution and sessional papers.*

CONTENTS OF VOLUME 23.

27. Report of the Department of Indian Affairs for the year ended March 31, 1915. Presented by Hon. Mr. Roche, January 19, 1916..*Printed for distribution and sessional papers.*

28. Report of the Royal Northwest Mounted Police, 1915. Presented by Sir Robert Borden, January 19, 1916.. .. ..*Printed for distribution and sessional papers.*

CONTENTS OF VOLUME 24.

29. Report of the Secretary of State of Canada for the year ended March 31, 1915. Presented by Hon. Mr. Blondin, February 28, 1916.
Printed for distribution and sessional papers.

29a. Report of the work of the Public Archives for the year 1914. Presented, 1916.
Printed for distribution and sessional papers.

CONTENTS OF VOLUME 25.

30. The Civil Service List of Canada for 1915. Presented by Hon. Mr. Patenaude 1916.
Printed for distribution. ana sessional papers.

31. Annual Report of the Civil Service Commission of Canada for the year ended August 31, 1915. Presented by Hon. Mr. Patenaude, 1916.
Printed for distribution and sessional papers.

CONTENTS OF VOLUME 26.

32. Annual Report of the Department of Public Printing and Stationery for the fiscal year ended March 31, 1915. Presented by Hon. Mr. Blondin, March 20, 1916.
Printed for distribution and sessional papers.

33. Report of the Secretary of State for External Affairs for the year ended March 31, 1915. Presented by Sir Robert Borden, February 23, 1916.
Printed for distribution and sessional papers.

34. Report of the Minister of Justice as to Penitentiaries of Canada for the fiscal year ending March 31, 1915.. .. ..*Printed for distribution and sessional papers.*

35. Report of the Militia Council for the Dominion of Canada, for the fiscal year ending March 31, 1915. Presented by Sir Sam Hughes, February 21, 1916.
Printed for distribution and sessional papers.

35a. Employment for the Expeditionary Forces after the war. Presented, 1916.
Printed for distribution and sessional papers.

36. Report of the Department of Labour for the fiscal year ending March 31, 1915. Presented by Hon. Mr. Crothers, January 25, 1916.
Printed for distribution and sessional papers.

36a. Eighth Report of the Registrar of Boards of Conciliation and Investigations of the proceedings under " The Industrial Disputes Investigation Act, 1907," for the fiscal year ending March 31, 1915. Presented by Hon. Mr. Crothers, January 25, 1916.
Printed for distribution and sessional papers.

CONTENTS OF VOLUME 27.

37. Eleventh Annual Report of the Commissioners of the Transcontinental Railway, for the year ended March 31, 1914. Presented by Hon. Mr. Cochrane. February 2, 1916.
Printed for distribution and sessional papers.

38. Report of the Department of the Naval Service, for the fiscal year ending March 31, 1915. Presented by Hon. Mr. Hazen, January 13, 1916.
Printed for distribution and sessional papers.

38a. Supplement to the Report of the Naval Service—Contributions to Canadian Biology, 1914-15. Presented by Hon. Mr. Hazen, 1916.
Printed for distribution and sessional papers.

38b. Natural History of the Herring. Presented, 1916.
Printed for distribution and sessional papers.

39. Forty-eighth Annual Report of the Fisheries Branch of the Department of the Naval Service, 1914-1915. Presented by Hon. Mr. Hazen, January 13, 1916.
Printed for distribution and sessional papers.

40. The Report of the Joint Librarians of Parliament. Presented by Hon. Mr. Speaker, January 13, 1916.. .. ..Not printed.

CONTENTS OF VOLUME 28.

41. Copies of Orders in Council authorizing Regulations for the Department of Naval Service in accordance with Section 47, Chapter 43, 9-10 Edward VII, as follows:—

P.C. 2864, dated the 4th December, 1915, Payment of Separation Allowance in the case of Warrant Officers.

P.C. 3009, dated 21st December, 1915, with reference to application of the Naval Discipline Act, etc., for the Government of the Naval Volunteer Force.

P.C. 63/422, dated 15th October, 1915, with reference to appointment of Assistant Paymasters in charge.

P.C. 2267, dated 25th September, 1915, with reference to regulations for payment of " Detained Pay."

P.C. 93/2151, dated 17th September, 1915, with reference to allowances to officers and men employed on coding and decoding duties, etc.

P.C. 1712, dated 21st July, 1915, with reference to scheme of pensions for officers and men of the Royal Canadian Forces, etc.

CONTENTS OF VOLUME 28—*Continued.*

P.C. 748, dated 13th April, 1915, with reference to institution of the ratings of rangetaker first and second class in the Royal Canadian Navy.

P.C. 58/1470, dated 24th June, 1915, with reference to increase in amount of Separation Allowance to a motherless child from 3s. to 5s.

P.C. 85/1158, dated 20th May, 1915, with reference to revision of amounts payable on account of Separation Allowance to dependents of Royal Canadian Naval Permanent Ratings.

P.C. 756, dated 13th April, 1915, with reference to payment of Allowances to officers of the Royal Naval Canadian Volunteer Reserve for performance of duties which carry with them an Allowance to officers of the Royal Canadian Navy. Presented by Hon. Mr. Hazen, January 17, 1916.. .. ..*Not printed.*

42. Copies of Proclamations, Orders in Council and Documents relating to the European War. Presented by Sir Robert Borden, January 18, 1916.. .. ..*Not printed.*

42a. First Supplement to Copies of Proclamations, Orders in Council and Documents relating to the European War. Presented by Sir Robert Borden, January 18, 1916..*Not printed.*

43. Orders in Council relating to the European War, from 29th April, 1915, to 12th January, 1916, both inclusive. Presented by Sir Robert Borden, January 18, 1916..*Not printed.*

44. Copy of New Rules of Court passed by the Judges of the Supreme Court of Alberta, under the authority of Section 576 of the Criminal Code, at meeting of 27th November, 1915. Presented by Hon. Mr. Meighen, January 20, 1916.. .. ..*Not printed.*

45. Account of the average number of men employed on the Dominion Police Force during each month of the year 1915, and of their pay and travelling expenses, pursuant to Chapter 92, Section 6, Subsection 2, of the Revised Statutes of Canada. Presented by Hon. Mr. Doherty, January 20, 1916.. .. ..*Not printed.*

46. Regulations under "The Destructive Insect and Pest Act," pursuant to Section 9, Chapter 31 of 9-10 Edward VII. Presented by Hon. Mr. Burrell, January 24, 1916...*Not printed.*

47. Return of Orders in Council which have been published in the *Canada Gazette* and in the British Columbia *Gazette*, between 12th January, 1915, and the 31st December, 1915, in accordance with provisions of Subsection (d) of Section 38 of the regulations for the survey, administration, disposal and management of Dominion Lands within the 40-mile Railway Belt in the Province of British Columbia. Presented by Hon. Mr. Roche, January 25, 1916.. .. ..*Not printed.*

48. Return of Orders in Council which have been published in the *Canada Gazette*, between 12th January, 1915, and the 31st December, 1915, in accordance with the provisions of Section 77 of "The Dominion Lands Act," Chapter 20 of the Statutes of Canada, 1908. Presented by Hon. Mr. Roche, January 25, 1916.. .. ..*Not printed.*

49. Return of Orders in Council which have been published in the *Canada Gazette*, between the 16th January, 1915, and the 31st December, 1915, in accordance with the provisions of "The Forest Reserves and Park Act," Section 19 of Chapter 10, 1-2 George V. Presented by Hon. Mr. Roche, January 25, 1916.. .. ..*Not printed.*

50. Return of Orders in Council which have been published in the *Canada Gazette*, between the 12th January, 1915, and the 31st December, 1915, in accordance with the provisions of Section 5 of "The Dominion Lands Survey Act," Chapter 21, 7-8 Edward VII. Presented by Hon. Mr. Roche, January 25, 1916.. .. ..*Not printed.*

51. Return of Orders in Council which have been published in the *Canada Gazette*, between the 12th January, 1915, and the 31st December, 1915, in accordance with the provisions of Chapter 47, 2 George V, entitled "The Railway Belt Water Act." Presented by Hon. Mr. Roche, January 25, 1916.. .. ..*Not printed.*

52. Return of Orders in Council passed between the 16th January, 1915, and the 31st December, 1915, approving of regulations and forms prescribed in accordance with the provisions of Section 57 of the Irrigation Act, Chapter 61, Revised Statutes of Canada, 1906, as amended by Chapter 38, 7-8 Edward VII. Presented by Hon. Mr. Roche, January 25, 1916.. .. ..*Not printed.*

53. Return of Orders in Council passed under the provisions of Section 18 of Chapter 63, Revised Statutes of Canada, "An Act to provide for the Government of the Yukon Territory." Presented by Hon. Mr. Roche, January 25, 1916.. .. ..*Not printed.*

54. Return showing lands sold by the Canadian Pacific Railway Company during the year which ended on the 30th September, 1915. Presented January 25, 1916...*Not printed.*

CONTENTS OF VOLUME 28—*Continued.*

CONTENTS OF VOLUME 28—*Continued.*

72. Certified copy of a report of the Committee of the Privy Council, approved by His Royal Highness the Governor General on the 7th February, 1916, appointing Robert A. Pringle, of the city of Ottawa, one of His Majesty's counsel learned in the law, and His Honour D. B. MacTavish, Judge of the County Court for the County of Carleton, a Commission, under the Inquiries Act, to conduct an inquiry into and concerning the origin of the recent disastrous fire which destroyed the Parliament Buildings at Ottawa. Presented by Sir Robert Borden, February 7, 1916.. .. ..*Not printed.*

72a. Report of the Royal Commission appointed to inquire into the origin of the fire which destroyed the Central Parliament Building at Ottawa, on Thursday, 3rd February, 1916. Also copy of evidence taken before the Royal Commission appointed to inquire into the origin of the fire which destroyed the Central Parliament Building at Ottawa, on Thursday, 3rd February, 1916. Presented by Hon. Mr. Rogers, May 16, 1915.
Printed for sessional papers only.

73. Copy of Order in Council, *No.* P.C. 162, dated 29th January, 1916,—Establishment of the rank of wireless operator in the Royal Naval Canadian Volunteer Reserve and regulations for the proper government thereof. Presented by Hon. Mr. Hazen, February 7, 1916.. .. ..*Not printed.*

74. Copy of Orders in Council, *No.* P.C. 183, dated 31st January, 1916,—Regulations governing the·payment of allowance to officers of the Royal Canadian Naval Service acting as interpreters. Presented by Hon. Mr. Hazen, February 7, 1916.. .. ..*Not printed.*

74a. Copy of Order in Council *No.* P.C. 54/601, dated .16th March, 1916, authorizing payment of messing allowance to Royal Naval Reserve Officers. Presented by Hon. Mr. Hazen, March 29, 1916.. .. ..*Not printed.*

75. Communication from the Acting High Commissioner for Canada in London, Sir George Perley, enclosing a report on the Canadian Hospital at Dinard by Dr. Rallier du Baty, Chief Surgeon at the said hospital. Presented by Sir Robert Borden, February 7, 1916.
Printed for sessional papers only.

76. A communication from the Right Honourable A. Bonar Law, Colonial Secretary, to His Royal Highness the Governor General, enclosing a copy of the Imperial Parliamentary Debates (House of Commons, 10th January) on a resolution which was adopted by that House, as follows:—" That with a view to increasing the power of the Allies in the prosecution of the war, His Majesty's Government should enter into immediate consultation with the Governments of the Dominions in order with their aid to bring the whole economic strength of the Empire into co-operation with our Allies in a policy directed against the enemy." Presented by Sir Robert Borden, February 7, 1916.
Printed for distribution and sessional papers

77. Correspondence between the Canadian Manufacturers' Association and the Prime Minister. 1914-1915. Presented by Sir Robert Borden, February 7, 1916.. .. ..*Not printed.*

78. Correspondence between ·the International Nickel Company and the Prime Minister. Presented by Sir Robert Borden, February 7, 1916.. .. ..*Not printed.*

79. Return to an Order of the House of the 7th February, 1916, for a copy of all correspondence and reports on the claims of Sealers of British Columbia under the last treaty with the American Republic. Presented February 9, 1916.
Printed for sessional papers only.

80. Certified copy of a report of the Committee of the Privy Council, approved by His Royal Highness the Governor General on the 15th April, 1915, giving authority for the renewal, from the 31st March, 1916, of the agreement between the Dominion Government and the Province of Alberta for the service of the Royal Northwest Mounted Police in that province. Presented by Sir Robert Borden, February 10, 1916.
Printed for sessional papers only.

81. Certified copy of a report of the Committee of the Privy Council, approved by His Royal Highness the Governor General on the 21st May, 1915, giving authority for the renewal, from the 31st March, 1916, of the agreement between the Dominion Government and the province of Saskatchewan, for the services of the Royal Northwest Mounted Police in that province. Presented by Sir Robert Borden, February 10, 1916.
Printed for sessional papers only.

82. Return to an Order of the House of the 8th February, 1916, for a copy of all letters, papers and other documents relating to the application of Wasyl Pinianski for the patent of the southwest quarter section 5, township 25, range 4, west second principal meridian, Office File *No.* 1752484. Presented February 16, 1916.—*Mr. MacNutt...* ..*Not printed.*

CONTENTS OF VOLUME 28—*Continued.*

CONTENTS OF VOLUME 28—*Continued*.

94. Return to an Order of the House of the 8th April, 1915, for a return showing:—1. The names of the persons who have successfully passed the Civil Service examination in the province of Quebec since the establishment of the Civil Service Commission. 2. The number of such persons who have been called upon to enter the Civil Service. 3. The number in each grade of those who have passed such examinations with success. Presented February 24, 1916.—*Mr. Boulay*.. .. ..*Not printed*.

95. Return to an Order of the House of the 3rd February, 1916, for a copy of all documents, papers and telegrams in any way referring to the application of Aenas McKinnon, of Iron Mines, Inverness County, for the Fenian Raid Veteran Bounty. Presented February 24, 1916.—*Mr. Chisholm (Inverness)*.. .. ..*Not printed*.

95a. Return to an Order of the House of the 14th February, 1916, for a copy of all telegrams, letters, petitions and documents of any kind, referring in any way to the application of Anes or Angus McKinnon, of Iron Mines or Orangedale, Inverness County, for the Fenian Raid Bounty. Presented March 3, 1916.—*Mr. Chisholm (Inverness)*.

Not printed.

96. Return to an Order of the House of the 15th March, 1915, for a copy of the claim of Captain Stephen Paul, owner of the steamer *Rhoda*, for the destruction of his ship, as a wreckage, by the Department of Marine, and of all correspondence with regard to the same. Presented February 24, 1916.—*Sir Wilfrid Laurier*.. .. ..*Not printed*.

97. Return to an Order of the House of the 29th March, 1915, for a copy of all letters and telegrams, or any other written communications which passed between the Minister of Railways and Canals and J. C. Douglas, Esq., M.P.P., of Glace Bay, Nova Scotia, between the 1st of January and the last of December, 1914, and of all letters and telegrams between the Minister of Customs and Public Works, and the Postmaster General, and the said J. C. Douglas during the above period, in respect to the dismissal, appointment or restoration to office of Government officials. Presented February 24, 1916.—*Mr. McKenzie*.. .. ..*Not printed*.

98. Return to an Order of the House of the 3rd February, 1916, for a copy of all reports upon the depths of water in the different locks in the East River of Pictou, improvements, and of all correspondence and recommendations in regard to changes on the plans therefor. Presented February 24, 1916.—*Mr. Macdonald*.. .. ..*Not printed*.

98a. Supplementary return to an Order of the House of the 3rd February, 1916, for a copy of all reports upon the depths of water in the different locks in the East River of Pictou, improvements, and of all correspondence and recommendations in regard to changes on the plans therefor. Presented March 13, 1916.—*Mr. Macdonald*.. .. .. ..*Not printed*.

99. Return to an Order of the House of the 3rd February, 1916, for a copy of all letters, telegrams, petitions and other papers relative to the granting of a Conciliation Board to the employees of the Acadia Coal Company, in the county of Pictou, in the autumn of 1915. Presented February 24, 1916.—*Mr. Macdonald*.. .. ..*Not printed*.

100. Return to an Order of the House of the 1st March, 1915, for a return showing the number of miles of telegraph lines, and the locations, erected in the county of Inverness, each year since 1896, to the present day, with the cost of each line. Presented February 24, 1916.—*Mr. Chisholm (Inverness)*.. .. ..*Not printed*.

101. Return to an Order of the House of the 3rd February, 1916, for a copy of all tenders, letters, telegrams and contracts relative to a mail contract from *Noel* to *Maitland*, in the county of Hants, and relative to the warding of the same under contract. Presented February 24, 1916.—*Mr. Macdonald*.. .. ..*Not printed*.

102. Return to an Order of the House of the 22nd March, 1915, for a copy of the petition addressed to the Post Office Department for the establishment of the rural mail delivery route in the county of Shefford, known as Warden No. 1, and of all letters, telegrams reports and other communications connected therewith. Presented February 24, 1916.—*Mr. Boivin*.. .. ..*Not printed*.

103. Return to an Order of the House of the 9th February, 1916, for a return showing the different rural mail routes in the Strathcona constituency, their location and date of establishment, and all rural routes under consideration at the present time. Presented February 24, 1916.—*Mr. Douglas*.. .. .. :. .. ..*Not printed*.

103a. Return to an Order of the House of the 16th February, 1916, for a return showing the location of all rural mail routes in the present constituency of Strathcona, the date of their inception, and the location of routes at present under consideration. Presented February 24, 1916.—*Mr. Douglas*.. .. ..*Not printed*.

104. Return to an Order of the House of the 25th March, 1915, for a copy of all letters, papers, petitions, reports and other documents relating to the establishment of a rural mail delivery route, for the purpose of giving postal service to the districts of Hodson and Toney Mills, county of Pictou. Presented February 24, 1916.—*Mr. Macdonald*.

Not printed.

CONTENTS OF VOLUME 28—*Continued.*

CONTENTS OF VOLUME 28—*Continued.*

CONTENTS OF VOLUME 28—*Continued.*

131. Return to an Order of the House of the 7th February, 1916, for a copy of all letters, telegrams, evidence of witnesses at the investigation, and reports thereon, in relation to the claim of Alexandre D. Doucet, of Beresford, N.B., for cattle killed on the Intercolonial Railroad on May 25, 1915. Presented March 1, 1916.—*Mr. Turgeon.*
Not printed.

132. Return to an Order of the House of the 3rd February, 1916, for a copy of all letters, telegrams, correspondence and agreements between the Department of Railways and Canals, and any official thereof, including the officials of the Intercolonial Railway, regarding the installation of the McQueen Siding, so-called, at Shediac, in the province of New Brunswick, and the subsequent removal thereof. Presented March 1, 1916.— *Mr. Carvell.. .. ..Not printed.*

132a. Supplementary Return to an Order of the House of the 3rd February, 1916, for a copy of all letters, telegrams, correspondence and agreements between the Department of Railways and Canals, and any official thereof, including the officials of the Intercolonial Railway, regarding the installation of the McQueen Siding, so-called, at Shediac, in the province of New Brunswick, and the subsequent removal thereof. Presented March 23, 1916.—*Mr. Carvell.. .. ..Not printed.*

133. Return to an Order of the House of the 7th February, 1916, for a return showing:—1. The names, post office addresses, rate of wages and gross amount paid during the year 1915, to all engineers and employees of every description, engaged in connection with the survey of a branch line of the Intercolonial Railway in Guysborough County. 2. The gross expenditure in any way connected with the survey referred to in paragraph one since October, 1911. Presented March 1, 1916.—*Mr. Sinclair.. .. ..Not printed.*

134. Return to an Order of the House of the 3rd February, 1916, for a copy of all documents, letters and petitions in the possession of the Railway Department relating to the dismissal of Wm. P. Mills, Bridge and Building Master of District Number 4, Intercolonial Railway; and also a copy of all letters, telegrams, petitions and documents of all kinds in the possession of the Government either in Ottawa or at Moncton, relating in any way to the application of said Wm. P. Mills for an investigation into the causes which led to his dismissal. Presented March 1, 1916.—*Mr. Chisholm (Inverness).*
Not printed.

135. Return to an Order of the House of the 7th February, 1916, for a return showing the names and salaries of all the officials, assistants and clerks employed in the Intercolonial Railway offices in Moncton, including the assistant superintendent's office, dispatcher's office, station and freight house, the names and salaries of the foremen employed in each of the shops, and also the names of all officials, clerks, engine drivers and conductors who have been retired and placed on the pension list since the first of January, 1915, with the amount of the annual retiring allowance to each. Presented March 1, 1916.—*Mr. Copp.. .. ..Not printed.*

136. Return to an Order of the House of the 3rd February, 1916, for a copy of all letters, papers, evidence, reports and all other documents relating to the investigation into certain alleged irregularities in the weighing of freight on the Intercolonial Railway at Stellarton and New Glasgow in 1914 and 1915, and the dismissal of Arthur McLean in connection therewith. Presented March 1, 1916.—*Mr. Macdonald.. .. .. ..Not printed.*

137. Return to an Order of the House of 3rd February, 1916, for a copy of all telegrams, letters and other documents in connection with repairs to wharf at Shag Harbour, Shelburne County, N.S., during the years 1915 and 1916. Presented March 1, 1916.—*Mr. Law.. .. ..Not printed.*

138. Return to an Order of the House of the 7th February, 1916, for a copy of all letters, telegrams and other papers or documents in the possession of the Department of Public Works relating to a request made by the Nova Scotia Historical Society for permission to place a memorial tablet commemorating the late Reverend Dr. James MacGregor, on the post office building, New Glasgow, N.S. Presented March 1, 1916.—*Mr. Sinclair.*

139. Return to an Order of the House of the 8th February, 1916, for a return showing:—1. Who had the contract or contracts for supplies, meats and other provisions required for the dredges of the Department of Public Works, working in the East River of Pictou or elsewhere in Pictou County, during the years 1914 and 1915, respectively. 2. Amounts paid respectively to each of said tenderers. Presented March 1, 1916.—*Mr. Macdonald.. .. ..Not printed.*

140. Return to an Order of the House of the 7th February, 1916, for a return showing all sums of money expended during the present fiscal year to December 31, 1915, by the Department of Public Works, respectively, for public buildings, harbours and rivers, roads and bridges, telegraph and telephone lines, dredging, and for miscellaneous purposes, chargeable to income, showing said expenditure under the above headings and by provinces. Presented March 1, 1916.—*Mr. Maclean (Halifax).. .. ..Not printed.*

CONTENTS OF VOLUME 28—*Continued.*

CONTENTS OF VOLUME 28—*Continued.*

CONTENTS OF VOLUME 28—*Continued.*

CONTENTS OF VOLUME 28—*Continued.*

183. Return to an Address to His Royal Highness the Governor General of the 7th February, 1916, for a copy of the Order in Council or departmental order dismissing Mr. Bayfield from the position of Superintendent of Dredging in British Columbia; and also a copy of the Order in Council or departmental order appointing J. L. Nelson in his place. Presented March 13, 1916.—*Mr. Pugsley*.. .. ..*Not printed.*

184. Return to an Order of the House of the 23rd February, 1916, for a copy of all reports and documents concerning the surveys made by the Federal Government during the autumn of 1914 of Lake Matapedia and the river of the same name down to the village of Amqui. Presented March 13, 1916.—*Mr. Lapointe (Kamouraska)*.. ..*Not printed.*

185. Return to an Order of the House of the 13th March, 1916, for a copy of the pension list in force in Canada for disabled soldiers and of all petitions, letters or other documents relating to the amendment or readjustment of the same. Presented March 14, 1916.— *Printed for distribution and sessional papers.*

186. Return to an Order of the House of the 16th February, 1916, for a copy of all letters, petitions, correspondence and telegrams between the Government, the engineers, and all other persons concerning the building of the post office at Rigaud; also of the amounts of money paid to divers persons for such building, furnishing, the land, the care of the grounds and other works. Presented March 15, 1916.—*Mr. Boyer*.. .. .. ..*Not printed.*

187. Return to an Order of the House of the 6th March, 1916, for a return showing the different rural mail routes in the constituency of Medicine Hat, with their location and date of establishment; and also all rural mail routes now being established or under consideration at the present time in the same constituency. Presented March 15, 1916. —*Mr. Buchanan*.. .. ..*Not* printed.

187a. Return to an Order of the House of the 20th March, 1916, for a return showing:—1. The reason for the delay in the establishment of the rural mail routes, reported under consideration, in the constituency of Medicine Hat. 2. When these routes were first applied for. 3. If the applications possessed the required number of signatures. 4. If tenders have been invited. If so, for what routes. 5. Why the lowest tenders were not accepted, and the routes established. 6. If any tenders are being invited for these routes. 7. If there is a likelihood of any of these routes being operated immediately. Presented March 27, 1916.—*Mr. Buchanan*.. .. ..*Not printed.*

188. Return to an Order of the House of the 21st February, 1916, for a copy of all letters, telegrams, investigations and reports relating to the dismissal of Joseph Fleming, conductor Intercolonial Railway, and in regard to his reinstatement. Presented March 16, 1916.—*Mr. Macdonald*.. .. ..*Not printed.*

189. Return to an Order of the House of the 18th March, 1915, for a copy of all petitions, telegrams, communications and other documents relating to the dismissal of Mr. Hubert Paquin, postmaster of St. Gilbert de Portneuf. Presented March 16, 1916.—*Mr. Delisle.* *Not printed.*

190. Return to an Order of the House of the 16th February, 1916, for a copy of all letters, petitions, correspondence and telegrams, exchanged between the Government, its Inquiry Commissioner, Mr. G. H. Bergeron, and all other persons, concerning the inquiry, the dismissal and replacing of the postmasters of the different post offices mentioned below; and of all correspondence relating to the appointments of the present postmasters who replace the former ones, who had been either dismissed or replaced for one reason or another:—St. Lazare Village, Vaudreuil Station, Pointe Fortune, Val des Eboulis, Mont Oscar, St. Justine de Newton, Ste. Marthe. Presented March 16, 1916.—*Mr. Boyer.* *Not printed.*

191. Dismissal of Mr. Chisholm, Inspector of Indian Agencies, Saskatchewan.—(*Senate*). *Not printed.*

192. Return to an Order of the House of the 28th February, 1916, for a return showing:—1. The names, rank and military qualifications of the officers on the Headquarters Staff of the 1st, 2nd and 3rd Divisional Areas, including those on Staffs of Camps and Schools of Instruction, on October 1, 1915. 2. The names of those of the above who on that date had volunteered, taken the oath and been attested for overseas service. Presented March 20, 1916.—*Mr. Proulx*.. .. ..*Not printed.*

193. Return to an Order of the House of the 21st February, 1916, for a return showing:—1. How many persons have been employed by the Department of Militia since the beginning of the war in the examining, appraising or testing of materials, such as clothing, harness, etc., purchased for military purposes. 2. How many of such employees are practical trades people, experts, or otherwise experienced persons in the respective callings connected with the various materials as purchased. Presented March 20, 1916.— *Mr. Verville*.. .. ..*Not printed.*

CONTENTS OF VOLUME 28—*Continued.*

194. Return to an Order of the House of the 6th March, 1916, for a copy of all telegrams, letters, petitions and documents of all kinds referring in any way to the application of Mrs. Flora McIntyre, of River Dennis, Inverness County, N.S., for the Fenian Raid Veteran Bounty of her late husband, Angus McIntyre, late of River Dennis. Presented March 20, 1916.—*Mr. Chisholm (Inverness)* . . . . *Not printed.*

195. Return to an Order of the House of the 13th March, 1916, for a return showing :—1. The names, dates of appointment, post office addresses at time of appointment, and former occupations of the censors employed by the Militia Department at Louisburg and North Sydney, Nova Scotia. 2. The names of all the said censors who are also decoders, and the names and addresses of all who are employed in the censorship service at the above points. 3. The amount paid to each censor or decoder since the 4th of August, 1914, up to the 1st February, 1916, or to any party or person in connection with the censorship or decoding services at the above places. Presented March 20, 1916.—*Mr. McKenie.*
Not printed.

196. Return to an Order of the House of the 3rd February, 1916, for a copy of all letters, telegrams, agreements and all other papers relative to the creation of a Board of Conciliation, during the year 1915, under the Industrial Disputes Investigation Act in regard to the employees of the Nova Scotia Steel Company, in the county of Pictou. Presented March 20, 1916.—*Mr. Macdonald* . . . . *Not printed.*

197. Return to an Order of the House of the 6th March, 1916, for a list of the employees in the Dominion Police Force, with the salary of each of them. Presented March 20, 1916. —*Mr. Boulay* . . . . *Not printed.*

198. Return showing :—1. Whether the Government have taken cognizance of the following article published in the Montreal "Gazette" on November 1, 1915 :—"Canadian Help Comes from Sale of Gift Flour. Foodstuffs not Needed by the English Poor were Bought for Belgian Relief.—Funds to Aid East Coast.—Hon. Walter Long Suggested to Canadian Government that $750,000 be Allotted, and Latter Agreed.—(Special cable from the "Gazette's" resident staff correspondent.)

"London, October 31,—'Canada's aid to the east coast towns of England, which are suffering through the war, is the subject of some misconception,' said Sir George Perley to-day. In a statement in the Commons, Hon. Walter Long said that the necessary funds for a Government scheme of help for hotel and lodging house keepers had been generously provided by the Canadian Government. This gave rise to the idea that the Dominion was taking a new step, but the fact is that no money is coming from Canada. Of the flour sent by Canada a year ago to relieve distress in England, very little was distributed, as poverty was in no way abnormal. Some 400,000 bags of this flour were transferred to the American committee for Belgian relief, which purchased them. The money paid for this flour being in the hands of the Local Government Board, Hon. Walter Long, as President of the Board, suggested to Sir George Perley that this might be utilized for the relief of the east coast towns where the season had been ruined owing to the lack of railway facilities and the disinclination of the public to visit the east coast because of the possibility of German naval or aerial raids. The Dominion Government acquiesced in this proposal, and the sum of $750,000, part of the proceeds of the sale of the flour, has now been allotted for this purpose. Canada's generosity will therefore go to alleviate the distress of a large number of better-class people, who are direct sufferers from the war, instead of the destitute poor, for whom it was intended, but who, it develops, were not in need of it." 2. Whether the said article is accurate. If not, in what respect it is inaccurate. Presented March 20, 1916.—*Mr. Papineau.*
Not printed.

198a. Return showing :—1. Whether the Government is aware that the following extract from an article was published on the 12th January, 1915, in the Montreal "Gazette" :—

" Distress Caused in England by War is Negligible.—Comparatively Small Portion of Colonial Gifts Used for National Relief.—Much Went to Belgians.—War Office also took Large Share.—Salvation Army has Scheme Requiring Canadian Co-operation.— (Special cable from the "Gazette's" resident staff correspondent.)

"London, January 11.—Very satisfactory evidence of the comparative absence in England of any distress caused by the war is furnished by a report on the special work of the Local Government Board arising out of the war, which was issued to-day as a White Paper. The action by Noel Kershaw, dealing with the disposition of the gifts from the Colonies, shows that only a small part of the goods allocated has been required for relieving the distress of civilians.

"The following is the disposition of the 940,530 bags of flour received from Canada : To the local committees for the relief of distress, 90,474 ; to the Belgian Refugees Committees, 1,691 ; transferred to the War Office, 99,760 ; further offer to the War Office, 300,000 ; to the Belgian Relief Commission, 443,886 ; sold, owing to damage, 4,719." 2. Who had charge of accepting delivery and the shipping of this flour. 3. Whether the Government have any information of the shortage of 59,430 bags of flour, alleged in said article. If not, what became of the flour that was short. Presented March 20, 1916.—*Mr. Papineau* . . . . *Not printed.*

CONTENTS OF VOLUME 28—*Continued.*

199. Return to an Order of the House of the 6th March, 1916, for a return showing the amounts contributed from the constituency of Medicine Hat for machine guns, and by whom contributed or forwarded. Presented March 21, 1916.—*Mr. Buchanan.. ..Not printed.*

200. Return to an Order of the House of the 13th March, 1916, for a copy of all letters, petitions, recommendations and other documents in the possession of the Post Office Department relating to the appointment of the postmaster at West Roachdale, Guysborough County, Nova Scotia, to take the place of J. H. McGuire, deceased. Presented March 21, 1916.—*Mr. Sinclair,.. .. ..Not printed.*

201. Return to an Order of the House of the 28th February, 1916, for a return showing in detail the payment or payments amounting to $647.50, paid to P. A. Stoddart, fishery guardian, Shelburne County, N.S., during the year ending March 31, 1915. Presented March 21, 1916.—*Mr. Kyte.. .. ..Not printed.*

202. Return to an Order of the House of the 28th February, 1916, for a copy of all correspondence, letters, telegrams and documents of all kinds relating to the chartering of the vessel *Starling*, by the Department of Marine and Fisheries. Presented March 21, 1916. *Mr. Kyte.. .. .. i.. .. ..Not printed.*

203. Return to an Order of the House of the 7th February, 1916, for a copy of all documents, letters, messages, correspondence and reports concerning a conference between the Minister of Agriculture and certain representatives of the Mennonite Church in or about July, 1873, and referred to in a certain letter dated 23rd July, 1873, signed by P. M. Lowe, Secretary of the Department of Agriculture, and addressed to Messrs. David Klassen, Jacob Peters, Heinrich Wiebe and Cornelius Toews ,delegates from Southern Russia. Presented March 21, 1916.—*Mr. McCraney.. .. ..Not printed.*

204. Return to an Order of the House of the 13th March, 1916, for a copy of all letters, telegrams, petitions, memorials and other documents relating to the subsidizing by the Government of the construction of ships in British Columbia, or of ships when built; or as to the laying down or constructing or assisting in the construction in British Columbia of twenty-five ships by the Government, or as to assisting by subsidies or otherwise in the construction of ships in the Dominion. Presented March 23, 1916.—*Mr. Macdonald. Not printed.*

205. Return to an Order of the House of the 13th March, 1916, for a copy of the affidavit of David W. McLean, Windsor, N.S., to whom Warrant No. 25737 was issued for Fenian Raid Bounty, and also a copy of all correspondence and other documents relating to the payment of the same. Presented March 23, 1916.—*Mr. Macdonald.. .. ..Not printed.*

206. Return to an Order of the House of the 9th March, 1916, for a return showing:—1. The amount collected in wharfage on goods landed on Government wharves in the county of Victoria, at Neils Harbour, Ingonish, Englishtown, South Gut, Baddeck, Little Narrows, Nyaiga, and Big Bras d'Or. 2. The amount collected at each of the above places, by whom collected, and how much returned to the Government in each case. Presented March 27, 1916.—*Mr. McKenzie.. .. ..Not printed.*

207. Return to an Order of the House of the 20th March, 1916, for a return showing:—The names of the 54 Canadian officers employed in the Canadian Pay and Record Office, London, and amounts per month paid to each of them. Presented March 27, 1916.— *Mr. Macdonald.: .. ..Not printed.*

208. Return to an Order of the House of the 3rd February, 1916, for a copy of all letters, telegrams, petitions, directions and other documents relative to the surveys for a railway under the Railway Department, which have been carried on during the past summer, at points east and west from Sunnybrae, in the county of Pictou. Presented March 27, 1916.—*Mr. Macdonald.. .. ..Not printed.*

209. Return to an Order of the House of the 21st February, 1916, for a copy of all papers, agreements, letters, telegrams and other documents relating to the proposal to purchase, lease, or use of, the railway known as the Vale Railway, county of Pictou, and to the operation of the same by the Railway Department. Presented March 27, 1916.—*Mr. Macdonald.. .. ..Not printed.*

210. Return to an Order of the House of the 7th February, 1916, for a return showing the number and purpose of all commissions appointed by the Government since 1911, and the cost of each, together with names of the various members of such commissions. Presented March 27, 1916.—*Mr. Pardee.. .. ..Not printed.*

211. Return to an Order of the House of the 6th March, 1916, for a copy of all correspondence, letters, telegrams and documents relating to the dismissal or resignation of Dr. W. T. Patton from the service of the Veterinary Inspection Branch of the Department of the Interior, and his re-appointment and his later dismissal or resignation. Presented March 27, 1916.—*Mr. Buchanan.. .. ..Not printed.*

CONTENTS OF VOLUME 28—*Continued.*

CONTENTS OF VOLUME 28—*Continued.*

CONTENTS OF VOLUME 28—*Continued.*

CONTENTS OF VOLUME 28—*Continued.*

CONTENTS OF VOLUME 28—*Continued.*

CONTENTS OF VOLUME 28—*Continued.*

CONTENTS OF VOLUME 28—*Continued.*

CONTENTS OF VOLUME 28—*Continued.*

CONTENTS OF VOLUME 28—*Concluded.*

REPORT

OF THE

DEPARTMENT OF CUSTOMS

CONTAINING THE

TABLES OF IMPORTS, EXPORTS AND NAVIGATION

OF THE

DOMINION OF CANADA

FOR

THE FISCAL YEAR ENDED MARCH 31

1915

COMPILED FROM OFFICIAL RETURNS

PRINTED BY ORDER OF PARLIAMENT

OTTAWA
PRINTED BY J. de L. TACHÉ, PRINTER TO THE KING'S MOST
EXCELLENT MAJESTY
1915

No. 11—1916.]

To Field Marshal His Royal Highness Prince Arthur William Patrick Albert,
Duke of Connaught and Strathearn, K.G., K.T., K.P., etc., etc., etc., Governor
General and Commander in Chief of the Dominion of Canada.

MAY IT PLEASE YOUR ROYAL HIGHNESS:—

The undersigned has the honour to present to Your Royal Highness the
Annual Report of the Department of Customs, containing Tables of Imports,
Exports and Navigation of the Dominion of Canada for the Fiscal Year ended
March 31, 1915, as prepared from official returns and laid before me by the
Commissioner of Customs.

All of which is respectfully submitted.

J. D. REID,
Minister of Customs.

OTTAWA, October 15, 1915.

CUSTOMS DEPARTMENT,
OTTAWA, May 31, 1915.

Hon. J. D. REID,
Minister of Customs.

I have the honour to hand you the Annual Report of the Department of Customs, containing Tables of Imports, Exports and Navigation of the Dominion of Canada for the fiscal year ended March 31, 1915.

I have the honour to be, sir,

Your obedient servant,

JOHN McDOUGALD,
Commissioner of Customs.

INDEX TO TABLES.

INDEX TO TABLES—*Concluded.*

EXPLANATORY NOTES

In General Statement No. 1 (Pt. II) of Imports and Goods entered for Consumption, the term "Entered for consumption" is the technical term in use at the custom-house, and does not imply that the goods have been actually consumed in Canada, but that they have passed into the possession of the importer and that duty has been paid on that portion liable for duty.

The value of goods imported is governed by section 40 of the Customs Act, which provides that the value of imported goods subject to ad valorem duty "shall be the fair market value thereof, when sold for home consumption, in the principal markets of the country whence and at the time when the same were exported directly to Canada."

In General Statement No. 3 (Pt. ii) of Exports, the term "The Produce of Canada" includes all imported articles which have been changed in form or enhanced in value by further manufacture in Canada, such as sugar refined in Canada from imported raw sugar, flour ground from imported wheat, and articles constructed or manufactured from imported materials. "Goods not the produce of Canada" shows the exports of foreign goods which had been previously imported.

Under the Regulations commencing July 1, 1900, all *Export* entries are delivered at the "*frontier port of exit*," and the totals thereof are credited to the respective ports where the goods pass outwards from Canada. In view of the more complete returns obtained under this system the additions heretofore made to the exports statistics (prior to July 1, 1900) under the head of "Short returns" are now omitted.

In this report, the tables of imports and exports at the several ports of entry indicate that merchandise of the value stated was *entered inwards* or *passed outwards* at the ports mentioned, but do not imply that the imports were all for consumption at such ports or that the exports originated there.

The trade by Countries, with the Dominion as a whole, is recorded in the General Statements of Imports and Exports.

The value of "Goods the Produce of Canada" is their value at the time of exportation at the ports of Canada whence shipped.

The value of "Goods not the Produce of Canada" is the actual cost of such goods.

The initials n.e.s. mean "not elsewhere specified."

The initials n.o.p. mean "not otherwise provided for."

The expression " ton" means two thousand pounds, and " cwt." one hundred pounds.

The expression 'standard hundred" when applied to deals, means 2,750 feet board measure.

The expression "ton," applied to square timber, means 40 cubic feet.

In the shipping tables the tonnage is given in net tons.

ERRATA.

Part II, page 28, 6th item, " Freight Wagons " general consumption quantity should read 964.

Part II, page 86, 1st item, "Lobsters, fresh."   Total duty should read 662.50.

PART I

TABLES

OF THE

TRADE AND NAVIGATION

No. 1.—Value of Total Exports, Imports and Goods entered for Consumption in the Dominion with the duty collected thereon, for the undermentioned years.

		Total Exports.	Total Imports.	Entered for Consumption.	Duty.
		$	$	$	$ cts.
Fiscal year ended June 30,	1868.............	57,567,888	73,459,644	71,985,306	8,819,431 63
" "	1869.............	60,474,781	70,415,165	67,402,170	8,298,909 71
" "	1870.............	73,573,490	74,814,339	71,237,603	9,462,940 44
" "	1871.............	74,173,618	96,092,971	86,947,482	11,843,655 75
" "	1872.............	82,639,663	111,430,527	107,709,116	13,045,493 50
" "	1873.............	89,789,922	128,011,281	127,514,594	13,017,730 17
" "	1874.............	89,351,928	128,213,582	127,404,169	14,421,882 67
" "	1875.............	77,886,979	123,070,283	119,618,657	15,361,382 12
" "	1876.............	80,966,435	93,210,346	94,733,218	12,833,114 48
" "	1877.............	75,875,393	99,327,962	96,300,483	12,548,451 09
" "	1878.............	79,323,667	93,081,787	91,199,577	12,795,693 17
" "	1879.............	71,491,255	81,964,427	80,341,608	12,939,540 66
" "	1880.............	87,911,458	86,489,747	71,782,349	14,138,849 22
" "	1881.............	98,290,823	105,330,840	91,611,604	18,500,785 97
" "	1882.............	102,137,203	119,419,500	112,648,927	21,708,837 43
" "	1883.............	98,085,804	132,254,022	123,137,019	23,172,308 97
" "	1884.............	91,406,496	116,397,043	108,180,644	20,164,963 37
" "	1885.............	89,238,361	108,941,486	102,710,019	19,133,558 99
" "	1886.............	85,251,314	104,424,561	99,602,694	19,448,123 70
" "	1887.............	89,515,811	112,892,236	105,639,428	22,469,705 83
" "	1888.............	90,203,000	110,894,630	102,847,100	22,209,641 53
" "	1889.............	89,189,167	115,224,931	109,673,447	23,784,523 23
" "	1890.............	96,749,149	121,858,241	112,765,584	24,014,908 07
" "	1891.............	98,417,296	119,967,638	113,345,124	23,481,069 13
" "	1892.............	113,963,372	127,406,068	116,978,943	20,550,581 53
" "	1893.............	118,564,352	129,074,268	121,705,030	21,161,710 93
" "	1894.............	117,524,949	123,474,940	113,093,983	19,379,822 32
" "	1895.............	113,638,803	110,781,682	105,252,511	17,887,269 47
" "	1896.............	121,013,852	118,011,508	110,587,480	20,219,037 32
" "	1897.............	137,950,253	119,218,609	111,294,021	19,891,996 77
" "	1898.............	164,152,683	140,323,053	130,698,006	22,157,788 49
" "	1899.............	158,896,905	162,764,308	154,051,593	25,734,228 75
" "	1900.............	191,894,723	189,622,513	180,804,316	28,889,110 13
" "	1901.............	196,487,632	190,415,525	181,237,988	29,106,979 89
" "	1902.............	211,640,286	212,270,158	202,791,595	32,425,532 31
" "	1903.............	225,849,724	241,214,961	233,790,516	37,110,354 59
" "	1904.............	213,521,235	259,211,803	251,464,332	40,954,349 14
" "	1905.............	203,316,872	266,834,417	261,925,554	42,024,339 92
" "	1906.............	256,586,630	294,286,015	290,360,807	46,671,101 18
" March 31,	*1907.............	205,277,197	259,786,007	257,254,882	40,290,171 70
" "	1908.............	280,006,606	370,786,525	358,428,616	58,331,074 04
" "	1909.............	261,512,159	309,756,608	298,205,957	48,059,791 93
" "	1910.............	301,358,529	391,852,692	375,833,016	61,024,239 21
" "	1911.............	297,196,365	472,247,540	461,951,318	73,312,367 59
" "	1912.............	315,317,250	559,320,544	547,482,190	87,576,036 52
" "	1913.............	393,232,057	692,032,392	675,517,045	115,063,687 93
" "	1914.............	478,997,928	650,746,797	633,692,449	107,180,578 33
" "	1915.............	490,808,877	629,444,894	587,439,304	79,205,910 27

*9 months, change of fiscal ve

11—i—1½

No. 2.—Aggregate Trade of the Dominion by Countries on the basis of Goods entered for Consumption and Exported.

Fiscal Year.	United Kingdom.	United States.	France.	Germany.	Spain.	Portugal.	Italy.	Holland.
	$	$.	$	$	$	$	$	$
1873........	107,266,624	89,808,204	2,055,195	1,176,478	502,966	266,188	229,657	229,770
1874........	108,083,642	90,524,060	2,569,712	1,022,428	459,027	294,007	236,296	271,043
1875........	100,379,969	80,717,803	2,154,065	839,442	390,784	236,790	214,366	260,503
1876........	81,457,737	78,003,492	2,394,812	608,355	445,151	199,195	183,199	297,895
1877........	81,139,708	77,087,914	1,730,062	404,918	340,757	175,425	242,942	296,860
1878........	83,372,719	73,876,437	1,754,394	521,590	325,245	145,941	205,171	266,764
1879........	67,288,848	70,904,720	2,247,066	552,999	394,445	161,258	181,933	210,288
1880........	80,307,286	62,696,857	1,928,670	532,028	297,245	201,652	623,295	273,837
1881........	97,335,378	73,570,337	2,294,043	1,019,198	446,337	165,487	234,723	440,944
1882........	95,871,802	96,229,763	2,922,931	1,633,118	570,301	201,656	256,841	613,241
1883........	99,197,682	97,701,056	2,934,210	1,942,851	749,897	243,192	322,554	324,800
1884........	87,154,242	89,333,366	2,160,804	2,171,346	648,569	240,235	322,499	333,977
1885........	83,284,482	86,903,935	2,239,890	2,385,344	481,910	227,096	255,712	361,879
1886........	82,143,828	81,436,808	2,509,581	2,408,821	432,540	301,927	215,298	309,559
1887........	89,534,079	82,767,265	2,415,001	3,672,985	481,289	204,671	245,560	309,920
1888........	79,383,705	91,053,913	2,642,557	3,563,106	427,249	230,397	235,816	332,169
1889........	80,422,515	94,059,844	2,562,893	3,836,173	420,794	238,106	186,186	414,302
1890........	91,743,935	92,814,783	2,894,154	4,286,136	392,294	291,811	244,545	423,309
1891........	91,328,384	94,824,352	2,565,877	4,336,232	555,917	191,148	322,808	404,532
1892........	106,254,984	92,125,599	2,770,173	6,526,228	489,652	155,479	490,839	846,167
1893........	107,228,906	102,144,986	3,096,164	4,576,224	387,861	135,482	661,403	656,427
1894........	107,256,123	88,844,040	3,081,950	7,887,594	445,567	126,469	511,631	625,764
1895........	92,988,727	95,932,197	2,920,456	5,421,135	436,580	115,921	415,919	348,164
1896........	99,670,030	103,022,434	3,392,482	6,688,990	445,592	88,262	287,676	439,680
1897........	106,639,690	111,022,513	3,292,047	7,538,800	436,984	82,337	333,512	480,531
1898........	137,499,735	124,410,926	5,000,613	7,421,462	578,462	135,154	495,023	750,486
1899........	136,151,978	138,140,687	5,447,017	9,613,025	593,660	92,937	520,684	872,941
1900........	152,526,098	178,463,401	5,743,272	10,099,401	647,157	187,801	405,029	767,781
1901........	148,347,120	182,867,238	6,979,352	9,162,957	897,893	181,707	642,424	984,840
1902........	166,533,983	192,004,734	8,061,042	13,515,747	856,793	234,874	963,641	1,195,856
1903........	190,099,222	209,389,119	7,921,647	14,380,336	962,497	293,376	837,555	1,889,869
1904........	179,368,950	223,599,447	7,804,453	9,994,827	963,674	210,053	642,891	1,951,398
1905........	162,301,480	240,142,642	8,570,437	7,842,068	779,482	227,281	819,610	1,505,474
1906........	202,289,527	273,668,593	9,788,078	8,859,871	984,477	218,202	769,610	2,004,640
*1907.......	169,717,174	234,964,509	8,108,984	6,541,513	934,469	282,622	807,347	1,816,967
1908........	229,443,627	324,173,325	11,708,641	10,537,654	1,233,571	194,121	1,131,336	2,281,420
1909........	204,428,319	272,631,127	11,373,531	7,536,917	979,536	171,116	2,382,112	2,515,851
1910........	244,984,407	336,652,587	12,750,192	10,436,421	1,071,719	200,253	1,722,906	3,947,842
1911........	246,901,573	404,331,540	14,345,865	12,710,357	1,182,690	274,468	1,341,418	3,217,597
1912........	268,760,435	476,889,112	13,868,369	14,904,919	1,387,775	329,932	1,431,913	4,206,628
1913........	316,732,000	608,251,944	17,944,367	17,616,941	1,307,598	392,391	2,319,304	5,851,267
1914........	354,393,642	611,245,464	18,087,097	19,019,959	1,416,132	332,862	2,745,643	8,524,262
1915........	301,919,644	644,026,253	23,044,891	7,248,996	1,467,128	1,004,093	3,313,709	7,024,085

*9 months.

SESSIONAL PAPER No. 11

No. 2.—Aggregate Trade of the Dominion by Countries on the basis of Goods entered for Consumption and Exported—*Continued.*

Fiscal Year.	Belgium.	New-foundland	West Indies.	South America.	China and Japan.	Switzer-land.	Other Countries.	Total.
	$	$	$	$	$	$	$	$
1873.........	364,456	4,609,552	1,163,425	1,701,633	1,709,856	120,514	1,099,998	217,304,516
1874.........	534,153	2,657,547	6,086,529	1,686,508	1,263,728	139,674	927,743	216,756,097
1875.........	337,674	2,806,055	6,139,910	1,064,593	694,472	116,128	1,153,082	197,505,636
1876.........	374,880	2,675,477	5,291,433	975,762	971,314	56,168	1,764,483	175,699,653
1877.........	318,724	2,753,748	5,031,667	656,591	455,755	69,066	1,471,734	172,175,876
1878.........	805,692	2,767,347	4,397,996	669,804	436,244	61,178	1,366,532	170,523,244
1879.........	219,461	2,280,823	4,753,099	745,830	505,513	94,781	1,291,709	151,832,863
1880.........	837,897	2,002,261	6,489,257	1,073,421	931,457	94,225	1,314,429	159,693,807
1881.........	671,267	2,175,773	6,962,516	1,369,731	1,430,734	141,789	1,644,170	189,902,427
1882.........	645,568	2,468,432	7,018,956	2,314,779	1,635,717	268,093	2,134,932	214,786,130
1883.........	611,112	2,953,273	7,494,291	2,954,628	1,750,642	336,040	1,706,595	221,222,823
1884.........	746,528	2,701,120	6,726,486	2,756,371	1,970,541	242,380	2,079,676	199,537,140
1885.........	551,645	2,022,073	5,698,057	2,802,042	2,528,369	217,666	1,989,280	191,948,380
1886.........	517,472	2,139,301	5,266,042	2,111,029	2,495,703	203,085	2,363,014	184,854,008
1887.........	927,580	2,072,946	4,017,593	2,625,066	2,819,534	219,777	2,841,913	195,155,239
1888.........	505,800	1,945,426	5,870,149	2,487,240	2,261,155	194,938	2,016,480	193,050,100
1889.........	595,496	1,791,496	6,138,109	2,813,587	2,048,712	166,905	3,167,496	198,862,814
1890.........	763,146	1,655,400	5,808,189	2,555,849	2,161,816	316,923	3,162,393	209,514,733
1891.........	728,120	2,218,911	6,360,926	1,782,950	2,202,102	244,319	3,685,842	211,762,420
1892.........	573,244	2,503,963	7,638,846	1,905,346	3,300,108	193,033	5,168,657	230,942,318
1893.........	1,268,551	3,247,903	7,390,377	2,099,356	2,766,712	253,464	4,465,666	240,269,382
1894.........	1,253,692	3,633,154	7,121,172	2,264,677	3,065,768	276,065	4,220,266	230,618,932
1895.........	693,019	3,065,046	8,681,622	1,610.470	2,906,574	260,040	3,059,444	218,891,314
1896.........	1,018,789	2,333,721	4,707,243	2,063,145	3,339,429	332,405	3,771,454	231,601,332
1897.........	1,518,218	2,144,874	4,322,230	2,026,085	3,300,331	223,192	5,882,830	249,244,274
1898.........	2,204.054	2,632,184	3,829,346	2,505,195	2,829,890	357,003	4,201,156	294,850,689
1899.........	3,168,136	2,335,323	4,398,902	2,631,635	3,194,849	571,526	5,215,018	312,948,498
1900...:.....	4,421,716	2,804.748	4,202,119	2,423,994	2,749,759	529,976	6,726,187	372,699,039
1901.........	6,634,592	2,886,067	4,707,677	2,567,278	3,149,591	603,397	7,113,487	377,725,620
1902.........	4,156,049	3,498,482	5,472,747	3,440,987	2,555,462	780,183	11,161,301	414,431,881
1903.........	4,950,732	3,714,157	6,021,294	4,532,008	2,440,999	952,326	11,255,103	459,640,240
1904.........	4,255,930	3,975,418	8,397,290	5,613,612	3,134,959	1,392,895	13,679,770	464,985,567
1905.........	3,514,994	4,528,326	10,039,302	6,916,171	3,900,776	1,776,405	12,288,038	465,242,426
1906.........	4,175,238	4,972,281	9,944,179	9,425,735	3,634,769	2,042,635	14,119,602	546,947,437
*1907.........	3,553,137	3,708,200	6,935,876	8,814,147	3,001,144	1,609,063	11,736,927	462,532,079
1908.........	5,758,128	5,185,987	12,844,390	7,555,644	4,611,199	2,752,443	19,023,736	638,435,222
1909.........	5,829,033	5,190,721	12,626,749	8,262,369	4,405,402	2,195,342	19,189,991	559,718,116
1910.........	6,139,980	5,438,571	13,284,809	10,961,629	4,892,218	2,614,038	22,093,973	677,191,545
1911.........	6,387,798	5,693,035	15,603,170	12,482,760	4,255,948	3,125,533	27,293,881	759,147,683
1912.........	7,418,641	6,126,200	15,391,818	15,363,540	4,015,357	3,477,524	29,227,277	862,799,440
1913.........	8,829,175	6,785,116	16,814,434	14,881,135	6,137,859	4,312,054	40,573,517	1,068,749,102
1914.........	9,310,319	6,611,551	18,501,695	13,046,555	5,579,724	4,361,520	39,513,952	1,112,690,377
1915.........	5,135,322	5,726,336	17,507,373	11,708,498	5,159,252	3,995,701	39,966,900	1,078,248,181

*9 months.

6 GEORGE V, A. 1916

No. 3.—Showing the grand aggregate trade from 1868 to 1915 inclusive on the basis of "Total Exports and Imports."

Years.	Total Exports.	Total Imports.	Grand Total, Imports and Exports.
	$	$	$
1868	57,567,888	73,459,644	131,027,532
1869	60,474,781	70,415,165	130,889,946
1870	73,573,490	74,814,339	148,387,829
1871	74,173,618	96,092,971	170,266,589
1872	82,639,663	111,430,527	194,070,190
1873	89,789,922	128,011,281	217,801,203
1874	89,351,928	128,213,582	217,565,510
1875	77,886,979	123,070,283	200,957,262
1876	80,966,435	93,210,346	174,176,781
1877	75,875,393	99,327,962	175,203,355
1878	79,323,667	93,081,787	172,405,454
1879	71,491,255	81,964,427	153,455,682
1880	87,911,458	86,489,747	174,401,205
1881	98,290,823	105,330,840	203,621,663
1882	102,137,203	119,419,500	221,556,703
1883	98,085,804	132,254,022	230,339,826
1884	91,406,496	116,397,043	207,803,539
1885	89,238,361	108,941,486	198,179,847
1886	85,251,314	104,424,561	189,675,875
1887	89,515,811	112,892,236	202,408,047
1888	90,203,000	110,894,630	201,097,630
1889	89,189,167	115,224,931	204,414,098
1890	96,749,149	121,858,241	218,607,390
1891	98,417,296	119,967,638	218,384,934
1892	113,963,375	127,406,068	241,369,443
1893	118,564,352	129,074,268	247,638,620
1894	117,524,949	123,474,940	240,999,889
1895	113,638,803	110,781,682	224,420,485
1896	121,013,852	118,011,508	239,025,360
1897	137,950,253	119,218,609	257,168,862
1898	164,152,683	140,323,053	304,475,736
1899	158,896,905	162,764,308	321,661,213
1900	191,894,723	189,622,513	381,517,236
1901	196,487,632	190,415,525	386,903,157
1902	211,640,286	212,270,158	423,910,444
1903	225,849,724	241,214,961	467,064,685
1904	213,521,235	259,211,803	472,733,038
1905	203,316,872	266,834,417	470,151,289
1906	256,586,630	294,286,015	550,872,645
*1907	205,277,197	259,786,007	465,063,204
1908	280,006,606	370,786,525	650,793,131
1909	261,512,159	309,756,608	571,268,767
1910	301,358,529	391,852,692	693,211,221
1911	297,196,365	472,247,540	769,443,905
1912	315,317,250	559,320,544	874,637,794
1913	393,232,057	692,032,392	1,058,264,449
1914	478,997,928	650,746,797	1,129,744,725
1915	490,808,877	629,444,894	1,120,253,771

*9 months.

No. 4.—Value of Exports by Countries.

Fiscal Year.	United Kingdom.	United States.	France.	Germany.	Spain.	Portugal.	Italy.	Holland.
	$	$	$	$	$	$	$	$
1873.........	38,743,848	42,072,526	31,907	76,553	25,080	191,156	177,232	13,142
1874.........	45.003,882	36,244,311	267,212	65,511	960	193,463	190,211	14,905
1875.........	40,032:902	29,911,983	212,767	91,019	7,300	170,784	170,408	28,724
1876.........	40,723,477	31,933,450	553,935	125,768	9,417	127,540	142,787	30,816
1877.........	41,567,469	25,775,245	319,330	34,324	62,659	129,960	213,692	94,303
1878.........	45,941,530	25,244,808	369.391	122,254	47,816	104,028	151,861	53,750
1879.........	36,295,718	27,165,501	714,875	112,090	50,596	135,748	148,472	9,713
1880.........	45,846,062	33,349,909	812,829	82,237	60,727	165,885	163,787	102,592
1881.........	53,571,570	36,866,225	662,711	84,932	46,653	108,594	145,997	215,754
1882.........	45,274,461	47,940,711	825,573	153,114	108,082	149,744	163,755	365,198
1883.........	47,145,217	41,668,723	617,730	133,697	164,925	179,843	218,113	27,599
1884......'..	43,736,227	38,840,540	390,955	195,575	144,092	172,252	247,151	15,500
1885.........	41,877,705	39,752,734	303,309	264,075	132,695	166,730	147,550	24,094
1886.........	41,542,629	36,578,769	534,363	253,298	53,075	245,450	108,601	7,587
1887.........	44,571,846	37,660,199	341,531	437,536	72,020	146,528	125,681	14,859
1888.........	40,084,984	42,572,065	397,773	198,543	52,317	155,821	55,090	378
1889.........	38,105.126	43,522,404	334,210	143,603	13,526	166,021	60,062	1,222
1890.........	48,353,694	40,522,810	278,552	507,143	69,788	207,777	81,059	1,042
1891.........	49,280,858	41,138,695	253,734	532,142	67,110	120,611	90,999	14,741
1892.........	64,906,549	38,988,027	367,539	942,698	93,476	102,370	149,280	567,879
1893.........	64,080,493	43,923,010	264,047	750,461	44,355	83,001	87,387	282,569
1894.........	68,538,856	35,809,940	544,986	2,046,052	56,274	79,363	109,188	281,053
1895.........	61,856,990	41,297,676	335,282	620,976	34,101	58,781	34,325	140,264
1896.........	66,690,288	44,448,410	531,540	757,531	83,814	41,666	56,759	139,828
1897.........	77,227,502	49,373,472	690,696	1,045.432	50,452	36,745	108,627	104,422
1898.........	104,998,818	45,705,336	1,025,262	1,837,448	89,675	87,835	73,765	376,439
1899.........	99,091,855	45,133,521	1,557,722	2,219,569	59,178	29,641	125,265	372,548
1900.........	107.736,368	68,619,023	1,374,770	1,715,903	86,456	115,016	260,456	· 188,199
1901.........	105,328,956	72,382,230	1,581,331	2,141,552	155,354	85,403	315,063	187,378
1902.........	117,320,221	71,197,684	1,388,848	2,692,578	161,823	105,495	236,899	320,241
1903.........	131,202,321	71,783,924	1,341,618	2,097,699	138,553	164,184	295,770	619,329
1904.........	117,591,376	72,772,932	1,597,928	1,819,223	98,578	109,340	240,963	1,035,327
1905.........	101,958,771	77,404,071	1,511,298	1,146,654	50,223	128,993	198,973	550,821
1906.........	133,094,937	97,806,552	2,120,091	1,872,557	55,686	89,598	215,855	824,768
*1907.........	105,135,801	79,021,480	1,409,572	1,066,605	48,315	154,438	352,842	814,977
1908.........	134,484,156	113,520,500	1,806,732	2,374,607	106,594	46,865	349.839	855,085
1909.........	133,745,375	92,604,357	3,176,096	1,476,552	45,682	48,833	1,620,773	1,242,730
1910.........	149,634,107	113,150,778	2,640,648	2,501,191	51,944	59,731	829,508	1,937,852
1911.........	136,965,111	119,396,801	2,782,092	2,663,017	27,943	88,088	379,270	1,397,019
1912.........	151,853,413	120,534,634	2,123,705	3,814,914	114,564	70,390	285,091	1,782,726
1913.........	177,982,002	167,110,382	2,564,603	3,402,394	48,628	49,142	605,719	2,741,713
1914.........	222,322,766	200,459,373	3,810,562	4,433,736	63,999	55,481	655,256	5,508,806
1915.........	211,753,863	215,409,326	14,595,705	2,162,010	489,680	738,485	1,840,910	5,254,829

*9 months.

6 GEORGE V, A. 1916

No. 4.—Value of Exports by Countries—*Continued.*

Fiscal Year.	Belgium.	New-foundland	West Indies.	South America.	China and Japan.	Australia.	Other Countries.	Total.
	$	$	$	$	$	$	$	$
1873............	17,754	2,800,555	3,988,493	1,285,434	*46,466	41,822	277,954	89,789,922
1874............	240,494	1,569,079	3,778,796	1,212,978	39,222	98,733	432,171	89,351,928
1875............	59,503	1,901,831	3,945,506	785,797	37,046	181,938	349,411	77,886,979
1876............	13,825	1,900,891	3,675,320	688,209	23,075	79,643	938,273	80,966,435
1877............	66,912	2,112,106	3,788,858	651,625	37,149	185,610	836,151	75,875,393
1878............	49,998	2,094,682	3,414,147	654,357	102,568	370,723	651,655	79,323,667
1879............	40,430	1,641,417	3,500,670	741,442	56,551	290,762	587,270	71,491,255
1880............	688,811	1,510,300	3,544,103	789,940	37,546	139,901	616,829	87,911,458
1881............	258,433	1,523,469	3,147,369	732,111	19,761	146,363	580,881	98,290,823
1882............	142,358	1,974,923	2,995,572	941,162	106,675	340,608	655,267	102,137,203
1883............	195,705	2,187,338	3,125,031	1,489,957	105,388	375,065	451,473	98,085,804
1884............	287,378	1,920,450	3,119,569	1,277,383	60,979	502,181	496,264	91,406,496
1885............	72,385	1,670,968	2,535,283	1,461.206	29,918	415,887	383,822	89,238,361
1886............	6,565	1,754,980	2,121,570	1,010,034	63,118	259,960	711,315	85,251,314
1887............	223,729	1,718,604	2,075,411	1,426,660	69,196	269,471	362,540	89,515,811
1888............	17,057	1,523,827	2,601,486	1,510,637	132,448	446,019	454,555	90,203,000
1889............	64,756	1,303,335	2,759,455	1,488,999	84,174	661,208	481,051	89,189,167
1890............	41,814	1,185,739	2,719,141	1,551,887	61,751	471,028	695,924	96,749,149
1891............	72,672	1,467,908	3,122,770	1,063,172	78,791	589,100	523,993	98,417,296
1892............	56.212	1,750,714	3,546,559	1,027,525	283,251	436,603	744,693	113,963,375
1893............	669,040	2,594,633	3,145,708	1,326,743	341,140	288,352	683,413	118,564,352
1894............	708,455	2,818,592	3,443,761	1,392,285	540,849	322,745	832,545	117,524,949
1895............	251,402	2,325,196	3,725,426	1,303,474	378,160	417,124	853,626	113,638,803
1896............	98,031	1,782,309	2,810,817	1,496,118	668,011	517,258	841,472	121,013,852
1897............	354,584	1,692,798	2,643,360	1,405,359	903,922	1,418,289	894,593	137,950,253
1898.:.........	973,944	2,167,860	2,749,080	1,060,420	511,919	1,630,714	864,168	164,152,683
1899............	849,413	1,808,317	3,043,963	1,456,051	425,350	1,506,138	1,218,374	153,896,905
1900............	1,197,798	2,144,070	2,870,343	1,431,107	368,615	1,626,441	2,160,158	191,894,723
1901............	2,806,142	2,260,499	2,905,937	1,519,190	699,569	2,311,405	1,807,623	196,487,632
1902............	2,444,450	2,381,082	3,298,912	1,781,913	570,586	2,586,554	5,153,000	211,640,286
1903............	2,150,505	2,516,576	3,642,176	2,542,056	501,057	2,929,861	3,924,050	225,849,724
1904............	1,126,417	2,898,751	3,583,475	2,456,608	568,983	2,622,756	4,898,578	213,521,235
1905............	1,739,807	3,473,713	4,401,115	2,880,552	1,520,053	2,194,223	4,157,605	203,316,872
1906............	1,565,166	3,213,856	4,575,212	3,623,065	1,467,252	2,082,219	3,979,816	256,586,630
*1907..........	1,857,958	2,244,469	3,527,153	3,584,329	890,425	1,998,968	3,169,865	205,277,197
1908............	3,377,479	3,408,518	4,543,889	4,467,584	1,705,901	2,873,461	6,085,396	280,006,606
1909............	3,927,445	3,552,293	4,534,446	3,478,476	1,778,666	2,769,049	7,511,386	261,512,159
1910............	2,900,092	3,970,952	5,948,245	4,744,524	1,910,724	3,583,447	7,494,786	301,353,529
1911............	2,773,444	3,874,775	6,567,307	5,149,771	1,149,810	3,925,592	10,056,325	297,196,365
1912............	3,732,222	4,284,313	6,900,940	4,825,030	902,375	3,947,015	10,145,918	315,317,250
1913............	4,808,997	4,723,142	6,237,468	4,352,278	1,881,558	3,996,387	12,722,644	393,232,057
1914............	4,819,843	4,770,200	6,997,711	4,026,398	2,062,246	4,705,822	14,305,729	478,997,928
1915............	3,259,359	4,481,176	6,418,479	2,114,370	1,333,404	5,552,686	15,349,595	490,808,877

*9 months.

SESSIONAL PAPER No. 11

No. 5.—Value of Goods entered for Consumption, by Countries.

Fiscal Year.	United Kingdom.	United States.	France.	Germany.	Spain.	Portugal.	Italy.	Holland.
	$	$	$	$	$	$	$	$″
1873.......	68,522,776	47,735,678	2,023,288	1,099,925	477,886	75,032	52,425	216,628
1874.......	63,076,437	54,283,072	2,302,500	956,917	458,067	100,544	46,085	256,138
1875.......	60,347,067	50,805,820	1,941,298	748,423	383,484	66,006	43,958	231,779
1876.......	40,734,260	46,070,033	1,840,877	482,587	436,034	71,655	40,412	267.079
1877.......	39,572.239	51,312.669	1,410,732	370,594	278,098	45,465	29,250	202,557
1878...-...	37,431,180	48,631,739	1,385,003	399,326	277,429	41,913	53,310	213,014
1879.......	30,993,130	43,739,219	1,532,191	440,909	343,849	25,510	33,461	200,575
1880.......	34,461,224	29,346,948	1,115,841	449,791	236,518	35,767	459,508	171,245
1881.......	43,583,808	36,704,112	1,631,332	934,266	399,684	56,893	88,726	225,190
1882.......	50,597,341	48,289,052	2,097,358	1,480,004	462,219	51,912	93,086	248,043
1883.......	52,052,465	58,032,333	2,316,480	1,809,154	554,972	63,349	104,441	297,201
1884.......	43,418,015	50,492,826	1,769,849	1,975,771	504,477	67,983	75,348	318,477
1885.......	41,406,777	47,151,201	1,935,581	2,121,269	349,215	60,366	108,162	337,785
1886.......	40,601,199	44,858,039	1,975,218	2,155,523	379,465	56,477	106,697	301,972
1887.......	44,962,233	45,107,066	2,073,470	3,235,449	409,269	58,143	119,889	295,061
1888.......	39,298,721	48,481,848	2,244,784	3,364,563	374,932	74,576	180,726	331,791
1889.......	42,317,389	50,537,440	2,228,683	3,692,570	407,268	72,085	126,124	414,080
1890.......	43,390,241	52,291,973	2,615,602	3,778,993	322,506	84,034	163,486	232,267
1891.......	42,047,526	53,685,657	2,312,143	3,804,090	488,807	70,537	241,809	389,791
1892.......	41,348,435	53,137,572	2,402,634	5,593,530	396,176	53,109	341,559	278,288
1893.......	43,148,413	58,221,976	2,832,117	3,825,763	343,506	52,481	170,564	373,858
1894.......	38,717,267	53,034,100	2,536,964	5,841,542	389,293	47,106	402,443	344,706
1895.......	31,131,737	54,634,521	2,585,174	4,794,159	402,479	57,140	381,594	243,900
1896.......	32,979,742	58,574,024	2,810,942	5,931,459	361,778	46,696	230,917	299,852
1897.......	29,412,188	61,649,041	2,601,351	6,493,368	386,532	45,592	224,885	376,109
1898.......	32,500,917	78,705,590	3,975,351	5,584,014	488,787	47,319	421,258	374,047
1899.......	37,060,123	93,007,166	3,889,295	7,393.456	534,482	63,296	395,599	500,393
1900.......	44,789,730	109,844,378	4,368,502	8,383,498	560,701	72,785	144,573	579,582
1901.......	43,018,164	110,485.008	5,398,021	7,021,405	742,539	96,304	327,361	797,462
1902.......	49,213,762	120,807,050	6,672,194	10,823,169	694,970	129,379	726,742	875,615
1903.......	53,896,901	137,605,195	6,580,029	12,282,637	823,944	129,192	541,785	1,270,540
1904.......	61,777,574	150,826,515	6,206,525	8,175.604	865,096	100,713	401,928	916.071
1905.......	60,342,709	162,738,571	7,059,139	6,695,414	729,259	98,288	620,637	954,653
1906.......	69,194,588	175,862,071	7,667,987	6,987,314	928,791	128,604	553,755	1,179,892
*1907.......	64,581,373	155,943.029	6,699,412	5,474,908	886,154	128,084	454,505	1,001,990
1908.......	94,959,471	210,652,825	9,901,909	8,163,047	1,126,977	147,256	781,497	1,426,335
1909.......	70,682,944	180,026,550	8,197,435	6,050,365	933,854	122,283	761,339	1,273,121
1910.......	95,350,300	223,501,809	10,109,544	7,935,230	1,019,775	140,522	893,398	2,009,990
1911.......	109,936,462	284,934,739	11,563,773	10,047,340	1,154,747	186,380	962,148	1,820,578
1912.......	116,907,022	358,354,478	11,744,664	11,090,005	1,273,211	259,542	1,146,822	2,423,902
1913.......	138,749,998	441,141,562	15,379,764	14,214,547	1,253,970	343,249	1,713,585	3,109,554
1914.......	132,070,876	410,786,091	14,276,535	14,586,223	1,352,133	277,381	2,090,387	3,015,456
1915.......	90,160,781	428,616,927	8,449,186	5,086,986	977,448	215,608	1,472,799	1,769,256

*9 months.

6 GEORGE V, A. 1916

No. 5.—Value of Goods entered for Consumption, by Countries—*Continued.*

Fiscal Year.	Belgium.	New-found-land.	West Indies.	South America.	China and Japan.	Switzer-land.	Other Countries.	Total.
	$	$	$	$	$	$	$	$
1873	346,702	1,808,997	2,174,932	416,199	1,663,390	120,514	780,222	127,514,594
1874	293,659	1,088,468	2,307,733	473,530	1,224,506	139,674	396,839	127,404,169
1875	278,311	904,224	2,194,404	278,796	657,426	116,128	621,733	119,618,857
1876	361,055	774,586	1,616,113	287,553	948,239	56,168	746,567	94,733,218
1877	251,812	641,642	1,242,809	4,971	418,606	69,066	449,973	96,300,483
1878	255,694	672,665	1,033,849	15,447	383,676	61,178	344,154	91,199,577
1879	179,031	639,406	1,252,429	4,388	448,962	94,781	413,767	80,341,608
1880	149,086	581,961	2,945,154	283,431	893,911	94,225	557,689	71,782,349
1881	412,834	652,304	3,815,147	637,620	1,410,973	141,789	916,926	91,611,604
1882	503,210	493,509	4,023,384	1,373,617	1,529,042	268,093	1,139,057	112,648,927
1883	415,407	765,935	4,369,260	1,464,671	1,645,254	336,040	880,057	123,137,019
1884	459,150	780,670	3,606,917	1,478,988	1,909,562	242,380	1,080,231	108,180,644
1885	479,260	351,105	3,162,774	1,340,836	2,493,451	217,666	1,189,571	102,710,019
1886	510,907	384,321	3,144,472	1,100,995	2,432,585	203,085	1,391,739	99,602,694
1887	703,851	354,342	1,942,182	1,198,406	2,750,388	219,777	2,209,902	105,639,428
1888	488,743	421,599	3,268,663	876,603	2,128,707	193,838	1,117,006	102,847,100
1889	530,740	488,161	3,378,654	1,324,588	1,964,538	166,890	2,025,237	109,673,447
1890	721,332	469,711	3,089,048	1,003,962	2,100,065	316,523	1,995,841	112,765,584
1891	655,448	751,003	3,238,156	719,778	2,123,311	244,319	2,572,749	113,345,124
1892	517,032	753,249	4,092,287	877,821	3,016,857	192,365	3,988,029	116,978,943
1893	599,511	653,270	4,244,669	772,613	2,425,572	258,464	3,782,253	121,705,030
1894	550,237	814,562	3,677,411	872,392	2,524,919	274,825	3,066,216	113,093,983
1895	441,617	739,850	4,794,020	469,172	2,528,414	259,400	1,789,334	105,252,511
1896	920,758	551,412	1,896,426	567,027	2,671,418	332,120	2,413,009	110,587,480
1897	1,163,632	452,076	1,678,870	620,250	2,396,409	222,173	3,571,545	111,294,021
1898	1,230,110	464,324	1,080,266	1,425,653	2,317,971	349,678	1,732,721	130,698,006
1899	2,318,723	527,006	1,354,939	1,175,534	2,769,499	568,768	2,493,264	154,051,593
1900	3,223,918	660,678	1,331,776	992,887	2,381,144	529,176	2,940,988	180,804,316
1901	3,828,450	625,568	1,801,740	1,048,088	2,450,022	602,653	2,995,198	181,237,988
1902	1,711,599	1,117,400	2,173,835	1,659,074	1,984,876	765,010	3,436,920	202,791,595
1903	2,800,182	1,197,581	2,379,275	1,989,952	1,939,942	944,727	4,408,634	233,790,516
1904	3,129,513	1,076,667	4,813,815	3,157,004	2,565,976	1,389,000	6,062,331	251,464,332
1905	1,775,187	1,054,613	5,638,187	4,035,619	2,470,723	1,766,991	5,945,564	261,925,554
1906	2,610.072	1,758,425	6,591,083	5,869,075	2,217,517	2,012,405	6,799,228	290,360,807
*1907	1,695,179	1,463,731	3,406,723	5,229,818	2,110,719	1,604,692	6,574,479	257,254,882
1908	2,380,649	1,777,469	8,300,501	3,088,060	2,905,298	2,734,779	10,082,543	358,428,616
1909	1,901,588	1,638,428	8,092,303	4,783,893	2,626,736	2,188,265	8,926,853	298,205,957
1910	3,239,888	1,467,619	7,336,564	6,217,105	2,981,494	2,603,853	11,025,920	375,833,016
1911	3,614,354	1,818,260	9,035,863	7,334,136	3,106,138	3,102,910	13,333,490	461,951,318
1912	3,686,419	1,841,887	8,490,878	10,533,310	3,112,982	3,458,006	15,159,062	547,482,190
1913	4,020,178	2,056,974	10,576,966	10,528,857	4,256,301	4,296,702	23,869,838	675,517,045
1914	4.490,476	1,841,351	11,503,984	9,020,157	3,517,478	4,314,805	20,549,116	633,692,449
1915	1,875,963	1,245,160	11,088,894	9,594,128	3,825,848	3,979,256	19,081,064	587,439,304

*9 months.

SESSIONAL PAPER No. 11

No. 6.—Duty Collected.

Fiscal Year.	United Kingdom.	United States.	France.	Germany.	Spain.	Portugal.	Italy.	Holland.
	$ cts.	$ cts.	$ cts.	$ cts.	$ cts.	$ cts.	$ cts.	$ cts.
1873....	7,398,460 17	2,960,119 34	627,831 95	334,415 51	102,711 21	21,245 21	9,320 80	294,569 02
1874....	7,867,481 41	3,695,564 03	744,059 19	272,234 68	112,918 73	27,674 63	13,626 76	361,153 47
1875....	8,881,997 81	3,860,877 10	604,092 47	173,427 65	113,599 78	28,421 97	8,502 45	394,017 97
1876....	6,075,759 82	4,117,223 40	723,368 24	134,282 11	157,287 53	29,302 21	24,629 25	459,887 63
1877....	6,377,596 23	4,426,394 79	480,340 56	75,762 93	79,515 38	20,322 20	15,783 10	316,156 00
1878....	6,445,995 38	4,794,599 63	400,600 04	79,673 10	87,755 88	13,452 55	19,652 43	308,153 30
1879....	5,561,933 02	5,529,150 64	501,747 90	104,211 80	120,385 81	7,970 14	19,474 58	329,634 07
1880....	6,737,997 05	4,521,311 08	427,937 89	103,156 82	106,720 56	14,935 79	30,031 12	301,570 50
1881....	8,772,949 97	5,657,292 75	597,948 79	215,108 04	167,412 55	25,307 99	40,956 25	372,335 63
1882....	10,011,811 00	7,082,722 29	742,774 93	338,691 39	210,766 86	29,105 63	34,283 98	420,607 91
1883....	9 897,785 16	8,158,023 35	824,963 17	388,556 85	231,866 95	38,135 50	44,340 03	535,741 81
1884....	8,001,370 74	7,420,461 79	645,152 71	554,181 88	192,946 21	34,228 80	32,186 80	493,807 39
1885....	7,617,249 45	6,636,405 83	650,515 29	572,947 24	154,680 24	29,345 65	33,380 25	521,318 20
1886....	7,817,357 45	6,790,080 76	735,666 52	598,168 44	150,268 47	30,510 74	35,667 84	602,570 19
1887....	9,318,920 08	7,299,591 68	699,840 07	1,190,267 30	176,449 17	33,329 81	31,404 53	623,894 26
1888....	8 972,739 84	7,131,006 28	796,242 70	1,214,748 15	171,790 38	36,621 03	42,004 78	704,034 45
1889....	9,450,243 70	7,413,354 83	854,805 00	1,266,638 56	185,969 33	36,805 32	32,456 70	756,785 89
1890....	9,576,965 75	8,220,299 55	957,312 22	1,165,158 67	170,028 06	36,528 91	37,938 11	806,261 40
1891....	9,114,271 75	7,709,318 12	932,032 53	1,320,583 23	217,612 94	30,680 47	44,888 90	741,462 43
1892....	9,074,200 71	7,814,666 93	931,044 99	783,740 50	186,168 39	27,446 98	35,846 83	697,184 17
1893....	9,498,747 08	7,636,075 81	1,058,095 75	857,264 35	180,132 25	27,171 69	30,816 89	815,200 70
1894....	8,245,845 87	6,960,950 68	1,019,568 12	978,224 53	207,724 63	22,894 36	49,073 63	879,107 85
1895....	7,006,676 58	6,897,395 04	985,945 87	892,547 04	187,788 45	24,361 92	46,697 12	755,251 48
1896....	7,358,514 15	7,767,992 63	1,020,804 74	1,329,186 36	162,118 81	22,269 68	39,386 02	792,609 63
1897....	6,205,366 80	8,147,075 10	969,539 64	1,489,755 60	150,587 43	23,191 61	33,474 05	920,096 46
1898....	6,649,428 60	9,941,624 48	1,183,890 30	1,364,159 04	176 764 64	20,606 24	46,466 82	908,046 37
1899....	7,328,191 92	11,713,858 94	1,300,876 33	1,903,223 16	181,346 14	25,559 36	52,842 44	1,061,622 69
1900....	8,074,541 07	13,491,872 86	1,428,019 46	2,189,798 17	183,147 69	28,548 59	26,842 73	1,171,550 06
1901....	7,845,406 49	13,411,749 58	1,794,455 55	1,811.974 55	191,527 27	37,138 80	45,171 84	1,350,098 08
1902....	8,424,693 04	15,155,136 39	2,163,016 40	2,741,263 29	205,803 43	42,700 86	88,174 27	1,306,967 57
1903....	9.841,627 33	17,069,881 19	2,098,633 61	3,255,121 88	212,104 39	45,912 40	87,457 75	1,527,113 35
1904....	10,838,017 31	19,554,585 54	2,113,667 94	2,172,571 04	228,532 66	41,226 25	88,831 12	1,726,681 98
1905....	11,171,010 04	20,580,301 56	2,224,967 73	1,826,789 33	216,933 42	39,295 27	123,388 07	1,570,378 88
1906....	12,944,249 35	22,187,102 94	2,520,034 97	1,852,538 47	289,363 62	44,716 82	118,725 17	1,620,711 72
*1907...	11,823,197 06	19,084,738 46	2,219,577 38	1,521,946 23	197,483 36	43,941 45	91,853 92	1,309,895 96
1908....	17,265,293 25	27,132,543 26	3,331,350 36	2,434,631 34	301,055 23	54,079 21	126,376 10	1,812,404 99
1909....	13,449 341 99	22,526,806 65	2,801,383 52	1,709 641 79	255,514 39	48,470 49	112,251 96	1,731,470 46
1910....	18,032,629 10	29,515,836 43	3,269,278 92	1,934.523 03	290,268 99	45,590 34	156,168 96	1,875,408 97
1911....	20,756,810 71	37,854,727 80	3,342,954 67	2,153,180 04	237,265 35	75,334 02	175,984 52	2,052,451 84
1912....	22,367,039 82	49,177,584 32	3,436.947 88	2,246,745 17	334,321 59	90,568 14	197,252 39	2,254,024 52
1913....	27,158,162 29	68,929,805 04	4,141,150 64	2,881,497 00	245,919 50	119 061 09	315 391 84	2,570,778 05
1914....	25,816,854 15	61,895,167 68	4,223,138 30	3,114,324 84	250,904 64	113,335 74	373,037 75	2,755,883 50
1915....	18,447,534 18	42,335,574 74	2,900,280 46	1,039,038 74	189,612 71	87,207 21	279,181 33	2,277,291 85

*9 months.

No. 6—DUTY COLLECTED—Concluded.

Fiscal Year.	Belgium.	New-foundland.	West Indies.	South America.	China and Japan.	Switzer-land.	Other Countries.	Additional duties, post entries, over collections, War Tax, &c.	Total.
	$ cts.	$ cts.	$ cts.	$ cts.	$ cts.	$ cts.	$ cts.	$ cts.	$ cts.
1873	94,504 87	97,147 31	831,930 86	182,660 79	157 95	15,994 95	40,660 23		13,017,730 17
1874	51,171 82	54,929 33	935,653 11	194,325 88	26,185 10	21,960 85	42,953 77		14,421,882 67
1875	42,489 19	12,584 62	926,463 33	124,963 29	83,469 42	20,917 93	85,557 14		15,361,382 12
1876	61,407 14	4,890 45	603,819 86	120,843 58	132,042 28	10,274 57	178,096 41		12,833,114 48
1877	50,106 96	9,735 83	435,718 43	1,834 11	68,261 35	12,387 96	178,535 96		12,548,451 09
1878	45,144 82	4,921 33	341,240 58	6,874 10	113,447 24	9,855 02	124,338 17		12,795,693 17
1879	45,107 35	3,230 76	454,872 58	2,591 84	127,283 34	16,597 54	115,349 29		12,939,540 66
1880	41,686 44	3,168 48	1,305,495 00	161,936 81	207,920 61	18,764 19	156,016 88		14,138,849 22
1881	90,250 84	3,251 22	1,584,622 00	280,009 74	348,466 71	33,740 02	311,133 47		18,500,785 97
1882	119,492 16	1,781 73	1,615,945 44	504,255 74	178,499 40	65,780 72	352,318 25		21,708,837 43
1883	106,234 50	7,365 17	1,770,682 99	692,562 12	157,516 29	83,492 95	239,042 13		23,172,308 97
1884	103,953 96	4,158 34	1,397,926 95	688,702 68	273,798 27	56,966 92	265,210 33		20,164,963 37
1885	121,660 61	2,268 61	1,327,363 99	655,708 66	450,153 25	51,863 04	308,698 01		19,133,558 99
1886	132,116 62	2,467 90	1,384,327 91	503,735 53	148,088 67	49,052 66	478,033 91		19,448,123 70
1887	166,445 16	1,624 70	968,496 12	843,562 83	222,799 93	59,393 20	828,686 99		22,469,705 83
1888	117,228 84	3,211 68	1,831,368 64	641,854 29	162,844 61	43,778 82	340,166 62		23,209,641 53
1889	122,116 44	1,087 36	1,727,816 27	849,431 97	185,782 89	38,653 78	845,532 61	7,952 63	23,784,523 23
1890	150,349 40	3,386 14	1,223,589 61	559,312 13	216,956 50	79,331 47	804,400 21	7,089 94	24,014,908 07
1891	126,180 23	3,452 92	1,337,754 14	260,102 71	265,198 43	63,161 46	1,215,178 05	9,190 73	23,481,069 13
1892	104,003 88	4,191 49	272,167 34	75,439 20	273,256 10	49,388 15	201,113 48	20,723 00	20,550,581 53
1893	112,081 99	1,494 56	314,148 32	78,592 25	313,798 23	70,418 15	160,133 95	7,533 96	19,379,822 33
1894	102,178 54	1,623 12	292,464 66	73,489 61	273,712 90	73,695 14	172,318 72	10,108 33	21,161,710 93
1895	93,303 46	1,053 95	380,955 12	68,786 81	230,890 41	72,742 85	231,349 72	14,523 65	17,887,269 47
1896	192,457 64	1,197 81	478,829 02	106,494 83	285,572 02	93,877 02	521,413 34	64,312 97	20,219,037 32
1897	250,770 38	1,274 89	454,418 06	109,914 69	267,575 35	64,153 55	757,363 19	47,439 87	19,891,996 77
1898	287,411 60	1,670 86	304,971 01	209,761 63	291,747 74	91,525 82	328,978 26	*350,715 08	22,157,788 49
1899	663,398 07	1,669 28	374,161 69	97,167 56	349,381 86	156,108 44	414,930 52	109,390 35	25,734,228 75
1900	915,374 13	2,740 46	363,563 81	120,148 16	279,351 20	143,983 86	414,866 20	53,760 91	28,889,110 13
1901	1,081,162 82	1,180 88	471,923 66	205,344 97	341,473 58	159,147 86	416,207 47	43,006 49	29,106,979 89
1902	387,008 06	7,023 17	550,252 39	199,921 53	370,966 45	199,638 08	509,973 06	72,994 33	37,110,354 59
1903	602,178 47	1,914 12	684,985 96	303,880 29	355,971 99	255,250 00	680,547 56	87,773 38	40,954,349 14
1904	444,514 69	2,780 11	1,202,659 24	731,277 80	444,747 26	376,616 33	873,447 83	114,191 98	42,024,339 92
1905	321,677 65	2,435 99	1,184,429 25	501,607 60	489,814 72	469,943 27	982,112 49	229,747 00	46,671,101 18
1906	511,894 66	1,092 68	1,531,148 25	712,435 40	486,583 62	546,901 63	1,070,251 65	233,660 83	40,290,171 70
*1907	261,362 94	1,153 35	692,072 47	809,020 77	376,798 58	415,707 02	977,657 28	163,894 53	58,331,074 04
1908	375,296 31	4,146 91	615,082 44	700,185 39	525,328 90	733,350 11	2,846,353 13	286,708 68	48,059,791 93
1909	357,745 34	2,549 89	1,642,462 43	831,853 03	416,616 80	591,501 16	1,458,936 73	254,912 94	61,024,239 21
1910	520,726 06	8,364 10	1,575,328 09	882,791 71	435,600 94	630,135 47	1,578,994 86	314,531 92	73,312,367 59
1911	539,675 14	3,077 98	1,054,632 33	1,238,183 43	430,014 83	644,991 93	1,829,013 33	376,728 67	87,576,036 52
1912	521,234 65	2,781 43	2,070,708 91	1,100,637 88	451,158 58	718,809 23	2,045,932 94	522,446 97	115,063,687 93
1913	574,815 34	2,781 38	2,370,130 38	1,095,047 81	708,201 11	882,861 51	2,500,478 11	562,016 72	107,180,578 33
1914	618,893 63	4,313 81	2,755,823 67	1,806,369 45	563,856 80	900,781 99	2,123,206 25	586,008 77	79,205,910 27
1915	266,119 46	3,491 70	3,187,995 15		439,642 65	845,898 52	1,933,070 02	3,117,602 10	

*9 months.

SESSIONAL PAPER No. 11

No. 7.—Percentage of Duty on Total Value of Goods imported and entered for
Consumption, Dutiable and Free; and percentage of expenses of collection
of Customs Revenue in the Dominion of Canada, during each year from
1868 to 1915, inclusive.

Year.	Percentage of duty on Total Value of Goods Imported, Dutiable and Free.	Percentage of duty on Total Value of Goods entered for Consumption, Dutiable and Free.	Percentage Expense of Collection of Customs Revenue.
	p.c.	p.c.	p.c.
1868	12·00	12·25	05·99
1869	11·78	12·31	07·09
1870	12·65	13·28	05·41
1871	12·32	13·62	04·21
1872	11·70	12·11	04·04
1873	10·17	10·20	04·35
1874	11·25	11·32	04·55
1875	12·48	12·83	04·44
1876	13·76	13·44	05·61
1877	12·63	13·03	05·75
1878	13·74	14·03	05·58
1879	15·78	16·10	05·56
1880	16·34	19·70	05·04
1881	17·56	20·19	03·87
1882	18·18	19·27	03·33
1883	17·52	18·82	03·26
1884	17·32	18·64	03·96
1885	17·55	18·61	04·14
1886	18·60	19·50	04·10
1887	19·87	21·24	03·64
1888	20·03	21·57	03·81
1889	20·60	21·65	03·62
1890	19·63	21·21	03·63
1891	19·52	20·06	03·83
1892	16·13	17·56	04·39
1893	16·39	17·38	04·26
1894	15·69	17·13	04·75
1895	16·14	16·99	05·13
1896	17·13	18·28	04·43
1897	16·68	17·87	04·75
1898	15·79	16·95	04·37
1899	15·81	16·70	04·02
1900	15·23	15·98	03·71
1901	15·28	16·06	03·86
1902	15·28	15·99	03·62
1903	15·38	15·87	03·31
1904	15·80	16·28	03·31
1905	15·75	16·04	03·49
1906	15·85	16·07	03·31
*1907	15·51	15·66	03·04
1908	15·73	16·27	03·30
1909	15·51	16·11	04·15
1910	15·57	16·24	03·32
1911	15·52	15·87	02·98
1912	15·66	16·00	02·78
1913	16·63	17·03	02·74
1914	16·47	16·91	03·59
†1915	15·92	17·39	04·77

*9 months.   †Exclusive of Coin and Bullion.

6 GEORGE V, A. 1916

No. 8.—COMPARATIVE STATEMENT of the Values of the Imports and Exports into also percentage excess of Imports over Exports

| Fiscal Year. | IMPORTS. | | | | EXPORTS. | | | |
| | Merchandise. | | Coin and Bullion. | Totals. | Merchandise. | | Coin. | Totals. |
	Dutiable.	Free.			Home Produce.	Foreign Produce.		
	$	$	$	$	$	$	$	$
1868....	45,250,395	23,314,102	4,895,147	73,459,644	48,504,899	4,196,821	4,866,168	57,567,888
1869....	44,081,563	22,086,373	4,247,229	70,415,165	52,400,772	3,855,801	4,218,208	60,474,781
1870....	48,665,547	21,813,263	4,335,529	74,814,339	59,043,590	6,527,622	8,002,278	73,573,490
1871....	70,295,223	23,064,654	2,733,094	96,092,971	57,630,024	9,853,244	6,690,350	74,173,618
1872....	72,157,423	36,519,355	2,753,749	111,430,527	65,831,083	12,798,182	4,010,398	82,639,663
1873....	74,217,954	50,787,862	3,005,465	128,011,281	76,538,025	9,405,910	3,845,987	89,789,922
1874....	77,070,460	46,919,840	4,223,282	128,213,582	76,741,997	10,614,096	1,995,835	89,351,928
1875....	81,504,477	39,355,717	2,210,089	123,070,283	69,709,823	7,137,319	1,039,837	77,886,979
1876....	58,794,777	32,195,458	2,220,111	93,210,346	72,491,437	7,234,961	1,240,037	80,966,435
1877....	63,986,376	33,167,497	2,174,089	99,327,962	68,030,546	7,111,108	733,739	75,875,393
1878....	61,700.190	30,577,871	803,726	93,081,787	67,989,800	11,164,878	168,989	79,323,667
1879....	57,052,042	23,273,296	1,639,089	81,964,427	62,431,025	8,355,644	704,586	71,491,255
1880....	68,895,483	15,712,457	1,881,807	86,489,747	72,899,697	13,240,006	1,771,755	87,911,458
1881....	85,516,908	18,690,657	1,123,275	105,330,840	83,944,701	13,375,117	971,005	98,290,823
1882....	93,339,930	24,575,827	1,503,743	119,419,500	94,137,657	7,628,453	371,093	102,137,203
1883....	100,827,816	30,150,683	1,275,523	132,254,022	87,702,431	9,751,773	631,600	98,085,804
1884....	88,349,492	25,839,885	2,207,666	116,397,043	79,833,098	9,389,106	2,184,292	91,406,496
1885....	79,614,108	26,373,134	2,954,244	108,941,486	79,131,735	8,079,646	2,026,980	89,238,361
1886....	75,536,758	25,277,246	3,610,557	104,424,561	77,756,704	7,438,079	56,531	85,251,314
1887....	85,479,400	26,880,618	532,218	112,892,236	80,960,909	8,549,333	5,569	89,515,811
1888....	77,784,037	30,935,121	2,175,472	110,894,630	81,382,072	8,803,394	17,534	90,203,000
1889....	80,059,966	34,589,714	575,251	115,224,931	80,272,456	6,938,455	1,978,256	89,189,167
1890....	86,258,633	34,516,597	1,083,011	121,858,241	85,257,586	9,051,781	2,439,782	96,749,149
.891....	81,286,372	36,870,096	1,811,170	119,967,638	88,671,738	8,798,631	946,927	98,417,296
1892....	81,190,844	44,396,694	1,818,530	127,406,068	99,032,466	13,121,791	1,809,118	113,963,375
1893....	77,378,091	45,161,977	6,534,200	129,074,268	105,488,798	8,941,856	4,133,698	118,564,352
1894....	73,341,506	46,110,362	4,023,072	123,474,940	103,851,764	11,833,805	1,839,380	117,524,949
1895....	64,064,587	42,140,475	4,576,620	110,781,682	102,828,441	6,485,043	4,325,319	113,638,803
1896....	74,229,940	38,525,249	5,226,319	118,011,508	109,707,805	6,606,738	4,699,309	121,013,852
1897....	74,108,590	40,433,825	4,676,194	119,218,609	123,632,540	10,825,163	3,492,550	137,950,253
1898....	84,141,104	51,791,105	4,390,844	140,323,053	144,548,662	14,980,883	4,623,138	164,152,683
1899....	98,349,633	59,709,541	4,705,134	162,764,308	137,360,792	17,520,088	4,016,025	158,896,905
1900....	112,943,896	68,381,179	8,297,438	189,622,513	168,972,301	14,265,254	8,657,168	191,894,723
1901....	115,574,658	71,303,573	3,537,294	190,415,525	177,431,386	17,077,757	1,978,489	196,487,632
1902 ...	127,955,254	78,003,499	6,311,405	212,270,158	196,019,763	13,951,101	1,669,422	211,640,286
1903....	143,839,632	88,398,532	8,976,797	241,214,961	214,401,674	10,828,087	619,963	225,849,724
1904....	156,108,453	95,229,037	7,874,313	259,211,803	198,414,439	12,641,239	2,465,557	213,521,235
1905....	157,164,975	99,361,007	10,308,435	266,834,417	190,854,946	10,617,115	1,844,811	203,316.872
1906....	176,790,332	110,417,080	7,078,603	294,286,015	235,483,956	11,173,846	9,928,828	256,586,630
*1907...	154,856.659	97,412,340	7,517,008	259,786,007	180,545,306	11,541,927	13,189,964	205,277,197,
1908....	230,917,914	133,319,950	6,548,661	370,786,525	246,960,968	16,407,984	16,637,654	280,006,606
1909....	185,329,094	114,439,072	9,988,442	309,756,608	242,603,584	17,318,782	1,589,793	261,512,159
1910....	241,961,556	143,873,547	6,017,589	391,852,692	279,247,551	19,516,442	2,594,536	301,358,529
1911....	291,818,801	170,222,529	10,206,210	472,247,540	274,316,553	15,683,657	7,196,155	297,196,365
1912....	343,370,082	189,916,581	26,033,881	559,320,544	290,223,857	17,492,294	7,601,099	315,317,250
1913....	456,086,187	230,518,226	5,247,979	692,032,392	355,754,600	21,313,755	16,163,702	393,232,057
1914....	425,324,576	210,186,916	15,235,305	650,746,797	431,588,439	23,848,785	23,560,704	478,997,928
1915....	318,951,094	178,500,808	131,992,992	629,444,894	409,418,836	52,023,673	29,366,368	490,808,877

*9 months.

and from the Dominion of Canada in each Fiscal Year from 1868 to 1915; showing or of Exports over Imports in each Year.

Excess Value of Merchandise Imported over.		Excess of total Exports over total Imports, including Coin and Bullion.	Percentage Excess of total Imp'ts over total Exports, including Coin and Bullion.	Percentage Excess of total Exp'ts over total Imports, including Coin and Bullion.	Percentage, Increase or Decrease.			
					Gross Imports compared with preceding year.		Gross Exports compared with preceding year.	
Canadian Merchandise Exported.	Canadian and Foreign Merchandise Exported.				Increase.	D'creas	Increase.	D'creas
$	$	$	p.c.	p.c.	p.c.	p.c.	p.c.	p.c.
20,059,598	15,862,777		27·6					
13,767,164	9,911,363		16·4			04·1	05·05	
11,435,220	4,907,598		01·7		06·2		21·6	
35,729,853	25,876,609		29·5		28·4		00·8	
42,845,695	30,047,513		34·8		15·0		11·4	
48,467,791	39,061,881		32·5		14·9		08·6	
47,248,303	36,634,207		43·5		00·16			00·5
51,150,371	44,013,052		58·0			00·4		12·8
18,498,798	11,263,837		15·1			24·2	03·9	
29,123,327	22,012,219		30·9		06·5			06·3
24,288,261	13,123,383		17·3			06·3	04·5	
17,894,313	9,438,669		14·6			11·9		09·6
11,708,243		1,421,711		01·6	05·5		22·9	
20,262,864	6,887,747		07·1		21·8		11·8	
23,778,100	16,149,647		14·5		13·3		03·9	
43,276,068	33,524,295		28·8		10·7			03·9
34,356,279	24,967,173		21·4			11·9		06·8
26,855,507	18,775,861		18·0			06·4		02·3
23,057,300	15,619,221		18·3			04·1		04·3
31,399,109	22,849,776		20·7		08·1		05·0	
27,337,086	18,533,692		18·6			01·8	00·7	
34,377,224	27,438,769		22·6		03·9			01·1
35,517,644	26,465,863		20·6		05·4		07·8	
29,484,730	20,686,099		17·9			01·5	01·7	
26,555,072	13,433,281		10·5		06·2		16·0	
17,051,270	8,109,414		08·1		01·3		04·0	
15,600,104	3,766,299	2,857,121	04·8			04·3		00·8
3,376,621				02·21	09·95			03·3
3,077,384		3,002,344		02·54	06·14		6·49	
		18,731,644		15·71	01·02		14·00	
		23,829,630		16·98	17·70		18·99	
20,698,382	3,178,294		02·4		16·00			03·2
12,352,774		2,272,210		01·2	14·16		20·77	
9,446,845		6,072,107		03·2	00·42		02·39	
9,938,990			00·3		11·47		07·71	
17,836,490	7,008,403		06·4		13·63		06·29	
52,923,051	40,281,812		21·4		7·46			05·4
65,671,036	55,053,921		31·2		02·94			04·77
51,723,456	40,549,610		14·69		10·29		26·2	
71,723,693	60,181,766							
117,276,796	100,868,912		32·42					
57,164,582	39,845,800		18·44			16·45		06·60
106,587,552	87,071,110		30·03		26·50		15·24	
187,724,777	172,041,120		58·90		20·51			01·04
269,096,687	251,604,393		77·38		18·44		06·09	
330,849,813	309,536,058		75·99		23·73		24·71	
203,923,053	180,074,268		35·86			05·97	21·81	
88,033,066	36,009,393		28·25			03·27	02·47	

No. 9.—COMPARATIVE STATEMENT showing the Tonnage of all Vessels entered Inwards and. Outwards in the Dominion of Canada, during each Fiscal Year, from 1868 to 1915, inclusive.

NAVIGATION.

Fiscal Year.	Tonnage of Vessels built.	Tonnage of Vessels registered.	Tonnage of Vessels entered Inwards and Outwards (Sea-going and Inland Navigation exclusive of Coasting).	Tonnage of Vessels employed in the Coasting Trade entered Inwards and Outwards.	Tonnage and value of vessels sold to other countries.	
					Tonnage.	Value.
	Tons.	Tons.	Tons.	Tons.	Tons.	$
1868	87,230	113,692	12,982,825			
1869	96,439	125,408	10,461,044			
1870	93,166	110,852	11,415,870			
1871	106,101	121,724	13,126 028			
1872	114,065	127,371	12,808,160			
1873	140,370	152,226	11,748,997			
1874	174,404	163,016	11,399,857			
1875	188,098	204,002	9,537,155			
1876	165,041	144,422	9,911,199	10,300,939	64,134	2,189,270
1877	127,297	126,160	11,091,244	8,968,862	46,329	1,576,244
1878	106,976	100,089	12,054,890	11,047,661	35,039	1,218,145
1879	103,551	94,882	11,646,812	12,066,683	19,318	529,824
1880	68,756	64,982	13,577,845	14,053,013	16;208	464,327
1881	79,364	70,210	13,802,432	15,116,766	16,808	348,018
1882	68,240	78,076	13,379,882	14,791,064	16,161	402,311
1883	73,576	78,229	13,770,735	15,683,566	23,896	506,538
1884	70,287	80,822	14,359,026	15,473,707	17,368	416,756
1885	57,486	65,962	14,084,712	15,944,422	13,177	246,977
1886	37,531	40,872	13,969,232	16,368,274	14,343	266,363
1887	26,798	67,662	14,090,998	17,513,677	9,263	143,772
1888	22,698	33,298	15,217,308	18,789,279	14,479	289,969
1889	23,835	31,998	16,054,221	19,834,577	16,173	266,817
1890	39,434	53,853	18,446,100	22,797,115	22,844	442,781

SESSIONAL PAPER No. 11

No. 9.—COMPARATIVE STATEMENT showing the Tonnage of all Vessels entered Inwards and Outwards., etc.—*Concluded.*

NAVIGATION.

Fiscal Year.	Tonnage of Vessels built.	Tonnage of Vessels registered.	Tonnage of Vessels entered Inwards and Outwards (Sea-going and Inland Navigation exclusive of Coasting).	Tonnage of Vessels employed in the Coasting Trade entered Inwards and Outwards.	Tonnage and value of vessels sold to other countries.	
					Tonnage.	Value.
	Tons.	Tons.	Tons.	Tons.	Tons.	$
1891	55,477	52,506	18,303,648	24,694,580	15,143	280,474
1892	44,321	61,457	18,692,455	24,783,844	36,399	506,747
1893	38,521	45,796	18,539,534	24,579,123	31,317	363,916
1894	23,497	29,878	20,353,081	26,560,968	21,960	243,429
1895	18,728	26,125	19,100,963	25,473,434	16,567	172,563
1896	10,753	14,144	21,870,473	27,431,753	12,203	99,392
1897	12,058	22,959	23,373,933	27,267,979	9,158	105,164
1898	22,426	27,716	24,746,116	29,663,950	17,210	191,069
1899	22,085	28,257	25,420,110	30,212,496	7,562	126,466
1900	28,544	40,443	26,914,095	33,631,730	13,354	205,618
1901	20,156	35,156	26,029,808	34,444,796	4,490	66,468
1902	28,288	34,236	30,025,404	40,700,907	11,360	235,865
1903	30,856	41,405	33,655,043	44,990,358	11,172	220,602
1904	28,397	33,192	31,202,205	45,505,122	7,208	87,115
1905	21,865	27,583	32,277,820	44,377,261	3,696	100,363
1906	18,724	37,639	34,732,172	46,324,062	9,487	187,725
*1907	33,205	31,635	30,595,891	31,691,420	3,855	68,190
1908	49,928	78,144	39,575,031	50,529,835	4,515	132,900
1909	29,023	32,899	40,701,603	52,670,198	3,644	98,643
1910	24,059	33,383	44,567,991	56,750,928	5,047	133 800
1911	22 812	50 006	47 429,545	66,627,934	5,885	201,526
1912	31,065	30,021	52,973,127	66,267,662	4,265	140,350
1913	24,325	30,225	57,849,783	73,644,713	7,976	610,650
1914	46,887	46,909	61,919,483	78,356,809	8,258	169,618
1915	45·721	55,384	53,604,153	73,099,982	17,044	1,150,950

*9 months.

6 GEORGE V, A. 1916

No. 10.—STATEMENT (by Provinces) of the Values of Exports, of Total Imports, Port in the Dominion of Canada during the Fiscal

PROVINCE OF

| Number. | Ports. | Fiscal Year ended March 31, 1913. | | | | Fiscal |
		Exports.	Imports.	Entered for Consumption.	Duty.	Exports.
		$	$	$	$ cts.	$
1	Amherstburg	431,665	553,812	511,642	80,755 89	463,033
2	Belleville	572	1,185,703	1,186,524	140,407 02	190
3	Berlin		4,555,989	4,534,428	407,880 65	
4	Bowmanville		1,429,979	1,429,979	101,345 31	
5	Brantford		4,608,537	4,595,135	679,266 59	
6	Bridgeburg	16,306,556	2,904,452	2,839,457	634,300 78	20,584,103
7	Brockville	94,170	946,483	948,035	131,343 76	184,981
8	Chatham	36,051	2,078,380	1,956,472	355,237 73	9,975
9	Cobourg	244,921	1,202,796	1,069,708	177,607 18	424,147
10	Collingwood		1,457,290	1,453,417	85,419 82	
11	Cornwall	1,509,344	1,538,407	1,538,407	79,412 93	2,767,760
12	Deseronto	41,198	260,185	260,185	19,433 25	12,710
13	Fort William	41,325,154	14,002,930	13,200,524	2,064,383 61	62,098,116
14	Galt		3,199,375	3,199,375	340,165 06	
15	Gananoque	11,531	531,770	531,770	70,648 83	41,463
16	Goderich		975,883	953,862	110,370 73	
17	Guelph		2,484,117	2,484,117	247,267 94	
18	Hamilton	1,767	25,439,203	25,199,359	3,509,763 25	1,631
19	Ingersoll	114	1,203,206	1,211,795	210,379 79	10,219
20	Kenora	24,976	485,878	483,517	44,955 99	35,624
21	Kingston	211,851	3,226,867	3,222,312	369,173 36	288,112
22	Lindsay		410,796	410,796	39,811 43	
23	London		10,770,565	10,727,465	1,303,534 00	
24	Midland	212,646	2,093,314	2,021,537	91,339 18	307,409
25	Morrisburg	26,208	139,007	138,707	10,725 47	81,729
26	Napanee		259,738	259,738	24,534 10	
27	Niagara Falls	23,289,370	3,557,568	3,552,242	539,245 29	24,293,037
28	North Bay		3,357,709	3,358,581	495,699 79	
29	Orillia		5,065,914	5,065,914	156,936 83	
30	Oshawa		2,568,225	2,566,658	376,799 24	
31	Ottawa	24,423	10,479,417	10,394,593	1,819,162 87	5,002
32	Owen Sound	16,868	864,374	871,116	77,977 54	4
33	Paris		1,063,141	1,063,141	75,697 09	
34	Parry Sound	241,289	1,255,487	1,085,603	250,070 63	
35	Peterborough		4,522,645	3,900,148	478,884 87	
36	Picton	1,502	192,015	191,726	23,071 91	6,198
37	Port Arthur	18,965,466	6,323,499	6,149,848	887,293 45	38,282,894
38	Port Hope		401,266	401,266	38,837 44	100
39	Port McNicholl	118,974	77,592	78,769	11,687 38	122,357
40	Prescott	8,624,858	2,022,003	2,027,611	208,022 88	9,177,805
41	St. Catharines	40,934	4,534,920	4,533,101	662,371 35	59,863
42	St. Thomas		2,267,970	2,226,475	380,455 53	
43	Sarnia	5,622,710	6,323,222	6,160,799	539,296 57	8,569,528
44	Sault Ste. Marie	7,373,465	7,726,949	7,215,177	1,122,953 40	8,180,663
45	Simcoe	6,610	965,365	955,769	64,124 48	15,676
46	Stratford		2,136,350	2,136,097	237,499 86	
47	Sudbury					
48	Tillsonburg		298,914	298,914	37,843 44	
49	Toronto	57,683	121,099,797	119,923,722	20,243,662 83	1,235
50	Trenton		308,273	307,580	49,551 59	
51	Wallaceburg	6,872	2,050,951	2,050,791	319,784 80	5,938
52	Welland		4,574,789	4,574,789	362,603 77	
53	Whitby		185,504	185,504	11,561 88	
54	Windsor	7,886 784	18,321,437	18,387,260	3,915,835 62	10,379,341
55	Woodstock		1,161,370	1,161,370	92,195 22	
	Total	132,756,532	301,651,328	297,192,227	44,808,591 20	186,410,843

of Imports entered for Consumption and of the Amount of Duty Collected at each Years ended March 31, 1913, 1914, and 1915.

ONTARIO.

Imports.	Entered for Consumption.	Duty.		Exports.	Imports.	Entered for Consumption.	Duty.		Number.
	Year ended March 31, 1914.				Fiscal Year ended March 31, 1915.				
$	$	$	cts.	$	$	$	$	cts.	
726,971	701,049	103,737	25	803,030	533,640	518,348	69,767	80	1
1,067,240	1,068,897	134,900	51	1,113	935,260	928,060	107,464	54	2
4,207,368	4,218,827	451,787	73	....	4,876,219	4,903,060	430,477	75	3
934,569	934,569	44,490	76	....	674,967	674,967	51,156	37	4
4,381,364	4,386,005	647,487	96	....	2,977,624	2,988,427	395,863	30	5
3,686,333	3,400,069	742,170	11	26,184,656	3,215,522	3,183,439	654,704	04	6
964,297	953,143	125,564	15	128,954	695,024	703,688	90,565	45	7
2,127,211	1,916,544	337,587	47	2,486	1,741,433	1,647,140	330,387	54	8
1,111,065	1,133,352	201,707	90	634,072	689,252	774,506	112,187	91	9
987,066	984,107	51,139	19	....	557,471	555,574	39,935	56	10
1,456,049	1,456,049	116,740	58	27,390,253	1,537,940	1,525,940	250,811	38	11
202,986	202,986	11,885	00	41,064	64,351	64,351	4,338	63	12
13,225,046	12,140,050	1,890,319	11	20,295,564	5,564,514	6,014,815	745,216	68	13
3,123,371	3,123,365	331,677	35	....	2,376,154	2,375,927	222,043	89	14
507,319	507,319	65,260	48	31,784	388,622	388,622	42,775	04	15
873,347	865,557	104,053	77	142,737	872,838	872,776	101,984	25	16
2,327,592	2,324,245	238,254	66	....	1,539,454	1,539,454	174,995	25	17
23,670,555	23,482,870	3,410,242	95	871	15,749,530	15,896,238	2,459,169	98	18
1,511,566	1,514,018	271,083	54	24,739	1,074,451	1,067,924	173,190	72	19
130,384	129,115	34,474	76	42,833	69,078	71,321	19,981	89	20
2,655,792	2,634,432	293,199	65	213,996	1,959,048	1,966,604	211,058	99	21
375,003	375,003	38,014	47	....	432,803	432,803	32,139	41	22
9,677,796	9,551,293	1,318,484	34	....	8,103,687	8,037,709	1,011,353	10	23
1,277,196	1,356,127	137,667	82	317,301	1,527,236	1,497,157	141,510	71	24
113,236	113,236	8,253	97	67,347	107,065	107,065	4,539	76	25
205,623	205,623	19,526	06	....	186,209	186,209	11,682	30	26
3,732,985	3,728,233	556,465	80	29,955,392	2,635,605	2,630,719	294,652	67	27
2,029,145	2,027,282	319,433	36	....	2,063,958	2,061,100	403,710	33	28
3,697,181	3,697,181	86,585	35	....	4,787,483	4,787,483	127,958	07	29
1,945,433	1,914,299	257,054	70	....	2,045,690	2,076,365	344,847	97	30
10,033,627	10,020,886	1,855,575	82	71,988	130,473,783	130,472,681	1,515,599	72	31
784,637	788,071	58,914	83	56	548,631	555,685	47,426	45	32
1,171,460	1,171,310	96,938	16	....	797,432	800,666	44,388	76	33
1,903,454	1,744,647	377,464	47	580,561	1,231,184	1,158,004	230,047	64	34
3,019,555	3,032,122	468,172	39	....	3,246,435	3,232,348	409,016	37	35
167,392	167,804	20,046	46	402	135,843	133,097	15,157	62	36
7,242,599	6,680,215	1,043,465	26	23,009,332	4,109,587	3,927,924	615,631	40	37
280,535	289,535	26,489	05	....	235,678	235,678	22,031	98	38
73,866	79,173	6,423	83	118,398	42,061	59,919	1,777	07	39
2,407,044	2,347,962	245,548	94	8,153,486	1,606,322	1,589,522	147,592	05	40
4,968,843	4,884,053	761,039	77	363,577	5,449,823	5,485,809	776,118	32	41
2,362,538	2,377,112	468,032	61	110,311	1,706,076	1,712,454	362,621	18	42
6,994,844	6,923,776	605,834	58	10,688,948	5,071,232	5,145,476	365,237	05	43
5,740,216	5,937,117	737,661	14	7,428,232	3,702,679	3,812,928	554,296	00	44
882,010	880,576	57,464	90	10,649	712,178	709,613	56,120	93	45
1,912,366	1,911,860	221,825	93	....	1,591,285	1,576,085	205,363	27	46
1,813,107	1,806,696	274,844	17	....	995,019	990,486	132,375	90	47
217,434	217,434	30,533	93	....	198,714	198,714	28,954	92	48
119,150,282	118,308,642	19,924,464	89	190,230	96,129,026	94,698,903	15,806,033	97	49
411,800	411,800	43,159	87	....	200,784	200,876	19,509	09	50
1,824,074	1,824,074	364,955	41	14,373	1,988,407	1,988,407	586,063	40	51
5,459,715	5,428,241	493,367	21	35,000	4,303,038	4,299,138	281,930	67	52
183,775	183,775	13,241	14	....	238,300	238,300	13,753	36	53
17,668,183	17,516,574	3,753,650	07	10,631,875	10,198,835	10,122,965	1,834,351	58	54
1,033,990	1,033,990	108,273	48	....	870,528	870,418	86,890	90	55
290,647,435	287,012,290	44,406,539	06	167,685,610	345,765,008	344,693,885	33,218,760	88	

No. 10.—STATEMENT of the Value of Exports·

PROVINCE

Number.	Ports.	Fiscal Year ended March 31, 1913.				Fiscal
		Exports.	Imports.	Entered for Consumption.	Duty.	Exports.
		$	$	$	$ cts.	$
1	Abercorn........................	4,969,633	156,389	156,389	20,370 36	5,263,077
2	Athelstan.......................	4,355,034	1,175,588	1,175,588	55,680 49	5,000,268
3	Beebe Junction.................	4,634,932	1,371,189	1,367,764	138,914 57	4,277,214
4	Coaticook.......................	12,050,030	288,491	288,491	29,525 58	14,627,734
5	Cookshire....·.................	506,192	133,275	132,650	14,721 09	1,128,837
6	Gaspe..........................	168,099	21,206	22,151	5,336 33	118,190
7	Hemmingford....................	8,546	39,274	39,274	2,855 88	25,266
8	Highwater.......·.............	1,232	17,199	17,199	3,703 87	313
9	Hull...........................	....	661,152	630,115	66,943 96	....
10	Mansonville....................	122,383	7,814	7,814	936 85	118,729
11	Montreal.......................	85,080,238	155,909,428	145,629,791	25,655,340 42	99,238,107
12	Paspebiac......................	264,051	82,908	82,965	11,459 04	359,276
13	Perce..........................	120,901	12,990	12,990	786 70	143,265
14	Port Burwell...................	....	....	....	....	....
15	Quebec....·.................	8,592,177	14,778,587	14,719,547	2,181,736 67	9,603,192
16	Rimouski.......................	....	55,465	55,465	8,275 90	....
17	Saint Armand..................	2,995,508	113,835	113,515	10,094 12	3,682,997
18	Saint Hyacinthe................	....	784,434	791,368	75,857 32	....
19	Saint Johns....................	23,854,951	3,889,664	3,888,314	301,678 37	33,654,297
20	Sherbrooke.....................	....	2,328,298	2,332,061	401,925 36	....
21	Sorel..........................	....	252,151	253,074	45,487 73	77,838
22	Three Rivers...................	....	3,674,352	3,677,676	362,279 94	238,184
23	Valleyfield....................	....	1,547,804	1,558,835	137,604 68	....
	Total...................	147,723,907	187,301,493	176,953,036	29,531,515 25	177,556,784

and Imports at each Port, etc.—*Continued.*

OF QUEBEC.

Year ended March 31, 1914.			Fiscal Year ended March 31, 1915.				
Imports.	Entered for Con- sumption.	Duty.	Exports.	Imports.	Entered for Con- sumption.	Duty.	Number.
$	$	$ cts.	$	$	$	$ cts.	
169,115	169,115	23,036 90	5,494,836	116,390	116,390	14,995 36	1
1,091,517	1,091,217	67,069 67	4,699,421	1,176,140	1,176,140	44,901 13	2
1,605,568	1,595,599	189,238 86	4,182,297	846,321	846,518	112,425 09	3
340,106	340,106	33,695 36	18,857,500	231,870	229,120	19,366 40	4
137,490	137,165	15,616 36	544,125	198,822	198,347	31,576 80	5
28,946	29,699	4,690 88	336,541	41,709	41,916	10,399 43	6
29,894	29,894	3,113 93	56,380	41,760	41,760	2,833 37	7
9,037	9,037	1,093 10	140,969	211,987	211,987	2,606 10	8
758,570	755,302	75,848 11	....	802,089	798,160	72,665 15	9
14,113	14,113	1,671 42	91,792	15,724	15,724	1,766 31	10
152,635,805	141,728,705	24,732,198 57	119,349,025	141,189,498	102,198,355	19,420,723 12	11
63,804	63,916	8,572 47	287,962	52,943	52,999	7,435 35	12
79,524	79,524	19,481 90	144,985	334,815	334,815	77,836 42	13
5,558	5,558	1,102 74	....	21,231	21,231	2,368 52	14
14,623,364	14,599,652	2,176,822 18	7,310,185	11,782,355	11,801,600	1,859,600 30	15
56,221	56,254	9,611 38	....	58,118	58,118	9,401 92	16
181,498	181,011	15,781 39	3,536,116	218,055	218,055	13,069 63	17
850,158	851,125	87,398 25	....	760,887	776,993	82,871 77	18
3,787,993	3,790,721	289,331 75	16,729,078	3,480,145	3,484,371	228,207 48	19
2,311,855	2,307,726	422,686 64	....	2,181,381	2,162,617	304,687 21	20
331,283	333,019	47,082 54	40,806	222,692	224,235	42,546 19	21
4,239,222	4,244,186	458,501 22	180 736	3,227,153	3,228,268	286,693 02	22
1,977,629	1,976,704	169,753 24	....	1,752,926	1,750,917	270,089 08	23
185,328,270	174,389,348	28,853,398 86	181,982,754	168,965,016	129,988,636	22,919 065 15	

6 GEORGE V, A. 1916

No. 10.—STATEMENT of the Value of Exports

PROVINCE OF

Number.	Ports.	Fiscal Year ended March 31, 1913.				Fiscal
		Exports.	Imports.	Entered for Consumption.	Duty.	Exports.
		$	$	$	$ cts.	$
1	Amherst	404,168	1,268,728	1,269,333	154,826 21	447,250
2	Annapolis	342,542	116,769	117,319	9,478 30	219,246
3	Antigonish	6,057	34,558	34,558	5,346 01	....
4	Arichat	....	10,719	11,860	2,410 14	....
5	Baddeck	39,504	8,771	8,771	1,569 39	43,303
6	Barrington Passage	11,485	20,368	20,368	915 48	53,568
7	Bridgewater	637,497	52,789	53,754	7,701 90	875,220
8	Canso	172,465	33,013	33,023	3,138 76	118,582
9	Digby	141,843	53,206	53,206	6,740 00	180,827
10	Glace Bay	2,946	318,382	318,559	63,137 72	1,012
11	Halifax	15,173,250	12,404,055	12,196,236	2,197,805 00	19,157,170
12	Kentville	37,828	215,055	215,179	36,642 81	37,214
13	Liverpool	209,925	56,950	57,575	10,020 99	239,196
14	Lockeport	24,073	15,266	15,300	1,309 82	27,633
15	Lunenburg	442,664	167,099	182,098	11,377 20	516,017
16	Middleton	....	21,857	21,867	3,685 01	....
17	New Glasgow	....	769,797	770,494	129,262 72	....
18	North Sydney	1,240,250	715,536	722,003	121,875 20	1,404,454
19	Parrsboro'	667,803	4,180	4,312	640 07	563,498
20	Pictou	....	305,355	305,355	12,871 88	45,000
21	Port Hawkesbury	142,910	23,072	21,881	5,127 80	133,309
22	Port Hood	301	23,277	23,475	3,993 05	2
23	Shelburne	81,801	16,406	16,449	1,968 26	44,936
24	Sydney	1,590,283	2,426,819	2,427,718	287,788 58	1,179,323
25	Truro	....	581,674	579,675	82,679 09	....
26	Weymouth	217,684	19,995	20,412	2,299 76	248,811
27	Windsor	705,998	159,826	159,965	14,183 72	642,715
28	Yarmouth	1,908,196	909,797	908,465	86,583 27	1,803,083
	Total	24,201,473	20,753,369	20,569,210	3,265,378 14	27,981,369

PROVINCE OF

Number.	Ports.	Exports.	Imports.	Entered for Consumption.	Duty.	Exports.
1	Bathurst	....	86,604	84,337	34,243 14	134,264
2	Campbellton	934,014	75,713	76,449	12,061 76	1,200,717
3	Chatham	1,320,297	151,452	151,452	11,257 99	1,436,210
4	Dalhousie	489,225	19,643	19,941	3,557 01	549,884
5	Fredericton	12,179	799,839	793,537	85,587 36	....
6	McAdam Junction	4,349,936	254,728	250,639	56,247 89	4,807,090
7	Moncton	496,379	911,030	908,891	113,165 05	639,405
8	Newcastle	795,523	60,006	60,037	8,087 38	662,117
9	Sackville	122,220	110,086	110,086	14,162 01	162,560
10	St. Andrews	173,688	296,655	297,363	47,790 36	97,056
11	St. John	25,594,721	9,873,026	9,845,221	1,752,692 27	21,359,760
12	St. Stephen	200,346	1,186,368	1,186,192	62,490 02	216,326
13	Woodstock	145,628	620,661	626,261	91,904 10	186,416
	Total	34,634,156	14,445,811	14,410,406	2,303,246 34	31,451,805

SESSIONAL PAPER No. 11

and Imports at each Port, etc.—*Continued*.

NOVA SCOTIA.

	Year ended March 31, 1914.			Fiscal Year ended March 31, 1915.			Number
Imports.	Entered for Consumption.	Duty.	Exports.	Imports.	Entered for Consumption.	Duty.	
$	$	$ cts.	$	$	$	$ cts.	
1,062,304	1,062,585	150,198 58	395,582	414,935	414,935	68,979 26	1
60,138	60,409	4,917 09	46,323	39,929	39,879	4,214 70	2
41,899	41,899	4,933 89	....	21,190	21,190	4,234 13	3
5,412	6,277	438 06	....	5,571	6,614	585 80	4
6,639	6,639	1,070 07	91,068	18,884	18,884	3,590 96	5
16,070	16,070	1.453 17	60,929	28,866	28,866	2,042 91	6
66,133	67,453	13,085 43	689,416	58,281	59,312	9,787 46	7
43,528	43,314	4,424 38	64,227	39,887	39,567	5,545 61	8
53,751	53,742	6,541 96	179,732	46,294	46,267	6,364 66	9
316,202	316,805	73,384 17	2,260	134,834	135,287	37,552 57	10
12,139,606	11,546,554	2,222,171 24	17,247,719	10,712,585	10,709,544	2,224,024 23	11
153,938	154,117	21,265 95	92,896	208,590	208,674	21,788 80	12
55,278	55,698	9,322 58	172,164	59,395	59,770	6,287 49	13
14,806	14,892	1,251 53	35,056	24,390	24,506	1,308 39	14
172,773	175,764	10,395 80	396,849	147,051	153,862	8,068 87	15
26,236	26,296	4,386 79	....	21,489	21,489	2,373 84	16
1,302,819	1,303,215	190,405 50	....	461,986	461,986	87,243 90	17
801,543	807,537	120,320 95	1,530,799	505,160	510,568	93,610 24	18
6,842	6,918	838 33	839,996	2,764	2,807	703 98	19
339,681	339,681	12,362 55	117,872	417,000	417,000	13,660 45	20
37,943	37,952	8,870 14	164,376	12,835	11,892	2,788 95	21
49,119	49,295	12,815 03	4,847	15,205	15,205	2,820 29	22
12,411	12,517	1,641 04	72,572	17,689	17,828	2,308 42	23
2,436,627	2,435,819	249,907 34	4,783,717	1,458,027	1,372,580	167,483 48	24
659,049	659,148	102,221 13	19,293	664,630	664,630	77,988 49	25
21,878	22,052	3,095 88	207,551	26,460	26,708	3,009 24	26
254,883	254,969	14,829 23	566,182	184,101	184,175	12,745 80	27
1,100,717	1,101,646	77,422 90	1,931,192	579,758	583,280	58,892 28	28
21,258,225	20,679,263	3,323,970 71	29,712,618	16,327,786	16,257,305	2,930,005 20	

NEW BRUNSWICK.

94,737	99,355	41,520 66	415,613	225,976	227,552	67,043 77	1
110,251	110,606	16,009 78	830,118	78,696	80,841	29,031 69	2
254,008	253,803	27,037 20	987,911	111,834	111,834	10,896 20	3
16,303	16,464	2,999 65	420,713	11,773	12,005	5,241 39	4
836,347	836,347	75,421 50	....	592,897	592,889	69,754 88	5
98,807	98,807	12,716 59	5,391,834	69,488	69,488	9,920 28	6
1,054,034	1,054,186	111,080 70	617,985	780,845	780,859	91,382 69	7
175,006	175,021	28,503 33	852,163	44,812	44,861	7,872 05	8
130,108	130,108	10,390 04	21,522	117,968	117,968	11,160 78	9
130,047	130,047	18,594 72	348,058	132,340	132,340	12,015 01	10
9,433,220	9,373,675	1,668,664 02	43,872,932	9,112,916	8,847,049	1,670,957 65	11
1,326,092	1,326,269	54,649 93	369,921	1,063,557	1,063,557	59,031 15	12
725,599	740,117	142,556 54	193,720	640,267	655,465	118,463 14	13
14,384,559	14,344,805	2,210,144 66	54,322,490	12,983,369	12,736,708	2,162,770 68	

6 GEORGE V, A. 1916

No. 10.—STATEMENT of the Value of Exports

PROVINCE OF

Number.	Ports.	Fiscal Year ended March 31, 1913.				Fiscal
		Exports.	Imports.	Entered for Consumption.	Duty.	Exports.
		$	$	$	$ cts.	$
1	Abbotsford......................	3,122,511	1,107,709	1,057,713	97,885 84	4,537,052
2	Cranbrook.....................	736,711	654,111	599,396	93,062 79	733,558
3	Fernie.......................	1,804,174	522,737	523,871	106,047 05	1,682,030
4	Grand Forks..., ...	2,997,849	697,235	697,235	74,585 26	3,071,512
5	Greenwood.....................	800,928	657,297	660,268	84,488 67	792,564
6	Nanaimo.......................	2,597,900	901,747	905,830	162,152 54	1,325,064
7	Nelson........................	16,463	723,266	723,048	157,014 22	24,599
8	New Westminster................	2,065,457	3,098,617	2,960,199	633,826 90	2,916,865
9	Prince Rupert...................	121,213	720,656	735,164	131,163 33	30,344
10	Revelstoke......................	....	1,007,939	1,036,748	260,330 87	....
11	Rossland......................	368,771	649,622	652,636	57,780 12	173,777
12	Vancouver.....................	11,077,421	44,361,962	43,475,412	9,286,661 74	17,058,893
13	Victoria.......................	1,377,971	11,493,581	11,409,033	2,618,025 13	1,572,001
	Total.....................	27,087,369	66,596,479	65,436,553	13,763,024 46	33,918,259

PROVINCE OF

Number	Ports					
1	Brandon........................	37,756	2,133,064	2,082,474	409,720 66	1,076,931
2	Emerson........................	4,591,968	3,902,363	3,901,350	736,845 70	6,958,131
3	Gretna.........................	263,015	568,537	564,537	52,503 63	972,363
4	Portage la Prairie................	....	1,121,942	1,104,397	200,403 79	....
5	Winnipeg.......................	366,697	51,172,378	50,928,829	11,075,636 34	59,584
	Total.....................	5,259,436	58,898,284	58,581,587	12,475,110 12	9,067,009

PROVINCE OF

Number	Ports					
1	Charlottetown...................	536,496	741,130	743,446	118,589 52	549,381
2	Summerside.....................	36,582	234,553	234,609	28,856 28	24,247
	Total.....................	573,078	975,683	978,055	147,445 80	573,628

PROVINCE OF

Number	Ports					
1	Calgary........................	....	11,542,937	11,492,877	2,801,072 55	....
2	Edmonton......................	....	6,881,998	6,838,102	1,682,971 27	....
3	Lethbridge.....................	162,171	2,653,844	2,593,925	486,715 13	283,359
4	Medicine Hat...................	....	....	....	....	....
	Total.....................	162,171	21,078,779	20,924,904	4,970,758 95	283,359

and Imports, at each Port, etc.—*Continued.*

BRITISH COLUMBIA.

Year ended March 31, 1914.			Fiscal Year ended March 31, 1915.				
Imports.	Entered for Consumption.	Duty.	Exports.	Imports.	Entered for Consumption.	Duty.	Number.
$	$	$ cts.	$	$	$	$ cts.	
681,987	681,987	58,070 91	6,262,577	214,187	214,387	26,481 22	1
521,883	487,920	71,442 37	723,497	222,747	227,165	33,791 53	2
793,694	796,041	187,990 84	1,308,382	247,778	244,148	56,754 97	3
724,941	724,941	61,127 50	1,417,884	332,423	332,396	55,612 76	4
781,669	785,437	65,633 54	703,161	400,669	404,797	53,324 85	5
941,923	935,995	151,983 24	2,101,615	425,059	432,971	104,815 53	6
663,418	665,787	155,272 62	61.915	398,707	372,194	96,033 07	7
2,107,040	1,938,375	450,855 72	2,684,932	1,555,199	850,960	196,213 43	8
1,524,040	1,530,499	314,674 18	1,552,115	757,111	761,174	156,663 24	9
1,081,700	1,117,313	302,525 49	....	479,972	503,582	151,496 41	10
748,172	753,245	60,618 66	105,916	604,088	604,866	54,122 36	11
38,411 379	37,628,156	7,470,044 55	15,172,233	25,705,360	25,055,487	5,146,896 89	12
8,940,635	8,819,275	2,016,683 47	1,532,782	4,879,780	4,972,708	1,240,893 55	13
57,922,481	56,864,971	11,366,923 15	33,627,009	36,223,080	34,976,835	7,373,099 81	

MANITOBA.

1,935,458	1,894,182	330,674 25	1,026,891	1,302,744	1,306,775	236,765 31	1
1,588,093	1,216,653	49,716 73	8,889,233	1,142,548	792,548	22,136 93	2
431,168	427,168	44,749 94	1,058,975	216,064	216,064	19,096 94	3
765,383	786,906	119,232 85	....	545,632	531,408	77,632 12	4
41,733,292	41,414,842	9,202,391 20	583,366	26,640,659	26,601,723	6,057.957 92	5
46,453,394	45,739,751	9,746,764 97	11,558,465	29,847,647	29,448,519	6,413,589 22	

PRINCE EDWARD ISLAND.

757,951	750,248	135,660 27	507,543	719,379	716,004	127,522 66	1
256,319	256,319	33,529 74	34,544	214,463	214,463	32,703 03	2
1,014,270	1,006,567	169,190,01	542,087	933,842	930,467	160,225 69	

ALBERTA.

9,203,423	9,205,219	2,209,616 31	....	4,672,686	4,690,106	1,168,112 75	1
7,365,010	7,379,717	1,780,360 73	....	3,798,375	3,770,907	1,000,574 91	2
1,739,401	1,745,329	338,426 86	469,183	1,013,196	1,019,613	199,632 26	3
....	....	....	....	469,038	472,420	116,618 85	4
18,307,834	18,330,265	4,328,403 90	469,183	9,953,295	9,953,046	2,484,938 77	

No. 10.—STATEMENT of the Value of Exports

PROVINCE OF

| Number. | Ports. | Fiscal Year ended March 31, 1913. | | | | Fiscal |
		Exports.	Imports.	Entered for Consumption.	Duty.	Exports.
		$	$	$	$ cts.	$
1	Moosejaw........................	....	4,649,577	4,768,218	925,008 14	....
2	North Portal....................	17,153,688	2,642,140	2,642,395	160,208 04	8,111,337
3	Prince Albert....................	....	....	....	....	....
4	Regina..........................	....	5,175,767	5,185,323	1,117,052 74	....
5	Saskatoon.......................	....	6,543,521	6,542,571	1,408,761 78	....
	Total........................	17,153,688	19,011,005	19,138,507	3,611,030 70	8,111,337

YU

1	Dawson.........................	134,612	1,017,661	1,029,937	121,098 92	34,431
2	Whitehorse......................	3,545,635	213,623	213,746	41,956 04	3,609,104
	Total........................	3,630,247	1,231,284	1,243,683	163,054 96	3,643,535

TERRI

| 1 | Fullerton........................ | .... | .... | .... | .... | .... |
| | Total........................ | .... | .... | .... | .... | .... |

and Imports, at each Port, etc.—*Concluded.*

SASKATCHEWAN.

| Year ended March 31, 1914. | | | Fiscal Year ended March 31, 1915. | | | | |
Imports.	Entered for Consumption.	Duty.	Exports.	Imports.	Entered for Consumption.	Duty.	Number.
$	$	$ cts.	$	$	$	$ cts.	
2,625,210	2,628,707	506,860 58	....	1,825,992	1,829,923	371,181 97	1
2,509,142	2,509,970	155,263 86	7,057,324	1,351,147	1,352,169	75,957 21	2
....	....	....	....	222,138	226,273	66,014 67	3
4,559,079	4,518,704	996,818 85	128,033	2,195,036	2,193,464	482,068 60	4
4,574,586	4,519,416	884,363 39	....	1,956,104	1,940,339	361,122 92	5
14,268,017	14,176,797	2,543,306 68	7,185,357	7,550,417	7,542,168	1,356,345 37	

KON.

Imports.	Entered for Consumption.	Duty.	Exports.	Imports.	Entered for Consumption.	Duty.	Number.
810,658	796,738	152,481 79	18,170	664,000	680,302	131,719 02	1
223,384	223,384	43,521 26	3,705,134	156,493	156,493	33,001 85	2
1,034,042	1,020,122	196,003 05	3,723,304	820,493	836,795	164,720 87	

TORIES.

Imports.	Entered for Consumption.	Duty.	Exports.	Imports.	Entered for Consumption.	Duty.	Number.
....	....	....	....	....	....	1,126 17	1
....	....	....	....	....	....	1,126 17	

6 GEORGE V, A. 1916

No. 10.—STATEMENT (by Provinces) showing the Value of Exports, of Total
collected by the Dominion of Canada during the

Number.	PROVINCES.	Fiscal Year ended March 31, 1913.				Fiscal
		Exports.	Imports.	Entered for Consumption.	Duty.	Exports.
		$	$	$	$ cts.	$
1	Ontario.............................	132,756,532	301,651,328	297,192,227	44,808,591 20	186,410,843
2	Quebec.............................	147,723,907	187,301,493	176,953,036	29,531,515 25	177,556,784
3	Nova Scotia......................	24,201,473	20,753,369	· 20,569,210	3,265,378 14	27,981,369
4	New Brunswick..................	34,634,156	14,445,811	14,410,406	2,303,246 34	31,451,805
5	Manitoba.........................	5,259,436	58,898,284	58,581,587	12,475,110 12	9,067,009
6	British Columbia................	27,087,369	66,596,479	65,436,553	13,763,024 46	33,918,259
7	Prince Edward Island............	573,078	975,683	978,055	147,445 80	573,628
8	Alberta...........................	162,171	21,078,779	20,924,904	4,970,758 95	283,359
9	Saskatchewan....................	17,153,688	19,011,005	19,138,507	3,611,030 70	8,111,337
10	Yukon............................	3,680,247	1,231,284	1,243,683	163,054 96	3,643,535
11	Territories.......................	....	....	....	....	....
	Total.........................	393,232,057	691,943,515	675,428,168	115,039,155 92	478,997,928
	Prepaid postal parcels duty received ·through P.O. Department......................	....	88,877	88,877	24,532 01	....
	Grand total....................	393,232,057	692,032,392	675,517,045	115,063,687 93	478,997,928

SESSIONAL PAPER No. 11

Imports and of Imports entered for Consumption, and the Amount of Duty
Fiscal Years ended March 31, 1913, 1914, and 1915.

Year ended March 31, 1914.			Fiscal Year ended March 31, 1915.				Number.
Imports.	Entered for Consumption.	Duty.	Exports.	Imports.	Entered for Consumption.	Duty.	
$	$	$ cts.	$	$	$	$ cts.	
290,647,435	287,012,290	44,406,539 06	167,685,610	345,765,008	344,693,885	33,218,760 88	1
185,328,270	174,389,348	28,853,398 86	181,982,754	168,965,016	129,988,636	22,919,065 15	2
21,258,225	20,679,263	3,323,970 71	29,712,618	16,327,786	16,257,305	2,930,005 20	3
14,384,559	14,344,805	2,210,144 66	54,322,490	12,983,369	12,736,708	2,162,770 69	4
46,453,394	45,739,751	9,746,764 97	11,558,465	29,847,647	29,448,518	6,413,589 22	5
57,922,481	56,864,971	11,366,923 15	33,627,009	36,223,080	34,976,835	7,373,099 81	6
1,014,270	1,006,567	169,190 01	542,087	933,842	930,467	160,225 69	7
18,307,834	18,330,265	4,328,403 90	469,183	9,953,295	9,953,046	2,484,938 77	8
14,268,017	14,176,797	2,543,306 68	7,185,357	7,550,417	7,542,168	1,356,345 37	9
1,034,042	1,020,122	196,003 05	3,723,304	820,493	836,795	164,720 87	10
....	....	....	....	....	....	1,126 17	11
650,618,527	633,564,179	107,144,645 05	490,808,877	629,369,953	587,364,363	79,184,647 81	
128,270	128,270	35,933 28	....	74,941	74,941	21,262 46	
650,746,797	633,692,449	107,180,578 33	490,808,877	629,444,894	587,439,304	79,205,910 27	

6 GEORGE V, A. 1916

No. 11.—STATEMENT showing the Value of Goods entered for Consumption at the eighteen undermentioned Ports during the Fiscal Year ended March 31, 1915.

Dutiable Goods.	Brantford.	Calgary.	Dawson.	Halifax.	Hamilton.	London.	Montreal.	Ottawa.	Quebec.
Ale, beer and porter	564	18,436	19,293	20,142	6,674	1,906	97,968	14,295	4,828
Animals, living	53	5,933	1,953	2,331	5,613	1,333	24,717	3,426	8,376
Antiseptic ... and dressings		1,339		4,616	1,589	1,228	140,987	7,608	1,126
Bagatelle tables		153			35		275	526	
Bags which contained cement	4	10	1,510	38	20	105	86	67	100
... powder				3			81,949		258
Balls, cues and racks for bagatelle tables	14				1,249		2,434	339	161
Baskets	568	1,894	63	1,667	8,242	640	19,115	5,811	810
Baths, bath tubs, etc	457	5,500	15	4,716	3,919	11,243	61,421	9,818	6,783
Belting, all kinds, except rubber and leather		3,413	274	4,145	588	380	82,438	3,295	66
Belts, all kinds, n.o.p	489	844	7	382	744	291	17,048	1,126	94
Bells	19	423	153	633	35	631	7,672	379	470
Billiard tables	73			357	3,768	45	7,345	128	125
Blacking, shoe and shoemakers' ink	75	1,773	57	3,098	374	3,026	22,392	2,345	7,777
... red, ... sisal or other material, except textile or paper	489			63			662	344	300
Blue, laundry, all kinds	236	25	30	1,038	2,465	2,779	7,248	850	2,326
Boats		82	350	940	31	80	2,202	1,811	
Books, peri... and ... printed matter	31,340	64,828	2,837	52,247	79,430	74,746	727,274	85,556	45,148
Boot, shoe and stay laces	461	1,092		1,443	2,525	2,939	58,808	702	8,020
Boots, shoes and slippers, except rubber and leather	29	1,148	888	5,591	37,060	5,450	62,558	3,430	2,075
Braces and suspenders and ... of	32	1,160	205	420	497	555	16,346	611	1,120
Brass and ... of	18,881	26,180	1,047	24,750	78,605	19,705	519,484	60,046	36,390
Breadstuffs, viz.—									
Arrowroot, ... rice, macaroni, sago and tapioca	4,984	12,803	484	27,662	24,486	29,487	294,621	11,965	16,462
..., flour and meal	10,128	23,858	12,700	23,828	79,337	85,923	477,865	11,306	19,269
Bricks, tiles and manufactures of clay, n.o.p	6,931	12,406		2,660	42,628	36,553	289,508	18,381	33,440
British gum, dextrine, sizing cream, &c	450		17	17	1,001		2,310	63	65
Brooms and ...	786	3,603	136	2,070	8,025	2,069	116,639	5,336	3,310
Buttons	653	1,831	93	2,756	16,108	4,047	205,188	4,759	10,155
Candles	39	30	500	1,147	9,285	783	28,350	1,163	6,814
Cane, reed or rattan, split, and manufactures of	32	55		45	108	102	712	372	195
... of all kinds, railway cars, trucks and parts of	44,765	170,227	8,939	49,212	692,070	98,334	811,056	122,743	83,790
Carpets, n.o.p							84		
Carpet linings and stair ...	49			25	97		340	81	67
Carpet sweepers	132	360		188	1,205	698	11,316	145	39
... registers	539	157		26	101	22	515	244	
Celluloid, manufactures of	140	421		218	2,099	1,126	16,807	458	364

Cement	43	40		20,216	1,650	791	12,463	644	4,250
Chalk, prepared	124	299		735	1,575	200	9,072	572	499
Charcoal	724	160		26	9,547	8,326	32,434	123	6,952
Church vestments		136		497	217	297	7,162	234	52
Cider		398		269	26	323	8,613	251	9,408
Clocks, clock ...s, ...'s and				20	88	71	431	42	66
...th, coated or ... for manufacture of blue or black print cloth	307	6,608	382	4,350	6,421	6,598	89,150	5,779	7,343
Clothes wringers							4,612		
Coal, ...als and dust		49		405	819	584	3,404	351	74
Cocoa carpeting, ...ats and matting	55,120	224	4,304	4,518	367,243	73,662	1,298,650	269,941	274,001
Cocoa nuts		20	9	160	1,810	201	2,816	101	228
Cocoa ...t, desiccated	39	343	13	1,735	5	25	3,826	843	543
...a paste, chocolate paste, shells, nibs and other preparations		48		2	4		8,244	4	
Coffee, all kinds, n.o.p. (see Free Goods)	4,381	26,606	1,111	73,308	6,177	7,257	593,642	4,709	29,644
Collars	198	6,601	8,611	4,119	51,621	10,338	309,945	17,249	1,475
Combs, dress and toilet	468	283	207	2,937	820	16,518	26,301	4,195	2,068
Copper and manufactures of	273	925	89	2,163	1,545	813	49,428	480	3,312
Cordage of all kinds	1,310	6,263	5,372	11,995	17,643	879	44,940	5,566	3,500
Corks and other manufactures of cork wood	687	23,861	1,566	17,123	11,003	3,523	124,363	5,775	5,730
Corsets, clasps, etc	676	551	1	975	6,568	1,616	72,389	1,430	12,161
...es and scenery, theatrical	3,695	11,555	229	4,864	13,554	1,652	91,771	19,818	11,174
Crape, black		15				7,586	499	228	
Cuffs	94,892	165,464	13,331	218,626	424,124	25	4,925,559	314,092	491,046
Curtains, made up				69	1	371,942	33	118	1,153
...rs and pedometers				4		33	43	11	40
Drugs, ...es, chemicals and medicines	1,082	1,175	22	3,693	9,149		5,539		8,843
Earthenware and china	728	249		6	82	14,253	1,895	4,273	
Eggs	31,791	72,399	1,288	50,387	125,961	236	104,945	8	37,742
Elastic	5,523	21,532	556	36,213	33,414	40,822	1,734,721	63,672	49,675
Electric light, ...ms and points	5,108	63,383	16,738		1,097	53,210	531,112	40,186	9,787
Electric apparatus, motors, etc	145	1,914	20	1,453	1,419	1,503	34,186	10,973	4,991
Embroideries, n.o.p		101	71	2,444	644	1,721	12,428	1,947	440
Emery ...els and manufactures of emery	12,074	61,211	7, 04	89,765	407,550	76	1,418,825	617	54,280
Express parcels	525	1,104		95	1,754	32,577	9,792	66,200	649
Fancy goods	584	1,209	101	516	2,791	364	16,998	296	1,473
Feathers, bed, etc	11,346	32,276	2,025	17,831	56,826	1,147	213,511	1,293	34,044
Featherbone	8,409	37,796	1,090	37,820	47,677	36,562	820,674	53,723	68,628
Fertilizers					45	43,339	12,541	46,600	9,746
Fibreware, n.o.p	1,623	64		41,342	5,841	1,171	9,893	33	38,249
Fireworks (see Free Goods)	59	238	154	1,653	10,167	10,531	26,894	3,081	7,671
Flax, ...mp, jute and manufactures of	523	23		165	4,396	1,576	2,756	1,228	605
Foundry facings	1,668	5,025	4,814	11,822	32,649	311	347,505	983	11,895
Fruits and nuts (see Free Goods)	8,460	18,365	865	35,025	61,807	20,087	1,575,606	19,953	54,129
Furniture, ...ed, iron or other (...lls)	285				58	62,447	4,272	72,234	88
Furs and manufactures of furs (see Free ...	55,409	293,828	25,877	244,356	260,122	109	1,298,528	253	96,712
...lls	4,890	50,582	1,734	17,078	35,805	244,540	215,816	181,522	24,316
	518	3,641	117	3,245	9,345	20,183	260,064	43,593	86,872
				2,189		21,573	39,724	14,039	233
								31	

IMPORTS for Consumption by Ports.—*Continued.*

Dutiable Goods.	Brantford.	Calgary.	Dawson.	Halifax.	Hamilton.	London.	Montreal.	Ottawa.	Quebec.
Glass and manufactures of	10,259	35,795	1,170	66,708	80,577	124,862	975,108	67,089	109,659
Gloves and mitts, ...s of	24,342	12,994	1,054	10,263	6,036	16,780	967,815	12,986	13,733
Glue, ... and	878	9,037	992	11,245	4,256	6,155	187,177	12,249	10,094
Grease, axle	145		3,020	675	6,747	1,339	14,920	514	165
Gunpowder and other explosives, etc.		11,701	2,811	15,462	11,551	5,172	71,750	47,301	217,069
Gutta percha, India-rubber and manufactures of	7,163	50,358	27,332	56,737	68,530	50,439	943,179	31,035	35,140
Hair and ...s of	64	886	445	638	3,798	63	29,492	31,783	1,841
... caps and bonnets	5,470	55,418	2,098	32,105	58,484	79,233	768,729	53,438	56,194
Hay			32,355				11	81	
Honey	442	3,647	328	99	6,318	11	752	106	183
Hops	216	4,349	263	16,132	3,277	9,324	83,370	4,734	11,680
Ink		1,363	12	3,101		3,255	38,635		902
Iron and steel and manufactures of (see Free Goods)	643,007	947,007	52,086	683,246	2,709,270	774,699	10,875,820	1,095,507	747,609
Ivory		15	89	17	17		727		
Jellies, jams and preserves	420	3,979	272	11,855	1,581	828	72,675	12,158	15,072
Jewellery	3,659	15,075	851	8,265	47,689	12,095	256,943	16,793	15,043
Knitted goods		491			576	2,604	28,430	3,818	1,536
Launches—pleasure, steam, gasolene and other motor power	18		217		150		4,668	936	388
Lead and manufactures of	54,315	529		14,822	48,106	9,669	379,660	1,881	5,074
Leather and manufactures of	6,021	153,167	8,788	49,550	261,228	151,828	1,721,527	154,188	336,589
Lime	32	150	424	23	7,798	1,355	23,119	7,853	
... lime and other fruit juices		11,904		7,136	5,575	2,476	25,923	1,278	769
Lithographic ..., not ...oved	1,428	77,885	15	339	39	659	245	185	
Machine card ...	26	3,612	327	402	401		5,743	4,992	1,085
... lanterns and ... therefor		1,616		106	194	233	506,130	283	670
Malt	321	2,101		31		2,299	14,645	119	333
Malt extract, ...p		65		3,563	574	24	16,131	17	110
Marble and ...tures of				85	2,184	1,408	83,071	8,849	15,674
Mattresses					23	16	1,272	62	100
Mats, door or carriage, other than metal, n.o.p							313	35	
Metals and manufactures of	10,455	36,950	2,849	28,662	213,693	45,541	665,436	51,353	56,402
Milk, condensed and fresh			1,082	1,190			265		40
Mineral substances, ...p	4,541	2,586		12,184	12,894	4,779	119,062	11,735	2,922
Mineral and aerated waters		2,173	54	1,597	3,073	83	116,417	7,244	16,254
Mucilage	127	398	20	751	2,250	990	1,442	351	610
Musical instruments	3,475	42,932	1,797	14,701	2,699	7,697	388,185	28,406	22,815
Mustard	1,502	195		4,030	10,301	13,625	42,954	7,309	8,984
Oils, all kinds, n.o.p	9,677	28,595	5,818	75,137	74,857	39,660	492,211	39,954	17,189
Oiled cloths of all kinds, cork matting and linoleum	8,609	22,386	1,507	29,034	24,906	38,545	364,608	31,115	44,304
Optical, philosophical, photographic and mathematical instruments	1,304	5,767	591	11,354	14,318	7,217	144,305	187,060	8,176

Article	(1)	(2)	(3)	(4)	(5)	(6)	(7)	(8)	(9)
Packages	6,332	35,001	7,489	66,572	37,204	24,786	588,209	48,829	111,688
Paints and ...	4,947	5,551	191	45,719	19,952	9,234	369,929	33,120	7,205
Paintings in oil or water colours and pastels, less than $20.		24			24	6	417	76	
Paper and manufactures of.	88,698	55,519	2,836	62,087	248,962	125,166	1,285,398	183,701	80,660
Pencils, lead.	2,154	3,076	187	4,958	9,654	4,499	59,908	13,661	7,475
Pens, penholders and ...	409	1,081	145	3,485	3,210	979	19,335	5,049	2,051
Perfumery, non-alcoholic.	736	7,790	21	5,676	8,860	5,282	172,646	9,132	5,997
Photographic dry plates	157	328	12	14	149	217	17,457	639	777
... and photograph frames	287	4,955	896	1,561	2,530	1,120	18,834	2,605	2,606
Pickles	706	1,932	91	15,492	15,492	16,912	59,177	11,300	9,779
Plants and trees	14	897	128	3,151	10,284	5,743	48,290	5,936	5,454
Plaster of Paris.	459	179	48	153	468	2,099	3,205	242	356
Plates, engraved on wood or metal	184	191	7,474	136	5,896	4,428	7,750	29,237	10,314
Pocketbooks, purses	9,252	5,984	141	3,418	6,694	3,337	84,076	9,278	2,710
Polish or composition, knife or other.		1,197		1,765	37,557	24,331	41,493	1,804	31,653
Post office parcels		52,207		24,870	9,916	1,038	93,450	46,211	871
Precious stones, n.o.p.—	36	140			3,900	8,987	27,658	308	9,130
Provisions, viz:—									
Butter, cheese and lard.	319	566	9,094	10,706	34,234	20,758	132,794	23,821	259,692
Meats, all kinds	1,548	17,921	58,240	87,444	3,160	323	533,654	57,600	130
Pulleys, etc. for power.	799	1,075	706	1,290	555	496	7,026	520	530
Regalia and badges.	146	1,830	336	1,331	12,343	18,685	4,607	1,852	15,651
Ribbons	4,222	13,418	98	17,917	6,966	1,980	744,945	17,613	2,899
Sails	1,600	26		98	3,157	1,419	86	1,500	3,506
Salt (see Free list)	469	5,508	752	1,163	4,276	2,714	2,958	1,147	1,912
Sand, glass, emery and flint paper	150	420	182	8,437	17,901	295	32,352	5,023	385
Sauces, catsups and soy.	3,144	9,122	52	930	62,068	55,127	42,929	3,378	74,032
Sausage casings, cleaned.	20,744	107		6,083	40,820	1,234	71,660	16,060	56,233
Seeds, n.o.p.—				8,300	3,780	33,587	319,547	1,983	830
Ships and vessels and materials on.	199	5,598	65	839	202,188	9,769	46,932	103,029	49,980
Signs of any material and letters for signs	19,556	4,430	2,093	35,463	5,934	23,874	36,862	3,586	3,017
Silk and manufactures of	2,630	57,033	1,278	3,161	50,290	18,113	2,252,813	35,115	9,565
Slate	3,817	1,729	98	19,156	68,841	28,197	30,744	2,303	6,828
Soaps	232	24,125	10,222	25,272	55,904	3,135	313,831	145,568	241,178
Spices	5,514	3,470	1,071	202,607	5,381	1,837	67,238	18,699	38,867
Spirits, wine, not sparkling.	392	134,233	4,963	11,799	3,377	1,908	1,257,139	7,927	3,886
Spirits, wine, sparkling.	23	8,861	2	4,764	1,974	1,673	235,679	1,556	676
Sponges	17	18,027	53	1,535	23,814	11,300	170,411	26,844	974
Starch	4,330	739	354	2,164	1,170	934	30,195	1,445	21,016
Soles for manufacture of rubber boots.	118	728	91	9,857	5,421	3,344	23,596	489	292
Stone and manufactures of	739	4,123	2,009	542	10,289	2,218	8,919	2,132	92,313
Straw and	92	337	245	3,317,725	12,033	13,365	141,065	10,095	357
Sugars and syrups	2,285	3	70	10,289	1,126	10,983	9,475	742	9,317
Sugars, molasses	87	41	30	11,015	41	341	16,605	841	2,001
Sugar, candy and confectionery	150	9,849		3,561			126,784	373	428
Sugar, maple sugar and syrup.	6	42		383			20,956		7
Surgical trusses, pessaries and suspensory bandages.		966		2,635			3,968		
Tallow		16					476		

CUSTOMS DEPARTMENT

IMPORTS for Consumption by Ports.—Continued.

Dutiable Goods.	Brantford.	Calgary.	Dawson.	Halifax.	Hamilton.	London.	Montreal.	Ottawa.	Quebec.
Tape lines	7	11	......	79	133	108	2,300	264	354
Tea (see Free Goods)	......	180	184	4,414	754	47	45,442	2,650	730
Tin and manufactures of	1,996	5,635	50	10,266	10,851	11,353	134,585	6,778	10,175
...o and ...es of	217	17,611	12,391	21,886	5,143	2,052	588,097	3,342	5,745
...co pipes	395	1,487	401	6,003	4,638	875	203,947	4,649	9,095
Trawls and trawling ...ps	124	1,009	......	653	443	339	4,201	957	1,774
Trunks, ...s, hat b x ...te.	178	2,420	43	539	1,462	1,212	8,936	2,855	2,071
...c, manufactures of	266	883	171	139	2,738	1,189	7,821	866	392
Umbrellas, parasols and sunshades	106	367	......	329	851	528	11,698	2,500	2,283
Unenumerated articles	1,360	6,342	195	9,542	26,525	8,533	156,095	5,227	5,594
Varnish, lacquers, japans, etc	1,618	201	20	718	111,339	1,278	27,768	1,351	4,112
Vegetables	19,595	91,608	21,065	63,153	111,129	18,740	699,987	61,765	56,123
Vinegar	98	2,508	199	786	1,712	450	13,541	2,224	507
...le or shoddy from cotton, wol or other material	1,048	3,600	59	2,874	6,021	20,688	89,617	20,419	3,318
Watches, ...h ...ees, movements, glasses, etc	15	8,630	464	6,095	22,693	4,380	493,062	3,251	3,370
Wax and manufactures of	1,305	782	6	1,555	38,797	1,232	51,660	5,556	5,291
...king	760	23	......	18	38	341	21,149	1,535	12,768
...hs, thongs and lashes ...ue pol...	......	1,994	11	421	1,065	1,493	2,691	414	1,221
...aw ...ees and	29	664	......	......	72	44	......	103	......
Window shades and rollers	428	428	......	963	85	961	4,623	505	403
Wil and ...es of	12,299	41,711	2,448	21,266	85,986	54,420	406,403	43,288	29,766
Wol and ...es of	96,650	171,326	14,757	191,346	821,207	317,819	6,838,916	355,866	354,075
Zinc and manufactures of	263	218	......	58	1,141	976	5,671	779	538
Damaged goods	......	138	......	......	......	......	2,480	13,613	......
Total dutiable goods	1,557,203	3,632,234	462,459	6,754,618	9,096,279	3,887,689	68,063,198	5,035,584	5,242,781

FREE GOODS.

	1	2	3	4	5	6	7	8	9
PRODUCE OF THE MINE.									
Clay	1,563	104	51	428	15,707	923	43,911	10,841	2,043
Coal, anthracite	211,887			243,040	767,417	557,176	1,838,934	1,248,377	557,384
Minerals	9,354	290		1,076	11,163	5,423	27,506	3,364	1,622
Ores					1,718	60	2,245		
Diamonds		325		45	39,077	228	588,576	35	61,827
Salt		5	903	48,774	196		112,058	12	56,216
Whiting	123	42		1,906	654	185	52,142	1,406	208
Other articles				374	33,239	2,334	53,261	3,286	456
Total	222,627	766	954	295,643	869,171	566,329	2,718,635	1,267,321	679,756
FISHERIES.									
Fish of all kinds	22			434,581	76	403	17,073	54	5,658
Fish oil				3,427		1,522	12,918		
Other articles		35	35	4,205	135	6	757	289	51
Total	22	35	35	442,213	211	1,931	30,748	343	5,709
FOREST.									
Corkwood				1,582	6,564	1,220	11,106		45
Logs and round unmanufactured timber	131,047	460		1,079	261,420	154,055	2,355	1,858	
Lumber and timber, planks, etc., sawn, not shaped	18,639	53,186	35	37,921	9,153	108,120	639,732	91,745	672,736
Other articles		1,509		1,037			29,053	15,991	1,127
Total	149,686	55,155	35	41,619	277,137	263,395	682,246	109,594	673,908
ANIMALS AND THEIR PRODUCE.									
Animals for improvement of stock	1,554	9,785		3,274	9,947	9,482	31,983	9,862	9,784
Bristles	90	153		227	32,971	324	5,032	22	9
Fur skins, not dressed		110	9,553	1,309		1,246	717,973	16,247	171,045
Grease	1,810	8,506			59,383	36,071	45,296	18	2,687
Hair, unmanufactured and horse hair	3,380	32		179	4,985	142	9,401	607	335
Hides and skins, undressed	660	28		24,670	218,061	777,630	474,653		217,427
Silk, raw	10,986				9,065	31,351	293,055	537,347	
Wool	106,649				85,425	1,635	38,335	2,826	13
Other articles	27	325		77,581	929		97,222		6,406
Total	125,156	18,939	9,553	107,240	420,766	857,881	1,712,950	566,929	407,706

6 GEORGE V, A. 1916

IMPORTS for Consumption by Ports.—*Continued.*

Free Goods	Brantford	Calgary	Dawson	Halifax	Hamilton	London	Montreal	Ottawa	Quebec
AGRICULTURAL PRODUCTS.									
Broom corn	404			900	23,143	10,112	19,570	9,283	7,860
Gum beans				55,582		677	56,467		
Cocoanuts	455			14,357	5,370	1,546	11,676	42,657	
Cotton wool, or raw, not dyed	9,465	121	5,099	36,984	843,452	147,833	1,787,266	14,596	512,443
Fibres, Mexican and vegetable	348	125,211		528	7,014		6,411		25
Fruits, green	88,879			206,294	195,022		1,243,482	355,430	216,850
Hemp and Manila grass	357,436	19,369		167,813	63,628	44,603	178,741	58,980	251,308
Indian corn	116,955		15	241,271			605,902		
Rice, uncleaned	41	531		294	14,056	774	258,335	1,760	559
Seeds	12,262	19,701		1,115	360,088	346,397	6,470	947	110,809
Tobacco leaf for ... purposes	2,971	5,466	89	8,866	16,303	9,453	3,176,462	2,555	6,140
...fiber articles							46,323		
Total	589,276	170,399	5,803	734,004	1,638,076	561,395	7,397,105	486,258	1,106,000
MANUFACTURED AND PARTIALLY MANUFACTURED ARTICLES.									
Asphalt	22,426	444		284	56,855	10,611	234,612	38,671	1,180
Bells for churches				89	287	603	7,581	197	
Binder twine	3,829	12,480	105	14,250	19,263	32,108	87,911	64,904	21,503
Fire brick	3,774	1,459		1,208	28,403	7,594	67,565	13,318	38,313
Plaits, straw, tuscan and grass	445	43	2	976	2,873	344	131,646	371	13,702
Pitch and tar, pine		529		18,358			81,086	680	40
Coke	21,386	791		548		11,441	56,833	7,895	2,335
Duck for belting and hose					230,352		21,330		6,095
Drugs, dyes and chemicals	18,986	13,957	36	90,992	220,590	1,030,246	1,626,710	79,020	156,800
Fish hooks, nets, seines, etc.		34	194	114,724	7,510		20,284	126	11,123
Jute cloth and yarn	883	33	207	8,458	70	20	850,489	1,013	324
Metals:—									
Brass	4,216	207	52	7,809	32,513	45,217	193,239	7,676	22,492
Copper	1,788	1,730		17,020	460,651	57,428	1,509,302	17,151	93,377
Iron and steel	26,798	286,113	176,009	92,477	948,057	175,221	2,726,511	108,533	672,661
Tin	7,590			42,107	497,786	78,701	767,396	4,259	37,783
Zinc		1,990		10,657	89,750	32,876	260,218	969	22,976
Other	744	140		14,676	41,979	2,364	277,191	1,606	9,743
Oakum		20		5,104	784	244	13,107	155	2,076
Newspapers and magazines	935	56	227	42,882	5,185	2,970	203,823	30,368	1,358
Oil-cake meal and cotton seed cake and meal	3,488	368	4	470	14,514	11,397	9,084	16,489	

Molasses	3,436			351,093	2,414		282,574	61,267	249,709
Noils	17,559	27,552			8,109	9,859	5,027	2,755	
Oil, cocoanut and palm	2,736	117,474	3,694		62,032	57,550	22,708	100,435	
Crude petroleum	31,520	593		199,542	20,720	15,985	379,895	9,311	63,500
Rags and waste	5,439	644		12,963	13,788	2,494	170,402	11,822	14,805
Resin or rosin	52	10,196		260	38,812	1,533	361,852	13,483	2,552
Silk, crude	2,702	95		3,959	90,614		70,629	216	11,762
Gutta percha, crude, rubber, etc	8,575	5,476	24	521	5,981	4,380	754,880	26,089	1,518
Surgical instruments				4,203	188,030	43,293	51,347	2,053	7,124
Yarn, cotton					95,675	45,144	301,825		3,991
Other articles	49,918	40,288	271	102,651			1,381,636	136,895	88,006
Total	290,233	522,709	180,825	1,158,281	3,183,597	1,681,627	12,929,293	757,727	1,556,850
MISCELLANEOUS ARTICLES.									
Coffee, green (see Dutiable)	858	12,396		3,224	58,556	27,203	207,506	11,407	
Models of inventions	500	2	39	20	3,250	2,912	9,119	1,311	126
Paintings in oil or water colours	27,821	2,210	3,487	396	5,718	4,573	180,437	42,836	8,311
Settlers' effects	22,738	172,277		34,141	98,383	49,728	603,251	70,518	1,958,282
Tea, (see Dutiable)	7	41,588	10,225	430,442	187,035	110,987	1,496,871	96,647	102,178
Coin and bullion	2,300	222	6,922	192,415	80,283	7,767	4,320,848	121,907,260	2,657
Other articles		11,174		515,286	86,774	14,292	1,846,145	118,946	57,336
Total	54,224	239,869	20,673	1,175,926	520,990	217,462	8,664,180	22,248,925	2,128,890
Total Free	1,431,224	1,007,872	217,843	3,954,926	6,799,957	4,150,020	34,135,157	125,437,097	6,558,819
Total Dutiable	1,557,203	3,682,234	462,459	6,754,618	9,096,279	3,887,689	68,063,198	5,035,584	5,242,781
Grand total	2,988,427	4,690,106	680,302	10,709,544	15,896,236	8,037,709	102,198,355	130,472,681	11,801,600

No. 11—STATEMENT showing the value of Goods entered for Consumption at the eighteen undermentioned Ports during the Fiscal Year ended March 31, 1915.

Dutiable Goods.	Sault Ste. Marie.	St. John, N.B.	St. Johns, Que.	Sydney.	Toronto.	Vancouver.	Victoria.	Windsor, Ont.	Winnipeg.
	$	$	$	$	$	$	$	$	$
Ale, beer and porter	2,484	34,209	17	8,341	49,578	135,670	56,614	13,312	79,135
Animals, living	1,229	3,431	355	930	40,790	68,019	13,022	3,039	50,446
Antiseptic surgical dressings		3,980			46,127	11,942	4,255	130	19,263
Bagatelle tables		142			2,231	185	55		2,055
Bags which contained cement	4,215		1		565	457	194	150	545
Baking powder					291	47,510		127	15,885
Balls, cues and racks for bagatelle tables	45	785	36	55	15,045	176			1,340
Baskets	53	6,205	155	66	21,860	8,596	3,125	225	9,425
Baths, bath tubs, etc.	343	15,373	123	77	73,969	31,041	5,575	10,484	38,942
Belting, all kinds, except rubber and leather	10	472	193	1	39,767	22,444	3,966	4,044	32,176
Belts, all kinds, n.o.p.	30	582	43		26,531	1,358	1,189	14	10,052
Bells	23				11,902	2,041	309	45	6,853
Billiard tables		2,187		285	16,835	9,542	285	89	1,467
Blacking, shoe and shoemakers' ink		120			38,601	135	909		12,553
Blinds, of wood, metal or other material, except textile or paper		749	5	45	106	8,509			773
Blue, laundry, all kinds		126	25	131	9,267	1,372	584	2,782	8,143
Boats	380	1,469	9,424	3,828	902	134,382	173	157	2,030
Books, periodicals and other printed matter	26,542	34,270	6	91	1,747,205	3,892	33,706	779	320,124
Boot, shoe and stay laces	19				38,096	26,318	450	51,431	14,273
Boots, shoes and slippers, except rubber and leather	2	10,889	4		73,315	3,658	4,133	33	13,074
Braces and suspenders, and parts of	15	1,288			10,210	69,988	1,100	600	11,189
Brass and manufactures of	16,134	24,759	2,249	2,233	358,884		13,828	35	100,933
Breadstuffs, viz.:—								104,770	
Arrowroot, biscuits, rice, macaroni, sago and tapioca	2,993	20,821	201	8,952	211,241	158,925	21,047	1,096	104,937
... flour and meal	4,206	29,694	131	6,141	200,606	454,001	167,980	248,845	146,677
Bricks, tiles and ... of clay, n.o.p.	23,648	6,912	552	7,656	226,210	64,536	24,343	54,927	150,803
British gum, dextrine, sizing cream, etc.	3,946	604	249		2,026	20		34	280
Brushes and brooms	618	4,503	219	613	150,664	30,501	3,377	1,564	45,710
Buttons	139	3,933	7,216	127	183,222	11,480	1,933	13,028	31,891
Candles	4	5,147		5	8,385	4,514	2,840	706	12,404
Cane, reed or rattan, split, and ...		409	21	271	612	2,316	931	1,730,017	24
Carriages of all kinds, railway cars, ... and parts of	20,477	66,057	10,792	1,916	1,373,571	421,508	124,887		747,618
Carpets, n.o.p.		107						21	
Carpet, linings and stair pads		204		29	613	428	104	85	189
Carpet sweepers		262			19,404	175	40	534	1,834
Cash registers and manufactures of	66	70	42		116,117	547	180	960	1,190
Cement	14,496	846	29	26	27,766	1,799	540	2,224	5,139
Chalk, prepared	131	7,842	4		7,591	1,812	1,034		5,262
...		637			18,131	851	42		2,812
...	1	441	2	2	19,067	553	243	80	5,017

Article									
Chicory	3,564		61	1,126	3,509	66	398		10
Church vestments	4,003		261	130	3,071	30	81		25
Cider	170	112	662	160	14	1	136		29
Clocks, clock cases, keys and movements	45,103	422	5,383	12,395	125,774	76	9,042	46	604
Cloth, coated or sized for manufacture of blue or black print cloth	819				1,029				
Clothes wringers	3,050	100	132	471	12,994		900	29	
Coal, bituminous, and dust	211,337	457,530	86,414	56,711	1,336,330	55	6,438	12,320	884,273
Cocoa carpeting, mats and matting	1,331	1,558	15	1,507	2,577		94		6
Cocoa nuts	834	186	373	717	1,422	96			
Cocoanut, desiccated	9,912	28	1,202	10,286	24,952	1,091	9,655	15	2,283
Cocoa paste, chocolate paste, shells, nibs and other preparations	127,723	12,837	8,441	95,704	644,806	276	16,523	91	354
Coffee, all kinds, n.o.p. (see Free Goods)	183,992	20,499	7,768	99,072	299,319	11	3,304		
Collars	7,244	62	1,494	2,603	61,482	221	1,405	1,474	2,238
Combs dress and toilet	11,502	18	607	2,751	48,449	877	5,826	11	
...er and ...es of	22,176	2,029	2,463	6,732	23,985	6	14,698	123	685
Cordage of all kinds	59,593	2,043	12,648	28,358	104,865	304	2,716	1,252	824
...ks and ...her ...es of cork wood	19,133	17,417	696	9,335	143,282		3,865	29	95
...s, ...ps, etc.	95,007	330	330	33,592	149,715			40	694
...es and ...ry, ...trical	80	145	145	16	5,872		199		
...n, manufacture of	2,194,792	144,863	126,339	540,316	6,822,090	19,933	241,511	145,581	37,266
Crape, black	416	8	73	52	783		32		
Cuffs				14	164	169	17		171
Curling stones and handles therefor					74				
Curtains, made up									
Cyclometers and pedometers	31,561	1,446	1,128	9,724	163,106	8,183	5,513	39	28,502
Drugs, dyes, chemicals, medicines	4,406	17,474	191	1,087	12,880	812	65	8	8,941
Earthenware and china	353,184	75,543	28,742	215,738	1,181,008	31	66,738	93,262	15,601
Eggs	210,990	9,890	30,119	92,337	487,730	30	100,539	688	4
Elastic	68,964	6,161	62,852	262,996	274,034	25	42	32	89
Electric light carbons and points	18,047	11	1,187	3,729	6,957	4,013	144	28	674
Electric apparatus, motors, etc.	2,116	458	80	2,515	10,487	208	674		15,464
Embroideries, n.o.p.	295,686	274,116	18,548	139,799	962,658	4,355	74,664	5,792	7
Emery wheels and manufactures of emery	5,166	48	48	1,716	20,632	2,421	2,497	150	631
Express parcels	6,302	3,803	620	6,090	22,544	135	28,676	126	11,336
Fancy goods	100,873	165,871	26,235	71,355	222,714	206	77,437	5,486	1,153
Feathers, ...al, etc.	257,808	7,019	24,137	93,672	1,404,512	16		1,276	
Fertilizers	318	4	7,133	6,333	16,119	454	46,436	7,221	1,422
Fireware, n.o.p.	65	14,172	141	1,429	35,374	29,121	577	117	58
Fireworks	1,651	953	1,795	2,526	21,768	22,335	101	53	1,582
Fish (see Free Goods)	1,007	129	49,712	138,355	5,239	1,420	16,043	292	1,732
Flax, hemp, jute and manufactures of	144,765	3,679	46,578	121,739	223,912	614	37,323	481	181
Foundry facings	808,980	18,201	4	61	1,097,199	1,350	104		18,976
Fruits and nuts (see Free Goods)	345	25,151	178,397	737,956	1,335	662	231,467	1,069	3,053
Furniture, ...d, iron, or ...ber material	1,100,946	40,760	29,316	127,990	1,469,957	185	12,712	3,078	78
Furs and manufactures of furs (see Free Goods)	164,509	1,256	3,469	9,786	395,094		3,158		
Fuses	81,791	5	153	16,185	245,544		507		
Glass and manufactures of	341,300	97,122	35,330	192,939	863,792		110,307	4,569	5,020
Gloves and mitts	192,874	2,440	10,853	38,953	358,250		23,914	58	455
Gold, silver and manufactures of	63,365	1,078	12,217	24,588	147,042		6,931	296	5

CUSTOMS DEPARTMENT

6 GEORGE V, A. 1916

IMPORTS for Consumption by Ports.—Continued.

Dutiable Goods.	Sault Ste. Marie.	St. John, N.B.	St. Johns, Que.	Sydney.	Toronto.	Vancouver.	Victoria.	Windsor, Ont.	Winnipeg.
	$	$	$	$	$	$	$	$	$
Grease, axle	280	272	13	2,052	76,464	4,990	789	250	60
Gunpowder and other explosives, etc.	772	10,306	17	67	15,534	62,550	18,948	137,180	214,275
Gutta percha, India rubber and manufactures of	13,204	60,916	4,808	2,723	945,964	273,533	51,918	30,606	246,351
Hair and manufactures of		814		161	36,758	3,034	1,094		13,750
Hats, caps and bonnets	2,353	84,393	1,521	3,356	1,254,611	126,981	32,422	3,204	260,612
Hay	63,096	280			899	5,361	17,716		1,654
Honey	175	7,514			36,312	277	1,692	20	3,321
Hops	2,734	1,244			48,921		2,750	9,678	20,285
Ink	126		43	293		10,627	2,705	347	9,102
Iron and steel and manufactures of (see Free Goods)	414,683	758,638	233,394	94,763	6,908,362	2,065,533	345,592	1,727,334	3,930,596
Ivory					1,189	151	10	171	70
Jellies, jams and preserves	368	7,626	9	2,624	57,518	63,898	14,188	5,461	95,359
Jewellery	265	9,271	1,496	1,168	300,234	27,544	9,717		86,883
Knitted goods		1,847			56,415	9,450	3,758		10,971
Launches, gasoline or other motor power	3,431				817		950	3,042	1,935
Lead and manufactures of	200	12,264	30	298	198,563	17,544	10,568	25,176	11,780
Leather and manufactures of	3,038	95,077	3,692	13,411	1,720,242	362,281	100,457	20,808	560,954
Lime	4,648	234	1,163	382	36,334	114	1,031	8,989	24,112
Lime juice and other fruit juices	281	7,023	36	496	28,971	27,274	3,084	480	31,558
Lithographic stones, etc.		118			1,223	10			198
Machine card clothing		190			7,491				
Magic lanterns and slides therefor				412	429,238	91,104	892	1,923	91,032
Malt	546	4,288			24,816	7,288	7,621	181	4,083
Malt extract	51	126			45,127	44	44		4,466
Marble and manufactures of	167	186	9,098	396	103,495	8,099	11,231	2,048	24,669
Mattresses		1,183	9		47	28,702	235		41
Mats, door or carriage, other than metal, n.o.p.	59,148				1,086,103	255	19,407		286,366
Metals and manufactures of		34,827	5,511	31,794		164,902	1,458	65,082	20,549
Milk	2,130			178		40,34.	2,298		42,660
Meats, salted and fresh	23	9,447	16	2,048	170	24,784	8,167	6,470	7,478
Meats, n.o.p.	6	1,431	980	18	117,783	9,824	284	212	2,297
Mineral and aerated waters	1,754	794	69	38	15,940	569	8,175	1,001	127,927
Mucilage	107	29,438	750	740	17,422	69,937	5,445	12,770	39,127
Musical instruments	12,885	4,969		513	461,746	14,085	43,596	398	215,049
Mustard		50,605	2,062	12,756	47,656	636,405	1,536	43,626	127,219
Oils, all kinds, n.o.p.	107	4,969	750	513	654,171	636,405	43,596		215,049
Oiled cloths, of all kinds, cork matting and linoleum	12,885	50,605	2,062	12,756	283,312	44,405	1,536	43,626	127,219
Optical, philosophical, photographic and mathematical instruments	1,100	32,733	620	2,153	258,215	30,365	12,038	47,062	50,145
Packages	1,149	10,904	267	461	389,074	158,327	65,716	13,028	191,094
Paints and colours	2,016	82,460	4,992	9,035	329,717	37,852	23,683	17,865	73,917
Paintings in oils or water colours and pastels, less than $20	2,738	10,214	4,644	2,127	1,265	122	18	36,072	12

Article									
Paper and manufactures of	9,692	71,124	13,194	4,206	1,797,880	289,142	53,713	161,269	515,017
Pencils, lead	679	3,885	18	31	78,684	10,684	1,987	736	34,259
Pens, ... and rulers	150	2,301	1	245	70,080	3,027	784	47	12,742
Perfumery, on-alcoholic	315	8,216	38	490	104,104	22,634	4,304	8,142	43,670
Photographic dry plates		119			23,152	6,807	844		3,419
Picture and ... frames	82	2,098	73	26	44,079	3,624	1,412	987	8,869
Pickles and ...tes	81	17,783	624	6,195	48,423	19,215	4,615	639	25,496
Plants and ...	21	3,607	96	77	41,210	16,175	3,891	12,402	42,402
Plaster of Paris	87	18			1,274	19,976	8,204	5,141	233
Pla..., engraved on ... or metal	4	53			20,308	12,415	348	3,022	7,957
Pocket ..., purses	2,301	6,033	66	402	151,477	12,271	4,316	539	52,580
Polish or ..., knife or other	97	2,764	91	204	72,951	17,553	1,747	3,706	6,455
Pomades								472	
Post ...	7,34	18,646	2,288	7,933	201,271	92,854	42,110	5,259	85,63
Provisions, viz.:—		1,384			115,685	1,381	12		3,
Butter, cheese and lard	3,442	2,328	11	6,112	134,354	1,291,977	241,735	4,510	31,408
...s all ...	16,488	86,728	167	10,452	325,030	471,608	179,950	14,520	167,643
Pulleys, ..., dr ...	87	3,015	185		5,546	5,281	1,702	2,734	2,934
Regalia and dies	1,933	692	89		9,476	2,337	1,708	248	657
Ribbons	638	56,599	79	2,007	592,680	41,171	9,478	2,911	138,991
Sails	64	445	61	70	2,556	215	10	5,633	26,08
Salt (see Free Goods)	81	1,311	3,46	68	21,940	17,412	5,157	1,106	4,80
Sand, g..., ...ry and flint paper	98	7,168		494	48,656	3,692	256	731	33,42
..., ...s and ...y				70	50,825	67,824	16,451	23	10,08
Sausage casings, cleaned	44	2,365	85		15,485	3,611	134	45,062	36,87
Seeds, n.o.p.	36,352	5,675		4,882	1,083,115	55,198	22,749	621	
...s and vessels and repairs on	94	69,800			7,557	4,299	6,319	2,481	11,527
...ns of any ... m... and letters for signs	1,242	1,443	62		29,009	2,764	841	12,43	522,508
Silk and ...s of	1,019	67,135	3,441	13,768	3,703,484	241,398	51,980	892	6,560
Slate	2,876	3,626	20	20	58,910	6,312	7,469	8,36	156,471
Soaps	6	14,927	633	958	302,827	97,132	20,733	421	42,003
Spices	4,669	280,297		172	85,527	33,229	2,372	3,63	355,969
Spirits, ...e, on-sparkling	202	9,106	5,480	24,479	542,137	289,805	257,689	352	30,256
Spirits, ..., m. sparkling		152	49	1,071	60,423	123,151	33,453		27,109
Sponges		2,364	26	50	27,043	30,740	30,418	392	6,119
Starch	250	1,913	2,248	68	15,535	2,895	30,418	1,248	18,281
...s for ... of rubber boots		5,724	11,80		15,879	10,699	4,117		
Stone and manufactures of	912	6,64	2,143	40	15,040	5,29	2,300	13,065	14,177
Straw and ...s of	67	1,57	231		131,699	14,01	1,230	4,408	4,576
Sugars and syrups		82,254	3	123	25,962	33,60	34,460	287	16,408
Sugars, ...		129	1,053	796	72,296	9,67	979	1,442	21,649
Sugar candy and ...	917	10,91	253	771	36,172	68,84	12,361	3,918	143,503
Sugar ..., ...s and ... spry ...	158	87	6,809	66	197,501	10,36	338	148	17,145
Tallow		98	57	82	11,005	2,703	323	74	6,341
Tape lines	65	83		7	13,383	250	112		1,028
Tea (see Free ...)	201	6,61	3	58	8,336	232	25	403	1,222
...	728	5,83		36	2,067	1,330	133	1,253	1,734
Tin and ...s of	262		60,800		13,647	22,601	498	30,172	56,191
					135,552				

IMPORTS for Consumption by Ports.—*Continued.*

Dutiable Goods.	Sault Ste. Marie	St. John, N.B.	St. Johns, Que.	Sydney	Toronto	Vancouver	Victoria	Windsor, Ont.	Winnipeg.
	$	$	$	$	$	$	$	$	$
Tobacco and manufactures of	183	7,477	809	1,309	154,552	96,245	20,715	1,188	71,648
Tobacco pipes	91	5,696	10,662	421	91,906	11,509	2,176	552	29,110
...s and trawling spoons	72	1,211		123	14,071	9,977	1,171		3,476
Trunks, valises, etc	83	1,287	2	12	13,482	5,602	2,324	976	11,149
Twine, manufactures of	35	2,409		59	18,468	1,249	333	101	3,562
Umbrellas, ...s and	146	780		70	39,581	4,846	699	188	8,900
Unenumerated articles	274	5,049	2,183	271	207,540	56,993	18,360	10,360	62,491
Varnish, lacquers, &c	168	2,146	257	22	45,092	2,670	381	3,543	2,512
Vegetables	18,153	56,701	124	17,546	577,159	232,936	69,134	21,228	388,530
Vinegar	28	547		212	15,122	10,644	3,659	165	4,955
Waste or ...ly from cotton, wool, or other material	9	6,314	6	2,779	44,999	16,779	4,102	3,095	13,458
...s, ...a, movements, glasses, etc	53	2,324	5,030	40	243,730	7,901	1,125	210	64,637
Wax and...	125	757	431	34	58,320	4,796	1,759	2,507	10,334
...ing		1,844			51,253	551	246	224	5,881
...s, thongs and...		301			1,919	558	17		7,746
W...dw ...es and ...ne pol..e	13	901		12	116	232	23		2,143
Window ...s and rollers		94			31,481	3,045	70,590	454	339,300
Wood and ...s of	15,774	24,948	40,342	486	506,000	82,037	162,731	124,297	1,555,688
Wool and ...s d	9,108	265,411	21,171	18,742	6,019,376	528,552	1,278	70,084	5,005
Zinc and ...ts of		187		120	6,488	2,879		16	31
Damaged ...d						3,645			41
Total dutiable goods	1,897,202	4,358,758	791,322	455,704	59,364,781	17,523,409	3,597,530	6,499,679	21,500,249

FREE GOODS.

PRODUCE OF THE MINE.

Clay	15,538	2,123	15,123	8,962	22,852	499	760	2,285	1,9 0
Coal, anthracite	120,079	407,073	1,769,154	4,509	3,809,293	232		74,063	857, 88
Minerals	315	1,440	6,249	8,497	46,699	2,053	14,916	64,065	823 4
Ores	913,474	713		308,613	13	10,638			
Diamonds	820	100		13	797,104	12,419		6,819	85,350
Salt		35,371	155	314	10,071	55,816	3,714	1,199	247
Whiting		599		84	32,756	772	1,159		6,61
Other articles	78,278	89	1,504	98,440		156	1,667	58,521	1,22
Total	1,128,504	447,508	1,792,185	429,362	4,718,788	82,595	22,216	206,952	187,232

FISHERIES.

Fish of all kinds		4,679		3,144	605	474	112		226
Fish oil		199			8,355				
Other articles	2,400	2,400	3		7,999	383	2,289	8,737	25
Total		7,278	3	3,144	16,959	857	2,401	8,737	251

FOREST.

Corkwood					6,690				413
Logs and round unmanufactured timber	47,600	1,438		539	642	36,992	8,555	2,688	84,194
Lumber and timber, planks, etc., sawn, not shaped	85,350	211,707	46,849	7,545	959,115	91,859	13,647	356,150	390,406
Other articles	39,366	172	1,617		391,864	281	285	228,890	222,119
Total	172,316	213,317	48,466	8,084	1,258,311	129,132	22,487	587,728	697,132

ANIMALS AND THEIR PRODUCE.

Animals for improvement of stock	1,005	10,908	219	1,432	42,930	3,699	2,379	2,652	15,340
Bristles		29,510			32,012	187			79
Fur skins, not dressed	265	263		21	336,913	12,553	14,830	191	13,027
Hair, cleaned or ..., but not curled, dyed or otherwise manufactured; and h..se hair not further manufactured than simply cleaned and dipped or dyed					365,046	6,447	9,354	42	16,634
Skins, undressed		6,579	10,664	46	30,995	96	89	15,967	3,111
Silk, raw		85,577	52,171		3,272,733	12,923	2,547	480	267
Wool					4,100				
Wool					761,533				
Other ...cks	33	4,942	8		59,432	17,782		1,204	1,197
Total	1,303	195,356	63,062	1,499	4,905,703	53,687	29,199	20,536	49,655

IMPORTS for Consumption by Ports.—*Concluded.*

Free Goods.	Sault Ste. Marie	St. John, N.B.	St. Johns, Que.	Sydney.	Toronto.	Vancouver.	Victoria.	Windsor, Ont.	Winnipeg.
	$	$	$	$	$	$	$	$	$
AGRICULTURAL PRODUCTS.									
Broom corn		39,779	1,489		21,754	14,455	1,337	1,750	9,695
Cocoa beans, not roasted, crushed or ground		4,321			191,150				
Cocoanuts		11,349			26,930	1,389	295	25	259
Cotton wool or raw cotton not dyed		135,981			263,976				
Fibres, Mexican and vegetable		10,052	203		19,920	387	387	32,641	1,104
Fruits, green	38,023	213,320	44,926	39,554	1,147,451	381,853	122,809	84,452	462,802
Indian corn	11,905	228,703	66,741	8,845	479,170	134,852	54,601	1,042,563	194,319
Rice, uncleaned		503	4	12	65,453	809,945	137,360	130,213	3,405
Seeds	468	3,555	193,778	868	239,326	1,823	1,809	27,005	12,108
Tobacco leaf for excise purposes	377	3,615	4,776	11	153,176	17,490	8,182	1,417	9,646
Other articles						23,525	10,694		
Total	50,773	651,178	311,917	49,296	2,608,306	1,385,712	237,067	1,320,066	693,338
MANUFACTURED AND PARTIALLY MANUFACTURED ARTICLES.									
Salt	29	7,467	245		104,157	19,326	13,647	14,527	16,379
Bells for churches			931		10,381	112		85	1,516
Binder twine		11,105			56,111	1,765	344	3,719	119,797
Plaits, straw, etc.		1,972	15,090	235	123,442	382	48	9	2,658
Fire brick of a class or kind not made in Canada	37,489	1,822	340	99,621	16,264	3,731	900	4,568	3,246
Pitch and tar, pine	185	4,946	12		25,501	1,545		7,995	15,591
Coke	575	1,037	1,004		145,280	12,720	933	15,655	30,842
Duck for belting and etc.	35,585	29			46,263				
Drugs, dyes and chemicals	4,791	170,971	130,864	61,215	2,224,014	182,913	232,714	89,770	125,785
Fish hooks, nets, seines, etc.		84,532	126	19	216,033	517,154	3,193	1,943	43,644
Jute, yarn, etc.		3,535			272,755	42,788	14	6,505	357,921
Metals:—									
Brass	309	14,057	593	373	90,167	11,772	2,421	59,827	5,032
Copper	934	65,923	591	7,553	744,197	16,886	7,404	39,304	43,768
Iron and steel	320,330	180,646	20,468	168,370	1,280,995	103,844	51,403	321,595	301,576
Tin	3,510	27,005	7,517	96	952,163	547,158	36,053	4,754	75,052
Zinc		19,078		64,706	200,440	5,531	1,881	9,382	10,781
Other	169	1,135	25	4,472	168,928	4,624	1,208	82,811	25,564
Newspapers and magazines	748	5,284		12	6,689	3,764	857	186	2,440
Oil cake meal and cotton seed cake and meal	299	37,356		508	733,035	135,610	11,689	5,864	121,381
		11,313	14,556		22,041	12,047	9,693	59	4,618

Articles									
Ms, being the short wool ... with falls from the ... its in ... wl				246,010					
Ms, and wl tops, n.o.p.									
Oil, cocoanut and palm	892	9			424,429	28,827	1,045	12	90,916
Gasoline 1 udr .725 ... ity at 60 degrees temperature			103,514	110	138,727	210,644	782	24,117	392,443
Crude ... fuel and gas oil, .8255 ... gravity or havier		471	21,821		442,240				
at 60 degrees			2,108	30	309,659	1,978,387	128,187	14,661	18,006
Rags and waste		4,169		540	280,748	7,109	1,296	965	32,090
Resin or rosin	55	1,500			145,833	7,593	5,555	6,998	28,746
Rubber, crude		346	201,805		2,127,571	60,361			101
Surgical and dental ... of metal; surgical needles; X-ray ... surgical operating tables for use in									
... and parts ... valued at not less than $50 each by retail; and	343	1,330	12,617	328	168,112	18,583	3,669	5,541	42,595
Yarn, No. 40 and fi n					80,497				
Other articles	18,380	78,692	15,165	79,596	2,419,751	219,861	35,858	81,208	306,795
Total	424,530	1,077,777	446,532	409,704	13,987,040	4,162,014	550,803	802,060	2,219,283

MISCELLANEOUS ARTICLES.

Articles									
Coffee, green (see Dutiable)		25,263			222,910	165,338	8,711		145,752
Models of inventions		115			5,011	554	210		102
Paintings in oil or water colours, etc.		271			100,437	25,357	7,882	2,205	53,587
Settlers' effects	32,986	36,973	29,533	75	488,318	240,965	102,463	2,437	216,661
Tea (see Dutiable)	1,598	1,668,870		10,514	1,314,276	786,526	55,641	196,028	587,147
Coin and bullion		8,671	86	3,687	4,765,043	361,843	204,153	10,363	39,630
Other articles	103,656	155,714	1,265	1,517	943,020	137,498	31,925	466,046	211,704
Total	138,240	1,896,877	30,884	15,793	7,839,015	1,718,081	410,985	677,207	1,254,583
Total Free	1,915,726	4,488,291	2,693,049	916,876	35,334,122	7,532,078	1,375,178	3,623,286	5,101,474
Total Dutiable	1,897,202	4,358,758	791,322	455,704	59,364,781	17,523,409	3,597,530	6,499,679	21,500,249
Grand total	3,812,928	8,847,049	3,484,371	1,372,580	94,698,903	25,055,487	4,972,708	10,122,965	26,601,723

No. 12.—Exports of Canadian Produce from the twenty undermentioned Ports during Fiscal Year ended March 31, 1915.

Exports.	Abercorn.	Bridge-burg.	Coaticook.	Fort William.	Halifax.	Athelstan.	Montreal.	Nanaimo.	New West-minster.	Niagara Falls.
	$	$	$	$	$	$	$	$	$	$
THE MINE.										
Arsenic		31,194	172,614			273,448	191,354			22,400
Asbestos	20	22,908				8,124	12,635			3,068
Asbestos sand		3,564	1,434							
Coal	3,988		561		29,610		5,201	1,499,772	2,131	1,35
Felspar		2,900								82
Goldbearing quartz, dust, nuggets, etc.		4,136,790	510,078		14,823	629	97,332		94	46,06
Metals, viz.:—										
Copper, fine, contained in ore, matte, regulus, etc.		4,515			80,633		331,159			7
Lead in ore			1,615							2,224
Nickel, fine, contained in ore, matte or speiss		170			166,686		606,412			
Platinum, in concentrates or other form	600									996
Silver, metallic, contained in ore, concentrates, etc.		998,385	2,828		1,363,279	21,607	3,215,886			832,447
Mica	484	814	1,098		2		18,611			1,080
Mineral, pigment, iron oxide, ochres, etc.		424					6,606			
Mineral water	2		10		235					
Coal oil, refined										
Ores, viz.:—										
Iron	459	3,183				10,671	15,155			75
Corundum		2,150				1,979				28,36
Other ores		36,784			18,285		203,188		1,115	188,23
Plumbago, crude ore, concentrates, etc.	1,407	2,990					2,630			16,94
Pyrites				323,280	154					
Salt		21,542								2,100
Sand and gravel		9,162					592		4	4,88
Stone, unwrought		18,037								
Other articles	2,779		417		82	112	4,904		351	21,386
Total	9,739	5,296,307	690,655	323,280	1,673,789	316,570	4,711,665	1,499,772	3,695	1,171,637
THE FISHERIES.										
Codfish, fresh	2				1,788	4,027				
" dry, salted	5,215	9,050	30		2,471,280	358,913	142,943	80	476	
" wet, salted			1,538		70,736	237				
" tongues and sounds			1,382		2,706					
Mackerel, fresh		610			12,548	11,808				
" pickled		160	18		154,042					

SESSIONAL PAPER No. 11

Halibut, f sh	52,608	8,548			1,354		1,700		81,471	189
Herring, fresh or frozen	8,014	28,243	16	195,881	10	127,902	1,538	4,941	31,393
" pickled		6,102	104	222				3,368	
" canned				5,072	55,243			2,311	12,362
" smoked	100	5,249	5	10,469	112,587			336	
Seafish, fresh			287	45,967	1,764	4,728		2,217	37
" smoked	2	1,623	909	3,955	5,914		704	3,132	73
preserved		10		40	68		136		64
Oysters, sh		202		50,928	1,401				46
Lobsters, canned		8,540	4,104	1,370,118	61,982	492,094			
Cl ms				1,985				47,453	
Sal ron, fresh	12,837	106	1,061	5,991	4,107	62,792		177	
" smoked	19			22	7			32,062	
" dog				4,654		323,641		35,998	
" pickled							14,480	1,556	
or l ale		15,212	1,045	16,427	6,440	448			1,430
Fish, all fresh	447	467,300	751		32			368	237,272
" pickled	1,155	7,414		171	8,257				
Fish oil, od	6,442	971		70,020	1,023				
" al	414			1,406	3,393				
" whale	660								
" other		1,661		748		2,726		28,238	123
Furs or skins, the articles of fish or marine animals	15			1,941	21				
th articles		3,302		800	2,145			1,074	301
Total	87,930	564,303	11,250	4,501,271	639,571	1,027,184	148,728	245,185	283,253

THE FOREST.

A, pt ard parl	3,944	8,910	1,700	504	47	16,287			10,623
" all other	246	3,398	916		139				
Bark dr ing		1,652	774						
Firewood			1,178	33	41			1,992	104
Knees and					1,741				
Logs, cedar	160	250	1,159			3,336	244,273	18,136	
" elm	1,275					9,916	13,376	47,477	119
" spruce	4,382	2,796	1,458	88			19,645	7,619	
" all other					90	11,154			
Lumber, viz.—	1,192	14,547	4,490	808		1,064,313			394
Basswood		11,617	27,663	841,308	8,588	156,993			
Deals, pine				10,705		72,832	4,630	8,673	317
Spruce ard	870	77,563	287	32,986	60,789	21,099	53		17,389
Deal vds	77	9,684			4,397	24,503	47,096	269,288	265,274
Lths	185,833	469,395	125,996	374,849	749,419	847,226			
Pickets	251	989	1,402	82,154	1,875			555,650	6,243
Shingles	123,964	10,431	23,930	1,330	63,801	11,493	41,503		

6 GEORGE V, A. 1916

Exports of Canadian Produce by Ports.—*Continued.*

Exports	Abercorn	Bridge-burg	Coaticook	Fort-William	Halifax	Athelstan	Montreal	Nanaimo	New West minster	Niagara Falls
	$	$	$	$	$	$	$	$	$	$
THE FOREST—*Con.*										
Lumber—*Con.*										
Logs, lbr					67,189	49	7,751			4,275
Staves and headings	2,753	625	6,321		2,783		29,030	883		2,146
All other lumber, n.e.s		2,189	5,100		240		923			·
Match blocks		4,267			1,437					
Masts and spars										
Piling	204	1,250	124					1,700	6,879	
Poles, hop, &c telegraph and tbr	321	336	13,859			1,904	1,601	8,082	16,024	536
Rails, and all railway ties	5,597				4,542				595	
Shingle bolts									21,251	
Wood, square, viz.:—										
Ash							866			
Birch		603	732		4,053		52,674			564
Elm			375				14,661			531
Pine, white							1,108			
All other		982	575		75	51,498			1,398	67,503
Wood, ids and other, for pulp	25,573	65,246	1,371,947				672,059			553
Other art ids of the forest	95	1,135	312			2,150				
Total	356,727	687,865	1,500,208	53,802	1,425,002	946,616	3,019,825	381,241	955,096	376,571
ANIMALS AND THEIR PRODUCE.										
Animals, horses one year old or less	40	600			557,650					18,320
" horses over one year old	16,865	53,974	39,399			8,785	293,638		12,915	3,·
" cattle one year old or less	10,176	175,052	520		25	25	5,041			1,166,283
" cattle over one year old	72,032	2,831,088	90		3,853	950	15,075		275	118,213
" swine	1,206	599,687			241					17,468
" sheep, one year old or less	30,921	72,948	1,572			4			30	10,827
" sheep over one year old	149	24,960	270		262	983	20		459	16,536
Poultry	198	217,636	131		90	699			2,366	3,757
Animals, all other	11,793	3,353	149				10,028		630	6,948
Bones	17,512	3,060	25,642		114,440	28,413	163,381		45	27,317
Butter		3,630								168
Casein	371	3,383								
Cheese	22,270	7,846	632,992		260,207	29,917	17,698,887			35,354
Eggs	1,656	7,452	65,109		20,194	16	469,227		98	85,193
Furs, dressed						222	3,903			1,398
Furs, undressed	2,484	33,556	4,114		34,947	12,310	198,617		39,346	126,920

Article	1	2	3	4	5	6	7	8	9
Grease and grease scraps	18,016	340		268	15	1,073		13,999	1,371
Glue, stock	1,539	71		32	341		385	7,533	
Hair	81,399	99,894	3,723	19,903	47,640		34,698	71,359	3,568
Hides and skins, other than fur	401,161		3,615	242,996	217		3	1,132,283	352,604
Horns and hoofs	664		4	8	5		16,674	1,076	2,106
Honey	109			456	486			183	21
Lard	65,313		86,180					20,103	9,437
Meats, viz:—									
Bacon	5,329,725	12,277	1,801,053	15,820	100,990		1,705,046	166,353	7,222
Beef	399,667		7,896	85	24,095		60,901	266,576	52,862
Hams	722,388		342,011	4,358	16,355		45,933	266,049	39,250
Mutton	22,664			1,349	2,086			12,674	5,600
Pork	116,595	5,387	108,021	9,312	9,081		197,206	263,325	3,084
Poultry, dressed or undressed	64,598	3	11,893	139	3,841		2,525	52,273	9,455
Game, dressed or undressed	16			48	197			621	25
Canned	1,263,865		136,736	165	61,339		381,318	162,729	102,658
All other, n.e.s.	52,295		7,039		752		8,341	72,665	1,494
Milk and cream, n.e.s.								109,215	
Sweet milk	350,530		1,011	129,378	28,489		384,372	13,135	63,018
Sweet cream	3,512			9,383	2,045		24,041	10,290	7,983
Oil, meat's foot and other animal, n.e.s.	3,978		4,250	20,700	240		40,285	17,488	431,979
Sausage casings	113,962		32,569	12,952	96			25,242	490
Sheep pelts	95,904	2,135	47,379	531	772			15,474	8,533
Tails	1,452	7,671		739	21,777			2,057	666
Tallow	14,773		125	195	245			10,571	
Wool	146,498	59,151	490	2,203		29,735	270	33,725	277,012
Other articles	3,807	177		1,046			486	8,652	1,093
Total	10,912,036	243,270	21,451,812	554,979	1,313,013	30,815	3,672,539	6,793,865	1,569,204

AGRICULTURAL PRODUCTS.

Article	1	2	3	4	5	6	7	8	9
Balsam	101			3,230					2,578
Cider	10,430		2,420		15		190	801	
Flax	130,615		1,530		2,962		1,299	59,201	11,706
Apples, dried	56,677						900	676	32
Apples, green or ripe	957	2	527	54	15,661		65,269	52,259	71
Berries, of all kinds	89,774	23	15,376	50			174,837	6,064	1
Fruits, all other, n.e.s., canned or preserved	10,342		527,271	167	1,472,612		7,877		
Grain and pelts of, viz:—									
Barley	83,848		105,660	4	2,756	228,013	78,053	16,209	2,657
Beans	53,404		31,270	950	17,321		9,341	7,543	2,331
Buckwheat	199,883				4,277		270,545	18,899	55
Indian corn	1,375		2,092,870		108		3	8,346	74,032
Oats	463,917		3,374,097		206,205	902,129	8,640	49,770	36
Pease	276,607		24,513		15,491		198,888	85,615	2,200
Pease, split	68,398		3,096					10,290	
Rye	73,110		5,915	3,309	8,465		18,002	63,802	

11—i—4

Exports of Canadian Produce by Ports.—*Continued.*

Exports	Abercorn	Bridge-burg.	Coaticook	Fort William.	Halifax.	Athelstan.	Montreal.	Nanaimo.	New West-minster.	Niagara Falls.
	$	$	$	$	$	$	$	$	$	$
AGRICULTURAL PRODUCTS—*Con.*										
Wheat	652,886	1,662,922	6,603,472	13,546,481	657,344		27,637,142			1,823,960
Bran	119,921	279,299	5,410	68,330	62,307	540	38,714			80,318
Flour of wheat	221,071	981,369	961,205	814,375	2,212,257	136,714	8,515,223			5,531,898
Oatmeal	19,361		69,867	8,805	6,320		91,769			1,452
Indian meal					7,530		615			622
Meal, all other			4		1,169					
Cereal foods, prepared, all kinds	417,016	44,788	97,505	1,510	26,233	145	481,749			501,912
Hay	126,711	6,252	4,272		24,511	55,749	752,421		77	3,358
Hops					20					
Honey					550					1,536
Maple sugar	469	11	2,816		156	4,672	2,055			17
Maple syrup	481	176	331		176	103	3,470			118
Nuts		419			464		1,696			122
Seeds:—										
Clover	2,467	75,402	16,265		93	1,608	41,564			111,224
Flax	255	1,360	1,250	4,099,758	21	11	178,025			9,464
Grass	6,124	17,732	51			4,596	7,853			903
All other	154	974	477				28			
Straw	63	698	311				358		37	
Tobacco leaf					171	13,623	313		50	2,748
fbs, shrubs and plants		8,242	15			28	22		34	2,120
Vegetables:—										
Canned or preserved	2,955	23,522	92,776		14,298	4	21,256		16	8,664
Potatoes	36	91	25		371,968		1,441		277	88
Turnips	20,944	93,018	1,351		495				300	48,438
All other vegetables	82	665	12		14,848	29	550			4,477
other articles	208	14,929	267	168,758	1,231	3,030	24			6,384
Total	1,686,903	3,591,353	8,691,526	19,838,159	5,153,633	228,616	43,956,922		816	9,659,261
MANUFACTURES.										
Agricultural implements, viz:—					49	124				
Mowing machines		91,597					8,697			110,965
Reapers		11,288					2,887			21,110
Drills		80,117					22,545			104,939

SESSIONAL PAPER No. 11

Harvesters	156,040	3,009		1,490	25	158,576	136	249,179	61
Ploughs	18,137	3,629		245		120,518		164,667
Harrows	24,283					28,940		23,590
Hay rakes	10,722					17,137		4,220
Threshing machines	100,070	9,914				274,670		104,766
Cultivators	63,042	725			274	18,594		47,815
All other	55,470				12	24,629	12	90,250
Parts of	74,917			3,582		152,896		249,934
Baking powders		45,570		21,638	8,650	3,478		
Binder twine	41,108	3,904		10,697	101	114,290	5,753	19,255
Books, pamphlets, maps, etc.	1,252			17,153	132	59,333		44,624
Biscuits and bread		267		236		130		453
Bricks	799			1,075	80	3,501		
Brooms and whisks		197		546		1,699	99	
Brushes of all kinds	73			32		1,967		
Buttons	213			4	13	22		72
Candles		18			2,313	53,420		13
Cartridges	764			3,203		1,932		
Charcoal	22		35		95	721,351	9,627	
Cement	4,114	57,497		305	13,992	927		325,852
Clothing and wearing apparel				518,634		35,925		28,673
Coke	64	15,386		29,660	6	54,004		435
Cordage, rope and twine	26	3,761		17,178	7,196			17,002
Cotton	191	64		1,917	11,017	79,425		4,117
Cotton waste	354	5,120		38	33,638	186,317		1,932
Cotton, other	4,208					1,184		44,392
Acetate of lime	15,422			1,211	95,118	1,000		197,635
Calcium carbide	242					56,573		613
Senega root	66,126			670		97,346		24,887
Lye	1,260	10,986		23,997	53,465	1,046	4,318	
Phosphorus	187,450			482	2,759	307		388,339
Drugs, chemicals and medicines, n.c.s.	3,220			317	687	8,710	1,364	13,974
Dyestuffs	1,914	200		7,092	4,075	19	261	16,087
Earthenware and all manufactures	30,663	1,240		20	47	660	175	709
Electrical apparatus	747	3		16,764		260		
Electrotypes	686		15,120	54,066	2,009	465	4,743	
Extract of hemlock	2,613			1,313	90	3,483		1,208
Felt, manufactures of all kinds	248	1,187		5,743	32,838		10,039	624,427
Fertilizers	4	8,723		210	1,301	5,549	963	1,560
Films for photos	221			1,207	70	4,049	175	268
Fur, manufactures of	10,621			1,847	2,289	1,955	249	1,278
Glass and glassware, n.e.s.	906	271		263	627	4,600		
Grindstones, manufactured	865	353		61,662	2,970	1,245	71	414
Guns, rifles and firearms, all kinds	116			445			45	234
Hats and caps	1,635	72		3,362	25			
Household, o. s.	109	239	1,000	27,844	69,606	192,610	145,654	235,634
	130,838	35,859		27,844				275,099

CUSTOMS DEPARTMENT

Exports of Canadian Produce by Ports.—*Continued.*

Exports	Abercorn.	Bridge-burg.	Coaticook.	Fort William.	Halifax.	Atholstan.	Montreal.	Nanaimo.	New West-minster.	Niagara Falls.
	$	$	$	$	$	$	$	$	$	$
MANUFACTURES—*Con.*										
Ice		4,100								
India-rubber, manufactures of	30,783	76,482	57,789		49,415	3,467	132,476		1,428	82,717
Iron and steel, and manufactures of, viz.:—										
Stoves	137	170	93		2,935	163	868		20	129
Buoys, gas, and parts of							3,850			1,000
Castings, n.e.s	65	2,467	353		4,440	1,282	1,226			4,691
Ferro-silicon		156,992			480	128				30,475
Machinery, viz.: type machines		1,160								
Machines, n.e.s	14,604	41,421	4,975		67,790	4,542	27,792		4,997	61,678
Sewing machines	355	1,782	845		230	195	1,696		190	1,145
Typewriters	18	1,480	35		11,065	10,062	65,866		85	
Scrap iron or steel	3,109	184,645			946	6,230	5,181		4,326	34,110
Hardware:—										
Tools, hand or machine	1,220	8,094	4,042		3,360	121	31,051		322	20,350
Hardware, n.e.s	3,275	13,690	12,307		13,478	15,541	59,973		159	11,373
Steel and manufactures of	11,701	48,660	29,939	58	73,732	11,092	264,191	5,078	4,859	275,191
Jewellery, all kinds	1,381	1,876	44		16,449	904	9,053		341	3,838
Jewellers' sweepings	6,637	38,069	3,000		428	1,575	19,512			49,576
Junk	13,862	17,018	3,144		785	4,672	690		783	21,838
Lamps and lanterns	158	1,672	835		184	14	4,097			2,628
Leather, viz.:—										
Sole	377,818	32,009	491,530		77,878	513	1,220,267			155,100
Upper	34,359	48,991	105,375		140	341	79,927		185	295,320
Leather, n.e.s	21,141	63,558	55,653		4,803	9,044	31,378		275	94,869
Boots and shoes	3,564	5,565	5,170		10,496	32,773	3,353		600	9,181
Harness and saddlery	441	12,890	634,186		32,471	156	105,603		93	63,869
other	3,557	2,962	6,039		5,849	641	4,575			10,776
Lime					119					6,308
Liquors, viz.:—										
Ale and beer		1,440	30		1,563	8	32		20	1,059
Gin	282				20	53				
Whisky	1,483	44,107		6	256		13,353			127,383
Wines					497	12	284			273
Wood alcohol		56,533				33,195	60,883			45,147
Rum in pigs, bars, etc		495,159	175		16,800	232,435	779,053			397,302
" ... ages of		1,868				16				120
Metals, n.o.p	17,734	137,672	53,145		24,759	36,885	159,690		18,918	126,0 7

Musical instruments, viz.:—								
Organs	350	502	850	285		20,509	801	590
Pianos	3,140	2,675		1,570	100	9,840		3,370
Other	1,351	6,067	26	523	337	18,954	371	50,951
Oakum				50				
Oil cake	342	5,148	7,515	12,300	7,602	207,805		8,654
Oilcloths, all kinds		960		1,157	7,591	4,327		
Oils, crude	459			508				4,150
Oils, naptha and gasolene		27,489		8,759	4,669	4,683		159
Oils, n.e.s.		D1		3,043	4,635	17,001		7,440
Paper, wall		705		7,099	5	3,181		1,688
Paper, felt		11,428		37,248		51,921		194
Paper, wrapping	26,262	168,648	24,380	1,575	181,714	198,909	835	
Paper, n.e.s.	234,128	681,013	1,105	18,725	325,404	749,042	424	33,425
Paper, printing	605	3,789	1,920	2,443	1,101	41,473		17,505
Paintings	832	21,984	333	815	6,378	15		5,946
Paints and varnishes, all kinds	17	1,423	37	53,588	658			6,889
Photographs		6,615		251		4,340	2,746	523
Plumbago, manufactures of	32,196	226,727	52,468	14,142	38,329	183,467		19,402
Rags		3,189	11	540	72	3,617		140,557
Silk and ...				1,928	107	13,758		7
Soap	60	1,478	445	776	709	958	191	109
Starch			270	5,681	370	10,893		15,758
Stationery				119				
Stone, ornamental, viz.:—Granite, etc.	2	1,476	50	68	53	3,790	15	53
Sugar of all kinds, n.e.s.			3,716	35,941			3,647	
Confectionery, sweetened				11,582			329	
Sugarhouse syrup				3,463			5	
Tar	579	8,382	82	885	75	2,085		20,338
Tin, manufactures of		236						2,087
Tobacco, viz.:—								
Cigarettes		48		361	18	83		8,120
Stems and ...		549	289	118	7,930	6,320		460
All other, n.e.s.	99	300		886	97	904		37
Trunks and ..., all kinds		539	143	11,130	75	1,229		214
Vehicles, viz.:—								
Automobiles	2,835	445,144	2,150	15,800	1,003	824,498	600	419,327
Automobiles, parts of	3	51,372	2	1,205		156,469	285	111,040
Carriages		206		632		1,085		423
Carts, parts of		593		727		24,228		4,361
Wagons	25	158	100	165	300	302,820		14,699
Bicycles		23	50	60	14	1,625		1,336
Bicycles, parts of				6,926				7
All other	391	1,285	1,126	5	4,218	4,632	37	21,821
Vinegar								
Wood, viz.:—								
Barrels	4	1,503	298	6,680	19	364		137
Household furniture	972	3,587	225	13,906	6,319	84,311	10	35,754

Exports of Canadian Produce by Ports.—*Continued.*

Exports	Abercorn.	Bridge-burg.	Coaticook.	Fort William.	Halifax.	Athelstan.	Montreal.	Nanaimo.	New West-minster.	Niagara Falls.
	$	$	$	$	$	$	$	$	$	$
MANUFACTURES—Con.										
Wood—*Con.*										
Doors, sashes and blds..					1,210		1,078			
Matches and ath splints..		584	1,950		422	1,012				48
Mouldings, trimmings and ther furnishings..					95					
Pails, tubs, s, etc..		64	26		417		1,121			648
Spool wood and spools..	265	8,617	1,015,797	1,953	11,665		12,318			165
Wood pulp, ly prepared..	146,731	41,930	280,922		89,321	115,696	29,735		31,132	110,843
„ mechanically ground..	80,967	8,433	15,962		72,130	23,081	125,409			152,502
ther manufactures of..	9,603	12,227	29,819		7,379	392	74,744		1,322	26,757
Woollens..	12,437	48,290	17,624			3,613	250,304		348	11,160
Other articles..	13,411				257,429	22,692	69,984		7,165	263,097
Total..	1,402,391	5,349,933	3,136,609	30,153	1,981,297	1,568,528	9,160,914	21,233	271,473	6,622,172
MISCELLANEOUS.										
Rice meal..					1,762	2,667	2,475		2,320	
Coffee..	136	81			1,145	133	24			6,155
Fruits, dried, n.e.s..			46				158,500			
Other miscellaneous articles..	231	5,340			16,493	54			2,747	4,461
Total..	367	5,421	46	46	19,400	2,854	160,999		5,067	10,616
Grand total..	5,113,261	22,289,047	17,792,923	20,276,207	16,067,405	4,247,734	83,489,321	2,050,974	1,724,602	29,035,546

No. 12.—Exports of Canadian Produce from the twenty undermentioned Ports during the Fiscal Year ended March 31, 1915.

Exports.	Prescott.	Quebec.	Rossland. F. B.C.N	St. Armand.	St. Johns Que.	St. John N.B.	Sault Ste Marie.	Sydney.	Vancouver.	Winnipeg.
	$	$	$	$	$	$	$	$	$	$
THE MINE.										
Asbestos....	100	34,680		100,942	262,564	221,322			9,346	
...os sand...				2,974	10,574	4,635			64	
Gal....		4								
Felspar....				250	480	465			30	
Gold-bearing, quartz, dust, nuggets, etc....	2,899				2,374		38,336	1,528,482		
...s, viz:—					254,155	278,875			2,180,165	
...fr. fine, contained in ore, matte, regulus, etc.	1,156,050	163,233			198,816	546,931			964,208	
Lead-pig...									96,803	
...el fine, contained in ore, matte or speiss.	3,439,539	302,473	95,680	250	138,326	2,521,888	801,760			
Silver, metallic, contained in ore, concentrates, etc...		2,044,262							315,682	
Mica...	861			225	176	11,879				
...al pigment, iron oxides, ochres, etc.						2,440				
Mineral water...	3,573									
a, Iron.	90			40	99	40			1,500	
Corundum.					11,560	5,055				
Other...	*				6,097	38,808			215	
Sand and gravel.			324		100		4,760			
Stone, unwrought.		83	472		704		8,763		26,390	
...her articles...	991			742	6,923	1,988	4,458		340	1,056
Total....	4,604,103	2,544,735	96,476	105,423	892,948	3,631,306	858,077	1,528,482	3,594,743	1,056
THE FISHERIES.										
Codfish, including haddock, ling and pollock, fresh...				8	366	520	8			
" dry salted...		157,293		116,766	2,578	58,153	1,646	3,250	477	
" wet salted...		36,436		166				4,775	14,438	
" tongues and sounds...				30		7,158				
Mackerel, fresh...				8	1,230	2,764				
Mackerel, pickled...					177	51,652	21		448	
Halibut, fresh...				207	3,170	13,143			487	
Herring, fresh or frozen...	1,511				82	154,760			9,113	
" pickled.		30,780		296	208	1,553	2,368		334,575	

6 GEORGE V, A. 1916

Exports of Canadian Produce by Ports.—*Continued.*

Exports.	Prescott	Quebec.	Rossland.	St. Armand.	St. Johns Que.	St. John N.B.	Sault Ste Marie.	Sydney.	Vancouver.	Winnipeg.
	$	$	$	$	$	$	$	$	$	$
THE FISHERIES—*Con.*										
Herring, canned		8,500		1,450	2,536	44,599				
" smoked				74	88,293	10,198			1,865	
Fish, fresh		21,718			70	4,124				
Fish, pickled		48			120	4,723				
Fish, preserved				12	213	3,108				
Oysters, fresh				14	263	36			1,374	
Lobsters, fresh						2,231	2,022		1,706	
Lobsters, canned					19,697	228,277	380			
Clams		14,253		991		31,651		425	114	
Salmon, fresh	10,668	11,150		15,269	14,232	80,764			4,103	
" smoked		45			10		9		10	
" canned		153							4,215,303	
" dog		20		338	234	202,786			3,219	
" fed or lake trout	125,079				988	52	53,479		81,882	
Fish, all fresh	51,902	117		11,997	15,025	4,115	21,275		118	285
Fish, pickled	1,826	1,957		815	1,198		358			
Fish oil, cod		64,737		23,224	6,472	11,078				
Fish oil, whale					116	909			8,652	312
Fish oil, other						3,660			735	104
Furs or skins, the ule of fish or marine animals	214	555				1,780			12,475	
other articles					4,331					
Total	191,200	347,762		171,635	161,618	923,784	81,566	8,450	4,691,094	701
THE FOREST.										
Ashes, pot and pearl	375			320	6,625	4,147				
Ashes, all other				812	183		1,223			
Bark for tanning							725			
Firewood	1,184			1,360	24,004	4,193	4,127			
Logs, cedar, capable of being made into shingle bolts									165,681	
" elm				90	2,445	4,286			5,874	
" hemlock				200	406		517		17,596	
" spruce				475	574	11,450	408		4,725	
" pine					331		32,427		6,418	
" all other		1,285		178	4,370	9,259	34			

Lumber, viz:—										
Basswood	2,280	2,385		726	350					
Deals, pine	1,804	39			10,604	8,042				
Spruce and other	182	390,155		15,116	40,621	1,799,318				
Deal ends						59,006				
Laths	45,014			14,163	107,486	294,019	150,640		7,099	
Pickets	8,976			319	11,168		16,592		5,566	
Planks and boards	1,220,080	102,031		143,907	2,579,891	543,738	2,868,112		305,955	189
Scantling				2,219	3,632	255,744				
Shingles	23,317			67,933	119,497	42,412	5	19	55,738	
Shooks	2,400					37,134	11,741		24,809	
Staves, other and heading	1,075	1,745				13,197			7,274	
All other lumber, n.e.s.		38,177		350	450	19,066				
Masts and spars						99				
Piling						12,225			3,779	70
Poles, hop, hoop, telegraph and other	371			222	39	1,592	5,726		65,736	
Posts and railway ties	462		42	2,642	16,794		10,233		100,889	3,869
Shingle bolts of pine or cedar									75	
Timber, square, viz:—										
Ash		220								
Birch		49,484				12,443				
Elm		83,349								
Oak		71,578								
Pine, white		235,548								
All other						296				
Wood, blocks and other for pulp	18,508	160,748		42,892	1,646,505	71,497	161,000			
Other articles of the forest	95			505						
Total	1,326,123	1,136,744	42	294,429	4,575,975	3,203,163	3,263,510	19	777,214	4,128
ANIMALS AND THEIR PRODUCE.										
Animals, horses one year old or less	192			50						
" horses over one year old	16,230			29,730	31,141	483,735	14,715	1,329	5,350	575
" cattle, one year old or less	142,102			347	13,249					
" cattle, over one year	424,608			57,845	85,960		1,140			1,585
" swine				650						
" sheep, one year old or less	6,940			4,470	6,450					
" sheep, over one year	717			8,277	75		50			
Poultry	1,026	9		2,053	2,233	5	138		575	
All other	443	560		583	7,732	130	117		898	
Bones	19	1,465		1,653	1,511				2,525	36
Butter	1,052			322	18,941	26,711	119	821	83	
Casein	84			800	4,516					
Cheese	80	131,601		463	14,777	350,075	5		6,628	
Eggs	344			205	783	189,962	4		247	
Furs, dressed		1,900			16,232	4,553				
Furs, undressed	7,333	53,027		344	210,459	47,057	2,391	60	4,259	561,906

Exports of Canadian Produce by Ports.—_Continued._

Exports.	Prescott.	Quebec.	Rossland.	St. Armand.	St. Johns, Que.	St. John, N.B.	Sault Ste. Marie.	Sydney.	Vancouver.	Winnipeg.
	$	$	$	$	$	$	$	$	$	$
ANIMALS AND THEIR PRODUCE—Con.										
Glue and grease scraps	2			595	15,349	5,734			3,012	
Live stock					46		20		3,744	
Hair	1,204	35	1,825	3,039	24,933	103			2,065	
Hides and skins other than fur	50,654			358,696	431,226	114,975	17,527		321,518	
Skins and hides				352	1,292				5	
Hay				32	13					
Lard		2,650			4,251	39,228			2,494	
Meats, viz:—										
Bacon	24,508	37,606		6,024	184,884	2,041,224	2,105	88	511	
Beef	341	9,759		325,218	140,545	72,379	350	4,866	547	64
Hams	21,943	13,773		23,305	45,743	435,357	27	475	52	
Mutton					6,300	310		920		
Pork	107	74,242		13,375	24,109	399,073	100		6,546	
Poultry, dressed or undressed	1,344			5,071	17,853	18,497			20	
Game				10	359	50	142			
Canned	43	11,750			7,534					
All other, n.e.s.	655	71,620		23,626	35,240	203,461	98	14	2,106	183
Milk and cream, condensed				636	189,778	6,319			252	
Milk, cream and milk	26,318	3		42,647	167,657	8,045			190,180	
Oil—Neat's foot and other animal, n.e.s.						983				
Sausage casings	128			2,094	28,803	17,797	15		8,939	
Sheep pelts	771			3,831	6,436	35,887			13,918	
Tails				1,095	618	97	97	135	1,782	
Tallow	6,665			357	329,770	26,573	7,723		23,518	138
Wool	14,059			13,467					55,899	
Other articles	122	95	19	1,608	3,718	959	71	15	1,030	623
Total	750,034	410,096	1,844	933,146	2,060,416	4,529,182	46,954	8,723	663,028	565,110
AGRICULTURAL PRODUCTS.										
Balsam		16		1,082	9,337	804				
Cider		513				9,366				
Flax				265	13,850		1,705		12	
Fruits, viz:—										
Apples, dried					13,888	32,116				
Apples, green or ripe	12	837		2,630	45,547	199,585	210	22	56,905	

	1	2	3	4	5	6	7	8	9	10
Berries, of all kinds	888									14
Canned or preserved		1,337	49	48			4,196	175	4,435	
All other, n.e.s.	193	85	6	74			12		256	
Grain and products of, viz:—							31			
Barley	2,204			2,421	3,112	1,115,492				
Beans			9	720	9,218	3,131				
Buckwheat				6,596	17,995	76,431		17,456	19,468	
Indian corn	1,218			14,612	28,317	875	2			
corn meal	59			287,833	4,660	99,624				
Peas, whole	26,565	192,035		200	374,335	1,584,223		2,662	159,117	10
Wheat		34,347		10,291	16,204	3,077	112	46,464	198	
Bran				292,243	794,282	6,974,550			353,316	
Flour of wheat	74,601				53,199	16,421				
Meal, all other					203,476	3,100,698				
Cereal food preprepared, all kinds	10,499	1,975		1,099	4,159	51,745		79	1,516	
Hay	100	8,724		154,870	4	70		23		
Hops					174,253	134,384	78	5,586		
Malt sugar	14	84		196	235,865	752,250	183		35	
Maple syrup	77	150		213		28,430			13	
Seeds:—										
Clover				14	1,367	808				
Flax					85	897				
Grass						55,822			9	
All other	852	6		207	5	3,944	8	45		16
Straw				105	7,637	1,654			7	
Tobacco leaf	11			7,096	639	64			299	
Trees, shrubs and plants		5		3,148	658	397				
Vegetables, viz:—				16						
Canned or preserved				26	4,612	130,401	3		649	
Potatoes				263	38,805	117,957	12			
Turnips	184	15		257	2,855	85			340	5
All other vegetables	57				1,055	63,622	74	244	279	
Other articles						3,820				1,769
Total	117,534	240,132	64	786,559	2,059,423	13,562,972	6,626	72,756	596,854	1,814
MANUFACTURES.										
Agricultural implements:—										
Mowing machines	20,114			387	12,016	23,347	1,115	10	3,829	
Reapers	11,162			303	62	430			1,364	
Harvesters	41,699				60	69,771				
Ploughs	363					16,879			330	
Harrows	105				3,170	5,319			2,162	
Hay rakes	3,090	16,282		258	9,304	1,869				
Threshing machines										
Cultivators	150				7,148	2,436			450	

Exports of Canadian Produce by Ports.—Continued.

Exports.	Prescott.	Quebec.	Rossland.	St. Armand.	St. Johns, Que.	St. John, N.B.	Sault Ste. Marie	Sydney.	Vancouver.	Winnipeg.
	$	$	$	$	$	$	$	$	$	$
MANUFACTURES—Con.										
Agricultural implements.—										
All other	294	773			10,300	43,618	151	89	15,446	100
Parts of	2,260	3,300			28,991	77,672			22,632	
Binder twine		5,399				3,871				
Books, pamphlets, maps, etc	571	12,393	10	16	13,667	60,415	2,124	765	25,132	
...ins and bead				25,121	139	5,384	408		382	
Brooms and whisks				7	50	10,697				
Brushes of all kinds		2		2					10	
Cartridges		534			439	2,149		899		
Cement					170	61,136		42		
Clothing and ...g apparel	25,306	40,575	84	22,891	44,659	5,392,299	687	705	60,070	45
&c										
Cordage, rope and twine				300	229	576	150	149	614	
Cotton ...s				38	22,206	52,834		103	1,709	
..., other	29	1,562		1,538	2,519	16,111	4,920		1,048	
... of lime	755			580	11,645					
... carbide		5,250		20,240	51,103	117,923	4,800		3,427	
Senega root	18,001			30		1,326				
Phosphorous	18,942									
Drugs, chemicals and medicines, n.e.s	19,705			6,825	22,877	27,885	371	2,645	12,589	
Dyestuffs	275	192		516	3,561	32,234				
Earthenware and manufactures of	220			89	1,174	1,501		16	508	
Electrical apparatus		817		796	5,187	11,959	495	1,172	932	
Electrotypes				13	74		133		90	76
Extract of hemlock bark	64,000			6		13,140	140			
Explosives and fulminates of all kinds	258			95	95	25			8,048	
Felt, ...res of					209	61				
Fertilizers	31,465	10,100		12,873	45,952	139	73,248	167,339	56,360	
...ns for ...nto use		696		640	1,314	699			379	
Fur, manufactures of	108	5,270		120	3,271	5,928	60		1,302	
Glass and glassware, n.e.s	20	1,398		266	500	11,236	75		21,878	1,292
Guns, rifles and firearms		3,114		40	617	88,150	35			
Gypsum or ... ground						4,151	7		267	
Hats and ...	4	59		7	144	177			263	
Household effects, n.e.s	25,928	8,581	1,944	93,475	132,164	125,608	54,820	4,604	233,746	6,204

Ice	13,079	788	185	120 / 43,220	644 / 31,062	53,957	698	543	47,999
India-rubber, manufactures of									
Iron and steel and manufactures of, viz.:—									
Stoves	12	259		111	68	1,174	46	1,564	878
Gas buoys and parts of									220
Castings, n.e.s	11,000			90	803	127,212	147	133	
Ferro-silicon							17,361	107,565	
Linotype machines	842	2,631		2,699	98	20,488	7,583	2,370	1,674
Machinery, n.e.s	2,486	175		1,357	17,578	1,103	170		11,884
Sewing machines	110	65		190	14,455	77,750	175		325
Typewriters				707	110	516			710
Scrap iron or steel	1,760				3,533		141,814		6,496
Hardware, viz.:—									
Tools, etc	127	360		1,080	1,381	31,793	940		1,259
Hardware, n.e.s., ...es of	5,759	336		899	1,108	41,485	427	226	2,180
Steel and ...	75	6,721	89	12,642	15,681	3,793,659	4,195	2,854,369	10,200
Jewellery, all l ...ds, n.o.p	780	5,628		537	18,273	1,533	102		1,340
Jewellers' sweepings				16,680	7,865	8,734			3,612
Junk	2,463			23,215	23,283	1,448	25		1,444
Lamps and ...		6		360	12	1,303		80	146
..., viz.:—									
Sole	257	35,664		181,414	298,109	409,679	286	7,612	15,297
Upper	580	13,579		163,034	199,722	289,947	263		95
Leather, n.e.s	110	663		34,786	18,955	22,172	3,748		3,289
Boots and sh...		107		6,049	5,479	33,403	2,177		1,032,626
Harness and saddlery		55		382	10,073	1,869,921	51		43
...her manufactures of				4,638	6,125	18,637	144		6,280
Lime						144			
Liquors, viz:—									
Ale and beer				26	30	7			31
Gin					13				
Whisky	537	2,152		318	17	11,104	50		9,956
Wines	235			7	3,417	4,195			
W...d alcohol					31,363				
Or spirits, n.e.s					264		28		
Aluminum	13,903	16,800	305	5,936	7,438	724,142	3,218	30	67,558
Metals, n.o.p		7,700		17,600	57,124	90,566			33,773
Musical instruments, viz:—									
Organs				910	130	15,245	70		4,054
Pianos	10,911	10,745		132	2,465	6,273	400	424	8,997
Other		116			909	9,189	8		1,514
Oil cake	250	19,079		4,035	1,029	81,354	2,206	560	20
Oil, n.e.s	22,460				23,169	5,136	1,179		
Oil, creosote					1,210	75,232			
Paper, wrapping		34,807		77,411	19	20,434	6	1,275	1,385,841
...el	22,605	34,068		16,005	358,548	529,251	2,487,472		1,023
" printing	2	7		318	17,540	154,925	15	951	441
" n.e.s	194	4,686		10,150	313	26,881	50		663
Paints and varnishes				3,263	3,263	2,728			
Paintings									

Exports of Canadian Produce by Ports.—*Concluded.*

Exports	Prescott. $	Quebec. $	Rossland. $	St. Armand. $	St. Johns, Que. $	St. John, N.B. $	Sault Ste. Marie $	Sydney. $	Vancouver. $	Winnipeg $
MANUFACTURES—*Con.*										
Photographs.... mfs of....	72	644		146	679	567	66		324	
Plumbago,	6,833			30,975	92,619	5,838	199			
Rags,	3,492					12,073			7,276	
Ships,						7,000				
Silk and mfs of....		1,067		4	70	2,863			17,323	
Soap....				224	310	17,859	30	14	15	
fnery.		310		1,288	955	9,412			952	854
Stone, ornamental: Granite, marble, etc., dressed...	6									
Sugar of all kinds, n.e.s....										
Confectionery....		28		12	828	24,060	9	72	30	
Tar....				85	10			324	2,548	
Tin, manufactures of....				375	7	79,188		2,034	5,364	
do., viz....								406		
Cigarettes....				906		1,242				
Stems and cuttings....		117		50	5	3,619	65			
All other, n.e.s....				33	109	3,027				
Tow.... mfr, n.e.s....		185		222	49	100	20		2	
Trunks and valises, all kinds....										
mfs, viz....		1,000		110	218	851,624			23,787	
mfs, parts of....	157	207		193	694	52,028	2	25	7,164	82
Carriages....				1	44	150			95	
Carriages, parts of....					79	3,671			8,822	
Carts....										
Wagons....										
Bicycles....		40		5	20	6,775	1		485	
Bicycles, parts of....						437			2,458	
All other....				369	942	7,886	80		289	
Wood, viz:—										
Barrels, empty....	95			6	561	748		1,740	137	
empty mfe....	689	35		3,820	42,273	46,734	182	183	4,246	
Doors, sashes and blinds....		1,450				1,180	52	22	4,453	
Pails, tubs, churns, etc....				40		15,193				
Wood up, chemically prepared....	92,948				715,514	2,094	84,676		308,655	
Wood pulp, mechanically ground....	287,236	1,727,455		14,979	516,544	82,410	176,448		2,128	
other mfs of....	846	1,155		4,381	16,285	110,358	2,826	1,153	2,064	

Woollens...........	2,391	2,742	......	3,696	17,031	918,875	290	461	535	......
Other articles.....	1,570	9,712	204	36,209	139,037	92,426	3,165	921	30,399	439
Total..........	791,696	2,059,641	2,821	·912,681	3,163,383	17,211,856	3,087,283	3,163,595	3,587,262	9,238
MISCELLANEOUS ARTICLES.										
Coffee...........	......	......	......	......	......	......	......	210	79,063	......
Rice............	1,767	......	......	3,275	3,476	......	......	......	95,390	......
Rice meal.........	60	......	......	166	1,247	19,666	......	......	28,520	......
Other miscellaneous articles...	......	......	......	......	......	......	......	......	......	......
Total.........	1,827	......	......	3,441	4,723	19,666	......	210	203,003	......
Grand total........	7,782,517	6,739,109	101,247	3,207,284	12,938,486	43,081,929	7,344,016	4,782,235	14,113,198	582,047

6 GEORGE V, A. 1916

No. 13.—STATEMENT of Customs and other Revenues collected throughout the Dominion by Chief Ports and Outports during the fiscal year ended March 31, 1915.

NOVA SCOTIA.

Chief Port.	Outports.	Customs Duties.	Other Revenues.	Total Revenues.	Remarks.
		$ cts.	$ cts.	$ cts.	
Amherst............		61,028 42	2 68		
	Joggin's Mines......	2,023 00			
	Northport...........	6 97			
	Oxford.............	1,598 84			
	Pugwash...........	412 79	425 00		
	River Hebert.......	325 80			
	Springhill..........	3,285 37			
	Tidnish.............	4 89			
	Wallace............	293 18			
		68,979 26	427 68	69,406 94	
Annapolis Royal......	....	2,143 73			
	Bridgetown.........	1,655 77			
	Clementsport.......	379 86			
	Port Wade.........	35 34			
		4,214 70	....	4,214 70	
Antigonish..........	....	4,106 02			
	Bayfield............	62 36			
	Harbour au Bouche.	65 75			
		4,234 13	....	4,234 13	
Arichat..............	....	247 20			
	Descouse..........	59 41			
	Irish Cove.........	Nil.			
	L'Ardoise..:.......	34 47			
	Petit de Grat......	10 91			
	River Bourgeoise...	Nil.			
	St. Peter's.........	226 00			
	West Arichat.......	7 81	....	....	Closed Nov. 30, 1914 File 73647.
		585 80	....	585 80	
Baddeck.............	....	915 17			
	Aspey Bay.........	14 35			
	Ingonish...........	31 16			
	Iona...............	2,603 09			
	Little Narrows.....	Nil.			
	Neil's Harbour.....	Nil.			
	New Campbellton..	15 23			
	St. Anne's.........	11 96			
		3,590 96	....	3,590 96	
Barrington Passage...	....	685 87			
	Clark's Harbour....	860 41			
	Port La Tour.......	359 42			
	Wood's Harbour....	137 21			
		2,042 91	....	2,042 91	
Bridgewater.........	....	9,787 46	....	9,787 46	

SESSIONAL PAPER No. 11

No. 13.—STATEMENT of Customs and other Revenues collected, &c.—Nova Scotia—*Continued.*

Chief Port.	Outports.	Customs Duties.	Other Revenues.	Total Revenues.	Remarks.
		$ cts.	$ cts.	$ cts.	
Canso..................	....	2,353 20	8 33		
	Guysboro...........	139 12			
	Isaac's Harbour.....	171 63			
	Liscomb............	8 87			
	Port Mulgrave......	2,311 27			
	Queensport.........	380 73			
	Sherbrooke........	180 79			
		5,545 61	8 33	5,553 94	
Digby...............	....	4,377 65			
	Bear River........	1,313 19			
	Freeport...........	119 39			
	Sandy Cove........	176 11			
	Tiverton...........	174 92			
	Westport...........	203 40			
		6,364 66	....	6,364 66	
Glace Bay............	....	37,552 57	200 59	37,753 16	
Halifax..............	....	2,223,749 43	482 98		
	Hubbard's.........	121 85			
	Ingramport.........	57 95			
	Sheet Harbour......	95 00			
		2,224,024 23	482 98	2,224,507 21	
Kentville............	....	9,307 21			
	Aylesford Station...	357 35			
	Berwick............	1,231 05			
	Canning.............	500 73			
	Harbourville.......	3 96			
	Kingsport..........	3,146 15			
	Port Williams......	1,504 51			
	Wolfville...........	5,737 84			
		21,788 80	....	21,788 80	
Liverpool............	....	6,001 27			
	Caledonia..........	158 52			
	Port Medway......	127 70			
		6,287 49	....	6,287 49	
Lockeport............	....	1,308 39	....	1,308 39	
Lunenburg...........	....	5,362 31			
	Chester.............	848 70			
	Lahave.............	1,275 83			
	Mabone Bay........	582 03			
		8,068 87	....	8,068 87	
Middleton...........	....	2,237 53			
	Margaretsville......	24 78			
	Port George.......	8 98			
	Springfield........	102 55	....	....	Opened July 1, 1914.
		2,373 84	....	2,373 84	
New Glasgow........	....	87,178 44			
	Merigomish.........	65 46			
		87,243 90	....	87,243 90	

6 GEORGE V, A. 1916

No. 13.—STATEMENT of Customs and other Revenues collected, &c.—Nova Scotia—*Continued.*

Chief Port.	Outports.	Customs Duties.	Other Revenues.	Total Revenues.	Remarks.
		$ cts.	$ cts.	$ cts.	
North Sydney........	....	71,632 94	92 66		
	Grand Narrows.....	22 52			
	Little Bras d'Or....	47 84			
	Sydney Mines.......	21,906 94			
		93,610 24	92 66	93,702 90	
Parrsboro............	....	595 29	50 00		
	Advocate Harbour..	55 11			
	Apple River........	12 34			
	Five Islands.......	10 96			
	Port Greville.....	30 28			
		703 98	50 00	753 98	
Pictou..............	....	13,233 17	3 10		
	River John.........	287 16			
	Tatamagouche.....	140 12			
		13,660 45	3 10	13,663 55	
Port Hawkesbury.....	....	2,092 85			
	Marble Mountain....	16 22			
	Orangedale........	277 69			
	Port Hastings......	207 32			
	West Bay..........	135 17			
	Whycocomagh.....	59 70			
		2,788 95	....	2,788 95	
Port Hood...........	....	222 95			
	Cheticamp.........	284 45			
	Grand Etang.......	75 14			
	Inverness..........	2,035 43			
	Mabou.............	115 46			
	Margaree..........	86 86			
		2,820 29	....	2,820 29	
Shelburne..........	....	2,083 32			
	Jordan Bay........	1 13			
	North East Harbour	13 69			
	Port Clyde........	210 28			
	Sandy Point.......	Nil			
		2,308 42	....	2,308 42	
Sydney..............	....	166,474 04	199 90		
	Gaberouse..........	6 72			
	Louisburg..........	733 80	10 00		
	Main à Dieu........	2 83			
	Port Morien........	266 09			
		167,483 48	209 90	167,693 38	
Truro..............	....	76,461 11			
	Bass River........	13 26			
	Economy...........	27 01			
	Little Bass River...	5 54			
	Londonderry.......	1,481 57			
		77,988 49	....	77,988 49	

No. 13.—STATEMENT of Customs and other Revenues collected, &c.—Nova Scotia—*Concluded.*

Chief Port.	Outports.	Customs. Duties.	Other Revenues.	Total Revenues.	Remarks.
		$ cts.	$ cts.	$ cts.	
Weymouth...........		915 30	400 00		
	Barton.............	745 21			
	Belliveau's Cove....	5 87			
	Church Point.......	238 10			
	Little River........	17 00			
	Meteghan...........	168 75			
	Meteghan River....	919 01			
		3,009 24	400 00	3,409 24	
Windsor.............		11,355 38			
	Cheverie............	26 07			
	Hantsport..........	879 71			
	Maitland............	450 15			
	Noel................	11 09			
	Walton.............	23 40			
		12,745 80	....	12,745 80	
Yarmouth...........		57,710 22	332 70		
	Lower East Pubnico	606 21			
	Salmon River......	311 46			
	Tusket.............	246 38			
	Wedgeport.........	18 01			
		58,892 28	332 70	59,224 98	
	Nova Scotia, total..	2,930,005 20	2,207 94	2,932,213 14	

PRINCE EDWARD ISLAND.

Chief Port.	Outports.	Customs. Duties.	Other Revenues.	Total Revenues.	Remarks.
Charlottetown........		123,464 46	122 82		
	Cardigan...........	309 18			
	Crapaud............	261 65			
	Georgetown.........	140 65			
	Grand River........	2 43			
	Montague Bridge....	824 60			
	Murray River......	42 32	....	....	Opened July 1, '14·
	Murray Harbour....	171 36			
	New London.......	37 84			
	Rustico.............	19 86			
	Souris..............	2,103 74			
	St. Peter's.........	67 30			
	Vernon River.......	77 27			
		127,522 66	122 82	127,645 48	
Summerside..........		28,074 97			
	Alberton............	1,503 21			
	Malpeque...........	12 22			
	Port Hill...........	6 44			
	Tignish.............	3,106 19			
		32,703 03	....	32,703 03	
	P. E. I., total.......	160,225 69	122 82	160,348 51	

NEW BRUNSWICK.

Chief Port.	Outports.	Customs. Duties.	Other Revenues.	Total Revenues.	Remarks.
Bathurst.............		65,312 26	27 71	....	
	Caraquet...........	1,509 33	....	....	
	Shippegan..........	150 52	....	....	....
	Tracadie...........	71 66	....	....	....
		67,043 77	27 71	67,071 48	

No. 13.—STATEMENT of Customs and other Revenues collected, &c.—New Brunswick—*Continued.*

Chief Port.	Outports.	Customs Duties.	Other Revenues.	Total Revenues.	Remarks.
		$ cts.	$ cts.	$ cts.	
Campbellton.........	....	29,031 69	....	29,031 69	
Chatham............		9,279 76	....	....	
	Buctouche........	421 95	....	....	
	Richibucto........	1,194 49	....	....	
		10,896 20	....	10,896 20	
Dalhousie...........	....	5,241 39	....	5,241 39	
Fredericton.........	....	69,754 88	50 00	69,804 88	
McAdam Junction.....	....	9,920 28	1,015 69	10,935 97	
Moncton............		78,998 32	....	....	
	Albert.............	521 18	....	....	
	Alma..............	100,25	....	....	
	Cocagne...........	2 05	....	....	
	Dorchester........	939 00	....	....	
	Hillsboro..........	1,086 09	....	....	
	Shediac............	9,735 80	....	....	
	Waterside........	Nil.	....	....	
		91,382 69	....	91,382 69	
Newcastle...........	....	7,872 05	....	7,872 05	
St. Andrews.........		8,167 85	2 00	....	
	Campobello........	925 25	....	....	
	Grand Harbour.....	230 51	....	....	
	Indian Island......	32 35	....	....	
	Lord's Cove.......	1,047 22	....	....	
	North Head.......	1,331 64	....	....	
	Wilson's Beach.....	280 19	....	....	
		12,015 01	2 00	12,017 01	
St. John............		1,658 378 64	125 17	....	
	Back Bay..........	58 05	....	....	
	Beaver Harbour....	465 32	....	....	
	Lepreaux..........	215 25	....	....	
	Lorneville.........	Nil.	....	....	
	Musquash.........	Nil.	....	....	
	St. George.........	962 17	....	....	
	St. Martin's........	284 98	....	....	
	Sussex.............	10,593 24	....	....	
		1,670 957 65	125 17	1,671 082 82	
St. Stephen..........		50,695 44	1,033 39	....	
	Grand Falls........	176 94	....	....	
	Milltown...........	8,061 95	....	....	
	Upper Mills........	96 82	....	....	
		59,031 15	1,033 39	60 064 54	
Sackville............		9,908 98	....	....	
	Baie Verte.........	1,251 80	....	....	
		11,160 78	....	11,160 78	
Woodstock...........	....	27,180 20	10,010 50	....	
	Andover...........	921 80	353 50	....	Formerly lower Andover, Memo 1831
	Aroostook Junction..	6,719 63	345 00	....	B
	Bath..............	172 69	....	....	
	Bloomfield........	130 27	....	....	
	Centreville........	463 40	....	....	
	Clair..............	10,712 40	100 63	....	

No. 13.—STATEMENT of Customs and other Revenues collected, &c.—N
Brunswick—*Concluded.*

Chief Port.	Outports.	Customs Duties.	Other Revenues.	Total Revenues.	
		$ cts.	$ cts.	$ cts.	
	Debec Junction.....	5,046 79	2 40	....	
	Edmunston........	25,666 28	175 00	....	
	Grand Falls........	5,532 79	405 10	....	
	Green River........	694 67	....	....	
	Richmond Road....	802 43	600 00	....	
	St. Hilaire.........	180 52	....	....	
	St. Leonard's.......	34,239 27	62 20	....	
		118,463 14	12,054 33	130,517 47	
New Brunswick, total	....	2,162,770 68	14,308 29	2,177,078 97	
Abercorn............	....	14,995 36	307 50	15,302 86	
Athelstan............	....	44,901 13	....	44,901 13	
Beebe Junction.......		38,167 38	876 00	....	
	Georgeville........	948 51	1,800 00	....	
	Magog............	24,061 35	....	....	
	Rock Island.......	49,247 85	3,143 55	....	
		112,425 09	5,819 55	118,244 64	
Coaticook..........	....	19,181 53	105 00	....	
	Stanhope..........	184 87	....	....	
		19,366 40	105 00	19,471 40	
Cookshire............		25,901 39	....	....	
	Comin's Mills......	3,867 36	....	....	Formerly Hall's
	Hereford Road.....	54 58	....	....	Stream Memo.
	Lake Megantic......	1,753 47	....	....	1794B.
		31,576 80	....	31,576 80	
Gaspe..............		10,385 80	....	....	
	Esquimaux Point...	13 63	....	....	
		10,399 43	....	10,399 43	
Hemmingford........		2,101 05	....	....	
	Franklin Centre.....	403 24	....	....	
	Huntingdon........	131 70	....	....	
	Roxham............	69 02	....	....	
	Vicars............	128 36	....	....	
		2,833 37	....	2,833 37	
Highwater............	....	2,606 10	146 00	2,752 10	
Hull........ :........		45,057 14	....	....	
	Lachute..........	27,608 01	....	....	
		72,665 15	....	· 72,665 15	
Mansonville..........	....	1,766 31	140 35	1,906 66	
Montreal...........		19,277,341 78	26,192 73	....	
	Dundee............	1,831 50	....	....	
	Joliette............	63,712 86	....	....	
	Marieville.........	17,679 13	....	....	
	St. Agnes de Dundee	42,523 18	....	....	
	St. Jerome.........	17,541 12	....	....	
	Trout River........	93,55	....	....	
		19,420,723 12	26,192 73	19,446,915 85	

No. 13.—STATEMENT of Customs and other Revenues collected, &c.
Quebec—*Continued.*

Chief Port.	Outports.	Customs. Duties.	Other Revenues.	Total Revenues.	Remarks.
		$ cts.	$ cts.	$ cts.	
Paspébiac.............		6,527 71	....	....	
	New Richmond.....	907 64	....	....	
		7,435 35	....	7,435 35	
Perce.................		435 84	....	....	
	Chandler...........	66,984 83	....	....	Opened July 1, 14.
	Grand River.......	10,415 75	....	....	Memo 1794B.
					Closed July 1, 14.
		77,836 42	....	77,836 42	Memo 1794B.
Port Burwell..........	....	2,368 52	....	2,368 52	File 82950.
Quebec...............	....	1,594,952 35	1,211 82		
	Beauceville........	4,403 92			
	Bradore Bay.......	293 21			
	Chicoutimi........	23,741 03			
	Ellis Bay...........	47 02			
	Jonquiere..........	10,155 09			
	La Tuque..........	9,122 34			
	Levis..............	162,043 77			
	Magdalen Islands...	131 48			
	Montmagny........	6,416 63			
	Murray Bay.......	1,595 24			
	Riviere du Loup....	7,286 04			
	Seven Islands......	0 70			
	St. Anselme........	2,491 67			
	Tadousac..........	29 27			
	Trois Pistoles......	1,469 80			
	Victoriaville.......	35,420 74			
		1,859,600 30	1,211 82	1,860,812 12	
Rimouski............	....	9,339 89			
	Matane............	62 03			
		9,401 92	....	9,401 92	
St. Armand..........	....	9,421 06	5 00		
	Phillipsburg.......	3,648 57			
		13,069 63	5 00	13,074 63	
St. Hyacinthe.......	....	63,514 92			
	Drummondville....	19,356 85			
		82,871 77		82,871 77	
St. John's...........	....	136,833 68	54 55		
	Clarenceville........	479 13			
	Frelighsburg........	1,590 79			
	Granby............	79,005 74			
	Lacolle............	9,109 52			
	Lacolle Junction....	54 85			
	Noyan Junction....	1,133 77			
		228,207 48	54 55	228,262 03	
Sherbrooke..........	....	253,659 23	400 00		
	Richmond..........	25,896 90			
	Thetford Mines.....	17,010 25			
	Windsor Mills.......	8,120 83			
		304,687 21	400 00	305,087 21	
Sorel...............	....	42,546 19		42,546 19	

SESSIONAL PAPER No. 11

No. 13.—STATEMENT of Customs and other Revenues collected, &c., Quebec—
Concluded.

Chief Port.	Outports.	Customs Duties.	Other Revenues.	Total Revenues.	Remarks.
		$ cts.	$ cts.	$ cts.	
Three Rivers.........		124,152 00			
	Grand Mere........	88,418 53			
	Nicolet............	1,114 98			
	Shawinigan Falls....	73,007 51			
		286,693 02	....	286,693 02	
Valleyfield.........	....	270,089 08	....	270,089 08	
	Quebec, total...	22,919,065 15	34,382 50	22,953,447 65	

ONTARIO.

Amherstburg........	....	12,066 05	34 65		
	Essex Centre.......	7,118 64			
	Kingsville.........	8,800 87			
	Leamington........	40,827 62			
	West Dock.........	954 62			
		69,767 80	34 65	69,802 45	
Belleville...........	....	93,667 01	8 40		
	Campbellford......	13,797 53			
		107,464 54	8 40	107,472 94	
Berlin.............	....	361,163 16			
	Elmira............	10,184 68			
	New Hamburg.....	6,255 70			
	Waterloo..........	52,874 21			
		430,477 75	....	430,477 75	
Bowmanville.......	....	51,105 79			
	Newcastle.........	50 58			
		51,156 37	....	51,156 37	
Brantford..........	....	395,863 30	....	395,863 30	
Bridgeburg.........	....	654,704 04	4,966 23	659,670 27	
Brockville..........	....	90,565 45	....	90,565 45	
Chatham...........	....	145,336 82	3 10		
	Blenheim..........	40,927 33			
	Dresden...........	47 31			
	Glencoe...........	5,930 30			
	Ridgetown.........	11,740 92			
	Rondeau..........	109,160 45			
	Tilbury...........	17,244 41			
		330,387 54	3 10	330,390 64	
Cobourg...........	....	105,382 28			
	Brighton..........	5,146 04			
	Colbourne.........	1,659 59			
		112,187 91	....	112,187 91	
Collingwood........	....	31,585 21			
	Meaford..........	8,350 35			
		39,935 56	....	39,935 56	

No. 13.—STATEMENT of Customs and other Revenues collected, &c.—Ontario—
Continued.

Chief Port.	Outports.	Customs Duties.	Other Revenues.	Total Revenues.	Remarks.
		$ cts.	$ cts.	$ cts.	
Cornwall............	....	250,660 93	25 00		
	St. Regis..........	150 45	10 00		
		250,811 38	35 00	250,846 38	
Deseronto...........	....	4,338 63	....	4,338 63	
Fort William........	....	742,479 03	40 12		
	Dryden...........	2,737 65	....	....	Opened April 13, '14. Memo 1778B.
		745,216 68	40 12	745,256 80	
Galt...............	....	124,936 84	0 75		
	Ayr...............	818 76			
	Preston...........	96,288 29			
		222,043 89	0 75	222,044 64	
Gananoque.........	....	40,846 66			
	Ivy Lea..........	31 05			
	Landsdowne.......	985 08			
	Mallorytown L'd'g.	1 00			
	Rockport..........	911 25			
		42,775 04	....	42,775 04	
Goderich...........	....	45,750 33	0 07		
	Clinton...........	26,077 35			
	Kincardine........	7,631 20			
	Lucknow..........	22 37			
	Seaforth..........	7,354 04			
	Southampton......	6,322 54			
	Wingham..........	8,826 42			
		101,984 25	0 07	101,984 32	
Guelph.............	....	166,726 46			
	Durham..........	44 12			
	Harriston..........	9 27			
	Mount Forest......	99 17			
	Walkerton.........	8,116 23			
		174,995 25	....	174,995 25	
Hamilton..........	....	2,369,832 00	803 75		
	Burlington........	8,122 02			
	Dundas...........	49,133 88			
	Dunnville.........	20,636 92			
	Oakville..........	11,445 16			
		2,459,169,98	803 75	2,459,973 73	
Ingersoll..........	....	43,191 07			
	Port Burwell.......	129,999 65			
		173,190 72	....	173,190 72	
Kenora............	....	19,981 89	....	19,981 89	
Kingston..........	....	210,513 16	186 46		
	Bath.............	115 70			
	Collin's Bay.......	103 82			
	Wolfe Island.......	326 31			
		211,058 99	186 46	211,245 45	
Lindsay...........	....	32,139 41	....	32,139 41	

No. 13.—STATEMENT of Customs and other Revenues collected, &c.—Ontario—
Continued.

˙Chief Port.	Outports.	Customs. Duties.	Other Revenues.	Total Revenues.	Remarks.
		$ cts.	$ cts.	$ cts.	
London..............		995,522 38	1,041 67		
	Parkhill...........	5,282 91			
	Strathroy.........	10,547 81			
		1,011,353 10	1,041 67	1,012,394 77	
Midland.............	....	125,871 31			
	Penetanguishene....	15,639 40			
		141,510 71	....	141,510 71	
Morrisburg...........	....	2,361 32	44 00		
	Aultsville..........	872 23			
	Iroquois...........	1,306 21			
		4,539 76	44 00	4,583 76	
Napanee..............	......	11,682 30	....	11,682 30	
Niagara Falls........	....	289,476 57	848 01		
	Chippewa..........	2,735 42			
	Niagara...........	2,333 53	....	....	or Niagara-on-the-lake.
	Queenston..........	107 15			
		294,652 67	848 01	295,500 68	
North Bay....	....	142,222 85	1 00		
	Cobalt.............	185,658 88			
	Cochrane..........	13,341 86			
	Haileybury........	622 64			
	South Porcupine....	47,835 23			
	Sturgeon Falls.....	14,014 87			
	Temagami.........	14 00			
		403,710 33	1 00	403,711 33	
Orillia.............	....	50,562 80			
	Bracebridge.......	77,387 92			
	Burk's Falls........	Nil.			
	Gravenhurst.......	Nil.			
	Huntsville..........	7 35			
		127,958 07	....	127,958 07	
Oshawa..............	....	344,847 97	....	344,847 97	
Ottawa..............	....	1,351,447 20	56 05		
	Alexandria.........	7,412 64			
	Almonte...........	10,249 50			
	Arnprior..........	6,079 38			
	Carleton Place.....	10,243 64			
	Hawkesbury.......	16,398 94			
	Pembroke..........	33,027 75			
	Perth..............	20,318 12			
	Renfrew...........	23,406 31			
	Smith's Falls.......	36,596 62			
	Ville Marie........	419 62			
		1,515,599 72	56 05	1,515,655 77	
Owen Sound........	....	47,332 28			
	Chesley............	94 17			
		47,426 45	....	47,426 45	

6 GEORGE V, A. 1916

No. 13.—STATEMENT of Customs and other Revenues collected, &c.—Ontario
—*Continued.*

Chief Port.	Outports.	Customs Duties.	Other Revenues.	Total Revenues.	Remarks.
		$ cts.	$ cts.	$ cts.	
Paris................	....	39,949 56			
	St. George..........	4,439 20			
		44,388 76	....	44,388 76	
Parry Sound.........	....	9,973 20	40 00		
	Byng Inlet..........	116,196 17			
	Depot Harbour.....	77,116 75			
	French River.......	227 47			
	Key Harbour.......	26,534 05			
		230,047 64	40 00	230,087 64	
Peterboro.............	....	409,016 37	749 30	409,765 67	
Picton...............	....	13,977 39			
	Wellington..........	1,180 23			
		15,157 62	....	15,157 62	
Port Arthur..........	....	442,585 32	4 05		
	Fort Francis.......	155,765 29			
	North Lake.........	Nil.			
	Rainy River........	17,280 79	19 24		
		615,631 40	23 29	615,654 69	
Port Hope.............	....	22,031 98	....	22,031 98	
Port McNicoll........	....	1,777 07	....	1,777 07	
Prescott..............	....	141,195 19	41 17		
	Cardinal............	6,396 86			
		147,592 05	41 17	147,633 22	
St. Catharines........	....	405,613 24	100 00		
	Port Colborne......	147,567 88			
	Port Dalhousie.....	10,833 33			
	Thorold............	212,103 87			
		776,118 32	100 00	776,218 32	
St. Thomas...........	....	221,128 11			
	Aylmer.............	10,539 25			
	Port Stanley........	130,953 82			
		362,621 18	....	362,621 18	
Sarnia................	Courtwright........	321,803 00	495 00		
	Courtwright........	7,743 92			
	Petrolia............	25,182 39			
	Point Edward......	10,427 60			
	Stag Island........	80 14			
		365,237 05	495 00	365,732 05	

No. 13.—STATEMENT of Customs and other Revenues collected, &c.—Ontario
—*Continued.*

Chief Port.	Outports.	Customs Duties.	Other Revenues.	Total Revenues.	Remarks.
		$ cts.	$ cts.	$ cts.	
Sault Ste. Marie......		498,029 74	426 81		
	Blind River........	6,091 04			
	Bruce Mines........	4,945 71			
	Cockburn Island....	476 05			
	Cutler.............	4,978 81			
	Gore Bay...........	688 71			
	Little Current......	36,504 23			
	Manitowaning.......	393 29			
	Michipicoten Harb'r	107 93			
	Providence Bay.....	23 35			
	Richards Landing...	286 13			
	Thessalon..........	1,771 01			
		554,296 00	426 81	554,722 81	
Simcoe..............		52,188 15			
	Port Dover........	3,433 20			
	Port Rowan.......	499 58			
		56,120 93	....	56,120 93	
Stratford............		115,424 44	17 10		
	Hanover...........	17,502 56			
	Listowel...........	22,789 26			
	Mitchell..........	12,168 93			
	St. Mary's.........	32,302 33			
	Wiarton...........	5,175 75			
		205,363 27	17 10	205,380 37	
Sudbury.............		93,341 00			
	Conniston..........	9,039 53			
	Copper Cliff.......	24,060 59			
	Espanola...........	5,934 78	....	....	Opened Oct. 1, '14. Memo 1815 B.
		132,375 90	....	132,375 90	
Tillsonburg..........		28,954 92	....	28,954 92	
Toronto.............		15,037,456 04	15,063 41		
	Acton.............	28,013 13			
	Alliston...........	6,927 45			
	Aurora and New-market..........	28,714 92			
	Bala..............	Nil.			
	Barrie.............	18,599 62			
	Brampton..........	23,690 21			
	Georgetown........	26,956 96			
	Markdale..........	102 05			
	Milton West........	51 74			
	Orangeville........	24,483 93			
	Port Credit........	27,340 07			
	Streetsville........	16,261 27			
	West Toronto......	567,436 58	330 86		
	Lake Joseph........	Nil.	....	....	Opened May 14, '15. Summer season.
		15,806,033 97	15,394 27	15,821,428 24	
Trenton.............		19,509 09	....	19,509 09	
Wallaceburg.........		583,874 31			
	Port Lambton......	841 46			
	Sombra............	1,119 28			
	Walpole Island......	228 35			
		586,063 40	....	586,063 40	

No. 13.—STATEMENT of Customs and other Revenues collected, &c.—Ontario
—*Concluded.*

Chief Port.	Outports.	Customs Duties.	Other Revenues.	Total Revenues.	Remarks.
		$ cts.	$ cts.	$ cts.	
Welland...............	....	281,930 67	1 99	281,932 66	
Whitby...............	....	13,753 36	....	13,753 36	
Windsor...............		956,913 33	4,123 74		
	Belle River.........	1,500 84			
	Sandwich...........	8,921 16			
	Walkerville........	867,016 25	681 92		
		1,834,351 58	4,805 66	1,839,157 24	
Woodstock...........	....	79,642 05			
	Norwich............	7,248 85			
		86,890 90	....	86,890 90	
	Ontario total.......	33,218,760 88	30,163 85	33,248,924 73	

MANITOBA.

Brandon...............	....	204,673 03	37 75		
	Boissevain.........	2,139 00			
	Bannerman........	1,892 95			
	Carberry..........	1,860 62			
	Cartwright........	181 36	....	....	Opened Oct. 1, 1914.
	Deloraine.........	1,788 13			Memo. 1815B.
	Killarney..........	1,567 74			
	Melita............	2,487 33			
	Oak Lake..........	119 60			
	Souris.............	8,065 33	20 00		
	Virden............	11,990 22			
		236,765 31	57 75	236,823 06	
Emerson...............	....	22,136 93	867 70	23,004 63	
Gretna...............	....	16,516 57	57 26		
	Haskett...........	2,580 37			
		19 096 94	57 26	19,154 20	
Portage la Prairie.....	....	49,246 61			
	Birtle..............	481 01			
	Gladstone.........	148 47			
	Dauphin...........	19,595 96			
	Minnedosa.........	3,596 26			
	Neepawa..........	4,439 19			
	Rapid City........	124 62			
		77,632 12	....	77,632 12	
Winnipeg.............	....	5,988,995 54	7,979 49	....	$42.35 transferred
	Crystal City.......	1,047 00			from Other Rev-
	Manitou...........	76 98			enues to Customs
	Moose Factory.....	22,298 20			Duties as per in-
	Morden............	3,788 65			structions from
	Pilot Mound.......	44 28			Dept. of Finance.
	Selkirk............	10,677 34			File 61,198.
	Snowflake.........	1,181 69	128 00		
	Sprague...........	8,625 92			
	The Pas...........	11,911 85	....	....	Formerly Le Pas,
	York Factory......	9,310 47			O.C. June 2, 1914.
		6,057,957 92	8,107 49	6,066,065 41	
	Manitoba total.....	6,413,589 22	9,090 20	6,422,679 42	

SESSIONAL PAPER No. 11

No. 13.—STATEMENT of Customs and other Revenues collected, &c.

SASKATCHEWAN.

Chief Port.	Outports.	Customs Duties.	Other Revenues.	Total Revenues.	Remarks.
		$ cts.	$ cts.	$ cts.	
Moosejaw.............	....	248,238 30	2,106 70		
	Big Muddy.........	1,096 20	56 00		
	East Poplar River..	574 80			
	Gull Lake..........	3,822 99			
	Harlem Trail.......	438 28	....	....	Opened May 1, 1914.
	Maple Creek.......	7,420 97			File 71076
	Swift Current......	50,679 11			
	Weyburn...........	46,710 61			
	Willow Creek.......	2,998 53			
	Wood Mountain....	9,202 18			
		371,131 97	2,162 70	373,344 67	
North Portal........	....	27,853 80	135 55		
	Estevan...........	43,804 38			
	Marienthal........	4,299 03	17 60		
		75,957 21	153 15	76,110 36	
Prince Albert.......	....	66,014 67	....	66,014 67	
Regina..............	....	471,803 43	65 91		
	Arcola............	120 23			
	Boundary Line.....	3,112 97			
	Broadview.........	138 44			
	Fort Q'Appelle.....	185 45			
	Grenfell...........	154 46			
	Indian Head.......	574 77			
	Moosomin..........	5,118 90			
	Q'Appelle..........	310 39			
	Wapella...........	97 04			
	Whitewood........	81 72			
	Wolseley..........	370 80			
		482,068 60	65 91	482,134 51	
Saskatoon...........	....	297,558 16	217 38		
	Battleford........	512 00	....	....	Opened May 1, 1914.
	Humboldt.........	7,486 52			
	Lloydminster......	0 94	....	....	Closed Sept. 30, 1914
	Melfort...........	2,801 53			
	North Battleford...	32,257 99			
	Rosthern..........	2,242 43			
	Yorkton...........	18,263 35	26 00		
		361,122 92	243 38	361,366 30	
	Saskatchewan total.	1,356,345 37	2,625 14	1,358,970 51	

6 GEORGE V, A. 1916

No. 13.—STATEMENT of Customs and other Revenues collected, &c.

ALBERTA.

Chief Port.	Outports.	Customs Duties.	Other Revenues.	Total Revenues.	Remarks.
		$ cts.	$ cts.	$ cts.	
Calgary...............	....	1,140,623 03	6,034 31	....	
	Banff...............	Nil.	....	....	
	Banff. P.O.........	764 40	....	....	
	Burdett.............	3,140 45	21 00	....	
	Canmore............	179 12	....	....	
	Claresholm.........	329 39	....	....	
	Field...............	Nil.	....	....	Opened May 28, 1914
	Lake Louise........	Nil.	....	.......•....	Tourist season.
	Red Deer...........	18,149 82	....	....	
	Medicine Hat.......	4,926 54	....	....	April 1914, only.
		1,168,112 75	6,055 31	1,174,168 06	
Edmonton...........	....	⁀939,006 07	1,958 97	....	
	Athabasca Landing.	2,759 10	406 25	....	
	Edson..............	8,564 72	....	....	
	Grand Prairie......	128 00	....	....	
	Grouard............	71 29	....	....	
	Peace River Crossing..............	154 78	....	....	
	Shandro............	4 73	....	....	
	Vermillion.........	3,970 98	....	....	
	Vegreville..........	18,760 35	....	....	
	Wainwright.........	2,459 57	....	....	
	Wetaskiwin.........	24,695 32	....	....	
	Wostoc.............	Nil.	....	....	Closed Sept. 5, 1914
		1,000,574 91	2,365 22	1,002,940 13	
Lethbridge..........	....	115,091 23	46 35	....	
	Blairmore..........	18,198 55	....	....	
	Cardston...........	2,803 72	....	....	
	Coutts..............	37,315 53	640 85	....	
	Macleod............	20,450 59	67 20	.........⁄....	
	Pinhorn............	3,048 41	144 05	....	
	Pincher Creek......	481 63	....	....	
	St. Kilda...........	187 94	....	....	Opened for summer
	Twin Lakes........	1,344 15	....	....	season of 1914.
	Wild Horse........	86 75	....	....	
		199,008 50	898 45	199,906 95	
Medicine Hat........	....	116,618 85	75 38	116,694 23	
	Alberta total........	2,484,315 01	9,394 36	2,493 709 37	

No. 13.—STATEMENT of Customs and other Revenues collected, &c.

BRITISH COLUMBIA.

Chief Port.	Outports.	Customs Duties.	Other Revenues.	Total Revenues.	Remarks.
		$ cts.	$ cts.	$ cts.	
Abbotsford..........		18,438 92	110 33	....	
	Aldergrove........	1,246 52	178 50	....	
	Huntingdon........	6,210 33	....	....	
	Upper Sumas......	585 45	....	....	
		26,481 22	288 83	26,770 05	
Cranbrook..........		27,279 02	....	....	
	Athalmer.........	726 82	....	....	
	Creston...........	271 58	....	....	
	Fort Steele........	140 51	....	....	
	Kingsgate.........	4,708 96	....	....	
	Rykerts...........	664 64	....	....	
		33,791 53	....	33,791 53	
Fernie.............		39,078 13	40 47	....	Opened May 26, '14. File 61235.
	Flathead..........	1,956 27	....	....	
	Michel............	9,124 59	....	....	
	Newgate..........	6,510 45	15 00	....	Formerly Gateway, Memo 1831B.
	Phillips...........	85 53	....	....	Opened May 26, '14. File 61235.
		56,754 97	55 47	56,810 44	
Grand Forks........	....	43,393 12	999 11	....	
	Carson............	811 10	....	....	
	Cascade City......	658 90	....	....	
	Phœnix...........	10,749 64	....	....	
		55 612 76	999 11	56,611 87	
Greenwood..........		6,133 00	....	....	
	Bridesville........	1,780 33	....	....	
	Keremeos.........	33,597 72	....	....	
	Midway....	9,171 85	774 75	....	
	Myncaster.........	1,100 41	....	....	
	Osoyoos...........	1,541 54	....	....	
		53,324 85	774 75	54,099 60	
Nanaimo...........	....	62,242 74	34 22	....	
	Alberni...........	314 11	....	....	
	Chemainus........	4,554 44	....	....	
	Comox P.O........	244 09	....	....	
	Courtney..........	582 33	....	....	
	Cumberland.......	15,023 42	61 15	....	
	Duncan's Station....	8,158 75	....	....	
	Ladysmith........	4,231 67	....	....	
	Port Alberni.......	1,519 43	....	....	
	Uchuckleset.......	787 22	....	....	
	Union Bay.........	7,157 33	....	....	Opened July 1, '14. File 72879.
		104,815 53	95 37	104,910 90	

6 GEORGE V, A. 1916

No. 13.—STATEMENT of Customs and other Revenues collected, &c.—British Columbia—*Continued.*

Chief Port.	Outports.	Customs Duties.	Other Revenues.	Total Revenues.	Remarks.
		$ cts.	$ cts.	$ cts.	
Nelson..............		90,162 97	8 50	....	
	Kaslo..............	2,111 12	....	....	
	Waneta............	3,758 98	3 90	....	
		96,033 07	12 40	96,045 47	
New Westminster.....	....	139,770 18	1,822 25	....	
	Chilliwack.........	1,205 57	....	....	
	Douglas............	2,892 16	....	....	
	Ladner.............	1,614 18	....	....	
	Pacific Highway....	1,774 76	78 73	....	
	Steveston..........	3,556 47	....	....	
	White Rock........	45,400 11	80 00	....	
		196,213 43	1,980 98	198,194 41	
Prince Rupert........	....	132,289 81	30 00	....	
	Anyox.............	21,623 43	....	....	
	Hazelton..........	560 14	....	....	
	Massette Inlet.....	179 52	....	....	
	Nass Harbour.....	55 43	....	....	Opened Aug. 1, '14·
	Port Essington.....	77 26	....	....	
	Port Simpson......	278 36	....	....	
	Stewart............	139 63	....	....	
	Stickeen...........	1,459 66	....	....	
		156,663 24	30 00	156,693 24	
Revelstoke..........	....	28,113 47	3 85	....	
	Armstrong..........	682 28	....	....	
	Ashcroft...........	16,041 51	....	....	
	Barkerville........	132 83	....	....	
	Clinton............	465 87	....	....	
	Enderby............	408 04	....	....	
	Fort George.......	902 08	....	....	
	Golden.............	27,900 22	....	....	
	Kamloops..........	28,019 60	....	....	
	Kelowna...........	8,744 11	....	....	
	Lilloet.............	326 49	....	....	
	150 Mile House.....	734 63	....	....	
	Merrit.............	599 03	....	....	
	Penticton..........	1,289 05	....	....	
	Quesnel............	489 44	....	....	
	Soda Creek........	22 81	....	....	
	Summerland.......	676 45	....	....	
	Vernon............	35,948 50	5 40	....	
		151,496 41	9 25	151,505 66	
Rossland............	....	32,293 35	171 85	....	
	Paterson..........	316 10	....	....	
	Trail..............	21,512 91	....	....	
		54,122 36	171 85	54,294 21	
Vancouver..........	....	5,089,994 88	10,517 03		
	Alert Bay..........	256 93	....	....	
	Bella Coola........	303 72	....	....	
	Newport...........	25,175 92	....	....	
	Powell River.......	31,165 44	....	....	
		5,146,896 89	10,517 03	5,157,413 92	

No. 13.—STATEMENT of Customs and other Revenues collected, &c.—British Columbia—*Concluded.*

Chief Port.	Outports.	Customs. Duties.	Other Revenues.	Total Revenues.	Remarks.
		$ cts.	$ cts.	$ cts.	
Victoria.............		1,234,679 56	1,321 86	....	
	Barnfield.........:..	295 63	....	....	
	Clayoquot..........	67 53	....	....	
	Ganges............	649 43	....	....	
	Ganges Harbour....	Nil.	....	....	
	Port Renfrew......	43 75	....	....	
	Sidney.............	5,049 49	....	....	
	Quatsino...........	108 16	....	....	
		1,240,893 55	1,321 86	1,242,215 41	
	British Columbia total.............	7,373,099 81	16,256 90	7,389,356 71	

YUKON.

Dawson.............	.......:..........	129,045 57	69 87		
	Forty Mile.........	1,106 55			
	Herschel Island.....	931 10			
	Rampart House.....	635 80			
		131,719 02	69 87	131,788 89	
White Horse.........	....	25,017 56	8 40		
	Atlin..............	575 18			
	Carcross...........	5,117 86			
	White Pass........	2,291 25			
		33,001 85	8 40	33,010 25	
	Yukon, total.......	164,720 87	78 27	164,799 14	

RECAPITULATION.

Province.	Customs Duties.	Other Revenues.	Total Revenues.
	$ cts.	$ cts.	$ cts.
Nova Scotia..	2,930,005 20	2,207 94	2,932,213 14
Prince Edward Island..	160,225 69	122 82	160,348 51
New Brunswick..	2,162,770 68	14,308 29	2,177,078 97
Quebec..	22,919,065 15	34,382 50	22,953,447 65
Ontario..	33,218,760 88	30,163 85	33,248,924 73
Manitoba..	6,413,589 22	9,090 20	6,422,679 42
Saskatchewan..	1,356,345 37	2,625 14	1,358,970 51
Alberta.....:.	2,484,315 01	9,394 36	2,493,709 37
British Columbia..	7,373,099 81	16,256 90	7,389,356 71
Yukon Territory..	164,720 87	78 27	164,799 14
North West Territories..	1,126 17		1,126 17
British Post Office Parcels..	21,262 46	....	21,262 46
Grand totals..	79,205,286 51	118,630 27	79,323,916 78

6 GEORGE V, A. 1916

No. 14.—SUMMARY STATEMENT of Foreign Merchandise Imported into Canada; and Treaty Tariffs; the Duty Collected by Articles under each Consumption and Amount of Duty Collected

ARTICLES.	TOTAL IMPORTS.		General Tariff.		
	Quantity.	Value.	Quantity.	Value.	Duty.
DUTIABLE GOODS.		$		$	$ cts.
1 Ale, porter, lager and other beer in bottles. Gal.	920,982	642,907	935,930	660,780	278,614 14
2 Ale, porter, lager and other beer in casks.. "	124,732	36,910	125,135	36,355	24,077 82
Total, ales............................	1,045,714	679,817	1,061,065	697,135	302,691 96
3 Ginger ale................................ $	....	27,764	....	1,997	· 349 51
Animals, living, viz.—					
4 Hogs.................................Lb.	3,830	795	3,830	795	57 45
5 Horned cattle.........................No.	1,683	42,255	1,683	42,255	10,563 75
6 Horses over one year old valued at $50 or less per head........................ "	91	3,978	92	4,028	1,150 00
7 Horses, n.o.p............................ "	24,912	2,515,267	2,800	261,353	65,338 25
8 Sheep................................. "	110,663	362,051	110,663	362,051	90,512 75
9 All other, not elsewhere specified....... $	....	55,917	....	54,250	13,562 50
Total, animals......................	....	2,980,263	....	724,732	181,184 70
10 Antiseptic surgical dressings, such as absorbent cotton, cotton wool, lint, lamb's wool, tow, jute, gauzes and oakum, prepared for use as surgical dressings, plain or medicated................ $	....	251,706	....	189,205	37,841 00
11 Bagatelle and other game tables or boards $	....	7,633	....	6,305	2,206 75
12 Bags which contained cement, etc........ $	....	15,123	....	15,123	3,024 60
13 Baking powder..........................Lb.	528,365	150,516	520,100	149,501	31,206 00
14 Balls, cues and racks and cue-tips for bagatelle boards and billiard tables......... $	....	19,921	....	16,569	5,799 15
15 Baskets of all kinds, n.o.p............... $	....	94,126	....	58,170	17,451 00
16 Baths, bath-tubs, basins, closets, lavatories, urinals, sinks and laundry-tubs of any material........................... $	....	316,107	....	202,655	70,929 25
17 Belting of all kinds except rubber and leather................................ $	....	246,217	....	92,988	25,572 36
18 Belts of all kinds, n.o.p., except silk....... $	....	70,373	....	56,664	19,832 40
19 Bells and gongs, n.o.p.................... $	....	33,767	....	31,854	9,556 20
20 Billiard tables...........................No.	254	30,736	121	5,299	1,854 65
21 Blacking, shoe and shoemakers' ink, shoe, harness and leather dressing, n.o.p....... $	....	127,617	....	92,553	25,453 28
22 Blinds, of wood, metal or other material, not textile or paper..................... $	....	3,497	....	3,454	1,036 20
23 Blueing, laundry blueing................ $	....	45,792	....	5,703	1,283 50
24 Boats, open, pleasure, sail boats, skiffs and canoes.......................No.	802	30,015	769	26,554	6,638 50
25 Books, printed, periodicals and pamphlets, or parts thereof, n.o.p................. $	....	1,567,393	....	966,339	96,633 90
26 Books—Novels or works of fiction, or literature of a similar character, unbound or paper bound, or in sheets, not including Christmas annuals or publications commonly known as juvenile or toy books.. $	....	72,533	....	45,989	11,497 25
27 Freight rates for railways, and telegraph rates, bound in book or pamphlet form, and time tables of railways outside of Canada............................. $	....	21,582	....	21,456	5,364 00
28 Bank notes, bonds, bills of exchange, cheques, promissory notes, drafts and all similar work unsigned, and cards or other commercial blank forms printed or lithographed or printed from steel or copper or other plates, and other printed matter, n.o.p..................... $	....	259,214	....	221,834	77,641 90

Quantity and value entered for Consumption under the General, Preferential Tariff, the Total Quantity and Value of each Article entered for thereon during the Fiscal Year ended March 31, 1915.

			ENTERED FOR HOME CONSUMPTION.						
Preferential Tariff.			Treaty Rates.			Total.			
Quantity.	Value.	Duty.	Quantity.	Value.	Duty.	Quantity.	Value.	DutyColl'd.	
	$	$ cts.		$	$ cts.		$	$ cts.	
						935,930	660,780	278,614 14	1
						125,135	36,355	24,077 82	2
						1,061,065	697,135	302,691 96	
	25,746	3,861 90					27,743	4,211 41	3
						3,830	795	57 45	4
						1,683	42,255	10,563 75	5
2	487	73 05				92	4,028	1,150 00	6
						2,802	261,840	65,411 30	7
						110,663	362,051	90,512 75	8
	2,112	316 80					56,362	13,879 30	9
	2,599	389 85					727,331	181,574 55	
	61,501	7,687 98		757	132 49		251,463	45,661 47	10
	1,328	298 87					7,633	2,505 62	11
							15,123	3,024 60	12
8,377	1,048	335 08				528,477	150,549	31,541 08	13
	3,352	754 29					19,921	6,553 44	14
	12,253	2,450 60		23,500	6,462 64		93,923	26,364 24	15
	113,760	22,752 00					316,415	93,681 25	16
	154,924	30,984 80					247,912	56,557 16	17
	13,841	3,114 54					70,505	22,946 94	18
	4,712	942 40		58	15 96		36,624	10,514 56	19
133	25,421	5,719 82				254	30,720	7,574 47	20
	35,670	5,350 50					128,223	30,803 78	21
	43	8 60					3,497	1,044 80	22
	40,940	6,141 00					46,643	7,424 50	23
33	3,312	496 80				802	29,866	7,135 30	24
	540,947	27,047 35		60,004	3,000 20		1,567,290	126,681 45	25
	21,442	3,216 30		5,119	767 85		72,550	15,481 40	26
	126	18 90					21,582	5,382 90	27
	35,268	7,935 73					257,102	85,577 63	28

No. 14.—Summary Statement of Foreign Merchandise

		Total Imports.		General Tariff.		
	Articles.	Quantity.	Value.	Quantity.	Value.	Duty.
			$		$	$ cts.
	Dutiable Goods—*Con.*					
	Books, &c.—*Con.*					
1	Posters, advertising bills and folders.... Lb.	51,915	14,553	47,978	13,275	7,196 70
2	Labels for cigar boxes, fruits, vegetables, meats, fish, confectionery and other goods and wares; also shipping, price or other tags, tickets or labels; and railroad or other tickets whether lithographed or printed or partly printed, n.o.p................................ $	....	255,677	....	232,768	81,468 80
3	Maps and charts, n.o.p................. $	....	38,252	....	27,023	6,080 82
4	Newspapers or supplemental editions or parts thereof partly printed and intended to be completed and published in Canada................................ $	....	9,674	....	9,237	2,309 25
5	Advertising pamphlets, advertising show cards, illustrated advertising periodicals, price books, catalogues and price lists, advertising calendars and almanacs; patent medicine or other advertising circulars, fly sheets or pamphlets...................... Lb.	2,592,615	755,304	2,279,646	680,689	341,946 90
6	Advertising chromos, chromotypes, oleographs or like work produced by any process other than hand painting or drawing, and having any advertisement or advertising matter printed, lithographed or stamped thereon, or attached thereto, or other similar artistic work, lithographed, printed or stamped on paper or cardboard, for business or advertising purposes, n.o.p. "	12,752	6,489	12,183	6,434	1,827 45
7	Printed music, bound or in sheets, and music for mechanical players......... $	....	247,285	....	200,235	20,023 50
8	Photographs, chromos, chromotypes, artotypes, oleographs, paintings, drawings, pictures, engravings or prints, decalcomania transfers of all kinds, or proofs therefrom and similar works of art, n.o.p.; blue prints and building plans................................ $	....	761,289	....	541,889	121,927 86
	Total, books, &c.....................	....	4,009,245	....	2,967,168	773,918 33
9	Boot, shoe, shirt, and stay laces of any material........................... $	....	141,231	....	52,677	15,803 10
10	Boots, shoes, slippers, and insoles of all kinds, except rubber and leather....... $	....	267,233	....	85,667	25,700 10
11	Braces or suspenders and finished parts of. $	....	55,659	....	41,056	14,369 60
	Brass and manufactures of—					
12	Brass in strips, sheets or plates, not polished, planished, or coated........... $	....	189,582	....	186,360	18,636 00
13	Brass in bars and rods, in coils or otherwise, not less than 6 feet in length.... $	....	156,952	....	154,713	15,471 30
14	Nails, tacks, rivets, and burrs or washers $	....	6,443	....	6,199	1,859 70
15	Pumps, hand, n.o.p..................... $	....	10,107	....	9,942	2,982 60
16	Wire, plain.............................Lb.	446,842	70,792	443,698	70,232	8,779 40
17	Wire cloth, or woven wire of brass, n.o.p. $	....	117,159	....	91,593	22,898 25
18	Manufactures of, n.o.p................. $	....	1,378,825	....	1,208,999	362,699 70
	Total, brass............................	....	1,929,860	....	1,723,038	433,326 95
	Breadstuffs, &c., viz.—					
19	Arrowroot...........................Lb.	91,420	5,649	14,571	858	145 71
20	Biscuits, not sweetened................ "	1,243,010	93,371	855,658	61,650	15,412 50
21	Biscuits, sweetened................... "	1,391,301	193,269	168,247	18,864	5,359 49
22	Macaroni and vermicelli.............. "	6,700,390	313,010	1,622,681	90,007	20,284 01
23	Rice, cleaned......................... "	13,289,170	369,955	7,626,434	207,798	57,198 37

SESSIONAL PAPER No. 11

Imported into Canada, &c.—*Continued.*

				ENTERED FOR HOME CONSUMPTION.					
Preferential Tariff.			Treaty Rates.			Total.			
Quantity.	Value.	Duty.	Quantity.	Value.	Duty.	Quantity.	Value.	DutyColl'd.	
	$	$ cts.		$	$ cts.		$	$ cts.	
3,943	1,280	394 30	....	....	....	51,921	14,555	7,591 00	1
....	22,403	5,041 11	....	....	....	....	255,171	86,509 91	2
....	8,929	1,339 35	....	....	....	....	35,952	7,420 17	3
....	437	65 55	....	....	....	....	9,674	2,374 80	4
303,149	73,772	30,314 90	....	....	....	2,582,795	754,461	372,261 80	5
569	55	56 90	....	....	....	12,752	6,489	1,884 35	6
....	47,046	2,352 30	....	....	....	....	247,281	22,375 80	7
....	166,564	24,984 60	....	....	....	....	708,453	146,912 46	8
....	918,269	102,767 29	....	65,123	3,768 05	....	3,950,560	880,453 67	
....	56,646	11,329 20	....	33,212	9,133 55	....	142,535	36,265 85	9
....	163,427	32,685 40	....	16,810	4,622 86	....	265,904	63,008 36	10
....	6,655	1,497 59	....	7,334	2,200 20	....	55,045	18,067 39	11
....	3,222	161 10	....	....	....	....	189,582	18,797 10	12
....	2,101	105 05	....	....	....	....	156,814	15,576 35	13
....	244	48 80	....	....	....	....	6,443	1,908 50	14
....	141	28 20	....	....	....	....	10,083	3,010 80	15
2,294	522	39 16	....	....	....	445,992	70,754	8,818 56	16
....	18,284	3,199 75	....	7,282	1,638 48	....	117,159	27,736 48	17
....	150,517	30,103 40	....	22,227	6,112 64	....	1,381,743	398,915 74	18
....	175,031	33,685 46	....	29,509	7,751 12	....	1,932,578	474,763 53	
76,932	4,801	384 71	....	....	....	91,503	5,659	530 42	19
385,457	31,430	4,714 50	....	....	....	1,241,115	93,080	20,127 00	20
1,237,452	175,991	32,416 82	....	....	....	1,405,699	194,855	37,776 31	21
218	20	1 64	5,078,782	217,117	50,787 82	6,701,681	307,144	71,073 47	22
5,457,420	157,601	27,287 11	....	....	....	13,083,854	365,399	84,485 48	23

.6. GEORGE V, A. 1916

No. 14.—Summary Statement of Foreign Merchandise

	ARTICLES.		TOTAL IMPORTS.		General Tariff.		
			Quantity.	Value.	Quantity.	Value.	Duty.
				$		$	$ cts.
	DUTIABLE GOODS—*Con.*						
	Breadstuffs, &c.—*Con.*						
1	Rice and sago flour, cassava flour, and rice meal	Lb.	845,193	30,888	234,197	11,047	2,341 97
2	Rice bran	"	120	5	120	5	0 88
3	Sago and tapioca	"	2,983,256	69,193	188,631	5,609	1,542 53
4	Tapioca flour	"	594,253	18,559	593,803	18,539	5,938 03
	Total, breadstuffs		27,138,113	1,093,899	11,304,342	414,377	108,223 49
	Grain and products of, viz.—						
5	Barley, n.o.p	Bush.	1,076,640	537,966	44,277	27,519	6,641 55
6	Barley, pot, pearl, rolled, roasted or ground	Lb.	647,442	33,533	119,057	3,239	971 70
7	Beans, n.o.p	Bush.	175,314	332,991	169,651	322,946	42,412 75
8	Buckwheat	"	2,779	2,366	2,779	2,366	416 85
9	Indian corn for purposes of distillation.	"	903,401	690,355	903,401	690,355	67,755 04
10	Oats	"	3,118,119	1,383,453	1,409,121	699,203	140,912 10
11	Peas, n.o.p	"	68,531	144,095	64,243	135,168	9,636 45
12	Rye	"	439,161	282,115	52,671	50,046	5,267 10
13	Wheat	"	35,982,280	35,909,675	1,870,174	1,803,338	224,420 88
	Total, grain		....	39,316,549	....	3,734,180	498,434 42
14	Bran, mill feed, etc	$	....	56,709	....	51,145	8,950 74
15	Buckwheat meal or flour	Cwt.	1,879	7,162	1,868	7,104	934 00
16	Indian or corn meal	Brl.	61,371	217,126	61,367	217,108	15,341 75
17	Oat meal and rolled oats	Lb.	35,752	1,959	9,451	459	56 71
18	Rye flour	Brl.	11,549	43,900	11,549	43,900	5,774 50
19	Wheat flour	"	55,148	258,340	54,678	256,388	32,806 80
20	Hominy, cracked, evaporated or dried corn	$	....	26,956	....	26,946	4,715 68
21	Cattle food containing molasses	$	....	44,083	....	2,486	497 20
22	Cereal foods, prepared, n.o.p	$	....	61,846	....	55,364	11,072 80
23	Cereal foods, prepared, in packages not exceeding 25 lbs. weight each	Lb.	4,420,512	198,590	3,310,581	189,990	50,098 79
24	All other breadstuffs, n.o.p	$	....	127,969	....	117,334	20,533 87
25	Grain, flour and meal, etc., of all kinds when damaged by water in transit or prior to importation into Canada	$	....	1,360	....	1,360	340 00
	Total, grain products		....	1,046,000	....	969,584	151,122 84
	Bricks and tiles. *See* Earthenware.						
26	Bath brick	$	....	1,613	....	65	17 88
27	Building blocks, partition hollow and fire proof building tile	$	....	263,271	....	244,845	55,090 42
28	Building brick	M.	26,329	307,658	24,543	287,407	64,667 04
29	Fire brick, n.o.p	$	....	149,520	....	122,358	27,531 04
30	Paving brick	M.	9,172	146,647	6,514	105,681	23,775 42
31	Drain tiles, not glazed	$	....	2,832	....	2,168	433 60
32	Drain pipes, sewer pipes and earthenware fittings therefor, chimney linings or vents, chimney tops and inverted blocks, glazed or unglazed	$	....	301,433	....	268,230	93,880 50
33	Manufactures of clay, n.o.p	$	....	165,997	....	154,400	34,740 71
	Tota , bricks, &c		....	1,338,971	....	1,185,154	300,139 61
34	British gum, dry sizing cream and enamel sizing	Lb.	1,188,761	36,174	881,907	28,276	2,827 60
35	Brooms and whisks	$	....	15,166	....	13,953	2,790 60
36	Brushes of all kinds	$	....	391,777	....	193,406	53,188 60
37	Buttons, shoe, n.o.p	$	....	1,392	....	1,385	346 25.
38	Buttons of vegetable ivory	Gross	27,718	15,515	16,197	11,806	4,351 65

SESSIONAL PAPER No. 11

Imported into Canada, &c.—*Continued.*

			ENTERED FOR HOME CONSUMPTION.						
Preferential Tariff.			Treaty Rates.			Total.			
Quantity.	Value.	Duty.	Quantity.	Value.	Duty.	Quantity.	Value.	DutyColl'd.	
	$	$ cts.		$	$ cts.		$	$ cts.	
534,430	13,432	4,008 24	....	....	....	768,627	24,479	6,350 21	1
						120	5	0 88	2
2,907,161	66,425	11,624 52				3,095,792	72,034	13,167 05	3
450	20	3 38				594 253	18,559	5,941 41	4
10,599,520	449,720	80,440 92	5,078,782	217,117	50,787 82	26,982,644	1,081,214	239,452 23	
10	22	1 00	....	....	....	44,287	27,541	6,642 55	5
536,503	30,489	6,097 80				655,560	33,728	7,069 50	6
622	1,045	93 30				170,273	323,991	42,506 05	7
....						2,779	2,366	416 85	8
						903,401	690,355	67,755 04	9
2,279	2,162	159,53				1,411,400	701,365	141,071 63	10
4,216	8,926	421 60				68,459	144,094	10,058 05	11
						52,671	50,046	5,267 10	12
						1,870,174	1,803,338	224,420 88	13
....	42,644	6,773 23				....	3,776,824	505,207 65	
....	5,565	834 75				....	56,710	9,785 49	14
8	36	2 80				1,876	7,140	936 80	15
						61,367	217,108	15,341 75	16
25,101	1,460	100 37				34,552	1,919	157 08	17
....						11,549	43,900	5,774 50	18
27	145	10 80				54,705	256,533	32,817 60	19
....	10	1 50					26,956	4,717 18	20
....	41,611	6,241 65					44,097	6,738 85	21
	6,396	959 40					61,760	12,032 20	22
121,680	9,337	1,743 69				3,432,261	199,327	51,842 48	23
....	11,125	1,668 75					128,459	22,202 62	24
....	....	....				....	1,360	340 00	25
....	75,685	11,563 71	....	....	....	....	1,045,269	162,686 55	
...........,	1,571	235 65	....	....	....		1,636	253 53	26
	18,426	2,303 22					263,271	57,393 64	27
1,786	20,251	2,531 40				26,329	307,658	67,198 44	28
....	27,164	3,395 67					149,522	30,926 71	29
2,658	40,966	5,120 75				9,172	146,647	28,899 17	30
....	664	99 60					2,832	533 20	31
....	30,755	7,688 75					298,985	101,569 25	32
....	11,595	1,449 67					165,995	36,190 38	33
....	151,392	22,824 71	....	....	....	....	1,336,546	322,964 32	
306,854	7,898	394 90	....	....	....	1,188,761	36,174	3,222 50	34
....	1,109	166 35					15,062	2,956 95	35
....	67,914	11,885 69	....	133,551	33,387 75	....	394,871	98,462 04	36
....	7	1 23	....	....	....	....	1,392	347 48	38
11,521	3,709	1,317 85				27,718	15,515	5,669 50	37

6 GEORGE V, A. 1916

No. 14.—Summary Statement of Foreign Merchandise

		Total Imports.		General Tariff.		
	Articles.	Quantity.	Value.	Quantity.	Value.	Duty.
			$		$	$ cts.
	Dutiable Goods—*Con.*					
	Buttons—*Con.*					
1	Buttons, all kinds, covered or not, n.o.p., including recognition buttons, and collar and cuff buttons............... $	....	517,314	....	379,174	132,710 90
2	Button blanks of animal shell, in the rough................................... $	....	8,788	....	8,788	878 80
	Total, buttons.....................	....	543,009	....	401,153	138,287 60
	Candles—					
3	Paraffine wax......................... Lb.	375,962	44,526	268,916	35,138	8,784 50
4	All other, n.o.p......................... "	414,491	52,000	369,238	46,799	11,699 75
	Total, candles.....................	790,453	96,526	638,154	81,937	20,484 25
5	Cane, reed or rattan, not further manufactured than split, n.o.p................. $	....	8,844	....	8,823	882 30
	Carriages and vehicles—					
6	Automobiles and motor vehicles of all kinds................................No.	5,457	4,813,310	5,179	4,625,790	1,619,026 50
7	Automobiles and motor vehicles, parts of, n.o.p............................. $	....	2,162,218	....	2,146,387	637,519 94
8	Buggies, carriages, pleasure carts and vehicles, n.o.p.........................No.	873	44,050	861	43,895	15,363 25
9	Cutters................................. "	36	708	36	708	247 80
10	Farm wagons......................... "	2,061	66,069	2,061	66,069	16,517 25
11	Freight wagons and drays.............. "	975	81,106	964	79,891	19,972 75
12	Complete parts of farm and freight wagons, drays and sleighs............ $	....	40,604	....	40,377	10,094 25
13	Complete parts of buggies, carriages and vehicles, n.o.p., including parts of cutters, children's carriages, and sleds, n.o.p................................. $	....	23,167	....	23,009	8,053 15
14	Cars, railway, passenger.................No.	34	257,149	34	257,149	77,144 70
15	Cars, railway, box and flat.............. "	120	58,697	120	58,697	17,609 10
16	Cars, other, n.o.p........................ "	2,095	262,552	1,914	256,505	76,951 50
17	Cars, railway, parts of.................. $	....	93,679	....	91,474	27,442 20
18	Scrapers, railway or road............... $	....	34,877	....	34,877	10,463 10
19	Sleighs................................No.	97	2,238	97	2,238	559 50
20	Wheelbarrows, trucks and hand-carts... "	9,108	49,060	9,001	46,916	14,074 80
21	Bicycles and tricycles, n.o.p........... "	7,643	100,404	2,582	23,153	6,945 90
22	Bicycles and tricycles, parts of, including nickel or electro plated parts for the manufacture of bicycles................. $	....	44,941	....	18,099	5,429 70
23	Children's carriages and sleds......... $	....	311,616	....	306,257	107,189 95
	Total, carriages, &c.................	....	8,446,445	....	8,121,491	2,670,605 34
24	Carpets, n.o.p. (see woollens)...........Yd.	1,092	216	552	131	45 85
25	Carpet linings and stair pads............. $	....	2,274	....	1,736	434 00
26	Carpet sweepers.......................No.	8,001	37,323	9,249	43,905	13,171 50
27	Cash registers and parts of................ $	....	121,323	....	121,177	36,353,10
28	Celluloid, moulded into sizes for handles of knives and forks, not bored or otherwise manufactured; moulded celluloid balls and cylinders coated with tin-foil or not, but not finished or further manufactured, and celluloid lamp shade blanks and comb blanks................. $	....	79	....	7	0 70
29	Celluloid, manufactures of, n.o.p......... $	....	57,795	....	48,699	8,523 19
30	Celluloid, xylonite or xyolite in sheets, lumps, blocks, rods or bars, not further manufactured then moulded or pressed $	....	3,420	....	3,420	171 00
	Total, celluloid.....................	....	61,294	....	52,126	8,694 89

Imported into Canada, &c.—*Continued.*

	Preferential Tariff.			Treaty Rates.			Total.		
Quantity.	Value.	Duty.	Quantity.	Value.	Duty.	Quantity.	Value.	DutyColl'd.	
	$	$ cts.		$	$ cts.		$	$ cts.	
....	41,620	9,365 25	....	98,986	29,695 80	....	519,780	171,771 95	1
....	....	....	....	....	....	....	8,788	878 80	2
....	45,336	10,684 33	....	98,986	29,695 80	....	545,475	178,667 73	
99,798	8,799	1,319 85				368,714	43,937	10,104 35	3
47,083	5,427	814 05				416,321	52,226	12,513 80	4
146,881	14,226	2,133 90				785,035	96,163	22,618 15	
....	21	1 57	....			....	8,844	883 87	5
280	221,190	49,767 91	17	41,724	12,517 20	5,476	4,888,704	1,681,311 61	6
....	19,757	4,130 53	....	49	12 25	....	2,166,193	641,662 72	7
8	281	63 23				869	44,176	15,426 48	8
....						36	708	247 80	9
....						2,061	66,069	16,517 25	10
1	130	22 75				965	80,021	19,995 50	11
....	238	41 66				....	40,615	10,135 91	12
....	243	54 70				....	23,252	8,107 85	13
						34	257,149	77,144 70	14
						120	58,697	17,609 10	15
212	6,875	1,375 00				2,126	263,380	78,326 50	16
....	3,032	606 40				....	94,506	28,048 60	17
....						....	34,877	10,463 10	18
....						97	2,238	559 50	19
105	2,121	424 20				9,106	49,037	14,499 00	20
4,989	76,838	15,367 60				7,571	99,991	22,313 50	21
....	23,398	4,679 60				....	41,497	10,109 30	22
....	6,048	1,360 93				....	312,305	108,550 88	23
....	360,151	77,894 51	....	41,773	12,529 45	....	8,523,415	2,761,029 30	
540	85	21 25				1,092	216	67 10	24
....	552	96 61				....	2,288	530 61	25
6	35	7 00				9,255	43,940	13,178 50	26
....	....	....				....	121,177	36,353 10	27
....	72	3 60	....			....	79	4 30	28
....	9,095	1,364 25	....			....	57,794	9,887 44	29
....	....	....				....	3,420	171 00	30
....	9,167	1,367 85	....			....	61,293	10,062 74	

6 GEORGE V, A. 1916

No. 14.—Summary Statement of Foreign Merchandise

		Total Imports.		General Tariff.		
	Articles.	Quantity.	Value.	Quantity.	Value.	Duty.
			$		$	$ cts.
	Dutiable Goods—*Con.*					
1	Cement, Portland and hydraulic or water-lime............................Cwt.	289,414	124,325	197,202	89,651	19,720 20
2	Cement, n.o.p., and manufactures of, n.o.p $	....	8,879	....	8,242	1,854 68
	Total, cement......................	....	133,204	....	97,893	21,574 88
3	Chalk, prepared........................... $	....	39,823	....	39,081	6,839 70
4	Charcoal................................ $	....	95,949	....	95,900	16,783 12
5	Chicory, raw or green..................Lb.	41,647	1,917	11,512	715	345 36
6	Chicory, kiln-dried, roasted or ground.... "	264,410	14,966	156,204	10,007	4,686 12
	Total, chicory.......................	306,057	16,883	167,716	10,722	5,031 48
7	Church vestments of any material........ $	....	30,935	....	5,467	1,093 40
8	Cider, clarified or refined................Gal.	3,305	2,652	2,835	2,167	283 50
9	Cider, not clarified or refined............ "	669	251	759	347	37 95
	Total, cider........................	3,974	2,903	3,594	2,514	321 45
10	Clocks, time recorders, clock and watch keys, clock movements and clock cases. $	....	366,116	....	335,634	100,690 20
11	Cloth, coated or sized, for manufacture of sensitized, blue or black print cloth..... $	....	6,460	....	3,703	555 45
12	Clothes wringers and parts thereof for domestic use........................... $	....	26,144	....	26,101	9,135 35
13	Coal, bituminous slack, such as will pass through a ¾-inch screen................Ton.	2,312,601	3,246,856	2,283,520	3,214,736	319,692 86
14	Coal, bituminous, round, and run of the mine—and coal, n.o.p.................. "	7,154,405	13,271,784	6,829,839	12,883,315	3,619,814 67
	Total, coal...........................	9,467,006	16,518,640	9,113,359	16,098,051	3,939,507 53
15	Cocoa carpeting, mats, rugs, and matting. $	....	14,633	....	4,144	1,036 00
16	Cocoanuts, imported from the place of growth by vessel direct to a Canadian port....................................No.	85,016	2,115	85,016	2,115	425 08
17	Cocoanuts, n.o.p........................ "	341,762	10,829	325,762	10,397	2,443 38
	Total, cocoanuts.....................	426,778	12,944	410,778	12,512	2,868 46
18	Cocoanut, desiccated, sweetened or not... Lb	675,392	62,376	28,466	3,196	1,270 70
19	Cocoa butter............................. "	1,468,144	429,879	1,250,815	362,585	25,016 30
20	Cocoa paste, or liquor, chocolate paste or liquor not sweetened, in blocks or cakes. "	53,817	10,407	47,757	9,880	1,910 28
21	Cocoa paste or liquor, chocolate paste or liquor, sweetened, in blocks or cakes, not less than two pounds in weight...... "	385,226	83,695	382,965	82,988	16,465 42
22	Cocoa or chocolate, preparations of, in powdered form........................ "	1,396,956	320,575	182,987	40,061	10,533 22
23	Cocoa beans not roasted, crushed or ground. Cwt	30,619	383,840	30,605	383,659	22,953 95
24	Cocoa shells and nibs..................... Lb.	344	12	....	....	....
25	Cocoa or chocolate, preparations of, n.o.p. and confectionery coated with or containing chocolate...................... "	2,648,013	565,687	497,349	111,853	42,971 37
	Total, cocoa, &c.....................	....	1,794,095	....	991,026	119,850 54

Imported into Canada, &c.—Continued.

	Preferential Tariff.			Treaty Rates.			Total.		
Quantity.	Value.	Duty.	Quantity.	Value.	Duty.	Quantity.	Value.	DutyColl'd.	
	$	$ cts.		$	$ cts.		$	$ cts.	
90,200	33,962	6,314 00	....	....	....	287,402	123,613	26,034 20	1
....	637	79 63	....	....	....	....	8,879	1,934 31	2
....	34,599	6,393 63	....	....	....	....	132,492	27,968 51	
....	780	114 00	....	....	....	....	39,841	6,953 70	3
....	25	3 75	....	....	....	....	95,925	16,786 87	4
31,377	1,260	627 54	....	....	....	42,889	1,975	972 90	5
147,365	6,604	2,947 30	....	....	....	303,569	16,611	7,633 42	6
178,742	7,864	3,574 84	....	....	....	346,458	18,586	8,606 32	
....	4,114	514 44	....	21,354	3,737 10	....	30,935	5,344 94	7
....	....	....	....	....	....	2,835	2,167	283 50	8
....	....	....	....	....	....	759	347	37 95	9
....	....	....	....	....	....	3,594	2,514	321 45	
....	26,508	5,301 60	....	4,227	1,162 50	....	366,369	107,154 30	10
....	2,757	275 70	....	....	....	....	6,460	831 15	11
....	43	9 68	....	....	....	....	26,144	9,145 03	12
....	....	....	....	....	....	2,283,520	3,214,736	319,692 86	13
11,140	37,869	3,899 00	....	....	....	6,840,979	12,921,184	3,623,713 67	14
11,140	37,869	3,899 00	....	....	....	9,124,499	16,135,920	3,943,406 53	
....	6,920	1,211 13	....	2,955	664 88	....	14,019	2,912 01	15
....	....	....	....	....	....	85,016	2,115	425 08	16
16,000	432	40 00	....	....	....	341,762	10,829	2,483 38	17
16,000	432	40 00	....	....	....	426,778	12,944	2,908 46	
644,371	59,079	18,348 91	....	....	....	672,837	62,275	19,619 61	18
217,325	67,218	3,259 91	....	....	....	1,468,140	429,803	28,276 21	19
10,116	1,109	354 06	....	....	....	57,873	10,989	2,264 34	20
16,890	3,496	655 69	....	....	....	399,855	86 484	17,121 11	21
1,244,457	290,877	63,111 59	....	....	....	1,427,444	330,938	73,644 81	22
....	....	....	....	....	....	30,605	383,659	22,953 95	23
344	12	0 90	....	....	....	344	12	0 90	24
2,177,922	459,814	118,862 38	....	....	....	2,675,271	571,667	161,833 75	25
....	822,526	186,244 53	....	....	....	....	1,813,552	306,095 07	

6 GEORGE V, A. 1916

No. 14.—Summary Statement of Foreign Merchandise

Articles.		Total Imports.		General Tariff.		
		Quantity.	Value.	Quantity.	Value.	Duty.
	Dutiable Goods—*Con.*		$		$	$ cts.
1	Coffee, green, n.o.p........................ Lb.	641,216	66,579	640,925	66,555	23,398 44
2	Coffee, green, imported direct from the country of growth and production or purchased in bond in the United Kingdom (from August 22nd, see Free Goods) "	7,112,887	810,348	6,648,545	752,973	199,456 35
3	Coffee, extract of, n.o.p., or substitute therefor of all kinds.................. "	142,866	46,808	57,777	26,479	2,524 32
4	Coffee, roasted or ground, when not imported direct from the country of growth and production................. "	470,452	109,075	465,167	107,531	28,178 82
5	Coffee, roasted or ground, and all imitations thereof and substitutes therefor, including acorn nuts, n.o.p............. "	219,342	32,970	218,033	32,691	8,766 31
6	Coffee, condensed with milk............. "	1,485	358	....	....	....
	Total, coffee.....................	8,588,248	1,066,138	8,030,447	986,229	262,324 24
7	Collars of cotton or linen, xylonite, xyolite or celluloid...........................Doz.	109,805	123,253	80,465	95,077	35,654 08
8	Combs.................................. $	....	127,053	....	55,327	19,364 45
	Copper and manufactures of—					
9	Copper nails, tacks, rivets and burrs or washers........................... $	....	4,371	....	4,059	1,217 70
10	Copper wire, plain, tinned or plated.....Lb.	103,285	24,801	93,383	22,400	2,800 25
11	Copper wire cloth, or woven wire of copper.................................. $	....	4,328	....	2,937	734 25
12	Copper, all other manufactures of, n.o.p. $	....	179,093	....	162,327	48,698 10
	Total, copper.....................	....	212,593	....	191,723	53,450 30
13	Cordage, cotton of all kinds...............Lb.	257,633	35,199	84,830	15,530	3,882 50
14	Cordage and twines of all kinds, n.o.p..... "	4,145,375	458,488	1,429,995	182,645	45,661 25
	Total, cordage and twines...........	4,403,008	493,687	1,514,825	198,175	49,543 75
15	Corks, manufactured from corkwood, over three-fourths of an inch in diameter measured at the larger end........... "	212,708	84,340	206,273	79,341	10,313 65
16	Corks, manufactured from corkwood, three-fourths of an inch and less in diameter measured at the larger end...... "	54,134	24,776	52,084	23,713	4,166 72
17	Cork slabs, boards, planks and tiles produced from cork waste or granulated or ground cork........................... $	....	53,266	....	49,167	14,750 10
18	Manufactures of corkwood or cork bark, n.o.p., including strips, shives, shells and washers of cork........................ $	....	149,979	....	139,886	27,977 20
	Total, cork.........................	....	312,361	....	292,107	57,207 67
19	Corsets of all kinds...................... $	....	525,000	....	508,761	178,066 35
20	Corset clasps, busks, blanks and steels and covered corset wires cut to length, tipped or untipped, reed, rattan and horn covered......................... $	....	12,815	....	12,613	4,414 55
21	Costumes and scenery, theatrical........ $	....	13,247	....	8,301	1,921 84
	Cotton, manufactures of—					
22	Duck, grey or white, n.o.p., weighing over 8 oz. per square yard............Yd.	1,986,019	562,368	1,163,606	392,271	78,454 20
23	Embroideries white and cream coloured $	....	789,470	....	235,589	47,117 80
24	Gray, unbleached cotton fabrics........ Yd.	9,239,003	576,890	1,856,962	122,738	30,684 50

Imported into Canada, &c.—*Continued.*

	ENTERED FOR HOME CONSUMPTION.								
Preferential Tariff.			Treaty Rates.			Total.			
Quantity.	Value.	Duty.	Quantity.	Value.	Duty.	Quantity.	Value.	DutyColl'd.	
	$	$ cts.		$	$ cts.		$	$ cts.	
....	....	....	....	....	....	640,925	66,555	23,398 44	1
363,358	· 38,845	8,175 53	....	....	....	7,011,903	791,818	207,631 88	2
86,430	20,463	2,558 91	....	....	....	144,207	46,942	5,083 23	3
1,922	486	97 16	....	....	....	467,089	108,017	28,275 98	4
840	207	21 15	....	....	....	218,873	32,898	8,787 46	5
1,485	358	82 20	....	....	....	1,485	358	82 20	
454,035	60,359	10,934 95	....	....	....	8,484,482	1,046,588	273,259 19	
29,696	28,621	7,155 25	....	....	....	110,161	123,698	42,809 33	7
....	60,779	13,675 59	....	10,581	3,439 01	....	126,687	36,479 05	8
....	288	57 60	....	24	6 60	....	4,371	1,281 90	9
10,247	2,267	170 02	....	....	....	103,630	24,667	2,970 27	10
....	1,069	187 13	....	322	72 45	....	4,328	993 83	11
....	15,842	3,168 40	....	1,789	491 99	....	179,958	52,358 49	12
....	19,466	3,583 15	....	2,135	571 04	....	213,324	57,604 49	
166,821	18,809	3,761 80	....	....	....	251,651	34,339	7,644 30	13
2,706,414	275,017	55,003 40	....	....	....	4,136,409	457,662	100,664 65	14
2,873,235	293,826	58,765 20	....	....	....	4,388,060	492,001	108,308 95	
2,199	1,202	87 96	....	....	....	208,472	80,543	10,401 61	15
1,157	956	69 42	....	....	....	53,241	24,669	4,236 14	16
....	1,004	200 80	....	....	....	....	50,171	14,950 90	17
....	9,964	1,494 60	....	....	....	....	149,850	29,471 80	18
....	13,126	1,852 78	....	....	....	....	305,233	59,060 45	
....	10,853	2,713 25	....	4,052	1,316 91	....	523,666	182,096 51	19
....	160	36 02	....	....	....	....	12,773	4,450 57	20
....	21	3 15	....	....	....	....	8,322	1,924 99	21
837,185	188,159	28,223 85	....	....	....	2,000,791	580,430	106,678 05	22
....	17,642	2,205 59	....	574,598	100,555 15	....	827,829	149,878 54	23
7,386,344	461,481	69,222 15	....	....	....	9,243,306	584,219	99,906 65	24

6 GEORGE V, A. 1916

No. 14.—SUMMARY STATEMENT of Foreign Merchandise

ARTICLES.	TOTAL IMPORTS.		General Tariff.		
	Quantity.	Value.	Quantity.	Value.	Duty.
		$		$	$ cts.
DUTIABLE GOODS—*Con.*					
Cotton, mfrs of—*Con.*					
1 White or bleached cotton fabrics........Yd.	31,263,665	2,595,696	8,013,509	730,487	182,621 75
2 Towelling in the web.................. "	3,193,214	223,380	61,668	5,430	1,357 50
3 Fabrics, printed, dyed or coloured, n.o.p. "	53,295,618	5,278,532	16,337,610	1,783,819	579,744 26
4 Jeans, coutilles and sateens, imported by corset and dress·stay manufacturers, for use exclusively for the manufacture of such articles in their own factories. "	1,886,704	224,259	226,501	30,777	6,155·40
5 Handkerchiefs......................... $	....	482,916	....	27,845	9,745 75
6 Batts, batting and sheet wadding......Lb.	294,826	32,053	288,393	31,135	7,783 75
7 Bobbinet (white cotton) plain, in the web................................Yd.	317,758	37,190	14,386	1,831	457↓75
8 Knitting yarn, hosiery yarn or other cotton yarn, dyed or not, n.o.p.......Lb.	851,740	200,461	589,688	132,374	33,093 50
9 Cotton warps......................... $	....	4,268	....	3,475	868 75
10 Seamless bags......................... $	....	28,383	....	14,769	2,953 80
11 Sheets, bed quilts, pillow cases and damask of cotton in the piece, including uncoloured table cloths or napkins of cotton............................... $	....	817,236	....	105,497	31,649 10
12 Shirts of cotton.......................Doz.	83,962	441,136	67,487	344,176	120,461 60
13 Sewing thread on spools............... $	....	215,814	....	98,182	24,545 50
14 Sewing cotton thread in hanks.........Lb.	486,667	248,486	143,434	69,998	6,999 80
15 Crochet and knitting cotton........... "	165,393	68,317	93,755	38,451	9,612 75
16 All other cotton thread, n.o.p. .... "	214,583	136,780	110,101	63,943	15,985 75
17 Clothing, n.o.p........................ $	....	2,175,976	....	1,570,063	549,522 05
18 Blouses and shirt waists............... $	....	190,338	....	164,000	57,400 00
19 Cotton bags made up by the use of the needle, not otherwise provided for.... $	....	127,084	....	46,987	16,445 45
20 Lampwicks........................... $	....	25,750	....	20,457	5,114 25
21 Lace, white and cream coloured........ $	....	808,888	....	103,053	20,610 60
22 Shawls................................ $	....	4,263	....	2,712	949 20
23 Socks and stockings..................Doz. pairs	529,123	634,816	339,378	398,502	139,475 70
24 Tape of cotton not over 1¼" in width.... $	....	19,852	....	7,627	2,669 45
25 Tape, not dyed or coloured............. $	....	24,214	....	10,625	2,656 25
26 Tape, dyed or coloured................. $	....	33,896	....	8,100	2,632 68
27 Towels.............. .... $	....	360,246	....	36,412	10,923 60
28 Undershirts and drawers............... $	....	87,244	....	74,747	26,161 45
29 Uncoloured cotton fabrics, bleached, viz:— Scrims and window scrims, cambric cloths, muslin apron checks, brilliants, cords piques, diapers, lenos, Swiss jaconet and cambric muslins, and plain striped or checked lawns..Yd.	848,089	27,793	125,952	6,350	1,587 50
30 Velvets, velveteens, and plush fabrics, n.o.p...................... "	3,490,094	983,175	430,886	109,379	32,813 70
31 Manufactures of cotton of which cotton is component material of chief value, n.o.p............................... $	....	977,889	....	725,281	253,848 35
Total cottons......................	....	19,445,059	....	7,517,082	2,313,103 44
32 Crapes, black, mourning................. $	....	8,434	....	566	113 20
33 Cuffs of cotton, linen, xylonite, xyloite, or celluloid...........................Pairs.	2,822	349	1,965	253	94 88
34 Curling stones and handles therefor....... "	10	74	10	74	7 40
35 Curtains and shams when made up, trimmed or untrimmed.................. $	....	389,868	....	85,465	29,912 75
36 Cyclometers, pedometers, and speedometers.................................. $	....	50,435	....	50,099	12,524 75
Drugs, Dyes, Chemicals, Medicines—					
37 Acetone and amyl acetate.............. $	....	31,450	....	31,418	9,425 40
38 Acids—Acetic and pyroligneous, n.o.p., not exceeding proof strength..........Gal	1,691	1,192	1,684	1,178	

SESSIONAL PAPER No. 11

Imported into Canada, &c.—*Continued.*

				ENTERED FOR HOME CONSUMPTION.					
Preferential Tariff.			Treaty Rates.			Total.			
Quantity.	Value.	Duty.	Quantity.	Value.	Duty.	Quantity.	Value.	DutyColl'd.	
	$	$ cts.		$	$ cts.		$	$ cts.	
23,670,821	1,892,305	331,154 93	....	....	....	31,684,330	2,622,792	513,776 68	1
3,124,077	217,007	37,977 32	....	....	....	3,185,745	222,437	39,334 82	2
36,672,686	3,516,050	879,012 50	....	....	....	53,010,296	5,299,869	1,458,756 76	3
1,656,408	192,622	24,077 93	....	....	....	1,882,909	223,399	30,233 33	4
....	398,281	99,570 25	....	55,357	17,991 31	....	481,483	127,307 31	5
6,433	918	160 67	....	....	....	294,826	32,053	7,944 42	6
317,345	37,441	5,616 15	856	262	58 95	332,587	39,534	6,132 85	7
262,052	68,087	11,915 46	....	....	....	851,740	200,461	45,008 96	8
....	793	138 78	....	....	....	....	4,268	1,007 53	9
....	13,614	2,042 10	....	....	....	....	28,383	4,995 90	10
....	713,881	142,776 20	....	....	....	819,378	174,425 30	11	
16,085	92,950	23,237 50	760	5,429	1,764 56	84,332	442,555	145,463 66	12
....	114,489	20,035 79	....	3,331	749 49	....	216,002	45,330 78	13
343,233	178,488	13,386 58	....	....	....	486,667	248,486	20,386 38	14
67,930	28,390	4,968 40	3,708	1,476	332 11	165,393	68,317	14,913 26	15
102,220	71,621	12,533 91	4,648	1,678	377 56	216,969	137,242	28,897 22	16
....	539,212	134,803 00	....	73,101	23,758 05	....	2,182,376	708,083 10	17
....	22,196	5,549 00	....	3,763	1,223 00	....	189,959	64,172 00	18
....	80,095	20,023 75	....	....	....	....	127,082	36,469 20	19
....	5,282	924 39	....	....	....	....	25,739	6,038 64	20
....	589,610	73,702 37	....	125,756	22,007 93	....	818,419	116,320 90	21
....	1,426	356 50	....	91	29 58	....	4,229	1,335 28	22
189,360	240,508	60,127 00	....	....	....	528,738	639,010	199,602 70	23
....	12,211	3,052 75	....	....	....	....	19,838	5,722 20	24
....	13,565	2,374 07	....	....	....	....	24,190	5,030 32	25
....	26,422	6,605 50	....	....	....	....	34,522	9,238 18	26
....	322,642	64,528 40	....	....	....	....	359,054	75,452 00	27
....	11,904	2,678 56	....	....	....	....	86,651	28,840 01	28
741,131	21,903	3,833 21	....	....	....	867,083	28,253	5,420 71	29
2,732,498	726,652	127,164 98	311,270	143,932	'39,581 55	3,474,654	979,963	199,560 23	30
....	249,746	62,436 50	....	....	....	....	975,027	316,284 85	31
....	11,067,593	2,276,416 04	....	988,774	208,429 24	....	19,573,449	4,797,948 72	
....	5,725	715 70	....	2,143	375 07	....	8,434	1,203 97	32
857	96	24 00	....	....	....	2,822	349	118 88	33
....	....	....	....	....	....	10	74	7 40	34
....	260,449	65,112 25	....	43,358	14,091 51	....	389,272	109,116 51	35
....	163	28 54	....	....	....	....	50,262	12,553 29	36
....	....	....	....	....	....	....	31,418	9,425 40	37
7	14	0 70	....	....	....	1,691	1,192	253 30	38

6 GEORGE V, A. 1916

No. 14.—SUMMARY STATEMENT of Foreign Merchandise

	ARTICLES.	TOTAL IMPORTS.		General Tariff.		
		Quantity.	Value.	Quantity.	Value.	Duty.
			$		$	$ cts.
	DUTIABLE GOODS—*Con.*					
	Drugs, dyes, &c.—*Con.*					
1	Acids—Acetic and pyroligneous, in excess of strength of proof...........Gal.	1,703	1,870	572	710	712 90
2	Acid, acetic and pyroligneous, crude, of any strength not exceeding 30 per cent. "	1,931	443	1,920	433	108 25
3	Acid phosphate, not medicinal..........Lb.	1,838,945	100,804	1,691,393	94,590	18,918 00
4	Acid, Muriatic......................... "	153,740	3,101	153,740	3,101	384 38
5	Nitric......................... "	233,423	10,043	71,538	4,799	1,079 92
6	Stearic......................... "	163,700	14,549	163,300	14,452	2,890 40
7	Sulphuric..................... "	315,484	6,357	315,484	6,357	788 73
8	Other, n.o.p.................... "	593,989	96,387	421,940	48,751	10,969 57
9	Albumen blood, egg albumen and egg yolk...................... $	....	23,149	....	22,402	2,240 20
10	Alum, in bulk, ground or unground, but not calcined: and sulphate of alumina, or alum cake......................Lb.	17,748,033	158,304	17,748,033	158,304	15,830 40
11	Aniline dyes, in packages of less than 1 lb. in weight..................... "	11,772	3,267	1,749	810	141 79
12	Carbon dioxide or carbonic acid gas.... $	....	8,552	....	8,015	1,402 79
13	Casein.................... $	....	4,650	....	4,245	1,167 48
14	Cloride and hypochlorite of lime, in pkgs. of not less than 25 lbs...............Lb.	8,905,545	79,940	6,136,786	52,964	9,205 05
15	Chloride and hypochloride of lime in pkges less than 25 lbs................ "	139,840	6,985	130,390	6,476	1,619 00
16	Cocaine.................... Oz.	50	144	50	144	25 20
17	Collodion for use in films for photo-engravings and for engraving copper rollers, when imported by photo engravers and manufacturers of copper rollers.............................Gal.	1,048	1,703	1,048	1,703	298 06
18	Dextrine, dry........................Lb.	2,556,229	82,416	2,572,773	82,496	8,249 60
19	Gelatine and isinglass.................. "	678,807	155,276	297,256	83,695	23,016 47
20	Glue, powdered or sheet................ "	2,899,266	258,120	677,491	57,849	15,909 02
21	Glue, liquid......................... $	....	54,944	....	38,242	10,517 59
22	Glycerine, n.o.p.......................Lb.	108,166	20,440	102,455	19,201	3,360 34
23	Gums—Camphor..................... "	56,767	21,184	52,827	18,794	3,288 98
24	" Opium (crude)................. "	6,279	29,315	7,248	32,134	7,248 00
25	" Other, n.o.p................. "	8,518	1,827	8,202	1,718	300 71
26	Liquorice, in paste, rolls, and sticks, not sweetened, n.o.p................. "	1,792,613	155,343	2,059,133	175,960	39,591 03
27	Magnesia............................. "	190,743	14,403	140,831	10,309	1,804 16
28	Medicinal, chemical, and pharmaceutical preparations, including proprietary preparations (dry)................ $	....	994,416	....	609,377	152,344 25
29	Medicinal, chemical and pharmaceutical preparations, including proprietary preparations (all other)............ $	....	102,801	....	97,346	53,702 50
30	Medicinal (all other) non-alcoholic..... $	....	84,316	....	....	....
31	Liquid preparations, non-alcoholic, for disinfecting, dipping, or spraying, n.o.p $	....	75,578	....	63,011	15,752 75
32	Milk food, and other similar preparations............................. $	....	353,336	....	217,713	57,566 46
33	Morphine............................Oz.	259	708	59	294	51 45
34	Opium, powdered......................Lb.	267	1,398	267	1,398	360 45
35	Potash or potassa, bicarbonate of......Lb.	3,688	385	3,088	332	58 11
36	Potash and pearl ash, in packages less then 25 lbs. each................... "	4,022	150	4,022	150	22 50
37	Potash caustic, in packages less than 25 lbs. each....................... "	19,467	1,379	19,240	1,361	204 15
38	Pyroxylin and wood naphtha, preparations of, for coating imitation leather, and for the manufacture of leather belting............................. $	....	19,190	....	19,190	1,919 00
39	Salts, glauber...........................Lb.	665,504	2,692	100,040	529	92 59
40	Soda, bicarbonate of.-................ "	7,336,280	69,125	2,066,020	19,407	3,396 37
41	Soda, caustic, when in packages less than 25 lbs. each................... "	435,537	10,711	422,947	10,455	1,944 95

Imported into Canada, &c.—*Continued.*

			ENTERED FOR HOME CONSUMPTION.						
Preferential Tariff.			Treaty Rates.			Total.			
Quantity.	Value.	Duty.	Quantity.	Value.	Duty.	Quantity.	Value.	DutyColl'd.	
,	$	$ cts.		$	$ cts.		$	$ cts.	
1,215	1,350	1,546 34	15	17	26 33	1,802	2,077	2,285 57	1
11	10	1 50	....	....	....	1,931	443	109 75	2
147,552	6,214	776 87	....	....	....	1,838,945	100,804	19,694 87	3
....	....	....	....	....	....	153,740	3,101	384 38	4
....	....	....	....	....	....	71,538	4,799	1,079 92	5
400	97	12 13	....	....	....	163,700	14,549	2,902 53	6
....	....	....	....	....	....	315,484	6,357	788 73	7
174,991	47,982	7,197 30	....	....	....	596,931	96,733	18,166 87	8
....	11	0 55	....	....	....	....	22,413	2,240 75	9
....	....	....	....	....	....	17,748,033	158,304	15,830 40	10
10,023	2,457	368 55	....	....	....	11,772	3,267	510 34	11
....	74	11 10	....	....	....	....	8,089	1,413 89	12
....	411	71 93	....	....	....	....	4,656	1,239 41	13
2,768,759	26,976	2,768 70	....	....	....	8,905,545	79,940	11,973 75	14
9,450	509	89 09	....	....	....	139,840	6,985	1,708 09	15
....	....	....	....	....	....	50	144	25 20	16
....	....	....	....	....	....	1,048	1,703	298 06	17
10,196	318	15 90	....	....	....	2,582,969	82,814	8,265 50	18
313,474	58,884	10,304 88	87,412	15,249	3,812 25	698,142	157,828	37,133 60	19
2,143,911	182,109	31,869 36	216,857	21,458	5,364 50	3,038,259	261,416	53,142 88	20
....	17,273	3,022 86	....	145	36 25		55,660	13,576 70	21
5,711	1,239	185 85	....	....	....	108,166	20,440	3,546 19	22
2,576	1,199	179 85	....	....	....	55,403	19,993	3,468 83	23
....	....	....	....	....	....	7,248	32,134	7,248 00	24
316	109	16 35	....	....	....	8,518	1,827	317 06	25
4,274	326	48 90	....	....	....	2,063,407	176,286	39,639 93	26
47,912	3,823	573 45	....	....	....	188,743	14,132	2,377 61	27
....	393,020	78,604 00	....	....	....	....	1,002,397	230,948 25	28
....	....	....	....	....	....	....	97,346	53,702 50	29
....	....	....	....	84,235	21,058 75	....	84,235	21,058 75	30
....	11,759	2,351 80	....	....	....	....	74,770	18,104 55	31
....	139,738	26,389 57	....	....	....	....	357,451	83,956 03	32
200	414	62 10	....	....	....	259	708	113 55	33
....	....	....	....	....	....	267	1,398	360 45	34
600	53	7 95	....	....	....	3,688	385	66 06	35
....	....	....	....	....	....	4,022	150	22 50	36
227	18	1 80	....	....	....	19,467	1,379	205 95	37
....	....	....	....	....	....	....	19,190	1,919 00	38
565,464	2,163	324 45	....	....	....	665,504	2,692	417 04	39
5,270,260	49,718	7,457 70	....	....	....	7,336,280	69,125	10,854 07	40
12,590	256	30 54	....	....	....	435,537	10,711	1,975 49	41

6 GEORGE V, A. 1916

No. 14.—Summary Statement of Foreign Merchandise

ARTICLES.		Total Imports.		General Tariff.		
		Quantity.	Value.	Quantity.	Value.	Duty.
			$		$	$ cts.
	Dutiable Goods—*Con.*					
	Drugs, dyes, &c.—*Con.*					
1	Soda, caustic, when in packages of 25 lbs. and over.................... Lb.	2,600,249	46,781	2,536,773	45,346	7,825 48
2	Sodium, hyposulphite................ $	....	2,703	....	2,476	433,29
3	Sulphuric ether, chloroform, and solutions of peroxide of hydrogen........ $	....	67,314	....	38,358	9,589 50
4	Thorium nitrate..................... $	....	542	....	542	94 84
5	Vaseline and all similar preparations of petroleum, for toilet, medicinal or other purposes...................... $	....	23,217	....	22,925	5,731 25
6	Yeast cakes................... Lb.	464	86	474	93	28 44
7	Yeast, compressed, in packages weighing less than 50 lbs............... "	6,690	1,167	6,681	1,166	400 86
8	Yeast, compressed, in bulk or mass of not less than 50 lbs............... "	1,617,660	423,071	1,616,204	422,908	48,486 12
9	All other drugs, dyes, and chemicals, etc., not otherwise provided for...... $	....	992,858	....	765,604	133,982 49
	Total, drugs....................	....	4,620,088	....	3,321,231	684,733 82
	Earthen and Chinaware. (See Bricks and Tiles.)—					
10	Brown or coloured earthen and stoneware, and Rockingham ware........ $	....	63,706	....	45,753	13,725 90
11	C. C. or cream coloured ware, decorated, printed or sponged, and all earthenware, n.o.p....................... $	....	148,911	....	57,670	17,301 00
12	Demijohns, churns or crocks............ $	....	25,145	....	23,894	7,168 20
13	Table ware of china, porcelain, white granite or ironstoneware............ $	....	1,260,355	....	406,931	111,907 11
14	Chinaware, to be silver mounted, imported by manufacturers of silverware $	....	750	....	713	160 49
15	China and porcelain ware, n.o.p........ $	....	26,316	....	18,684	5,605 20
16	Tiles or blocks of earthenware or stone prepared for mosaic flooring......... $	....	83,761	....	75,175	22,552 50
17	Earthenware tiles, n.o.p............... $	....	160,055	....	99,191	34,716 85
18	Manufactures of earthenware, n.o.p...... $	....	164,803	....	99,988	29,996 40
	Total, earthenware................	....	1,933,802	....	827,999	243,133 65
19	Eggs............................ Doz.	5,599,096	1,181,876	4,493,396	994,919	134,801 88
20	Elastic, round or flat, including garter elastic......................... $	....	133,255	....	21,499	7,524 65
21	Electric light carbons and carbon points, of all kinds, n.o.p................... $	....	46,030	....	42,803	14,981 05
22	Electrodes, carbon, over 35 inches in circumference......................... $	....	2,736	....	2,736	547 20
23	Incandescent lamp bulbs and glass tubing for use in the manufacture of incandescent lamps and mantle stockings for gas light............................ $	....	69,764	....	71,415	7,141 50
24	Electric apparatus, n.o.p., insulators of all kinds and sockets, etc., and electric galvanic batteries; telegraph and telephone instruments.................. $	....	4,355,613	....	3,782,239	1,040,120 23
25	Electric motors, generators and dynamos. $	....	1,348,957	....	1,160,315	319,087 79
	Total, electric apparatus...............	....	5,704,570	....	4,942,554	1,359,208 02
26	Embroideries, not otherwise provided for $	....	47,953	....	25,574	8,950 90
27	Emery and carborundum wheels and manufactures of emery or carborundum..... $	....	86,030	....	85,497	21,374 25
28	Express parcels of small value............ $	....	1,825,184	....	1,823,353	514,875 25

Imported into Canada, &c.—*Continued.*

				ENTERED FOR HOME CONSUMPTION.					
	Preferential Tariff.			Treaty Rates.			Total.		
Quant ty.	Value.	Duty.	Quantity.	Value.	Duty.	Quantity.	Value.	DutyColl'd.	
	$	$ cts.		$	$ cts.		$	$ cts.	
62,476	1,435	248 90	....	....	....	2,599,249	46,781	8,074 38	1
....	227	34 05	....	....	....	....	2,703	467 34	2
....	28,956	4,343 40	....	....	....	....	67,314	13,932 90	3
....	....	....	....	....	....	....	542	94 84	4
....	287	43 05	....	....	....	....	23,212	5,774 30	5
....	....	....	....	....	....	474	93	28 44	6
9	1	0 36	....	....	....	6,690	1,167	401 22	7
1,456	163	29 12	....	....	....	1,617,660	423,071	48,515 24	8
....	213,490	32,023 50	....	....	....	....	979,094	166,005 99	9
....	1,193,083	211,014 45	....	121,104	30,298 08	....	4,635,418	926,046 35	
....	17,560	3,512 00	....	....	....	....	63,313	17,237 90	10
....	93,537	18,707 40	....	....	....	....	151,207	36,008 40	11
....	1,251	250 20	....	....	....	....	25,145	7,418 40	12
....	857,999	128,699 85	....	....	....	....	1,264,930	240,606 96	13
....	37	5 55	....	....	....	....	750	166 04	14
....	7,465	1,493 00	....	....	....	....	26,149	7,098 20	15
....	9,298	1,859 60	....	....	....	....	84,473	24,412 10	16
....	60,981	15,245 25	....	....	....	....	160,172	49,962 10	17
....	64,638	12,927 60	....	....	....	....	164,626	42,924 00	18
....	1,112,766	182,700 45	....	....	....	....	1,940,765	425,834 10	
41,215	11,057	824 30	....	....	....	4,534,611	1,005,976	135,626 18	19
....	112,805	28,201 25	....	2	0 65	....	134,306	35,726 55	20
....	594	133 68	....	971	315 58	....	44,368	15,430 31	21
....	....	....	....	....	....	....	2,736	547 20	22
....	350	17 50	....	....	....	....	71,765	7,159 00	23
....	511,896	76,784 40	....	49,891	12,472 75	....	4,344,026	1,129,377 38	24
....	171,229	25,684 35	....	17,942	4,485 50	....	1,349,486	349,257 64	25
....	683,125	102,468 75	....	67,833	16,958 25	....	5,693,512	1,478,635 02	
....	4,039	1,009 75	....	18,704	5,215 36	....	48,317	15,176 01	26
....	530	92 77	....	....	....	....	86,027	21,467 02	27
....	1,831	418 33	....	....	....	....	1,825,184	515,293 58	28

6 GEORGE V, A. 1916

No. 14.—Summary Statement of Foreign Merchandise

ARTICLES.		TOTAL IMPORTS.		General Tariff.		
		Quantity.	Value.	Quantity.	Value.	Duty.
			$		$	$　cts.
	DUTIABLE GOODS—*Con.*					
	Fancy Goods, viz.—					
1	Alabaster, spar, amber, terra cotta, or composition ornaments.............. $	....	38,059	....	31,555	9,466 50
2	Bead ornaments....................... $	....	15,484	....	10,960	3,288 00
3	Boxes, fancy, ornamental cases and writing desks, etc................. $	....	215,326	....	125,972	44,090 20
4	Braids, cords, fringes, tassels, n.o.p..... $	....	307,562	....	191,268	66,943 80
5	Tinsel thread and tinsel wire, for the manufacture of braids, cords, tassels, ribbons or trimmings................. $	....	10,082	....	10,082	1,008 20
6	Cases for jewellery, watches, silverware, plated ware and cutlery.............. $	....	29,743	....	24,992	8,747 20
7	Fans............................. $	....	5,313	....	2,830	849 00
8	Feathers, fruits, grains, leaves and flowers, artificial, suitable for ornamenting hats......................... $	....	496,468	....	387,560	106,580 38
9	Feathers, fancy, undressed........... $	....	136,930	....	88,871	13,330 65
10	Feathers, fancy, n.o.p. and manufactures of feathers, n.o.p................... $	....	216,121	....	162,769	44,762 21
11	Feathers, ostrich and vulture, dressed.. $	....	122,338	....	41,070	11,294 38
12	Ivory or bone dice, draughts, chessmen, etc......................... $	....	350	....	165	28 91
13	Lace, n.o.p., lace collars and all manufactures of lace; nets and nettings of cotton, linen, silk or other material, n.o.p...................... $	....	815,402	....	253,623	88,768 05
14	Statues and statuettes of any material..	....	78,978	....	48,479	14,543 70
15	Toilet and manicure sets................	....	25,294	....	21,417	7,495 95
16	Toys, and dolls of all kinds............ $	....	655,946	....	556,021	166,806 30
	Total, fancy goods...................	....	3,169,396	....	1,957,634	588,003 43
17	Feathers, bed and other, undressed, n.o.p. $	....	26,833	....	24,357	3,653 55
18	Feathers, bed and other, dressed, n.o.p.... $	....	12,487	....	1,855	510 17
	Total, feathers, n.o.p.................	....	39,320	....	26,212	4,163 72
19	Featherbone, plain or covered, in coils.... $	....	1,204	....	1,204	240 80
20	Fertilizers, compounded or manufactured. $	....	714,584	....	664,708	66,470 80
21	Fibre, Kartavert, indurated fibre, vulcanized fibre and like material and manufactures of, n.o.p.................. $	....	101,976	....	97,502	24,375 50
22	Fireworks, firecrackers and torpedoes, all kinds................................ $	....	24,670	....	22,949	5,737 25
	Fish—					
23	Cod, haddock, ling and pollock, fresh imported otherwise than in barrels, etc................................ Lb.	213,304	10,577	213,304	10,577	2,133 04
24	Cod, haddock, ling, and pollock, dry salted............................. "	802,807	49,141	55,077	5,240	550 77
25	Cod, haddock, ling and pollock, wet salted............................ "	276	19	276	19	2 76
26	Cod, haddock, ling and pollock, smoked "	368	26	....	....	....
27	Halibut, fresh, not in barrels.......... "	3,245,192	159,443	1,396,328	69,547	13,963 28
28	Halibut, pickled, in barrels............ "	400	16	400	16	4 00
29	Herrings, fresh, not in barrels.......... "	12,295	547	10,795	504	107 95
30	Herrings, pickled or salted............. "	2,327,646	111,782	992,645	54,859	4,963 26
31	Herrings, smoked....................... "	720	77	720	77	7 20
32	Mackerel, fresh........................ "	768	81	768	408	4 08
33	Mackerel, pickled...................... "	4,649	463	2,244	341	22 44
34	Sea fish, other, fresh, not in barrels..... "	28,233	1,962	28,195	1,948	281 95
35	Sea fish, other, pickled, in barrels...... "	3,488	239	3,488	239	34 88
36	Sea fish, other, preserved, n.o.p......... "	134,004	11,525	65,013	5,110	1,533 00

SESSIONAL PAPER No. 11 .

Imported into Canada, &c.—*Continued*. -

		ENTERED FOR HOME CONSUMPTION.							
Preferential Tariff.			Treaty Rates.			Total.			
Quantity.	Value.	Duty.	Quantity.	Value.	Duty.	Quantity.	Value.	DutyColl'd.	
	$	$ cts.		$	$ cts.		$.	$ cts.	
....	1,390	278 00	....	5,343	1,469 43	....	38,288	11,213 93	1
....	1,115	223 00	....	3,417	939 73	....	15,492	4,450 73	2
....	79,026	17,781 37	....	10,107	3,032 10	....	215,105	64,903 67	3
....	80,018	20,004 50	....	35,504	11,539 16	....	306,790	98,487 46	4
....	....			....	....	....	10,082	1,008 20	5
....	7,294	1,641 22	....	99	29 70	....	32,385	10,418 12	6
....	21	4 20	....	2,481	682 34	....	5,332	1,535 54	7
....	108,737	21,747 40	....			....	496,297	128,327 78	8
....	42,569	4,256 90	....	6,953	869 14	....	138,393	18,456 69	9
....	53,351	10,670 20	....			....	216,120	55,432 41	10
....	81,293	16,258 60	....			....	122,363	27,552 98	11
....	185	27 75	....			....	350	56 66	12
....	398,158	99,539 50	....	166,109	46,816 59	....	817,890	235,124 14	13
....	1,222	244 40	....	27,786	7,641 45	....	77,487	22,429 55	14
....	4,477	1,007 40	....	35	10 50	....	25,929	8,513 85	15
....	60,267	12,053 40	....	40,975	11,268 33	....	657,263	190,128 03	16
....	919,123	205,737 84	....	298,809	84,298 47	....	3,175,566	878,039 74	
....	2,476	247 60	....			....	26,833	3,901 15	17
....	10,632	2,126 40	....			....	12,487	2,636 57	18
....	13,108	2,374 00	....			....	39,320	6,537 72	
....			....			....	1,204	240 80	19
....	49,876	2,493 80	....			....	714,584	68,964 60	20
....	4,598	804 68	....			....	102,100	25,180 18	21
....	1,721	301 18	....			....	24,670	6,038 43	22
....	....			....	....	213,304	10,577	2,133 04	23
112	. 8	0 56	....			55,189	5,248	551 33	24
....	....					276	19	2 76	25
....	....								26
....	....					1,396,328	69,547	13,963 28	27
....	....					400	16	4 00	28
....	....					10,795	504	107 95	29
1,336,461	56,978	4,677 63	....			2,329,106	111,837	9,640 89	30
....						720	77	7 20	31
360	28	1 80	....			768	81	5 88	32
....	....					2,244	341	22 44	33
38	14	0 19	....			28,233	1,962	282 14	34
....	....					3,488	239	34 88	35
63,926	6,209	1,086 64	....			128,939	11,319	2,619 64	36

No. 14.—Summary Statement of Foreign Merchandise

	ARTICLES.		TOTAL IMPORTS.		General Tariff.		
			Quantity.	Value.	Quantity.	Value.	Duty.
	DUTIABLE .GOODS—*Con.*			$		$	$ cts.
	Fish—*Con.* . .						
1	Oysters, fresh, in shell.................Brl.		3,385	17,745	3,385	17,745	4,436 25
2	Oysters, shelled, in bulk...............Gal.		173,958	210,839	173,958	210,839	17,395 80
3	Oysters, canned, in cans not over one pint.................................Cans		231,728	21,926	235,308	23,899	7,059 24
4	Oysters, canned, in cans over one pint and not over one quart.............. "		3,094	1,451	2,554	1,180	127 70
5	Oysters, canned, in cans exceeding one quart (provided that a fraction over a quart shall be computed as a quart for duty purposes)......................Qt.		484	246	436	223	21 80
6	Oysters, prepared or preserved, n.o.p.... Lb.		26,085	4,971	30,700	5,177	1,553 10
7	Lobsters, fresh......................... $			2,650		2,650	662 50
8	Lobsters, canned, n.o.p.............·.... Lb.		2,153	481	....	....	....
9	Bait fish, fresh, not in barrels.......... "		165,055	4,061	74,647	1,741	746 47
10	Bait fish, salted, not in barrels......... "		4,000	120	4,000	120	40 00
11	Salmon, fresh......................... "		105,933	5,296	117,384	5,869	1,173 84
12	Salmon, smoked....................... "		1,867	371	1,867	371	18 67
13	Salmon, canned, prepared or preserved, n.o.p................................. $		....	457	....	597	179 10
14	Salmon, pickled or salted............... Lb.		9,957	1,018	10,407	1,074	104 07
15	Fish, smoked or boneless.............. "		34,858	2,379	20,218	1,432	202 18
16	Anchovies, sardines, sprats and other fish, packed in oil or otherwise, in tin boxes weighing over 20 ounces and not over 36 ounces each.................Boxes		13,470	2,547	11,537	2,297	692 22
17	Anchovies, sardines, etc., in tin boxes weighing over 12 ounces and not over 20 ounces each...................... "		48,216	7,087	32,008	5,238	1,440 36
18	Anchovies, sardines, etc., when packed in tin boxes weighing over 8 ounces and not over 12 ounces................... "		189,124	13,630	30,719	3,636	1,075 17
19	Anchovies, sardines, etc., when packed in tin boxes weighing 8 ounces or less.. " .		5,361,799	301,999	519,954	32,676	12,998 86
20	Fish preserved in oil, n.o.p............. $		....	9,081	....	6,067	2,123 45
21	Fish, all other, not in barrels or half barrels.........................Lb.		480,042	33,686	478,846	33,433	4,788 46
22	Fish, all other, not in barrels or half barrels.................... "		65,209	5,950	68,118	6,238	681 18
23	Fish, fresh or dried, n.o.p., imported in barrels or half barrels.............. "		951,453	77,606	946,478	77,184	9,464 78
24	Fish, all other, pickled or salted, in barrels.............................. "		133,923	10,388	115,439	9,873	1,154 39
25	Fish, prepared or preserved, n.o.p....... $		....	145,106	....	76,715	23,014 50
26	Fish oil, cod, n.o.p....................,Gal.		1,484	654	1,484	654	147 18
27	Fish oil, cod liver..................... "		18,006	11,943	20,379	13,891	3,125 57
28	Fish oil, whale and spermaceti.......... "		6,531	3,441	1,683	1,145	257 63
29	Fish oil, other, n.o.p................... "		33,955	15,422	27,274	11,433	2,572 52
30	Other articles the produce of the fish-eries, not specially provided for....... $		....	43,198	....	41,306	10,326 50
	Total, fish............................		....	1,301,647	....	743,233	131,192 10
	Flax, hemp and jute, manufactures of, viz:—			?			
31	Bags or sacks of hemp, linen or jute..... $		....	249,985	....	108,543	21,708 60
32	Canvas of hemp or flax, for ship's sails.. $		......,....	7,210	....	6,627	331 35
33	Carpeting, rugs, matting and mats of hemp or jute........................ $		....	40,813	....	5,150	1,287 50
34	Embroideries and lace of linen, white and cream coloured.................. $		....	2,327	....	535	107 00
35	Sail twine of flax or hemp to be used for boats, and ships' sails...............Lb.		5,399	1,440	5,399	1,440	72 00
36	Uncoloured damask of linen, in the piece, stair linen, diaper, doylies, tray cloths, uncoloured table cloths, or napkins of linen, quilts, counterpanes, pillow cases of linen and sheets................... $		....	824,814	....	82,689	24,806 70
37	Handkerchiefs.......................... $		....	251,491	....	13,469	4,714 15

SESSIONAL PAPER No. 11

Imported into Canada, &c.—*Continued*.

	ENTERED FOR HOME CONSUMPTION.								
Preferential Tariff.			Treaty Rates.			Total.			
Quantity.	Value.	Duty.	Quantity.	Value.	Duty.	Quantity.	Value.	DutyColl'd.	
	$	$ cts.		$	$ cts.	$	$	$ cts.	
....	....	....	....	....	....	3,385	17,745	4,436 25	1
....	....	....	....	....	....	173,958	210,839	17,395 80	2
....	....	....	....	....	....	235,308	23,899	7,059 24	3
....	....	....	....	....	....	2,554	1,180	127 70	4
....	....	....	....	....	....	436	223	21 80	5
....	....	....	....	....	....	30,700	5,177	1,553 10	6
....	....	....	....	....	....	2,650	670	662 50	7
·2,837	670	117 24	....	....	....	2,837	670	117 24	8
....	....	....	....	....	....	74,647	1,741	746 47	9
....	....	....	....	....	....	4,000	120	40 00	10
....	....	....	....	....	....	117,384	5,869	1,173 84	11
....	....	....	....	....	....	1,867	371	18 67	12
....	....	....	....	....	....	597	....	179 10	13
14,040	917	70 20	....	....	....	10,407	1,074	104 07	14
....	....	....	....	....	....	34,258	2,349	272 38	15
1,683	171	58 90	250	79	12 50	13,470	2,547	763 62	16
1,856	145	46 41	9,714	2,160	388 56	43,578	7,543	1,875 33	17
23,696	1,648	473 92	144,668	9,023	2,893 36	199,083	14,307	4,442 45	18
506,967	22,641	6,337 09	4,268,846	237,961	85,376 92	5,295,767	293,278	104,712 87	19
....	322	64 40	....	2,371	711 30	....	8,760	2,899 15	20
1,396	316	6 98	....	....	....	480,242	33,749	4,795 44	21
477	38	2 39	....	....	....	68,595	6,276	683 57	22
2,825	262	14 13	....	....	....	949,303	77,446	9,478 91	23
425	30	2 13	....	....	....	115,864	9,903	1,156 52	24
....	63,430	11,100 82	....	....	....	140,145	34,115 32		25
....	....	....	....	....	....	1,484	654	147 18	26
63	54	6 76	....	....	....	20,442	13,945	3,132 33	27
4,848	2,296	287 01	....	....	....	6,531	3,441	544 64	28
6,681	3,989	498 63	....	....	....	33,955	15,422	3,071 15	29
....	193	28 95	....	....	....	....	41,499	10,355 45	30
....	160,359	24,882 78	....	251,594	89,382 64	....	1,155,186	245,457 52	
....	133,375	20,006 25	....	....	....	....	241,918	41,714 85	31
....	....	....	....	....	....	....	6,627	331 35	32
....	30,848	5,398 53	....	4,965	1,117 13	....	40,963	7,803 16	33
....	1,412	176 52	....	380	66 52	....	2,327	350 04	34
....	....	....	....	....	....	....	5,399	1,440	72 00	35
....	740,663	148,132 60	....	....	....	....	823,352	172,939 30	36
....	229,846	57,461 50	....	9,685	3,147 71	....	253,000	65,323 36	37

6 GEORGE V, A. 1916

No. 14.—SUMMARY STATEMENT of Foreign Merchandise

| ARTICLES. | TOTAL IMPORTS. | | General Tariff. | | |
	Quantity.	Value.	Quantity.	Value.	Duty.
DUTIABLE GOODS—*Con.*		$		$	$ cts.
Flax, hemp and jute, mfrs of—*Con.*					
1 Horse clothing of jute, shaped or otherwise manufactured.................... $	....	1,152	....	823	246 90
2 Towels................................ $	....	157,066	....	10,105	3,031 50
3 Fabrics, brown or bleached............. Yd.	872,227	117,585	32,981	4,625	1,156 25
4 Fabrics of flax, unbleached, n.o.p....... "	3,642,380	326,884	568,279	41,042	10,260 50
5 Tailors' hollands of linen and towelling in the web.......................... "	3,124,902	228,483	36,436	3,537	884 25
6 Linen clothing, n.o.p................... $	....	10,868	....	5,566	1,948 10
7 Linen blouses and shir' waists.......... $	....	431	....	259	90 65
8 Linen thread, n.o.p.................... Lb.	332,758	224,781	9,644	7,908	1,977 00
9 Shirts of linen................... ..... Doz.	58	828	12	276	96 60
10 Linen tape, not over 1¼ inches in width.. $	....	984	....	253	88 55
11 Tapestry, jute........................ $	....	49	....	49	12 25
12 Jute cloth, or jute canvas, uncoloured, not further finished than cropped, bleached, mangled or calendered..... Yd.	35,978,424	1,630,460	9,449,567	505,343	50,534 30
13 Fabrics of flax, printed, dyed or coloured, n.o.p............................ "	344,259	50,282	68,423	7,618	2,475 99
14 Other manufactures of hemp, or flax, or of which hemp or flax is the component material of chief value, n.o.p......... $	....	47,715	....	28,824	10,088 40
15 Manufactures of jute, n.o.p............. $	....	193,330	....	18,850	4,712 50
Total, flax, hemp and jute............	....	4,368,978	....	853,531	140,631 04
16 Foundry facings of all kinds............. $	....	9,746	....	9,541	2,385 25
Fruits, including nuts, viz:—					
17 Dried apples......................... Lb.	118,158	7,905	115,366	7,336	1,834 00
18 Bananas, dried or evaporated........ .. "	529	63	63	63	2 65
19 Currants............................. "	10,853,360	579,635	10,928,471	583,157	72,856 27
20 Dates................................ "	3,207,840	208,741	3,199,934	208,017	17,599 49
21 Figs.................................. "	3,286,538	188,907	3,279,142	188,665	18,035 20
22 Prunes and plums unpitted.............. "	8,164,636	525,141	8,263,172	528,242	55,087 81
23 Raisins............................... "	22,404,937	1,434,585	22,617,937	1,441,780	150,786 18
24 All other, n.o.p., dried fruits........... "	4,058,591	253,108	4,115,517	256,586	64,146 50
25 Almonds, shelled...................... "	850,114	258,553	166,855	50,662	6,674 20
26 Almonds, not shelled.................. "	651,639	77,834	632,615	76,302	12,652 30
27 Brazil nuts, not shelled................ "	1,117,420	82,494	1,111,781	82,210	22,235 62
28 Pecans, not shelled and shelled peanuts, n.o.p............................ "	4,887,820	280,524	4,921,420	284,179	98,428 40
29 Walnuts, not shelled.................. "	1,180,848	109,793	1,153,060	108,613	23,061 20
30 All other nuts, n.o.p., not shelled....... "	6,364,914	394,621	6,373,744	397,224	127,474 88
31 All other nuts, shelled.......:.......... "	2,151,926	520,022	447,877	118,413	17,915 08
32 Green apples......................Brl.	269,797	648,499	269,359	646,994	107,743 60
33 Blackberries, gooseberries, raspberries and strawberries, n.o.p.............. Lb.	6,457,109	589,275	6,457,356	589,107	129,147 12
34 Cherries............................. "	942,317	102,732	938,659	102,394	18,773 18
35 Cranberries........................Brl.	28,297	109,669	28,256	109,500	27,375 00
36 Currants............................. Lb.	12,920	1,075	12,920	1,075	258 40
37 Grapes............................... "	6,205,132	317,641	6,200,160	317,183	124,003 20
38 Limes................................ $	....	3,758	....	3,758	375 80
39 Peaches............................. Lb.	12,737,063	340,825	12,733,661	340,739	127,336 61
40 Plums..............................Bush.	104,978	251,941	104,904	251,791	31,471 20
41 Quinces, apricots, pears and nectarines, n.o.p............................ Lb.	11,798,317	384,850	11,780,751	384,160	58,903 98
42 All other, n.o.p....................... $	....	33,475	....	33,144	8,286 00
43 Fruits in air-tight cans or other air-tight packages......................... Lb.	7,761,096	449,336	5,589,202	358,332	136,761 11
44 Fruits, preserved in brandy or preserved in other spirits, and containing not more than 40 p.c. of proof spirits, etc..Gal.	76	314	76	314	166 30
45 Fruits preserved in brandy, etc., etc., containing more than 40 p.c. of proof spirits............................ "	22	221	22	221	131 10
Total, fruits and nuts...............	....	8,155,537	....	7,470,141	1,459,522 38

Imported into Canada, &c.—*Continued.*

				ENTERED FOR HOME CONSUMPTION.					
Preferential Tariff.			Treaty Rates.			Total.			
Quantity.	Value.	Duty.	Quantity.	Value.	Duty.	Quantity.	Value.	DutyColl'd.	
	$	$ cts.		$	$ cts.		$	$ cts.	
....	329	65 80	....	....	....	....	1,152	312 70	1
....	146,234	29,246 80	....	....	....	....	156,339	32,278 30	2
846,782	113,487	19,860 84	....	....	....	879,763	118,112	21,017 09	3
3,131,733	290,014	43,502 10	....	....	....	3,700,012	331,056	53,762 60	4
3,032,633	-224,961	39,369 28	....	....	....	3,069,069	228,498	40,253 53	5
....	5,290	1,322 50	....	12	3 90	....	10,868	3,274 50	6
....	172	43 00					431	133 65	7
320,921	215,301	37,677 60	2,023	1,466	329 86	332,588	224,675	39,984 46	8
46	552	138 00	....	....	....	58	828	234 60	9
....	731	182 75	....	....	....		984	271 30	10
....	....	....	....	....	....		49	12 25	11
26,573,707	1,125,451	84,409 13	....	....	....	36,023,274	1,630,794	134,943 43	12
274,027	42,348	10,587 00	....	....	....	342,450	49,966	13,062 99	13
....	18,319	4,579 75					47,143	14,668 15	14
....	155,751	23,362 65					174,601	28,075 15	15
....	3,475,084	525,522 60	....	16,508	4,665 12	....	4,345,123	670,818 76	
....	205	30 75	....	....	....	....	9,746	2,416 00	16
....	....	....	....	....	....	115,366	7,336	1,834 00	17
....	....	....	....	....	....	529	63	2 65	18
170	10	0 86	....	....	....	10,928,641	583,167	72,857 13	19
....	....	....	....	....	....	3,199,934	208,017	17,599 49	20
280	31	1 12	....	....	....	3,279,422	188,696	18,036 32	21
200	20	1 00	....	....	....	8,263,372	528,262	55,088 81	22
133	11	0 66	....	....	....	22,618,070	1,441,771	150,786 84	23
234	20	3 50	....	....	....	4,115,751	256,606	64,150 00	24
13,811	4,584	414 33	651,261	198,063	21,708 77	831,927	253,309	28,797 30	25
....	....	....	....	....	....	632,615	76,302	12,652 30	26
....	....	....	....	....	....	1,111,781	82,210	22,235 62	27
52,425	2,230	524 25	....	....	....	4,973,845	286,409	98,952 65	28
730	106	7 30	....	....	....	1,153,790	108,719	23,068 50	29
47,036	1,935	470 36	....	....	....	6,420,780	399,159	127,945 24	30
27,763	3,627	832 89	1,641,232	393,532	54,707 44	2,116,872	515,572	73,455 41	31
....	....	....	....	....	....	269,359	646,994	107,743 60	32
....	....	....	....	....	....	6,457,356	589,107	129,147 12	33
45	3	0 68	....	....	....	938,704	102,397	18,773 86	34-
....	....	....	....	....	....	28,256	109,500	27,375 00	35
....	....	....	....	....	....	12,920	1,075	258 40	36
....	....	....	....	....	....	6,200,160	317,183	124,003 20	37
....	....	....	....	....	....	3,758		375 80	38
....	....	....	....	....	....	12,733,661	340,739	127,336 61	39
....	....	....	....	....	....	104,904	251,791	31,471 20	40
....	....	....	....	....	....	11,780,751	384,160	58,903 98	41
....	211	36 93	....	....	....		33,355	8,322 93	42
2,111,674	85,006	33,928 27	275,074	21,328	5,501 48	7,975,950	464,666	176,190 86	43
....	....	....	....	....	....	76	314	166 30	44
....	....	....	....	....	....	22	221	131 10	45
....	97,794	36,222 15	....	612,923	81,917 69	....	8,180,858	1,577,662 22	

6 GEORGE V, A. 1916

No. 14.—Summary Statement of Foreign Merchandise

ARTICLES.		TOTAL IMPORTS.		General Tariff.		
		Quantity.	Value.	Quantity.	Value.	Duty.
	DUTIABLE GOODS—Con.		$		$	$ cts.
1	Furniture, house, office, cabinet or store furniture of wood, iron or other material, in parts or finished.................... $	....	1,514,628	....	1,360,503	408,150 90
	Furs and manufactures of, viz.:—					
2	Fur skins wholly or partly dressed,n.o.p. $	....	375,434	....	350,797	52,619 55
3	Caps, hats, muffs, tippets, capes, coats and cloaks of fur and other manufactures of fur, n.o.p................... $	....	401,443	....	192,163	57,648 90
	Total, furs..................	....	776,877	....	542,960	110,268 45
4	Fuses, non-metallic...................... $	....	89,632	....	20,702	4,140 40
	Glass and manufactures of—					
5	Glass carboys or demijohns, bottles, decanters, flasks, jars and phials...... $	....	388,943	....	348,856	113,380 96
6	Glass balls, and cut. pressed or moulded, crystal glass tableware, blown glass tableware, and other cut glass ware... $	....	381,017	....	369,368	120,047 54
7	Lamp chimneys, glass shades or globes. $	....	212,451	....	210,641	68,460 32
8	Ornamental figured and enamelled coloured glass and memorial or other ornamental window glass, n.o.p....... $	....	8,121	....	2,988	747 00
9	Painted or vitrified, chipped, figured, enamelled and obscured white glass... $	....	4,950	....	1,326	331 50
10	Common and colourless window glass..Sq.ft	38,444,337	1,247,873	31,184,884	1,020,349	127,544 49
11	Plain, coloured, opaque, stained or tinted or muffled glass in sheets...... $	....	63,735	....	36,410	9,102 50
12	Plate glass, not bevelled, in sheets or panes, not exceeding 7 sq. ft. each, n.o.p...........................Sq. ft.	944,484	191,272	638,236	133,708	13,370 80
13	Plate glass, not bevelled, in sheets or panes exceeding 7 sq. ft. each, and not exceeding 25 sq. ft. each, n.o.p........ "	807,134	186,080	202,068	52,241	14,366 46
14	Plate glass, n.o.p..... :............. "	1,053,721	269,906	461,391	118,084	41,329 40
15	Plate glass, bevelled, n.o.p............ "	11,589	3,376	11,470	3,334	1,166 90
16	German looking glass (thin plate), unsilvered or for silvering............... $	....	892	....	892	178 40
17	Silvered glass, bevelled or not, framed or not framed.................. $	....	104,868	....	49,680	17,388 00
18	Stained or ornamental glass windows.... $	....	27,158	....	12,550	3,765 00
19	Glass in sheets and bent plate glass, n.o.p.......................... $	....	60,154	....	43,972	10,993 00
20	Articles of glass, not plate or sheet, designed to be cut or mounted, and manufactures of glass, n.o.p.......... $	....	338,147	....	285,869	64,322 43
	Total, glass....................	....	3,488,943	....	2,690,268	606,494 70
21	Gloves and mitts of all kinds............. $	....	1,796,942	....	611,281	213,948 35
	Gold and silver, manufactures of—					
22	Gold, silver and Dutch or Schlag metal leaf........................ $	....	43,784	....	30,205	8,306 68
23	Manufactures of gold and silver, n.o.p... $	....	12,961	....	6,549	2,292 15
24	Electro-plated ware and gilt ware, n.o.p. $	....	269,807	....	102,565	35,897 75
25	Sterling or other silverware, n.o.p....... $	....	231,540	....	91,684	32,089 40
26	Silver and other coin, foreign, except gold........................ $	....	39	....	39	13 65
	Total gold and silver...............	....	558,131	....	231,042	78,599 63
27	Grease, axle........................ Lb.	3,240,258	137,291	3,182,552	134,826	26,965 20

Imported into Canada, &c.—*Continued.*

				ENTERED FOR HOME CONSUMPTION.					
Preferential Tariff.			Treaty Rates.			Total.			
Quantity.	Value.	Duty.	Quantity.	Value.	Duty.	Quantity.	Value.	DutyColl'd.	
	$	$ cts.		$	$ cts.		$	$ cts.	
....	94,364	18,872 80	....	51,889	14,269 69	....	1,506,756	441,293 39	1
....	24,878	2,487 80	....	....	....	....	375,675	55,107 35	2
....	209,726	41,945 20	....			....	401,889	99,594 10	3
....	234,604	44,433 00	....	....	....	....	777,564	154,701 45	
....	69,501	8,687 68	....			....	90,203	12,828 08	4
....	43,240	8,648 00	....			....	392,096	122,028 96	5
....	17,175	3,435 00	....			....	386,543	123,482 54	
....	2,095	419 00					212,736	68,879 32	6
....	5,133	898 34	....			....	8,121	1,645 34	8
....	3,624	634 23	....				4,950	965 73	9
7,259,440	227,522	17,064 27	....			38,444,324	1,247,871	144,608 76	10
....	27,325	4,781 98	....				63,735	13,884 48	11
307,946	57,859	4,339 65	....			946,182	191,567	17,710 45	12
364,295	82,893	12,433 95	240,771	50,946	12,736 50	807,134	186,080	39,536 91	13
592,672	151,661	34,124 03	....			1,054,063	269,745	75,453 43	14
119	42	9 45	....			11,589	3,376	1,176 35	15
....	....	....	....				892	178 40	16
....	40,518	9,116 96	....	14,335	4,300 50	....	104,533	30,805 46	17
....	14,608	2,921 60	....			....	27,158	6,686 60	18
....	16,182	2,831 91	....				60,154	13,824 91	19
....	23,162	3,474 30	....	29,285	5,857 00	....	338,316	73,653 73	20
....	713,039	105,132 67	....	94,566	22,894 00	....	3,497 873	734,521 37	
....	608,818	136,985 26	....	548,007	164,402 10	....	1,768,106	515,335 71	21
....	13,060	1,959 00	....	519	129 75	....	43,784	10,395 43	22
....	4,827	1,086 21		1,579	473 70	....	12,955	3,852 06	23
....	163,986	36,897 35	....	2,991	897 30	....	269,542	73,692 40	24
....	138,814	31,233 83	....	3,948	1,184 40	....	234,446	64,507 63	25
....	....	....	....	....	....	....	39	13 65	26
....	320,687	71,176 39	....	9,037	2,685 15	....	560,766	152,461 17	
45,770	1,548	193 49	....	....	....	3,228,322	136,374	27,158 69	27

6 GEORGE V, A. 1916

No. 14.—SUMMARY STATEMENT of Foreign Merchandise

ARTICLES.	TOTAL IMPORTS.		General Tariff.		
	Quantity.	Value.	Quantity.	Value.	Duty.
		$		$	$ cts
DUTIABLE GOODS—*Con.*					
Gunpowder and other explosives, &c.—					
1 Gun, rifle, sporting, cannon, musket and cannister powder.................... Lb.	211,608	147,782	153,922	121,943	4,617 66
2 Blasting and mining powder............ "	148,125	15,784	13,325	1,551	266 50
3 Giant powder, nitro, nitro-glycerine and other explosives, n.o.p............... "	567,820	118,031	549,410	97,974	13,735 30
4 Gun, rifle and pistol cartridges, or other ammunition, n.o.p................... $	....	705,973	....	463,780	139,134 00
5 Gun wads, percussion caps, primers and cartridge cases........................ $	....	29,106	....	26,392	7,917 60
6 Gun or pistol covers or cases, game bags, loading tools, and cartridge belts of any material............................. $	....	34,995	....	30,019	9,005 70
Total, gunpowder and explosives......	....	1,051,671	....	741,659	174,676 76
Gutta-percha and India-rubber, manufactures of—					
7 Boots and shoes........................ $	....	128,842	....	100,714	25,178 50
8 Belting............................... $	....	82,065	....	77,532	21,321 85
9 Clothing, and clothing made waterproof with india-rubber................... $	....	801,516	....	57,516	20,130 60
10 Hose, including cotton or linen, lined with rubber........................ $	....	91,083	....	88,202	30,870 70
11 Packing, mats and matting............ $	....	69,664	....	66,570	23,299 50
12 Tires of rubber for vehicles of all kinds. $	....	1,199,077	....	1,164,718	407,651 30
13 Rubber cement and all manufactures of india-rubber and gutta-percha, n.o.p. $	....	878,176	....	656,835	180,633 64
14 Rubber, hard, unfinished, in tubes, for the manufacture of fountain pens...... $	....	5,957	....	5,957	595 70
Total, gutta-percha...................	....	3,256,380	....	2,218,044	709,681 79
Hair and manufactures of, not otherwise provided for—					
15 Braids, chains or cords.....'........... $	....	640	....	625	218 75
16 Curled or dyed, n.o.p.................. $	....	29,201	....	24,515	4,903 00
17 Hair cloth of all kinds................ $	....	37,645	....	1,909	572 70
18 Other manufactures of, n.o.p.......... $	....	33,211	....	30,248	10,586 80
Total, hair..........................	....	100,697	....	57,297	16,281 25
Hats, caps and bonnets, n.o.p.—					
19 Beaver, silk or felt.................... $	....	959,037	....	517,132	180,996 20
20 Straw, grass, chip or other material, n.o.p............................. $	....	2,076,992	....	1,290,284	451,599 40
21 Hat, cap and bonnet shapes, and hat and bonnet crowns...................... $	....	66,791	....	52,760	18,466 00
Total, hats, caps, &c.................	....	3,102,820	....	1,860,176	651,061 60
22 Hay.................................Ton.	16,092	208,593	16,078	208,294	32,156 00
23 Honey, in the comb or otherwise, and imitations thereof....................Lb.	165,898	19,793	132,817	17,357	3,984 51
24 Hops.................................. "	1,366,071	278,114	1,231,268	246,848	86,188 76
25 Ink, writing........................... $	....	35,056	....	15,584	3,896 00
26 Ink, printing.......................... $	....	95,523	....	81,858	16,371 60
Total. ink...........................	....	130,579	....	97,442	20,267 60

Imported into Canàda, &c.—*Continued.*

	ENTERED FOR HOME CONSUMPTION.								
Preferential Tariff.				Treaty Rates.		Total.			
Quantity.	Value.	Duty.	Quantity.	Value.	Duty.	Quantity.	Value.	DutyColl'd.	
	$	$ cts.		$	$ cts.		$	$ cts.	
57,761	25,857	1,155 22				211,683	147,800	5,772 88	1
134,800	14,233	1,797 33				148,125	15,784	2,063 83	2
18,410	20,057	322 18				567,820	118,031	14,057 48	3
....	239,470	47,894 00				....	703,250	187,028 00	4
....	2,577	515 40				....	28,969	8,433 00	5
....	4,976	995 20				....	34,995	10,000 90	6
....	307,170	52,679 33				....	1,048,829	227,356 09	
....	25,692	3,853 80				....	126,406	29,032 30	7
....	4,523	904 60				....	82,055	22,226 45	8
....	747,299	168,143 90				....	804,815	188,274 50	9
....	3,089	695 05				....	91,291	31,565 75	10
....	3,200	720 08				....	69,770	24,019 58	11
....	39,739	8,941 44				....	1,204,457	416,592 74	12
....	213,173	31,975 95	....	6,501	1,625 25	....	876 509	214,234 84	13
....	....	....				....	5,957	595 70	14
....	1,036,715	215,234 82	....	6,501	1,625 25	....	3,261,260	926,541 86	
....	15	3 38				....	640	222 13	15
....	4,686	585 80				....	29,201	5,488 80	16
....	35,418	7,083 60				....	37,327	7,656 30	17
....	3,290	740 40				....	33,538	11,327 20	18
....	43,409	8,413 18				....	100,706	24,694 43	
....	450,429	101,347 51				....	967 561	282,343 71	19
....	788,502	177,414 40				....	2,078,786	629,013 80	20
....	13,700	3,082 68				....	66,460	21,548 68	21
....	1,252,631	281,844 59				....	3,112,807	932,906 19	
....	....	....				16,078	208,294	32,156 00	22
31,010	2,304	620 20				163,827	19,661	4,604 71	23
135,838	31,462	5,433 52				1,367,106	278,310	91,622 28	24
....	18,863	2,829 45	....	609	137 01	....	35,056	6,862 46	25
....	14,664	1,833 29	....	409	71 59	....	96,931	18,276 48	26
....	33,527	4,662 74	....	1,018	208 60	....	131,987	25,138 94	

No. 14.—SUMMARY STATEMENT of Foreign Merchandise

	ARTICLES.	TOTAL IMPORTS.		General Tariff.		
		Quantity.	Value.	Quantity.	Value.	Duty.
			$		$	$ cts.
	DUTIABLE GOODS—Con.					
	Iron and manufactures of, steel and manu-					
	tures of, or both combined—					
	Agricultural implements, n.o.p., viz.:—					
1	Binding attachments.................$	....	2,485	....	2,389	323 20
2	Cultivators and weeders and parts of $	....	53,114	....	52,996	10,599 20
3	Drills, seed.....................:.......No.	5,114	63,880	5,114	63,880	12,776 00
4	Farm, road or field rollers........... "	234	116,257	173	85,450	21,362 50
5	Forks, pronged.................... "	8,931	4,671	5,637	3,441	774 51
6	Harrows and parts of.............·.. $	....	67,268	....	67,174	13,434 80
7	Harvesters, self-binding.............No.	1,635	177,158	1,635	177,158	22,241 24
8	Hay loaders......................... "	228	11,270	228	11,270	2,817 50
9	Hay tedders........................ "	14	570	14	570	142 50
10	Hoes.............................. "	8,693	2,341	7,874	2,130	479 38
11	Horse rakes........................ "	754	13,979	754	13,979	2,795 80
12	Knives, hay or straw............... "	3,409	934	2,937	800	180 03
13	Knives, edging..................... "	90	78	72	66	14 85
14	Lawn mowers..................... "	10,750	49,639	10,642	47,543	15,452 93
15	Manure spreaders.................. "	905	57,333	903	57,254	11,450 80
16	Mowing machines.................. "	1,198	43,607	1,198	43,607	5,584 95
17	Ploughs and parts of................$	....	498,103	....	497,849	99,569 80
18	Post hole diggers....................No.	3,989	4,163	3,989	4,163	1,040 75
19	Potato diggers..................... "	1,439	44,185	1,410	42,847	10,711 75
20	Rakes, n.o.p....................... "	18,869	3,905	18,620	3,823	860 30
21	Reapers........................... "	432	32,094	432	32,094	4,011 77
22	Scythes...........................Doz.	3,046	15,287	2,542	13,021	2,929 80
23	Sickles or reaping hooks............. "	282	615	75	207	46 60
24	Snaths............................ "	248	1,042	248	1,042	260 50
25	Spades and shovels of iron or steel, n.o.p..... "	5,013	18,886	2,531	8,346	2,713 02
26	Spade and shovel blanks, and iron or steel cut to shape for the same...... "	1,331	2,492	23	80	26 01
27	Parts of agricultural implements pay- ing 12½ p.c., 12½ p.c. and 12½ p.c..... $	....	83,460	....	82,616	11,250 74
28	Parts of agricultural implements pay- ing 12½ p.c., 17½ p.c. and 20 p.c., n.o.p. $	....	142,525	....	142,490	28,498 00
29	All other agricultural implements, n.o.p....................... $	....	82,800	....	77,080	19,270 00
30	Anvils and vises..................... $	....	46,107	....	28,843	8,652 90
1	Cart or wagon skeins or boxes........Lb.	358,867	20,182	358,092	20,182	5,045 50
32	Springs, n.o.p., and parts thereof, of iron or steel, for railway, tramway or other vehicles................... $	....	71,361	....	74,432	26,051 20
33	Axles and axle parts, n.o.p., and axle blanks and parts thereof of iron or steel, for railway, tramway or other vehicles...................... $	....	214,236	....	201,325	70,463 75
34	Bar iron or steel, rolled, whether in coils, bundles, rods or bars, com- prising rounds, ovals, squares and flats, n.o.p.......................Cwt.	853,908	1,223,439	783,009	1,088,635	274,053 15
35	Butts and hinges, n.o.p............. $	....	77,117	....	75,213	22,563 90
36	Canada plates, Russia iron, terne plate, and rolled sheets of iron or steel coated with zinc, spelter or other metal, of all widths or· thicknesses, n.o.p'.......:..................Cwt.	175,823	443,899	175,823	443,899	22,194 95
37	Castings, iron or steel, n.o.p.......... $	....	609,639	....	567,570	156,084 50
38	Castings, malleable iron, when im- ported by manufacturers of mowers, binding attachments, harvesters and reapers for use exclusively in their own factories..................... $	....	93,007	....	93,007	16,276 04
39	Cast iron pipe of every description...Cwt.	267,241	325,563	220,267	265,053	88,106 80
40	Cast scrap iron......................Ton.	5,720	63,563	5,538	61,277	13,845 00
41	Chains, coil chain, chain links, includ- ing repair links, and chain shackles, of iron or steel, 1½ of an inch in dia- meter and over....................Cwt.	10,572	46,282	9,554	42,876	2·816 50

SESSIONAL PAPER No. 11

Imported into Canada, &c.—*Continued.*

	Entered for Home Consumption.								
Preferential Tariff.			Treaty Rates.			Total.			
Quantity.	Value.	Duty.	Quantity.	Value.	Duty.	Quantity.	Value.	DutyColl'd.	
	$	$ cts.		$	$ cts.		$	$ cts.	
....	118	14 76	....	....	....	....	2,389	323 20	1
....			....	....	....	....	53,114	10,613 96	2
....			....	....	....	5,114	63,880	12,776 00	3
62	33,077	4,961 55	....	....	....	235	118,527	26,324 05	4
3,294	1,230	184 50	....	....	....	8,931	4,671	959 01	5
....	94	11 75	....	....	....	....	67,268	13,446 55	6
....			....	....	....	1,635	177,158	22,241 24	7
....			....	....	....	228	11,270	2,817 50	8
....			....	....	....	14	570	142 50	9
819	211	31 65	....	....	....	8,693	2,341	511 03	10
....			....	....	....	754	13,979	2,795 80	11
472	134	20 10	....	....	....	3,409	934	200 13	12
18	12	1 80	....	....	....	90	78	16 65	13
108	2,096	419 20	....	....	....	10,750	49,639	15,872 13	14
2	79	9 88	....	....	....	905	57,333	11,460 68	15
....			....	....	....	1,198	43,607	5,584 95	16
....	32	4 00	....	....	....	....	497,881	99,573 80	17
....			....	....	....	3,989	4,163	1,040 75	18
23	1,164	174 60	....	....	....	1,433	44,011	10,886 35	19
249	82	12 30	....	....	....	18,869	3,905	872 60	20
....			....	....	....	432	32,094	4,011 77	21
509	2,287	343 05	....	....	....	3,051	15,308	3,272 83	22
207	408	61 20	....	....	....	282	615	107 80	23
....			....	....	....	248	1,042	260 50	24
2,472	10,422	2,084 40	....	....	....	5,003	18,768	4,797 42	25
1,308	2,412	482 40	....	....	....	1,331	2,492	508 41	26
....	744	92 99	....	....	....	....	83,360	11,343 73	27
....	11	1 38	....	....	....	....	142,501	28,499 38	28
....	5,620	843 00	....	....	....	....	82,700	20,113 00	29
....	17,384	3,476 80	....	....	....	....	46,227	12,129 70	30
....			....	....	....	358,092	20,182	5,045 50	31
....	5,114	1,150 65	....	....	....	....	79,546	27,201 85	32
....	22,739	5,116 32	....	....	....	....	224,064	75,580 07	33
70,872	134,746	15,060 31	....	....	....	853,881	1,223,381	289,113 46	34
....	943	188 60	....	948	260 71	....	77,104	23,013 21	35
....			....	....	....	175,823	443,899	22,194 95	36
....	41,086	6,162 90	....	....	....	....	608,656	162,247 40	37
....			....	....	....	....	93,007	16,276 04	38
46,974	60,510	14,092 20	....	....	....	267,241	325,563	102,199 00	39
184	2,304	276 00	....	....	....	5,722	63,581	14,121 00	40
1,005	3,404	170 20	....	....	....	10,559	46,280	2,986 70	41

6 GEORGE V, A. 1916

No. 14.—SUMMARY STATEMENT of Foreign Merchandise

		TOTAL IMPORTS.		General Tariff.		
ARTICLES.		Quantity.	Value.	Quantity.	Value.	Duty.
			$		$	$ ts.
	DUTIABLE GOODS—Con.					
	Iron and steel—Con.					
1	Chains, coil chains and links, including repair links and chain shackles of iron and steel, n.o.p..........Cwt.	19,693	75,724	11,982	44,300	8,860 00
2	Chains, n.o.p................$	....	86,005	....	72,015	21,604 50
3	Tacks, shoe...................Lb.	34,637	2,498	28,044	2,155	754 25
4	Nails, brads, spikes and tacks of all kinds, n.o.p.................... "	530,219	32,424	458,036	29,030	10,160 50
	Engines, &c.—					
5	Locomotives for railways..........No.	70	162,427	69	158,777	55,571 95
6	Locomotive parts................$	....	81,618	....	81,618	28,566 30
7	Motor cars for railways and tramways No.	25	50,404	25	50,404	17,641 40
8	Engines, fire.................... "	26	99,465	26	99,465	34,812 75
9	Engines, gasoline and gas.......... "	14,668	2,034,310	14,306	1,917,721	527,376 87
10	Engines, steam................... "	296	237,344	271	170,117	46,782 43
11	Boilers, steam, and parts of........$	....	203,789	....	163,447	44,948 20
12	Boilers, n.o.p., and parts of........$	....	240,044	....	225,372	61,978 14
13	Fire extinguishing machines, including sprinklers for fire protection........$	....	102,309	....	101,655	35,579 25
14	Fittings, iron or steel, for iron or steel pipe of every description..........$	....	729,472	....	710,569	213,170 70
15	Flat eye bar blanks, not punched nor drilled, for use exclusively in the manufacture of bridges, or of steel structural work, or in car construction................Ton	4,717	315,422	4,717	315,422	14,151 00
16	Ferro-silicon, containing not more than 15 p.c. silicon............... "	317	13,353	289	11,923	722 50
17	Ferro-silicon containing more than 15 p.c. silicon.................... "	2	171	2	171	9 00
18	Spiegeleisen and ferro manganese containing not more than 15 p.c. manganese................ "	310	15,195	1,955	50,731	4,887 50
19	Forgings of iron or steel, of whatever shape or size, or in whatever stage of manufacture, n.o.p., and hammered, drawn or cold rolled iron or steel bars or shapes, n.o.p..............Lb.	4,679,986	323,012	4,635,325	319,711	95,913 30
20	Hardware, viz.:—Builders', cabinetmakers',upholsterers',harnessmakers', saddlers' and carriage hardware, including curry-combs, n.o.p..........$	....	578,653	....	475,912	142,773 60
21	Horse, mule and ox shoes.............$	....	29,919	....	27,455	8,236 50
22	Iron or steel billets, weighing not less than 60 lbs. per lineal yard..........Cwt.	230,104	226,114	228,987	216,845	28,623 42
23	Iron or steel ingots, cogged ingots, blooms, slabs, puddled bars, and loops or other forms, n.o.p., less finished than iron or steel bars, but more advanced than pig iron, except castings................ "	7,660	12,166	7,148	11,442	893·53
24	Iron or steel bridges or parts thereof, iron or steel structural work, columns, shapes or sections, drilled, punched, or in any further state of manufacture than as rolled or cast, n.o.p..........$	....	267,661	....	253,841	88,844 35
25	Iron in pig....................Ton	54,874	673,374	50,434	621,035	126,085 00
26	Iron in pig, charcoal.................. "	25	275	25	275	62 50
27	Iron ore.................... "	4,391	11,689	4,391	11,689	351 28
28	Locks of all kinds.....z.............$	....	215,172	....	203,189	60,956 70
	Machines, machinery, &c.—					
29	Cranes and derricks.................No.	127	364,782	116	338,235	93,014 80
30	Dental engines (electric)............. "	66	5,800	66	5,800	1,595 02
31	Fanning mills...................... "	780	16,980	780	16,980	4,245 00
32	Grain crushers..................... "	369	6,928	369	6,928	1,732 00
33	Hay presses...................... "	168	29,278	168	29,278	8,051 53
34	Windmills and complete parts thereof. $	....	45,653	....	45,653	9,130 60

Imported into Canada, &c.—*Continued.*

	ENTERED FOR HOME CONSUMPTION.								
Preferential Tariff.			Treaty Rates.			Total.			
Quantity.	Value.	Duty.	Quantity.	Value.	Duty.	Quantity.	Value.	DutyColl'd.	
	$	$ cts.		$	$ cts.		$	$ cts.	
7,711	31,424	4,713 60	....	....	....	19,693	75,724	13,573 60	1
....	13,421	2,684 20	....	422	116 07	....	85,858	24,404 77	2
6,593	343	68 60	....	....	....	34,637	2,498	822 85	3
71,335	3,357	671 40	....	....	....	529,371	32,387	10,831 90	4
1	3,650	821 25	....	....	....	70	162,427	56,393 20	5
....	....	....	....	....	....	....	81,618	28,566 30	6
....	....	....	....	....	....	25	50,404	17,641 40	7
....	....	....	....	....	....	26	99,465	34,812 75	8
362	84,964	12,744 60	....	....	....	14,668	2,002,685	540,121 47	9
25	67,227	10,084 05	....	....	....	296	237,344	56,866 48	10
....	34,964	5,244 60	....	....	....	....	198,411	50,192 80	11
....	4,766	714 90	....	....	....	....	230,138	62,693 04	12
....	250	56 26	....	....	....	....	101,905	35,635 51	13
....	18,878	3,775 60	....	....	....	....	729,447	216,946 30	14
....	....	....	....	....	....	4,717	315,422	14,151 00	15
28	1,430	42 00	....	....	....	317	13,353	764 50	16
....	....	....	....	....	....	2	171	9 00	17
420	17,714	630 00	....	....	....	2,375	68,445	5,517 50	18
44,767	3,307	661 40	....	....	....	4,680,092	323,018	96,574 70	19
....	99,850	19,970 00	....	2,418	664 96	....	578,180	163,408 56	20
....	2,464	492 80	....	....	....	....	29,919	8,729 30	21
1,117	9,269	83 85	....	....	....	230,104	226,114	28,707 27	22
512	724	38 40	....	....	....	7,660	12,166	931 93	23
....	13,820	3,109 57	....	....	....	267,661	91,953 92	24	
8,477	104,954	12,715 50	....	....	....	58,911	725,989	138,800 50	25
....	....	....	....	....	....	25	275	62 50	26
....	....	....	....	....	....	4,391	11,689	351 28	27
....	11,461	2,292 20	....	671	184 53	....	215,321	63,433 43	28
10	26,507	3,976 05	....	....	....	126	364,742	96,990 85	29
....	....	....	....	....	....	66	5,800	1,595 02	30
....	....	....	....	....	....	780	16,980	4,245 00	31
....	....	....	....	....	....	369	6,928	1,732 00	32
....	....	....	....	....	....	168	29,278	8,051 53	33
....	....	....	....	....	....	....	45,653	9,130 60	34

No. 14.—Summary Statement of Foreign Merchandise

Articles.	Total Imports.		General Tariff.		
	Quantity.	Value.	Quantity.	Value.	Duty.
Dutiable Goods—Con.		$		$	$ cts.
Iron and steel—*Con.*					
1 Ore crushers and rock crushers, stamp mills, Cornish and belted rolls, rock drills, air compressors, and percussion coal cutters................ $	....	417,988	....	371,011	102,028 79
2 Fodder or feed cutters....:........... No.	725	10,833	725	10,833	2,708 25
3 Horse powers, for farm purposes...... "	4	116	4	116	23 20
4 Portable engines with boilers in combination, 'and traction engines for farm purposes..................... "	476	710,398	464	691,120	138,224 00
5 Portable saw-mills and planing mills.. "	19	4,797	19	4,797	1,319 23
6 Steam shovels and electric shovels... "	21	154,796	21	154,796	42,569 42
7 Threshing machine separators....... "	615	318,124	597	302,495	60,499 00
8 Threshing machine separators. parts of, including wind stackers, baggers, weighers and self-feeders. therefor and finished parts thereof for repairs, when imported separately.......... $	....	212,768	....	212,293	42,458 60
9 All other portable machines, n.o.p., and parts of..................... $	....	118,564	....	118,186	32,501 28
10 Concrete mixing-machines........... No.	131	62,208	132	63,300	17,407 61
11 Sewing machines.................... "	15,912	319,139	14,870	303,129	90,938 70
12 Sewing machines, parts of............ $	....	69,738	....	67,412	20,223 60
13 Machines, adding................... No.	1,130	199,985	1,133	201,403	50,350 75
14 Machines, typewriting.............. "	7,296	405,122	7,236	401,241	100,310 25
15 Machines specially designed for ruling, folding, binding, embossing, creasing or cutting paper or cardboard, when for use exclusively by printers, bookbinders and by manufacturers of articles made from paper or cardboard, including parts thereof, composed wholly or in part of iron, steel, brass or wood..................... $	....	164,002	....	158,918	15,891 80
16 Printing presses and lithographic presses...................... $	....	230,826	....	223,292	22,329 20
17 Type making accessories for printing presses..... .... $	....	31,750	....	31,750	3,175 00
18 Cement making, machines......... .. $	....	45,185	....	43,425	11,941 93
19 Coal handling, machines:........... $	....	141,863	....	136,581	37,559 89
20 Paper and pulp mill, machines...... .. $	....	406,678	....	385,224	105,936 69
21 Rolling mill, machines............. $	....	118,910	....	108,943	29,959 42
22 Saw mill, machines............. .... $	....	139,497	....	137,148	37,716 00
23 Machinery of a class or kind not made in Canada and parts thereof adapted for carding, spinning, weaving, braiding or knitting fibrous material, when imported by manufacturers for such purposes................... $	....	484,054	....	484,101	48,410 10
24 All machinery composed wholly or in part of iron or steel, n.o.p., and iron or steel integral parts of............ $	....	9,304,006	....	8,291,778	2,280,246 20
25 Machines, washing, domestic....... No.	7,798	63,731	7,667	62,665	17,233 18
26 Nails and spikes, composition and sheathing nails........................... Lb.	134,126	3,711	131,782	3,445	516 75
27 Nails and spikes, cut (ordinary builders) Cwt	4,689	8,585	4,684	8,560	2,342 00
28 Railway spikes....... .... "	54,900	82,850	54,671	82,355	27,335 50
29 Nails, wire, of all kinds, n.o.p.......... "	18,038	50,739	18,000	50,630	10,800 00
30 Pumps, hand, n.o.p................ No.	19,122	104,230	18,787	102,999	30,899 70
31 Pumps, power and parts............... "	3,186	490,033	3,044	448,587	123,362 86
32 Iron and steel railway bars or rails of any form, punched or not, n.o.p., for railways, which term for the purposes of this item shall include all kinds of railway, street railways and tramways, even although they are used for private purposes only, and even although they are not used or intended to be used in connection with the business of common carrying of goods or passengers........................ Ton.	27,726	710,268	27,666	706,888	193,662 00

Imported into Canada, &c.—*Continued.*

			ENTERED FOR HOME CONSUMPTION.					
Preferential Tariff.			Treaty Rates.			Total.		
Quantity.	Value.	Duty.	Quantity.	Value.	Duty.	Quantity.	Value.	DutyColl'd.
	$	$ cts.		$	$ cts.		$	$ cts.
....	46,977	7,046 55	....	....	....	....	417,988	109,075 34	1
....	....	....	....	....	....	725	10,833	2,708 25	2
....	....	....	....	....	....	4	116	23 20	.3
13	21,345	3,201 75	....	....	....	477	712,465	141,425 75	4
....	....	....	....	....	....	19	4,797	1,319 23	5
....	....	....	....	....	....	21	154,796	42,569 42	6
2	2,706	405 90	....	....	....	599	305,201	60,904 90	7
....	475	71 25	....	....	....	....	212,768	42,529 85	8
....	....	....	....	....	....	....	118,186	32,501 28	9
....	....	....	....	....	....	132	63,300	17,407 61	10
1,072	16,215	3,243 00	....	....	....	15,942	319,344	94,181 70	11
....	2,360	472 00	....	....	....	....	69,772	20,695 60	12
....	....	....	....	....	....	1,133	201,403	50,350 75	13
33	1,405	245 91	....	....	....	7,269	402,646	100,556 16	14
....	5,037	251 85	....	....	....	....	163,955	16,143 65	15
....	7,534	376 70	....	....	....	....	230,826	22,705 90	16
....	....	....	....	....	....	....	31,750	3,175 00	17
....	1,760	264 00	....	....	....	....	45,185	12,205 93	18
....	5,282	792 30	....	....	....	....	141,863	38,352 19	19
....	21,454	3,218 10	....	....	....	....	406,678	109,154 79	20
....	2,314	347 10	....	....	....	....	111,257	30,306 52	21
....	2,349	352 35	....	....	....	....	139,497	38,008 35	22
....	....	....	....	....	....	....	484,101	48,410 10	23
....	973,279	145,991 85	....	....	....	....	9,265,057	2,426,238 05	24
17	.42	6 30	....	....	....	7,684	62,707	17,239 48	25
3,016	411	41 10	....	....	....	134,798	3,856	557 85	26
5	25	1 50	....	....	....	4,689	8,585	2,343 50	27
129	292	38 70	....	....	....	54,800	82,647	27,374 20	28
29	90	11 60	....	....	....	18,029	50,720	10,811 60	29
226	884	176 80	....	....	....	19,013	103,883	31,076 50	30
133	41,288	6,193 20	....	....	....	3,177	489,875	129,556 06	31
37	1,917	166 50	....	....	....	27,703	708,805	193,828 50	32

6 GEORGE V, A. 1916

No. 14.—SUMMARY STATEMENT of Foreign Merchandise

ARTICLES.	TOTAL IMPORTS.		General Tariff.		
	Quantity.	Value.	Quantity.	Value.	Duty.
DUTIABLE GOODS—*Con.*		$		$	$ cts.
Iron and steel—*Con.*					
1 Railway fish plates....................Ton.	2,955	113,970	2,938	112,853	23,504 00
2 Railway tie-plates........................ "	490	18,023	490	18,023	3,920 00
3 Rolled iron or steel angles, tees, beams, channels, girders and other rolled shapes or sections, not punched, drilled or further manufactured than rolled, n.o.p........................Cwt.	542,432	723,182	524,882	696,094	183,708 70
4 Rolled iron or steel beams, channels, angles, and other rolled shapes of iron or steel, not punched, drilled, or further manufactured than rolled, weighing not less than 35 lbs. per lineal yard, not being square, flat, oval or round shapes, and not being railway bars or rails............................... "	1,299,625	1,664,337	1,268,013	1,619,106	190,201 93
5 Rolled iron or steel hoop, band, scroll or strip, 12 inches or less in width, No. 13 gauge and thicker, n.o.p....... "	59,008	96,272	55,978	89,692	19,592 30
6 Rolled hoop iron or hoop steel (galvanized) Nos. 12 and 13 gauge............ "	1,275	3,053	572	1,507	200 20
7 Rolled iron or steel, hoop, band, scroll or strip, No. 14 gauge and thinner, galvanized or coated with other metal or not, n.o.p., including drawn iron or steel of this description for the manufacture of mats................. "	196,455	416,883	194,265	413,390	20,669 50
8 Rolled iron or steel sheets or plates, sheared or unsheared, and skelp iron or steel, sheared or rolled in grooves, n.o.p.............................., "	286,699	424,950	280,302	414,162	98,105 70
9 Rolled iron or steel plates, not less than 30 inches in width and not less than ½-inch in thickness, n.o.p............. "	444,629	655,309	438,364	646,580	65,754 61
10 Rolled iron or steel sheets, polished or not, No. 14 gauge and thinner, n.o.p... "	581,130	1,248,261	581,792	1,250,021	62,501 05
11 Rolls of chilled iron or steel............ "	769	2,403	569	1,658	497 40
12 Rolled round wire rods in the coil of iron or steel not over ¼-inch in diameter when imported by wire manufacturers for use in making wire in the coil in their own factories.................. "	611,792	660,379	597,942	644,801	104,639 89
13 Rolled round rods in the coil of iron or steel for the manufacture of chains.... "	6,194	7,468	6,194	7,468	1,083 96
14 Sad or smoothing, hatters' and tailors' irons not plated........................ $	....	3,608	....	3,507	1,052 10
15 Safes, doors for safes and vaults........ $	....	165,891	....	165,746	49,723 80
16 Screws, iron and steel, commonly called "wood screws" n.o.p., including lag or coach screws, plated or not, and machine or other screws, n.o.p....... $	....	37,061	....	36,921	12,922 35
17 Scales, balances, weighing beams and strength testing machines of all kinds. $	....	90,468	....	88,213	26,463 90
18 Shafting, round, steel, in bars not exceeding 2½ inches in diameter........... Cwt.	20,563	38,159	19,758	36,208	9,052 00
19 Shafting, steel, turned, compressed or polished................................ $	....	14,599	....	12,620	3,786 00
20 Sheets or plates of steel, cold rolled, sheared edges, over 14 gauge, not less than 1½ inches wide, for manufacture of mower bars, hinges, typewriters, and sewing machines............... Cwt.	7,435	16,432	7,435	16,432	1,643 20
21 Sheets, flat, of galvanized iron or steel.. "	301,451	819,394	301,451	819,394	40,969 70
22 Sheets, iron or steel corrugated, galvanized................................. "	1,140	2,998	1,082	2,821	846 30
23 Sheets, iron or steel corrugated, not galvanized............................. "	138	484	138	484	145 20
24 Skates of all kinds, roller or other, and parts thereof......................... $	....	38,203	....	37,673	13,185 55

SESSIONAL PAPER No. 11

Imported into Canada, &c.—*Continued.*

	Entered for Home Consumption.								
Preferential Tariff.			Treaty Rates.			Total.			
Quantity.	Value.	Duty.	Quantity.	Value.	Duty.	Quantity.	Value.	DutyColl'd.	
	$	$ cts.		$	$ cts.		$	$ cts.	
4	443	20 00	....	....	....	2,942	113,296	23,524 00	1
....	....	....	....	....	....	490	18,023	3,920 00	2
17,571	27,127	3,733 80	....	....	....	542,453	723,221	187,442 50	
31,612	45,231	3,161 20	....	....	....	1,299,625	1,664,337	193,363 13	4
3,030	6,580	643 87	....	....	....	59,008	96,272	20,236 17	5
703	1,546	149 39	....	....	....	1,275	3,053	349 59	6
....	....	....	....	....	....	194,265	413,390	20,669 50	7
6,687	11,153	1,420 94	....	....	....	286,989	425,315	99,526 64	8
6,265	8,729	626 50	....	....	....	444,629	655,309	66,381 11	9
....	....	....	....	....	....	581,792	1,250,021	62,501 05	10
200	745	149 00	....	....	....	769	2,403	646 40	11
....	....	....	....	....	....	597,942	644,801	104,639 89	12
....	....	....	....	....	....	6,194	7,468	1,083 96	13
....	101	20 20	....	....	....	....	3,608	1,072 30	14
....	145	29 00	....	....	....	....	165,891	49,752 80	15
....	276	62 12	....	....	....	....	37,197	12,984 47	16
....	2,274	454 80	....	....	....	....	90,487	26,918 70	17
784	1,901	332 67	....	....	....	20,542	38,109	9,384 67	18
....	2,026	405 20	....	....	....	....	14,646	4,191 20	19
....	....	....	....	....	....	7,435	16,432	1,643 20	20
....	....	....	....	....	....	301,451	819,394	40,969 70	21
58	177	35 40	....	....	....	1,140	2,998	881 70	22
....	....	....	....	....	....	138	484	145 20	23
....	530	119 26	....	....	....	....	38,203	13,304 81	24

6 GEORGE V, A. 1916

No. 14.—Summary Statement of Foreign Merchandise

	ARTICLES.	TOTAL IMPORTS.		General Tariff.		
		Quantity.	Value.	Quantity.	Value.	Duty.
			$		$	$ cts.
	DUTIABLE GOODS—*Con.*					
	Iron and steel—*Con.*					
1	Skelp iron or steel, sheared or rolled in grooves, imported by manufacturers of wrought iron or steel pipe, for use exclusively in the manufacture of wrought iron or steel pipe in their own factories........................... Cwt.	1,886,340	2,104,205	1,886,340	2,104,205	105,210 25
2	Steel billets, n.o.p.................... "	12,246	14,413	11,811	13,873	4,133 85
3	Stoves of all kinds, for coal, wood, oil, spirits or gas....................... $	....	488,042	....	483,514	120,878 50
4	Stove urns of metal, and dovetails, chaplet and hinge tubes of tin for use in the manufacture of stoves......... $	....	11,169	....	11,169	1,116 90
5	Swtiches, frogs, crossings and intersections for railways.................... $	....	135,659	....	104,149	33,848 81
6	Wrought or seamless iron or steel tubing, plain or galvanized, threaded and coupled or not, over 10 inches in diameter, n.o.p........................ $	....	193,921	....	189,192	28,378 80
	Tubing—.					
7	Wrought or seamless tubing, iron or steel, plain or galvanized, threaded and coupled or not, over 4 inches in diameter, but not exceeding 10 inches in diameter, n.o.p........... $	....	190,201	....	175,572	51,724 20
8	Wrought or seamless tubing, iron or steel, plain or galvanized, threaded and coupled or not, 4 inches or less in diameter, n.o.p................. $	....	144,309	....	135,356	47,374 60
9	Seamless steel tubing, valued at not less than 3½ cents per lb......... Cwt.	4,035	30,866	4,038	30,868	1,543 40
10	Rolled or drawn square tubing of iron or steel, adapted for use in the manufacture of agricultural implements... $	....	2,785	....	2,785	139 25
11	Iron or steel pipe or tubing, plain or galvanized, riveted, corrugated or otherwise specially manufactured, including lock joint pipe, n.o.p....... $	....	395,026	....	324,533	97,359 90
12	Iron or steel pipe, not butt or lap welded, and wirebound wooden pipe, not less than thirty inches internal diameter, when for use exclusively in alluvial gold mining............. $	....	1,716	....	1,716	171 60
13	Ware—Agate, granite or enamelled iron or steel ware.................... $	....	185,083	....	168,746	59,061 10
14	Ware—Iron or steel hollow-ware, plain black or coated, n.o.p., and nickel and aluminium kitchen or household hollow-ware, n.o.p.................... $	....	206,525	....	198,109	59,432 70
15	Wire bale ties....................... $	....	8,656	....	8,656	2,596 80
16	Wire cloth or wove wire and netting of iron or steel........................ Lb.	4,235,171	233,432	2,587,726	134,480	40,344 00
17	Wire, crucible cast steel, valued at not less than 6 cents per lb.............. "	170,330	27,135	170,330	27,135	1,356 75
18	Wire screens, doors and windows........ $	....	35,508	....	34,257	10,277 10
19	Wire buckthorn strip, fencing, woven wire fencing and wire fencing of iron or steel, n.o.p., not to include woven wire or netting made from wire smaller than No. 14 gauge, not to include fencing of wire larger than No. 9 gauge. Lb.	1,822,933	72,485	1,455,859	51,476	7,721 40
20	Wire, single or several, covered with cotton, linen, silk, rubber or other material, including cable so covered.. $	....	340,025	....	181,037	54,311 10
21	Wire of iron and steel, all kinds, n.o.p... Lb.	6,870,401	169,927	6,665,072	161,908	32,381 60
22	Wire, rope, stranded or twisted wire, clothes lines, picture or other twisted wire, and wire cables, n.o.p.......... "	5,213,711	377,212	1,528,567	132,379	33,094 75

SESSIONAL PAPER No. 11

Imported into Canada, &c.—*Continued.*

			ENTERED FOR HOME CONSUMPTION.						
Preferential Tariff.			Treaty Rates.			Total.			
Quantity.	Value.	Duty.	Quantity.	Value.	Duty.	Quantity.	Value.	DutyColl'd.	
	$	$ cts.		$	$ cts.		$	$ cts.	
435	540	92 43				1,886,340	2,104,205	105,210 25	1
						12,246	14,413	4,226 28	2
	4,055	608 25					487,569	121,486 75	3
						11,169		1,116 90	4
	28,655	5,731 00					132,804	39,579 81	5
	4,729	472 90					193,921	28,851 70	6
	14,629	2,905 90					190,201	54,630 10	7
	8,875	1,775 00					144,231	49,149 60	8
						4,038	30,868	1,543 40	9
							2,785	139 25	10
	70,492	14,098 40					395,025	111,458 30	11
							1,716	171 60	12
	15,951	3,589 17					184,697	62,650 27	13
	8,701	1,740 20					206,810	61,172 90	14
							8,656	2,596 80	15
1,648,305	99,000	19,800 00				4,236,031	233,480	60,144 00	16
						170,330	27,135	1,356 75	17
	1,185	237 00		66	18 15		35,508	10,532 25	18
367,074	21,009	2,100 90				1,822,933	72,485	9,822 30	19
	157,100	31,420 00					338,137	85,731 10	20
207,946	8,276	1,241 40				6,873,018	170,184	33,623 00	21
3,659,880	£45,865	43,026 62				5,188,447	378,244	76,121 37	22

6 GEORGE V, A. 1916

No. 14.—Summary Statement of Foreign Merchandise

	Articles.	Total Imports.		General Tariff.		
		Quantity.	Value.	Quantity.	Value.	Duty.
			$		$	$ cts.
	Dutiable Goods—*Con.*					
	Iron and steel—*Con.*					
1	Iron or steel nuts, rivets and bolts, with or without threads; nut, bolt and hinge blanks; and T and strap hinges of all kinds, n.o.p............... Cwt.	36,648	142,235	34,248	135,439	59,545 77
2	Iron or steel scrap, wrought, being waste or refuse, including punchings, cuttings and clippings of iron or steel plates or sheets, having been in actual use; crop ends of tin plate bars, blooms and rails, the same not having been in actual use............... "	223,786	143,076	222,114	142,268	11,105 70
3	Pen-knives. jack-knives and pocket-knives of all kinds.............. $	....	87,957	....	10,390	3,117 00
4	Knives and forks of steel, plated or not, n.o.p........................ $	....	188,265	....	62,155	18,646 50
5	All other cutlery, n.o.p............. $	....	464,625	....	260,489	78,146 70
6	Guns, rifles, including air guns and air rifles (not being toys) muskets, cannons, pistols, revolvers, or other firearms............................. $	....	727,023	....	598,306	179,491 80
7	Bayonets, swords, fencing foils and masks.......................... $	....	7,632	....	4,273	1,281 90
8	Needles, of any material or kind, n.o.p. $	....	115,423	....	55,105	16,531 50
9	Steel, chrome steel................Cwt.	1,980	9,123	1,980	9,123	1,368 45
10	Steel plate, universal mill or rolled edge plates of steel over 12 inches wide, imported by manufacturers of bridges or of structural work or in car construction........................ "	444,379	646,962	444,379	646,962	66,656 85
11	Steel, in bars or sheets, to be used exclusively in the manufacture of shovels, when imported by manufacturers of shovels.......................... "	19,249	23,753	19,243	23,734	2,886 45
12	Rolled iron or steel, and cast steel in bars, bands, hoops, scroll or strip, sheet or plate, of any size, thickness or width, galvanized or coated with any material or not, and steel blanks for the manufacture of milling cutters, when of greater value than 3¼ cents per lb...................... "	106,294	687,722	106,326	682,614	34,130 70
13	Steel balls adapted for use on bearings of machinery and vehicles.......... $	....	14,734	....	14,712	1,471 20
14	Flat steel, cold rolled, not over ½ inch thick, for the manufacture of cups and cones for ball bearings.........Cwt.	151	418	151	418	20 90
15	Steel wool.......................... $	....	4,095	....	4,095	409 50
	Tools and implements—					
16	Adzes, cleavers, hatchets, wedges, sledges, hammers, crowbars, cant-dogs and track tools; picks, mattocks and eyes or poles for the same $	....	37,838	....	31,375	9,412 50
17	Axes...........................Doz.	2,852	19,390	2,856	19,458	4,378 38
18	Saws............................. $	....	77,235	....	74,554	22,366 20
19	Files and rasps, n.o.p.............. $	....	90,014	....	70,739	21,221 70
20	Tools, hand, of all kinds, n.o.p....... $	....	536,710	....	506,634	151,990 20
21	Knife blades, or blanks, and table forks of iron or steel, in the rough, not handled, filed, ground or otherwise manufactured.................... $	....	101	....	87	8 70
22	Manufactures, articles or wares of iron or steel, or of which iron or steel, (or either) are the component materials of chief value, n.o.p................. $	....	7,120,756	....	6,510,399	1,953,119 70
	Total, iron and steel...............	....	51,478,634	....	47,330,076	10,870,675 69

Imported into Canada, &c.—*Continued.*

	Preferential Tariff.			Treaty Rates.			Total.		
Quantity.	Value.	Duty.	Quantity.	Value.	Duty.	Quantity.	Value.	DutyColl'd.	
	$	$ cts.		$	$ cts.		$	$ cts.	
2,394	7,627	2,558 20	....	....	....	36,642	143,066	62,103 97	1
1,692	954	42 30	....	....	....	223,806	143,222	11,148 00	2
....	77,237	15,447 40	....	497	136 70	....	88,124	18,701 10	3
....	125,889	25,177 80	....	788	216 72	....	188,832	44,041 02	4
....	201,469	40,293 80	....	3,061	841 84	....	465,019	119,282 34	5
....	125,270	25,054 00	....	....	....	....	723,576	204,545 80	6
....	3,698	739 60	....	....	....	....	7,971	2,021 50	7
....	60,184	12,036 80	....	194	53 36	....	115,483	28,621 66	8
....	....	....	....	....	....	1,980	9,123	1,368 45	9
....	....	....	....	....	....	444,379	646,962	66,656 85	10
6	19	0 60	....	....	....	19,249	23,753	2,887 05	11
....	....	....	....	....	....	106,326	682,614	34,130 70	12
....	....	....	....	....	....	....	14,712	1,471 20	13
....	....	....	....	....	....	151	418	20 90	14
....	....	....	....	....	....	....	4,095	409 50	15
....	6,463	1,292 60	....	....	....	....	37,838	10,705 10	16
6	30	4 50	....	249	68 48	2,862	19,488	4,382 88	17
....	2,432	486 40	....	....	....	....	77,235	22,921 08	18
....	17,491	3,498 20	....	1,784	490 65	....	90,014	25,210 55	19
....	29,081	5,816 20	....	994	273 48	....	536,709	158,079 88	20
....	14	0 70	....	....	....	....	101	9 40	21
....	594,748	118,949 20	....	11,577	3,183 88	....	7,116,722	2,075,252 78	22
....	4,109,298	705,556 45	....	23,669	6,509 53	....	51,463,043	11,582,741 67	

6 GEORGE V, A. 1916

No. 14.—Summary Statement of Foreign Merchandise

	ARTICLES.	TOTAL IMPORTS.		General Tariff.		
		Quantity.	Value.	Quantity.	Value.	Duty.
	. DUTIABLE GOODS—*Con.*		$		$	$ cts.
1	Ivory, manufactures of, n.o.p............ $	....	2,274	....	2,229	390 15
2	Jellies, jams and preserves, n.o.p., and condensed mince meat................. Lb.	4,584,548	398,609	162,728	23,943	5,858 78
3	Jewellery, n.o.p....................:........ $	....	901,310	....	655,898	229,564 30
4	Knitted goods of every description, n.o.p. $	....	122,552	....	47,863	16,752 05
5	Launches, pleasure, steam, gasoline or other motive power...................No.	120	35,309	118	34,512	8,628 00
	Lead and manufactures of—					
6	Old, scrap, pig and block..............Cwt.	166,159	631,754	147,521	555,142	83,271 30
7	Bars and sheets..................... "	7,885	34,537	1,861	8,773	2,193 25
8	Pipe................................Lb.	546,140	25,492	132,851	7,993	2,397 90
9	Shot and bullets..................... "	163,523	9,743	20,327	1,364	409 20
10	Manufactures of, n.o.p................. $	....	112,568	....	38,853	11,655 90
	Total, lead......................	....	814,094	....	612,125	99,927 55
	Leather, and manufactures of—					
11	Sole leather.......................... $	....	91,595	....	56,086	9,815 27
12	Leather, belting leather of all kinds..... $	....	92,352	....	10,232	1,534 80
13	Upper leather, not dressed, waxed or glazed......................... $	....	12,426	....	11,019	1,652 85
14	Calf, kid, or goat, lamb and sheep skins, tanned.................... $	....	111,289	....	106,750	16,012 50
15	Calf, kid, or goat, lamb and sheep skins, dressed, waxed or glazed............ $	....	1,002,519	....	878,460	131,769 00
16	Glove leathers, tanned or dressed, coloured or uncoloured, imported by glove manufacturers for use exclusively in their own factories in the manufacture of gloves........................ $	....	541,582	....	522,796	52,279 60
17	Harness leather....................... $	....	58,599	....	50,113	7,516 95
18	Tanners' scrap leather................ $	....	16,331	....	10,993	1,648 95
19	Upper leather, including dongola, cordovan, kangaroo, alligator and all leather, dressed, waxed or glazed, or further finished than tanned, n.o.p., and chamois skins.................. $	....	392,020	....	292,163	43,824 45
20	Japanned, patent or enamelled leather and Morocco leather, and leather in imitation of Morocco leather.......... $	....	31,460	....	28,920	7,230 00
21	Skins for Morocco leather, tanned but not further manufactured............. $	....	13,852	....	10,345	1,551 75
22	All other leather and skins, n.o.p........ $	....	225,050	....	202,857	30,428 55
23	All other leather, dressed, waxed or glazed, etc., n.o.p................. $	....	269,361	....	159,180	23,877 00
24	Boots and shoes, slippers and insoles of leather, n.o.p...................... $	....	3,403,042	....	2,913,677	874,103 10
25	Boots and shoes, pegged or wire fastened, with unstitched soles, close edged.... $	....	78,294	....	20,226	5,056 50
26	Harness and saddlery, including horse boots............................... $	....	141,399	....	94,018	28,205 40
27	Leather belting....................... $	....	72,591	....	60,669	13,651 28
28	All other manufactures of leather and raw hide, n.o.p...................... $	....	534,726	....	464,068	116,017 00
	Total, leather......................	....	7,088 488	....	5,892,572	1,366,174 95
29	Lime.................................Cwt.	596,614	186,787	594,032	185,447	32,453 77
30	Lime juice, crude only.................. Gal.	5,876	1,723	5,876	1,723	293 80
31	Lime juice, and fruit juices, fortified with or containing not more than twenty-five per cent of proof spirits........... "	1,349	1,750	1,156	1,551	752 40

SESSIONAL PAPER No. 11

Imported into Canada, &c.—*Continued.*

| | ENTERED FOR HOME CONSUMPTION. | | | | | | | |
| Preferential Tariff. | | | Treaty Rates. | | | Total. | | |
Quantity.	Value.	Duty.	Quantity.	Value.	Duty.	Quantity.	Value.	DutyColl'd.	
	$	$ cts.		$	$ cts.		$	$ cts.	
....	45	6 75	....			....	2,274	396 90	1
4,477,400	378,202	113,677 78				4,640,128	402,145	119,536 56	2
....	161,636	36,369 20		80,542	24,162 60		898,076	290,096 10	3
....	75,104	16,898 77					122,967	33,650 82	4
2	797	119 55				120	35,309	8,747 55	5
18,638	76,612	7,661 20				166,159	631,754	90,932 50	6
6,020	25,690	3,853 50				7,881	34,463	6,046 75	7
419,489	17,812	3,562 40				552,340	25,805	5,960 30	8
143,196	8,379	1,675 80				163,523	9,743	2,085 00	9
....	26,560	5,312 00		29,892	8,220 48		95,305	25,188 38	10
....	155,053	22,064 90	....	29,892	8,220 48		797,070	130,212 93	
....	35,509	4,438 68					91,595	14,253 95	11
....	83,754	8,375 40					93,986	9,910 20	12
....	1,407	140 70					12,426	1,793 55	13
....	3,999	399 90					110,749	16,412 40	14
....	117,556	14,694 80					996,016	146,463 80	15
....	18,786	939 30					541,582	53,218 90	16
....	8,486	1,060 75					58,599	8,577 70	17
....	5,338	533 80					16,331	2,182 75	18
....	98,827	12,353 64					390,990	56,178 09	19
....../..	2,540	381 00					31,460	7,611 00	20
....	3,507	350 70					13,852	1,902 45	21
....	22,193	2,219 30					225,050	32,647 85	22
....	92,566	11,570 89					251,746	35,447 89	23
....	484,656	96,931 20		2,324	639 12		3,400,657	971,673 42	24
....	58,068	10,162 09					78,294	15,218 59	25
....	46,839	9,367 80					140,857	37,573 20	26
....	11,922	1,788 30					72,591	15,439 58	27
....	68,063	10,209 45					532,131	126,226 45	28
....	1,164,016	185,917 70	....	2,324	639 12	....	7,058,912	1,552,731 77	
332	145	21 75				594,364	185,592	32,475 52	29
....						5,876	1,723	293 80	30
....						1,156	1,551	752 40	31

6 GEORGE V, A. 1916

No. 14.—SUMMARY STATEMENT of Foreign Merchandise

		TOTAL IMPORTS.		General Tariff.		
	ARTICLES.	Quantity.	Value.	Quantity.	Value.	Duty.
			$		$	$ cts.
	DUTIABLE GOODS—*Con.*					
	Lime juice, &c.—*Con.*					
1	Lime juice, and fruit juices, containing more than twenty-five per cent of proof spirits..............................Gal.	146	1,603	170	1,671	950 10
2	Lime juice and other fruit syrups and fruit juices, n.o.p..................... "	174,717	195,714	125,649	130,663	26,535 10
	Total, lime juice....................	182,088	200,790	132,851	135,608	28,531 40
3	Lithographic stones, not engraved........ $	....	3,014	....	2,914	582 80
4	Machine card clothing.................. $	....	37,175	....	15,228	3,807 00
5	Magic lanterns and slides therefor and moving picture machines............... $	....	1,310,337	....	1,260,243	315,060 75
6	Malt, whole, crushed or ground...........Lb	3,165,896	80,414	3,168,066	80,375	14,256 39
7	Malt flour, containing not less than 50 p.c. of malt.............................. "	80,921	3,127	80,921	3,127	364 14
8	Malt flour, containing less than 50 p.c. in weight of malt........................ "	27,030	1,284	27,030	1,284	835 53
9	Malt, extract of, fluid or not, including grain molasses, to August 21st, 1914... $	....	35,510	....	36,157	12,654 95
10	Malt, extract of, fluid or not, including grain molasses, from August 21st, 1914..Lb	789,593	41,680	795,478	41,938	38,542 63
	Marble, and manufactures of—					
11	Marble, sawn or sand rubbed, not polished.............. .. .. $	....	178,777	....	178,709	35,741 80
12	Rough, not hammered or chiselled.... $	....	104,261	....	104,261	15,639 15
13	Manufactures of, n.o.p.................. $	....	124,697	....	122,032	42,711 20
	Total, marble........................	....	407,735	....	405,002	94,092 15
14	Mattresses, hair, spring and other........ $	....	4,645	....	4,390	1,317 00
15	Mats, door or carriage, other than metal, n.o.p................................... $	....	530		356	124 60
	Metals, n.o.p., and manufactures of—					
16	Aluminum, manufactures of, n.o.p...... $	....	87,449	....	80,350	20,087 50
17	Anodes of nickel, zinc, copper, silver or gold..... .... $	....	12,350	....	11,491	1,149 10
18	Babbit metal in blocks, bars, plates and sheets.... ..:.... .... $	....	19,080	....	14,597	2,189 55
19	Britannia metal, manufactures of, not plated.........................'........ $	....	14,923	....	14,243	4,272 90
20	Buckles and clasps of iron, steel, brass or copper, of all kinds, n.o.p. (not being jewellery)...................... $	....	120,266	....	113,046	33,913 80
21	Cages,—Bird, parrot, squirrel and rat, of wire, and metal parts thereof...... $	....	6,106	....	5,855	2,049 25
22	Composition metal and plated metal; in bars, ingots or cores, for the manufacture of watch cases, jewellery, filled gold and silver seamless wire . $	....	3,898	....	3,898	389 80
23	Frames not more than 10 inches in width, clasps and fasteners, adapted for use in the manufacture of purses and chatelaine bags or reticules.......... $	....	22,637	....	22,637	4,527 40
24	Furniture springs...................... $	....	15,923	....	15,845	4,753 50
25	Phosphor tin and phosphor bronze, in blocks, bars, plates, sheets and wire.. $	....	18,734	....	13,182	1,318 20
26	Gas, coal oil or other lighting fixtures, including electric light fixtures or parts thereof of metal, lava or other tips, burners, collars, galleries, shades and shade holders................. $	....	438,238	....	418,348	125,504 40
27	Gas mantles and incandescent gas burners............................. $	....	69,994	....	71,877	21,563 10
28	Gas meters and finished parts thereof.. $	....	39,879	....	33,990	11,896 50

Imported into Canada, &c.—*Continued.*

				ENTERED FOR HOME CONSUMPTION.					
Preferential Tariff.			Treaty Rates.			Total.			
Quantity.	Value.	Duty.	Quantity.	Value.	Duty.	Quantity.	Value.	DutyColl'd.	
	$	$ cts.		$	$ cts.		$	$ cts.	
....	....	....	....	....	....	170	1,671	950 10	1
41,366	59,458	9,045 57	....	....	....	167,015	190,121	35,580 67	2
41,366	59,458	9,045 57	....	....	....	174,217	195,066	37,576 97	
....	100	12 50	....	....	....	....	3,014	595 30	
....	21,947	3,840 86	....	....	....	....	37,175	7,647 86	3
....	40,325	7,057 21	....	5,003	1,125 70	....	323,243 66		
....	....	....	....	....	....	3,168,066	80,375	14,256 39	6
....	....	....	....	....	....	80,921	3,127	364 14	7
....	....	....	....	....	....	27,030	1,284	835 53	8
....	....	....	....	....	....	....	36,157	12,654 95	9
....	....	....	....	....	....	795,478	41,938	38,542 63	10
....	64	9 60	....	....	....	....	178,773	35,751 40	11
....	....	....	....	....	....	....	104,261	15,639 15	12
....	2,487	746 10	....	....	....	....	124,519	43,457 30	13
....	2,551	755 70	....	....	....	....	407,553	94,847 85	
....	250	50 00	....	....	....	....	4,640	1,367 00	14
....	174	43 50	....	....	....	....	530	168 10	15
....	2,600	390 00	....	4,292	965 78	....	87,242	21,443 28	16
....	796	39 80	....	....	....	....	12,287	1,188 90	17
....	4,483	448 30	....	....	....	....	19,080	2,637 85	18
....	702	122 88	....	....	....	....	14,945	4,395 78	19
....	6,806	1,361 20	....	558	153 50	....	120,410	35,428 50	20
....	251	56 48	....	....	....	....	6,106	2,105 73	21
....	....	....	....	....	....	....	3,898	389 80	22
....	....	....	....	....	....	....	22,637	4,527 40	23
....	76	15 20	....	2	0 55	....	15,923	4,769 25	24
....	5,552	277 60	....	....	....	....	18,734	1,595 80	25
....	9,884	1,976 80	....	....	....	....	428,232	127,481 20	26
....	3,372	674 40	....	....	....	....	75,249	22,237 50	27
....	5,889	1,325 05	....	....	....	....	39,879	13,221 55	28

6 GEORGE V, A. 1916

No. 14.—Summary Statement of Foreign Merchandise

	ARTICLES.		TOTAL IMPORTS.		General Tariff.		
			Quantity.	Value.	Quantity.	Value.	Duty.
				$		$	$ cts.
	DUTIABLE GOODS—*Con.*						
	Metals and mfrs. of—*Con.*						
1	German, Nevada and nickel silver, manufactures of, not plated	$		84,430	•	66,079	19,823 70
2	Ingot moulds, glass moulds of metal	$		187,562		91,971	9,197 10
3	Lamp springs and clock springs	$		1,596		1,581	158 10
4	Lamps, side lights and head lights, lanterns, chandeliers	$		1,005,123		922,785	276,835 50
5	Metal parts adapted for the manufacture of covered buttons	$		27,222		27,194	5,438 80
6	Nickel plated ware, n.o.p	$		880,761		793,526	277,734 10
7	Patterns of brass, iron, steel or other metal, not being models	$		14,734		14,631	4,389 30
8	Pins, n.o.p	$		87,823		15,868	4,760 40
9	Screws, brass or other metal, except iron or steel, n.o.p	$		17,807		17,482	6,118 70
10	Stereotypes, electrotypes and celluloids for almanacs, calendars, illustrated pamphlets, newspaper or other advertisements, n.o.p., and matrices or copper shells for such stereotypes, electrotypes and celluloids........Sq. in.		1,645,859	56,270	1,629,184	55,079	24,437 99
11	Stereotypes, electrotypes and celluloids and bases for the same composed wholly or partly of metal or celluloid, n.o.p., and copper shells for such stereotypes, electrotypes and celluloids	"	328,401	8,671	323,529	8,537	404 45
12	Matrices for stereotypes, electrotypes and celluloids specified in preceding item	"	1,086,725	14,239	1,086,725	14,239	5,433 64
13	Type for printing, including chases, quoins and slugs of all kinds	$		75,543		58,567	11,713 40
14	Type metal in blocks, bars, plates and sheets	$		1,062		780	117 00
15	Wire of all kinds, n.o.p	$		35,826		34,866	6,973 20
16	Wire, twisted, etc., except iron or steel, n.o.p	$		727		727	181 75
	Total, metals			3,368,873		2,943,271	887,332 13
17	Milk, condensed	Lb.	132,223	10,344	109,937	8,434	3,767 62
18	Milk and cream, fresh	$		77,413		77,413	13,547 59
	Total, milk and cream, fresh and condensed			87,757		85,847	17,315 21
	Mineral and bituminous substances not otherwise provided for—						
19	Asbestos, in any form other than crude, and all manufactures of	$		226,694		194,758	48,689 50
20	Asphalt, not solid	$		29,709		29,695	5,196 72
21	Blacklead	$		5,295		532	133 00
22	Mineral and bituminous substances, other, not otherwise provided for	$		146,668		132,601	23,205 72
23	Plumbago, not ground or otherwise manufactured	$		1,464		1,452	145 20
24	Plumbago, ground and manufactures of, n.o.p	$		40,499		33,572	8,393 00
	Total mineral and bituminous substances			450,329		392,610	' 85,763 14
25	Mineral and aerated waters, n.o.p	$		201,197		170,744	29,880 66
26	Mucilage and adhesive paste	$		35,894		31,879	8,767 68

Imported into Canada, &c.—*Continued.*

	Preferential Tariff.			Treaty Rates.			Total.		
Quantity.	Value.	Duty.	Quantity.	Value.	Duty.	Quantity.	Value.	Duty Coll'd.	
	$	$ cts.		$	$ cts.		$	$ cts.	
....	18,696	3,271 94	....	....	....	....	84,775	23,095 64	1
....	39,892	1,994 60	....	....	....	....	131,863	11,191 70	2
....	15	1 12	....	....	....	....	1,596	159 22	3
....	103,488	20,697 60	....	....	....	....	1,026,273	297,533 10	4
....	28	3 50	....	....	....	....	27,222	5,442 30	
....	75,540	16,997 22	....	5,869	1,760 70	....	874,935	296,492 02	5
....	153	30 60	....	....	....	....	14,784	4,419 90	7
....	71,717	14,343 40	....	807	221 97	....	88,392	19,325 77	8
....	314	70 69	....	....	....	....	17,796	6,189 39	9
14,153	1,128	141 53	....	....	....	1,643,337	56,207	24,579 52	10
4,872	134	6 09	....	....	....	328,401	8,671	410 54	11
....	....	....	....	....	....	1,086,725	14,239	5,433 64	12
....	16,978	2,122 11	....	....	....	....	75,543	13,835 51	13
....	282	28 20	....	....	....	....	1,062	145 20	14
....	960	144 00	....	....	....	....	35,826	7,117 20	1c
....	....	....	....	....	....	....	727	181 75	16
....	369,734	66,540 31	....	11,528	3,102 50	....	3,324,533	956,974 94	
10,908	1,051	253 92	....	....	....	120,845	9,485	4,021 54	17
....	....	....	....	....	....	....	77,413	13,547 59	18
....	1,051	253 92	....	....	....	....	86,898	. 17,569 13	
....	31,757	4,763 55	....	....	....	....	226,515	53,453 05	19
....	14	1 75	....	....	....	....	29,709	5,198 47	20
....	4,763	714 45	....	....	....	....	5,295	847 45	21
....	11,447	1,717 05	....	....	....	....	144,048	24,922 77	22
....	12	0 60	....	....	....	....	1,464	145 80	23
....	4,446	666 90	....	....	....	....	38,018	9,059 90	24
....	52,439	7,864 30	....	....	....	....	445,049	93,627 44	
....	22,830	3,424 50	....	....	....	....	193,574	33,305 16	25
....	3,954	692 03	....	....	....	....	35,833	9,459 71	26

No. 14.—Summary Statement of Foreign Merchandise

ARTICLES.	TOTAL IMPORTS.		General Tariff.		
	Quantity.	Value.	Quantity.	Value.	Duty.
		$		$	$ cts.
DUTIABLE GOODS—*Con.*					
Musical instruments, viz.—					
1 Brass band instruments and bagpipes... $	....	59,768	....	24,116	6,029 00
2 Cabinet organs...........................No.	353	20,033	352	19,962	5,988 60
3 Pipe organs.................................."	2	1,400	2	1,400	420 00
4 Parts of organs.......................... $	....	9,494	....	8,811	2,202 75
5 Pianofortes............................No.	1,365	235,307	1,302	226,815	68,044 50
6 Pianos, parts of.......................... $	....	152,079	....	146,630	36,657 50
7 Piano and organ players, mechanical....No.	47	10,232	.47	10,232	3,069 60
8 Phonographs, graphophones, gramophones and finished parts thereof, including cylinders and records therefor................................... $	....	755,166	....	697,461	209,238 30
9 Other musical instruments, n.o.p........ $	....	121,132	....	127,951	38,385 30
Total musical instruments.............	....	1,364,611	....	1,263,378	370,035 55
10 Mustard, ground...........................Lb.	892,878	185,051	294,529	23,521	6,468 53
11 Mustard, French, liquid................... $	....	20,987	....	18,924	6,623 40
Total mustard......................	....	206,038	....	42,445	13,091 93
Oils—					
Mineral—					
12 Coal and kerosene, distilled, purified or refined...........................Gal.	8,821,531	605,573	9,587,159	653,401	239,680 01
13 Petroleum, products of, n.o.p........ "	5,312,409	562,343	5,729,172	588,886	143,230 14
14 Crude petroleum; gas oils other than naphtha, benzine and gasoline, lighter than ·8235 but not less than ·775 specific gravity at 60 degrees....... "	64,057	5,418	64,057	5,418	960 90
15 Illuminating oils composed wholly or in part of the products of petroleum, coal, shale or lignite, costing more than 30 cents per gallon........... "	125,138	50,691	120,826	48,888	9,777 60
Animal—					
16 Lard oil............................ "	32,415	15,271	27,701	13,574	3,393 50
17 Neatsfoot........................... "	10,061	7,306	10,061	7,306	1,826 50
18 Other animal oil, n.o.p.............. "	9,648	5,280	8,154	4,726	827 06
Vegetable—					
19 Castor.............................. "	80,217	44,388	4,480	3,054	534 51
20 Cocoanut, n.o.p.....;............... "	48,421	49,991	4,501	5,289	925 73
21 Cotton seed......................... "	232,574	113,415	231,974	112,998	19,775 04
22 Flaxseed or linseed, raw or boiled..... Lb.	253,387	16,597	79,937	6,004	1,319 18
23 Olive, n.o.p..........................Gal	253,641	328,350	147,824	172,806	34,561 20
24 Sesame seed......................... "	1,517	1,438	1,517	1,438	359 50
25 Vegetable oil, not otherwise provided for................................... "	141,440	93,611	132,795	86,002	15,050 76
26 Lubricating oils composed wholly or in part of petroleum and costing less than 25 cents per gallon............. "	4,435,900	577,681	4,366,796	571,862	109,170 49
27 Lubricating oils, n.o.p............... "	987,997	306,044	871,847	266,358	53,271 60
28 Essential, n.o.p......................Lb.	211,558	303,294	195,352	282,186	21,164 37
29 Peppermint........................ "	7,542	17,560	6,872	15,570	1,167 81
30 All other oils, nor elsewhere specified..Gal.	208,467	71,148	196,345	64,325	11,257 54
Total oils...........................	....	3,175,399	....	2,910,091	668,253 44
31 Oiled silk, oiled cloth, and tape or other textile, india-rubbered, flocked or coated n.o.p.,........................... $	....	410,420	....	228,906	68,671 80
32 Oil cloth, enamelled carriage, floor, shelf and table oil cloth, cork matting or carpet and linoleum.................Sq. yd.	2,814,435	875,489	514,356	112,184	39,264 40
Total oil cloth, &c...................	....	1,285,909	....	341,090	107,936 20

Imported into Canada, etc.—*Continued.*

	ENTERED FOR HOME CONSUMPTION.								
Preferential Tariff.			Treaty Rates.			Total.			
Quantity.	Value.	Duty.	Quantity.	Value.	Duty.	Quantity.	Value.	DutyColl'd.	
	$	$ cts.		$	$ cts.		$	$ cts.	
	18,125	2,718 75		17,409	3,917 17		59,650	12,664 92	1
1	71	14 20				353	20,033	6,002 80	
						2	1,400	420 00	
	630	94 50		53	11 93		9,494	2,309 18	
70	7,405	1,481 00	2	358	98 46	1,374	234,578	69,623 96	
	2,078	311 70		3,514	790 67		152,222	37,759 87	
						47	10,232	3,069 60	
	19,233	3,846 60		11,928	3,280 30		728,622	216,365 20	8
	7,141	1,428 20		7,190	1,977 29		142,282	41,790 79	9
	54,683	9,894 95		40,452	10,075 82		1,358,513	390,006 32	
619,136	167,889	29,381 08				913,665	191,410	35,849 61	10
	378	94 50		830	269 80		20,132	6,987 70	11
	168,267	29,475 58			269 80		211,542	42,837 31	
						9,587,159	653,401	239,680 01	12
38,865	7,706	582 99				5,768,037	596,592	143,813 13	13
						64,057	5,418	960 90	14
3,775	1,615	242 25				124,601	50,503	10,019 85	15
4,714	1,697	254 55				32,415	15,271	3,648 05	16
						10,061	7,306	1,826 50	17
1,494	554	83 10				9,648	5,280	910 16	18
76,031	41,534	6,230 10				80,511	44,588	6,764 61	19
44,161	44,637	5,579 69				48,662	49,926	6,505 42	20
						231,974	112,998	19,775 04	21
151,815	9,921	1,897 71				217,975	15,925	3,216 89	22
14,583	26,327	3,949 05	55,568	92,169	13,825 35	231,752	291,302	52,335 60	23
						1,517	1,438	359 50	24
8,982	7,810	1,171 50				141,777	93,812	16,222 26	25
2,497	513	37 45				4,369,293	572,375	109,207 94	26
85,049	28,585	3,573 18				956,896	294,943	56,844 78	27
13,997	16,360	818 00				209,349	298,546	21,982 37	28
270	990	49 50				7,142	16,560	1,217 31	29
11,965	6,724	1,008 60				208,310	71,049	12,266 14	30
	194,973	25,477 67		92,169	13,825 35		3,197,233	707,556 46	
	186,933	37,386 60					415,839	106,058 40	31
2,305,264	764,797	191,199 25				2,819,620	876,981	230,463 65	32
	951,730	228,585 85					1,292,820	336,522 05	

No. 14.—Summary Statement of Foreign Merchandise

		Total Imports.		General Tariff.		
	Articles.	Quantity.	Value.	Quantity.	Value.	Duty.
	Dutiable Goods—*Con.*		$		$	$ cts.
1	Optical, philosophical, photographic and mathematical instruments, n.o.p........ $	....	744,535	....	547,054	136,763 50
2	Parts, brass and aluminum, of cameras and kodaks, including special parts of metal in the rough, when imported by manufacturers of cameras and kodaks for the use only in the manufacture of cameras and kodaks................... $	....	3,081	....	3,081	231 08
3	Spectacles, eye-glasses and ground or finished spectacle or eye-glass lenses.. $	....	33,426	....	32,382	9,714 60
4	Spectacle frames, eye-glass frames, and metal parts of..................... $	....	66,128	....	65,861	13,172 20
5	Silvered lenses for automobile lamps.... $	....	2,986	....	2,986	447 90
	Total optical instruments, etc.......	....	850,156	....	651,364	160,329 28
6	Packages, usual coverings, containing goods subject to any *ad valorem* duty, not included in the invoice value of the goods they contained.................. $	....	1,218,854	....	456,535	91,307 00
7	Packages paying 17½, 22½ and 25 per cent.. $	....	234,267	....	114,096	28,524 00
8	Packages paying 20, 30 and 32½ per cent... $	....	687,169	....	356,573	115,889 23
	Total packages......................	....	2,140,290	....	927,204	235,720 23
	Paints and colours—					
9	Brocade and bronze powders......,..... $	......	16,013	....	15,721	4,323 61
10	Gold liquid paint........................ $		8,900	....	8,800	2,200 00
11	Lead, white, dry.......................Lb.	284,486	15,189	130,758	6,890	2,067 00
12	Lead, white, ground in oil............ "	451,289	25,631	54,125	2,761	1,035 54
13	Lead, red, dry, and orange mineral..... "	762,566	33,850	762,566	33,850	1,692 50
14	Ochres, ochrey earths, siennas, and umbers.............................. "	2,802,148	28,341	2,458,334	22,743	3,411 45
15	Zinc white............................ "	8,990,837	392,947	8,990,837	392,947	19,647 35
16	Oxides, fire proofs, rough stuffs, fillers, and colours, dry, n.o.p.............. "	6,706,295	236,663	5,558,249	177,782	40,001 69
17	Liquid fillers, anti-corrosive and anti-fouling paints, and ground and liquid paints, n.o.p........................ "	3,983,097	342,906	2,821,172	221,001	66,300 30
18	Paris green, dry........................ "	361,932	53,657	55,032	8,201	820 10
19	Paints and colours ground in spirits, and all spirit varnishes and lacquers....... Gal.	3,866	9,428	3,902	9,480	4,365 00
20	Putty.................................Lb.	437,539	9,024	387,803	8,217	2,054 25
	Total, paints and colours............	....	1,172,549	....	908,393	147,918 79
21	Paintings in oil or watercolours and pastels, when valued at less than $20 each................................No.	1,548	2,285	1,375	1,425	356 25
	Paper and manufactures of—					
22	Albumenized and other papers and films, chemically prepared for photographers' use .... $	....	195,141	....	111,827	33,548 10
23	Bags or sacks, printed or not.......... $	....	46,702	....	33,480	9,207 49
24	Cards for playing.....................Packs	966,379	109,064	360,057	45,656	28,804 56
25	Cardboard, not pasted or coated........ $	....	98,796	....	95,139	23,784 75
26	Envelopes.............................M.	89,469	110,251	76,316	89,520	31,332 00
27	Feltboard.............................. $	....	4,998	....	5,217	1,304 25
28	Hangings of wall paper, including borders Rolls	2,926,449	264,945	2,724,936	233,028	81,559 80
29	Leather board, leatheroid, and manufactures of, n.o.p..................... $	....	16,095	....	16,079	4,019 75
30	Millboard not coated or pasted......... $	....	120,153	....	118,316	29,579 00
31	Union collar cloth paper in rolls or sheets not glossed or finished................ $	....	628	....	628	94 20
32	Union collar cloth paper in rolls or sheets glossed or finished..................... $	....	15,437	....	15,437	3,087 40

Imported into Canada, etc.—*Continued.*

	ENTERED FOR HOME CONSUMPTION.								
Preferential Tariff.			Treaty Rates.			Total.			
Quantity.	Value.	Duty.	Quantity.	Value.	Duty.	Quantity.	Value.	DutyColl'd.	
	$	$ cts.		$	$ cts.		$	$ cts.	
....	162,447	28,428 94	....	28,648	6,446 01	....	738,149	171,638 45	1
....	....		....	....	....	....	3,081	231 08	2
....	1,044	208 80	....	....	....	....	33,426	9,923 40	3
....	267	40 05	....	....	....	....	66,128	13,212 25	4
....	....	....	....	....	....	....	2,986	447 90	5
....	163,758	28,677 79	....	28,648	6,446 01	....	843,770	195,453 08	
....	766,900	115,035 00	....	....	....	....	1,223,435	206,342 00	6
....	64,330	11,259 99	....	56,334	12,676 37	....	234,760	52,460 36	7
....	308,765	61,753 00	....	....	....	....	665,338	177,642 23	8
....	1,139,995	188,047 99	....	56,334	12,676 37	....	2,123,533	436,444 59	
....	179	26 85				....	15,900	4,350 46	9
....	111	16 65				....	8,911	2,216 65	10
156,528	8,420	1,684 00				287,286	15,310	3,751 00	11
418,559	24,203	7,260 90				472,684	26,964	8,296 44	12
....	....	....				762,566	33,850	1,692 50	13
367,624	6,015	601 50				2,825,958	28,758	4,012 95	14
....	....	....				8,990,837	392,947	19,647 35	15
1,153,258	59,408	8,911 20				6,711,507	237,190	48,912 89	16
1,124,098	121,176	24,235 20				3,945,270	342,177	90,535 50	17
314,100	46,607	2,330 35	....	....		369,132	54,808	3,150 45	18
....	....	....				3,902	9,480	4,365 00	19
49,736	807	141 24				437,539	9,024	2,195 49	20
....	266,926	45,207 89	....	....	....	....	1,175,319	193,126 68	
'173	860	129 00	....	....	....	1,548	2,285	485 25	21
....	82,664	12,399 60	....	....	....	....	194,491	45,947 70	22
....	13,222	1,983 30	....	....	....	....	46,702	11,190 79	23
581,498	60,912	29,074 90	....	....	....	941,555	106,568	57,879 46	24
....	3,657	548 55	....	....	....	....	98,796	24,333 30	25
13,284	20,364	4,582 15	....	....	....	89,600	109,884	35,914 15	26
....	....	....	....	....	....	....	5,217	1,304 25	27
199,919	31,214	7,023 37	....	....	....	2,924,855	264,242	88,583 17	28
....	16	2 40	....	....	....	....	16,095	4,022 15	29
....	1,837	275 55	....	....	....	....	120,153	29,854 55	30
....	....	....	....	....	....	....	628	94 20	31
....	....	....	....	....	....	....	15,437	3,087 40	32

6 GEORGE V, A. 1916

No. 14.—SUMMARY STATEMENT of Foreign Merchandise

	ARTICLES.	TOTAL IMPORTS.		General Tariff.		
		Quantity.	Value.	Quantity.	Value.	Duty.
			$		$	$. cts.
	DUTIABLE GOODS—Con.					
	Paper and mfrs. of—Con.					
1	Pads not printed, papier mache ware, n.o.p............................... $	....	12,017	....	10,840	3,794 00
2	Paper, manufactures of, n.o.p............. $	....	1,920,778	....	1,558,269	545,394 15
3	Paper matting, when for use in Canadian manufactures...................... $	....	2,570	....	2,570	642 50
4	Patterns, boot and shoe, manufactures of paper............................ $	....	13,684	....	13,684	2,052 60
5	Printing paper (for newspapers) in sheets or rolls, valued at not more than 2¼ c. per pound......................Lb.	1,476,869	29,596	1,427,014	28,602	4,290 30
6	Printing paper, n.o.p................ "	7,945,534	429,078	4,886,109	263,411	65,852 75
7	Ruled and border and coated papers ; boxed papers and papeteries.......... $	....	252,477	....	199,820	69,937 00
8	Straw board not pasted or coated......Lb.	5,405,753	75,414	5,405,753	75,414	18,853 50
9	Tarred and other building papers, n.o.p. $	....	317,200	....	317,349	79,337 25
10	Window blinds of paper of all kinds..... $	....	20	....	20	7 00
11	Wrapping paper.........................Lb.	7,815,939	194,792	7,471,830	176,446	44,111 50
12	All kinds, n.o.p........................ $	....	1,429,294	....	1,083,956	270,989 00
	Total, paper......................	....	5,659,130	....	4,494,708	1,351,582 85
13	Pencils, lead........................... $	....	261,384	....	226,850	62,384 73
14	Pens, penholders, and rulers of all kinds... $	....	132,895	....	72,346	19,895 98
	Perfumery, non-alcoholic, viz.—					
15	Hair oil, tooth and other powders and washes, pomatums, pastes and all other perfumed preparations. n.o.p., used for the hair, mouth, or skin...... $	....	451,324	....	413,306	134,327 73
16	Photographic dry plates................. $	....	55,588	....	14,948	4,484 40
17	Picture and photograph frames of any material........................... $	....	111,100	....	87,079	26,123 70
	Pickles, viz.—					
18	Pickles in bottles, jars, or similar vessels Gal.	224,318	222,043	16,985	17,000	5,950 00
19	Pickles in bulk........................ "	24,039	6,328	21,721	5,644	1,975 40
20	Olives, in brine, not bottled........... "	53,637	27,814	57,750	28,050	8,415 00
21	Olives, in brine, by manufacturers, for the manufacture of pickles................ "	58,186	33,815	54,384	33,516	6,703 20
	Total, pickles.......................	360,180	290,000	150,840	84,210	23,043 60
	Plants and trees, viz.—					
	Apple trees.........................No.	132,421	14,871	131,958	14,774	3,958 74
	Cherry trees........................ "	62,395	12,266	62,383	12,264	1,871 49
	Currant bushes...................... "	53,362	1,471	52,832	1,452	290 40
22-25	Florist stock, viz.: palms, ferns, rubber plants (ficus), gladiolus, cannas, dahlias, and pæonies...................... $	....	37,406	....	32,167	8,041 75
26	Gooseberry bushes....................No.	68,558	3,115	44,468	2,337	467 40
27	Grape vines......................... "	89,526	2,374	89,514	2,343	468 60
28	Peach trees and June buds............ "	51,504	4,737	51,489	4,724	1,544 67
29	Pear trees.......................... "	24,705	3,910	24,587	3,871	737 61
30	Plum trees.......................... "	49,693	16,579	48,622	16,555	1,488 66
31	Raspberry bushes.................... "	208,378	2,915	208,378	2,915	583 00
32	Rose bushes......................... "	200,336	17,669	129,699	11,420	2,284 00
33	Quince trees........................ "	1,857	432	1,857	432	55 71
34	Fruit plants, n.o.p.................. "	146,351	2,080	146,111	2,067	413 40
35	Trees, plants, and shrubs known as nursery stock, n.o.p.................... $	....	92,501	....	83,975	16,795 00
36	Cut flowers......................... $	....	97,497	....	97,405	17,046 81
	Total, plants and trees...............	....	309,823	....	288,701	56,047 24

Imported into Canada, etc.—*Continued.*

| | | | ENTERED FOR HOME CONSUMPTION. | | | | | |
| Preferential Tariff. | | | Treaty Rates. | | | Total. | | |
Quantity.	Value.	Duty.	Quantity.	Value.	Duty.	Quantity.	.Value.	DutyColl'd.
	$	$ cts.		$	$ cts.		$	$ cts.
....	1,177	264 86	....	....	....	....	12,017	4,058 86
....	361,379	81,311 47	....	....	....	....	1,919,648	626,705 62
....	....	....	....	....	....	....	2,570	642 50
....	....	....	....	....	....	....	13,684	2,052 60
5,300	103	10 30	....	....	....	1,432,314	28,705	4,300 60	5
3,061,645	165,894	24,884 10	....	....	....	7,947,754	429,305	90,736 85	6
....	53,349	12,004 04	....	....	....		253,169	81,941 04	7
....	....	....	....	....	....	5,405,753	75,414	18,853 50	8
....	407	61 05	....	....	....		317,756	79,398 30	9
							20	7 00	10
272,448	16,324	2,448 60	....	....	....	7,744,278	192,770	46,560 10	11
....	371,116	55,667 40	....	....	....		1,455,072	326,656 40	12
....	1,183,635	232,541 64	....	....	....	....	5,678,343	1,584,124 49
....	17,569	2,635 35	....	17,129	4,282 25	....	261,548	69,302 33	13
....	59,825	8,973 75	....	785	196 25	....	132,956	29,065 98	14
....	36,272	9,068 00	....	....	....	....	449,578	143,395 73	15
....	40,644	8,128 80	....	....	....	....	55,592	12,613 20	16
....	20,478	4,095 60	....	3,296	906 49	....	110,853	31,125 79	17
203,721	201,509	50,377 25	1,755	2,478	805 44	222,461	220,987	57,132 69	18
....	....	....	2,425	713	231 72	24,146	6,357	2,207 12	19
....	....	....	....	....	....	57,750	28,050	8,415 00	20
....	....	....	....	....	....	54,384	33,516	6,703 20	21
203,721	201,509	50,377 25	4,180	3,191	1,037 16	358,741	288,910	74,458 01
444	95	8 88	19	2	0 48	132,421	14,871	3,968 10	22
....	....	....	12	2	0 30	62,395	12,266	1,871 79	23
30	1	0 13	500	18	3 15	53,362	1,471	293 68	24
....	1,012	151 80	....	4,227	951 11	....	37,406	9,144 66	25
24,084	775	96 89	36	3	0 55	68,588	3,115	564 84	26
12	31	3 88	....	....	....	89,526	2,374	472 48	27
15	13	0 30	....	....	....	51,504	4,737	1,544 97	28
118	39	2 86	....	....	....	24,705	3,910	739 97	29
71	24	1 42	....	....	....	49,693	16,579	1,490 08	30
....	....	....	....	....	....	208,378	2,915	583 00	31
68,804	6,092	761 56	1,833	157	27 49	200,336	17,669	3,073 05	32
....	....	....	....	....	....	1,857	432	55 71	33
240	13	1 63	....	....	....	146,351	2,080	415 03	34
....	4,569	571 26	....	3,957	692 53	....	92,501	18,058 79	35
....	92	13 80	....	....	....	....	97,497	17,060 61	36
....	12,756	1,613 91	....	8,366	1,675 61	....	309,823	59,336 76

No. 14.—Summary Statement of Foreign Merchandise

	Articles.	Total Imports.		General Tariff.		
		Quantity.	Value.	Quantity.	Value.	Duty.
			$		$	$ cts.
	Dutiable Goods—*Con.*					
1	Plaster of Paris, or gypsum, ground, not calcined...................Cwt.	4,971	3,300	3,322	1,814	272 10
2	Plaster of Paris, or gypsum, calcined, and prepared wall plaster................ "	127,141	45,302	126,924	45,168	15,866 02
	Total, plaster of Paris...............	132,112	48,602	130,246	46,982	16,138 12
3	Plates engraved on wood, steel, or other metal, and transfers taken from the same, engravers' plates, of steel or other metal polished for engraving thereon.............................. $	....	88,039	....	79,488	15,897 60
4	Pocket books, portfolios, purses, reticules, satchels, card cases, fly books, and musical instrument cases............... $	....	369,836	....	295,054	103,268 90
5	Polish or composition, knife or other, n.o.p...................... $	....	175,492	....	77,569	21,332 69
6	Pomades, French, or flower odours, etc., imported in tins of not less than ten pounds each...........................Lb.	250	472	....	....	....
7	Post office parcels and packages........... $	....	1,419,934	....	1,133,661	327,882 27
8	Precious stones and imitations thereof, not mounted or set, and pearls and imitations thereof, pierced, split, strung or not, but not set or mounted........... $	....	167,544	....	101,000	10,100 00
	Provisions, not otherwise specified—					
9	Butter................................Lb.	6,759,409	1,673,717	2,060,874	508,312	82,434 96
10	Cheese................................ "	1,285,895	249,285	1,135,621	222,952	34,068 63
11	Lard...................................... "	735,816	78,922	699,079	75,396	13,981 58
12	Lard compound and similar substances, cottolene, and animal stearine of all kinds, n.o.p......................... "	2,371,962	217,033	2,277,884	206,172	45,557 68
	Total, provisions....................	11,153,082	2,218,957	6,173,458	1,012,832	176,042 85
	Meats, viz.—					
13	Bacon and hams, shoulders and sides, cured...............................Lb.	1,497,250	242,823	1,505,380	241,964	30,107 60
14	Beef, fresh, chilled or frozen............ "	577,507	54,052	535,574	54,322	16,067 22
15	Beef salted, in barrels.................. "	1,504,981	119,252	1,012,541	79,640	20,250 82
16	Canned meats and canned poultry and game............................... "	1,480,292	256,594	379,908	61,533	16,922 10
17	Extracts of meats and fluid beef, not medicated, and soups of all kinds...... $	....	468,550	....	277,881	76,418 33
18	Mutton and lamb, fresh, chilled or frozen...........................Lb.	3,468,076	377,618	3,446,876	369,967	103,406 28
19	Pork, barrelled, in brine................ "	8,440,569	819,402	8,475,605	818,304	169,512 10
20	Pork, fresh, chilled or frozen............ "	114,683	14,282	23,900	3,107	717 00
21	Poultry and game, n.o.p................ $	....	86,127	....	86,570	17,314 00
22	Dried or smoked meats, and meats preserved in any other way than salted or pickled, n.o.p.............. Lb.	670,550	143,150	720,523	155,082	14,410 46
23	Other meats, fresh, chilled or frozen.... "	512,609	68,890	595,173	77,261	17,855 19
24	Other meats, salted, n.o.p.......... "	534,236	93,102	461,683	85,698	9,233 66
	Total, meats.....................	....	2,743,842	....	2,311,329	492,214 76
25	Pulleys, belt, of all kinds for power transmission........................ $	....	54,541	....	50,026	13,757 96
26	Regalia and badges...................... $	....	47,072	....	28,146	9,851 10
27	Ribbons of all kinds and materials........ $	....	1,780,693	....	258,328	90,414 80
28	Ribbons, undyed, for the manufacture of typewriter ribbons.................... $	....	10,794	....	7,200	1,080 00
	Total, ribbons.......................	....	1,791,487	....	265,528	91,494 80

SESSIONAL PAPER No. 11

Imported into Canada, etc.—*Continued.*

			ENTERED FOR HOME CONSUMPTION.						
Preferential Tariff.			Treaty Rates.			Total.			
Quantity.	Value.	Duty.	Quantity.	Value.	Duty.	Quantity.	Value.	DutyColl'd.	
	$	$ cts.		$	$ cts.		$	$ cts.	
1,649	1,486	148 60	....	....	....	4,971	3,300	420 70	1
217	134	17 36	....	....	....	127,141	45,302	15,883 38	2
1,866	1,620	165 96	....	....	....	132,112	48,602	16,304 08	
....	8,551	1,282 65	....	....	....	....	88,039	17,180 25	3
....	50,486	11,359 92	....	24,835	7,450 50	....	370,375	122,079 32	4
....	97,872	14,680 80	....	....	....	....	175,441	36,013 49	5
....	....	....	250	472	59 01	250	472	59 01	6
....	285,381	67,618 56	....	892	208 65	....	1,419,934	395,709 48	7
....	66,544	4,990 81	....	....	....	....	167,544	15,090 81	8
4,761,666	1,169,744	142,849 98				6,822,540	1,678,056	225,284 94	9
26,844	6,142	536 88				1,162,465	229,094	34,605 51	10
4,803	648	72 05				703,882	76,044	14,053 63	11
255,483	23,814	3,832 26				2,533,367	229,986	49,389 94	12
5,048,796	1,200,348	147,291 17				11,222,254	2,213,180	323,334 02	
6,706	1,519	100 59				1,512,086	243,483	30,208 19	13
235,721	16,508	4,714 42				771,295	70,830	20,781 64	14
100	8	1 50				1,012,641	79,648	20,252 32	15
164,309	41,434	7,251 11	922,339	141,379	35,344 75	1,466,556	244,346	59,517 96	16
....	152,288	26,650 65	....	42,035	10,508 75	....	472,204	113,577 73	17
4,936	363	98 72				3,451,812	370,330	103,505 00	18
....	....	....				8,475,605	818,304	169,512 10	19
....	....	....				23,900	3,107	717 00	20
....	4,142	517 77				....	90,712	17,831 77	21
1,313	334	19 70				721,836	155,416	14,430 16	22
40,597	1,792	811 94				635,770	79,053	18,667 13	23
37,879	3,207	568 20				499,562	88,905	9,801 86	24
....	221,595	40,734 60	....	183,414	45,853 50	....	2,716,338	578,802 86	
....	4,444	666 60				....	54,470	14,424 56	25
....	18,392	4,138 60				....	46,538	13,989 70	26
....	16,418	3,694 52	....	1,476,378	369,413 84	....	1,751,124	463,523 16	27
....	3,533	353 30				....	10,733	1,433 30	28
....	19,951	4,047 82	....	1,476,378	369,413 84	....	1,761,857	464,956 46	

6 GEORGE V, A. 1916

No. 14.—SUMMARY.STATEMENT of Foreign Merchandise

ARTICLES.	TOTAL IMPORTS.		General Tariff.		
	Quantity.	Value.	Quantity.	Value.	Duty.
DUTIABLE GOODS—*Con.*		$		$	$ cts.
1 Sails for boats and ships.................. $	....	4,907	....	1,780	445 00
2 Salt, in bulk, n.o.p.....................Cwt.	546,696	85,548	546,696	85,548	27,334 80
3 Salt, n.o.p., in bags, barrels, and other coverings............................... "	157,867	67,750	154,246	67,212	11,568 68
Total, salt..................	704,563	153,298	700,942	152,760	38,903 48
4 Bags, barrels and other coverings used in the importation of salt specified in preceding item......................... $	....	20,629	....	20,524	5,131 00
5 Sandpaper, glass, flint and emery paper or emery cloth......................... $	....	126,195	....	119,382	29,845 50
6 Sauces and catsups, in bottles............ Gal	178,671	230,153	80,546	102,963	36,037 05
7 Sauces and catsups, in bulk............... "	46,209	14,106	42,569	13,131	4,595 85
8 Sauces, soy................................. "	89,519	29,858	87,157	28,909	10,118 15
Total, sauces...................	314,399	274,117	210,272	145,003	50,751 05
9 Sausage casings, n.o.p..................... $	....	201,771	....	107,437	18,801 72
Seeds, viz.—					
10 Clover and timothy..................... $	....	1,675,120	....	1,459,802	145,980 20
11 Flax.............................Bush.	221	366	221	366	22 10
12 Garden, field and other seeds for agricultural or other purposes, n.o.p., sunflower, canary, hemp and millet seed, when in packages weighing over one pound each...................... $	....	416,515	....	375,103	37,510 30
13 Garden, field and other seeds for agricultural or other purposes, n.o.p., sunflower, canary, hemp and millet seed, when in packages weighing one pound each or less...................... $	....	29,070	....	15,931	3,982 75
14 Garden and field seeds not specified as free, valued at not less than $5 per pound in packages of not less than one oz. each............................... $	....	347	....	261	26 10
Total, seeds..........................	....	2,121,418	....	1,851,463	187,521 45
15 Ships and other vessels built in any foreign country, if British registered since September 1, 1902, on application for license to engage in the Canadian coasting trade; on the fair market value of the hull, rigging, machinery, boilers, furniture and appurtenances thereof, as provided in an Act respecting the coasting trade of Canada...................No.	8	237,500	6	212,500	53,125 00
16 Vessels, dredges, scows, yachts, boats and other water-borne craft, built outside of Canada, of any material, destined for use or service in Canadian waters (not to include registered vessels entitled to engage in the coasting trade, nor vessels in transit between Canada and any place outside thereof), n.o.p., on the fair market value of the hull, rigging, machinery, boilers, furniture and appurtenances thereof, on arrival in Canada.. $	....	409,176	....	409,176	102,294 00
17 Ships and vessels, repairs on.............. $	....	85,770	....	85,770	21,442 50
Total, ships......................	....	732,446	....	707,446	176,861 50

Imported into Canada, etc.—*Continued.*

			ENTERED FOR HOME CONSUMPTION.						
Preferential Tariff.			Treaty Rates.			Total.			
Quantity.	Value.	Duty.	Quantity.	Value.	Duty.	Quantity.	Value.	DutyColl'd.	
	$ 3,127	$ cts. 469 05		$	$ cts.		$ 4,907	$ cts. 914 05	1
....	....	....	....	....	....	546,696	85,548	27,334 80	2
....	....	....	....	....	....	154,246	67,212	11,568 68	3
....	....	....	....	....	....	700,942	152,760	38,903 48	
....	....	....	....	....	....	20,524	5,131 00		4
....	6,788	1,018 20	....	....	....	126,170	30,863 70		5
96,025	129,637	32,409 25	894	530	172 29	177,465	233 130	68,618 59	6
1,719	507	126 75	49	15	4 88	44,337	13,653	4,727 48	7
....	....	....	2,187	878	285 39	89,344	29,787	10,403 54	8
97,744	130,144	32,536 00	3,130	1,423	462 56	311,146	276,570	83,749 61	
....	67,008	10,051 20	....	....	....	174,445	28,852 92		9
....	154,227	7,711 35	....	....	....	1,614,029	153,691 55		10
....	....	....	....	....	....	221	366	22 10	11
....	40,694	2,034 70	....	....	....	415,797	39,545 00		12
....	12,332	1,849 80	....	....	....	28,263	5,832 55		13
....	86	4 30	....	....	....	347	30 40		14
....	207,339	11,600 15	....	....	....	2,058,802	199,121 60		
....	....	....	....	....	....	6	212,500	53,125 00	15
....	....	....	....	....	....	409,176	102,294 00		16
....	....	....	....	....	....	85,770	21,442 50		17
....	....	....	....	....	....	707,446	176,861 50		

No. 14.—SUMMARY STATEMENT of Foreign Merchandise

ARTICLES.	TOTAL IMPORTS.		General Tariff.		
	Quantity.	Value.	Quantity.	Value.	Duty.
DUTIABLE GOODS—*Con.*		$		$	$ cts.
1 Signs of any material other than paper, framed or not; letters or numerals of any material other than paper......... $	....	114,633	....	· 89,480	26,844 00
Silk and manufactures of—					
2 Fabrics, n.o.p.......................... $	....	5,286,952	....	674,243	202,272 90
3 Silk fabrics of which silk is the component material of chief value, for the manufacture of neckties............... $	....	382,354	....	360,998	72,199 60
4 Handkerchiefs......................	....	74,516	....	4,865	1,702 75
5 Blouses and shirt waists............... $	....	87,972	....	38,574	14,465 32
6 Clothing.............................. $	....	734,095	....	351,272	131,727 15
7 Silk, spun, not coloured, n.o.p., silk in the gum not more advanced than single; tram or thrown organzine, not coloured............................ Lb.	3,593	6,383	2,025	4,340	651 00
8 Silk in the gum or spun, imported by the manufacturers of ribbons and shoe laces.................................. $	....	1,522	....	1,522	152 20
9 Sewing and embroidery silk, silk twist, and silk floss........................ $	....	118,519	....	72,507	18,126 75
10 Shawls................................ $	....	1,691	....	1,056	396 03
11 Shirts............................... Doz.	618	10,153	117	2,564	961 52
12 Silk and all manufactures of, not otherwise provided for, or of which silk is the component part of chief value, n.o.p... $	....	235,489	....	65,889	24,708 29
13 Socks and stockings.............. Doz. prs.	91,481	284,860	94,312	303,466	106,213 10
14 Undershirts and drawers.............. $	....	10,181	....	8,678	3,037 30
15 Velvets, and plush fabrics, n.o.p....... Yd.	481,324	399,584	87,679	68,843	20,652 90
Total, silk.....................	....	7,634,271	......:..	1,958,817	597,266 81
Slate and manufactures of—					
16 Mantles............................. $	....	598	....	598	179 40
17 Roofing slate........Squares of 100 sq. ft.	16,394	81,212	14,944	71,204	11,208 00
18 School writing slates.................. $	....	52,160	....	51,649	12,912 25
19 Slate pencils......................... $	....	5,107	....	5,105	1,276 25
20 Slate and manufactures of, n.o.p........ $	....	49,003	....	45,018	13,505 40
Total, slate...................	....	188,080	....	173,574	39,081 30
Soap—					
21 Common or laundry................... Lb.	7,797,815	404,986	7,462,700	387,328	74,627 00
22 Castile.......................... "	1,896,393	138,041	60,916	7,271	1,218 32
23 Common soft and liquid.............. "	271,862	11,590	199,278	8,244	2,679 52
24 Harness.......................... "	8,887	863	7,145	644	209 31
25 Toilet.............................. $	....	448,242	....	381,436	123,969 79
26 Soap, n.o.p., including pumice, silver and mineral soaps, sapolio and like articles $	....	87,537	....	70,386	22,876 04
27 Pearline and other soap powders........ Lb.	2,480,245	97,972	2,405,576	95,519	31,044 19
Total, soap.........................	....	1,189,231	....	950,828	256,624 17
Spices—					
28 Ginger and spices, n.o.p., unground...... "	3,488,795	· 296,237	1,413,560	118,885	14,861 09
29 Ginger and spices, n.o.p., ground........ "	145,393	30,081	120,615	23,557	5,974 15
30 Ginger, preserved.................... "	275,971	20,755	258,804	17,439	5,642 65
31 Nutmegs and mace, whole or unground. "	228,670	28,370	· 33,443	5,172	1,034 40
32 Nutmegs and mace, ground............ "	10,075	· 3,417	9,876	3,349	1,004 70
Total, spices......................	4,148,904	378,860	1,836,298	168,402	28,516 99
Spirits and wines, viz.—					
33 Amyl alcohol or fusil oil, or any substance known as potato spirit or potato oil................................. Gal.	8	25	8	25	19 80

Imported into Canada, etc.—*Continued.*

			ENTERED FOR HOME CONSUMPTION.						
Preferential Tariff.			Treaty Rates.			Total.			
Quantity.	Value.	Duty.	Quantity.	Value.	Duty.	Quantity.	Value.	DutyColl'd.	
	$	$ cts.		$	$ cts.	.	$	$ cts.	
....	24,394	4,878 80	....	....	....	....	113,874	31,722 80	1
....	237,873	41,628 71	....	4,408,227	887,271 05	....	5,320,343	1,131,172 66	2
....	9,333	1,633 33	....			....	370,331	73,832 93	3
....	24,872	6,218 00	....	44,336	14,409 25	....	74,073	22,330 00	4
....	45,660	13,698 00	....	3,660	1,192 65	....	87,894	29,355 97	5
....	295,825	88,747 50	....	86,187	28,045 67	....	733,284	248,520 32	6
1,568	2,043	204 30	....	....	....	3,593	6,383	855 30	7
....			....	....	....		1,522	152 20	8
....	45,895	8,031 72	....			....	118,402	26,158 47	9
....	80	24 00	....	495	172 48	....	1,631	592 51	10
168	2,815	844 50	333	4,774	1,551 57	618	10,153	3,357 59	11
....	78,296	23,488 80	....	90,743	29,524 28	....	234,928	77,721 37	12
3,907	14,928	3,732 00	....	....	....	98,219	318,394	109,945 10	13
....	1,503	338 21	....			....	10,181	3,375 51	14
291,051	245,604	42,981 89	96,279	82,214	20,911 73	475,009	396,661	84,546 52	15
....	1,004,727	231,570 96	....	4,720,636	983,078 68	....	7,684,180	1,811,916 45	
....	10,008	725 00	....	....	....	....	598	179 40	16
1,450	10,008	725 00	....	....	....	16,394	81,212	11,933 00	17
....	511	76 65	....	....	....	....	52,160	12,988 90	18
....	2	0 30	....	....	....	....	5,107	1,276 55	19
....	3,985	797 00	....	....	....	....	49,003	14,302 40	20
....	14,506	1,598 95	....	....	....	....	188,080	40,680 25	
301,641	16,411	1,960 77	....	....	....	7,764,341	403,739	76,587 77	21
24,679	1,676	246 79	1,825,175	128,803	18,251 75	1,910,770	137,750	19,716 86	22
67,178	3,158	710 61	....	....	....	266,456	11,402	3,390 13	23
1,742	219	49 29	....	....	....	8,887	863	258 60	24
....	68,960	15,516 30	....	....	....	....	450,396	139,486 09	25
....	17,087	3,844 72	....	....	....	....	87,473	26,720 76	26
116,217	4,565	1,027 16	....	....	....	2,521,793	100,084	32,071 35	27
....	112,076	23,355 64	....	128,803	18,251 75	....	1,191,707	298,231 56	
2,037,302	178,892	17,889 20	....	....	....	3,450,862	297,777	32,750 29	28
24,358	6,577	1,224 19	....	....	....	144,973	30,134	7,198 34	29
19,625	3,421	782 15	....	....	....	278,429	20,860	6,424 80	30
182,736	22,001	2,750 22	....	....	....	216,179	27,173	3,784 62	31
1,720	220	44 00	....	....	....	11,596	3,569	1,048 70	32
2,265,741	211,111	22,689 76	....	....	....	4,102,039	379,513	51,206 75	
....	....	....	....	....	....	8	25	19 80	33

6 GEORGE V, A. 1916

No. 14. —Summary Statement of Foreign Merchandise

ARTICLES.	TOTAL IMPORTS.		General Tariff.		
	Quantity.	Value.	Quantity.	Value.	Duty.
DUTIABLE GOODS—*Con.*		$		$	$ cts.
Spirits and wines—*Con.*					
1 Ethyl alcohol or the substance known as alcohol, hydrated oxide of ethyl, or spirits of wine..........................Gal.	37,368	9,236	4,630	1,203	12,783 60
2 Methyl alcohol, wood alcohol, wood naptha, pyroxylic spirits, or any substance known as wood spirits, or methylated spirits......................... "	34	44	34	44	96 00
Absinthe.............................. "	4,578	8,336	6,039	10,648	16,078 72
3 Arrack or palm spirits.................. "	257	361	358	342	887 40
6 Brandy, including artificial brandy. and imitations of brandy, n.o.p........... "	450,198	885,076	462,864	896,513	1,251,750 11
6 Cordials and liqueurs of all kinds, n.o.p., mescal, pulque, rum shrub, scheidam and other schnapps; tafia, angostura and similar alcoholic bitters or beverages.................................. "	74,101	178,103	64,578	161,851	172,392 17
7 Gin of all kinds, n.o.p.................. "	1,094,277	795,896	926,988	704,316	2,491,572 60
8 Rum.................................... "	184,770	94,610	186,065	101,167	517,044 59
9 Whiskey................................ "	1,252,944	2,402,975	1,275,050	2,390,742	3,491,669 16
10 All spirituous or alcoholic liquors, n.o.p. "	5,871	9,650	5,936	10,297	16,350 60
11 Spirits and strong waters of any kind, mixed with any ingredient or ingredients, and being known or designated as anodynes, elixirs, essences, extracts, lotions, tinctures or medicines, or ethereal and spirituous fruit essences, n.o.p................................ "	7,065	49,983	6,566	48,952	32,422 35
12 Medicinal, or medicated wines, containing not more than 40 per cent of proof spirit.......................... "	14,504	35,339	15,700	38,795	21,248 20
13 Alcoholic perfumes and perfumed spirits, bay rum, Cologne and lavender waters, hair, tooth and skin washes, and other toilet preparations containing not more than 4 ounces each.... .... "	6,273	61,741	6,085	61,999	33,949 70
14 Alcoholic perfumes and perfumed spirits, bay rum, Cologne and lavender waters, hair, tooth and skin washes, and other toilet preparations containing more than 4 ounces each.................... "	5,470	79,851	5,675	81,838	47,730 40
15 Vermouth containing not more than 40 per cent of proof spirits............. "	40,430	50,742	39,427	48,323	26,252 00
16 Vermouth containing more than 40 per cent of proof spirits.................. "	....	....	2	8	4 80
17 Nitrous ether, sweet spirits of nitre and aromatic spirits of ammonia.......... "	532	2,713	552	2,774	2,301 00
18 Wines, ginger, containing not more than 40 per cent of proof spirits............. "	4,423	3,705	4,327	3,769	2,064 40
Total, spirits.......................	3,183,103	4,668,386	3,010,884	4,563,606	8,136,617 60
Wines of all kinds, n.o.p., including orange, lemon, strawberry, raspberry, elder and currant wines—					
19 Containing 20 p.c. or less of proof spirits. Gal.	137,458	102,266	....	....	....
20 Containing over 20 p.c. and not over 23 p.c................................ "	35,059	28,463	....	....	....
21 Containing 26 p.c. or less of proof spirits "	228,674	128,660	53,830	40,794	25,095 70
22 Containing over 26 p.c. and not over 27 p.c................................ "	22,320	12,380	5,153	3,557	2,509 94
23 Containing over 27 p.c. and not over 28 p.c................................ "	25,678	19,269	11,375	9,435	6,356 75
24 Containing over 28 p.c. and not over 29 p.c................................ "	38,284	32,628	21,133	17,422	12,411 82
25 Containing over 29 p.c. and not over 30 p.c................................ "	65,654	57,668	46,048	38,242	28,510 36

SESSIONAL PAPER No. 11

Imported into Canada, etc.—*Continued.*

	ENTERED FOR HOME CONSUMPTION.								
	Preferential Tariff.			Treaty Rates.			Total.		
Quantity.	Value.	Duty.	Quantity.	Value.	Duty.	Quantity.'	Value.	DutyColl'd.	
	$	$ cts.		$	$ cts.		$	$ cts.	
....	....	....	....	....	....	4,630	1,203	12,783 60	1
....	....	....	....	....	....	34	44	96 00	2
....	....	....	....	....	....	6,039	10,648	16,078 72	3
....	....	....	....	....	....	358	342	887 40	4
....	....	....	....	....	....	462,864	896,513	1,251,750 11	5
....	....	....	....	....	....	64,578	161,851	172,392 17	6
....	....	....	....	....	....	926,988	704,316	2,491,572 60	7
....	....	....	....	....	....	186,065	101,167	517,044 59	8
....	....	....	....	....	....	1,275,050	2,390,742	3,491,669 16	9
....	....	....	....	....	....	5,936	10,297	16,350 60	10
....	....	....	....	....	....	6,566	48,952	32,422,35	11
....	....	....	....	....	....	15,700	38,795	21,248 20	12
....	....	....	....	....	....	6,085	61,999	33,949 70	13
....	....	....	....	....	....	5,675	81,838	47,730 40	14
....	....	....	....	....	....	39,427	48,323	26,252 00	15
....	....	....	....	....	....	2	8	4 80	16
....	....	....	....	....	....	552	2,774	2,301 00	17
....	....	....	....	....	....	4,327	3,769	2,064 40	18
....	....	....	....	....	....	3,010,884	4,563,606	8,136,617 60	
....	....	....	147,638	116,651	22,145 70	147,638	116,651	22,145 70	19
....	....	....	56,905	41,015	11,381 00	56,905	41,015	11,381 00	20
....	....	....	151,518	78,717	37,879 50	205,348	119,511	63,575 20	21
....	....	....	14,019	7,309	3,925 32	19,172	10,866	6,435 26	22
....	....	....	12,909	8,840	4,001 79	24,284	18,275	10,358 54	23
....	....	....	12,369	11,905	4,205 46	.33,502	29,327	16,617 28	24
....	....	....	19,050	19,758	7,048 50	65,098	58,000	35,558 86	25

No. 14.—SUMMARY STATEMENT of Foreign Merchandise

		TOTAL IMPORTS.		General Tariff.		
	ARTICLES.	Quantity.	Value.	Quantity.	Value.	Duty.
			$		$	$ cts.
	· DUTIABLE GOODS—*Con.*					
	Spirits and wines—*Con.*					
1	Containing over 30 p.c. and not over 31 p.c............................Gal.	50,409	44,298	30,614	26,062	20,064 20
2	Containing over 31 p.c. and not over 32 p.c.,........................ "	40,708	48,756	22,860	27,672	18,131 40
3	Containing over 32 p.c. and not over 33 p.c............................ "	35,714	41,901	24,716	28,668	19,969 76
4	Containing over 33 p.c. and not over 34 p.c............................ "	21,490	31,258	19,014	29,129	18,055 56
5	Containing over 34 p.c. and not over 35 p.c.,... "	8,101	13,081	8,641	˙ 12,629	8,282 02
6	Containing over 35 p.c. and not over 36 p.c.......................... "	6,055	15,258	4,957	11,797	6,265 45
7	Containing over 36 p.c. and not over 37 p.c........................... "	2,261	4,467	1,818	3,771	2,185 74
8	Containing over 37 p.c. and not over 38 p.c........................... "	966	1,473	906	1,452	988 26
9	Containing over 38 p.c. and not over 39 p.c............................ "	787	1,326	736	1,279	854 74
10	Containing over 39 p.c. and not over 40 p.c...................-........ "	1,151	1,502	185	166	173 75
11	Containing more than 40 p.c. of proof spirits, n.o.p......................... "	22,961	35,761	20,928	32,739	56,817 60
	Total, wines, non-sparkling..........	743,730	620,415	272,914	284,814	227,273 05
	Champagne and all other sparkling wines—					
12	In bottles containing each not more than a quart but more than a pint, old wine measure.............................Doz.	7,117	102,605	673	5,178	3,774 30
13	In bottles containing not more than a pint, each, but more than half a pint, old wine measure...................... "	15,887	141,723	1,050	4,686	3,138 30
14	In bottles containing one-half pint each or less......................... "	1,345	2,694	....	....	....
15	In bottles containing over one quart each Gal	110	989	2	˙ 16	7 80
	Total, wines, sparkling................	....	248,011	....	9,880	6,920 40
16	Sponges of marine production.............. $	....	73,441	....	66,711	11,675 14
17	Starch, including farina, corn starch, etc., etc...................................Lb.	2,941,065	107,585	2,358,203	81,588	35,373 35
18	Stockinettes for the manufacture of rubber boots and shoes when imported by manfacturers of rubber boots and shoes for use exclusively in the manufacture of such articles in their own factories.... $	....	76,659	....	54,714	8,207 10
	Stone and manufactures of—					
19	Building stone other than marble or granite, sawn on more than two sides but not sawn on more than four sides.....Cwt	11,571	3,549	11,571	3,549	1,735 65
20	Building stone other than marble or granite, planed, turned, cut or further manufactured than sawn on four sides. "	18,163	19,965	18,163	19,965	8,173 35
21	Flagstone, granite, rough sandstone, and all building stone, not hammered, sawn or chiselled...................... $	....	˙74,619	....	74,193	11,128 95
22	Flagstone and all other building stone sawn on not more than two sides...... $	....	170,712	....	169,523	33,904 60
23	Granite, sawn only.................... $	....	3,840	....	3,076	615 20
24	Granite, manufactures of, n.o.p........ $	....	196,208	....	19,740	6,909 00
25	Grindstones, not mounted and not less than 36 inches in diameter............ $	....	79,270	....	56,317	8,447 55

Imported into Canada, etc.—*Continued.*

			ENTERED FOR HOME CONSUMPTION.						
Preferential Tariff.			Treaty Rates.			Total.			
Quantity.	Value.	Duty.	Quantity.	Value.	Duty.	Quantity.	Value.	DutyColl'd.	
	$	$ cts.		$	$ cts.		$	$ cts.	
....	....	....	17,580	18,059	7,032 00	48,194	44,121	27,096 20	1
....	....	....	15,517	18,959	6,672 31	38,377	46,631	24,803 71	2
....	....	....	11,144	13,291	5,126 24	35,860	41,959	25,096 00	3
....	....	....	4,030	7,417	1,974 70	23,044	36,546	20,030 26	4
....	....	....	1,067	2,677	554 84	9,708	15,306	8,836 86	5
....	....	....	554	951	304 70	5,511	12,748	6,570 15	6
....	....	....	625	919	362 50	2,443	4,690	2,548 24	7
....	....	....	126	254	76 86	1,032	1,706	1,065 12	8
....	....	....	....	....	....	736	1,279	854 74	9
....	....	....	380	739	254 60	565	905	428 35	10
....	....	....	....	....	....	20,928	32,739	56,817 60	11
....	....	....	465,431	347,461	112,946 02	738,345	632,275	340,219 07	
....	....	....	7,520	128,662	24,816 00	8,193	133,840	28,590 30	12
....	....	....	21,918	220,141	36,164 70	22,968	224,827	39,303 00	13
....	....	....	1,091	3,738	894 62	1,091	3,738	894 62	14
....	....	....	104	988	156 00	106	1,004	163 80	15
....	....	....	....	353,529	62,031 32	....	363,409	68,951 72	
....	6,217	777 36	....	....	....	....	72,928	12,452 50	16
558,214	25,152	5,582 14	....	....	....	2,916,417	106,740	40,955 49	17
....	21,945	2,194 50	....	....	....	....	76,659	10,401 60	18
....	....	....	....	....	....	11,571	3,549	1,735 65	19
....	....	....	....	....	....	18,163	19,965	8,173 35	20
....	426	42 60	....	....	....	....	74,619	11,171 55	21
....	1,189	178 35	....	....	....	....	170,712	34,082 95	22
....	764	114 60	....	....	....	....	3,840	729 80	23
....	174,829	52,448 70	....	....	....	....	194,569	59,357 70	24
....	22,112	2,211 20	....	....	....	....	78,429	10,658 75	25

6 GEORGE V, A. 1916

No. 14.—SUMMARY STATEMENT of Foreign Merchandise

ARTICLES.		TOTAL IMPORTS.		General Tariff.		
		Quantity.	Value.	Quantity.	Value.	Duty.
DUTIABLE GOODS—*Con.*			$		$	$ cts.
Stone, mfrs. of—*Con.*						
1 Grindstones, n.o.p................... $		....	15,962	....	15,054	3,763 50
2 Paving blocks................... $		....	4,428	.....\.....	4,428	885 60
3 Manufactures of stone, n.o.p........... $		....	29,097	....	25,558	7,667 40
Total, stone..................		....	597,650	....	391,403	83,230 80
4 Straw.....................Ton.		198	2,955	198	2,955	396 00
5 Straw, carpeting, rugs, mats and matting. $		....	52,509	....	26,675	6,668 75
6 Straw, manufactures of, n.o.p........... $		....	15,994	....	17,392	3,043 83
Total, straw..................		....	71,458	....	47,022	10,108 58
Sugars, syrups and molasses—						
7 Sugar, above No. 16 D. S. in colour, and all refined sugars of whatever kinds, grades or standards.................Lb.		6,124,459	196,247	2,959,223	103,110	42,753 89
8 Sugar, n.o.p., not above No. 16 D. S. in colour, sugar drainings, or pumpings drained in transit, melado or concentrated melado, tank bottoms and sugar concrete................ "		657,162,676	17,036,419	283,010,963	7,254,783	2,653,796 86
9 Raw sugar as described in preceding item, when imported to be refined in Canada by Canadian sugar refiners under provisions of Tariff Item No. 135A. (This item does not include the amount of sugar entered for consumption under Tariff Item 135, on which a refund of duty was subsequently obtained under Item 135A)................. "		18,086,716	350,147	18,086,716	350,147	80,403 51
Total sugars..................		681,373,851	17,582,813	304,056,902	7,708,040	2,776,954 26
10 Syrups and molasses of all kinds, the product of the sugar cane or beet, n.o.p., and all imitations thereof or substitutes therefor................ "		3,366,159	89,405	2,720,196	56,775	13,601 17
11 Molasses of cane, testing by polariscope under 35 degrees but not less than 20 degrees.......................Gal.		296,633	24,591	296,633	24,591	4,449 55
12 Molasses, testing over 56 degrees and not more than 75 degrees by the polariscope......................Lb.		19,787	239	....	....	....
13 Molasses produced in the process of the manufacture of cane sugar from the juice of the cane without any admixture with any other ingredient, when imported direct from the place of production, or its shipping port, in the original package in which it was placed at the point of production and not afterwards subjected to any process of treating or mixing, testing by polariscope not less than 35 degrees nor more than 56 degrees...............Gal.		35,869	6,441	35,869	6,441	1,076 07
Total, syrups and molasses..........		....	120,676	....	87,807	19,126 79
14 Sugar cane, shredded.................. $		....	1,277	....	1,277	· 223 49
15 Sugar candy,and confectionery of all kinds n.o.p.,including sweetened gums, candied peel, candied pop corn, candied fruit, candied nuts, flavouring powders, custard powders, jelly powders, sweetmeats, sweetened breads, cakes, pies, puddings and all other confections containing sugar. (To August 21, 1914)... $		....	267,662	....	115,277	40,346 95·

Imported into Canada, etc.—*Continued.*

			ENTERED FOR HOME CONSUMPTION.						
Preferential Tariff.			Treaty Rates.			Total.			
Quantity.	Value.	Duty.	Quantity.	Value.	Duty.	Quantity.	Value.	DutyColl'd.	
	$	$ cts.		$	$ cts.		$	$ cts.	
....	908	158 91	....	....	....	....	15,962	3,922 41	1
....							4,428	885 60	2
....	3,540	708 00	....	....	....	....	29,098	8,375 40	3
....	203,768	55,862 36	....	....	....	....	595,171	139,093 16	
....	....	....	....	....	....	198	2,955	396 00	4
....	395	69 14	....	25,439	5,723 83	....	52,509	12,461 72	5
....	455	68 25	....			....	17,847	3,112 08	6
....	850	137 39	....	25,439	5,723 83	....	73,311	15,969 80	
2,889,800	82,405	24,856 77	....	....	....	5,849,023	185,515	67,610 66	7
370,542,158	8,991,308	2,599,280 04	....	....	....	653,553,121	16,246,091	5,253,076 90	8
....	....	....	....	....	....	18,086,716	350,147	80,403 51	9
373,431,958	9,073,713	2,624,136 81	....	....	....	677,488,860	16,781,753	5,401,091 07	
652,737	32,965	2,284 53	....	....	....	3,372,933	89,740	15,885 70	10
....						296,633	24,591	4,449 55	11
....									12
....	....	....	....	....	....	35,869	6,441	1,076 07	13
....	32,965	2,284 53	....	....	....	....	120,772	21,411 32	
....	....	....	....	....	....	....	1,277	223 49	14
....	153,319	34,497 11	....	....	....	....	268,596	74,844 06	15

No. 14.—Summary Statement of Foreign Merchandis^e

ARTICLES.		Total Imports.		General Tariff.		
		Quantity.	Value.	Quantity.	Value.	Duty.
			$		$	$ cts.
	Dutiable Goods—*Con.*					
	Sugar, syrups and molasses—*Con.*					
1	Sugar candy, and confectionery of all kinds, n.o.p., including sweetened gums, candied peel, candied pop corn, candied fruit, candied nuts, flavouring powders, custard powders, jelly powders, sweetmeats, sweetened breads, cakes, pies, puddings and all other confections containing sugar. (From August 21, 1914)..................... Lb.	4,338,680	458,981	1,440,783	153,474	60,928 46
2	Glucose or grape sugar, glucose syrup and corn syrup or any syrups containing any admixture thereof................... "	4,426,435	118,531	4,390,234	116,719	27,438 99
3	Sugar, maple, and maple syrup.......... "	37,947	3,983	20,564	2,099	419 80
4	Surgical trusses, pessaries and suspensory bandages.............................. $	....	44,183	....	38,249	7,649 80
5	Tallow....:........................... Lb.	161,363	17,199	58,334	4,363	872 60
6	Tape lines of any material................ $	....	8,141	....	4,827	1,206 75
7	Tape lines measuring. yarn of linen or cotton for the manufacture of................ Lb.	1,611	390	1,611	390	39 00
	Total tape lines, yarns, etc..........	....	8,531	....	5,217	1,245 75
8	Tea of Ceylon, black..................... Lb.	63,319	15,253	53,450	12,554	1,255 40
9	Tea of Ceylon, green..................... "	28,077	4,851	28,077	4,851	485 10
10	Tea of India, black...................... "	7,378	1,250	7,378	1,250	125 00
11	Tea of India, green...................... "	800	188	800	188	18 80
12	Tea of China, black...................... "	62,946	9,158	62,946	9,158	915 80
13	Tea of China, green...................... "	295,570	36,523	297,644	36,699	3,669 90
14	Tea of Japan, green...................... "	85,614	15,046	85,614	15,046	1,504 60
15	Tea of other countries, black............ "	40,491	8,614	40,024	8,309	830 90
16	Tea of other countries, green............ "	8,308	1,516	8,308	1,516	151 60
	Total, teas...........................	592,503	92,399	584,241	89,571	8,957 10
17	Tinware, japanned or not, and all manufactures of tin, n.o.p................... $	....	574,912	....	476,920	119,230 00
	Tobacco and manufactures of—					
18	Cigarettes............................. Lb.	45,948	106,219	44,339	103,800	168,755 50
19	Cigars....... .... "	102,731	416,412	99,257	409,077	424,002 25
20	Tobacco, cut........................... "	559,812	465,366	575,530	481,203	343,939 00
21	Snuff.................................. "	6,279	2,948	6,281	2,902	3,436 60
22	All other manufactures of tobacco, n.o.p. "	132,433	86,293	127,341	85,908	69,064 10
	Total, tobacco.......................	847,203	1,077,238	852,748	1,082,890	1,009,197 45
23	Tobacco pipes of all kinds, pipe mounts, cigar and cigarette holders and cases for the same, smokers' sets and cases therefor, and tobacco pouches............ $	....	386,381	....	75,435	26,402 25
24	Trawls, trawling spoons, hooks, sinkers, swivels and sportsman fishing bait, and fish hooks, n.o.p....................... $	....	46,799	....	22,885	8,009 75
25	Trunks, valises, hat-boxes, carpet bags, and tool bags....................... $	....	66,138	....	49,393	14,817 90
26	Twine, manufactures of, viz.: hammocks and lawn tennis nets, sportsman's fish nets and other articles, n.o.p........... $	....	46,584	....	35,336	10,600 80
27	Umbrellas, parasols and sunshades, of all kinds and materials.................... $	....	77,287	....	22,522	7,882 70
28	Unenumerated articles................ $	....	673,218	....	605,099	105,895 07
29	Varnish, lacquers, japans, japan dryers, liquid dryers and oil finish, n.o.p...... Gal.	64,767	125,373	47,204	87,743	29,183 89

Imported into Canada, etc.—*Continued.*

| | ENTERED FOR HOME CONSUMPTION. | | | | | | | | |
| Preferential Tariff. | | | Treaty Rates. | | | Total. | | | |
Quantity.	Value.	Duty.	Quantity.	Value.	Duty.	Quantity.	Value.	DutyColl'd.	
	$	$ cts.		$	$ cts.		$	$ cts.	
2,891.140	302,034	82,413 55	....	....	....	4,331,923	455,508	143,342 01	1
36,201	1,812	144 81	....	....	....	4,426,435	118,531	27,583 80	2
....	....	....	....	....	....	20,564	2,099	419 80	3
....	5,377	672 19	....	557	97 47	....	44,183	8,419 46	4
98,030	12,153	1,822 95	....	....	....	156,364	16,516	2,695 55	5
....	3,314	580 14	....	....	....	....	8,141	1,786 89	6
....	....	....	....	....	....	1,611	390	39 00	7
....	3,314	580 14	....	....	....	....	8,531	1,825 89	
....	....	....	....	....	....	53,450	12,554	1,255 40	8
....	....	....	....	....	....	28,077	4,851	485 10	9
....	....	....	....	....	....	7,378	1,250	125 00	10
....	....	....	....	....	....	800	188	18 80	11
....	....	....	....	....	....	62,946	9,158	915 80	12
....	....	....	....	....	....	297,644	36,699	3,669 90	13
....	....	....	....	....	....	85,614	15,046	1,504 60	14
....	....	....	....	....	....	40,024	8,309	830 90	15
....	....	....	....	....	....	8,308	1,516	151 60	16
....	....	....	....	....	....	584,241	89,571	8,957 10	
....	114,896	17,234 40	....	....	....	....	591,816	136,464 40	17
....	....	....	....	....	....	44,339	103,800	168,755 50	18
....	....	....	....	....	....	99,257	409,077	424,002 25	19
....	....	....	....	....	....	575,530	481,203	343,939 00	20
....	....	....	....	....	....	6,281	2,902	3,436 60	21
....	....	....	....	....	....	127,341	85,908	69,064 10	22
....	....	....	....	....	....	852,748	1,082,890	1,009,197,45	
....	160,474	36,107 14	....	164,170	53,355 56	....	400,079	115,864 95	23
....	24,014	5,403 52	....	....	....	....	46,899	13,413 27	24
....	15,221	3,044 20	....	1,407	386 93	....	66,021	18,249 03	25
....	11,235	2,247 00	....	....	....	....	46,571	12,847 80	26
....	55,081	12,393 53	....	....	....	....	77,603	20,276 23	27
....	66,678	10,001 70	....	....	....	....	671,777	115,896 77	28
17,532	37,621	9,149 57	....	....	....	64,736	125,364	38,333 46	29

11—i—10½

No. 14.—SUMMARY STATEMENT of Foreign Merchandise

ARTICLES.	TOTAL IMPORTS.		General Tariff.		
	Quantity.	Value.	Quantity.	Value.	Duty.
		$		$	$ cts.
DUTIABLE GOODS—*Con.*					
Vegetables—					
1 Melons..................................No.	2,321,164	223,898	2,315,509	223,558	69,465 27
2 Potatoes, n.o.p.......................Bush	671,108	531,509	668,927	530,162	133,785 40
3 Potatoes, sweet and yams.............. "	50,995	52,744	50,933	52,648	5,093 30
4 Tomatoes, and cooked corn in cans or other air-tight packages..............Lb.	537,338	40,685	396,865	25,092	5,953 00
5 Tomatoes, fresh.................. ....Bush	298,982	450,208	297,708	449,151	134,745 30
6 Vegetables and baked beans in cans or other air-tight packages, n.o.p..:....Lb.	4,022,899	299,852	2,326,990	166,435	34,905 13
7 Vegetables, n.o.p.......................$	....	1,410,472	....	1,395,259	418,577 70
Total, vegetables.....................	....	3,009,368	....	2,842,305	802,525 10
8 Vinegar, of any strength not exceeding strength of proof.......................Gal.	172,307	62,516	28,489	4,807	4,273 35
9 Vinegar, above strength of proof.......... "	6,115	2,042	6,001	1,887	1,272 85
Total, vinegar.......................	178,422	64,558	· 34,490	6,694	5,546 20
10 Waste or shoddy from cotton, woollen or other fabrics or from yarn or thread, machined, garnetted or prepared for use Lb.	4,498,072	·292,535	2,741,653	185,283	23,161 27
11 Watches.............................$	....	73,938	....	32,806	9,841 80
12 Watch cases and parts thereof, finished or unfinished..........................$	....	95,024	....	92,792	27,837 60
13 Watch actions and movements and parts thereof, finished or unfinished, including winding bars and sleeves................$	....	707,211	....	706,711	88,339 30
Total, watches, cases, movements, etc.	....	876,173	....	832,309	126,018 70
14 Wax, bees..............................Lb.	77,737	28,243	70,824	25,544	2,554 40
15 Wax, paraffine........................... "	1,003,422	48,681	732,140	34,883	8,720 75
16 Wax, sealing.............................$		13,262		3,387	846 75
17 Wax, vegetable and mineral, n.o.p........Lb.	640,706	83,562	620,683	81,115	8,111 50
18 Wax, and manufactures of, n.o.p..........$	....	50,271	....	46,852	8,199 84
Total, wax..........................	....	224,019	....	191,781	28,433 24
19 Webbing, elastic, over one inch wide...... $	....	163,188	....	144,581	28,916 20
20 Webbing, non-elastic, when imported by manufacturers of suspenders for use exclusively in the manufacture of such articles in their own factories...........$	....	4,091	....	4,070	814 00
Total, webbing, elastic, etc..........	....	167,279	....	148,651	29,730 20
21 Whips of all kinds, including thongs and lashes..................................$	....	25,803	....	21,668	6,500 40
22 Window cornices and cornice poles of all kinds..................................$	....	5,562	....	5,336	1,600 80
23 Window shade or blind rollers............$	....	12,419	....	11,687	4,090 45
24 Window shades cut to size or hemmed or mounted on rollers, n.o.p., and window shade cloth in the piece................$	....	35,279	....	3,213	1,124 55
Total, window cornices, rollers, shades, etc................	....	53,260	....	20,236	6,815 80

Imported into Canada, etc.—*Continued.*

	ENTERED FOR HOME CONSUMPTION.									
Preferential Tariff.			Treaty Rates.			Total.			
Quantity.	Value.	Duty.	Quantity.	Value.	Duty.	Quantity.	Value.	DutyColl'd.	
	$	$ cts.		$	$ cts.		$	$ cts.	
....	240	22 01	....	....	....	2,315,509	223,558	69,465 27	1
176						669,103	530,402	133,807 41	2
31	33	2 17	....	....	....	50,964	52,681	5,095 47	3
....	....	....	242,717	20,289	3,033 94	639,582	45,381	8,986 94	4
1,166	595	119 00	....	....	....	298,874	449,746	134,864 30	5
85,947	5,940	859 47	1,925,456	159,503	22,067 92	4,338,393	331,878	57,832 52	6
....	10,454	1,568 10	....	....	....	....	1,405,713	420,145 80	7
....	17,262	2,570 75	....	179,792	25,101 86	....	3,039,359	830,197 71	
140,593	57,461	14,059 30	5,825	1,567	728 18	174,907	63,835	19,060 83	8
424	415	409 33	....	....	....	6,425	2,302	1,682 18	9
141,017	57,876	14,468 63	5,825	1,567	728 18	181,332	66,137	20,743 01	
1,818,270	103,567	7,767 71	....	....	....	4,559,923	288,850	30,928 98	10
....	2,791	558 20	....	38,743	10,654 50	....	74,340	21,054 50	11
....	1,902	380 40				....	94,694	28,218 00	12
....	434	43 40	....	....	....	....	707,145	88,382 70	13
....	5,127	982 00	....	38,743	10,654 50	....	876,179	137,655 20	
7,980	3,156	157 80	....	....	....	78,804	28,700	2,712 20	14
271,282	13,798	2,070 10				1,003,422	48,681	10,790 85	15
....	9,881	1,482 15				....	13,268	2,328 90	16
20,023	2,447	122 35				640,706	83,562	8,233 85	17
....	3,450	517 50				....	50,302	8,717 34	18
....	32,732	4,349 90	....	....	....	....	224,513	32,783 14	
....	18,223	2,278 01	....	....	....	....	162,804	31,194 21	19
....	21	2 63	....	....	....	....	4,091	816 63	20
....	18,244	2,280 64	....	....	....	....	166,895	32,010 84	
....	4,135	827 00	....	....	....	....	25,803	7,327 40	21
....	226	45 20	....	....	....	....	5,562	1,646 00	22
....	732	164 71	....	....	....	....	12,419	4,255 16	23
....	32,338	7,276 14	....	....	....	....	35,551	8,400 69	24
....	33,296	7,486 05	....	....	....	....	53,532	14,301 85	

6 GEORGE V, A. 1916

No. 14.—Summary Statement of Foreign Merchandise

ARTICLES.		TOTAL IMPORTS.		General Tariff.		
		Quantity.	Value.	Quantity.	Value.	Duty.
			$		$	$ cts.
	DUTIABLE GOODS—*Con.*					
	Wood and manufactures of—					
1	Barrels containing petroleum or its products, or any mixture of which petroleum forms a part, when such contents are chargeable with a specific duty... No.	30,041	29,486	28,001	27,440	6,860 00
2	Barrels, empty.......................... "	46,559	35,578	46,460	35,393	8,848 25
3	Caskets and coffins and metal parts thereof......................... $	....	48,924	....	48,924	12,231 00
4	Curtain stretchers..................... $	....	5,679	....	4,708	1,412 40
5	Doors of wood....................... $	....	236,239	....	235,944	58,986 00
6	Fishing rods........................ $	....	29,604	....	22,691	6,807 30
7	Handles, D. shovel, wholly of wood and wood handles for manufacture of D. shovel handles.... $	....	36,056	....	36,009	5,401 35
8	Handles of all kinds, ash.............. $	....	22,449	....	22,434	5,608 50
9	Handles of all kinds, hickory.......... $	....	48,880	....	48,649	12,162 25
10	Heading and stave bolts and staves in the rough of poplar................... $	....	1,025	....	1,025	205 00
11	Lasts of wood......................... $	....	65,839	....	65,706	16,426 50
12	Matches of wood...................... $	....	40,405	....	33,370	8,342 50
13	Mouldings, plain, gilded or otherwise further manufactured................ $	....	72,691	....	72,745	18,186 25
14	Rakes, hay........................... No.	691	242	688	241	54 24
15	Refrigerators........................ "	1,402	31,477	1,397	31,107	9,332 10
16	Show cases of all kinds and metal parts thereof......................... $	....	20,365	....	16,483	5,769 05
17	Window sash.......................... $	....	26,543	....	26,543	6,635 75
18	Woodenware, churns, n.o.p., washboards, pounders and rolling pins............. $	....	21,109	....	20,811	4,162 20
19	Woodenware pails and tubs............. $	....	22,807	....	22,635	5,658 75
20	Manufactures of wood, n.o.p........... $	....	1,338,623	....	1,222,916	305,729 00
21	Sawed boards, planks, deals, planed or dressed on one or both sides, when the edges thereof are jointed or tongued and grooved..................... M. ft.	22,509	330,652	22,481	328,675	82,168 75
22	Umbrella, parasol and sunshade sticks or handles, n.o.p................... $	....	10,868	....	7,995	1,599 00
23	Veneers of oak, rosewood, mahogany, Spanish cedar and walnut, not over ³/₃₂ of an inch in thickness................ $	....	148,087	....	148,044	11,103 77
24	Veneers of wood, n.o.p. not over ³/₃₂ of an inch in thickness,............... $	....	31,679	....	31,679	4,751 85
25	Walking sticks and walking canes of all kinds........................... $	....	27,301	....	12,255	3,676 50
26	Wood pulp............................ $	....	456,820	....	480,393	120,098 25
	Total, wood, etc.....................	....	3,139,428	....	3,004,815	722,216 51
	Wool, manufactures of—					
27	Blankets composed wholly of pure wool Pr.	27,771	91,134	7,533	20,623	7,218 05
28	Cassimeres, cloths and doeskins....... Yd.	1,849,966	1,661,120	299,517	299,978	104,992 30
29	Coatings and overcoatings...........: "	1,240,700	1,012,050	86,764	67,870	23,754 50
30	Tweeds............................. "	1,745,918	1,027,470	172,032	198,793	69,577 55
31	Felt cloth, n.o.p..................... "	55,352	50,557	43,727	35,912	12,569 20
32	Flannels, plain, not fancy.............. "	2,237,165	668,604	1,434,175	544,513	190,579 55
33	Knitted goods, n.o.p.................. $	....	512,370	....	123,982	43,393 70
34	Bed comforters...................... No.	265	625	162	153	53 55
35	Railway rugs......................... $	....	45,952	....	2,806	982 10
36	Shawls............................. $	....	63,859	....	8,327	2,914 45
37	Shirts.............................. Doz.	3,453	31,879	665	5,457	1,909 95
38	Socks and stockings............. Doz. pr.	676,903	1,231,882	37,811	75,957	26,584 95
39	Undershirts and drawers, n.o.p........ $	....	393,382	....	63,868	22,353 80

Imported into Canada, etc.—*Continued.*

			ENTERED FOR HOME CONSUMPTION.						
Preferential Tariff.			Treaty Rates.			Total.			
Quantity.	Value.	Duty.	Quantity.	Value.	Duty.	Quantity.	Value.	DutyColl'd.	
	$	$ cts.		$	$ cts.		$	$ cts.	
356	362	63 37				28,357	27,802	6,92 7	1
82	153	26 79				46,542	35,546	8,873 64	2
....	....	....				48,924	12,231 00		3
....	....	....				4,708	1,412 40		4
....	295	51 63				236,239	59,037 63		5
....	6,927	1,385 40				29,618	8,192 70		6
....	47	4 70				36,056	5,406 05		7
....	15	2 62				22,449	5,611 12		8
....	217	37 98				48,866	12,200 23		9
....						1,025	205 00		10
....	133	23 28				65,839	16,449 78		11
....	563	98 53		7,853	1,767 17	41,786	10,208 20		12
3	1	0 15				72,745	18,186 25		13
2	30	6 00				691	242 54 39		14
						1,399	31,137 9,338 10		15
....	3,882	873 57				20,365	6,642 62		16
....	....	....				26,543	6,635 75		17
....	298	44 70				21,109	4,206 90		18
....	66	11 55		106	23 85	22,807	5,694 15		19
....	81,189	14,208 62		36,483	8,208 96	1,340,588	328,146 58		20
28	1,977	345 98				22,509	330,652	82,514 73	21
....	2,873	430 95					10,868	2,029 95	22
	43	2 15					148,087	11,105 92	23
....	....	....					31,679	4,751 85	24
....	14,909	2,981 80					27,164	6,658 30	25
....	88	13 20					480,481	120,111 45	26
....	114,068	20,612 97	....	44,442	9,999 98	....	3,163,325	752,829 46	
19,911	69,036	15,533 56				27,444	89,659	22,751 61	27
1,544,845	1,358,185	407,455 50				1,844,362	1,658,163	512,447 80	28
1,163,933	951,144	285,343 20				1,250,697	1,019,014	309,097 70	29
1,567,939	819,187	245,756 10				1,739,971	1,017,980	315,333 65	30
11,645	14,667	4,400 10				55,372	50,579	16,969 30	31
783,974	122,082	27,469 32				2,218,149	666,595	218,048 87	32
....	386,457	86,954 77				....	510,439	130,348 47	33
103	472	141 60				265	625	195 15	34
....	43,292	12,987 60				....	46,098	13,969 70	35
....	55,300	16,590 00				....	63,627	19,504 45	36
2,891	27,219	8,165 70				3,556	32,676	10,075 65	37
639,957	1,159,825	289,956 25				677,668	1,235,782	316,541 20	38
....	328,280	73,863 45				....	392,148	96,217 25	39

6 GEORGE V, A. 1916

No. 14.—SUMMARY STATEMENT of Foreign Merchandise

	ARTICLES.	TOTAL IMPORTS.		General Tariff.		
		Quantity.	Value.	Quantity.	Value.	Duty.
			$		$	$ cts.
	DUTIABLE GOODS—*Con.*					
	Wool, mfrs. of—*Con.*					
1	Yarns, composed wholly or in part of wool, worsted, the hair of the goat or like animal, n.o.p., costing thirty cents per pound or over, when imported on the cop, cone, or tube, or in the hank, by manufacturers of woollen goods, for use exclusively in their own factories................................Lb.	1,906,980	1,197,291	86,846	54,631	10,926 20
2	Yarns, woollen and worsted, n.o.p....... "	404,521	250,779	62,058	37,696	11,308 80
3	All fabrics and manufactures composed wholly or in part of wool, worsted, etc., n.o.p.......................... $	....	6,872,476	....	1,491,401	521,990 35
4	Fabrics of wool, or of cotton and wool, commonly described and sold as lustres, mohairs, alpaca and Italian linings.............................Yd.	2,697,983	783,183	18,113	6,321	2,212 35
5	Women's and children's dress goods, coat linings, Italian cloths, alpacas, orleans, cashmeres, henriettas, serges, buntings, nun's cloth, bengalines, whip cords, twills, plains or jacquards of similar fabrics, composed wholly or in part of wool, worsted, the hair of the camel, alpaca, goat or like animal, not exceeding in weight six ounces to the square yard, when imported in the gray or unfinished state for the purpose of being dyed or finished in Canada. Sq.yd.	1,236,731	327,897	3,271	1,480	370 00
6	Clothing, women's and children's outside garments........................ $	....	568,697	....	388,527	135,984 45
7	Clothing, ready-made, and wearing apparel, composed wholly or in part of wool worsted, etc., n.o.p.............. $	....	1,291,012	....	594,379	208,032 65
8	Carpets, Axminster, including Abusson, Savonerie and Moqnette............Yd.	133,478	138,518	5,741	6,962	2,436 70
9	Carpets, Brussels, including Wilton and Teprac................................. "	148,331	169,488	3,250	3,829	1,340 15
10	Carpets, Tapestry, including drum printed or machine printed, and velvet.... "	391,491	202,871	6,830	3,403	1,191 05
11	Carpets, Ingrain, 2 and 3 ply all wool or union................................. "	22,245	17,718	3,529	3,886	1,360 10
12	Whole carpets, including tufted, hand made or Oriental, Turkish, Persian, Japanese, Indian or Smyrna.......Sq. yd.	277,967	312,916	27,976	72,627	25,419 45
13	Mats and rugs, including hearth sizes 30 sq. ft. and smaller wool, n.o.p........ $	....	393,166	....	80,461	28,161 35
14	Felt, pressed, of all kinds not filled or covered by or with any woven fabric.Lb.	1,057,743	296,582	707,227	153,372	38,343 00
	Wool, viz.—					
15	Leicester, Cotswold, Lincolnshire, South Down combing wools, or wools known as lustre wools and other like combing wools, such as are grown in Canada.. "	1,506	444	1,506	444	45 18
	Total, wool, etc.....	....	19,613,922	....	4,347,658	1,496,005 43
16	Zinc, manufactures of, n.o.p............ $	....	31,573	....	29,382	7,345 50
17	Damaged goods, under sections 49 to 53 of Rev. Stat., cap. 32.................... $	....	51,046	....	49,132	11,796 22
18	Prepaid postal parcels from Great Britain $	....	74,941	....	74,941	21,262 46
19	Special duty on articles shipped to Canada at lower than usual home trade price.... $	....	....	....	....	68,296 47
20	Additional duties, post entries, over collections, etc........................... $	....	....	....	....	410,832 60
21	War tax................................	....	....	....	....	2,236,290 16
	Total, dutiable goods.........:........	....	318,951,094	....	198,401,802	60,903,163 73

SESSIONAL PAPER No. 11

Imported into Canada, etc.—*Continued.*

			ENTERED FOR HOME CONSUMPTION.						
Preferential Tariff.			Treaty Rates.			Total.			
Quantity.	Value.	Duty.	Quantity.	Value.	Duty.	Quantity.	Value.	DutyColl'd.	
	$	$ cts.		$	$ cts.		$	$ cts.	
1,821,815	1,143,826	142,978 64	....	....	....	1,908,661	1,198,457	153,904 84	1
341,501	211,343	42,268 60	....	....	....	403,559	249,039	53,577 40	2
....	5,473,639	1,642,091 70	....	....	....	....	6,965,040	2,164,082 05	3
2,672,501	793,107	178,450 36	....	....	....	2,690,614	799,428	180,662 71	4
1,223,589	323,028	48,454 20	10,272	3,619	814 26	1,237,132	328,127	49,638 46	5
....	180,147	54,044 10	....	....	....	....	568,674	190,028 55	6
....	692,885	207,865 50	....	....	....	....	1,287,264	415,898 15	7
129,964	134,060	33,515 00	....	....	....	135,705	141,022	35,951 70	8
147,327	167,427	41,856 75	....	....	....	150,577	171,256	43,196 90	9
383,958	200,112	50,028 00	....	....	....	390,788	203,515	51,219 05	10
18,716	13,832	3,458 00	....	....	....	2,245	17,718	4,818 10	11
252,804	242,187	60,546 75	....	....	....	280,780	314,814	85,966 20	12
....	318,034	79,508 50	....	....	....	....	398,495	107,669 85	13
351,166	143,112	21,466 80	....	....	....	1,058,393	296,484	59,809 80	14
....	....	....	....	....	....	1,506	444	45 18	15
....	15,371,885	4,081,150 05	....	3,619	814 26	....	19,723,162	5,577,969 74	
....	1,004	150 60	....	....	....	....	30,386	7,496 10	16
....	2,480	80 72	....	....	....	....	51,612	11,876 94	17
....	....	....	....	....	....	....	74,941	21,262 46	18
....	....	....	....	....	....	....	....	68,296 47	19
....	....	....	....	....	....	....	....	410,832 60	20
....	....	402,182 87	....	....	....	....	....	2,638,473 03	21
....	69,441,881	15,587,565 52	....	11,948,512	2,715,181 02	....	279,792,195	79,205,910 27	

6 GEORGE V, A. 1916

No. 14.—Summary Statement of Imports—*Continued.*

ARTICLES.	IMPORTED.		ENTERED FOR HOME CONSUMPTION.	
	Quantity.	Value.	Quantity.	Value.
FREE GOODS.		$		$
PRODUCE OF THE MINE.				
Burrstones in blocks, rough or unmanufactured, not bound up or prepared for binding into mill stones............. .. .No.	4	30	4	30
Chalk, China or Cornwall stone, cliff stone, and felspar, fluorspar, magnesite and mica schist ground or unground $	....	107,238	....	107,238
Clays, viz.:—				
China clay, ground or unground.................... Cwt.	365,744	130,845	365,744	130,845
Fire clay, ground or unground......................... $	....	90,723	....	90,723
Pipe clay, ground or unground....................... $	....	587	....	587
Clays, all other, n.o.p................................ $	....	45,733	....	45,733
Total, clays........................	....	267,888	....	267,888
Coal, anthracite, and anthracite dust.............. Ton.	4,383,407	20,927,539	4,383,407	20,927,539
Earths, crude only................................ $	....	4,306	....	4,306
Emery, in bulk, crushed or ground................. $	....	28,150	....	28,150
Flint, and ground flint stones................ Cwt.	90,021	54,704	90,021	54,704
Fossils......... .... $	....	5,266	....	5,266
Fuller's earth, in bulk only........................ $	....	11,808	....	11,808
Gannister............................... Cwt.	1,641	441	1,641	441
Gravel and sand........................ Ton.	258,062	215,933	258,062	215,933
Gypsum, crude (sulphate of lime)............. "	3,317	14,898	3,317	14,898
Pumice and pumice stone, lava and calcareous tufa, not further manufactured than ground................ $	....	16,560	....	16,560
Minerals—				
Alumina................................ Cwt.	250,805	501,807	250,805	501,807
Cinnabar................................. Lb.	760	451	760	451
Cryolite or kryolite............................ Cwt.	10,748	44,683	10,748	44,683
Litharge................................. "	10,547	49,920	10,547	49,920
Total, minerals.............	....	596,861	....	596,861
Mineral waters, natural, not in bottles............ Gal.	2,565	551	2,565	551
Meerschaum, crude or raw...................... Lb.	59	355	59	355
Ores of metals, n.o.p............: .... Cwt.	766,568	469,945	766,568	469,945
Ore, iron (to Feb. 12th see Dutiable Goods).......... Ton.	1,051,333	2,126,709	1,051,333	2,126,709
Total, ores.................	....	2,596,654	....	2,596,654
Phosphate rock (fertilizer).......................... $	....	17,122	....	17,122
Diamonds, unset.............................. $	....	1,593,440	....	1,593,440
Diamond dust or bort, and black diamonds for borers.... $	....	89,183	....	89,183
Salt, imported from the United Kingdom, or any British Possession; or imported for the use of the sea or gulf fisheries.......................... Cwt.	1,980,949	364,850	1,980,949	364,850
Stone, refuse, not sawn, hammered or chiselled, nor fit for flagstone, building stone or paving.................. Ton.	389,518	211,676	389,518	211,676
Silex or crystallized quartz, ground or unground....... Cwt.	12,824	10,373	12,824	10,373
Talc, ground, bolted or precipitated, not for toilet use.... "	8,275	6,546	8,275	6,546
Whiting, gilders' whiting and Paris white............... "	234,166	87,499	234,166	87,499
Total, mine............................	....	27,229,871	....	27,229,871

SESSIONAL PAPER No. 11

No, 14.—Summary Statement of Imports—*Continued.*

ARTICLES.	IMPORTED.		ENTERED FOR HOME CONSUMPTION.	
	Quantity.	Value.	Quantity.	Value.
Free Goods—The Fisheries.		$		$
Ambergris..	....	222	....	222
Fish offal or refuse...................................	....	28,836	....	28,836
Fur skins, undressed, the produce of marine animals.....	....	6,361	....	6,361
Pearl, mother of, unmanufactured......................	....	2,804	....	2,804
Squid..	....	7,181	....	7,181
Tortoise and other shells, unmanufactured........ $	....	12,514	....	12,514
Turtles.. $	....	2,650	....	2,650
Whale bone, unmanufactured................ Lb.	152	171	152	171
Seed and breeding oysters, imported for the purpose of being planted in Canadian waters,............... $	....	7,167	....	7,167
Live fish and fish eggs for propagating purposes.......... $	....	665	....	665
SPECIAL FROM NEWFOUNDLAND.				
Fish—				
Cod, haddock, ling and pollock, fresh................ Lb.	82,251	2,799	82,251	2,799
Cod, haddock, ling and pollock, dry, salted or smoked Cwt.	69,453	345,229	69,453	345,229
Cod, haddock, ling and pollock, wet, salted............ "	1,037	2,598	1,037	2,598
Cod, haddock, ling and pollock, pickled............... "	394	1,563	394	1,563
Halibut, fresh.. Lb.	147,952	10,405	147,952	10,405
Herring, fresh.. "	560,489	· 13,776	560,489	13,776
Herring, pickled...................................... "	6,701,270	124,656	6,701,270	124,656
Herring, smoked...................................... "	214,080	8,167	214,080	8,167
Sea fish, other, fresh................................. "	18,445	740	18,445	740
Sea fish, other, pickled............................... "	281,910	10,134	281,910	10,134
Lobsters, preserved, in cans........................... "	31,020	8,630	31,020	8,630
Bait—fish, clams or other, fresh or salted.......... Brl.	201	1,291	201	1,291
Salmon, fresh.. Lb.	174,942	16,101	174,942	16,101
Salmon, smoked..................................... "	1,650	215	1,650	215
Salmon, canned..................................... "	16,379	1,753	16,379	1,753
Salmon, pickled..................................... "	408,375	20,823	408,375	20,823
Total, fish from Newfoundland.................	....	568,880	....	568,880
Fish oil, viz.—				
Cod.. Gal.	135,244	54,045	135,244	54,045
Seal... "	10,836	4,909	10,836	4,909 ·
Other... "	9,382	4,130	9,382	4,130
Total, fish oil from Newfoundland...............	155,462	63,084	155,462	63,084
Other articles, produce of the fisheries, n.o.p............ $	....	577	....	577
Total, fisheries.................................	....	701,112	....	701,112
THE FOREST.				
Corkwood, unmanufactured............................ $	....	21,252	....	21,252
Bark, hemlock.................................Cords	· 152	968	· 152	968
Felloes of hickory or oak, not further manufactured than rough sawn or bent to shape...................... $	....	41,381	....	41,381
Handle, heading, stave and shingle bolts, n.o.p........... $	....	141,006	....	141,006
Hickory billets.. $	....	34,914	....	34,914
Hickory and oak spokes, not further manufactured than rough turned and not tenoned, mitred or sized......... $	....	185,414	....	185,414
Hub, last, wagon, oar and gun blocks and all like blocks or sticks, rough hewn or sawn only, and scale board for cheese boxes..................................... $	....	67,892	....	67,892
Ivory nuts (vegetable)................................. ‡	....	23,067	....	23,067
Fence posts and railroad ties......................... $	....	1,255,137	....	1,255,137
Logs, and round unmanufactured timber................. $	....	487,103	....	485,953
Lumber and timber, planks and boards, when not otherwise manufactured than rough sawn or split or creosoted, vulcanized, or treated by any other preserving process, viz.—				
Cherry, chestnut, gumwood, hickory and whitewood. M ft.	13,663	462,729	13,663	462,729
Mahogany.. Feet	1,383,224	152,769	·1,383,224	152,769

6 GEORGE V, A. 1916

No. 14.—Summary Statement of Imports—*Continued.*

ARTICLES.	IMPORTED.		ENTERED FOR HOME CONSUMPTION.	
	Quantity.	Value.	Quantity.	Value.
FREE GOODS—THE FOREST—*Con.*		$		$
Lumber and timber—*Con.*				
Oak...................................... M ft.	34,454	1,437,924	34,454	1,437,924
Pitch pine................................. "	95,182	1,608,788	95,182	1,608,788
Redwood................................ Feet	691,305	20,576	691,305	20,576
Rosewood................................ "	8,749	2,336	8,749	♭2,336
Spanish cedar............................ "	354,102	38,595	354,102	38,595
Walnut................................... "	384,283	27,561	384,283	27,561
White ash................................ "	1,370,260	71,443	1,370,260	71,443
African teak, amaranth, black heart, ebony, boxwood, cocoboral, dogwood, lignum vitae, persimmon, red cedar and satin wood................................ $	....	21,518	....	21,518
Timber, hewn or sawn, squared or sided, or creosoted, etc. $	....	544,483	....	544,483
Planks, boards and other lumber of wood, sawn, split or cut, and dressed on one side only, but not further manufactured................................ M ft.	135,375	2,322,368	135,375	2,322,368
Pine and spruce clapboards............................ "	49	698	49	698
Laths................................... M	20,291	46,853	20,291	46,853
Pickets................................. $	....	8,267	....	8,267
Shingles................................ M	16,606	29,494	16,606	29,494
Staves of oak, sawn, split or cut, not further manufactured, than listed or jointed................................ "	3,177	122,727	3,177	122,727
Total, lumber........................	....	6,919,129	....	6,919,129
Sawdust of wood, of all kinds............................ $	....	6,085	....	6,085
Treenails................................ M	2	104	2	104
Wood for fuel............................ Cords	23,145	63,856	23,145	63,856
Total, forest........................	....	9,247,308	....	9,246,158
ANIMALS AND THEIR PRODUCE.				
Animals for improvement of stock, viz.:—				
Horses................................... No.	444	198,724	458	205,334
Cattle................................... "	331	57,333	331	57,333
Sheep................................... "	343	6,108	343	6,108
Swine................................... "	68	1,964	68	1,964
Dogs................................... "	636	28,337	636	28,337
Goats................................... "	4	110	4	110
Fowls, domestic, pure bred.......................... $	76,148	45,370	76,148	45,370
Animals, all other, n.o.p................................ $	....	152,919	....	152,919
Total, animals for improvement of stock..........	77,974	490,865	77,988	497,475
Animals brought into Canada temporarily, and for a period not exceeding three months, for the purpose of exhibition or competition for prizes offered by any agricultural or other association, viz.:—				
Horses................................... No.	4,639	1,612,375	....	....
Cattle................................... "	156	86,410	....	....
Swine................................... "	1	25	....	....
All other, n.o.p.......................... $	....	41,013	....	....
Total, animals for exhibition......................	....	1,739,823	....	....
Bees................................... $	....	4,775	....	4,775
Bones, crude............................ Cwt.	13,106	19,787	13,106	19,787
Bone dust, charred bone, and bone ash.................. "	96,283	200,663	96,283	200,663
Bone pitch, crude only................................ $	....	1,250	....	1,250
Bristles................................. Lb.	138,956	132,040	138,956	132,040
Cat-gut or worm gut unmanufactured, adapted for the manufacture of whip or other cord or of ligatures........ $	....	4,670	....	4,670
Fur skins of all kinds, not dressed in any manner, n.o.p.. $	....	1,328,864	....	1,328,864
Fur tails in the raw state.......................... $	....	615	....	615

No. 14.—Summary Statements of Imports—*Continued.*

ARTICLES.	IMPORTED.		ENTERED FOR HOME CONSUMPTION.	
	Quantity.	Value.	Quantity.	Value.
FREE GOODS—ANIMALS AND THEIR PRODUCE—*Con.*		$		$
Grease and degras for stuffing or dressing leather........Lb.	1,916,816	94,457	1,916,816	94,457
Grease, rough, the refuse of animal fat, for the manufacture of soap and oils only.............................. "	11,869,101	751,756	11,869,101	751,756
Total, grease...................................	13,785,917	846,213	13,785,917	846,213
Guano and other animal manures.......................Cwt.	63,582	93,747	63,582	93,747
Hair, cleaned or uncleaned, not dyed, curled or otherwise manufactured.................................. $	....	72,428	....	72,428
Horse hair, not further manufactured than simply cleaned, and dipped or dyed......................Lb.	67,401	59,622	67,401	59,622
Hatters' furs, not on the skin...................... $	....	105,976	....	105,976
Hides and skins, raw, whether dry salted or pickled...Lb.	59,110,483	12,828,215	59,110,483	12,828,215
Hoofs, horn strips, horn and horn tips, in the rough, not polished or otherwise manufactured than cleaned... $	....	105	....	105
Ivory, unmanufactured............................Lb.	566	2,358	566	2,358
Leeches................................... $	....	357	....	357
Musk in pods or in grains...........................Oz.	67	1,006	67	1,006
Pelts, raw... $	....	14,238	....	14,238
Pigeons, homing and messenger, pheasants and quails.. $	....	3,679	....	3,679
Quills in their natural state or unplumed................ $	....	557	....	557
Rennet, raw and prepared........................... $	....	72,564	....	72,564
Silk, raw, or as reeled from the cocoon, not being doubled, twisted, or advanced in manufacture in any way...Lb.	94,458	314,480	94,458	314,480
Silk, in the gum, or spun, when imported by manufacturers of silk underwear or of woven labels, and spun silk for manufacture of silk thread, for use exclusively for the manufacture of such articles in their own factories....................................... "	37,383	119,369	37,333	119,236
Silk cocoons and silk waste........................... $	....	23	....	23
Sausage skins or casings, not cleaned................. $	....	98	....	98
Wool and the hair of the camel, alpaca, goat and other like animals, not further prepared than washed, n.o.p..Lb.	13,420,809	3,761,025	13,193,986	3,717,039
Total, animals and their produce..................	....	22,219,412	....	20,442,080
AGRICULTURAL PRODUCTS.				
Bamboo-reed, not further manufactured than cut into suitable lengths for walking sticks or canes, or for sticks for umbrellas, parasols, or sunshades, and bamboos unmanufactured.................................... $	....	3,331	....	3,331
Bristles, n.o.p.....................................Lb.	4,718	1,878	4,718	1,878
Broom corn... $	....	285,574	....	285,574
Cane and rattans not manufactured and not further manufactured than split, when for use in Canadian manufactures... $	....	50,101	....	50,101
Cassava root, unground................................ $	....	1,312	....	1,312
Citron, lemon and orange rinds, in brine.................. $	....	613	....	613
Cocoa beans, not roasted, crushed, or ground.............Lb.	2,700,373	326,748	2,700,373	326,748
Cocoanuts imported from the place of growth by vessel direct to a Canadian port...........................No.	3,482,039	70,814	3,482,039	70,814
Cotton wool or raw cotton, not dyed...................Lb.	73,032,453	6,533,631	73,032,453	6,533,631
Esparto or Spanish grass, and other grasses and pulp of, including fancy grasses dried but not coloured or otherwise manufactured, n.o.p............................ $	....	1,530	....	1,530
Fibre, Mexican, istle, or tampico........................Cwt	960	13,004	960	13,004
Fibrilla, flax fibre and flax tow......................... "	2,710	14,806	2,710	14,806
Fibre, vegetable, n.o.p.............................. "	8,128	90,382	8,128	90,382
Total, fibre...................................	11,798	118,192	11,798	118,192

No. 14.—Summary Statement of Imports—*Continued.*

Articles.	Imported.		Entered for Home Consumption.	
	Quantity.	Value.	Quantity.	Value.
		$		$
FREE GOODS—AGRICULTURAL PRODUCTS—*Con.*				
Florist stock, viz.: azaleas, rhododendrons, pot grown lilacs, seedling carnation stock, rose stock, and other stock for grafting, n.o.p.; araucaria, bulbs, corms, tubers, rhizomes, and dormant roots, n.o.p., and rooted carnation cuttings in their first year of introduction..............$	....	285,539	....	285,539
Fruit, green, viz.—				
Bananas............................Bunches	2,549,926	2,296,381	2,549,926	2,296,381
Berries, viz.: wild blueberries, wild strawberries, wild raspberries, and wild edible berries, n.o.p...........$	....	18,212	....	18,212
Guavas, mangoes, plantains, pomegranates.............$	....	1,738	....	1,738
Lemons and limes......................................$	....	718,307	....	718,307
Oranges and shaddocks or grape fruit..................$	....	3,524,606	....	3,524,554
Pine-apples...$	....	305,372	....	305,372
Total, fruit, green...............................	....	6,864,616	....	6,864,564
Foots, being the refuse of the cotton seed or olives after the oil has been pressed out.......................Cwt.	3,018	14,103	3,018	14,103
Hemp, dressed or undressed........................."	55,370	318,914	55,370	318,914
Indian corn, not for purposes of distillation...........Bush.	9,361,826	6,734,199	9,361,826	6,734,199
Jute butts and jute...................................Cwt.	839	6,736	839	6,736
Locust beans and locust bean meal.....................Lb.	1,975	81	1,975	81
Manila grass.......................................Cwt.	283,660	1,883,551	283,660	1,883,551
Manures, vegetable....................."	65	101	65	101
Osiers or willows, unmanufactured.....................$	....	8,190	....	8,190
Palm leaf, unmanufactured...........................$	....	3,926	....	3,926
Rice, uncleaned, unhulled, or paddy....................Lb.	59,807,991	1,205,833	59,807,991	1,205,833
Seedling stock for grafting, viz.:				
Plum, pear, peach, and other fruit trees..............$	....	3,622	....	3,622
Seeds, viz.—				
Beet and mangold..................................Lb.	1,056,060	90,413	1,056,060	90,413
Carrot............................."	35,091	9,581	35,091	9,581
Turnip............................"	1,927,313	146,571	1,927,313	146,571
Mustard..........................."	207,081	10,145	207,081	10,145
Beans (seed) from the United Kingdom..............."	17,993	1,513	17,993	1,513
Peas (seed) from the United Kingdom................"	53,714	4,707	53,714	4,707
Rape, sowing......................................"	450,029	26,801	386,832	22,994
Mushroom spawn...................................$	....	3,775	....	3,775
Total, seeds.....................................	....	293,506	....	* 289,699
Teasels...$	....	664	....	664
Tobacco, unmanufactured, for excise purposes, under conditions of Inland Revenue Act.......................Lb.	17,562,139	4,584,183	18,595,957	4,718,488
Trees, n.o.p.......................................$	....	2,474	....	2,474
Total, agricultural products.......................	....	29,603,962	....	29,734,408
MANUFACTURED AND PARTIALLY MANUFACTURED ARTICLES.				
Admiralty charts..................................$	....	1,655	....	1,655
Album insides, made of paper......................$	....	495	....	495
Artificial abrasives in bulk, crushed or ground, when imported for use in the manufacture of abrasive wheels and polishing composition...............................$	....	11,427	....	11,427
Artificial limbs, articles for manufacture of, pressed felt, elastic web, and hollow wood blocks..................$	....	701	....	701
Artificial limbs and parts thereof.....................$	....	39,422	....	39,422
Artificial teeth, not mounted.........................$	....	167,086	....	167,086
Asphaltum or asphalt, solid........................Cwt.	841,265	635,061	841,377	635,204
Astrachan or Russian hare skins and China goat skins, plates, or rugs, wholly or partially dressed but not dyed $	....	126,045	....	126,045
Bells when imported for use of churches only...........$	....	60,063	....	60,063
Binder twine.......................................Lb.	28,577,030	2,738,224	28,577,030	2,738,274

No. 14.—Summary Statement of Imports—*Continued.*

ARTICLES.	IMPORTED.		ENTERED FOR HOME CONSUMPTION.	
	Quantity.	Value.	Quantity.	Value.
FREE GOODS—MANUFACTURED ARTICLES, ETC.—*Con.*		$		$
Binder twine, articles which enter into the cost of the manufacture of binder twine or twine for harvest binders when imported for such use exclusively by manufacturers who manufacture such twine only...... $	....	9,947	....	9,947
Blanc fixe and satin white............Lb.	4,194,987	44,823	4,194,987	44,823
Blanketing and lapping and discs for mills for engraving copper rollers, imported by cotton manufacturers, calico printers, and wallpaper manufacturers for use in their own factories only............ $	....	8,962	....	8,962
Blast furnace slag............ $	....	11,788	....	11,788
Bolting cloth, not made up............ $	....	21,440	....	21,400
Books, viz.: Bibles, prayer books, psalm and hymn books religious tracts, and Sunday school lesson pictures...... $	....	265,030	....	265,030
Books, printed by any government or by any association for the promotion of science or letters, and official annual reports of religious or benevolent associations and issued in the proceedings of said associations, to their members and not for the purpose of sale or trade............ $	....	11,324	....	11,324
Books, embossed and grooved cards for the blind and books for the instruction of the deaf and dumb and blind $	....	720	....	720
Maps and charts for the use of schools for the blind;..... $	....	23	....	23
Books, not printed or reprinted in Canada, which are included and used as text books in the curriculum of any university, college, or school in Canada; books especially imported for the bona fide use of incorporated mechanics' institutes, public libraries, libraries of universities, colleges, and schools, or for the library of any incorporated medical, law, literary, scientific or art association or society, and being the property of the organized authority of such library, and not in any case the property of individuals............ $	....	635,101	....	635,101
Books, bound or unbound, which have been printed and manufactured more than twelve years............ $	....	15,145	....	15,145
Books on the application of science to industries of all kinds, also books printed in any language other than the English and French languages, or in any two languages not being English or French, or in any three or more languages............ $	....	171,914	....	171,914
Book manuscript and insurance maps............ $	....	80,752	....	80,752
Total, books and maps............	....	1,180,009	....	1,180,009
Bookbinder's cloth............ $	....	102,335	....	102,335
Brick, fire, of a class or kind not made in Canada........ $	....	482,763	....	482,763
Buckram, adapted for the manufacture of hat and bonnet shapes............ $	....	60,845	....	60,845
Braids or plaits of chip, palm leaf, manila, willow, osier, rattan, straw, Tuscan or grass, suitable for making or ormanenting hats, and plait braids or plaits of glazed cotton thread not over ¼-in. wide, when imported by manufacturers of hats for use only in the manufacture of hat bodies............ $	....	292,685	....	292,685
Bullion or gold fringe............ $	....	7,087	....	7,087
Buttons, shoe, papier mache............ $	....	16,021	....	16,021
Carbons over three inches in circumference and not exceeding 35 inches............ $	....	223,294	....	223,294
Celluloid, xylonite or xyolite in sheets, lumps, blocks, rods or bars, not further manufactured than moulded or pressed............ $	....	114,988	....	114,988
Chronometers and compasses for ships............ $	....	8,685	....	8,685
Coal and pine pitch............Gal.	1,064,269	58,374	1,064,269	58,374
Coal and pine tar, crude, in packages of not less than 15 gallons............ "	2,937,062	124,065	2,937,062	124,065
Coal tar base or salt (paranitraniline)............Lb.	20,264	3,994	20,264	3,994
Coke............Ton	506,799	1,445,836	506,799	1,445,836

No. 14.—Summary Statement of Imports—*Continued.*

Articles.	Imported.		Entered for Home Consumption.	
	Quantity.	Value.	Quantity.	Value.
FREE GOODS—MANUFACTURED ARTICLES, ETC.—*Con.*		$		$
Coke, ground, when imported by manufacturers of electric batteries, for use in their own factories in the manufacture of such batteries.........................Cwt.	11,280	14,420	11,280	14,420
Colours, metallic, viz.: oxide of cobalt, tin, and copper, n.o.p...Lb.	284,032	65,165	284,032	65,165
Colours, dry red lead and orange mineral.............. "	416,272	18,883	416,272	18,883
Colours, zinc white.. "	861,500	27,293	861,500	27,293
Communion sets of metal, glass or wood................ $	....	22,755	....	22,755
Coir and coir yarn..Lb.	283,972	13,233	283,972	13,233
Cotton or linen duck, seamless, in circular form, of a class or kind not made in Canada, for use in the manufacture of hose pipe....................................... $	....	74,425	....	74,425
Cotton thread, nitrate of thorium and nitrate of cerium, for use in the manufacture of incandescent gas mantles, when imported by manufacturers of such mantles or of stockings for such mantles.............................. $	....	5,527	....	5,527
Crucibles, clay, sand or plumbago....................... $	....	50,846	....	50,846
Crucibles, platinum...................................... $	....	9,496	....	9,496
Curling stones and handles therefor....................No.	1,599	8,928	1,599	8,928
Drugs, dyes, chemicals, and medicines:—				
Acid boracic, in packages of not less than 25 pounds.....Lb.	403,538	27,322	386,738	25,978
" hydro-fluo-silicic................................... "	1,110,079	32,980	1,110,079	32,980
" oxalic... "	274,302	23,124	274,302	23,124
" tannic.. "	19,513	6,865	19,513	6,865
Alum, in bulk, ground or unground but not calcined..... "	1,947,938	20,196	1,947,938	20,196
Alumina, sulphate of, or alum cake..................... "	1,611,863	9,629	1,611,863	9,629
Ammonia, nitrate of.................................... "	1,998,850	109,498	1,998,850	109,498
Ammonia, sulphate of................................... "	952,864	25,979	952,864	25,979
Aniline and coal tar dyes, soluble in water, in bulk or packages of not less than one pound weight, including alizarine and artificial alizarine.................... "	1,768,788	514,248	1,768,788	514,248
Aniline oil, crude...................................... "	340	103	340	103
" salts... "	59,139	10,410	59,139	10,410
Annatto, liquid or solid. .... "	66,466	8,460	66,466	8,460
Antimony, or regulus of, not ground, pulverized, or otherwise manufactured................................. "	1,543,018	164,471	1,543,018	164,471
Antimony salts, viz.: tartar emetic, chlorine and lactate (antimonine)..................................... "	72,951	14,179	72,951	14,179
Antimony salts for dyeing.............................. "	28	2	28	2
Arsenious oxide.. "	5,233	266	5,233	266
Arsenic, sulphide of................................... "	11,881	868	11,881	868
Barium, peroxide of, non-alcoholic, for use in the manufacture of peroxide of hydrogen when imported by manufacturers of peroxide of hydrogen................ "	78,078	5,573	78,078	5,573
Beans, viz.—				
Tonquin, crude only................................. "	1,262	1,776	1,262	1,776
Vanilla, crude only................................. "	17,127	52,387	17,127	52,387
Binitrotoluol, trinitrotoluol, and perchlorate of ammonia, when imported by manufacturers of explosives for use exclusively in the manufacture of such articles in their own factories................................. "	437,034	52,412	437,034	52,412
Borax, in bulk, of not less than 25 pounds............. "	2,971,101	122,910	3,036,341	126,068
Brimstone, crude, or in roll or flour, and sulphur in roll or flour... "	86,864,409	894,815	86,864,409	894,815
Bromides, crude.. "	3,112	890	3,112	890
Bromine... "	786	419	786	419
Burgundy pitch... "	135,829	5,472	135,829	5,472
Camwood and sumac and extract thereof................ "	808,697	25,194	808,697	25,194
Carbon bisulphide...................................... "	10,941	582	10,941	582
Chloride of lime and hypo-chlorite of lime, in packages of not less than 25 pounds (to July 1st. See Dutiable Goods.).. "	5,390,899	45,829	5,390,899	45,829
Cochineal.. "	1,873	969	1,873	969
Cream of tartar, in crystals or argols................ "	1,141,830	257,833	1,139,215	257,204
Cyanide of potassium, cyanide of sodium, and cyanogen bromide for reducing metals in mining operations.... "	1,862,869	331,530	1,862,869	331,530
Dragon's blood.. "	546	537	546	537

No. 14.—Summary Statement of Imports—*Continued.*

ARTICLES.	IMPORTED.		ENTERED FOR HOME CONSUMPTION.	
	Quantity.	Value.	Quantity.	Value.
		$		$
FREE GOODS—MANUFACTURED ARTICLES, ETC.—*Con.*				
Drugs, dyes, &c.—*Con.*				
Dyeing or tanning articles in a crude state, used in dyeing or tanning, n.o.p..........Lb.	9,343,606	206,246	9,343,606	206,246
Extract of logwood, fustic, oak, and oak bark and quebracho.......... "	38,219,142	1,066,031	38,219,142	1,066,031
Ferment cultures to be used in butter-making.......... $	....	164	....	164
Glycerine, crude, when imported by manufacturers for use only in their own factories in the manufacture of refined glycerine.......... "	322,033	45,279	322,033	45,279
Glycerine, when imported by manufacturers of explosives, for use exclusively for the manufacture of such articles in their own factories.......... "	2,166,027	393,368	2,166,027	393,368
Roots, medicinal, viz.: Alkanet, crude, crushed or ground, aconite, calumba, foliæ digitalis, gentian, ginseng, jalap, ipecacuanha, iris, orris root, liquorice, sarsaparilla, squills, taraxacum, rhubarb, and valerian, unground.......... $	....	18,944	....	18,944
Gums, viz.—				
Amber, arabic, australian, copal, damar, elemy, kaurie, mastic, sandarac, senegal, tragacanth, gedda, barberry, pontianac and lac, crude, seed, button, stick, and shell.......... $	....	360,467	....	360,467
Balata, crude, unmanufactured..........Lb.	384	304	384	304
Chicle or Sappato gum, crude.......... "	5,903,911	1,990,917	5,393,392	1,809,794
Indigo.......... "	14,485	2,681	14,485	2,681
Indigo, paste and extract of.......... "	111,405	18,354	111,405	18,354
Iodine, crude.......... "	7.732	21,400	7,732	21,400
Iron liquor, being solution of acetate or nitrate of iron, adapted for dyeing and calico printing.......... $	....	2,925	....	2,925
Kainite and other crude German potash salts for fertilizers..........Lb.	760,902	13,370	760,902	13,370
Lead, nitrate and acetate of, not ground.......... "	240,762	15,131	240,762	15,131
Litmus and all lichens, prepared or not.......... "	149	54	149	54
Logwood and fustic, ground, and ground oak bark..... "	28,269	476	28,269	476
Madder and munjeet, or Indian madder, ground or prepared, and all extracts of.......... $	....	122	....	122
Manganese, oxide of..........Lb.	3,527,316	48,430	3,527,316	48,430
Moss, Iceland, and other mosses.......... "	1,347,091	32,402	1,347,091	32,402
Nitrate compounds adapted for use in the manufacture of explosives.......... "	62,726	7,074	62,726	7,074
Nut galls and extracts thereof.......... "	21,128	2,716	21,128	2,716
Nicotine sulphate.......... "	1,596	1,431	1,596	1,431
Persis, or extract of archill and cudbear.......... "	2,174	325	2,174	325
Phosphorus.......... "	44,393	15,453	44,393	15,453
Potash, caustic, in packages of not less than 25 lbs. each. "	501,394	36,451	501,394	36,451
Potash, chlorate of, not further prepared than ground.. "	808,685	70,195	808,685	70,195
Potash, bichromate.......... "	102,750	8,608	102,750	8,608
Potash, muriate and sulphate of, crude.......... "	7,485,715	146,061	7,485,715	146,061
Potash, red and yellow prussiate of.......... "	134,760	22,351	134,760	22,351
Potash and pearl ash in packages of not less than 25 pounds each.......... "	62,518	6,226	62,518	6,226
Quicksilver.......... "	147,537	71,838	147,537	71,838
Quinine, salts of..........Oz.	79,501	22,779	79,501	22,779
Radium.......... $	....	1,553	....	1,553
Red liquor, being a crude acetate of aluminum prepared from pyroligneous acid, and adapted for dyeing and calico printing.......... $	....	81	....	81
Saffron, saffron cake, safflower, and extracts of.......Lb.	271	1,062	271	1,062
Sal ammoniac.......... "	948,128	50,362	948,128	50,362
Saltpetre, or nitrate of potash.......... "	2,308,377	142,639	2,279,772	140,231
Seeds, aromatic, crude, not edible, and not advanced in value or condition by grinding or refining or by any other process or manufacture, viz.: anise, anise-star, caraway, coriander, cardamon, cumin, fenugreek, and fennel.......... "	224,964	16,497	224,964	16,497
Soda ash or barilla.......... "	58,474,285	392,399	58,474,285	392,399
Soda, bichromate of.......... "	600,348	29,007	600,348	29,007
Soda, bisulphite of.......... "	752,378	12,615	752,378	12,615

No: 14.—Summary Statement of Imports—*Continued.*

Articles.		Imported.		Entered for Home Consumption.	
		Quantity.	Value.	Quantity.	Value.
			$		$
FREE GOODS—MANUFACTURED ARTICLES, ETC.—*Con.*					
Drugs, dyes. &c.—*Con.*					
Soda, caustic, in packages of not less than 25 pounds (to July 1st, see Dutiable Goods)	Lb.	13,524,587	223,077	13,524,587	223,077
Soda, chlorate of	"	324,401	17,503	324,401	17,503
Soda hyposulphite, when imported by tanners for use in their own factories in the tanning of leather	"	262,648	2,993	262,648	2,993
Soda nitrate of or cubic nitre	"	26,559,516	581,399	26,559,516	581,399
Soda, nitrite of	"	434,236	9,503	434,236	9,503
Soda, peroxide of	"	23,152	6,490	23,152	6,490
Soda sal	"	9,361,953	55,022	9,361,953	55,022
Soda, silicate of, in crystals or in solution	"	12,911,877	77,636	12,911,877	77,636
Soda, sulphate of, crude, known as salt cake	"	37,730,558	167,263	37,730,558	167,263
Soda, arseniate, binarseniate, and stannate of	"	14,327	587	14,327	587
Soda, prussiate and sulphite of	"	211,503	20,132	211,503	20,132
Sodium, sulphide of	"	1,660,038	30,308	1,660,038	30,308
Sulphate of iron (copperas)	"	738,843	5,344	738,843	5,344
Sulphate of copper (blue vitriol)	"	1,576,334	70,578	1,576,334	70,578
Tartaric acid crystals	"	237,138	67,952	237,138	67,952
Terra japonica, gambier, or cutch	"	2,881,707	95,893	2,881,707	95,893
Tin, bichloride of	Lb.	200	29	200	29
Tin crystals	$		7,856		7,856
Turmeric	Lb.	45,494	2,507	45,494	2,507
Ultramarine blue, dry, or in pulp	"	351,235	22,265	351,235	22,265
Verdigris, or sub-acetate of copper, dry	"	4,138	927	4,138	927
Zinc dust	"	393,839	38,304	393,839	38,304
Zinc, sulphate and chloride of	"	360,452	10,985	360,452	10,985
Drugs, crude, such as barks, flowers, roots, beans, berries, balsams, bulbs, fruits, insects, grains, gums and gum resins, herbs, leaves, nuts, fruit and stem seeds— which are not edible and which are in a crude state and not advanced in value by refining or grinding or any other process of manufacture, n.o.p	$	....	92,635	....	92,635
Total, drugs		....	9,669,704	....	9,487,358
Fashion plates. tailors', milliners' and mantle makers', when imported in single copies in sheet form with magazines, etc	$	....	18,630	....	18,630
Felt, adhesive, for sheathing vessels	$	....	1,409	....	1,409
Fertilizers, unmanufactured, n.o.p	$	....	752	....	752
Fillets of cotton and rubber, not exceeding seven inches wide when imported by manufacturers of card clothing, for use exclusively in the manufacture of card clothing in their own factories	$	....	22	....	22
Fisheries, for the use of, viz.: Fish hooks for deep sea or lake fishing not smaller in size than No. 2.0, not including hooks commonly used for sportsman's purposes	$	....	21,989	....	21,989
Bank, cod, pollock and mackerel fish lines; and mackerel, herring, salmon, seal, seine, mullet, net and trawl twine in hanks or coils, barked or not, in variety of sizes and threads, including gilling thread in balls, and head ropes for fishing nets, manilla rope not exceeding 1½ inches in circumference for holding traps in the lobster fishery; barked marline, and net norsels of cotton, hemp or flax, and fishing nets or seines, when used exclusively for the fisheries, and not including lines or nets commonly used for sportsman's purposes.	$	....	1,346,162	....	1,346,162
Total, fish hooks, seines, etc		....	1,368,151	....	1,368,151
Fuse heads of metal, foil and cardboard, when imported by manufacturers of electric fuses, for use in their own factories in the manufacture of such fuses	$	....	14	....	14
Glass, cut to size for manufacture of dry plates for photographic purposes when imported by the manufacturers of such dry plates for use exclusively in the manufacture thereof in their own factories	$	....	21,734	....	21,734

No. 14.—Summary Statement of Imports—*Continued.*

ARTICLES.	IMPORTED.		ENTERED FOR HOME CONSUMPTION.	
	Quantity.	Value.	Quantity.	Value.
FREE GOODS—MANUFACTURED ARTICLES, ETC.—*Con.*		$		$
Glass plates or discs, rough cut or unwrought, for use in the manufacture of optical instruments, when imported by manufacturers of such optical instruments........... $				
Glove fasteners, metal, shoe eyelets, corset eyelets, shoe eyelet hooks, shoe lace wire fasteners.................. $	....	4,745	....	4,745
Globes, geographical, topographical and astronomical.... $	....	200,893	....	200,893
Gold beaters' moulds and gold beaters' skins............. $	....	4,567	....	4,567
Gold and silver sweepings............................. $	....	2,359	....	2,359
Hatters' bands (not cords), bindings and hat sweats; hatters' tips and sides when cut to shape, and cashmere when cut to shape for under brims and hat covers, when imported by manufacturers of hats and caps for use exclusively in the manufacture of these articles in their own factories.. $	....	121,082	....	121,082
Hatters' plush of silk or cotton......................... $	....	90,741		92,051
Hemp paper, made on four cylinder machines and calendered to between .006 and .008 thickness, adapted for the manufacture of shot shells; and felt board sized and hydraulic pressed and covered with paper or uncovered, adapted for the manufacture of gun wads............... $	....	27,031	....	27,031
Hoods, unfinished, composed of 'Leghorn,' 'Manilla,' palm leaf, grass, willow or chip, not bleached or blocked $	....	4,409	....	4,015
Iron sand or globules or iron shot, and dry putty adapted for polishing glass or granite or for sawing stone........ $	....	13,049	....	13,049
Ivories, piano key...................................... $	....	80,699	....	80,699
Junk, old..Cwt.	3,671	18,348	8,671	18,348
Jute cloth as taken from the loom, not coloured, cropped, mangled, pressed, calendered, nor finished in any way..Yd.	17,451,582	963,025	17,451,582	963,025
Jute or hemp yarn, plain, dyed or coloured, for weaving purposes for insulating wire and for the manufacture of hammocks or twines..................................Lb.	2,172,095	205,126	2,172,095	205,126
Jute canvas, as taken from the loom, not coloured, cropped, mangled, pressed, calendered nor finished in any way...Yd.	6,383,879	468,011	6,383,879	468,011
Kelp, sea grass and sea weed in their natural state or cleaned only, n.o.p.................................Lb.	31,835	2,252	34,835	2,252
Lamp black, bone black, ivory black and carbon black.. "	1,750,757	80,470	1,750,757	80,470
Lenses and shutters for manufacturing cameras.......... $	....	32,654	....	32,654
Life boats and life-saving apparatus specially imported by societies to encourage the saving of human life.......... $	....	3,114	....	3,114
Life saving appliances, miners rescue and automatic resuscitation apparatus for artificial breathing.............. $	....	20,801	....	20,801
Lime juice, crude only................................Gal.	66.603	20,663	66,603	20,663
Lastings, mohair cloth, or other manufactures of cloth, woven or made in patterns of such size, shape or form or cut in any such manner as to be fit only for covering buttons, when imported by manufacturers of buttons... $	....	4,943	....	4,943
Medals of gold, silver or copper, and other metallic articles, actually bestowed as trophies or prizes and received and accepted as honorary distinctions, and cups or other metallic prizes won in bona fide competitions........... $	....	9,691	....	9,626
'Mexican saddle trees and stirrups of wood................ $	....	12,997	....	12,997
Metals, viz.:—				
Aluminum leaf or foil.................................. $	....	5,786	....	5,786
Aluminium in ingots, blocks, bars, rods, strips, sheets or plates...Lb.	3,295,223	660,152	3,295,223	660,152
Aluminium tubing in lengths of not less than 6 feet, not bent, etc... "	15,099	6,589	15,099	6,589
Anchors for vessels...............................Cwt.	8,320	30,424	8,320	30,424
Bismuth, metallic, in its natural state................Lb.	1,915	3,555	1,915	3,555
Brass caps adapted for use in the manufacture of electric batteries.. $	....	5,948	....	5,948
Brass cups, being rough blanks, for the manufacture of paper shells or cartridges, when imported by manufacturers of brass and paper shells and cartridges for use exclusively in the manufacture of such articles in their own factories.................................. $	....	168,832	....	168,832

11—i—11½

No. 14.—Summary Statement of Imports—*Continued*,

Articles.		Imported.		Entered for Home Consumption.	
		Quantity.	Value.	Quantity.	Value.
FREE GOODS—MANUFACTURED ARTICLES, ETC.—*Con.*			$		$
Metals—*Con.*					
Brass, old and scrap................................Cwt.		12,461	132,484	12,461	132,484
Brass in blocks, ingots or pigs............................ "		8 929	102,067	8,929	102,067
Brass tubing not polished, bent or otherwise manufactured in lengths not less than 6 feet...................Lb.		1,615,018	312,517	1,615,018	312,517
Brass in bars or rods, not less than 6 feet in length, and brass in strips, sheets or plates, not polished, etc., for use in Canadian manufacture (to July 1st see Dutiable Goods)......................................Cwt.		5,440	93,500	5,440	93,500
Total, brass..............................		....	815,348	....	815,348
Britannia metal, in pigs, blocks, or bars............... "		368	13.056	368	13,056
Canada plates; Russia iron; terne plates and rolled sheets of iron or steel coated with zinc, spelter or other metal, of all widths or thicknesses, n.o.p............. "		114,654	269,178	114,654	269 178
Chain coil, coil chain links including repair links and chain shackles of iron or steel 1¼ inches in diameter and over.. "		5,417	20,178	5,417	20,178
Chain, malleable sprocket or link belting, imported by manufacturers of agricultural implements for use in the manufacture of such implements in their own factories $		....	79,719	....	79,719
Copper, old and scrap................................Cwt.		1,023	11,719	1,023	11,719
Copper, in blocks, pigs or ingots...................... "		44,226	585,610	44,226	585,610
Copper, in bars and rods in coil or otherwise, in lengths of not less than 6 feet, unmanufactured............. "		144,782	2,056,510	144,782	2,056,510
Copper, in strips, sheets or plates, not polished, planished or coated, etc.. "		33,576	552,890	33,576	552,890
Copper, tubing in lengths of not less than 6 feet, and not polished, bent or otherwise manufactured............Lb.		622,326	137,491	622,326	137,491
Copper rollers adapted for use in calico printing........ $		....	3,311	....	3,311
Total, copper..........................		....	3,347,531	....	3,347,531
Cream separators and steel bowls for.................. $		....	408,702	....	408,702
Cream separators—materials, which enter into the construction and form part of, when imported by manufacturers of cream separators to be used in the manufacture thereof and articles of metal for use in the manufacture of cream separator parts.................. $		....	197,571	....	198,116
Ferromanganese and spiegeleisen containing more than 15% manganese....................................Ton.		17,508	476,466	17,508	476,466
Gas buoys:— The following articles and materials when imported by manufacturers of automatic gas buoys and automatic gas beacons, for use in the manufacture of such buoys and beacons for the Government of Canada or for export, viz.: Iron or steel tubes over 16 inches in diameter; flanged and dished steel heads made from boiler plate, over 5 feet in diameter; hardened steel balls, not less than 3 inches in diameter; acetylene gas 'lanterns and parts thereof and tobin bronze in bars or rods...... $		....	26,510	....	26,510
Iron or steel rods over 5-16 in. for manufacture of chains..Cwt.		933	1,041	933	1,041
Iron or steel, rolled round wire rods, in the coil, not over ⅜ inch in diameter, when imported by wire manufacturers for use in making wire in the coil in their own factories (to July 1st, see Dutiable Goods).......... "		699,958	805,414	699,958	805,414
Boiler plate of iron or steel not less than 30 inches in width and not less than ¼ inch in thickness, for use exclusively in the manufacture of boilers............. "		104,664	146,915	104,664	146,915
Rolled iron or steel, and cast steel in bars, band, hoop, scroll or strip, sheet or plate of any size, thickness or width, galvanized or coated with any material, or not, and steel blanks for the manufacture of milling cutters when of greater value than 3⅓ cents per pound. "		40,341	326,813	40,341	326,813
Rolled iron or steel sheets in strips, polished or not, 14 gauge and thinner, n.o.p........—................. "		145,200	318,939	145,200	318,939

No. 14.—Summary Statement of Imports—*Continued.*

Articles.	Imported.		Entered for Home Consumption.	
	Quantity.	Value.	Quantity.	Value.
FREE GOODS—MANUFACTURED ARTICLES, ETC.—*Con.*		$		$
Rolled iron or steel hoop, band, scroll or strip, No. 14 gauge and thinner, galvanized, or coated with other metal or not, n.o.p....................................Cwt	8,382	18,961	8,382	18,961
Sheets, flat, of galvanized iron........................ "	403,704	1,197,223	403,704	1,197,223
Metallic elements and tungstic acid when imported by manufacturers for use only in their own factories in the manufacture of metal filaments for electric lamps..... $	....	32,108	....	32,108
Iron tubing, brass covered, not over 3 inches in diameter, and brass trimmings not polished, lacquered, or otherwise manufactured, when imported by manufacturers of iron or brass bedsteads for use exclusively in the manufacture of such articles in their own factories.... $	....	115,538	....	115,538
Iron tubing, brass covered, not over 2 inches in diameter, in the rough, when imported by manufacturers for use only in their own factories in the manufacture of towel bars, bathtub rails and clothes carriers.............. $	....	224	....	224
Iron tubing, lacquered or brass covered, not over 2 inches in diameter, brass cased rods and brass trimmings, when imported by manufacturers of carriage rails for use exclusively in the manufacture of such articles in their own factories.................................. $	....	1,938	....	1,938
Iron tubing, lacquered or brass covered, for manufacturing extension rods for windows...................... $	....	3,879	....	3,879
Iron or steel beams, sheets, plates, angles, knees, masts or parts thereof, and cable chains for wooden, iron, steel or composite ships or vessels...................Cwt.	310,702	416,402	310,702	416,402
Iron or steel bands, strips or sheets, No. 14 gauge or thinner, coated, polished or not, and rolled iron or steel sections, not being ordinary square, flat, or round bars, when imported by manufacturers of saddlery and hames, for use exclusively in the manufacture of such articles in their own factories.......... $	....	14,676	....	14,676
Locomotive and car wheel tires of steel in the rough.Cwt.	123,037	314,629	123,037	314,629
Manufactured articles of iron or steel or brass which at the time of their importation are of a class or kind not manufactured in Canada, imported for use in the construction or equipment of ships or vessels.............. $	....	97,310	....	97,310
Scrap iron and scrap steel, old, and fit only to be remanufactured, being part of or recovered from any vessel wrecked in waters subject to the jurisdiction of Canada..Cwt.	9,604	2,190	9,604	2,190
Skelp iron or steel sheared or rolled in grooves, not over 4¼ inches wide, for the manufacture of rolled iron tubes not over 1½ inches in diameter................ "	7,447	9,988	7,447	9,988
Lead, tea..Lb.	1,362,341	89,167	1,362,341	89,167
Machinery, viz.:—				
Articles of metal as follows, when for use exclusively in mining or metallurgical operations, viz.: coal cutting machines, except percussion coal cutters; coal heading machines; coal augers; rotary coal drills; core drills; miners' safety lamps and parts thereof, also accessories for cleaning, filling and testing such lamps; electric or magnetic machines for separating or concentrating iron ores; furnaces for the smelting of copper, zinc and nickel ores; converting apparatus for metallurgical processes in metals; copper plates, plated or not; machinery for extraction of precious metals by the chlorination or cyanide processes; amalgam safes; automatic ore samplers; automatic feeders; retorts; mercury pumps; pyrometers; bullion furnaces; amalgam cleaners; blast furnace blowing engines; and integral parts of all machinery mentioned in this item; blowers of iron or steel for use in the smelting of ores, or in the reduction, separation or refining of metals; rotary kilns, revolving roasters and furnaces of metal designed for roasting ore, mineral, rock or clay; furnace slag trucks and slag pots of a class or kind not made in Canada; buddles, vanners and slime tables adapted for use in gold mining................... $	....	450,503	....	465,515

6 GEORGE V, A. 1916

No. 14.—Summary Statement of Imports—*Continued.*

ARTICLES.	IMPORTED.		ENTERED FOR HOME CONSUMPTION.	
	Quantity.	Value.	Quantity.	Value.
		$		$
FREE GOODS—MANUFACTURED ARTICLES, ETC.—*Con.*				
Diamond drills and parts of, not to include motive power...... $	....	41,117	....	41,117
Appliances of iron or steel, of a class or kind not made in Canada, and elevators and machinery of floating dredges, when for use exclusively in alluvial gold mining....... $	....	183,655	....	183,655
Well-drilling, and apparatus of a class or kind not made in Canada for drilling for water, natural gas or oil and for prospecting for minerals, not to include motive power...... $	....	214,379	....	214,379
Briquette making machines............ $	....	2,906	....	2,906
Newspaper printing presses, of not less value by retail than $1,500 each, of a class or kind not made in Canada.No.	57	343,018	57	343,018
Machinery and tools not manufactured in Canada up to the required standard necessary for any factory to be established in Canada for the manufacture of rifles for the Government of Canada,...... $	....	271,718	....	271,718
All materials or parts in the rough, unfinished, and screws, nuts, bands and springs, and steel for rough unfinished parts, to be used in rifles to be manufactured at any such factory for the Government of Canada....... $	....	341,647	....	·341,647
Machines, typecasting and typesetting and parts thereof, adapted for use in printing offices...... $	....	479,178	....	479,178
Machinery of every kind and structural iron and steel, for use in the construction and equipment of factories for the manufacture of sugar from beet root....... $	....	2,683	....	2,683
Machinery of a class or kind not made in Canada and parts thereof, for the manufacture of twine, cordage, or linen or for the preparation of flax fibre...... $	....	38,684	....	38,684
Machines, traction ditching (not being ploughs), adapted for tile drainage on farms, valued by retail at not more than $3,000 each, and parts thereof for repairs..No.	31	78,768	31	78,768
Mould boards or shares, or plough plates, land sides, and other plates for agricultural implements, when cut to shape from rolled plates of steel, but not moulded, punched, polished or otherwise manufactured......Cwt.	50,681	135,425	50,681	135,425
Material to be used in Canada for the construction of bridges and tunnels crossing the boundary between Canada and the United States, when similar materials are admitted free under similar circumstances into the United States, under regulations prescribed by the Minister of Customs....... $	....	20,097	....	20,097
Metal tips, studs and eyes for the manufacture of corset clasps and corset wires...... $	....	5,504	....	5,504
Nickel, nickel silver and German silver, in bars and rods, and also in strips, sheets or plates. Lb.	584,631	139,640	584,631	139,640
Nickel, nickel silver and German silver, in ingots or blocks, n.o.p. "	90,396	32,397	90,396	32,397
Platinum retorts, pans, condensers, tubing and pipe, and preparations of platinum, when imported by manufacturers of sulphuric acid for use exclusively in the manufacture or concentration of sulphuric acid in their own factories....... $	....	59	....	59
Platinum wire and platinum in bars, strips, sheets or plates....... $	....	55,453	....	55,453
Ribs of brass, iron or steel, runners, rings, caps, notches, ferrules, mounts and sticks or canes in the rough, or not further manufactured than cut into lengths, suitable for umbrella, parasol or sunshade or walking sticks, when imported by manufacturers of such articles for use exclusively in their own factories...... $	....	98,564	....	98,443
Sewing machine attachments...... $	....	26,450	....	26,450
Steel balls adapted for use on bearings on machinery and vehicles...... $	....	4,317	....	4,317
Steel rolled for saws and straw cutters not tempered or ground nor further manufactured than cut to shape, without indented edges......Cwt.	16,924	124,299	16,924	124,299

No. 14.—Summary Statement of Imports—*Continued.*

Articles.	Imported.		Entered for Home Consumption.	
	Quantity.	Value.	Quantity.	Value.
FREE GOODS—MANUFACTURED ARTICLES, ETC.—*Con.*		$		°
Steel wire Bessemer soft drawn spring of Nos. 10, 12 and 13 gauge, respectively, and homo steel spring wire of Nos. 11 and 12 gauge, respectively, when imported by manufacturers of wire mattresses to be used exclusively in their own factories in the manufacture of such articles........Cwt.	10,511	25,338	511	25,338
Steel, crucible sheet, 11 to 16 gauge, 2½ to 18 inches wide for the manufacture of mower and reaper knives when imported by manufacturers thereof for use exclusively in the manufacture of such articles in their own factories........ "	6,776	24,468	6,776	24,468
Steel of No. 20 gauge and thinner, but not thinner than No. 30 gauge, for the manufacture of corset steels, clock springs and shoe shanks, imported by manufacturers of such articles for exclusive use in the manufacture of such articles in their own factories........ "	864	4,078	864	4,078
Steel wire flat, of 16 gauge or thinner imported by the manufacturers of crinoline or corset wires and dress stays, for use exclusively in the manufacture of such articles in their own factories........ "	6,237	48,003	6,237	48,003
Steel of No. 12 gauge and thinner, but not thinner than No. 30 gauge, for the manufacture of buckle clasps, bed fasts, furniture casters and ice creepers, imported by the manufacturers of such articles, for use exclusively in the manufacture of such articles in their own factories........ "	1,551	4,351	1,551	4,351
Steel No. 24 and 17 gauge, in sheets 63 inches long, and from 18 to 32 inches wide when imported by the manufacturers of tubular bow sockets for use exclusively in the manufacture of such articles in their own factories........ "	1,620	3,951	1,620	3,951
Steel springs for the manufacture of surgical trusses when imported by manufacturers of surgical trusses for use exclusively in the manufacture thereof in their own factories........Lb.	388	187	388	187
Stereotypes, electrotypes and celluloids of newspaper columns in any language other than English and French and of books, and bases and matrices and copper shells for the same, whether composed wholly or in part of metal or celluloid........Sq.in.	672,545	11,555	672.545	11,555
Rolled iron and rolled steel nail rods, under half an inch in diameter, for the manufacture of horse shoe nails. Cwt.	31 688	72,097	31,688	72,097
Tagging metal plain, japanned or coated, in coils, not over 1½ inches wide, when imported by the manufacturers of shoe and corset laces for use exclusively in the manufacture of such articles in their own factories........ "	121	1.553	121	1,553
Tin in blocks, pigs and bars........ "	29,402	1,003,800	29,402	1,003,800
Tin plates and sheets........ "	985.103	3,032,224	985,103	3,032,224
Tin foil........Lb.	1,126,382	155,268	1,126,382	155,268
Steel seamless tubing valued at not less than 3½ cents per pound ....Cwt.	550	4,842	550	4,842
Steel or iron tubes, rolled, not joined or welded, not more than 1½ inches in diameter, n.o.p........$	....	37,882	....	37,882
Seamless steel or wrought iron boiler tubes, including flues and corrugated tubes for marine boilers........ $	....	356,992	....	356,992
Barbed fence wire of iron or steel........Cwt.	325,390	627,203	325,390	627,203
Wire, crucible cast steel, valued at not less than 6 cents per pound........Lb.	23,402	2,765	23,402	2,765
Wire of brass, zinc, iron or steel, screwed or twisted, or flattened or corrugated, for use in connection with nailing machines for the manufacture of boots and shoes, when imported by the manufacturers of boots and shoes to be used exclusively for such purposes in their own factories........ "	116,894	40,721	116,894	40,721

No. 14.—SUMMARY STATEMENT OF IMPORTS—*Continued.*

ARTICLES.	IMPORTED.		ENTERED FOR HOME CONSUMPTION.	
	Quantity.	Value.	Quantity.	Value.
FREE GOODS—MANUFACTURED ARTICLES, ETC.—*Con.*		$		$
Wire, curved or not, galvanized iron or steel, Nos. 9, 12, and 13 gauge, with variations not exceeding 4-1000 of an inch, but not for use in telegraph or telephone lines....Cwt.	758,258	1,306,942	758,258	1,306,942
Wire rope, for use exclusively for rigging of ships and vessels "	748	4,352	748	4,352
Wire, steel, valued at not less than 2¼ cents per pound, when imported by manufacturers of rope for use exclusively in the manufacture of rope............ "	55,535	218,197	55,535	218,197
Yellow metal, in bars, bolts, and sheets, for use in the construction or repairs of vessels........ "	500	6,373	500	6,373
Zinc, in blocks, pigs, bars, rods, sheets, and plates....... "	30,240	199,619	30,240	199,619
Zinc spelter............ "	129,119	711,809	129,119	711,809
Total, zinc......................	159,359	911,428	159,359	911,428
Molasses, not testing more than 56 degrees by the polariscope, the produce of any British country entitled to the benefits of the British Preferential Tariff when produced from sugar cane and imported direct by ship from the country of production, or from any British country, in the original package in which it was placed at the point of production and not afterwards subjected to any process of treating or mixing............Gal.	7,314,669	1,284,246	7,314,669	1,284,246
Newspapers, and quarterly, monthly, and semi-monthly magazines, and weekly literary papers, unbound...... $	....	1,425,848	....	1,425,848
Noils, being the short wool that falls from the combs in worsted factories; and worsted tops, n.o.p............ $	•	1,312,885	....	1,312,885
Oakum of jute or hemp............Cwt	11,858	48,630	11,858	48,630
Oil cake, linseed and linseed oil cake and meal, cotton seed cake and meal, palm nut cake and meal............. "	255,374	331,639	255,374	331,639
Soya beans and soya bean cake, for use in the manufacture of cattle food and of fertilizers, when imported by manufacturers of such cattle food and fertilizers............. "	2,206	2,930	2,206	2,930
Oils, viz.—				
Carbolic or heavy oil............Gal.	736,539	97,448	·736,539	97,448
Cocoanut palm, and palm kernel, not edible, peanut and soya bean, for manufacture of soap.... ·........... "	411,797	353,285	411,797	353,285
Cotton seed, refined, edible, and peanut, for canning fish "	32,000	20,309	32,000	20,309
Cotton seed, crude, for the manufacture of refined cotton seed oil............ "	2,938,492	1,327,386	2,938,492	1,327,386
Gasoline under ·725 specific gravity at 60 degrees temperature............ "	26,504,649	2,828,383	26,504,649	2,828,383
Palm bleached and Shea butter............Lb.	73,091	15,732	73,091	15,732
Asphaltum oil............ $	....	35,802	....	35,802
Olive, for manufacturing soap or tobacco or for canning fish............Gal.	2,022	1,712	2,022	1,712
Petroleum, crude, fuel and gas oils (8235 specific gravity or heavier) at 60 degrees temperature............ "	196,848,287	5,253,527	196,203,287	5,230,497
Rosin oil and Chinawood oil............ $	....	.140,989	....	140,989
Total, oil............		10.074,573	....	10,051,543
Paper, matrix, not being tissue paper, for use in printing.. $	....	13,538	... .	13,538
Paper tubes and cones of all sizes, adapted for winding yarn thereon............ $	....	15,591	....	15,591
Paper and materials of paper, gutta percha, and rubber for the manufacture of music rolls for piano players...... $	....	4,062	....	4,062
Paper, photographic, plain basic, baryta coated, adapted for use exclusively in the manufacture of albumenized or sensitized paper............ $	....	48,557	....	48,557
Paper decalcomania, not printed, when imported by manufacturers of decalcomania transfers, to be used in their own factories in the manufacture of such transfers...... $	....	3,227	....	3,227

No. 14.—Summary Statement of Imports—*Continued.*

Articles.	Imported.		Entered for Home Consumption.	
	Quantity.	Value.	Quantity.	Value.
		$		$
FREE GOODS—MANUFACTURED ARTICLES, ETC.—*Con.*				
Philosophical and scientific apparatus, utensils, instruments, and preparations, including boxes and bottles containing the same, maps, photographic reproductions, casts as models, etchings, lithographic prints or charts, when specially imported in good faith for use and by order of any society or institution, incorporated or established solely for religious, philosophical, educational, scientific or literary purposes, or for the encouragement of the fine arts or for the use or by order of any college, academy, school, or seminary of learning in Canada, and not for sale...$	....	226,890	....	226,890
Piano and organ parts:—key pins, damper springs. jack springs, rail springs, regulating screws, spoons, bridle wires, damper wires, back check wires, dowel wires, German centre pins, brass pins, rail hooks, brass brackets, plates, damper rod nuts, damper sockets and screws, shell, brass capstan screws, brass flange plates and screws, brass flanges, brass whitened spring wire, hammer wires, felt, butt felt, damper felt, hammer rail cloth, back check felt, catch felt, thin damper felt, whip cloth, bushing cloth, hammer felt, back hammer felt,p bridle leather and buckskin, when imported by manufacturers of piano keys, actions, hammers, base dampers, and organ keys,. for use exclusively in the manufacture of such articles in their own factories......$	....	59,763	....	59,763
Prunella cloth of wool...................................$	....	42,997	....	42,997
Rags of cotton, jute, hemp, and wool; paper waste clippings, and waste of all kinds, n.o.p., except metallic ; broken glass or glass cullet.......................Cwt.	540,922	1,244,469	540,922	1,244,469
Resin or rosin in packages of not less than 100 lbs........ "	251,941	444,601	251,941	444,601
Rubber and gutta percha, crude caoutchouc, or Indian rubber, umanufactured.....................................Lb.	7,481,962	4,100,272	6,504,476	3,604,025
Rubber, recovered, rubber substitute and hard rubber in sheets, but not further manufactured, also hard rubber in strips or rods, but not further manufactured, when imported for use in Canadian manufactures........... "	5,781,516	781,444	5,781,516	781,444
Rubber, powdered, and rubber or gutta percha waste or junk... "	658,351	83,951	658,351	83,951
Rubber thread not covered............................. "	24,032	35,855	24,032	35,855
Total, rubber...............................	13,945,861	5,001,522	12,968,375	4,505,275
Soap, whale oil.. "	135,334	5,283	135,334	5,283
Spirits, amyl alcohol or refined fusil oil, when imported by the Department of Inland Revenue or by a person licensed by the Minister of Inland Revenue, to be denatured for use in the manufacture of metal varnishes or lacquers.......................................Gal.	42	135	42	135
Spirits, ethyl alcohol, when imported by the Department of Inland Revenue or by a person licensed by the Minister of Inland Revenue, to be denatured for use in the arts and industries, and for fuel, light and power....... "	7,464	3,544	7,464	3,544
Spurs and stilts adapted for use in the manufacture of earthenware.......................................$	....	288	....	288
Square or round reeds and raw hide centres, textile leather or rubber heads, thumbs and tips, and steel, iron, or nickel caps for whip ends, imported by whip manufacturers for use exclusively in the manufacture of whips in their own factories...................................$	....	25,281	....	25,281
Scientific apparatus, glassware and other for laboratory work,also apparatus for sterilizing purposes. not including washing or laundry machines, all for use in public hospitals...$	....	18,324	....	18,324
Surgical and dental instruments of metal and surgical needles, and surgical operating tables for use in hospitals, X-ray apparatus and parts thereof, and microscopes valued at not less than $50 each by retail.............$	....	393,341	....	393,341

No. 14.—Summary Statement of Imports—*Continued.*

ARTICLES.	IMPORTED.		ENTERED FOR HOME CONSUMPTION.	
	Quantity.	Value.	Quantity.	Value.
		$		$
FREE GOODS—MANUFACTURED ARTICLES, ETC.—*Con.*				
Turpentine, raw or crude...............Lb.	59,473	1,956	59,473	1,956
Turpentine, spirits of....................Gal.	905,437	459,143	905,437	459,143
Twine or yarn of paper imported by manufacturers for the purpose of being woven into fabrics................ $	....	291	....	291
Twine or yarn of paper for use in the manufacture of furniture... $	....	275	....	275
Typewriters, type tablets with movable figures, and musical instruments, when imported by and for use of schools for the blind............................. $	....	40	....	40
Wool waste in the white, garnetted, for the manufacture of woollen goods................................Lb.	103,789	30,530	103,789	30,530
Yarn, cotton, No. 40 and finer......................... "	1,902,654	848,210	1,890,713	843,473
Yarn, cotton, polished or glazed, when imported by manufacturers of shoe laces for use exclusively for the manufacture of such articles in their own factories.......... "	67,158	23,388	67,158	23,388
Yarn, linen, for the manufacture of towels, damask, or seamless linen, fire hose duck, when imported by the manufacturers of such articles for use exclusively in the manufacture of such articles in their own factories...... "	353,393	103,487	353,393	103,487
Yarn, mohair....................................... "	5,872	3,572	5,872	3,572
Yarn, wool or worsted, when genapped, dyed or finished, and imported by manufacturers of braid, cords, tassels, buttons, and fringes for use exclusively in the manufacture of such articles in their own factories.......... "	17,177	8,503	17,177	8,503
Yarns, thread, and filaments of artificial and imitation silk, produced from a form cellulose obtained by chemical processes from cotton or wool when imported by manufacturers of knitted, woven or braided fabrics, for use only in their own factories in the manufacture of such knitted, woven or braided fabrics.................. "	128,148	190,289	128,148	190,289
Total, yarn...	2,474,402	1,177,449	2,462,461	1,172,712
Total, manufactures................................	....	66,755,876	....	66,065,946
MISCELLANEOUS ARTICLES.				
Anatomical preparations and skeletons or parts thereof... $	....	2,480	....	2,480
Apparel, wearing, and other personal and household effects not merchandise, of British subjects dying abroad, but domiciled in Canada; books, pictures, family plate or furniture, personal effects and heirlooms left by bequest $	....	39,107	....	39,107
Articles and other goods, the growth, produce, or manufacture of Canada, returned within five years after having been exported............................... $	....	718,652	....	718,652
Articles brought into Canada temporarily and for a period not exceeding three months for the purpose of exhibition or of competition for prizes offered by any agricultural or other association................................. $	....	415,662	....	....
Articles for the use of the Governor-General.............. $	....	9,874	....	9,874
Articles for the personal or official use of Consuls General who are natives or citizens of the Country they represent, and who are not engaged in any other business or profession...................................... $	....	7,749	....	7,765
Articles for the use of the Army and Navy, viz.: arms, military stores, munitions of war, and other articles the property of the Imperial Government and to remain the property of such Government; articles consigned direct to officers and men of His Majesty's Imperial Navy, for their own personal use or consumption, on board their own ships................................. $	....	3,205,295	....	3,210,698
Articles ex-warehoused for ship's stores................. $	....	....	....	967,173

No. 14.—Summary Statement of Imports—*Continued.*

Articles.		Imported.		Entered for Home Consumption.	
		Quantity.	Value.	Quantity.	Value.
FREE GOODS—MISCELLANEOUS ARTICLES—*Con.*			$		$
Articles for the Anglo-American Telegraph Company....	$	....	16	....	16
Articles presented from abroad in recognition of the saving of human life....................................	$	....	1,739	....	1,739
Bacteriological products or serum for subcutaneous injection..	$	....	107,568	....	107,568
Barrels or packages of Canadian manufacture which have been exported filled with Canadian products, when returned, or exported empty and returned filled with foreign products....................................	$	....	213,225	....	213,225
Bird skins and skins of animals not native to Canada, and fish skins for taxidermic purposes, not further manufactured than prepared for preservation................	$	....	723	....	723
Botanical, entomological, and mineralogical specimens...	$	....	2,276	....	2,276
Cabinets of coins, collections of medals, and collections of postage stamps..	$	....	2,577	....	2,577
Collections of antiquities when imported for or by public museums, public libraries, universities, colleges, or schools, and which are to be placed in such institutions	$	....	5,894	....	5,894
Clothing and books, donations of, for charitable purposes.	$	....	66,048	....	66,048
Casual donations from abroad sent by friends, not being advertising matter, tobacco, articles containing spirits or merchandise for sale—when the duty otherwise payable thereon does not exceed fifty cents in any one case —under regulations by the Minister of Customs........	$	....	414	....	414
Coffee, green, imported direct from the country of growth and production or purchased in bond in the United Kingdom (to August 22nd—See Dutiable Goods.)......Lb.		6,836,794	893,437	6,836,794	893,437
Ice...	$	....	17,561	....	.17,561
Models of inventions and other improvements in the Arts, but no article shall be deemed a model which can be fitted for use......................................	$	....	34,176	....	34,176
Paintings in oil or water colours, and pastels, valued at not less than twenty dollars each; paintings and sculptures by artists domiciled in Canada but residing temporarily abroad for purposes of study, under regulations by the Minister of Customs............................	$	....	452,981	....	452,981
Passover bread......................................	$	....	52,951	....	52,951
Photographs, press, for use only as newspaper pictures....	$	....	125	....	125
Settlers' effects.....................................	$	....	7,864,092	....	7,864,092
Specimens, models, and wall diagrams for illustrations of natural history for universities and public museums.....	$	....	7,084	....	7,084
Menageries, horses, cattle, carriages, and harness of......	$	....	1,068,296	....	2,641
Vaccine and ivory vaccine points.......................	$	....	13,471	....	13,471
Works of art in bronze cast from models made in Canada and designed by sculptors domiciled therein...........	$	....	22,100	....	22,100
Tea of Ceylon, black, imported direct or purchased in bond in the United Kingdom......................Lb.		15,282,407	2,999,434	15,282,407	2,999,434
Tea of Ceylon, green, imported direct or purchased in bond in the United Kingdom.....................	"	1,419,058	285,144	1,419,058	285,144
Tea of China, black, imported direct or purchased in bond in the United Kingdom............................	"	2,006,954	269,516	2,006,954	269,516
Tea of China, green, imported direct or purchased in bond in the United Kingdom........................	"	1,120,487	143,569	1,120,487	143,569
Tea of India, black, imported direct or purchased in bond in the United Kingdom............................	"	15,268,234	2,696,759	15,268,234	2,696,759
Tea of India, green, imported direct or purchased in bond in the United Kingdom............................	"	291,149	54,796	291,149	54,796
Tea of Japan, green, imported direct or purchased in bond in the United Kingdom............................	"	4,237,971	719,174	4,237,971	719,174
Tea of other countries, black, imported direct or purchased in bond in the United Kingdom......................	"	613,648	105,190	613,648	105,190
Tea of other countries, green, imported direct or purchased in bond in the United Kingdom...............	"	6,552	1,097	6,552	1,097
Total, tea......................................		40,246,460	7,274,679	40,246,460	7,274,679

No. 14.—Summary Statement of Imports—*Concluded.*

Articles.	Imported.		Entered for Home Consumption.	
	Quantity.	Value.	Quantity.	Value.
FREE GOODS—MISCELLANEOUS ARTICLES—*Con.*		$		$
Coins, British and Canadian and foreign gold coins....... $	....	117,055,024	....	117,055,024
Gold bullion in bars, blocks, ingots, drops, sheets or plates, unmanufactured.................................... $	....	14,428,372	....	14,428,372
Silver bullion, in bars, blocks, ingots, drops, sheets, or plates, unmanufactured............................ $	....	509,596	....	509,596
Total, coin and bullion............................	....	131,992,992	....	131,992,992
Rifles and cartridges for home guard................... $	....	67,942	....	67,942
Other free articles.................................. $	....	175,073	....	175,073
Total, miscellaneous................................	....	154,736,259	....	154,227,534
Total, Free goods..................................	....	310,493,800	....	307,647,109

No. 15.—STATEMENT showing the Value and Duty of Goods entered for Consumption in Canada during the twelve months ending March 31, 1914 and 1915 respectively; also the Value and Duty collected on Goods entered for Consumption from the "British Empire" and from "Other Countries," during the twelve months ending March 31, 1915.

COMPARATIVE AND BRITISH EMPIRE.

ARTICLES.	ENTERED FOR CONSUMPTION. Twelve months ending March 31, 1914.		Twelve months ending March 31, 1915.		ENTERED FOR CONSUMPTION DURING THE TWELVE Months ending March 31, 1915. From British Empire.		From Other Countries.	
	Value. $	Duty. $ cts.	Value. $	Duty. $ cts.	Value. $	Duty. $ cts.	Value. $	Duty. $ cts.
DUTIABLE GOODS.								
Ale, beer and porter	1,338,893	476,258 88	697,135	302,691 96	242,719	87,457 15	454,416	215,234 81
" ginger	34,014	5,150 93	27,743	4,211 41	25,972	3,901 45	1,771	309 96
Animals, living	1,552,390	387,733 98	727,331	181,574 55	5,753	1,265 85	721,578	180,308 70
Antiseptic surgical dressing	241,544	43,132 53	251,463	45,661 47	65,039	8,382 78	186,424	37,278 69
Bagatelle tables	10,700	3,442 29	7,633	2,505 62	1,360	310 07	6,273	2,195 55
Bags, cotton, containing cement, etc.	62,478	12,495 60	15,123	3,024 60			15,123	3,024 60
Baking powder	207,323	44,084 92	150,549	31,541 08	1,051	335 80	149,498	31,205 28
Balls, cues and racks for billiard tables	28,784	9,491 81	19,921	6,553 44	3,677	868 04	16,244	5,685 40
Baskets	159,548	45,490 98	93,923	26,364 24	14,139	2,993 51	79,784	23,370 73
Baths, bath tubs, basins closets, etc.	452,748	134,290 05	316,415	93,681 25	117,242	23,970 70	199,173	69,710 55
Belting, all kinds, except rubber and leather	478,388	110,753 69	247,912	56,557 16	156,028	31,288 40	91,884	25,268 76
Belts of all kinds, n.o.p., except silk	94,957	30,666 13	70,505	22,946 94	14,106	3,207 29	56,399	19,739 65
Bells and gongs, n.o.p.	53,520	15,736 63	35,624	10,514 56	4,936	1,009 60	31,688	9,504 96
Billiard tables	103,804	27,861 79	30,720	7,574 47	25,704	5,818 87	5,016	1,755 60
Blacking, shoe, leather dressing, etc., n.o.p.	133,047	32,731 45	128,223	30,803 78	35,987	5,437 68	92,236	25,366 10
Blinds of wood, etc., except textile or paper	6,656	1,973 90	3,497	1,044 80	43	8 60	3,454	1,036 20
Blueing, laundry	55,448	8,738 39	46,643	7,424 50	40,940	6,141 00	5,703	1,283 50
Boats, open, the, sail, skiffs and canoes	35,659	8,479 15	29,866	7,135 30	3,395	517 55	26,471	6,617 75
Books, periodicals and other printed matter	5,214,606	1,105,603 28	3,950,560	880,453 67	964,212	113,914 32	2,986,348	766,539 35
Boot, shoe, shirt and stay laces	248,891	61,879 66	142,535	36,265 85	59,953	12,259 47	82,582	24,006 38
Boots, shoes and slippers, except rubber, etc.	317,644	75,997 05	265,904	63,008 36	177,938	36,907 37	87,966	26,100 99
Braces or suspenders, and parts of	89,181	29,325 49	55,045	18,067 30	9,072	2,233 59	45,973	15,833 80
Brass and manufactures of	2,352,090	652,358 83	1,932,578	474,763 53	180,892	35,346 61	1,751,686	439,416 92
Breadstuffs, etc., viz.—								
Grain, flour and meal, etc.	1,409,226	288,295 57	1,081,214	239,452 23	601,309	126,921 68	479,905	112,530 55
Bricks, tiles and manufactures of clay, n.o.p.	2,620,177	349,324 34	4,822,093	667,894 30	183,774	27,879 61	4,638,319	640,014 59
British gum, dextrine, etc.	2,097,444	496,212 08	1,336,546	322,964 32	152,372	23,037 69	1,184,174	299,926 63
Brooms and brushes	54,991	4,912 60	36,174	3,222 60	7,898	394 90	28,276	2,827 60
Buttons	691,215	172,032 44	409,933	101,418 99	77,692	14,295 66	332,241	87,123 33
......	843,783	209,650 03	545,475	178,667 73	87,910	24,348 13	457,565	154,319 60
Cane, reed or rattan, split	91,268	20,958 60	96,163	22,618 15	14,697	2,251 65	81,466	20,366 50
......	6,977	697 70	8,844	883 87	3,710	370 47	5,131	513 40

No. 15.—STATEMENT showing the Value and Duty of Goods entered for Consumption, in Canada, &c.—Continued.

ARTICLES.	ENTERED FOR CONSUMPTION				ENTERED FOR CONSUMPTION DURING THE TWELVE MONTHS ENDING MARCH 31, 1915.			
	Twelve months ending March 31, 1914.		Twelve months ending March 31, 1915.		From British Empire.		From Other Countries.	
	Value.	Duty.	Value.	Duty.	Value.	Duty.	Value.	Duty.
	$	$ cts.	$	$ cts.	$	$ cts.	$	$ cts.
DUTIABLE GOODS.								
Carriages, all kinds, railway cars and parts, etc.	20,097,851	6,256,367 88	8,523,415	2,761,029 30	396,680	90,548 46	8,126,735	2,670,480 84
Carpets, n.o.p.	3,491	957 65	216	67 10	85	21 25	131	45 85
Carpet linings and stair pads	2,892	688 00	2,288	530 61	552	96 61	1,736	434 00
Carpet sweepers	23,702	7,103 70	43,940	13,178 50	35	7 00	43,905	13,171 50
Cash registers	210,260	63,078 00	121,177	36,353 10	.....	.....	121,177	36,353 10
... lied and manufactures of	79,794	13,176 46	61,293	10,062 74	11,294	1,737 28	49,999	8,325 46
Cement	352,134	74,035 24	132,492	27,968 51	35,054	6,413 66	97,438	21,554 85
..., prepared	46,982	8,201 06	39,841	6,953 70	1,105	174 38	38,736	6,779 32
Charcoal	86,562	15,148 57	95,925	16,786 87	1,143	24 23	95,783	16,762 64
Chicory	25,765	12,593 44	18,586	8,606 32	9,212	4,482 04	9,374	4,124 28
Church vestments	59,469	10,273 15	30,035	5,344 94	5,484	761 94	25,451	4,583 00
Cider	3,341	482 45	2,514	321 45	1,301	140 30	1,213	181 15
Clocks, clock keys and ...ments	679,382	198,459 61	366,369	107,154 30	33,978	7,527 98	332,391	99,626 32
Cloth, coated, for manufacture of sensitized cloth	11,451	1,550 05	6,460	831 15	2,757	275 70	3,703	555 45
Clothes wringers	34,215	11,962 38	26,144	9,145 63	43	9 68	26,101	9,135 35
Coal, ...nus and dust	26,140,676	6,144,582 56	16,135,920	3,943,406 53	38,230	3,963 14	16,097,690	3,939,443 39
Coa... mats and matting	32,780	6,499 05	14,019	2,912 01	7,827	1,435 73	6,192	1,476 28
Cocoanuts, etc.	22,853	3,428 76	12,944	2,908 46	2,713	508 02	10,231	2,400 44
Cocoanut, dessicated, etc.	102,304	21,581 66	62,275	19,619 61	61,000	19,330 36	1,275	289 25
Coco... chocolate paste, etc.	2,285,020	396,370 13	1,813,552	306,095 07	857,377	189,634 23	956,175	116,460 84
Coffee (see Free Goods)	316,222	41,041 49	1,046,588	273,259 19	133,580	25,408 34	913,008	247,850 85
Collars	211,615	70,963 16	123,608	42,809 33	33,337	8,923 75	90,361	33,885 58
Combs	174,646	53,713 06	126,687	36,479 05	63,486	14,568 19	63,201	21,910 86
...er and manufactures of	441,577	108,196 41	213,324	57,604 49	20,619	3,919 15	192,705	53,685 34
Cordage and twines of all ...	577,938	125,963 30	492,001	108,308 95	299,156	60,097 70	192,845	48,211 25
...ks and ther manufactures of cork wood	522,957	94,421 83	305,233	59,060 45	29,625	3,003 10	275,608	56,057 35
Corsets, clasps, etc.	668,336	233,080 01	536,439	186,547 08	14,117	3,786 50	522,322	182,760 58
Costumes and ... theatrical	7,205	1,901 83	8,322	1,924 99	21	3 15	8,301	1,921 84
Cotton, manufactures of	26,131,590	6,312,243 14	19,573,449	4,797,048 72	11,656,694	2,424,761 47	7,916,755	2,373,187 25
Crapes	11,612	1,638 75	8,434	1,203 97	7,435	1,019 20	999	184 77
Cuffs	993	345 90	.....	118 88	217	69 38	132	49 50
Curling stones	7,100	710 00	349	7 40	.....	.....	74	7 40
..., trimmed or untrimmed	594,841	167,297 71	389,272	109,116 51	253,067	72,572 03	106,205	36,544 48

Article								
Cyclometers and pedometers	70,065	17,511 61	50,262	12,553 29	204	38 79	50,058	12,514 50
Drugs, dyes, chemicals and medicines	4,778,071	967,479 59	4,635,418	926,046 35	1,322,368	246,496 36	3,313,050	679,549 99
Earthenware and china	3,131,305	681,662 31	1,940,765	425,834 10	1,136,326	189,412 68	804,439	236,421 42
Eggs	2,630,364	338,121 80	1,005,976	135,626 18	20,277	2,695 58	985,699	132,930 60
Elastic	148,249	40,047 23	134,306	35,726 55	113,341	28,388 85	20,965	7,337 70
Electric light carbons and carbon points	58,844	30,934 56	47,104	15,977 51	1,032	279 08	46,072	15,698 43
Incandescent lamp, lbs, etc.	131,565	13,086 10	71,765	7,159 00	1,396	122 10	70,369	7,036 90
Electric apparatus, bars, &c.	8,404,501	2,193,622 19	5,693,512	1,478,635 00	712,567	110,535 46	4,980,945	1,368,099 56
Embroideries	121,174	37,898 25	48,317	15,176 01	11,521	3,205 50	36,796	11,970 51
Emery and manufactures of emery	124,353	31,065 39	86,027	21,467 02	798	159 77	85,229	21,307 25
Express parcels	2,103,138	593,580 21	1,825,184	515,293 58	2,426	520 19	1,822,758	514,773 39
Fancy goods	4,870,431	1,362,172 15	3,175,566	878,039 74	1,254,562	303,970 44	1,921,004	574,069 30
Feathers, bed	121,070	23,896 37	39,320	6,537 72	16,331	2,872 45	22,989	3,665 27
Featherbone	37	4 78	1,204	240 80	33	6 60	1,171	234 20
Fertilizers	602,142	58,248 15	714,584	68,964 60	51,023	2,608 50	663,561	66,356 10
Fibreware	159,714	39,569 46	102,100	25,180 18	4,649	817 43	97,451	24,362 75
Silks	28,727	6,820 87	24,670	6,038 43	7,830	1,828 43	16,840	4,210 00
Fish	1,558,663	337,695 07	1,155,186	245,457 52	230,768	46,126 16	904,418	199,331 36
Flax, hemp, jute, and manufactures of	3,298,599	649,443 09	4,345,123	670,818 76	3,581,991	544,596 47	763,132	126,222 29
Foundry facings	19,556	4,801 30	9,746	2,416 00	205	30 75	9,541	2,385 25
Fruits and nuts	9,281,475	1,753,864 03	8,180,858	1,577,662 22	336,645	92,348 76	7,844,213	1,485,313 46
Fur, iron and other material	3,049,874	890,111 67	1,506,756	441,293 39	141,251	32,225 19	1,365,505	409,068 20
Furs and manufactures of	1,419,575	275,226 55	777,564	154,701 45	282,367	53,001 15	495,197	101,700 30
Fuses, n.o.p.	140,718	19,572 47	90,203	12,828 08	69,501	8,687 08	20,702	4,140 40
Glass and	5,045,262	1,103,626 35	3,497,873	734,531 37	758,380	115,663 74	2,739,493	618,857 63
Gloves and mitts, manufactures of	2,722,130	792,831 85	1,768,106	515,335 71	763,064	186,364 56	1,005,022	328,971 15
Gold and silver, manufactures of	969,182	265,983 02	560,786	152,461 07	331,735	74,769 89	229,031	77,691 28
Grease, axle, and other	206,392	41,008 30	136,374	27,158 60	1,707	225 29	134,667	26,933 40
Gunpowder and other	1,113,972	240,552 60	1,048,829	227,356 09	307,466	52,757 75	741,363	174,598 34
Gutta percha and india rubber, manufactures of	4,690,292	1,290,546 67	3,261,260	926,541 86	1,058,813	222,068 05	2,292,447	704,473 81
Hair and manufactures of, not otherwise provided for	163,215	39,875 44	100,706	24,694 43	51,897	11,363 18	48,809	13,331 25
Hats, caps and bonnets	4,862,790	1,408,017 29	3,112,807	932,906 19	1,303,166	299,531 84	1,809,641	633,374 35
Hay	288,023	39,846 00	208,294	32,156 00			208,294	32,156 00
Honey in the comb or otherwise and imitations thereof	55,985	13,485 97	19,661	4,604 71	2,405	668 65	17,256	3,936 06
Hops	579,871	133,455 28	278,310	91,622 28	31,973	5,561 97	246,337	86,060 31
Inks	158,739	30,692 98	131,987	25,138 94	33,810	4,717 81	98,177	20,421 13
Iron and steel and manufactures of (see also Free Goods)	99,070,033	21,412,742 64	51,463,043	11,582,741 67	4,398,957	759,474 46	47,064,086	10,823,267 21
Iron, manufactures of	2,091	358 03	2,274	396 90	60	9 38	2,214	387 52
Jellies, jams and preserves	580,490	147,226 67	402,145	119,536 56	379,616	114,234 64	22,529	5,301 92
Jewellery	1,755,131	558,054 35	898,076	290,096 10	196,749	47,562 10	701,327	242,534 00
Knitted goods of every description	180,540	46,830 08	122,967	33,050 82	78,505	18,089 12	44,462	15,561 70
steam, gasoline or other motive power	89,351	22,337 75	35,309	8,747 55	797	119 55	34,512	8,628 00
Lead, and	709,591	108,084 70	797,070	130,212 93	156,873	22,570 98	640,197	107,641 95
Leather, and manufactures of	8,454,176	1,886,479 15	7,058,912	1,552,731 77	1,186,806	191,005 78	5,872,106	1,361,725 99
Lime	243,700	42,641 18	185,592	32,475 52	145	21 75	185,447	32,453 77
Lime juice	177,430	33,816 81	195,066	37,676 97	64,047	10,232 43	131,019	27,544 54

No. 15.—STATEMENT showing the Value and Duty of Goods entered for Consumption in Canada, &c.—Continued.

ARTICLES.	ENTERED FOR CONSUMPTION.				ENTERED FOR CONSUMPTION DURING THE TWELVE MONTHS ENDING MARCH 31, 1915.			
	Twelve months ending March 31, 1914.		Twelve months ending March 31, 1915.		From British Empire.		From Other Countries.	
	Value.	Duty.	Value.	Duty.	Value.	Duty.	Value.	Duty.
DUTIABLE GOODS.	$	$ cts.	$	$ cts.	$	$ cts.	$	$ cts.
Lithographic stones, not engraved	7,336	1,460 15	3,014	595 30	100	12 50	2,914	582 80
Machine c...d clothing	47,407	9,735 99	37,175	7,647 86	21,978	3,848 61	15,197	3,799 25
Magic lanterns and slides therefor	1,214,428	301,271 26	1,305,571	323,243 66	43,049	7,737 44	1,262,522	315,506 22
Malt, malt flour, etc	244,051	47,063 94	84,786	15,456 06	8,036	1,770 13	76,750	13,685 93
" extract, ...tes of	64,665	22,632 75	78,095	51,197 58	16,087	10,247 87	62,008	40,949 71
Marble and ...tes of	531,329	126,862 20	407,553	94,847 85	13,150	4,304 70	394,403	90,543 15
Mattresses	7,694	2,248 20	4,640	1,367 00	475	117 50	4,165	1,249 50
Mats, door or carriage, other than metal, n.o.p.	21,618	7,515 30	530	168 10	184	47 00	346	121 10
...is and...es of	5,196,756	1,452,888 97	3,324,533	956,974 94	391,998	73,186 92	2,932,535	883,788 02
Milk and cream, fresh and condensed	275,188	55,188 64	86,898	17,569 13	1,531	404 17	85,367	17,164 96
Mineral and...his...	758,744	166,291 22	445,049	93,627 44	55,141	8,477 32	389,908	85,150 12
Mineral and...bars	258,798	44,361 74	193,574	33,305 16	25,270	3,851 50	168,304	29,453 66
Mucilage	34,306	8,907 38	35,833	9,459 71	3,978	698 63	31,855	8,761 08
...al instruments	2,038,559	582,894 43	1,358,513	390,006 32	74,659	15,458 94	1,283,854	374,547 38
Mustard and mustard cake	224,863	44,940 51	211,542	42,837 31	169,153	29,723 84	42,389	13,113 47
Oils, all kinds	4,369,635	998,947 73	3,197,233	707,556 46	280,565	35,257 86	2,936,668	672,298 60
Oilcloths of all kinds, cork matting and linoleum	2,314,378	591,351 05	1,292,890	336,522 05	955,172	229,682 75	337,648	106,839 30
Optical, philosophical, photographic and mathematical instruments	1,069,454	242,306 15	843,770	195,453 08	178,821	32,338 84	664,949	163,114 24
Packages	3,144,972	654,822 99	2,123,533	436,444 59	1,219,176	206,500 33	904,357	229,944 26
Paints and colours	1,673,027	270,596 29	1,175,319	193,136 68	302,690	48,620 81	872,629	144,505 87
Paintings, oil, or water colours and pastels	4,273	875 35	2,285	485 25	1,106	190 50	1,179	294 75
Paper and manufactures of	7,897,919	2,192,009 44	5,678,343	1,584,124 49	1,258,482	255,540 04	4,419,861	1,328,584 45
Pencils, lead	360,218	96,114 38	261,548	69,302 33	33,796	6,842 80	227,752	62,459 53
Pens, penholders and rulers	213,954	46,484 62	132,956	29,065 98	62,579	9,724 89	70,377	19,341 09
Perfumery, non-alcoholic	539,491	172,605 09	449,578	143,395 73	413 45	10,716 72	408,233	132,679 01
Photographic dry plates	62,364	14,423 80	55,592	12,613 20	41,830	8,454 60	13,762	4,128 60
Picture and photograph frames	169,157	47,710 09	110,853	31,125 79	21,545	4,413 29	89,308	26,712 50
Pickles	424,576	110,729 02	288,910	74,458 01	204,370	51,343 55	84,540	23,114 46
Plants and trees	445,919	88,227 05	309,823	59,336 76	16,067	2,297 09	293,756	57,039 67
Plaster of Paris	138,321	42,605 71	43,602	16,304 08	1,624	166 66	46,978	16,137 42
Plates, ...ed on wood or metal	67,470	12,923 80	88,039	17,180 25	9,324	1,437 25	78,715	15,743 00
Pocket-books, purses, ...co pouches, etc	665,039	217,920 72	370,375	122,079 32	61,253	15,013 17	309,122	107,066 15

Article								
Polish or composition, knife or other	229,517	48,886 45	175,441	36,013 49	98,521	14,859 27	76,920	21,154 22
Pomades	346	43 26	472	59 01			472	59 01
Post office parcels	1,569,506	429,786 46	1,419,934	395,709 48	310,018	76,794 97	1,109,916	318,914 51
Precious stones	346,653	30,625 10	167,544	15,090 81	83,226	6,659 01	84,318	8,431 80
Provisions:—								
Butter, cheese and lard	2,915,242	412,646 98	2,213,180	323,334 02	1,363,240	175,020 72	849,940	148,313 30
Meats, all kinds	5,267,853	1,081,044 59	2,716,338	578,802 86	513,851	121,620 93	2,202,487	457,181 93
Pulleys, belt	105,031	28,008 64	54,470	14,424 56	4,500	682 00	49,970	13,742 56
Regalia and badges	67,304	21,404 04	46,538	13,989 70	19,229	4,431 55	27,309	9,558 15
Ribbons	1,820,037	476,165 86	1,761,857	464,914 05	670,057	169,051 48	1,091,800	295,904 98
Sails	6,079	1,265 65	4,907	914 05	3,134	470 80	1,773	443 25
Salt	149,043	36,089 32	152,760				152,760	38,903 48
ags, barrels, etc., containing salt	17,993	4,398 25	20,524				20,524	5,131 00
Sand paper, glass, flint and emery papers	172,427	41,835 75	126,170	30,863 70	7,468	1,188 20	118,702	29,675 50
Sauces, catsups and soy	324,214	96,626 59	276,570	83,749 61	145,259	37,825 56	131,311	45,924 05
Sausage casings	162,376	26,800 37	174,445	28,852 92	91,706	14,373 36	82,739	14,479 56
Seeds	1,369,891	136,833 30	2,058,802	199,121 60	223,799	13,282 00	1,835,003	185,839 60
Ships, vessels and repairs on	1,001,764	250,441 00	707,446	31,722 80			707,446	176,861 50
ies of any material and letters for signs	172,007	48,660 10	113,874		25,425	5,188 10	88,449	26,534 70
Silk and manufactures of	9,250,996	2,196,680 58	7,684,180	1,811,916 44	2,544,421	557,775 23	5,139,759	1,254,141 22
Slate	236,038	53,821 05	188,080	40,680 25	15,273	1,823 75	172,807	38,856 50
Soap	1,320,872	338,603 29	1,191,707	298,231 56	121,082	25,450 17	1,070,625	272,781 39
Spices	403,079	51,563 40	379,513	51,206 75	248,077	29,632 71	131,436	21,574 04
Spirits	5,820,463	9,125,364 60	4,563,606	340,219 07	2,767,195	4,476,451 77	1,796,451	3,660,165 83
" wines, non-sparkling	809,479	409,281 38	632,275	68,951 72	80,034	78,765 24	552,241	66,217 00
ms, sparkling	762,393	146,743 01	363,409	12,452 50	13,847	2,734 72	349,562	11,163 26
Sponges of marine production	95,927	16,402 67	72,928	40,955 64	9,142	1,289 24	63,786	34,028 23
Starch	104,080	38,264 42	106,740		28,498	6,927 26	78,242	
Stockinettes, for the manufacture of rubber boots	70,474	9,230 90	6,659	10,401 60	21,945	2,194 50	54,714	8,207 10
Stone and manufactures of	1,002,261	213,950 35	595,171	139,093 16	206,291	56,621 26	388,880	82,471 90
Straw and manufactures of	91,382	19,900 67	73,311	15,969 80	3,573	716 00	69,738	15,253 80
Sugars	15,062,627	3,693,226 67	16,781,753	5,401,091 07	9,181,166	2,668,073 81	7,600,587	2,733,017 26
" syrups and molasses	138,687	21,694 86	120,772	21,411 32	35,678	2,793 82	85,094	18,617 50
" sugar cane, shredded	1,959	342 85	1,277	223 49	1,180	206 51	97	16 98
" candy, confectionery, etc	1,043,115	280,476 18	724,104	218,186 07	472,381	123,332 82	251,723	94,853 25
" glucose, maple sugar and syrup	107,052	28,463 11	120,630	28,003 60	1,812	144 81	118,818	27,838 79
Surgical trusses, pessaries and bandages	63,252	12,000 80	44,183	8,419 46	5,928	778 16	38,255	7,641 30
Tallow	23,875	3,956 00	16,516	2,695 55	12,676	1,927 55	3,840	768 00
he lines of any material and yarn for the manufacture of	13,933	2,655 12	8,531	1,825 89	4,018	756 14	4,513	1,069 75
Tea (see Free Goods)	55,038	5,505 80	89,571	8,957 10	9,261	926 10	80,310	8,031 00
Tin and manufactures of	659,586	152,535 10	591,816	136,464 40	117,092	17,783 40	474,724	118,681 00
bacco, pipes, etc	1,289,537	1,532,023 35	1,082,890	1,009,197 45	442,967	337,166 95	639,923	622,030 50
trawling spoons, etc	808,802	257,375 54	400,079	115,864 95	205,985	51,164 39	194,094	64,700 56
Tes, valises, hat bs, etc	56,688	15,831 95	46,899	13,413 03	24,738	5,663 92	22,141	7,749 35
Twine and manufactures of	149,870	41,878 22	66,021	18,249 03	16,899	3,547 25	49,122	14,701 78
ms, parasols and sunshades	76,591	19,576 60	46,521	12,847 80	11,298	2,265 90	35,273	10,581 90
Unenumerated articles	98,376	25,407 50	77,603	20,276 23	55,677	12,602 13	21,926	7,674 10
	866,788	149,131 88	671,777	115,896 77	97,799	15,447 88	573,978	100,448 89

11—i—12

No. 15.—STATEMENT showing the Value and Duty of Goods entered for Consumption in Canada, &c.—*Continued.*

ARTICLES	ENTERED FOR CONSUMPTION				ENTERED FOR CONSUMPTION DURING THE TWELVE MONTHS ENDING MARCH 31, 1915.			
	Twelve months ending March 31, 1914.		Twelve months ending March 31, 1915.		From British Empire.		From Other Countries.	
	Value.	Duty.	Value.	Duty.	Value.	Duty.	Value.	Duty.
	$	$ cts.	$	$ cts.	$	$ cts.	$	$ cts.
DUTIABLE GOODS.								
Varnish, lacquers, japans, &c	167,326	52,193 83	125,364	38,333 46	37,880	9,235 64	87,484	29,097 82
Vegetables	3,306,930	886,839 02	3,039,359	830,197 71	208,663	58,671 74	2,830,696	771,525 97
Vinegar	83,001	24,895 00	66,137	20,743 01	58,931	14,990 30	7,206	5,752 71
Waste or shoddy of cotton, wool, etc	466,438	48,270 42	288,850	30,928 98	110,432	8,625 84	178,418	22,303 14
Watches, watch cases, garments, etc	1,574,261	251,154 08	876,179	137,655 20	96,059	17,824 21	780,120	119,830 99
Wax and manufactures of	295,244	44,439 93	224,513	32,783 14	33,846	4,496 48	190,667	28,286 66
Wig	235,038	44,138 46	166,895	32,010 84	18,540	2,339 84	148,355	29,671 00
Whips, thongs and lashes	26,010	7,360 80	25,803	7,327 40	4,282	871 10	21,521	6,456 30
Window ...ils, poles, etc	92,192	24,356 80	53,532	14,301 85	33,342	7,499 85	20,190	6,802 0
Wood and ...es of	4,630,187	1,099,407 94	3,163,325	752,829 46	136,515	26,046 74	3,026,810	726,782 72
Wool and ...es of	28,459,250	7,934,461 92	19,723,162	5,577,969 74	16,069,294	4,323,285 05	3,653,878	1,254,684 69
Zinc and manufactures of	49,455	12,218 65	30,386	7,496 10	2,356	438 60	28,030	7,007 50
Damaged goods	53,384	11,817 34	51,612	11,876 94	3,313	361 24	48,299	11,515 70
Prepaid p stal packages, duty received by ...ns from Post Office Department	128,270	35,933 28	74,941	21,262 46	74,941	21,262 46		
Total	410,258,744	106,594,569 56	279,792,19	76,088,308 17	80,410,450	22,057,155 38	199,381,745	54,031,152 79
Special duty on articles shipped to Canada at lower than usual home trade price		92,425 87		68,296 47				68,296 47
Additional duties		493,582 90		410,832 60				410,832 60
War tax				2,638,473 03		402,182 87		2,236,290 16
Grand total	410,258,744	107,180,578 33	279,792,195	79,205,910 27	80,410,450	22,459,338 25	199,381,745	56,746,572 02

SESSIONAL PAPER No. 11

No. 15.—Free Goods.

ARTICLES.	Entered for Consumption.		Entered for Consumption during the twelve months ending March 31st, 1915.	
	Twelve months ending March 31st, 1914.	Twelve months ending March 31st, 1915.	From British Empire.	From other Countries.
	Value.	Value.	Value.	Value.
FREE GOODS.	$	$	$	$
PRODUCE OF THE MINE.				
Clay.................................	319,985	267,888	66,642	201,246
Coal, anthracite........................	20,734,126	20,927,539	129,885	20,797,654
Gravel and sand........................	419,720	215,933	6,757	209,176
Minerals...............................	708,566	596,861	17,756	579,105
Ores..................................	5,010,880	2,596,654	374,331	2,222,323
Precious stones, viz:—				
Diamonds unset, diamond dust, etc...............	2,986,507	1,682,623	1,210,829	471,794
Salt..................................	414,825	364,850	258,883	105,967
Whiting...............................	102,993	87,499	22,400	65,099
Other articles.........................	575,373	490,024	144,584	345,440
Total........................	31,272,975	27,229,871	2,232,067	24,997,804
THE FISHERIES.				
Fish from Newfoundland................	635,231	568,880	568,880	....
Fish-oil from Newfoundland............	64,633	63,084	63,084	....
Other articles.........................	73,245	69,148	3,571	65,577
Total...........................	773,109	701,112	635,535	65,577
THE FOREST.				
Cork wood............................	34,212	21,252	539	20,713
Ivory nuts............................	70,222	23,067	....	23,067
Fence posts and railroad ties..........	2,326,843	1,255,137	10	1,255,127
Logs and round unmanufactured timber............	679,816	485,953	10,892	475,061
Lumber and timber, planks, boards, etc............	12,306,865	6,919,129	14,643	6,904,486
Other articles.........................	783,654	541,620	59	541,561
Total...........................	16,201,612	9,246,158	26,143	9,220,015
ANIMALS AND THEIR PRODUCE.				
Animals, for improvement of stock...........	959,195	497,475	137,909	359,566
Bristles...............................	214,998	132,040	61,019	71,021
Fur skins, not dressed.................	2,241,877	1,328,864	83,062	1,245,802
Grease................................	881,544	846,213	14,377	831,836
Hides and skins, undressed............	8,777,694	12,828,215	3,746,205	9,082,010
Pelts, raw............................	53,297	14,238	4,022	10,216
Silk, raw.............................	335,385	314,480	....	314,480
Wool.................................	1,872,089	3,717,039	1,506,545	2,210,494
Other articles.........................	771,014	763,516	186,404	577,112
Total...........................	16,107,093	20,442,080	5,739,543	14,702,537
AGRICULTURAL PRODUCTS.				
Broom corn...........................	324,590	285,574	61	285,513
Cocoa beans, not roasted, crushed or ground.........	447,026	326,748	326,748	....
Cotton wool, or raw cotton, not dyed...............	9,752,437	6,533,631	183	6,533,448
Fibre, Mexican and vegetable................	123,302	118,192	16,049	102,143
Fruits, green..........................	7,351,282	6,864,564	69,572	6,794,992
Hemp.................................	448,970	318,914	42,165	276,749
Indian corn...........................	3,950,934	6,734,199	66	6,734,133
Manila grass..........................	1,384,031	1,883,551	39,579	1,843,972
Rice, uncleaned, unhulled or paddy............	1,137,009	1,205,833	862,171	343,662
Seeds.................................	285,426	289,699	139,594	150,105
Tobacco (for Excise)..................	5,109,641	4,718,488	30,226	4,688,262
Other articles.........................	583,329	455,015	102,285	352,730
Total...........................	30,897,977	29,734,408	1,628,699	28,105,709

6 GEORGE V, A. 1916

No. 15.—Free Goods—*Concluded.*

ARTICLES.	Entered for Consumption.		Entered for Consumption during the twelve months ending March 31st, 1915.	
	Twelve months ending March 31st, 1914.	Twelve months ending March 31st, 1915.	From British Empire.	From other Countries.
	Value.	Value.	Value.	Value.
	$	$	$	$
FREE GOODS—*Concluded.*				
MANUFACTURED AND PARTIALLY MANUFACTURED ARTICLES.				
Artificial teeth, not mounted........................	182,725	167,086	12,598	154,488
Asphaltum or asphalt..............................	833,622	635,204	2,297	632,907
Bells, for churches.................................	73,545	60,063	13,279	46,784
Binder twine......................................	3,779,589	2,738,274	86,823	2,651,451
Books, maps, etc..................................	1,248,497	1,180,009	406,616	773,393
Brick, fire, for manufactures.......................	850,718	482,763	48,375	434,388
Coke..	2,074,474	1,445,836	844	1,444,992
Drugs, dyes and chemicals.........................	10,548,541	9,487,358	1,804,747	7,682,611
Fish hooks, nets, seines, etc.......................	1,333,737	1,368,151	691,998	676,153
Jute cloth, yarn and canvas........................	5,122,932	1,636,162	1,498,328	137,834
Metals, viz.:—				
Brass...	1,843,469	815,348	40,923	774,425
Copper..	6,139,908	3,347,531	15,093	3,332,438
Iron and steel.................................	15,654,542	10,822,381	2,981,633	7,840,748
Tin...	2,146,860	1,159,068	503,395	655,673
Zinc..	869,963	911,428	24,595	886,833
Other (items made up of more than one metal).....	5,018,701	4,223,045	807,124	3,415,921
Molasses..	1,595,956	1,284,246	1,284,246	....
Newspapers and magazines.........................	1,297,399	1,425,848	82,137	1,343,711
Noils...	1,072,066	1,312,885	1,033,504	279,381
Oil cake and meal, cotton seed cake and meal, palm nut cake and meal..............................	138,224	331,639	10,554	321,085
Oil, cocoanut and palm............................	365,796	353,285	140,993	212,292
Oil, crude cotton seed, for manufacture of refined cotton seed oil.................................	1,316,958	1,327,386	....	1,327,386
Oil, gasoline, under ·725 specific gravity.............	4,466,986	2,828,383	....	2,828,383
Oil, petroleum, crude, fuel and gas.................	5,994,318	5,230,497	276	5,230,221
Rags..	1,423,458	1,244,469	141,797	1,102,672
Resin or rosin.....................................	572,062	444,601	27,848	416,753
Rubber, etc.......................................	4,303,751	4,505,275	1,512,574	2,992,701
Surgical and dental instruments, operating tables, etc.	533,273	393,341	30,032	363,309
Turpentine, crude and spirits of....................	479,883	461,099	582	460,517
Yarns, n.o.p......................................	1,271,730	1,172,712	845,154	327,558
Other articles.....................................	3,948,238	3,270,573	713,040	2,557,533
Total..............................	86,501,921	66,065,946	14,761,405	51,304,541
MISCELLANEOUS.				
Articles, Canadian, returned within five years........	694,688	718,652	149,114	569,538
Articles, for Army and Navy.......................	372	3,210,698	483,393	2,727,305
Articles, Ex-warehoused, for ships' stores............	1,041,782	967,173	39,565	927,608
Coffee (see dutiable goods)........................	2,060,231	893,437	172,167	721,270
Models of inventions..............................	50,294	34,176	6,289	27,887
Paintings in oil and water colours..................	927,999	452,981	173,401	279,580
Settlers' effects...................................	14,348,441	7,864,092	2,487,426	5,376,666
Tea (see dutiable goods)...........................	6,594,658	7,274,679	6,168,067	1,106,612
Coin and bullion..................................	15,235,305	131,992,992	5,022	131,987,970
Other articles.....................................	725,248	818,654	229,442	589,212
Total..............................	41,679,018	154,227,534	9,913,886	144,313,648
Total Free.......................	223,433,705	307,647,109	34,937,278	272,709,831
Total Dutiable...................	410,258,744	279,792,195	80,410,450	199,381,745
Grand Total......................	633,692,449	587,439,304	115,347,728	472,091,576.

No. 16.—STATEMENT of Goods Imported from British and Foreign West Indies (including Guiana) during the Fiscal Year ended March 31, 1915.

DUITABLE GOODS.	FROM BRITISH WEST INDIES AND BRITISH GUIANA.		FROM FOREIGN WEST INDIES AND FOREIGN GUIANA.		TOTAL FROM WEST INDIES AND GUIANA.	
	Quantity.	Value.	Quantity.	Value.	Quantity.	Value.
		$		$		$
Animals, viz:—						
" Horses, n.o.p........ No.	1	85	....	....	1	· 85
" living all other, n.o.p...... $	....	25	....	....		25
Baskets, all kinds, n.o.p............ $	....	43	....	....	....	43
Advertising pamphlets, show cards, price lists, etc................... Lb	40	5	....	....	40	5
Arrowroot.......................... "	51,510	2,683	....	....	51,510	2,683
Biscuits, sweetened................ "	348	31	....	....	348	31
Rice and sago flour, cassava flour, and rice meal................... "	244	5	....	....	244	5
Cattle food containing molasses..... $	....	193	....	....		193
Cereal foods prepared, in packages, not exceeding 25 lbs, each........ Lb	207	10	....	....	207	10
Bicycles and tricycles, n.o.p.......No.	2	24	....	....	2	24
Cider, clarified or refined.........Gal	....	....	14	14	14	14
Cocoanuts:—						
" imported direct.........No.	84,270	2,091	746	24	85,016	2,115
" n.o.p.................... "	- 22,223	622	....	....	22,223	622
Cocoa beans, not roasted, crushed or ground..................... Cwt	255	2,267	....	....	255	2,267
Coffee, green, n.o.p............... Lb	64	15	....	....	64	15
" green, imported direct..... "	181,649	21,370	....	....	181,649	21,370
" roasted or ground and imitations thereof, etc, n.o.p......... "	72	18	....	....	72	18
Cotton, handkerchiefs.............. $	....	3	....	....		3
" sheets, bed quilts, etc..... $	....	1	....	....		1
C. C. or cream coloured ware, etc., n.o.p............................. $	....	2	....	....		2
Tableware of china, etc............. $	....	24	....	....		24
Fancy Goods, viz:—						
" boxes..................... $	....	21	....	....		21
" ians...................... $	....	2	....	....		2
" feathers, undressed......... $	....	....	....	180	....	180
" " and manufactures of, n.o.p..................... $	....	25	....	....		25
Feathers bed, undressed........... $	....	756	....	....		756
Bags or sacks of hemp, linen or jute.. $	....	160	....	....	....	160
Uncoloured damask of linen, etc.... $	....	112	....	....		112
Handkerchiefs of linen............. $	....	3	....	....		3
Fruits, including nuts, viz:—						
Figs............................Lb	123	7	....	....	123	· 7
Raisins.......................... "	96,919	· 3,896	....	....	96,919	3,896
All other, n.o.p., dried frutis....... "	214	18	....	....	214	18
Pecans not shelled, and shelled peanuts, n.o.p.................... "	260	8	26,499	1,241	26,759	1,249
All other nuts, n.o.p., not shelled.. "	358	20	....	....	358	20
" " shelled............. "	460	104	....	....	460	104
" green fruits, n.o.p......... "		211	....	....		211
Fruits in air-tight cans, etc....... Lb	87,963	6,585	....	....	87,963	6,585
Furniture........................ $	....	249		2	....	251
Gas carboys and demijohns........ $	....	548	....	....		548
Hats, beaver, silk or felt........... $	....	33	....	....		33
" grass, straw, etc.............. $	....	4,425	....	....		4,425
Honey in the comb................ Lb	21,715	1,054	....	....	21,715	1,054
Iron, ploughs and parts of.......... $	....	....		35	....	35
Iron, cast scrap iron................Ton	38	558	....	....	38	558
Iron·or steel tubing, plain or galvanized, etc., n.o.p............. $	....	610	....	....		610
Iron or steel scrap, wrought, crop ends, etc......................Cwt	2,002	1,020	....	....	2,002	1,020
Jellies and jams...................Lb	976	167	....	....	976	167

6 GEORGE V, A. 1916

No. 16.—STATEMENT of Goods Imported from British and Foreign West Indies,
&c.—*Continued.*

DUTIABLE GOODS.	FROM BRITISH WEST INDIES AND BRITISH GUIANA.		FROM FOREIGN WEST INDIES AND FOREIGN GUIANA.		TOTAL FROM WEST INDIES AND GUIANA.	
	Quantity.	Value.	Quantity.	Value.	Quantity.	Value.
		$		$		$
Lime juice, crude................ Gal.	3,907	1,111	....	....	3,907	1,111
" etc., n.o.p.............. "	11	8	....	....	11	8
Mineral and aerated waters, n.o.p... $	....	115	....	....	....	115
Oils, cotton seed, n.o.p............ Gal	387	432	....	....	387	432
" essential, n.o.p.............. "	240	430	....	....	240	430
Packages......................... $	....	6,373	....	2,328	....	8,701
Pickles, in bottles............... Gal.	13	24	....	....	13	24
Precious stones and imitations there-of.......................... $	....	30	....	....		30
Extracts of meats, fluid beef, etc., Soups of all kinds.............. $	....	3	....	....		3
Sauces and catsups in bottles...... Gal	....	1	....	....		1
Silk fabrics, n.o.p................ $	....	13	....	....		13
" handkerchiefs............... $	....	10	....	....		10
" manufactures of, n.o.p........ $	....	212	....	....		212
Soap, n.o.p., sapolio, etc.......... $	....	45	....	....		45
Spices, ginger, n.o.p., unground...... Lb.	369,317	15,340	....	....	369,317	15,340
" " preserved............ "	34	12	....	....	34	12
" nutmegs and mace, whole or unground................ "	76,151	8,122	....	....	76,151	8,122
Spirits, cordials and liqueurs, etc., n.o.p...................... Gal	122	739	....	....	122	739
" rum..................... "	124,645	44,100	....	....	124,645	44,100
" alcoholic, perfumes, etc.,under 4 ounces............... "	5	121	....	....	5	121
" alcoholic perfumes, etc., over 4 ounces............... "	35	59	124	177	169	236
Sponges of marine production....... $	....	....	....	566		566
Starch, etc...................... Lb.	11,258	487	....	....	11,258	487
Straw, carpeting, rugs........... $	....	2	....	....		2
Sugar..........................Lb.	283,786,077	7,042,387	192,718,704	4,923,281	476,504,781	11,965,668
Molasses........................ $	....	2,576	....	1		2,577
Sugar candy, and confectionery of all kinds......................... Lb.	19	5	....	....	19	5
Tobacco, cigarettes............... "	252	217	571	1,732	823	1,949
" cigars................... "	391	1,450	91,291	377,036	91,682	378,486
" cut..................... "	....	....	306	94	306	94
Trunks, valises, etc.............. $	....	....	....	5		5
Unenumerated articles............ $	....	152	....	....		152
Vegetables, potatoes, n.o.p........Bush	151	222	....	....	151	222
" " sweet and yams.. "	12	8	....	....	12	8
" tomatoes fresh........... "	1,166	595	....	....	1,166	595
" n.o.p................. $	....	756	....	....		756
Wood, barrels, empty.............No.	421	253	....	....	421	253
" manufactures of............. $	....	3	....	....		3
" walking sticks, canes, etc..... $	....	7	....	....		7
Total, Dutiable Goods............	....	7,176,529	....	5,306,716	....	12,483,245

SESSIONAL PAPER No. 11

No. 16.—STATEMENT of Goods Imported from British and Foreign West Indies &c.—*Concluded.*

FREE GOODS.	FROM BRITISH WEST INDIES AND BRITISH GUIANA.		FROM FOREIGN WEST INDIES AND FOREIGN GUIANA.		TOTAL FROM WEST INDIES AND GUIANA.	
	Quantity.	Value.	Quantity.	Value.	Quantity.	Value.
		$		$		$
Salt.............................Cwt	232,107	21,153	....	....	232,107	21,153
Tortoise and other shells unmanufactured..............................$	....	86	....	....	....	86
Logs and round unmanufactured timber...........................$	....	3,106	....	....	....	3,106
Lumber:—						
" mahogany...................$	....	....	....	16	....	16
" african, teak, etc..........$	....	630	....	....	....	630
Fur skins of all kinds not dressed, n.o.p...............................$	....	2,287	....	....	....	2,287
Hides and skins, raw...............Lb.	556,143	76,005	....	....	556,143	76,005
Cocoa beans not roasted, etc........ "	1,822,253	205,328	....	....	1,822,253	205,328
Cocoanuts, imported direct..........No	3,482,039	70,814	....	....	3,482,039	70,814
Bananas.......................Bunch	800	452	400	237	1,200	689
Lemons and limes..................$	....	140	....	....	....	140
Oranges and shaddocks.............$	....	17,384	....	13,240	....	30,624
Pineapples........................$	....	120	....	2,421	....	2,541
Foots, refuse of the cotton seed or olives.........................Cwt.	....	....	389	681	389	681
Tobacco, unmanufactured for excise purposes.........................Lb.	....	....	400,549	165,340	400,549	165,340
Dyeing or tanning articles, crude n.o.p.............................. "	1,320	8	....	....	1,320	8
Drugs, crude, barks, flowers, etc....$	....	1,631	....	....	....	1,631
Hatters' bands, imported by manufacturera.........................$	....	198	....	....	....	198
Hoods, unfinished, leghorn, etc., not bleached, etc..................$	....	4,335	....	....	....	4,335
Junk, old........................Cwt	90	90	....	....	90	90
Lime juice, crude only.... ....Gal.	66,403	20,594	....	....	66,403	20,594
Molasses, not over 56 degrees imported direct......................... "	7,312,464	1,283,915	....	....	7,312,464	1,283,915
Canadian articles returned...........$	....	9,223	....	....	....	9,223
Articles for exhibition...............$	....	1,024	....	....	....	1,024
Barrels, returned after exportation...$	....	18	....	....	....	18
Clothing and books, donations of....$	....	15	....	....	....	15
Coffee, green, imported direct.....Lb.	505,496	64,799	....	....	505,496	64,799
Settlers' effects....................$	....	2,820	....	1,650	....	4,470
Tea, black of other countries.......Lb.	25	6	....	....	25	6
Total, Free Goods.............	....	1,786,181	....	183,585	....	1,969,766
Total, Duitable and Free...........	....	8,962,710	....	5,490,301	....	14,453,011
Imported through Foreign Countries............................	....	1,520,201	....	965,993	....	2,486,194
Imported direct..................	....	7,442,509	....	4,524,308	....	11,966,817

6 GEORGE V, A. 1916

No. 16.—STATEMENT of Goods, Exported to British and Foreign West Indies.

ARTICLES.	To British West Indies and British Guiana.		To Foreign West Indies and Foreign Guiana.		Total to West Indies and Guiana.	
	Quantity.	Value.	Quantity.	Value.	Quantity.	Value.
THE MINE.		$		$		$
Asbestos sand................Ton	30	75	....	....	30	75
Coal............................"	421	1,545	486	1,461	907	3,006
Salt.........................Cwt.	300	112	....	....	300	112
Total.....................	....	1,732	....	1,461	....	3,193
THE FISHERIES.						
Codfish, fresh.................Lb.	200	11	....	....	200	11
" dry, salted.........Cwt.	117,571	751,465	147,827	993,454	265,398	1,744,919
" tongues and sounds....Lb.	310	16	....	....	310	16
Mackerel, pickled..............Brl.	6,881	65,607	341	3,120	7,222	68,727
Herring, pickled................."	33,426	146,658	3,560	15,997	36,986	162,655
" canned.................Lb.	50	9	....	....	50	9
" smoked.................."	236,291	7,734	106,923	3,371	343,214	11,105
Sea fish, other, fresh............	1,600	469	....	....	1,600	69
" pickled..........Brl.	9,034	44,726	179	957	9,213	45,683
" preserved........Lb.	2,216	146	....	....	2,216	146
Lobsters, canned................."	4,485	1,713	367	135	4,852	1,848
Salmon, canned................."	42,676	5,143	....	....	42,676	5,143
" pickled...............Brl.	858	10,398	197	2,338	1,055	12,736
Fish, all other pickled............"	16	160	2	11	18	171
Fish oil, cod..................Gal.	985	338	....	....	985	338
Total.....................	....	1,034,193	....	1,019,383	....	2,053,576
THE FOREST.						
Laths...........................M	191	689	....	....	191	689
Planks and boards............M.ft	9,926	203,255	18,886	342,652	28,812	545,907
Scantling......................."	5	148	....	....	5	148
Shingles........................."	18,019	23,831	80	210	18,099	24,041
Shooks..........................$	....	2,475	....	....	....	2,475
Staves and headings............$	....	9,613	....	....	....	9,613
Masts and spars................No.	68	1,239	....	....	68	1,239
Poles...........................$	....	1,500	....	....	....	1,500
Timber, square, pine, white......$	....	....	....	564	....	564
Total.....................	....	242,750	....	343,426	....	586,176
ANIMALS AND THEIR PRODUCE.						
Sheep, over one year old........No.	25	202	....	....	25	202
Poultry.........................$	....	28	....	....	....	28
Butter.........................Lb.	146,490	45,571	6,652	1,913	153,142	47,484
Cheese.........................."	209,443	36,048	24,834	4,082	234,277	40,130
Cream and milk, condensed......."	144,074	12,424	....	....	144,074	12,424
Grease and grease scraps.........."	....	....	37,748	1,887	37,748	1,887
Lard............................"	517	60	....	....	517	60
Meats, bacon...................."	219	46	461	99	680	145
" beef...................."	10,000	817	....	....	10,000	817
" hams...................."	952	105	1,093	220	2,045	325
" mutton.................."	1,454	265	....	....	1,454	265
" pork....................."	66,137	3,816	200	18	66,337	3,834
" poultry, dressed or undressed $	....	8	....	....	....	8
" canned.................Lb.	900	87	56,615	7,349	57,515	7,436
" all other, n.o.p........."	123,868	5,836	63,900	3,435	187,768	9,271
Tallow..........................$	....	....	72,170	3,609	72,170	3,609
Other articles..................$	....	....	....	275	....	275
Total.....................	....	105,313	....	22,887	....	128,200

No. 16.—STATEMENT of Goods Exported to British and Foreign West Indies— Continued.

ARTICLES.	To British West Indies and British Guiana.		To Foreign West Indies and Foreign Guiana.		Total to West Indies and Guiana.	
	Quantity.	Value.	Quantity.	Value.	Quantity.	Value.
AGRICULTURAL PRODUCTS.		$		$		$
Cider........................ Gal.	29	6	....	....	29	6
Fruits, apples, green or ripe....... Brl.	1,407	2,956	1,618	3,950	3,025	6,906
" berries of all kinds........ $	....	7	....	....	....	7
" canned or preserved...... $	....	90	....	....	....	90
" all other, n.o.p........... $	....	132	....	....	....	132
Grain, barley.................. Bush.	81	71	....	....	81	71
" beans................... "	68	159	811	2,592	879	2,751
" Indian corn............. "	3,376	1,911	....	....	3,376	1,911
.. oats.................... "	408,018	231,670	203,889	95,695	611,907	327,365
" pease, whole............. "	4,470	9,763	14	33	4,484	9,796
" pease, split............. "	24,690	60,621	....	....	24,690	60,621
" wheat................... "	5	6	....	....	5	6
Bran........................... Cwt.	25,019	34,230	41	98	25,060	34,328
Flour.......................... Brl.	585,655	2,733,039	6,813	31,861	592,468	2,764,900
Indian meal.................... "	6	20	....	....	6	20
Oatmeal....................... "	95	332	....	....	95	332
Meal, all other................ "	39	188	....	....	39	188
Cereal foods, prepared, all kinds $	....	27,703	....	71,885	....	99,588
Hay........................... Ton.	1,077	16,239	872	7,998	1,949	24,237
Nuts.......................... Lb.	195	20	....	....	195	20
Tobacco, leaf.................. "	....	....	11,849	14,840	11,849	14,840
Vegetables, canned or preserved $	....	1,572	....	....	....	1,572
" potatoes............. Bush	130,151	88,895	617,698	382,179	747,849	471,074
" turnips.............. "	32	14	....	....	32	14
" other............... $	....	1,647	....	57	....	1,704
Other articles.................. $	....	60	....	....	....	60
Total......................	....	3,211,351	....	611,188	....	3,822,539
MANUFACTURED ARTICLES.						
Agricultural implements:—						
Cultivators.................... No.	....	....	60	261	60	261
Ploughs....................... "	12	87	44	1,558	56	1,645
Harrows....................... "	....	....	1	87	1	87
All other..................... $	....	60	....	....	....	60
Parts of..................... $	....	31	....	65	....	96
Asbestos, manufactures of....... $	....	207	....	....	....	207
Books, pamphlets, maps, etc..... $	....	4,988	....	9,528	....	14,516
Biscuits and bread.............. Cwt.	450	4,895	....	....	450	4,895
Brooms and whisks.............. $	....	10,670	....	115	....	10,785
Brushes of all kinds............ $	....	1,151	....	....	....	1,151
Cartridges..................... $	....	....	....	171	....	171
Cement........................ $	....	5	....	....	....	5
Clothing and wearing apparel..... $	....	6,859	....	358	....	7,217
Confectionery.................. $	....	169	....	....	....	169
Cordage, ropes and twine........ $	....	24,589	....	51	....	24,640
Cotton fabrics.................. Yd.	411	113	1,118	174	1,529	287
Cotton, other.................. $	....	155	....	....	....	155
Drugs and chemicals:—						
Calcium carbide.............. Lb.	119,460	3,602	....	....	119,460	3,602
All other, n.o.p.............. $	....	7,093	....	492	....	7,585
Earthenware................... $	....	....	....	449	....	449
Electrical apparatus............ $	....	1,341	....	....	....	1,341
Felt, manufactures of........... $	....	88	....	....	....	88
Fertilizers..................... $	....	138,809	....	120	....	138,929
Glass and glassware, n.o.p....... $	....	253	....	....	....	253
Grindstones, manufactured...... $	....	8	....	....	....	8
Guns, rifles, and firearms........ $	....	88	....	....	....	88
Hats and caps.................. $	....	20	....	....	....	20

No. 16.—STATEMENT of Goods Exported to British and Foreign West Indies—
Continued.

ARTICLES.		To British West Indies and British Guiana.		To Foreign West Indies and Foreign Guiana.		Total to West Indies and Guiana.	
		Quantity.	Value.	Quantity.	Value.	Quantity.	Value.
MANUFACTURES—*Con.*			$		$		$
Household effects, n.o.p	$	....	4,890	....	1,370	....	6,260
India-rubber, hose	$	....	8	....	....	....	8
" boots and shoes....	$	....	1,348	....	87	....	1,435
" other manufactures.	$	....	2,000	....	....	....	2,000
Iron and steel:—Stoves	No.	7	116	....	....	7	116
Castings	$	....	....	....	87	....	87
Wire and wire nails	Cwt.	9,097	19,200	1,237	3,984	10,334	23,184
Machinery, n.o.p	$	....	400	....	250	....	650
Sewing machines	No.	1	30	....	....	1	30
Washing machines, domestic and wringers	$	....	15	....	....	....	15
Tools, hand or machine	$	....	9	....	....	....	9
Hardware, n.o.p	$	....	818	....	572	....	1,390
All other, n.o.p	$	....	10,327	....	264	....	10,591
Jewellery of all kinds, n.o.p	$	....	1,633	....	1,646	....	3,279
Jewellers' sweepings	$	....	228	....	....	....	228
Lamps and lanterns	$	....	107	....	....	....	107
Leather, sole	Lb.	1,321	409	....	....	1,321	409
" all other, n.o.p	"	542	132	....	....	542	132
" harness and saddlery....	$	....	65	....	....	....	65
" other, manufactures of...	$	....	50	....	....	....	50
Liquors, ale and beer	Gal.	368	126	....	....	368	126
" gin	"	90	53	....	....	90	53
" whiskey	"	1,053	3,353	1,186	3,886	2,239	7,239
" wines	"	830	655	80	38	910	693
" other spirits, n.o.p	"	29	20	....	....	29	20
Metallic shingles and laths and corrugated roofing	$	....	986	....	....	....	986
Metals, n.o.p	$	....	367	....	450	....	817
Mineral waters in bottles	$	....	66	....	....	....	66
Musical instruments:—							
Organs	No.	2	285	....	....	2	285
Pianos	"	1	285	....	....	1	285
Oilcake	Cwt.	13,164	19,896	....	....	13,164	19,896
Oilcloths, all kinds	Sq.yd	8,546	960	....	....	8,546	960
Oils, n.o.p	Gal.	20,651	3,740	....	....	20,651	3,740
Paper, wall	Roll	7,386	2,194	....	....	7,386	2,194
" wrapping	Lb.	89,206	3,124	....	....	89,206	3,124
" printing	Cwt.	3,119	6,164	22,422	42,796	25,541	48,960
" n.o.p	$	....	2,351	....	....	....	2,351
Paints and varnishes	$	....	19,446	....	2,061	....	21,507
Photographs	$	....	17	....	....	....	17
Philosophical apparatus	$	....	50	....	....	....	50
Ships sold to other countries	No. & ton	3— 716	44,000	....	....	3— 716	44,000
Silk and manufactures of	$	....	276	....	....	....	276
Soap	Lb.	375,624	16,568	....	....	375,624	16,568
Stationery	$	....	4,564	....	7,557	....	12,121
Stone, ornamental, dressed	$	....	14	....	....	....	14
Sugar, of all kinds, n.o.p	Lb.	2,000	87	....	....	2,000	87
Tar	$	....	68	....	....	....	68
Tin, manufactures of	$	....	597	....	....	....	597
Tobacco, cigars	M	2	50	....	....	2	50
Trunks and valises	$	....	9,395	....	....	....	9,395
Vehicles, automobiles,	No.	60	27,675	3	7,700	63	35,375
" " parts of....	$	....	4,974	....	....	....	4,974
" carriages	No.	11	1,071	....	....	11	1,071
" " parts of	$	....	245	....	....	....	245
" carts	No.	1	102	....	....	1	102
Wood, barrels, empty	"	5,276	7,833	....	....	5,276	7,833
" household furniture	$	....	12,994	....	820	....	13,814
" doors, sashes and blinds...	$	....	215	....	....	....	215

SESSIONAL PAPER No. 11

No. 16.—STATEMENT of Goods Exported to British and Foreign West Indies—Concluded.

ARTICLES.		To British West Indies and British Guiana.		To Foreign West Indies and Foreign Guiana.		Total to West Indies and Guiana.	
		Quantity.	Value.	Quantity.	Value.	Quantity	Value.
MANUFACTURES.— con.			$		$		$
Wood—con:							
Matches.........................	$	....	198	....	....	....	198
Mouldings, trimmings and other house furnishings.............	$	....	24	....	....	....	24
Pails, tubs, churns and other hollow woodenware.........	$	....	62	....	....	....	62
Other manufactures of..........	$	....	4,465	....	70	....	4,535
Woollens.........................	$	....	10	....	....	....	10
Other articles...................	$	....	2,576	....	3,015	....	5,591
Total................		....	449,267	....	90,082	....	539,349
MISCELLANEOUS ARTICLES.							
Dried fruits, n.o.p...............	Lb.	52	5	....	....	52	5
Rice...........................	"	4,386	121	198,000	6,582	201,386	6,703
Tea.............................	"	3,277	857	....	....	3,277	857
Total................		....	983	....	6,582	....	7,565
Grand total................		....	5,045,589	....	2,095,009	....	7,140,598

6 GEORGE V, A. 1916

No. 17.—STATEMENT showing the Total Value of Imports and Exports of the Dominion of Canada, from and to each Country, during the Twelve Months ended March 31, 1915.

Countries.	IMPORTS.			EXPORTS.		
	Dutiable Goods.	Free Goods.	Total.	Produce of Canada.	Foreign. Produce.	Total.
	$	$	$	$	$	$
British Empire.						
United Kingdom..........	67,867,733	22,490,554	90,358,287	186,668,599	25,090,264	211,758,863
Aden.....................	3,437	14,531	17,968	9,014	....	9,014
Australia................	157,484	227,990	385,474	5,521,594	30,092	5,551,686
Bermuda.................	51	23,863	23,914	357,712	10,551	368,263
British E. Africa.........	7,558	15,169	22,727	59,838	....	59,838
" S. Africa.............	7,668	307,467	315,135	4,585,791	59,798	4,645,589
" W. Africa............	....	....	....	40,927	....	40,927
" Guiana..............	2,909,514	13,601	2,923,115	675,660	3,137	678,797
" Honduras............	....	552,450	552,450	9,450	....	9,450
" India................	829,265	3,307,137	4,136,402	415,105	575	415,680
" East Indies, other....	62,647	1,622,417	1,685,064	23,905	....	23,905
" West Indies..........	4,267,015	1,772,580	6,039,595	4,333,095	33,697	4,366,792
" Oceania, other.......	1,715	7,709	9,424	8,244	....	8,244
" Straits Settlements...	206,370	788,232	994,602	246,355	101	246,456
Fiji Islands..............	1,996,924	....	1,996,924	112,355	324	112,679
Gibraltar................	....	150	150	210,303	1,226,011	1,436,314
Hong Kong..............	651,959	616,801	1,268,760	653,878	1,215	655,093
Malta and Cyprus Islands..	821	....	821	23,313	42,770	66,083
Newfoundland............	14,767	1,230,913	1,245,680	3,976,160	505,016	4,481,176
New Zealand.............	1,298,969	2,607,493	3,906,462	2,619,556	4,299	2,623,855
Total, British Empire.	80,283,897	35,599,057	115,882,954	210,550,854	27,007,850	237,558,704
Other Countries.						
Alaska...................	109,053	21,073	130,126	297,282	26,595	323,877
Argentina................	10,226	3,354,561	3,364,787	634,387	5,082	639,469
Austria-Hungary..........	581,670	31,501	613,171	220,654	59,134	279,788
Azores and Madeira........	2,089	....	2,089	6,279	....	6,279
Belgium..................	1,204,517	651,050	1,855,567	2,220,709	1,038,650	3,259,359
Brazil...................	728,180	425,797	1,153,977	541,998	517	542,515
Bulgaria.................	1,725	....	1,725	....	....	....
Canary Islands...........	....	....	....	29,841	328	30,169
Chili....................	190	....	190	55,302	45	55,347
China...................	311,868	813,113	1,124,981	333,733	5,306	339,039
Costa Rica...............	2,407	15,026	17,433	36,045	37	36,082
Cuba....................	1,520,619	183,585	1,704,204	1,443,167	36,188	1,479,355
Denmark.................	10,403	33,729	44,132	527,008	190,230	717,238
Danish West Indies.......	117,687	....	117,687	16,218	35	16,253
Dutch East Indies........	47,000	81,589	128,589	25,927	....	25,927
" West Indies........	....	....	....	6,715	....	6,715
" Guiana..............	203,898	....	203,898	40,453	495	40,948
Ecuador.................	1,155	....	1,155	8,646	....	8,646
Egypt and Soudan.........	20,845	8,820	29,665	26,484	....	26,484
France...................	6,995,425	1,256,185	8,251,610	10,499,680	4,096,025	14,595,705
French Africa............	3,216	5,478	8,694	4,103	....	4,103
" Guiana.............	....	....	....	2,374	....	2,374
" Oceania............	....	....	....	1,488	....	1,488
" West Indies........	....	....	....	32,546	....	32,546
Germany.................	3,760,566	1,149,289	4,909,855	1,447,391	714,619	2,162,010
German Africa...........	....	113,305	113,305	....	....	....
" Oceania...........	....	....	....	4,800	....	4,800
Greece..................	414,173	1,958	416,131	87,485	....	87,485
Greenland and Iceland, etc.	....	208	208	1,668	....	1,668
Guatemala...............	38,722	45,591	84,313	27,295	....	27,295
Hawaii..................	22,106	9,395	31,501	70,723	700	71,423
Hayti...................	....	....	....	4,163	....	4,163
Holland..................	1,335,815	589,013	1,924,828	1,623,405	3,631,424	5,254,829
Honduras................	....	....	....	5,587	20	5,607
Italy....................	1,090,291	417,257	1,507,548	521,802	1,319,108	1,840,910
Japan...................	1,331,297	1,481,323	2,812,620	963,631	73,370	1,037,001
Kongo Free State.........	....	12,952	12,952	....	....	....
Korea...................	75	....	75	1,712	....	1,712

SESSIONAL PAPER No. 11

No. 17.—STATEMENT showing the Total Value of Imports and Exports of the Dominion of Canada, from and to each Country—*Concluded.*

Countries.	IMPORTS.			EXPORTS.		
	Dutiable Goods.	Free Goods.	Total.	Produce of Canada.	Foreign Produce.	Total.
	$	$	$	$	$	$
Other Countries—Con.						
Liberia....................				63		63
Madagascar...............	138	4,122	4,260			
Mexico...................	58,497	1,267,736	1,326,233	18,551		18,551
Miquelon and St. Pierre....	40,264	2,022	42,286	141,097	14,235	155,332
Morocco..................		89	89			
Nicaragua.................				1,618		1,618
Norway...................	319,931	68,878	388,809	1,000,715	75	1,000,790
Panama...................				125,630	3,406	129,036
Persia....................	6,015	509	6,524			
Peru.....................	1,359,940	86,696	1,446,636	13,141		13,141
Philippines...............	1,399	3,976	5,375	41,574		41,574
Porto Rico................				468,698		468,698
Portugal..................	200,072	19,177	219,249	25,206	763,279	788,485
Portuguese Africa.........				79,611		79,611
Roumania.................	4,379	185	4,564	3,150		3,150
Russia....................	61,013	42,941	103,954	1,270,941	60,250	1,331,191
Salvador..................	9,650	6,789	16,439	2,215		2,215
San Domingo..............	3,464,512		3,464,512	3,938		3,938
Servia....................		140	140	8		8
Siam.....................	494	12,178	12,672	16,322		16,322
Spain.....................	902,908	76,097	979,005	243,001	246,679	489,680
Sweden...................	412,153	134,547	546,700	172,796	500	173,296
Switzerland...............	3,943,913	58,869	4,002,782	11,853	4,592	16,445
Turkey...................	279,119	16,378	295,497	3,979	1,982	5,961
U.S. of Colombia.........	67,963	114,425	182,388	24,027	90	24,117
United States.............	207,614,812	262,107,254	469,722,066	173,320,798	42,088,528	215,409,326
Uruguay..................	1,415	11,347	12,762	52,820		52,820
Venezuela.................	53,392	158,590	211,982	56,196		56,196
Total, Other Countries.	238,667,197	274,894,743	513,561,940	198,868,649	54,381,524	253,250,173
Grand Total..........	318,951,094	310,493,800	629,444,894	409,419,503	81,389,374	490,808,877

6 GEORGE V, A. 1916

No. 18.—Abstract by Countries

Number.	Countries.	Imports.			General Tariff.	
		Dutiable.	Free.	Total.		
		Value.	Value.	Value.	Value.	Duty.
		$	$	$	$	$ cts.
1	United Kingdom	67,867,733	22,490,554	90,358,287	6,788,775	5,453,340 38
2	Aden	3,437	14,531	17,968	3,437	535 95
3	Bermuda	51	23,863	23,914	51	20 30
4	British East Africa	7,558	15,169	22,727	6,628	839 38
5	" South Africa	7,668	307,467	315,135	301	312 50
6	" India	829,265	3,307,137	4,136,402	68,955	8,405 30
7	" Straits Settlements	206,370	788,232	994,602	6,241	1,405 82
8	" East Indies, other	62,647	1,622,417	1,685,064	17,016	4,082 07
9	" Guiana	2,909,514	13,601	2,923,115	43,868	248,984 67
10	" Honduras		552,450	552,450		
11	" West Indies	4,267,015	1,772,580	6,039,595	54,075	87,804 51
12	" Oceania: Australia and Tasmania	157,484	227,990	385,474	183,641	50,960 56
13	" Oceania: New Zealand	1,298,969	2,607,493	3,906,462	87,571	14,261 27
14	" Oceania: All other	1,715	7,709	9,424	1,715	91 50
15	Fiji Islands	1,996,924		1,996,924		
16	Gibraltar		150	150		
17	Hong Kong	651,959	616,801	1,268,760	603,057	291,346 67
18	Malta		821	821	858	1,350 85
19	Newfoundland	14,767	1,230,913	1,245,680	14,183	3,486 54
	Total British Empire	80,283,897	35,599,057	115,882,954	7,880,372	6,167,228 27
20	Alaska	109,053	21,073	130,126	20,768	3,851 86
21	Argentina	10,226	3,354,561	3,364,787	1,532	283 18
22	Austria-Hungary	581,670	31,501	613,171	349,762	96,742 62
23	Azores and Madeira Islands	2,089		2,089	1,865	645,44
24	Belgium	1,204,517	651,050	1,855,567	1,050,777	224,621 24
25	Brazil	728,180	425,797	1,153,977	723,754	235,694 59
26	Bulgaria	1,725		1,725	1,725	269 50
27	Cen. Am. States: Costa Rica	2,407	15,026	17,433	453	95 60
28	" " Guatemala	38,722	45,591	84,313	46,558	12,812 43
29	" " Salvador	9,650	6,789	16,439	3,600	856 08
30	Chili	190		190	190	9 20
31	China	311,868	813,113	1,124,981	228,927	79,177 50
32	Cuba	1,520,619	183,585	1,704,204	1,384,407	770,799 00
33	Denmark	10,403	33,729	44,132	10,398	2,106 14
34	Danish West Indies	117,687		117,687	115,469	75,626 31
35	Dutch East Indies	47,000	81,589	128,589	116,153	40,184 18
36	" Guiana	203,898		203,898	186,376	72,217 62
37	Ecuador	1,155		1,155	1,155	404 25
38	Egypt and Soudan	20,845	8,820	29,665	21,652	27,825 98
39	France	6,995,425	1,256,185	8,251,610	3,539,598	2,099,784 48
40	French Africa	3,216	5,478	8,694	1,899	876 17
41	Germany	3,760,566	1,149,289	4,909,855	3,887,906	1,089,038 74
42	German Africa		113,305	113,305		
43	Greece	414,173	1,958	416,131	415,953	60,827 80
44	Greenland, Iceland, etc		208	208		
45	Hawaii	22,106	9,395	31,501	23,217	9,366 92
46	Holland	1,335,815	589,013	1,924,828	1,206,806	2,271,650 17
47	Italy	1,090,291	417,257	1,507,548	734,251	198,853 73
48	Japan	1,331,297	1,481,323	2,812,620	660,811	198,633 45
49	Kongo Free State		12,952	12,952		
50	Korea	75		75	75	22 50
51	Madagascar	138	4,122	4,260	203	53 30
52	Mexico	58,497	1,267,736	1,326,233	52,055	12,291 12
53	Miquelon and St. Pierre	40,264	2,022	42,286	1,260	732 41
54	Morocco		89	89		
55	Norway	319,931	68,878	388,809	112,045	31,135 84

SESSIONAL PAPER No. 11

DUTIABLE AND FREE.

ENTERED FOR CONSUMPTION.

Preferential Tariff.		Treaty Rates.		Total Dutiable.	Total Free.	Grand Total.		Number.
Value.	Duty.	Value.	Duty.	Value.	Value.	Value.	Duty.	
$	$ cts.	$	$ cts.	$	$	$	$ cts.	
58,170,806	12,299,501 61	3,051,676	694,692 19	68,011,257	22,149,524	90,160,781	18,447,534 18	1
				3,437	14,531	17,968	535 95	2
				51	23,872	23,923	20 30	3
1,719	171 90			8,347	15,169	23,516	1,011 28	4
7,119	714 10			7,420	307,467	314,887	1,026 60	5
757,745	66,167 91			826,700	3,307,147	4,133,847	74,573 21	6
196,447	44,605 34			202,688	573,028	775,716	46,011 16	7
45,975	13,930 18			62,991	1,574,994	1,637,985	18,012 25	8
2,936,246	824,595 16	1	0 23	2,980,115	13,419	2,993,534	1,073,580 06	9
					497,786	497,780		10
4,336,684	1,150,311 78	5	1 13	4,390,764	1,771,574	6,162,338	1,238,117 42	11
		7,679	1,918 00	191,320	220,885	412,205	52,878 56	12
1,208,772	150,679 40			1,296,343	2,612,273	3,908,616	164,940 67	13
				1,715	7,709	9,424	91 50	14
1,780,368	634,705 27			1,780,368		1,780,368	634,705 27	15
					150	150		16
		28,717	7,904 90	631,774	616,801	1,248,575	299,251 57	17
		78	22 85	936	13	949	1,373 70	18
		41	5 16	14,224	1,230,936	1,245,160	3,491 70	19
69,441,881	15,185,382 65	3,088,197	704,544 46	80,410,450	34,937,278	115,347,728	22,057,155 38	
				20,768	21,073	41,841	3,851 86	20
		8,694	2,173 50	10,226	3,354,561	3,364,787	2,456 68	21
		260,919	67,624 90	610,681	31,501	642,182	164,367 52	22
				1,865		1,865	645 44	23
		173,042	41,498 22	1,223,819	652,144	1,875,963	266,119 46	24
				723,754	425,797	1,149,551	235,694 59	25
				1,725		1,725	269 50	26
				453	15,026	15,479	95 60	27
				46,558	45,591	92,149	12,812 43	28
				3,600	6,789	10,389	856 08	29
				190		190	9 20	30
				228,927	813,456	1,042,383	79,177 50	31
				1,384,407	232,884	1,617,291	770,799 00	32
		217	49 63	10,615	33,729	44,344	2,155 77	33
				115,469		115,469	75,626 31	34
				116,153	81,589	197,742	40,184 18	35
				186,376		186,376	72,217 62	36
				1,155		1,155	404 25	37
				21,652	8,830	30,482	27,825 98	38
		3,651,585	800,495 98	7,191,183	1,258,003	8,449,186	2,900,280 46	39
		984	295 75	2,883	5,478	8,361	1,171 92	40
				3,887,906	1,199,080	5,086,986	1,089,038 74	41
					113,305	113,305		42
				415,953	1,958	417,911	60,827 80	43
					208	208		44
				23,217	9,438	32,655	9,366 92	45
		22,699	5,641 68	1,229,505	539,751	1,769,256	2,277,291 85	46
		321,265	80,327 60	1,055,516	417,283	1,472,799	279,181 33	47
		641,181	161,831 70	1,301,992	1,481,473	2,783,465	360,465 15	48
					12,952	12,952		49
				75		75	22 50	50
				203	4,122	4,325	53 30	51
				52,055	1,177,922	1,229,977	12,291 12	52
		962	254 97	2,222	2,022	4,244	987 38	53
					89	89		54
		204,699	75,969 52	316,744	68,903	385,647	107,105 36	55

6 GEORGE V, A. 1916

No. 18.—ABSTRACT BY COUNTRIES

Number.	Countries.	IMPORTS.			General Tariff.	
		Dutiable.	Free.	Total.		
		Value.	Value.	Value.	Value.	Duty.
		$	$	$	$	$ cts.
56	Peru..........................	1,359,940	86,696	1,446,636	1,407,350	395,404 70
57	Persia..........................	6,015	509	6,524	6,015	2,104 05
58	Philippines.....................	1,399	3,976	5,375	2,177	6,995 35
59	Portugal........................	200,072	19,177	219,249	196,395	87,207 21
60	Roumania..........	4,379	185	4,564	6,960	1,694 13
61	Russia..........................	61,013	42,941	103,954	61,868	22,075 72
62	San Domingo....................	3,464,512		3,464,512	3,193,796	1,103,452 42
63	Servia..........................		140	140		
64	Siam...........................	494	12,178	12,672	494	148,75
65	Spain..........................	902,908	76,097	979,005	477,561	81,864 42
66	Sweden.........................	412,153	134,547	546,700	347,979	86,731 20
67	Switzerland.....................	3,943,913	58,869	4,002,782	833,960	195,230 79
68	Turkey.........................	279,119	16,378	295,497	306,849	57,941 05
69	Uruguay........................	1,415	11,347	12,762	1,434	391 62
70	U. S. of Colombia...............	67,963	114,425	182,388	67,657	14,590 68
71	United States...................	207,614,812	262,107,254	469,722,066	168,658,299	42,335,574 74
72	Venezuela.:....................	53,392	158,590	211,982	51,036	11,620 05
	Total other countries.....	238,667,197	274,894,743	513,561,940	190,521,430	52,020,516 23
	Duty on articles lower than home trade price.....................					68,296 47
	Additional duties................					410,832 60
	War tax........................					2,236,290 16
	Grand total.............	318,951,094	310,493,800	629,444,894	198,401,802	60,903,163 73

DUTIABLE AND FREE.

Preferential Tariff		Treaty Rates		Total Dutiable	Total Free	Grand Total		Number
Value	Duty	Value	Duty	Value	Value	Value	Duty	
$	$ cts.	$	$ cts.	$	$	$	$ cts.	
				1,407,350	86,696	1,494,046	395,404 70	56
				6,015	509	6,524	2,104 05	57
				2,177	4,027	6,204	6,995 35	58
				196,395	19,213	215,608	87,207 21	59
				6,960	185	7,145	1,694 13	60
		646	148 05	62,514	42,941	105,455	22,223 77	61
				3,193,796		3,193,796	1,103,452 42	62
					140	140		63
				494	12,178	12,672	148 75	64
		423,686	107,748 29	901,247	76,201	977,448	189,612 71	65
		63,309	15,909 04	411,288	134,547	545,835	102,640 24	66
		3,086,427	650,667 73	3,920,387	58,869	3,979,256	845,898 52	67
				306,849	16,378	323,227	57,941 05	68
				1,434	11,347	12,781	391 62	69
				67,657	114,425	182,082	14,590 68	70
				168,658,299	259,958,628	428,616,927	42,335,574 74	71
				51,036	158,590	209,626	11,620 05	72
		8,860,315	2,010,636 56	199,381,745	272,709,831	472,091,576	54,031,152 79	
							68,296 47	
	402,182 87						410,832 60	
							2,638,473 03	
69,441,881	15,587,565 52	11,948,512	2,715,181 02	279,792,195	307,647,109	587,439,304	79,205,910 27	

ENTERED FOR CONSUMPTION.

11—i—13

6 GEORGE V, A. 1916

No. 19.—ABSTRACT of the Total Value of Goods Exported from the

Number	Countries.	THE MINE.		THE FISHERIES.		THE FOREST.		ANIMALS AND THIER PRODUCE.	
		Produce.	Not Produce	Produce.	Not Produce	Produce.	Not Produce	Produce	Not Produce
		$	$	$	$	$	$	$	$
1	United Kingdom.......	12,219,937	106	5,448,902	7,695	9,914,548	458,465	38,222,698	1,378,635
2	Aden..............								
3	Australia..............	125,903	......	395,023	......	110,205	......	25,673	......
4	Burmuda..............	......	......	26,411	454	28,743	......	69,289	1,634
5	B. E. Africa..........								
6	B. S. Africa..........	8,092	......	1,139	......	202,033	......	77,693	......
7	B. W. Africa..........								
8	B. Guiana..............	......	......	68,105	2,260	38,077	......	19,835	......
9	B. Honduras..........			91				956	......
10	B. India...............	612	......	13,040		97,375	200	......	......
11	B. E. Indies, other.....	4,404							
12	B. W. Indies..........	1,552	180	939,380	24,448	204,673	......	84,796	682
13	B. Oceania, other......			8,008	......	80	......		
14	B. Straits Settlements..	......		144,991				510	......
15	Fiji Islands..............			51,812		36,689		16	......
16	Gibraltar.............	1,974							
17	Hong Kong............	213,254	......	198,216		3,102	......	11,730	45
18	Malta.................							3,050	......
19	Newfoundland..........	516,756	32,673	64,817	680	10,016	276	420,657	27,159
20	New Zealand...........	130	......	172,909	......	28,025	......	4,500	......
	Total, British Empire.	13,092,614	32,959	7,532,844	35,537	10,673,566	458,941	38,941,403	1,408,155
21	Alaska.................	243,231	......	13,658	......	334	644	7,311	17
22	Argentina..............	3,447	......	2,988	......	435,606	......		......
23	Austria-Hungary.......	37,124	......					2,435	78
24	Azores and Madeira....					6,244	......		
25	Belgium..............	45,668	......	98,415	......	8,188	......	76,419	81
26	Brazil.................	3,159	......	487,494	517	......	......		
27	Canary Islands........					13,301			
28	Chili..................					10,192			
29	China.................	94,203	......	117,057	......	2,111	......	32,781	730
30	Costa Rica............			23,364	37			499	......
31	Cuba..................	1,461	......	504,691	21,451	303,661	......	15,959	......
32	Denmark..............	611	......	55,085	......	......	......	17,822	......
33	Danish W. Indies......	......	......	4,830	17	439	......	5,728	18
34	Dutch E. Indies.......			16,267	......				
35	Dutch W. Indies.......								
36	Dutch Guiana.........			39,751	495				
37	Ecuador...............			570	......				
38	Egypt and Soudan.....								
39	France................	91,857	......	689,462	......	20,737	......	655,067	108,605
40	French Africa.........								
41	French Guiana........			172	......	1,432	......	770	......
42	French Oceania.......			1,488					
43	French W. Indies......	......	......	300	......	21,562	......	412	......
44	Germany..............	290,276	......	196,819	......	725	......	144,823	7,081
45	German Oceania......			4,800					
46	Greece................								
47	Greenland, Iceland, etc								
48	Guatemala.............								
49	Hawaii................	26,262	......	11,223	......	607	......		
50	Hayti.................			710	......	2,218	......		
51	Holland...............	87,207	......	36,756	......	5,350	......	61,317	......
52	Honduras.............								
53	Italy.................	41,353	......	346,595	750	......			
54	Japan.................	69,483	......	255,867	144	31,054	......	153,506	......
55	Korea.................			1,250	......				
56	Liberia...............								
57	Mexico................	1,928						985	......
58	Miquelon and St. Pierre	36,519	932	1,002	......	9,855	193	44,417	1,400
59	Nicaragua..............			55				422	......
60	Norway...............	2,662	......	87,624	......			30,499	......
61	Panama...............	3,891	......	79,614	3,301			4,888	......
62	Peru..................					597	......		
63	Philippines............	5,257	......			549	......	746	......

Dominion of Canada during the Twelve Months ended March 31, 1915.

| Agricultural Products. | | Manufacturers. | | Miscellaneous. | | Totals. | | Grand Totals. | Number. |
Produce.	Not Produce	Produce	Not Produce	Produce	Not Produce	Produce	Not Produce		
$	$	$	$	$	$	$	$	$	
95,834,460	22,128,753	24,848,359	1,103,835	179,650	11,675	186,668,554	25,089,164	211,757,718	1
	9,014					9,014		9,014	2
79,120	2,240	4,786,670	27,852			5,522,594	30,092	5,552,686	3
198,408	1,579	34,849	1,183	12	5,701	357,712	10,551	368,263	4
7,634		52,204				59,838		59,838	5
1,872,400	59,143	2,424,434	655			4,585,791	59,798	4,645,589	6
13,552		27,375				40,927		40,927	7
507,922		41,721	877			675,660	3,137	678,797	8
		8,403				9,450		9,450	9
45		304,033	375			415,105	575	415,680	10
		19,501				23,905		23,905	11
2,703,275	154	399,419	7,250		983	4,333,095	33,697	4,366,792	12
		156				8,244		8,244	13
		99,854	101			245,355	101	245,456	14
13,510	324	10,328				112,355	324	112,679	15
208,329	1,226,011					210,303	1,226,011	1,436,314	16
218,411	176	9,125	994			653,838	1,215	655,053	17
17,804	42,764	2,459	6			23,313	42,770	66,083	18
1,895,803	13,799	1,050,534	116,670	17,577	25,046	3,976,160	216,303	4,192,463	19
658,558	478	1,755,434	3,821			2,619,556	4,299	2,623,855	20
104,229,231	23,475,421	35,883,872	1,263,619	197,239	43,405	210,550,769	26,718,037	237,268,806	
1,949	1,375	27,063	14,432	3,736	127	297,282	16,595	313,877	21
6,756		185,590	5,082			634,387	5,082	639,469	22
141,385	58,065	39,710	991			220,654	59,134	279,788	23
		35				6,279		6,279	24
1,333,809	1,030,685	655,480	7,884	2,730		2,220,709	1,038,650	3,259,359	25
2,851		48,494				541,998	517	542,515	26
16,540			328			29,841	328	30,169	27
		45,110	45			55,302	45	55,347	28
12,022		36,077	1,422			294,251	2,152	296,403	29
		12,182				36,045	37	36,082	30
572,473	14,840	77,822	3,051	6,582		1,482,649	39,342	1,521,991	31
386,810	188,396	69,362	1,834			529,690	190,230	719,920	32
2,501		38				13,536	35	13,571	33
		9,660				25,927		25,927	34
5,829		886				6,715		6,715	35
249		453				40,453	495	40,948	36
3,622		4,454				8,646		8,646	37
17,016		9,468				26,484		26,484	38
5,493,748	3,878,193	3,548,809	109,227			10,499,680	4,096,025	14,595,705	39
345		3,825				4,170		4,170	40
						2,374		2,374	41
						1,488		1,488	42
10,175		30				32,479		32,479	43
493,373	626,218	321,375	81,320			1,447,391	714,619	2,162,010	44
						4,800		4,800	45
82,124		5,361				87,485		87,485	46
1,518		150				1,668		1,668	47
		27,295				27,295		27,295	48
		32,499	700			70,591	700	71,291	49
1,367						4,295		4,295	50
1,208,893	3,626,146	223,882	5,278			1,623,405	3,631,424	5,254,829	51
200		5,387	20			5,587	20	5,607	52
101	1,311,769	133,753	6,589			521,802	1,319,108	1,840,910	53
32,798	366	420,623	72,860	300		963,631	73,370	1,037,001	54
		462				1,712		1,712	55
63						63		63	56
500		15,138				18,551		18,551	57
24,165	3,561	25,097	6,241	42	1,908	141,097	14,235	155,332	58
		1,141				1,618		1,618	59
862,040		17,890	75			1,000,715	75	1,000,790	60
10,646		26,591	105			125,630	3,406	129,036	61
		12,544				13,141		13,141	62
18,717		16,305				41,574		41,574	63

11—i—13½

6 GEORGE V, A. 1916

No. 19.—Abstract of the Total Value of Goods Exported from the

Number	Countries	The Mine.		The Fisheries.		The Forest.		Animals and Their Produce.	
		Produce.	Not Produce	Produce.	Not Produce	Produce.	Not Produce	Produce.	Not Produce
		$	$	$	$	$	$	$	$
64	Porto Rico	....	....	446,966	....	14,114	....	....	....
65	Portugal	633	....	20,242	....	....	....	....	....
66	Portuguese Africa	....	....	....	....	....	....	....	....
67	Roumania	....	....	....	....	....	....	....	....
68	Russia	2,678	....	81	....	....	....	40	....
69	Salvador	....	....	....	....	....	....	....	....
70	San Domingo	....	....	....	....	....	....	....	....
71	Servia	....	....	....	....	....	....	....	....
72	Siam	....	....	12,280	....	....	....	....	....
73	Spain	911	....	....	....	19,583	....	1,706	....
74	Sweden	345	....	69,078	....	....	....	2,240	....
75	Switzerland	....	....	....	....	....	....	260	....
76	Turkey	....	....	....	....	....	....	....	....
77	U. S. of Colombia	....	....	4,677	90	....	....	2,232	....
78	United States	37,558,209	291,657	8,521,901	69,330	31,030,873	26,320	34,186,056	1,039,094
79	Uruguay	....	....	1,012	....	37,785	....	....	....
80	Venezuela	....	....	80	....	....	....	....	....
	Total, other countries	38,648,375	292,589	12,154,224	96,132	31,977,117	27,157	35,449,340	1,157,104
	Grand total	51,740,989	325,548	19,687,068	131,669	42,650,683	486,098	74,390,743	2,565,259

```
To Great Britain—Coin, produce $  45;  not produce  $      1,100
   Hong Kong        "        "     40;     "
   Newfoundland     "                      "              288,713
   Alaska           "                      "               10,000
   United States    "        "    582      "           29,065,888
                                  ───                  ──────────
                                  667                  29,365,701
```

Grand Total Exports..

Dominion of Canada during the Twelve Months ended March 31, 1915—*Con.*

AGRICULTURAL PRODUCTS.		MANUFACTURES.		MISCELLANEOUS.		TOTALS.		Grand TOTALS.	Number.
Produce.	Not Produce	Produce	Not Produce	Produce	Not Produce	Produce	Not Produce		
$	$	$	$	$	$	$	$	$	
1,195	....	6,423	....	....	....	468,698	....	468,698	64
73	763,279	4,258	....	....	....	25,206	763,279	788,485	65
70,155	....	9,456	....	....	....	79,611	....	79,611	66
....	....	3,150	....	....	....	3,150	....	3,150	67
29,337	....	1,238,805	60,250	....	....	1,270,941	60,250	1,331,191	68
....	....	2,215	....	....	....	2,215	....	2,215	69
2,559	....	1,379	....	....	....	3,938	....	3,938	70
....	....	8	....	....	....	8	....	8	71
....	....	4,042	....	....	....	16,322	....	16,322	72
176,283	246,500	44,518	....	....	179	243,001	246,679	489,680	73
56,518	....	44,615	500	....	....	172,796	500	173,296	74
....	....	11,593	4,592	....	....	11,853	4,592	16,445	75
1,630	....	2,349	1,982	....	....	3,979	1,982	5,961	76
....	....	17,118	....	....	....	24,027	90	24,117	77
19,405,251	379,200	42,164,753	7,880,597	453,173	3,336,442	173,320,216	13,022,640	186,342,856	78
....	....	14,023	....	....	....	52,820	....	52,820	79
29,233	....	26,883	....	....	....	56,196	....	56,196	80
30,516,819	12,128,593	49,655,629	8,265,405	466,563	3,338,656	198,868,067	25,305,636	224,173,703	
134,746,050	35,604,014	85,539,501	9,529,024	663,802	3,382,061	409,418,836	52,023,673	461,442,509	
						667	29,365,701	29,366,368	
						409,419,503	81,389,374	490,808,877	

6 GEORGE V, A. 1916

No. 20.—STATEMENT showing the Value of Goods (dutiable and free), imported into Canada during the Fiscal Year ended March 31, 1915, classified under the following heads and countries.

Articles.	UNITED KINGDOM.	BRITISH POSSESSIONS, ALL OTHER.	FOREIGN COUNTRIES.
	$	$	$
Food, drink and tobacco..................................	11,084,584	17,982,349	94,425,121
Raw materials and articles mainly unmanufactured.........	8,359,490	6,184,454	102,076,927
Articles wholly or mainly manufactured...................	70,349,549	1,287,052	177,530,114
Miscellaneous articles...................................	562,002	68,452	7,541,808
Coin and specie..	2,662	2,360	131,987,970
Total...	90,358,287	25,524,667	513,561,940

No. 21.—STATEMENT showing the Value of Goods Exported from the Dominion of Canada during the Fiscal Year ended March 31, 1915, classified under the following heads and countries:—

	UNITED KINGDOM.		BRITISH POSSESSIONS ALL OTHER.		FOREIGN COUNTRIES.	
	Canadian Produce.	Foreign Produce.	Canadian Produce.	Foreign Produce.	Canadian Produce.	Foreign Produce.
	$	$	$	$	$	$
Food, drink and tobacco...	135,480,712	22,458,934	10,939,548	1,492,910	53,577,606	13,495,826
Raw materials and articles mainly unmanufactured..	15,684,576	565,474	1,331,797	7,720	72,036,114	595,372
Articles wholly or mainly manufactured.............	33,935,598	868,797	11,577,068	128,204	72,166,908	8,413,167
Miscellaneous articles......	1,567,668	1,195,959	33,802	39	1,087,439	2,801,271
Coin and specie.............	45	1,100	40	288,713	582	29,075,888
Total..............	186,668,599	25,090,264	23,882,255	1,917,586	198,868,649	54,381,524

SESSIONAL PAPER No. 11

No. 22.—SUMMARY STATEMENT of Goods Exported from the Dominion of Canada distinguishing Canadian Produce and Manufactures from those of other Countries, during the Twelve Months ended March 31, 1915.

Articles.	Goods THE PRODUCE OF CANADA.		Goods NOT THE PRODUCE OF CANADA.		TOTAL EXPORTS.	
	Quantity.	Value.	Quantity.	Value.	Quantity.	Value.
THE MINE.		$		$		$
Arsenic.................... Cwt.	32,655	120,242			32,655	120,242
Asbestos................... Ton.	74,904	2,227,387			74,904	2,227,387
Asbestos sand................ "	19,928	111,727			19,928	111,727
Coal........................ "	1,512,487	4,466,258	88,642	169,164	1,601,129	4,635,422
Chromite (chromic Iron)....... "	79	878			79	878
Felspar..................... "	13,649	56,668			13,649	56,668
Gold bearing quartz, dust, nuggets, etc............... $		15,406,510		2,509		15,409,019
Gypsum or plaster—crude....... Ton.	322,680	378,648			322,680	378,648
Metals, viz:—						
*Copper, fine, contained in ore, matte, regulus, etc.......... Lb.	62,677,038	6,173,357			62,677,038	6,173,357
Copper, black or coarse cement copper and copper in pigs..... "	9,861,780	1,371,889			9,861,780	1,371,889
*Lead, metallic, contained in ore, etc.................... "	723,100	12,534			723,100	12,534
Lead, pig.................. "	2,534,502	97,286			2,534,502	97,286
*Nickel, fine, contained in ore, matte or speiss............... "	45,412,017	5,063,656			45,412,017	5,063,656
*Platinum, contained in concentrates, or other forms........ Oz.	46	2,171	98	4,656	144	6,827
*Silver, metallic, contained in ore, concentrates, etc......... "	25,355,305	13,516,390			25,355,305	13,516,390
Mica........................ Lb.	852,752	217,800	377	59	853,129	217,859
Mineral pigment, iron oxides, ochres, etc................ Cwt.	32,767	20,744			32,767	20,744
Mineral water, natural, not in bottles.................... Gal.	981	82			981	82
Oil, mineral:—						
Coal and kerosene, crude....... "	17,120	1,177	201,780	4,216	218,900	5,393
" " refined.......... "	1,256	235	162,164	12,458	163,420	12,693
Total..................	18,376	1,412	363,944	16,674	382,320	18,086
Ores, viz:—						
Antimony.................... Ton.	337	19,769			337	19,769
Corundum.................... "	933	82,358			933	82,358
Iron........................ "	130,496	345,119			130,496	345,119
Manganese................... "	90	1,950			90	1,950
Other....................... "	12,764	645,873			12,764	645,873
Total, ores...................	144,620	1,095,069			144,620	1,095,069
Phosphates.................... "	60	180			60	180
Plumbago, crude ore and concentrates.................... Cwt	9,944	24,120			9,944	24,120
Pyrites...................... Ton	95,901	393,085			95,901	393,085
Salt........................ Cwt	9,519	5,509	55,434	23,646	64,953	29,155
Sand and gravel................ Ton	959,039	808,012			959,039	808,012
Stone:—						
Ornamental, granite, marble, etc., unwrought.................. "	95	399	13	420	108	819
Building, freestone, limestone, etc. unwrought.................. "	62,600	45,950			62,600	45,950
Crushed..................... "	28,995	20,080			28,995	20,080
For manufacture of grindstones, rough........................ "	54	294			54	294
Total, stone...................	91,744	66,723	13	420	91,757	67,143
Other articles of the mine.......... $		102,652		108,420		211,072
Total, mine...................		51,740,989		325,548		52,066,537

*These items to show the weight and value of the copper, lead, nickel, platinum and silver respectively, not the gross weight of ore, matte, concentrates, etc.

6 GEORGE V, A. 1916

No. 22.—SUMMARY STATEMENT OF EXPORTS—*Continued*.

Articles.	GOODS THE PRODUCE OF CANADA.		GOODS NOT THE PRODUCE OF CANADA.		TOTAL EXPORTS.	
	Quantity.	Value.	Quantity.	Value.	Quantity.	Value.
THE FISHERIES.		$		$		$
Codfish, including haddock, ling and pollock—fresh......... Lb.	3,403,157	111,004	13,525	632	3,416,682	111,636
"　　dry salted.............. Cwt	659,903	4,121,962	9,284	50,892	669,187	4,172,854
"　　wet salted................ "	67,217	268,976	2,527	8,057	69,744	277,033
"　　pickled.................. "	34,386	128,910	....	....	34,386	128,910
"　　tongues and sounds......... Lb.	138,723	30,786	9,735	568	148,458	31,354
Total, codfish................	....	4,661,638	....	60,149	....	4,721,787
Mackerel, fresh................. "	3,229,558	156,487	....	....	3,229,558	156,487
"　　pickled................Brl.	27,776	299,208	435	3,058	28,211	302,266
Total, mackerel...............	....	455,695	....	3,058	....	458,753
Halibut, fresh.............. Lb	7,270,514	451,912	473,475	23,678	7,743,989	475,590
"　　pickled................ Brl.	163	2,296	....	....	163	2,296
Total, halibut................	....	454,208	....	23,678	....	477,886
Herring, fresh or frozen.......... Lb.	30,725,723	506,536	130,000	1,300	30,855,723	507,836
"　　pickled................Brl.	331,056	821,252	4,964	19,695	336,020	840,947
"　　canned................Lb.	619,934	53,338	1,900	131	621,834	53,469
"　　smoked................ "	4,193,419	141,963	....	....	4,193,419	141,963
Total, herring...............	....	1,523,089	....	21,126	....	1,544,215
Smelts................... "	7,073,036	427,873	....	....	7,073,036	427,873
Sea fish, other, fresh............ "	1,619,084	81,684	....	....	1,619,084	81,684
"　"　pickled......... Brl.	11,867	68,058	5	51	11,872	68,109
"　"　preserved........... Lb.	1,726,892	118,284	20,080	2,303	1,746,972	120,587
Total, sea fish, other..........	....	268,026	....	2,354	....	270,380
Oysters, fresh................Brl.	623	6,857	....	....	623	6,857
"　　preserved in cans.......... Lb.	170	40	....	....	170	40
Total, oysters...............	....	6,897	....	....	....	6,897
Lobsters, fresh................. "	5,500,586	849,368	....	....	5,500,586	849,368
"　　canned................ "	7,518,741	3,013,782	20,976	6,635	7,539,717	3,020,417
Total, lobsters...............	13,019,327	3,863,150	20,976	6,635	13,040,303	3,869,785
Bait, fish...................... Brl.	234	459	....	....	234	459
Clams...................... "	29,148	67,274	....	....	29,148	67,274
Salmon, fresh................. Lb.	5,569,545	387,543	150	15	5,569,695	387,558
"　　smoked................ "	2,160	313	....	....	2,160	313
"　　canned................ "	34,655,108	4,948,723	....	....	34,655,108	4,948,723
"　　pickled................Brl.	40,692	306,438	106	1,293	40,798	307,731
"　　dog................ Lb.	6,312,230	53,667	....	....	6,312,230	53,667
Total, salmon................	....	5,696,684	....	1,308	....	5,697,992
Salmon or lake trout............ "	1,360,875	76,947	....	....	1,360,875	76,947
Fish, all other, fresh............ $	....	1,735,943	....	....	....	1,735,943
"　　"　pickled........... Brl	4,441	19,058	....	....	4,441	19,058
Total, fish, other...... $	....	1,755,001	....	....	....	1,755,001
Fish oil, cod..................... Gal.	596,137	188,798	32,570	10,940	628,707	199,738
"　　seal.................... "	9,686	2,426	1,335	375	11,021	2,801
"　　whale.................. "	334,223	144,388	....	....	334,223	144,388
"　　other.................. "	50,636	12,994	145	57	50,781	13,051
Total, fish oil..............	990,682	348,606	34,050	11,372	1,024,732	359,978

No. 22.—Summary Statement of Exports—*Continued.*

Articles.	Goods the Produce of Canada.		Goods not the Produce of Canada.		Total Exports.	
	Quantity.	Value.	Quantity.	Value.	Quantity.	Value.
THE FISHERIES.		$		$		$
Furs or skins, the produce of fish or marine animals............ $	....	12,574	....	189	....	12,763
Other articles of the fisheries..... $	....	68,947	....	1,800	....	70,747
Total, fisheries...............	....	19,687,068	....	131,669	....	19,818,737
THE FOREST.						
Ashes, pot and pearl.............. Brl.	453	22,685	116	3,487	569	26,172
" all other................. $	....	34,359	....	....	....	34,359
Total, ashes..................	....	57,044	....	3,487	....	60,531
Bark for tanning.................Cord.	5,675	42,370	....	....	5,675	42,370
Firewood........................ "	23,296	80,776	....	....	23,296	80,776
Knees and futtocks............... No.	11,364	15,877	....	....	11,364	15,877
Lathwood........................Cord.	12	42	....	....	12	42
Logs, cedar, capable of being made into shingle bolts... $	....	471,165	....	....	....	471,165
" elm...................... $	....	13,758	....	....	....	13,758
" hemlock.................. $	....	63,822	....	....	....	63,822
" oak...................... $	....	238	....	....	....	238
" pine..................... $	....	100,715	....	....	....	100,715
" spruce................... $	....	491,209	....	....	....	491,209
" tamarac.................. $	....	278	....	....	....	278
" all other................ $	....	117,748	....	....	....	117,748
Total, logs....................	....	1,258,933	....	....	....	1,258,933
Lumber, viz.: Battens.............. $	....	4,379	....	....	....	4,379
Basswood....................M ft.	1,283	38,053	....	....	1,283	38,053
Deals, pine..............St. hund	14,399	1,148,738	....	....	14,399	1,148,738
" spruce and other........... "	138,500	6,393,420	....	....	138,500	6,393,420
Deal ends........................ "	6,582	269,849	....	....	6,582	269,849
Hickory......................M ft.	8	355	8	545	16	900
Laths.......................... M	635,974	1,798,219	....	....	635,974	1,798,219
Pickets....... $	....	114,122	....	....	....	114,122
Planks and boards...............M ft.	975,420	18,921,445	454	17,850	975,874	18,939,295
Scantling........................ "	76,565	1,196,559	....	....	76,565	1,196,559
Shingles........................ M	1,359,069	2,987,764	....	....	1,359,069	2,987,764
Shooks .... $	....	158,397	....	2,350	....	160,747
Staves—other and headings...... $	....	77,762	....	1,215	....	78,977
All other lumber, n.o.p........... $	....	108,463	....	194	....	108,657
Total, lumber................	....	33,217,525	....	22,154	....	33,239,679
Match blocks.................. $	....	5,190	....	....	....	5,190
Masts and spars.................No.	168	2,416	15	683	183	3,099
Piling........ $	....	171,758	....	....	....	171,758
Poles, hop, hoop, telegraph and other............ $	....	162,153	....	404	....	162,557
Posts, sleepers and railroad ties..... $	....	247,862	....	77	....	247,939
Shingle bolts, of pine or cedar.....Cord	7,769	24,780	....	....	7,769	24,780
Timber, square, viz.:—						
Ash.............. $	....	1,086	....	....	....	1,086
Birch........................ $	....	119,386	....	....	....	119,386
Elm.......................... $	....	98,988	....	163,770	....	262,758
Maple........................ $	....	10	....	....	....	10
Oak.......................... $	....	73,251	....	143,389	....	216,640
Pine, red.................... $	....	....	....	940	....	940
Pine, white.................. $	....	237,220	....	151,004	....	388,224
All other.................... $	....	3,014	....	188	....	3,202
Total, timber, square........	....	532,955	....	459,291	....	992,246

6 GEORGE V, A. 1916

No. 22.—Summary Statement of Exports—*Continued.*

Articles.	Goods the Produce of Canada.		Goods not the Produce of Canada.		Total Exports.	
	Quantity.	Value.	Quantity.	Value.	Quantity.	Value.
		$		$		$
THE FOREST—*Con.*						
Wood, blocks and other, for pulp..Cord	1,010,914	6,817,311	....	....	1,010,914	6,817,311
Other articles of the forest.......... $	....	13,691	....	2	....	13,693
Total, forest...................	....	42,650,683	....	486,098	....	43,136,781
ANIMALS AND THEIR PRODUCE.						
Animals—						
Horses, one year old or less......No.	16	1,272	....	....	16	1,272
" over one year old........ "	10,398	1,841,095	14,800	1,935,421	25,198	3,776,516
Cattle, one year old or less...... "	34,082	416,038	1	200	34,083	416,238
" over one year old........ "	151,821	8,851,496	20	4,850	151,841	8,856,346
Swine...................... "	243,311	3,117,005	1	50	243,312	3,117,055
Sheep, one year old or less...... "	35,293	211,714	....	....	35,293	211,714
" over one year old......... "	7,539	74,898	460	9,380	7,999	84,278
Poultry........................ "	....	335,454	....	2,632	....	338,086
Other...................... $	....	82,020	....	11,157	....	93,177
Total, animals living........	....	14,930,992	....	1,963,690	....	16,894,682
Bones......................... Cwt.	72,790	95,665	2,195	2,426	74,985	98,091
Butter....................... Lb.	2,724,913	639,625	45,411	9,663	2,770,324	649,288
Casein........................ "	230,045	13,923	....	....	230,045	13,923
Cheese........................ "	137,601,661	19,213,501	179,223	34,102	137,780,884	19,247,603
Cream, fresh...................Gal.	1,895,575	1,836,006	....	....	1,895,575	1,836,006
Milk, fresh.................... "	477,692	68,205	....	....	477,692	68,205
Cream and milk, condensed, canned						
or preserved............... Lb	18,355,975	1,181,300	....	....	18,355,975	1,181,300
Eggs......................Doz.	3,592,899	965,640	1,117,130	240,878	4,710,029	1,206,518
Furs,—dressed.................. $	....	29,862	....	12,997	....	42,859
" undressed.................. $	....	2,726,961	....	85,973	....	2,812,934
Total, furs...................	....	2,756,823	....	98,970	....	2,855,793
Grease and grease scraps........... Lb.	2,411,238	77,947	78,678	3,071	2,489,916	81,018
Glue stock...................... $	....	41,350	....	....	....	41,350
Hair........................... $	....	283,191	....	16,947	....	300,138
Hides and skins, other than fur..... $	....	7,434,210	....	36,571	....	7,470,781
Horns and hoofs.................. $	....	16,186	....	81	....	16,267
Honey.......................... Lb.	6,929	792	675	48	7,604	840
Lard........................... "	2,689,036	305,933	3,698	401	2,692,734	306,334
Meats, viz.:—						
Bacon........................ "	76,801,419	11,811,825	2,410	361	76,803,829	11,812,186
Beef......................... "	18,828,257	1,988,489	841,444	72,941	19,669,701	2,061,430
Hams........................ "	17,958,874	2,652,917	7,576	1,147	17,966,450	2,654,064
Mutton...................... "	1,064,963	124,087	....	....	1,064,963	124,087
Pork........................ "	21,288,226	2,599,844	120,857	10,932	21,409,083	2,610,776
Poultry, dressed or undressed..... $	....	212,992	....	....	....	212,992
Game, dressed or undressed...... $	....	2,340	....	....	....	2,340
Tongues...................... Lb.	192,469	24,703	....	....	192,469	24,703
Canned...................... "	9,882,662	2,340,081	8,707	1,354	9,891,369	2,341,435
All other, n.o.p.................. "	4,403,437	310,663	31,465	3,943	4,434,902	314,606
Total, meats................	....	22,067,941	....	90,678	....	22,158,619
Oil, Neat's foot and other animal,						
n.o.p...................... Gal.	228,126	239,638	206	273	228,332	239,911
Sausage casings.................... $	....	441,587	....	12,276	....	453,863
Sheep pelts....................... $	....	265,332	....	7,356	....	272,688
Tails............................. $	....	14,192	....	....	....	14,192
Tallow........................ Lb.	1,039,872	64,842	....	....	1,039,872	64,842
Wool........................... "	5,659,970	1,359,741	137,188	38,304	5,797,158	1,398,045
Other articles of the animals........ $	....	76,181	....	9,524	....	85,705
Total, animals and produce...	....	74,390,743	....	2,565,259	....	76,956,002

SESSIONAL PAPER No. 11

No. 22.—Summary Statement of Exports—*Continued.*

Articles.	Goods the Produce of Canada.		Goods not the Produce of Canada.		Total Exports.	
	Quantity.	Value.	Quantity.	Value.	Quantity.	Value.
		$		$		$
AGRICULTURAL PRODUCTS.						
Balsam.......................... $	....	23,954	....	950	....	24,904
Cider........................Gal.	88,736	15,715	215	72	88,951	15,787
Flax..........................Cwt	6,729	34,230	....	....	6,729	34,230
Fruits, viz.:—						
Apples, dried...................Lb.	4,488,050	276,060	....	....	4,488,050	276,060
" green or ripe........... Brl	1,117,336	2,657,115	1,488	4,277	1,118,824	2,661,392
Berries of all kinds.............. $	....	106,545	....	3,042	....	109,587
Canned or preserved........... $	....	476,497	....	3,266	....	479,763
All other, n.o.p................. $	....	80,804	....	159,413	....	240,217
Total, fruits..................	....	3,597,021	....	169,998	....	3,767,019
Grain and products of, viz.:—						
Barley........................Bush	5,576,646	3,262,025	1,014,607	589,874	6,591,253	3,851,899
Beans........................ "	28,661	73,508	4,262	7,422	32,923	80,930
Buckwheat.................... "	343,349	272,516	....	....	343,349	272,516
Indian corn.................... "	376,663	256,090	34,030	21,954	410,693	278,044
Oats.......................... "	17,768,166	8,961,126	2,616,207	1,180,018	20,384,373	10,141,144
Pease, whole.................. "	261,354	532,171	252	388	261,606	532,559
" split.................. "	41,624	107,677	201	150	41,825	107,827
Rye.......................... "	263,422	259,622	358,572	277,691	621,994	537,313
Wheat........................ "	71,913,385	74,293,548	33,522,079	33,042,368	105,435,464	107,335,916
Total, grain..................	96,573,270	88,018,283	37,550,210	35,119,865	134,123,480	123,138,148
Bran..........................Cwt.	1,038,134	946,331	220	407	1,038,354	946,738
Flour of wheat.................Brl.	4,952,337	24,610,946	1,125	3,726	4,953,462	24,614,672
Indian meal................... "	2,560	9,549	....	....	2,560	9,549
Oatmeal...................... "	60,320	287,844	....	....	60,320	287,844
Meal, all other, n.o.p.......... "	432	1,616	....	....	432	1,616
Total, flour and meal........	5,015,649	24,909,955	1,125	3,726	5,016,774	24,913,681
Cereal foods, prepared, of all kinds. $	....	1,970,402	....	3,732	....	1,974,134
Hay..........................Ton	131,875	2,232,558	72	1,444	131,947	2,234,002
Hemp.....,....................Cwt.	....	....	460	2,090	460	2,090
Hops.........................Lb.	170,226	35,892	1,200	276	171,426	36,168
Malt..........................Bush.	4,481	4,141	2,000	2,069	6,481	6,210
Maple sugar...................Lb.	1,462,416	131,477	....	....	1,462,416	131,477
Maple syrup...................Gal.	6,165	6,687	....	....	6,165	6,687
Nuts..........................Lb.	36,951	2,246	141,313	7,312	178,264	9,558
Seeds—Clover..................Bush	44,735	375,205	1,207	9,745	45,942	384,950
Flax.......................... "	7,689,525	10,359,703	58,983	88,475	7,748,508	10,448,178
Grass......................... "	73,806	69,118	235	438	74,041	69,556
All other...................... $	....	5,755	....	80,058	....	85,813
Total, seeds..................	....	10,809,781	....	178,716	....	10,988,497
Straw........................Ton	4,962	29,618	....	....	4,962	29,618
Tobacco, leaf..................Lb.	36,445	21,644	139,857	92,690	176,302	114,334
Trees, shrubs and plants........... $	....	22,538	....	3,791	....	26,329
Vegetables,—canned or preserved... $	....	299,412	....	1,072	....	300,484
Potatoes......................Bush	1,192,258	696,783	72	118	1,192,330	696,901
Turnips....................... "	2,150,399	286,461	....	....	2,150,399	286,461
All other vegetables.............. $	....	217,627	....	10,363	....	227,990
Total, vegetables..............	....	1,500,283	....	11,553	....	1,511,836
Other articles of agriculture......... $	....	433,294	....	5,323	....	438,617
Total, agriculture products.....	....	134,746,050	....	35,604,014	....	170,350,064

No. 22.—Summary Statement of Exports—*Continued.*

Articles.	Goods the Produce of Canada.		Goods not the Produce of Canada.		Total Exports.	
	Quantity.	Value.	Quantity.	Value.	Quantity.	Value.
MANUFACTURES.		$		$		$
Agricultural Implements and Machines, viz.:—						
Mowing machines..............No.	7,512	260,709	....	....	7,512	260,709
Cultivators..................... "	5,831	143,807	....	....	5,831	143,807
Reapers......................... "	902	48,301	....	....	902	48,301
Drills........................... "	3,996	260,318	4	1,862	4,000	262,180
Harvesters and binders.......... "	6,799	695,858	2	3,540	6,801	699,398
Ploughs......................... "	13,573	339,301	65	7,450	13,638	346,751
Harrows......................... "	6,164	92,691	29	2,479	6,193	95,170
Hay rakes....................... "	2,055	47,773	....	....	2,055	47,773
Seeders.......................... "	11	670	....	....	11	670
Threshing machines.............. "	2,043	866,993	8	9,824	2,051	876,817
All other........................ $	....	263,776	....	11,939	....	275,715
Parts of......................... $	....	648,892	....	20,164	....	669,056
Asbestos, manufactures of........ $	....	78,329	....	964	....	79,293
Baking powders..................Lb.	84,777	13,096	1,380	194	86,157	13,290
Binder twine.................... "	12,281,708	1,077,021	35,850	3,050	12,317,558	1,080,071
Books, pamphlets, maps, etc...... $	....	420,026	....	233,741	....	653,767
Biscuits and bread..............Cwt.	3,032	26,452	29	415	3,061	26,867
Bricks...........................M.	1,482	12,020	22	224	1,504	12,244
Brooms and whisks............... $	....	14,471	....	3	....	14,474
Brushes of all kinds............. $	....	9,569	....	1,335	....	10,904
Buttons.......................... $	....	394	....	2,771	....	3,165
Candles.........................Lb.	652	89	1,379	207	2,031	296
Cartridges, gun, rifle and pistol..... $	....	221,137	....	1,905	....	223,042
Charcoal......................... $	....	3,878	....	....	....	3,878
Cement.......................... $	....	1,065	....	1,296	....	2,361
Cinders.......................... $	....	885	....	....	....	885
Clay, manufactures of............ $	....	17,396	....	985	....	18,381
Clothing and wearing apparel....... $	....	7,344,388	....	139,951	....	7,484,339
Coke............................Ton.	52,874	240,818	....	....	52,874	240,818
Confectionery.................... $	....	82,702	....	6,160	....	88,862
Cordage, ropes and twine.......... $	....	47,180	....	21,077	....	68,257
Cotton fabrics...................Yd	1,222,964	282,828	104,287	12,757	1,327,251	295,585
Cottons, other................... $	....	151,343	....	455,453	....	606,796
Cotton waste....................Lb.	1,606,881	72,736	195,758	9,180	1,802,639	81,916
Cream separators................. $	....	49,819	....	16,389	....	66,208
Drugs, Chemicals and Medicines, viz.:—						
Acetate of lime.................Lb.	15,139,007	269,591	....	....	15,139,007	269,591
Acid, sulphuric................. "	6,409,835	41,335	360	9	6,410,195	41,344
Calcium carbide................ "	36,342,719	1,117,118	....	....	36,342,719	1,117,118
Gum chicle..................... "	1,897,872	921,804	333,093	130,972	2,230,965	1,052,776
Lye............................. $	....	110,818	....	....	....	110,818
Phosphorus.....................Lb.	558,050	84,458	....	....	558,050	84,458
Senega root..................... "	373,843	171,319	....	....	373,843	171,319
All other, n.o.p................. $	....	757,789	....	358,532	....	1,116,321
Dye stuffs....................... $	....	24,734	....	46,019	....	70,753
Earthenware and all manufactures of......................... $	....	7,098	....	7,175	....	14,273
Electrical apparatus............. $	....	97,890	....	224,581	....	322,471
Electrotypes and stereotypes...... $	....	6,287	....	7,269	....	13,556
Extract of hemlock bark.........Brl.	2,550	30,812	....	....	2,550	30,812
Explosives and fulminates, n.o.p.... $	....	265,578	....	18,035	....	283,613
Felt, manufactures of............. $	....	6,927	....	2,345	....	9,272
Fertilizers....................... $	....	2,163,917	....	7,255	....	2,171,172
Films for photographers' use and for moving pictures........... $	....	31,244	....	56,945	....	88,189
Fur, manufactures of............. $	....	29,808	....	8,220	....	38,028
Gasoline engines..................No.	894	116,607	447	92,697	1,341	209,304
Gasoline launches................. "	11	6,467	10	7,543	21	14,010
Glass and glassware, n.o.p........ $	....	55,553	....	22,341	....	77,894
Grindstones, manufactured........ $	....	45,889	....	1,858	....	47,747
Guns, rifles and firearms of all kinds........................... $	....	211,324	....	21,473	....	232,797
Gypsum or plaster, ground........ $	....	31,878	....	....	....	31,878
Hats and caps.................... $	....	16,203	....	15,515	....	31,718
Household effects, n.o.p........... $	....	3,681,709	....	347,745	....	4,029,454
Ice.............................. $	....	7,515	....	....	....	7,515

SESSIONAL PAPER No. 11

No. 22.—Summary Statement of Exports—*Continued.*

Articles.	Goods The Produce of Canada.		Goods not the Produce of Canada.		Total Exports.	
	Quality.	Value.	Quantity.	Value.	Quantity.	Value.
		$		$		$
MANUFACTURES—*Con.*						
India-rubber, manufactures of, viz.:—						
Belting................................ $	....	2,274	....	1,336	....	3,610
Hose.................................. $	....	16,476	....	2,772	....	19,248
Boots and shoes..................... $	....	197,104	....	1,208	....	198,312
Mats and matting................... $	....	34	....	....	....	34
Clothing.............................. $	....	730	....	1,160	....	1,890
Waste............................Lb.	4,221,476	276,128	14,134	2,314	4,235,610	278,442
All other, n.o.p.................... $	....	230,159	....	1,292,268	....	1,522,427
Total, India-rubber, mfrs. of....	....	722,905	....	1,301,058	....	2,023,963
Iron and steel and manufactures of, viz.:						
Stoves...........................No.	4,225	24,708	2,356	7,035	6,581	31,743
Gas buoys and parts of........... $	....	20,080	....	607	....	20,687
Castings, n.o.p.................... $	....	148,145	....	18,033	....	166,178
Pig iron........................Ton.	10,477	126,975	1,115	12,452	11,592	139,427
Ferro-silicon and ferro-compounds "	6,901	398,488	....	....	6,901	398,488
Wire and wire nails.............Cwt.	446,909	870,319	22,355	11,364	469,264	881,683
Machinery, viz.: Linotype machines, and parts of................... $	....	6,035	....	29,759	....	35,794
Machinery, n.o.p.................. $	....	313,780	....	524,090	....	837,870
Sewing machines.................No.	3,026	33,244	343	14,090	3,369	47,334
Washing machines, domestic and wringers.......................... $	....	31,252	....	1,264	....	32,516
Typewriters......................No.	2,674	173,211	1,220	56,811	3,894	230,022
Scrap iron or steel..............Cwt.	858,855	534,946	9,083	4,750	867,938	539,696
Hardware, viz.: tools, hand or machine.......................... $	....	119,779	....	51,303	....	171,082
Hardware, n.o.p................... $	....	249,935	....	85,159	....	335,094
All other, n.o.p................... $	....	7,111,529	....	355,739	....	7,467,268
Total, iron and steel..............	....	10,162,426	....	1,172,456	....	11,334,882
Jewellery of all kinds, n.o.p......... $	....	80,714	....	403,407	....	484,121
Jeweller's sweepings............... $	....	170,720	....	18,330	....	189,050
Junk, except metallic and rubber..Cwt.	78,508	161,221	465	1,476	78,973	162,697
Lamps and lanterns............... $	....	14,294	....	8,235	....	22,529
Leather—Sole.....................Lb.	13,758,727	4,096,081	4,834	2,128	13,763,561	4,098,209
Upper.............................. "	2,179,021	1,450,910	15,087	12,668	2,194,108	1,463,578
All other, n.o.p.................... "	3,013,799	1,014,490	19,112	8,018	3,032,911	1,022,508
Boots and shoes.................... $	....	188,084	....	48,802	....	236,886
Harness and saddlery............. $	....	3,981,959	....	6,090	....	3,988,049
Other manufactures of............ $	....	75,765	....	19,865	....	95,630
Total, leather and manuf. of........	....	10,807,289	....	97,571	....	10,904,860
Lime................................. $	....	17,137	....	....	....	17,137
Liquors—Ale and beer............Gal.	11,215	4,401	10,440	8,193	21,655	12,594
Brandy........................... "	3	28	724	2,934	727	2,962
Gin............................... "	147	133	11,928	9,337	12,075	9,470
Rum.............................. "	....	....	5,953	2,060	5,953	2,060
Whiskey........................... "	282,867	860,932	2,273	5,753	285,140	866,685
Wines.:........................... "	2,779	3,298	6,218	49,302	8,997	52,600
Wood alcohol...................... "	500,338	231,283	5	3	500,343	231,286
Other spirits, n.o.p.............. "	982	1,538	900	1,938	1,882	3,476
Total, liquors.....................	798,331	1,101,613	38,441	79,520	836,772	1,181,133

6 GEORGE V, A. 1916

No. 22.—Summary Statement of Exports—*Continued.*

Articles.	Goods The Produce of Canada. Quality.	Value.	Goods Not the Produce of Canada. Quantity.	Value.	Total Exports. Quantity.	Value.
MANUFACTURES—*Con.*		$		$		$
Metals, viz.:—						
Aluminum in bars, blocks, etc...Cwt	140,441	2,318,800	435	10,643	140,876	2,329,443
Aluminum, manufactures of.......$	....	452,708	....	2,024	....	454,732
Brass, old and scrap.............Cwt.	27,342	258,531	294	2,508	27,636	261,039
Copper, old and scrap........... "	21,119	241,050	....	....	21,119	241,050
Metallic shingles and laths and corrugated roofing..............$	....	88,348	....	1,295	....	89,643
Metals, n.o.p....................$	....	402,906	....	121,315	....	524,221
Total, metals......................	....	3,762,343	....	137,785	....	3,900,128
Mineral and aerated waters in bottles......................$	....	1,805	....	56	....	1,861
Molasses......................Gal.	....	....	202,094	51,388	202,094	51,388
Musical Instruments, viz.:—						
Organs.........................No.	1,093	63,199	27	592	1,120	63,791
Pianos.......................... "	239	61,547	44	14,758	283	76,305
Other, and parts of..............$	....	100,829	....	31,988	....	132,817
Total, musical instruments........	....	225,575	....	47,338	....	272,913
Oakum...........................Cwt.	10	50	25	168	35	218
Oil cake........................ "	279,334	392,330	....	....	279,334	392,330
Oilcloths, all kinds..............Sq.yd	60,042	8,417	400	120	60,442	8,537
Oil, creosote....................Gal.	632,563	45,392	....	....	632,563	45,392
Oil, gasoline and naphtha........... "	37,849	10,319	136,646	30,210	174,495	40,529
Oil, n.o.p........................ "	424,632	100,380	323,214	111,218	747,846	211,598
Total, oils........................	1,095,044	156,091	459,860	141,428	1,554,904	297,519
Paper, viz.:—						
Wall............................Roll	783,895	53,916	25,190	3,647	809,085	57,563
Felt.......................... "	78,793	85,066	877	2,110	79,670	87,176
Wrapping.....................Lb.	13,539,646	408,360	783	90	13,540,429	408,450
Printing.....................Cwt.	7,292,047	14,091,662	....	....	7,292,047	14,091,662
Paper, n.o.p....................$	....	839,334	....	15,879	....	855,213
Total, paper......................	....	15,478,338	....	21,726	....	15,500,064
Paints and varnishes of all kinds....$	....	169,454	....	21,969	....	191,423
Paintings.......................$	....	66,346	....	222,458	....	288,804
Photographs....................$	....	10,137	....	3,555	....	13,692
Philosophical and scientific apparatus and instruments............$	....	46,625	....	106,530	....	153,155
Plumbago, manufactures of........$	....	62,138	....	2,523	....	64,661
Rags.........................Cwt.	659,922	1,080,769	240	369	660,162	1,081,138
Sails, awnings, tents and tarpaulins.$	....	1,902	....	13,813	....	15,715
Ships sold to other countries.No. & Ton	15—14,303	448,900	2— 4,977	616,000	17—19,280	1,064,900
Silk and manufactures of..........$	....	30,933	....	41,049	....	71,982
Soap.......................Lb.	584,337	34,118	54,545	2,779	638,882	36,897
Starch....................... "	76,158	2,439	925	70	77,083	2,509
Stationery......................$	....	63,780	....	7,954	....	71,734
Stone, ornamental, viz.: granite, marble, etc., dressed............$	....	1,462	....	2,067	....	3,529
Stone, building, dressed...........$	....	370	....	....	....	370
Sugar of all kinds, n.o.p..........Lb.	12,550	640	4,775,375	238,771	4,787,925	239,411
Sugar house syrup...........Gal.	134,908	16,775	11,932	1,790	146,840	18,565
Tar............................$	....	41,736	....	351	....	42,087
Tin, manufactures of.............$	....	98,870	....	99,098	....	197,968

No. 22.—Summary Statement of Exports—*Continued.*

Articles.	Goods The Produce of Canada.		Goods not the Produce of Canada.		Total Exports.	
	Quality.	Value.	Quantity.	Value.	Quantity.	Value.
MANUFACTURES—*Con.*		$		$		$
Tobacco, viz.:—						
Cigars...................... M	18	762	2	43	20	805
Cigarettes...................... "	185	1,754	222	1,235	407	2,989
Stems and cuttings..............Lb.	293,963	27,515	5,986	548	299,949	28,063
All other, n.o.p.............. "	13,293	8,308	12,300	10,762	25,593	19,070
Total, tobacco...................	....	38,339	....	12,588	....	50,927
Tow................Cwt.	1,356	1,947	....		1,356	1,947
Trunks and valises............. $		16,363	....	1,799		18,162
Vehicles, viz.:—						
Automobiles.................No.	5,238	2,645,824	341	644,410	5,579	3,290,234
Automobile, parts of........... $	....	408,629	....	198,702	....	607,331
Carriages...................No.	59	4,438	12	1,656	71	6,094
" parts of.............. $	....	43,527		1,389		44,916
Carts.......................No.	598	15,769	....		598	15,769
Wagons...................... "	2,142	313,174	29	3,071	2,171	316,245
Bicycles................... "	118	10,648	125	18,152	243	28,800
" parts of.............. $	....	3,226	....	2,160	....	5,386
Other vehicles............. $	....	52,535	....	135,580	....	188,115
Total, vehicles...............	....	3,497,770	....	1,005,120	....	4,502,890
Vinegar...................Gal.	20	5	27	6	47	11
Wood, viz.:—						
Barrels, empty.................No.	14,330	16,913	15,236	24,077	29,566	40,990
Household furniture........... $	....	299,679	....	24,627	....	324,306
Doors, sashes and blinds........ $	....	12,440	....	213	....	12,653
Matches...................... $	....	470	....	207	....	677
Match splints.................. $	....	12,893	....		....	12,893
Mouldings, trimmings and other house furnishings.............. $	....	4,731	....	1,714	....	6,445
Pails, tubs, churns and other hollow woodenware........... $	....	4,046	....	588	....	4,634
Spool wood and spools.......... $	....	98,247	....	3,901	....	102,148
Wood pulp, chemically prepared.Cwt.	2,424,328	4,806,622	....		2,424,328	4,806,622
" mechanically ground.. "	6,163,702	4,459,539	....		6,163,702	4,459,539
Other manufactures of........... $	....	360,372	....	76,556	....	436,928
Total, wood....................	....	10,075,952	....	131,883	....	10,207,835
Woollens...................... $	....	1,301,671	....	86,949	....	1,388,620
Other articles of manufacture....... $	....	1,018,389	....	1,085,627	....	2,104,016
Total, manufactures.............	....	85,539,501	....	9,529,024	....	95,068,525
MISCELLANEOUS ARTICLES.						
Contractor's outfits............. $	....	186,831	....	220,345	....	407,176
Coffee......................Lb.	107,397	21,117	37,834	6,025	145,231	27,142
Dried fruits, n.o.p.............. "	3,329	105	210,968	15,078	214,297	15,183
Menageries, etc................ $	....	7,480	....	1,998,132	....	2,005,612
Rice.......................Lb.	2,207,680	84,498	636,902	23,726	2,844,582	108,224
Rice meal..................... "	4,310,910	109,242	....		4,310,910	109,242
Tea.......................... "	....		3,762,671	1,071,688	3,762,671	1,071,688
Other miscellaneous articles....... $	....	254,529	....	47,067	....	301,596
Total, miscellaneous...........	....	663,802	....	3,382,061	....	4,045,863

6 GEORGE V, A. 1916

No. 22.—Summary Statement of Exports—*Concluded.*

Articles.	Goods The Produce of Canada.		Goods Not the Produce of Canada.		Total Exports.	
	Quality.	Value.	Quantity.	Value.	Quantity.	Value.
		$		$		$
COIN.						
Gold coin.......................... $	....	100	....	28,234,873	....	28,234,973
Silver coin........................ $	....	467	....	1,121,927	....	1,122,394
Copper coin....................... $	....	100	....	8,901	....	9,001
Total, coin.....................	....	667	....	29,365,701	....	29,366,368
RECAPITULATION.						
Produce of mine.....................	....	51,740,989	....	325,548	....	52,066,537
Produce of fisheries.................	....	19,687,068	....	131,669	....	19,818,737
Produce of forest...................	....	42,650,683	....	486,098	....	43,136,781
Animals and their produce............	....	74,390,743	....	2,565,259	....	76,956,002
Agricultural products...............	....	134,746,050	....	35,604,014	....	170,350,064
Manufacturers......................	....	85,539,501	....	9,529,024	....	95,068,525
Miscellaneous articles................	....	663,802	....	3,382,061	....	4,045,863
Total..........................	....	409,418,836	....	52,023,673	....	461,442,509
Coin..............................	....	667	....	29,365,701	....	29,366,368
Grand total exports...............	....	409,419,503	....	81,389,374	....	490,808,877

No. 23.—STATEMENT showing the Value of Goods Exported from Canada during the Twelve Months ended March 31, 1914 and 1915, respectively; the Value of Goods exported to countries embraced in the "British Empire", and to "All Other Countries" during the Twelve Months ended March 31, 1915.

Articles.	TWELVE MONTHS ENDED MARCH 31, 1914.		TWELVE MONTHS ENDED MARCH 31, 1915.		TWELVE MONTHS ENDED MARCH, 1915.			
					British Empire.		All other Countries.	
	Quantity.	Value.	Quantity.	Value.	Quantity.	Value.	Quantity.	Value.
		$		$		$		$
CLASSIFICATION OF THE MINE.								
Arsenic......................Cwt.	29,487	117,497	32,655	120,242			32,655	120,242
Asbestos........................Ton	105,971	2,891,669	74,904	2,227,387	14,726	513,877	60,178	1,713,510
Asbestos sand................."	28,433	162,767	19,928	111,727	997	12,298	18,931	99,429
Coal............................"	1,553,013	3,794,882	1,601,129	4,635,422	236,788	752,834	1,364,341	3,882,588
Chromite (chromic iron)......."			79	878			79	878
Felspar........................"	18,898	75,988	13,649	56,666	22	176	13,627	56,492
Gold bearing quartz, dust, nuggets, etc....$		13,376,735		15,409,019		105,324		15,303,695
Gypsum or plaster—crude........Ton	395,962	480,779	322,680	378,648			322,680	378,648
Metals, viz:—								
*Copper, fine, contained in ore, matte, regulus, etc....Lb.	83,250,198	9,489,729	62,677,038	6,173,357	11,062,501	853,900	51,614,537	5,319,457
Copper black or coarse, cement copper and copper in pigs.Lb.			9,861,780	1,371,889			9,861,780	1,371,889
*Lead, metallic, contained in ore, etc....	274,760	7,562	723,100	12,534			723,100	12,534
*Lead, pig....	200	7	2,534,502	97,286			2,534,502	97,286
*Nickel, fine, contained in ore, matte or speiss....	50,580,536	5,374,738	45,412,017	5,063,656	10,838,477	1,601,251	34,573,540	3,462,405
*Platinum, contained in concentrates, or other forms....Oz.	289	14,578	144	6,827			144	6,827
*Silver, metallic, contained in ore, concentrates, etc....	36,758,276	20,971,538	25,355,305	13,516,390	16,918,426	9,061,318	8,436,879	4,455,072
Mica..........................Lb.	714,567	210,178	853,129	217,859	130,171	32,468	722,958	185,391
Mineral pigment, iron oxides, ochres, etc........Cwt	39,519	19,638	32,767	20,744	9,826	5,942	22,941	14,802
Mineral water, natural, not in bottles........Gal.	1,757	610	981	82	800	40	181	42
Oil—Mineral, coal and kerosene, crude.... "	3,650	379	218,900	5,393	9,000	600	209,900	4,793
Oil—Mineral, coal and kerosene, refined.... "	191,238	19,979	163,420	12,693	153,458	11,754	9,962	939
Total, oils.................	194,888	20,358	382,320	18,086	162,458	12,354	219,862	5,732
Ores, viz:—								
Antimony..................Ton			337	19,769	332	18,285	5	1,484
Corundum.................."	831	99,744	933	82,358	142	14,970	791	67,388
Iron......................."	113,650	398,023	130,496	345,119			130,496	345,119
Manganese.................."			90	1,950			90	1,950
Other......................"	11,437	734,993	12,764	645,873	112	113,249	12,652	532,624
Total, ores................	125,918	1,232,760	144,620	1,095,069	586	146,504	144,034	948,565

*These items show the weight and value of the copper, lead, nickel, platinum and silver respectively, not the gross weight of ore, matte, concentrates, etc.

11—i—14

No. 23.—STATEMENT showing the Value of Goods Exported from Canada—*Continued.*

Articles.	Twelve months ended March 31, 1914.		Twelve months ended March 31, 1915.		British Empire.		All other Countries.	
	Quantity.	Value.	Quantity.	Value.	Quantity.	Value.	Quantity.	Value.
THE MINE—*Con.*		$		$		$		$
Phosphates..........................Ton.	187	497	60	180			60	180
Plumbago, crude ore and concentrates......Cwt.	30,127	81,209	9,944	24,120			9,944	24,120
Pyrites..............................Ton.	46,293	212,220	95,901	393,085			95,901	393,085
Salt.................................Cwt.	76,588	29,915	64,953	29,155	43,912	20,586	21,041	8,569
Sand and gravel......................Ton.	685,893	485,873	959,039	808,012			959,039	808,012
Stone—Ornamental, granite, marble, etc., unwrought....Ton.	166	5,471	62,108	819			108	819
" Building, freestone, limestone, etc., unwrought.. "	187,484	89,862	28,600	45,950			62,600	45,950
" Crushed......................... "	4,843	3,145	995	20,080			28,995	20,080
" For manufacture of grindstones, rough... "			54	294			54	294
Total, stone...................	192,493	98,478	91,757	67,143			91,757	67,143
Other articles of the mine........$		83,701		211,072		6,701		204,371
Total, mine....................		59,233,906		52,066,537		13,125,573		38,940,964
THE FISHERIES.								
Codfish, including haddock, ling and pollock, fresh......Lb.	2,052,064	66,149	3,416,682	111,636	500	20	3,416,182	111,616
" dry salted...................Cwt.	749,701	4,582,933	669,187	4,172,854	139,018	856,263	530,169	3,316,591
" wet salt....................... "	12,927	54,139	69,744	277,033	18,922	83,636	50,822	193,347
" pickled........................ "	6,135	23,215	34,386	128,910			34,386	128,910
" tongues and sounds...........Lb.	200,735	34,938	148,458	31,354	1,000	61	147,458	31,293
Total, codfish.................		4,761,374		4,721,787		940,030		3,781,757
Mackerel, fresh..................	4,027,141	216,516	3,229,558	156,487			3,229,558	156,487
" pickled.....................Brl.	30,628	353,211	28,211	302,266	7,000	66,957	21,211	235,309
Total, mackerel...............		569,727		458,753		66,957		391,796
Halibut, fresh....................Lb.	4,639,008	283,775	7,743,989	475,590	198,489	14,749	7,545,500	460,841
" pickled.....................Brl.	5	24	163	2,296			163	2,296
Total, halibut................		283,799		477,886		14,749		463,137

'SESSIONAL PAPER No. 11

Item	Unit								
Herring, fresh or frozen	Lb.	11,270,576	155,929	30,855,723	507,836	250	15	30,855,473	507,821
" pickled	Brl.	346,621	832,701	336,020	840,947	130,517	318,612	205,503	522,335
" canned	Lb.	32,640	1,834	621,834	53,469	71,409	9,649	550,425	43,820
" smoked	"	3,617,825	90,511	4,193,419	141,963	256,051	8,723	3,937,368	133,240
Total, herring		6,023,034	1,070,975	7,073,036	1,544,215		336,999	7,073,036	1,207,216
Smelts	"		332,792		427,873				427,873
Sea fish, other fresh	Brl.	1,960,857	96,109	1,619,084	81,684	3,400	105	1,615,684	81,579
" pickled	Brl.	21,669	114,390	11,872	68,109	9,295	45,705	2,577	22,404
" preserved	Lb.	3,206,820	155,904	1,746,972	120,587	160,567	26,107	1,586,405	94,480
Total, sea fish, other			366,403		270,380		71,917		198,463
Oysters, fresh	Brl.	343	2,522	623	6,857	25	259	598	6,598
" preserved in cans	Lb.	4,193	1,552	170	40			170	40
Total, oysters			4,074		6,897		259		6,638
Lobsters, fresh	"	4,943,930	707,486	5,500,586	849,368		1,140,471	5,500,586	849,368
" canned	"	8,318,654	3,005,029	7,539,717	3,020,417	2,842,862		4,696,855	1,879,946
Total, lobsters		13,262,584	3,712,515	13,040,303	3,869,785	2,842,862	1,140,471	10,197,441	2,729,314
Bait, fish	Brl.	36,663	36,663	234	459	200	425	34	34
Clams	"	49,205	103,904	29,148	67,274	252	1,766	28,896	65,508
Salmon, fresh	Lb.	4,439,747	364,923	5,569,695	387,558	872,739	93,849	4,696,956	203,709
" smoked	"	45,100	7,116	2,180	313	230	28	1,930	285
" canned	Brl.	61,099,004	6,631,562	34,655,108	4,948,723	32,614,643	4,805,769	2,040,465	142,954
" pickled	Brl.	48,169	373,130	40,798	307,731	12,910	27,888		259,377
dog	Lb.	3,403,658	42,193	6,312,230	53,667		48,354	6,312,230	53,667
Total, salmon	"		7,418,924		5,607,992		4,948,000		749,992
Salmon or lake trout	"	712,045	39,035	1,360,875	76,947			1,360,875	76,947
Fish, all other, fresh			1,477,449		1,735,943				1,735,943
" pickled	Brl.	701	8,388	4,441	19,058	43	277	4,398	18,781
Total, fish, other			1,485,837		1,755,001		277		1,754,724
Fish Oil, cod	Gal	384,855	116,432	628,707	199,738	18,209	4,820	610,498	194,918
seal	"	858	269	11,021	2,801	3,120	312	7,901	2,489
" whale	"	662,451	293,894	334,223	144,388	25,633	8,934	308,590	135,454
" other	"	129,822	40,810	50,781	13,051	35,795	8,572	14,936	4,479
Total, fish oils		1,177,986	451,405	1,024,732	359,978	82,757	22,638	941,975	337,340

No. 23.—STATEMENT showing the Value of Goods Exported from Canada—*Continued.*

Articles.	Unit	Twelve months ended March 31, 1914. Quantity.	Value.	Twelve months ended March 31, 1915. Quantity.	Value.	British Empire. Quantity.	Value.	All other Countries. Quantity.	Value.
THE FISHERIES—Con.									
Furs or skins, the produce of fish or marine animals	$		45,203		12,763		7,532		5,231
Other articles of the fisheries	$		52,219		70,747		16,361		54,386
Total, fisheries			20,734,849		19,818,737		7,568,381		12,250,356
THE FOREST.									
Ashes, pot and pearl	Brl.	434	19,218	569	26,172	436	22,081	133	4,091
" all other	$		29,644		34,359				34,359
Total, ashes			48,862		60,531		22,081		38,450
Bark for tanning	Cord	4,833	25,577	5,675	42,370			5,675	42,370
Firewood	"	16,403	49,608	23,296	80,776			23,296	80,776
Knees and futtocks	No.	30,526	33,404	11,364	15,877			11,364	15,877
Lathwood	Cord	72	258	12	42			12	42
Logs, cedar, capable of being made into shingle bolts	$		376,046		471,165				471,105
" elm	$		33,721		13,735		8,132		5,626
" hemlock	$		11,276		63,822				63,822
" oak	$		811		238				238
" pine	$		62,743		100,715				100,715
" spruce	$		95,483		491,209		471		490,738
" tamarac	$		25,473		278				278
" all other	$		212,836		117,748		17,953		99,795
Total, logs			818,389		1,258,933		26,556		1,232,377
Lumber, viz.:—									
Battens	M ft.	687	5,426	1,283	4,379	197	4,379	1,086	
Basswood	"	20,382	14,992	14,399	38,053	13,425	7,195	974	30,858
Deals, pine	St. hund.	149,638	1,408,709	138,500	1,148,738	127,156	1,083,420	11,344	65,318
" spruce and other	"	7,124	6,547,854	6,582	6,393,420	6,281	5,806,449	301	526,971
Deal ends	"	59	294,195		269,849		258,808		11,041
Hickory	M ft.		2,993	16	900			16	900
Laths	M	608,921	1,609,221	635,974	1,798,219	6,617	12,712	629,357	1,785,507
Palings	"	2,909	20,657						
Pickets	$		206,573		114,122		31,022		83,100
Planks and boards	M ft.	999,311	19,522,675	975,874	18,939,295	99,273	2,058,744	876,601	16,880,561
Scantling	"	87,233	1,264,881	76,565	1,196,559	25,824	381,912	50,741	814,647
Shingles	M	689,150	1,775,619	1,359,069	2,987,764	25,314	41,065	1,333,755	2,946,099

Article	Unit	Quantity	Value	Quantity	Value	Quantity	Value	Quantity	Value
Lumber, shooks	$		191,001		160,747		136,717		24,030
" staves and headings	$		70,918		78,977		31,352		47,625
" all other lumber, n.o.p.	$		260,630		108,657		89,675		18,963
Total, lumber	$		33,286,344		33,239,679		10,003,450		23,236,229
Match blocks	No.	299	6,739		5,190		923		4,267
Masts and spars	$		3,499		3,099		1,564		1,535
Piling	No.		176,959	183	171,758	75		108	171,758
Poles—hop, hoop, telegraph and other	$		127,438		162,557		1,542		161,015
Posts, sleepers and railroad ties	$		269,365		247,939		98,680		149,259
Shingle bolts, of pine or cedar	Cord	13,582	47,132	7,769	24,780			7,760	24,780
Timber, square, viz.:—									
Ash	$		3,414		1,086		1,086		
Birch	$		134,276		119,386		113,874		5,512
Elm	$		319,797		262,758		259,735		3,023
Maple	$				10				10
Oak	$		260,223		216,640		214,967		1,673
Pine, red	$		31,343		940				940
Pine, white	$		315,509		388,224		387,660		564
All other	$		30,645		3,202		86		3,116
Total, timber, square			1,096,207		992,246		977,408		14,838
Wood, blocks and other, for pulp	Cord	1,089,384	7,388,770	1,010,914	6,817,311			1,010,914	6,817,311
Other articles of the forest	$		8,536		13,693		303		13,390
Total, forest			43,386,087		43,136,781		11,132,507		32,004,274
ANIMALS AND THEIR PRODUCE.									
Animals—									
Horses, one year old or less	No.	85	4,367	16	1,272			16	1,272
" over one year old	"	5,601	1,427,236	25,198	3,776,516	19,396	2,594,273	5,802	1,182,243
Cattle, one year old or less	"	20,782	252,078	34,083	416,238	2	25	34,081	416,213
" over one year old	"	199,066	7,676,938	151,841	8,856,346	1,886	101,542	149,955	8,754,804
Swine	"	28,207	446,430	243,312	3,117,055	186	2,801,079	243,126	315,976
Sheep, one year old or less	"	13,324	70,719	35,293	211,714			35,293	211,714
" over one year old	"	7,387	61,689	7,999	84,278	919	5,244	7,080	79,034
Poultry	$		137,493		333,086		797		337,289
Other	$		73,569		93,177		11,125		82,052
Total, animals living			10,150,519		16,894,682		2,714,085		14,180,597
Bones	Cwt.	65,183	94,586	74,985	98,091	455	500	74,530	97,591
Butter	Lb.	1,352,875	342,953	2,770,324	649,288	1,271,490	347,420	1,498,834	301,868
Casein	"	270,486	11,071	230,045	13,923			230,045	13,923
Cheese	"	144,910,780	18,948,511	137,780,884	19,247,603	137,208,857	19,146,854	572,027	100,749
Cream, fresh	Gal.	1,324,017	1,289,768	1,895,575	1,836,006			1,895,575	1,836,006
Milk, fresh	"	307,188	47,645	477,692	68,205			477,692	68,205
Cream and milk, condensed, canned or preserved	Lb.	9,379,382	671,042	18,355,975	1,181,300	690,027	60,533	17,675,948	1,130,767
Eggs	Doz.	485,202	92,322	4,710,029	1,206,518	3,731,817	1,029,936	978,212	176,692

6 GEORGE V, A. 1916

No. 23.—STATEMENT showing the value of Goods Exported from Canada—Continued.

Articles		TWELVE MONTHS ENDED MARCH 31, 1914.		TWELVE MONTHS ENDED MARCH 31, 1915.		TWELVE MONTHS ENDED MARCH 31, 1915.			
						British Empire.		All other Countries.	
		Quantity.	Value.	Quantity.	Value.	Quantity.	Value.	Quantity.	Value.
ANIMALS AND THEIR PRODUCTS—Con.			$		$		$		$
Furs, dressed	$		21,814		42,859		9,329		33,530
Furs, undressed	$		5,682,469		2,812,934		1,302,206		1,510,728
Total, furs			5,704,273		2,855,793		1,311,535		1,544,258
Grease and grease scraps	Lb.	4,113,580	116,363	2,489,916	81,018	85,689	4,033	2,404,227	76,995
Glue stock	$		286,719		41,359		341		41,009
Hair	$		243,150		300,138		14,410		285,728
Hides and skins, other than fur	$		9,221,150		7,470,781		10,392		7,460,389
Horns and hoofs	$		16,634		16,267				16,267
Honey	Lb.	19,508	2,063	7,604	840	201	30	7,403	810
Lard	Lb.	193,222	18,399	2,692,734	306,334	1,816,644	214,305	876,090	92,029
Meats, viz.:—									
Bacon		23,860,536	3,763,330	76,803,829	11,812,186	72,071,409	11,085,835	4,732,490	726,351
Beef	"	13,617,707	1,165,295	19,669,701	2,061,430	1,955,789	239,510	17,713,912	1,821,920
Hams	"	1,890,658	270,049	17,966,450	2,654,064	9,213,274	1,378,745	8,753,176	1,275,319
Mutton	"	65,167	10,804	1,064,963	124,087	32,178	3,623	1,032,785	120,464
Pork	"	1,968,941	216,810	21,409,083	2,610,776	6,165,727	809,992	15,243,356	1,800,784
Poultry, dressed or undressed	$		74,270		212,992		73,775		139,217
Game, dressed or undressed	$		4,973		2,340				2,340
lbs.	Lb.			192,469	24,703	12,272	2,369	180,197	22,334
Canned		654,681	97,031	9,891,369	2,341,435	6,077,066	1,630,535	3,814,283	710,900
All other, n.o.p.	"	2,850,642	267,177	4,434,902	314,606	1,162,756	105,388	3,272,140	209,218
Total, meats			5,869,739		22,158,619		15,329,772		6,828,847
Oil, Neatsfoot and other animal, n.o.p.	Gal.	240,358	247,143	228,332	239,911	38,579	42,912	189,753	196,999
Sausage casings	$		372,121		453,863		126,359		327,504
Sheep pelts	$		145,686		272,688				272,688
Tails	$		17,963		14,192				14,192
Tallow	Lb.	2,349,450	158,055	1,039,872	64,842	19,056	1,243	1,020,816	63,599
Wool	$	2,878,029	688,428	5,797,158	1,398,045	14,845	2,520	5,782,313	1,395,525
Other articles of the animals	$		145,703		85,705		2,358		83,317
Total, animals and products			54,612,072		76,956,002		40,349,558		36,606,444
AGRICULTURAL PRODUCTS.									
Balsam	Gal.	151,073	22,708	88,951	24,904	85,421	2,893	3,530	22,011
Cider	Gal.		19,737		15,787	1,110	15,182		605
Flax	Cwt.	6,065	46,309	6,729	34,230		7,022	5,619	27,208

Article		Quantity	Value	Quantity	Value	Quantity	Value	Quantity	Value
Fruits, viz.:—									
Apples, dried	Lb.	6,084,976	411,980	4,488,050	276,060	2,362,946	142,880	2,125,104	133,180
Apples, green or ripe	Brl.	948,098	3,467,838	1,118,824	2,661,392	1,082,386	2,580,503	38,438	80,889
Berries of all kinds	$		107,780		109,587		65		109,522
Canned or preserved	$		407,302		479,763		444,994		34,769
All other, n.o.p.	$		407,741		240,217		53,782		186,435
Total, fruits			4,802,641		3,767,019		3,222,224		544,795
Grain and products of, viz.:—									
Barley	Bush.	13,596,322	6,799,527	6,591,253	3,851,899	5,250,260	3,027,618	1,340,993	824,281
Beans	"	13,332	32,134	32,923	80,930	3,841	7,129	29,082	73,801
Buckwheat	"	172,802	120,353	343,349	272,516	225,309	176,845	118,040	95,671
Indian corn	"	64,216	43,592	410,693	278,044	149,568	113,486	261,125	164,558
Oats	"	35,042,845	13,403,456	20,384,373	10,141,144	11,274,855	5,385,450	9,109,518	4,755,694
Pease, whole	"	121,924	241,381	261,606	532,559	38,029	93,564	223,577	438,995
Pease, split	"	21,563	23,294	41,825	107,827	27,668	67,880	14,157	39,947
Rye	"	228,039	145,244	621,994	537,313	104,424	105,290	517,570	432,023
Wheat	"	126,478,585	123,627,058	105,435,464	107,335,916	87,271,364	89,287,453	18,164,100	18,002,000
Other grain	"	10,611	10,377						46,463
Total, grain		175,750,229	144,446,416	134,123,480	123,138,148	104,345,318	98,264,715	29,778,162	24,873,433
Bran	Cwt.	2,078,213	1,790,312	1,038,354	946,738	160,214	161,469	878,140	785,209
Flour of wheat	Brl.	4,832,310	20,581,682	4,953,462	24,614,672	4,377,069	21,960,200	576,393	2,654,472
Indian meal	"	3,939	14,639	2,560	9,549	2,180	8,126	380	1,423
Oatmeal	"	111,537	488,643	60,320	287,844	58,479	280,524	1,841	7,320
Meal, all other, n.o.p.	"	2,042	7,534	432	1,616	331	1,243	101	373
Total, flour and meal			21,092,498		24,913,681		22,250,093		2,663,588
Cereal foods, prepared, of all kinds	$		2,171,689		1,974,134		1,715,099		259,035
Hay	Ton	191,560	1,791,017	131,947	2,234,002	14,488	203,554	117,459	2,030,448
Hemp	Cwt.	200	190	460	2,090			460	2,090
Hops	Lb.	284,979	64,353	171,426	36,168	169,015	35,650	2,411	518
Malt	Bush.	4,337	4,256	6,481	6,210	4,881	4,674	1,600	1,536
Maple sugar	Lb.	1,925,343	159,619	1,462,416	131,477	80,626	6,733	1,381,790	124,744
Maple syrup	Gal.	5,205	5,284	6,165	6,687	2,492	2,680	3,673	4,007
Nuts	Lb.	99,833	9,750	178,264	9,558	46,162	2,058	132,102	7,500
Seeds, clover	Bush.	120,155	1,109,015	45,942	384,950	21,019	178,493	24,923	206,457
" flax	"	22,186,355	26,734,601	7,748,508	10,448,178	734,301	1,016,821	7,014,207	9,431,357
" grass	"	110,894	106,756	74,041	69,556	7,038	10,139	67,003	59,417
" all other	$		103,333		85,813		1,245		84,568
Total, seeds			28,053,705		10,988,497		1,206,698		9,781,799
Straw	Ton	5,118	28,964	4,962	29,618	132	1,006	4,830	28,612
Tobacco, leaf	Lb.	250,412	102,219	176,302	114,334	1,419	624	174,883	113,710
Trees, shrubs and plants	$		35,646		26,329		4,538		21,791

No. 23.—STATEMENT showing the value of Goods Exported from Canada—Continued.

Articles.	Twelve Months Ended March 31, 1914.		Twelve Months Ended March 31, 1915.		Twelve Months Ended March 31, 1915.			
					British Empire.		All other Countries.	
	Quantity.	Value.	Quantity.	Value.	Quantity.	Value.	Quantity.	Value.
AGRICULTURAL PRODUCTS—Con.		$		$		$		$
Vegetables, canned or preserved......$		21,927		300,484		277,612		22,872
" potatoes......Bush.	1,980,869	1,127,561	1,192,330	696,901	370,624	225,465	821,706	471,436
" turnips......	1,707,062	309,582	2,150,399	286,461	9,611	1,895	2,140,788	284,566
" all other vegetables......$		127,256		227,990		86,870		141,120
Total, vegetables......		1,586,326		1,511,836		591,842		919,994
Other articles of agriculture......		582,019		438,617		5,898		432,719
Total, agricultural products......		206,815,718		170,350,064		127,704,652		42,645,412
MANUFACTURES.								
Agricultural implements and machines, viz.:—								
Mowing machines......No	26,510	904,083	7,512	260,709	2,325	77,877	5,187	182,832
Cultivators......	7,202	183,165	5,831	143,807	4,276	106,281	1,555	37,526
Reapers......	5,293	301,610	902	48,301	22	1,347	880	46,954
Drills......	11,116	679,280	4,000	262,180	3,280	220,128	720	42,052
Harvesters and binders......	29,340	3,078,023	6,801	699,398	3,682	374,900	3,119	324,498
Ploughs......	14,907	449,992	13,638	346,751	11,110	254,695	2,528	92,056
Harrows......	7,463	128,470	6,193	95,170	5,235	67,533	958	27,637
Hay rakes......	9,764	293,788	2,055	47,773	1,268	26,111	787	21,662
Seeders......	21	1,140	11	670	1	11	10	659
Threshing machines......	1,931	714,102	2,051	876,817	1,760	547,627	291	329,190
All other......$		414,345		275,715		86,319		189,396
Parts of......$		915,239		669,056		435,389		233,667
Total, agricultural machinery......		8,063,237		3,726,347		2,198,218		1,528,129
Asbestos, manufactures of......$		98,718		79,293		60,350		18,943
Baking powders......Lb.	82,724	15,386	86,157	13,290	84,702	13,079	1,455	211
Binder twine......	4,690,820	453,530	12,317,558	1,080,071	2,508,560	180,401	9,808,998	899,670
Books, pamphlets, maps, etc......		671,336		653,767		236,488		417,279
Biscuits and bread......Cwt.	2,029	16,227	3,061	26,867	1,835	16,756	1,226	10,111
Bricks......M	1,048	8,454	1,504	12,244	51	478	1,453	11,766
Brooms and whisks......		17,056		14,474		14,171		303
Brushes of all kinds......		15,128		10,904		9,291		1,613
Buttons......		4,532		3,165		147		3,018
Candles......Lb.	1,806	4,238	713	296	713	96		200
Cartridges, gun, rifle and pistol......$		20,300		223,042		119,656	1,318	103,386
Charcoal......$		3,073		3,878		1,887		1,991

Article	Unit	C1	C2	C3	C4	C5	C6	C7
Cement	$		2,907	2,361		1,640		721
Cinders	$		627	885				885
Clay, manufactures of	$		37,281	18,381				18,304
Clothing and wearing apparel	$		586,596	7,484,339		6,520,578		963,761
Coke	Ton	73,299	332,635	940,818			52,874	240,818
Confectionery	$		54,944	88,862		72,316		16,546
Cordage, ropes and twine	Yd	424,761	70,149	68,257		36,216		32,041
Con fabrics	$		92,791	295,585	1,060,028	231,202	267,223	64,383
Cottons, thr	Lb	600,670	121,832	606,796	1,802,639	64,883	1,563,206	541,913
Con waste	$		30,069	81,916		12,604		69,312
Cream separators	$		27,049	66,208		4,604		61,604
Drugs, chemicals and medicines, viz:—								
ate of lime	Lb	14,709,568	316,481	269,591	7,667,068	130,519	7,471,039	139,072
Acid, sulphuric	"	6,245,086	37,413	41,344	360	9	6,409,835	41,335
rm carbide	"	5,441,061	161,026	1,117,118	10,912,462	328,423	25,430,257	788,695
Gum chicle	$	,613,861	2,850,132	1,052,776	25,823	13,028	2,205,142	1,039,748
Lye	Lb		70,584	110,818		1,670		109,148
Phosphorus	"	629,390	88,521	84,453	558,050	84,458		167,755
Senega root	$	405,039	245,870	171,319	6,647	3,564	367,196	722,354
All ber n.o.p	$		926,368	1,116,321		393,967		67,581
Dye stuffs	$		15,663	70,753		3,172		11,340
Earthenware and all manufactures of	$		17,809	14,273		2,933		266,172
al apparatus	$		303,553	322,471		56,299		13,261
Electrotypes nd				13,556		295		908
Extract of hemlock bark	Brl	2,040	8,926	30,812	2,487	29,904	63	187,465
Explosives and ful ates, n.o.p	$		24,618	283,613		96,148		5,137
Felt, manufactures of	$		261,579	9,272		4,135		2,023,003
Fertilizers	$		5,787	2,171,172		148,169		84,339
Films for photographers' use and for moving pictures	$		2,543,671	88,189		3,950		13,918
Fur, manufactures of	$		62,394	38,028		24,110		101,046
Gasoline engines	No.	995	74,826	209,304	870	108,258	471	13,910
Gasoline launches	"	30	161,049	14,010	1	100	20	36,266
Glass and glassware, n.o.p	$		18,403	77,894		41,628		
Glucose	Lb	8,143	54,932					47,419
Grindstones, manufactured	$		294	47,747		328		45,865
Guns, rifles and ns of all kinds	$		54,614	232,797		186,932		24,045
m or per, ground	$		143,644	31,878		7,833		13,227
Hats and caps	$		14,225	31,718		18,491		50
Household effects, n.o.p	$		33,251			477,524		7,515
Ice	$		15,922	7,515				
India-rubber, manufactures of, viz:—								
Belting	$		11,081	3,610		2,448		1,162
Hose	$		9,716	19,248		6,844		12,404
Boots and shoes	$		174,414	198,312		185,466		12,846
Mats and matting	$			34		34		
Clothing	$		11,643	1,890		1,639		51
Waste	Lb	432,877		278,442				278,442
All other n.o.p	$		506,121	1,522,427		143,835		1,378,592
Total, India-rubber, and manufactures of		5,125,901	1,135,852	2,023,963		340,466	4,235,610	1,683,497

6 GEORGE V, A. 1916

No. 23.—STATEMENT showing the Value of Goods Exported from Canada—*Continued.*

Articles.	Twelve Months Ended March 31, 1914. Quantity.	Value.	Twelve Months Ended March 31, 1915. Quantity.	Value.	Twelve Months Ended March 31, 1915. British Empire. Quantity.	Value.	All other Countries. Quantity.	Value.
		$		$		$		$
MANUFACTURES—Con.								
Iron and steel and manufactures of, viz.:—								
Stoves............No.	1,439	23,352	6,581	31,743	1,050	15,617	5,531	16,126
Gas buoys and parts of............$		18,966		20,687		13,331		7,356
Castings, n.o.p............$		64,903		166,178		133,716		32,462
Pig iron............Ton	9,330	347,597	11,592	139,427	1,813	22,531	9,779	116,896
Ferro silicon and ferro............Cwt.			6,901	398,488	124	9,032	6,777	389,456
Wire and wire............Cwt.			469,264	881,683	396,836	760,411	72,428	121,272
Pipe machines and parts of............		19,878		35,704		1,835		33,939
Machinery, n.o.p............No.	7,411	985,587	3,309	837,870	505	107,354	2,864	736,516
Sewing machines............$		111,356		47,334		8,954		38,380
Washing machines, domestic, and wringers............No.	4,426	27,953	3,894	32,516	1,891	25,967	2,003	6,549
Typewriters............$		259,861		230,022		122,218		107,804
Scrap iron or steel............Cwt.	1,024,288	591,201	867,938	539,696	20,553	8,922	847,385	530,774
Hard ware, viz.: Tools, hand or machine............$		154,508		171,082		76,420		94,662
Hardware, n.o.p............$		125,851		335,094		137,157		197,937
All mfr. n.o.p............$		1,515,926		7,467,268		6,321,671		1,145,597
Total, iron and steel, and manufactures of......		4,246,939		11,334,882		7,765,136		3,569,746
Jewellery of all kinds, n.o.p............$		273,577		484,121		154,828		329,293
Jeweller's sweepings............$		213,034		189,050		29,969		159,081
Junk, except metallic and rubber............Cwt.	102,295	208,540	78,973	162,697	1,250	1,412	77,723	161,285
Lamps and lanterns............$		25,118		22,529		7,211		15,318
Leather, viz.:—								
Sole............Lb.	8,309,960	2,419,893	13,673,561	4,096,209	7,793,594	2,383,009	5,969,967	1,715,200
Upper............"	377,292	120,290	2,194,108	1,463,578	901,631	534,202	1,292,477	929,376
All other, n.o.p............"	2,652,583	630,377	3,032,911	1,022,508	472,921	140,586	2,559,990	881,922
Boots and shoes............$		116,710		236,886		45,521		191,365
Harness and saddlery............$		27,574		3,983,049		1,653,282		2,334,767
Other manufactures of............$		73,252		95,630		40,724		54,906
Total, leather and manufactures of......		3,388,096		10,904,860		4,797,324		6,107,536
Lime............$		28,610		17,137		133		17,004
Liquors, viz.:—								
Ale and beer............Gal	12,468	5,220	21,655	12,594	7,193	3,685	14,462	8,900
Brandy............"	358	1,889	727	2,962			727	2,962
Gin............"	17,724	13,973	12,075	9,470	205	268	11,870	9,202
Rum............"	4,996	1,910	5,953	2,060	149	52	5,804	2,008

Whiskey....................."	340,553	1,048,028	285,140	866,685	14,504	44,357	270,636	822,328
Wines......................."	11,379	19,897	8,997	52,600	2,789	2,792	6,208	49,808
Wood alcohol..............."	457,757	256,869	500,343	231,286	131,184	79,000	369,159	152,286
Other spirits, n.o.p......."	1,408	3,312	1,882	3,476	192	654	1,690	2,822
Total, liquors............	846,643	1,351,098	836,772	1,181,133	156,216	130,808	680,556	1,050,325
Metals, viz.:—								
Aluminum in bars, blocks, etc.....Cwt.	130,845	1,885,074	140,876	2,329,443	52,023	814,259	88,853	1,515,184
Aluminum, manufactures of........$		54,168		454,732		448,127		6,605
Brass, old and scrap.............Cwt.	40,838	378,076	27,636	261,039	5,041	54,282	22,595	206,757
Copper, old and scrap............$	29,923	390,336	21,119	241,050	3,655	45,258	17,464	195,792
Metallic shingles and laths and corrugated roofing....$		163,008		89,643		71,150		18,493
Metals, n.o.p....................$		601,512		524,221		181,070		343,151
Total, metals............		3,472,174		3,900,128		1,614,146		2,285,982
Mineral and aerated water in bottles......$	69,506	1,572		1,861		1,043		818
Molasses..........................Gal.		23,706	202,094	51,388	108,654	29,643	93,440	21,745
Musical instruments, viz.:—								
Organs............................No.	2,228	147,543	1,120	63,791	1,039	59,284	81	4,507
Pianos............................No.	245	70,492	283	76,305	86	25,149	197	51,156
Other, and parts of..............$		107,186		132,817		76,443		56,374
Total, musical instruments.......		325,221		272,913		160,876		112,037
Oakum............................Cwt.	61	461	35	218	35	218		
Oil cake.........................Cwt.	605,305	833,287	279,334	392,330	172,446	242,477	106,888	149,853
Oilcloths, all kinds............Sq. yd.	64,180	9,670	60,442	8,537	59,658	8,347	784	190
Oil, resote......................Gal.	1,008,808	65,575	632,563	45,392			632,563	45,392
Oil, saline and naphtha..........Gal.	173,977	39,641	174,495	40,239	160,148	36,777	14,347	3,752
Oil, n.o.p.......................$	655,712	221,324	747,846	211,598	122,767	30,267	625,079	181,331
Paper, viz.:—								
Wall.............................Roll.	560,750	47,817	809,085	57,563	712,390	48,881	96,695	8,682
Felt.............................Lb.	49,316	50,159	79,670	87,176	51,357	65,037	28,313	22,139
Printing.........................Cwt.	18,253,112	615,337	13,540,429	408,450	4,328,973	128,853	9,211,456	279,567
Paper, n.o.p.....................$	5,851,579	11,386,845	7,292,047	14,091,662	928,302	1,822,177	6,363,745	12,269,485
		590,391		855,213		407,780		447,433
Total, paper.............		12,690,549	638,882	15,500,064	627,956	2,472,758		13,027,306
Paints and varnishes of all kinds........$		156,085		191,123		146,141		45,282
Paintings................................$		430,182		288,804		137,046		151,758
Photographs..............................$		10,277		13,692		1,341		12,351
Philosophical and scientific apparatus and instruments...$		96,908		153,155		33,474		119,681
Plumbago, manufactures of................$		40,104		64,661		8,458		56,203
Raps.....................................Cwt.	549,041	822,319	660,162	1,081,138	52,178	388,908	607,984	692,230
Sails, awnings, tents and tarpaulins.....$		13,256		15,715		636		15,079
Ships sold to other countries......No. and Ton	22—12,225	17—625,843	19,280	7—1,064,900	1,066	10—57,400	18,214	1,007,503
Silk and manufactures of.................$		87,707		71,982		39,825		32,157
Soap.....................................Lb.	457,883	28,569	638,882	36,897	627,956	35,855	10,926	1,042

No. 23.—STATEMENT showing the value of Goods Exported from Canada—*Concluded*.

Articles.		Twelve Months Ended March 31, 1914.		Twelve Months Ended March 31, 1915.		Twelve Months Ended March, 31, 1915.			
						British Empire.		All other Countries.	
		Quantity.	Value.	Quantity.	Value.	Quantity.	Value.	Quantity.	Value.
MANUFACTURES—Con.			$		$		$		$
Starch	Lb.	160,473	7,927	77,083	2,509	71,308	2,279	5,775	230
Stationery	$		71,800		71,734		39,160		32,565
Stone, ornamental, viz.: granite, marble, etc., dressed	$		7,331		3,529		119		3,410
" building, viz.: freestone, limestone, etc., dressed	$				370				370
Total, stone.			7,331		3,899		119		3,780
Sugar of all kinds, n.o.p	Lb.	141,195	5,555	4,787,925	239,411	4,692,722	235,532	95,203	3,879
Sugar house syrup	Gal.	153,520	10,779	146,840	18,565	88,650	13,372	58,190	5,193
Tar	$		35,836		42,087		5,679		36,408
Tin, manufactures of	$		240,032		197,968		87,107		110,861
Tobacco, viz.:—									
Cigars	M	32	1,382	20	805	17	747	3	58
Cigarettes	"	110	566	407	2,989	189	1,747	218	1,242
Stems and cuttings	Lb.	912,307	68,512	299,949	28,063			299,949	28,063
All other, n.o.p	"	20,033	13,305	25,593	19,070	12,236	9,807	13,357	9,263
Total, tobacco.			83,765		50,927		12,301		38,626
Tow	Cwt.	1,275	3,267	1,356	1,947			1,356	1,947
Trunks and valises	$		24,348		18,162		13,602		4,560
Vehicles, viz.:—									
Automobiles	No.	6,691	4,321,369	5,579	3,290,234	5,059	2,516,484	520	773,750
Automobile, parts of	$		454,296		607,331		383,782		223,549
Carriages	No.	574	41,141	71	6,094	33	2,717	38	3,377
" parts of	$		36,632		44,916		41,890		3,026
Carts	No.	1,704	51,368	598	15,769	5	342	593	15,427
Wagons	"	244	13,064	2,171	316,245	2,064	310,030	107	6,215
Bicycles	"	200	22,998	243	28,800	31	3,622	212	25,178
" parts of	$		12,978		5,386		3,039		2,347
Other vehicles	$		127,680		188,115		26,159		161,956
Total, vehicles.			5,081,526		4,502,890		3,288,065		1,214,825
Vinegar	Gal.	330	82	47	11	47	11		
Wood, viz.:—									
Barrels, empty	No.	37,457	53,593	29,566	40,990	9,359	13,363	20,207	27,627
Household furniture	$		437,775		324,306		214,423		109,883
Doors, sashes and blinds	$		20,728		12,653		11,790		863

Article	Unit	Qty.	(1)	(2)	Qty.	(3)	(4)
Matches	$		338			224	453
Match splints	$			12,893		12,893	4,782
Mouldings, trimmings and other house furnishings	$		6,652	6,445		1,663	1,050
Pails, tubs, churns and other hollow woodenware	$		5,896			3,584	14,669
Spool wood and spools	Cwt.	1,515,633	29,525			87,479	
Wood pulp, chemically prepared	Cwt.	4,816,170	2,923,083	2,424,328	2,423,180	1,495,521	4,803,728
Wood pulp, mechanically ground	"		3,441,741	6,163,702	3,965,666	2,894	2,964,018
Other manufactures of	$		467,033	436,928		262,834	174,094
Total, wood		7,386,364		10,207,835		2,106,668	8,101,167
Woollens	$	145,094	1,388,620		188,673		1,199,947
Other articles of manufactures	$	1,123,774	2,104,016		521,106		1,582,910
Total, manufactures		67,602,238		95,068,525		37,147,468	57,921,057

MISCELLANEOUS ARTICLES.

Article	Unit	Qty.	(1)	(2)	Qty.	(3)	(4)
Contractors' outfits	$		132,936	407,176		15,904	391,272
Coffee	Lb.	227,109	35,991	27,142	12,390	3,188	23,954
Dried fruits, n.o.p.	"	200,204	11,121	15,183	57,868	3,624	11,559
Menageries, etc.	$		1,581,725	2,005,612		313	2,005,612
Rice	Lb.	675,663	19,015	108,224	2,832,244		107,911
Rice meal	"	2,713,800	48,240	109,242	4,310,910	39,370	109,242
Tea	"	3,593,184	1,019,391	1,071,688	3,562,380	178,245	1,032,318
Other miscellaneous articles	$		203,935	301,596			123,351
Total, miscellaneous articles		3,052,354		4,045,863		240,644	3,805,219

COIN.

Article	Unit	(1)	(2)	(3)	(4)
Gold coin	$	22,221,147	28,234,973	285,926	27,949,047
Silver coin	$	1,327,085	1,122,394	3,972	1,118,422
Copper coin	$	12,472	9,001		9,001
Total, coin		23,560,704	29,366,368	289,898	29,076,470
Grand total		478,997,928	490,808,877	237,558,681	253,250,196

RECAPITULATION.

	(1)	(2)	(3)	(4)
Produce of the mine	59,233,906	52,066,537	13,125,573	38,940,964
" " fisheries	20,734,849	19,818,737	7,568,381	12,250,356
" " forest	43,386,087	43,136,781	11,132,507	32,004,274
Animals and their produce	54,612,072	76,956,002	40,349,558	36,606,444
Agricultural products	206,815,718	170,350,064	127,704,652	42,645,412
Manufactures	67,602,238	95,068,525	37,147,491	57,921,034
Miscellaneous	3,052,354	4,045,863	240,644	3,805,219
Total	455,437,224	461,442,509	237,268,806	224,173,703
Coin	23,560,704	29,366,368	289,898	29,076,470
Grand total exports	478,997,928	490,808,877	237,558,704	253,250,173

6 GEORGE V, A. 1916

No. 24.—STATEMENT showing the value of Merchandise imported into and exported from Canada through the United States from and to Foreign Countries, distinguishing the countries whence imported and to which exported, during the Fiscal Year ended March 31, 1915.

Countries whence imported and to which exported.	Value of Merchandise Imported from Foreign Countries through the United States.	Value of Merchandise Exported to Foreign Countries through the United States.
	$	$
United Kingdom	4,853,119	60,433,803
Aden		9,014
Australia and Tasmania	16,790	1,322,414
Bermuda	3,183	21,622
British East Africa	13,068	55,286
" South Africa	280,367	400,490
" West Africa		36,738
" Guiana	735,390	103,576
' Honduras	79,596	9,450
" India	1,257,848	289,373
" East Indies, other	960,383	19,262
" West Indies	784,811	1,346,956
" Straits Settlements	67,440	98,781
Fiji Islands		678
Gibraltar		40,703
Hong Kong	9,600	1,285
Malta		15,407
Newfoundland		85,659
New Zealand	95,520	260,815
Total British Empire	9,157,115	64,551,312
Argentina	1,500,270	328,489
Austria-Hungary	28,835	34,658
Azores and Madeira		27
Belgium	134,711	67,860
Brazil	631,306	258,041
Canary Islands		16,465
Chili	190	43,653
China	534,678	9,054
Costa Rica	1,080	34,187
Cuba	372,421	465,028
Denmark	10,448	391,054
Danish West Indies	69	13,549
Dutch East Indies	37,300	9,660
" West Indies		6,715
" Guiana	68,809	32,958
Ecuador		6,911
Egypt and Soudan	19,526	6,940
France	672,859	3,059,963
French Africa	7,155	4,170
" Guiana		2,202
" West Indies		32,479
Germany	818,240	505,597
German Africa	105,040	
Greece	96,403	84,469
Greenland, Iceland, etc.		1,518
Guatemala	8,212	27,295
Hawaii	620	3,049
Hayti		3,815
Holland	326,382	807,386
Honduras		5,587
Italy	555,965	507,199
Japan	130,996	114,962

No. 24.—STATEMENT showing the value of Merchandise imported into and exported from Canada through the United States from and to Foreign Countries, during the Fiscal Year ended March 31, 1915—*Concluded.*

Countries whence imported and to which exported.	Value of Merchandise Imported from Foreign Countries through the United States.	Value of Merchandise Exported to Foreign Countries through the United States.
	$	$
Korea...	....	75
Liberia...	....	63
Mexico..	206,554	16,306
Nicaragua...	....	1,268
Norway..	33,567	856,890
Panama..	....	100,517
Persia..	758	....
Peru..		12,506
Philippines...	762	828
Porto Rico..	....	251,601
Portugal..	29,069	6,688
Portuguese Africa...		48,603
Roumania..	90	3,150
Russia..	26,104	121,673
Salvador..		2,215
San Domingo...	524,694	2,791
Siam..	....	4,026
Spain...	147,929	46,647
Sweden..	155,861	111,053
Switzerland...	173,926	9,740
Turkey..	128,802	1,757
U. S. of Colombia...	96,989	23,785
Uruguay...	6,152	19,338
Venezuela...	45,566	54,058
Total other countries..................	7,638,338	8,580,518
Grand total...................................	16,795,453	73,130,830

No. 25.—COMPARATIVE STATEMENT of Goods remaining in Warehouse in 1913, 1914 and 1915.

Articles	REMAINING IN WAREHOUSE, MARCH 31, 1913.		REMAINING IN WAREHOUSE, MARCH 31, 1914.		REMAINING IN WAREHOUSE, MARCH 31, 1915.	
	Quantity.	Value.	Quantity.	Value.	Quantity.	Value.
		$		$		$
Breadstuffs—						
Wheat.......................Bush.	217,032	195,764	72,975	72,975	68,222	68,222
Other breadstuffs................ $	....	35,350	....	122,441	....	74,760
Coal, bituminous.................Tons..	1,162,353	1,679,296	1,550,056	2,653,646	1,273,347	2,500,366
Cotton and manufactures of........ $	....	342,743	....	349,919	....	202,633
Drugs............................. $	....	142,364	....	146,606	....	97,157
Fancy goods...................... $	....	18,072	....	31,958	....	13,553
Fish.............................. $	....	92,347	....	110,234	....	90,082
Flax and manufactures of.......... $	....	37,843	....	39,085	....	35,756
Fruits and nuts....'.............. $	....	214,924	....	175,524	....	165,451
Glass and manufactures of......... $	....	13,823	....	21,968	....	11,066
Iron and steel.................... $	....	1,712,826	....	1,181,783	....	998,031
Leather........................... $	....	49,852	....	29,950	....	30,408
Oils.............................. $	....	142,291	....	29,923	....	80,682
Paper and manufactures of......... $	....	53,975	....	50,282	....	30,992
Silk.............................. $	....	112,652	....	135,728	....	103,169
Spirits and wines—						
Brandy........................Gal.	232,034	445,960	538,783	1,150,003	189,371	438,603
Gin............................. "	342,802	217,124	293,164	194,732	421,528	277,627
Rum............................ "	74,438	47,489	62,091	47,511	53,910	40,286
Whiskey........................ "	521,983	982,265	565,305	1,286,552	551,947	1,279,859
Wines of all kinds, except sparkling "	257,209	283,707	398,109	387,715	356,901	348,097
Wines, sparkling............... $	....	333,567	....	361,782	....	342,936
Sugar above No. 16 D.S...........Lb.	5,015,146	125,871	4,860,494	214,492	4,860,167	124,578
Sugar not above No. 16 D.S........ "	64,231,739	1,505,710	57,372,309	1,299,096	67,078,555	1,890,470
Molasses.......................Gal.	31,133	4,398	51,521	2,037	41,975	1,618
Tobacco, manufactures of—						
Cigars...........................Lb.	30,345	103,261	27,041	92,897	27,781	93,309
Cigarettes..................... "	6,640	18,765	5,163	10,205	4,853	9,572
All other........................ $	....	81,978	....	109,269	....	69,005
Woollens......................... $	....	320,223	....	377,336	....	277,223
All other articles................. $	....	3,348,152	....	3,780,766	....	3,412,025
Grand totals..................	....	12,662,592	....	14,466,415	....	13,107,536

SESSIONAL PAPER No. 11

No. 26.—STATEMENT showing the quantity and value of merchandise received from foreign countries for immediate transit through Canada, and trans-shipped at the port of Montreal for United States and other countries during the fiscal year ended March 31st, 1915.

ARTICLES.	COUNTRIES.	RECEIVED FROM		SHIPPED TO	
		Quantity.	Value.	Quantity.	Value.
THE MINE.			$		$
Ore and other articles of the mine..................	Great Britain......	....	21,465	....	
	Australia..........	....	....	....	14
	B. South Africa.....	....	....	....	22,072
	France...........	....	255	....	
	United States......	....	22,686	....	21,720
	Total..........	....	44,406	....	44,406
THE FISHERIES.					
Salmon and other articles of the fisheries....................	Great Britain......	....	46,955	....	97,075
	Newfoundland......	....	2,300	....	
	Belgium...........	....	528	....	43,300
	France...........	....	....	....	10,192
	Germany..........	....	1,000	....	
	Holland..........	....	300	....	
	Norway...........	....	5,003	....	
	Turkey...........	....	44	....	
	United States......	....	150,567	....	56,130
	Total..........	....	206,697	....	206,697
THE FOREST.		M ft.		M ft.	
Planks and boards.............	Great Britain......	....	....	5,131	126,025
	B. South Africa....	....	....	223	5,390
	United States......	5,354	131,415	....	
	Total..........	5,354	131,415	5,354	131,415
Lumber and timber............	Great Britain......	....	1,274	....	43,637
	B. South Africa.....	....	....	....	14,617
	United States......	....	57,630	....	650
	Total...........	....	58,904	....	58,904
Total, products of the forest....	....	....	190,319	....	190,319
ANIMALS AND PRODUCE.		No.		No.	
Horses.......................	Great Britain......	....	....	850	85,700
	France...........	....	....	1,748	263,920
	United States......	2,598	349,620	....	
	Total..........	2,598	349,620	2,598	349,620
Sheep.........................	B. South Africa.....	....	....	146	800
	United States......	146	800	....	
	Total..........	146	800	146	800
Furs and skins..................	Great Britain......	....	25,451	....	6,222
	United States......	....	6,072	....	25,301
	Total..........	....	31,523	....	31,523
Cheese.......................		Lb.		Lb.	
	Great Britain......	659	158	129,485	16,722
	Germany..........	660	100	....	
	United States......	129,485	16,722	1,319	258
	Total..........	130,804	16,980	130,804	16,980

6 GEORGE V, A. 1916

No. 26.—STATEMENT showing the quantity and value of merchandise received from and shipped to foreign countries—*Continued.*

ARTICLES.	COUNTRIES.	RECEIVED FROM		SHIPPED TO	
		Quantity.	Value.	Quantity.	Value.
ANIMALS AND PRODUCE—*Con.*		Lb.	$	Lb.	$
Lard........................	Great Britain.......	1,656,550	163,819	30,713,156	3,881,885
	B. South Africa.....	35,914	3,765	13,214	1,440
	Newfoundland......	....	....	158,657	14,955
	Germany..........	....	....	138,880	10,500
	United States.......	29,360,043	3,744,196	28,600	3,000
	Total..........	31,052,507	3,911,780	31,052,507	3,911,780
Bacon and Hams...............	Great Britain.......	....	....	274,039	36,429
	Newfoundland......	....	....	4,800	421
	Belgium...........	....	....	1,287	166
	United States......	280,126	37,016	....	....
	Total..........	280,126	37,016	280,126	37,016
Pork......................	Great Britain.......	122,349	17,322	3,147,510	472,015
	B. South Africa....	....	....	101,440	15,216
	Newfoundland......	....	....	310,584	43,493
	New Zealand......	....	....	134,743	17,506
	United States.......	3,571,928	530,908	....	....
	Total..........	3,694,277	548,230	3,694,277	548,230
Meats, all other...............	Great Britain.......	2,003,363	254,660	43,998,571	6,141,558
	B. South Africa.....	3,700	897	247,550	39,188
	Newfoundland......	....	....	654,366	97,362
	United States.......	42,983,021	6,035,391	89,597	12,840
	Total..........	44,990,084	6,290,948	44,990,084	6,290,948
Other articles of animals........	Great Britain.......	....	7,085	....	30,948
	United States......	....	30,948	....	7,085
	Total..........	....	38,033	....	38,033
Total, animals and produce....	....	....	11,224,930	....	11,224,930
AGRICULTURAL PRODUCTS					
Fruits and nuts................	Great Britain.......	....	13,950	....	39,175
	B. South Africa.....	....	....	....	31,805
	Belgium...........	....	1,000	....	....
	United States.....	....	62,580	....	6,550
	Total..........	....	77,530	....	77,530
		Brl.		Brl.	
Flour of wheat................	Great Britain.......	280	1,250	39,045	193,544
	B. South Africa....	....	....	8,332	23,070
	Newfoundland.....	....	....	2,401	11,480
	Belgium...........	....	....	1,420	7,490
	United States.......	50,918	234,334	....	....
	Total........	51,198	235,584	51,198	235,584
Seeds......................	Great Britain.......	....	14,300	....	....
	Australia..........	....	....	....	6,388
	Belgium...........	....	1,700	....	....
	France............	....	442	....	....
	Germany..........	....	663	....	....
	Holland...........	....	1,000	....	....
	United States......	....	6,388	....	18,105
	Total..........	....	24,493	....	24,493
Other agricultural products......	Great Britain......	....	271,015	....	....
	United States......	....	....	....	271,015
	Total..........	....	271,015	....	271,015
TOTAL, AGRICULTURAL PRODUCTS.	....	....	608,622	....	608,622

No. 26.—STATEMENT showing the quantity and value of merchandise received from and shipped to foreign countries—*Continued.*

ARTICLES.	COUNTRIES.	RECEIVED FROM		SHIPPED TO	
		Quantity.	Value.	Quantity.	Value.
MANUFACTURES.			$		$
Cottons and manufactures......	Great Britain......	....	10,846	....	7,020
	Belgium............	....	250	....	....
	Cuba..............	....	....	....	371
	Germany..........	....	78	....	....
	Switzerland........	....	300	....	....
	United States......	....	1,984	....	6,067
	Total........	....	13,458	....	13,458
Drugs, dyes and chemicals......	Great Britain......	....	16,257	....	47,301
	B. South Africa....	....	....	....	784
	Aust.-Hungary.....	....	....	....	1,740
	Chili..............	....	260,000	....	....
	France............	....	423	....	317
	Switzerland........	....	519	....	....
	United States......	....	51,611	....	278,668
	Total..........	....	328,810	....	328,810
Earthenware........	Great Britain......	....	51,144	..:........	20
	B. South Africa....	....	....	....	1,770
	Newfoundland.....	....	....	....	1,740
	New Zealand.....	....	....	....	4,980
	Belgium............	....	40,546	....	50
	Germany..........	....	2,240	....	....
	Holland...........	....	1,010	....	....
	United States.....	....	8,358	....	94,738
	Total.........	....	103,298	....	103,298
Glass and glassware..........	Great Britain.....	....	69,418	....	1,710
	Australia..........	....	....	....	11,325
	B. South Africa....	....	....	....	105,360
	New Foundland....	....	....	....	215
	New Zealand......	....	....	....	2,660
	Belgium............	....	104,514	....	....
	Holland...........	....	4,350	....	....
	Germany..........	....	2,090	....	300
	United States......	....	119,847	....	178,649
	Total.........	....	300,219	....	300,219
Iron and steel................	Great Britain......	..·........	41,001	....	118,462
	Australia..........	....	....	....	300
	B. South Africa:..	....	....	....	125
	Newfoundland.....	....	25	....	750
	Belgium............	....	2,219	....	....
	Germany..........	....	1,278	....	919
	United States.....	....	120,730	....	44,697
	Total.........	....	165,253	....	165,253
Leather and manufactures......	Great Britain......	....	11,163	....	19,937
	B. South Africa.....	....	....	....	150
	Italy..............	....	900	....	....
	United States......	....	20,145	....	12,121
	Total..........	....	32,208	....	32,208
Oil cake,......................	Great Britain......	Cwt. 6,720	8,400	Cwt. 4,480	6,830
	Belgium............	....	....	12,249	13,920
	United States......	10,009	12,350	....	....
	Total..........	16,729	20,750	16,729	20,750

6 GEORGE V, A. 1916

No. 26.—STATEMENT showing the quantity and value of merchandise received
from and shipped to foreign countries—*Continued.*

ARTICLES.	COUNTRIES.	RECEIVED FROM		SHIPPED TO	
		Quantity.	Value.	Quantity.	Value.
			$		$
MANUFACTURES—*Con.*					
Oils of all kinds...............	Great Britain......	....	10,765	....	56,528
	B. South Africa.....	....	....	....	120
	New Zealand......	....	....	....	23,415
	Belgium...........	....	1,890	....	13,000
	Germany..........	....	1,250	....	....
	United States......	....	89,648	....	10,490
	Total..........	....	103,553	....	103,553
Paper and manufactures........	Great Britain......	....	7,782	....	305
	B. South Africa.....	....	....	....	650
	Aust.-Hungary.....	....	....	....	100
	Belgium...........	....	400	....	....
	France............	....	15	....	....
	Germany..........	....	1,515	....	5
	United States......	....	1,089	....	9,741
	Total..........	....	10,801	....	10,801
		Gal.		Gal.	
Spirits and wines...............	Great Britain......	265,898	549,976	76,940	47,042
	Newfoundland.....	....	....	13,600	7,025
	Belgium...........	30,171	63,970	......	....
	France............	8,920	16,410	100	1,950
	Germany..........	6,160	15,660	....	....
	Holland...........	15,298	31,654	....	....
	Italy..............	1,095	4,367	....	....
	Spain.............	100	60	....	....
	United States......	92,075	54,590	329,077	680,670
	Total..........	419,717	736,687	419,717	736,687
Sugar and glucose..............	Great Britain......	....	125	....	10
	Germany..........	....	1,500	....	....
	United States......	....	10	....	1,625
	Total..........	....	1,635	....	1,635
Tobacco and manufactures.....	Great Britain......	....	90	....	31,247
	Aust.-Hungary.....	....	375	....	....
	Egypt.............	....	....	....	200
	Holland...........	....	....	....	1,550
	United States......	....	34,440	....	1,908
	Total..........	....	34,905	....	34,905
		Lb.		Lb.	
Tea..........................	Great Britain......	718,220	168,426	....	....
	Belgium...........	120,544	22,087	....	....
	United States......	....	....	838,764	190,513
	Total..........	838,764	190,513	838,764	190,513
Wood and manufactures........	Great Britain......	....	7,460	....	50,596
	B. South Africa.....	....	....	....	13,646
	Newfoundland.....	....	....	....	240
	New Zealand......	....	....	....	1,929
	Belgium...........	....	3,140	....	....
	France............	....	....	....	301
	Holland...........	....	250	....	....
	United States......	....	66,712	....	10,850
	Total..........	....	77,562	....	77,562

No. 26.—STATEMENT showing the quantity and value of merchandise received from and shipped to foreign countries—*Concluded.*.

ARTICLES.	COUNTRIES.	RECEIVED FROM		SHIPPED TO	
		Quantity.	Value.	Quantity.	Value.
MANUFACTURES—*Con.*			$		$
Woollens......................	Great Britain.......	....	51,955	....	26,141
	Belgium.............	....	4,215	....	200
	France..............	....	400	....	51
	Germany............	....	....	....	425
	United States.......	....	25,203	....	54,956
	Total..........	....	81,773	....	81,773
Other articles of manufactures...	Great Britain.......	....	1,148,290	....	2,593,831
	Australia...........	....	....	....	93,274
	B. South Africa.....	....	20,316	....	183,286
	Newfoundland......	....	8,014	....	8,374
	New Zealand.......	....	17,200	....	231,181
	Argentina..........	....	15,339	....	....
	Aust.-Hungary......	....	3,852	....	7,000
	Belgium............	....	192,671	....	56,066
	France..............	....	9,698	....	10,802
	Germany............	....	11,530	....	4,084
	Hawaii.............	....	....	....	10
	Holland............	....	22,241	....	950
	Italy...............	....	8,435	....	1,085
	Japan..............	....	225	....	378
	Switzerland........	....	1,050	....	62
	United States.......	....	3,105,016	....	1,373,494
	Total..........	....	4,563,877	....	4,563,877
Total manufactures.........		....	6,765,302	....	6,765,302

6 GEORGE V, A. 1916

SUMMARY STATEMENT of the value of merchandise received from foreign countries
Montreal for the United States and other countries

COUNTRIES

	Great Britain.	British South Africa.	New-foundland	New Zealand.	Aust-Hun-gary.	Ar-gentina.	Bel-gium.	Chili.
	$	$	$	$	$	$	$	$
Produce of the mine......	21,465	....	....	....	....	....	....	....
" fisheries...	46,955	....	2,300	....	....	....	528	....
" forest......	1,274	....	....	....	....	....	....	....
Animals and produce.....	492,358	4,662	....	....	....	....	....	....
Agricultural products.....	300,515	....	....	....	....	....	2,700	....
Manufactures..............	2,153,098	20,316	8,039	17,200	4,227	15,339	435,902	260,000
Total.........	3,015,665	24,978	10,339	17,200	4,227	15,339	439,130	260,000

COUNTRIES

	Great Britain.	Austra-lia.	British South Africa.	Egypt.	New-found-land.	New Zealand	Aust.-Hun-gary.	Bel-gium.
	$	$	$	$	$	$	$	$
Produce of the mine......	....	14	22,672	....	....	....	....	43,300
" fisheries...	97,075	....	....	....	....	....	....	....
" forest......	169,662	....	20,007	....	....	....	....	166
Animals and produce.......	10,671,479	....	56,644	....	156,231	17,506	....	....
Agricultural products......	232,719	6,388	54,875	....	11,480	....	....	7,490
Manufactures..............	3,006,980	104,899	305,891	200	18,344	264,165	8,840	83,236
Total.........	14,177,915	111,301	460,089	200	186,055	281,671	8,840	134,192

for immediate transit through Canada, and transhipped at the port of
during the fiscal year ended March 31, 1915.

RECEIVED FROM.

France.	Germany.	Holland.	Italy.	Japan.	Norway.	Spain.	Switzerland.	Turkey	United States.	Total.
$	$	$	$	$	$	$	$	$	$	$
255	....	300	....	....	5,003	....	....	....	22,686	44,406
....	1,000	....	....	....	....	....	....	44	150,567	206,697
....	....	....	....	....	....	....	....	....	189,045	190,319
....	100	....	....	....	....	....	....	....	10,727,810	11,224,930
442	663	1,000	....	....	....	....	....	....	303,302	608,622
26,946	37,141	59,505	13,702	225	....	60	1,869	....	3,711,733	6,765,302
27,643	38,004	60,805	13,702	225	5,003	60	1,869	44	15,105,143	19,040,276

SHIPPED TO.

Cuba.	France.	Germany.	Holland.	Hawaii.	Italy.	Japan.	Switzerland.	United States.	Total.
$	$	$	$	$	$	$	$	$	$
....	10,192	....	....	....	....	....	....	21,720	44,406
....	....	....	....	....	....	....	....	56,130	206,697
....	....	....	....	....	....	....	....	650	190,319
....	263,920	10,500	....	....	....	....	....	48,484	11,224,930
....	....	....	....	....	....	....	....	295,670	608,622
371	13,421	5,733	2,500	10	1,085	378	62	2,949,187	6,765,302
371	287,533	16,233	2,500	10	1,085	378	62	3,371,841	19,040,276

6 GEORGE V, A. 1916

STATEMENT by Years showing the Value of Goods transhipped at the Port of Montreal for Foreign Countries from 1886 to 1915, inclusive.

	Total Value of Goods in Transit through Montreal for Transhipment to Foreign Countries.
	$
Fiscal year ending June 30, 1886	5,745,606
" " 1887	7,645,393
" " 1888	8,058,888
" " 1889	10,314,396
" " 1890	12,714,705
" " 1891	13,202,292
" " 1892	9,423,862
" " 1893	9,313,904
" " 1894	8,186,145
" " 1895	8,027,366
" " 1896	14,191,628
" " 1897	11,077,825
" " 1898	9,378,657
" " 1899	10,485,519
" " 1900	13,160,009
" " 1901	10,707,379
" " 1902	11,382,567
" " 1903	11,689,912
" " 1904	15,224,361
" " 1905	14,095,449
" " 1906	22,114,464
9 months ending March 31, 1907	15,233,092
Fiscal year ending March 31, 1908	18,955,468
" " 1909	20,881,570
" " 1910	21,705,210
" " 1911	18,510,807
" " 1912	21,506,933
" " 1913	21,670,616
" " 1914	26,665,697
" " 1915	19,040,276

No. 27.—STATEMENT showing the Trade via St. Lawrence River (Sea-going Vessels) Inwards and Outwards, during the Fiscal year ended March 31, 1915.

	VESSELS.		FREIGHT.	
	No.	Tons Register.	Tons Weight.	Tons Measurement.
Inwards	987	3,549,346	602,132	229,360
Outwards	869	2,833,746	2,620,761	282,282
Total trade	1,856	6,383,092	3,222,893	511,642

PART II

GENERAL STATEMENTS

Imports, Exports and Shipping of the Dominion of Canada

FOR THE

FISCAL YEAR ENDED MARCH 31, 1915

6 GEORGE V, A. 1916

No. 1.—GENERAL STATEMENT (by Countries) of the Total Quantities and Values for Consumption and the Duties Collected thereon in the Dominion

(*Abbreviations: B. E., British East; B. W., British West; F. W.,*

| Articles Imported. | Countries. | TOTAL IMPORTS. | | ENTERED | | |
| | | Quantity. | Value. | General Tariff. | | |
				Quantity.	Value.	Duty.
DUTIABLE GOODS		Gal.	$	Gal.	$	$ cts.
Ale, porter, lager and other beer in bottles.	Unit'd Kingdom	252,027	215,359	269,374	238,249	84,717 89
	Belgium........	344	83	344	83	82 56
	Denmark.......	280	130	460	190	160 80
	France..........	48	43	48	43	20 16
	Germany.......	13,021	11,548	11,675	10,087	3,142 56
	Holland........	6	7	180	179	43 20
	Sweden........	2,020	1,282	1,482	1,107	496 08
	United States...	653,236	414,455	652,367	410,842	189,950 89
	Total.......	920,982	642,907	935,930	660,780	278,614 14
Ale, porter, lager and other beer in casks.	Unit'd Kingdom	11,453	4,003	12,279	4,470	2,739 26
	Aust.-Hungary.	2,750	684	3,359	840	588 19
	Belgium........	286	38	286	38	45 76
	Germany.......	22,679	9,042	22,030	7,885	3,820 41
	United States..	87,564	23,143	87,181	23,122	16,884 20
	Total.......	124,732	36,910	125,135	36,355	24,077 82
Ginger ale.................	Unit'd Kingdom	....	25,923	....	226	39 55
	Japan..........	....	88	....	18	3 15
	United States...	....	1,753	....	1,753	306 81
	Total.......	....	27,764	....	1,997	349 51
		Lb.		Lb.		
Animals, living, viz.:— Hogs......................	United States...	3,830	795	3,830	795	57 45
		No.		No.		
Horned cattle.................	United States...	1,683	42,255	1,683	42,255	10,563 75
Horses over one year old valued at $50 or less per head.	Newfoundland..	32	1,250	32	1,250	400 00
	United States..	59	2,728	60	2,778	750 00
	Total.......	91	3,978	92	4,028	1,150 00
Horses, n.o.p.................	Unit'd Kingdom	5	972	2	285	71 25
	B. W. Indies....	1	85	1	85	21 25
	Newfoundland ..	21	1,107	21	1,107	276 75
	Belgium........	7	7,876	7	7,876	1,969 00
	United States...	24,878	2,505,227	2,769	252,000	63,000 00
	Total.......	24,912	2,515,267	2,800	261,353	65,338 25
Sheep......................	United States...	110,663	362,051	110,663	362 051	90,512 75
All other ,not elsewhere specified	Unit'd Kingdom	....	2,413	....	311	77 75
	Australia.......	....	15	....	15	3 75
	B. India........	....	5	....	5	1 25
	B. W. Indies....	....	25	....	15	3 75
	Hong Kong.....	....	53	....	53	13 25
	Newfoundland..	....	28	....	28	7 00
	Holland........	....	21	....	21	5 25
	Japan..........	....	19	....	19	4 75
	United States...	....	53,338	....	53,783	13,445 75
	Total.......	....	55,917	....	54,250	13,562 50

'of Merchandise imported; also of the Quantities and Values of the same entered of Canada during the Fiscal Year ended March 31, 1915.

French West; Dan. W., Danish West; N. E. S., not elsewhere specified).

FOR HOME CONSUMPTION.

Preferential Tariff.			Treaty Rates.			Total.		
Quantity.	Value.	Duty.	Quantity.	Value.	Duty.	Quantity.	Value.	Duty Coll'd
Gal.	$	$ cts.	Gal.	$	$ cts.	Gal.	$	$ cts.
....	....	....	....	....	....	269,374	238,249	84,717 89
....	....	....	....	....	....	344	83	82 56
....	....	....	....	....	....	460	190	160 80
....	....	....	....	....	....	48	43	20 16
....	....	....	....	....	....	11,675	10,087	3,142 56
....	....	....	....	....	....	180	179	43 20
....	....	....	....	....	....	1,482	1,107	496 08
....	....	....	....	....	....	652,367	410,842	189,950 89
....	.'......	....	....	....	..'.....	935,930	660,780	278,614 14
....	....	....	....	....	....	12,279	4,470	2,739 26
....	....	....	....	....	....	3,359	840	588 19
....	....	....	....	....	....	286	38	45 76
....	....	....	....	....	....	22,030	7,885	3,820 41
....	....	....	....	....	....	87,181	23,122	16,884 20
....	....	....	....	....	....	125,135	36,355	24,077 82
....	25,746	3,861 90	....	....	....	....	25,972	3,901 45
....	....	....	....	....	....	....	18	3 15
....	....	....	....	....	....	....	1,753	306 81
....	25,746	3,861 90	....	....	....	....	27,743	4,211 41
Lb.			Lb.			Lb.		
....	....	....	....	....	....	3,830	795	57 45
No.			No.			No.		
....	....	....	....	....	....	1,683	42,255	10,563 75
....	....	....	....	....	....	32	1,250	400 00
....	....	....	....	....	....	60	2,778	750 00
....	....	....	....	....	....	92	4,028	1,150 00
2	487	73 05	....	....	....	4	772	144 30
....	....	....	....	....	....	1	85	21 25
....	....	....	....	....	....	21	1,107	276 75
....	....	....	....	....	....	7	7,876	1,969 00
....	....	....	....	....	....	2,769	252,000	63,000 00
2	487	73 05	....	....	....	2,802	261,840	65,411 30
....	....	....	....	....	....	110,663	362,051	90,512 75
....	2,102	315 30	....	....	....	....	2,413	393 05
....	....	....	....	....	....	....	15	3 75
....	....	....	....	....	....	....	5	1 25
....	10	1 50	....	....	....	....	25	5 25
....	....	....	....	....	....	....	53	13 25
....	....	....	....	....	....	....	28	7 00
....	....	....	....	....	....	....	21	5 25
....	....	....	....	....	....	....	19	4 75
....	....	....	....	....	....	....	53,783	13,445 75
....	2,112	316 80	....	....	....	....	56,362	13,879 30

6 GEORGE V, A. 1916

No. 1.—General Statement

Articles Imported.	Countries.	Total Imports.		Entered		
		Quantity.	Value.	General Tariff.		
				Quantity.	Value.	Duty.
DUTIABLE GOODS—*Còn.*			$		$	$ cts.
Antiseptic surgical dressings, such as absorbent cotton, cotton wool, lint, lamb's wool, tow, jute, gauzes and oakum, prepared for use as surgical dressings, plain or medicated.	Unit'd Kingdom	....	65,282	....	3,026	605 20
	Belgium........	....	131	....	131	26 20
	France.........	....	128	....	....	....
	Germany.......	....	114	....	114	22 80
	Holland........	....	213	....	213	42 60
	Japan..........	....	30	....	23	4 60
	Switzerland.....	....	110	....	....	....
	United States...	....	185,698	....	185,698	37,139 60
	Total......	....	251,706	....	189,205	37,841 00
Bagatelle and other game tables or boards.	Unit'd Kingdom	....	1,360	....	32	11 20
	France.........	....	16	....	16	5 60
	Japan..........	....	8	....	8	2 80
	United States...	....	6,249	....	6,249	2,187 15
	Total......	....	7,633	....	6,305	2,206 75
Bags which contained cement, etc.	Belgium........	....	100	....	100	20 00
	United States...	....	15,023	....	15,023	3,004 60
	Total......	....	15,123	....	15,123	3,024 60
		Lb.		Lb.		
Baking powder..................	Unit'd Kingdom	8,389	1,051	12	3	0 72
	United States...	519,976	149,465	520,088	149,498	31,205 28
	Total......	528,365	150,516	520,100	149,501	31,206 00
Balls, cues and racks and cue-tips for bagatelle boards and billiard tables.	Unit'd Kingdom	....	3,677	....	325	113 75
	France.........	....	5,187	....	5,187	1,815 45
	Germany.......	....	145	....	145	50 75
	United States...	....	10,912	....	10,912	3,819 20
	Total......	....	19,921	....	16,569	5,799 15
Baskets of all kinds, n.o.p........	Unit'd Kingdom	....	13,928	....	805	241 50
	B. W. Indies....	....	43	....	....	....
	Hong Kong.....	....	168	....	165	49 50
	Aust.-Hungary.	....	574	....	353	105 90
	Belgium........	....	10,874	....	5,384	1,615 20
	China..........	....	19	....	19	5 70
	France.........	....	1,427	....	31	9 30
	Germany.......	....	5,953	....	5,953	1,785 90
	Holland.·......	....	20	....	8	2 40
	Italy..........	....	396	....	396	118 80
	Japan..........	....	17,710	....	2,103	630 90
	Spain..·.......	....	159	....	....	....
	United States...	....	42,855	....	42,953	12,885 90
	Total......	....	94,126	....	58,170	17,451 00
Baths, bath-tubs, basins, closets, lavatories, urinals, sinks and laundry tubs of any material.	Unit'd Kingdom	....	117,024	....	3,482	1,218 70
	Belgium........	....	....	....	35	12 25
	France.........	....	211	....	428	149 80
	Germany.......	....	94	....	5	1 75
	United States...	....	198,778	....	198,705	69,546 75
	Total......	....	316 107	....	202,655	70,929 25

OF IMPORTS—*Continued.*

FOR HOME CONSUMPTION.

	Preferential Tariff.			Treaty Rates.			Total.	
Quantity.	Value.	Duty.	Quantity.	Value.	Duty.	Quantity.	Value.	Duty Coll'd
	$	$ cts.		$	$ cts.		$	$ cts.
....	61,501	7,687 98	....	512	89 60	....	65,039	8,382 78
....	....	....	....	....	....	....	131	26 20
....	....	....	....	128	22 40	....	128	22 40
....	....	....	....	....	....	....	114	22 80
....	....	....	....	....	....	....	213	42 60
....	....	....	....	7	1 23	....	30	5 83
....	....	....	....	110	19 26	....	110	19 26
....	....	....	....	....	....	....	185,698	37,139 60
....	61,501	7,687 98	....	757	132 49	....	251,463	45,661 47
....	1,328	298 87	....	....	....	....	1,360	310 07
....	....	....	....	....	....	....	16	5 60
....	....	....	....	....	....	....	8	2 80
....	....	....	....	....	....	....	6,249	2,187 15
....	1,328	298 87	....	....	....	....	7,633	2,505 62
....	....	....	....	....	....	....	100	−20 00
....	....	....	....	....	....	....	15,023	3,004 60
....	....	....	....	....	....	....	15,123	3,024 60
Lb. 8,377	1,048	335 08	Lb.			Lb. 8,389	1,051	335 80
....	....	....	....	....	....	520,088	149,498	31,205 28
8,377	1,048	335 08	....	....	....	528,477	150,549	31,541 08
....	3,352	754 29	....	....	....	....	3,677	868 04
....	....	....	....	....	....	....	5,187	1,815 45
....	....	....	....	....	....	....	145	50 75
....	....	....	....	....	....	....	10,912	3,819 20
....	3,352	754 29	....	....	....	....	19,921	6,553 44
....	12,210	2,442 00	....	913	251 08	....	13,928	2,934 58
....	43	8 60	....	....	....	....	43	8 60
....	....	....	....	3	0 83	....	168	50 33
....	....	....	....	221	60 78	....	574	166 68
....	....	....	....	5,490	1,509 75	....	10,874	3,124 95
....	....	....	....	....	....	....	19	5 70
....	....	....	....	1,396	383 90	....	1,427	393 20
....	....	....	....	....	....	....	5,953	1,785 90
....	....	....	....	12	3 30	....	20	5 70
....	....	....	....	....	....	....	396	118 80
....	....	....	....	15,306	4,209 27	....	17,409	4,840 17
....	....	....	....	159	43 73	....	159	43 73
....	....	....	....	....	....	....	42,953	12,885 90
....	12,253	2,450 60	....	23,500	6,462 64	....	93,923	26,364 24
....	113,760	22,752 00	....	....	....	....	117,242	23,970 70
....	....	....	....	....	....	....	35	12 25
....	....	....	....	....	....	....	428	149 80
....	....	....	....	....	....	....	5	1 75
....	....	....	....	....	....	....	198,705	69,546 75
....	113,760	22,752 00	....	....	....	....	316,415	93,681 25

No. 1.—General Statement

Articles Imported.	Countries.	Total Imports.		Entered		
				General Tariff.		
		Quantity.	Value.	Quantity.	Value.	Duty.
DUTIABLE GOODS—*Con.*			$		$	$ cts.
Belting of all kinds except rubber and leather.	Unit'd Kingdom	....	152,577	....	1,104	303 60
	Belgium........	....	143	....	143	39 33
	France.........	....	451	....	451	124 03
	Germany......	....	2,715	....	2,177	598 68
	United States...	....	90,331	....	89,113	24,506 72
	Total......	....	246,217	....	92,988	25,572 36
Belts, of all kinds, n.o.p., except silk.	Unit'd Kingdom	....	13,992	....	265	92 75
	France........	....	472	....	490	171 50
	Germany......	....	122	....	122	42 70
	Japan.........	....	15	....	15	5 25
	United States...	....	55,772	....	55,772	19,520 20
	Total......	....	70,373	....	56,664	19,832 40
Bells and gongs, n.o.p.............	Unit'd Kingdom	....	2,074	....	224	67 20
	France........	....	58	....	....	....
	Germany......	....	252	....	252	75 60
	United States...	....	31,383	....	31,378	9,413 40
	Total......	....	33,767	....	31,854	9,556 20
		No.		No.		
Billiard tables..................	Unit'd Kingdom	134	25,717	1	283	99 05
	United States...	120	5,019	120	5,016	1,755 60
	Total......	254	30,736	121	5,299	1,854 65
Blacking, shoe and shoemakers' ink, shoe, harness and leather dressing, n.o.p.	Unit'd Kingdom	....	36,106	....	317	87 18
	Belgium........	....	1	....	1	0 28
	Germany......	....	222	....	222	61 05
	United States...	....	91,288	....	92,013	25,304 77
	Total......	....	127,617	....	92,553	25,453 28
Blinds, of wood, metal or other material, not textile or paper.	Unit'd Kingdom	....	43	....	....	....
	Germany......	....	138	....	138	41 40
	Japan.........	....	538	....	538	161 40
	Sweden........	....	34	....	34	10 20
	United States...	....	2,744	....	2,744	823 20
	Total......	....	3,497	....	3,454	1,036 20
Blueing, laundry blueing.........	Unit'd Kingdom	....	40,089	....	....	....
	Germany......	....	213	....	213	47 93
	United States...	....	5,490	....	5,490	1,235 57
	Total......	....	45,792	....	5,703	1,283 50
Boats, open, pleasure, sail boats, skiffs and canoes.	Unit'd Kingdom	35	3,469	2	8	2 00
	Hong Kong.....	1	75	1	75	18 75
	United States...	766	26,471	766	26,471	6,617 75
	Total......	802	30,015	769	26,554	6,638 50

OF IMPORTS—*Continued.*

FOR HOME CONSUMPTION.

Preferential Tariff.			Treaty Rates.			Total.		
Quantity.	Value.	Duty.	Quantity.	Value.	Duty.	Quantity.	Value.	Duty Coll'd
	$	$ cts.		$	$ cts.		$	$ cts.
....	154,924	30,984 80	....	....	....	....	156,028	31,288 40
....	....	....	....	....	....	....	143	39 33
....	....	....	....	....	....	....	451	124 03
....	....	....	....	....	....	....	2,177	598 68
....	....	....	....	....	....	....	89,113	24,506 72
....	154,924	30,984 80	....	....	....	....	247,912	56,557 16
....	13,841	3,114 54	....			....	14,106	3,207 29
....	....	....				....	490	171 50
....	....	....				....	122	42 70
....	....	....				....	15	5 25
....	....	....				....	55,772	19,520 20
....	13,841	3,114 54	....			....	70,505	22,946 94
....	4,712	942 40	....			....	4,936	1,009 60
....	....	....		58	15 96	....	58	15 96
....	....	....				....	252	75 60
....	....	....				....	31,378	9,413 40
....	4,712	942 40	....	58	15 96	....	36,624	10,514 56
No.			No.			No.		
133	25,421	5,719 82	....	....	....	134	25,704	5,818 87
....	....	....	....	....	....	120	5,016	1,755 60
133	25,421	5,719 82	....	....	....	254	30,720	7,574 47
....	35,670	5,350 50	....	....	....	....	35,987	5,437 68
....	....	....	....	....	....	....	1	0 28
....	....	....	....	....	....	....	222	61 05
....	....	....	....	....	....	....	92,013	25,304 77
....	35,670	5,350 50	....	....	....	....	128 223	30,803 78
....	43	8 60	....	....	....	....	43	8 60
....	....	....	....	....	....	....	138	41 40
....	....	....	....	....	....	....	538	161 40
....	....	....	....	....	....	....	34	10 20
....	....	....	....	....	....	....	2,744	823 20
....	43	8 60	....	....	....	....	3,497	1,044 80
....	40,940	6,141 00	....	....	....	....	40,940	6,141 00
....	....	....	....	....	....	....	213	47 93
....	....	....	....	....	....	....	5,490	1,235 57
....	40,940	6,141 00	....	....	....	....	46,643	7,424 50
33	3,312	496 80	....	....	....	35	3,320	498 80
....	....	....	....	....	....	1	75	18 75
....	....	....	....	....	....	766	26,471	6,617 75
33	3,312	496 80	....	....	....	802	29,866	7,135 30

6 GEORGE V, A. 1916

No. 1.—General Statement

Articles Imported.	Countries.	Total Imports.		Entered		
				General Tariff.		
		Quantity.	Value.	Quantity.	Value.	Duty.
			$		$	$ cts.
DUTIABLE GOODS—*Con.*						
Books, printed, periodicals and pamphlets, or parts thereof, n.o.p.	Unit'd Kingdom	....	549,882	....	8,409	840 90
	Australia........	....	10	....	10	1 00
	Hong Kong.....	....	44	....	44	4 40
	Newfoundland..	....	30	....	30	3 00
	Belgium........	....	9,530	....	9,530	953 00
	China..........	....	34	....	34	3 40
	France....,....	....	68,547	....	8,871	887 10
	Germany.......	....	2,674	....	2,674	267 40
	Holland........	....	345	....	345	34 50
	Italy..........	....	78	....	78	7 80
	Japan..........	....	41	....	41	4 10
	United States...	....	936,178	....	936,273	93,627 30
	Total......	....	1,567,393	....	966,339	96,633 90
Books—Novels or works of fiction, or literature of a similar character, unbound or paper bound, or in sheets, not including Christmas annuals or publications commonly known as juvenile or toy books.	Unit'd Kingdom	....	21,623	....	183	45 75
	France.........	....	5,435	....	331	82 75
	Japan..........	....	4	....	4	1 00
	United States...	....	45,471	....	45,471	11,367 75
	Total......	....	72,533	....	45,989	11,497 25
Freight rates for railways, and telegraph rates, bound in book or pamphlet form, and time tables of railways outside of Canada.	Unit'd Kingdom	....	207	....	83	20 75
	New Zealand...	....	2	....	....	....
	France.........	....	5	....	5	1 25
	United States...	....	21,368	....	21,368	5,342 00
	Total......	....	21,582	....	21,456	5,364 00
Bank notes, bonds, bills of exchange, cheques, promissory notes, drafts and all similar work unsigned, and cards or other commercial blank forms printed or lithographed or printed from steel or copper or other plates, and other printed matter, n.o.p.	Unit'd Kingdom	....	38,405	....	2,143	750 05
	Hong Kong.....	....	367	....	367	128 45
	Newfoundland..	....	20	....	20	7 00
	New Zealand...	....	11	....	....	....
	China..........	....	43	....	43	15 05
	France.........	....	379	....	389	136 15
	Germany.......	....	973	....	973	340 55
	Japan..........	....	157	....	157	54 95
	United States...	....	218,859	....	217,742	76,209 70
	Total......	....	259,214	....	221,834	77,641 90
		Lb.		Lb.		
Posters, advertising bills and folders................	Unit'd Kingdom	4,192	1,338	255	60	38 25
	France.........	120	31	120	31	18 00
	United States...	47,603	13,184	47,603	13,184	7,140 45
	Total......	51,915	14,553	47,978	13,275	7,196 70
Labels for cigar boxes, fruits, vegetables, meats, fish, confectionery and other goods and wares; also shipping, price or other tags, tickets or labels; and railroad or other tickets whether lithographed or printed or partly printed, n.o.p.	Unit'd Kingdom	....	26,442	....	4,084	1,429 40
	B.E. Indies, other.	....	35	....	....	....
	Belgium........	....	16	....	16	5 60
	France.........	....	859	....	847	296 45
	Germany.......	....	14,707	....	14,547	5,091 45
	Holland........	....	113	....	113	39 55
	Italy..........	....	20	....	6	2 10
	Japan..........	....	76	....	81	28 35
	Portugal.......	....	33	....	33	11 55
	Spain..........	....	3	....	5	1 75
	Switzerland....	....	20	....	20	7 00
	Turkey........	....	100	....	100	35 00
	United States...	....	213,253	....	212,916	74,520 60
	Total......	....	255,677	....	232,768	81,468 80

OF IMPORTS—*Continued.*

FOR HOME CONSUMPTION.

Preferential Tariff.			Treaty Rates.			Total.		
Quantity.	Value.	Duty.	Quantity.	Value.	Duty.	Quantity.	Value.	Duty Coll'd.
	$	$ cts.		$	$ cts.		$	$ cts.
....	540,947	27,047 35	....	313	15 65	....	549,669	27,903 90
....	....	....	....	....	....	....	10	1 00
....	....	....	....	....	....	....	44	4 40
....	....	....	....	....	....	....	30	3 00
....	....	....	....	....	....	....	9,530	953 00
....	....	....	....	....	....	....	34	3 40
....	....	....	....	59,691	2,984 55	....	68,562	3,871 65
....	....	....	....	....	....	....	2,674	267 40
....	....	....	....	....	....	....	345	34 50
....	....	....	....	....	....	....	78	7 80
....	....	....	....	....	....	....	41	4 10
....	....	....	....	....	....	....	936,273	93,627 30
....	540,947	27,047 35	....	60,004	3,000 20	....	1,567,290	126,681 45
....	21,442	3,216 30	....	....	....	....	21 625	3,262 05
....	....	....	....	5,119	767 85	....	5,450	850 60
....	....	....	....	....	....	....	4	1 00
....	....	....	....	....	....	....	45,471	11,367 75
....	21,442	3,216 30	....	5,119	767 85	....	72,550	15,481 40
....	124	18 60	....	....	....	....	207	39 35
....	2	0 30	....	....	....	....	2	0 30
....	....	....	....	....	....	....	5	1 25
....	....	....	....	....	....	....	21,368	5,342 00
....	126	18 90	....	....	....	....	21,582	5,382 90
....	35,257	7,933 25	....	....	....	....	37,400	8,683 30
....	....	....	....	....	....	....	367	128 45
....	....	....	....	....	....	....	20	7 00
....	11	2 48	....	....	....	....	11	2 48
....	....	....	....	....	....	....	43	15 05
....	....	....	....	....	....	....	389	136 15
....	....	....	....	....	....	....	973	340 55
....	....	....	....	....	....	....	157	54 95
....	....	....	....	....	....	....	217,742	76,209 70
....	35,268	7,935 73	....	....	....	....	257,102	85,577 63
Lb. 3,943	1,280	394 30	Lb.	....	....	Lb. 4,198	1,340	432 55
....	....	....	....	....	....	120	31	18 00
....	....	....	....	....	....	47,603	13,184	7,140 45
3,943	1,280	394.30	....	....	....	51,921	14,555	7,591 00
....	22,403	5,041 11	....	....	....	....	26,487	6,470 51
....	....	....	....	....	....	....	16	5 60
....	....	....	....	....	....	....	847	296 45
....	....	....	....	....	....	....	14,547	5,091 45
....	....	....	....	....	....	....	113	39 55
....	....	....	....	....	....	....	6	2 10
....	....	....	....	....	....	....	81	28 35
....	....	....	....	....	....	....	33	11 55
....	....	....	....	....	....	....	5	1 75
....	....	....	....	....	....	....	20	7 00
....	....	....	....	....	....	....	100	35 00
....	....	....	....	....	....	....	212,916	74,520 60
....	22,403	5,041 11	....	....	....	....	255,171	86,509 91

6 GEORGE V, A. 1916

No. 1.—General Statement

Articles Imported.	Countries.	Total Imports.		Entered		
				General Tariff.		
		Quantity.	Value.	Quantity.	Value.	Duty.
DUTIABLE GOODS—*Con.*			$		$	$ cts.
Books, &c.—*Con.*						
Maps and charts, n.o.p.........	Unit'd Kingdom	....	11,758	....	529	119 03
	China...........	....	30	....	- 30	6 75
	France...........	....	455	....	455	101 78
	Japan...........	....	4	....	4	0 90
	United States...	....	26,005	....	26,005	5,852 36
	Total......	....	38,252	....	27,023	6,080 82
Newspapers or supplemental editions or parts thereof partly printed and intended to be completed and published in Canada.	Unit'd Kingdom	....	437	....	....	....
	United States...	....	9,237	....	9,237	2,309 25
	Total......	....	9,674	....	9,237	2,309 25
		Lb.		Lb.		
Advertising pamphlets, advertising show cards, illustrated advertising periodicals, price books, catalogues and price lists, advertising calendars and almanacs; patent medicine or other advertising circulars, fly sheets or pamphlets.	Unit'd Kingdom	328,970	79,613	19,448	5,838	2,917 20
	Australia.......	376	55	376	55	56 40
	B. W. Indies....	40	5	6	1	0 90
	Hong Kong....	94	33	94	33	14 10
	Aust.-Hungary..	150	38	....	....	....
	Belgium........	445	96	445	96	66 75
	China...........	110	25	110	25	16 50
	Cuba...........	....	....	82	....	12 30
	Denmark.......	50	41	50	41	7 50
	France.........	6,740	1,576	5,514	1,247	827 10
	Germany.......	23,085	8,006	22,975	7,883	3,446 25
	Holland........	2,118	515	2,126	515	318 90
	Italy...........	187	34	72	24	10 80
	Japan..........	1,835	378	1,835	378	275 25
	Russia.........	10	8	10	8	1 50
	Sweden........	35	10	35	10	5 25
	Switzerland.....	457	32	50	10	7 50
	United States...	2,227,913	664,839	2,226,418	664,525	333,962 70
	Total......	2,592,615	755,304	2,279,646	680,689	341,946 90
Advertising chromos, chromotypes, oleographs or like work produced by any process other than hand painting or drawing, and having any advertisement or advertising matter printed, lithographed or stamped thereon, or attached thereto, or other similar artistic work, lithographed, printed or stamped on paper or cardboard, for business or advertising purposes, n.o.p.	Unit'd Kingdom	596	56	27	1	4 05
	Germany.......	1,175	557	1,175	557	176 25
	Switzerland.....	28	7	28	7	4 20
	United States...	10,953	5,869	10,953	5,869	1,642 95
	Total......	12,752	6,489	12,183	6,434	1,827 45
Printed music, bound or in sheets, and music for mechanical players.	Unit'd Kingdom	....	51,776	....	4,726	472 60
	Belgium........	....	155	....	155	15 50
	China...........	....	3	....	3	0 30
	France..........	....	3,455	....	3,455	345 50
	French Africa...	....	200	....	200	20 00
	Germany.......	....	833	....	833	83 30
	Switzerland....	....	48	....	48	4 80
	United States...	....	190,815	....	190,815	19,081 50
	Total......	....	247,285	....	200,235	20,023 50
Photographs, chromos, chromotypes, artotypes, oleographs, paintings, drawings, pictures, engravings, or prints, decalcomania transfers of all kinds, or proofs therefrom and similar works of art, n. o. p.; blue prints and building plans.	Unit'd Kingdom	....	192,913	....	18,856	4,242 60
	Hong Kong.....	....	8	....	8	1 80
	Newfoundland..	....	4	....	4	0 90
	New Zealand...	....	146	....	146	32 85
	Aust.-Hungary..	....	469	....	469	105 53
	Belgium........	....	348	....	348	78 30
	France.........	....	7,315	....	6,947	1,563 09
	Germany.......	....	40,261	....	41,189	9,267 52

OF IMPORTS—*Continued.*

FOR HOME CONSUMPTION.

	Preferential Tariff.			Treaty Rates.			Total.	
Quantity.	Value.	Duty.	Quantity.	Value.	Duty.	Quantity.	Value.	Duty Coll'd.
	$	$ cts.		$	$ cts.		$	$ cts.
....	8,929	1,339 35	....	....	....	....	9,458	1,458 38
....	....	....	....	....	....	....	30	6 75
....	....	....	....	....	....	....	455	101 78
....	....	....	....	....	....	....	4	0 90
....	....	....	....	....	....	....	26,005	5,852 36
....	8,929	1,339 35	....	....	....	....	35,952	7,420 17
....	437	65 55	....	....	....	....	437	65 55
....	....	....	....	....	....	....	9,237	2,309 25
....	437	65 55	....	....	....	....	9,674	2,374 80
Lb. 303,109	73,767	30,310 90	Lb.	....	....	Lb. 322,557	79,605	33,228 10
....	....	....	....	....	....	376	55	56 40
40	5	4 00	....	....	....	46	6	4 90
....	....	....	....	....	....	94	33	14 10
....	....	....	....	....	....	445	96	66 75
....	....	....	....	....	....	110	25	16 50
....	....	....	....	....	....	82	....	12 30
....	....	....	....	....	....	50	41	7 50
....	....	....	....	....	....	5,514	1,247	827 10
....	....	....	....	....	....	22,975	7,883	3,446 25
....	....	....	....	....	....	2,126	515	318 90
....	....	....	....	....	....	72	24	10 80
....	....	....	....	....	....	1,835	378	275 25
....	....	....	....	....	....	10	8	1 50
....	....	....	....	....	....	35	10	5 25
....	....	....	....	....	....	50	10	7 50
....	....	....	....	....	....	2,226,418	664,525	333,962 70
303,149	73,772	30,314 90	....	....	....	2,582,795	754,461	372,261 80
569	55	56 90	....	....	....	596	56	60 95
....	....	....	....	....	....	1,175	557	176 25
....	....	....	....	....	....	28	7	4 20
....	....	....	....	....	....	10,953	5,869	1,642 95
569	55	56 90	....	....	....	12,752	6,489	1,884 35
....	47,046	2,352 30	....	....	....	....	51,772	2,824 90
....	....	....	....	....	....	....	155	15 50
....	....	....	....	....	....	....	3	0 30
....	....	....	....	....	....	....	3,455	345 50
....	....	....	....	....	....	....	200	20 00
....	....	....	....	....	....	....	833	83 30
....	....	....	....	....	....	....	48	4 80
....	....	....	....	....	....	....	190,815	19,081 50
....	47,046	2,352 30	....	....	....	....	247,281	22,375 80
....	166,564	24,984 60	....	....	....	....	185,420	29,227 20
....	....	....	....	....	....	....	8	1 80
....	....	....	....	....	....	....	4	0 90
....	....	....	....	....	....	....	146	32 85
....	....	....	....	....	....	....	469	105 53
....	....	....	....	....	....	....	348	78 30
....	....	....	....	....	....	....	6,947	1,563 09
....	....	....	....	....	....	....	41,189	9,267 52

6 GEORGE V, A. 1916

No. 1—General Statement

Articles Imported.	Countries.	Total Imports.		Entered		
				General Tariff.		
		Quantity.	Value.	Quantity.	Value.	Duty.
DUTIABLE GOODS—*Con.*			$		$	$ cts.
Books, &c.—*Con.*						
Photographs, chromos, chromo-	Holland........	....	293	....	293	65 93
types, artotypes, oleographs,	Italy.........	....	90	....	90	20 25
paintings, &c.—*Con.*	Japan..........	....	542	....	476	107 10
	Sweden.........	....	78	....	78	17 55
	Switzerland....	....	330	....	330	74 25
	United States...	....	518,492	....	472,655	106,350 19
	Total......	....	761,289	....	541,889	121,927 86
Boot, shoe, shirt and stay laces	Unit'd Kingdom	....	59,362	....	834	250 20
of any material................	Aust.-Hungary..	....	317	....	....	....
	Belgium.......	....	24,616	....	1,425	427 50
	France........	....	6,073	....	30	9 00
	Germany......	....	478	....	478	143 40
	Switzerland....	....	336	....	....	....
	United States...	....	50,049	....	49,910	14,973 00
	Total......	....	141,231	....	52,677	15,803 10
Boots,shoes, slippers, and insoles	Unit'd Kingdom	....	170,529	....	553	165 90
of all kinds, except rubber and	Hong Kong....	....	8,707	....	8,702	2,610 60
leather.....................	Aust.-Hungary .	....	2,344	....	110	33 00
	China..........	....	1,793	....	1,793	537 90
	France........	....	3,774	....	228	68 40
	Germany......	....	12,511	....	12,511	3,753 30
	Holland.......	....	4	....	4	1 20
	Japan..........	....	1,677	....	133	39 90
	Miquelon and St. Pierre.....	....	1	....	....	....
	Norway.......	....	562	....	....	....
	Switzerland....	....	3,698	....	....	....
	Turkey........	....	21	....	21	6 30
	United States...	....	61,612	....	61,612	18,483 60
	Total......	....	267,233	....	85,667	25,700 10
Braces or suspenders and finished	Unit'd Kingdom	....	9,088	....	218	76 30
parts of.....................	France........	....	9,115	....	3,336	1,167 60
	Germany......	....	5	....	5	1 75
	Japan..........	....	2	....	2	0 70
	United States...	....	37,449	....	37,495	13,123 25
	Total......	....	55,659	....	41,056	14,369 60
Brass and manufactures of—						
Brass in strips, sheets or plates,	Unit'd Kingdom	....	3,247	....	25	2 50
not polished, planished or	Germany......	....	106	....	106	10 60
coated.......	United States...	....	186,229	....	186,229	18,622 90
	Total......	....	189,582	....	186,360	18,636 00
Brass in bars and rods, in coils	Unit'd Kingdom	....	2,468	....	229	22 90
or otherwise, not less than 6	United States...	....	154,484	....	154,484	15,448 40
feet in length.	Total......	....	156,952	....	154,713	15,471 30
Nails, tacks, rivets and burrs	Unit'd Kingdom	....	245	....	1	0 30
or washers.	Germany......	....	255	....	255	76 50
	United States...	....	5,943	....	5,943	1,782 90
	Total......	....	6,443	....	6,199	1,859 70

OF IMPORTS—*Continued.*

FOR HOME CONSUMPTION.

	Preferential Tariff.			Treaty Rates.			Total.	
Quantity.	Value.	Duty.	Quantity.	Value.	Duty.	Quantity.	Value.	Duty Coll'd
	$	$ cts.		$	$ cts.		$	$ cts.
....	....	....	....	....	....	....	293	65 93
....	....	....	....	....	....	....	90	20 25
....	....	....	....	....	....	....	476	107 10
....	....	....	....	....	....	....	78	17 55
....	....	....	....	....	....	....	330	74 25
....	....	....	....	....	....	....	472,655	106,350 19
....	166,564	24,984 60	....	....	....	....	708,453	146,912 46
....	56,646	11,329 20	....	2,473	680 07	....	59,953	12,259 47
....	....	....	....	317	87 17	....	317	87 17
....	....	....	....	23,883	6,567 82	....	25,308	6,995 32
....	....	....	....	6,203	1,705 82	....	6,233	1,714 82
....	....	....	....	....	....	....	478	143 40
....	....	....	....	336	92 67	....	336	92 67
....	....	....	....	....	....	....	49,910	14,973 00
....	56,646	11,329 20	....	33,212	9,133 55	....	142,535	36,265 85
....	163,427	32,685 40	....	5,251	1,444 09	....	169,231	34,295 39
....	....	....	....	5	1 38	....	8,707	2,611 98
....	....	....	....	2,234	614 35	....	2,344	647 35
....	....	....	....	....	....	....	1,793	537 90
....	....	....	....	3,547	975 42	....	3,775	1,043 82
....	....	....	....	....	....	....	12,511	3,753 30
....	....	....	....	....	....	....	4	1 20
....	....	....	....	1,512	415 80	....	1,645	455 70
....	....	....	....	1	0 28	....	1	0 28
....	....	....	....	562	154 55	....	562	154 55
....	....	....	....	3,698	1,016 99	....	3,698	1,016 99
....	....	....	....	....	....	....	21	6 30
....	....	....	....	....	....	....	61,612	18,483 60
....	163,427	32,685 40	....	16,810	4,622 86	....	265,904	63,008 36
....	6,655	1,497 59	....	2,199	659 70	....	9,072	2,233 59
....	....	....	....	5,135	1,540 50	....	8,471	2,708 10
....	....	....	....	....	....	....	5	1 75
....	....	....	....	....	....	....	2	0 70
....	....	....	....	....	....	....	37,495	13,123 25
....	6,655	1,497 59	....	7,334	2,200 20	....	55,045	18,067 39
....	3,222	161 10	....	....	....	....	3,247	163 60
....	....	....	....	....	....	....	106	10 60
....	....	....	....	....	....	....	186,229	18,622 90
....	3,222	161 10	....	....	....	....	189,582	18,797 10
....	2,101	105 05	....	....	....	....	2,330	127 95
....	....	....	....	....	....	....	154,484	15,448 40
....	2,101	105 05	....	....	....	....	156,814	15,576 35
....	244	48 80	....	....	....	....	245	49 10
....	....	....	....	....	....	....	255	76 50
....	....	....	....	....	....	....	5,943	1,782 90
....	244	48 80	....	....	....	....	6,443	1,908 50

6 GEORGE V, A. 1916

No. 1.—GENERAL STATEMENT

Articles Imported.	Countries.	TOTAL IMPORTS.		ENTERED		
		Quantity.	Value.	General Tariff.		
				Quantity.	Value.	Duty.
DUTIABLE GOODS—*Con.*			$		$	$ cts.
Brass and manufactures of—*Con.*						
Pumps, hand, n.o.p	Unit'd Kingdom	....	141	....	68	20 40
	Germany	....	68	....	68	20 40
	United States	....	9,898	....	9,874	2,962 20
	Total	....	10,107	....	9,942	2,982 60
		Lb.		Lb.		
Wire, plain	Unit'd Kingdom	2,294	522	....	....	.....
	Hong Kong	8	2	8	2	0 25
	Germany	150	59	150	59	7 38
	United States	444,390	70,209	443,540	70,171	8,771 77
	Total	446,842	70,792	443,698	70,232	8,779 40
Wire cloth, or woven wire of brass, n.o.p	Unit'd Kingdom	....	18,714	....	280	70 00
	Aust.-Hungary	....	248	....	248	62 00
	Belgium	....	2,297	....	2,297	574 25
	France	....	7,132	....	....	.....
	Germany	....	16,015	....	16,015	4,003 75
	Sweden	....	428	....	428	107 00
	United States	....	72,325	....	72,325	18,081 25
	Total	....	117,159	....	91,593	22,898 25
Manufactures of, n.o.p	Unit'd Kingdom	....	151,749	....	4,187	1,256 10
	Hong Kong	....	153	....	153	45 90
	Newfoundland	....	4	....	4	1 20
	Aust.-Hungary	....	645	....	225	67 50
	Belgium	....	117	....	55	16 50
	China	....	20	....	20	6 00
	Egypt & Soudan	....	122	....	122	36 60
	France	....	12,622	....	2,305	691 50
	Germany	....	9,734	....	9,666	2,899 80
	Holland	....	10,751	....	5,539	1,661 70
	Italy	....	146	....	158	47 40
	Japan	....	5,928	....	501	150 30
	Korea	....	75	....	75	22 50
	Norway	....	61	....	61	18 30
	Sweden	....	33	....	....	.....
	Switzerland	....	1	....	....	.....
	Turkey	....	102	....	102	30 60
	United States	....	1,186,562	....	1,185,826	355,747 80
	Total	....	1,378,825	....	1,208,999	362,699 70
Breadstuffs, &c., viz.—						
Arrowroot	Unit'd Kingdom	30,417	2,441	1,015	103	10 15
	B. W. Indies	51,510	2,683	9,313	493	93 13
	B. Straits Settlements	5,250	263	....	....	.....
	Hong Kong	660	19	660	19	6 60
	Japan	310	13	310	13	3 10
	United States	3,273	230	3,273	230	32 73
	Total	91,420	5,649	14,571	858	145 71
Biscuits, not sweetened	Unit'd Kingdom	410,654	33,579	22,228	1,770	442 50
	Hong Kong	1,266	91	1,266	91	22 75
	Newfoundland	12,306	724	12,306	724	181 00
	China	60	4	60	4	1 00
	France	500	152	500	152	38 00
	Germany	1,310	108	1,310	108	27 00
	Holland	80	5	80	5	1 25
	Japan	22,503	2,134	22,503	2,134	533 50
	Turkey	294	9	294	9	2 25
	United States	794,037	56,565	795,111	56,653	14,163 25
	Total	1,243,010	93,371	855,658	61,650	15,412 50

OF IMPORTS—*Continued.*

ron HOME CONSUMPTION.

Preferential Tariff.			Treaty Rates.			Total.		
Quantity.	Value.	Duty.	Quantity.	Value.	Duty.	Quantity.	Value.	Duty Coll'd
	$	$ cts.		$	$ cts.		$	$ cts.
....	141	28 20	....	....	....	....	141	28 20
....	....	....	....	....	....	....	68	20 40
....	....	....	....	....	....	....	9,874	2,962 20
....	141	28 20	....	....	....	....	10,083	3,010 80
Lb. 2,294	522	39 16	Lb.	....	....	Lb. 2,294	522	39 16
....	....	....	....	....	....	8	2	0 25
....	....	....	....	....	....	150	59	7 38
....	....	....	....	....	....	443,540	70,171	8,771 77
2,294	522	39 16	....	....	....	445,992	70,754	8,818 56
....	18,284	3,199 75	....	150	33 75	....	18,714	3,303 50
....	....	....	....	....	....	....	248	62 00
....	....	....	....	....	....	....	2,297	574 25
....	....	....	....	7,132	1,604 73	....	7,132	1,604 73
....	....	....	....	....	....	....	16,015	4,003 75
....	....	....	....	....	....	....	428	107 00
....	....	....	....	....	....	....	72,325	18,081 25
....	18,284	3,199 75	....	7,282	1,638 48	....	117,159	27,736 48
....	150,517	30,103 40	....	830	228 25	....	155,534	31,587 75
....	....	....	....	....	....	....	153	45 90
....	....	....	....	....	....	....	4	1 20
....	....	....	....	420	115 50	....	645	183 00
....	....	....	....	62	17 05	....	117	33 55
....	....	....	....	....	....	....	20	6 00
....	....	....	....	....	....	....	122	36 60
....	....	....	....	10,237	2,815 38	....	12,542	3,506 88
....	....	....	....	....	....	....	9,666	2,899 80
....	....	....	....	5,212	1,433 30	....	10,751	3,095 00
....	....	....	....	....	....	....	158	47 40
....	....	....	....	5,432	1,493 80	....	5,933	1,644 10
....	....	....	....	....	....	....	75	22 50
....	....	....	....	33	9 08	....	61	18 30
....	....	....	....	....	....	....	33	9 08
....	....	....	....	1	0 28	....	1	0 28
....	....	....	....	....	....	....	102	30 60
....	....	....	....	....	....	....	1,185,826	355,747 80
....	150,517	30,103 40	....	22,227	6,112 64	....	1,381,743	398,915 74
29,485	2,348	147 48	....	....	....	30,500	2,451	157 63
42,197	2,190	210 98	....	....	....	51,510	2,683	304 11
5,250	263	26 25	....	....	....	5,250	263	26 25
....	....	....	....	....	....	660	19	6 60
....	....	....	....	....	....	310	13	3 10
....	....	....	....	....	....	3,273	230	32 73
76,932	4,801	384 71	....	....	....	91,503	5,659	.530 42
385,457	31,430	4,714 50	....	....	....	407,685	33,200	5,157 00
....	....	....	....	....	....	1,266	91	22 75
....	....	....	....	....	....	12,306	724	181 00
....	....	....	....	....	....	60	4	1 00
....	....	....	....	....	....	500	152	38 00
....	....	....	....	....	....	1,310	108	27 00
....	....	....	....	....	....	80	5	1 25
....	....	....	....	....	....	22,503	2,134	533 50
....	....	....	....	....	....	294	9	2 25
....	....	....	....	....	....	795,111	56,653	14,163 25
385,457	31,430	4,714 50	....	....	....	1,241,115	93,080	20,127 00

6 GEORGE V, A. 1916

No. 1.—General Statement

Articles Imported.	Countries.	Total Imports.		Entered		
				General Tariff.		
		Quantity.	Value.	Quantity.	Value.	Duty.
DUTIABLE GOODS—*Con.*		Lb.	$	Lb.	$	$ cts.
Breadstuffs, &c., viz—*Con.*						
Biscuits, sweetened	Unit'd Kingdom	1,242,087	176,842	14,765	1,852	510 12
	B. W. Indies....	348	31	348	31	9 30
	Hong Kong.....	6,551	561	6,551	561	160 93
	Newfoundland..	1,705	87	1,705	87	24 28
	China..........	367	26	367	26	7 47
	France.........	1,579	244	1,579	244	72 85
	Holland........	20,295	2,726	24,506	3,303	924 31
	Japan..........	8,364	861	8,364	861	245 15
	United States...	110,005	11,891	110,062	11,899	3,405 08
	Total.:.....	1,391,301	193,269	168,247	18,864	5,359 49
Macaroni and vermicelli........	Unit'd Kingdom	125,636	7,497	28,187	2,058	351 34
	Hong Kong.....	36,810	2,131	36,810	2,131	460 12
	China..........	7,468	444	7,468	444	93 35
	France..	1,260,251	58,732	14,500	738	181 25
	Germany......	653	59	653	59	8 16
	Italy..........	4,137,033	181,570	441,521	23,538	5,519 01
	Japan...•......	24,820	1,125	1,061	80	13 26
	Switzerland....	5,006	313	....	....	....
	United States..	1,102,713	61,139	1,092,481	60,959	13,657 52
	Total......	6,700,390	313,010	1,622,681	90,007	20,284 01
Rice, cleaned..................	Unit'd Kingdom	5,726,418	169,601	727,180	24,195	5,453 85
	B. India.......	406,756	12,809	27,412	913	205 59
	B. E. Indies, other	2,000	109	2,000	109	15 00
	Hong Kong.....	5,165,079	113,116	4,845.079	106,524	36,338 18
	Belgium........	46,300	1,524	46,300	1,524	347 25
	China..........	104,595	2,515	104,595	2,515	784 49
	Dutch E. Indies	20,160	645	20,160	645	151 20
	Germany.......	98,800	2,845	98,800	•2,845	741 00
	Holland........	627,276	20,415	632,838	20,670	4,746 28
	Italy.....•....	95,761	3,357	106,761	3,764	800 71
	Japan..........	24,145	1,255	33,105	1,619	248 29
	Siam...•......	19,700	489	19,700	489	147 75
	United States...	952,180	41,275	962,504	41,986	7,218 78
	Total......	13,289,170	369,955	7,626,434	207,798	57,198 37
Rice and sago flour, cassava flour and rice meal.	Unit'd Kingdom	144,012	4,794	1,442	107	14 42
	B. W. Indies....	244	5	....	....	....
	B. Straits Settlements......	424,374	9,532	....	....	....
	Hong Kong.....	39,191	1,547	39,191	1,547	391 91
	China..........	11,936	372	11,936	372	119 36
	Holland........	3,640	84	3,640	84	36 40
	Italy..........	4,134	188	4,134	185	41 34
	Japan..........	13,562	667	13,562	667	135 62
	United States...	204,100	13,699	160,292	8,082	1,602 92
	Total......	845,193	30,888	234,197	11,047	2,341 97
Rice bran....................	United States...	120	5	120	5	0 88
Sago and tapioca..............	Unit'd Kingdom	50,200	1,817	2,549	101	27 78
	B. E. Indies, other	66,649	1,410	....	....	....
	B. Straits Settlements......	2,826,735	63,653	125,535	2,821	775 77
	Hong Kong.....	680	63	680	63	17 33
	China..........	196	14	196	14	3 85
	France.........	255	9	255	9	2 48
	United States...	38,541	2,227	59,416	2,601	715 32
	Total......	2,983,256	69,193	188,631	5,609	1,542 53

OF IMPORTS—*Continued.*

FOR HOME CONSUMPTION.

Preferential Tariff.			Treaty Rates.			Total.		
Quantity.	Value.	Duty.	Quantity.	Value.	Duty.	Quantity.	Value.	Duty Coll'd
Lb.	$	$ cts.	Lb.	$	$ cts.	Lb.	$	$ cts.
1,237,452	175,991	32,416 82	....	....	....	1,252,217	177,843	32,926 94
....	....	....	....	....	....	348	31	9 30
....	....	....	....	....	....	6,551	561	160 93
....	....	....	....	....	....	1,705	87	24 28
....	....	....	....	....	....	367	26	7 47
....	....	....	....	....	....	1,579	244	72 85
....	....	....	....	....	....	24,506	3,303	924 31
....	....	....	....	....	....	8,364	861	245 15
....	....	....	....	....	....	110,062	11,899	3,405 08
1,237,452	175,991	32,416 82	....	....	....	1,405,699	194,855	37,776 31
218	20	1 64	94,431	5,203	944 31	122,836	7,281	1,297 29
....	....	....	....	....	....	36,810	2,131	460 12
....	....	....	1,262,879	61,096	12,628 79	7,468	444	93 35
....	....	....	....	....	....	1,277,379	61,834	12,810 04
....	....	....	....	....	....	653	59	8 16
....	....	....	3,692,707	149,460	36,927 07	4,134,228	172,998	42,446 08
....	....	....	23,759	1,045	237 59	24,820	1,125	250 85
....	....	....	5,006	313	50 06	5,006	313	50 06
....	....	....	....	....	....	1,092,481	60,959	13,657 52
218	20	1 64	5,078,782	217,117	50,787 82	6,701,681	307,144	71,073 47
5,140,482	147,897	25,702 41	....	....	....	5,867,662	172,092	31,156 26
316,938	9,704	1,584 70	....	....	....	344,350	10,617	1,790 29
....	....	....	....	....	....	2,000	109	.15 00
....	....	....	....	....	....	4,845,079	106,524	36,338 18
....	....	....	....	....	....	46,300	1,524	347 25
....	....	....	....	....	....	104,595	2,515	784 49
....	....	....	....	....	....	20,160	645	151 20
....	....	....	....	....	....	98,800	2,845	741 00
....	....	....	....	....	....	632,838	20,670	4,746 28
....	....	....	....	....	....	106,761	3,764	800 71
....	....	....	....	....	....	33,105	1,619	248 29
....	....	....	....	....	....	19,700	489	147 75
....	....	....	....	....	....	962,504	41,986	7,218 78
5,457,420	157,601	27,287 11	....	....	....	13,083,854	365,399	84,485 48
142,714	4,695	1,070 35	....	....	....	144,156	4,802	1,084 77
244	5	1 83	....	....	....	244	5	1 83
391,472	8,732	2,936 06	....	....	....	391,472	8,732	2,936 06
....	....	....	....	....	....	39,191	1,547	391 91
....	....	....	....	....	....	11,936	372	119 36
....	....	....	....	....	....	3,640	84	36 40
....	....	....	....	....	....	4,134	188	41 34
....	....	....	....	....	....	13,562	667	135 62
....	....	....	....	....	....	160,292	8,082	1,602 92
534,430	13,432	4,008 24	....	....	....	768,627	24,479	6,350 21
....	....	....	....	....	....	120	5	0 88
58,911	2,097	366 95	....	....	....	61,460	2,198	394 73
66,649	1,410	246 75	....	....	....	66,649	1,410	246 75
2,781,601	62,918	11,010 82	....	....	....	2,907,136	65,739	11,786 59
....	....	....	....	....	....	680	63	17 33
....	....	....	....	....	....	196	14	3 85
....	....	....	....	....	....	255	9	2 48
....	....	....	....	....	....	59,416	2,601	715 32
2,907,161	66,425	11,624 52	....	....	....	3,095,792	72,034	13,167 05

6 GEORGE V, A. 1916

No. 1.—General Statement

Articles Imported.	Countries.	Total Imports.		Entered		
				General Tariff.		
		Quantity.	Value.	Quantity.	Value.	Duty.
DUTIABLE GOODS—*Con.*		Lb.	$	Lb.	$	$ cts.
Breadstuffs, &c., viz.—*Con.*						
Tapioca flour..............	Unit'd Kingdom	450	20	....	....	
	Hong Kong....	2,440	86	2,440	86	24 40
	China..........	240	16	240	16	2 40
	France..........	396	35	396	35	3 96
	Holland........	53,847	1,292	53,847	1,292	538 47
	United States...	536,880	17,110	536,880	17,110	5,368 80
	Total......	594,253	18,559	593,803	18,539	5,938 03
Grain and products of, viz.—		Bush.		Bush.		
Barley, n.o.p..............	Unit'd Kingdom	10	22	....	....	
	Japan...........	1	1	1	1	0 15
	Sweden.........	401	773	401	773	60 15
	United States...	1,076,228	537,170	43,875	26,745	6,581 25
	Total......	1,076,640	537,966	44,277	27,519	6,641 55
		Lb.		Lb.		
Barley, pot, pearl, rolled,	Unit'd Kingdom	574,599	31,652	46,310	1,364	409 20
roasted or ground.	Hong Kong.....	346	17	346	17	5 10
	Belgium.........	12,300	325	12,300	325	97 50
	Holland........	17,125	526	17,125	526	157 80
	Japan...........	365	16	365	16	4 80
	United States...	42,707	997	42,611	991	297 30
	Total......	647,442	33,533	119,057	3,239	971 70
		Bush.		Bush.		
Beans, n.o.p..............	Unit'd Kingdom	27,711	49,964	26,787	48,780	6,696 75
	Hong Kong.....	3,469	4,592	3,553	4,769	888 25
	New Zealand...	30	112	30	112	7 50
	Aust.-Hungary..	23,609	36,274	23,589	36,118	5,897 25
	Belgium........	7,186	12,280	7,236	12,352	1,809 00
	Bulgaria........	1,078	1,725	1,078	1,725	269 50
	China..........	389	357	389	357	97 25
	France..........	212	613	226	660	56 50
	French Africa...	5,838	9,337	6,008	9,619	1,502 00
	Germany.......	2,562	5,774	2,599	5,878	649 75
	Holland........	546	1,345	604	1,456	151 00
	Italy...........	64,920	119,340	59,541	109,807	14,885 25
	Japan..........			20	65	5 00
	Madagascar....	....	....	443	1,238	110 75
	Peru...........	457	1,278	2,317	3,521	579 25
	Roumania.:....	2,135	3,360	29,581	76,722	7,395 25
	United States...	29,522	76,873			
	Total......	175,314	332,991	169,651	322,946	42,412 75
Buckwheat.................	Japan..........	543	378	543	378	81 45
	United States...	2,236	1,988	2,236	1,988	335 40
	Total......	2,779	2,366	2,779	2,366	416 85
Indian corn for purposes of dis-	Unit'd Kingdom	1,000	600	1,000	600	75 00
tillation.	Argentina.......	1,000	775	1,000	775	75 00
	United States...	901,401	688,980	901,401	688,980	67,605 04
	Total......	903,401	690,355	903,401	690,355	67,755 04
Oats......................	Unit'd Kingdom	2,282	2,167	3	5	0 30
	New Zealand...	2	5	2	5	0 20
	Japan..........	9	5	9	5	0 90
	Sweden.........	1,974	3,021	1,974	3,021	197 40
	United States...	3,113,852	1,378,255	1,407,133	696,167	140,713 30
	Total......	3,118,119	1,383,453	1,409,121	699,203	140,912 10

OF IMPORTS—*Continued.*

FOR HOME CONSUMPTION.

Preferential Tariff.			Treaty Rates.			Total.		
Quantity.	Value.	Duty.	Quantity.	Value.	Duty.	Quantity.	Value.	Duty Coll'd
Lb.	$	$ cts.	Lb.	$	$ cts.	Lb.	$	$ cts.
450	20	3 38	....	....	....	450	20	3 38
....	....	....	....	....	....	2,440	86	24 40
....	....	....	....	....	....	240	16	2 40
....	....	....	....	....	....	396	35	3 96
....	....	....	....	....	....	53,847	1,292	538 47
....	....	....	....	....	....	536,880	17,110	5,368 80
450	20	3 38	....	....	....	594,253	18,559	5,941 41
Bush.			Bush.			Bush.		
10	22	1 00				10	22	1 00
....	....	....	....	....	....	1	1	0 15
....	....	....	....	....	....	401	773	60 15
....	....	....	....	....	....	43,875	26,745	6,581 25
10	22	1 00	....	....	....	44,287	27,541	6,642 55
Lb.			Lb.			Lb.		
536,503	30,489	6,097 80	....	....	....	582,813	31,853	6,507 00
....	....	....	....	....	....	346	17	5 10
....	....	....	....	....	....	12,300	325	97 50
....	....	....	....	....	....	17,125	526	157 80
....	....	....	....	....	....	365	16	4 80
....	....	....	....	....	....	42,611	991	297 30
536,503	30,480	6,097 80	....	....	....	655,560	33,728	7,069 50
Bush.			Bush.			Bush.		
622	1,045	93 30	....	....	....	27,409	49,825	6,790 05
....	....	....	....	....	....	3,553	4,769	888 25
....	....	....	....	....	....	30	112	7 50
....	....	....	....	....	....	23,589	36,118	5,897 25
....	....	....	....	....	....	7,236	12,352	1,809 00
....	....	....	....	....	....	1,078	1,725	269 50
....	....	....	....	....	....	389	357	97 25
....	....	....	....	....	....	5,650	9,767	1,412 50
....	....	....	....	....	....	226	660	56 50
....	....	....	....	....	....	6,008	9,619	1,502 00
....	....	....	....	....	....	2,599	5,878	649 75
....	....	....	....	....	....	604	1,456	151 00
....	....	....	....	....	....	59,541	109,807	14,885 25
....	....	....	....	....	....	20	65	5 00
....	....	....	....	....	....	443	1,238	110 75
....	....	....	....	....	....	2,317	3,521	579 25
....	....	....	....	....	....	29,581	76,722	7,395 25
622	1,045	93 30	....	....	....	170,273	323,991	42,506 05
....	....	....	....	....	....	543	378	81 45
....	....	....	....	....	....	2,236	1,988	335 40
....	....	....	....	....	....	2,779	2,366	416 85
....	....	....	....	....	....	1,000	600	75 00
....	....	....	....	....	....	1,000	775	75 00
....	....	....	....	....	....	901,401	688,980	67,605 04
....	....	....	....	....	....	903,401	690,355	67,755 04
2,279	2,162	159 53	....	....	....	2,282	2,167	159 83
....	....	....	....	....	....	2	5	0 20
....	....	....	....	....	....	9	5	0 90
....	....	....	....	....	....	1,974	3,021	197 40
....	....	....	....	....	....	1,407,133	696,167	140,713 30
2,279	2,162	159 53	....	....	....	1,411,400	701,365	141,071 63

11—ii—2½

6 GEORGE V, A. 1916

No. 1.—General Statement

Articles Imported.	Countries.	Total Imports.		Entered		
				General Tariff.		
		Quantity.	Value.	Quantity.	Value.	Duty.
DUTIABLE GOODS—*Con.*						
Breadstuffs, &c., viz—*Con.*						
Grain and products of—*Con.*		Bush.	$	Bush.	$	$ cts.
Pease, n.o.p.	Unit'd Kingdom	4,239	8,249	1,419	2,311	212 85
	Hong Kong	328	441	328	441	49 20
	Newfoundland	8	22	8	22	1 20
	New Zealand	1,672	3,620	167	521	25 05
	Belgium	1,007	1,760	1,035	1,796	155 25
	China	39	62	48	78	7 20
	France	367	801	374	813	56 10
	Germany	23,624	37,138	23,670	37,214	3,550 50
	Holland	818	1,367	888	1,514	133 20
	Japan	6,889	8,972	6,735	8,794	1,010 25
	Russia	455	740	455	740	68 25
	Sweden	110	281	110	281	16 50
	Turkey	241	224	241	224	36 15
	United States	28,734	80,418	28,765	80,419	4,314 75
	Total	68,531	144,095	64,243	135,168	9,636 45
Rye	Sweden	4	8	4	8	0 40
	United States	439,157	282,107	52,667	50,038	5,266 70
	Total	439,161	282,115	52,671	50,046	5,267 10
Wheat	United States	35,982,280	35,909,675	1,870,174	1,803,338	224,420 88
Bran, mill feed, etc	Unit'd Kingdom		5,565			
	Japan		3,367		3,367	589 10
	United States		47,777		47,778	8,361 64
	Total		56,709		51,145	8,950 74
		Cwt.		Cwt.		
Buckwheat meal or flour	Unit'd Kingdom	8	36			1 50
	China	3	16	3	16	1 50
	Japan	11	36	11	36	5 50
	United States	1,857	7,074	1,854	7,052	927 00
	Total	1,879	7,162	1,868	7,104	934 00
		Brl.		Brl.		
Indian or corn meal	United States	61,371	217,126	61,367	217,108	15,341 75
		Lb.		Lb.		
Oat meal and rolled oats	Unit'd Kingdom	25,201	1,465	100	5	6 00
	United States	10,551	494	9,351	454	50 71
	Total	35,752	1,959	9,451	459	56 71
		Brl.		Brl.		
Rye flour	United States	11,549	43,900	11,549	43,900	5,774 50
Wheat flour	Unit'd Kingdom	38	211	11	66	6 60
	Australia	19	64	19	64	11 40
	Hong Kong	4	34	4	34	2 40
	Newfoundland	79	465	79	465	47 40
	China	3	4	3	4	1 80
	Norway	4	24	4	24	2 40
	United States	55,001	257,538	54,558	255,731	32,734 80
	Total	55,148	258,340	54,678	256,388	32,806 80
Hominy, cracked, evaporated or dried corn	Unit'd Kingdom		10			
	United States		26,946		26,946	4,715 68
	Total		26,956		26,946	4,715 68

OF IMPORTS—*Continued*.

FOR HOME CONSUMPTION.

Preferential Tariff.				Treaty Rates.			Total.		
Quantity.	Value.	Duty.	Quantity.	Value.	Duty.		Quantity.	Value.	Duty Coll'd
Bush.	$	$ cts.	Bush.	$	$ cts.		Bush.	$	$ cts.
2,711	5,827	271 10	....	....	....		4,130	8,138	483 95
....	....	....	....	....	....		328	441	49 20
....	....	....	....	....	....		8	22	1 20
1,505	3,099	150 50	....	....	....		1,672	3,620	175 55
....	....	....	....	....	....		1,035	1,796	155 25
....	....	....	....	....	....		48	78	7 20
....	....	....	....	....	....		374	813	56 10
....	....	....	....	....	....		23,670	37,214	3,550 50
....	....	....	....	....	....		888	1,514	133 20
....	....	....	....	....	....		6,735	8,794	1,010 25
....	....	....	....	....	....		455	740	68 25
....	....	....	....	....	....		110	281	16 50
....	....	....	....	....	....		241	224	36 15
....	....	....	....	....	....		28,765	80,419	4,314 75
4,216	8,926	421 60	....	....	....		68,459	144,094	10,058 05
....	....	....	....	....	....		4	8	0 40
....	....	....	....	....	....		52,667	50,038	5,266 70
....	....	....	....	....	....		52,671	50,046	5,267 10
....	....	....	....	....	....		1,870,174	1,803,338	224,420 88
....	5,565	834 75	....	....	....		....	5,565	834 75
....	....	....	....	....	....		....	3,367	589 10
....	....	....	....	....	....		....	47,778	8,361 64
....	5,565	834 75	....	....	....		....	56,710	9,785 49
Cwt.			Cwt.				Cwt.		
8	36	2 80	....	....	....		8	36	2 80
....	....	....	....	....	....		3	16	1 50
....	....	....	....	....	....		11	36	5 50
....	....	....	....	....	....		1,854	7,052	927 00
8	36	2 80	....	....	....		1,876	7,140	936 80
Brl.			Brl.				Brl.		
....	....	....	....	....	....		61,367	217,108	15,341 75
Lb.			Lb.				Lb.		
25,101	1,460	100 37	....	....	....		25,201	1,465	106 37
....	....	....	....	....	....		9,351	454	50 71
25,101	1,460	100 37	....	....	....		34,552	1,919	157 08
Brl.			Brl.				Brl.		
....	....	....	....	....	....		11,549	43,900	5,774 50
27	145	10 80	....	....	....		38	211	17 40
....	....	....	....	....	....		19	64	11 40
....	....	....	....	....	....		4	34	2 40
....	....	....	....	....	....		79	465	47 40
....	....	....	....	....	....		3	4	1 80
....	....	....	....	....	....		4	24	2 40
....	....	....	....	....	....		54,558	255,731	32,734 80
27	145	10 80	....	....	....		54,705	256,533	32,817 60
....	10	1 50	....	....	....		....	10	1 50
....	....	....	....	....	....		....	26,946	4,715 68
....	10	1 50	....	....	....		....	26,956	4,717 18

6 GEORGE V, A. 1916

No. 1.—General Statement

Articles Imported.	Countries.	Total Imports.		Entered		
				General Tariff.		
		Quantity.	Value.	Quantity.	Value.	Duty.
DUTIABLE GOODS—*Con.*			$		$	$ cts.
Breadstuffs, &c., viz.—*Con.*						
Grain and products of—*Con.*						
Cattle food containing molasses.	Unit'd Kingdom	....	41,474	....	70	14 00
	B. Guiana......	....	193	....	....	....
	United States...	....	2,416	....	2,416	433 20
	Total......	....	44,083	....	2,486	497 20
Cereal foods prepared, n. o. p.	Unit'd Kingdom	....	7,344	....	799	159 80
	Hong Kong....	....	1,594	....	1,594	318 80
	Newfoundland..	....	3	....	3	0 60
	China..........	....	69	....	69	13 80
	France..........	....	102	....	147	29 40
	Japan..........	....	147	....	147	29 40
	Sweden........	....	51	....	51	10 20
	Turkey.........	....	243	....	243	48 60
	United States...	....	52,293	....	52,311	10,462 20
	Total......	....	61,846	....	55,364	11,072 80
		Lb.		Lb.		
Cereal foods prepared, in packages not exceeding 25 lb weight each.	Unit'd Kingdom	115,057	8,913	155	12	3 00
	B. W. Indies....	207	10	....	....	....
	B. Straits Settlements......	7,000	494	....	....	....
	Hong Kong....	1,500	115	1,500	115	29 71
	China..........	100	5	100	5	1 30
	France..........	224	29	224	29	7 25
	Germany.......	1,536	48	1,536	48	12 00
	Japan..........	5,961	352	5,961	352	94 92
	Sweden........	15	2	15	2	0 55
	United States...	4,288,912	188,622	3,301,090	189,427	49,950 06
	Total......	4,420,512	198,590	3,310,581	189,990	50,098 79
All other breadstuffs, n. o. p....	Unit'd Kingdom	....	11,379	....	693	121 28
	Hong Kong....	....	2,507	....	2,507	438 65
	Newfoundland..	....	71	....	71	12 43
	China..........	....	586	....	589	103 08
	France..........	....	588	....	872	152 60
	Germany.......	....	1,188	....	1,188	207 90
	Greece..........	....	250	....	....	....
	Holland........	....	....	....	66	11 55
	Italy...........	....	63	....	63	11 03
	Japan..........	....	873	....	873	152 78
	United States...	....	110,464	....	110,412	19,322 57
	Total......	....	127,969	....	117,334	20,533 87
Grain, flour and meal, etc., of all kinds when damaged by water in transit or prior to importation into Canada.	United States...	....	1,360	....	1,360	340 00
Bricks and tiles. *See* Earthenware						
Bath brick.....................	Unit'd Kingdom	....	1,548	....	....	....
	United States...	....	65	....	65	17 88
	Total......	....	1,613	....	65	17 88
Building blocks, partition hollow and fire proof building tile......	Unit'd Kingdom	....	18,426	....	....	....
	United States...	....	244,845	....	244,845	55,090 42
	Total......	....	263,271	....	244,845	55,090 42

OF IMPORTS—*Continued.*

FOR HOME CONSUMPTION.

Preferential Tariff.			Treaty Rates.			Total.		
Quantity.	Value.	Duty.	Quantity.	Value.	Duty.	Quantity.	Value.	Duty Coll'd
	$	$ cts.		$	$ cts.		$	$ cts.
....	41,418	6,212 70	....	....	....	....	41,488	6,226 70
....	193	28 95	....	....	....	....	193	28 95
....	....	....	....	....	....	....	2,416	483 20
....	41,611	6,241 65	....	....	....	....	44,097	6,738 85
....	6,396	959 40	....	....	....	....	7,195	1,119 20
....	....	....	....	....	....	....	1,594	318 80
....	....	....	....	....	....	....	3	0 60
....	....	....	....	....	....	....	69	13 80
....	....	....	....	....	....	....	147	29 40
....	....	....	....	....	....	....	147	29 40
....	....	....	....	....	....	....	51	10 20
....	....	....	....	....	....	....	243	48 60
....	....	....	....	....	....	....	52,311	10,462 20
....	6,396	959 40	....	....	....	....	61,760	12,032 20
Lb. 114,473	8,833	1,655 49	Lb.	....	....	Lb. 114,628	8,845	1,655 49
207	10	1 75	....	....	....	207	10	1 75
7,000	494	86 45	....	....	....	7,000	494	86 45
....	....	....	....	....	....	1,500	115	29 71
....	....	....	....	....	....	100	5	1 30
....	....	....	....	....	....	224	29	7 25
....	....	....	....	....	....	1,536	48	12 00
....	....	....	....	....	....	5,961	352	94 92
....	....	....	....	....	....	15	2	0 55
....	....	....	....	....	....	3,301,090	189,427	49,950 06
121,680	9,337	1,743 69	....	....	....	3,432,261	199,327	51,842 48
....	11,125	1,668 75	....	....	....	....	11,818	1,790 03
....	....	....	....	....	....	....	2,507	438 65
....	....	....	....	....	....	....	71	12 43
....	....	....	....	....	....	....	589	103 08
....	....	....	....	....	....	....	872	152 60
....	....	....	....	....	....	....	1,188	207 90
....	....	....	....	....	....	....	66	11 55
....	....	....	....	....	....	....	63	11 03
....	....	....	....	....	....	....	873	152 78
....	....	....	....	....	....	....	110,412	19,322 57
....	11,125	1,668 75	....	....	....	....	128,459	22,202 62
....	....	....	....	....	....	....	1,360	340 00
....	1,571	235 65	....	....	....	....	1,571	235 65
....	....	....	....	....	....	....	65	17 88
....	1,571	235 65	....	....	....	....	1,636	253 53
....	18,426	2,303 22	....	....	....	....	18,426	2,303 22
....	....	....	....	....	....	....	244,845	55,090 42
....	18,426	2,303 22	....	....	....	....	263,271	57,393 64

6 GEORGE V, A. 1916

No. 1.—General Statement

Articles Imported.	Countries.	Total Imports.		Entered		
				General Tariff.		
		Quantity.	Value.	Quantity.	Value.	Duty.
DUTIABLE GOODS—*Con.*		M.	$	M.	$	$ cts.
Bricks and tiles—*Con.*						
Building brick..............	Unit'd Kingdom	1,793	20,434	7	183	41 18
	United States...	24,536	287,224	24,536	287,224	64,625 86
	Total......	26,329	307,658	24,543	287,407	64,667 04
Fire brick, n.o.p............	Unit'd Kingdom	....	27,629	....	465	104 60
	Germany......	....	1,647	....	1,647	370 57
	United States...	....	120,244	....	120,246	27,055 87
	Total......	....	149,520	....	122,358	27,531 04
Paving brick...............	Unit'd Kingdom	2,658	40,966	....	23,779	23,778 42
	United States...	6,514	105,681	6,514	105,681	23,778 42
	Total......	9,172	146,647	6,514	105,681	23,778 42
Drain tiles, not glazed........	Unit'd Kingdom	....	964	....	300	60 00
	United States...	....	1,868	....	1,868	373 60
	Total......	....	2,832	....	2,168	433 60
Drain pipes, sewer pipes and	Unit'd Kingdom	....	31,135	....	....	....
earthenware fittings therefor,	France.........	....	121	....	121	42 35
chimney linings or vents,	United States..	....	270,177	....	268,109	93,838 15
chimney tops and inverted						
blocks, glazed or unglazed.	Total......	....	301,433	....	268,230	93,880 50
Manufactures of clay, n.o.p.....	Unit'd Kingdom	....	11,624	....	32	7 20
	France.........	....	122	....	122	27 45
	Germany......	....	170	....	170	38 25
	Japan.........	....	18	....	18	4 05
	United States..	....	154,063	....	154,058	34,663 76
	Total......	....	165,997	....	154,400	34,740 71
British gum, dry sizing cream and	Unit'd Kingdom	Lb. · 306,854	7,898	Lb.	....	....
enamel sizing.	Germany......	3,250	100	3,250	100	10 00
	United States..	878,657	28,176	878,657	28,176	2,817 60
	Total......	1,188,761	36,174	881,907	28,276	2,827 60
Brooms and whisks.............	Unit'd Kingdom	....	1,281	....	172	34 40
	Hong Kong.....	....	124	....	124	24 80
	China.........	....	4	....	4	0 80
	Germany......	....	3	....	3	0 60
	Japan.........	....	1,137	....	1,137	227 40
	United States..	....	12,617	....	12,513	2,502 60
	Total......	....	15,166	....	13,953	2,790 60
Brushes of all kinds.............	Unit'd Kingdom	....	75,753	....	2,895	796 12
	Hong Kong.....	....	761	....	752	206 80
	Aust.-Hungary..	....	502	....	287	78 92
	Belgium.......	....	380	....	94	25 85
	China.........	....	147	....	147	40 43
	France.........	....	52,719	....	6,142	1,689 05
	Germany......	....	15,967	....	16,063	4,417 32
	Japan.........	....	81,373	....	2,869	788,97
	Miquelon and St. Pierre.....	....	3	....	3	0 83
	Sweden........	....	10	....	....	....
	Switzerland....	....	199	....	192	52 80
	United States..	....	163,963	....	163,962	45,091 51
	Total......	....	391,777	....	193,406	53,188 60

OF IMPORTS—*Continued.*

FOR HOME CONSUMPTION.

Preferential Tariff.			Treaty Rates.			Total.		
Quantity.	Value.	Duty.	Quantity.	Value.	Duty.	Quantity.	Value.	Duty Coll'd
M. 1,786	$ 20|251	$ cts. 2,531 40	M.	$	$ cts.	M. 1,793	$ 20,434	$ cts. 2,572 58
						24,536	287,224	64,625 86
1,786	20,251	2,531 40				26,329	307,658	67,198 44
	27,164	3,395 67					27,629	3,500 27
							1,647	370 57
							120,246	27,055 87
	27,164	3,395 67					149,522	30,926 71
2,658	40,966	5,120 75				2,658	40,966	5,120 75
						6,514	105,681	23,778 42
2,658	40,966	5,120 75				9,172	146,647	28,899 17
	664	99 60					964	159 60
							1,868	373 60
	664	99 60					2,832	533 20
	30,755	7,688 75					30,755	7,688 75
							121	42 35
							268,109	93,838 15
	30,755	7,688 75					298,985	101,569 25
	11,595	1,449 67					11,627	1,456 87
							122	27 45
							170	38 25
							18	4 05
							154,058	34,663 76
	11,595	1,449 67					165,995	36,190 38
Lb. 306,854	7,898	394 90	Lb.			Lb. 306,854	7,898	394 90
						3,250	100	10 00
						878,657	28,176	2,817 60
306,854	7,898	394 90				1,188,761	36,174	3,222 50
	1,109	166 35					1,281	200 75
							124	24 80
							4	0 80
							3	0 60
							1,137	227 40
							12,513	2,502 60
	1,109	166 35					15,062	2,956 95
	67,914	11,885 69		4,717	1,179 25		75,526	13,861 06
				9	2 25		761	209 05
				215	53 75		502	132 67
				286	71 50		380	97 35
							147	40 43
				47,398	11,849 50		53,540	13,538 55
							16,063	4,417 32
				80,909	20,227 25		83,778	21,016 22
							3	0 83
				10	2 50		10	2 50
				7	1 75		199	54 55
							163,962	45,091 51
	67,914	11,885 69		133,551	33,387 75		394,871	98,462 04

6 GEORGE V, A. 1916

No. 1.—General Statement

Articles Imported.	Countries.	Total Imports.		Entered		
		Quantity.	Value.	General Tariff.		
				Quantity.	Value.	Duty.
DUTIABLE GOODS—*Con.*			$		$	$ cts.
Buttons, shoe, n.o.p.	Unit'd Kingdom	....	81	....	74	18 50
	United States..	....	1,311	....	1,311	327 75
	Total.......	....	1,392	....	1,385	346 25
		Gross.		Gross.		
Buttons, of vegetable ivory	Unit'd Kingdom	11,971	4,187	450	478	165 90
	Aust.-Hungary..	2,546	1,374	2,546	1,374	539 50
	Germany.......	312	216	312	216	80 40
	Italy..;.......	6,487	2,367	6,487	2,367	1,034 45
	Japan...........	222	71	222	71	32 40
	United States..	6,180	7,300	6,180	7,300	2,499 00
	Total.......	27,718	15,515	16,197	11,806	4,351 65
Buttons, all kinds, covered or not, n.o.p., including recognition buttons, and collar and cuff buttons.	Unit'd Kingdom	....	82,175	....	17,452	6,108 20
	Hong Kong.....	....	4	....	4	1 40
	Aust.-Hungary..	....	17,465	....	1,499	524 65
	Belgium.......	....	4,852	....	1,213	424 55
	France.........	....	9,965	....	4,297	1,503 95
	Germany.......	....	18,972	....	19,797	6,928 95
	Italy..........	....	3,540	....	3,204	1,121 40
	Japan..........	....	50,807	....	2,113	739 55
	United States..	....	329,534	....	329,595	115,358 25
	Total.......	....	517,314	....	379,174	132,710 90
Button blanks of animal shell, in the rough.	Japan..........	....	5	....	5	0 50
	United States..	....	8,783	....	8,783	878 30
	Total.......	....	8,788	....	8,788	878 80
		Lb..		Lb.		
Candles, paraffine wax	Unit'd Kingdom	107,862	9,477	652	80	20 00
	Belgium........	650	49	650	49	12 25
	France.........	484	83	484	83	20 75
	Germany.......	879	102	879	102	25 50
	Japan..........	10	1	10	1	0 25
	United States..	266,077	34,814	266,241	34,823	8,705 75
	Total.......	375,962	44,526	268,916	35,138	8,784 50
Candles, all other, n.o.p	United Kingdom	49,190	5,547	4,317	375	93 75
	Hong Kong.....	297	16	297	16	4 00
	France..........	2,848	447	2,848	447	111 75
	Germany.......	3,725	401	3,725	401	100 25
	Holland........	200	19	200	19	4 75
	Japan..........	97	8	97	8	2 00
	United States..	358,134	45,562	357,754	45,533	11,383 25
	Total.......	414,491	52,000	369,238	46,799	11,699 75
Cane, reed or rattan, not further manufactured than split, n.o.p.	Unit'd Kingdom	....	252	....	231	23 10
	Hong Kong.....	....	3,458	....	3,458	345 80
	Japan..........	....	2	....	2	0 20
	United States..	....	5,132	....	5,132	513 20
	Total.......	....	8,844	....	8,823	882 30

of Imports—*Continued.*

for Home Consumption.

Preferential Tariff.			Treaty Rates.			Total.		
Quantity.	Value.	Duty.	Quantity.	Value.	Duty.	Quantity.	Value.	Duty Coll'd
	$	$ cts.		$	$ cts.		$	$ cts.
....	7	1 23	....	....	....	....	81	19 73
....	....	....	....	....	....	....	1,311	327 75
....	7	1 23	....	....	....	....	1,392	347 48
Gross.			Gross.			Gross.		
11,521	3,709	1,317 85	....	....	....	11,971	4,187	1,483 75
....	....	....	....	....	....	2,546	1,374	539 50
....	....	....	....	....	....	312	216	80 40
....	....	....	....	....	....	6,487	2,367	1,034 45
....	....	....	....	....	....	222	71	32 40
....	....	....	....	....	....	6,180	7,300	2,499 00
11,521	3,709	1,317 85	....	....	....	27,718	15,515	5,669 50
....	41,620	9,365 25	....	24,566	7,369 80	....	83,638	22,843 25
....	....	....	....	....	....	....	4	1 40
....	....	....	....	16,293	4,887 90	....	17,792	5,412 55
....	....	....	....	3,639	1,091 70	....	4,852	1,516 25
....	....	....	....	5,992	1,797 60	....	10,289	3,301 55
....	....	....	....	....	....	....	19,797	6,928 95
....	....	....	....	336	100 80	....	3,540	1,222 20
....	....	....	....	48,160	14,448 00	....	50,273	15,187 55
....	....	....	....	....	....	....	329,595	115,358 25
....	41,620	9,365 25	....	98,986	29,695 80	....	519,780	171,771 95
....	....	....	....	....	....	....	5	0 50
....	....	....	....	....	....	....	8,783	878 30
....	....	....	....	....	....	....	8,788	878 80
Lb.			Lb.			Lb.		
99,798	8,799	1,319 85	....	....	....	100,450	8,879	1,339 85
....	....	....	....	....	....	650	49	12 25
....	....	....	....	....	....	484	83	20 75
....	....	....	....	....	....	879	102	25 50
....	....	....	....	....	....	10	1	0 25
....	....	....	....	....	....	266,241	34,823	8,705 75
99,798	8,799	1,319 85	....	....	....	368,714	43,937	10,104 35
47,083	5,427	814 05	....	....	....	51,400	5,802	907 80
....	....	....	....	....	....	297	16	4 00
....	....	....	....	....	....	2,848	447	111 75
....	....	....	....	....	....	3,725	401	100 25
....	....	....	....	....	....	200	19	4 75
....	....	....	....	....	....	97	8	2 00
....	....	....	....	....	....	357,754	45,533	11,383 25
47,083	5,427	814 05	....	....	....	416,321	52,226	12,513 80
....	21	1 57	....	....	....	....	252	24 67
....	....	....	....	....	....	....	3,458	345 80
....	....	....	....	....	....	....	2	0 20
....	....	....	....	....	....	....	5,132	513 20
....	21	1 57	....	....	....	....	8,844	883 87

6 GEORGE V, A. 1916

No. 1.—General Statement

Articles Imported.	Countries.	Total Imports.		Entered		
		Quantity.	Value.	General Tariff.		
				Quantity.	Value.	Duty.
DUTIABLE GOODS—*Con.*		No.	$	No.	$	$ cts.
Carriages and vehicles— Automobiles and motor vehicles of all kinds.	Unit'd Kingdom	299	247,849	19	31,708	11,097 80
	Belgium........	1	900	1	900	315 00
	France.........	14	32,423	1	2,000	700 00
	United States..	5,143	4,532,138	5,158	4,591,182	1,606,913 70
	Total......	5,457	4,813,310	5,179	4,625,790	1,619,026 50
Automobiles and motor vehicles, parts of, n.o.p.	Unit'd Kingdom	....	22,442	....	2,580	872 80
	France.........	....	132	....	820	283 55
	Germany.......	....	92	....	92	32 20
	United States,.	....	2,139,552	....	2,142,895	636,331 39
	Total......	....	2,162,218	....	2,146,387	637,519 94
Buggies, carriages, pleasure carts and vehicles, n.o.p.....	Unit'd Kingdom	8	281	....	....	....
	United States...	865	43,769	861	43,895	15,363 25
	Total......	873	44,050	861	43,895	15,363 25
Cutters.....................	United States...	36	708	36	708	247 80
Farm wagons..................	United States...	2,061	66,069	2,061	66,069	16,517 25
Freight wagons and drays......	Unit'd Kingdom	1	130	....	....	....
	United States...	974	80,976	964	79,891	19,972 75
	Total......	975	81,106	946	79,891	19,972 75
Complete parts of farm and freight wagons, drays and sleighs.	Unit'd Kingdom	....	375	....	137	34 25
	United States...	....	40,229	....	40,240	10,060 00
	Total......	....	40,604	....	40,377	10,094 25
Complete parts of buggies, carriages and vehicles, n.o.p., including parts of cutters, children's carriages, and sleds, n.o.p.	Unit'd Kingdom	....	243	....	....	....
	United States...	....	22,924	....	23,009	8,053 15
	Total......	....	23,167	....	23,009	8,053 15
Cars, railway, passenger........	United States...	34	257,149	34	257,149	77,144 70
Cars, railway, box and flat.....	United States...	120	58,697	120	58,697	17,609 10
Cars, other, n.o.p..............	Unit'd Kingdom	188	6,047	....	....	....
	United States...	1,907	256,505	1,914	256,505	76,951 50
	Total......	2,095	262,552	1,914	256,505	76,951 50
Cars, railway, parts of.........	Unit'd Kingdon	....	3,032	....	....	....
	Belgium.......	....	3,202	....	3,202	960,60
	Germany......	....	2,475	....	2,475	742 50
	United States...	....	84,970	....	85,797	25,739 10
	Total......	....	93,679	....	91,474	27,442 20
Scrapers, railway or road.......	United States...	....	34,877	....	34,877	10,463 10
Sleighs........................	United States...	97	2,238	97	2,238	559 50

SESSIONAL PAPER No. 11

OF IMPORTS—*Continued.*

FOR HOME CONSUMPTION.

Preferential Tariff.			Treaty Rates.			Total.		
Quantity.	Value.	Duty.	Quantity.	Value.	Duty.	Quantity.	Value.	Duty Coll'd
No.	$	$ cts.	No.	$	$ cts.	No.	$	$ cts.
280	221,190	49,767 91	....	....	....	299	252,898	60,865 71
....	....	....	....	....	....	1	900	315 00
....	....	....	17	41,724	12,517 20	18	43,724	13,217 20
....	....	....	....	....	....	5,158	4,591,182	1,606,913 70
280	221,190	49,767 91	17	41,724	12,517 20	5,476	4,888,704	1,681,311 61
....	19,757	4,130 53	....	....	....	....	22,337	5,003 33
....	....	....	....	49	12 25	....	869	295 80
....	....	....	....	....	....	....	92	32 20
....	....	....	....	....	....	....	2,142,895	636,331 39
....	19,757	4,130 53	....	49	12 25	....	2,166,193	641,662 72
8	281	63 23	....	....	....	8	281	63 23
....	....	....	....	....	....	861	43,895	15,363 25
8	281	63 23	....	....	....	869	44,176	15,426 48
....	....	....				36	708	247 80
....	....	....				2,061	66,069	16,517 25
1	130	2 75	....	....	....	1	130	22 75
....	....	....	....	....	....	964	79,891	19,972 75
1	130	22 75	....	....	....	965	80,021	19,995 50
....	238	41 66	....	....	....	....	375	75 91
....	....	....	....	....	....	....	40,240	10,060 00
....	238	41 66	....	....	....	....	40,615	10,135 91
....	243	54 70	....	....	....	....	243	54 70
....	....	....	....	....	....	....	23,009	8,053 15
....	243	54 70	....	....	....	....	23,252	8,107 85
....	....	....	....	....	....	34	257,149	77,144 70
....	....	....	....	....	....	120	58,697	17,609 10
212	6,875	1,375 00	....	....	....	212	6,875	1,375 00
....	....	....	....	....	....	1,914	256,505	76,951 50
212	6,875	1,375 00	....	....	....	2,126	263,380	78,326 50
....	3,032	606 40	....	....	....	....	3,032	606 40
....	....	....	....	....	....	....	3,202	960 60
....	....	....	....	....	....	....	2,475	742 50
....	....	....	....	....	....	....	85,797	25,739 10
....	3,032	606 40	....	....	....	....	94,506	28,048 60
....	....	....	....	....	....	....	34,877	10,463 10
....	....	....	....	....	....	97	2,238	559 50

6 GEORGE V, A. 1916

No. 1.—General Statement

Articles Imported.	Countries.	Total Imports.		Entered		
				General Tariff.		
		Quantity.	Value.	Quantity.	Value.	Duty.
DUTIABLE GOODS—*Con*.		No.	$	No.	$	$ cts.
Carriages and vehicles—*Con*.						
Wheelbarrows, trucks and hand-carts.	Unit'd Kingdom	121	2,162	16	41	12 30
	United States...	8,987	46,899	8,985	46,875	14,062 50
	Total......	9,108	49,060	9,001	46,916	14,074 80
Bicycles and tricycles, n.o.p....	Unit'd Kingdom	5,114	78,116	54	870	261,00
	B. W. Indies....	2	24	2	24	7 20
	Belgium........	8	102	8	102	30 60
	United States...	2,519	22,162	2,518	22,157	6,647 10
	Total......	7,643	100,404	2,582	23,153	6,945 90
Bicycles and tricycles, parts of, including nickel or electro-plated parts for the manufacture of bicycles.............	Unit'd Kingdom	....	28,473	....	811	243 30
	United States...	....	16,468	....	17,288	5,186 40
	Total......	....	44,941	....	18,099	5,429 70
Children's carriages and sleds..	Unit'd Kingdom	....	5,808	....	358	125 30
	Germany......	....	8	....	9	3 15
	Japan..........	....	4	....	4	1 40
	United States...	....	305,799	....	305,886	107,060 10
	Total......	....	311,610	....	306,257	107,189 95
		Yd.		Yd.		
Carpets, n.o.p. (see woollens).....	Unit'd Kingdom	540	85	....	....	....
	United States...	552	131	552	131	45 85
	Total......	1,092	216	552	131	45 85
Carpet linings and stair pads....	Unit'd Kingdom	....	552	....	....	....
	United States..	....	1,722	....	1,736	434 00
	Total......	....	2,274	....	1,736	434 00
		No.		No.		
Carpet sweepers.................	Unit'd Kingdom	6	35	....	....	....
	United States...	7,995	37,288	9,249	43,905	13,171 50
	Total......	8,001	37,323	9,249	43,905	13,171 50
Cash registers and parts of.......	Unit'd Kingdom	....	146	....	....	....
	United States...	....	121,177	....	121,177	36,353 10
	Total......	....	121,323	....	121,177	36,353 10
Celluloid, moulded into sizes for handles of knives and forks, not bored or otherwise manufactured; moulded celluloid balls and cylinders coated with tin-foil or not, but not finished or further manufactured, and celluloid lamp shade blanks and comb blanks.	Unit'd Kingdom	....	72	....	....	....
	United States...	....	7	....	7	0 70
	Total......	....	79	....	7	0 70
Celluloid, manufactures of, n.o.p..	Unit'd Kingdom	....	11,201	....	2,105	368 33
	Aust.-Hungary..	....	1,897	....	1,897	331 95
	France..........	....	2,822	....	2,822	493 85
	Germany........	....	2,654	....	2,654	464 45
	Switzerland....	....	105	....	105	18 35
	United States...	....	39,116	....	39,116	6,846 26
	Total......	....	57,795	....	48,699	8,523 19

OF IMPORTS—*Continued.*

ron HOME CONSUMPTION.

Preferential Tariff.			Treaty Rates.			Total.		
Quantity.	Value.	Duty.	Quantity.	Value.	Duty.	Quantity.	Value.	Duty Coll'd
No.	$	$ cts.	No.	$	$ cts.	No.	$	$ cts.
105	2,121	424 20	....	....	....	121	2,162	436 50
....	....	....	....	....	....	8,985	46,875	14,062 50
105	2,121	424 20	....	....	....	9,106	49,037	14,499 00
4,989	76,838	15,367 60	....	....	....	5,043	77,708	15,628 60
....	....	....	....	....	....	2	24	7 20.
....	....	....	....	....	....	8	102	30 60
....	....	....	....	....	....	2,518	22,157	6,647 10
4,989	76,838	15,367 60	....	....	....	7,571	99,991	22,313 50
....	23,398	4,679 60	....	....	....	....	24,209	4,922 90
....	....	....	....	....	....	....	17,288	5,186 40
....	23,398	4,679 60	....	....	....	....	41,497	10,109 30
....	6,048	1,360 93	....	....	....	....	6,406	1,486 23
....	....	....	....	....	....	....	9	3 15
....	....	....	....	....	....	....	4	1 40
....	....	....	....	....	....	....	305,886	107,060 10
....	6,048	1,360 93	....	....	....	....	312,305	108,550 88
Yd. 540	85	21 25	Yd.	....	....	Yd. 540	85	21 25
....	....	....	....	....	....	552	131	45 85
540	85	21 25	....	....	....	1,092	216	67 10
....	552	96 61	....	....	....	....	552	96 61
....	....	....	....	....	....	....	1,736	434 00
....	552	96 61	....	....	....	....	2,288	530 61
No. 6	35	7 00	No.	....	....	No. 6	35	7 00
....	....	....	....	....	....	9,249	43,905	13,171 50
6	35	7 00	....	....	....	9,255	43,940	13,178 50
....	....	....	....	....	....	121,177	36,353 10
....	....	....	....	....	....	121,177	36,353 10
....	72	3 60	....	....	....	....	72	3 60
....	....	....	....	....	....	....	7	0 70
....	72	3 60	....	....	....	....	79	4 30
....	9,095	1,364 25	....	....	....	....	11,200	1,732 58
....	....	....	....	....	....	....	1,897	331 95
....	....	....	....	....	....	....	2,822	493 85
....	....	....	....	....	....	....	2,654	464 45
....	....	....	....	....	....	....	105	18 35
....	....	....	....	....	....	....	39,116	6,846 26
....	9,095	1,364 25	....	....	....	....	57,794	9,887 44

6 GEORGE V, A. 1916

No. 1.—General Statement

Articles Imported.	Countries.	Total Imports.		Entered		
				General Tariff.		
		Quantity.	Value.	Quantity.	Value.	Duty.
DUTIABLE GOODS—*Con.*			$		$	$ cts.
Celluloid, xylonite or xyolite in sheets, lumps, blocks, rods or bars, not further manufactured than moulded or pressed	Unit'd Kingdom	....	22	....	22	1 10
	France..........	....	681	....	681	34 05
	Germany......	....	93	....	93	4 65
	United States...	....	2,624	....	2,624	131 20
	Total......	....	3,420	....	3,420	171 00
		Cwt.		Cwt.		
Cement, Portland and hydraulic or water-lime..................	Unit'd Kingdom	92,347	35,100	135	426	·13 50
	Belgium........	6,803	2,695	6,803	2,695	680 30
	Japan...........	40	20	40	20	· 4 00
	United States...	190,224	·86,510	190,224	86,510	19,022 40
	Total......	289,414	124,325	197,202	89,651	19,720 20
Cement, n.o.p., and manufactures of, n.o.p.	Unit'd Kingdom	....	666	....	29	6 53
	Belgium........	....	392	....	392	88 20
	France.........	....	204	....	204	45 90
	United States...	....	7,617	....	7,617	1,714 05
	Total......	....	8,879	....	8,242	1,854 68
Chalk, prepared..................	Unit'd Kingdom	....	1,113	....	345	60 38
	Aust.-Hungary..	....	256	....	·256	44 80
	France..........	....	556	....	556	97 30
	Germany......	....	1,016	..+......	1,016	177 80
	Holland........	....	231	....	231	40 43
	United States...	....	36,651	....	36,677	6,418 99
	Total......	....	39,823	....	39,081	6,839 70
Charcoal.......................	Unit'd Kingdom	....	142	....	117	20 48
	France..........	........•.	208	....	208	36 40
	Germany......	....	259	....	259	· 45 33
	Japan.....•....	.•........	101	....	101	17 68
	Turkey..........	....	8	....	8	1 40
	United States...	....	95,231	....	95,207	16,661 83
	Total......	....	95,949	....	95,900	16,783 12
		Lb.		Lb.		
Chicory, raw or green...........	Unit'd Kingdom	35,409	1,443	4,032	183	120 96
	Belgium........	1,120	53	2,362	111	70 86
	France.........	300	16	·300	16	9 00
	United States...	4,818	405	· 4,818	405	144 54
	Total......	41,647	1,917	11,512	715	345 36
Chicory, kiln-dried, roasted or ground.	Unit'd Kingdom	174,275	7,796	26,208	1,165	786 24
	Belgium........	1,779	76	41,610	1,741	1,248 30
	France.........	450	25	480	32	14 40
	Germany......	1,215	82	1,215	82	36 45
	Holland........	4,480	208	4,480	208	134 40
	United States...	82,211	6,779	82,211	6,779	2,466 33
	Total......	264,410	14,966	156,204	10,007	4,686 12
Church vestments of any material	Unit'd Kingdom	....	5,484	....	310	62 00
	Aust.-Hungary..	....	93	....	93	18 60
	Belgium........•	....	152	....	10	2 00
	France..........	....	21,619	....	1,641	328 20
	Italy.....•....	....	1,399	....	1,225	245 00
	United States...	....	2,188	....	2,188	437 60
	Total......	....	30,935	....	5,467	1,093 40

OF IMPORTS—*Continued.*

FOR HOME CONSUMPTION.

	Preferential Tariff.			Treaty Rates.			Total.	
Quantity.	Value.	Duty.	Quantity.	Value.	Duty.	Quantity.	Value.	Duty Coll'd
	$	$ cts.		$	$ cts.		$	$ cts.
....	....	....	....	....	....	....	22	1 10
....	....	....	....	....	....	....	681	34 05
....	....	....	....	....	....	....	93	4 65
....	....	....	....	....	....	....	2,624	131 20
....	....	....	....	....	....	....	3,420	171 00
Cwt. 90,200	33,962	6,314 00	Cwt.	....	....	Cwt. 90,335	34,388	6,327 50
....	....	....	....	....	....	6,803	2,695	680 30
....	....	....	....	....	....	40	20	4 00
....	....	....	....	....	....	190,224	86,510	19,022 40
90,200	33,962	6,314 00	....	....	....	287,402	123,613	26,034 20
....	637	79 63	....	....	....	....	666	86 16
....	....	....	....	....	....	....	392	88 20
....	....	....	....	....	....	....	204	45 90
....	....	....	....	....	....	....	7,617	1,714 05
....	637	79 63	....	....	....	....	8,879	1,934 31
....	760	114 00	....	....	....	....	1,105	174 38
....	....	....	....	....	....	....	256	44 80
....	....	....	....	....	....	....	556	97 30
....	....	....	....	....	....	....	1,016	177 80
....	....	....	....	....	....	....	231	40 43
....	....	....	....	....	....	....	36,677	6,418 99
....	760	114 00	....	....	....	....	39,841	6,953 70
....	25	3 75	....	....	....	....	142	24 23
....	....	....	....	....	....	....	208	36 40
....	....	....	....	....	....	....	259	45 33
....	....	....	....	....	....	....	101	17 68
....	....	....	....	....	....	....	8	1 40
....	....	....	....	....	....	....	95,207	16,661 83
....	25	3 75	....	....	....	....	95,925	16,786 87
Lb. 31,377	1,260	627 54	Lb.	....	....	Lb. 35,409	1,443	748 50
....	....	....	....	....	....	2,362	111	70 86
....	....	....	....	....	....	300	16	9 00
....	....	....	....	....	....	4,818	405	144 54
31,377	1,260	627 54	....	....	....	42,889	1,975	972 90
147,365	6,604	2,947 30	....	....	....	173,573	7,769	3,733 54
....	....	....	....	....	....	41,610	1,741	1,248 30
....	....	....	....	....	....	480	32	14 40
....	....	....	....	....	....	1,215	82	36 45
....	....	....	....	....	....	4,480	208	134 40
....	....	....	....	....	....	82,211	6,779	2,466 33
147,365	6,604	2,947 30	....	....	....	303,569	16,611	7,633 42
....	4,114	514 44	....	1,060	185 50	....	5,484	761 94
....	....	....	....	....	....	....	93	18 60
....	....	....	....	142	24 85	....	152	26 85
....	....	....	....	19,978	3,496 30	....	21,619	3,824 50
....	....	....	....	174	30 45	....	1,399	275 45
....	....	....	....	....	....	....	2,188	437 60
....	4,114	514 44	....	21,354	3,737 10	....	30,935	5,344 94

6 GEORGE V, A. 1916

No. 1.—General Statement

Articles Imported.	Countries.	Total Imports.		Entered		
		Quantity.	Value.	General Tariff.		
				Quantity.	Value.	Duty.
DUTIABLE GOODS—*Con.*		Gal.	$	Gal.	$	$ cts.
Cider, clarified or refined........	Unit'd Kingdom	1,834	1,721	1,322	1,192	132 20
	Cuba............	14	14	14	14	1 40
	France.........	26	34	26	34	2 60
	Germany.......	30	51	30	51	3 00
	United States...	1,401	832	1,443	876	144 30
	Total......	3,305	2,652	2,835	2,167	283 50
Cider, not clarified or refined.....	Unit'd Kingdom	72	13	162	109	8 10
	France.........	97	13	97	13	4 85
	United States...	500	225	500	225	25 00
	Total......	669	251	759	347	37 95
Clocks, time recorders, clock and watch keys, clock movements and clock cases.	Unit'd Kingdom	....	34,012	....	6,885	2,065 50
	Aust.-Hungary.	....	555	....	553	165 90
	Belgium.......	....	747	....	689	206 70
	France.........	....	3,375	....	751	225 30
	Germany......	....	38,233	....	40,211	12,063 30
	Holland........	....	135	....	135	40 50
	Japan..........	....	63	....	....	....
	Switzerland....	....	3,891	....	2,996	898 80
	United States...	....	285,105	....	283,414	85,024 20
	Total......	....	366,116	....	335,634	100,690 20
Cloth, coated or sized, for manufacture of sensitized, blue or black print cloth.	Unit'd Kingdom	....	2,757	....	....	....
	United States...	....	3,703	....	3,703	555 45
	Total......	....	6,460	....	3,703	555 45
Clothes wringers and parts thereof for domestic use.	Unit'd Kingdom	....	43	....	....	....
	United States...	....	26,101	....	26,101	9,135 35
	Total......	....	26,144	....	26,101	9,135 35
Coal, bituminous slack, such as will pass through a ¾ inch screen.	United States...	Tons. 2,312,601	3,246,856	Tons. 2,283,520	3,214,736	319,692 86
Coal, bituminous, round, and run of the mine—and coal n.o.p.	Unit'd Kingdom	13,050	44,333	121	361	64 14
	Alaska.........	73	195	73	195	38 69
	United States...	7,141,282	13,227,256	6,829,645	12,882,759	3,619,711 84
	Total......	7,154,405	13,271,784	6,829,839	12,883,315	3,619,814 67
Cocoa carpeting, mats, rugs, and matting.	Unit'd Kingdom	....	6,631	....	77	19 25
	B. India.......	....	1,036	....	741	185 25
	Hong Kong....	....	3	....	3	0 75
	Belgium.......	....	3,557	....	1,127	281 75
	China..........	....	6	....	6	1 50
	Holland........	....	239	....	....	....
	Japan..........	....	143	....	....	....
	United States...	....	3,018	....	2,190	547 50
	Total......	....	14,633	....	4,144	1,036 00
Cocoanuts, imported from the place of growth by vessel direct to a Canadian port.	B. Guiana......	No. 16,500	330	No. 16,500	330	82 50
	B. W. Indies....	67,770	1,761	67,770	1,761	338 85
	San Domingo...	746	24	746	24	3 73
	Total......	85,016	2,115	85,016	2,115	425 08

SESSIONAL PAPER No. 11

OF IMPORTS—*Continued.*

FOR HOME CONSUMPTION.

Preferential Tariff.			Treaty Rates.			Total.		
Quantity.	Value.	Duty.	Quantity.	Value.	Duty.	Quantity.	Value.	Duty Coll'd
Gal.	$	$ cts.	Gal.	$	$ cts.	Gal.	$	$ cts.
....	....	....	....	....	....	1,322	1,192	132 20
....	....	....	....	....	....	14	14	1 40
....	....	....	....	....	....	26	34	2 60
....	....	....	....	....	....	30	51	3 00
....	....	....	....	....	....	1,443	876	144 30
....	....	....	....	....	....	2,835	2,167	283 50
....	....	....	....	....	....	162	109	8 10
....	....	....	....	....	....	97	13	4 85
....	....	....	....	....	....	500	225	25 00
....	....	....	....	....	....	759	347	37 95
....	. 26,508	5,301 60	....	585	160 88	....	33,978	7,527 98
....	....	....	....	2	0 55	....	555	166 45
....	....	....	....	58	15 95	....	747	222 65
....	....	....	....	2,624	721 60	....	3,375	946 90
....	....	....	....	....	....	....	40,211	12,063 30
....	....	....	....	....	....	....	135	40 50
....	....	....	....	63	17 33	....	63	17 33
....	....	....	....	895	246 19	....	3,891	1,144 99
....	....	....	....	....	....	....	283,414	85,024 20
....	26,508	5,301 60	....	4,227	1,162 50	....	366,369	107,154 30
....	.2,757	275 70	....	....	....	....	2,757	275 70
....	....	....	....	....	....	....	3,703	555 45
....	2,757	275 70	....	....	....	....	6,460	831 15
....	43	9 68	....	....	....	....	43	9 68
....	....	....	....	....	....	....	26,101	9,135 35
....	43	9 68	....	....	....	....	26,144	9,145 03
Tons.			Tons.			Tons.		
....	....	....	....	....	....	2,283,520	3,214,736	319,692 86
11,140	37,869	3,899 00	....	....	....	11,261	38,230	3,963 14
....	....	....	....	....	....	73	195	38 69
....	....	....	....	....	....	6,829,645	12,882,759	3,619,711 84
11,140	37,869	3,899 00	....	....	....	6,840,979	12,921,184	3,623,713 67
....	5,838	1,021 65	....	86	19 35	....	6,001	1,060 25
....	1,082	189 48	....	....	....	....	1,823	374 73
....	....	....	....	....	....	....	3	0 75
....	....	....	....	2,487	559 37	....	3,614	841 12
....	....	....	....	....	....	....	6	1 50
....	....	....	....	239	53 78	....	239	53 78
....	....	....	....	143	32 38	....	143	32 38
....	....	....	....	....	....	....	2,190	547 50
....	6,920	1,211 13	....	2,955	664 88	....	14,019	2,912 01
No.			No.			No.		
....	....	....	....	....	....	16,500	330	82 50
....	....	....	....	....	....	67,770	1,761	338 85
....	....	....	....	....	....	746	24	3 73
....	....	....	....	....	....	85,016	2,115	425 08

6 GEORGE V, A. 1916

No. 1.—General Statement

Articles Imported.	Countries.	Total Imports.		Entered		
				General Tariff.		
		Quantity.	Value.	Quantity.	Value.	Duty.
DUTIABLE GOODS—*Con.*		No.	$	No.	$	$ cts.
Cocoanuts, n.o.p..............	B. W. Indies....	22,223	622	6,223	190	46 67
	United States..	319,539	10,207	319,539	10,207	2,396 71
	Total......	341,762	10,829	325,762	10,397	2,443 38
		Lb.		Lb.		
Cocoanut, desiccated, sweetened	Unit'd Kingdom	193,477	18,389	....	....	....
or not.	B. E. Indies, other	475,164	42,708	21,700	1,914	976 50
	Hong Kong.,..	110	7	110	7	4 95
	Holland........	2,500	438	2,500	438	112 50
	United States...	4,141	834	4,156	837	176 75
	Total......	675,392	62,376	28,466	3,196	1,270 70
Cocoa butter....................	Unit'd Kingdom	219,565	68,007	2,240	789	44 80
	Germany.......	217,176	62,536	217,176	62,536	4,343 52
	Holland......	340,055	99,834	342,275	100,445	6,845 50
	United States...	691,348	199,502	689,124	198,815	13,782 48
	Total......	1,468,144	429,879	1,250,815	362,585	25,016 30
Cocoa paste, or liquor, chocolate	Unit'd Kingdom	11,297	2,529	10,407	2,354	416 28
paste or liquor, not sweetened,	B. E. Indies, other	6,170	552	....	....	....
in blocks or cakes.	France..........	2,240	545	2,240	545	89 60
	Holland.........	1,665	291	1,665	291	66 60
	Switzerland.....	1,908	383	2,908	583	116 32
	Unite : States...	30,537	6,107	30,537	6,107	1,221 48
	Total......	53,817	10,407	47,757	9,880	1,910 28
Cocoa paste or liquor, chocolate	Unit'd Kingdom	11,363	2,640	1,279	341	55 71
paste or liquor, sweetened, in	Belgium.........	....	....	33	4	1 32
blocks or cakes, not less than	Holland........	2,600	684	7,100	1,587	297 00
two pounds in weight.	Switzerland.....	4,585	1,109	7,475	1,690	323 10
	United States...	366,678	79,262	367,078	79,366	15,788 29
	Total......	385,226	83,695	382,965	82,988	16,465 42
Cocoa or chocolate, preparations	Unit'd Kingdom	1,224,998	284,902	5,446	1,594	418 78
of, in powdered form.	B. W. Indies....	....	....	125	29	7 97
	Germany.......	3,510	429	3,510	429	117 32
	Holland........	62,439	16,815	67,275	19,393	5,096 72
	Switzerland.....	2,620	590	2,782	628	160 43
	United States...	103,380	17,839	103,869	17,988	4,732 00
	Total......	1,396,956	320,575	182,987	40,061	10,533 22
		Cwt.		Cwt.		
Cocoa beans not roasted, crushed	Unit'd Kingdom	1,693	23,517	1,693	23,517	1,209 75
or ground.	B. W. Indies....	255	2,267	255	2,267	191 25
	B. Oceania,					
	other....	122	1,715	122	1,715	91 50
	France..........	559	8,244	559	8,244	419 25
	Holland........	133	2,466	133	2,466	99 75
	United States...	27,857	345,631	27,843	345,450	20,882 45
	Total......	30,619	383,840	30,605	383,659	22,953 95
		Lb.		Lb.		
Cocoa shells and nibs.............	Unit'd Kingdom	344	12	....	....	....

OF IMPORTS—*Continued.*

FOR HOME CONSUMPTION.

Preferential Tariff.			Treaty Rates.			Total.		
Quantity.	Value.	Duty.	Quantity.	Value.	Duty.	Quantity.	Value.	Duty Coll'd
No.	$	$ cts.	No.	$	$ cts.	No.	$	$ cts.
16,000	432	40 00	....	....	....	22,223	622	86 67
....	....	....	....	....	....	319,539	10,207	2,396 71
16,000	432	40 00	....	....	....	341,762	10,829	2,483 38
Lb.			Lb.			Lb.		
203,877	19,191	5,417 50	....	....	....	203,877	19,191	5,417 50
440,494	39,888	12,931 41	....	....	....	462,194	41,802	13,907 91
....	....	....	....	....	....	110	7	4 95
....	....	....	....	....	....	2,500	438	112 50
....	....	....	....	....	....	4,156	837	176 75
644,371	59,079	18,348 91	....	....	....	672,837	62,275	19,619 61
Lb.			Lb.			Lb.		
217,325	67,218	3,259 91	....	....	....	219,565	68,007	3,304 71
....	....	....	....	....	....	217,176	62,536	4,343 52
....	....	....	....	....	....	342,275	100,445	6,845 50
....	....	....	....	....	....	689,124	198,815	13,782 48
217,325	67,218	3,259 91	....	....	....	1,468,140	429,803	28,276 21
1,986	354	69 51	....	....	....	12,393	2,708	485 79
8,130	755	284 55	....	....	....	8,130	755	284 55
....	....	....	....	....	....	2,240	545	89 60
....	....	....	....	....	....	1,665	291	66 60
....	....	....	....	....	....	2,908	583	116 32
....	....	....	....	....	....	30,537	6,107	1,221 48
10,116	1,109	354 06	....	....	....	57,873	10,989	2,264 34
16,890	3,496	655 69	....	....	....	18,169	3,837	711 40
....	....	....	....	....	....	33	4	1 32
....	....	....	....	....	....	7,100	1,587	297 0b
....	....	....	....	....	....	7,475	1,690	323 10
....	....	....	....	....	....	367,078	79,366	15,788 29
16,890	3,496	655 69	....	....	....	399,855	86,484	17,121 11
1,244,457	290,877	63,111 59	....	....	....	1,249,903	292,471	63,530 37
....	....	....	....	....	....	125	29	7 97
....	....	....	....	....	....	3,510	429	117 32
....	....	....	....	....	....	67,275	19,393	5,096 72
....	....	....	....	....	....	2,762	628	160 43
....	....	....	....	....	....	103,869	17,988	4,732 00
1,244,457	290,877	63,111 59	....	....	....	1,427,444	330,938	73,644 81
Cwt.			Cwt.		.	Cwt.		
....	....	....	....	....	....	1,693	23,517	1,269 75
....	....	....	....	....	....	255	2,267	191 25
....	....	....	....	....	....	122	1,715	91 50
....	....	....	....	....	....	559	8,244	419 25
....	....	....	....	....	....	133	2,466	99 75
....	....	....	....	....	....	27,843	345,450	20,882 45
....	....	....	....	....	....	30,605	383,659	22,953 95
Lb.			Lb.		-	Lb.		
344	12	0 90	....	....	....	344	12	0 90

6 GEORGE V, A. 1916

No. 1.—GENERAL STATEMENT

Articles Imported.	Countries.	Total Imports.		Entered		
				General Tariff.		
		Quantity.	Value.	Quantity.	Value.	Duty.
DUTIABLE GOODS—*Con.*		Lb.	$	Lb.	$	$ cts.
Cocoa or chocolate, preparations of, n.o.p. and confectionery coated with or containing chocolate.	Unit'd Kingdom	2,191,899	462,819	11,125	2,245	893 66
	Belgium........	412	52	1,094	156	60 07
	France..........	713	256	430	175	64 25
	Germany......	1,418	303	21	3	1 16
	Holland	6,644	1,472	5,894	1,343	512 39
	Switzerland....	299,229	66,600	324,286	72,322	27,719 69
	United States...	147,698	34,185	154,499	35,609	13,720 15
	Total......	2,648,013	565,687	497,349	111,853	42,971 37
Coffee, green, n.o.p..............	Unit'd Kingdom	5,693	975	5,693	975	170 79
	B. E. Indies, other........	12	1	12	1	0 46
	B. W. Indies....	64	15	64	15	1 50
	Belgium........	60	12	60	12	3 00
	Brazil..........	480	48	480	48	19 20
	Costa Rica....	450	68	450	68	6 80
	France..........	2,592	304	2,301	280	44 83
	United States...	631,865	65,156	631,865	65,156	23,151 86
	Total......	641,216	66,579	640,925	66,555	23,398 44
Coffee, green, imported direct from the country of growth and production or purchased in bond in the United Kingdom (From August 22. See Free Goods)...	Unit'd Kingdom	456,147	64,398	271,213	43,337	8,136 39
	Aden...........	17,865	3,437	17,865	3,437	535 95
	B. India........	8,400	1,597	8,400	1,597	252 00
	B. E. Indies, other........	80,452	9,748	80,452	9,748	2,413 56
	B. W. Indies....	181,649	21,370	77,917	10,828	2,337 51
	Brazil..........	4,910,713	507,459	4,862,242	498,859	145,867 26
	Costa Rica....	17,760	2,339	2,960	385	88 80
	Dutch E. Indies	41,870	8,807	41,870	8,807	1,256 10
	Guatemala......	19,019	2,730	19,019	2,730	570 57
	Hawaii..........	22,700	3,119	21,500	2,943	645 00
	Mexico..........	373,769	52,140	331,141	45,810	9,934 23
	Salvador........	75,884	9,650	28,536	3,600	856 08
	Turkey.........	12,400	2,282	12,400	2,282	372 00
	U.S.of Colombia	488,962	67,963	486,356	67,657	14,590 68
	Venezuela.......	405,297	53,309	386,674	50,953	11,600 22
	Total......	7,112,887	810,348	6,648,545	752,973	199,456 35
Coffee, extract of, n.o.p., or substitute therefor of all kinds.....	Unit'd Kingdom	86,933	20,631	1,844	302	63 75
	Germany.......	606	58	606	58	18 18
	United States...	55327	26,119	55,327	26,119	2,442 39
	Total......	142,866	46,808	57,777	26,479	2,524 32
Coffee, roasted or ground, when not imported direct from the country of growth and production.	Unit'd Kingdom	2,968	768	1,046	282	58 30
	Holland	105	105	105	29	5 00
	United States...	467,379	108,278	464,016	107,220	28,115 52
	Total......	470,452	109,075	465,167	107,531	28,178 82
Coffee, roasted or ground, and all imitations thereof and substitutes therefor, including acorn nuts, n.o.p.	Unit'd Kingdom	12,162	2,981	10,777	2,685	500 18
	B. W. Indies....	72	18	60	14	3 00
	Germany......	88	9	88	9	1 76
	United States...	207,020	29,962	207,108	29,983	8,261 37
	Total......	219,342	32,970	218,033	32,691	8,766 31
Coffee, condensed with milk......	Unit'd Kingdom	1,485	358	....	....	....

OF IMPORTS—*Continued.*

FOR HOME CONSUMPTION.

Preferential Tariff.			Treaty Rates.			Total.		
Quantity.	Value.	Duty.	Quantity.	Value.	Duty.	Quantity.	Value.	Duty Coll'd
Lb. 2,177,922	$ 459,814	$ cts. 118,862 38	Lb.	$	$ cts.	Lb. 2,189,047	$ 462,059	$ cts. 119,756 04
....	....	....	....	....	....	1,094	156	60 07
....	....	....	....	....	....	430	175	64 25
....	....	....	....	....	....	21	3	1 16
....	....	....	....	....	....	5,894	1,343	512 39
....	....	....	....	....	....	324,286	72,322	27,719 69
....	....	....	....	....	....	154,499	35,609	13,720 15
2,177,922	459,814	118,862 38	....	....	....	2,675,271	571,667	161,833 75
....	....	....	....	....	....	5,693	975	170 79
....	....	....	....	....	....	12	1	0 46
....	....	....	....	....	....	64	15	1 50
....	....	....	....	....	....	60	12	3 00
....	....	....	....	....	....	480	48	19 20
....	....	....	....	....	....	450	68	6 80
....	....	....	....	....	....	2,301	280	44 83
....	....	....	....	....	....	631,865	65,156	23,151 86
....	....	....	....	....	....	640,925	66,555	23,398 44
183,807	20,935	4,135 63	....	....	....	455,020	64,272	12,272 02
....	....	....	....	....	....	17,865	3,437	535 95
....	....	....	....	....	....	8,400	1,597	252 00
....	....	....	....	....	....	80,452	9,748	2,413 56
179,551	17,910	4,039 90	....	....	....	257,468	28,738	6,377 41
....	....	....	....	....	....	4,862,242	498,859	145,867 26
....	....	....	....	....	....	2,960	385	88 80
....	....	....	....	....	....	41,870	8,807	1,256 10
....	....	....	....	....	....	19,019	2,730	570 57
....	....	....	....	....	....	21,500	2,943	645 00
....	....	....	....	....	....	331,141	45,810	9,934 23
....	....	....	....	....	....	28,536	3,600	856 08
....	....	....	....	....	....	12,400	2,282	372 00
....	....	....	....	....	....	486,356	67,657	14,590 68
....	....	....	....	....	....	386,674	50,953	11,600 22
363,358	38,845	8,175 53	....	....	....	7,011,903	791,818	207,631 88
86,430	20,463	2,558 91	....	....	....	88,274	20,765	2,622 66
....	....	....	....	....	....	606	58	18 18
....	....	....	....	....	....	55,327	26,119	2,442 39
86,430	20,463	2,558 91	....	....	....	144,207	46,942	5,083 23
1,922	486	97 16	....	....	....	2,968	768	155 46
....	....	....	....	....	....	105	29	5 00
....	....	....	....	....	....	464,016	107,220	28,115 52
1,922	486	97 16	....	....	....	467,089	108,017	28,275 98
828	203	20 67	....	....	....	11,605	2,888	520 85
12	4	0 48	....	....	....	72	18	3 48
....	....	....	....	....	....	88	9	1 76
....	....	....	....	....	....	207,108	29,983	8,261 37
840	207	21 15	....	....	....	218,873	32,898	8,787 46
1,485	358	82 20	....	....	....	1,485	358	82 20

6 GEORGE V, A. 1916

No. 1.—General Statement

Articles Imported.	Countries.	Total Imports.		Entered		
				General Tariff.		
		Quantity.	Value.	Quantity.	Value.	Duty.
DUTIABLE GOODS—*Con.*		Doz.	$	Doz.	$	$ cts.
Collars of cotton or linen, xylonite, xyolite or celluloid.	Unit'd Kingdom	32,965	33,276	3,542	4,716	1,768 50
	Aust.-Hungary..	5,697	4,932	5,697	4,932	1,849 50
	France..........	221	366	257	398	149 25
	Germany......	1,244	1,703	1,244	1,703	638 63
	Japan..........	6	8	6	8	3 00
—	Switzerland....	6,518	9,261	6,518	9,261	3,472 88
	United States...	63,154	73,707	63,201	74,059	27,772 32
	Total.......	109,805	123,253	80,465	95,077	35,654 08
Combs......................	Unit'd Kingdom	....	64,213	....	467	163 45
	Hong Kong.....	....	46	....	46	16 10
	Aust-Hungary...	....	1,054	....	711	248 85
	China...........	....	3	....	3	1 05
	France..........	....	9,202	....	1,824	638 40
	Germany......	....	24,971	....	24,971	8,739 85
	Italy...........	....	72	....	72	25 20
	Japan..........	....	69	....	....	....
	Switzerland....	....	848	....	658	230 30
	United States..	....	26,575	....	26,575	9,301 25
	Total.......	....	127,053	....	55,327	19,364 45
Copper and manufactures of— Copper nails, tacks, rivets and burrs or washers.	Unit'd Kingdom	....	293	....	5	1 50
	Belgium........	....	24	....	....	....
	United States..	....	4,054	....	4,054	1,216 20
	Total.......	....	4,371	....	4,059	1,217 70
		Lb.		Lb.		
Copper wire, plain, tinned or plated.	Unit'd Kingdom	10,253	2,270	....	....	....
	United States..	93,032	22,531	93,383	22,400	2,800 25
	Total.......	103,285	24,801	93,383	22,400	2,800 25
Copper wire cloth, or woven wire of copper.	Unit'd Kingdom	....	1,201	....	....	....
	France........	....	190	....	....	....
	United States..	....	2,937	....	2,937	734 25
	Total.......	....	4,328	....	2,937	734 25
Copper, all other manufactures of, n.o.p.	Unit'd Kingdom	....	16,607	....	725	217 50
	B. India.......	....	130	....	130	39 00
	Hong Kong....	....	161	....	161	48 30
	Belgium......	....	18	....	13	3 90
	China..........	....	30	....	30	9 00
	France.........	....	1,484	....	....	....
	Germany......	....	755	....	755	226 50
	Japan..........	....	306	....	6	1 80
	United States..	....	159,602	....	160,507	48,152 10
	Total.......	....	179,093	....	162,327	48,698 10
Cordage, cotton of all kinds......	Unit'd Kingdom	178,862	21,699	10,300	2,579	644 75
	Germany......	60	59	60	59	14 75
	United States..	78,711	13,441	74,470	12,892	3,223 00
	Total.......	257,633	35,199	84,830	15,530	3,882 50

OF IMPORTS—*Continued.*

FOR HOME CONSUMPTION.

	Preferential Tariff.			Treaty Rates.			Total.	
Quantity.	Value.	Duty.	Quantity.	Value.	Duty.	Quantity.	Value.	Duty Coll'd
Doz.	$	$ cts.	Doz.	$	$ cts.	Doz.	$	$ cts.
29,696	28,621	7,155 25	....	....	....	33,238	33,337	8,923 75
....	....	....	....	....	....	5,697	4,932	1,849 50
....	....	....	....	....	....	257	398	149 25
....	....	....	....	....	....	1,244	1,703	638 63
....	....	....	....	....	....	6	8	3 00
....	....	....	....	....	....c.....	6,518	9,261	3,472 88
....	....	....	....	....	....	63,201	74,059	27,772 32
29,696	28,621	7,155 25	....	....	....	110,161	123,698	42,809 33
....	60,779	13,675 59	....	2,194	713 05	....	63,440	14,552 09
....	....	....	....	....	....	46		16 10
....	....	....	....	343	111 48	....	1,054	360 33
....	....	....	....	....	....	3		1 05
....	....	....	....	7,785	2,530 30	...,.....	9,609	3,168 70
....	....	....	....	....	....	24,971		8,739 85
....	....	....	....	....	....	72		25 20
....	....	....	....	69	22 43	....	69	22 43
....	....	....	....	190	61 75	....	848	292 05
....	....	....	....	....	....	26,575		9,301 25
....	60,779	13,675 59	....	10,581	3,439 01	....	126,687	36,479 05
....	288	57 60	....	....	....	....	293	59 10
....	....	....	....	24	6 60	....	24	6 60
....	....	....	....	....	....	4,054		1,216 20
....	288	57 60	....	24	6 60	....	4,371	1,281 90
Lb.			Lb.			Lb.		
10,247	2,267	170 02	....	....	....	10,247	2,267	170 02
....	....	....	....	....	....	93,383	22,400	2,800 25
10,247	2,267	170 02	....	....	....	103,630	24,667	2,970 27
....	1,069	187 13	....	132	29 70	....	1,201	216 83
....	....	....	....	190	42 75	....	190	42 75
....	....	....	....	....	....	2,937		734 25
....	1,069	187 13	....	322	72 45	....	4,328	993 83
....	15,842	3,168 40	....	....	....	....	16,567	3,385 90
....	....	....	....	....	....	130		39 00
....	....	....	....	....	....	161		48 30
....	....	....	....	5	1 39	....	18	5 29
....	....	....	....	....	....	30		9 00
....	....	....	....	1,484	408 10	....	1,484	408 10
....	....	....	....	....	....	755		226 50
....	....	....	....	300	82 50	....	306	84 30
....	....	....	....	....	....	160,507		48,152 10
....	15,842	3,168 40	....	1,789	491 99	....	179,958	52,358 49
166,821	18,809	3,761 80	....	....	....	177,121	21,388	4,406 55
....	....	....	....	....	....	60	59	14 75
....	....	....	....	....	....	74,470	12,892	3,223 00
166,821	18,809	3,761 80	....	....	....	251,651	34,339	7,644 30

6 GEORGE V, A. 1916

No. 1.—General Statement

Articles Imported.	Countries.	Total Imports.		Entered		
				General Tariff.		
		Quantity.	Value.	Quantity.	Value.	Duty.
DUTIABLE GOODS—*Con.*		Lb.	$	Lb.	$	$ cts.
Cordage and twines of all kinds,	Unit'd Kingdom	2,740,856	278,443	26,005	2,662	665 50
n.o.p.	Hong Kong.....	886	.89	886	89	22 25
	Aust.-Hungary..	2,562	. 680	2,562	680	170 00
	France..........	685	264	685	264	66 00
	Germany.......	206	135	206	135	33 75
	Norway..,.....	12,879	1,065	12,879	1,065	266 25
	Japan..........	222	29	222	29	7 25
	Switzerland.....	25	7	25	7	1 75
	United States..	1,387,054	177,776	1,386,525	177,714	44,428 50
	Total.......	4,145,375	458,488	1,429,995	182,645	45,661 25
Corks, manufactured from cork-	Unit'd Kingdom	27,095	20,727	21,348	15,972	1,067 40
wood, over three-fourths of an	France.........	237	399	227	159	11 35
inch in diameter measured at	Germany.......	897	101	897	101	44 85
the larger end.	Portugal.......	85,077	23,863	84,411	23,863	4,220 55
	Spain..........	48,064	14,597	48,064	14,597	2,403 20
	United States..	51,338	24,653	51,326	24,649	2,566 30
	Total.......	212,708	84,340	206,273	79,341	10,313 65
Corks, manufactured from cork-	Unit'd Kingdom	1,681	1,336	409	276	32 72
wood, three-fourths of an inch	France.........	129	32	99	29	7 92
and less in diameter measured	Portugal.......	26,921	9,419	26,173	9,419	2,093 84
at the larger end.	Spain..........	10,649	4,865	10,649	4,865	851 92
	United States..	14,754	. 9,124	14,754	9,124	1,180 32
	Total.......	54,134	. 24,776	52,084	23,713	4,166 72
Cork slabs, boards, planks and	Unit'd Kingdom	....	1,004	....	....	.... ..
tiles produced from cork.waste	Spain..........	....	8,859	....	6,042	1,812 60
or granulated or ground cork.	United States..	....	43,403	....	43,125	12,937 50
	Total......	....	53,266	....	49,167	14,750 10
Manufactures of corkwood or cork	Unit'd Kingdom	....	10,215	....	251	50 20
bark, n.o.p., including strips,	France.........	....	384	....	255	51 00
shives, shells and washers of	Germany.......	....	152	....	152	30 40
cork.	Holland........	....	226	....	226	45 20
	Portugal.......	....	19,682	....	19,682	3,936 40
	Spain..........	....	41,598	....	41,598	8,319 60
	United States..	....	77,722	....	77,722	15,544 40
	Total......	....	149,979	...:.....	139,886	27,977 20
Corsets of all kinds..............	Unit'dKingdom	....	13,880	....	1,060	371 00
	Belgium........	....	456	....	....	.... ..
	France.........	....	1,673	....	44	15 40
	Germany......	....	77	....	77	26 95
	United States..	....	508,914	....	507,580	177,653 00
	Total......	....	525,000	....	508,761	178,066 35
Corset clasps, busks, blanks and	Unit'd Kingdom	....	237	....	77	26 95
steels, and covered corset wires	Germany......	....	498	....	498	174 30
cut to length, tipped or untipped,	United States..	....	12,080	....	12,038	4,213 30
reed, rattan and horn covered.	Total.......	....	12,815	....	12,613	4,414 55

OF IMPORTS—*Continued*.

FOR HOME CONSUMPTION.

Preferential Tariff.			Treaty Rates.			Total.		
Quantity.	Value.	Duty.	Quantity.	Value.	Duty.	Quantity.	Value.	Duty Coll'd
Lb.	$	$ cts.	Lb.	$	$ cts.	Lb.	$	$ cts.
2,706,414	275,017	55,003 40	....	....	....	2,732,419	277,679	55,668 90
....	....	....	....	....	....	886	89	22 25
....	....	....	....	....	....	2,562	680	170 00
....	....	....	....	....	....	685	264	66 00
....	....	....	....	....	....	206	135	33 75
....	....	....	....	....	....	12,879	1,065	266 25
....	....	....	....	....	....	222	29	7 25
....	....	....	....	....	....	25	7	1 75
....	....	....	....	....	....	1,386,525	177,714	44,428 50
2,706,414	275,017	55,003 40	....	....	....	4,136,409	457,662	100,664 65
2,199	1,202	87 96	....	....	....	23,547	17,174	1,155 36
....	....	....	....	....	....	227	159	11 35
....	....	....	....	....	....	897	101	44 85
....	....	....	....	....	....	84,411	23,863	4,220 55
....	....	....	....	....	....	48,064	14,597	2,403 20
....	....	....	....	....	....	51,326	24,649	2,566 30
2,199	1,202	87 96	....	....	....	208,472	80,543	10,401 61
1,157	956	69 42	....	....	....	1,566	1,232	102 14
....	....	....	....	....	....	99	29	7 92
....	....	....	....	....	....	26,173	9,419	2,093 84
....	....	....	....	....	....	10,649	4,865	851 92
....	....	....	....	....	....	14,754	9,124	1,180 32
1,157	956	69 42	....	....	....	53,241	24,669	4,236 14
....	1,004	200 80	....	....	....	....	1,004	200 80
....	....	....	....	....	....	....	6,042	1,812 60
....	....	....	....	....	....	....	43,125	12,937 50
....	1,004	200 80	....	....	....	....	50,171	14,950 90
....	9,964	1,494 60	....	....	....	....	10,215	1,544 80
....	....	....	....	....	....	....	255	51 00
....	....	....	....	....	....	....	152	30 40
....	....	....	....	....	....	....	226	45 20
....	....	....	....	....	....	....	19,682	3,936 40
....	....	....	....	....	....	....	41,598	8,319 60
....	....	....	....	....	....	....	77,722	15,544 40
....	9,964	1,494 60	....	....	....	....	149,850	29,471 80
....	10,853	2,713 25	....	1,967	639 28	....	13,880	3,723 53
....	....	....	....	456	148 20	....	456	148 20
....	....	....	....	1,629	529 43	....	1,673	544 83
....	....	....	....	....	....	....	77	26 95
....	....	....	....	....	....	....	507,580	177,653 00
....	10,853	2,713 25	....	4,052	1,316 91	....	523,666	182,096 51
....	160	36 02	....	....	....	....	237	62 97
....	....	....	....	....	....	....	498	174 30
....	....	....	....	....	....	....	12,038	4,213 30
....	160	36 02	....	....	....	....	12,773	4,450 57

6 GEORGE V, A. 1916

No. 1.—General Statement

Articles Imported.	Countries.	Total Imports.		Entered		
				General Tariff.		
		Quantity.	Value.	Quantity.	Value.	Duty.
DUTIABLE GOODS—*Con.*			$		$	$ cts.
Costumes and scenery, theatrical.	Unit'd Kingdom	....	1,821	....	....	....
	France	....	54	....	54	12 15
	United States	....	11,372	....	8,247	1,909 69
	Total	....	13,247	....	8,301	1,921 84
		Yd.		Yd.		
Cotton, manufactures of—	Unit'd Kingdom	820,602	170,048	1,026	300	60 00
Duck, grey or white, n.o.p.,	Newfoundland	111	12	111	12	2 40
weighing over 8 oz. per square	Aust.-Hungary	2,817	1,274	2,817	1,274	254 80
yard	Belgium	696	212	696	212	42 40
	United States	1,161,793	390,822	1,158,956	390,473	78,094 60
	Total	1,986,019	562,368	1,163,606	392,271	78,454 20
Embroideries, white and cream	Unit'd Kingdom	....	186,471	....	2,182	436 40
coloured.	Aust.-Hungary	....	1,170	....	64	12 80
	Azores and Madeira	....	269	....	269	53 80
	Belgium	....	506	....	199	39 80
	France	....	19,964	....	1,687	337 40
	Germany	....	4,647	....	5,867	1,173 40
	Holland	....	2,814	....	619	123 80
	Italy	....	286	....	155	31 00
	Japan	....	63	....	....	....
	Switzerland	....	428,003	....	79,270	15,854 00
	United States	....	145,277	....	145,277	29,055 40
	Total	....	789,470	....	235,589	47,117 80
Gray, unbleached cotton fabrics	Unit'd Kingdom	7,408,622	456,954	36,608	4,139	1,034 75
	Belgium	3,505	1,280	3,505	1,280	320 00
	France	850	153	850	153	38 25
	Germany	3,442	596	3,222	441	110 25
	Switzerland	20	4	20	4	1 00
	United States	1,822,564	117,903	1,812,757	116,721	29,180 25
	Total	9,239,003	576,890	1,856,962	122,738	30,684 50
White or bleached cotton fabrics	Unit'd Kingdom	23,552,448	1,902,482	290,852	34,784	8,696 00
	Hong Kong	1,100	61	1,100	61	15 25
	Aust.-Hungary	1,500	162	1,500	162	40 50
	Belgium	688	112	688	112	28 00
	France	44,185	9,139	45,336	9,613	2,403 25
	Germany	51,015	5,107	45,370	4,880	1,220 00
	Holland	148	15	148	15	3 75
	Japan	58,502	4,908	56,077	4,901	1,225 25
	Switzerland	101,298	18,376	101,298	18,376	4,594 00
	United States	7,452,781	655,334	7,471,140	657,583	164,395 75
	Total	31,263,665	2,595,696	8,013,509	730,487	182,621 75
Towelling in the webb	Unit'd Kingdom	3,163,583	220,110	32,167	2,170	542 50
	Aust.-Hungary	665	58	665	58	14 50
	Germany	130	10	....	....	....
	Holland	4,191	191	4,191	191	47 75
	Russia	96	9	96	9	2 25
	United States	24,549	3,002	24,549	3,002	750 50
	Total	3,193,214	223,380	61,668	5,430	1,357 50

OF IMPORTS—*Continued.*

FOR HOME CONSUMPTION.

Preferential Tariff.			Treaty Rates.			Total.		
Quantity.	Value.	Duty.	Quantity.	Value.	Duty.	Quantity.	Value.	Duty Coll'd
	$ 21	$ cts. 3 15		$	$ cts.		$ 21	$ cts. 3 15
....	....	....	....	....	....	....	54	12 15
....	....	....	....	....	....	....	8,247	1,909 69
....	21	3 15	....	....	....	....	8,322	1,924 99
Yd. 837,185	188,159	28,223 85	Yd.	....	....	Yd. 838,211	188,459	28,283 85
....	....	....	....	....	....	111	12	2 40
....	....	....	....	....	....	2,817	1,274	254 80
....	....	....	....	....	....	696	212	42 40
....	....	....	....	....	....	1,158,956	390,473	78,094 60
837,185	188,159	28,223 85	....	....	....	2,000,791	580,430	106,678 05
....	17,642	2,205 59	....	173,713	30,399 78	....	193,537	33,041 77
....	....	....	....	1,258	220 15	....	1,322	232 95
....	....	....	....	....	....	....	269	53 80
....	....	....	....	307	53 73	....	506	93 53
....	....	....	....	18,801	3,290 18	....	20,488	3,627 58
....	....	....	....	....	....	....	5,867	1,173 40
....	....	....	....	2,195	384 13	....	2,814	507 93
....	....	....	....	131	22 93	....	286	53 93
....	....	....	....	63	11 03	....	63	11 03
....	....	....	....	378,130	66,173 22	....	457 400	82,027 22
....	....	....	....	....	....	....	145,277	29,055 40
....	17,642	2,205 59	....	574,598	100,555 15	....	827,829	149,878 54
7,386,344	461,481	69,222 15	....	....	....	7,422,952	465,620	70,256 90
....	....	....	....	....	....	3,505	1,280	320 00
....	....	....	....	....	....	850	153	38 25
....	....	....	....	....	....	3,222	441	110 25
....	....	....	....	....	....	20	4	1 00
....	....	....	....	....	....	1,812,757	116 721	29,180 25
7,386,344	461,481	69,222 15	....	....	....	9,243,306	584,219	99,906 65
23,670,821	1,892,305	331,154 93	....	....	....	23,961,673	1,927,089	339,850 93
....	....	....	....	....	....	1,100	61	15 25
....	....	....	....	....	....	1,500	162	40 50
....	....	....	....	....	....	688	112	28 00
....	....	....	....	....	....	45,336	9,613	2,403 25
....	....	....	....	....	....	45,370	4,880	1,220 00
....	....	....	....	....	....	148	15	3 75
....	....	....	....	....	....	56,077	4,901	1,225 25
....	....	....	....	....	....	101,298	18,376	4,594 00
....	....	....	....	....	....	7,471,140	657,583	164,395 75
23,670,821	1,892,305	331,154 93	....	....	....	31,684,330	2,622,792	513,776 68
3,124,077	217,007	37,977 32	....	....	....	3,156,244	219,177	38,519 82
....	....	....	....	....	....	665	58	14 50
....	....	....	....	....	....	....	....	....
....	....	....	....	....	....	4,191	191	47 75
....	....	....	....	....	....	96	9	2 25
....	....	....	....	....	....	24,549	3,002	750 50
3,124,077	217,007	37,977 32	....	....	....	3,185,745	222,437	39,334 82

6 GEORGE V, A. 1916

No. 1.—General Statement

Articles Imported.	Countries.	Total Imports.		Entered		
				General Tariff.		
		Quantity.	Value.	Quantity.	Value.	Duty.
DUTIABLE GOODS—*Con.*		Yd.	$	Yd.	$	$ cts.
Cotton, mfrs of—*Con.*						
Fabrics, printed, dyed or coloured, n.o.p.	Unit'd Kingdom	37,401,077	3,587,339	497,425	98,824	32,117 80
	Hong Kong.....	434	91	434	91	29 58
	Aust.-Hungary .	2,873	905	2,873	905	294 13
	Belgium........	12,587	5,265	12,587	5,265	1,711 13
	France.........	155,677	34,080	156,641	34,104	11,083 80
	Germany......	311,473	47,448	311,672	47,424	15,412 80
	Holland.......	569	46	569	46	14 95
	Italy..........	12,022	2,754	12,022	2,754	895 05
	Japan..........	109,265	10,661	109,606	10,685	3,472 63
	Switzerland.....	18,217	3,319	18,275	3,335	1,083 88
	United States...	15,271,424	1,586,624	15,215,506	1,580,386	513,628 51
	Total......	53,295,618	5,278,532	16,337,610	1,783,819	579,744 26
Jeans, coutilles and sateens, imported by corset and dress stay manufacturers, for use exclusively for the manufacture of such articles in their own factories.	Unit'd Kingdom	1,661,251	193,990	1,559	958	191 60
	France.........	3,947	1,324	2,780	651	130 20
	Germany......	387	466	1,043	689	137,80
	United States...	221,119	28,479	221,119	28,479	5,695 80
	Total......	1,886,704	224,259	226,501	30,777	6,155 40
Handkerchiefs.................	Unit'd Kingdom	....	419,246	....	1,964	687 40
	B. W. Indies....	....	3	....	3	1 05
	Hong-Kong.....	....	286	....	286	100 10
	Azores and Madeira	....	4	....	4	1 40
	Belgium........	....	39	....	39	13 65
	China..........	....	83	....	83	29 05
	France.........	....	2,368	....	186	65 10
	Germany.......	....	420	....	572	200 20
	Holland........	....	1,753	....	1,753	613 55
	Japan..........	....	2,607	....	71	24.85
	Portugal.......	....	51	....	51	17 85
	Switzerland.....	....	45,006	....	11,781	4,123 35
	Turkey.........	....	3	....	3	1 05
	United States...	....	11,047	....	11,049	3,867 15
	Total......	....	482,916	....	27,845	9,745 75
		Lb.		Lb.		
Batts, batting and sheet wadding.	Unit'd Kingdom	7,683	1,035	1,250	117	29 25
	Aust.-Hungary .	52	18	52	18	4 50
	Germany......	699	51	699	51	12 75
	Japan..........	3,884	443	3,884	443	110 75
	United States...	282,508	30,506	282,508	30,506	7,626 50
	Total......	294,826	32,053	288,393	31,135	7,783 75
		Yd.		Yd.		
Bobbinet, (white cotton) plain, in the web.	Unit'd Kingdom	315,321	36,713	12,624	1,605	401 25
	France.........	675	251	....	....	....
	United States...	1,762	226	1,762	226	56,50
	Total......	317,758	37,190	14,386	1,831	457 75
		Lb.		Lb.		
Knitting yarn, hoisery yarn or other cotton yarn, dyed or not n.o.p.	Unit'd Kingdom	262,593	68,368	541	281	70 25
	France.........	30,925	14,312	30,925	14,312	3,578 00
	Germany......	1,307	746	1,307	746	186 50
	Switzerland....	3,778	4,349	3,778	4,349	1,087 25
	United States...	553,137	112,686	553,137	112,686	28,171 50
	Total......	851,740	200,461	589,688	132,374	33,093 50

OF Imports—*Continued.*

FOR HOME CONSUMPTION.

Preferential Tariff.			Treaty Rates.			Total.		
Quantity.	Value.	Duty.	Quantity.	Value.	Duty.	Quantity.	Value.	Duty Coll'd
Yd.	$	$ cts.	Yd.	$	$ cts.	Yd.	$	$ cts.
36,672,686	3,516,050	879,012 50	....	....	....	37,170,111	3,614,874	911,130 30
....	....	....	....	....	....	434	91	29 58
....	....	....	....	....	....	2,873	905	294 13
....	....	....	....	....	....	12,587	5,265	1,711 13
....	....	....	....	....	....	156,641	34,104	11,083 80
....	....	....	....	....	....	311,672	47,424	15,412 80
....	....	....	....	....	....	569	46	14 95
....	....	....	....	....	....	12,022	2,754	895 05
....	....	....	....	....	....	109,606	10,685	3,472 63
....	....	....	....	....	....	18,275	3,335	1,083 88
....	....	....	....	....	....	15,215,506	1,580,386	513,628 51
36,672,686	3,516,050	879,012 50	...:......	....	....	53,010,296	5,299,869	1,458,756 76
1,656,408	192,622	24,077 93	....	....	....	1,657,967	193,580	24,269 53
....	....	....	....	....	....	2,780	651	130 20
....	....	....	....	....	....	1,043	689	137 80
....	....	....	....	....	....	221,119	28,479	5,695 80
1,656,408	192,622	24,077 93	....	....	....	1,882,909	223,399	30,233 33
....	398,281	99,570 25	....	16,139	5,245 18	....	416,384	105,502 83
....	....	....	....	....	....	....	3	1 05
....	....	....	....	....	....	....	286	100 10
....	....	....	....	....	....	....	4	1 40
....	....	....	....	....	....	....	39	13 65
....	....	....	....	....	....	....	83	29 05
....	....	....	....	1,597	519 03	....	1,783	584 13
....	....	....	....	....	....	....	572	200 20
....	....	....	....	....	....	....	1,753	613 55
....	....	....	....	2,536	824 20	....	2,607	849 05
....	....	....	....	....	....	....	51	17 85
....	....	....	....	35,085	11,402 90	....	46,866	15,526 25
....	....	....	....	....	....	....	3	1 05
....	....	....	....	....	....	....	11,049	3,867 15
....	398,281	99,570 25	....	55,357	17,991 31	....	481,483	127,307 31
Lb.			Lb.			Lb.		
6,433	918	160 67	....	....	....	7,683	1,035	189 92
....	....	....	....	....	....	52	18	4 50
....	....	....	....	....	....	699	51	12 75
....	....	....	....	....	....	3,884	443	110 75
....	....	....	....	....	....	282,508	30,506	7,626 50
6,433	918	160 67	....	....	....	294,826	32,053	7,944 42
Yd.			Yd.			Yd.		
317,845	37,441	5,616 15	181	11	2 48	330,150	39,057	6,019 88
....	....	....	675	251	56 47	675	251	56 47
....	....	....	....	....	....	1,762	226	56 50
317,345	37,441	5,616 15	856	262	58 95	332,587	39,534	6,132 85
Lb.			Lb.			Lb.		
262,052	68,087	11,915 46	....	....	....	262,593	68,368	11,985 71
....	....	....	....	....	....	30,925	14,312	3,578 00
....	....	....	....	....	....	1,307	746	186 50
....	....	....	....	....	....	3,778	4,349	1,087 25
....	....	....	....	....	....	553,137	112,686	28,171 50
262,052	68,087	11,915 46	....	....	....	851,740	200,461	45,008 96

6 GEORGE V, A. 1916

No. 1.—General Statement

Articles Imported.	Countries.	Total Imports.		Entered General Tariff.		
		Quantity.	Value.	Quantity.	Value.	Duty.
			$		$	$ cts.
DUTIABLE GOODS—*Con.*						
Cotton, mfrs of—*Con.*						
Cotton warps..............	Unit'd Kingdom	....	793	....	....	....
	United States...	....	3,475	....	3,475	868 75
Total......		....	4,268	....	3,475	868 75
Seamless bags.................	Unit'd Kingdom	....	13,614	....	....	....
	United States...	....	14,769	....	14,769	2,953 80
Total......		....	28,383	....	14,769	2,953 80 -
Sheets, bed quilts, pillow cases and damask of cotton in the piece, including uncoloured table cloths or napkins of cotton.	Unit'd Kingdom	....	725,364	....	14,538	4,361 40
	B. W. Indies....	....	1	....	1	0 30
	Hong Kong....	....	700	....	700	210 00
	Aust.-Hungary	....	860	....	860	258 00
	Azores and Madeira	....	35	....	35	10 50
	Belgium........	....	264	....	264	79 20
	China..........	....	96	....	96	28 80
	France..........	....	2,445	....	2,445	733 50
	Germany.......	....	7,369	....	6,998	2,099 40
	Japan...........	....	23,041	....	22,356	6,706 80
	Portugal.......	....	3,511	....	3,511	1,053 30
	Switzerland....	....	2,216	....	2,216	664 80
	Turkey.........	....	28	....	28	8 40
	United States...	....	51,306	....	51,449	15,434 70
Total......		....	817,236	....	105,497	31,649 10
		Doz.		Doz.		
Shirts of cotton.................	Unit'd Kingdom	16,184	94,433	194	1,308	457 80
	Hong Kong.....	5	31	5	31	10 85
	Aust-Hungary..	643	4.718	24	162	56 70
	France..........	80	470	80	470	164 50
	Germany.......	171	637	171	637	222 95
	Japan...........	108	580	....	....	....
	Switzerland....	1	11	....	....	....
	United States...	66,770	340,256	67,013	341,568	119,548 80
T tal......		83,962	441,136	67,487	344,176	120,461 60
Sewing thread on spools.......	Unit'd Kingdom	....	115,385	....	719	179 75
	Belgium........	....	2,005	....	132	33 00
	France..........	....	1,188	....	164	41 00
	Germany.......	....	1,161	....	1,161	290 25
	Japan...........	....	11	....	1	0 25
	Switzerland....	....	59	....	....	....
	United States...	....	96,005	....	96,005	24,001 25
Total......		....	215,814	....	98,182	24,545 50
		Lb.		Lb.		
Sewing cotton thread in hanks..	Unit'd Kingdom	352,960	183,508	9,727	5,020	502 00
	France..........	325	163	325	163	16 30
	United States...	133,382	64,815	133,382	64,815	6,481 50
Total......		486,667	248,486	143,434	69,998	6,999 80
Crochet and knitting cotton......	Unit'd Kingdom	69,283	29,158	774	516	129 00
	France..........	10,055	4,662	6,926	3,438	859 50
	Germany.......	736	503	736	503	125 75
	United States...	85,319	33,994	85,319	33,994	8,498 50
Total......		165,393	68,317	93,755	38,451	9,612 75

SESSIONAL PAPER No. 11

OF Imports—*Continued.*

FOR HOME CONSUMPTION.

	Preferential Tariff.			Treaty Rates.			Total.	
Quantity.	Value.	Duty.	Quantity.	Value.	Duty.	Quantity.	Value.	Duty Coll'd
	$	$ cts.		$	$ cts.		$	$. cts.
....	793	138 78	....	....	....	....	793	138 78
....	....	....	....	....	....	....	3,475	868 75
....	793	138 78	....	....	....	....	4,268	1,007 53
....	13,614	2,042 10	....	....	....	....	13,614	2,042 10
....	....	....	....	....	....	....	14,769	2,953 80
....	13,614	2,042 10	....	....	....	....	28,383	4,995 90
....	713,881	142,776 20	....	....	....	....	728,419	147,137 60
....	....	....	....	....	....	....	1	0 30
....	....	....	....	....	....	....	700	210 00
....	....	....	....	....	....	....	860	258 00
....	....	....	....	....	....	....	35	10 50
....	....	....	....	....	....	....	264	79 20
....	....	....	....	....	....	....	96	28 80
....	....	....	....	....	....	....	2,445	733 50
....	....	....	....	....	....	....	6,998	2,099 40
....	....	....	....	....	....	....	22,356	6,706 80
....	....	....	....	....	....	....	3,511	1,053 30
....	....	....	....	....	....	....	2,216	664 80
....	....	....	....	....	....	....	28	8 40
....	....	....	....	....	....	....	51,449	15,434 70
....	713,881	142,776 20	....	....	....	....	819,378	174,425 30
Doz. 16,085	92,950	23,237 50	Doz. 34	297	96 53	Doz. 16,313	94,555	23,791 83
....	....	....	....	....	....	5	31	10 85
....	....	....	619	4,556	1,480 82	643	4,718	1,537 52
....	....	....	....	....	....	80	470	164 50
....	....	....	....	....	....	171	637	222 95
....	....	....	106	565	183 63	106	565	183 63
....	....	....	1	11	3 58	1	11	3 58
....	....	....	....	....	....	67,013	341,568	119,548 80
16,085	92,950	23,237 50	760	5,429	1,764 56	84,332	442,555	145,463 66
....	114,489	20,035 79	....	301	67 73	....	115,509	20,283 27
....	....	....	....	1,873	421 43	....	2,005	454 43
....	....	....	....	1,088	244 80	....	1,252	285 80
....	....	....	....	....	....	....	1,161	290 25
....	....	....	....	10	2 25	....	11	2 50
....	....	....	....	59	13 28	....	59	13 28
....	....	....	....	....	....	....	96,005	24,001 25
....	114,489	20,035 79	....	3,331	749 49	....	216,002	45,330 78
Lb. 343,233	178,488	13,386 58	Lb.	....	....	Lb. 352,960	183,508	13,888 58
....	....	....	....	....	....	325	163	16 30
....	....	....	....	....	....	133,382	64,815	6,481 50
343,233	178,488	13,386 58	....	....	....	486,667	248,486	20,386 38
67,930	28,390	4,968 40	579	252	56 70	69,283	29,158	5,154 10
....	....	....	3,129	1,224	275 41	10,055	4,662	1,134 91
....	....	....	....	....	....	736	503	125 75
....	....	....	....	....	....	85,319	33,994	8,498 50
67,930	28,390	4,968 40	3,708	1,476	332 11	165,393	68,317	14,913 26

6 GEORGE V, A. 1916

No. 1—General Statement

Articles Imported.	Countries.	Total Imports.		Entered		
				General Tariff.		
		Quantity.	Value.	Quantity.	Value.	Duty.
DUTIABLE GOODS—*Con.*		Lb.	$	Lb.	$	$ cts.
Cotton, Mfrs. of—*Con.*	Unit'd Kingdom	102,993	72,151	156	27	6 75
All other cotton thread, n. o. p.	Hong Kong.....	10	2	10	2	0 50
	France.........	4,147	1,326	2	1	0 25
	Germany.......	10,985	8,725	13,485	9,337	2,334 25
	Switzerland....	842	615	842	615	153 75
	United States...	95,606	53,961	95,606	53,961	13,490 25
	Total......	214,583	136,780	110,101	63,943	15,985 75
Clothing, n.o.p.................	Unit'd Kingdom	....	560,263	....	15,273	5,345 55
	B. W. Indies....	....	....	....	40	14 00
	Hong Kong....	....	337	....	337	117 95
	Malta..........	....	28	....	....	....
	Aust.-Hungary..	....	5,625	....	180	63 00
	Azores and Madeira......	....	40	....	40	14 00
	Belgium.......	....	1,650	....	777	271 95
	China..........	....	1,083	....	193	67 55
	France.........	....	46,292	....	7,326	2,564 10
	French Africa...	....	150	....	150	52 50
	Germany.......	....	19,528	....	19,518	6,831 30
	Holland........	....	443	....	171	59 85
	Japan..........	....	14,779	....	1,509	528 15
	Portugal.......	....	344	....	344	120 40
	Russia.........	....	13	....	13	4 55
	Sweden........	....	2	....	2	0 70
	Switzerland....	....	3,323	....	2,369	829 15
	United States...	....	1,522,076	....	1,521,821	532,637 35
	Total......	....	2,175,976	....	1,570,063	549,522 05
Blouses and shirt waists.........	Unit'd Kingdom	....	22,551	....	151	52 85
	Belgium.......	....	542	....	....	....
	France.........	....	3,708	....	1,053	368 55
	Germany......	....	1,314	....	1,314	459 90
	Japan..........	....	12	....	....	....
	Switzerland....	....	17	....	....	....
	United States...	....	162,194	....	161,482	56,518 70
	Total......	....	190,338	....	164,000	57,400 00
Cotton bags made up by the use of the needle, not otherwise provided for.	Unit'd Kingdom	....	80,120	....	25	8 75
	Germany......	....	28	....	28	9 80
	Japan..........	....	18	....	18	6 30
	Switzerland....	....	17	....	17	5 95
	United States...	....	46,901	....	46,899	16,414 65
	Total......	....	127,084	....	46,987	16,445 45
Lampwicks.....................	Unit'd Kingdom	....	5,310	....	28	7 00
	Aust.-Hungary..	....	2	....	2	0 50
	France.........	....	220	....	220	55 00
	Germany......	....	9	....	9	2 25
	United States...	....	20,209	....	20,198	5,049 50
	Total......	....	25,750	....	20,457	5,114 25
Lace, white and cream coloured..	Unit'd Kingdom	....	656,195	....	18,952	3,790 40
	Malta..........	....	10	....	10	2 00
	Aust.-Hungary..	....	230	....	22	4 40
	Belgium.......	....	2,361	....	427	85 40
	China..........	....	364	....	364	72 80
	France.........	....	27,223	....	2,522	504 40

SESSIONAL PAPER No. 11

OF IMPORTS—*Continued.*

FOR HOME CONSUMPTION.

Preferential Tariff.			Treaty Rates.			Total.		
Quantity.	Value.	Duty.	Quantity.	Value.	Duty.	Quantity.	Value.	Duty Coll'd
Lb.	$	$ cts.	Lb.	$	$ cts.	Lb.	$	$ cts.
102,220	71,621	12,533 91	503	353	79 43	102,879	72,001	12,620 09
						10	2	0 50
			4,145	1,325	298 13	4,147	1,326	298 38
						13,485	9,337	2,334 25
						842	615	153 75
						95,606	53,961	13,490 25
102,220	71,621	12,533 91	4,648	1,678	377 56	216,969	137,242	28,897 22
	539,212	134,803 00		12,527	4,071 28		567,012	144,219 83
							40	14 00
							337	117 95
				28	9 10		28	9 10
				5,445	1,769 63		5,625	1,832 63
							40	14 00
				873	283 73		1,650	555 68
							193	67 55
				39,280	12,766 21		46,606	15,330 31
							150	52 50
							19,518	6,831 30
				272	88 40		443	148 25
				13,734	4,463 55		15,243	4,991 70
							344	120 40
							13	4 55
							2	0 70
				942	306 15		3,311	1,135 30
							1,521,821	532,637 35
	539,212	134,803 00		73,101	23,758 05		2,182,376	708,083 10
	22,196	5,549 00		243	78 98		22,590	5,680 83
				836	271 70		836	271 70
				2,655	862 89		3,708	1,231 44
							1,314	459 90
				12	3 90		12	3 90
				17	5 53		17	5 53
							161,482	56,518 70
	22,196	5,549 00		3,763	1,223 00		189,959	64,172 00
	80,095	20,023 75					80,120	20,032 50
							28	9 80
							18	6 30
							17	5 95
							46,899	16,414 65
	80,095	20,023 75					127,082	36,469 20
	5,282	924 39					5,310	931 39
							2	0 50
							220	55 00
							9	2 25
							20,198	5,049 50
	5,282	924 39					25,739	6,038 64
	589,610	73,702 37		53,959	9,443 45		662,521	86,936 22
							10	2 00
				208	36 40		230	40 80
				1,934	338 45		2,361	423 85
							364	72 80
				24,546	4,295 55		27,068	4,799 95

6 GEORGE V, A. 1916

No. 1.—GENERAL STATEMENT

Articles Imported.	Countries.	TOTAL IMPORTS.		ENTERED		
		Quantity.	Value.	General Tariff.		
				Quantity.	Value.	Duty.
DUTIABLE GOODS—*Con.*			$		$	$ cts.
Cotton, Mfrs. of—*Con.*	Germany	....	31,720	....	33,756	6,751 20
Lace, white and cream coloured	Holland	....	1,175	....	1,175	235 00
—*Con.*	Italy	....	151	....	151	30 20
	Japan	....	639	....	639	127 80
	Portugal	....	391	....	391	78 20
	Switzerland	....	49,302	....	5,598	1,119 60
	Turkey	....	250	....	250	50 00
	United States	....	38,877	....	38,796	7,759 20
	Total	....	808,888	....	103,053	20,610 60
Shawls	Unit'd Kingdom	....	2,335	....	784	274 40
	Aust.-Hungary	....	362	....	362	126 70
	Germany	....	757	....	757	264 95
	Russia	....	744	....	744	260 40
	Switzerland	....	7	....	7	2 45
	United States	....	58	....	58	20 30
	Total	....	4,263	....	2,712	949 20
		Doz. pairs		Doz. pairs		
Socks and stockings	Unit'd Kingdom	202,760	255,142	12,486	15,852	5,548 20
	Hong Kong	56	47	56	47	16 45
	Aust.-Hungary	147	318	147	318	111 30
	Belgium	....	....	729	840	294 00
	China	50	35	50	35	12 25
	France	830	916	830	916	320 60
	Germany	74,545	98,707	76,705	101,670	35,584 50
	Japan	1,642	1,213	1,634	1,208	422 80
	Switzerland	627	700	627	700	245 00
	United States	248,466	277,738	246,114	276,916	96,920 60
	Total	529,123	634,816	339,378	398,502	139,475 70
Tape of cotton not over 1¼ inch	Unit'd Kingdom	....	12,610	....	391	136 85
in width.	France	....	131	....	131	45 85
	Germany	....	410	....	410	143 50
	Japan	....	16	....	16	5 60
	United States	....	6,685	....	6,679	2,337 65
	Total	....	19,852	....	7,627	2,669 45
Tape, not dyed or coloured	Unit'd Kingdom	....	15,142	....	1,553	388 25
	Germany	....	947	....	947	236 75
	Sweden	....	122	....	122	30 50
	United States	....	8,003	....	8,003	2,000 75
	Total	....	24,214	....	10,625	2,656 25
Tape, dyed or coloured	Unit'd Kingdom	....	26,459	....	614	199 55
	Aust.-Hungary	....	152	....	152	49 40
	France	....	1,167	....	1,216	395 20
	Germany	....	1,113	....	1,113	361 73
	United States	....	5,005	....	5,005	1,626 80
	Total	....	33,896	....	8,100	2,632 68
Towels	Unit'd Kingdom	....	328,683	....	4,430	1,329 00
	B. India	....	9	....	9	2 70
	Hong Kong	....	14	....	14	4 20
	Aust.-Hungary	....	66	....	66	19 80
	China	....	4	....	4	1 20

SESSIONAL PAPER No. 11

OF IMPORTS—*Continued.*

FOR HOME CONSUMPTION.

	Preferential Tariff.			Treaty Rates.			Total.	
Quantity.	Value.	Duty.	Quantity.	Value.	Duty.	Quantity.	Value.	Duty Coll'd
	$	$ cts.		$	$ cts.		$	$ cts.
....	....	....	....	....	....	....	33,756	6,751 20
....	....	....	....	....	....	....	1,175	235 00
....	....	....	....	....	....	....	151	30 20
....	....	....	....	....	....	....	639	127 80
....	....	....	....	....	....	....	391	78 20
....	....	....	....	45,109	7,894 08	....	50,707	9,013 68
....	....	....	....	....	....	....	250	50 00
....	....	....	....	....	....	....	38,796	7,759 20
....	589,610	73,702 37	....	125,756	22,007 93	....	818,419	116,320 90
....	1,426	356 50	....	91	29 58	....	2,301	660 48
....	....	....	....	....	....	....	362	126 70
....	....	....	....	....	....	....	757	264 95
....	....	....	....	....	....	....	744	260 40
....	....	....	....	....	....	....	7	2 45
....	....	....	....	....	....	....	58	20 30
....	1,426	356 50	....	91	29 58	....	4,229	1,335 28
Doz. pairs 189,360	240,508	60,127 00	Doz. pairs	....	....	Doz. pairs 201,846	256,360	65,675 20
....	....	....	....	....	....	56	47	16 45
....	....	....	....	....	....	147	318	111 30
....	....	....	....	....	....	729	840	294 00
....	....	....	....	....	....	50	35	12 25
....	....	....	....	....	....	830	916	320 60
....	....	....	....	....	....	76,705	101,670	35,584 50
....	....	....	....	....	....	1,634	1,208	422 80
....	....	....	....	....	....	627	700	245 00
....	....	....	....	....	....	246,114	270,916	96,920 60
189,360	240,508	60,127 00	....	....	....	528,738	639,010	199,602 70
....	12,211	3,052 75	....	....	....	....	12,602	3,189 60
....	....	....	....	....	....	....	131	45 85
....	....	....	....	....	....	....	410	143 50
....	....	....	....	....	....	....	16	5 60
....	....	....	....	....	....	....	6,679	2,337 65
....	12,211	3,052 75	....	....	....	....	19,838	5,722 20
....	13,565	2,374 07	....	....	....	....	15,118	2,762 32
....	....	....	....	....	....	....	947	236 75
....	....	....	....	....	....	....	122	30 50
....	....	....	....	....	....	....	8,003	2,000 75
....	13,565	2,374 07	....	....	....	....	24,190	5,030 32
....	26,422	6,605 50	....	....	....	....	27,036	6,805 05
....	....	....	....	....	....	....	152	49 40
....	....	....	....	....	....	....	1,216	395 20
....	....	....	....	....	....	....	1,113	361 73
....	....	....	....	....	....	....	5,005	1,626 80
....	26,422	6,605 50	....	....	....	....	34,522	9,238 18
....	322,642	64,528 40	....	....	....	....	327,072	65,857 40
....	....	....	....	....	....	....	9	2 70
....	....	....	....	....	....	....	14	4 20
....	....	....	....	....	....	....	66	19 80
....	....	....	....	....	....	....	4	1 20

6 GEORGE V, A. 1916

No. 1.—General Statement

Articles Imported.	Countries.	Total Imports.		Entered		
				General Tariff.		
		Quantity.	Value.	Quantity.	Value.	Duty.
DUTIABLE GOODS—*Con.*			$		$	$ cts.
Cotton, Mfrs. of—*Con.*	France.........		66	....	66	19 80
Towels—*Con.*	Germany........		1,248	....	1,668	500 40
	Japan...........		276	....	276	82 80
	Portugal........		18	....	18	5 40
	Spain...........		24	....	24	7 20
	United States...	....	29,838	....	29,837	8,951 10
	Total......	....	360,246	....	36,412	10,923 60
Undershirts and drawers.......	Unit'd Kingdom	....	15,065	....	3,183	1,114 05
	France.........	....	4,416	....	4,416	1,545 60
	Germany,......	....	1,011	....	1,011	353 85
	Japan...........	....	111	....	111	38 85
	Switzerland....	....	1,904	....	1,904	666 40
	United States...	....	64,737	....	64,122	22,442 70
	Total......	....	87,244	....	74,747	26,161 45
Uncoloured cotton fabrics, bleached, viz.:—		Yd.		Yd.		
Scrims and window scrims, cambric cloths, muslin apron checks, brilliants, cords, piques, diapers, lenos, Swiss jaconet and cambric muslins and plain, striped or check-ed lawns.	Unit'd Kingdom	728,796	22,046	6,659	603	150 75
	Japan...........	150	31	150	31	7 75
	Switzerland....	320	84	320	84	21 00
	United States...	118,823	5,632	118,823	5,632	1,408 00
	Total......	848,089	27,793	125,952	6,350	1,587 50
Velvets, velveteens, and plush fabrics, n.o.p.	Unit'd Kingdom	3,022,679	797,444	201,579	27,290	8,187 00
	Aust.-Hungary .	1,429	739	....		
	Belgium........	5,500	2,881	2,662	1,083	324 90
	France,.........	246,979	110,043	15,755	10,188	3,056 40
	Germany......	69,835	28,680	68,749	28,053	8,415 90
	Japan...........	45	22	....		
	Switzerland....	1,494	605	8	4	1 20
	United States...	142,133	42,761	142,133	42,761	12,828 30
	Total......	3,490,094	983,175	430,886	109,379	32,813 70
Manufactures of cotton of which cotton is component material of chief value, n.o.p	Unit'd Kingdom	....	279,625	....	30,361	10,626 35
	Hong Kong....	....	130	....	130	45 50
	Aust.-Hungary .	....	1,230	....	1,230	430 50
	Azores and Ma-deira.	....	675	....	675	236 25
	Belgium........	....	7,122	....	7,092	2,482 20
	China..........	....	158	....	709	248 15
	France.........	....	26,878	....	27,066	9,473 10
	Germany......	....	18,871	....	18,971	6,639 85
	Holland........	....	43	....	43	15 05
	Italy...........	....	1,473	....	1,473	515 55
	Japan..........	....	14;578	....	12,992	4,547 20
	Portugal........	....	1,320	....	1,320	462 00
	Switzerland....	....	1,129	....	1,129	395 15
	Turkey.........	....	20	....	20	7 00
	United States...	....	624,637	....	622,070	217,724 50
	Total......	....	977,889	....	725,281	253,848 35
Crapes, black, mourning........	Unit'd Kingdom	....	7,435	....	168	33 60
	France.........	....	601	....		
	Japan..........	....	73	....	73	14 60
	United States...	....	325	....	325	65 00
	Total.	....	8,434	....	566	113 20

OF IMPORTS—*Continued.*

FOR HOME CONSUMPTION.

Preferential Tariff.			Treaty Rates.			Total.		
Quantity.	Value.	Duty.	Quantity.	Value.	Duty.	Quantity.	Value.	DutyColl'd.
	$	$ cts.		$	$ cts.		$	$ cts.
....	....	....	....	....	....	....	66	19 80
....	....	....	....	....	....	....	1,668	500 40
....	....	....	....	....	....	....	276	82 80
....	....	....	....	....	....	....	18	5 40
....	....	....	....	....	....	....	24	7 20
....	....	....	....	....	....	....	29,837	8,951 10
....	322,642	64,528 40	....	....	....	....	359,054	75,452 00
....	11,904	2,678 56	....	....	....	....	15,087	3,792 61
....	....	....	....	....	....	....	4,416	1,545 60
....	....	....	....	....	....	....	1,011	353 85
....	....	....	....	....	....	....	111	38 85
....	....	....	....	....	....	....	1,904	666 40
....	....	....	....	....	....	....	64,122	22,442 70
....	11,904	2,678 56	....	....	....	....	86,651	28,840 01
Yd. 741,131	21,903	3,833 21	Yd.	....	....	Yd. 747,790	22,506	3,983 96
....	....	....	....	....	....	150	31	7 75
....	....	....	....	....	....	320	. 84	21 00
....	....	....	....	....	....	118,823	5,632	1,408 00
741,131	21,903	3,833 21	....	....	....	867,083	28,253	5,420 71
2,732,498	726,652	127,164 98	73,657	· 40,471	11,129,53	3,007,734	794,413	146,481 51
....	....	....	1,429	739	392 98	1,429	739	392 98
....	....	....	2.838	1,798	780 45	5,500	2,881	1,105 35
....	....	....	· 231,815	100,301	26,857 56	247,570	110,489	29,913 96
....	....	....	....	....	....	68,749	28,053	8,415 90
....	....	....	45	22	12 38	45	22	12 38
....	....	.	1,486	601	· 408 65	1,494	605	409 85
....	....	....	....	....	....	142 133	42,761	12,828 30
2,732,498	726,652	127,164 98	311,270	143,932	39,581 55	3,474,654	979,963	199,560 23
....	249,746	62,436 50	....	....	....	....	280,107	73,062 85
....	....	....	....	....	....	....	130	45 50
....	....	....	....	....	....	....	1,230	430 50
....	....	....	....	....	....	....	675	236 25
....	....	....	....	....	....	....	7,092	2,482 20
....	....	....	....	....	....	....	709	248 15
....	....	....	....	....	....	....	27,066	9,473 10
....	....	....	....	....	....	....	18,971	6,639 85
....	....	....	....	....	....	....	43	15 05
....	....	....	....	....	....	....	1,473	515 55
....	....	....	....	....	....	....	12,992	4,547 20
....	....	....	....	....	....	....	1,320	462 00
....	....	....	....	....	....	....	1,129	395 15
....	....	....	....	....	....	....	20	7 00
....	....	....	....	....	....	....	622,070	217,724 50
....	249,746	62,436 50	....	....	....	·	975,027	316,284 85
.... '	5,725	715 70	....	1,542	269 90	....	7,435	1,019 20
....	....	....	....	601	105 17	....	601	105 17
....	....	....	....	....	....	....	73	14 60
....	....	....	....	....	....	....	325	65 00
....	5,725	715 70	....	2,143	˙375 07	....	8,434	1,203 97

6 GEORGE V, A. 1916

No: 1.—General Statement

Articles Imported.	Countries.	Total Imports.		Entered		
		Quantity.	Value.	General Tariff.		
				Quantity.	Value.	Duty.
DUTIABLE GOODS—*Con.*		Pairs.	$	Pairs.	$	$ cts.
Cotton, mfrs. of—*Con.*						
Cuffs of cotton, linen, xylonite, xyolite or celluloid..........	Unit'd Kingdom	1,635	217	778	121	45 38
	United States...	1,187	132	1,187	132	49 50
	Total.......	2,822	349	1,965	253	94 88
Curling stones and handles therefor.	United States...	10	74	10	74	7 40
Curtains and shams when made up, trimmed or untrimmed.....	Unit'd Kingdom	....	284,143	....	4,357	1,524 95
	Aust.-Hungary..	....	21	....	....	....
	Belgium........	....	250	....	....	....
	France.........	....	11,181	....	4,201	1,470 35
	Germany......	....	69	....	69	24 15
	Holland.......	....	56	....	56	19 60
	Italy..........	....	108	....	108	37 80
	Japan.........	....	29	....	....	....
	Switzerland....	....	19,737	....	2,275	796 25
	United States...	....	74,274	....	74,399	26,039 65
	Total......	....	389,868	....	85,465	29,912 75
Cyclometers, pedometers and speedometers.	Unit'd Kingdom	....	204	....	41	10 25
	Germany......	....	51	....	51	12 75
	United States...	....	50,180	....	50,007	12,501 75
	Total......	....	50,435	....	50,099	12,524 75
Drugs, dyes Chemicals, medicines—						
Acetone and amyl acetate......	Unit'd Kindgom	....	203	....	203	60 90
	Germany......	....	212	....	180	54 00
	United States...	....	31,035	....	31,035	9,310 50
	Total.......	....	31,450	....	31,418	9,425 40
Acids—Acetic and pyroligneous, n.o.p., not exceeding proof strength.	Unit'd Kingdom	Gal. 18	29	Gal. 11	15	1 65
	United States...	1,673	1,163	1,673	1,163	250 95
	Total.......	1,691	1,192	1,684	1,178	252 60
Acids—Acetic and pyroligneous, in excess of strength of proof.	Unit'd Kingdom	1,223	1,350	92	190	84 85
	United States...	480	520	480	520	628 05
	Total.......	1,703	1,870	572	710	712 90
Acid acetic and pyroligneous, crude, of any strength not exceeding 30 per cent.	Unit'd Kingdom	11	10	....	....	....
	Sweden.........	10	2	10	2	0 50
	United States...	1,910	431	1,910	431	107 75
	Total.......	1,931	443	1,920	433	108 25
Acid phosphate, not medicinal..	Unit'd Kingdom	Lb. 150,252	6,349	Lb. 2,700	135	27 00
	United States...	1,688,693	94,455	1,688,693	94,455	18,891 00
	Total.......	1,838,945	100,804	1,691,393	94,590	18,918 00
Muriatic Acid...	United States...	153,740	3,101	153,740	3,101	384 38
Nitric Acid....................	United States...	233,423	10,043	71,538	4,799	1,079 92

OF IMPORTS—Continued.

FOR HOME CONSUMPTION.

Preferential Tariff.			Treaty Rates.			Total.		
Quantity.	Value.	Duty.	Quantity.	Value.	Duty.	Quantity.	Value.	DutyColl'd.
Pairs.	$	$ cts.	Pairs.	$	$ cts.	Pairs.	$	$ cts.
857	96	24 00	....	....	....	1,635	217	69 38
....	....	....	....	....	....	1,187	132	49 50
857	96	24 00	....	....	....	2,822	349	118 88
....	....	....	....	....	....	10	74	7 40
....	260,449	65,112 25	....	18,261	5,934 83	....	283,067	72,572 03
....	....	....	....	21	6 83	....	21	6 83
....	....	....	....	250	81 25	....	250	81 25
....	....	....	....	7,430	2,414 75	....	11,631	3,885 10
....	....	....	....	....	....	....	69	24 15
....	....	....	....	....	....	....	56	19 60
....	....	....	....	....	....	....	108	37 80
....	....	....	....	29	9 43	....	29	9 43
....	....	....	....	17,367	5,644 42	....	19,642	6,440 67
....	....	....	....	....	....	....	74,399	26,039 65
....	260,449	65,112 25	....	43,358	14,091 51	....	389,272	109,116 51
....	163	28 54	....	....	....	....	204	38 79
....	....	....	....	....	....	....	51	12 75
....	....	....	....	....	....	....	50,007	12,501 75
....	163	28 54	....	....	....	....	50,262	12,553 29
....	....	....	....	....	....	....	203	60 90
....	....	....	....	....	....	....	180	54 00
....	....	....	....	....	....	....	31,035	9,310 50
....	....	....	....	....	....	....	31,418	9,425 40
Gal. 7	14	0 70	Gal.	....	....	Gal. 18	29	2 35
....	....	....	....	....	....	1,673	1,163	250 95
7	14	0 70	....	....	....	1 691	1,192	253 30
1,215	1,350	1,546 34	15	17	26 33	1,322	1,557	1,657 52
....	....	....	....	....	....	480	520	628 05
1,215	1,350	1,546 34	15	17	26 33	1,802	2,077	2,285 57
11	10	1 50	....	....	....	11	10	1 50
....	....	....	....	....	....	10	2	0 50
....	....	....	....	....	....	1,910	431	107 75
11	10	1 50	....	....	....	1,931	443	109 75
Lb. 147,552	6,214	776 87	Lb.			Lb. 150,252	6,349	803 87
....	....	....	....	....	....	1,688,693	94,455	18,891 00
147,552	6,214	776 87	....	....	....	1,838,945	100,804	19,694 87
....	....	....	....	....	....	153,740	3,101	384 38
....	....	....	....	....	....	71,538	4,799	1,079 92

6 GEORGE V, A. 1916

No. 1.—General Statement

Articles Imported.	Countries.	Total Imports.		Entered		
				General Tariff.		
		Quantity.	Value.	Quantity.	Value.	Duty.
DUTIABLE GOODS—*Con.*		Lb.	$	Lb.	$	$ cts.
Drugs, dyes, &c.—*Con.*						
Stearic acid	Unit'd Kingdom	3,100	235	2,700	138	27 60
	France	550	127	550	127	25 40
	United States	160,050	14,187	160,050	14,187	2,837 40
	Total	163,700	14,549	163,300	14,452	2,890 40
Sulphuric acid	United States	315,484	6,357	315,484	6,357	788 73
Other acid, n.o.p	Unit'd Kingdom	175,535	46,851	7,250	1,163	261 68
	Belgium	1,604	82	1,604	82	18 45
	France	130	60	130	60	13 50
	Germany	11,746	4,270	11,839	4,560	1,026 00
	Italy	2,204	1,279	551	320	72 00
	Switzerland	100	39	100	39	8 78
	United States	402,670	43,806	400,466	42,527	9,569 16
	Total	593,989	96,387	421,940	48,751	10,969 57
Albumen blood, egg albumen and egg yolk.	Unit'd Kingdom	....	41	....	30	3 00
	Belgium	....	236	....	236	23 60
	China	....	1,759	....	1,640	164 00
	Germany	....	43	....	43	4 30
	United States	....	21,070	....	20,453	2,045 30
	Total	....	23,149	....	22,402	2,240 20
Alum, in bulk, ground or un-ground, but not calcined; and sulphate of alumina, or alum cake.	Unit'd Kingdom	47,936	333	47,936	333	33 30
	Germany	1,072,867	10,994	1,072,867	10,994	1,099 40
	United States	16,627,230	146,977	16,627,230	146,977	14,697 70
	Total	17,748 033	158,304	17,748,033	158,304	15,830 40
Aniline dyes, in packages of less than 1 lb. in weight.	Unit'd Kingdom	10,023	2,457	....	....	....
	France	30	28	30	28	4 90
	United States	1,719	782	1,719	782	136 89
	Total	11,772	3,267	1,749	810	141 79
Carbon dioxide or carbonic acid gas.	Unit'd Kingdom	....	74	....	....	....
	United States	....	8,478	....	8,015	1,402 79
	Total	....	8,552	....	8,015	1,402 79
Casein	Unit'd Kingdom	....	411	....	....	....
	United States	....	4,245	....	4,245	1,167 48
	Total	....	4,656	....	4,245	1,167 48
Chloride and hypochlorite of lime in packages of not less than 25 lbs.	Unit'd Kingdom	2,774,009	27,009	5,250	33	7 88
	Belgium	48,902	464	48,902	464	73 35
	Germany	65,719	587	65,719	587	98 58
	United States	6,016,915	51,880	6,016,915	51,880	9,025 24
	Total	8,905,545	79,940	6,136,786	52,964	9,205 05

OF IMPORTS—*Continued.*

FOR HOME CONSUMPTION.

Preferential Tariff.			Treaty Rates.			Total.		
Quantity.	Value.	Duty.	Quantity.	Value.	Duty.	Quantity.	Value.	DutyColl'd.
Lb.	$	$ cts.	Lb.	$	$ cts.	Lb.	$	$ cts.
400	97	12 13	....	....	....	3,100	235	39 73
....	....	....	....	....	....	550	127	25 40
....	....	....	....	....	....	160,050	14,187	2,837 40
400	97	12 13	....	....	....	163,700	14,549	2,902 53
....	....	....	....	....	....	315,484	6,357	788 73
174,991	47,982	7,197 30	....	....	....	182,241	49,145	7,458 98
....	....	....	....	....	....	1,604	82	18 45
....	....	....	....	....	....	130	60	13 50
....	....	....	....	....	....	11,839	4,560	1,026 00
....	....	....	....	....	....	551	320	72 00
....	....	....	....	....	....	100	39	8 78
....	....	....	....	....	....	400,466	42,527	9,569 16
174,991	47,982	7,197 30	....	....	....	596,931	96,733	18,166 87
....	11	0 55	....	....	....	....	41	3 55
....	....	....	....	....	....	....	236	23 60
....	....	....	....	....	....	....	1,640	164 00
....	....	....	....	....	....	....	43	4 30
....	....	....	....	....	....	....	20,453	2,045 30
....	11	0 55	....	....	....	....	22,413	2,240 75
....	....	....	....	....	....	47,936	333	33 30
....	....	....	....	....	....	1,072,867	10,994	1,099 40
....	....	....	....	....	....	16,627,230	146,977	14,697 70
....	....	....	....	....	....	17,748,033	158,304	15,830 40
10,023	2,457	368 55	....	....	....	10,023	2,457	368 55
....	....	....	....	....	....	30	28	4 90
....	....	....	....	....	....	1,719	782	136 89
10,023	2,457	368 55	....	....	....	11,772	3,267	510 34
....	74	11 10	....	....	....	....	74	11 10
....	....	....	....	....	....	....	8,015	1,402 79
....	74	11 10	....	....	....	....	8,089	1,413 89
....	411	71 93	....	....	....	....	411	71 93
....	....	....	....	....	....	....	4,245	1,167 48
....	411	71 93	....	....	....	....	4,656	1,239 41
2,768,759	26,976	2,768 70	....	....	....	2,774,009	27,009	2,776 58
....	....	....	....	....	....	48,902	464	73 35
....	....	....	....	....	....	65,719	587	98 58
....	....	....	....	....	....	6,016,915	51,880	9,025 24
2,768,759	26,976	2,768 70	....	....	....	8,905,545	79,940	11,973 75

6 GEORGE V, A. 1916

No. 1.—General Statement

Articles Imported.	Countries.	Total Imports.		Entered		
				General Tariff.		
		Quantity.	Value.	Quantity.	Value.	Duty.
DUTIABLE GOODS—*Con.*		Lb.	$	Lb.	$	$ cts.
Drugs, dyes, &c.—*Con.*						
Chloride and hypochlorite of lime in packages less than 25 lbs.	Unit'd Kingdom	9,450	509	....	....	....
	Germany	200	9	200	9	2 25
	United States	130,190	6,467	130,190	6,467	.1,616 75
	Total	139,840	6,985	130,390	6,476	1,619 00
		Oz.		Oz.		
Cocaine	United States	50	144	50	144	25 20
		Gal.	-	Gal.		
Collodion for use in films for photo engravings and for engraving copper rollers, when imported by photo engravers and manufacturers of copper rollers.	Germany	28	53	28	53	9 28
	United States	1,020	1,650	1,020	1,650	288 78
	Total	1,048	1,703	1,048	1,703	298 06
		Lb.		Lb.		
Dextrine, dry	Unit'd Kingdom	12,196	383	2,000	65	6 50
	Germany	29,546	1,131	29,546	1,131	113 10
	Holland	378,945	9,620	405,685	10,018	1,001 80
	United States	2,135,542	71,282	2,135,542	·71,282	7,128 20
	Total	2,556,229	82,416	2,572,773	82,496	8,249 60
Gelatine and insinglass	Unit'd Kingdom	341,378	64,939	15,425	3,609	992 48
	Hong Kong	53	10	53	10	2 75
	Belgium	20,876	4,018	1,120	248	68 20
	China	60	21	60	21	5 78
	France	36,994	6,704	14,175	2,940	808 50
	Germany	47,090	15,622	48,930	16,040	4,411 00
	Japan	8,440	2,426	5,152	1,527	419 93
	Spain	4	1	4	1	0 28
	Switzerland	30,979	5,301	20,679	3,740	1,028 50
	United States	192,933	56,234	191,658	55,559	15,279 05
	Total	678,807	155,276	297,256	83,695	23,016 47
Glue, powdered or sheet	Unit'd Kingdom	2,132,139	189,677	24,353	2,385	655 88
	Aust.-Hungary	....	....	13,288	776	213 40
	Belgium	23,396	3,233	....	....	....
	France	133,673	12,052	....	....	....
	Germany	149,056	10,768	137,856	9,968	2,741 20
	Roumania	....	....	40,992	2,330	640 75
	Sweden	....				
	United States	461,002	42,390	461,002	42,390	11,657 79
	Total	2,899,266	258,120	677,491	57,849	15,909 02
Glue, liquid	Unit'd Kingdom	....	17,584	....	227	62 43
	Hong Kong	....	65	....	65	17 88
	France	....	145	....		
	Germany	....	39	....	839	230 73
	United States	....	37,111	....	37,111	10,206 55
	Total	....	54,944	....	38,242	10,517 59
Glycerine, n.o.p	Unit'd Kingdom	5,791	1,252	80	13	2 28
	France	57,300	10,500	57,300	10,500	1,837 66
	United States	45,075	8,688	45,075	8,688	1,520 40
	Total	108,166	20,440	102,455	19,201	3,360 34

SESSIONAL PAPER No. 11

OF IMPORTS—*Continued.*

FOR HOME CONSUMPTION.

Preferential Tariff.			Treaty Rates.			Total.		
Quantity.	Value.	Duty.	Quantity.	Value.	Duty.	Quantity.	Value.	DutyColl'd.
Lb.	$	$ cts.	Lb.	$	$ cts.	Lb.	$	$ cts.
9,450	509	89 09	....	....	....	9,450	509	89 09
....	....	....	....	....	....	200	9	2 25
....	....	....	....	....	....	130,190	6,467	1,616 75
9,450	509	89 09	....	....	....	139,840	6,985	1,708 09
Oz.			Oz.			Oz.		
....	....	....	....	....	....	50	144	25 20
Gal.			Gal.			Gal.		
....	....	....	....	....	....	28	53	9 28
....	....	....	....	....	....	1,020	1,650	288 78
....	....	....	....	....	....	1,048	1,703	298 06
Lb.			Lb.			Lb.		
10,196	318	15 90	....	....	....	12,196	383	22 40
....	....	....	....	....	....	29,546	1,131	113 10
....	....	....	....	....	....	405,685	10,018	1,001 80
....	....	....	....	....	....	2,135,542	71,282	7,128 20
10,196	318	15 90	....	....	....	2,582,969	82,814	8,265 50
313,474	58,884	10,304 88	13,543	2,328	582 00	342,442	64,821	11,879 36
....	....	....	....	....	....	53	10	2 75
....	....	....	21,506	4,041	1,010 25	22,626	4,289	1,078 45
....	....	....	....	....	....	60	21	5 78
....	....	....	35,677	5,255	1,313 75	49,852	8,195	2,122 25
....	....	....	....	....	....	48,930	16,040	4,411 00
....	....	....	6,386	2,064	516 00	11,538	3,591	935 93
....	....	....	....	....	....	4	1	0 28
....	....	....	10,300	1,561	390 25	30,979	5,301	1,418 75
....	....	....	....	....	....	191,658	55,559	15,279 05
313,474	58,884	10,304 88	87,412	15,249	3,812 25	698,142	157,828	37,133 60
2,143,911	182,109	31,869 36	21,317	2,040	510 00	2,189,581	186,534	33,035 24
....	....	....	6,601	438	109 50	19,889	1,214	322 90
....	....	....	34,940	4,650	1,162 50	34,940	4,650	1,162 50
....	....	....	145,039	13,659	3,414 75	145,039	13,659	3,414 75
....	....	....	....	....	....	137,856	9,968	2,741 20
....	....	....	....	....	....	40,992	2,330	640 75
....	....	....	8,960	671	167 75	8,960	671	167 75
....	....	....	....	....	....	461,002	42,390	11,657 79
2,143,911	182,109	31,869 36	216,857	21,458	5,364 50	3,038,259	261,416	53,142 88
....	17,273	3,022 86	....	....	....	....	17,500	3,085 29
....	....	....	....	....	....	....	65	17 88
....	....	....	....	145	36 25	....	145	36 25
....	....	....	....	....	....	....	839	230 73
....	....	....	....	....	....	....	37,111	10,206 55
....	17,273	3,022 86	....	145	36 25	....	55,660	13,576 70
5,711	1,239	185 85	....	....	....	5,791	1,252	188 13
....	....	....	....	....	....	57,300	10,500	1,837 66
....	....	....	....	....	....	45,075	8,688	1,520 40
5,711	1,239	185 85	....	....	....	108,166	20,440	3,546 19

6 GEORGE V, A. 1916

No. 1.—GENERAL STATEMENT

Articles Imported.	Countries.	TOTAL IMPORTS.		ENTERED		
		Quantity.	Value.	General Tariff.		
				Quantity.	Value.	Duty.
DUTIABLE GOODS—*Con.*		Lb.	$	Lb.	$	$ cts.
Drugs, dyes, &c.—*Con.*						
Gums-Camphor...............	Unit'd Kingdom	2,774	1,248	610	283	49 53
	Germany......	....	....	224	101	17 68
	Japan...........	51,400	18,751	48,700	17,001	2,975 19
	United States...	2,593	1,185	3,293	1,409	246 58
	Total......	56,767	21,184	52,827	18,794	3,288 98
Opium (crude)..............	Unit'd Kingdom	1,571	8,541	1,879	9,843	1,879 00
	Germany......	25	84	25	84	25 00
	Turkey.........	2,721	9,668	3,521	11,897	3,521 00
	United States..	1,962	11,022	1,823	10,310	1,823 00
	Total......	6,279	29,315	7,248	32,134	7,248 00
Other, n.o.p................	Unit'd Kingdom	316	109	....	....	....
	United States...	8,202	1,718	8,202	1,718	300 71
	Total......	8,518	1,827	8,202	1,718	300 71
Liquorice, in paste, rolls and	Unit'd Kingdom	7,941	930	3,667	604	135 90
sticks, not sweetened, n.o.p.	France.........	24,887	2,336	24,887	2,336	525 60
	Italy..........	11,605	1,521	11,605	1,521	342 23
	Turkey.........	810,373	64,811	1,081,167	85,754	19,294 67
	United States...	937,807	85,745	937,807	85,745	19,292 63
	Total......	1,792,613	155,343	2,059,133	175,960	39,591 03
Magnesia.....................	Unit'd Kingdom	50,032	4,101	120	7	1 23
	Germany......	3,345	416	3,345	416	72 80
	United States..	137,366	9,886	137,366	9,886	1,730 13
	Total......	190,743	14,403	140,831	10,309	1,804 16
Medicinal, chemical and phar-	Unit'd Kingdom	....	417,526	....	27,134	6,783 50
maceutical preparations, in-	Hong Kong.....	....	10,826	....	10,826	2,706 50
cluding proprietary prepar-	Aust-.Hungary.	....	393	....	....	....
ations (dry).	Belgium........	....	330	....	330	82 50
	China..........	....	3,960	....	3,960	990 00
	France.........	....	79,859	....	79,912	19,978 00
	Germany.......	....	30,646	....	37,517	9,379 25
	Holland........	....	165	....	165	41 25
	Italy...........	....	1,130	....	970	242 50
	Japan..........	....	2,477	....	2,450	612 50
	Sweden........	....	58	....	58	14 50
	Switzerland....	....	111	....	111	27 75
	United States...	....	446,935	....	445,944	111,486 00
	Total......	....	994,416	....	609,377	152,344 25
Medicinal, chemical and phar-	Unit'd Kingdom	....	19,239	....	15,480	8,501 40
maceutical preparations, in-	Hong Kong.....	....	701	....	701	380 70
including proprietary prepara-	Belgium........	....	33	....	33	16 50
tions (all other).	China..........	....	45	....	45	24 60
	France.........	....	23,303	....	20,536	11,323 40
	Germany.......	....	1,585	....	1,680	849 70
	Holland........	....	772	....	772	444 30
	Japan..........	....	75	....	75	44 60
	Sweden........	....	232	....	232	139 20
	Switzerland....	....	221	....	221	131 50
	United States...	....	56,595	....	57,571	31,846 60
	Total......	....	102,801	....	97,346	53,702 50

SESSIONAL PAPER No. 11

OF IMPORTS—*Continued.*

FOR HOME CONSUMPTION.

Preferential Tariff.			Treaty Rates.			Total.		
Quantity.	Value.	Duty.	Quantity.	Value.	Duty.	Quantity.	Value.	DutyColl'd.
Lb.	$	$ cts.	Lb.	$	$ cts.	Lb.	$	$ cts.
2,576	1,199	179 85	....	....	....	3,186	1,482	229 38
....	....	....	....	....	....	224	101	17 68
....	....	....	....	....	....	48,700	17,001	2,975 19
....	....	....	....	....	....	3,293	1,409	246 58
2,576	1,199	179 85	....	....	....	55,403	19,993	3,468 83
....	....	....	....	....	....	1,879	9,843	1,879 00
....	....	....	....	....	....	25	84	25 00
....	....	....	....	....	....	3,521	11,897	3,521 00
....	....	....	....	....	....	1,823	10,310	1,823 00
....	......	....	....	....	....	7,248	32,134	7,248 00
316	109	16 35	....	....	....	316	109	16 35
....	....	....	....	....	....	8,202	1,718	300 71
316	109	16 35	....	....	....	8,518	1,827	317 06
4,274	326	48 90	....	....	....	7,941	930	184 80
....	....	....	....	....	....	24,887	2,336	525 60
....	....	....	....	....	....	11,605	1,521	342 23
....	....	....	....	....	....	1,081,167	85,754	19,294 67
....	....	....	....	....	....	937,807	85,745	19,292 63
4,274	326	48 90	....	....	....	2,063,407	176,286	39,639 93
47,912	3,823	573 45	....	....	....	48,032	3,830	574 68
....	....	....	....	....	....	3,345	416	72 80
....	....	....	....	....	....	137,366	9,886	1,730 13
47,912	3,823	573 45	....•...	....	....	188,743	14,132	2,377 61
....	393,020	78,604 00	....	....	....	420,154	85,387 50	
....	....	....	....	....	....	10,826	2,706 50	
....	....	....	....	....	....	330	82 50	
....	....	....	....	....	....	3,960	990 00	
....	....	....	....	....	....	79,912	19,978 00	
....	....	....	....	....	....	37,517	9,379 25	
....	....	....	....	....	....	165	41 25	
....	....	....	....	....	....	970	242 50	
....	....	....	....	....	....	2,450	612 50	
....	....	....	....	....	....	58	14 50	
....	....	....	....	....	....	111	27 75	
....	....	....	....	....	....	445,944	111,486 00	
....	393,020	78,604 00	....	....	....	1,002,397	230,948 25	
....	....	....	....	....	....	15,480	8,501 40	
....	....	....	....	....	....	701	380 70	
....	....	....	....	....	....	33	16 50	
....	....	....	....	....	....	45	24 60	
....	....	....	....	....	....	20,536	11,323 40	
....	....	....	....	....	....	1,680	849 70	
....	....	....	....	....	....	772	444 30	
....	....	....	....	....	....	75	44 60	
....	....	....	....	....	....	232	139 20	
....	....	....	....	....	....	221	131 50	
....	....	....	....	....	....	57,571	31,846 60	
....	....	....	....	....	....	97,346	53,702 50	

6 GEORGE V, A. 1916

No. 1.—General Statement

Articles Imported.	Countries.	Total Imports.		Entered		
		Quantity.	Value.	General Tariff.		
				Quantity.	Value.	Duty.
DUTIABLE GOODS—*Con.*			$		$	$ cts.
Drugs, dyes, &c.—*Con.*						
Medicinal, chemical and pharmaceutical preparations, including proprietary preparations (all other) non-alcholic.	Unit'd Kingdom	....	27,055	....	....	....
	France..........	....	57,261	....	....	....
	Total......	....	84,316	....	....	....
Liquid preparations, non-alcoholic for disinfecting, dipping or spraying, n.o.p.	Unit'd Kingdom	....	16,292	....	3,661	915 25
	Belgium........	....	14	....	14	3 50
	France..	....	837	....	948	237 00
	Germany......	....	662	....	662	165 50
	Switzerland....	....	47	....	47	11 75
	United States...	....	57,726	....	57,679	14,419 75
	Total......	....	75,578	....	63,011	15,752 75
Milk food, and other similar preparations.	Unit'd Kingdom	....	139,395	....	306	76 65
	Newfoundland..	....	8	....	8	2 20
	Belgium........	....	1,378	....	1,378	344 50
	France........	....	144	....	19	5 23
	Germany......	....	23	....	23	5 75
	Holland.......	....	148	....	148	40 06
	Switzerland....	....	22,006	....	28,421	7,345 25
	United States...	....	190,234	....	187,410	49,746 82
	Total......	....	353,336	....	217,713	57,566 46
		Oz.		Oz.		
Morphine......................	Unit'd Kingdom	200	414	....		
	United States...	59	294	59	294	51 45
	Total......	259	708	59	294	51 45
		Lb.		Lb.		
Opium, powdered..............	Unit'd Kingdom	228	1,154	228	1,154	307 80
	Germany......	25	100	25	100	33 75
	United States...	14	144	14	144	18 90
	Total......	267	1,398	267	1,398	360 45
Potash or potassa, bicarbonate of.	Unit'd Kingdom	600	53	....	....	....
	United States...	3,088	332	3,088	332	58 11
	Total......	3,688	385	3,088	332	58 11
Potash and pearl ash, in packages less than 25 lbs. each.	United States...	4,022	150	4,022	150	22 50
Potash caustic, in packages less than 25 lbs. each.	Unit'd Kingdom	227	18	....	....	....
	Germany......	1,060	144	1,060	144	21 60
	Sweden........	500	73	500	73	10 95
	United States...	17,680	1,144	17,680	1,144	171 60
	Total......	19,467	1,379	19,240	1,361	204 15
Pyroxylin and wood naptha, preparations of, for coating imitation leather, and for the manufacture of leather belting	United States...	....	19,190	....	19,190	1,919 00
Salts, glauber.................	Unit'd Kingdom	610,264	2,363	44,800	200	35 00
	United States...	55,240	329	55,240	329	57 59
	Total......	665,504	2,692	100,040	529	92 59

OF IMPORTS—*Continued.*

FOR HOME CONSUMPTION.

Preferential Tariff.			Treaty Rates.			Total.		
Quantity.	Value.	Duty.	Quantity.	Value.	Duty.	Quantity.	Value.	DutyColl'd.
	$	$ cts.		$	$ cts.		$	$ cts.
....	....	....	....	30,188	7,547 00	....	30,188	7,547 00
....	....	....	....	54,047	13,511 75	....	54,047	13,511 75
....	....	....	....	84,235	21,058 75	....	84,235	21,058 75
....	11,759	2,351 80	....	....	....		15,420	3,267 05
....	....	....	....	....	....		14	3 50
....	....	....	....	....	....		948	237 00
....	....	....	....	....	....		662	165 50
....	....	....	....	....	....		47	11 75
....	....	....	....	....	....		57,679	14,419 75
....	11,759	2,351 80	....	....	....	....	74,770	18,104 55
....	139,738	26,389 57	....	....	....		140,044	26,466 22
....	....	....	....	....	....		8	2 20
....	....	....	....	....	....		1,378	344 50
....	....	....	....	....	....		19	5 23
....	....	....	....	....	....		23	5 75
....	....	....	....	....	....		148	40 06
....	....	....	....	....	....		28,421	7,345 25
....	....	....	....	....	....		187,410	49,746 82
....	139,738	26,389 57	....	....	....	....	357,451	83,956 03
Oz. 200	414	62 10	Oz.	....	....	Oz. 200	414	62 10
....	....	....	....	....	....	59	294	51 45
200	414	62 10	....	....	....	259	708	113 55
Lbs.	....	....	Lbs.	....	....	Lbs. 228	1,154	307 80
....	....	....	....	....	....	25	100	33 75
....	....	....	....	....	....	14	144	18 90
....	....	....	....	....	....	67	1,398	360 45
600	53	7 95	....	....	....	600	53	7 95
....	....	....	....	....	....	3,088	332	58 11
600	53	7 95	....	....	....	3,688	385	66 06
....	....	....	....	....	....	4,022	150	22 50
227	18	1 80	....	....	....	227	18	1 80
....	....	....	....	....	....	1,060	144	21 60
....	....	....	....	....	....	500	73	10 95
....	....	....	....	....	....	17,680	1,144	171 60
227	18	1 80	....	....	....	19,467	1,379	205 95
....	....	....	....	....	....	....	19,190	1,919 00
565,464	2,163	324 45	....	....	....	610,264	2,363	359 45
....	....	....	....	....	....	55,240	329	57 59
565,464	2,163	324 45	....	....	....	665,504	2,692	417 04

6 GEORGE V, A. 1916

No. 1.—General Statement

Articles Imported.	Countries.	Total Imports.		Entered		
				General Tariff.		
		Quantity.	Value.	Quantity.	Value.	Duty.
DUTIABLE GOODS—*Con.*		Lb.	$	Lb.	$	$ cts.
Drugs, dyes, &c.—*Con.*						
Soda, bicarbonate of...........	Unit'd Kingdom	5,298,860	49,991	28,600	273	47 78
	United States..	2,037,420	19,134	2,037,420	19,134	3,348 59
	Total.......	7,336,280	69,125	2,066,020	19,407	3,396 37
Soda caustic, when in packages	Unit'd Kingdom	12,590	256	....	....	....
less than 25 lbs. each.	United States...	422,947	10,455	422,947	10,455	1,944 95
	Total.......	435,537	10,711	422,947	10,455	1,944 95
Soda caustic when in packages	Unit'd Kingdom	63,726	1,453	250	18	4 50
of 25 lbs. and over...........	Hong Kong.....	180	6	180	6	0 54
	United States..	2,536,343	45,322	2,536,343	45,322	7,820 44
	Total......	2,600,249	46,781	2,536,773	45,346	7,825 48
Sodium, hyposulphite.........	Unit'd Kingdom	....	388	....	161	28 18
	United States...	....	2,315	....	2,315	405 11
	Total.......	....	2,703	....	2,476	433 29
Sulphuric ether, chloroform and	Unit'd Kingdom	....	29,105	....	149	377 25
solutions of peroxide of hydro-	Germany.......	....	1,856	....	1,856	464 00
gen.	United States...	....	36,353	....	36,353	9,088 25
	Total......	....	67,314	....	38,358	9,589 50
Thorium nitrate...............	United States...	....	542	....	542	94 84
Vaseline and all similar prepara-	Unit'd Kingdom	....	299	....	12	3 00
tions of petroleum, for toilet,	Belgium........	....	220	....	220	55 00
medicinal or other purposes.	France..........	....	24	....	24	6 00
	Germany.......	....	545	....	545	136 25
	United States..	....	22,129	....	22,124	5,531 00
	Total......	....	23,217	....	22,925	5,731 25
Yeast cakes...................	United States..	464	86	474	93	28 44
Yeast, compressed, in packages	Unit'd Kingdom	9	1	....	....	....
weighing less than 50 lbs.	United States..	6,681	1,166	6,681	1,166	400 86
	Total.......	6,690	1,167	6,681	1,166	400 86
Yeast, compressed, in bulk or	Unit'd Kingdom	1,456	163	....	....	....
mass of not less than 50 lbs.	United States..	1,616,204	422,908	1,616,204	422,908	48,486 12
	Total.......	1,617,660	423,071	1,616,204	422,908	48,486 12
All other drugs, dyes and	Unit'd Kingdom	....	229,152	....	14,678	2,568 65
chemicals, etc., not otherwise	Australia......	....	279	....	279	48 83
provided for.	Hong Kong.....	....	315	....	315	55 13
	Aust.-Hungary..	....	349	....	349	61 08
	Belgium........	....	762	....	762	133 35
	China..........	....	50	....	50	8 75
	France.........	....	19,304	....	15,588	2,727 90
	Germany......	....	42,910	....	43,659	7,640 33

OF IMPORTS—*Continued.*

FOR HOME CONSUMPTION.

Preferential Tariff.			Treaty Rates.			Total.		
Quantity.	Value.	Duty.	Quantity.	Value.	Duty.	Quantity.	Value.	DutyColl'd.
Lb.	$	$ cts.	Lb.	$	$ cts.	Lb.	$	$ cts.
5,270,260	49,718	7,457 70	....	....	....	5,298,860	49,991	7,505 48
....	....	....	....	....	....	2,037,420	19,134	3,348 59
5,270,260	49,718	7,457 70	....	....	....	7,336,280	69,125	10,854 07
12,590	256	30 54	....	....	....	12,590	256	30 54
....	....	....	....	....	....	422,947	10,455	1,944 95
12,590	256	30,54	....	....	....	435,537	10,711	1,975 49
62,476	1,435	248 90	....	....	....	62,726	1,453	253 40
....	....	....	....	....	....	180	6	0 54
....	....	....	....	....	....	2,536,343	45,322	7,820 44
62,476	1,435	248 90	....	....	....	2,599,249	46,781	8,074 38
....	227	34 05	....	....	....	....	388	62 23
....	....	....	....	....	....	....	2,315	405 11
....	227	34 05	....	....	....	....	2,703	467 34
....	28,956	4,343 40	....	....	....	....	29,105	4,380 65
....	....	....	....	....	....	....	1,856	464 00
....	....	....	....	....	....	....	36,353	9,088 25
....	28,956	4,343 40	....	....	....	....	67,314	13,932 90
....	....	....	....	....	....	....	542	94 84
....	287	43 05	....	....	....	....	299	46 05
....	....	....	..\.....	....	....	....	220	55 00
....	....	....	....	....	....	....	24	6 00
....	....	....	....	....	....	....	545	136 25
....	....	....	....	....	....	....	22,124	5,531 00
....	287	43 05	....	....	....	....	23,212	5,774 30
....	....	....	....	....	....	....	474	93	28 44
9	1	0 36	....	....	....	9	1	0 36
....	....	....	....	....	....	6,681	1,166	400 86
9	1	0 36	....	....	....	6,690	1,167	401 22
1,456	163	29 12	....	....	....	1,456	163	29 12
....	....	....	....	....	....	1,616,204	422,908	48,486 12
1,456	163	29 12	....	....	....	1,617,660	423,071	48,515 24
....	213,490	32,023 50	....	....	....	....	228,168	34,592 15
....	....	....	....	....	....	....	279	48 83
....	....	....	....	....	....	....	315	55 13
....	....	....	....	....	....	....	349	61 08
....	....	....	....	....	....	....	782	133 35
....	....	....	....	....	....	....	50	8 75
....	....	....	....	....	....	....	15,588	2,727 90
....	....	....	....	....	....	....	43,659	7,640 33

6 GEORGE V, A. 1916

No. 1.—General Statement

Articles Imported.	Countries.	Total Imports.		Entered		
		Quantity.	Value.	General Tariff.		
				Quantity.	Value.	Duty.
			$		$	$ cts.
DUTIABLE GOODS—*Con.*						
Drugs, dyes, &c.—*Con.*						
All other drugs, etc.—*Con.*	Greece...........	....	7,404	....	7,404	1,295 70
	Holland........	....	1,887	....	1,887	330 23
	Japan...........	....	6,738	....	5,992	1,048 60
	Switzerland.....	....	6,586	....	6,586	1,152 55
	Turkey.........	....	17	....	17	2 98
	United States..	....	677,105	....	668,038	116,908 41
	Total......	....	992,858	....	765,604	133,982 49
Earthenware and Chinaware— (See Bricks and Tiles.)						
Brown or coloured earthen and stoneware, and Rockingham ware.	Unit'd Kingdom	....	18,477	....	907	272 10
	Hong Kong....	....	74	....	74	22 20
	France........	....	106	....	36	10 80
	Germany.......	....	76	....	76	22 80
	Holland........	....	37	....	4	1 20
	Italy.........	....	259	....		....
	Japan.........	....	619	....	619	185 70
	United States..	....	44,058	....	44,037	13,211 10
	Total......	....	63,706	....	45,753	13,725 90
C. C. or cream-coloured ware, decorated, printed or sponged, and all earthenware, n.o.p.	Unit'd Kingdom	....	94,494	....	3,111	933 30
	B. W. Indies....	....	2	....	2	0 60
	Hong Kong....	....	239	....	239	71 70
	Aust.-Hungary..	....	1,040	....	1,040	312 00
	Belgium.......	....	67	....	67	20 10
	China..........	....	381	....	264	79 20
	France.........	....	2,425	....	2,439	731 70
	Germany......	....	6,646	....	6,684	2,005 20
	Holland.......	....	640	....	626	187 80
	Italy..........	....	23	....	282	84 60
	Japan..........	....	7,913	....	7,921	2,376 30
	United States..	....	35,041	....	34,995	10,498 50
	Total......	....	148,911	....	57,670	17,301 00
Demijohns, churns or crocks....	Unit'd Kingdom	....	1,502	....	251	75 30
	Hong Kong.....	....	2	....	2	0 60
	Germany......	....	19	....	19	5 70
	United States..	....	23,622	....	23,622	7,086 60
	Total......	....	25,145	....	23,894	7,168 20
Table ware of china, porcelain, white granite or iron-stoneware.	Unit'd Kingdom	....	865,893	....	12,881	3,542 28
	B. W. Indies....	....	24	....	24	6 60
	Hong Kong.....	....	2,290	....	2,290	629 75
	Aust.-Hungary..	....	25,368	....	25,368	6,976 20
	Belgium.......	....	679	....	679	186 73
	China..........	....	849	....	849	233 48
	Denmark......	....	80	....	80	22 00
	Egypt & Soudan	....	39	....	39	10 73
	France........	....	143,407	....	143,604	39,491 88
	Germany......	....	121,718	....	121,970	33,541 75
	Holland.......	....	4,757	....	4,757	1,308 18
	Italy..........	....	2,395	....	2,437	670 18
	Japan.........	....	63,410	....	63,256	17,395 40
	Norway.......	....	34	....	34	9 35
	Spain.........	....	89	....	89	24 75
	Sweden.......	....	130	....	130	35 75
	United States..	....	29,193	....	28,444	7,822 10
	Total......	....	1,260,355	....	406,931	111,907 11

OF IMPORTS—*Continued.*

FOR HOME CONSUMPTION.

Preferential Tariff.			Treaty Rates.			Total.		
Quantity.	Value.	Duty.	Quantity.	Value.	Duty.	Quantity.	Value.	DutyColl'd.
	$	$ cts.		$	$ cts.		$	$ cts.
....	....	....	....	....	....	....	7,404	1,295 70
....	....	....	....	....	....	....	1,887	330 23
....	....	....	....	....	....	....	5,992	1,048 60
....	....	....	....	....	....	....	6,586	1,152 55
....	....	....	....	....	....	....	17	2 98
....	....	....	....	....	....	....	668,038	116,908 41
....	213,490	32,023 50	....	....	....	....	979,094	166,005 99
....	17,560	3,512 00	....	....	....	....	18,467	3,784 10
....	....	....	....	....	....	....	74	22 20
....	....	....	....	....	....	....	36	10 80
....	....	....	....	....	....	....	76	22 80
....	....	....	....	....	....	....	4	1 20
....	....	....	....	....	....	....	....	....
....	....	....	....	....	....	....	619	185 70
....	....	....	....	....	....	....	44,037	13,211 10
....	17,560	3,512 00	....	....	....	....	63,313	17,237 90
....	93,537	18,707 40	....	....	....	....	96,648	19,640 70
....	....	....	....	....	....	....	2	0 60
....	....	....	....	....	....	....	239	71 70
....	....	....	....	....	....	....	1,040	312 00
....	....	....	....	....	....	....	67	20 10
....	....	....	....	....	....	....	264	79 20
....	....	....	....	....	....	....	2,439	731 70
....	....	....	....	....	....	....	6,684	2,005 20
....	....	....	....	....	....	....	626	187 80
....	....	....	....	....	....	....	282	84 60
....	....	....	....	....	....	....	7,921	2,376 30
....	....	....	....	....	....	....	34,995	10,498 50
....	93,537	18,707 40	....	....	....	....	151,207	36,008 40
....	1,251	250 20	....	....	....	....	1,502	325 50
....	....	....	....	....	....	....	2	0 60
....	....	....	....	....	....	....	19	5 70
....	....	....	....	....	....	....	23,622	7,086 60
....	1,251	250 20	....	....	....	....	25,145	7,418 40
....	857,999	128,699 85	....	....	....	....	870,880	132,242 13
....	....	....	....	....	....	....	24	6 60
....	....	....	....	....	....	....	2,290	629 75
....	....	....	....	....	....	....	25,368	6,976 20
....	....	....	....	....	....	....	679	186 73
....	....	....	....	....	....	....	849	233 48
....	....	....	....	....	....	....	80	22 00
....	....	....	....	....	....	....	39	10 73
....	....	....	....	....	....	....	143,604	39,491 88
....	....	....	....	....	....	....	121,970	33,541 75
....	....	....	....	....	....	....	4,757	1,308 18
....	....	....	....	....	....	....	2,437	670 18
....	....	....	....	....	....	....	63,256	17,395 40
....	....	....	....	....	....	....	34	9 35
....	....	....	....	....	....	....	89	24 75
....	....	....	....	....	....	....	130	35 75
....	....	....	....	....	....	....	28,444	7,822 10
....	857,999	128,699 85	....	....	....	....	1,264,930	240,606 96

6 GEORGE V, A. 1916

No. 1.—GENERAL STATEMENT

Articles Imported.	Countries.	Total Imports.		Entered		
				General Tariff.		
		Quantity.	Value.	Quantity.	Value.	Duty.
			$		$	$ cts.
DUTIABLE GOODS—*Con.*						
Earthenware, &c.—*Con.*						
Chinaware, to be silver mount-ed, imported by manufac-turers of silverware.	Unit'd Kingdom	....	37	....	....	....
	France	....	597	....	597	134 39
	United States	....	116	....	116	26 10
	Total	....	750	....	713	160 49
China and porcelain ware,n.o.p.	Unit'd Kingdom	....	8,570	....	912	273 60
	Hong Kong	....	84	....	84	25 20
	Aust.-Hungary	....	181	....	181	54 30
	China	....	34	....	34	10 20
	France	....	302	....	302	90 60
	Germany	....	3,537	....	3,563	1,068 90
	Holland	....	185	....	185	55 50
	Japan	....	2,827	....	2,827	848 10
	Portugal	....	52	....	52	15 60
	United States	....	10,544	....	10,544	3,163 20
	Total	....	26,316	....	18,684	5,605 20
Tiles or blocks of earthenware or stone prepared for mosaic flooring.	Unit'd Kingdom	....	9,973	....	675	202 50
	France	....	757	....	757	227 10
	Germany	....	18	....	18	5 40
	Italy	....	955	....	608	182 40
	United States	....	72,058	....	73,117	21,935 10
	Total	....	83,761	....	75,175	22,552 50
Earthenware tiles, n.o.p.	Unit'd Kingdom	....	61,490	....	482	168 70
	France	....	2	....	2	0 70
	Germany	....	293	....	293	102 55
	United States	....	98,270	....	98,414	34,444 90
	Total	....	160,055	....	99,191	34,716 85
Manufactures of earthenware, n.o.p.	Unit'd Kingdom	....	66,190	....	1,347	404 10
	Hong Kong	....	279	....	279	83 70
	Aust.-Hungary	....	601	....	601	180 30
	Belgium	....	126	....	126	37 80
	China	....	155	....	278	83 40
	France	....	1,325	....	1,325	397 50
	Germany	....	10,474	....	10,474	3,142 20
	Holland	....	525	....	525	157 50
	Italy	....	136	....	136	40 80
	Japan	....	1,428	....	1,341	402 30
	United States	....	83,564	....	83,556	25,066 80
	Total	....	164,803	....	99,988	29,996 40
		Doz.		Doz.		
Eggs	Unit'd Kingdom	1,143	337	1,118	256	33 54
	Hong Kong	64,498	8,385	53,098	7,017	1,592 94
	New Zealand	49,350	12,923	8,160	1,947	244 80
	China	950,502	132,425	235,452	34,226	7,063 56
	Japan	21,600	2,958	3,600	618	108 00
	United States	4,512,003	1,024,848	4,191,968	950,855	125,759 04
	Total	5,599,096	1,181,876	4,493,396	994,919	134,801 88

OF IMPORTS—*Continued.*

FOR HOME CONSUMPTION.

Preferential Tariff.			Treaty Rates.			Total.		
Quantity.	Value.	Duty.	Quantity.	Value.	Duty.	Quantity.	Value.	DutyColl'd.
	$	$ cts.		$	$ cts.		$	$ cts.
....	37	5 55	....	....	....	....	37	5 55
....	....	....	....	....	....	....	597	134 39
....	....	....	....	....	....	....	116	26 10
....	37	5 55	....	....	....	....	750	166 04
....	7,465	1,493 00	....	....	....	....	8,377	1,766 60
....	....	....	....	....	....	....	84	25 20
....	....	....	....	....	....	....	181	54 30
....	....	....	....	....	....	....	34	10 20
....	....	....	....	....	....	....	302	90 60
....	....	....	....	....	....	....	3,563	1,068 90
....	....	....	....	....	....	....	185	55 50
....	....	....	....	....	....	....	2,827	848 10
....	....	....	....	....	....	....	52	15 60
....	....	....	....	....	....	....	10,544	3,163 20
....	7,465	1,493 00	....	....	....	....	26,149	7,098 20
....	9,298	1,859 60	....	....	....	....	9,973	2,062 10
....	....	....	....	....	....	....	757	227 10
....	....	....	....	....	....	....	18	5 40
....	....	....	....	....	....	....	608	182 40
....	....	....	....	....	....	....	73,117	21,935 10
....	9,298	1,859 60	....	....	....	....	84,473	24,412 10
....	60,981	15,245 25	....	....	....	....	61,463	15,413 95
....	....	....	....	....	....	....	2	0 70
....	....	....	....	....	....	....	293	102 55
....	....	....	....	....	....	....	98,414	34,444 90
....	60,981	15,245 25	....	....	....	....	160,172	49,962 10
....	64,638	12,927 60	....	....	....	....	65,985	13,331 70
....	....	....	....	....	....	....	279	83 70
....	....	....	....	....	....	....	601	180 30
....	....	....	....	....	....	....	126	37 80
....	....	....	....	....	....	....	278	83 40
....	....	....	....	....	....	....	1,325	397 50
....	....	....	....	....	....	....	10,474	3,142 20
....	....	....	....	....	....	....	525	157 50
....	....	....	....	....	....	....	136	40 80
....	....	....	....	....	....	....	1,341	402 30
....	....	....	....	....	....	....	83,556	25,066 80
....	64,638	12,927 60	....	....	....	....	164,626	42,924 00
Doz. 25	81	0 50	Doz.			Doz. 1,143	337	34 04
....	....	....	....	....	....	53,098	7,017	1,592 94
41,190	10,976	823 80	....	....	....	49,350	12,923	1,068 60
....	....	....	....	....	....	235,452	34,226	7,063 56
....	....	....	....	....	....	3,600	618	108 00
....	....	....	....	....	....	4,191,968	950,855	125,759 04
41,215	11,057	824 30	....	....	....	4,534,611	1,005,976	135,626 18

6 GEORGE V, A. 1916

No. 1.—General Statement

Articles Imported.	Countries.	Total Imports.		Entered		
		Quantity.	Value.	General Tariff.		
				Quantity.	Value.	Duty.
DUTIABLE GOODS—*Con.*			$		$	$ cts.
Elastic, round or flat, including garter elastic	Unit'd Kingdom	....	112,290	....	536	187 60
	France..........	....	241	....	239	83 65
	Germany......	....	337	....	337	117 95
	Switzerland....	....	404	....	404	141 40
	United States .	....	19,983	....	19,983	6,994 05
	Total......	....	133,255	....	21,499	7,524 65
Electric light carbons and carbon points, of all kinds, n.o.p.	Unit'd Kingdom	....	1,032	....	122	42 70
	Aust.-Hungary.	....	507	....	....	....
	Germany......	....	8,099	....	6,305	2,206 75
	Japan..........	....	3	....	3	1 05
	Spain..........	....	261	....	261	91 35
	Switzerland...	....	306	....	....	....
	United States .	....	35,822	....	36,112	12,639 20
	Total......	....	46,030	....	42,803	14,981 05
Electrodes, carbon, over 35 inches in circumference.	United States .	....	2,736	....	2,736	547 20
Incandescent lamp bulbs and glass tubing for use in the manufacture of incandescent lamps and mantle stockings for gas light.	Unit'd Kingdom	....	1,396	....	1,046	104 60
	Aust.-Hungary.	....	8,500	....	10,344	1,034 40
	France..........	....	1,372	....	1,372	137 20
	Germany......	....	4,118	....	4,234	423 40
	United States .	....	54,378	....	54,419	5,441 90
	Total......	....	69,764	....	71,415	7,141 50
Electric apparatus, n.o.p., insulators of all kinds and sockets, etc., and electric galvanic batteries; telegraph and telephone instruments.	Unit'd Kingdom	....	549,651	....	24,436	6,719 90
	Newfoundland..	....	49	....	89	24 48
	Aust.-Hungary.	....	2,185	....	711	195 53
	Belgium......	....	300	....	300	82 50
	Denmark......	....	133	....	133	36 58
	France..........	....	9,049	....	2,945	809 88
	Germany......	....	68,268	....	67,352	18,521 80
	Italy.........	....	8,175	....	7,613	2,093 58
	Japan.........	....	255	....	....	....
	Sweden........	....	41,098	....	1,309	359 98
	Switzerland...	....	1,978	....	1,975	543 13
	United States .	....	3,674,472	....	3,675,376	1,010,732 87
	Total......	....	4,355,613	....	3,782,239	1,040,120 23
Electric motors, generators and dynamos.	Unit'd Kingdom	....	174,896	....	3,708	1,019 70
	Newfoundland..	....	15	....	15	4 13
	Denmark......	....	66	....	66	18 15
	France.........	....	2,196	....	....	....
	Germany......	....	1,217	....	1,418	389 95
	Italy........	....	....	....	809	222 48
	Sweden........	....	24,759	....	8,520	2,343 00
	Switzerland...	....	222	....	41	11 28
	United States .	....	1,145,586	....	1,145,738	315,079 10
	Total......	....	1,348,957	....	1,160,315	319,087 79
Embroideries, not otherwise provided for.	Unit'd Kingdom	....	11,505	....	1,861	651 35
	Aust.-Hungary.	....	54	....	....	....
	Belgium.......	....	100	....	....	....
	France..........	....	7,747	....	2,625	918 75
	Germany......	....	3,020	....	3,020	1,057 00
	Holland.......	....	58	....	....	....
	Japan..........	....	834	....	92	32 20

OF IMPORTS—*Continued.*

FOR HOME CONSUMPTION.

	Preferential Tariff.			Treaty Rates.			Total.	
Quantity.	Value.	Duty.	Quantity.	Value.	Duty.	Quantity.	Value.	DutyColl'd.
	$	$ cts.		$	$ cts.		$	$ cts.
....	112,805	28,201 25	....			....	113,341	28,388 85
....	....	....		2	0 65	....	241	84 30
....	....	....	....	....	....	....	337	117 95
....	....	....	....	....	....	....	404	141 40
....	....	....	....	....	....	....	19,983	6,994 05
....	112,805	28,201 25	....	2	0 65	....	134,306	35,726 55
....	594	133 68	....	316	102 70	....	1,032	279 08
....	....	....	....	349	113 43	....	349	113 43
....	....	....	....	....	....	....	6,305	2,206 75
....	....	....	....	....	....	....	3	1 05
....	....	....	....	....	....	....	261	91 35
....	....	....	....	306	99 45	....	306	99 45
....	....	....	....	....	....	....	36,112	12,639 20
....	594	133 68	....	971	315 58	....	44,368	15,430 31
....	....	....	....	....	....	....	2,736	547 20
....	350	17 50	....	....	....	....	1,396	122 10
....	....	....	....	....	....	....	10,344	1,034 40
....	....	....	....	....	....	....	1,372	137 20
....	....	....	....	....	....	....	4,234	423 40
....	....	....	....	....	....	....	54,419	5,441 90
....	350	17 50	....	....	....	....	71,765	7,159 00
....	511,896	76,784 40	....	1,194	298 50	....	537,526	83,802 80
....	....	....	....	....	....	....	89	24 48
....	....	....	....	1,949	487 25	....	2,660	682 78
....	....	....	....	....	....	....	300	82 50
....	....	....	....	....	....	....	133	36 58
....	....	....	....	6,592	1,648 00	....	9,537	2,457 88
....	....	....	....	....	....	....	67,352	18,521 80
....	....	....	....	113	28 25	....	7,726	2,121 83
....	....	....	....	90	22 50	....	90	22 50
....	....	....	....	39,950	9,987 50	....	41,259	10,347 48
....	....	....	....	3	0 75	....	1,978	543 88
....	....	....	....	....	....	....	3,675,376	1,010,732 87
....	511,896	76,784 40	....	49,891	12,472 75	....	4,344,026	1,129,377 38
....	171,229	25,684 35	....	....	....	....	174,937	26,704 05
....	....	....	....	....	....	....	15	4 13
....	....	....	....	....	....	....	66	18 15
....	....	....	....	2,196	549 00	....	2,196	549 00
....	....	....	....	....	....	....	1,418	389 95
....	....	....	....	....	....	....	809	222 48
....	....	....	....	15,565	3,891 25	....	24,085	6,234 25
....	....	....	....	181	45 25	....	222	56 53
....	....	....	....	....	....	....	1,145,738	315,079 10
....	171,229	25,684 35	....	17,942	4,485 50	....	1,349,486	349,257 64
....	4,039	1,009 75	....	5,621	1,544 40	....	11,521	3,205 50
....	....	....	....	402	110 55	....	402	110 55
....	....	....	....	100	27 50	....	100	27 50
....	....	....	....	5,122	1,411 77	....	7,747	2,330 52
....	....	....	....	....	....	....	3,020	1,057 00
....	....	....	....	58	15 95	....	58	15 95
....	....	....	....	742	209 50	....	834	241 70

6 GEORGE V, A. 1916

No. 1.—General Statement

Articles Imported.	Countries.	Total Imports.		Entered		
		Quantity.	Value.	General Tariff.		
				Quantity.	Value.	Duty.
DUTIABLE GOODS—*Con.*			$		$	$ cts.
Embroideries not otherwise pro-	Sweden.........	....	3	....		
vided for—*Con.*	Switzerland ...	....	7,943	....	1,287	450 45
	United States...	....	16,689	....	16,689	5,841 15
	Total......	....	47,953	....	25,574	8,950 90
Emery and carborundum wheels	Unit'd Kingdom	....	798	....	268	67 00
and manufactures of emery or	France..........	....	76	....	76	19 00
carborundum.	Germany.......	....	133	....	133	33 25
	United States...	....	85,023	....	85,020	21,255 00
	Total......	....	86,030	....	85,497	21,374 25
Express parcels of small value.....	Unit'd Kingdom	....	1,836	....	5	1 50
	Newfoundland..	....	590	....	590	100 36
	United States...	....	1,822,758	....	1,822,758	514,773 39
	Total......	....	1,825,184	....	1,823,353	514,875 25
Fancy Goods, viz.:—						
Alabaster, spar, amber, terra	Unit'd Kingdom	....	4,018	....	531	159 30
cotta, or composition orna-	Australia........	....	10	....	10	3 00
ments.	France..........	....	2,340	....	234	70 20
	Germany.......	....	1,190	....	1,190	357 00
	Italy...........	....	1,360	....	487	146 10
	Switzerland....	....	38	....		
	United States...	....	29,103	....	29,103	8,730 90
	Total......	....	38,059	....	31,555	9,466 50
Bead ornaments..............	Unit'd Kingdom	....	4,471	....	1,534	460 20
	Hong Kong.....	....	12	....	12	3 60
	Aust.-Hungary.	....	174	....	6	1 80
	Belgium........	....	131	....		
	France..........	....	1,247	....	243	72 90
	Germany.......	....	1,172	....	1,172	351 60
	Italy...........	....	284	....		
	Japan..........	....	9	....	9	2 70
	United States...	....	7,984	....	7,984	2,395 20
	Total......	....	15,484	....	10,960	3,288 00
Boxes, fancy, ornamental cases	Unit'd Kingdom	....	83,185	....	3,880	1,358 00
and writing desks, etc.	B. W. Indies....	....	21	....		
	Hong Kong.....	....	85	....	85	29 75
	Aust.-Hungary.	....	506	....	175	61 25
	Belgium........	....	357	....	203	71 05
	China...........	....	16	....	16	5 60
	France..........	....	4,444	....	865	302 75
	Germany.......	....	23,304	....	23,319	8,161 65
	Italy,.........	....	3	....	3	1 05
	Japan.........	....	6,102	....	196	68 60
	Portugal.......	....	448	....	448	156 80
	Sweden.........	....	10	....	10	3 50
	Switzerland....	....	196	....	39	13 65
	Turkey.........	....	2	....	2	0 70
	United States...	....	96,647	....	96,731	33,855 85
	Total......	....	215,326	....	125,972	44,090 20

OF IMPORTS—*Continued.*

FOR HOME CONSUMPTION.

Preferential Tariff.			Treaty Rates.			Total.		
Quantity.	Value.	Duty.	Quantity.	Value.	Duty.	Quantity.	Value.	DutyColl'd.
	$	$ cts.		$	$ cts.		$	$ cts.
....	....	....	....	3	0 84	....	3	0 84
....	....	....	....	6,656	1,894 85	....	7,943	2,345 30
....	....	....	....	....	....	....	16,689	5,841 15
—........	4,039	1,009 75	....	18,704	5,215 36	....	48,317	15,176 01
....	530	92 77	....	....	....	....	798	159 77
....	....	....	....	....	....	....	76	19 00
....	....	....	....	....	....	....	133	33 25
....	....	....	....	....	....	....	85,020	21,255 00
....	530	92 77	....	....	....	....	86,027	21,467 02
....	1,831	418 33	....	....	....	....	1,836	419 83
....	....	....	....	....	....	....	590	100 36
....	....	....	....	....	....	....	1,822,758	514,773 39
....	1,831	418 33	....	....	....	....	1,825,184	515,293 58
....	1,390	278 00	....	2,09	576 67	....	4,018	1,013 97
....	....	....	....	....	....	....	10	3 00
....	....	....	....	2,106	579 26	....	2,340	649 46
....	....	....	....	....	....	....	1,190	357 00
....	....	....	....	1,102	303 05	....	1,589	449 15
....	....	....	....	38	10 45	....	38	10 45
....	....	....	....	....	....	....	29,103	8,730 90
....	1,390	278 00	....	5,343	1,469 43	....	38,288	11,213 93
....	1,115	223 00	....	1,822	501 11	....	4,471	1,184 31
....	....	....	....	....	....	....	12	3 60
....	....	....	....	168	46 20	....	174	48 00
....	....	....	....	131	36 0	....	131	36 02
....	....	....	....	1,004	276 10	....	1,247	349 00
....	....	....	....	....	....	....	1,172	351 60
....	....	....	....	284	78 10	....	284	78 10
....	....	....	....	8	2 20	....	17	4 90
....	....	....	....	....	....	....	7,984	2,395 20
....	1,115	223 00	....	3,417	939 73	....	15,492	4,450 73
....	79,005	17,776 65	....	302	90 60	....	83,187	19,225 25
....	21	4 72	....	....	....	....	21	4 72
....	....	....	....	....	....	....	85	29 75
....	....	....	....	331	99 30	....	506	160 55
....	....	....	....	154	46 20	....	357	11 25
....	....	....	....	....	....	....	..16	5 60
....	....	....	....	3,579	1,073 70	....	4,444	1,376 45
....	....	....	....	....	....	....	23,319	8,161 65
....	....	....	....	....	....	....	3	1 05
....	....	....	....	5,584	1,675 20	....	5,780	1,743 80
....	....	....	....	....	....	....	448	156 80
....	....	....	....	....	....	....	10	3 50
....	....	....	....	157	47 10	....	196	60 75
....	....	....	....	....	....	....	2	0 70
....	....	....	....	....	....	....	96,731	33,855 85
....	79,026	17,781 37	....	10,107	3,032 10	....	215,105	64,903 67

6 GEORGE V, A. 1916

No. 1.—General Statement

Articles Imported.	Countries.	Total Imports.		Entered		
		Quantity.	Value.	General Tariff.		
				Quantity.	Value.	Duty.
DUTIABLE GOODS—*Con.*			$		$	$ cts.
Fancy goods—*Con.*						
Braids, cords, fringes, tassels, n.o.p.	Unit'd Kingdom	....	123,120	....	27,475	9,616 25
	Hong Kong.....	....	56	....	56	19 60
	Aust.-Hungary .	....	862	....	325	113 75
	Belgium........	....	1,716	....	1,387	485 45
	China.......	....	2	....	2	0 70
	France.........	...●.....	23,827	....	6,160	2,156 00
	Germany......	....	23,368	....	23,475	8,216 25
	Holland.......	....	594	....	589	206 15
	Japan.........	....	3	....	1	0 35
	Switzerland....	....	1,374	....	179	62 65
	Turkey........	....	3	....	3	1 05
	United States..	....	132,637	....	131,616	46,065 60
	Total......	....	307,562	....	191,268	66,943 80
Tinsel thread and tinsel wire, for the manufacture of braids, cords, tassels, ribbons or trimmings	France..........	....	440	....	· 440	44 00
	United States...	....	9,642	....	9,642	964 20
	Total......	....	10,082	....	10,082	1,008 20
Cases for jewellery, watches, silverware, plated ware and cutlery	Unit'd Kingdom	....	8,358	....	1,062	371 70
	Germany.	....	12,735	....	15,377	5,381 95
	Switzerland....	....	96	....	....	....
	United States...	....	8,553	....	8,553	2,993 55
	Total......	....	29,743	....	24,992	8,747 20
Fans	Unit'd Kingdom	....	120	....	22	6 60
	B. W. Indies....	....	2	....	....	....
	Hong Kong....	....	91	....	91	27 30
	Aust.-Hungary .	....	257	....	....	....
	China..........	....	94	....	94	28 20
	France.........	....	341	....	1	0 30
	Germany......	....	238	....	238	71 40
	Japan.........	....	1,756	.....:...	376	112 80
	Spain.....	....	406	....	....	....
	United States...	....	2,008	....	2,008	602 40
	Total......	....	5,313	....	2,830	849 00
Feathers, fruits, grains, leaves and flowers, artificial, suitable for ornamenting hats.	Unit'd Kingdom	....	165,583	....	57,106	15,704 35
	Hong Kong.....	....	2	....	2	0 55
	Aust.-Hungary .	....	614	....	401	110 27
	Belgium........	....	300	....	300	82 50
	China..........	....	172	..·....	172	47 30
	France.........	....	69,062	....	69,041	18,986 47
	Germany......	....	19,999	....	19,810	5,447 95
	Japan.........	....	209	....	201	55 27
	Switzerland....	....	26	....	26	7 15
	United States...	....	240,501	....	240,501	66,138 57
	Total......	....	496,468	....	387,560	106,580 38
Feathers, fancy, undressed.....	Unit'd Kingdom	....	57,285	....	16,278	2,441 70
	B. S. Africa....	....	7,125	....	50	7 50
	B. India.......	....	2,373	....	2,373	355 95
	B. E. Indies, other	....	75	....	....	....
	Aust.-Hungary .	....	1,507	....	904	135 60
	Belgium........	....	100	......:...	100	15 00
	China..........	....	2,495	....	3,913	586 95
	Cuba..........	....	180	....	225	33,75
	Denmark......	....	128	....	128	19 20

SESSIONAL PAPER No. 11

OF IMPORTS—*Continued.*

FOR HOME CONSUMPTION.

	Preferential Tariff.			Treaty Rates.			Total.	
Quantity.	Value.	Duty.	Quantity.	Value.	Duty.	Quantity.	Value.	DutyColl'd.
	$	$ cts.		$	$ cts.		$	$ cts.
....	80,018	20,004 50	....	15,700	5,102 50	....	123,193	34,723 25
....	....	....	....	....	....	....	56	19 60
....	....	....	....	806	261 95	....	1,131	375 70
....	....	....	....	329	106 92	....	1,716	592 37
....	....	....	....	....	....	....	2	0 70
....	....	....	....	17,467	-5,677 15	....	23,627	7,833 15
....	....	....	....	....	....	....	23,475	8,216 25
....	....	....	....	5	1 62	....	594	207 77
....	....	....	....	2	0 65	....	3	1 00
....	....	....	....	1,195	383 37	....	1,374	451 02
....	....	....	....	....	....	....	3	1 05
....	....	....	....	....	....	....	131,616	46,065 60
....	80,018	20,004 51	....	35,504	11,539 16	....	306,790	98,487 46
....	....	....	....	....	....	....	440	44 00
....	....	....	....	....	....	....	9,642	964 20
....	....	....	....	....	....	....	10,082	1,008 20
....	7,294	1,641 22	....	....	....	....	8,356	2,012 92
....	....	....	....	....	....	....	15,377	5,381 95
....	....	....	....	99	29 70	....	99	29 70
....	....	....	....	....	....	....	8,553	2,993 55
....	7,294	1,641 22	....	99	29 70	....	32,385	10,418 12
....	19	3 80	....	79	21 72	....	120	32 12
....	2	0 40	....	....	....	....	2	0 40
....	....	....	....	....	....	....	91	27 30
....	....	....	....	257	70 67	....	257	70 67
....	....	....	....	....	....	....	94	28 20
....	....	....	....	340	93 50	....	341	93 80
....	....	....	....	....	....	....	238	71 40
....	....	....	....	1,399	384 80	....	1,775	· 497 60
....	....	....	....	406	111 65	....	406	111 65
....	....	....	....	....	....	....	2,008	602 40
....	21	4 20	....	2,481	682 34	....	5,332	1,535 54
....	108,737	21,747 40	....	....	....	....	165,843	37,451 75
....	....	....	....	....	....	....	2	0 55
....	....	....	....	....	....	....	401	110 27
....	....	....	....	....	....	....	300	82 50
....	....	....	....	....	....	....	172	47 30
....	....	....	....	....	....	....	69,041	18,986 47
....	....	....	....	....	....	....	19,810	5,447 95
....	....	....	....	....	....	....	201	55 27
....	....	....	....	....	....	....	26	7 15
....	....	....	....	....	....	....	240,501	66,138 57
....	108,737	21,747 40	....	....	....	....	496,297	128,327 78
....	35,419	3,541 90	....	5,588	698 53	....	57,285	6,682 13
....	7,075	707 50	....	....	....	....	7,125	715 00
....	....	....	....	....	....	....	2,373	355 95
....	75	7 50	....	....	....	....	75	7 50
....	....	....	....	603	75 36	....	1,507	210 96
....	....	....	....	....	....	....	100	15 00
....	....	....	....	....	....	....	3,913	586 95
....	....	....	....	....	....	....	225	33 75
....	....	....	....	....	....	....	123	19 20

No. 1.—General Statement

Articles Imported.	Countries.	Total Imports.		Entered		
				General Tariff.		
		Quantity.	Value.	Quantity.	Value.	Duty.
			$		$	$ cts.
DUTIABLE GOODS—*Con.*						
Fancy goods—*Con.*						
Feathers, fancy, undressed—*Con.*	France..........	....	27,811	....	27,049	4,057 35
	Germany.........	....	3,210	....	3,210	481 50
	Mexico..........	....	180	....	180	27 00
	Russia..........	....	44	....	44	6 60
	United States...	....	34,417	....	34,417	5,162 55
	Total......	....	136,930	....	88,871	13,330 65
Feathers, fancy, n.o.p. and manufactures of feathers, n.o.p	Unit'd Kingdom	....	87,808	....	34,533	9,496 77
	B W Indies....	....	25	....	....	....
	Hong Kong.....	....	7	....	7	1 92
	Aust.-Hungary.	....	54	....	54	14 85
	Belgium........	....	121	....	121	33 27
	China..........	....	40	....	40	11 00
	France..........	....	51,005	....	50,955	14,012 82
	Germany......	....	3,302	....	3,302	908 05
	Japan..........	....	42	....	42	11 55
	United States...	....	73,717	....	73,715	20,271 98
	Total......	....	216,121	....	162,769	44,762 21
Feathers, ostrich and vulture, dressed.	Unit'd Kingdom	....	87,679	....	6,411	1,763 02
	Belgium........	....	138	....	138	37 95
	France..........	....	18,969	....	18,969	5,216 60
	Germany.	....	2,570	....	2,570	706 75
	Italy..........	....	20	....	20	5 50
	United States...	....	12,962	....	12,962	3,564 56
	Total......	....	122,338	....	41,070	11,294 38
Ivory or bone dice, draughts, chessmen, etc.	Unit'd Kingdom	....	194	....	9	1 57
	Hong Kong.....	....	18	....	18	3 15
	France..........	....	82	....	82	14 39
	United States...	....	56	....	56	9 80
	Total......	....	350	....	165	28 91
Lace, n.o.p., lace collars and all manufactures of lace; nets and nettings of cotton, linen, silk or other material, n.o.p.	Unit'd Kingdom	....	540,259	....	62,897	22,013 95
	B. India.......	....	300	....	51	17 85
	Hong Kong....	....	16	....	16	5 60
	Malta..........	....	186	....	136	47 60
	Aust.-Hungary.	....	548	....	484	169 40
	Azores and Madeira	....	226	....	226	79 10
	Belgium........	....	884	....	402	140 70
	China.........	....	250	....	250	87 50
	France..........	....	107,509	....	42,360	14,826 00
	Germany......	....	43,961	....	44,273	15,495 55
	Holland.......	....	102	....	102	35 70
	Italy..........	....	129	....	129	45 15
	Japan..........	....	5,043	....	123	-43 05
	Portugal.......	....	18	....	18	6 30
	Switzerland....	....	16,357	....	2,542	889 70
	Turkey........	....	492	....	492	172 20
	United States...	....	99,122	....	99,122	34,692 70
	Total......	....	815,402	....	253,623	88,768 05
Statues and statuettes of any material.	Unit'd Kingdom	....	2,995	....	957	287 10
	Hong Kong.....	....	16	....	16	4 80
	Aust.-Hungary.	....	89	....	84	25 20
	Belgium........	....	206	....	120	36 00
	France..........	....	26,355	....	5,083	1,524 90

OF IMPORTS—*Continued.*

FOR HOME CONSUMPTION.

	Preferential Tariff.			Treaty Rates.			Total.	
Quantity.	Value.	Duty.	Quantity.	Value.	Duty.	Quantity.	Value.	DutyColl'd.
	$	$ cts.		$	$ cts.		$	$ cts.
....	....	....	....	762	95 25	....	27,811	4,152 60
....	....	....	....	....	....	....	3,210	481 50
....	....	....	....	....	....	....	180	27 00
....	....	....	....	....	....	....	44	6 60
....	....	....	....	....	....	....	34,417	5,102 55
....	42,569	4,256 90	....	6,953	869 14	....	138,393	18,456 69
....	53,351	10,670 20	....	....	....	....	87,884	20,166 97
....	....	....	....	....	....	....	7	1 92
....	....	....	....	....	....	....	54	14 85
....	....	....	....	....	....	....	121	33 27
....	....	....	....	....	....	....	40	11 00
....	....	....	....	....	....	....	50,955	14,012 12
....	....	....	....	....	....	....	3,302	908 05
....	....	....	....	....	....	....	42	11 55
....	....	....	....	....	....	....	73,715	20,271 98
....	53,351	10,670 20	....	....	....	....	216,120	55,432 41
....	81,293	16,258 60	....	....	....	....	87,704	18,021 62
....	....	....	....	....	....	....	138	37 95
....	....	....	....	....	....	....	18,969	5,216 60
....	....	....	....	....	....	....	2,570	706 75
....	....	....	....	....	....	....	20	5 50
....	....	....	....	....	....	....	12,962	3,564 56
....	81,293	16,258 60	....	....	....	....	122,363	27,552 98
....	185	27 75	....	....	....	....	194	29 32
....	....	....	....	....	....	....	18	3 15
....	....	....	....	....	....	....	82	14 39
....	....	....	....	....	....	....	56	9 80
....	185	27 75	....	....	....	....	350	56 66
....	397,909	99,477 25	....	80,724	23,014 95	....	541,530	144,506 15
....	249	62 25	....	....	....	....	300	80 10
....	....	....	....	....	....	....	16	5 60
....	....	....	....	50	13 75	....	186	61 35
....	....	....	....	64	17 60	....	548	187 .0
....	....	....	....	....	....	....	226	79 10
....	....	....	....	482	156 64	....	884	297 34
....	....	....	....	....	....	....	250	87 50
....	....	....	....	67,660	18,858 21	....	110,020	33,684 21
....	....	....	....	....	....	....	44,273	15,495 55
....	....	....	....	....	....	....	102	35 70
....	....	....	....	....	....	....	129	45 15
....	....	....	....	3,986	1,110 04	....	4,109	1,153 09
....	....	....	....	....	....	....	18	6 30
....	....	....	....	13,143	3,645 40	...	15,685	4,535 10
....	....	....	....	....	....	....	492	172 20
....	....	....	....	....	....	....	99,122	34,692 70
....	398,158	99,539 50	....	166,109	46,816 59	....	817,890	235,124 14
....	1,222	244 40	....	616	169 40	....	2,795	700 90
....	....	....	....	....	....	....	16	4 80
....	....	....	....	5	1 37	....	89	26 57
....	....	....	....	86	23 65	....	206	59 65
....	....	....	....	20,170	5,547 17	....	25,253	7,072 07

6 GEORGE V, A. 1916

No. 1.—General Statement

Articles Imported.	Countries.	Total Imports.		Entered		
		Quantity.	Value.	General Tariff.		
				Quantity.	Value.	Duty.
			$		$	$ cts.
DUTIABLE GOODS—*Con.*						
Fancy goods—*Con.*						
Statues and statuettes of any material—*Con.*	Germany	....	5,270	....	5,098	1,529 40
	Greece	....	425	....	425	127 50
	Holland	....	11	....	....	....
	Italy	....	16,923	....	10,731	3,219 30
	Japan	....	663	....	4	1 20
	Portugal	....	70	....	70	21 00
	Switzerland	....	64	....	....	....
	United States	....	25,891	....	25,891	7,767 30
	Total	....	78,978	....	48,479	14,543 70
Toilet and manicure sets	Unit'd Kingdom	....	5,148	....	675	236 25
	France	....	91	....	56	19 60
	Germany	....	1,040	....	1,040	364 00
	United States	....	19,015	....	19,646	6,876 10
	Total	....	25,294	....	21,417	7,495 95
Toys, and dolls of all kinds	Unit'd Kingdom	....	72,045	....	9,988	2,996 40
	Hong Kong	....	1,085	....	102	30 60
	Aust.-Hungary	....	4,896	....	3,507	1,052 10
	Belgium	....	2,231	....	2,174	652 20
	China	....	15	....	15	4 50
	France	....	13,713	....	3,480	1,044 00
	Germany	....	245,294	....	247,044	74,113 20
	Holland	....	2,111	....	2,071	621 30
	Italy	....	67	....	67	20 10
	Japan	....	28,679	....	1,633	489 90
	Spain	....	24	....	24	7 20
	Switzerland	....	46	....	6	1 80
	United States	....	285,740	....	285,910	85,773 00
	Total	....	655,946	....	556,021	166,806 30
Feathers, bed and other, undressed, n.o.p.	Unit'd Kingdom	....	4,823	....	3,103	465 45
	B. W. Indies	....	756	....	....	3 00
	Aust.-Hungary	....	20	....	20	3 00
	France	....	2,358	....	2,358	353 70
	Germany	....	330	....	330	49 50
	Russia	....	30	....	30	4 50
	United States	....	18,516	....	18,516	2,777 40
	Total	....	26,833	....	24,357	3,653 55
Feathers, bed and other, dressed, n.o.p.	Unit'd Kingdom	....	10,752	....	120	33 00
	France	....	393	....	393	108 07
	Germany	....	461	....	461	126 77
	United States	....	881	....	881	242 33
	Total	....	12,487	....	1,855	510 17
Featherbone, plain or covered, in coils.	Unit'd Kingdom	....	33	....	33	6 60
	United States	....	1,171	....	1,171	234 20
	Total	....	1,204	....	1,204	240 80
Fertilizers, compounded or manufactured.	Unit'd Kingdom	....	51,023	....	1,147	114 70
	Belgium	....	13,144	....	13,144	1,314 40
	Germany	....	471	....	471	47 10
	Holland	....	3,652	....	3,652	365 20
	Norway	....	163	....	163	16 30
	United States	....	646,131	....	646,131	64,613 10
	Total	....	714,584	....	664,708	66,470 80

SESSIONAL PAPER No. 11

OF IMPORTS—*Continued.*

FOR]HOME CONSUMPTION.

Preferential Tariff.			Treaty Rates.			Total.		
Quantity.	Value.	Duty.	Quantity.	Value.	Duty.	Quantity.	Value.	DutyColl'd.
	$	$ cts.		$	$ cts.		$	$ cts.
....	....	....	....	....	....	....	5,098	1,529 40
....	....	....	....	....	....	....	425	127 50
....	....	...	....	11	3 02	....	11	3 02
....	....	....	....	6 175	1,698 12	....	16,906	4,917 42
....	....	....	....	659	181 12	....	663	182 32
....	....	....	....	....	....	....	70	21 00
....	....	.	....	64	17 60	....	64	17 60
....	....	....	....	....	....	....	25,891	7,767 30
....	1,222	244 40	....	27,786	7,641 45	.....	77,487	22,429 55
....	4,477	1,007 40	....	....	....	....	5,152	1,243 65
....	....	....	....	35	10 50	....	91	30 10
....	....	....	....	....	....	....	1,040	364 00
....	....	....	....	....	....	....	19,646	6,876 10
....	4,477	1,007 40	....	35	10 50	....	25,929	8,513 85
....	60,267	12,053 40	....	1,095	301 12	....	71,350	15,350 92
....	....	....	....	983	270 32	....	1,085	300 92
....	....	....	....	1,501	412 77	....	5,008	1,464 87
....	....	....	....	57	15 67	....	2,231	667 87
....	....	....	....	....	....	....	15	4 50
....	....	....	....	10,233	2,814 27	....	13,713	3,858 27
....	....	....	....	....	....	....	247 044	74,113 20
....	....	....	....	40	11 00	....	2,111	632 30
....	....	....	....	....	....	....	67	20 10
....	....	....	....	27,026	7,432 18	....	28,659	7,922 08
....	....	....	....	....	....	....	24	7 20
....	....	....	....	40	11 00	....	46	12 80
....	....	....	....	....	....	....	285,910	85,773 00
....	60,267	12,053 40	....	40,975	11,268 33	....	657,263	190,128 03
....	1,720	172 00	....	....	....	....	4,823	637 45
....	756	75 60	....	....	....	....	756	75 60
....	....	....	....	....	....	....	20	3 00
....	....	....	....	....	....	....	2,358	353 70
....	....	....	....	....	....	....	330	49 50
....	....	....	....	....	....	....	30	4 50
....	....	....	....	....	....	....	18,516	2,777 40
....	2,476	247 60	....	....	....	....	26,833	3,901 15
....	10,632	2,126 40	....	....	....	....	10,752	2,159 40
....	....	....	....	....	....	....	393	108 07
....	....	....	....	....	....	....	461	126 77
....	....	....	....	....	....	....	881	242 33
....	10,632	2,126 40	....	....	....	....	12,487	2,636 57
....	....	....	....	....	....	....	33	6 60
....	....	....	....	....	....	....	1,171	234 20
....	....	....	....	....	....	....	1,204	240 80
....	49,876	2,493 80	....	....	....	....	51,023	2,608 50
....	....	....	....	....	....	....	13,144	1,314 40
....	....	....	....	....	....	....	471	47 10
....	....	....	....	....	....	....	3,652	365 20
....	....	....	....	....	....	....	163	16 30
....	....	....	....	....	....	....	646,131	64,613 10
....	49,876	2,493 80	....	....	....	....	714,584	68,964 60

11—ii—6

6 GEORGE V, A. 1916

No. 1.—GENERAL STATEMENT

Articles Imported.	Countries.	Total Imports.		Entered		
		Quantity.	Value.	General Tariff.		
				Quantity.	Value.	Duty.
			$		$	$ cts.
DUTIABLE GOODS—*Con.*						
Fibre, Kartavert, indurated fibre'	Unit'd Kingdom	....	4,649	....	51	12 75
vulcanized fibre and like ma	Italy..........	....	1	....	1	0 25
terial and manufactures of, n.o.p'	United States...	....	97,326	....	97,450	24,362 50
	Total.......	....	101,976	....	97,502	24,375 50
Fireworks, firecrackers and tor-	Unit'd Kingdom	....	1,792	....	71	17 75
pedoes, all kinds.	Hong Kong.....	....	6,038	....	6,038	1,509 50
	China,..........	....	3,412	....	3,412	853 00
	France..........	....	49	....	49	12 25
	Germany......	....	4	....	4	1 00
	Japan..........	....	473	....	473	118 25
	United States..	....	12,902	....	12,902	3,225 50
	Total......	....	24,670	....	22,949	5,737 25
Fish—		Lb.		Lb.		
Cod, haddock, ling and pollock,	Newfoundland..	25	2	25	2	0 25
fresh imported otherwise than	United States...	213,279	10,575	213,279	10,575	2,132 79
in barrels, &c.	Total......	213,304	10,577	213,304	10,577	2,133 04
Cod, haddock, ling and pollock,	Unit'd Kingdom	45,849	2,888	....	....	....
dry salted.	Newfoundland..	240	32	240	32	2 40
	Alaska..........	150	15	150	15	1 50
	Japan..........	519	44	519	44	5 19
	Miquelon and					
	St-Pierre......	657,958	37,935	95	4	0 95
	United States...	98,091	8,227	54,073	5,145	540 73
	Total......	802,807	49,141	55,077	5,240	550 77
Cod, haddock, ling and pollock,	United States...	276	19	276	19	2 76
wet salted.						
Cod, haddock, ling and pollock,	United States...	368	26	....	....	....
Smoked.						
Halibut, fresh, not in barrels...	Alaska..........	2,113,768	103,951	291,666	15,093	2,916 66
	United States...	1,131,424	55,492	1,104,662	54,454	11,046 62
	Total......	3,245,192	159,443	1,396,328	69,547	13,963 28
Halibut, pickled, in barrels.....	United States...	400	16	400	16	4 00
Herrings, fresh, not in barrels..	United States...	12,295	547	10,795	504	107 95
Herrings, pickled or salted.....	Unit'd Kingdom	1,494,699	64,854	158,598	7,905	792 99
	Hong Kong.....	974	116	974	116	4 87
	Belgium........	53	2	53	2	0 26
	China..........	2,840	329	2,840	329	14 20
	Holland........	531,222	29,962	531,222	29,962	2,656 15
	Japan..........	380	19	380	19	1 90
	Norway........	47,280	2,114	48,380	2,140	241 90
	Sweden........	120	7	120	7	0 60
	United States...	250,078	14,379	250,078	14,879	1,250 39
	Total......	2,327,646	111,782	992,645	54,859	4,963 26
Herrings, smoked..............	United States...	720	77	720	77	7 20

SESSIONAL PAPER No. 11

OF IMPORTS—*Continued.*

FOR HOME CONSUMPTION.

Preferential Tariff.			Treaty Rates.			Total.		
Quantity.	Value.	Duty.	Quantity.	Value.	Duty.	Quantity.	Value.	DutyColl'd.
	$ 4,598	$ cts. 804 68		$	$ cts.		$ 4,649	$ cts. 817 43
....	....	....	....	....	....	....	1	0 25
....	....	....	....	....	....	....	97,450	24,362 50
....	4,598	804 68	....	....	....	....	102,100	25,180 18
....	1,721	301 18	....	....	....	....	1,792	318 93
....	....	....	....	....	....	....	6,038	1,509 50
....	....	....	....	....	....	....	3,412	853 00
....	....	....	....	....	....	....	49	12 25
....	....	....	....	....	....	....	4	1 00
....	....	....	....	....	....	....	473	118 25
....	....	....	....	....	....	....	12,902	3,225 50
....	1,721	301 18	....	....	....	....	24,670	6,038 43
Lb.			Lb.			Lb.		
....	....	....	....	....	....	25	2	0 25
....	....	....	....	....	....	213,279	10,575	2,132 79
....	....	....	....	....	....	213,304	10,577	2,133 04
112	8	0 50	....	....	....	112	8	0 56
....	....	....	....	....	....	240	32	2 40
....	....	....	....	....	....	150	15	1 50
....	....	....	....	....	....	519	44	5 19
....	....	....	....	....	....	95	4	0 95
....	....	....	....	....	....	54,073	5,145	540 73
112	8	0 56	....	....	....	55,189	5,248	551 33
....	....	....	....	....	....	276	19	2 76
....	....	....	....	....	....	....	....	....
....	....	....	....	....	....	291,666	15,093	2,916 66
....	....	....	....	....	....	1,104,662	54,454	11,046 62
....	....	....	....	....	....	1,396,328	69,547	13,963 28
....	....	....	....	....	....	400	16	4 00
....	....	....	....	....	....	10,795	504	107 95
1,336,461	56,978	4,677 63	....	....	....	1,495,059	64,883	5,470 62
....	....	....	....	....	....	974	116	4 87
....	....	....	....	....	....	53	2	0 26
....	....	....	....	....	....	2,840	329	14 20
....	....	....	....	....	....	531,222	29,962	2,656 15
....	....	....	....	....	....	380	19	1 90
....	....	....	....	....	....	48,380	2,140	241 90
....	....	....	....	....	....	120	7	0 60
....	....	....	....	....	....	250,078	14,379	1,250 39
1,336,461	56,978	4,677 63	....	....	....	2,329,106	111,837	9,640 89
....	....	....	....	....	....	720	77	7 20

No. 1.—GENERAL STATEMENT

Articles Imported.	Countries.	TOTAL IMPORTS.		ENTERED		
		Quantity.	Value.	General Tariff.		
				Quantity.	Value.	Duty.
DUTIABLE GOODS—*Con.*		Lb.	$	Lb.	$	$ cts.
Fish—*Con.*						
Mackerel, fresh..............	Unit'd Kingdom	360	28	....	....	....
	United States...	408	53	408	53	4 08
	Total.......	768	81	408	53	4 08
Mackerel, pickled..............	Unit'd Kingdom	2,000	73	....	....	....
	United States...	2,649	390	2,244	341	22 44
	Total.......	4,649	463	2,244	341	22 44
Sea fish, other, fresh, not in barrels.	Unit'd Kingdom	38	14	....	....	4 00
	Hong Kong.....	400	35	400	35	
	China..........	120	36	120	36	1 20
	Miquelon and St. Pierre....	50	2	50	2	0 50
	United States...	27,625	1,875	27,625	1,875	276 25
	Total.......	28,233	1,962	28,195	1,948	281 95
Sea fish, other, pickled, in barrels	United States...	3,488	239	3,488	239	34 88
Sea fish. other, preserved, n.o.p.	Unit'd Kingdom	67,485	6,403	180	7	2 10
	Hong Kong.....	120	5	120	5	1 50
	China..........	412	26	412	26	7 80
	France..........	100	13	100	13	3 90
	Norway........	47,007	2,761	45,321	2,742	822 60
	United States...	18,880	2,317	18,880	2,317	695 10
	Total.......	134,004	11,525	65,013	5,110	1,533 00
		Brl.		Brl.		
Oysters, fresh, in shell..........	United States...	3,385	17,745	3,385	17,745	4,436 25
		Gal.		Gal.		
Oysters, shelled, in bulk........	United States...	173,958	210,839	173,958	210,839	17,395 80
		Cans.		Cans.		
Oysters, canned, in cans not over one pint.	Unit'd Kingdom	240	21	240	21	7 20
	Japan..........	384	22	384	22	11 52
	United States...	231,104	21,883	234,684	23,856	7,040 52
	Total.......	231,728	21,926	235,308	23,899	7,059 24
Oysters, canned, in cans over one pint and not over one quart.	United States...	3,094	1,451	2,554	1,180	127 70
		Qt.		Qt.		
Oysters, canned, in cans exceeding one quart (provided that a fraction over a quart shall be computed as a quart for duty purposes).	United States...	484	246	436	223	21 80
		Lb.		Lb.		
Oysters, prepared or preserved, n.o.p.	Hong Kong.....	8,721	2,800	8,721	2,800	840 00
	China..........	1,800	158	1,800	158	47 40
	Japan..........	28	14	28	14	4 20
	United States...	15,536	1,999	20,151	2,205	661 50
	Total.......	26,085	4,971	30,700	5,177	1,553 10

SESSIONAL PAPER No. 11

OF IMPORTS—*Continued.*

FOR HOME CONSUMPTION.

Preferential Tariff.			Treaty Rates.			Total.		
Quantity.	Value.	Duty.	Quantity.	Value.	Duty.	Quantity.	Value.	DutyColl'd.
Lb.	$	$ cts.	Lb.	$	$ cts.	Lb.	$	$ cts.
360	28	1 80	....	....	....	360	28	1 80
....	....	....	....	....	....	408	53	4 08
360	28	1 80	....	....	....	768	81	5 88
....	....	....	....	....	....	2,244	341	22 44
....	....	....	....	....	....	2,244	341	22 44
38	14	0 19	....	....	....	38	14	0 19
....	....	....	....	....	....	400	35	4 00
....	....	....	....	....	....	120	36	1 20
....	....	....	....	....	....	50	2	0 50
....	....	....	....	....	....	27,625	1,875	276 25
38	14	0 19	....	....	....	28,233	1,962	282 14
....	....	....	....	....	....	3,488	239	34 88
63,926	6,209	1,086 64	....	....	....	64,106	6,216	1,088 74
....	....	....	....	....	....	120	5	1 50
....	....	....	....	....	....	412	26	7 80
....	....	....	....	....	....	100	13	3 90
....	....	....	....	....	....	45,321	2,742	822 60
....	....	....	....	....	....	18,880	2,317	695 10
63,926	6,209	1,086 64	....	....	....	128,939	11,319	2,619 64
Brl.			Brl.			Brl.		
....	....	....	....	....	....	3,385	17,745	4,436 25
Gal.			Gal.			Gal.		
....	....	....	....	....	....	173,958	210,839	17,395 80
Cans			Cans.			Cans.		
....	....	....	....	....	....	240	21	7 20
....	....	....	....	....	....	384	22	11 52
....	....	....	....	....	....	234,684	23,856	7,040 52
....	....	....	....	....	....	235,308	23,899	7,059 24
....	....	....	....	....	....	2,554	1,180	127 70
Qt.			Qt.			Qt.		
....	....	....	....	....	....	436	223	21 80
Lb.			Lb.			Lb.		
....	....	....	....	....	....	8,721	2,800	840 00
....	....	....	....	....	....	1,800	158	47 40
....	....	....	....	....	....	28	14	4 20
....	....	....	....	....	....	20,151	2,205	661 50
....	....	....	....	....	....	30,700	5,177	1,553 10

. 6 GEORGE V, A. 1916

No. 1.—General Statement

Articles Imported.	Countries.	Total Imports.		Entered		
		Quantity.	Value.	General Tariff.		
				Quantity.	Value.	Duty.
DUTIABLE GOODS—*Con.*			$		$	$ cts.
Fish—*Con.*						
Lobsters, fresh	United States...	....	2,650	....	2,650	662 50
		Lb.		Lb.		
Lobsters, canned, n.o.p.	New Zealand...	2,153	481	....	....	....
Bait fish, fresh, not in barrels.	United States...	165,055	4,061	74,647	1,741	746 47
Bait fish, salted, not in barrels.	United States...	4,000	120	1,000	120	40 00
Salmon, fresh	Alaska	....	....	11,451	573	114 51
	United States...	105,933	5,296	105,933	5,296	1,059 33
	Total......	105,933	5,296	117,384	5,869	1,173 84
Salmon, smoked	United States...	1,867	371	1,867	371	18 67
Salmon, canned, prepared or preserved, n.o.p.	Unit'd Kingdom	....	28	....	28	8 40
	United States...	....	429	....	569	170 70
	Total......	....	457	....	597	179 10
Salmon, pickled or salted	United States...	9,957	1,018	10,407	1,074	104 07
Fish, smoked or boneless	Unit'd Kingdom	25,065	1,651	11,025	734	110 25
	Kong Kong	190	24	190	24	1 90
	Norway	2,625	146	2,625	146	26 25
	United States...	6,978	558	6,378	528	63 78
	Total......	34,858	2,379	20,218	1,432	202 18
		Boxes.		Boxes.		
Anchovies, sardines, sprats and other fish, packed in oil or otherwise, in tin boxes weighing over 20 ounces and not over 36 ounces each.	Unit'd Kingdom	1,683	171	....	....	....
	Hong Kong	8,958	1,860	8,958	1,860	537 48
	China	914	144	914	144	54 84
	France	250	79	....	....	....
	Italy	1,200	177	1,200	177	72 00
	United States...	465	116	465	116	27 90
	Total......	13,470	2,547	11,537	2,297	692 22
Anchovies, sardines, etc., in tin boxes weighing over 12 ounces and not over 20 ounces each.	Unit'd Kingdom	12,066	1,022	186	35	8 37
	Hong Kong	14,126	2,464	14,126	2,464	635 67
	China	1,896	255	1,896	255	85 32
	France	6,072	1,406	1,500	277	67 50
	Italy	3,900	631	4,900	824	220 50
	Japan	2,496	224	2,112	184	95 04
	Norway	500	41	....	....	....
	Sweden	200	23	....	....	....
	United States...	6,960	1,021	7,288	1,199	327 96
	Total......	48,216	7,087	32,003	5,238	1,440 36

SESSIONAL PAPER No. 11

OF IMPORTS—*Continued.*

FOR HOME CONSUMPTION.

Preferential Tariff.			Treaty Rates.			Total.		
Quantity.	Value.	Duty.	Quantity.	Value.	Duty.	Quantity.	Value.	DutyColl'd.
	$	$. cts.		$	$ cts.		$	$ cts.
....	....	....	....	....	....	....	2,650	622 50
Lb. 2,837	670	117 24	Lb.	....	....	Lb. 2,837	670	117 24
....	....	....	....	....	....	74,647	1,741	746 47
....	....	....	....	....	....	4,000	120	40 00
....	....	....	....	....	....	11,451	573	114 51
....	....	....	....	....	....	105,933	5,296	1,059 33
....	....	....	....	....	....	117,384	5,869	1,173 84
....	....	....	....	....	....	1,867	371	18 67
....	....	....	....	....	....	....	28	8 40
....	....	....	....	....	....	....	569	170 70
....	....	....	....	....	....	....	597	179 10
....	....	....	....	....	....	10,407	1,074	104 07
14,040	917	70 20	....	....	....	25,065	1,651	180 45
....	....	....	....	....	....	190	24	1 90
....	....	....	....	....	....	2,625	146	26 25
....	....	....	....	....	....	6,378	528	63 78
14,040	917	70 20	....	....	....	34,258	2,349	272 38
Boxes. 1,683	171	58 90	Boxes.	....	....	Boxes. 1,683	171	58 90
....	....	....	....	....	....	8,958	1,860	537 48
....	....	....	....	....	....	914	144	54 84
....	....	....	250	79	12 50	250	79	12 50
....	....	....	....	....	....	1,200	177	72 00
....	....	....	....	....	....	465	116	27 90
1,683	171	58 90	250	79	12 50	13,470	2,547	763 62
1,856	145	46 41	1,358	309	54 32	3,400	489	109 10
....	....	....	....	....	....	14,126	2,464	635 67
....	....	....	....	....	....	1,896	255	85 32
....	....	....	7,172	1,740	286 88	8,672	2,017	354 38
....	....	....	....	....	....	4,900	824	220 50
....	....	....	384	40	15 36	2,496	224	110 40
....	....	....	600	48	24 00	600	48	24 00
....	....	....	200	23	8 00	200	23	8 00
....	....	....	....	....	....	7,288	1,199	327 96
1,856	145	46 41	9,714	2,160	388 56	43,578	7,543	1,875 33

6 GEORGE V, A. 19'6

No. 1.—GENERAL STATEMENT

Articles Imported.	Countries.	TOTAL IMPORTS.		ENTERED		
				General Tariff.		
		Quantity.	Value.	Quantity.	Value.	Duty.
DUTIABLE GOODS—*Con.*		Boxes.	$	Boxes.	$	$ cts.
Fish—*Con.*						
Anchovies, sardines, etc., when packed in tin boxes weighing over 8 ounces and not over 12 ounces.	Unit'd Kingdom	31,708	2,300	3,012	336	105 42
	Hong Kong.....	33	6	33	6	1 15
	Belgium........	4,000	251	....	....	....
	China..........	144	17	144	17	5 04
	France.........	18,260	2,340	2,787	284	97 54
	Germany.......	200	24	200	24	7 00
	Japan..........	144	14	144	14	5 04
	Norway........	108,900	5,569	200	10	7 00
	Portugal.......	6,500	815	6,500	815	227 50
	Sweden........	52	6	52	6	1 82
	United States...	19,183	2,288	17,647	2,124	617 66
	Total......	189,124	13,630	30,719	3,636	1,075 17
Anchovies, sardines, etc., when packed in tin boxes weighing 8 ounces or less.	Unit'd Kingdom	949,190	54,040	124,609	8,021	3,115 22
	Hong Kong.....	192	26	192	26	4 75
	Belgium........	110,754	5,121	704	53	17 60
	France.........	217,546	20,732	10,524	950	263 10
	Germany.......	28,400	1,489	18,900	988	472 50
	Holland........	8,700	416	8,700	416	217 50
	Italy...........	28,400	2,170	28,100	2,032	702 50
	Japan..........	240	27	....	....	....
	Norway........	3,778,710	202,729	111,200	5,903	2,780 00
	Portugal.......	142,640	9,031	156,040	9,867	3,901 06
	Spain..........	7,000	286	....	....	....
	Sweden........	22,484	1,018	84	6	2 10
	United States.:.	67,543	4,914	60,901	4,414	1,522 53
	Total......	5,361,799	301,999	519,954	32,676	12,998 86
Fish preserved in oil, n.o.p........	Unit'd Kingdom	....	1,892	....	42	14 70
	Hong Kong....	....	4,463	....	4,435	1,552 25
	China..........	....	451	....	451	157 85
	France.........	....	865	....	....	....
	Italy...........	....	....	....	506	177 10
	Japan..........	....	404	....	84	29 40
	Norway........	....	548	....	91	31 85
	Sweden........	....	5	....	5	1 75
	United States...	....	453	....	453	158 55
	Total......	....	9,081	....	6,067	2,123 45
		Lb.		Lb.		
Fish, all other, not in barrels or half barrels, fresh.	Unit'd Kingdom	1,749	445	353	129	3 53
	Hong Kong....	700	100	700	100	7 00
	China..........	274	45	274	45	2 74
	Italy...........	....	....	569	73	5 69
	Spain..........	....	....	325	18	3 25
	United States...	477,319	33,096	476,625	33,068	4,766 25
	Total......	480,042	33,686	478,846	33,433	4,788 46
Fish, all other, not in barrels or half barrels, pickled.	Unit'd Kingdom	477	38	....	....	....
	Hong-Kong....	14,140	1,122	14,140	1,122	141 40
	Alaska........—	25	3	25	3	0 25
	China..........	3,510	516	3,510	516	35 10
	Italy...........	14,528	1,232	17,318	1,392	173 18
	Japan..........	300	27	300	27	3 00
	Venezuela......	1,623	65	1,623	65	16 23
	United States...	30,606	2,947	31,202	3,113	312 02
	Total......	65,209	5,950	68,118	6,238	681 18

OF IMPORTS—*Continued.*

FOR HOME CONSUMPTION.

	Preferential Tariff.			Treaty Rates.			Total.	
Quantity.	Value.	Duty.	Quantity.	Value.	Duty.	Quantity.	Value.	DutyColl'd.
Boxes.	$	$ cts.	Boxes.	$	$ cts.	Boxes.	$	$ cts.
23,696	1,648	473 92	8,500	706	170 00	35,208	2,690	749 34
....	....	....	....	....	....	33	6	1 15
....	....	....	4,000	251	80.00	4,000	251	80 00
....	....	....	....	....	....	144	17	5 04
....	....	....	12,468	1,607	249 36	15,255	1,891	346 90
....	....	....	....	....	....	200	24	7 00
....	....	....	....	....	....	144	14	5 04
....	....	....	119,700	6,459	2,394 00	119,900	6,469	2,401 00
....	....	....	....	....	....	6,500	815	227 50
....	....	....	....	....	....	52	6	1 82
....	....	....	....	....	....	17,647	2,124	617 66
23,696	1,648	473 92	144,668	9,023	2,893 36	199,083	14,307	4,442 45
506,967	22,641	6,337 09	330,262	22,579	6,605 24	961,838	53,241	16,057 55
....	....	....	....	....	....	192	26	4 75
....	....	....	73,600	3,528	1,472 00	74,304	3,581	1,489 80
....	....	....	207,398	16,415	4,147 96	217,922	17,365	4,411 06
....	....	....	....	....	....	18,900	988	472 50
....	....	....	700	70	14 00	8,700	416	217 50
....	....	....	240	27	4 80	28,800	2,102	716 50
....	....	....	3,626,446	194,000	72,528 92	240	27	4 80
....	....	....	....	....	....	3,737,646	199,903	75,308 92
....	....	....	....	....	....	156,040	9,867	3,901 06
....	....	....	7,800	330	156 00	7,800	330	156 00
....	....	....	22,400	1,012	448 00	22,484	1,018	450 10
....	....	....	....	....	....	60,901	4,414	1,522 53
506,967	22,641	6,337 09	4,268,846	237,961	85,376 92	5,295,767	293,278	104,712 87
....	322	64 40	....	682	204 60	....	1,046	283 70
....	....	....	28	8 40	....	4,463	1,560 65	
....	....	....	....	....	....	451	157 85	
....	....	....	884	265 20	....	884	265 20	
....	....	....	....	....	....	506	177 10	
....	....	....	320	96 00	....	404	125 40	
....	....	....	457	137 10	....	548	168 95	
....	....	....	....	....	....	5	1 75	
....	....	....	....	....	....	453	158 55	
....	322	64 40	....	2,371	711 30	....	8,760	2,899 15
Lb.			Lb.			Lb.		
1,396	316	6 98	....	....	....	1,749	445	10 51
....	....	....	....	....	....	700	100	7 00
....	....	....	....	....	....	274	45	2 74
....	....	....	....	....	....	569	73	5 69
....	....	....	....	....	....	325	18	3 25
....	....	....	....	....	....	476,625	33,068	4,766 25
1,396	316	6 98	....	....	....	480,242	33,749	4,795 44
477	38	2 39	....	....	....	477	38	2 39
....	....	....	....	....	....	14,140	1,122	141 40
....	....	....	....	....	....	25	3	0 25
....	....	....	....	....	....	3,510	516	35 10
....	....	....	....	....	....	17,318	1,392	173 18
....	....	....	....	....	....	300	27	3 00
....	....	....	....	....	....	1,623	65	16 23
....	....	....	....	....	....	31,202	3,113	312 02
477	38	2 39	....	....	....	68,595	6,276	683 57

No. 1.—General Statement

Articles Imported.	Countries.	Total Imports.		Entered		
				General Tariff.		
		Quantity.	Value.	Quantity.	Value.	Duty?
DUTIABLE GOODS—Con. Fish—Con.		Lb.	$	Lb.	$	$ - cts.
Fish, fresh or dried, n.o.p., imported in barrels or half barrels.	Unit'd Kingdom	2,825	262			
	Hong Kong.....	130,178	16,680	130,178	16,680	1,301 78
	China..........	18,754	2,660	18,754	2,660	187 54
	Japan..........	115,810	14,121	119,810	14,334	1,198 10
	Miquelon and St. Pierre.....	160	8	160	8	1 60
	Norway........	5,500	541	5,500	541	55 00
	United States...	678,226	43,334	672,076	42,961	6,720 76
	Total......	951,453	77,606	946,478	77,184	9,464 78
Fish, all other, pickled or salted, in barrels.	Unit'd Kingdom	425	30			
	Hong Kong....	16,525	2,099	16,525	2,099	165 25
	China..........	2,466	220	2,766	264	27 66
	Italy..........	13,130	1,179	13,636	1,219	136 36
	Japan..........	2,322	251	3,322	303	33 22
	Norway........	200	46	200	46	200
	Sweden...:....	1,098	125	1,098	125	10 98
	United States...	97,757	6,438	77,892	5,817	778 92
	Total......	133,923	10,388	115,439	9,873	1,154 39
Fish, prepared or preserved, n.o.p.	Unit'd Kingdom	....	70,964	....	5,857	1,757 10
	B. Straits Settlements...	....	360	....		
	Hong Kong.....	....	6,032	....	6,032	1,809 60
	New Zealand...	....		....		
	China..........	....	2,049	....	2,049	614 70
	France..........	....	967	....	866	259 80
	Germany..:....	....	756	....	756	226 80
	Italy..........	....	108	....	238	71 40
	Japan...........	....	13,497	....	12,110	3,633 00
	Norway........	....	17,260	....	16,993	5,097 90
	Sweden........	....	212	....	212	63 60
	Turkey.........	....	52	....	52	15 60
	United States...	....	32,849	....	31,550	9,465 00
	Total....:...	....	145,106	....	76,715	23,014 50
Fish oil, cod, n.o.p.............	Unit'd Kingdom	Gal. 90	92	Gal. 90	92	20 70
	United States..	1,394	562	1,394	562	126 48
	Total......	1,484	654	1,484	654	147 18
Fish, oil, cod liver..............	Unit'd Kingdom	2,561	1,719	1,123	825	185 62
	Miquelon and St. Pierre.....	6	10	6	10	2 25
	Norway........	9,227	5,673	13,038	8,515	1,915 98
	United States...	6,212	4,541	6,212	4,541	1,021 72
	Total......	18,006	11,943	20,379	13,891	3,125 57
Fish oil, whale and spermaceti....	Unit'd Kingdom	4,848	2,296	....	....	....
	United States...	1,683	1,145	1,683	1,145	257 63
	Total......	6,531	3,441	1,683	1,145	257 63
Fish oil, other, n.o.p.............	Unit'd Kingdom	6,681	3,989	....	....	....
	Hong Kong....	24	31	24	31	6 97
	United States...	27,250	11,402	27,250	11,402	2,565 55
	Total......	33,955	15,422	27,274	11,433	2,572 52

SESSIONAL PAPER No. 11

OF IMPORTS—*Continued.*

FOR HOME CONSUMPTION.

Preferential Tariff.			Treaty Rates.			Total.		
Quantity.	Value.	Duty.	Quantity.	Value.	Duty.	Quantity.	Value.	DutyColl'd.
Lb.	$	$ cts.	Lb.	$	$ cts.	Lb.	$	$ cts.
2,825	262	14 13	....	....	....	2,825	262	14 13
....	....	....	....	....	....	130,178	16,680	1,301 78
....	....	....	....	....	....	18,754	2,660	187 54
....	....	....	....	....	....	119,810	14,334	1,198 10
....	....	....	....	....	....	160	8	1 60
....	....	....	....	....	....	5,500	541	55 00
....	....	....	....	....	....	672,076	42,961	6,720 76
2,825	262	14 13	....	....	....	949,303	77,446	9,478 91
425	30	2 13	....	....	....	425	30	2 13
....	....	....	....	....	....	16,525	2,099	165 25
....	....	....	....	....	....	2,766	264	27 66
....	....	....	....	....	....	13,636	1,219	136 36
....	....	....	....	....	....	3,322	303	33 22
....	....	....	....	....	....	200	46	2 00
....	....	....	....	....	....	1,098	125	10 98
....	....	....	....	....	....	77,892	5,817	778 92
425	30	2 13	....	....	....	115,864	9,903	1,156 52
....	62,982	11,022 42	....	....	....	....	68,839	12,779 52
....	360	63 00	....	....	....	....	360	63 00
....	....	....	....	....	....	....	6,032	1,809 60
....	88	15 40	....	....	....	....	88	15 40
....	....	....	....	....	....	....	2,049	614 70
....	....	....	....	....	....	....	866	259 80
....	....	....	....	....	....	....	756	226 80
....	....	....	....	....	....	....	238	71 40
....	....	....	....	....	....	....	12,110	3,633 00
....	....	....	....	....	....	....	16,093	5,097 90
....	....	....	....	....	....	....	212	63 60
....	....	....	....	....	....	....	52	15 60
....	....	....	....	....	....	....	31,550	9,465 00
....	63,430	11,100 82	....	....	....	....	140,145	34,115 32
Gal.			Gal.			Gal.		
....	....	....	....	....	....	90	92	20 70
....	....	....	....	....	....	1,394	562	126 48
....	....	....	....	....	....	1,484	654	147 18
63	54	6 76	....	....	....	1,186	879	192 38
....	....	....	....	....	....	6	10	2 25
....	....	....	....	....	....	13,038	8,515	1,915 98
....	....	....	....	....	....	6,212	4,541	1,021 72
63	54	6 76	....	....	....	20,442	13,945	3,132 33
4,848	2,296	287 01	....	....	....	4,848	2,296	287 01
....	....	....	....	....	....	1,683	1,145	257 63
4,848	2,296	287 01	....	....	....	6,531	3,441	544 64
6,681	3,989	498 63	....	....	....	6,681	3,989	498 63
....	....	....	....	....	....	24	31	6 97
....	....	....	....	....	....	27,250	11,402	2,565 55
6,681	3,989	498 63	....	....	....	33,955	15,422	3,071 15

6 GEORGE V, A. 1916

No. 1.—General Statement

Articles Imported.	Countries.	Total Imports.		Entered		
		Quantity.	Value.	General Tariff.		
				Quantity.	Value.	Duty.
DUTIABLE GOODS—*Con.*			$		$	$ cts.
Fish—*Con.*						
Other articles the produce of the	Unit'd Kingdom	....	414	....	210	52 50
fisheries, not specially provided	Hong Kong.....	....	3,994	....	3,994	998 50
for.	China..........	....	656	....	656	164 00
	France..........	....	10	....	415	103 75
	Germany.......	....	171	....	171	42 75
	Japan..........	....	9,966	....	9,959	2,489 75
	Norway........	....	506	....	506	126 50
	Russia.........	....	3,233	....	3,233	808 25
	Sweden........	....	5	....	5	1 25
	United States...	....	24,243	....	22,157	5,539 25
	Total......	....	43,198	....	41,306	10,326 50
Flax, hemp and jute, manufactures of, viz.—						
Bags or sacks of hemp, linen or	Unit'd Kingdom	....	50,439	....	2,796	559 20
jute.	B. India........	....	92,758	....	2,824	564 80
	B. W. Indies....	....	160	....	160	32 00
	United States...	....	106,628	....	102,763	20,552 60
	Total......	....	249,985	....	108,543	21,708 60
Canvas of hemp or flax, for	Unit'd Kingdom	....	5,561	....	5,561	278 05
ship's sails.	United States...	....	1,649	....	1,066	53 30
	Total......	....	7,210	....	6,627	331 35
Carpeting, rugs, matting and	Unit'd Kingdom	....	32,647	....	1,232	308 00
mats of hemp or jute.	Hong Kong.....	....	30	....	30	7 50
	Aust.-Hungary..	....	1,176	....	....	....
	Belgium........	....	98	....	98	24 50
	China..........	....	32	....	32	8 00
	France.........	....	80	....	13	3 25
	Germany.......	....	545	....	545	136 25
	Holland........	....	10	....	10	2 50
	Japan..........	....	3,000	....	85	21 25
	United States...	....	3,105	....	3,105	776 25
	Total......	....	40,813	....	5,150	1,287 50
Embroideries and lace of linen,	Unit'd Kingdom	....	1,818	....	26	5 20
white and cream coloured....	Germany.......	....	61	....	61	12 20
	United States...	....	448	....	448	89 60
	Total......	....	2,327	....	535	107 00
		Lb.		Lb.		
Sail twine of flax or hemp to be	Unit'd Kingdom	4,752	1,287	4,752	1,287	64 35
used for boats' and ships'	United States...	647	153	647	153	7 65
sails.	Total......	5,399	1,440	5,399	1,440	72 00
Uncoloured damask of linen,	Unit'd Kingdom	....	758,559	....	20,639	6,191 70
in the piece, stair linen, diaper,	B. India........	....	69	....	69	20 70
doylies, tray cloths, uncolour-	B. W. Indies....	....	112	....	....	....
ed table cloths, or napkins of	Hong Kong.....	....	358	....	358	107 40
linen, quilts, counterpanes,	Aust.-Hungary .	....	1,473	....	1,473	441 90
pillow cases of linen, and sheets	Azores and Madeira.....	....	335	....	335	100 50
	Belgium........	....	238	....	238	71 40
	China..........	....	78	....	12	3 60
	France.........	....	13,259	....	10,711	3,213 30
	Germany.......	....	11,657	....	11,946	3,583 80
	Italy..........	....	1,171	....	1,171	351 30

OF IMPORTS—*Continued.*

FOR HOME CONSUMPTION.

Preferential Tariff.			Treaty Rates.			Total.		
Quantity.	Value.	Duty.	Quantity.	Value.	Duty.	Quantity.	Value.	Duty Coll'd.
	$	$ cts.		$	$ cts.		$	$ cts.
....	193	28 95	....	....	....	....	403	81 45
....	....	....	....	....	....	....	3,994	998 50
....	....	....	....	....	....	....	656	164 00
....	....	....	....	....	....	....	415	103 75
....	....	....	....	....	....	....	171	42 75
....	....	....	....	....	....	....	9,959	2,489 75
....	....	....	....	....	....	....	506	126 50
....	....	....	....	....	....	....	3,233	808 25
....	....	....	....	....	....	....	5	1 25
....	....	....	....	....	....	....	22,157	5,539 25
....	193	28 95	....	....	....	....	41,499	10,355 45
....	43,030	6,454 50	....	....	....	....	45,826	7,013 70
....	90,345	13,551 75	....	....	....	....	93,169	14,116 55
....	....	....	....	....	....	....	160	32 00
....	....	....	....	....	....	....	102,763	20,552 60
....	133,375	20,006 25	....	....	....	....	241,918	41,714 85
....	....	....	....	....	....	....	5,561	278 05
....	....	....	....	....	....	....	1,066	53 30
....	....	....	....	....	....	....	6,627	331 35
:..........	30,848	5,398 53	....	717	161 32	....	32,797	5,867 85
....	....	....	....	....	....	....	30	7 50
....	....	....	....	1,176	264 60	....	1,176	264 60
....	....	....	....	....	....	....	98	24 50
....	....	....	....	....	....	....	32	8 00
....	....	....	....	67	15 07	....	80	18 32
....	....	....	....	....	....	....	545	136 25
....	....	....	....	....	....	....	10	2 50
....	....	....	....	3,005	676 14	....	3,090	697 39
....	....	....	....	....	....	....	3,105	776 25
....	30,848	5,398 53	....	4,965	1,117 13	....	40,963	7,803 16
....	1,412	176 52	....	380	66 52	....	1,818	248 24
....	....	....	....	....	....	....	61	12 20
....	....	....	....	....	....	....	448	89 60
....	1,412	176 52	....	380	66 52	....	2,327	350 04
Lb.			Lb.			Lb.		
....	....	....	....	....	....	4,752	1,287	64 35
....	....	....	....	....	....	647	153	7 65
....	....	....	....	....	....	5,399	1,440	72 00
....	740,657	148,131 40	....	....	....	....	761,296	154,323 10
....	....	....	....	....	....	....	69	20 70
....	6	1 20	....	....	....	....	6	1 20
....	....	....	....	....	....	....	358	107 40
....	....	....	....	....	....	....	1,473	441 90
....	....	....	....	....	....	....	335	100 50
....	....	....	....	....	....	....	238	71 40
....	....	....	....	....	....	....	12	3 60
....	....	....	....	....	....	....	10,711	3,213 30
....	....	....	....	....	....	....	11,946	3,583 80
....	....	....	....	....	....	....	1,171	351 30

No. 1.—General Statement

Articles Imported.	Countries.	Total Imports.		Entered		
				General Tariff.		
		Quantity.	Value.	Quantity.	Value.	Duty.
DUTIABLE GOODS—*Con.*			$		$	$ cts.
Flax, hemp and jute—*Con.*						
Uncoloured damask of linen, in the piece, &c.—*Con.*	Japan..........	....	22,22	....	20,453	6,135 90
	Portugal........	....	4.10	.	4,101	1,230 30
	Switzerland.....	....	1.270	....	1,270	381 00
	United States...	....	9,913	....	9,913	2,973 90
	Total......	....	824,812	....	82,689	24,806 70
Handkerchiefs...............	Unit'd Kingdom	....	231,330	....	1,117	390 95
	B. India........	....	3	....	33	11 55
	B. W. Indies....	....				
	HongKong-....	....	2	....	22	7 70
	Belgium........	....	25			
	China..........	....	20	....	20	7 00
	France.........	....	43	....	142	49 70
	Germany.......	....	20	....	202	70 70
	Holland........	....	1,14	....	1,142	399 70
	Japan..........	....	96	....		
	Portugal........	....	74	....	541	189 35
	Switzerland....	....	14,564	....	8,101	2,835 35
	Turkey........	....	1,19	....	1,199	419 65
	United States...	....	950	....	950	332 50
	Total......	....	271,497	....	13,469	4,714 15
Horse clothing of jute, shaped or otherwise manufactured.	Unit'd Kingdom	....	40	....	74	22 20
	United States...	....	749	....	749	224 70
	Total......	....	1,15	....	823	246 90
Towels........................	Unit'd Kingdom	....	149,274	....	2,276	682 80
	Aust.-Hungary .	....	137	....	137	41 10
	Belgium........	....	661	....	661	198 30
	Germany.....	....	4,057	....	4,094	1,228 20
	Switzerland....	....	19	....	19	5 70
	United States...	....	2,918	....	2,918	875 40
	Total......	....	157,066	....	10,105	3,031 50
		Yd.		Yd.		
Fabrics, brown or bleached....	Unit'd Kingdom	849,667	114,687	10,421	1,727	431 75
	Belgium........	771	107	771	107	26 75
	France.........	10	8	10	8	2 00
	Germany.......	1,22	534	1,225	534	133 50
	United States...	20,554	2,249	20,554	2,249	562 25
	Total.......	872,227	117,535	32,981	4,625	1,156 25
Fabrics of flax, unbleached, n.o.p.	Unit'd Kingdom	3,100,110	288,132	26,009	2,290	572 50
	Belgium........	48	7	48	7	1 75
	France.........	387	75	387	75	18 75
	Germany.......	6,619	899	6,619	899	224 75
	United States...	535,216	37,771	535,216	37,771	9,442 75
	Total.......	3,642,380	326,884	568,279	41,042	10,260 50
Tailors' hollands of linen and towelling in the web.	Unit'd Kingdom	3,093,774	225,464	5,225	502	125 50
	Belgium........	420	84	420	84	21 00
	Germany.......	649	120	732	136	34 00
	United States...	30,059	2,815	30,059	2,815	703 75
	Total.......	3,124,902	228,483	36,436	3,537	884 25

OF IMPORTS—*Continued.*

FOR HOME CONSUMPTION.

Preferential Tariff.			Treaty Rates.			Total.		
Quantity.	Value.	Duty.	Quantity.	Value.	Duty.	Quantity.	Value.	Duty Coll'd.
	$	$ cts.		$	$ cts.		$	$ cts.
....	....	....	....	....	....	....	20,453	6,135 90
....	....	....	....	....	....	....	4,101	1,230 30
....	....	....	....	....	....	....	1,270	381 00
....	....	....	....	....	....	....	9,913	2,973 90
....	740,663	148,132 60	....	....	....	....	823,352	172,939 30
....	229,843	57,460 75	....	2,663	865 47	....	233,623	58,717 17
....	....	....	....	....	....	....	33	11 55
....	3	0 75	....	....	....	....	3	0 75
....	....	....	....	....	....	....	22	7 70
....	....	....	....	28	9 10	....	28	9 10
....	....	....	....	....	....	....	20	7 00
....	....	....	....	346	112 45	....	488	162 15
....	....	....	....	....	....	....	202	70 70
....	....	....	....	....	....	....	1,142	399 70
....	....	....	....	940	305 50	....	940	305 50
....	....	....	....	....	....	....	541	189 35
....	....	....	....	5,708	1,855 19	....	13,809	4,690 54
....	....	....	....	....	....	....	1,199	419 65
....	....	....	....	....	....	....	950	332 50
....	229,846	57,461 50	....	9,685	3,147 71	....	253,000	65,323 36
....	329	65 80	....	....	....	....	403	88 00
....	....	....	....	....	....	....	749	224 70
....	329	65 80	....	....	....	....	1,152	312 70
....	146,234	29,246 80	....	....	....	....	148,510	29,929 60
....	....	....	....	....	....	....	137	41 10
....	....	....	....	....	....	....	661	198 30
....	....	....	....	....	....	....	4,094	1,228 20
....	....	....	....	....	....	....	19	5 70
....	....	....	....	....	....	....	2,918	875 40
....	146,234	29,246 80	....	....	....	....	156,339	32,278 30
Yd. 846,782	113,487	19,860 84	. Yd.	....	....	857,203	Yd. 115,214	20,292 59
....	....	....	....	....	....	771	107	26 75
....	....	....	....	....	....	10	8	2 00
....	....	....	....	....	....	1,225	534	133 50
....	....	....	....	....	....	20,554	2,249	562 25
846,782	113,487	19,860 84	....	....	....	879,763	118,112	21,017 09
3,131,733	290,014	43,502 10	....	....	....	3,157,742	292,304	44,074 60
....	....	....	....	....	....	48	7	1 75
....	....	....	....	....	....	387	75	18 75
....	....	....	....	....	....	6,619	899	224 75
....	....	....	....	....	....	535,216	37,771	9,442 75
3,131,733	290,014	43,502 10	....	....	....	3,700,012	331,056	53,762 60
3,032,633	224,961	39,369 28	....	....	....	3,037,858	225,463	39,494 78
....	....	....	....	....	....	420	84	21 00
....	....	....	....	....	....	732	136	34 00
....	....	....	....	....	....	30,059	2,815	703 75
3,032,633	224,961	39,369 28	....	....	....	3,069,069	228,498	40,253 53

6 GEORGE V, A. 1916

No. 1.—General Statement

Articles Imported.	Countries.	Total Imports.		Entered		
		Quantity.	Value.	General Tariff..		
				Quantity.	Value.	Duty.
			$		$	$ cts.
DUTIABLE GOODS—*Con.*						
Flax, hemp and jute—*Con.*						
Linen clothing, no.p...........	Unit'd Kingdom	....	5,907	....	617	215 95
	Australia........		4	....	4	1 40
	Aust.-Hungary..	....	76	....	76	26 60
	Belgium........	....	379	....	379	132 65
	France........,..	....	283	....	271	94 85
	Germany.......	....	364	....	364	127 40
	Japan...........	....	201	....	201	70 35
	United States..	....	3,654	....	3,654	1,278 90
	Total......	....	10,868	....	5,566	1,948 10
Linen blouses and shirt waists..	Unit'd Kingdom	....	172	....	....	....
	United States...	....	259	....	259	90 65
	Total......	....	431	....	259	90 65
		Lb.			Lb.	
Linen thread, n.o.p.............	Unit'd Kingdom	322,003	216,009	433	277	69 25
	Belgium........	997	807	....	....	....
	France.........	407	252	30	24	6 00
	Germany.......	382	238	212	132	33 00
	United States..	8,969	7,475	8,969	7,475	1,868 75
	Total......	332,758	224,781	9,644	7,908	1,977 00
		Doz.		Doz.		
Shirts of linen.................	Unit'd Kingdom	48	655	2	103	36 05
	United States..	10	173	10	173	60 55
	Total......	58	828	12	276	96 60
Linen tape, not over 1½ inches in width.	Unit'd Kingdom	....	731	....	....	....
	France.........	....	22	....	22	7 70
	United States..	....	231	....	231	80 85
	Total......	....	984	....	253	88 55
Tapestry jute,.................	United States..	....	49	....	49	12 25
		Yd.		Yd.		
Jute cloth, or jute canvas, un-coloured, not further finished than cropped, bleached, mang-led or calendered.	Unit'd Kingdom	8,294,432	514,957	28,284	1,845	184 50
	B. India.......	19,296,371	662,511	1,033,662	50,506	5,050 60
	Belgium........	15,293	2,125	15,293	2,125	212 50
	Germany.......	228	121	228	121	12 10
	United States..	8,372,100	450,746	8,372,100	450,746	45,074 60
	Total......	35,978,424	1,630,460	9,449,567	505,343	50,534 30
Fabrics of flax, printed, dyed or coloured, n.o.p.	Unit'd Kingdom	307,095	45,691	34,162	3,453	1,122 29
	Belgium........	2,231	753	2,231	753	244 72
	France..........	130	38	130	38	12 35
	Germany.......	293	103	293	103	33 47
	Switzerland....	23	9	23	9	2 92
	United States..	34,487	3,688	31,584	3,262	1,060 24
	Total......	344,259	50,282	68,423	7,618	2,475 99

OF IMPORTS.—*Continued.*

FOR HOME CONSUMPTION.

Preferential Tariff.			Treaty Rates.			Total.		
Quantity.	Value.	Duty.	Quantity.	Value.	Duty.	Quantity.	Value.	DutyColl'd
	$	$ cts.		$	$ cts.	-	$	$ cts.
....	5,290	1,322 50	....	....	....	....	5,907	1,538 45
....	....	....	....	....	....	....	4	1 40
....	....	....	....	....	....	....	76	26 60
....	....	....	....	....	....	....	379	132 65
....	....	....	....	12	3 90	....	283	98 75
....	....	....	....	....	....	....	364	127 40
....	....	....	....	....	....	....	201	70 35
....	....	....	....	....	....	....	3,654	1,278 90
....	5,290	1,322 50	....	12	3 90	....	10,868	3,274 50
....	172	43 00	....	....	....	....	172	43 00
....	....	....	....	....	....	....	259	90 65
....	172	43 00	....	....	....	....	431	133 65
Lb. 320,921	215,301	37,677 60	649	Lb. 431	96 97	Lb. 322,003	216,009	37,843 82
....	....	....	.997	807	181 59	997	807	181 59
....	....	....	377	228	51 30	407	252	57 30
....	....	....	....	....	....	212	132	33 00
....	....	....	....	....	....	8,969	7,475	1,868 75
320,921	215,301	37,677 60	2,023	1,466	329 86	332,588	224,675	39,984 46
Doz. 46	552	138 00	Doz.			Doz. 48	655	174 05
....	....	....	....	....	....	10	173	60 55
46	552	138 00	....	....	....	58	828	234 60
....	731	182 75	....	....	....	....	731	182 75
....	....	....	....	....	....	....	22	7 70
....	....	....	....	....	....	....	231	80 85
....	731	182 75	....	....	....	....	984	271 30
....	....	....	....	....	....	....	49	12 25
Yd. 8,309,998	513,446	38,508 45	Yd.			Yd. 8,338,282	515,291	38,692 95
18,263,709	612,005	45,900 68	....	....	....	19,297,371	662,511	50,951 28
....	....	....	....	....	....	15,293	2,125	212 50
....	....	....	....	....	....	228	121	12 10
....	....	....	....	....	....	8,372,100	450,746	45,074 60
26,573,707	1,125,451	84,409 13	....	....	....	36,023,274	1,630,794	134,943 43
274,027	42,348	10,587 00	....	....	....	308,189	45,801	11,709 29
....	....	....	....	....	....	2,231	753	244 72
....	....	....	....	....	....	130	38	12 35
....	....	....	....	....	....	293	103	33 47
....	....	....	....	....	....	23	9	2 92
....	....	....	....	....	....	31,584	3,262	1,060 24
274,027	42,348	10,587 00	....	....	....	342,450	49,966	13,062 99

6 GEORGE V, A. 1916

No. 1.—General Statement

Articles Imported.	Countries.	Total Imports.		Entered		
		Quantity.	Value.	General Tariff.		
				Quantity.	Value.	Duty.
			$		$	$ cts.
DUTIABLE GOODS—Con.						
Flax, hemp and jute—Con.						
Other manufactures of hemp, or flax, or of which hemp or flax is the component material of chief value, n.o.p.	Unit'd Kingdom	....	19,868	....	977	341 95
	Aust.-Hungary..	....	231	....	231	80 85
	France..........	....	45	....	45	15 75
	Germany.......	....	933	....	933	326 55
	Japan...........	....	530	....	530	185 50
	Portugal........	....	39	....	39	13 65
	Turkey.........	....	23	....	23	8 05
	United States..	....	26,046	....	26,046	9,116 10
	Total......	....	47,715	....	28,824	10,088 40
Manufactures of jute, n.o.p.....	Unit'd Kingdom	....	159,991	....	1,876	469 00
	Hong Kong.....	....	35	....	35	8 75
	Belgium.......	....	800	....	800	200 00
	Germany.......	....	3,403	....	2,721	680 25
	Japan...........	....	6	....	6	1 50
	United States..	....	29,095	....	13,412	3,353 00
	Total......	....	193,330	....	18,850	4,712 50
Foundry facings of all kinds......	Unit'd Kingdom	....	205	....	....	....
	United States..	....	9,541	....	9,541	2,385 25
	Total......	....	9,746	....	9,541	2,385 25
Fruits, including nuts, viz.:—		Lb.		Lb.		
Dried apples..................	United States..	118,158	7,905	115,366	7,336	1,834 00
Bananas, dried or evaporated...	United States..	529	63	529	63	2 65
Currants......................	Unit'd Kingdom	88,273	4,519	88,103	4,509	587 35
	Australia.......	109,030	6,095	109,030	6,095	726 87
	Greece.........	7,757,192	370,023	7,802,188	372,433	52,014 72
	United States:..	2,898,865	198,998	2,929,150	200,120	19,527 33
	Total......	10,853,360	579,635	10,928,471	583,157	72,856 27
Dates.......................	Unit'd Kingdom	290,056	8,858	309,949	9,616	1,704 71
	Hong Kong.....	2,704	111	2,704	111	14 87
	China..........	1,222	67	1,222	67	6 72
	France.........	12,276	1,613	12,276	1,613	67 51
	Turkey.........	36,240	942	36,340	942	199 87
	United States..	2,865,342	197,150	2,837,443	195,668	15,605 81
	Total......	3,207,840	208,741	3,199,934	208,017	17,599 49
Figs.........................	Unit'd Kingdom	158,325	7,840	158,429	7,836	871 35
	B. W. Indies....	123	7	123	7	0 67
	Hong Kong.....	160	8	160	8	0 88
	China..........	25	3	25	3	0 13
	France.........	7,308	619	7,308	619	40 19
	Greece.........	1,928	200	1,928	200	10 60
	Portugal........	352,921	10,143	347,637	10,053	1,911 99
	Spain...........	51,218	1,684	51,218	1,684	281 69
	Turkey.........	1,318,604	77,075	1,317,816	76,932	7,247 98
	United States..	1,395,926	91,328	1,394,498	91,323	7,669 72
	Total......	3,286,538	188,907	3,279,142	188,665	18,035 20

OF IMPORTS—*Continued.*

FOR HOME CONSUMPTION.

Preferential Tariff.			Treaty Rates.			Total.		
Quantity.	Value.	Duty.	Quantity.	Value.	Duty.	Quantity.	Value.	DutyColl'd
	$	$ cts.		$	$ cts.		$	$ cts.
....	18,319	4,579 75	....	....	....	....	19,296	4,921 70
....	....	....	....	....	....	....	231	80 85
....	....	....	....	....	....	....	45	15 75
....	....	....	....	....	....	....	933	326 55
....	....	....	....	....	....	....	530	185 50
....	....	....	....	....	....	....	39	13 65
....	....	....	....	....	....	....	23	8 05
....	....	....	....	....	....	....	26,046	9,116 10
....	18,319	4,579 75	....	....	....	....	47,143	14,668 15
....	155,751	23,362 65	....	....	....	....	157,627	23,831 65
....	....	....	....	....	....	....	35	8 75
....	....	....	....	....	....	....	800	200 00
....	....	....	....	....	....	....	2,721	680 25
....	....	....	....	....	....	....	6	1 50
....	....	....	....	....	....	....	13,412	3,353 00
....	155,751	23,362 65	....	....	....	....	174,601	28,075 15
....	205	30 75	....	....	....	....	205	30 75
....	....	....	....	....	....	....	9,541	2,385 25
....	205	30 75	....	....	....	....	9,746	2,416 00
Lb.			Lb.			Lb.		
....	....	....	....	....	....	115,366	7,336	1,834 00
....	....	....	....	....	....	529	63	2 65
170	10	0 86	....	....	....	88,273	4,519	588 21
....	....	....	....	....	....	109,030	6,095	726 87
....	....	....	....	....	....	7,802,188	372,433	52,014 72
....	....	....	....	....	....	2,929,150	200,120	19,527 33
170	10	0 86	....	....	....	10,928,641	583,167	72,857 13
....	....	....	....	....	....	309,949	9,616	1,704 71
....	....	....	....	....	....	2,704	111	14 87
....	....	....	....	....	....	1,222	67	6 72
....	....	....	....	....	....	12,276	1,613	67 51
....	....	....	....	....	....	36,340	942	199 87
....	....	....	....	....	....	2,837,443	195,668	15,605 81
....	....	....	....	....	....	3,199,934	208,017	17,599 49
280	31	1 12	....	....	....	158,709	7,867	872 47
....	....	....	....	....	....	123	7	0 67
....	....	....	....	....	....	160	8	0 88
....	....	....	....	....	....	25	3	0 13
....	....	....	....	....	....	7,308	619	40 19
....	....	....	....	....	....	1,928	200	10 60
....	....	....	....	....	....	347,637	10,053	1,911 99
....	....	....	....	....	....	51,218	1,684	281 69
....	....	....	....	....	....	1,317,816	76,932	7,247 98
....	....	....	....	....	....	1,394,498	91,323	7,669 72
280	31	1 12	....	....	....	3,279,422	188,696	18,036 32

6 GEORGE V, A. 1916

No. 1.—General Statement

Articles Imported.	Countries.	Total Imports.		Entered		
				General Tariff.		
		Quantity.	Value.	Quantity.	Value.	Duty.
DUTIABLE GOODS—*Con.*		Lb.	$	Lb.	$	$ cts.
Fruits—*Con.*						
Prunes and plums, unpitted.....	Unit'd Kingdom	22,408	1,268	23,208	1,301	154 72
	Hong Kong.....	122	8	122	8	0 81
	Aust.-Hungary..	113,437	6,570	113,176	6,556	754 50
	China..........	375	24	375	24	2 50
	France.........	57,005	3,780	57,029	3,786	380 19
	Spain..........	27,558	1,663	27,558	1,663	183 72
	Turkey.........	1,450	95	1,450	95	9 33
	United States..	7,942,281	511,733	8,040,254	514,809	53,602 04
	Total......	8,164,636	525,141	8,263,172	528,242	55,087 81
Raisins......................	Unit'd Kingdom	200,498	10,210	226,601	11,648	1,510 67
	Australia.......	253,840	14,351	242,560	13,799	1,617 06
	B. W. Indies....	96,919	3,896	96,919	3,896	646 12
	Chili..........	1,200	175	1,200	175	8 00
	France.........	....	......	2,466	165	16 44
	Greece.........	268,734	19,453	263,691	18,698	1,757 94
	Spain..........	3,956,063	244,632	4,099,927	252,636	27,332 84
	Turkey.........	1,602,597	81,388	1,584,289	80,368	10,561 92
	United States..	16,025,086	1,060,480	16,100,284	1,060,375	107,335 19
	Total......	22,404,937	1,434,585	22,617,937	1,441,760	150,786 18
All other, n.o.p., dried fruits....	Unit'd Kingdom	330	37	300	35	8 75
	Australia......	28	4	28	4	1 00
	B. W. Indies....	204	18	....	......	......
	Hong Kong.....	117,976	8,959	117,976	8,959	2,239 75
	China..........	17,718	1,106	17,718	1,106	276 50
	Germany.......	25	5	25	5	1 25
	Japan..........	8,275	233	8,275	233	58 25
	Spain..........	300	12	300	12	3 00
	United States..	3,913,735	242,734	3,970,895	246,232	61,558 00
	Total......	4,058,591	253,108	4,115,517	256,586	64,146 50
Almonds, shelled..............	Unit'd Kingdom	94,879	31,315	10,585	3,674	423 40
	Hong Kong.....	2,501	626	2,501	626	100 04
	China..........	107	24	107	24	4 28
	France.........	49,049	15,570	5,582	1,720	223 28
	Italy..........	26,222	7,606	26,222	7,606	1,048 88
	Spain..........	594,607	176,353	41,209	10,499	1,648 36
	United States.	82,749	27,059	80,649	26,513	3,225 96
	Total......	850,114	258,553	166,855	50,662	6,674 20
Almonds, not shelled..........	Unit'd Kingdom	5,497	717	5,497	717	109 94
	China..........	50	9	50	9	1 00
	France.........	29,408	3,411	29,408	3,411	588 16
	Italy..........	10,690	868	6,840	464	136 80
	Spain..........	350,044	37,786	330,666	36,091	6,613 32
	United States..	255,950	35,043	260,154	35,610	5,203 08
	Total......	651,639	77,834	632,615	76,302	12,652 30
Brazil nuts, not shelled........	Unit'd Kingdom	193	10	586	66	11 72
	Brazil.........	....	......	570	43	11 40
	France.........	570	40	570	40	11 40
	Japan..........	25,000	1,129	25,000	1,129	500 00
	United States...	1,091,657	81,315	1,085,055	80,932	21,701 10
	Total......	1,117,420	82,494	1,111,781	82,210	22,235 62

OF IMPORTS—*Continued.*

FOR HOME CONSUMPTION.

Preferential Tariff.			Treaty Rates.			Total.		
Quantity.	Value.	Duty.	Quantity.	Value.	Duty.	Quantity.	Value.	DutyColl'd.
Lb.	$	$ cts.	Lb.	$	$ cts.	Lb.	$	$ cts.
200	20	1 00	....	....	....	23,408	1,321	155,72
....	....	....	....	....	....	122	8	0 81
....	....	....	....	....	....	113,176	6,556	754 50
....	....	....	....	....	....	375	24	2 50
....	....	....	....	....	....	57,029	3,786	380 19
....	....	....	....	....	....	27,558	1,663	183 72
....	....	....	....	....	....	1,450	95	9 33
....	....	....	....	....	....	8,040,254	514,809	53,602 04
200	20	1 00	....	....	....	8,263,372	528,262	55,088 81
133	11	0 66	....	....	....	226,734	11,659	1,511 33
....	....	....	....	....	....	242,560	13,799	1,617 06
....	....	....	....	....	....	96,919	3,896	646 12
....	....	....	....	....	....	1,200	175	8 00
....	....	....	....	....	....	2,466	165	16 44
....	....	....	....	....	....	263,691	18,698	1,757 94
....	....	....	....	....	....	4,099,927	252,636	27,332 84
....	....	....	....	....	....	1,584,289	80,368	10,561 92
....	....	....	....	....	....	16,100,284	1,060,375	107,335 19
133	11	0 66	....	....	....	22,618,070	1,441,771	150,786 84
30	2	0 35	....	....	....	330	37	9 10
....	....	....	....	....	....	28	4	1 00
204	18	3 15	....	....	....	204	18	3 15
....	....	....	....	....	....	117,976	8,959	2,239 75
....	....	....	....	....	....	17,718	1,106	276 50
....	....	....	....	....	....	25	5	1 25
....	....	....	....	....	....	8,275	233	58 25
....	....	....	....	....	....	300	12	3 00
....	....	....	....	....	....	3,970,895	246,232	61,558 00
234	20	3 50	....	....	....	4,115,751	256,606	64,150 00
13,811	4,584	414 33	63,623	20,707	2,120 77	88,019	28,965	2,958 50
....	....	....	....	....	....	2,501	626	100 04
....	....	....	....	....	....	107	24	4 28
....	....	....	47,126	15,239	1,570 87	52,708	16,959	1,794 15
....	....	....	....	....	....	26,222	7,606	1,048 88
....	....	....	540,512	162,117	18,017 13	581,721	172,616	19,665 49
....	....	....	....	....	....	80,649	26,513	3,225 96
13,811	4,584	414 33	651,261	198,063	21,708 77	831,927	253,309	28,797 30
....	....	....	....	....	....	5,497	717	109 94
....	....	....	....	....	....	50	9	1 00
....	....	....	....	....	....	29,408	3,411	588 16
....	....	....	....	....	....	6,840	464	136 80
....	....	....	....	....	....	330,666	36,091	6,613 32
....	....	....	....	....	....	260,154	35,610	5,203 08
....	....	....	....	....	....	632,615	76,302	12,652 30
....	....	....	....	....	....	586	66	11 72
....	....	....	....	....	....	570	43	11 40
....	....	....	....	....	....	570	40	11 40
....	....	....	....	....	....	25,000	1,129	500 00
....	....	....	....	....	....	1,085,055	80,932	21,701 10
....	....	....	....	....	....	1,111,781	82,210	22,235 62

6 GEORGE V, A. 1916

No. 1.—General Statement

Articles Imported.	Countries.	Total Imports.		Entered		
				General Tariff.		
		Quantity.	Value.	Quantity.	Value.	Duty.
DUTIABLE GOODS—*Con.*		Lb.	$	Lb.	$	$ cts.
Fruits—*Con.*						
Pecans, not shelled and shelled	Unit'd Kingdom	162,246	7,677	143,267	6,734	2,865 34
peanuts, n.o.p.	B.E.Indies, other.	10,208	472	10,208	472	204 16
	B. W. Indies....	260	8	260	8	5 20
	Hong Kong....	194,155	8,255	188,778	7,974	3,775 56
	China..........	220,310	6,670	197,410	6,087	3,948 20
	Dutch E. Indies	767,245	35,672	709,098.	33,196	14,181 96
	Dutch Guiana.	26,499	1,241	26,499	1,241	529 98
	France..........	153,694	8,271	202,789	10,891	4,055 78
	Holland...:....	186,927	8,132	267,708	11,217	5,354 16
	Japan..........	715,483	28,879	639,511	26,472	12,790 22
	Spain..........	118,041	6,406	147,367	8,173	2,947 34
	United States...	2,332,752	168,841	2,388,525	171,714	47,770 50
	Total......	4,887,820	280,524	4,921,420	284,179	98,428 40
Walnuts, not shelled...........	Unit'd Kingdom	32,929	2,082	17,199	1,126	343 98
	Hong Kong....	87	5	87	5	1 74
	Aust.-Hungary .	2,973	247	2,806	247	56 12
	China...........	1,036	49	1,036	49	20 72
	France.........	654,657	51,599	640,090	51,281	12,801 80
	Italy...........	10,823	1,544	14,123	1,810	282 46
	Japan..........	160,515	11,563	161,531	11,653	3,230 62
	United States...	317,828	42,704	316,188	42,442	6,323 76
	Total......	1,180,848	109,793	1,153,060	108,613	23,061 20
All other nuts, n.o.p., not shelled	Unit'd Kingdom	235,589	11,472	188,652	8,748	3,773 04
	B. India........	12,871	538	.....	.....	.....
	B. W. Indies....	358	20	.....	.....	.....
	Hong Kong....	29,338	1,904	29,338	1,904	586 76
	China..........	24,158	1,584	33,649	2,318	672 98
	France..........	270,983	14,379	273,450	14,502	5,469 00
	Greece..........	10	1	10	1	0 20
	Italy...........	491,962	37,734	545,334	42,132	10,906 68
	Japan..........	453,792	18,796	447,472	18,669	8,949 44
	Spain..........	138,177	12,126	121,027	11,008	2,420 54
	Turkey..........	2,772	1,083	2,772	1,083	55 44
	United States..	4,704,904	294,984	4,732,040	296,859	94,640 80
	Total......	6,364,914	394,621	6,373,744	397,224	127,474 88
All other nuts, shelled..........	Unit'd Kingdom	102,453	20,759	6,574	1,702	262 96
	B. India........	23,627	3,715	9,039	1,896	361 56
	B. W. Indies....	460	104	306	68	12 24
	Hong Kong....	1,315	188	1,315	188	52 60
	Aust.-Hungary .	4,409	741	4,409	741	176,36
	Brazil..........	1,000	362	1,000	362	40 00
	China..........	887	104	887	104	35 48
	Dutch E. Indies	89	24	89	24	3 56
	France..........	1,276,698	316,014	77,209	18,297	3,088 36 •
	Germany.......	2,595	523	2,595	523	103 80
	Greece.......	2,420	200	1,614	133	64 56
	Italy..........	5,038	963	5,038	963	201 52
	Japan..........	7,931	1,706	98	3	3 92
	Spain..........	413,769	86,973	27,040	5,709	1,081 60
	Turkey........	33,533	6,808	34,339	6,875	1,373 56
	United States...	275,702	80,838	276,325	80,825	11,053 00
	Total......	2,151,926	520,022	447,877	118,413	17,915 08
		Brl.		Brl.		
Green apples.................	Unit'd Kingdom	1	4	1	4	0 40
	Newfoundland..	1	1	1	1	0 40
	New Zealand...	52	238	52	238	20 80
	United States...	269,743	648,256	269,305	646,751	107,722 00
	Total......	269,797	648,499	269,359	646,994	107,743 60

OF IMPORTS—*Continued.*

FOR HOME CONSUMPTION.

Preferential Tariff.			Treaty Rates.			Total.		
Quantity.	Value.	Duty.	Quantity.	Value.	Duty.	Quantity.	Value.	DutyColl'd.
Lb.	$	$ cts.	Lb.	$	$ cts.	Lb.	$	$ cts.
52,425	2,230	524 25	....	....	....	195,692	8,964	3,389 59
....	....	....	....	....	....	10,208	472	204 16
....	....	....	....	....	....	260	8	5 20
....	....	....	....	....	....	188,778	7,974	3,775 56
....	....	....	....	....	....	197,410	6,087	3,948 20
....	....	....	....	....	....	709,098	33,196	14,181 96
....	....	....	....	....	....	26,499	1,241	529 98
....	....	....	....	....	....	202,789	10,891	4,055 78
....	....	....	....	....	....	267,708	11,217	5,354 16
....	....	....	....	....	....	639,511	26,472	12,790 22
....	....	....	....	....	....	147,367	8,173	2,947 34
....	....	....	....	....	....	2,388,525	171,714	47,770 50
52,425	2,230	524 25	....	....	....	4,973,845	286,409	98,952 65
730	106	7 30	....	....	....	17,929	1,232	351 28
....	....	....	....	....	....	87	5	1 74
....	....	....	....	....	....	2,806	247	56 12
....	....	....	....	....	....	1,036	49	20 72
....	....	....	....	....	....	640,090	51,281	12,801 80
....	....	....	....	....	....	14,123	1,810	282 46
....	....	....	....	....	....	161,531	11,653	3,230 62
....	....	....	....	....	....	316 188	42,442	6,323 76
730	106	7 30	....	....	....	1,153,790	108,719	23,068 50
33,807	1,377	338 07	....	....	....	222,459	10,125	4,111 11
12,871	538	128 71	....	....	....	12,871	538	128 71
358	20	3 58	....	....	....	358	20	3 58
....	....	....	....	....	....	29,338	1,904	586 76
....	....	....	....	....	....	33,649	2,318	672 98
....	....	....	....	....	....	273,450	14,502	5,469 00
....	....	....	....	....	....	10	1	0 20
....	....	....	....	....	....	545,334	42,132	10,906 68
....	....	....	....	....	....	447,472	18,669	8,949 44
....	....	....	....	....	....	121,027	11,008	2,420 54
....	....	....	....	....	....	2,772	1,083	55 44
....	....	....	....	....	....	4,732,040	296,859	94,640 80
47,036	1,935	470 36	....	....	....	6,420,780	399 159	127,945 24
13,021	1,772	390 63	89,458	18,882	2,981 93	109,053	22,356	3,635 52
14,588	1,819	437 64	....	....	....	23,627	3,715	799 20
154	36	4 62	....	....	....	460	104	16 86
....	....	....	....	....	....	1,315	188	52 60
....	....	....	....	....	....	4,409	741	176 36
....	....	....	....	....	....	1,000	362	40 00
....	....	....	....	....	....	887	104	35 48
....	....	....	....	....	....	89	24	3 56
....	....	....	1,162,086	291,553	38,735 91	1,239,295	309,850	41,824 27
....	....	....	....	....	....	2,595	523	103 80
....	....	....	....	....	....	1,614	133	64 56
....	....	....	....	....	....	5,038	963	201 52
....	....	....	7,833	1,703	261 10	7,931	1,706	265 02
....	....	....	381,855	81,394	12,728 50	408,895	87,103	13,810 10
....	....	....	....	....	....	34,339	6,875	1,373 56
....	....	....	....	....	....	276,325	80,825	11,053 00
27,763	3,627	832 89	1,641,232	393,532	54,707 44	2,116,872	515,572	73,455 41
Brl.			Brl.			Brl.		
....	....	....	....	....	....	1	4	0 40
....	....	....	....	....	....	1	1	0 40
....	....	....	....	....	....	52	238	20 80
....	....	....	....	....	....	269,305	646,751	107,722 00
....	....	....	....	....	....	269,359	646,994	107,743 60

6 GEORGE V, A. 1916

No. 1.—General Statement

Articles Imported.	Countries.	Total Imports.		Entered		
				General Tariff.		
		Quantity.	Value.	Quantity.	Value.	Duty.
DUTIABLE GOODS—*Con.*		Lb.	$	Lb.	$	$ cts.
Fruits—*Con.*						
Blackberries, gooseberries, rasp-berries and strawberries, n.o.p	Unit'd Kingdom	900	113	900	113	18 00
	Newfoundland..	20	2	20	2	0 40
	United States...	6,456,189	589,160	6,456,436	588,992	129,128 72
	Total......	6,457,109	589,275	6,457,356	589,107	129,147 12
Cherries................	Unit'd Kingdom	45	3	....	....	....
	France..........	2,152	239	2,152	239	43 04
	United-States...	940,120	102,490	936,507	102,155	18,730 14
	Total......	942,317	102,732	938,659	102,394	18,773 18
		Brl.		Brl.		
Cranberries................	Newfoundland..	83	311	51	183	45 75
	Germany......	11	60	11	60	15 00
	United States...	28,203	109,298	28,194	109,257	27,314 25
	Total......	28,297	109,669	28,256	109,500	27,375 00
		Lb.		Lb.		
Currants................	United States...	12,920	1,075	12,920	1,075	258 40
Grapes................	Unit'd Kingdom	635,556	48,103	635,276	48,086	12,705 52
	Spain...........	31,244	2,211	31,244	2,211	624 88
	United States...	5,538,332	267,327	5,533,640	266,886	110,672 80
	Total......	6,205,132	317,641	6,200,160	317,183	124,003 20
Limes................	United States...	....	3,758	....	3,758	375 80
Peaches................	United States...	12,737,063	340,825	12,733,661	340,739	127,336 61
		Bush.		Bush.		
Plums................	China...........	8	29	8	29	2 40
	United States...	104,970	251,912	104,896	251,762	31,468 80
	Total......	104,978	251,941	104,904	251,791	31,471 20
		Lb.		Lb.		
Quinces, apricots, pears and nec-tarines, n.o.p.	New Zealand...	21,000	1,000	14,700	700	73 50
	Japan..........	6,158	139	6,158	139	30 79
	United States...	11,771,159	383,711	11,759,893	383,321	58,799 69
	Total......	11,798,317	384,850	11,780,751	384,160	58,903 98
All other, n.o.p................	B. W. Indies....	....	211	....	....	....
	Hong Kong.....	....	7	....	7	1 75
	Newfoundland..	....	36	....	36	9 00
	China...........	....	5	....	5	1 25
	Italy...........	....	13,640	....	13,640	3,410 00
	United States..	....	19,576	....	19,456	4,864 00
	Total......	....	33,475	....	33,144	8,286 00

OF IMPORTS—*Continued.*

FOR HOME CONSUMPTION.

Preferential Tariff.			Treaty Rates.			Total.		
Quantity.	Value.	Duty.	Quantity.	Value.	Duty.	Quantity.	Value.	DutyColl'd.
Lb.	$	$ cts.	Lb.	$	$ cts.	Lb.	$	$ cts.
....	....	....	....	....	....	900	113	18 00
....	....	....	....	....	....	20	2	0 40
....	....	....	....	....	....	6,456,436	588,992	129,128 72
....	....	....	....	....	....	6,457,356	589,107	129,147 12
45	3	0 68	....	....	....	45	3	0 68
....	....	....	....	....	....	2,152	239	43 04
....	....	....	....	....	....	936,507	102,155	18,730 14
45	3	0 68	....	....	....	938,704	102,397	18,773 86
Brl.			Brl.			Brl.		
....	....	....	....	....	....	51	183	45 75
....	....	....	....	....	....	11	60	15 00
....	....	....	....	....	....	28,194	109,257	27,314 25
....	....	....	....	....	....	28,256	109,500	27,375 00
Lb.			Lb.			Lb.		
....	....	....	....	....	....	12,920	1,075	258 40
....	....	....	....	....	....	635,276	48,086	12,705 52
....	....	....	....	....	....	31,244	2,211	624 88
....	....	....	....	....	....	5,533,640	266,886	110,672 80
....	....	....	....	....	....	6,200,160	317,183	124,003 20
....	....	....	....	....	....	....	3,758	375 80
....	....	....	....	....	....	12,733,661	340,739	127,336 61
Bush.			Bush.			Bush.		
....	....	....	....	....	....	8	29	2 40
....	....	....	....	....	....	104,896	251,762	31,468 80
....	....	....	....	....	....	104,904	251,791	31,471 20
Lb.			Lb.			Lb.		
....	....	....	....	....	....	14,700	700	73 50
....	....	....	....	....	....	6,158	139	30 79
....	....	....	....	....	....	11,759,893	383,321	58,799 69
....	....	....	....	....	....	11,780,751	384,160	58,903 98
....	211	36 93	....	....	....	....	211	36 93
....	....	....	....	....	....	....	7	1 75
....	....	....	....	....	....	....	36	9 00
....	....	....	....	....	....	....	5	1 25
....	....	....	....	....	....	....	13,640	3,410 00
....	....	....	....	....	....	....	19,456	4,864 00
....	211	36 93	....	....	....	....	33,355	8,322 93

6 GEORGE V, A. 1916

No. 1.—General Statement

Articles Imported.	Countries.	Total Imports.		Entered		
				General Tariff.		
		Quantity.	Value.	Quantity.	Value.	Duty.
DUTIABLE GOODS—Con.		Lb.	$	Lb.	$	$ cts.
Fruits—*Con.*						
Fruits in air-tight cans or other air-tight packages.	Unit'd Kingdom	966,414	47,694	368,586	26,016	9,131 86
	Australia	54,179	5,172	54,179	5,172	1,354 49
	B. India	2,880	93			
	B. W. Indies	87,963	6,585	60,926	4,803	1,440 66
	B. Straits Settlements	1,542,092	60,297	10,805	454	243 12
	Hong Kong	20,680	857	20,386	845	478 99
	Newfoundland	423	60	423	60	10 57
	Chili	48	15	48	15	1 20
	China	14,711	510	14,711	510	352 01
	France	132,026	12,304	82,651	6,740	2,062 08
	Hawaii	336,631	18,967	355,408	20,256	8,716 56
	Holland	37,110	2,320	26,085	1,479	652 12
	Italy	1,100	71	1,430	117	35 75
	Japan	1,274	78	340	26	8 26
	Spain	107,247	4,280	86,493	2,971	2,152 69
	United States	4,456,318	290,033	4,506,731	288,868	110,120 75
	Total	7,761,096	449,336	5,589,202	358,332	136,761 11
		Gal.		Gal.		
Fruits, preserved in brandy or preserved in other spirits, and containing not more than 40 p.c. of proof spirits, etc.	Unit'd Kingdom	13	63	13	63	37 80
	United States	63	251	63	251	128 50
	Total	76	314	76	314	166 30
Fruits preserved in brandy, etc., etc., containing more than 40 p.c. of proof spirits.	Unit'd Kingdom	7	73	7	73	42 90
	United States	15	148	15	148	88 20
	Total	22	221	22	221	131 10
Furniture, house, office, cabinet or store furniture of wood, iron or other material, in parts or finished.	Unit'd Kingdom		110,028		13,732	4,119 60
	B. India		34		34	10 20
	B. W. Indies		249			
	Hong Kong		31,577		4,563	1,368 90
	Aust.-Hungary		11,470		9,538	2,861 40
	Belgium		210		74	22 20
	China		1,445		1,445	433 50
	Cuba		2		2	0 60
	Egypt and Soudan		566		566	169 80
	France		24,378		7,392	2,217 60
	Germany		3,159		3,159	947 70
	Holland		119		52	15 60
	Italy		3,702		3,580	1,074 00
	Japan		7,426		2,371	711 30
	Norway		27		27	8 10
	Philippines		18		18	5 40
	Portugal		70		70	21 00
	Russia		146		92	27 60
	Spain		21		21	6 30
	Switzerland		129		78	23 40
	Turkey		197		197	59 10
	United States		1,319,655		1,313,492	394,047 60
	Total		1,514,628		1,360,503	408,150 90
Furs and manufactures, of, viz.:—						
Fur skins wholly or partially dressed, n.o.p.	Unit'd Kingdom		65,887		37,705	5,655 75
	Newfoundland		700		700	105 00
	Belgium		7,619		7,479	1,121 85
	China		4,015		4,015	602 25
	France		91,261		95,869	14,380 35
	Germany		60,389		67,351	10,102 65

SESSIONAL PAPER No. 11

OF IMPORTS—*Continued.*

FOR HOME CONSUMPTION.

Preferential Tariff.			Treaty Rates.			Total.		
Quantity.	Value.	Duty.	Quantity.	Value.	Duty.	Quantity.	Value.	DutyColl'd.
Lb.	$	$ cts.	Lb.	$	$ cts.	Lb.	$	$ cts.
635,144	27,850	9,913 77	121,465	8,659	2,429 30	1,125,195	62,525	21,474 93
....	....	....	....	....	....	54,179	5,172	1,354 49
2,880	93	43 20	....	....	....	2,880	93	43 20
27,057	1,783	406 67	....	....	....	87,983	6,586	1,847 33
1,446,593	55,280	23,564 63	....	....	....	1,457,398	55,734	23,807 75
....	....	....	144	7	2 88	20,530	852	481 87
....	....	....	....	....	....	423	60	10 57
....	....	....	....	....	....	48	15	1 20
....	....	....	....	....	....	14,711	510	352 01
....	....	....	93,084	8,923	1,861 68	175,735	15,663	3,923 76
....	....	....	....	....	....	355,408	20,256	8,716 56
....	....	....	15,025	1,201	300 50	41,110	2,680	952 62
....	....	....	....	....	....	1,430	117	35 75
....	....	....	934	52	18 68	1,274	78	26 94
....	....	....	44,422	2,486	888 44	130,915	5,457	3,041 13
....	....	....	....	....	....	4,506,731	288,868	110,120 75
2,111,674	85,006	33,928 27	275,074	21,328	5,501 48	7,975,950	464,666	176,190 86
Gal.			Gal.			Gal.		
....	....	....	....	....	....	13	63	37 80
....	....	....	....	....	....	63	251	128 50
....	....	....	....	....	....	76	314	166 30
....	....	....	....	....	....	7	73	42 90
....	....	....	....	....	....	15	148	88 20
....	....	....	....	....	....	22	221	131 10
....	94,115	18,823 00	....	1,544	424 60	....	109,391	23,367 20
....	....	....	....	....	....	....	34	10 20
....	249	49 80	....	....	....	....	249	49 80
....	....	....	....	27,014	7,429 09	....	31,577	8,797 99
....	....	....	....	1,932	531 30	....	11,470	3,392 70
....	....	....	....	136	37 40	....	210	59 60
....	....	....	....	....	....	....	1,445	433 50
....	....	....	....	....	....	....	-2	0 60
....	....	....	....	....	....	....	566	169 80
....	....	....	....	15,771	4,337 02	....	23,163	6,554 62
....	....	....	....	....	....	....	3,159	947 70
....	....	....	....	67	18 42	....	119	34 02
....	....	....	....	267	73 42	....	3,847	1,147 42
....	....	....	....	5,053	1,389 57	....	7,424	2,100 87
....	....	....	....	....	....	....	27	8 10
....	....	....	....	....	....	....	18	5 40
....	....	....	....	....	....	....	70	21 00
....	....	....	....	54	14 85	....	146	42 45
....	....	....	....	....	....	....	21	6 30
....	....	....	....	51	14 02	....	129	37 42
....	....	....	....	....	....	....	197	59 10
....	....	....	....	....	....	....	1,313,492	94,047 60
....	94,364	18,872 80	....	51,889	14,269 69	....	1,506,756	441,293 39
....	24,878	2,487 80	....	....	....	....	62,583	8,143 55
....	....	....	....	....	....	....	700	105 00
....	....	....	....	....	....	....	7,479	1,121 85
....	....	....	....	....	....	....	4,015	602 25
....	....	....	....	....	....	....	95,869	14,380 35
....	....	....	....	....	....	....	67,351	10,102 65

6 GEORGE V, A. 1916

No. 1.—General Statement

Articles Imported.	Countries.	Total Imports.		Entered		
				General Tariff.		
		Quantity.	Value.	Quantity.	Value.	Duty.
			$		$	$ cts.
Dutiable Goods—*Con.*						
Furs and mfrs. of—*Con.*						
Fur skins, wholly or partially	Russia	....	1,005	....	1,005	150 75
dressed, n.o.p.—*Con.*	Spain	....	680	....	680	102 00
	Switzerland	....	741	....	741	111 15
	United States	....	143,137	....	135,252	20,287 80
	Total	....	375,434	....	350,797	52,619 55
Caps, hats, muffs, tippets, capes,	Unit'd Kingdom	....	218,492	....	9,358	2,807 40
coats and cloaks of fur and	Newfoundland	....	40	....	....	....
other manufactures of fur,	Belgium	....	20	....	20	6 00
n.o.p.	France	....	10,644	....	10,644	3,193 20
	Germany	....	12,223	....	11,723	3,516 90
	Italy	....	586	....	586	175 80
	Japan	....	118	....	118	35 40
	Spain	....	9	....	9	2 70
	United States	....	159,311	....	159,705	47,911 50
	Total	....	401,443	....	192,163	57,648 90
Fuses, non-metallic	Unit'd Kingdom	....	68,930	....	....	....
	Germany	....	315	....	315	63 00
	United States	....	20,387	....	20,387	4,077 40
	Total	....	89,632	....	20,702	4,140 40
Glass and manufactures of—						
Glass carboys or demijohns,	Unit'd Kingdom	....	54,314	....	2,897	941 54
bottles, decanters, flasks, jars	Bermuda	....	44	....	44	14 30
and phials.	B. W. Indies	....	548	....	47	15 28
	Hong Kong	....	185	....	185	60 13
	Aust.-Hungary	....	6,696	....	6,696	2,176 20
	Belgium	....	1,000	....	1,000	325 00
	France	....	3,373	....	3,363	1,093 00
	Germany	....	30,435	....	38,742	12,591 15
	Holland	....	6,009	....	11,014	3,579 77
	Italy	....	104	....	104	33 80
	Japan	....	40	....	40	13 00
	Miquelon and					
	St. Pierre	....	20	....	20	6 50
	United States	....	286,175	....	284,704	92,531 29
	Total	....	388,943	....	348,856	113,380 96
Glass balls, and cut, pressed or	Unit'd Kingdom	....	27,971	....	10,713	3,481 75
moulded, crystal glass table-	Hong Kong	....	38	....	38	12 35
ware, blown glass tableware,	Newfoundland	....	90	....	....	....
and other cut glass ware.	Aust.-Hungary	....	15,500	....	15,608	5,072 65
	Belgium	....	22,281	....	27,318	8,878 35
	China	....	109	....	109	35 43
	France	....	8,825	....	8,678	2,820 35
	Germany	....	30,380	....	30,352	9,864 40
	Holland	....	4,894	....	4,917	1,598 05
	Italy	....	1,211	....	1,211	393 60
	Japan	....	40	....	40	13 00
	Norway	....	30	....	30	9 75
	Roumania	....	25	....	25	8 13
	Sweden	....	5,594	....	5,594	1,818 05
	United States	....	264,029	....	264,735	86,041 68
	Total	....	381,017	....	369,368	120,047 54

OF IMPORTS—*Continued.*

FOR HOME CONSUMPTION.

	Preferential Tariff.			Treaty Rates.			Total.	
Quantity.	Value.	Duty.	Quantity.	Value.	Duty.	Quantity.	Value.	DutyColl'd.
	$	$ cts.		$	$ cts.		$	$ cts.
....	....	....	....	....	....	....	1,005	150 75
....	....	....	....	....	....	....	680	102 00
....	....	....	....	....	....	....	741	111 15
....	....	....	....	....	....	....	135,252	20,287 80
....	24,878	2,487 80	....	....	....	....	375,675	55,107 35
....	209,726	41,945 20	....	....	....	....	219,084	44,752 60
....	....	....	....	....	....	....	20	6 00
....	....	....	....	....	....	....	10,644	3,193 20
....	....	....	....	....	....	....	11,723	3,516 90
....	....	....	....	....	....	....	586	175 80
....	....	....	....	....	....	....	118	35 40
....	....	....	....	....	....	....	9	2 70
....	....	....	....	....	....	....	159,705	47,911 50
....	209,726	41,945 20	....	....	....	....	401,889	99,594 10
....	69,501	8,687 68	....	....	....	....	69,501	8,687 68
....	....	....	....	....	....	....	315	63 00
....	....	....	....	....	....	....	20,387	4,077 40
....	69,501	8,687 68	....	....	....	....	90,203	12,828 08
....	42,737	8,547 40	....	....	....	....	45,634	9,488 94
....	....	....	....	....	....	....	44	14 30
....	503	100 60	....	....	....	....	550	115 88
....	....	....	....	....	....	....	185	60 13
....	....	....	....	....	....	....	6,696	2,176 20
....	....	....	....	....	....	....	1,000	325 00
....	....	....	....	....	....	....	3,363	1,093 00
....	....	....	....	....	....	....	38,742	12,591 15
....	....	....	....	....	....	....	11,014	3,579 77
....	....	....	....	....	....	....	104	33 80
....	....	....	....	....	....	....	40	13 00
....	....	....	....	....	....	....	20	6 50
....	....	....	....	....	....	....	284,704	92,531 29
....	43,240	8,648 00	....	....	....	....	392,096	122,028 96
....	17,475	3,435 00	....	....	....	....	27,888	6,916 75
....	....	....	....	....	....	....	38	12 35
....	....	....	....	....	....	....	15,608	5,072 65
....	....	....	....	....	....	....	27,318	8,878 35
....	....	....	....	....	....	....	109	35 43
....	....	....	....	....	....	....	8,678	2,820 35
....	....	....	....	....	....	....	30,352	9,864 40
....	....	....	....	....	....	....	4,917	1,598 05
....	....	....	....	....	....	....	1,211	393 60
....	....	....	....	....	....	....	40	13 00
....	....	....	....	....	....	....	30	9 75
....	....	....	....	....	....	....	25	8 13
....	....	....	....	....	....	....	5,594	1,818 05
....	....	....	....	....	....	....	264,735	86,041 68
....	17,175	3,435 00	....	....	....	....	386,543	123,482 54

6 GEORGE V, A. 1916

No. 1.—General Statement

Articles Imported.	Countries.	Total Imports.		Entered		
				General Tariff.		
		Quantity.	Value.	Quantity.	Value.	Duty.
			$		$	$ cts.
DUTIABLE GOODS—*Con.*						
Glass, mfrs. of—*Con.*						
Lamp chimneys, glass shades or globes.	Unit'd Kingdom	....	3,018	....	1,314	427 05
	Hong Kong.....	....	5	....	5	1 64
	Aust.-Hungary..	....	5,429	....	5,281	1,716 35
	Belgium........	....	28	....	28	9 10
	China..........	....	8	....	8	2 60
	France.........	....	929	....	959	311 70
	Germany.......	....	16,729	....	16,643	5,409 00
	Holland........	....	3	....	3	0 98
	Italy..........	....	10	....	10	3 25
	Japan..........	....	6	....	6	1 95
	United States...	....	186,286	....	186,384	60,576 70
	Total......	....	212,451	....	210,641	68,460 32
Ornamental figured and enamelled coloured glass and memorial or other ornamental window glass, n.o.p.	Unit'd Kingdom	....	5,208	....	75	18 75
	Belgium........	....	47	....	47	11 75
	United States...	....	2,866	....	2,866	716 50
	Total......	....	8,121	....	2,988	747 00
Painted or vitrified, chipped, figured, enamelled and obscured white glass.	Unit'd Kingdom	....	3,624	....	....	....
	Belgium........	....	46	....	46	11 50
	United States...	....	1,280	....	1,280	320 00
	Total......	....	4,950	....	1,326	331 50
		Sq. ft.		Sq. ft.		
Common and colourless window glass.	Unit'd Kingdom	7,593,930	237,813	334,490	10,291	1,286 38
	Belgium........	10,501,798	276,701	10,501,798	276,701	34,587 63
	France.........	20,000	565	20,000	565	70 63
	Germany.......	38,378	1,360	38,378	1,360	170 00
	Holland.......	6,100	191	6,100	191	23 88
	United States...	20,284,131	731,243	20,284,118	731,241	91,405 97
	Total......	38,444,337	1,247,873	31,184,884	1,020,349	127,544 49
Plain, coloured, opaque, stained or tinted, or muffled glass in sheets.	Unit'd Kingdom	....	27,707	....	382	95 50
	Aust.-Hungary..	....	41	....	41	10 25
	Belgium........	....	3,000	....	3,000	750 00
	France.........	....	379	....	379	94 75
	Germany.......	....	591	....	591	147 75
	United States...	....	32,017	....	32,017	8,004 25
	Total......	....	63,735	....	36,410	9,102 50
Plate glass, not bevelled, in sheets or panes, not exceeding 7 sq. ft. each, n.o.p.	Unit'd Kingdom	315,914	59,279	7,968	1,420	142 00
	Belgium........	312,218	61,299	313,916	61,594	6,159 40
	France.........	12,488	2,579	12,488	2,579	257 90
	United States...	303,864	68,115	303,864	68,115	6,811 50
	Total......	944,484	191,272	638,236	133,708	13,370 80
Plate glass, not bevelled, in sheets or panes exceeding 7 sq. ft. each., and not exceeding 25 sq. ft. each. n.o.p.	Unit'd Kingdom	364,295	82,893	....	....	....
	Belgium........	245,054	52,668	11,387	3,000	852 50
	France.........	7,104	1,378	....		
	United States..	190,681	49,141	190,681	49,141	13,513 96
	Total......	807,134	186,080	202,068	52,241	14,366 46

OF IMPORTS—*Continued.*

FOR HOME CONSUMPTION.

Preferential Tariff.			Treaty Rates.			Total.		
Quantity.	Value.	Duty.	Quantity.	Value.	Duty.	Quantity.	Value.	DutyColl'd.
	$	$ cts.		$	$ cts.		$	$ cts.
....	2,095	419 00	....	....	....	....	3,409	846 05
....	....	....	....	....	....	....	5	1 64
....	....	....	....	....	....	....	5,281	1,716 35
....	....	....	....	....	....	....	28	9 10
....	....	....	....	....	....	....	8	2 60
....	....	....	....	....	....	....	959	311 70
....	....	....	....	....	....	....	16,643	5,409 00
....	....	....	....	....	....	....	3	0 98
....	....	....	....	....	....	....	10	3 25
....	....	....	....	....	....	....	6	1 95
....	....	....	....	....	....	....	186,384	60,576 70
....	2,095	419 00	....	....	....	....	212,736	68,879 32
....	5,133	898 34	....	....	....	....	5,208	917 09
....	....	....	....	....	....	....	47	11 75
....	....	....	....	....	....	....	2,866	716 50
....	5,133	898 34	....	....	....	....	8,121	1,645 34
....	3,624	634 23	....	....	....	....	3,624	634 23
....	....	....	....	....	....	....	46	11 50
....	....	....	....	....	....	....	1,280	320 00
....	3,624	634 23	....	....	....	....	4,950	965 73
Sq. ft. 7,259,440	227,522	17,064 27	Sq. ft.	....	....	Sq. ft. 7,593,930	237,813	18,350 65
....	....	....	....	....	....	10,501,798	276,701	34,587 63
....	....	....	....	....	....	20,000	565	70 63
....	....	....	....	....	....	38,378	1,360	170 00
....	....	....	....	....	....	6,100	191	23 88
....	....	....	....	....	....	20,284,118	731,241	91,405 97
7,259,440	227,522	17,064 27	....	....	....	38,444,324	1,247,871	144,608 76
....	27,325	4,781 98	....	....	....	....	27,707	4,877 48
....	....	....	....	....	....	....	41	10 25
....	....	....	....	....	....	....	3,000	750 00
....	....	....	....	....	....	....	379	94 75
....	....	....	....	....	....	....	591	147 75
....	....	....	....	....	....	....	32,017	8,004 25
....	27,325	4,781 98	....	....	....	....	63,735	13,884 48
307,946	57,859	4,339 65	....	....	....	315,914	59,279	4,481 65
....	....	....	....	....	....	313,916	61,594	6,159 40
....	....	....	....	....	....	12,488	2,579	257 90
....	....	....	....	....	....	303,864	68,115	6,811 50
307,946	57,859	4,339 65	....	....	....	946,182	191,567	17,710 45
364,295	82,893	12,433 95	....	....	....	364,295	82,893	12,433 95
....	....	....	233,667	49,568	12,392 00	245,054	52,668	13,244 50
....	....	....	7,104	1,378	344 50	7,104	1,378	344 50
....	....	....	....	....	....	190,681	49,141	13,513 96
364,295	82,893	12,433 95	240,771	50,946	12,736 50	807,134	186,080	39,536 91

6 GEORGE V, A. 1916

No. 1.—General Statement

Articles Imported.	Countries.	Total Imports.		Entered		
				General Tariff.		
		Quantity.	Value.	Quantity.	Value.	Duty.
DUTIABLE GOODS—*Con.*		Sq. ft.	$	Sq. ft.	$	$ cts.
Glass, mfrs. of—*Con.*						
Plate glass, n.o.p...............	Unit'd Kingdom	592,672	151,661	....	....	....
	Belgium........	218,195	50,554	218,537	50,393	17,637 55
	France.........	6,027	1,244	6,027	1,244	435 40
	Germany.......	2,971	828	2,971	828	289 80
	Holland........	11,818	2,822	11,818	2,822	987 70
	United States...	222,038	62,797	222,038	62,797	21,978 95
	Total......	1,053,721	269,906	461,391	118,084	41,329 40
Plate glass, bevelled, n.o.p........	Unit'd Kingdom	119	42	....	....	....
	Belgium........	2,890	810	2,890	810	283 50
	United States...	8,580	2,524	8,580	2,524	883 40
	Total......	11,589	3,376	11,470	3,334	1,166 90
German looking glass (thin plate), unsilvered or for silvering.	Aust.-Hungary..	....	189	....	189	37 80
	Germany.......	....	637	....	637	127 40
	United States...	....	66	....	66	13 20
	Total......	....	892	....	892	178 40
Silvered glass, bevelled or not, framed or not framed.	Unit'd Kingdom	....	41,474	....	634	221 90
	Hong Kong.....	....	8	....	8	2 80
	Aust.-Hungary..	....	136	....	136	47 60
	Belgium........	....	763	....	656	229 60
	France.........	....	17,558	....	3,520	1,232 00
	Germany.......	....	10,301	....	10,311	3,608 85
	Holland........	....	1	....	1	0 35
	Italy..........	....	92	....	92	32 20
	Japan..........	....	180	....	52	18 20
	Spain..........	....	2	....	....	....
	Switzerland.....	....	2	....	2	0 70
	United States...	....	34,351	....	34,268	11,993 80
	Total......	....	104,868	....	49,680	17,388 00
Stained or ornamental glass windows.	Unit'd Kingdom	....	15,158	....	550	165 00
	Belgium........	....	49	....	49	14 70
	Germany.......	....	2,770	....	2,770	831 00
	United States...	....	9,181	....	9,181	2,754 30
	Total......	....	27,158	....	12,550	3,765 00
Glass in sheets and bent plate glass, n.o.p.	Unit'd Kingdom	....	16,182	....	201	50 25
	Aust.-Hungary.	....	201	....	4,004	1,001 00
	Belgium........	....	4,004	....	359	92 25
	France.........	....	369	....	1,152	288 00
	Germany.......	....	1,152	....	685	171 25
	Holland........	....	685	....	37,561	9,390 25
	United States...	....	37,561	....		
	Total......	....	60,154	....	43,972	10,993 00
Articles of glass, not plate or sheet, designed to be cut or mounted, and manufactures of glass, n.o.p.	Unit'd Kingdom	....	39,491	....	11,022	2,479 95
	Hong Kong.....	....	6	....	6	1 35
	Aust.-Hungary..	....	6,836	....	3,286	739 35
	Belgium........	....	7,979	....	559	125 78
	China..........	....	82	....	82	18 45
	France.........	....	13,708	....	2,100	472 50
	Germany.......	....	24,514	....	24,514	5,515 65
	Holland........	....	69	....	21	4 74

OF IMPORTS—*Continued.*

FOR HOME CONSUMPTION.

	Preferential Tariff.			Treaty Rates.			Total.	
Quantity.	Value.	Duty.	Quantity.	Value.	Duty.	Quantity.	Value.	DutyColl'd.
Sq. Ft.	$	$ cts.	Sq. Ft.	$	$ cts.	Sq. Ft.	$	$ cts.
592,672	151,661	34,124 03	....	....	....	592,672	151,661	34,124 03
....	....	....	....	....	....	218,537	50,393	17,637 55
....	....	....	....	....	....	6,027	1,244	435 40
....	....	....	....	....	....	2,971	828	289 80
....	....	....	....	....	....	11,818	2,822	987 70
....	....	....	....	....	....	222,038	62,797	21,978 95
592,672	151,661	34,124 03	....	....	....	1,054,063	269,745	75,453 43
119	42	9 45	....			119	42	9 45
....	....	....	....			2,890	810	283 50
....	....	....	....			8,580	2,524	883 40
119	42	9 45	....	....	....	11,589	3,376	1,176 35
....	....	....	....	....	....	189		37 80
....	....	....	....	....	....	637		127 40
....	....	....	....	....	....	66		13 20
....	....	....	....	....	....	892		178 40
....	40,518	9,116 96	....	214	64 20	....	41,366	9,403 06
....	....	....	....	....	....	8		2 80
....	....	....	....	....	....	136		47 60
....	....	....	....	107	32 10	....	763	261 70
....	....	....	....	13,886	4,165 80	....	17,406	5,397 80
....	....	....	....	....	....	10,311		3,608 85
....	....	....	....	....	....	1		0 35
....	....	....	....	128	38 40	....	92	32 20
....	....	....	....	....	....	180		56 60
....	....	....	....	....	....	2		0 70
....	....	....	....	....	....	34,268		11,993 80
....	40,518	9,116 96	....	14,335	4,300 50	....	104,533	30,805 46
....	14,608	2,921 60	....			15,155		3,086 60
....	....	....	....			49		14 70
....	....	....	....			2,770		831 00
....	....	....	....			9,181		2,754 30
....	14,608	2,921 60	....	....	....	27,158		6,686 60
....	16,182	2,831 91	....			16,182		2,831 91
....	....	....	....			201		50 25
....	....	....	....			4,004		1,001 00
....	....	....	....			369		92 25
....	....	....	....			1,152		288 00
....	....	....	....			685		171 25
....	....	....	....			37,561		9,390 25
....	16,182	2,831 91	....	....	....	60,154		13,824 91
....	23,162	3,474 30	....	5,496	1,099 20	....	39,680	7,053 45
....	....	....	....	....	....	6		1 35
....	....	....	....	3,550	710 00	....	6,836	1,449 35
....	....	....	....	7,420	1,484 00	....	7,979	1,609 78
....	....	....	....	....	....	82		18 45
....	....	....	....	11,807	2,361 40	....	13,907	2,833 90
....	....	....	....	....	....	24,514		5,515 65
....	....	....	....	48	9 60	....	69	14 34

6 GEORGE V, A. 1916

No. 1.—General Statement

Articles Imported.	Countries.	Total Imports.		Entered		
		Quantity.	Value.	General Tariff.		
				Quantity.	Value.	Duty.
DUTIABLE GOODS—*Con.*			$		$	$ cts.
Glass, mfrs. of—*Con.*						
Articles of glass, not plate or	Italy............	....	1,692	....	1,692	380 70
sheet, etc.—*Con.*	Japan..........	....	115	....	55	12 38
	Sweden........	....	1	....	2	0 45
	Switzerland....	....	6,011	....	5,107	1,149 08
	United States...	....	237,643	....	237,423	53,422 05
	Total......	....	338,147	....	285,869	64,322 43
Gloves and mitts of all kinds.....	Unit'd Kingdom	....	763,673	....	61,988	21,695 80
	Hong Kong.....	....	2	....	2	0 70
	Aust.-Hungary..	....	14,591	....	379	132 65
	Belgium.......	....	4,463	....	1,031	360 85
	France........	....	429,057	....	36,628	12,819 80
	Germany......	....	174,061	....	174,138	60,948 30
	Holland.......	....	202	....	202	70 70
	Italy..........	....	99,444	....	57,765	20,217 75
	Japan.........	....	187	....	....	....
	Miquelon and					
	St. Pierre.....	....	5	....	5	1 75
	Switzerland.....	....	1,203	....	71	24 85
	United States...	....	310,054	....	279,072	97,675 20
	Total......	....	1,796,942	....	611,281	213,948 35
Gold and silver, manufactures of:	Unit'd Kingdom	....	16,204	....	2,810	772 75
Gold, silver and Dutch or Schlag	France........	....	510	....	325	89 38
metal leaf.	Germany......	....	12,662	....	12,662	3,482 05
	United States...	....	14,408	....	14,408	3,962 50
	Total......	....	43,784	....	30,205	8,306 68
Manufactures of gold and silver,	Unit'd Kingdom	....	5,015	....	89	31 15
n.o.p.	Aust.-Hungary.	....	510	....	10	3 50
	France........	....	352	....	16	5 60
	Germany......	....	382	....	382	133 70
	Holland.......	....	644	....	....	....
	United States...	....	6,058	....	6,052	2,118 20
	Total......	....	12,961	....	6,549	2,292 15
Electro-plated ware and gilt	Unit'd Kingdom	....	167,657	....	3,071	1,074 85
ware, n.o.p.	Newfoundland..	....	5	....	5	1 75
	Aust.-Hungary..	....	18	....	....	....
	China.........	....	3	....	3	1 05
	France........	....	2,625	....	48	16 80
	Germany......	....	1,550	....	1,576	551 60
	Japan.........	....	291	....	....	....
	United States...	....	97,658	....	97,862	34,251 70
	Total......	....	269,807	....	102,565	35,897 75
Sterling or other silverware,	Unit'd Kingdom	....	139,170	....	3,015	1,055 25
n.o.p.	B. India......	....	1,136	....	1,136	397 60
	Hong Kong.....	....	5	....	5	1 75
	Aust.-Hungary.	....	93	....	76	26 60
	Denmark......	....	165	....	165	57 75
	France........	....	4,527	....	999	349 65
	Germany......	....	3,067	....	3,067	1,073 45
	Italy..........	....	212	....	212	74 20
	Japan.........	....	20	....	....	....
	United States...	....	83,145	....	83,009	29,053 15
	Total......	....	231,540	....	91,684	32,089 40

SESSIONAL PAPER No. 11

OF IMPORTS—*Continued.*

FOR HOME CONSUMPTION.

	Preferential Tariff.			Treaty Rates.			Total.	
Quantity.	Value.	Duty.	Quantity.	Value.	Duty.	Quantity.	Value.	DutyColl'd.
	$	$ cts.		$	$ cts.		$	$ cts.
....	....	....	....	....	12 00	....	1,692	380 70
....	....	....	....	60	....	....	115	24 38
....	....	....	....	....	....	....	2	0 45
....	....	....	....	904	180 80	....	6,011	1,329 88
....	....	....	....	....	....	....	237,423	53,422 05
....	23,162	3,474 30	....	29,285	5,857 00	....	338,316	73,653 73
....	608,818	136,985 26	....	92,276	27,682 80	....	763,082	186,363 86
....	....	....	....	....	....	....	2	0 70
....	....	....	....	15,507	4,652 10	....	15,886	4,784 75
....	....	....	....	3,432	1,029 60	....	4,463	1,390 45
....	....	....	....	390,845	117,253 50	....	427,473	130,073 30
....	....	....••...	....	....	....	....	174,138	60,948 30
....	....	....	....	....	....	....	202	70 70
....	....	....	....	44,628	13,388 40	....	102,393	33,606 15
....	....	....	....	187	56 10	....	187	56 10
....	....	....	....	....	....	....	5	1 75
....	....	....	....	1,132	339 60	....	1,203	364 45
....	....	....	....	....	....	....	279,072	97,675 20
....	608,818	136,985 26	....	548,007	164,402 10	....	1,768,106	515,335 71
....	13,060	1,959 00	....	334	83 50	....	16,204	2,815 25
....	....	....	....	185	46 25	....	510	135 63
....	....	....	....	....	....	....	12,662	3,482 05
....	....	....	....	....	....	....	14,408	3,962 50
....	13,060	1,959 00	....	519	129 75	....	43,784	10,395 43
....	4,827	1,086 21	....	99	29 70	....	5,015	1,147 06
....	....	....	....	500	150 00	....	510	153 50
....	....	....	....	336	100 80	....	352	106 40
....	....	....	....	....	....	....	382	133 70
....	....	....	....	644	193 20	....	644	193 20
....	....	....	....	....	....	....	6,052	2,118 20
....	4,827	1,086 21	....	1,579	473 70	....	12,955	3,852 06
....	163,986	36,897 35	....	103	30 90	....	167,160	38,003 10
....	....	....	....	....	....	....	5	1 75
....	....	....	....	10	3 00	....	10	3 00
....	....	....	....	....	....	....	3	1 05
....	....	....	....	2,587	776 10	....	2,635	792 90
....	....	....	....	....	....	....	1,576	551 60
....	....	....	....	291	87 30	....	291	87 30
....	....	....	....	....	....	....	97,862	34,251 70
....	163,986	36,897 35	....	2,991	897 30	....	269,542	73,692 40
....	138,814	31,233 83	....	381	114 30	....	142,210	32,403 38
....	....	....	....	....	....	....	1,136	397 60
....	....	....	....	....	....	....	5	1 75
....	....	....	....	17	5 10	....	93	31 70
....	....	....	....	....	....	....	165	57 75
....	....	....	....	3,530	1,059 00	....	4,529	1,408 65
....	....	....	....	....	....	....	3,067	1,073 45
....	....	....	....	....	....	....	212	74 20
....	....	....	....	20	6 00	....	20	6 00
....	....	....	....	....	....	....	83,009	29,053 15
....	138,814	31,233 83	....	3,948	1,184 40	....	234,446	64,507 63

11—ii—8½

6 GEORGE V, A. 1916

No. 1.—General Statement

Articles Imported.	Countries.	Total Imports.		Entered		
				General Tariff.		
		Quantity.	Value.	Quantity.	Value.	Duty.
DUTIABLE GOODS—*Con.*			$		$	$ cts.
Gold and silver—*Con.*						
Silver and other coin, foreign, except gold.	United States...	....	39	....	39	13 65
		Lb.		Lb.		
Grease, Axle....................	Unit'd Kingdom	47,250	1,707	1,480	159	31 80
	United States...	3,193,008	135,584	3,181,072	134,667	26,933 40
	Total.......	3,240,258	137,291	3,182,552	134,826	26,965 20
Gunpowder and other explosives, &c.—						
Gun ,rifle, sporting, cannon, musket and cannister powder.	Unit'd Kingdom	57,795	25,895	34	38	1 02
	United States...	153,813	121,887	153,813	121,887	4,614 39
	Uruguay.......	....	....	75	18	2 25
	Total.......	211,608	147,782	153,922	121,943	4,617 66
Blasting and mining powder....	Unit'd Kingdom	134,800	14,233	....	....	....
	United States...	13,325	1,551	13,325	1,551	266 50
	Total.......	148,125	15,784	13,325	1,551	266 50
Giant powder, nitro, nitro-glycerine and other explosives, no.p.	Unit'd Kingdom	18,410	20,057	....	....	....
	United States...	549,410	97,974	549,410	97,974	13,735 30
	Total.......	567,820	118,031	549,410	97,974	13,735 30
Gun, rifle and pistol cartridges, or other ammunition, n.o.p.	Unit'd Kingdom	....	242,351	....	196	58 80
	Newfoundland..	....	3	....	3	0 90
	Belgium.......	....	1,143	....	1,143	342 90
	France.........	....	316	....	316	94 80
	Germany......	....	1,222	....	1,222	366 60
	United States...	....	460,938	....	460,900	138,270 00
	Total.....:	....	705,973	....	463,780	139,134 0
Gun wads, percussion caps,primers and cartridge cases.	Unit'd Kingdom	....	2,577	....	....	....
	Germany......	....	14,912	....	14,912	4,473 60
	United States...	....	11,617	....	11,480	3,444 00
	Total.......	....	29,106	....	26,392	7,917 60
Gun or pistol covers or cases, game bags, loading tools, and cartridge belts of any material.	Unit'd Kingdom	....	5,035	....	59	17 70
	United States...	....	29,960	....	29,960	8,988 00
	Total.......	....	34,995	....	30,019	9,005 70
Gutta percha and india-rubber, manufactures of—						
Boots and shoes...............	Unit'd Kingdom	....	26,044	....	352	88 00
	Japan..........	....	10	....	10	2 50
	United States...	....	102,788	....	100,352	25,088 00
	Total.......	....	128,842	....	100,714	25,178 50
Belting......................	Unit'd Kingdom	....	4,523	....	....	....
	United States...	....	77,542	....	77,532	21,321 85
	Total.......	....	82,065	....	77,532	21,321 85

SESSIONAL PAPER No. 11

OF IMPORTS—*Continued*.

FOR HOME CONSUMPTION.

Preferential Tariff.			Treaty Rates.			Total.		
Quantity.	Value.	Duty.	Quantity.	Value.	Duty.	Quantity.	Value.	DutyColl'd.
	$	$ cts.		$	$ cts.		$	$ cts.
....	....	....	....	....	....	....	39	13 65
Lb. 45,770	1,548	193 49	Lb.	....	....	Lb. 47,250	1,707	225 29
....	....	....	....	....	....	3,181,072	134,667	26,933 40
45,770	1,548	193 49	....	....	....	3,228,322	136,374	27,158 69
57,761	25,857	1,155 22	....	....	....	57,795	25,895	1,156 24
....	....	....	....	....	....	153,813	121,887	4,614 39
....	....	....	....	....	....	75	18	2 25
57,761	25,857	1,155 22	....	....	....	211,683	147,800	5,772 88
134,800	14,233	1,797 33	....	....	....	134,800	14,233	1,797 33
....	....	....	....	....	....	13,325	1,551	266 50
134,800	14,233	1,797 33	....	....	....	148,125	15,784	2,063 83
18,410	20,057	322 18	....	....	....	18,410	20,057	322 18
....	....	....	....	....	....	549,410	97,974	13,735 30
18,410	20,057	322 18	....	....	....	567,820	118,031	14,057 48
....	239,470	47,894 00	....	....	....	....	239,666	47,952 80
....	....	....	....	....	....	....	3	0 90
....	....	....	....	....	....	....	1,143	342 90
....	....	....	....	....	....	....	316	94 80
....	....	....	....	....	....	....	1,222	366 60
....	....	....	....	....	....	....	460,900	138,270 00
....	239,470	47,894 00	....	....	....	....	703,250	187,028 00
....	2,577	515 40	....	....	....	....	2,577	515 40
....	....	....	....	....	....	....	14,912	4,473 60
....	....	....	....	....	....	....	11,480	3,444 00
....	2,577	515 40	....	....	....	....	28,969	8,433 00
....	4,976	995 20	....	....	....	....	5,035	1,012 90
....	....	....	....	....	....	....	29,960	8,988 00
....	4,976	995 20	....	....	....	....	34,995	10,000 90
....	25,692	3,853 80	....	....	....	....	26,044	3,941 80
....	....	....	....	....	....	....	10	2 50
....	....	....	....	....	....	....	100,352	25,088 00
....	25,692	3,853 80	....	....	....	....	126,406	29,032 30
....	4,523	904 60	....	....	....	....	4,523	904 60
....	....	....	....	....	....	....	77,532	21,321 85
....	4,523	904 60	....	....	....	....	82,055	22,226 45

6 GEORGE V, A. 1916

No. 1.—General Statement

Articles Imported.	Countries.	Total Imports.		Entered		
				General Tariff.		
		Quantity.	Value.	Quantity.	Value.	Duty.
DUTIABLE GOODS—*Con.*			$		$	$ cts.
ᴗGutta-percha—*Con.*						
Clothing, and clothing made waterproof with india-rubber.	Unit'd Kingdom	....	748,618	....	5,174	1,810 90
	Hong Kong.....	....	2	....	2	0 70
	Aust.-Hungary .	....	14	....	14	4 90
	France..........	....	60	....	55	19 25
	Germany......	....	208	....	488	170 80
	Japan..........	....	3	....	3	1 05
	United States...	....	52,611	....	51,780	18,123 00
	Total......	....	801,516	....	57,516	20,130 60
Hose, including cotton or linen, lined with rubber...........	Unit'd Kingdom	....	3,140	....	51	17 85
	United States...	....	87,943	....	88,151	30,852 85
	Total......	....	91,083	....	88,202	30,870 70
Packing, mats and matting....	Unit'd Kingdom	....	3,096	....	5	1 75
	Germany......	....	58	....	58	20 30
	United States...	....	66,510	....	66,507	23,277 45
	Total......	....	69,664	....	66,570	23,299 50
Tires of rubber for vehicles of all kinds.	Unit'd Kingdom	....	44,953	....	5,571	1,949 85
	Belgium........	....	2,191	....	2,191	766 85
	France.......	....	47,643	....	40,612	14,214 20
	Germany......	....	13,109	....	19,480	6,818 00
	Holland......	....	220	....	220	77 00
	Italy..........	....	3,283	....	3,283	1,149 05
	Russia.........	....	43,086	....	43,086	15,080 10
	United States...	....	1,044,592	....	1,050,275	367,596 25
–	Total......	....	1,199,077	....	1,164,718	407,651 30
Rubber cement and all manufactures of india-rubber and gutta-percha, n.o.p.	Unit'd Kingdom	....	225,023	....	9,112	2,505 80
	Newfoundland..	....	25	....	25	6 88
	Aust.-Hungary .	....	3,425	....	1,266	348 15
	Belgium.......	....	1,325	....	....	....
	France.......	....	3,212	....	1,298	356 40
	Germany......	....	24,226	....	24,105	6,628 90
	Holland......	....	5	....	5	1 38
	Italy..........	....	25	....	25	6 88
	Japan..........	....	224	....	5	1 38
	Russia.........	....	8	....	8	2 20
	Sweden........	....	2	....	....	....
	Switzerland....	....	14	....	14	3 85
	United States...	....	620,662	....	620,974	170,771 82
	Total......	....	878,176	....	656,835	180,633 64
Rubber, hard, unfinished, in tubes, for the manufacture oi fountain pens.	United States...	....	5,957	....	5,957	595 70
Hair and manufactures of, not otherwise provided for—						
Braids, chains or cords.........	Unit'd Kingdom	....	34	....	19	6 65
	France..........	....	103	....	103	36 05
	Germany......	....	56	....	56	19 60
	United States...	....	447	....	447	156 45
	Total......	....	640	....	625	218 75

OF IMPORTS—*Continued.*

FOR HOME CONSUMPTION.

	Preferential Tariff.			Treaty Rates.			Total.	
Quantity.	Value.	Duty.	Quantity.	Value.	Duty.	Quantity.	Value.	DutyColl'd.
	$	$ cts.		$	$ cts.		$	$ cts.
....	747,299	168,143 90	....	....	....	....	752,473	169,954 80
....	....	....	....	....	....	....	2	0 70
....	....	....	....	....	....	....	14	4 90
....	....	....	....	....	....	....	55	19 25
....	....	....	....	....	....	....	488	170 80
....	....	....	....	....	....	....	3	1 05
....	....	....	....	....	....	....	51,780	18,123 00
....	747,299	168,143 90	....	....	....	....	804,815	188,274 50
....	3,089	695 05	....	....	....	....	3,140	712 90
....	....	....	....	....	....	....	88,151	30,852 85
....	3,089	695 05	....	....	....	....	91,291	31,565 75
....	3,200	720 08	....	....	....	....	3,205	721 83
....	....	....	....	....	....	....	58	20 30
....	....	....	....	....	....	....	66,507	23,277 45
....	3,200	720 08	....	....	....	....	69,770	24,019 58
....	39,739	8,941 44	....	....	....	....	45,310	10,891 29
....	....	....	....	....	....	....	2,191	766 85
....	....	....	....	....	....	....	40,612	14,214 20
....	....	....	....	....	....	....	19,480	6,818 00
....	....	....	....	....	....	....	220	77 00
....	....	....	....	....	....	....	3,283	1,149 05
....	....	....	....	....	....	....	43,086	15,080 10
....	....	....	....	....	....	....	1,050,275	367,596 25
....	· 39,739	8,941 44	....	....	....	....	1,204,457	416,592 74
....	213,173	31,975 95	....	1,806	451 50	....	224,091	34,933 25
....	....	....	....	....	....	....	25	6 88
....	....	....	....	2,133	533 25	....	3,399	881 40
....	....	....	....	425	106 25	....	425	106 25
....	....	....	....	1,916	479 00	....	3,212	835 40
....	....	....	....	....	....	....	24,105	6,628 90
....	....	....	....	....	....	....	5	1 38
....	....	....	....	....	....	....	25	6 88
....	....	....	....	219	54 75	....	224	56 13
....	....	....	....	....	....	....	8	2 20
....	....	....	....	2	0 50	....	2	0 50
....	....	....	....	....	....	....	14	3 85
....	....	....	....	....	....	....	620,974	170,771 82
....	213,173	31,975 95	....	6,501	1,625 25	....	876,509	214,234 84
....	....	....	....	....	....	....	5,957	595 70
....	15	3 38	....	....	....	....	34	10 03
....	....	....	....	....	....	....	103	36 05
....	....	....	....	....	....	....	56	19 60
....	....	....	....	....	....	....	447	156 45
....	15	3 38	....	....	....	....	640	222 13

6 GEORGE V, A. 1916

No. 1.—General Statement

Articles Imported.	Countries.	Total Imports.		Entered		
		Quantity.	Value.	General Tariff.		
				Quantity.	Value.	Duty.
DUTIABLE GOODS—*Con.*			$		$	$ cts.
Hair, mfrs. of—*Con.*						
Curled or dyed, n.o.p..........	Unit'd Kingdom	....	4,717	....	31	6 20
	France..........	....	22	....	22	4 40
	Germany......	....	81	....	81	16 20
	Japan..........	....	20	....	20	4 00
	United States..	....	24,361	....	24,361	4,872 20
	Total......	....	29,201	....	24,515	4,903 00
Hair cloth of all kinds..........	Unit'd Kingdom	....	36,059	....	323	96 90
	Germany......	....	60	....	60	18 00
	United States..	....	1,526	....	1,526	457 80
	Total......	....	37,645	....	1,909	572 70
Other manufactures of, n.o.p....	Unit'd Kingdom	....	11,385	....	8,115	2,840 25
	Aust.-Hungary..	....	483	....	483	169 05
	France..........	....	3,244	....	3,244	1,135 40
	Germany......	....	665	....	665	232 75
	Japan..........	....	24	....	24	8 40
	United States..	....	17,410	....	17,717	6,200 95
	Total......	....	33,211	....	30,248	10,586 80
Hats, caps and bonnets, n.o.p.—						
Beaver, silk or felt.............	Unit'd Kingdom	....	457,298	....	13,970	4,889 50
	B. W. Indies....	....	33	....		
	Aust.-Hungary..	....	6,845	....	7,908	2,767 80
	Belgium........	....	1,827	....	1,802	630 70
	France..........	....	15,140	....	15,140	5,299 00
	Germany......	....	1,696	....	1,696	593 60
	Holland........	....	11	....	11	3 85
	Italy..........	....	68,898	....	68,681	24,038 35
	Japan..........	....	9	....	9	3 15
	United States..	....	407,280	....	407,915	142,770 25
	Total......	....	959,037	....	517,132	180,996 20
Straw, grass, chip or other material n.o.p.	Unit'd Kingdom	....	816,601	....	35,261	12,341 35
	B. W. Indies....	....	4,425	....		
	Hong Kong....	....	12	....	12	4 20
	Newfoundland..	....	262	....	262	91 70
	Aust.-Hungary..	....	10,194	....	8,922	3,122 70
	Belgium........	....	304	....	304	106 40
	China..........	....	1	....	1	0 35
	Ecuador........	....	1,155	....	1,155	404 25
	France..........	....	50,638	....	50,561	17,696 35
	Germany......	....	8,232	....	8,232	2,881 20
	Italy..........	....	43,534	....	42,832	14,991 20
	Japan..........	....	12,071	....	11,617	4,065 95
	Madagascar,....	....	138	....	138	48 30
	Mexico........	....	370	....	370	129 50
	Portugal.......	....	47	....	47	16 45
	Switzerland....	....	692	....	692	242 20
	United States..	....	1,128,316	....	1,129,878	395,457 30
	Total......	....	2,076,992	....	1,290,284	451,599 40
Hat, cap and bonnet shapes, and hat and bonnet crowns.	Unit'd Kingdom	....	15,060	....	1'030	360 50
	France..........	....	497	....	497	173 95
	Japan..........	....	1	....		
	United States..	....	51,233	....	51,233	17,931 55
	Total......	....	66,791	....	52,760	18,466 00

OF IMPORTS—*Continued.*

FOR HOME CONSUMPTION.

Preferential Tariff.			Treaty Rates.			Total.		
Quantity.	Value.	Duty.	Quantity.	Value.	Duty.	Quantity.	Value.	DutyColl'd.
	$	$ cts.		$	$ cts.		$	$ cts.
....	4,686	585 80	....	....	....	....	4,717	592 00
....	....	....	....	....	....	....	22	4 40
....	....	....	....	....	....	....	81	16 20
....	....	....	....	....	....	....	20	4 00
....	....	....	....	....	....	....	24,361	4,872 20
....	4,686	585 80	....	....	....	....	29,201	5,488 80
....	35,418	7,083 60	....	....	....	....	35,741	7,180 50
....	....	....	....	....	....	....	60	18 00
....	....	....	....	....	....	....	1,526	457 80
....	35,418	7,083 60	....	....	....	....	37,327	7,656 30
....	3,290	740 40	....	....	....	....	11,405	3,580 65
....	....	....	....	....	....	....	483	169 05
....	....	....	....	....	....	....	3,244	1,135 40
....	....	....	....	....	....	....	665	232 75
....	....	....	....	....	....	....	24	8 40
....	....	....	....	....	....	....	17,717	6,200 95
....	3,290	740 40	....	....	....	....	33,538	11,327 20
....	450,429	101,347 51	....	....	....	....	464,399	106,237 01
....	....	....	....	....	....	....	7,908	2,767 80
....	....	....	....	....	....	....	1,802	630 70
....	....	....	....	....	....	....	15,140	5,299 00
....	....	....	....	....	....	....	1,696	593 60
....	....	....	....	....	....	....	11	3 85
....	....	....	....	....	....	....	68,681	24,038 35
....	....	....	....	....	....	....	9	3 15
....	....	....	....	....	....	....	407,915	142,770 25
....	450,429	101,347 51	....	....	....	....	967,561	282,343 71
....	783,908	176,380 65	....	....	....	....	819,169	188,722 00
....	4,594	1,033 75	....	....	....	....	4,594	1,033 75
....	....	....	....	....	....	....	12	4 20
....	....	....	....	....	....	....	262	91 70
....	....	....	....	....	....	....	8,922	3,122 70
....	....	....	....	....	....	....	304	106 40
....	....	....	....	....	....	....	1	0 35
....	....	....	....	....	....	....	1,155	404 25
....	....	....	....	....	....	....	50,561	17,696 35
....	....	....	....	....	....	....	8,232	2,881 20
....	....	....	....	....	....	....	42,832	14,991 20
....	....	....	....	....	....	....	11,617	4,065 95
....	....	....	....	....	....	....	138	48 30
....	....	....	....	....	....	....	370	129 50
....	....	....	....	....	....	....	47	16 45
....	....	....	....	....	....	....	692	242 20
....	....	....	....	....	....	....	1,129,878	395,457 30
....	788,502	177,414 40	....	....	....	....	2,078,786	629,013 80
....	13,700	3,082 68	....	....	....	....	14,730	3,443 18
....	....	....	....	....	....	....	497	173 95
....	....	....	....	....	....	....	51,233	17,931 55
....	13,700	3,082 68	....	....	....	....	66,460	21,548 68

6 GEORGE V, A. 1916

No. 1.—General Statement

Articles Imported.	Countries.	Total Imports.		Entered		
				General Tariff.		
		Quantity.	Value.	Quantity.	Value.	Duty.
DUTIABLE GOODS—*Con.*		Ton.	$	Ton.	$	$ cts.
Hay............................	United States..	16,092	208,593	16,078	208,294	32,156 00
		Lb.		Lb.		
Honey, in the comb or otherwise,	Unit'd Kingdom	10,902	1,351	126	26	3 78
and imitations thereof.	B. W. Indies....	21,715	1,054	356	21	10 68
	Hong Kong.....	1,133	54	1,133	54	33 99
	New Zealand...	896	71	....	....	....
	China..........	130	9	130	9	3 90
	Greece..........	20	2	20	2	0 60
	Japan..........	96	5	96	5	2 88
	United States..	131,006	17,247	~130,956	17,240	3,928 68
	Total.......	165,898	19,793	132,817	17,357	3,984 51
Hops............................	Unit'd Kingdom	137,803	32,002	1,835	511	128 45
	Aust.-Hungary..	20,506	11,108	20,506	11,108	1,435 42
	Germany......	23,732	14,036	23,732	14,036	1,661 24
	United States..	1,184,030	220,968	1,185,195	221,193	82,963 65
	Total.......	1,366,071	278,114	1,231,268	246,848	86,188 76
Ink, writing................	Unit'd Kingdom	....	18,889	....	23	5 75
	Hong Kong.....	....	29	....	29	7 25
	China..........	....	21	....	21	5 25
	France.........	....	600	....	106	26 50
	Germany......	....	406	....	406	101 50
	Holland........	....	286	....	286	71 50
	Japan..........	....	248	....	147	36 75
	Sweden........	....	11	....	....	....
	United States..	....	14,566	....	14,566	3,641 50
	Total.......	....	35,056	....	15,584	3,896 00
Ink, printing................	Unit'd Kingdom	....	13,702	....	54	10 80
	Newfoundland..	....	5	....	5	1 00
	France..........	....	276	....	36	7 20
	Germany......	....	1,582	....	1,582	316 40
	United States..	....	79,958	....	80,181	16,036 20
	Total.......	....	95,523	....	81,858	16,371 60
Iron and manufactures of, steel and manufactures of, or both combined— Agricultural implements, n.o.p., viz.:						
Binding attachments.........	United States..	....	2,485	....	2,389	323 20
Cultivators and weeders and	Unit'd Kingdom	....	118	....	....	....
parts of.	France...........	....	94	....	94	18 80
	United States..	....	52,902	....	52,902	10,580 40
	Total.......	....	53,114	....	52,996	10,599 20
		No.		No.		
Drills, seed................	Unit'd Kingdom	2	109	2	109	21 80
	United States..	5,112	63,771	5,112	63,771	12,754 20
	Total.......	5,114	63,880	5,114	63,880	12,776 00
Farm, road or field rollers....	Unit'd Kingdom	61	30,807	....	....	....
	United States..	173	85,450	173	85,450	21,362 50
	Total.......	234	116,257	173	85,450	21,362 50

SESSIONAL PAPER No. 11

OF IMPORTS—*Continued.*

FOR HOME CONSUMPTION.

Preferential Tariff.			Treaty Rates.			Total.		
Quantity.	Value.	Duty.	Quantity.	Value.	Duty.	Quantity.	Value.	DutyColl'd.
Ton.	$	$ cts.	Ton.	$	$ cts.	Ton.	$	$ cts.
....	....	....	....	....	....	16,078	208,294	32,156 00
Lb.			Lb.			Lb.		
10,776	1,325	215 52	....			• 10,902	1,351	219 30
19,338	908	386 76	....			19,694	929	397 44
....						1,133	54	33 99
896	71	17 92				896	71	17 92
....						130	9	3 90
....						20	2	0 60
....						96	5	2 88
....						130,956	17,240	3,928 68
31,010	2,304	620 20	....	....	....	163,827	19,661	4,604 71
135,838	31,462	5,433 52	....	....	....	137,673	31,973	5,561 97
....						20,506	11,108	1,435 42
....						23,732	14,036	1,661 24
....						1,185,195	221,193	82,963 65
135,838	31,462	5,433 52	....	....	....	1,367,106	278,310	91,622 28
....	18,863	2,829 45	....	3	0 68	....	18,889	2,835 88
....							29	7 25
....							21	5 25
....				494	111 12		600	137 62
....							406	101 50
....							286	71 50
....				101	22 73		248	59 48
....				• 11	2 48		11	2 48
....							14,566	3,641 50
....	18,863	2,829 45	....	609	137 01	....	35,056	6,862 46
....	14,664	1,833 29	....	169	29 59	....	14,887	1,873 68
....							5	1 00
....				240	42 00		276	49 20
....							1,582	316 40
....							80,181	16,036 20
....	14,664	1,833 29	....	409	71 59	....	96,931	18,276 48
......	....	....	....	....	....		2,889	323 20
....	118	14 76	....				118	14 76
....							94	18 80
....							52,902	10,580 40
....	118	14 76	....			....	53,114	10,613 96
No.			No.			No.		
....						2	109	21 80
....						5,112	63,771	12,754 20
....						5,114	63,880	12,776 00
62	33,077	4,961 55	....			62	33,077	4,961 55
....						173	85,450	21,362 50
• 62	33,077	4,961 55	....	....	....	235	118,527	26,324 03

6 GEORGE V, A. 1916

No. 1.—General Statement

Articles Imported.	Countries.	Total Imports.		Entered		
		Quantity.	Value.	General Tariff.		
				Quantity.	Value.	Duty.
DUTIABLE GOODS—*Con.*		No.	$	No.	$	$ cts.
Iron and steel—*Con.*						
Agricultural Implements—*Con.*	Unit'd Kingdom	3,363	1,252	69	22	4 95
Forks, pronged..................	United States..	5,568	3,419	5,568	3,419	769 56
	Total......	8,931	4,671	5,637	3,441	774 51
Harrows and parts of..........	Unit'd Kingdom	....	94	....	....	....
	United States...	....	67,174	....	67,174	13,434 80
	Total......	....	67,268	....	67,174	13,434 80
Harvesters, self-binding........	United States...	1,635	177,158	1,635	177,158	22,241 24
Hay loaders....................	United States...	228	11,270	228	11,270	2,817 50
Hay tedders....................	United States...	14	570	14	570	142 50
Hoes..........................	Unit'd Kingdom	1,082	275	263	64	14 40
	Holland........	48	5	48	5	1 13
	United States...	7,563	2,061	7,563	2,061	463 85
	Total......	8,693	2,341	7'874	2,130	479 38
Horse rakes....................	United States...	754	13,979	754	13,979	2,795 80
Knives, hay or straw..........	Unit'd Kingdom	472	134	....	....	....
	United States...	2,937	800	2,937	800	180 03
	Total......	3,409	934	2,937	800	180 03
Knives, edging.................	Unit'd Kingdom	18	12	....	....	....
	United States...	72	66	72	66	14 85
	Total......	90	78	72	66	14 85
Lawn mowers..................	Unit'd Kingdom	108	2,096	....	....	....
	United States...	10,642	47,543	10,642	47,543	15,452 93
	Total......	10,750	49,639	10,642	47,543	15,452 93
Manure spreaders..............	Unit'd Kingdom	2	79	....	....	....
	Germany.......	1	64	1	64	12 80
	United States...	902	57,190	902	57,190	11,438 00
	Total......	905	57,333	903	57,254	11,450 80
Mowing machines..............	United States...	1,198	43,607	1,198	43,607	5,584 95
Ploughs and parts of..........	Unit'd Kingdom	....	32	....	....	....
	Aust.-Hungary..	....	27	....	27	5 40
	Cuba...........	....	35	....	35	7 00
	United States...	....	498,009	....	497,787	99,557 40
	Total......	....	498,103	....	497,849	99,569 80

OF IMPORTS—*Continued.*

FOR HOME CONSUMPTION.

Preferential Tariff.			Treaty Rates.			Total.		
Quantity.	Value.	Duty.	Quantity.	Value.	Duty.	Quantity.	Value.	DutyColl'd.
No.	$	$ cts.	No.	$	$ cts.	No.	$	$ cts.
3,294	1,230	184 50	....	....	....	3,363	1,252	189 45
....	....	....	....	....	....	5,568	3,419	769 56
3,294	1,230	184 50	....	....	....	8,931	4,671	959 01
....	94	11 75	....	....	....	....	94	11 75
....	....	....	....	....	....	....	67,174	13,434 80
....	94	11 75	....	....	....	....	67,268	13,446 55
....	....	....	....	....	....	1,635	177,158	22,241 24
....	....	....	....	....	....	228	11,270	2,817 50
....	....	....	....	....	....	14	570	142 50
819	211	31 65	....	....	....	1,082	275	46 05
....	....	....	....	....	....	48	5	1 13
....	....	....	....	....	....	7,563	2,061	463 85
819	211	31 65	....	....	....	8,693	2,341	511 03
....	....	....	....	....	....	754	13,979	2,795 80
472	134	20 10	....	....	....	472	134	20 10
....	....	....	....	....	....	2,937	800	180 03
472	134	20 10	....	....	....	3,409	934	200 13
18	12	1 80	....	....	....	18	12	1 80
....	....	....	....	....	....	72	66	14 85
18	12	1 80	....	....	....	90	78	16 65
108	2,096	419 20	....	....	....	108	2,096	419 20
....	....	....	....	....	....	10,642	47,543	15,452 93
108	2,096	419 20	....	....	....	10,750	49,639	15,872 13
2	79	9 88	....	....	....	2	79	9 88
....	....	....	....	....	....	1	64	12 80
....	....	....	....	....	....	902	57,190	11,438 00
2	79	9 88	....	....	....	905	57,333	11,460 68
....	....	....	....	....	....	1,198	43,607	5,584 95
....	32	4 00	....	....	....	....	32	4 00
....	....	....	....	....	....	....	27	5 40
....	....	....	....	....	....	....	35	7 00
....	....	....	....	....	....	....	497,787	99,557 40
....	32	4 00	....	....	....	....	497,881	99,573 80

No. 1.—General Statement

Articles Imported.	Countries.	Total Imports.		Entered		
				General Tariff.		
		Quantity.	Value.	Quantity.	Value.	Duty.
DUTIABLE GOODS—*Con.*		No.	$	No.	$	$ cts.
Iron and steel—*Con.*						
Agricultural Implements—*Con.*						
Post hole diggers...............	United States...	3,989	4,163	3,989	4,163	1,040 75
Potato diggers................	Unit'd Kingdom	23	1,164	....	....	....
	United States...	1,416	43,021	1,410	42,847	10,711 75
	Total.........	1,439	44,185	1,410	42,847	10,711 75
Rakes, n.o.p...................	Unit'd Kingdom	259	84	10	2	0 45
	United States...	18,610	3,821	18,610	3,821	859 85
	Total......	18,869	3,905	18,620	3,823	860 30
Reapers......................	United States...	432	32,094	432	32,094	4,011 77
		Doz.		Doz.		
Scythes......................	Unit'd Kingdom	509	2,287	....	....	....
	Japan...........	1	2	1	2	0 45
	United States...	2,536	12,998	2,541	13,019	2,929 35
	Total......	3,046	15,287	2,542	13,021	2,929 80
Sickles or reaping hooks........	Unit'd Kingdom	207	408	....	....	....
	Hong Kong.....	6	5	6	5	1 13
	Japan..........	9	19	9	19	4 28
	United States...	60	183	60	183	41 19
	Total......	282	615	75	207	46 60
Snaths.......................	United States...	248	1,042	248	1,042	260 50
Spades and shovels of iron or steel, n.o.p.	Unit'd Kingdom	2,516	10,570	44	148	48 10
	Germany.......	138	168	138	168	54 60
	Holland........	3	7	3	7	2 28
	United States...	2,356	8,141	2,346	8,023	2,608 04
	Total......	5,013	18,886	2,531	8,346	2,713 02
Spade and shovel blanks, and iron or steel cut to shape for the same.	Unit'd Kingdom	1,308	2,412	....	....	....
	United States...	23	80	23	80	26 01.
	Total......	1,331	2,492	23	80	26 01
Parts of agricultural implements paying 12½ p.c., 12½ p.c. and 12½ p.c.	Unit'd Kingdom	....	744	....	....	....
	United States...	....	82,716	....	82,616	11,250 74
	Total......	....	83,460	....	82,616	11,250 74
Parts of agricultural implements paying 12½ p.c., 17½ p.c. and 20 p.c., n.o.p.	Unit'd Kingdom	....	11	....	....	....
	United States...	....	142,514	....	142,490	28,498 00
	Total......	....	142,525	....	142,490	28,498 00
All other agricultural implements, n.o.p................	Unit'd Kingdom	....	5,894	....	274	68 50
	Australia.......	....	100	....	....	....
	France.........	....	77	....	77	19 25
	Germany.......	....	476	....	476	119 00
	Holland........	....	12	....	12	3 00
	United States...	....	76,241	....	76,241	19,060 25
	Total......	....	82,800	....	77,080	19,270 00

OF IMPORTS—*Continued.*

FOR HOME CONSUMPTION.

Preferential Tariff.			Treaty Rates.			Total.		
Quantity.	Value.	Duty.	Quantity.	Value.	Duty.	Quantity.	Value.	DutyColl'd.
No.	$	$ cts.	No.	$	$ cts.	No.	$	$ cts.
....	....	....	....	....	....	3,989	4,163	1,040 75
23	1,164	174 60	....	....	....	23	1,164	174 60
....	....	....	....	....	....	1,410	42,847	10,711 75
23	1,164	174 60	....	....	....	1,433	44,011	10,886 35
249	82	12 30	....	....	....	259	84	12 75
....	....	....	....	....	....	18,610	3,821	859 85
249	82	12 30	....	....	....	18,869	3,905	872 60
....	....	....	....	....	....	432	32,094	4,011 77
Doz. 509	 2,287	343 05	Doz.	....	....	Doz. 509	2,287	343 05
....	....	....	....	....	....	1	2	0 45
....	....	....	....	....	....	2,541	13,019	2,929 35
509	2,287	343 05	....	....	....	3,051	15,308	3,272 85
207	408	61 20	....	....	....	207	408	61 20
....	....	....	....	....	....	6	5	1 13
....	....	....	....	....	....	9	19	4 28
....	....	....	....	....	....	60	183	41 19
207	408	61 20	....	....	....	282	615	107 80
....	....	....	....	....	....	248	1,042	260 50
2,472	10,422	2,084 40	....	....	....	2,516	10,570	2,132 50
....	....	....	....	....	....	138	168	54 60
....	....	....	....	....	....	3	7	2 28
....	....	....	....	....	....	2,346	8,023	2,608 04
2,472	10,422	2,084 40	....	....	....	5,003	18,768	4,797 42
1,308	2,412	482 40	....	....	....	1,308	2,412	482 40
....	....	....	....	....	....	23	80	26 01
1,308	2,412	482 40	....	....	....	1,331	2,492	508 41
....	744	92 99	....	....	....	....	744	92 99
....	....	....	....	....	....	....	82,616	11,250 74
....	744	92 99	....	....	....	....	83,360	11,343 73
....	11	1 38	....	....	....	....	11	1 38
....	....	....	....	....	....	....	142,490	28,498 00
....	11	1 38	....	....	....	....	142,501	28,499 38
....	5,620	843 00	....	....	....	....	5,894	911 50
....	....	....	....	....	....	....	77	19 25
....	....	....	....	....	....	....	476	119 00
....	....	....	....	....	....	....	12	3 00
....	....	....	....	....	....	....	76,241	19,060 25
....	5,620	843 00	....	....	....	....	82,700	20,113 00

6 GEORGE V, A. 1916

No. 1.—General Statement

Articles Imported.	Countries.	Total Imports.		Entered		
				General Tariff.		
		Quantity.	Value.	Quantity.	Value.	Duty.
			$		$	$ cts.
DUTIABLE GOODS—*Con.*						
Iron and steel—*Con.*						
Anvils and vises......	Unit'd Kingdom	....	19,169	....	1,785	535 50
	Germany.......	....	279	....	279	83 70
	Holland........	....	14	....	14	4 20
	Switzerland.....	....	....	....	113	33 90
	United States...	....	26,645	....	26,652	7,995 60
	Total.......	....	46,107	....	28,843	8,652 90
		Lb.		Lb.		
Cart or wagon skeins or boxes.....	United States...	358,867	20,182	358,092	20,182	5,045 50
Springs, n.o.p., and parts thereof,	Unit'd Kingdom	....	1,068	....	....	....
of iron or steel, for railway,	United States...	....	70,293	....	74,432	26,051 20
tramway or other vehicles.	Total.......	....	71,361	....	74,432	26,051 20
Axles and axle parts, n.o.p., and	Unit'd Kingdom	....	22,776	....	37	12 95
axle blanks and parts thereof of	Belgium........	....	6,643	....	6,643	325 05
iron of steel, for railway, tram-	France........	....	28	....	28	9 80
way or other vehicles.	Germany......	....	3,517	....	3,517	1,230 95
	United States...	....	181,272	....	191,100	66,885 00
	Total.......	....	214,236	....	201,325	70,463 75
		Cwt.		Cwt.		
Bar iron or steel, rolled, whether	Unit'd Kingdom	83,369	149,450	12,497	14,704	4,373 95
in coils, bundles, rods or bars,	New Zealand...	5	10	5	10	1 75
comprising rounds, ovals,squares	Belgium........	30,735	33,350	3C,735	33,350	10,757 25
and flats, n.o.p."	Germany.......	6,806	9,391	6,806	9,391	2,382 10
	Sweden........	4,717	11,152	4,717	11,152	1,650 95
	United States...	728,276	1,020,086	728,249	1,020,028	254,887 15
	Total.......	853,908	1,223,439	783,009	1,088,635	274,053 15
Butts and hinges, n.o.p..........	Unit'd Kingdom	....	1,391	....	176	52 80
	France.........	....	162	....	....	....
	Germany.......	....	18	....	18	5 40
	Sweden........	....	592	....	78	23 40
	United States...	....	74,954	....	74,941	22,482 30
	Total.......	....	77,117	....	75,213	22,563 90
Canada plates, Russia iron, terne	United States...	175,823	443,899	175,823	443,899	22,194 95
plate, and rolled sheets of iron						
or steel coated with zinc, spelter						
or other metal, of all widths or						
thickness, n.o.p.						
Castings, iron or steel, n.o.p.......	Unit'd Kingdom	....	41,858	....	201	55 27
	Newfoundland..	....	1,375	....	1,375	378 13
	Germany......	....	11	....	11	3 03
	United States...	....	566,395	....	565 983	155,648 07
	Total.......	....	609,639	....	567,570	156,084 50
Castings, malleable iron, when	United States...	....	93,007	....	93,007	16,276 04
imported by manufacturers of						
mowers, binding attachments,						
harvesters and reapers for use						
exclusively in their own factories						
Cast iron pipe of every description.	Unit'd Kingdom	50,484	64,094	3,510	3,584	1,404 00
	United States...	216,757	261,469	216,757	261,469	86,702 80
	Total.......	267,241	325,563	220,267	265,053	88,106 80

OF IMPORTS—*Continued.*

FOR HOME CONSUMPTION.

	Preferential Tariff.			Treaty Rates.			Total.	
Quantity.	Value.	Duty.	Quantity.	Value.	Duty.	Quantity.	Value	DutyColl'd.
	$	$ cts.			$ cts.		$	$ cts.
....	17,384	3,476 80	....	....	....	....	19,169	4,012 30
....	....	....	....	....	....	....	279	83 70
....	....	....	....	....	....	....	14	4 20
....	....	....	....	....	....	....	113	33 90
....	....	....	....	....	....	....	26,652	7,995 60
....	17,384	3,476 80	....	....	....	....	46,227	12,129 70
Lb.			Lb.			Lb.		
....	....	....	....	....	....	358,092	20,182	5,045 50
....	5,114	1,150 65	....	....	....	....	5,114	1,150 65
....	....	....	....	....	....	....	74,432	26,051 20
....	5,114	1,150 65	....	....	....	....	79,546	27,201 85
....	22,739	5,116 32	....	....	....	....	22,776	5,129 27
....	....	....	....	....	....	....	6,643	2,325 05
....	....	....	....	....	....	....	28	9 80
....	....	....	....	....	....	....	3,517	1,230 95
....	....	....	....	....	....	....	191,100	66,885 00
....	22,739	5,116 32	....	....	....	....	224,064	75,580 07
Cwt. 70,872	134,746	15,060 31	Cwt.			Cwt. 83,369	149,450	19,434 26
....	....	....	....	....	....	5	10	1 75
....	....	....	....	....	....	30,735	33,350	10,757 25
....	....	....	....	....	....	6,806	9,391	2,382 10
....	....	....	....	....	....	4,717	11,152	1,650 95
....	....	....	....	....	....	728,249	1,020,028	254,887 15
70,872	134,746	15,060 31	....	....	....	853,881	1,223,381	289,113 46
....	943	188 60	....	272	74 80	....	1,391	316 20
....	....	....	....	162	44 55	....	162	44 55
....	....	....	....	....	....	....	18	5 40
....	....	....	....	514	141 36	....	592	164 76
....	....	....	....	....	....	....	74,941	22,482 30
....	943	188 60	....	948	260 71	....	77,104	23,013 21
....	....	....	....	....	....	....	175,823	443,899	22,194 95
....	41,086	6,162 90	....	....	....	....	41,287	6,218 17
....	....	....	....	....	....	....	1,375	378 13
....	....	....	....	....	....	....	11	3 03
....	....	....	....	....	....	....	565,983	155,648 07
....	41,086	6,162 90	....	....	....	....	608,656	162,247 40
....	....	....	....	....	....	....	93,007	16,276 04
46,974	60,510	14,092 20	....	....	....	....	50,484	64,094	15,496 20
....	....	....	....	....	....	216,757	261,469	86,702 80
46,974	60,510	14,092 20	....	....	....	267,241	325,563	102,199 00

6 GEORGE V, A. 1916

No. 1.—General Statement

Articles Imported.	Countries.	Total Imports.		Entered		
		Quantity.	Value.	General Tariff.		
				Quantity.	Value.	Duty.
DUTIABLE GOODS—*Con.*		Ton.	$	Ton.	$	$ cts.
Iron and steel—*Con.*						
Cast scrap iron................	Unit'd Kingdom	177	2,083	28	319	70 00
	B. Guiana......	38	558	3	18	7 50
	United States...	5,505	60,922	5,507	60,940	13,767 50
	Total......	5,720	63,563	5,538	61,277	13,845 00
		Cwt.		Cwt.		
Chains, coil chain, chain links	Unit'd Kingdom	2,142	8,172	1,124	4,766	238 30
including repair links and chain	United States...	8,430	38,110	8,430	38,110	2,578 20
shackles, of iron or steel 1¼ of an						
inch in diameter and over.	Total......	10,572	46,282	9,554	42,876	2,816 50
Chains, coil chains and links in-	Unit'd Kingdom	7,783	31,876	72	452	90 40
cluding repair links and chain	Germany.......	3	11	3	11	2 20
shackles of iron and steel, n.o.p..	United States...	11,907	43,837	11,907	43,837	8,767 40
	Total......	19,693	75,724	11,982	44,300	8,860 00
Chains, n.o.p..................	Unit'd Kingdom	....	15,378	....	344	103 20
	Aust.-Hungary..	....	9	....	9	2 70
	France..........	....	478	....	84	25 20
	Germany.......	....	859	....	859	257 70
	United States...	....	69,281	....	70,719	21,215 70
	Total......	....	86,005	....	72,015	21,604 50
		Lb.		Lb.		
Tacks, shoe...................	Unit'd Kingdom	6,643	347	50	4	1 40
	Germany.......	355	88	355	88	30 80
	United States...	27,639	2,063	27,639	2,063	722 05
	Total......	34,637	2,498	28,044	2,155	754 25
Nails, brads, spikes and tacks of	Unit'd Kingdom	72,005	3,395	670	38	13 30
all kinds, n.o.p.	Aust.-Hungary..	105	35	105	35	12 25
	France..........	415	171	415	171	59 85
	Germany.......	9,055	1,205	9,055	1,205	421 75
	Norway........	8,250	417	8,250	417	145 95
	United States...	440,389	27,201	439,541	27,164	9,507 40
	Total......	530,219	32,424	458,036	29,030	10,160 50
Engines, etc.—		No.		No.		
Locomotives for railways.......	Unit'd Kingdom	1	3,650	....	....	....
	United States...	69	158,777	69	158,777	55,571 95
	Total......	70	162,427	69	158,777	55,571 95
Locomotive parts...............	United States...	....	81,618	....	81,618	28,566 30
Motor cars for railways and tram-	United States...	25	50,404	25	50,404	17,641 40
ways.						
Engines, fire....................	United States...	26	99,465	26	99,465	34,812 75
Engines, gasoline and gas........	Unit'd Kingdom	364	85,180	2	216	59 40
	Newfoundland..	4	235	7	485	133 38
	France..........	1	338	1	338	92 95
	Sweden........	4	43,196	4	43,196	11,878 90
	United States...	14,295	1,905,361	14,292	1,873,486	515,212 24
	Total......	14,668	2,034,310	14,306	1,917,721	527,376 87

OF IMPORTS.—*Continued.*

FOR HOME CONSUMPTION.

	Preferential Tariff.			Treaty Rates.			Total.	
Quantity.	Value.	Duty.	Quantity.	Value.	Duty.	Quantity.	Value.	DutyColl'd.
Ton.	$	$ cts.	Ton.	$	$ cts.	Ton.	$	$ cts.
149	1,764	223 50	....	....	....	177	2,083	293 50
35	540	52 50	....	....	....	38	558	60 00
....	....	....	....	....	....	5,507	60,940	13,767 50
184	2,304	276 00	....	....	....	5,722	63,581	14,121 00
Cwt.			Cwt.			Cwt.		
1,005	3,404	170 20	....			2,129	8,170	408 50
....	....	....				8,430	38,110	2,578 20
1,005	3,404	170 20	....			10,559	46,280	2,986 70
7,711	31,424	4,713 60	....	....	....	·7,783	31,876	4,804 00
....	....	....	....	....	....	3	11	2 20
....	....	....	....	....	....	11,907	43,837	8,767 40
7,711	31,424	4,713 60	....			19,693	75,724	13,573 60
....	13,421	2,684 20	....	28	7 70	....	13,793	2,795 10
....	....	....					9	2 70
....	....	....		394	108 37	....	478	133 57
....	....	....					859	257 70
....	....	....					70,719	21,215 70
....	13,421	2,684 20	....	422	116 07	....	85,858	24,404 77
Lb.			Lb.			Lb.		
6,593	343	68 60				6,643	347	70 00
....	....	....				355	88	30 80
....	....	....				27,639	2,063	722 05
6,593	343	68 60	....	....		34,637	2,498	822 85
71,335	3,357	671 40	....	....	....	72,005	3,395	684 70
....	....	....				105	35	12 25
....	....	....				415	171	59 85
....	....	....				9,055	1,205	421 75
....	....	....				8,250	417	145 95
....	....	....				439,541	27,164	9,507 40
71,335	3,357	671 40	....	....	....	529,371	32,387	10,831 90
No.			No.			No.		
1	3,650	821 25				1	3,650	821 25
....	....	....				69	158,777	55,571 95
1	3,650	821 25	....	....	....	70	162,427	56,393 20
....	....	....	....	....	....	....	81,618	28,566 30
....	....	....	....	....	....	25	50,404	17,641 40
....	....	....	....	....	....	26	99,465	34,812 75
362	84,964	12,744 60	....			364	85,180	12,804 00
....	....	....				7	485	133 38
....	....	....				1	338	92 95
....	....	....				4	43,196	11,878 90
....	....	....				14,292	1,873,486	515,212 24
362	84,964	12,744 60	....	....		14,668	2,002,685	540,121 47

11—ii—9½

6 GEORGE V, A. 1916

No. 1.—General Statement

Articles Imported.	Countries.	Total Imports.		Entered		
				General Tariff.		
		Quantity.	Value.	Quantity.	Value.	Duty.
DUTIABLE GOODS—*Con.*		No.	$	No.	$	$ cts.
Iron and steel—*Con.*						
Engines, steam...............	Unit'd Kingdom	25	67,227	....	....	....
	United States...	271	170,117	271	170,117	46,782 43
	Total......	296	237,344	271	170,117	46,782 43
Boilers, steam, and parts of.....	Unit'd Kingdom	....	35,429	....	465	127 90
	United States...	....	168,360	....	162,982	44,820 30
	Total.........	....	203,789	....	163,447	44,948 20
Boilers, n.o.p., and parts of.....	Unit'd Kingdom	....	5,782	....	1,016	279 40
	United States...	....	234,262	....	224,356	61,698 74
	Total......	....	240,044	....	225,372	61,978 14
Fire extinguishing machines, including sprinklers for fire protection.	Unit'd Kingdom	....	347	....	106	37 10
	Newfoundland..	....	18	....	18	6 30
	United States...	....	101,944	....	101,531	35,535 85
	Total......	....	102,309	....	101,655	35,579 25
Fittings, iron or steel, for iron or steel pipe of every description.	Unit'd Kingdom	....	19,074	....	171	51 30
	United States...	....	710,398	....	710,398	213,119 40
	Total......	....	729,472	....	710,569	213,170 70
Flat eye bar blanks, not punched nor drilled, for use exclusively in the manufacture of bridges, or of steel structural work, or in car construction.	United States...	Ton. 4,717	315,422	Ton. 4,717	315,422	14,151 00
Ferro-silicon, containing not more than 15 p.c. silicon.	Unit'd Kingdom	28	1,430	....	....	....
	United States...	289	11,923	289	11,923	722 50
	Total......	317	13,353	289	11,923	722 50
Ferro-silicon containing more than 15 p.c. silicon.	United States...	2	171	2	171	9 00
Spiegeleisen and ferro manganese containing not more than 15 p.c. manganese.	Unit'd Kingdom	310	15,195	37	1,275	92 50
	Germany.......	....	....	1,918	49,456	4,795 00
	Total......	310	15,195	1,955	50,731	4,887 50
Forging of iron or steel, of whatever shape or size, or in whatever stage of manufacture, n.o.p., and hammered, drawn or cold rolled iron or steel bars or shapes, n.o.p.	Unit'd Kingdom	Lb. 46,157	3,400	Lb. 1,390	93	27 90
	United States...	4,633,829	319,612	4,633,935	319,618	95,885 40
	Total......	4,679,986	323,012	4,635,325	319,711	95,913 30
Hardware, viz.:—Builders', cabinetmakers', upholsterers', harnessmakers', saddlers' and carriage hardware, including curry-combs, n.o.p.	Unit'd Kingdom	....	101,477	....	624	187 20
	Newfoundland..	....	66	....	66	19 80
	Belgium.......	....	57	....	57	17 10
	France.........	....	2,430	....	12	3 60
	Germany.......	....	1,738	....	1,738	521 40
	Japan..........	....	255	....	255	76 50
	United States...	....	472,630	....	473,160	141,948 00
	Total......	....	578,653	....	475,912	142,773 60

SESSIONAL PAPER No. 11

OF IMPORTS—*Continued.*

FOR HOME CONSUMPTION.

Preferential Tariff.			Treaty Rates.			Total.		
Quantity.	Value.	Duty.	Quantity.	Value.	Duty.	Quantity.	Value.	DutyColl'd.
No.	$	$ cts.	No.	$	$ cts.	No.	$	$ cts.
25	67,227	10,084 05	....	....	....	25	67,227	10,084 05
....	....	....	....	....	....	271	170,117	46,782 43
25	67,227	10,084 05	....	....	....	296	237,344	56,866 48
....	34,964	5,244 60	....	....	....	35,429	5,372 50	
....	....	....	....	....	....	162,982	44,820 30	
....	34,964	5,244 00	....	....	....	198,411	50,192 80	
....	4,766	714 90	....	....	....	5,782	994 30	
....	....	....	....	....	....	224,356	61,698 74	
....	4,766	714 90	....	....	....	230,138	62,693 04	
....	250	56 26	....	....	....	356	93 36	
....	....	....	....	....	....	18	6 30	
....	....	....	....	....	....	101,531	35,535 85	
....	250	56 26	....	....	....	101,905	35,635 51	
....	18,878	3,775 60	....	....	....	19,049	3,826 90	
....	....	....	....	....	....	710,398	213,119 40	
....	18,878	3,775 60	....	....	....	729,447	216,946 30	
Ton.			Ton.			Ton.		
....	....	....				4,717	315,422	14,151 00
28	1,430	42 00	....	....	....	28	1,430	42 00
....	....	....	....	....	....	289	11,923	722 50
28	1,430	42 00	....	....	....	317	13,353	764 50
....	....	....	....	....	....	2	171	9 00
420	17,714	630 00	....	....	....	457	18,989	722 50
....	....	....	....	....	....	1,918	49,456	4,795 00
420	17,714	630 00	....	....	....	2,375	68,445	5,517 50
Lb.			Lb.			Lb.		
44,767	3,307	661 40	....	....	....	46,157	3,400	689 30
....	....	....	....	....	....	4,633,935	319,618	95,885 40
44,767	3,307	661 40	....	....	....	4,680,092	323,018	96,574 70
....	99,850	19,970 00	....	....	....	100,474	20,157 20	
....	....	....	....	....	....	66	19 80	
....	....	....	....	....	....	57	17 10	
....	....	....	....	2,418	664 96	2,430	668 56	
....	....	....	....	....	....	1,738	521 40	
....	....	....	....	....	....	255	76 50	
....	....	....	....	....	....	473,160	141,948 00	
....	99,850	19,970 00	....	2,418	664 96	....	578,180	163,408 56

6 GEORGE V, A. 1916

No. 1.—General Statement

Articles Imported.	Countries.	Total Imports.		Entered		
		Quantity.	Value.	General Tariff.		
				Quantity.	Value.	Duty.
DUTIABLE GOODS—*Con.*			$		$	$ cts.
Iron and steel—*Con.*						
Horse mule and ox shoes......	Unit'd Kingdom	....	2,467	....	3	0 90
	United States...	....	27,452	....	27,452	8,235 60
	Total........	....	29,919	....	27,455	8,236 50
		Cwt.		Cwt.		
Iron or steel billets, weighing	Unit'd Kingdom	1,117	9,269	....	....	....
not less than 60 lbs. per lineal	Belgium........	30,287	26,920	30,287	26,920	3,785 90
yard.	United States...	198,700	189,925	198,700	189,925	24,837 52
	Total......	230,104	226,114	228,987	216,845	28,623 42
Iron or steel ingots, cogged in-	Unit'd Kingdom	512	724	....	....	....
gots, blooms, slabs, puddled	United States.	7,148	11,442	7,148	11,442	893 53
bars, and loops or other forms,						
n.o.p., less finished than iron	Total.......	7,660	12,166	7,148	11,442	893 53
or steel bars, but more ad-						
vanced than pig iron, except						
castings.						
Iron or steel bridges or parts	Unit'd Kingdom	....	13,820	....	....	....
thereof, iron or steel structural	Germany......	....	1,800	....	1,800	630 00
work, columns, shapes or sec-	United States...	....	252,041	....	252,041	88,214 35
tions, drilled, punched, or in	Total......	....	267,661	....	353,841	88,844 35
any further state of manufac-						
ture than as rolled or cast,						
n.o.p.						
		Ton.		Ton.		
Iron in pig...................	Unit'd Kingdom	8,533	105,842	56	888	140 00
	United States...	46,341	567,532	50,378	620,147	125,945 00
	Total......	54,874	673,374	50,434	621,035	126,085 00
Iron in pig, charcoal..........	United States...	25	275	25	275	62 50
Iron ore......................	United States...	4,391	11,689	4,391	11,689	351 28
Locks of all kinds............	Unit'd Kingdom	....	11,633	....	•192	57 60
	Hong Kong.....	....	9	....	9	2 70
	France.........	....	671	....	....	....
	Germany......	....	1,547	....	1,547	464 10
	Holland........	....	9	....	9	2 70
	United States...	....	201,303	....	201,432	60,429 60
	Total......	....	215,172	....	203,189	60,956 70
Machines, machinery, etc.—		No.		No.		
Cranes and derricks...........	Unit'd Kingdom	10	26,507	....	....	....
	United States...	117	338,275	116	338,235	93,014 80
	Total......	127	364,782	116	338,235	93,014 80
Dental engines (electric).......	United States...	66	5,800	66	5,800	1,595 02
Fanning mills.................	France.........	1	122	1	122	30 50
	United States:..	779	16,858	779	16,858	4,214 50
	Total......	780	16,980	780	16,980	4,245 00
Grain crushers................	United States...	369	6,928	369	6,928	1,732 00

OF IMPORTS—*Continued.*

FOR HOME CONSUMPTION.

Preferential Tariff.			Treaty Rates.			Total.		
Quantity.	Value.	Duty.	Quantity.	Value.	Duty.	Quantity.	Value.	DutyColl'd.
	$	$ cts.		$	$ cts.		$	$ cts.
....	2,464	492 80	....	....	....	....	2,467	493 70
....	....	....	....	....	....	....	27,452	8,235 60
....	2,464	492 80	....	....	....	....	29,919	8,729 30
Cwt. 1,117	9,269	83 85	Cwt.	....	....	Cwt. 1,117	9,269	83 85
....	....	....	....	....	....	30,287	26,920	3,785 90
....	....	....	....	....	....	198,700	189,925	24,837 52
1,117	9,269	83 85	....	....	....	230,104	226,114	28,707 27
512	724	38 40	....	....	....	512	724	38 40
....	....	....	....	....	....	7,148	11,442	893 53
512	724	38 40	....	....	....	7,660	12,166	931 93
....	13,820	3,109 57	....	....	....	....	13,820	3,109 57
....	....	....	....	....	....	....	1,800	630 00
....	....	....	....	....	....	....	252,041	88,214 35
....	13,820	3,109 57	....	....	....	....	267,661	91,953 92
Ton. 8,477	104,954	12,715 50	Ton.	....	....	Ton. 8,533	105,842	12,855 50
....	....	....	....	....	....	50,378	620,147	125,945 00
8,477	104,954	12,715 50	....	....	....	58,911	725,989	138,800 50
....	....	....	....	....	....	25	275	62 50
....	....	....	....	....	....	4,391	11,689	351 28
....	11,461	2,292 20	....	....	....	....	11,653	2,349 80
....	....	....	....	....	....	....	9	2 70
....	....	....	....	671	184 53	....	671	184 53
....	....	....	....	....	....	....	1,547	464 10
....	....	....	....	....	....	....	9	2 70
....	....	....	....	....	....	....	201,432	60,429 60
....	11,461	2,292 20	....	671	184 53	....	215,321	63,433 43
No. 10	26,507	3,976 05	No.	....	....	No. 10	26,507	3,976 05
....	....	....	....	....	....	116	338,235	93,014 80
10	26,507	3,976 05	....	....	....	126	364,742	96,990 85
....	....	....	....	....	....	66	5,800	1,595 02
....	....	....	....	....	....	1	122	30 50
....	....	....	....	....	....	779	16,858	4,214 50
....	....	....	....	....	....	780	16,980	4,245 00
....	....	....	....	....	....	369	6,928	1,732 00

6. GEORGE V, A. 1916

No. 1.—General Statement

Articles Imported.	Countries.	Total Imports.		Entered		
				General Tariff.		
		Quantity.	Value.	Quantity.	Value.	Duty.
DUTIABLE GOODS—*Con.*		No.	$	No.	$	$ cts.
Iron and steel—*Con.*						
Hay presses....................	United States..	168	29,278	168	29,278	8,051 53
Windmills and complete parts thereof.	United States..	....	45,653	....	45,653	9,130 60
Ore crushers and rock crushers, stamp mills, Cornish and belted rolls, rock drills, air compressors, and percussion coal cutters.	Unit'd Kingdom	....	47,508	....	531	146 03
	Germany.......		2,629		2,629	723 00
	United States..	....	367,851	....	367,851	101,159 76
	Total.......	....	417,988	....	371,011	102,028 79
Fodder or feed cutters..........	United States..	725	10,833	725	10,833	2,708 25
Horse powers, for farm purposes.	United States..	4	116	4	116	23 20
Portable engines with boilers in combination, and traction engines for farm purposes.	Unit'd Kingdom	13	21,345	....	....	....
	United States..	463	689,053	464	691,120	138,224 00
	Total.......	476	710,398	464	691,120	138,224 00
Portable saw-mills and planing mills.	United States..	19	4,797	19	4,797	1,319 23
Steam shovels and electric shovels.	United States..	21	154,796	21	154,796	42,569 42
Threshing machine separators..	Unit'd Kingdom	2	2,706	....	....	....
	United States..	613	315,418	597	302,495	60,499 00
	Total.......	615	318,124	597	302,495	60,499 00
Threshing machine separators, parts of, including wind stackers, baggers, weighers and self-feeders therefor and finished parts thereof for repairs, when imported separately.	Unit'd Kingdom	....	654	....	179	35 80
	United States..	....	212,114	....	212,114	42,422 80
	Total.......	....	212,768	....	212,293	42,458 60
All other portable machines, n.o.p., and parts of.	United States..	....	118,564	....	118,186	32,501 28
Concrete mixing machines......	United States..	131	62,208	132	63,300	17,407 61
Sewing machines..............	Unit'd Kingdom	1,099	16,686	27	471	141 30
	France..........	1	25	1	25	7 50
	Germany.......	75	1,574	75	1,574	472 20
	Miquelon and St. Pierre.....	1	5	1	5	1 50
	United States..	14,736	300,849	14,766	301,054	90,316 20
	Total.......	15,912	319,139	14,870	303,129	90,938 70
Sewing machines, parts of......	Unit'd Kingdom	....	2,584	....	224	67 20
	Germany.......	....	57	....	57	17 10
	United States..	....	67,097	....	67,131	20,139 30
	Total.......	....	69,738	....	67,412	20,223 60

SESSIONAL PAPER No. 11

OF IMPORTS—*Continued.*

FOR HOME CONSUMPTION.

Preferential Tariff.			Treaty Rates.			Total.		
Quantity.	Value.	Duty.	Quantity.	Value.	Duty.	Quantity.	Value.	DutyColl'd.
No.	$	$ cts.	No.	$	$ cts.	No.	$	$ cts.
....	....	....	....	....	....	..	168	29,278	8,051 53
....	....	....	....	....	....	....	45,653	9,130 60
....	46,977	7,046 55	....	....	....	....	47,508	7,192 58
....	....	....	....	....	....	....	2,629	723 00
....	....	....	....	....	....	....	367,851	101,159 76
....	46,977	7,046 55	....	....	....	....	417,988	109,075 34
....	....	....	....	....	....	725	10,833	2,708 25
....	....	....	....	....	....	4	116	23 20
13	21,345	3,201 75	....	....	....	13	21,345	3,201 75
....	....	....	....	....	....	464	691,120	138,224 00
13	21,345	3,201 75	....	....	....	477	712,465	141,425 75
....	....	....	....	....	....	19	4,797	1,319 23
....	....	....	....	....	....	21	154,796	42,569 42
2	2,706	405 90	....	....	....	2	2,706	405 90
....	....	....	....	....	....	597	302,495	60,499 00
2	2,706	405 90	....	....	....	599	305,201	60,904 90
....	475	71 25	....	....	....	....	654	107 05
....	....	....	....	....	....	....	212,114	42,422 80
....	475	71 25	....	....	....	....	212,768	42,529 85
....	....	....	....	....	....	....	118,186	32,501 28
....	....	....	....	....	....	132	63,300	17,407 61
1,072	16,215	3,243 00	....	....	....	1,099	16,686	3,384 30
....	....	....	....	....	....	1	25	7 50
....	....	....	....	....	....	75	1,574	472 20
....	....	....	....	....	....	1	5	1 50
....	....	....	....	....	....	14,766	301,054	90,316 20
1,072	16,215	3,243 00	....	....	....	15,942	319,344	94,181 70
....	2,360	472 00	....	....	....	....	2,584	539 20
....	....	....	....	....	....	....	57	17 10
....	....	....	....	....	....	....	67,131	20,139 30
....	2,360	472 00	....	....	....	....	69,772	20,695 60

6 GEORGE V, A. 1916

No. 1.—General Statement

Articles Imported.	Countries.	Total Imports.		Entered		
				General Tariff.		
		Quantity.	Value.	Quantity.	Value.	Duty.
DUTIABLE GOODS—*Con.*		No.	$	No.	$	$ cts.
Iron and steel—*Con.*						
Machines, adding............	Germany.......	20	2,962	20	2,962	740 50
	United States..	1,110	197,023	1,113	198,441	49,610 25
	Total......	1,130	199,985	1,133	201,403	50,350 75
Machines, typewriting.........	Unit'd Kingdom	35	1,510	2	105	26 25
	Newfoundland..	11	90	11	90	22 50
	United States..	7,250	403,522	7,223	401,046	100,261 50
	Total......	7,296	405,122	7,236	401,241	100,310 25
Machines specially designed for ruling, folding, binding, embossing, creasing or cutting paper or cardboard, when for use exclusively by printers, bookbinders and by manufacturers of articles made from paper or cardboard, including parts t h e r e o f, composed wholly or in part of iron, steel, brass or wood.	Unit'd Kingdom	....	7,808	....	2,724	272 40
	Germany......	....	4,771	....	4,771	477 10
	United States..	....	151,423	....	151,423	15,142 30
	Total......	....	164,002	....	158,918	15,891 80
Printing presses and lithographic presses.	Unit'd Kingdom	....	7,633	....	99	9 90
	Newfoundland..	....	3	....	3	0 30
	Germany......	....	2,696	....	2,696	269 60
	United States..	....	220,494	....	220,494	22,049 40
	Total......	....	230,826	....	223,292	22,329 20
Type making accessories for printing presses.	United States..	....	31,750	....	31,750	3,175 00
Cement making machines......	Unit'd Kingdom	....	1,760	....	....	....
	Germany.......	....	1,358	....	1,358	373 45
	United States..	....	42,067	....	42,067	11,568 48
	Total......	....	45,185	....	43,425	11,941 93
Coal handling machines.......	Unit'd Kingdom	....	5,282	....	....	....
	United States...	....	136,581	....	136,581	37,559 89
	Total......	....	141,863	....	136,581	37,559 89
Paper and pulp mill machines..	Unit'd Kingdom	....	21,454	....	....	....
	Norway.......	....	440	....	440	121 00
	Switzerland.....	....	994	....	994	273 35
	United States..	....	383,790	....	383,790	105,542 34
	Total......	....	406,678	....	385,224	105,936 69
Rolling mill machines.........	Unit'd Kingdom	....	· 2,314	....	....	....
	United States..	....	116,596	....	108,943	29,959 42
	Total......	....	118,910	....	108,943	29,959 42
Saw mill machines............	Unit'd Kingdom	....	2,349	....	....	....
	United States...	....	137,148	....	137,148	37,716 00
	Total......	....	139,497	....	137,148	37,716 00

SESSIONAL PAPER No. 11

OF IMPORTS—*Continued.*

FOR HOME CONSUMPTION.

Preferential Tariff.			Treaty Rates.			Total.		
Quantity.	Value.	Duty.	Quantity.	Value.	Duty.	Quantity.	Value.	DutyColl'd.
No.	$	$ cts.	No.	$	$ cts.	No.	$	$ cts.
....	....	....	....	....	....	⁻ 20	2,962	740 50
....	....	....	....	....	....	1,113	198,441	49,610 25
....	....	....	....	....	....	1,133	201,403	50,350 75
33	1,405	245 91	....	....	....	35	1,510	272 16
....	....	....	....	....	....	11	90	22 50
....	....	....	....	....	....	7,223	401,046	100,261 50
33	1,405	245 91	....	....	....	7,269	402,646	100,556 16
....	5,037	251 85	....	....	....	....	7,761	524 25
....	....	....	....	....	....	....	4,771	477 10
....	....	....	....	....	....	....	151,423	15,142 30
....	5,037	251 85	....	....	....	....	163,955	16,143 65
....	7,534	376 70	....	....	....	....	7,633	386 60
....	....	....	....	....	....	....	3	0 30
....	....	....	....	....	....	....	2,696	269 60
....	....	....	....	....	....	....	220,494	22,049 40
....	7,534	376 70	....	....	....	....	230,826	22,705 90
....	....	....	....	....	....	....	31,750	3,175 00
....	1,760	264 00	....	....	....	....	1,760	264 00
....	....	....	....	....	....	....	1,358	373 45
....	....	....	....	....	....	....	42,067	11,568 48
....	1,760	˙264 00	....	....	....	....	45,185	12,205 93
....	5,282	792 30	....	....	....	....	5,282	792 30
....	....	....	....	....	....	....	136,581	37,559 89
....	5,282	792 30	....	....	....	....	141,863	38,352 19
....	21,454	3,218 10	....	....	....	....	21,454	3,218 10
....	....	....	....	....	....	....	440	121 00
....	....	....	....	....	....	....	994	273 35
....	....	....	....	....	....	....	383,790	105,542 34
....	21,454	3,218 10	....	....	....	....	406,678	109,154 79
....	2,314	347 10	....	....	....	....	2,314	347 10
....	....	....	....	....	....	....	108,943	29,959 42
....	2,314	347 10	....	....	....	....	111,257	30,306 52
....	2,349	352 35	....	....	....	....	2,349	352 35
....	....	....	....	....	....	....	137,148	37,716 00
....	2,349	352 35	....	....	....	....	139,497	38,068 35

6 GEORGE V, A. 1916

No. 1.—General Statement

Articles Imported.	Countries.	Total Imports.		Entered		
				General Tariff.		
		Quantity.	Value.	Quantity.	Value.	Duty.
DUTIABLE GOODS—*Con.*			$		$	$ cts.
Iron and steel—*Con.*						
Machinery of a class or kind not made in Canada and parts thereof adapted for carding, spinning, weaving, braiding or knitting fibrous material, when imported by manufacturers for such purposes.	Unit'd Kingdom	....	128,965	....	129,012	12,901 20
	Belgium..........	....	97	....	97	9 70
	France..........	....	94	....	94	9 40
	Germany..........	....	25,904	....	25,904	2,590 40
	Switzerland.....	....	2,700	....	2,700	270 00
	United States...	....	326,294	....	326,294	32,629 40
	Total......	....	484,054	....	484,101	48,410 10
All machinery composed wholly or in part of iron or steel, n.o.p., and iron or steel integral parts of.	Unit'd Kingdom	....	992,003	....	18,802	5,170 55
	Australia......	....	810	....	810	222 75
	Newfoundland..	....	300	....	300	82 50
	Aust.-Hungary..	....	1,081	....	1,081	297 27
	Belgium......	....	49	....	49	13 47
	France..........	....	4,941	....	4,604	1,266 10
	Germany......	....	113,731	....	109,570	30,131 75
	Holland.......	....	711	....	711	195 55
	Italy..........	....	933	....	933	256 57
	Japan..........	....	136	....	136	37 40
	Miquelon and St. Pierre.....	....	5	....	5	1 37
	Sweden........	....	1,143	....	1,341	368 77
	Switzerland.....	....	97,922	....	62,395	17,158 62
	United States...	....	8,090,241	....	8,091,041	2225,043 53
	Total......	....	9,304,006	....	8,291,778	2280,246 20
		No.		No.		
Machines, washing, domestic...	Unit'd Kingdom	17	42	....	....	....
	United States...	7,781	63,689	7,667	62,665	17,233 18
	Total......	7,798	63,731	7,667	62,665	17,233 18
		Lb.		Lb.		
Nails and spikes, composition and sheathing nails..........	Unit'd Kingdom	2,344	266	....	....	....
	United States...	131,782	3,445	131,782	3,445	516 75
	Total........	134,126	3,711	131,782	3,445	516 75
		Cwt.		Cwt.		
Nails and spikes, cut (ordinary builders'.)	Unit'd Kingdom	5	25	....	....	....
	United States...	4,684	8,560	4,684	8,560	2,342 00
	Total......	4,689	8,585	4,684	8,560	2,342 00
Railway spikes.................	Unit'd Kingdom	229	495	....	....	....
	United States...	54,671	82,355	54,671	82,355	27,335 50
	Total......	54,900	82,850	54,671	82,355	27,335 50
Nails, wire, of all kinds, n.o.p...	Unit'd Kingdom	29	90	....	....	....
	United States...	18,009	50,649	18,000	50,630	10,800 00
	Total......	18,038	50,739	18,000	50,630	10,800 00
		No.		No.		
Pumps, hand, n.o.p.............	Unit'd Kingdom	239	1,045	13	161	48 30
	Germany.......	1,788	3,882	1,788	3,882	1,164 60
	Norway........	25	116	25	116	34 80
	United States...	17,070	99,187	16,961	98,840	29,652 00
	Total......	19,122	104,230	18,787	102,999	30,899 70

SESSIONAL PAPER No. 11

OF IMPORTS—*Continued.*

FOR HOME CONSUMPTION.

	Preferential Tariff.			Treaty Rates.			Total.	
Quantity.	Value.	Duty.	Quantity.	Value.	Duty.	Quantity.	Value.	DutyColl'd.
	$	$ cts.		$	$ cts.		$	$ cts.
....	....	....	....	....	....	....	129,012	12,901 20
....	....	....	....	....	....	....	97	9 70
....	....	....	....	....	....	....	94	9 40
....	....	....	....	....	....	....	25,904	2,590 40
....	....	....	....	....	....	....	2,700	270 00
....	....	....	....	....	....	....	326,294	32,629 40
....	....	....	....	....	....	....	484,101	48,410 10
....	973,279	145,991 85	....	....	....	....	992,081	151,162 40
....	....	....	....	....	....	....	810	222 75
....	....	....	....	....	....	....	300	82 50
....	....	....	....	....	....	....	1,081	297 27
....	....	....	....	....	....	....	49	13 47
....	....	....	....	....	....	....	4,604	1,266 10
....	....	....	....	....	....	....	109,570	30,131 75
....	....	....	....	....	....	....	711	195 55
....	....	....	....	....	....	....	933	256 57
....	....	....	....	....	....	....	136	37 40
....	....	....	....	....	....	....	5	1 37
....	....	....	....	....	....	....	1,341	368 77
....	....	....	....	....	....	....	62,395	17,158 62
....	....	....	....	....	....	....	8,091,041	2,225,043 53
....	973,279	145,991 85	....	....	....	....	9,265,057	2,426,238 05
No. 17	42	6 30	No.	....	....	No. 17	42	6 30
....	....	....	....	....	....	7,667	62,665	17,233 18
17	42	6 30	....	....	....	7,684	62,707	17,239 48
Lb. 3,016	411	41 10	Lb.	....	....	Lb. 3,016	411	41 10
....	....	....	....	....	....	131,782	3,445	516 75
3,016	411	41 10	....	....	....	134,798	3,856	557 85
Cwt. 5	25	1 50	Cwt.	....	....	Cwt. 5	25	1 50
....	....	....	....	....	....	4,684	8,560	2,342 00
5	25	1 50	....	....	....	4,689	8,585	2,343 50
129	292	38 70	....	....	....	129	292	38 70
....	....	....	....	....	....	54,671	82,355	27,335 50
129	292	38 70	....	....	....	54,800	82,647	27,374 20
29	90	11 60	....	....	....	29	90	11 60
....	....	....	....	....	....	18,000	50,630	10,800 00
29	90	11 60	....	....	....	18,029	50,720	10,811 60
No. 226	884	176 80	No.	....	....	No. 239	1,045	225 10
....	....	....	....	....	....	1,788	3,882	1,164 60
....	....	....	....	....	....	25	116	34 80
....	....	....	....	....	....	16,961	98,840	29,652 00
226	884	176 80	....	....	....	19,013	103,883	31,076 50

6 GEORGE V, A. 1916

No. 1.—General Statement

Articles Imported.	Countries.	Total Imports.		Entered		
				General Tariff.		
		Quantity.	Value.	Quantity.	Value.	Duty.
DUTIABLE GOODS—*Con.*		No.	$	No.	$	$ cts.
Iron and steel—*Con.*						
Pumps, power, and parts.......	Unit'd Kingdom	133	41,288	....	....	....
	Germany,......	2	7,925	2	7,925	2,179 47
	Sweden........	1	56	1	56	15 40
	United States...	3,050	440,764	3,041	440,606	121,167 99
	Total.......	3,186	490,033	3,044	448,587	123,362 86
		Ton.		Ton.		
Iron and steel railway bars or rails of any form, punched or not, n.o.p., for railways, which term for the purposes of this item shall include all kinds of railway, street railways and tramways, even although they are used for private purposes only, and even although they are not used or intended to be used in connection with the business of common carrying of goods or passengers.	Unit'd Kingdom	148	4,337	111	2,420	777 00
	United States...	27,578	705,931	27,555	704,468	192,885 00
	Total.......	27,726	710,268	27,666	706,888	193,662 00
Railway fish plates............	Unit'd Kingdom	4	443	....	....	....
	United States...	2,951	113,527	2,938	112,853	23,504 00
	Total.......	2,955	113,970	2,938	112,853	23,504 00
Railway tie-plates.............	United States...	490	18,023	490	18,023	3,920 00
		Cwt.		Cwt.		
Rolled iron or steel angles, tees, beams, channels, girders and other rolled shapes or sections, not punched, drilled or further manufactured than rolled, n.o.p.	Unit'd Kingdom	24,478	34,852	6,928	7,764	2,424 80
	Belgium........	4,005	4,801	4,005	4,801	1,401 75
	Germany.......	6,545	7,652	6,545	7,652	2,290 75
	United States...	507,404	675,877	507,404	675,877	177,591 40
	Total.......	542,432	723,182	524,882	696,094	183,708 70
Rolled iron or steel beams, channels, angles, and other rolled shapes of iron or steel, not punched, drilled, or further manufactured than rolled, weighing not less than 35 lbs. per lineal yard, not being square, flat, oval or round shapes, and not being railway bars or rails.	Unit'd Kingdom	36,882	51,982	5,270	6,751	790 50
	Belgium........	12,798	18,121	12,798	18,121	1,919 70
	Germany.......	16,339	17,524	16,290	17,465	2,443 50
	United States.	1,233,606	1,576,710	1,233,655	1,576,769	185,048 23
	Total.......	1,299,625	1,664,337	1,268,013	1,619,106	190,201 93
Rolled iron or steel hoop, band, scroll or strip, 12 inches or less in width, No. 13 gauge and thicker, n.o.p.	Unit'd Kingdom	3,075	6,674	45	94	15 75
	Belgium........	90	98	90	98	31 50
	Germany.......	71	83	71	83	24 85
	United States...	55,772	89,417	55,772	89,417	19,520 20
	Total.......	59,008	96,272	55,978	89,692	19,592 30
Rolled hoop iron or hoop steel (galvanized) Nos. 12 and 13 gauge.	Unit'd Kingdom	703	1,546	....	....	....
	United States...	572	1,507	572	1,507	200 20
	Total.......	1,275	3,053	572	1,507	200 20

SESSIONAL PAPER No. 11

OF IMPORTS—*Continued.*

FOR HOME CONSUMPTION.

Preferential Tariff.			Treaty Rates.			Total.		
Quantity.	Value.	Duty.	Quantity.	Value.	Duty.	Quantity.	Value.	DutyColl'd.
No.	$	$ cts.	No.	$	$ cts.	No.	$	$ cts.
133	41,288	6,193 20	....	....	....	133	41,288	6,193 20
....	....	....	....	....	....	2	7,925	2,179 47
....	....	....	....	....	....	1	56	15 40
....	....	....	....	....	....	3,041	440,606	121,167 99
133	41,288	6,193 20	....	....	....	3,177	489,875	129,556 06
Ton. 37	1,917	166 50	Ton.			Ton. 148	4,337	943 50
....			....			· 27,555	704,468	192,885 00
37	1,917	166 50	....			27,703	708,805	193,828 50
4	443	20 00	....	....	....	4	443	20 00
....	....	....	....	....	....	. 2,938	112,853	23,504 00
4	443	20 00	....	....	....	2,942	113,296	23,524 00
....		....	....	....	....	490	18,023	3,920 00
Cwt. 17,571	27,127	3,733 80	Cwt.			Cwt. 24,499	34,891	6,158 60
....	....	....	....	....	....	4,005	4,801	1,401 75
....	....	....	....	....	....	6,545	7,652	2,290,75
....	....	....	....	....	....	507,404	675,877	177,591 40
17,571	27,127	3,733 80	....		....	542,453	723,221	187,442 50
31,612	45,231	3,161 20	....	....	....	36,882	51,982	3,951 70
....	....	....	....	....	....	12,798	18,121	1,919 70
....	....	....	....	....	....	16,290	17,465	2,443 50
....	....	....	....	....	....	1,233,655	1,576,769	185,048 23
31,612	45,231	3,161 20	....		....	1,299,625	1,664,337	193,363 13
3,030	6,580	643 87	....	....	....	3,075	6,674	659 62
....	....	....	....	....	....	90	98	31 50
....	....	....	....	....	....	71	83	24 85
....	....	....	....	....	....	55,772	89,417	19,520 20
3,030	6,580	643 87	....	....	....	59,008	96,272	20,236 17
703	1,546	149 39	....	....	....	703	1,546	149 39
....	....	....	....	....	....	572	1,507	200 20
703	1,546	149 39	....	....	....	1,275	3,053	349 59

6 GEORGE V, A. 1916

No. 1.—GENERAL STATEMENT

Articles Imported.	Countries.	TOTAL IMPORTS.		ENTERED		
				General Tariff.		
		Quantity.	Value.	Quantity.	Value.	Duty.
DUTIABLE GOODS—*Con.*		Cwt.	$	Cwt.	$	$ cts.
Iron and steel—*Con.*						
Rolled iron or steel, hoop, band,	Unit'd Kingdom	890	2,082	915	2,114	105 70
scroll or strip, No. 14 gauge	Belgium........	1,019	1,431	1,019	1,431	71 55
and thinner, galvanized or	Germany......	3,621	6,677	1,414	3,133	156 65
coated with other metal or	United States...	190,925	406,693	190,917	406,712	20,335 60
not, n.o.p., including drawn						
iron or steel of this description	Total......	196,455	416,883	194,265	413,390	20,669 50
for the manufacture of mats.						
Rolled iron or steel sheets or	Unit'd Kingdom	9,291	14,095	2,604	2,942	911 40
plates, sheared or unsheared,	Belgium........	2,808	3,163	2,808	3,163	247 45
and skelp iron or steel, sheared	Germany......	417	495	707	860	982 80
or rolled in grooves, n.o.p.	United States...	274,183	407,197	274,183	407,197	95,964 05
	Total......	286,699	424,950	280,302	414,162	98,105 70
Rolled iron or steel plates, not	Unit'd Kingdom	11,717	14,882	5,452	6,153	817 80
less than 30 inches in width	Belgium........	1,553	1,604	1,553	1,604	232 95
and not less than ¼ inch in	Germany.....	60	67	60	67	9 00
thickness, n.o.p.	United States...	431,299	638,756	431,299	638,756	64,694 86
	Total........	444,629	655,309	438,364	646,580	·65,754 61
Rolled iron or steel sheets,	Unit'd Kingdom	664	1,350	664	1,350	67 50
polished or not, No. 14 gauge	Belgium........	1,572	2,567	1,572	2,567	128 35
and thinner, n.o.p.	France..........	60	146	60	146	7 30
	Germany......	588	865	1,614	2,625	131 25
	United States..	578,246	1,243,333	577,882	1,243,333	62,166 65
	Total......	581,130	1,248,261	581,792	1,250,021	62,501 05
Rolls of chilled iron or steel....	Unit'd Kingdom	200	745	....	....	....
	United States...	569	1,658	569	1,658	497 40
	Total......	769	2,403	569	1,658	497 40
Rolled round wire rods in the	Belgium........	51,516	52,643	51,516	52,643	9, 15 35
coil of iron or steel not over ⅜	United States...	560,276	607,736	546,426	592,158	95,624 54
inch in diameter when im-						
ported by wire manufacturers	Total......	611,792	660,379	597,942	644,801	104,639 89
for use in making wire in the						
coil in their own factories.						
Rolled round rods in the coil of	United States...	6,194	7,468	6,194	7,468	. 1,083 96
iron or steel for the manufac-						
ture of chains.						
Sad or smoothing, hatters' and	Unit'd Kingdom	....	141	....	40	12 00
tailors' irons not plated.	Germany......	....	17	....	17	5 10
	United States...	....	3,450	....	3,450	1,035 00
	Total......	....	3,608	....	3,507	1,052 10
Safes, doors for safes and vaults	Unit'd Kingdom	....	145	....	....	....
	United States...	....	165,746	....	165,746	49,723 80
	Total......	....	165,891	....	165,746	49,723 80
Screws iron and steel, commonly	Unit'd Kingdom	....	372	....	96	33 60
called 'wood screws' n.o.p., in-	Belgium........	....	291	....	291	101 85
cluding lag or coach screws,	Germany......	....	110	....	110	38 50
plated or not, and machine or	United States...	....	36,288	....	36,424	12,748 40
other screws, n.o.p.						
	Total......	....	37,061	....	36,921	12,922 35

OF IMPORTS—*Continued.*

FOR HOME CONSUMPTION.

Preferential Tariff.			Treaty Rates.			Total.		
Quantity.	Value.	Duty.	Quantity.	Value.	Duty.	Quantity.	Value.	DutyColl'd.
Cwt.	$	$ cts.	Cwt.	$	$ cts.	Cwt.	$	$ cts.
....	....	....	....	....	....	915	2,114	105 70
....	....	....	....	....	....	1,019	1,431	71 55
....	....	....	....	....	....	1,414	3,133	156 65
....	....	....	....	....	....	190,917	406,712	20,335 60
....	....	....	....	....	....	194,265	413,390	20,669 50
6,687	11,153	1,420 94	....	....	....	9,291	14,095	2,332 34
....	....	....	....	....	....	2,808	3,163	247 45
....	....	....	....	....	....	707	860	982 80
....	....	....	....	....	....	274,183	407,197	95,964 05
6,687	11,153	1,420 94	....	....	....	286,989	425,315	99,526 64
6,265	8,729	626 50	....	....	....	11,717	14,882	1,444 30
....	....	....	....	....	....	1,553	1,604	232 95
....	....	....	....	....	....	60	67	9 00
....	....	....	....	....	....	431,299	638,756	64,694 86
6,265	8,729	626 50	....	....	....	444,629	655,309	66,381 11
....	....	....	....	....	....	664	1,350	67 50
....	....	....	....	....	....	1,572	2,567	128 35
....	....	....	....	....	....	60	146	7 30
....	....	....	....	....	....	1,614	2,625	131 25
....	....	....	....	....	....	577,882	1,243,333	62,166 65
....	....	....	....	....	....	581,792	1,250,021	62,501 05
200	745	149 00	....	....	....	200	745	149 00
....	....	....	....	....	....	569	1,658	497 40
200	745	149 00	....	....	....	769	2,403	646 40
....	....	....	....	....	....	51,516	52,643	9,015 35
....	....	....	....	....	....	546,426	592,158	95,624 54
....	....	....	....	....	....	597,942	644,801	104,639 89
....	....	....	....	....	....	6,194	7,468	1,083 96
....	101	20 20	....	....	....	....	141	32 20
....	....	....	....	....	....	....	17	5 10
....	....	....	....	....	....	....	3,450	1,035 00
....	101	20 20	....	....	....	....	3,608	1,072 30
....	145	29 00	....	....	....	....	145	29 00
....	....	....	....	....	....	....	165,746	49,723 80
....	145	29 00	....	....	....	....	165,891	49,752 80
....	276	62 12	....	....	....	....	372	95 72
....	....	....	....	....	....	....	291	101 85
....	....	....	....	....	....	....	110	38 50
....	....	....	....	....	....	....	36,424	12,748 40
....	276	62 12	....	....	....	....	37,197	12,984 47

6 GEORGE V, A. 1916

No. 1.—General Statement

Articles Imported.	Countries.	Total Imports.		Entered		
				General Tariff.		
		Quantity.	Value.	Quantity.	Value.	Duty.
DUTIABLE GOODS—*Con.*			$		$	$ cts.
Iron and steel—*Con.*						
Scales, balances, weighing beams and strength testing machines of all kinds.	Unit'd Kingdom	....	2,455	....	245	73 50
	Hong Kong.....	....	41	....	41	12 30
	China..........	....	3	....	3	0 90
	France..........	....	225	....	188	56 40
	Germany......	....	862	....	862	258 60
	Holland........	....	726	....	726	217 80
	United States...	....	86,156	....	86,148	25,844 40
	Total......	....	90,468	....	88,213	26,463 90
		Cwt.		Cwt.		
Shafting, round, steel, in bars not exceeding 2½ inches in diameter.	Unit'd Kingdom	929	2,222	124	271	67 75
	Switzerland.....	20	80	20	80	20 00
	United States...	19,614	35,857	19,614	35,857	8,964 25
	Total......	20,563	38,159	19,758	36,208	9,052 00
Shafting, steel, turned, compressed or polished..........	Unit'd Kingdom	....	1,986	....	10	3 00
	United States...	....	12,613	....	12,610	3,783 00
	Total......	....	14,599	....	12,620	3,786 00
Sheets or plates of steel, cold rolled, sheared edges, over 14 gauge, not less than 1½ inches wide, for manufacture of mower bars, hinges, typewriters, and sewing machines.	United States...	7,435	16,432	7,435	16,432	1,643 20
Sheets, flat, of galvanized iron or steel.	Germany......	110	216	110	216	10 80
	United States...	301,341	819,178	301,341	819,178	40,958 90
	Total......	301,451	819,394	301,451	819,394	40,969 70
Sheets, iron or steel corrugated, galvanized.	Unit'd Kingdom	58	177	....	....	....
	United States...	1,082	2,821	1,082	2,821	846 30
	Total......	1,140	2,998	1,082	2,821	846 30
Sheets, iron or steel, corrugated, not galvanized.	United States...	138	484	138	484	145 20
Skates of all kinds, roller or other, and parts thereof.	Unit'd Kingdom	....	530	....	....	....
	Germany......	....	10,437	....	10,437	3,652 95
	Sweden......	....	491	....	491	171 85
	United States...	....	26,745	....	26,745	9,360 75
	Total......	....	38,203	....	37,673	13,185 55
Skelp iron or steel, sheared or rolled in grooves, imported by manufacturers of wrought iron or steel pipe, for use exclusively in the manufacture of wrought iron or steel pipe in their own factories.	Belgium........	558	610	558	610	30 50
	United States...	1,885,782	2,103,595	1,885,782	2,103,595	105,179 75
	Total......	1,886,340	2,104,205	1,886,340	2,104,205	105,210 25
Steel billets, n.o.p..............	Unit'd Kingdom	435	540	....	....	....
	United States...	11,811	13,873	11,811	13,873	4,133 85
	Total......	12,246	14,413	11,811	13,873	4,133 85

OF IMPORTS—*Continued.*

FOR HOME CONSUMPTION.

Preferential Tariff.			Treaty Rates.			Total.		
Quantity.	Value.	Duty.	Quantity.	Value.	Duty.	Quantity.	Value.	DutyColl'd.
	$	$ cts.		$	$ cts.		$	$ cts.
....	2,274	454 80	....	....	....	....	2,519	528 30
....	....	....	....	....	....	....	41	12 30
....	....	....	....	....	....	....	3	0 90
....	....	....	....	....	....	....	188	56 40
....	....	....	....	....	....	....	862	258 60
....	....	....	....	....	....	....	726	217 80
....	....	....	....	....	....	....	86,148	25,844 40
....	2,274	454 80	....			....	90,487	26,918 70
Cwt. 784	1,901	332 67	Cwt.	....	....	Cwt. 908	2,172	400 42
....	....	....	....	....	....	20	80	20 00
....	....	....	....	....	....	19,614	35,857	8,964 25
784	1,901	332 67	....			20,542	38,109	9,384 67
....	2,026	405 20	....	....	....	....	2,036	408 20
....	....	....	....	....	....	....	12,610	3,783 00
....	2,026	405 20	....	....	....	....	14,646	4,191 20
....	....	....	....	....	....	7,435	16,432	1,643 20
....	....	....	....	....	....	110	216	10 80
....	....	....	....	....	....	301,341	819,178	40,958 90
....	....	....	....	....	....	301,451	819,394	40,969 70
58	177	35 40	....	....	....	58	177	35 40
....	....	....	....	....	....	1,082	2,821	846 30
58	177	35 40	....	....	....	1,140	2,998	881 70
....	....	....	....	....	....	138	484	145 20
....	530	119 26	....	....	....	....	530	119 26
....	....	....	....	....	....	....	10,437	3,652 95
....	....	....	....	....	....	....	491	171 85
....	....	....	....	....	....	....	26,745	9,360 75
....	530	119 26	....	....	....	....	38,203	13,304 81
....	....	....	....	....	....	558	610	30 50
....	....	....	....	....	....	1,885,782	2,103,595	105,179 75
....	....	....	....	....	....	1,886,340	2,104,205	105,210 25
435	540	92 43	....	....	....	435	540	92 43
....	....	....	....	....	....	11,811	13,873	4,133 85
435	540	92 43	....	....	....	12,246	14,413	4,226 28

11—ii—10½

6 GEORGE V, A. 1916

No. 1.—General Statement

Articles Imported.	Countries.	Total Imports.		Entered		
				General Tariff.		
		Quantity.	Value.	Quantity.	Value.	Duty.
			$		$	$ cts.
DUTIABLE GOODS—*Con.*						
Iron and steel—*Con.*						
Stoves of all kinds, for coal, wood, oil, spirits or gas.	Unit'd Kingdom	....	6,667	....	2,610	652 50
	Aust.-Hungary..	....	295	....	295	73 75
	Belgium........	....	81	....	81	20 25
	China..........	....	5	....	5	1 25
	France.........	....	51	....	51	12 75
	Germany.......	....	6,750	....	5,250	1,312 50
	Sweden........	....	967	....	967	241 75
	United States..	....	473,226	....	474,255	118,563 75
	Total......	....	488,042	....	483,514	120,878 50
Stove urns of metal, and dove-tails, chaplet and hinge tubes of tin for use in the manufacture of stoves.	United States..	....	11,169	....	11,169	1,116 90
Switches, frogs, crossings and intersections for railways.	Unit'd Kingdom	....	28,655	....	....	....
	United States..	....	107,004	....	104,149	33,848 81
	Total......	....	135,659	....	104,149	33,848 81
Wrought or seamless iron or steel tubing, plain or galvanized threaded and coupled or not, over 10 inches in diameter n.o.p.	Unit'd Kingdom	....	4,729	....	....	....
	Germany	....	1,800	....	1,800	270 00
	United States.	....	187,392	....	187,392	28,108 80
	Total......	....	193,921	....	189,192	28,378 80
Tubing—						
Wrought or seamless tubing, iron or steel, plain or galvanized, threaded and coupled or not, over 4 inches in diameter, but not exceeding 10 inches in diameter, n.o.p.	Unit'd Kingdom	....	14,640	....	11	3 30
	Germany	....	257	....	257	63 60
	United States..	....	175,304	....	175,304	51,657 30
	Total.....	....	190,201	....	175,572	51,724 20
Wrought or seamless tubing, iron or steel, plain or galvanized, threaded and coupled or not, 4 inches or less in diameter, n.o.p.	Unit'd Kingdom	....	8,970	....	17	5 95
	France.........	....	31	....	31	10 85
	United States..	....	135,308	....	135,308	47,357 80
	Total......	....	144,309	....	135,356	47,374 60
		Cwt.		Cwt.		
Seamless steel tubing, valued at not less than 3½ cents per lb.	Unit'd Kingdom	27	154	27	154	7 70
	Sweden........	159	987	159	987	49 35
	United States..	3,849	29,725	3,852	29,727	1,486 35
	Total........	4,035	30,866	4,038	30,868	1,543 40
Rolled or drawn square tubing of iron or steel, adapted for use in the manufacture of agricultural implements.	United States..	....	2,785	....	2,785	139 25
Iron or steel pipe or tubing, plain or galvanized, riveted, corrugated or otherwise specially manufactured, including lock-joint pipe, n.o.p.	Unit'd Kingdom	....	72,350	....	1,858	557 40
	B. W. Indies....	....	610	....	610	183 00
	Belgium........	....	398	....	398	119 40
	France.........	....	31	....	31	9 30
	Germany.......	....	59,411	....	59,411	17,823 30
	United States..	....	262,226	....	262,225	78,667 50
	Total......	....	395,026	....	324,533	97,359 90

SESSIONAL PAPER No. 11

OF IMPORTS—*Continued.*

FOR HOME CONSUMPTION.

	Preferential Tariff.			Treaty Rates.			Total.	
Quantity.	Value.	Duty.	Quantity.	Value.	Duty.	Quantity.	Value.	DutyColl'd.
	$	$ cts.		$	$ cts.		$	$ cts.
....	4,055	608 25	....	....	....	....	6,665	1,260 75
....	....	....	....	....	....	....	295	73 75
....	....	....	....	....	....	....	81	20 25
....	....	....	....	....	....	....	5	1 25
....	....	....	....	....	....	....	51	12 75
....	....	....	....	....	....	....	5,250	1,312 50
....	....	....	....	....	....	....	967	241 75
....	....	....	....	....	....	....	474,255	118,563 75
....	4,055	608 25	....	....	....	....	487,569	121,486 75
....	....	....	....	....	....	....	11,169	1,116·90
....	28,655	5,731 00	....	....	....	....	28,655	5,731 00
....	....	....	....	....	....	....	104,149	33,848 81
....	28,655	5,731 00	....	....	....	....	132,804	39,579 81
....	4,729	472 90	....	....	....	....	4,729	472 90
....	....	....	....	....	....	....	1,800	270 00
....	....	....	....	....	....	....	187,392	28,108 80
....	4,729	472 90	....	....	....	....	193,921	28,851 70
....	14,629	2,905 90	....	....	....	....	14,640	2,909 20
....	....	....	....	....	....	....	257	63 60
....	....	....	....	....	....	....	175,304	51,657 30
....	14,629	2,905 90	....	....	....	....	190,201	54,630 10
....	8,875	1,775 00	....	....	....	....	8,892	1,780 95
....	....	....	....	....	....	....	31	10 85
....	....	....	....	....	....	....	135,308	47,357 80
....	8,875	1,775 00	....	....	....	....	144,231	49,149 60
Cwt.			Cwt.			Cwt.		
....	....	....	....	....	....	27	154	7 70
....	....	....	....	....	....	159	987	49 35
....	....	....	....	....	....	3,852	29,727	1,486 35
....	....	....	....	....	....	4,038	30,868	1,543 40
....	....	....	....	....	....	....	2,785	139 25
....	70,492	14,098 40	....	....	....	....	72,350	14,655 80
....	....	....	....	....	....	....	610	183 00
....	....	....	....	....	....	....	398	119 40
....	....	....	....	....	....	....	31	9 30
....	....	....	....	....	....	....	59,411	17,823 30
....	....	....	....	....	....	....	262,225	78,667 50
....	70,492	14,098 40	....	....	....	....	395,025	111,458 30

6 GEORGE V, A. 1916

No. 1—GENERAL STATEMENT

Articles Imported.	Countries.	Total Imports.		Entered		
				General Tariff.		
		Quantity.	Value.	Quantity.	Value.	Duty.
			$		$	$ cts.
DUTIABLE GOODS—*Con.*						
Iron and steel—*Con.*						
Iron or steel pipe, not butt or lap-welded, and wirebound wooden pipe, not less than 30 inches internal diameter, when for use exclusively in alluvial gold mining.	United States.	....	1,716	....	1,716	171 60
Ware—Agate, granite or enamelled iron or steel ware.	Unit'd Kingdom	....	22,031	....	5,833	2,041 55
	Hong Kong.....	....	6	....	6	2 10
	Aust.-Hungary..	....	5,303	....	5,303	1,856 05
	Belgium........	....	405	....	439	153 65
	France..........	....	976	....	978	342 30
	Germany.......	....	28,763	....	28,648	10,026 80
	Holland........	....	8	....	8	2 80
	Japan..........	....	3	....	3	1 05
	Sweden........	....	5,544	....	5,544	1,940 40
	United States..	....	122,044	....	121,984	42,694 40
	Total......	......*..	185,083	....	168,746	59,061 10
Ware—Iron or steel hollow-ware, plain black or coated, n.o.p., and nickel and aluminum kitchen or household hollow-ware, n.o.p.	Unit'd Kingdom	....	10,029	....	1,381	414 30
	Hong Kong....	....	406	....	406	121 80
	Aust.-Hungary..	....	580	....	580	174 00
	Belgium........	....	230	....	230	69 00
	France.........	....	4,079	....	4,079	1,223 70
	Germany.......	....	21,734	....	22,069	6,620 70
	Holland........	....	1,857	....	1,857	557 10
	Japan..........	....	292	....	292	87 60
	Switzerland.....	....	1,251	....	1,251	375 30
	United States..	....	166,067	....	165,964	49,789 20
	Total......	....	206,525	....	198,109	59,432 70
Wire bale ties.....,...........	United States..	....	8,656	....	8,656	2,596 80
		Lb.		Lb.		
Wire cloth or wove wire and netting of iron or steel.	Unit'd Kingdom	1,727,764	104,127	80,319	5,175	1,552 50
	Hong Kong.....	30	2	30	2	0 60
	Germany.......	34,516	3,689	34,516	3,689	1,106 70
	United States..	2,472,861	125,614	2,472,861	125,614	37,684 20
	Total.......	4,235,171	233,432	2,587,726	134,480	40,344 00
Wire, crucible cast steel, valued at not less than 6 cents per lb.	France.........	1,145	387	1,145	387	19 35
	Germany.......	84,595	11,197	84,595	11,197	559 85
	United States..	84,590	15,551	84,590	15,551	777 55
	. Total......	170,330	27,135	170,330	27,135	1,356 75
Wire screens, doors and windows	Unit'd Kingdom	....	1,185	....	....	....
	Hong Kong.....	....	9	....	9	2 70
	Japan..........	....	66	....	....	....
	United States..	....	34,248	....	34,248	10,274 40
	Total......	....	35,508	....	34,257	10,277 10
Wire buckthorn strip, fencing, woven wire fencing and wire fencing of iron or steel, n.o.p., not to include woven wire or netting made from wire smaller than No. 14 gauge, not to include fencing of wire larger than No. 9 gauge.	Unit'd Kingdom	384,074	21,467	17,000	458	68 70
	Germany.......	59,908	1,311	59,908	1,311	196 65
	United States..	1,378,951	49,707	1,378,951	49,707	7,456 05
	Total......	1,822,933	72,485	1,455,859	51,476	7,721 40

OF IMPORTS—*Continued.*

FOR HOME CONSUMPTION.

Preferential Tariff.			Treaty Rates.			Total.		
Quantity.	Value.	Duty.	Quantity.	Value.	Duty.	Quantity.	Value.	DutyColl'd.
	$	$ cts.		$	$ cts.		$	$ cts.
....	....	....	....	....	....	....	1,716	171 60
....	15,951	3,589 17	....	....	....	....	21,784	5,630 72
....	....	....	....	....	....	....	6	2 10
....	....	....	....	....	....	....	5,303	1,856 05
....	....	....	....	....	....	....	439	153 65
....	....	....	....	....	....	....	978	342 30
....	....	....	....	....	....	....	28,648	10,026 80
....	....	....	....	....	....	....	8	2 80
....	....	....	....	....	....	....	3	1 05
....	....	....	....	....	....	....	5,544	1,940 40
....	....	....	....	....	....	....	121,984	42,694 40
....	15,951	3,589 17	....	....	....	....	184,697	62,650 27
....	8,701	1,740 20	....	....	....	....	10,082	2,154 50
....	....	....	....	....	....	....	406	121 80
....	....	....	....	....	....	....	580	174 00
....	....	....	....	....	....	....	230	69 00
....	....	....	....	....	....	....	4,079	1,223 70
....	....	....	....	....	....	....	22,069	6,620 70
....	....	....	....	....	....	....	1,857	557 10
....	....	....	....	....	....	....	292	87 60
....	....	....	....	....	....	....	1,251	375 30
....	....	....	....	....	....	....	165,964	49,789 20
....	8,701	1,740 20	....	....	....	....	206,810	61,172 90
....	....	....	....	....	....	....	8,656	2,596 80
Lb 1,648,305	99,000	19,800 00	Lb.	....	....	Lb. 1,728,624	104,175	21,352 50
....	....	....	....	....	....	30	2	0 60
....	....	....	....	....	....	34,516	3,689	1,106 70
....	....	....	....	....	....	2,472,861	125,614	37,684 20
1,648,305	99,000	19,800 00	....	....	....	4,236,031	233,480	60,144 00
....	....	....	....	....	....	1,145	387	19 35
....	....	....	....	....	....	84,595	11,197	559 85
....	....	....	....	....	....	84,590	15,551	777 55
....	....	....	....	....	....	170,330	27,135	1,356 75
....	1,185	237 00	....	....	....	....	1,185	237 00
....	....	....	....	....	....	....	9	2 70
....	....	....	....	66	18 15	....	66	18 15
....	....	....	....	....	....	....	34,248	10,274 40
....	1,185	237 00	....	66	18 15	....	35,508	10,532 25
367,074	21,009	2,100 90	....	....	....	384,074	21,467	2,169 60
....	....	....	....	....	....	59,908	1,311	196 65
....	....	....	....	....	....	1,378,951	49,707	7,456 05
367,074	21,009	2,100 90	....	....	....	1,822,933	72,485	9,822 30

6 GEORGE V, A. 1916

No. 1.—General Statement

Articles Imported.	Countries.	Total Imports.		Entered		
				General Tariff.		
		Quantity.	Value.	Quantity.	Value.	Duty.
			$		$	$ cts.
DUTIABLE GOODS—*Con.*						
Iron and steel—*Con.*						
Wire, single or several, covered with cotton, linen, silk, rubber or other material, including cable so covered.	Unit'd Kingdom	....	158,823	....	1,737	521 10
	Hong Kong.....	....	4	....	4	1 20
	Belgium.......	....	384	....	384	115 20
	France........	....	1	....	1	0 30
	Germany......	....	3,931	....	3,881	1,164 30
	Italy.........	....	478	....	478	143 40
	United States..	....	176,404	....	174,552	52,365 60
	Total......	....	340,025	....	181,037	54,311 10
		Lb.		Lb.		
Wire of iron and steel, all kinds, n.o.p.	Unit'd Kingdom	226,760	8,669	18,814	564	112 80
	Belgium........	10,813	260	10,813	260	52 00
	France.........	18	5	2,413	105	21 00
	Germany.......	1,507,016	29,534	1,507,516	29,584	5,916 80
	United States..	5,125,794	131,459	5,125,516	131,395	26,279 00
	Total......	6,870,401	169,927	6,665,072	161,908	32,381 60
Wire, rope, stranded or twisted wire, clothes lines, picture or other twisted wire, and wire cables, n.o.p.	Unit'd Kingdom	3,663,350	242,414	4,499	414	103 50
	Australia.......	60	3	60	3	0 75
	France.........	45,130	4,375	45,475	4,390	1,097 50
	Germany.......	36,320	2,022	36,320	2,022	505 50
	United States..	1,468,851	128,398	1,442,213	125,550	31,387 50
	. Total......	5,213,711	377,212	1,528,567	132,379	33,094 75
		Cwt.		Cwt.		
Iron or steel nuts, rivets and bolts, with or without threads; nut, bolt and hinge blanks; and T and strap hinges of all kinds, n.o.p.	Unit'd Kingdom	2,410	7,645	....	....	....
	United States...	34,238	134,590	34,248	135,439	59,545 77
	Total.......	36,648	142,235	34,248	135,439	59,545 77
Iron or steel scrap, wrought, being waste or refuse, including punchings, cuttings and clippings of iron or steel plates or sheets, having been in actual use; crop ends of tin plate bars, blooms and rails, the same not having been in actual use.	Unit'd Kingdom	40	22	....	....	....
	B. Guiana......	818	180	350	88	17 50
	B. W. Indies....	1,184	840	....	....	....
	Newfoundland..	4,145	1,104	4,145	1,104	207 25
	Miquelon and St. Pierre:....	930	279	930	279	46 50
	United States...	216,669	140,651	216,689	140,797	10,834 45
	Total.......	223,786	143,076	222,114	142,268	11,105 70
Pen-knives, jack-knives and pocket-knives of all kinds.	Unit'd Kingdom	....	77,459	....	381	114 30
	Hong Kong.....	....	1	....	1	0 30
	Aust.-Hungary..	....	221	....	....	....
	France........	....	351	....	75	22 50
	Germany......	....	4,454	....	4,462	1,338 60
	Holland.......	....	92	....	92	27 60
	Sweden........	....	32	....	32	9 60
	United States...	....	5,347	....	5,347	1,604 10
	Total......	....	87,957	....	10,390	3,117 00
Knives and forks of steel, plated or not, n.o.p.	Unit'd Kingdom	....	128,148	....	2,310	693 00
	Hong Kong.....	....	22	....	22	6 60
	Aust.-Hungary..	....	88	....	....	....
	Belgium........	....	46	....	....	....
	France........	....	709	....	197	59 10
	Germany.......	....	22,869	....	23,389	7,016 70
	Spain.........	....	146	....	....	....
	United States..	....	36,237	....	36,237	10,871 10
	Total......	....	188,265	....	62,155	18,646 50

SESSIONAL PAPER No. 11

OF IMPORTS—*Continued.*

FOR HOME CONSUMPTION.

	Preferential Tariff.			Treaty Rates.			Total.	
Quantity.	Value.	Duty.	Quantity.	Value.	Duty.	Quantity.	Value.	DutyColl'd.
	$	$ cts.		$	$ cts.		$	$ cts.
....	157,100	31,420 00	......	......	......	......	158,837	31,941 10
....	....	....	....	....	....	....	4	1 20
....	....	....	....	....	....	....	384	115 20
....	....	....	....	....	....	....	1	0 30
....	....	....	....	....	....	....	3,881	1,164 30
....	....	....	....	....	....	....	478	143 40
....	....	....	....	....	....	....	174,552	52,365 60
....	157,100	31,420 00	....	....	....	....	338,137	85,731 10
Lb. 207,946	8,276	1,241 40	Lb.	......	......	Lb. 226,760	8,840	1,354 20
....	....	....	....	....	....	10,813	260	52 00
....	....	....	....	....	....	2,413	105	21 00
....	....	....	....	....	....	1,507,516	29,584	5,916 80
....	....	....	....	....	....	5,125,516	131,395	26,279 00
207,946	8,276	1,241 40	....	....	....	6,873,018	170,184	33,623 00
3,659,880	245,865	43,026 62	....	....	....	3,664,379	246,279	43,130 12
....	....	....	....	....	....	60	3	0 75
....	....	....	....	....	....	45,475	4,390	1,097 50
....	....	....	....	....	....	36,320	2,022	505 50
....	....	....	....	....	....	1,442,213	125,550	31,387 50
3,659,880	245,865	43,026 62	....	....	....	5,188,447	378,244	76,121 37
Cwt. 2,394	7,627	2,558 20	Cwt.			Cwt. 2,394	7,627	2,558 20
....	....	....	....			34,248	135,439	59,545 77
2,394	7,627	2,558 20	....	....	....	36,642	143,066	62,103 97
40	22	1 00	....	....	....	40	22	1 00
468	92	11 70	....	....	....	818	180	29 20
1,184	840	29 60	....	....	....	1,184	840	29 60
....	....	....	....	....	....	4,145	1,104	207 25
....	....	....	....	....	....	930	279	46 50
....	....	....	....	....	....	216,689	140,797	10,834 45
1,692	954	42 30	....	....	....	223,806	143,222	11,148 00
....	77,237	15,447 40	....	....	....	....	77,618	15,561 70
....	....	....	....	....	....	....	1	0 30
....	....	....	....	221	60 80	....	221	60 80
....	....	....	....	276	75 90	....	351	98 40
....	....	....	....	....	....	....	4,462	1,338 60
....	....	....	....	....	....	....	92	27 60
....	....	....	....	....	....	....	32	9 60
....	....	....	....	....	....	....	5,347	1,604 10
....	77,237	15,447 40	....	497	136 70	....	88,124	18,701 10
....	125,889	25,177 80	....	....	....	....	128,199	25,870 80
....	....	....	....	....	....	....	22	6 60
....	....	....	....	88	24 20	....	88	24 20
....	....	....	....	46	12 65	....	46	12 65
....	....	....	....	508	139 72	....	705	198 82
....	....	....	....	....	....	....	23,389	7,016 70
....	....	....	....	146	40 15	....	146	40 15
....	....	....	....	....	....	....	36,237	10,871 10
....	125,889	25,177 80	....	788	216 72	....	188,832	44,041 02

6 GEORGE V, A. 1916

No. 1.—General Statement

Articles Imported.	Countries.	Total Imports.		Entered		
		Quantity.	Value.	General Tariff.		
				Quantity.	Value.	Duty.
DUTIABLE GOODS—*Con.*			$		$	$ cts.
Iron and steel—*Con.*						
All other cutlery, n.o.p.	Unit'd Kingdom	....	207,739	....	6,452	1,935 60
	Hong Kong	....	119	....	119	35 70
	Newfoundland	....	20	....	20	6 00
	Aust.-Hungary	....	710	....	376	112 80
	Belgium	....	24	....	24	7 20
	China	....	36	....	36	10 80
	France	....	2,916	....	417	125 10
	Germany	....	91,172	....	91,571	27,471 30
	Holland	....	80	....	80	24 00
	Japan	....	61	....	10	3 00
	Sweden	....	185	....	177	53 10
	Switzerland	....	258	....	258	77 40
	United States	....	161,305	....	160,949	48,284 70
	Total	....	464,625	....	260,489	78,146 70
Guns, rifles, including air guns and air rifles, (not being toys), muskets, cannons, pistols, revolvers, or other firearms.	Unit'd Kingdom	....	126,554	....	1,284	385 20
	Hong Kong	....	18	....	18	5 40
	Belgium	....	38,327	....	37,685	11,305 50
	France	....	1,360	....	1,360	408 00
	Germany	....	6,514	....	3,729	1,118 70
	Spain	....	796	....	796	238 80
	United States	....	553,454	....	553,434	166,030 20
	Total	....	727,023	....	598,306	179,491 80
Bayonets, swords, fencing foils and masks.	Unit'd Kingdom	....	3,805	....	107	32 10
	Germany	....	182	....	182	54 60
	United States	....	3,645	....	3,984	1,195 20
	Total	....	7,632	....	4,273	1,281 90
Needles, of any material or kind, n.o.p.	Unit'd Kingdom	....	60,499	....	375	112 50 -
	Aust.-Hungary	....	181	....	....	....
	France	....	57	....	45	13 50
	Germany	....	3,176	....	3,176	952 80
	Japan	....	1	....	....	....
	United States	....	51,509	....	51,509	15,452 70
	Total	....	115,423	....	55,105	16,531 50
		Cwt.		Cwt.		
Steel, chrome steel	United States	1,980	9,123	1,980	9,123	1,368 45
Steel plate, universal mill or rolled edge plates of steel over 12 inches wide, imported by manufacturers of bridges or of structural work or in car construction.	Unit'd Kingdom	4,708	5,387	4,708	5,387	706 20
	United States	439,671	641,575	439,671	641,575	65,950 65
	Total	444,379	646,962	444,379	646,962	66,656 85
Steel, in bars or sheets, to be used exclusively in the manufacture of shovels, when imported by manufacturers of shovels.	Unit'd Kingdom	6	19	....	....	....
	United States	19,243	23,734	19,243	23,734	2,886 45
	Total	19,249	23,753	19,243	23,734	2,886 45
Rolled iron or steel, and cast steel in bars, bands, hoops, scroll or strip, sheet or plate, of any size, thickness or width, galvanized or coated with any material or not, and steel blanks for the manufacture of milling cutters, when of greater value than 3½ cents per lb.	Unit'd Kingdom	262	1,414	262	1,414	70 70
	Belgium	227	2,286	176	1,607	80 35
	France	31	243	31	243	12 15
	Germany	1,153	13,040	1,123	12,656	632 80
	Sweden	2,555	12,948	2,555	12,948	647 40
	Switzerland	743	22,664	630	18,124	906 20
	United States	101,323	635,127	101,549	635,622	31,781 10
	Total	106,294	687,722	106,326	682,614	34,130 70

SESSIONAL PAPER No. 11

OF IMPORTS—*Continued.*

FOR HOME CONSUMPTION.

	Preferential Tariff.			Treaty Rates.			Total.	
Quantity.	Value.	Duty.	Quantity.	Value.	Duty.	Quantity.	Value.	DutyColl'd.
	$	$ cts.		$	$ cts.		$	$ cts.
....	201,469	40,293 80	....	192	52 80	....	208,113	42,282 20
....	....	....	....	....	....	....	119	35 70
							20	6 00
				311	85 52		687	198 32
							24	7 20
							36	10 80
				2,499	687 30		2,916	812 40
							91,571	27,471 30
							80	24 00
				51	14 02		61	17 02
				8	2 20		185	55 30
							258	77 40
							160,949	48,284 70
....	201,469	40,293 80	....	3,061	841 84	....	465,019	119,282 34
....	125,270	25,054 00					126,554	25,439 20
							18	5 40
							37,685	11,305 50
							1,360	408 00
							3,729	1,118 70
							796	238 80
							553,434	166,030 20
....	125,270	25,054 00	....				723,576	204,545 80
....	3,698	739 60					3,805	771 70
							182	54 60
							3,984	1,195 20
....	3,698	739 60	....			....	7,971	2,021 50
....	60,184	12,036 80					60,559	12,149 30
				181	49 78		181	49 78
				12	3 30		57	16 80
							3,176	952 80
				1	0 28		1	0 28
							51,509	15,452 70
....	60,184	12,036 80	....	194	53 36	....	115,483	28,621 66
Cwt.		·	Cwt.			Cwt.		
....						1,980	9,123	1,368 45
						4,708	5,387	706 20
						439,671	641,575	65,950 65
....	....					444,379	646,962	66,656 85
6	19	0 60	....			6	19	0 60
....	....	....				19,243	23,734	2,886 45
6	19	0 60	....	....		19,249	23,753	2,887 05
....	....	....	....			262	1,414	70 70
						176	1,607	80 35
						31	243	12 15
						1,123	12,656	632 80
						2,555	12,948	647 40
						630	18,124	906 20
						101,549	635,622	31,781 10
....	....	....	....	....	....	106,326	682,614	34,130 70

6 GEORGE-V, A. 1916

No. 1.—General Statement

Articles Imported.	Countries.	Total Imports.		Entered		
				General Tariff.		
		Quantity.	Value.	Quantity.	Value.	Duty.
DUTIABLE GOODS—*Con.*			$		$	$ cts.
Iron and steel—*Con.*						
Steel balls adapted for use on bearings of machinery and vehicles.	Unit'd Kingdom	....	206	....	206	20 60
	Germany	....	685	....	685	68 50
	United States...	....	13,843	....	13,821	1,382 10
	Total......	....	14,734	....	14,712	1,471 20
		Cwt.		Cwt.		
Flat steel, cold rolled, not over ½ inch thick, for the manufacture of cups and cones for ball bearings.	United States...	151	418	151	418	20 90
Steel wool....................	Unit'd Kingdom	....	424	....	424	42 40
	Germany	....	317	....	317	31 70
	United States...	....	3,354	....	3,354	335 40
	Total......	....	4,095	....	4,095	409 50
Tools and implements—						
Adzes, cleavers, hatchets, wedges, sledges, hammers, crowbars, cantdogs and track tools, picks, mattocks and eyes or poles for the same.	Unit'd Kingdom	....	6,475	....	12	3 60
	Belgium	....	11	....	11	3 30
	Germany	....	89	....	89	26 70
	United States...	....	31,263	....	31,263	9,378 90
	Total......	....	37,838	....	31,375	9,412 50
		Doz.		Doz.		
Axes........................	Unit'd Kingdom	6	31	....	1	0 23
	France	7	43	7	43	9 69
	Sweden	25	108	25	108	24 40
	United States...	2,814	19,208	2,824	19,306	4,344 06
	Total......	2,852	19,390	2,856	19,458	4,378 38
Saws........................	Unit'd Kingdom	....	2,574	....	142	42 60
	France	....	299	....	50	15 00
	Germany	....	81	....	81	24 30
	Holland	....	4	....	4	1 20
	Sweden	....	959	....	959	287 70
	United States...	....	73,318	....	73,318	21,995 40
	Total......	....	77,235	....	74,554	22,366 20
Files and rasps, n.o.p..........	Unit'd Kingdom	....	17,700	....	93	27 90
	France	....	2,050	....	603	180 90
	Germany	....	2,310	....	2,310	693 00
	Japan	....	4	....	....	....
	Switzerland....	....	219	....	2	0 60
	United States...	....	67,731	....	67,731	20,319 30
	Total......	....	90,014	....	70,739	21,221 70
Tools, hand, of all kinds, n.o.p.	Unit'd Kingdom	....	35,641	....	6,345	1,903 50
	Aust.-Hungary..	....	3	....	....	....
	Belgium	....	386	....	386	115 80
	France	....	440	....	115	34 50
	Germany	....	15,435	....	15,435	4,630 50
	Holland	....	65	....	65	19 50
	Japan	....	190	....	....	....
	Sweden	....	25	....	....	....
	Switzerland....	....	3	....	....	....
	United States...	....	484,522	....	484,288	145,286 40
	Total......	....	536,710	....	506,634	151,990 20

OF IMPORTS—*Continued.*

FOR HOME CONSUMPTION.

Preferential Tariff.			Treaty Rates.			Total.		
Quantity.	Value.	Duty.	Quantity.	Value.	Duty.	Quantity.	Value.	DutyColl'd
	$	$ cts.		$	$ cts.		$	$ cts.
....	....	....	....	....	....	....	206	20 60
....	....	....	....	....	....	....	685	68 50
....	....	....	....	....	....	....	13,821	1,382 10
....	....	....	....	....	....	....	14,712	1,471 20
Cwt.			Cwt.			Cwt.		
....	....	....	....	....	....	151	418	20 90
....	....	....					424	42 40
....	....	....					317	31 70
....	....	....					3,354	335 40
....	....	....	....	....	....	....	4,095	409 50
....	6,463	1,292 60					6,475	1,296 20
....	....	....					11	3 30
....	....	....					89	26 70
....	....	....					31,263	9,378 90
....	6,463	1,292 60	....	....	....	....	37,838	10,705 10
Doz.			Doz.			Doz.		
6	30	4 50	....	....	....	6	31	4 73
....	....	....				7	43	9 69
....	....	....	....	....	....	25	108	24 40
....	....	....	....	....	....	2,824	19,306	4,344 06
6	30	4 50	....	....	....	2,862	19,488	4,382 88
....	2,432	486 40					2,574	529 00
....	....	....	249	68 48	....	....	299	83 48
....	....	....					81	24 30
....	....	....					4	1 20
....	....	....					959	287 70
....	....	....	....	....	....	....	73,318	21,995 40
....	2,432	486 40	....	249	68 48	....	77,235	22,921 08
....	17,491	3,498 20	....	116	31 90	....	17,700	3,558 00
....	....	....	1,447	397 97	....	....	2,050	578 87
....	....	....					2,310	693 00
....	....	....	4	1 10	....	....	4	1 10
....	....	....	217	59 68	....	....	219	60 28
........:.	....	....	....	....	....	....	67,731	20,319 30
....	17,491	3,498 20	....	1,784	490 65	....	90,014	25,210 55
....	29,081	5,816 20	....	448	123 25	....	35,874	7,842 95
....	....	....	3	0 83	....	....	3	0 83
....	....	....					386	115 80
....	....	....	325	89 44	....	....	440	123 94
....	....	....	....	....	....	....	15,435	4,630 50
....	....	....					65	19 50
....	....	....	190	52 25	....	....	190	52 25
....	....	....	25	6 88	....	....	25	6 88
....	....	....	3	0 83	....	....	3	0 83
....	....	....	....	....	....	....	484,288	145,286 40
....	29,081	5,816 20	....	994	273 48	....	536,709	158,079 88

6 GEORGE V, A. 1916

No. 1.—General Statement

Articles Imported.	Countries.	Total Imports.		Entered		
		Quantity.	Value.	General Tariff.		
				Quantity.	Value.	Duty.
DUTIABLE GOODS—*Con.*			$		$	$ cts.
Iron and steel—*Con.*						
Knife blades, or blanks, and table forks of iron or steel, in the rough, not handled, filed, ground or otherwise manufactured.	Unit'd Kingdom	....	14	....	....	....
	United States...	....	87	....	87	8 70
	Total......	....	101	....	87	8 70
Manufactures, articles or wares of iron or steel, or of which iron or steel, (or either) are the component materials of chief value, n.o.p.	Unit'd Kingdom	....	617,747	....	21,621	6,486 30
	Hong Kong.....	....	328	....	328	98 40
	Newfoundland..	....	36	....	36	10 80
	Alaska..........	....	308	....	308	92 40
	Aust.-Hungary..	....	589	....	197	59 10
	Belgium........	....	3,375	....	3,222	966 60
	China..........	....	55	....	55	16 50
	Denmark......	....	145	....	129	38 70
	France........	....	13,262	....	3,599	1,079 70
	Germany......	....	88,076	....	82,621	24,786 30
	Holland.......	....	147	....	163	48 90
	Italy..........	....	1,100	....	415	124 50
	Japan..........	....	723	....	85	25 50
	Miquelon and St. Pierre.....	....	189	....	186	55 80
	Norway.......	....	107	....	....	....
	Sweden.......	....	2,346	....	2,148	644 40
	Switzerland....	....	141	....	2	0 60
	Turkey........	....	23	....	23	6 90
	United States...	....	6,392,059	....	6,395,261	1,918,578 30
	Total......	....	7,120,756	....	6,510,399	1,953,119 70
Ivory, manufactures of, n.o.p......	Unit'd Kingdom	....	50	....	5	0 88
	Hong Kong.....	....	10	....	10	1 75
	France........	....	106	....	106	18 55
	Germany......	....	6	....	6	1 05
	Holland.......	....	4	....	4	0 70
	Japan..........	....	164	....	164	28 70
	United States...	....	1,934	....	1,934	338 52
	Total......	....	2,274	....	2,229	390 15
		Lb.		Lb.		
Jellies, jams and preserves, n.o.p., and condensed mince meat.	Unit'd Kingdom	4,412,839	374,227	11,755	1,124	416 33
	Australia........	1,890	80	1,890	80	70 87
	B. W. Indies....	976	167	653	110	24 49
	Hong Kong.....	1,241	100	1,241	100	45 17
	New Zealand...	21,945	1,785	....	....	....
	China..........	208	13	208	13	7 56
	Denmark......	10	2	10	2	0 33
	France........:	17,425	1,939	17,544	1,990	650 75
	Italy..........	23,252	4,108	22,044	3,708	815 64
	Japan..........	438	18	438	18	14 40
	Norway........	200	20	200	20	6 50
	Switzerland....	....	....	468	63	16 29
	United States...	104,124	16,150	106,277	16,715	3,790 45
	Total......	4,584,548	398,609	162,728	23,943	5,858 78
Jewellery, n.o.p.................	Unit'd Kingdom	....	199,808	....	13,113	4,589 55
	Hong Kong.....	....	91	....	67	23 45
	Aust.-Hungary..	....	28,069	....	4,586	1,605 10
	Belgium........	....	73	....	73	25 55
	China..........	....	43	....	43	15 05
	France.........	....	37,760	....	6,219	2,176 65
	Germany......	....	38,628	....	38,708	13,547 80
	Italy..........	....	982	....	982	343 70

OF IMPORTS—*Continued.*

FOR HOME CONSUMPTION.

	Preferential Tariff.			Treaty Rates.			Total.	
Quantity.	Value.	Duty.	Quantity.	Value.	Duty.	Quantity.	Value.	DutyColl'd.
	$	$ cts.		$	$ cts.		$	$ cts.
....	14	0 70	....	....	....	....	14	0 70
....	....	....	....	....	....	....	87	8 70
....	14	0 70	....	....	....	....	101	9 40
....	594,746	118,949 20	....	1,195	328 69	....	617,562	125,764 19
							328	98 40
							36	10 80
							308	92 40
				392	107 80		589	166 90
				153	42 08		3,375	1,008 68
							55	16 50
				16	4 40		145	43 10
				8,051	2,214 14		11,650	3,293 84
							82,621	24,786 30
							163	48 90
				685	188 38		1,100	312 88
				638	175 45		723	200 95
				3	0 83		189	56 63
				107	29 43		107	29 43
				198	54 45		2,346	698 85
				139	38 23		141	38 83
							23	6 90
							6,395,261	1,918,578 30
....	594,746	118,949 20	....	11,577	3,183 88	....	7,116,722	2,075,252 78
....	45	6 75	....			....	50	7 63
							10	1 75
							106	18 55
							6	1 05
							4	0 70
							164	28 70
							1,934	333 52
....	45	6 75	....			....	2,274	396 90
Lb. 4,452,327	376,137	113,002 36	Lb.			Lb. 4,464,082	377,261	113,418 69
						1,890	80	70 87
323	57	8 83				976	167	33 32
						1,241	100	45 17
24,750	2,008	666 59				24,750	2,008	666 59
						208	13	7 56
						10	2	0 33
						17,544	1,990	650 75
						22,044	3,708	815 64
						438	18	14 40
						200	20	6 50
						468	63	16 29
						106,277	16,715	3,790 45
4,477,400	378,202	113,677 78	....	....	....	4,640,128	402,145	119,536 56
....	161,636	36,369 20	....	21,909	6,572 70	....	196,658	47,531 45
				24	7 20		91	30 65
				23,679	7,103 70		28,265	8,708 80
							73	25 55
							43	15 05
				31,486	9,445 80		37,705	11,622 45
							38,708	13,547 80
							982	343 70

6 GEORGE V, A. 1916

No. 1.—General Statement

Articles Imported.	Countries.	Total Imports.		Entered		
				General Tariff.		
		Quantity.	Value.	Quantity.	Value.	Duty.
DUTIABLE GOODS—*Con.*			$		$	$ cts.
Jewellery, n.o.p.—*Con.*	Japan		925		48	16 80
	Norway		75			
	Portugal		6		6	2 10
	Switzerland		3,537		1,132	396 20
	Turkey		41		41	14 35
	United States		591,272		590,880	206,808 00
	Total		901,310		655,898	229,564 30
Knitted goods of every description, n.o.p.	Unit'd Kingdom		78,062		3,373	1,180 55
	Hong Kong		28		28	9 80
	Belgium		1,377		1,377	481 95
	France		418		418	146 30
	Germany		6,824		6,824	2,388 40
	Holland		216		216	75 60
	Italy		1,667		1,667	583 45
	Japan		89		89	31 15
	Switzerland		912		912	319 20
	United States		32,959		32,959	11,535 65
	Total		122,552		47,863	16,752 05
		No.		No.		
Launches, pleasure, steam, gasoline or other motive power.	Unit'd Kingdom	2	797			
	United States	118	34,512	118	34,512	8,628 00
	Total	120	35,309	118	34,512	8,628 00
Lead and manufactures of—		Cwt.		Cwt.		
Old, scrap, pig and block	Unit'd Kingdom	18,670	76,750	32	138	20 70
	Miquelon and St. Pierre	5	10	5	10	1 50
	United States	147,484	554,994	147,484	554,994	83,249 10
	Total	166,159	631,754	147,521	555,142	83,271 30
Bars and sheets	Unit'd Kingdom	6,028	25,786	4	22	5 50
	United States	1,857	8,751	1,857	8,751	2,187 75
	Total	7,885	34,537	1,861	8,773	2,193 25
		Lb.		Lb.		
Pipe	Unit'd Kingdom	420,329	17,793	7,040	294	88 20
	United States	125,811	7,699	125,811	7,699	2,309 70
	Total	546,140	25,492	132,851	7,993	2,397 90
Shot and bullets	Unit'd Kingdom	143,196	8,379			
	United States	20,327	1,364	20,327	1,364	409 20
	Total	163,523	9,743	20,327	1,364	409 20
Manufactures of, n.o.p.	Unit'd Kingdom		27,091		621	186 30
	Hong Kong		20		20	6 00
	Aust.-Hungary		101			
	Belgium		32			
	France		39,320		113	33 90
	Germany		2,475		2,475	742 50
	Holland		8,002		2,825	847 50
	Italy		99			
	Japan		1,683			
	Portugal		16		16	4 80
	Spain		812		37	11 10
	Sweden		3		11	3 30
	United States		32,914		32,735	9,820 50
	Total		112,568		38,853	11,655 90

OF IMPORTS—*Continued.*

FOR HOME CONSUMPTION.

Preferential Tariff.			Treaty Rates.			Total.		
Quantity.	Value.	Duty.	Quantity.	Value.	Duty.	Quantity.	Value.	DutyColl'd.
	$	$ cts.		$	$ cts.		$	$ cts.
....	....	....	....	877	263 10	....	925	279 90
....	....	....	....	75	22 50	....	75	22 50
....	....	....	....	....	....	....	6	2 10
....	....	....	....	2,492	747 60	....	3,624	1,143 80
....	....	....	....	....	....	....	41	14 35
....	....	....	....	....	....	....	590,880	206,808 00
....	161,636	36,369 20	....	80,542	24,162 60	....	898,076	290,096 10
....	75,104	16,898 77	....	....	....	....	78,477	18,079 32
....	....	....	....	....	....	....	28	9 80
....	....	....	....	....	....	....	1,377	481 95
....	....	....	....	....	....	....	418	146 30
....	....	....	....	....	....	....	6,824	2,388 40
....	....	....	....	....	....	....	216	75 60
....	....	....	....	....	....	....	1,667	583 45
....	....	....	....	....	....	....	89	31 15
....	....	....	....	....	....	....	912	319 20
....	....	....	....	....	....	....	32,959	11,535 65
....	75,104	16,898 77	....	....	....	....	122,967	33,650 82
No. 2	797	119 55	No.	....	....	No. 2	797	119 55
....	....	....	....	....	....	118	34,512	8,628 00
2	797	119 55	....	....	....	120	35,309	8,747 55
Cwt. 18,638	76,612	7,661 20	Cwt.	....	....	Cwt. 18,670	76,750	7,681 90
....	....	....	....	....	....	5	10	1 50
....	....	....	....	....	....	147,484	554,994	83,249 10
18,638	76,612	7,661 20	....	....	....	166,159	631,754	90,932 50
6,020	25,690	3,853 50	....	....	....	6,024	25,712	3,859 00
....	....	....	....	....	....	1,857	8,751	2,187 75
6,020	25,690	3,853 50	....	....	....	7,881	34,463	6,046 75
Lb. 419,489	17,812	3,562 40	Lb.	....	....	Lb. 426,529	18,106	3,650 60
....	....	....	....	....	....	125,811	7,699	2,309 70
419,489	17,812	3,562 40	....	....	....	552,340	25,805	5,960 39
143,196	8,379	1,675 80	....	....	....	143,196	8,379	1,675 80
....	....	....	....	....	....	20,327	1,364	409 20
143,196	8,379	1,675 80	....	....	....	163,523	9,743	2,085 00
....	26,560	5,312 00	....	725	199 38	....	27,906	5,697 68
....	....	....	....	....	....	....	20	6 00
....	....	....	....	101	27 78	....	101	27 28
....	....	....	....	29	7 98	....	29	7 98
....	....	....	....	21,324	5,864 25	....	21,437	5,898 15
....	....	....	....	....	....	....	2,475	742 50
....	....	....	....	5,177	1,423 68	....	8,002	2,271 18
....	....	....	....	99	27 23	....	99	27 23
....	....	....	....	1,683	462 83	....	1,683	462 83
....	....	....	....	....	....	....	16	4 80
....	....	....	....	754	207 35	....	791	218 45
....	....	....	....	....	....	....	11	3 30
....	....	....	....	....	....	....	32,735	9,820 50
....	26,560	5,312 00	....	29,892	8,220 48	....	95,305	25,188 38

6 GEORGE V, A. 1916

No. 1.—General Statement

Articles Imported.	Countries.	Total Imports.		Entered		
		Quantity.	Value.	General Tariff.		
				Quantity.	Value.	Duty.
			$		$	$ cts.
DUTIABLE GOODS—*Con.*						
Leather, and manufactures of—						
Sole leather....................	Unit'd Kingdom	....	35,769	....	260	45 50
	Belgium.........	....	761	....	761	133 19
	Germany........	....	90	....	90	15 75
	United States..	....	54,975	....	54,975	9,620 83
	Total......	....	91,595	....	56,086	9,815 27
Leather, belting leather of all kinds.	Unit'd Kingdom	....	83,508	....	1,388	208 20
	United States..	....	8,844	....	8,844	1,326 60
	Total......	....	92,352	....	10,232	1,534 80
Upper leather, not dressed, waxed or glazed.	Unit'd Kingdom	....	1,407	....		
	United States..	....	11,019	....	11,019	1,652 85
	Total......	....	12,426	....	11,019	1,652 85
Calf, kid, or goat, lamb and sheep skins, tanned.	Unit'd Kingdom	....	4,767	....	768	115 20
	United States..	....	106,522	....	105,982	15,897 30
	Total......	....	111,289	....	106,750	16,012 50
Calf, kid, or goat, lamb and sheep skins, dressed, waxed or glazed.	Unit'd Kingdom	....	127,129	....	3,278	491 70
	France.........	....	2,462	....	2,462	369 30
	Germany........	....	3,223	....	2,563	384 45
	United States..	....	869,705	....	870,157	130,523 55
	Total......	....	1,002,519	....	878,460	131,769 00
Glove leathers, tanned or dressed, coloured or uncoloured, imported by glove manufacturers for use exclusively in their own factories in the manufacture of gloves.	Unit'd Kingdom	....	19,225	....	439	43 90
	Germany........	....	4,710	....	4,710	471 00
	United States..	....	517,647	....	517,647	51,764 70
	Total......	....	541,582	....	522,796	52,279 60
Harness leather................	Unit'd Kingdom	....	8,541	....	55	8 25
	United States..	....	50,058	....	50,058	7,508 70
	Total......	....	58,599	....	50,113	7,516 95
Tanners' scrap leather..........	Unit'd Kingdom	....	5,338	....		
	France.........	....	17	....	17	2 55
	United States..	....	10,976	....	10,976	1,646 40
	Total......	....	16,331	....	10,993	1,648 95
Upper leather, including dongola, cordovan, kangaroo, alligator and all leather, dressed, waxed or glazed, or further finished than tanned, n.o.p., and chamois skins.	Unit'd Kingdom	....	100,902	....	699	104 85
	Newfoundland..	....	34	....	34	5 10
	France.........	....	138	....	138	20 70
	Holland........	....	216	....	216	32 40
	United States..	....	290,730	....	291,076	43,661 40
	Total......	....	392,020	....	292,163	43,824 45
Japanned, patent or enamelled leather and Morocco leather, and leather in imitation of Morocco leather.	Unit'd Kingdom	....	2,689	....	149	37 25
	Germany........	....	1,197	....	1,197	299 25
	United States..	....	27,574	....	27,574	6,893 50
	Total......	....	31,460	....	28,920	7,230 00

OF IMPORTS—*Continued.*

FOR HOME CONSUMPTION.

	Preferential Tariff.			Treaty Rates.			Total.	
Quantity.	Value.	Duty.	Quantity.	Value.	Duty.	Quantity.	Value.	DutyColl'd.
	$	$ cts.		$	$ cts.		$	$ cts.
....	35,509	4,438 68	....	....	....	....	35,769	4,484 18
....	....	....	....	....	....	....	761	133 19
....	....	....	....	....	....	....	90	15 75
....	....	....	....	....	....	....	54,975	9,620 83
....	35,509	4,438 68	....	....	....	....	91,595	14,253 95
....	83,754	8,375 40	....	....	....	....	85,142	8,583 60
....	....	....	....	....	....	....	8,844	1,326 60
....	83,754	8,375 40	....	....	....	....	93,986	9,910 20
....	1,407	140 70	....	....	....	....	1,407	140 70
....	....	....	....	....	....	....	11,019	1,652 85
....	1,407	140 70	....	....	....	....	12,426	1,793 55
....	3,999	399 90	....	....	....	....	4,767	515 10
....	....	....	....	....	....	....	105,982	15,897 30
....	3,999	399 90	....	....	....	....	110,749	16,412 40
....	117,556	14,694 80	....	....	....	....	120,834	15,186 50
....	....	....	....	....	....	....	2,462	369 30
....	....	....	....	....	....	....	2,563	384 45
....	....	....	....	....	....	....	870,157	130,523 55
....	117,556	14,694 80	....	....	....	....	996,016	146,463 80
....	18,786	939 30	....	....	....	....	19,225	983 20
....	....	....	....	....	....	....	4,710	471 00
....	....	....	....	....	....	....	517,647	51,764 70
....	18,786	939 30	....	....	....	....	541,582	53,218 90
....	8,486	1,060 75	....	....	....	....	8,541	1,069 00
....	....	....	....	....	....	....	50,058	7,508 70
....	8,486	1,060 75	....	....	....	....	58,599	8,577 70
....	5,338	533 80	....	....	....	....	5,338	533 80
....	....	....	....	....	....	....	17	2 55
....	....	....	....	....	....	....	10,976	1,646 40
....	5,338	533 80	....	....	....	....	16,331	2,182 75
....	98,827	12,353 64	....	....	....	....	99,526	12,458 49
....	....	....	....	....	....	....	34	5 10
....	....	....	....	....	....	....	138	20 70
....	....	....	....	....	....	....	216	32 40
....	....	....	....	....	....	....	291,076	43,661 40
....	98,827	12,353 64	....	....	....	....	390,990	56,178 09
....	2,540	381 00	....	....	....	....	2,689	418 25
....	....	....	....	....	....	....	1,197	299 25
....	....	....	....	....	....	....	27,574	6,893 50
....	2,540	381 00	....	....	....	....	31,460	7,611 00

6 GEORGE V, A. 1916

No. 1.—General Statement

Articles Imported.	Countries.	Total Imports.		Entered		
				General Tariff.		
		Quantity.	Value.	Quantity.	Value.	Duty.
DUTIABLE GOODS—*Con.*			$		$	$ cts.
Leather, and mfrs. of—*Con.*						
Skins for Morocco leather, tan-	Unit'd Kingdom	....	4,682	....	1,175	176 25
ned but not further manu-	United States..	....	9,170	....	9,170	1,375 50
factured.						
	Total......	....	13,852	....	10,345	1,551 75
All other leather and skins,	Unit'd Kingdom	.......:.	22,361	....	168	25 20
n.o.p.	Newfoundland..	....	11	....	11	1 65
	France..........	....	13	....	13	1 95
	United States..	....	202,665	....	202,665	30,399 75
	Total......	....	225,050	....	202,857	30,428 55
All other leather, dressed, wax-	Unit'd Kingdom	....	109,703	....	1,456	218 40
ed, or glazed, etc., n.o.p.	Newfoundland..	....	16	....	16	2 40
	Belgium........	....	302	....	302	45 30
	France..........	....	1,256	....	1,256	188 40
	Germany.......	....	5,186	....	3,598	539 70
	United States..	....	152,898	....	152,552	22,882 80
	Total......	....	269,361	....	159,180	,23,877 00
Boots and shoes, slippers and	Unit'd Kingdom	....	493,895	....	5,877	1,763 10
insoles of leather, n.o.p.	Hong Kong.....	....	539	....	539	161 70
	Newfoundland..	....	163	....	163	48 90
	Aust.-Hungary..	....	348	....	348	104 40
	Belgium........	....	347	....	347	104 10
	China..........	....	410	....	410	123 00
	France..........	....	799	....	607	182 10
	Germany.......	....	5,111	....	5,111	1,533 30
	Japan..........	....	108	....	39	11 70
	Miquelon and St. Pierre.....	....	2	....	....	....
	Norway........	....	121	....	....	....
	Switzerland....	....	1,052	....	102	30 60
	United States..	....	2,900,147	....	2,900,134	870,040 20
	Total......	....	3,403,042	....	2,913,677	874,103 10
Boots and shoes, pegged or wire	Unit'd Kingdom	....	59,692	....	1,624	406 00
fastened, with unstitched	Hong Kong.....	....	42	....	42	10 50
soles, close edged.	United States..	....	18,560	....	18,560	4,640 00
	Total......	....	78,294	....	20,226	5,056 50
Harness and saddlery, including	Unit'd Kingdom	....	46,646	....	767	230 10
horse boots.	Australia.......	....	59	....	59	17 70
	Newfoundland..	....	20	....	20	6 00
	New Zealand...	....	71	....	....	....
	France..........	....	63	....	63	18 90
	Germany.......	....	33	....	33	9 90
	United States..	....	94,507	....	93,076	27,922 80
	Total......	....	141,399	....	· 94,018	28,205 40
Leather belting...............	Unit'd Kingdom	....	12,535	....	613	137 98
	Germany.......	....	368	....	368	82 85
	United States..	....	59,688	....	59,688	13,430 45
	Total......	....	72,591	....	60,669	13,651 28

OF IMPORTS—*Continued.*

FOR HOME CONSUMPTION.

	Preferential Tariff.			Treaty Rates.			Total.	
Quantity.	Value.	Duty.	Quantity.	Value.	Duty.	Quantity.	Value.	DutyColl'd.
	$	$ cts.		$	$ cts.		$	$ cts.
....	3,507	350 70	....	....	....	....	4,682	526 95
....	....	....	....	....	....	....	9,170	1,375 50
....	3,507	350 70	....	....	....	....	13,852	1,902 45
....	22,193	2,219 30	....	....	....	....	22,361	2,244 50
....	....	....	....	....	....	....	11	1 65
....	....	....	....	....	....	....	13	1 95
....	....	....	....	....	....	....	202,665	30,399 75
....	22,193	2,219 30	....	....	....	....	225,050	32,647 85
....	92,566	11,570 89	....	....	....	....	94,022	11,789 29
....	....	....	....	....	....	....	16	2 40
....	....	....	....	....	....	....	302	45 30
....	....	....	....	....	....	....	1,256	188 40
....	....	....	....	....	....	....	3,598	539 70
....	....	....	....	....	....	....	152,552	22,882 80
....	92,566	11,570 89	....	....	....	....	251,746	35,447 89
....	484,656	96,931 20	....	990	272 25	....	491,523	98,966 55
....	....	....	....	....	....	....	539	161 70
....	....	....	....	....	....	....	163	48 90
....	....	....	....	....	....	....	348	104 40
....	....	....	....	....	....	....	347	104 10
....	....	....	....	....	....	....	410	123 00
....	....	....	....	192	52 80	....	799	234 90
....	....	....	....	....	....	....	5,111	1,533 30
....	....	....	....	69	18 98	....	108	30 68
....	....	....	....	2	0 55	....	2	0 55
....	....	....	....	121	33 28	....	121	33 28
....	....	....	....	950	261 26	....	1,052	291 86
....	....	....	....	....	....	....	2,900,134	870,040 20
....	484,656	96,931 20	....	2,324	639 12	....	3,400,657	971,673 42
....	58,068	10,162 09	....	....	....	....	59,692	10,568 09
....	....	....	....	....	....	....	42	10 50
....	....	....	....	....	....	....	18,560	4,640 00
....	58,068	10,162 09	....	....	....	....	78,294	15,218 59
....	46,768	9,353 60	....	....	....	....	47,535	9,583 70
....	....	....	....	....	....	....	59	17 70
....	....	....	....	....	....	....	20	6 00
....	71	14 20	....	....	....	....	71	14 20
....	....	....	....	....	....	....	63	18 90
....	....	....	....	....	....	....	33	9 90
....	....	....	....	....	....	....	93,076	27,922 80
....	46,839	9,367 80	....	....	....	....	140,857	37,573 20
....	11,922	1,788 30	....	....	....	....	12,535	1,926 28
....	....	....	....	....	....	....	368	82 85
....	....	....	....	....	....	....	59,688	13,430 45
....	11,922	1,788 30	....	....	....	....	72,591	15,439 58

6 GEORGE V, A. 1916

No. 1.—General Statement

Articles Imported.	Countries.	Total Imports.		Entered		
				General Tariff.		
		Quantity.	Value.	Quantity.	Value.	Duty.
			$		$	$ cts.
DUTIABLE GOODS—*Con.*						
Leather, and mfrs. of—*Con.*						
All other manufactures of leather and raw hide, n.o.p.	Unit'd Kingdom	....	70,510	....	2,200	550 00
	Aust.-Hungary..	....	283	....	283	70 75
	Belgium........	....	33	....	33	8 25
	China...........	....	4	....	4	1 00
	France.........	....	745	....	745	186 25
	Germany.......	....	1,139	....	1,139	284 75
	Japan..........	....	870	....	870	217 50
	Switzerland.....	....	90	....	90	22 50
	United States...	....	461,052	....	458,704	114,676 00
	Total......	....	534,726	....	464,068	116,017 00
		Cwt.		Cwt.		
Lime..........................	Unit'd Kingdom	2,702	1,512	....	....	....
	Aust.-Hungary..	15	4	.15	4	0 70
	United States...	593,897	185,271	594,017	185,443	32,453 07
	Total......	596,614	186,787	594,032	185,447	32,453 77
		Gal.		Gal.		
Lime juice, crude only............	B. W. Indies....	3,907	1,111	3,907	1,111	195 35
	United States...	1,969	612	1,969	612	98 45
	Total......	5,876	1,723	5,876	1,723	293 80
Lime juice, and fruit juices, fortified with or containing not more than twenty-five per cent of proof spirits.	Unit'd Kingdom	18	45	18	45	13 50
	France.........	167	320	95	222	60 45
	Germany.......	342	230	332	233	212 25
	United States...	822	1,155	711	1,051	466 20
	Total......	1,349	1,750	1,156	1,551	752 40
Lime juice, and fruit juices, containing more than twenty-five per cent of proof spirits.	Unit'd Kingdom	81	916	81	916	469 80
	Germany........	6	84	6	84	39 60
	Italy...........	....	....	24	68	85 20
	Sweden.........	5	5	5	5	16 50
	United States...	54	598	54	598	339 00
	Total......	146	1,603	170	1,671	950 10
Lime juice and other fruit syrups and fruit juices, n.o.p.	Unit'd Kingdom	51,481	68,511	3,310	2,315	463 00
	Australia.......	138	194	138	194	43 56
	B. W. Indies....	11	8	11	8	1 65
	Belgium........	1	5	1	5	1 00
	France.........	1,614	2,940	1,112	2,098	441 11
	Germany.......	39	40	39	40	8 00
	Holland........	251	440	157	292	59 87
	Norway........	16	50	....	....	....
	United States...	121,166	123,526	120,881	125,711	25,516 91
	Total......	174,717	195,714	125,649	130,663	26,535 10
Lithographic stones, not engraved	Unit'd Kingdom	....	100	....	....	....
	United States...	....	2,914	....	2,914	582 80
	Total......	....	3,014	....	2,914	582 80
Machine card clothing............	Unit'd Kingdom	....	21,978	....	31	7 75
	Germany.......	....	1,165	....	1,165	291 25
	United States...	....	14,032	....	14,032	3,508 00
	Total.....	....	37,175	....	15,228	3,807 00

SESSIONAL PAPER No. 11

OF IMPORTS—*Continued.*

FOR HOME CONSUMPTION.

Preferential Tariff.			Treaty Rates.			Total.		
Quantity.	Value.	Duty.	Quantity.	Value.	Duty.	Quantity.	Value.	Duty Coll'd.
	$	$ cts.		$	$ cts.		$	$ cts.
....	68,063	10,209 45	....	....	....	....	70,263	10,759 45
....	....	....	....	....	....	....	283	70 75
....	....	....	....	....	....	....	33	8 25
....	....	....	....	....	....	....	4	1 00
....	....	....	....	....	....	....	745	186 25
....	....	....	....	....	....	....	1,139	284 75
....	....	....	....	....	....	....	870	217 50
....	....	....	....	....	....	....	90	22 50
....	....	....	....	....	....	....	458,704	114,676 00
....	68,063	10,209 45	....			....	532,131	126,226 45
Cwt. 332	145	21 75	Cwt.	....	....	Cwt. 332	145	21 75
....	....	....				15	4	0 70
....	....	....				594,017	185,443	32,453 07
332	145	21 75	....	....	....	594,364	185,592	32,475 52
Gal.			Gal.			Gal. 3,907	1,111	195 35
....	....	....	....	....	....	1,969	612	98 45
....	....	....	....	....	....	5,876	1,723	293 80
....	....	....	....	....	....	18	45	13 50
....	....	....	....	....	....	95	222	60 45
....	....	....	....	....	....	332	233	212 25
....	....	....	....	....	....	711	1,051	466 20
....	....	....	....	....	....	1,156	1,551	752 40
....	....	....	....	....	....	81	916	469 80
....	....	....	....	....	....	6	84	39 60
....	....	....	....	....	....	24	68	85 20
....	....	....	....	....	....	5	5	16 50
....	....	....	....	....	....	54	598	339 00
....	....	....	....	....	....	170	1,671	950 10
41,366	59,458	9,045 57	....	....	....	44,676	61,773	9,508 57
....	....	....	....	....	....	138	194	43 56
....	....	....	....	....	....	11	8	1 65
....	....	....	....	....	....	1	5	1 00
....	....	....	....	....	....	1,112	2,098	441 11
....	....	....	....	....	....	39	40	8 00
....	....	....	....	....	....	157	292	59 87
....	....	....	....	....	....	120,881	125,711	25,516 91
41,366	59,458	9,045 57	....	....	....	167,015	190,121	35,580 67
....	100	12 50	....	....	....	....	100	12 50
....	....	....	....	....	....	....	2,914	582 80
....	100	12 50	....	....	....	....	3,014	595 30
....	21,947	3,840 86	....	....	....	....	21,978	3,848 61
....	....	....	....	....	....	....	1,165	291 25
....	....	....	....	....	....	....	14,032	3,508 00
....	21,947	3,840 86	....	....	....	....	37,175	7,647 86

6 GEORGE V, A. 1916

No. 1.—GENERAL STATEMENT

Articles Imported.	Countries.	TOTAL IMPORTS.		ENTERED		
				General Tariff.		
		Quantity.	Value.	Quantity.	Value.	Duty.
DUTIABLE GOODS—*Con.*			$		$	$ cts.
Magic lanterns and slides therefor	Unit'd Kingdom	....	44,761	....	2,593	648 25
and moving picture machines.	Newfoundland..	....	100	....	100	25 0o
	Denmark......	....	201	....	....	....
	France........	....	6,442	....	1,671	417 75
	French Africa...	....	5	....	5	1 25
	Germany......	....	2,712	....	1,712	428 00
	Holland.......	....	32	....	32	8 00
	Italy.........	....	2,437	....	2,437	609 25
	Japan.........	....	25	....	25	6 25
	United States...	....	1,253 622	....	1,251,668	312,917 00
	Total......	....	1,310,337	....	1,260,243	315,060 75
		Lb.		Lb.		
Malt, whole, crushed or ground...	Unit'd Kingdom	137,879	4,090	137,879	4,090	620 46
	Germany.......	140,140	4,397	140,140	4,397	630 63
	Holland.......	165,000	4,907	165,000	4,907	742 50
	United States...	2,722,877	67,020	2,725,047	66,981	12,262 80
	Total.......	3,165,896	80,414	3,168,066	80,375	14,256 39
Malt flour, containing not less than	Unit'd Kingdom	69,921	2,663	69,921	2,663	314 64
50 p. c. of malt.	Germany.......	11,000	464	11,000	464	49 50
	Total.......	80,921	3,127	80,921	3,127	364 1á
Malt flour, containing less than	Unit'd Kingdom	27,025	1,283	27,025	1,283	835 03
50 p.c. in weight of malt.	United States...	5	1	5	1	0 50
	Total......	27,030	1,284	27,030	1,284	835 53
Malt, extract of, fluid or not, in-	Unit'd Kingdom	....	6,369	....	6,369	2,229 15
cluding grain molasses (to Au-	Germany.......	....	567	....	567	198 45
gust 21st, 1914)..	Mexico........	....	3	....	3	1 05
	United States...	....	28,571	....	29,218	10,226 30
	Total......	....	35,510	....	36,157	12,654 95
Malt, extract of, fluid or not, in-	Unit'd Kingdom	154,754	9,773	153,914	9,718	8,018 72
cluding grain molasses, (from	Japan...........	108	6	108	6	5 34
August 21st, 1914.)	Mexico.........	212	105	212	105	43 11
	United States...	634,519	31,796	641,244	32,109	30,475 46
	Total.......	789,593	41,680	795,478	41,938	38,542 63
Marble, and manufactures of—						
Marble, sawn or sand rubbed,	Unit'd Kingdom	....	1,135	....	1,071	214 20
not polished.	Belgium........	....	494	....	494	98 80
	Italy..........	....	26,770	....	26,770	5,354 00
	United States...	....	150,378	....	150,374	30,074 80
	Total......	....	178,777	....	178,709	35,741 80
Rough, not hammered or chis-	Alaska..........	....	4,568	....	4,568	685 20
elled.	Belgium........	....	851	....	851	127 65
	Italy..........	....	9,515	....	9,515	1,427 25
	United States...	....	89,327	....	89,327	13,399 05
	Total.	....	104,261	....	104,261	15,639 15

OF IMPORTS—*Continued*.

FOR HOME CONSUMPTION.

Preferential Tariff.			Treaty Rates.			Total.		
Quantity.	Value.	Duty.	Quantity.	Value.	Duty.	Quantity.	Value.	Duty Coll'd.
	$ 40,325	$ cts. 7,057 21		$ 31	$ cts. 6 98		$ 42,949	$ cts. 7,712 44
....	....	....	....	....	....	....	100	25 00
....	....	....	....	201	45 23	....	201	45 23
....	....	....	....	4,771	1,073 49	....	6,442	1,491 24
....	....	....	....	....	....	....	5	1 25
....	....	....	....	....	....	....	1,712	428 00
....	....	....	....	....	....	....	32	8 00
....	....	....	....	....	....	....	2,437	609 25
....	....	....	....	....	....	....	25	6 25
....	....	....	....	....	....	....	1,251,668	312,917 00
....	40,325	7,057 21	....	5,003	1,125 70	....	1,305,571	323,243 66
Lb.			Lb.			Lb. 137,879	4,090	620 46
....	....	....	....	....	....	140,140	4,397	630 63
....	....	....	....	....	....	165,000	4,907	742 50
....	....	....	....	....	....	2,725,047	66,981	12,262 80
....	....	....	....	....	....	3,168,066	80,375	14,256 39
....	....	....	....	....	....	69,921	2,663	314 64
....	....	....	....	....	....	11,000	464	49 50
....	....	....	....	....	....	80,921	3,127	364 14
....	....	....	....	....	....	27,025	1,283	835 03
....	....	....	....	....	....	5	1	0 50
....	....	....	....	....	....	27,030	1,284	835 53
....	....	....	....	....	....	....	6,369	2,229 15
....	....	....	....	....	....	....	567	198 45
....	....	....	....	....	....	....	3	1 05
....	....	....	....	....	....	....	29,218	10,226 30
....	....	....	....	....	....	....	36,157	12,654 95
....	....	....	....	....	....	153,914	9,718	8,018 72
....	....	....	....	....	....	108	6	5 34
....	....	....	....	....	....	212	105	43 11
....	....	....	....	....	....	641 244	32,109	30,475 46
....	....	....	....	....	....	795,478	41,938	38,542 63
....	64	9 60	....	....	....	....	1,135	223 80
....	....	....	....	....	....	....	494	98 80
....	....	....	....	....	....	....	26,770	5,354 00
....	....	....	....	....	....	....	150,374	30,074 80
....	64	9 60	....	....	....	....	178,773	35,751 40
....	....	....	....	....	....	....	4,568	685 20
....	....	....	....	....	....	....	851	127 65
....	....	....	....	....	....	....	9,515	1,427 25
....	....	....	....	....	....	....	89,327	13,399 05
....	....	....	....	....	....	....	104,261	15,639 15

6 GEORGE V, A. 1916

No. 1.—GENERAL STATEMENT

Articles Imported.	Countries.	TOTAL IMPORTS.		ENTERED		
		Quantity.	Value.	General Tariff.		
				Quantity.	Value.	Duty.
			$		$	$ cts.
DUTIABLE GOODS—*Con.*						
Marble, and mfrs. of—*Con.*						
Manufactures of, n.o.p.	Unit'd Kingdom	....	12,122	....	9,528	3,334 80
	Belgium	....	2,059	....	2,059	720 65
	France	....	328	....	328	114 80
	Germany	....	70	....	70	24 50
	Italy	....	9,121	....	9,121	3,192 35
	Sweden	....	649	....	649	227 15
	United States...	....	100,348	....	100,277	35,096 95
	Total......	....	124,697	....	122,032	42,711 20
Mattresses, hair, spring and other	Unit'd Kingdom	....	340	....	90	27 00
	Hong Kong.....	....	135	....	135	40 50
·	United States...	....	4,170	....	4,165	1,249 50
	Total......	....	4,645	....	4,390	1,317 00
Mats, door or carriage, other than	Unit'd Kingdom	....	184	....	10	3 50
metal, n.o.p.	Germany	....	22	....	22	7 70
	United States...	....	324	....	324	113 40
	Total......	....	530	....	356	124 60
Metals, n.o.p., and manufactures of—						
Aluminum, manufactures of, n.o.p.	Unit'd Kingdom	....	3,187	....	545	136 25
	Aust.-Hungary..	....	74	....	27	6 75
	Belgium	....	47	....	47	11 75
	France	....	4,485	....	3	0 75
	Germany	....	4,144	....	4,144	1,036 00
	Holland	....	11	....	11	2 75
	Italy	....	188	....	188	47 00
	United States...	....	75,313	....	75,385	18,846 25
	Total......	....	87,449	....	80,350	20,087 50
Anodes of nickel, zinc, copper, silver or gold.	Unit'd Kingdom	....	796	....	....	....
	Germany	....	43	....	43	4 30
	United States...	....	11,511	....	11,448	1,144 80
	Total......	....	12,350	....	11,491	1,149 10
Babbit metal in blocks, bars, plates and sheets.	Unit'd Kingdom	....	4,483	....	....	....
	Belgium	....	1,494	....	1,494	224 10
	United States...	....	13,103	....	13,103	1,965 45
	Total......	....	19,080	....	14,597	2,189 55
Britannia metal, manufactures of, not plated.	Unit'd Kingdom	....	734	....	32	9 60
	Belgium	....	64	....	64	19 20
	France	....	11	....	11	3 30
	Germany	....	4	....	26	7 80
	Japan	....	51	....	51	15 30
	United States...	....	14,059	....	14,059	4,217 70
	Total......	....	14,923	....	14,243	4,272 90
Buckles and clasps of iron, steel, brass or copper, of all kinds, n.o.p. (not being jewellery).	Unit'd Kingdom	....	7,710	....	553	165 90
	Belgium	....	20	....	20	6 00
	France	....	463	....	312	93 60
	Germany	....	1,088	....	1,088	326 40
	United States...	....	110,985	....	111,073	33,321 90
	Total......	....	120,266	....	113,046	33,913 80

SESSIONAL PAPER No. 11

OF IMPORTS.—*Continued.*

FOR HOME CONSUMPTION.

Preferential Tariff.			Treaty Rates.			Total.		
Quantity.	Value.	Duty.	Quantity.	Value.	Duty.	Quantity.	Value.	DutyColl'd.
	$	$ cts.		$	$ cts.		$	$ cts.
....	2,487	746 10	....	....	....	....	12,015	4,080 90
....	....	....	....	....	....	....	2,059	720 65
....	....	....	....	....	....	....	328	114 80
....	....	....	....	....	....	....	70	24 50
....	....	....	....	....	....	....	9,121	3,192 35
....	....	....	....	....	....	....	649	227 15
....	....	....	....	....	....	....	100,277	35,096 95
....	2,487	746 10	....			....	124,519	43,457 30
....	250	50 00	....	....	....	....	340	77 00
....	....	....	....	....	....	....	135	40 50
....	....	....	....	....	....	....	4,165	1,249 50
....	250	50 00	....	....	....	....	4,640	1,367 00
....	174	43 50	....	....	....	....	184	47 00
....	....	....	....	....	....	....	22	7 70
....	....	....	....	....	....	....	324	113 40
....	174	43 50	....	....	....	....	530	168 10
....	2,600	390 00	....	39	8 78	....	3,184	535 03
....	....	....	....	47	10 58	....	74	17 33
....	....	....	....			....	47	11 75
....	....	....	....	4,206	946 42	....	4,209	947 17
....	....	....	....	....	....	....	4,144	1,036 00
....	....	....	....	....	....	....	11	2 75
....	....	....	....	....	....	....	188	47 00
....	....	....	....	....	....	....	75,385	18,846 25
....	2,600	390 00	....	4,292	965 78	....	87,242	21,443 28
....	796	39 80	....	....	....	....	796	39 80
....	....	....	....	....	....	....	43	4 30
....	....	....	....	....	....	....	11,448	1,144 80
....	796	39 80	....			....	12,287	1,188 90
....	4,483	448 30	....	....	....	....	4,483	448 30
....	....	....	....	....	....	....	1,494	224 10
....	....	....	....	....	....	....	13,103	1,965 45
....	4,483	448 30	....	....	....	....	19,080	2,637 85
....	702	122 88	....	....	....	....	734	132 48
....	....	....	....	....	....	....	64	19 20
....	....	....	....	....	....	....	11	3 30
....	....	....	....	....	....	....	26	7 80
....	....	....	....	....	....	....	51	15 30
....	....	....	....	....	....	....	14,059	4,217 70
....	702	122 88	....	....	....	....	14,945	4,395 78
....	6,806	1,361 20	....	406	111 70	....	7,765	1,638 80
....	....	....	....			....	20	6 00
....	....	....	....	152	41 80	....	464	135 40
....	....	....	....	....	....	....	1,088	326 40
....	....	....	....	....	....	....	111,073	33,321 90
....	6,806	1,361 20	....	558	153 50	....	120,410	35,428 50

6 GEORGE V, A. 1916

No. 1.—GENERAL STATEMENT

Articles Imported.	Countries.	TOTAL IMPORTS.		ENTERED		
				General Tariff.		
		Quantity.	Value.	Quantity.	Value.	Duty.
			$		$	$ cts.
DUTIABLE GOODS—*Con.*						
Metals—*Con.*						
Cages,—Bird, parrot, squirrel and rat, of wire, and metal parts thereof.	Unit'd Kingdom	....	255	....	4	1 40
	Germany	....	71	....	71	24 85
	United States...	....	5,780	....	5,780	2,023 00
	Total......	....	6,106	....	5,855	2,049 25
Composition metal and plated metal, in bars, ingots or cores, for the manufacture of watch cases, jewellery, filled gold and silver seamless wire.	United States...	....	3,898	....	3,898	389 80
Frames not more than 10 inches in width, clasps and fasteners, adapted for use in the manufacture of purses and chatelaine bags or reticules.	Unit'd Kingdom	....	101	....	101	20 20
	France	....	2	....	2	0 40
	Germany	....	237	....	237	47 40
	United States...	....	22,297	....	22,297	4,459 40
	Total......	....	22,637	....	22,637	4,527 40
Furniture springs	Unit'd Kingdom	....	76	....	....	....
	France	....	2	....	....	....
	United States...	....	15,845	....	15,845	4,753 50
	Total......	....	15,923	....	15,845	4,753 50
Phosphor tin and phosphor bronze, in blocks, bars, plates, sheets and wire.	Unit'd Kingdom	....	5,552	....	....	....
	Germany	....	30	....	30	3 00
	United States...	....	13,152	....	13,152	1,315 20
	Total......	....	18,734	....	13,182	1,318 20
Gas, coal oil or other lighting fixtures, including electric light fixtures or parts thereof of metal, lava or other tips, burners, collars, galleries, shades and shade holders.	Unit'd Kingdom	....	11,774	....	1,518	455 40
	Hong Kong	....	87	....	87	26 10
	Aust.-Hungary..	....	1,380	....	1,380	414 00
	France	....	2,834	....	2,834	850 20
	Germany	....	4,183	....	5,989	1,796 70
	Holland	....	1,717	....	1,798	539 40
	Italy	....	552	....	602	180 60
	Japan	....	3,160	....	3,157	947 10
	United States...	....	412,551	....	400,983	120,294 90
	Total......	....	438,238	....	418,348	125,504 40
Gas mantles and incandescent gas burners.	Unit'd Kingdom	....	3,566	....	208	62 40
	Aust.-Hungary..	....	1	....	377	113 10
	France	....	20	....	20	6 00
	Germany	....	10	....	372	111 60
	Holland	....	789	....	5,376	1,612 80
	Japan	....	92	....	92	27 60
	Sweden	....	7	....	7	2 10
	Switzerland	....	140	....	140	42 00
	United States...	....	65,369	....	65,285	19,585 50
	Total......	....	69,994	....	71,877	21,563 10
Gas meters and finished parts thereof.	Unit'd Kingdom	....	5,889	....	....	....
	United States...	....	33,990	....	33,990	11,896 50
	Total......	....	39,879	....	33,990	11,896 50

OF IMPORTS—*Continued.*

FOR HOME CONSUMPTION.

	Preferential Tariff.			Treaty Rates.			Total.	
Quantity.	Value.	Duty.	Quantity.	Value.	Duty.	Quantity.	Value.	Duty Coll'd.
	$	$ cts.		$	$ cts.		$	$ cts.
....	251	56 48	....	....	....	....	255	57 88
....	....	....	....	....	....	....	71	24 85
....	....	....	....	....	....	....	5,780	2,023 00
....	251	56 48	....	....	....	....	6,106	2,105 73
....	....	....	....	....	....	....	3,898	389 80
....	....	....	....	....	....	....	101	20 20
....	....	....	....	....	....	....	2	0 40
....	....	....	....	....	....	....	237	47 40
....	....	....	....	....	....	....	22,297	4,459 40
....	....	....	....	....	....	....	22,637	4,527 40
....	76	15 20	....	....	....	....	76	15 20
....	....	....	....	2	0 55	....	2	0 55
....	....	....	....	....	....	....	15,845	4,753 50
....	76	15 20	....	2	0 55	....	15,923	4,769 25
....	5,552	277 60	....	....	....	....	5,552	277 60
....	....	....	....	....	....	....	30	3 00
....	....	....	....	....	....	....	13,152	1,315 20
....	5,552	277 60	....	....	....	....	18,734	1,595 80
....	9,884	1,976 80	....	....	....	....	11,402	2,432 20
....	....	....	....	....	....	....	87	26 10
....	....	....	....	....	....	....	1,380	414 00
....	....	....	....	....	....	....	2,834	850 20
....	....	....	....	....	....	....	5,989	1,796 70
....	....	....	....	....	....	....	1,798	539 40
....	....	....	....	....	....	....	602	180 60
....	....	....	....	....	....	....	3,157	947 10
....	....	....	....	....	....	....	400,983	120,294 90
....	9,884	1,976 80	....	....	....	....	428,232	127,481 20
....	3,372	674 40	....	....	....	....	3,580	736 80
....	....	....	....	....	....	....	377	113 10
....	....	....	....	....	....	....	20	6 00
....	....	....	....	....	....	....	372	111 60
....	....	....	....	....	....	....	5,376	1,612 80
....	....	....	....	....	....	....	92	27 60
....	....	....	....	....	....	....	7	2 10
....	....	....	....	....	....	....	140	42 00
....	....	....	....	....	....	....	65,285	19,585 50
....	3,372	674 40	....	....	....	....	75,249	22,237 50
....	5,889	1,325 05	....	....	....	....	5,889	1,325 05
....	....	....	....	....	....	....	33,990	11,896 50
....	5,889	1,325 05	....	....	....	....	39,879	13,221 55

6 GEORGE V, A. 1916

No. 1—General Statement

Articles Imported.	Countries.	Total Imports.		Entered		
				General Tariff.		
		Quantity.	Value.	Quantity.	Value.	Duty.
DUTIABLE GOODS—*Con.*			$		$	$ cts.
Metals—*Con.*						
German, Nevada and nickel silver, manufactures of, not plated.	Unit'd Kingdom	....	18,752	....	66	19 80
	New Zealand...	....	10	....	....	....
	Aust.-Hungary..	....	792	....	792	237 60
	France..........	....	237	....	237	71 10
	Germany.......	....	847	....	858	257 40
	United States...	....	63,792	....	64,126	19,237 80
	Total......	....	84,430	....	66,079	19,823 70
Ingot moulds, glass moulds of metal.	Unit'd Kingdom	....	96,181	....	590	59 00
	United States...	....	91,381	....	91,381	9,138 10
	Total......	....	187,562	....	91,971	9,197 10
Lamp springs and clock springs.	Unit'd Kingdom	....	15	....	....	....
	United States...	....	1,581	....	1,581	158 10
	Total......	....	1,596	....	1,581	158 10
Lamps, side lights and head lights, lanterns, chandeliers.	Unit'd Kingdom	....	108,451	....	10,546	3,163 80
	Hong Kong.....	....	60	....	60	18 00
	Aust-.Hungary..	....	59,828	....	73,110	21,933 00
	Belgium........	....	7,381	....	4,291	1,287 30
	China..........	....	21	....	21	6 30
	France..........	....	10,094	....	10,086	3,025 80
	Germany.......	....	38,698	....	43,232	12,969 60
	Holland........	....	156,003	....	161,048	48,314 40
	Italy...........	....	1,040	....	1,119	335 70
	Japan..........	....	2,066	....	2,253	675 90
	Sweden........	....	5,377	....	5,377	1,613 10
	Switzerland....	....	276	....	276	82 80
	Turkey........	....	98	....	98	29 40
	United States...	....	615,730	....	611,268	183,380 40
	Total......	....	1,005,123	....	922,785	276,835 50
Metal parts adapted for the manufacture of covered buttons.	Unit'd Kingdom	....	41	....	13	2 60
	Germany.......	....	88	....	88	17 60
	United States...	....	27,093	....	27,093	5,418 60
	Total......	....	27,222	....	27,194	5,438 80
Nickel plated ware, n.o.p.......	Unit'd Kingdom	....	81,150	....	3,806	1,332 10
	Hong Kong.....	....	5	....	5	1 75
	Aust.-Hungary..	....	352	....	187	65 45
	Belgium........	....	20	....	20	7 00
	France..........	....	4,609	....	267	93 45
	Germany.......	....	12,477	....	12,510	4,378 50
	Holland........	....	929	....	652	228 20
	Italy...........	....	6	....	6	2 10
	Japan..........	....	180	....	27	9 45
	United States..	....	781,033	....	776,046	271,616 10
	Total......	....	880,761	....	793,526	277,734 10
Patterns of brass, iron, steel or other metal, not being models.	Unit'd Kingdom	....	153	....	....	....
	United States..	....	14,581	....	14,631	4,389 30
	Total......	....	14,734	....	14,631	4,389 30

OF IMPORTS—*Continued.*

FOR HOME CONSUMPTION.

Preferential Tariff.			Treaty Rates.			Total.		
Quantity.	Value.	Duty.	Quantity.	Value.	Duty.	Quantity.	Value.	DutyColl'd.
	$	$ cts.		$	$ cts.		$	$ cts.
....	18,686	3,270 19	....	....	....	....	18,752	3,289 99
....	10	1 75	....	....	....	....	10	1 75
....	....	....	....	....	....	....	792	237 60
....	....	....	....	....	....	....	237	71 10
....	....	....	....	....	....	....	858	257 40
....	....	....	....	....	....	....	64,126	19,237 80
....	18,696	3,271 94	....	....	....	....	84,775	23,095 64
....	39,892	1,994 60	....	....	....	....	40,482	2,053 60
....	....	....	....	....	....	....	91,381	9,138 10
....	39,892	1,994 60	....	....	....	....	131,863	11,191 70
....	15	·1 12	....	....	....	....	15	1 12
....	....	....	....	....	....	....	1,581	158 10
....	15	1 12	....	....	....	....	1,596	159 22
....	103,488	20,697 60	....	....	....	....	114,034	23,861 40
....	....	....	....	....	....	....	60	18 00
....	....	....	....	....	....	....	73,110	21,933 00
....	....	....	....	....	....	....	4,291	1,287 30
....	....	....	....	....	....	....	21	6 30
....	....	....	....	....	....	....	10,086	3,025 80
....	....	....	....	....	....	....	43,232	12,969 60
....	....	....	....	....	....	....	161,048	48,314 40
....	....	....	....	....	....	....	1,119	335 70
....	....	....	....	....	....	....	2,253	675 90
....	....	....	....	....	....	....	5,377	1,613 10
....	....	....	....	....	....	....	276	82 80
....	....	....	....	....	....	....	98	29 40.
....	....	....	....	....	....	....	611,268	183,380 40
....	103,488	20,697 60	....	....	....	....	1,026,273	297,533 10
....	28	3 50	....	....	....	....	41	6 10
....	....	....	....	....	....	....	88	17 60
....	....	....	....	....	....	....	27,093	5,418 60
....	28	3 50	....	....	....	....	27,222	5,442 30
....	75,540	16,997 22	....	808	242 40	....	80,154	18,571 72
....	....	....	....	....	....	....	5	1 75
....	....	....	....	297	89 10	....	484	154 55
....	....	....	....	....	....	....	20	7 00
....	....	....	....	4,334	1,300 20	....	4,601	1,393 65
....	....	....	....	....	....	....	12,510	4,378 50
....	....	....	....	277	83 10	....	929	311 30
....	....	....	....	....	....	....	6	2 10
....	....	....	....	153	45 90	....	180	55 35
....	....	....	....	....	....	....	776,046	271,616 10
....	75,540	16,997 22	....	5,869	1,760 70	....	874,935	296,492 02
....	153	30 60	....	....	....	....	153	30 60
....	....	....	....	....	....	....	14,631	4,389 30
....	153	30 60	....	....	....	....	14,784	4,419 90

6 GEORGE V, A. 1916

No. 1.—General Statement

Articles Imported.	Countries.	Total Imports.		Entered		
				General Tariff.		
		Quantity.	Value.	Quantity.	Value.	Duty.
			$		$	$ cts.
DUTIABLE GOODS—*Con.*						
Metals—*Con.*						
Pins, n.o.p.....................	Unit'd Kingdom	....	73,649	....	2,047	614 10
	Hong Kong.....	....	15	....	15	4 50
	Aust.-Hungary..	....	284	....	76	22 80
	Belgium.........	....	190	....	190	57 00
	France..........	....	554	....	411	123 30
	Germany........	....	1,241	....	1,241	372 30
	Japan...........	....	5	....	3	0 90
	United States..	....	11,885	....	11,885	3,565 50
	Total.......	....	87,823	....	15,868	4,760 40
Screws, brass or other metal,	Unit'd Kingdom	....	315	....	1	0 35
except iron or steel, n.o.p.	France.........	....	15	....	15	5 25
	United States..	....	17,477	....	17,466	6,113 10
	Total.......	....	17,807	....	17,482	6,118 70
		Sq. in.		Sq. in.		
Stereotypes, electrotypes and	Unit'd Kingdom	18,057	1,309	1,382	118	20 73
celluloids for almanacs, calen-	France..........	56	9	56	9	0 84
dars, illustrated pamphlets,	Germany.......	1,071	30	1,071	30	16 09
newspaper or other advertise-	Japan...........	329	24	329	24	4 95
ments, n.o.p., and matrices or	Switzerland.....	54	3	54	3	0 81
copper shells for such stereo-	United States..	1,626,292	54,895	1,626,292	54,895	24,394 57
types, electrotypes and cel-						
luloids.	Total.......	1,645,859	56,270	1,629,184	55,079	24,437 99
Stereotypes, electrotypes and	Unit'd Kingdom	5,547	159	675	25	0 85
celluloids and bases for	United States..	322,854	8,512	322,854	8,512	403 60
the same composed wholly or						
partly of metal or celluloid,	Total.......	328,401	8,671	323,529	8,537	404 45
· n.o.p. and copper shells for						
such stereotypes, electrotypes						
and celluloids.						
Matrices for stereotypes and	Unit'd Kingdom	480	4	480	4	2 40
electrotypes and celluloids	United States..	1,086,245	14,235	1,086,245	14,235	5,431 24
specified in preceding item.						
	Total.......	1,086,725	14,239	1,086,725	14,239	5,433 64
Type for printing, including	Unit'd Kingdom	....	17,186	....	210	42 00
chases, quoins and slugs of all	France..........	....	151	....	151	30 20
kinds.	United States..	....	58,206	....	58,206	11,641 20
	Total.......	....	75,543	....	58,567	11,713 40
Type metal in blocks, bars,	Unit'd Kingdom	....	282	....	....	....
plates and sheets.	United States..	....	780	....	780	117 00
	Total.......	....	1,062	....	780	117 00
Wire of all kinds, n.o.p.........	Unit'd Kingdom	....	976	....	16	3 20
	Germany......	....	2,441	....	2,441	488 20
	Sweden........	....	697	....	697	139 40
	United States..	....	31,712	....	31,712	6,342 40
	Total.......	....	35,826	....	34,866	6,973 20
Wire, twisted, etc., except iron	United States...	....	727	....	727	181 75
or steel, n.o.p.						

SESSIONAL PAPER No. 11

OF IMPORTS—*Continued.*

FOR HOME CONSUMPTION.

Preferential Tariff.			Treaty Rates.			Total.		
Quantity.	Value.	Duty.	Quantity.	Value.	Duty.	Quantity.	Value.	DutyColl'd.
	$	$ cts.		$	$ cts.		$	$ cts.
....	71,717	14,343 40	....	441	121 30	....	74,205	15,078 80
							15	4 50
				208	57 22		284	80 02
							190	57 00
				156	42 90		567	166 20
							1,241	372 30
				2	0 55		5	1 45
							11,885	3,565 50
....	71,717	14,343 40	....	807	221 97	....	88,392	19,325 77
....	314	70 69					315	71 04
							15	5 25
							17,466	6,113 10
..../..	314	70 69					17,796	6,189 39
Sq. in. 14,153	1,128	141 53	Sq. in.			Sq. in. 15,535	1,246	162 26
						56	9	0 84
						1,071	30	16 09
						329	24	4 95
						54	3	0 81
						1,626,292	54,895	24,394 57
14,153	1,128	141 53				1,643,337	56,207	24,579 52
4,872	134	6 09				5,547	159	6 94
						322,854	8,512	403 60
4,872	134	6 09				328,401	8,671	410 54
....						480	4	2 40
						1,086,245	14,235	5,431 24
						1,086,725	14,239	5,433 64
....	16,976	2,122 11					17,186	2,164 11
							151	30 20
							58,206	11,641 20
....	16,976	2,122 11					75,543	13,835 51
....	282	28 20					282	28 20
							780	117 00
....	282	28 20					1,062	145 20
....	960	144 00					976	147 20
							2,441	488 20
							697	139 40
							31,712	6,342 40
....	960	144 00					35,826	7,117 20
....							727	181 75

6 GEORGE V, A. 1916

No. 1.—General Statement

Articles Imported.	Countries.	Total Imports.		Entered		
				General Tariff.		
		Quantity.	Value.	Quantity.	Value.	Duty.
DUTIABLE GOODS—*Con.*		Lb.	$	Lb.	$	$ cts.
Milk, condensed..................	Unit'd Kingdom	15,095	1,515	4,324	480	150 25
	New Zealand...	137	16	....	....	....
	Holland........	7,129	975	7,129	975	234 37
	Norway........	144	8	144	8	4 68
	Switzerland.....	1,004	82	1,004	82	37 65
	United States..	108,714	7,748	97,336	6,889	3,340 67
	Total......	132,223	10,344	109,937	8,434	3,767 62
Milk and cream, fresh...........	United States..	....	77,413	....	77,413	13,547 59
Mineral and bituminous substances not otherwise provided for— Asbestos, in any form other than crude, and all manufactures of.	Unit'd Kingdom	....	33,501	....	1,744	436 00
	Newfoundland..	....	4	....	4	1 00
	Belgium........	....	1,734	....	1,734	433 50
	Germany.......	....	3,064	....	3,064	766 00
	Holland........	....	33	....	33	8 25
	Portugal.......	....	1	....	1	0 25
	United States..	....	188,357	....	188,178	47,044 50
	Total......	....	226,694	....	194,758	48,689 50
Asphalt, not solid..............	Unit'd Kingdom	....	14	....	....	....
	United States..	....	29,695	....	29,695	5,196 72
	Total......	....	29,709	....	29,695	5,196 72
Blacklead......................	Unit'd Kingdom	....	4,829	....	66	16 50
	United States..	....	466	....	466	116 50
	Total...'....	....	5,295	....	532	133 00
Mineral and bituminous substances, other, not otherwise provided for.	Unit'd Kingdom	....	10,748	....	833	145 77
	B. E. Indies, other........	....	503	....	....	....
	Aust.-Hungary..	....	137	....	137	23 97
	Belgium.......	....	289	....	289	50 57
	Denmark......	....	1,836	....	1,836	321 30
	France........	....	318	....	318	55 65
	Germany.......	....	2,842	....	2,842	497 35
	Holland.......	....	233	....	233	40 77
	United States..	....	129,762	....	126,113	22,070 34
	Total......	....	146,668	....	132,601	23,205 72
Plumbago, not ground or otherwise manufactured.	Unit'd Kingdom	....	12	....	....	....
	Germany.......	....	346	....	346	34 60
	United States..	....	1,106	....	1,106	110 60
	Total......	....	1,464	....	1,452	145 20
Plumbago, ground and manufactures of, n.o.p.	United Kingdom	....	4,501	....	55	13 75
	Germany.......	....	2,413	....	....	....
	United States..	....	33,585	....	33,517	8,379 25
	Total......	....	40,499	....	33,572	8,393 00

OF IMPORTS—*Continued.*

FOR HOME CONSUMPTION.

Preferential Tariff.			Treaty Rates.			Total.		
Quantity.	Value.	Duty.	Quantity.	Value.	Duty.	Quantity.	Value.	DutyColl'd.
Lb.	$	$ cts.	Lb.	$	$ cts.	Lb.	$	$ cts.
10,771	1,035	251 18	....	....	....	15,095	1,515	401 43
137	16	2 74	....	....	....	137	16	2 74
....	....	....	....	....	....	7,129	975	234 37
....	....	....	....	....	....	144	8	4 68
....	....	....	....	....	....	1,004	82	37 65
....	....	....	....	....	....	97,336	6,889	3,340 67
10,908	1,051	253 92	....	....	....	120,845	9,485	4,021 54
....	....	....	....	....	....	....	77,413	13,547 59
....	31,757	4,763 55	....	....	....	....	33,501	5,199 55
....	....	....	....	....	....	....	4	1 00
....	....	....	....	....	....	....	1,734	433 50
....	....	....	....	....	....	....	3,064	766 00
....	....	....	....	....	....	....	33	8 25
....	....	....	....	....	....	....	1	0 25
....	....	....	....	....	....	....	188,178	47,044 50
....	31,757	4,763 55	....	....	....	....	226,515	53,453 05
....	14	1 75	....	....	....	....	14	1 75
....	....	....	....	....	....	....	29,695	5,196 72
....	14	1 75	....	....	....	....	29,709	5,198 47
....	4,763	714 45	....	....	....	....	4,829	730 95
....	....	....	....	....	....	....	466	116 50
....	4,763	714 45	....	....	....	....	5,295	847 45
....	10,230	1,534 50	....	....	....	....	11,063	1,680 27
....	1,217	182 55	....	....	....	....	1,217	182 55
....	....	....	....	....	....	....	137	23 97
....	....	....	....	....	....	....	289	50 57
....	....	....	....	....	....	....	1,836	321 30
....	....	....	....	....	....	....	318	55 65
....	....	....	....	....	....	....	2,842	497 35
....	....	....	....	....	....	....	233	40 77
....	....	....	....	....	....	....	126,113	22,070 34
....	11,447	1,717 05	....	....	....	....	144,048	24,922 77
....	12	0 60	....	....	....	....	12	0 60
....	....	....	....	....	....	....	346	34 60
....	....	....	....	....	....	....	1,106	110 60
....	12	0 60	....	....	....	....	1,464	145 80
....	4,446	666 90	....	....	....	....	4,501	680 65
....	....	....	....	....	....	....	33,517	8,379 25
....	4,446	666 90	....	....	....	....	38,018	9,059 90

6 GEORGE V, A. 1916

No. 1.—General Statement

Articles Imported:	Countries.	Total Imports.		Entered		
				General Tariff.		
		Quantity.	Value.	Quantity.	Value.	Duty.
DUTIABLE GOODS—*Con.*			$		$	$. cts. .
Mineral and aerated waters, n.o.p.	Unit'd Kingdom	....	27,780	....	2,356	412 30
	B. Guiana......	....	115	....	....	....
	Hong Kong....	....	84	....	84	14 70
	Aust. Hungary..	....	2,816	....	2,816	492 80
	France..........	....	115,464	....	108,419	18,973 80
	Germany.......	....	15,316	....	15,923	2,786 52
	Holland........	....	93	....	93	16 27
	Italy..........	....	222	....	222	38 85
	Japan..........	....	2,271	....	2,859	500 32
	Spain..........	....	....	....	20	3 50
	United States...	....	37,036	....	37,952	6,641 60
	Total......	....	201,197	....	170,744	29,880 66
Mucilage and adhesive paste......	Unit'd Kingdom	....	3,950	....	24	6 60
	Germany.......	....	39	....	39	10 72
	Japan..........	....	1	....	1	0 27
	United States...	....	31,904	....	31,815	8,750 09
	Total......	....	35,894	....	31,879	8,767 68
Musical instruments, viz.—						
Brass band instruments and bag	Unit'd Kingdom	....	21,293	....	272	68 00
pipes.	Aust.-Hungary..	....	6,411	....	460	115 00
	Belgium........	....	196	....	196	49 00
	France..........	....	8,630	....	30	7 50
	Germany.......	....	188	....	205	51 25
	Holland........	....	38	....	38	9 50
	Italy..........	....	13	....	13	3 25
	Japan..........	....	28	....	28	7 00
	Switzerland.....	....	97	....	....	....
	United States...	....	22,874	....	22,874	5,718 50
	Total......	....	59,768	....	24,116	6,029 00
		No.		No.		
Cabinet organs.................	Unit'd Kingdom	1	71	....	....	....
	Italy..........	1	63	1	63	18 90
	Japan..........	1	25	1	25	7 50
	United States...	350	19,874	350	19,874	5,962 20
	Total......	353	20,033	. 352	19,962	5,988 60
Pipe organs.....................	United States...	2	1,400	2	1,400	420 00
Parts of organs.................	Unit'd Kingdom	....	635	....	5	1 25
	France.........	....	53	....	....	....
	United States...	....	8,806	....	8,806	2,201 50
	Total......	....	9,494	....	8,811	2,202 75
Pianofortes....................	Unit'd Kingdom	81	10,526	11	3,121	936 30
	Aust.-Hungary..	2	358	....	....	....
	Belgium........	3	1,166	3	1,166	349,80
	Germany.......	10	3,241	9	3,020	906 00
	United States...	1,269	220,016	1,279	219,508	65,852 40
	Total......	1,365	235,307	1,302	226,815	68,044 50
Pianos, parts of................	Unit'd Kingdom	....	2,158	....	61	15 25
	Aust.-Hungary..	....	11	....	....	....
	France..........	....	3,898	....	557	139 25
	Germany.......	....	2,744	....	2,744	686 00
	United States...	....	143,268	....	143,268	35,817 00
	Total......	....	152,079	....	146,630	36,657 50

OF IMPORTS—*Continued*.

FOR HOME CONSUMPTION.

Preferential Tariff.			Treaty Rates.			Total.		
Quantity.	Value.	Duty.	Quantity.	Value.	Duty.	Quantity.	Value.	DutyColl'd.
	$ 22,830	$ cts. 3,424 50		$	$ cts.		$ 25,186	$ cts. 3,836 80
....	....	....	....	....	....	....	84	14 70
....	....	....	....	....	....	....	2,816	492 80
....	....	....	....	....	....	....	108,419	18,973 80
....	....	....	....	....	....	....	15,923	2,786 52
....	....	....	....	....	....	....	93	16 27
....	....	....	....	....	....	....	222	38 85
....	....	....	....	....	....	....	2,859	500 32
....	....	....	....	....	....	....	20	3 50
....	....	....	....	....	....	....	37,952	6,641 60
....	22,830	3,424 50	....	....	....	....	193,574	33,305 16
....	3,954	692 03	....				3,978	698 63
....	....	....	....	....	....	....	39	10 72
....	....	....	....	....	....	....	1	0 27
....	....	....	....	....	....	....	31,815	8,750 09
....	3,954	692 03	....	....	....	....	35,833	9,459 71
....	18,125	2,718 75	....	2,896	651 60	....	21,293	3,438 35
....	....	....	....	5,951	1,338 88	....	6,411	1,453 88
....	....	....	....			....	196	49 00
....	....	....	....	8,465	1,904 86	....	8,495	1,912 36
....	....	....	....	....	....	....	205	51 25
....	....	....	....	....	....	....	38	9 50
....	....	....	....	....	....	....	13	3 25
....	....	....	....	....	....	....	28	7 00
....	....	....	....	97	21 83	....	97	21 83
....	....	....	....	....	....	....	22,874	5,718 50
....	18,125	2,718 75	....	17,409	3,917 17	....	59,650	12,664 92
No. 1	71	14 20	No.	....	....	No. 1	71	14 20
....	....	....	....	....	....	1	63	18 90
....	....	....	....	....	....	1	25	7 50
....	....	....	....	....	....	350	19,874	5,962 20
1	71	14 20	....	....	....	353	. 20,033	6,002 80
....	....	....	....	....	....	2	1,400	420 00
....	630	94 50	....	....	....	....	635	95 75
....	....	....	....	53	11 93	....	53	11 93
....	....	....	....	....	....	....	8,806	2,201 50
....	630	94 50	....	53	11 93	....	9,494	2,309 18
70	7,405	1,481 00	....	....	....	81	10,526	2,417 30
....	....	....	2	358	98 46	2	358	98 46
....	....	....	....	....	....	3	1,166	349 80
....	....	....	....	....	....	9	3,020	906 00
....	....	....	....	....	....	1,279	219,508	65,852 40
70	7,405	1,481 00	2	358	98 46	1,374	234,578	69,623 96
....	2,078	311 70	....	19	4 27	....	2,158	331 22
....	....	....	....	11	2 48	....	11	2 48
....	....	....	....	3,484	783 92	....	4,041	923 17
....	....	....	....	....	....	....	2,744	686 00
....	....	....	....	....	....	....	143,268	35,817 00
....	2,078	311 70	....	3,514	790 67	....	152,222	37,759 87

6 GEORGE V, A. 1916

No. 1.—GENERAL STATEMENT

Articles Imported.	Countries.	TOTAL IMPORTS.		ENTERED		
				General Tariff.		
		Quantity.	Value.	Quantity.	Value.	Duty.
DUTIABLE GOODS—*Con.*		No.	$	No.	$	$ cts.
Musical instruments—*Con.*						
Piano and organ players, mechanical.	United States...	47	10,232	47	10,232	3,069 60
Phonographs, graphophones, gramophones and finished parts thereof, including cylinders and records therefor.	Unit'd Kingdom	....	26,116	....	1,155	346 50
	Newfoundland..	....	20	....	20	6 00
	Aust.-Hungary..	....	359	....	131	39 30
	Belgium........	....	490	....	25	7 50
	France..........	....	6,840	....	1,220	366 00
	Germany.......	....	9,342	....	6,664	1,999 20
	Japan..........	....	345	....	195	58 50
	Switzerland....	....	170	....	29	8 70
	United States...	....	711,484	....	688,022	206,406 60
	Total......	....	755,166	....	697,461	209,238 30
Other musical instruments, n.o.p	Unit'd Kingdom	....	13,805	....	4,223	1,266 90
	Hong Kong.....	....	473	....	473	141 90
	Aust.-Hungary..	....	1,727	....	42	12 60
	China..........	....	199	....	199	59 70
	France..........	....	2,733	....	4,928	1,478 40
	Germany.......	....	47,366	....	63,527	19,058 10
	Holland........	....	72	....	28	8 40
	Italy...........	....	460	....	439	131 70
	Japan..........	....	20	....	....	....
	Norway........	....	5	....	5	1 50
	Russia.........	....	65	....	65	19 50
	Switzerland....	....	143	....	44	13 20
	United States...	....	54,064	....	53,978	16,193 40
	Total......	....	121,132	....	127,951	38,385 30
		Lb.		Lb.		
Mustard, ground..................	Unit'd Kingdom	602,037	162,323	3,688	793	218 07
	Germany.......	600	53	600	53	14 57
	United States...	290,241	22,675	290,241	22,675	6,235 89
	Total......	892,878	185,051	294,529	23,521	6,468 53
Mustard, French, liquid.,........	Unit'd Kingdom	....	471	....	....	....
	France..........	....	795	....	34	11 90
	Sweden........	....	1	....	1	0 35
	United States...	....	19,720	....	18,889	6,611 15
	Total......	....	20,987	....	18,924	6,623 40
Oils—		Gal.		Gal.		
Mineral—						
Coal and kerosene, distilled, purified or refined.	Unit'd Kingdom	110	18	110	18	2 75
	Newfoundland..	817	142	817	142	20 42
	United States...	8,820,604	605,413	9,586,232	653,241	239,656 84
	Total......	8,821,531	605,573	9,587,159	653,401	239,680 01
Petroleum, products of, n.o.p.	Unit'd Kingdom	20,751	5,228	5,906	648	147 65
	United States...	5,291,658	557,115	5,723,266	588,238	143,082 49
	Total.....:...	5,312,409	562,343	5,729,172	588,886	143,230 14
Crude petroleum, gas oils other than naphtha, benzine and gasoline lighter than ·8235 but not less than ·775 specific gravity at 60 degrees.	United States...	64,057	5,418	64,057	5,418	960 90

SESSIONAL PAPER No. 11

OF IMPORTS—*Continued.*

FOR HOME CONSUMPTION.

Preferential Tariff.			Treaty Rates.			Total.		
Quantity.	Value.	Duty.	Quantity.	Value.	Duty.	Quantity.	Value.	DutyColl'd.
No.	$	$ cts.	No.	$	$ cts.	No.	$	$ cts.
						47	10,232	3,069 60
	19,233	3,846 60		5,324	1,464 10		25,712	5,657 20
					62 70		20	6 00
				228			359	102 00
				465	127 87		490	135 37
				5,620	1,545 66		6,840	1,911 66
							6,664	1,999 20
				150	41 20		345	99 70
				141	38 77		170	47 47
							688,022	206,406 60
	19,233	3,846 60		11,928	3,280 30		728,622	216,365 20
	7,141	1,428 20		2,407	661 92		13,771	3,357 02
							473	141 90
				1,806	496 65		1,848	509 25
							199	59 75
				2,797	769 23		7,725	2,247 60
							63,527	19,058 13
				44	12 10		72	20 50
				21	5 77		460	137 40
				16	4 40		16	4 47
							5	1 50
							65	19 50
				99	27 22		143	40 40
							53,978	16,193 42
	7,141	1,428 20		7,190	1,977 29		142,282	41,790 79
Lb. 619,136	167,889	29,381 08	Lb.			Lb. 622,824	168,682	29,599 15
						600	53	14 57
						290,241	22,675	6,235 89
619,136	167,889	29,381 08				913,665	191,410	35,849 61
	378	94 50		93	30 19		471	124 69
				737	239 61		771	251 51
							1	0 35
							18,889	6,611 15
	378	94 50		830	269 80		20,132	6,987 70
Gal.			Gal.			Gal. 110	18	2 75
						817	142	20 42
						9,586,232	653,241	239,656 84
						9,587,159	653,401	239,680 01
38,865	7,706	582 99				44,771	8,354	730 64
						5,723,266	588,238	143,082 49
38,865	7,706	582 99				5,768,037	596,592	143,813 13
						64,057	5,418	960 90

6 GEORGE .V, A. 1916

No. 1.—General Statement

Articles Imported.	Countries.	Total Imports.		Entered		
				General Tariff.		
		Quantity.	Value.	Quantity.	Value.	Duty.
DUTIABLE GOODS—*Con.*		Gal.	$	Gal.	$	$ cts.
Oils—*Con.*						
Illuminating oils composed	Unit'd Kingdom	3,823	1,616	....	......	....
wholly or in part of the pro-	France..........	100	155	100	155	31 00
ducts of petroleum, coal,	United States...	121,215	48,920	120,726	48,733	9,746 60
shale or lignite, costing						
more than 30 cents per gallon	Total.......	125,138	50,691	120,826	48,888	9,777 60
Animal—						
Lard oil.....................	Unit'd Kingdom	4,799	1,774	85	77	19 25
	United States...	27,616	13,497	27,616	13,497	3,374 25
	Total.......	32,415	15,271	27,701	13,574	3,393 50
Neatsfoot...................	United States...	10,061	7,306	10,061	7,306	1,826 50
Other animal oil, n.o.p.......	Unit'd Kingdom	1,494	554	....	......	....
	United States...	8,154	4,726	8,154	4,726	827 06
	Total.......	9,648	5,280	8,154	4,726	827 06
Vegetable—						
Castor.....................	Unit'd Kingdom	76,464	41,853	727	519	90 82
	France..........	469	338	469	338	59 15
	Germany......	6	4	6	4	0 70
	Italy...........	1,840	1,135	1,840	1,135	198 69
	United States...	1,438	1,058	1,438	1,058	185 15
	Total.......	80,217	44,388	4,480	3,054	534 51
Cocoanut, n.o.p..............	Unit'd Kingdom	43,858	44,736	413	503	88 02
	B.E.Indies other	496	492	21	23	2 27
	France..........	830	770	830	770	134 75
	Germany......	205	179	205	179	31 32
	United States...	3,032	3,814	3,032	3,814	669 37
	Total.......	48,421	49,991	4,501	5,289	925 73
Cotton seed................	B. W. Indies....	387	432	387	432	75 60
	China..........	5,469	1,578	5,469	1,578	276 15
	France..........	186	89	186	89	15 57
	Japan..........	12	6	12	6	1 05
	United States...	226,520	111,310	225,920	110,893	19,406 67
	Total.......	232,574	113,415	231,974	112,998	19,775 04
		Lb.		Lb.		
Flaxseed or linseed, raw or	Unit'd Kingdom	176,012	10,746	2,562	153	42 27
boiled.	Belgium........	392	22	392	22	6 46
	United States...	76,983	5,829	76,983	5,829	1,270 45
	Total......	253,387	16,597	79,937	6,004	1,319 18
		Gal.		Gal.		
Olive, n.o.p.................	Unit'd Kingdom	19,385	33,461	4,540	6,818	1,363 60
	Belgium........	2	5	235	331	66 20
	France..........	57,928	95,481	3,321	5,852	1,170 40
	French Africa...	107	360	107	360	72 00
	Germany......	25	21	25	21	4 20
	Greece..........	3,117	4,464	3,133	4,474	894 80
	Italy..........	150,055	165,938	114,432	127,685	25,537 00
	Japan..........	6	18	....	......	....
	Spain..........	2,488	3,127	840	1,061	212 20
	Turkey..........	50	43	40	33	6 60
	United States...	20,478	25,492	21,151	26,171	5,234 20
	Total.......	253,641	328,350	147,824	172,806	34,561 20

OF IMPORTS—*Continued.*

FOR HOME CONSUMPTION.

Preferential Tariff.			Treaty Rates.			Total.		
Quantity.	Value.	Duty.	Quantity.	Value.	Duty..	Quantity.	Value.	DutyColl'd.
Gal.	$	$ cts.	Gal.	$	$ cts.	Gal.	$	$ cts.
3,775	1,615	242 25	....	....	....	3,775	1,615	242 25
....	....	....	....	....	....	100	155	31 00
....	....	....	....	....	....	120,726	48,733	9,746 60
3,775	1,615	242 25	....	....	....	124,601	50,503	10,019 85
4,714	1,697	254 55	......:	....	....	4,799	1,774	273 80
....	....	....	....	....	......:.	27,616	13,497	3,374 25
4,714	1,697	254 55	....	....	......:..	32,415	15,271	3,648 05
....	....	....				10,061	7,306	1,826 50
1,494	554	83 10	....	....	....	1,494	554	83 10
....	....	....	....	....	....	8,154	4,726	827 06
1,494	554	83 10	....	....	....	9,648	5,280	910 16
76,031	41,534	6,230 10				76,758	42,053	6,320 92
....	....	....	....	....	....	469	338	59 15
....	....	....	....	....	....	6	4	0 70
....	....	....	....	....	....	1,840	1,135	198 69
....	....	....	....	....	....	1,438	1,058	185 15
....	....	....	....	....	....	80,511	44,588	6,764 61
43,686	44,168	5,521 07	....	....	....	44,099	44,671	5,609 09
.475	469	58 62	....	....	....	496	492	60 89
....	....	....	....	....	....	830	770	134 75
....	....	....	....	....	....	205	179	31 32
....	....	....	....	....	....	3,032	3,814	669 37
44,161	44,637	5,579 69	....	....	....	48,662	49,926	6,505 42
....	....	....	....	....	....	387	432	75 60
....	....	....	....	....	....	5,469	1,578	276 15
....	....	....	....	....	....	186	89	15 57
....	....	....	....	....	....	12	6	1 05
....	....	....	....	....	....	225,920	110,893	19,406 67
....	....	....	....	....	....	231,974	112,998	19,775 04
Lb. 151,815	9,921	1,897 71	Lb.			Lb. 154,377	10,074	1,939 98
....	....	....	....	....	....	392	22	6 46
....	....	....	....	....	....	76,983	5,829	1,270 45
151,815	9,921	1,897 71	....	....	....	231,752	15,925	3,216 89
Gal. 14,583	26,327	3,949 05	Gal. 905	1,721	258 15	Gal. 20,028	34,866	5,570 80
....	....	....	....	....	....	235	331	66 20
....	....	....	53,009	88,364	13,254 60	56,330	94,216	14,425 00
....	....	....	....	....	....	107	360	72 00
....	....	....	....	....	....	25	21	4 20
....	....	....	....	....	....	3,133	4,474	894 80
....	....	....	....	....	....	114,432	127,685	25,537 00
....	....	....	6	18	2 70	6	18	2 70
....	....	....	1,648	2,066	309 90	2,488	3,127	522 10
....	....	....	....	....	....	40	33	6 60
....	....	....	....	....	....	21,151	26,171	5,234 20
14,583	26,327	3,949 05	55,568	92,169	13,825 35	217,975	291,302	52,335 60

6 GEORGE V, A. 1916

No. 1.—General Statement

Articles Imported.	Countries.	Total Imports.		Entered		
				General Tariff.		
		Quantity.	Value.	Quantity.	Value.	Duty.
DUTIABLE GOODS—*Con.*		Gal.	$	Gal.	$	$ cts.
Oils—*Con.*						
Sesame seed...............	Hong Kong.....	444	512	444	512	128 00
	China..........	14	14	14	14	3 50
	Holland.......	3	9	3	9	2 25
	Japan..........	584	469	584	469	117 25
	United States...	472	434	472	434	108 50
	Total.......	1,517	1,438	1,517	1,438	359 50
Vegetable oil, not otherwise provided for.	Unit'd Kingdom	9,940	8,668	161	158	27 65
	Hong Kong.....	42,026	30,207	42,026	30,207	5,286 22
	Belgium........	3,962	4,517	3,962	4,517	790 47
	China..........	3,483	2,033	3,483	2,033	355 77
	France.........	12,497	12,109	13,630	13,006	2,276 05
	Germany.......	636	249	636	249	43 57
	Japan..........	30	30	30	30	5 25
	Russia.........	1,300	1,398	1,300	1,398	244 65
	United States...	67,566	34,400	67,567	34,404	6,021 13
	Total.......	141,440	93,611	132,795	86,002	15,050 76
Lubricating oils composed wholly or in part of petroleum and costing less than 25 cents per gallon.	Unit'd Kingdom	3,287	696	790	183	19 75
	Germany.......	5,315	1,254	5,315	1,254	132 87
	Russia.........	253	61	253	61	6 32
	United States...	4,427,045	575,670	4,360,438	570,364	109,011 55
	Total.......	4,435,900	577,681	4,366,796	571,862	109,170 49
Lubricating oils, n.o.p........	Unit'd Kingdom	95,660	32,781	7,745	2,970	594 00
	B.E.Indies other	240	240	240	240	48 00
	Belgium........	1,057	278	1,057	278	55 60
	China..........	1,094	928	1,094	928	185 60
	France.........	652	342	652	342	68 40
	Germany.......	969	432	969	432	86 40
	Norway........	110	44	110	44	8 80
	Sweden.........	21	9	21	9	1 80
	United States...	888,194	270,990	859,959	261,115	52,223 00
	Total.......	987,997	306,044	871,847	266,358	53,271 60
		Lb.		Lb.		
Essential, n.o.p..............	Unit'd Kingdom	26,887	33,002	13,086	17,039	1,277 92
	Australia.......	840	271	840	271	20 32
	B. India........	300	158	300	158	11 85
	B.E.Indies other	4,632	1,761	4,632	1,761	132 07
	B. W. Indies....	240	430	40	30	2 25
	Hong Kong.....	1,349	799	617	521	39 07
	France.........	15,312	29,892	14,906	26,892	2,016 90
	Germany.......	4,572	8,889	4,572	8,889	666 67
	Holland.......	50	128	50	128	9 60
	Italy..........	7,435	15,225	7,235	14,498	1,087 35
	Japan..........	932	756	1,232	1,009	75 67
	Russia.........	51	18	51	18	1 35
	Switzerland....	220	1,178	220	1,178	88 35
	United States...	148,738	210,787	147,571	209,794	15,735 00
	Total.......	211,558	303,294	195,352	282,186	21,164 37
Peppermint.................	Unit'd Kingdom	270	990	....	....	....
	Hong Kong.....	26	31	26	31	2 32
	China..........	4	1	4	1	08
	United States...	7,242	16,538	6,842	15,538	1,165 41
	Total.......	7,542	17,560	6,872	15,570	1,167 81

OF IMPORTS—*Continued.*

ᶠᴼᴿ HOME CONSUMPTION.

Preferential Tariff.			Treaty Rates.			Total.		
Quantity.	Value.	Duty.	Quantity.	Value.	Duty.	Quantity.	Value.	DutyColl'd.
Gal.	$	$ cts.	Gal.	$	$ cts.	Gal.	$	$ cts.
....	....	....	....	....	....	444	512	128 00
....	....	....	....	....	....	14	14	3 50
....	....	....	....	....	....	3	9	2 25
....	....	....	....	....	....	584	469	117 25
....	....	....	....	....	....	472	434	108 50
....	....	....	....	....	....	1,517	1,438	359 50
8,982	7,810	1,171 50	....	....	....	9,143	7,968	1,199 15
....	....	....	....	....	....	42,026	30,207	5,286 22
....	....	....	....	....	....	3,962	4,517	790 47
....	....	....	....	....	....	3,483	2,033	355 77
....	....	....	....	....	....	13,630	13,006	2,276 05
....	....	....	....	....	....	636	249	43 57
....	....	....	....	....	....	30	30	5 25
....	....	....	....	....	....	1,300	1,398	244 65
....	....	....	....	....	....	67,567	34,404	6,021 13
8,982	7,810	1,171 50	....	....	....	141,777	93,812	16,222 26
2,497	513	37 45	....	....	....	3,287	696	57 20
....	....	....	....	....	....	5,315	1,254	132 87
....	....	....	....	....	....	253	61	6 32
....	....	....	....	....	....	4,360,438	570,364	109,011 55
2,497	513	37 45	....	....	....	4,369,293	572,375	109,207 94
85,049	28,585	3,573 18	....	....	....	92,794	31,555	4,167 18
....	....	....	....	....	....	240	240	48 00
....	....	....	....	....	....	1,057	278	55 60
....	....	....	....	....	....	1,094	928	185 60
....	....	....	....	....	....	652	342	68 40
....	....	....	....	....	....	969	432	86 40
....	....	....	....	....	....	110	44	8 80
....	....	....	....	....	....	21	9	1 80
....	....	....	....	....	....	859,959	261,115	52,223 00
85,049	28,585	3,573 18	....	....	....	956,896	294,943	56,844 78
Lb. 13,797	15,960	798 00	Lb.	....	....	Lb. 26,883	32,999	2,075 92
....	....	....	....	....	....	840	271	20 32
....	....	....	....	....	....	300	158	11 85
....	....	....	....	....	....	4,632	1,761	132 07
200	400	20 00	....	....	....	240	430	22 25
....	....	....	....	....	....	617	521	39 07
....	....	....	....	....	....	14,906	26,892	2,016 90
....	....	....	....	....	....	4,572	8,889	666 67
....	....	....	....	....	....	50	128	9 60
....	....	....	....	....	....	7,235	14,498	1,087 35
....	....	....	....	....	....	1,232	1,009	75 67
....	....	....	....	....	....	51	18	1 35
....	....	....	....	....	....	220	1,178	88 35
....	....	....	....	....	....	147,571	209,794	15,735 00
13,997 ·	16,360	818 00	....	....	....	209,349	· 298,546	21,982 37
270	990	49 50	....	....	....	270	990	49 50
....	....	....	....	....	....	26	31	2 32
....	....	....	....	....	....	4	1	08
....	....	....	....	....	....	6,842	15,538	1,165 41
270	990	49 50	....	....	....	7,142	16,560	1,217 31

No. 1.—General Statement

Articles Imported.	Countries.	Total Imports.		Entered		
				General Tariff.		
		Quantity.	Value.	Quantity.	Value.	Duty.
DUTIABLE GOODS—*Con.*		Gal.	$	Gal.	$	$ cts.
Oils—*Con.*						
All other oils, not elsewhere specified.	Unit'd Kingdom	·12,466	6,980	521	342	· 59 85
	Hong Kong.....	178	115	178	115	20 12
	Belgium........	3,810	7,511	3,810	7,511	1,314 42
	China.¨........	1,905	998	1,905	998	174 65
	France..........	1,218	817	1,218	817	142 97
	Germany.......	118	136	177	179	31 32
	Japan..........	212	146	212	146	25 55
	Switzerland.....	1,850	531	1,850	531	92 92
	United States...	186,710	53,914	186,474	53,686	9,395 74
	Total......	208,467	·71,148	196,345	64,325	11,257 54
Oiled silk, oiled cloth, and tape or other textile, india-rubbered, flocked or coated, n.o.p.	Unit'd Kingdom	....	182,834	....	2,156	646 80
	Aust.-Hungary .	....	1,604	....	1,604	481 20
	Belgium........	....	602	....	602	180 60
	France.........	....	128	....	237	71 10
	Germany.......	....	756	....	756	226 80
	Sweden........	....	31	....	31	9 30
	United States...	....	224,465	....	223,520	67,056 00
	Total......	....	410,420	....	228,906	68,671 80
		Sq. yd.		Sq. yd.		
Oil cloth, enamelled carriage, floor, shelf and table oil cloth, cork matting or carpet and linoleum.	Unit'd Kingdom	2,305,934	764,940	4,398	1,286	450 10
	Belgium........	. 2,869	410	2,869	410	143 50
	France	2	1	501	71	24 85
	Germany.......	215	219	215	219	76 65
	United States...	505,415	109,919	· 506,373	110,198	38,569 30
	Total......	2,814,435	875,489	514,356	112,184	39,264 40
Optical, philosophical, photographic and mathematical instruments, n.o.p.	Unit'd Kingdom	....	172,048	....	9,850	2,462 50
	France.........	....	31,735	....	10,251	2,562 75
	Germany.......	....	17,323	....	17,335	4,333 75
	Holland........	....	11	....	11	2 75
	Japan..........	....	47	....	3	0 75
	Switzerland....	....	3,297	....	483	120 75
	United States...	....	520,074	....	509,121	127,280 25
	Total......	....	744,535	....	547,054	136,763 50
Parts, brass and aluminum, of cameras and kodaks, including special parts of metal in the rough, when imported by manufacturers of cameras and kodaks for the use only in the manufacture of cameras and kodaks.	United States...	....	3,081	....	3,081	231 08
Spectacles, eye-glasses and ground or finished spectacle or eye-glass lenses...	Unit'd Kingdom	....	1,527	....	483	144 90
	Aust.-Hungary .	....	37	....	37	11 10
	China..........	....	6	....	6	1 80
	France.........	....	2,326	....	2,326	697 80
	Germany.......	....	516	....	516	154 80
	Japan..........	....	17	....	17	5 10
	United States...	....	28,997	....	28,997	8,699 10
	Total......	....	33,426	....	32,382	9,714 60
Spectacle frames, eye-glass frames, and metal parts of.	Unit'd Kingdom	....	691	....	424	84 80
	France.........	....	84	....	84	16 80
	Germany.......	....	575	....	575	115 00
	United States...	....	64,778	....	64,778	12,955 60
	Total......	....	66,128	....	·65,861	13,172 20

SESSIONAL PAPER No. 11

OF IMPORTS—*Continued.*

FOR HOME CONSUMPTION.

Preferential Tariff.			Treaty Rates.			Total.		
Quantity.	Value.	Duty.	Quantity.	Value.	Duty.	Quantity.	Value.	DutyColl'd.
Gal.	$	$ cts.	Gal.	$	$ cts.	Gal.	$	$ cts.
11,965	6,724	1,008 60	....	....	....	12,486	7,066	1,068 45
....	....	....	....	....	....	178	115	20 12
....	....	....	....	....	....	3,810	7,511	1,314 42
....	....	....	....	....	....	1,905	998	174 65
....	....	....	....	....	....	1,218	817	142 97
....	....	....	....	....	....	177	179	31 32
....	....	....	....	....	....	212	146	25 55
....	....	....	....	....	....	1,850	531	92 92
....	....	....	....	....	....	186,474	53,686	9,395 74
11,965	6,724	1,008 60	....			208,310	71,049	12,266 14
....	186,933	37,386 60	....	....	....	189,089	38,033 40	
....	....	....	....	.		1,604	481 20	
....	....	....	....			602	180 60	
....	....	....	....			237	71 10	
....	....	....	....			756	226 80	
....	....	....	....			31	9 30	
....	....	....	....			223,520	67,056 00	
....	186,933	37,386 60	....	....	....	415,839	106,058 40	
Sq. yd. 2,305,264	764,797	191,199 25	Sq. yd.	....	....	Sq. yd. 2,309,662	766,083	191,649 35
....	....	....	....			2,869	410	143 50
....	....	....	....			501	71	24 85
....	....	....	....			215	219	76 65
....	....	....	....			506,373	110,198	38,569 30
2,305,264	764,797	191,199 25	....	....	....	2,819,620	876,981	230,463 65
....	162,447	28,428 94	....	4,306	968 85	....	176,603	31,860 29
....	....	....	....	21,656	4,872 81	....	31,907	7,435 56
....	....	....	....	....	....	....	17,335	4,333 75
....	....	....	....			....	11	2 75
....	....	....	....	44	9 90	....	47	10 65
....	....	....	....	2,642	594 45	....	3,125	715 20
....	....	....	....	....	....	....	509,121	127,280 25
....	162,447	28,428 94	....	28,648	6,446 01	....	738,149	171,638 45
....	....	....	....	....	....	....	3,081	231 08
....	1,044	208 80	....	....	....	....	1,527	353 70
....	....	....	....	....	....	....	37	11 10
....	....	....	....	....	....	....	6	1 80
....	....	....	....	....	....	....	2,326	697 80
....	....	....	....	....	....	....	516	154 80
....	....	....	....	....	....	....	17	5 10
....	....	....	....	....	....	....	28,997	8,699 10
....	1,044	208 80	....	....	....	....	33,426	9,923 40
....	267	40 05	....	....	....	....	691	124 85
....	....	....	....	....	....	....	84	16 80
....	....	....	....	....	....	....	575	115 00
....	....	....	....	....	....	....	64,778	12,955 60
....	267	40 05	....	....	....	....	66,128	13,212 25

No. 1.—General Statement

Articles Imported.	Countries.	Total Imports.		Entered		
				General Tariff.		
		Quantity.	Value.	Quantity.	Value.	Duty.
DUTIABLE GOODS—*Con.*			$		$	$ cts.
Silvered lenses for automobile lamps.	United States...	....	2,986	....	2,986	447 90
Packages, usual coverings, containing goods subject to any *ad valorem* duty, not included in the invoice value of the goods they contained.	Unit'd Kingdom	....	807,763	....	41,828	8,365 60
	Australia......	....	5,697	....	6,217	1,243 40
	B. E. Africa....	....	145	....	145	29 00
	B. S. Africa....	....	44	....	....	....
	B. Guiana......	....	13	....	5	1 00
	B. India........	....	443	....	7	1 40
	B. E. Indies, other........	....	54	....	....	....
	B. W. Indies....	....	205	....	236	47 20
	B. Straits Settlements........	....	1,007	....	86	17 20
	Hong Kong....	....	7,512	....	7,499	1,499 80
	New Zealand...	....	1,350	....	16	3 20
	Alaska........	....	12	....	12	2 40
	Aust.-Hungary .	....	9,671	....	10,520	2,104 00
	Azores and Madeira..........	....	1	....	1	0 20
	Belgium........	....	28,688	....	28,782	5,756 40
	China.........	....	1,307	....	1,310	262 00
	Cuba.........	....	2,301	....	2,458	491 60
	Denmark......	....	101	....	101	20 20
	Dutch E. Indies	....	44	....	96	19 20
	Egypt and Soudan......	....	7	....	7	1 40
	France........	....	30,587	....	30,840	6,168 00
	French Africa...	....	3	....	3	0 60
	Germany......	....	62,395	....	64,559	12,911 80
	Greece........	....	46	....	76	15 20
	Hawaii........	....	7	....	5	1 00
	Holland.......	....	6,027	....	7,567	1,513 40
	Italy..........	....	4,746	....	6,011	1,202 20
	Japan.........	....	17,591	....	17,537	3,507 40
	Mexico........	....	1	....	1	0 20
	Norway........	....	1,491	....	1,495	299 00
	Persia.........	....	8	....	8	1 60
	Philippines.....	....	20	....	26	5 20
	Portugal.......	....	121	....	185	37 00
	Roumania.....	....	1	....	91	18 20
	Russia........	....	864	....	864	172 80
	Siam..........	....	5	....	5	1 00
	Spain.........	....	1,623	....	1,147	229 40
	Sweden.......	....	2,703	....	2,724	544 80
	Switzerland....	....	2,559	....	2,582	516 40
	Turkey.......	....	658	....	658	131 60
	United States...	....	221,015	....	220,807	44,161 40 .
	Venezuela......	....	18	....	18	3 60
	Total......	....	1,218,854	....	456,535	91,307 00
Packages paying 7½, 22½ and 25 per cent.	Unit'd Kingdom	....	60,480	.	1,275	318 75
	B. Guiana......	....	5,167	....	107	26 75
	B. India.......	....	72	....	4	1 00
	B. W. Indies....	....	928	....	132	33 00
	Hong Kong....	....	269	....	265	66 25
	Newfoundland..	....	5	....	5	1 25
	Alaska........	....	1	....	1	0 25
	Aust.-Hungary .	....	94	....	243	60 75
	Belgium........	....	158	....	154	38 50
	China.........	....	83	....	85	21 25
	Cuba.........	....	24	....	24	6 00
	Egypt and Soudan......	....	26	....	6	1 50
	France........	....	31,891	....	3,632	908 00

SESSIONAL PAPER No. 11

OF IMPORTS—*Continued.*

FOR HOME CONSUMPTION.

	Preferential Tariff.			Treaty Rates.			Total.	
Quantity.	Value.	Duty.	Quantity.	Value.	Duty.	Quantity.	Value.	DutyColl'd.
	$	$ cts.		$	$ cts.		$	$ cts.
....	....	....	....	....	....	....	2,986	447 90
....	764,124	114,618 60	....	....	....	....	805,952	122,984 20
....	....	....	....	....	....	....	6,217	1,243 40
....	....	....	....	....	....	....	145	29 00
....	44	6 60	....	....	....	....	44	6 60
....	....	....	....	....	....	....	5	1 00
....	436	65 40	....	....	....	....	443	66 80
....	54	8 10	....	....	....	....	54	8 10
....	73	10 95	....	....	....	....	309	58 15
....	872	130 80	....	....	....	....	958	148 00
....	....	....	....	....	....	....	7,499	1,499 80
....	1,297	194 55	....	....	....	....	1,313	197 75
....	....	....	....	....	....	....	12	2 40
....	....	....	....	....	....	....	10,520	2,104 00
....	....	....	....	....	....	....	1	0 20
....Ÿ...	....	....	....	....	....	....	28,782	5,756 40
....	....	....	....	....	....	....	1,310	262 00
....	....	....	....	....	....	....	2,458	491 60
....	....	....	....	....	....	....	101	20 20
....	....	....	....	....	....	....	96	19 20
....	....	....	....	....	....	....	7	1 40
....	....	....	....	....	....	....	30,840	6,168 00
....	....	....	....	....	....	....	3	0 60
....	....	....	....	....	....	....	64,559	12,911 80
....	....	....	....	....	....	....	76	15 20
....	....	....	....	....	....	....	5	1 00
....	....	....	....	....	....	....	7,567	1,513 40
....	....	....	....	....	....	....	6,011	1,202 20
....	....	....	....	....	....	....	17,537	3,507 40
....	....	....	....	....	....	....	1	0 20
....	....	....	....	....	....	....	1,495	299 00
....	....	....	....	....	....	....	8	1 60
....	....	....	....	....	....	....	26	5 20
....	....	....	....	....	....	....	185	37 00
....	....	....	....	....	....	....	91	18 20
....	....	....	....	....	....	....	864	172 80
....	....	....	....	....	....	....	5	1 00
....	....	....	....	....	....	....	1,147	229 40
....	....	....	....	....	....	....	2,724	544 80
....	....	....	....	....	....	....	2,582	516 40
....	....	....	....	....	....	....	658	131 60
....	....	....	....	....	....	....	220,807	44,161 40
....	....	....	....	....	....	....	18	3 60
....	766,900	115,035 00	....	....	....	....	1,223,435	206,342 00
....	59,114	10,347 20	....	1,419	319 27	....	61,808	10,985 22
....	4,188	732 90	....	1	0 23	....	4,296	759 88
....	71	12 42	....	....	....	....	75	13 42
....	957	167 47	....	5	1 13	....	1,094	201 60
....	....	....	....	....	....	....	265	66 25
....	....	....	....	....	....	....	5	1 25
....	....	....	....	....	....	....	1	0 25
....	....	....	....	26	5 85	....	269	66 60
....	....	....	....	3	67	....	157	39 17
....	....	....	....	....	....	....	85	21 25
....	....	....	....	....	....	....	24	6 00
....	....	....	....	....	....	....	6	1 50
....	....	....	....	30,088	6,771 03	....	33,720	7,679 03

6 GEORGE V, A. 1916

No. 1.—GENERAL STATEMENT

Articles Imported.	Countries.	Total Imports.		Entered		
		Quantity.	Value.	General Tariff.		
				Quantity.	Value.	Duty.
DUTIABLE GOODS—*Con.*			$		$	$ cts.
Packages—*Con*	French Africa...	....	134	....		
	Germany.......	....	1,389	....	1,431	357 75
	Greece........	....	26	....	39	9 75
	Holland.......	....	6,860	....	3,446	861 50
	Italy..........	....	1,882	....	2,030	507 50
	Japan.........	....	166	....	64	16 00
	Miquelon and St. Pierre.....	....	35	....	3	0 75
	Norway.......	....	113	....	118	29 50
	Portugal......	....	349	....	214	53 50
	Russia........	....		....	76	19 00
	Spain.........	....	20,896	....	335	83 75
	Sweden.......	....	20	....	20	5 00
	Turkey.......	....	9	....	12	3 00
	Uruguay.......	....		....	1	0 25
	United States...	....	103,190	....	100,374	25,093 50
	Total......	....	234,267	....	114,096	28,524 00
Packages paying 20, 30 and 32½ per cent.	Unit'd Kingdom	....	311,165	....	5,611	1,823 57
	Australia......	....	46	....	48	15 60
	B. Guiana.....	....	1	....	1	0 32
	B. W. Indies....	....	59	....	35	11 37
	B. Straits Settlements...	....	7	....		
	Hong Kong.....	....	15,958	....	14,234	4,626 05
	Aust. Hungary..	....		....	20	6 50
	Belgium........	....	18	....	51	16 57
	China..........	....	1,668	....	1,657	538 52
	Cuba..........	....	3	....	3	0 97
	Denmark...:...	....	60	....	102	33 15
	France.........	....	76,694	....	91,045	29,589 62
	French Africa...	....	36	....	41	13 32
	Germany.......	....	2,295	....	2,180	708 50
	Greece........	....	185	....	111	36 07
	Holland.......	....	152,726	....	115,158	37,426 35
	Italy..........	....	2,281	....	2,311	751 07
	Japan.........	....	502	....	480	156 00
	Miquelon and St. Pierre.....	....	71	....	68	22 10
	Norway.......	....	179	....	176	57 20
	Portugal......	....	154	....	132	42 90
	Russia........	....	12	....	43	13 97
	Spain.........	....	6,140	....	4,925	1,600 62
	Sweden.......	....	670	....	402	130 65
	Switzerland.....	....	4	....	6	1 95
	Turkey........	....	35	....	45	14 62
	United States..	....	116,200	....	117,688	38,251 67
	Total......	....	687,169	....	356,573	115,889 23
Paints and colours— Brocade and bronze powders....	Unit'd Kingdom	....	457	....	278	76 45
	Aust.-Hungary..	....	101	....	101	27 77
	Belgium........	....	143	....	143	39 32
	France.........	....	504	....	504	138 60
	Germany......	....	8,266	....	8,153	2,242 42
	United States..	....	6,542	....	6,542	1,799 05
	Total......	....	16,013	....	15,721	4,323 61
Gold liquid paint..............	Unit'd Kingdom	....	100	....		
	France........	....	4	....	4	1 00
	Germany......	....	915	....	915	228 75
	United States..	....	7,881	....	7,881	1,970 25
	Total......	....	8,900	....	8,800	2,200 00

OF IMPORTS—*Continued.*

FOR HOME CONSUMPTION.

	Preferential Tariff.			Treaty Rates.			Total.	
Quantity.	Value.	Duty.	Quantity.	Value.	Duty.	Quantity.	Value.	DutyColl'd.
	$	$ cts.		$	$ cts.		$	$ cts.
....	....	....	....	124	27 90	....	124	27 90
....	....	....	....	....	....	....	1,431	357 75
....	....	....	....	....	....	....	39	9 75
....	....	....	....	3,966	892 35	....	7,412	1,753 85
....	....	....	....	257	57 82	....	2,287	565 32
....	....	....	....	108	24 30	....	172	40 30
....	....	....	....	32	7 20	....	35	7 95
....	....	....	....	....	....	....	118	29 50
....	....	....	....	....	....	....	214	53 50
....	....	....	....	....	....	....	76	19 00
....	....	....	....	20,305	4,568 62	....	20,640	4,652 37
....	....	....	....	....	....	....	20	5 00
....	....	....	....	....	....	....	12	3 00
....	....	....	....	....	....	....	1	0 25
....	....	....	....	....	....	....	100,374	25,093 50
....	64,330	11,259 99	....	56,334	12,676 37	....	234,760	52,460 36
....	308,698	61,739 60	....	....	....	....	314,309	63,563 17
....	....	....	....	....	....	....	48	15 60
....	....	....	....	....	....	....	1	0 32
....	67	13 40	....	....	....	....	102	24 77
....	....	....	....	....	....	....	14,234	4,626 05
....	....	....	....	....	....	....	20	6 50
....	....	....	....	....	....	....	·51	. 16 57
....	....	....	....	....	....	....	1,657	538 52
....	....	....	....	....	....	....	3	0 97
....	....	....	....	....	....	....	102	33 15
....	....	....	....	....	....	....	91,045	29,589 62
....	....	....	....	....	....	....	41	13 32
....	....	....	....	....	....	....	2,180	708 50
....	....	....	....	....	....	....	111	36 07
....	....	....	....	....	....	....	115,158	37,426 35
....	....	....	....	....	....	....	2,311	751 07
....	....	....	....	....	....	....	480	156 00
....	....	....	....	....	....	....	68	22 10
....	....	....	....	....	....	....	176	57 20
....	....	....	....	....	....	....	132	42 90
....	....	....	....	....	....	....	43	13 97
....	....	....	....	....	....	....	4,925	1,600 62
....	....	....	....	....	....	....	402	130 65
....	....	....	....	....	....	....	6	1 95
....	....	....	....	....	....	....	45	14 62
....	....	....	....	....	....	....	117,688	38,251 67
....	308,765	61,753 00	....	....	....	....	665,338	177,642 23
....	179	26 85	....	....	....	....	457	103 30
....	....	....	....	....	....	....	101	27 77
....	....	....	....	....	....	....	143	39 32
....	....	....	....	....	....	....	504	138 60
....	....	....	....	....	....	....	8,153	2,242 42
....	....	....	....	....	....	....	6,542	1,799 05
....	179	26 85	....	....	....	....	15,900	4,350 46
....	111	16 65	....	....	....	....	111	16 65
....	....	....	....	....	....	....	4	1 00
....	....	....	....	....	....	....	915	228 75
....	....	....	....	....	....	....	7,881	1,970 25
....	111	16 65	....	....	....	....	8,911	2,216 65

6 GEORGE V, A. 1916

No. 1—General Statement

Articles Imported.	Countries.	Total Imports.		Entered		
				General Tariff.		
		Quantity.	Value.	Quantity.	Value.	Duty.
DUTIABLE GOODS—*Con.*		Lb.	$	Lb.	$	$ cts.
Paints and colours—*Con.*						
Lead, white, dry..............	Unit'd Kingdom	153,728	8,299	....	....	....
	Germany.......	2,210	226	2,210	226	67 80
	United States..	128,548	6,664	128,548	6,664	1,999 20
	Total......	284,486	15,189	130,758	6,890	2,067 00
Lead, white, ground in oil......	Unit'd Kingdom	397,164	22,870	....	....	....
	United States..	54,125	2,761	54,125	2,761	1,035 54
	Total......	451,289	25,631	54,125	2,761	1,035 54
Lead, red, dry and orange mineral.	Unit'd Kingdom	263,820	9,092	263,820	9,092	454 60
	Belgium........	4,480	141	4,480	141	7 05
	Germany.......	18,748	919	18,748	919	45 95
	Holland........	45,857	1,641	45,857	1,641	82 05
	United States..	429,661	22,057	429,661	22,057	1,102 85
	Total......	762,566	33,850	762,566	33,850	1,692 50
Ochres, ochrey earths, siennas and umbers.	Unit'd Kingdom	458,176	7,196	90,552	1,181	177 15
	France.........	243,561	1,790	243,561	1,790	268 50
	Germany.......	32,848	368	56,658	785	117 75
	Italy..........	61,688	1,092	61,688	1,092	163 80
	United States..	2,005,875	17,895	2,005,875	17,895	2,684 25
	Total......	2,802,148	28,341	2,458,334	22,743	3,411 45
Zinc white...................	Unit'd Kingdom	575,373	19,793	575,373	19,793	989 65
	Belgium........	606,751	19,055	606,751	19,055	952 75
	Germany.......	1,404,013	50,268	1,404,013	50,268	2,513 40
	Holland........	494,730	17,414	494,730	17,414	870 70
	United States..	5,909,970	286,417	5,909,970	286,417	14,320 85
	Total......	8,990,837	392,947	8,990,837	392,947	19,647 35
Oxides, fire proofs, rough stuffs, fillers and colours, dry, n.o.p.	Unit'd Kingdom	1,167,795	60,127	20,478	1,333	299 92
	France.........	417	104	417	104	23 40
	Germany.......	35,284	4,315	35,284	4,315	970 87
	Holland........	680	280	680	280	63 00
	Japan..........	12	1	12	1	0 23
	United States..	5,502,107	171,836	5,501,378	171,749	38,644 27
	Total......	6,706,295	236,663	5,558,249	177,782	40,001 69
Liquid fillers, anti-corrosive and anti-fouling paints, and ground and liquid paints, n.o.p.	Unit'd Kingdom	1,183,297	123,386	26,801	1,928	578 40
	Aust.-Hungary..	100	25	100	25	7 50
	Belgium........	90	11	90	11	3 30
	France.........	2,279	619	2,279	619	185 70
	Germany.......	5,567	1,365	5,567	1,365	409 50
	Holland........	11,758	2,204	11,758	2,204	661 20
	Norway........	6,700	755	1,700	135	40 50
	United States..	2,773,306	214,541	2,772,877	214,714	64,414 20
	Total......	3,983,097	342,906	2,821,172	221,001	66,300 30
Paris green, dry..............	Unit'd Kingdom	323,525	47,772	9,425	1,165	116 50
	Germany.......	7,500	1,195	7,500	1,195	119 50
	United States..	30,907	4,690	38,107	5,841	584 10
	Total......	361,932	53,657	55,032	8,201	820 10

OF ·IMPORTS—*Continued.*

ᵣₒᵣ HOME CONSUMPTION.

Preferential Tariff.			Treaty Rates.			Total.		
Quantity.	Value.	Duty.	Quantity.	Value.	Duty.	Quantity.	Value.	DutyColl'd.
Lb.	$	$ cts.	Lb.	$	$ cts.	Lb.	$	$ cts.
156,528	8,420	1,684 00	....	....	....	156,528	8,420	1,684 00
....	....	....	....	....	....	2 210	226	67 80
....	....	....	....	....	....	128,548	6,664	1,999 20
156,528	8,420	1,684 00	....	....	....	287,286	15,310	3,751 00
418,559	24,203	7,260 90	....	....	....	418,559	24,203	7,260 90
....	....	....	....	....	....	54,125	2,761	1,035 54
418,559	24,203	7,260 90	....	....	....	472,684	26,964	8,296 44
....	....	....	....	....	....	263,820	9,092	454 60
....	....	....	....	....	....	4,480	141	7 05
....	....	....	....	....	....	18,748	919	45 95
....	....	....	....	....	....	45,857	1,641	82 05
....	....	....	....	....	....	429,661	22,057	1,102 85
....	....	....	....	....	....	762,566	33,850	1,692 50
367,624	6,015	601 50	....	....	....	458,176	7,196	778 65
....	....	....	....	....	....	243,561	1,790	268 50
....	....	....	....	....	....	56,658	785	117 75
....	....	....	....	....	....	61,688	1,092	163 80
....	....	....	....	....	....	2,005,875	17,895	2,684 25
367,624	6,015	601 50	....	....	....	2,825,958	28,758	4,012 95
....	....	....	....	....	....	575,373	19,793	989 65
....	....	....	....	....	....	606,751	19,055	952 75
....	....	....	....	....	....	1,404,013	50,268	2,513 40
....	....	....	....	....	....	494,730	17,414	870 70
....	....	....	....	....	....	5,909,970	286,417	14,320 85
....	....	....	....	....	....	8,990,837	392,947	19,647 35
1,153,258	59,408	8,911 20	....	....	....	1,173,736	60,741	9,211 12
....	....	....	....	....	....	417	104	23 40
....	....	....	....	....	....	35,284	4,315	970 87
....	....	....	....	....	....	680	280	63 00
....	....	....	....	....	....	12	1	0 23
....	....	....	....	....	....	5,501,378	171,749	38,644 27
1,153,258	59,408	8,911 20	....	....	....	6,711,507	237,190	48,912 89
1,124,098	121,176	24,235 20	....	....	....	1,150,899	123,104	24,813 60
....	....	....	....	....	....	100	25	7 50
....	....	....	....	....	....	90	11	3 30
....	....	....	....	....	....	2,279	619	185 70
....	....	....	....	....	....	5,567	1,365	409 50
....	....	....	....	....	....	11,758	2,204	661 20
....	....	....	....	....	....	1,700	135	40 50
....	....	....	....	....	....	2,772,877	214,714	64,414 20
1,124,098	121,176	24,235 20	....	....	....	3,945,270	342,177	90,535 50
314,100	46,607	2,330 35	....	....	....	323,525	47,772	2,446 85
....	....	....	....	....	....	7,500	1,195	119 50
....	....	....	....	....	....	38,107	5,841	584 10
314,100	46,607	2,330 35	....	....	....	369,132	54,808	3,150 45

11—ii—13½

6 GEORGE V, A. 1916

No. 1.—GENERAL STATEMENT

Articles Imported.	Countries.	TOTAL IMPORTS.		ENTERED		
				General Tariff.		
		Quantity.	Value.	Quantity.	Value.	Duty.
DUTIABLE GOODS—*Con.*		Gal.	$	Gal.	$	$ cts.
Paints, and Colours—*Con.*						
Paints and colours ground in spirits, and all spirit varnishes and lacquers.	Unit'd Kingdom	641	895	677	947	708 50
	United States..	3,225	8,533	3,225	8,533	3,656 50
	Total......	3,866	9,428	3,902	9,480	4,365 00
		Lb.		Lb.		
Putty..........................	Unit'd Kingdom	50,184	854	448	47	11 75
	United States..	387,355	8,170	387,355	8,170	2,042 50
	Total......	437,539	9,024	387,803	8,217	2,054 25
		No.		No.		
Paintings in oil or water colours and pastels, when valued at less than $20 each.	Unit'd Kingdom	191	1,106	18	246	61 50
	Germany........	1	6	1	6	1 50
	Holland........	202	102	202	102	25 50
	Italy...........	16	19	16	19	4 75
	United States..	1,138	1,052	1,138	1,052	263 00
	Total......	1,548	2,285	1,375	1,425	356 25
Paper and manufactures of—						
Albumenized and other papers and films, chemically prepared for photographers' use.	Unit'd Kingdom	....	82,853	....	189	56 70
	France..........	....	230	....	230	69 00
	Germany........	....	325	....	325	97 50
	United States..	....	111,733	....	111,083	33,324 90
	Total......	....	195,141	....	111,827	33,548 10
Bags or sacks, printed or not....	Unit'd Kingdom	....	13,299	....	77	21 17
	France..........	....	8	....	8	2 20
	Germany........	....	1,266	....	1,266	348 15
	Holland........	....	103	....	103	28 32
	Japan..........	....	10	....	10	2 75
	United States...	....	32,016	....	32,016	8,804 90
	Total......	....	46,702	....	33,480	9,207 49
		Packs.		Packs.		
Cards for playing..............	Unit'd Kingdom	616,940	64,673	4,086	366	326 88
	Hong Kong.....	1,470	42	1,090	30	87 20
	China..........	30	1	30	1	2 40
	France..........	1,020	204	876	169	70 08
	Japan..........	7,840	454	7,840	454	627 20
	United States...	339,079	43,690	346,135	44,636	27,690 80
	Total......	966,379	109,064	360,057	45,656	28,804 56
Card board not pasted or coated	Unit'd Kingdom	....	3,722	....	65	16 25
	Holland........	....	653	....	653	163 25
	United States...	....	94,421	....	94,421	23,605 25
	Total......	....	98,796	....	95,139	23,784 75
		M.		M.		
Envelopes.....................	Unit'd Kingdom	13,553	21,142	157	308	107 80
	Hong Kong.....	152	79	152	79	27 65
	Germany.......	192	623	192	623	218 05
	Holland........	16	46	16	46	16 10
	Japan..........	12	15	12	15	5 25
	Switzerland.....	1	5	1	5	1 75
	United States...	75,543	88,341	75,786	88,444	30,955 40
	Total......	89,469	110,251	76,316	89,520	31,332 00

OF IMPORTS—*Continued.*

FOR HOME CONSUMPTION.

Preferential Tariff.			Treaty Rates.			Total.		
Quantity.	Value.	Duty.	Quantity.	Value.	Duty.	Quantity.	Value.	DutyColl'd.
Gal.	$	$ cts.	Gal.	$	$ cts.	Gal.	$	$ cts.
....	....	....	....	....	....	677	947	708 50
....	....	....	....	....	....	3,225	8,533	3,656 50
....	....	....	....	....	....	3,902	9,480	4,365 00
Lb. 49,736	807	141 24	Lb.			Lb. 50,184	854	152 99
....	....	....				387,355	8,170	2,042 50
49,736	807	141 24	....	....	....	437,539	9,024	2,195 49
No. 173	860	129 00	No.			No. 191	1,106	190 50
....	....	....				1	6	1 50
....	....	....				202	102	25 50
....	....	....				16	19	- 4 75
....	....	....				1,138	1,052	263 00
173	860	129 00	....	....	....	1,548	2,285	485 25
....	82,664	12,399 60	....	....	....	....	82,853	12,456 30
....	....	....					230	69 00
....	....	....					325	97 50
....	....	....					111,083	33,324 90
....	82,664	12,399 60	....	....	....	....	194,491	45,947 70
....	13,222	1,983 30					13,299	2,004 47
....	....	....					8	2 20
....	....	....					1,266	348 15
....	....	....					103	28 32
....	....	....					10	2 75
....	....	....					32 016	8,804 90
....	13,222	1,983 30	....				46,70:	11,190 79
Packs. 581,498	60,912	29,074 90	Packs.			Packs. 585,584	61,278	29,401 78
....	....	....				1,090	30	87 20
....	....	....				30	1	2 40
....	....	....				876	169	70 08
....	....	....				7,840	454	627 20
....	....	....				346,135	44,636	27,690 80
581,498	60,912	29,074 90	....	....	....	941,555	106,568	57,879 46
....	3,657	548 55	....			....	3,722	564 80
....	....	....					653	163 25
....	....	....					94,421	23,605 25
....	3,657	548 55	....	....	....	....	98,796	24,333 30
M. 13,284	20,364	4,582 15	M.			M. 13,441	20,672	4,689 95
....	....	....				152	79	27 65
....	....	....				192	623	218 05
....	....	....				16	46	16 10
....	....	....				12	15	5 25
....	....	....				1	5	1 75
....	....	....				75,786	88,444	30,955 40
13,284	20,364	4,582 15	....	....	....	89,600	109,884	35,914 15

6 GEORGE V, A. 1916

No. 1.—General Statement

Articles Imported.	Countries.	Total Imports.		Entered		
				General Tariff.		
		Quantity.	Value.	Quantity.	Value.	Duty.
			$		$	$ cts.
DUTIABLE GOODS—*Con.*						
Paper, and mfrs. of—*Con.*						
Felt board....................	United States...	....	4,998	....	5,217	1,304 25
		Rolls		Rolls		
Hangings of wall paper, includ-	Unit'd Kingdom	204,863	32,955	2,891	1,093	382 55
ing borders.	Belgium........	3,640	1,011	3,640	1,011	353 85
	France.........	1,207	493	1,207	493	172 55
	Germany.......	22,653	1,916	22,653	1,916	670 60
	Japan..........	1,830	2,570	2,289	2,515	880 25
	United States...	2,692,256	226,000	2,692,256	226,000	79,100 00
	Total.......	2,926,449	264,945	2,724,936	233,028	81,559 80
Leather board, leatheroid and	Unit'd Kingdom	....	16	....	....	....
manufactures of, n.o.p.	United States...	....	16,079	....	16,079	4,019 75
	Total......	....	16,095	....	16,079	4,019 75
Millboard not coated or pasted.	Unit'd Kingdom	....	2,050	....	213	53 25
	France.........	....	31	....	31	7 75
	Holland........	....	95	....	95	23 75
	United States...	....	117,977	....	117,977	29,494 25
	Total......	....	120,153	....	118,316	29,579 00
Union collar cloth paper in rolls	United States...	....	628	....	628	94 20
or sheets not glossed or finish-						
ed.						
Union collar cloth paper in rolls	United States...	....	15,437	....	15,437	3,087 40
or sheets glossed or finished..						
Pads not printed, papier mache	Unit'd Kingdom	....	1,245	....	68	23 80
ware, n.o.p.	Germany.......	....	130	....	130	45 50
	United States...	....	10,642	....	10,642	3,724 70
	Total......	....	12,017	....	10,840	3,794 00
Paper, manufactures of, n.o.p...	Unit'd Kingdom	....	389,632	....	27,130	9,495 50
	Hong Kong.....	....	7,561	....	7,590	2,656 50
	Aust.-Hungary..	....	2,970	....	3,214	1,124 90
	Belgium........	....	14,084	....	13,845	4,845 75
	China..........	....	902	....	902	315 70
	Denmark.......	....	4	....	4	1 40
	France.........	....	84,177	....	84,304	29,506 40
	Germany.......	....	86,375	....	86,862	30,401 70
	Holland........	....	173	....	173	60 55
	Italy..........	....	36	....	36	12 60
	Japan..........	....	7,351	....	7,064	2,472 40
	Norway........	....	1,369	....	1,369	479 15
	Spain..:......	....	....	....	3	1 05
	Sweden........	....	215	....	215	75 25
	Switzerland.....	....	120	....	81	28 35
	United States...	....	1,325,809	....	1,325,477	463,916 95
	Total......	....	1,920,778	....	1,558,269	545,394 15
Paper matting when for use in	United States...	....	2,570	....	2,570	642 50
Canadian manufactures.						
Patterns, boot and shoe, manu-	United States...	....	13,684	....	13,684	2,052 60
factures of paper.						

SESSIONAL PAPER No. 11

OF IMPORTS—*Continued.*

FOR HOME CONSUMPTION.

Preferential Tariff.			Treaty Rates.			Total.		
Quantity.	Value.	Duty.	Quantity.	Value.	Duty.	Quantity.	Value.	DutyColl'd.
	$	$ cts.		$	$ cts.		$	$ cts.
....	....	....	....	....	....	....	5,217	1,304 25
Rolls 199,919	31,214	7,023 37	Rolls		....	Rolls 202,810	32,307	7,405 92
....	....	....	....		....	3,640	1,011	353 85
....	....	....	....		....	1,207	493	172 55
....	....	....	....		....	22,653	1,916	670 60
....	....	....	....		....	2,289	2,515	880 25
....	....	....	....		....	2,692 256	226,000	79,100 00
199,919	31,214	7,023 37	....	....	....	2,924,855	264,242	88,583 17
....	16	2 40	....		....	....	16	2 40
....	....	....	....		....	....	16,079	4,019 75
....	16	2 40	....	....	....	....	16,095	4,022 15
....	1,837	275 55	....		....	....	2,050	328 80
....	....	....	....		....	....	31	7 75
....	....	....	....		....	....	95	23 75
....	....	....	....		....	....	117,977	29,494 25
....	1,837	275 55	....	....	....	....	120,153	29,854 55
....	....	....					628	94 20
....	....	....	....	....	....	....	15,437	3,087 40
....	1,177	264 86	....		....	....	1,245	288 66
....	....	....	....		....	....	130	45 50
....	....	....	....		....	....	10,642	3,724 70
....	1,177	264 86	....	....	....	....	12,017	4,058 86
....	361,379	81,311 47	....		....	....	388,509	90,806 97
....	....	....	....		....	....	7,590	2,656 50
....	....	....	....		....	....	3,214	1,124 90
....	....	....	....		....	....	13,845	4,845 75
....	....	....	....		....	....	902	315 70
....	....	....	....		....	....	4	1 40
....	....	....	....		....	....	84,304	29,506 40
....	....	....	....		....	....	86,862	30,401 70
....	....	....	....		....	....	173	60 55
....	....	....	....		....	....	36	12 60
....	....	....	....		....	....	7,064	2,472 40
....	....	....	....		....	....	1,369	479 15
....	....	....	....		....	....	3	1 05
....	....	....	....		....	....	215	75 25
....	....	....	....		....	....	81	28 35
....	....	....	....		....	....	1,325,477	463,916 95
....	361,379	81,311 47	....	....	....	....	1,919,648	626,705 62
....	....	....	....	....	....	....	2,570	642 50
....	....	....	....	....	....	....	13,684	2,052 60

6 GEORGE V, A. 1916

No. 1.—General Statement

Articles Imported.	Countries.	Total Imports.		Entered		
				General Tariff.		
		Quantity.	Value.	Quantity.	Value.	Duty.
DUTIABLE GOODS—*Con.*		Lb.	$	Lb.	$	$ cts.
Paper, and mfrs. of—*Con.*						
Printing paper (for newspapers) in sheets or rolls, valued at not more than 2½c. per pound.	Unit'd Kingdom	18,300	362	13,000	259	38 85
	United States...	1,458,569	29,234	1,414,014	28,343	4,251 45
	Total.......	1,476,869	29,596	1,427,014	28,602	4,290 30
Printing paper, n.o.p............	Unit'd Kingdom	3,157,118	169,153	97,693	3,486	871 50
	Belgium........	12,308	875	12,308	875	218 75
	France.........	250	11	250	11	2 75
	Germany.......	42,645	2,080	42,645	2,080	520 00
	Japan..........	484	42	484	42	10 50
	Norway........	7,300	205	7,300	205	51 25
	Sweden........	11,697	491	11,697	491	122 75
	United States...	4,713,732	256,221	4,713,732	256,221	64,055 25
	Total.......	7,945,534	429,078	4,886,109	263,411	65,852 75
Ruled and border and coated papers; boxed papers and pape-teries.	Unit'd Kingdom	....	56,222	....	3,541	1,239 35
	Hong Kong.....	....	52	....	52	18 20
	Belgium........	....	9,056	....	9,056	3,169 60
	China..........	....	187	....	187	65 45
	France.........	....	1,262	....	1,262	441 70
	Germany.......	....	4,502	...·......	4,502	1,575 70
	Holland........	....	108	....	108	37 80
	Japan..........	....	556	....	556	194 60
	United States...	....	180,532	....	180,556	63,194 60
	Total.......	....	252,477	....	199,820	69,937 00
Straw board not pasted or coated.	Unit'd Kingdom	14,166	178	14,166	178	44 50
	Aust.-Hungary..	22,880	320	22,880	320	80 00
	Holland........	40,460	596	40,460	596	149 00
	United States...	5,328,247	74,320	5,328,247	74,320	18,580 00
	Total.......	5,405,753	75,414	5,405,753	75,414	18,853 50
Tarred and other building papers, n.o.p.	Unit'd Kingdom	....	407	....	....	....
	United States...	....	316,793	....	317,349	79,337 25
	Total.......	....	317,200	....	317,349	79,337 25
Window blinds of paper of all kinds.	United States...	....	20	....	20	7 00
Wrapping paper................	Unit'd Kingdom	416,636	22,347	144,153	6,022	1,505 50
	Hong Kong.....	2,888	128	2,888	128	32 00
	Aust.-Hungary..	1,018	99	1,018	99	24 75
	Belgium........	79,374	4,404	79,374	4,404	1,101 00
	Denmark.......	72,485	1,854	72,485	1,854	463 50
	France.........	1,140	64	1,219	68	17 00
	Germany.......	159,263	8,639	159,263	8,639	2,159 75
	Holland........	10,663	555	10,663	555	138 75
	Japan..........	1,395	124	1,395	124	31 00
	Norway........	327,343	9,954	327,343	9,869	2,467 25
	Sweden........	526,682	15,981	462,417	14,310	3,577 50
	United States...	6,217,052	130,643	6,209,612	130,374	32,593 50
	Total.......	7,815,939	194,792	7,471,830	176,446	44,111 50

OF IMPORTS—*Continued.*

FOR HOME CONSUMPTION.

Preferential Tariff.			Treaty Rates.			Total.		
Quantity.	Value.	Duty.	Quantity.	Value.	Duty.	Quantity.	Value.	DutyColl'd.
Lb.	$	$ cts.	Lb.	$	$ cts.	Lb.	$	$ cts.
5,300	103	10 30	....	....	....	18,300	362	49 15
....	....	....	....	....	....	1,414,014	28,343	4,251 45
5,300	103	10 30	....	....	....	1,432,314	28,705	4,300 60
3,061,645	⁄165,894	24,884 10	....	....	....	3,159,338	169,380	25,755 60
....	....	....	....	....	....	12,308	875	218 75
....	....	....	....	....	....	250	11	2 75
....	....	....	....	....	....	42,645	2,080	520 00
....	....	....	....	....	....	484	42	10 50
....	....	....	....	....	....	7,300	205	51 25
....	....	....	....	....	....	11,697	491	122 75
....	....	....	....	....	....	4,713,732	256,221	64,055 25
3,061,645	165,894	24,884 10	....	....	....	7,947,754	429,305	90,736 85
....	53,349	12,004 04	....	....	....	....	56,890	13,243 39
....	....	....	....	....	....	....	52	18 20
....	....	....	....	....	....	....	9,056	3,169 60
....	....	....	....	....	....	....	187	65 45
....	....	....	....	....	....	....	1,262	441 70
....	....	....	....	....	....	....	4,502	1,575 70
....	....	....	....	....	....	....	108	37 80
....	....	....	....	....	....	....	556	194 60
....	....	....	....	....	....	....	180,556	63,194 60
....	53,349	12,004 04	....	....	....	....	253,169	81,941 04
....	....	....	....	....	....	14,166	178	44 50
....	....	....	....	....	....	22,880	320	80 00
....	....	....	....	....	....	40,460	596	149 00
....	....	....	....	....	....	5,328,247	74,320	18,580 00
....	....	....	....	....	....	5,405,753	75,414	18,853 50
....	407	61 05	....	....	....	....	407	61 05
....	....	....	....	....	....	....	317,349	79,337 25
....	407	61 05	....	....	....	....	317,756	79,398 30
....	....	....	....	....	....	....	20	7 00
272,448	16,324	2,448 60	....	....	....	416,601	22,346	3,954 10
....	....	....	....	....	....	2,888	128	32 00
....	....	....	....	....	....	1,018	99	24 75
....	....	....	....	....	....	79,374	4,404	1,101 00
....	....	....	....	....	....	72,485	1,854	463 50
....	....	....	....	....	....	1,219	68	17 00
....	....	....	....	....	....	159,263	8,639	2,159 75
....	....	....	....	....	....	10,663	555	138 75
....	....	....	....	....	....	1,395	124	31 00
....	....	....	....	....	....	327,343	9,869	2,467 25
....	....	....	....	....	....	462,417	14,310	3,577 50
....	....	....	....	....	....	6,209,612	130,374	32,593 50
272,448	16,324	2,448 60	....	....	....	7,744,278	192,770	46,560 10

6 GEORGE V, A. 1916

No. 1.—GENERAL STATEMENT

Articles Imported.	Countries.	Total Imports.		Entered		
		Quantity.	Value.	General Tariff.		
				Quantity.	Value.	Duty.
			$		$	$ cts.
DUTIABLE GOODS—*Con.*						
Paper and mfrs. of—*Con.*						
All kinds, n.o.p.	Unit'd Kingdom	....	393,167	....	23,759	5,939 75
	Hong Kong....	....	214	....	214	53 50
	Aust.-Hungary..	....	2,744	....	6,265	1,566 25
	Belgium........	....	33,366	....	33,366	8,341 50
	China..........	....	202	....	202	50 50
	Denmark......	....	631	....	631	157 75
	France........	....	18,578	....	39,132	9,783 00
	Germany......	....	43,295	....	41,739	10,434 75
	Holland.......	....	1,545	....	1,545	386 25
	Japan..........	....	4,157	....	4,649	1,162 25
	Norway.......	....	29,857	....	29,857	7,464 25
	Russia........	....	174	....	174	43 50
	Sweden.......	....	37,720	....	37,858	9,464 50
	Switzerland....	....	371	....	423	105 75
	United States...	....	863,273	....	864,142	216,035 50
	Total......	....	1,429,294	....	1,083,956	270,989 00
Pencils, lead...	Unit'd Kingdom	....	33,820	....	5,987	1,646 45
	Hong Kong.....	....	40	....	40	11 00
	Aust.-Hungary..	....	7,242	....	708	194 70
	Belgium........	....	343	....	316	86 90
	France........	....	472	....	198	54 44
	Germany......	....	34,797	....	34,736	9,552 40
	Holland.......	....	6	....	6	1 65
	Japan.........	....	25	....	....	
	Switzerland....	....	58	....		
	United States...	....	184,581	....	184,859	50,837 19
	Total......	....	261,384	....	226,850	62,384 73
Pens, penholders and rulers of all kinds.	Unit'd Kingdom	....	62,313	....	2,301	632 77
	Hong Kong.....	....	205	....	205	56 37
	Aust.-Hungary..	....	741	....	282	77 55
	Belgium........	....	265	....	265	72 87
	China..........	....	18	....	18	4 95
	France........	....	179	....	153	42 07
	Germany......	....	2,138	....	2,138	587 95
	Japan.........	....	53	....	1	0 27
	United States...	....	66,983	....	66,983	18,421 18
	Total......	....	132,895	....	72,346	19,895 98
Perfumery, non-alcoholic, viz.— Hair oil, tooth and other powders and washes, pomatums, pastes and all other perfumed preparations, D.O.P., used for the hair, mouth or skin.	Unit'd Kingdom	....	42,050	....	4,624	1,502 80
	Australia......			....	105	34 12
	Hong Kong.....	....	344	....	344	111 80
	Aust.-Hungary..	....	6	....	214	69 55
	Belgium........	....	250	....	250	81 25
	China..........	....	7	....	7	2 27
	France........	....	50,333	....	50,877	16,535 02
	Germany......	....	9,746	....	9,777	3,177 52
	Holland.......	....	36	....	36	11 70
	Japan.........	....	1,467	....	1,467	476 77
	Sweden.......	....	20	....	20	6 50
	United States...	....	347,065	....	345,585	112,318 43
	Total......	....	451,324	....	413,306	134,327 73
Photographic dry plates..........	Unit'd Kingdom	....	41,830	....	1,186	355 80
	France........	....	11	....	15	4 50
	Germany......	....	238	....	238	71 40
	United States...	....	13,509	....	13,509	4,052 70
	Total......	....	55,588	....	14,948	4,484 40

OF IMPORTS—*Continued.*

FOR HOME CONSUMPTION.

	Preferential Tariff.			Treaty Rates.			Total.	
Quantity.	Value.	Duty.	Quantity.	Value.	Duty.	Quantity.	Value.	DutyColl'd.
	$	$ cts.		$	$ cts.		$	$ cts.
....	371,116	55,667 40	....	....	....	....	394,875	61,607 15
....	....	....	....	....	....	....	214	53 50
....							6,265	1,566 25
....							33,366	8,341 50
....							202	50 50
....							631	157 75
....							39,132	9,783 00
....							41,739	10,434 75
....							1,545	386 25
....							4,649	1,162 25
....							29,857	7,464 25
....							174	43 50
....							37,858	9,464 50
....							423	105 75
....							864,142	216,035 50
....	371,116	55,667 40	....	....	....	....	1,455,072	326,656 40
....	17,569	2,635 35	....	10,200	2,550 00	....	33,756	6,831 80
....	....	....					40	11 00
....				6,534	1,633 50	...	7,242	1,828 20
....				27	6 75		343	93 65
....				285	71 25		483	125 69
....				....	....		34,736	9,552 40
....							6	1 65
....				25	6 25		25	6 25
....				58	14 50		58	14 50
....				....	....		184,859	50,837 19
....	17,569	2,635 35	....	17,129	4,282 25	....	261,548	69,302 33
....	59,825	8,973 75	....	248	62 00	....	62,374	9,668 52
....							205	56 37
....				459	114 75		741	192 30
....							265	72 87
....							18	4 95
....				26	6 50		179	48 57
....							2,138	587 95
....				52	13 00		53	13 27
....							66,983	18,421 18
....	59,825	8,973 75	....	785	196 25	....	132,956	29,065 98
....	36,272	9,068 00	....	....	....	....	40,896	10,570 80
....							105	34 12
....							344	111 80
....							214	69 55
....							250	81 25
....							7	2 27
....							50,877	16,535 02
....							9,777	3,177 52
....							36	11 70
....							1,467	476 77
....							20	6 50
....							345,585	112,318 43
....	36,272	9,068 00	....	....	....	....	449,578	143,395 73
....	40,644	8,128 80	....	....	....	....	41,830	8,484 60
....							15	4 50
....							238	71 40
....							13,509	4,052 70
....	40,644	8,128 80	....	....	....	....	55,592	12,613 20

6 GEORGE V, A. 1916

No. 1.—General Statement

Articles Imported.	Countries.	Total Imports.		Entered		
				General Tariff.		
		Quantity.	Value.	Quantity.	Value.	Duty.
DUTIABLE GOODS—*Con.*			$		$	$ cts.
Picture and photograph frames of any material.	Unit'd Kingdom	....	21,364	....	954	286 20
	B. India.........	....	9	....	....	....
	Hong Kong....	....	88	....	17	5 10
	Aust.-Hungary..	....	24	....	....	....
	China............	....	3	....	3	0 90
	France.........	....	1,518	....	236	70 80
	Germany......	....	1,505	....	1,505	451 50
	Holland.......	....	115	....	115	34 50
	Italy..........	....	139	....	139	41 70
	Japan..........	....	1,906	....	18	5 40
	Sweden.........	....	20	....	20	6 00
	United States...	....	84,409	....	84,072	25,221 60
	Total......	....	111,100	....	87,079	26,123 70
Pickles, viz.—		Gal.		Gal.		
Pickles in bottles, jars or similar vessels.	Unit'd Kingdom	205,464	202,526	447	482	168 70
	B. W. Indies....	13	24	13	24	8 40
	Hong Kong....	2,082	1,153	2,082	1,153	403 55
	Belgium.......	20	71	....	....	....
	China..........	729	278	729	278	97 30
	France.........	1,900	2,214	9	14	4 90
	Germany......	6	1	6	1	0 35
	Holland........	207	211	....	....	....
	Italy...........	704	597	604	597	208 95
	Japan..........	499	407	326	206	72 10
	United States...	12,694	14,561	12,769	14,245	4,985 75
	Total......	224,318	222,043	16,985	17,000	5,950 00
Pickles in bulk.................	Hong Kong.....	2,123	498	2,123	498	174 30
	China..........	39	17	39	17	5 95
	France.........	....	4	....	4	1 40
	Japan..........	3,366	1,014	941	301	105 35
	United States...	18,511	4,795	18,618	4,824	1,688 40
	Total......	24,039	6,328	21,721	5,644	1,975 40
Olives, in brine, not bottled....	Hong Kong.....	936	698	936	698	209 40
	China..........	38	24	38	24	7 20
	France.........	95	84	95	84	25 20
	Greece.........	9,485	4,787	12,996	6,280	1,884 00
	Italy..........	48	17	48	17	5 10
	Spain..........	22,593	9,098	24,490	9,267	2,780 10
	United States...	20,442	13,106	19,147	11,680	3,504 00
	Total......	53,637	27,814	57,750	28,050	8,415 00
Olives, in brine, by manufacturers, for the manufacture of pickles.	Spain..........	57,321	33,198	53,519	32,899	6,579 80
	United States...	865	617	865	617	123 40
	Total......	58,186	33,815	54,384	33,516	6,703 20
Plants and trees, viz.—		No.		No.		
Apple trees....................	Unit'd Kingdom	491	101	47	6	1 41
	Holland........	19	2	....	....	....
	United States...	131,911	14,768	131,911	14,768	3,957 33
	Total......	132,421	14,871	131,958	14,774	3,958 74
Cherry trees.................	Unit'd Kingdom	12	2	....	....	....
	United States...	62,383	12,264	62,383	12,264	1,871 49
	Total......	62,395	12,266	62,383	12,264	1,871 49

OF IMPORTS—*Continued.*

FOR HOME CONSUMPTION.

Preferential Tariff.			Treaty Rates.			Total.		
Quantity.	Value.	Duty.	Quantity.	Value.	Duty.	Quantity.	Value.	DutyColl'd.
	$	$ cts.		$	$ cts.		$	$ cts.
....	20,469	4,093 80	....	25	6 87	....	21,448	4,386 87
....	9	1 80	....	....	....	....	9	1 80
....	....	....	....	71	19 52	....	88	24 62
....	....	....	....	24	6 60	....	24	6 60
....	....	....	....	....	....	....	3	0 90
....	....	....	....	1,282	352 55	....	1,518	423 35
....	....	....	....	....	....	....	1,505	451 50
....	....	....	....	....	....	....	115	34 50
....	....	....	....	....	....	....	139	41 70
....	....	....	....	1,894	520 95	....	1,912	526 35
....	....	....	....	....	....	....	20	6 00
....	....	....	....	....	....	....	84,072	25,221 60
....	20,478	4,095 60	....	3,296	906 49	....	110,853	31,125 79
Gal. 203,721	201,509	50,377 25	Gal. 3	6	1 95	Gal. 204,171	201,997	50,547 90
....	....	....	....	....	....	13	24	8 40
....	....	....	....	....	....	2,082	1,153	403 55
....	....	....	20	71	23 07	20	71	23 07
....	....	....	....	....	....	729	278	97 30
....	....	....	1,352	1,989	646 53	1,361	2,003	651 43
....	....	....	....	....	....	6	1	0 35
....	....	....	207	211	68 57	207	211	68 57
....	....	....	....	....	....	604	597	208 95
....	....	....	173	201	65 32	499	407	137 42
....	....	....	....	....	....	12,769	14,245	4,985 75
203,721	201,509	50,377 25	1,755	2,478	805 44	222,461	220,987	57,132 69
....	....	....	....	....	....	2,123	498	174 30
....	....	....	....	....	....	39	17	5 95
....	....	....	....	....	....	4	....	1 40
....	....	....	2,425	713	231 72	3,366	1,014	337 07
....	....	....	....	....	....	18,618	4,824	1,688 40
....	....	....	2,425	713	231 72	24,146	6,357	2,207 12
....	....	....	....	....	....	936	698	209 40
....	....	....	....	....	....	38	24	7 20
....	....	....	....	....	....	95	84	25 20
....	....	....	....	....	....	12,996	6,280	1,884 00
....	....	....	....	....	....	48	17	5 10
....	....	....	....	....	....	24,490	9,267	2,780 10
....	....	....	....	....	....	19,147	11,680	3,504 00
....	....	....	....	....	....	57,750	28,050	8,415 00
....	....	....	....	....	....	53,519	32,899	6,579 80
....	....	....	....	....	....	865	617	123 40
....	....	....	....	....	....	54,384	33,516	6,703 20
No. 444	95	8 88	No.	....	....	No. 491	101	10 29
....	....	....	19	2	0 48	19	2	0 48
....	....	....	....	....	....	131,911	14,768	3,957 33
444	95	8 88	19	2	0 48	132,421	14,871	3,968 10
....	....	....	12	2	0 30	12	2	0 30
....	....	....	....	....	....	62,383	12,264	1,871 49
....	....	....	12	2	0 30	62,395	12,266	1,871 79

6 GEORGE V, A. 1916

No. 1.—GENERAL STATEMENT

Articles Imported.	Countries.	TOTAL IMPORTS.		ENTERED		
				General Tariff.		
		Quantity.	Value.	Quantity.	Value.	Duty.
DUTIABLE GOODS—*Con.*		No.	$	No.	$	$ cts.
Plants and trees—*Con.*						
Currant bushes................	Unit'd Kingdom	30	1	....	....	....
	France........	500	18	....	....	....
	Holland........	375	13	375	13	2 60
	United States...	52,457	1,439	52,457	1,439	287 80
	Total......	53,362	1,471	52,832	1,452	290 40
Florist stock, viz.: palms, ferns,	Unit'd Kingdom	....	1,509	....	226	56 50
rubber plants (ficus), gladiolus,	Belgium........	....	8,695	....	5,399	1,349 75
cannas, dahlias and paeonies.	France........	....	40	....	33	8 25
	Germany......	....	58	....	58	14 50
	Holland........	....	6,976	....	6,323	1,580 75
	Japan....	....	315	....	315	78 75
	United States...	....	19,813	....	19,813	4,953 25
	Total......	....	37,406	....	32,167	8,041 75
Gooseberry bushes.............	Unit'd Kingdom	27,320	934	3,200	156	31 20
	France........	25	2	25	2	0 40
	Holland........	100	7	100	7	1 40
	United States...	41,143	2,172	41,143	2,172	434 40
	Total......	68,588	3,115	44,468	2,337	467 40
Grape vines.....................	Unit'd Kingdom	12	31	....	....	....
	France........	388	44	388	44	8 80
	United States...	89,126	2,299	89,126	2,299	459 80
	Total......	89,526	2,374	89,514	2,343	468 60
Peach trees and June buds......	Unit'd Kingdom	15	13	....	....	....
	United States...	51,489	4,724	51,489	4,724	1,544 67
	Total......	51,504	4,737	51,489	4,724	1,544 67
Pear trees.....................	Unit'd Kingdom	1,021	154	903	115	27 09
	France........	39	4	39	4	1 17
	United States...	23,645	3,752	23,645	3,752	709 35
	Total......	24,705	3,910	24,587	3,871	737 61
Plum trees....................	Unit'd Kingdom	71	24	....	....	....
	United States...	49,622	16,555	49,622	16,555	1,488 66
	Total......	49,693	16,579	49,622	16,555	1,488 66.
Raspberry bushes..............	Holland........	1,000	21	1,000	21	4 20
	United States...	207,378	2,894	207,378	2,894	578 80
	Total......	208,378	2,915	208,378	2,915	583 00
Rose bushes...................	Unit'd Kingdom	73,636	6,903	4,832	811	162 20
	Belgium........	150	14	150	14	2 80
	France........	153	31	....	....	....
	Holland........	83,960	5,968	82,280	5,842	1,168 40
	United States...	42,437	4,753	42,437	4,753	950 60
	Total......	200,336	17,669	129,699	11,420	2,284 00

OF IMPORTS—*Continued.*

FOR HOME CONSUMPTION.

Preferential Tariff.			Treaty Rates.			Total.		
Quantity.	Value.	Duty.	Quantity.	Value.	Duty.	Quantity.	Value.	DutyColl'd.
No.	$	$ cts.	No.	$	$ cts.	No.	$	$ cts.
30	1	0 13	....	....	....	30	1	0 13
....	....	....	500	18	3 15	500	18	3 15
....	....	....	....	....	....	375	13	2 60
....	....	....	....	....	....	52,457	1,439	287 80
30	1	0 13	500	18	3 15	53,362	1,471	293 68
....	1,012	151 80	....	271	60 98	....	1,509	269 28
....	....	....	....	3,296	741 63	....	8,695	2,091 38
....	....	....	....	7	1 57	....	40	9 82
....	....	....	....	....	....	....	58	14 50
....	....	....	....	653	146 93	....	6,976	1,727 68
....	....	....	....	....	....	....	315	78 75
....	....	....	....	....	....	....	19,813	4,953 25
....	1,012	151 80	....	4,227	951 11	....	37,406	9,144 66
24,084	775	96 89	36	3	0 55	27,320	934	128 64
....	....	....	....	....	....	25	2	0 40
....	....	....	....	....	....	100	7	1 40
....	....	....	....	....	....	41,143	2,172	434 40
24,084	775	96 89	36	3	0 55	68,588	3,115	564 84
12	31	3 88	....	....	....	12	31	3 88
....	....	....	....	....	....	388	44	8 80
....	....	....	....	....	....	89,126	2,299	459 80
12	31	3 88	....	....	....	89,526	2,374	472 48
15	13	0 30	....	....	....	15	13	0 30
....	....	....	....	....	....	51,489	4,724	1,544 67
15	13	0 30	....	....	....	51,504	4,737	1,544 97
118	39	2 36	....	....	....	1,021	154	29 45
....	....	....	....	....	....	39	4	1 17
....	....	....	....	....	....	23,645	3,752	709 35
118	39	2 36	....	....	....	24,705	3,910	739 97
71	24	1 42	....	....	....	71	24	1 42
....	....	....	....	....	....	49,622	16,555	1,488 66
71	24	1 42	....	....	....	49,693	16,579	1,490 08
....	....	....	....	....	....	1,000	21	4 20
....	....	....	....	....	....	207,378	2,894	578 80
....	....	....	....	....	....	208,378	2,915	583 00
68,804	6,092	761 56	....	....	....	73,636	6,903	923 76
....	....	....	....	....	....	150	14	2 80
....	....	....	153	31	5 42	153	31	5 42
....	....	....	1,680	126	22 07	83,960	5,968	1,190 47
....	....	....	....	....	....	42,437	4,753	950 60
68,804	6,092	761 56	1,833	157	27 49	200,336	17,669	3,073 05

6 GEORGE V, A. 1916

No. 1.—General Statement

Articles Imported.	Countries.	Total Imports.		Entered		
		Quantity.	Value.	General Tariff.		
				Quantity.	Value.	Duty.
DUTIABLE GOODS—*Con.*		No.	$	No.	$	$ cts.
Plants and trees—*Con.*						
Quince trees...................	Holland.........	153	136	153	136	4 59
	United States...	1,704	296	1,704	296	51 12
	Total.......	1,857	432	1,857	432	55 71
Fruit plants, n.o.p.............	Unit'd Kingdom	240	13	....	....	....
	Holland.........	241	22	241	22	4 40
	United States...	145,870	2,045	145,870	2,045	409 00
	Total.......	146,351	2,080	146,111	2,067	413 40
Trees, plants and shrubs known	Unit'd Kingdom	....	6,223	....	1,604	320 80
as nursery stock, n.o.p.	Newfoundland..	....	67	....	67	13 40
	Belgium.........	....	2,052	....	1,641	328 20
	France..........	....	5,474	....	3,607	721 40
	Germany.......	....	840	....	840	168 00
	Japan...........	....	200	....	59	11 80
	Holland........	....	12,613	....	11,183	2,236 60
	Sweden.........	....	58	....	....	....
	United States...	....	64,974	....	64,974	12,994 80
	Total.......	....	92,501	....	83,975	16,795 00
Cut flowers...................	Unit'd Kingdom	....	92	....	....	....
	Belgium.........	....	17	....	17	2 97
	France..........	....	569	....	569	99 57
	Germany.......	....	466	....	466	81 55
	Holland........	....	3	....	3	0 53
	United States...	....	96,350	....	96,350	16,862 19
	Total.......	....	97,497	....	97,405	17,046 81
		Cwt.		Cwt.		
Plaster of Paris, or gypsum,	Unit'd Kingdom	1,649	1,486	....	....	....
ground not calcined.	Hong Kong.....	5	3	5	3	0 45
	United States...	3,317	1,811	3,317	1,811	271 65
	Total.......	4,971	3,300	3,322	1,814	272 10
Plaster of Paris, or gypsum,	Unit'd Kingdom	217	134	....	1	0 25
calcined and prepared wall	Hong Kong.....	2	1	....	....	....
plaster.	Germany.......	800	490	800	490	100 00
	United States...	126,122	44,677	126,122	44,677	15,765 77
	Total.......	127,141	45,302	126,924	45,168	15,866 02
Plates engraved on wood, steel	Unit'd Kingdom	....	9,324	....	773	154 60
or other metal, and transfers	Germany........	....	1,014	....	1,014	202 80
taken from the same, engravers'	United States...	....	77,701	....	77,701	15,540 20
plates, of steel or other metal polished for engraving thereon.	Total.......	....	88,039	....	79,488	15,897 60
Pocket books, portfolios, purses,	Unit'd Kingdom	....	60,908	....	8,463	2,962 05
reticules, satchels, card cases,	Hong Kong.....	....	1	....	....	....
fly books and musical instru-	Aust.-Hungary..	....	1,908	....	846	296 10
ment cases.	Belgium.........	....	1,325	....	1,266	443 10
	China..........	....	5	....	5	1 75
	France.........	....	22,301	....	4,161	1,456 35
	Germany.......	....	33,061	....	32,945	11,530 75
	Holland........	....	9	....	2	0 70
	Japan..........	....	4,176	....	780	273 00
	Switzerland....	....	412	....	359	125 65
	Turkey.........	....	8	....	8	2 80
	United States...	....	245,722	....	246,219	86,176 65
	Total.......	....	369,836	....	295,054	103,268 90

OF IMPORTS—*Continued.*

FOR HOME CONSUMPTION.

Preferential Tariff.			Treaty Rates.			Total.		
Quantity.	Value.	Duty.	Quantity.	Value.	Duty.	Quantity.	Value.	DutyColl'd.
No.	$	$ cts.	No.	$	$ cts.	No.	$	$ cts.
....	....	....	....	....	....	153	136	4 59
...'......	....	....	....	....	....	1,704	296	51 12
....	....	....	....	....	....	1,857	432	55 71
240	13	1 63	....	....	....	240	13	1 63
....	....	....	....	....	....	241	22	4 40
....	....	....	....	....	....	145,870	2,045	409 00
240	13	1 63	....	....	....	146,351	2,080	415 03
....	4,569	571 26	....	50	8 75	....	6,223	900 81
....	....	....	....	....	....	....	67	13 40
....	....	....	....	411	71 92	....	2,052	400 12
....	....	....	....	1,867	326 79	....	5,474	1,048 19
....	....	....	....	....	....	....	840	168 00
....	....	....	....	141	24 67	....	200	36 47
....	....	....	....	1,430	250 25	....	12,613	2,486 85
....	....	....	....	58	10 15	....	58	10 15
....	....	....	....	....	....	....	64,974	12,994 80
....	4,569	571 26	.'........	3,957	692 53	....	92,501	18,058 79
....	92	13 80	....	....	....	....	92	13 80
....	....	....	....	....	....	....	17	2 97
....	....	....	....	....	....	....	569	99 57
....	....	....	....	....	....	....	466	81 55
....	....	....	....	....	....	....	3	0 53
....	....	....	....	....	....	....	96,350	16,862 19
....	92	1,380	....	....	....	....	97,497	17,060 61
Cwt. 1,649	1,486	148 60	Cwt.			Cwt. 1,649	1,486	148 60
....	....	....	....	....	....	5	3	0 45
....	....	....	....	....	....	3,317	1,811	271 65
1,649	1,486	148 60	....	....	....	4,971	3,300	420 70
217	134	17 36	....	....	....	217	134	17 36
....	....	....	....	....	....	2	1	0 25
....	....	....	....	....	....	800	490	100 00
........./	....	....	....	....	....	126,122	44,677	15,765 77
217	134	17 36	....	....	....	127,141	45,302	15,883 38
....	8,551	1,282 65	....	....	....	....	9,324	1,437 25
....	....	....	....	....	....	....	1,014	202 80
....	....	....	....	....	....	....	77,701	15,540 20
....	8,551	1,282 65	....	....	....	....	88,039	17,180 25
....	50,486	11,359 92	....	2,303	690 90	....	61,252	15,012 87
....	....	....	....	1	0 30	....	1	0 30
....	....	....	....	1,062	318 60	....	1,908	614 70
....	....	....	....	59	17 70	....	1,325	460 80
....	....	....	....	....	....	....	5	1 75
....	....	....	....	18,378	5,513 40	....	22,539	6,969 75
....	....	....	....	....	....	....	32,945	11,530 75
....	....	....	....	7	2 10	....	9	2 80
....	....	....	....	2,972	891 60	....	3,752	1,164 60
....	....	....	....	53	15 90	....	412	141 55
....	....	....	....	....	....	....	8	2 80
....	....	....	....	....	....	....	246,219	86,176 65
....	50,486	11,359 92	....	24,835	7,450 50	....	370,375	122,079 32

6 GEORGE V, A. 1916

No. 1.—General Statement

Articles Imported.	Countries.	Total Imports.		Entered		
		Quantity.	Value.	General Tariff.		
				Quantity.	Value..	Duty.
DUTIABLE GOODS—*Con.*			$		$	$ cts.
Polish or composition, knife and other, n.o.p.	Unit'd Kingdom	....	99,291	....	649	178 47
	B. Straits Settlements...	....	....	....	....	5 22
	Aust.-Hungary..	....	19	....	19	5 22
	China..........	....	7	....	7	1 92
	France..........	....	144	....	883	242 82
	Germany........	....	1,008	....	1,008	277 20
	Holland........	....	16	....	16	4 40
	Japan..........	....	12	....	12	3 30
	United States..	....	74,995	....	74,975	20,619 36
	Total.:.....	....	175,492	....	77,569	21,332 69
		Lb.		Lb.		
Pomades, French, or flower odours, etc., imported in tins of not less than ten pounds each.	France..........	250	472	....	....	....
Post office parcels and packages...	Unit'd Kingdom	....	310,018	....	24,637	9,176 41
	France...,....	....	892	....	....	....
	Germany......	....	6	....	6	2 05
	Switzerland....	....	4	....	4	1 10
	United States..	....	1,109,014	....	1,109,014	318,702 71
	Total......	....	1,419,934	....	1,133,661	327,882 27
Precious stones and imitations thereof not mounted or set, and pearls and imitations thereof, pierced, split, strung or not, but not set or mounted.	Unit'd Kingdom	....	83,195	....	16,681	1,668 10
	B. W. Indies....	....	30	....	....	....
	Hong Kong....	....	1	....	1	0 10
	Aust.-Hungary..	....	7,210	....	7,210	721 00
	France....,....	....	23,087	....	23,087	2,308 70
	Germany......	....	10,806	....	10,806	1,080 60
	Holland........	....	1,840	....	1,840	184 00
	Italy..........	....	4,008	....	4,008	400 80
	Japan..........	....	697	....	697	69 70
	Switzerland....	....	128	....	128	12 80
	United States..	....	36,542	....	36,542	3,654 20
	Total......	....	167,544	....	101,000	10,100 00
Provisions not otherwise specified—						
Butter......................	Unit'd Kingdom	70,711	18,100	1,525	332	61 00
	Australia......	210,896	50,003	226,856	53,952	9,074 24
	New Zealand...	4,918,512	1,223,631	296,576	78,231	11,863 04
	Denmark......	840	235	840	235	33 60
	Holland.......	315	79	315	79	12 60
	Norway........	300	60	300	60	12 00
	Russia.........	130	29	130	29	5 20
	United States..	1,557,705	381,580	1,534,332	375,394	61,373 28
	Total......	6,759,409	1,673,717	2,060,874	508,312	82,434 96
Cheese......................	Unit'd Kingdom	35,524	8,322	14,004	2,859	420 12
	New Zealand...	5,541	676	321	41	9 63
	Belgium........	109	62	1,789	333	53 67
	France..........	110,436	22,399	83,939	17,238	2,518 17
	Germany......	6,328	1,834	6,168	1,786	185 04
	Greece.........	18,877	2,209	18,877	2,209	566 31
	Holland........	31,096	4,603	38,833	6,062	1,164 99
	Italy..........	533,109	109,839	490,176	102,049	14,705 28
	Norway...,....	9,044	1,579	6,607	1,197	198 21
	Sweden.........	220	24	220	24	6 60
	Switzerland....	115,852	20,311	46,853	8,114	1,405 59
	Turkey.........	2,274	228	2,274	228	68 22
	United States..	417,485	77,199	425,560	80,812	12,766 80
	Total......	1,285,895	249,285	1,135,621	222,952	34,068 63

OF IMPORTS—*Continued.*

FOR HOME CONSUMPTION.

Preferential Tariff.			Treaty Rates.			Total.		
Quantity.	Value.	Duty.	Quantity.	Value.	Duty.	Quantity.	Value.	DutyColl'd.
	$	$ cts.		$	$ cts.		$	$ cts.
....	97,852	14,677 80	....	....	....	....	98,501	14,856 27
....	20	3 00	....	....	....	....	20	3 00
....	....	....	....	....	....	....	19	5 22
....	....	....	....	....	....	....	7	1 92
....	....	....	....	....	....	....	883	242 82
....	....	....	....	....	....	....	1,008	277 20
....	....	....	....	....	....	....	16	4 40
....	....	....	....	....	....	....	12	3 30
....	....	....	....	....	....	....	74,975	20,619 36
....	97,872	14,680 80	....	....	....	....	175,441	36,013 49
Lb.			Lb.			Lb.		
....	....	....	250	472	59 01	250	472	59 01
....	285,381	67,618 56	....	....	....	....	310,018	76,794 97
....	....	....	—	892	208 65	....	892	208 65
....	....	....	....	....	....	....	6	2 05
....	....	....	....	....	....	....	4	1 10
....	....	....	....	....	....	....	1,109,014	318,702 71
....	285,381	67,618 56	....	892	208 65	....	1,419,934	395,709 48
....	66,514	4,988 55	....	....	....	....	83,195	6,656 65
....	30	2 26	....	....	....	....	30	2 26
....	....	....	....	....	....	....	1	0 10
....	....	....	....	....	....	....	7,210	721 00
....	....	....	....	....	....	....	23,087	2,308 70
....	....	....	....	....	....	....	10,806	1,080 60
....	....	....	....	....	....	....	1,840	184 00
....	....	....	....	....	....	....	4,008	400 80
....	....	....	....	....	....	....	697	69 70
....	....	....	....	....	....	....	128	12 80
....	....	....	....	....	....	....	36,542	3,654 20
....	66,544	4,990 81	....	....	....	....	167,544	15,090 81
64,734	16,617	1,942 02	....	....	....	66,259	16,949	2,003 02
....	....	....	....	....	....	226,856	53,952	9,074 24
4,696,932	1,153,127	140,907 96	....	....	....	4,993,508	1,231,358	152,771 00
....	....	....	....	....	....	840	235	33 60
....	....	....	....	....	....	315	79	12 60
....	....	....	....	....	....	300	60	12 00
....	....	....	....	....	....	130	29	5 20
....	....	....	....	....	....	1,534,332	375,394	61,373 28
4,761,666	1,169,744	142,849 98	....	....	....	6,822,540	1,678,056	225,284 94
21,624	·5,507	432 48	....	....	....	35,628	8,366	852 60
5,220	635	104 40	....	....	....	5,541	676	114 03
....	....	....	....	....	....	1,789	333	53 67
....	....	....	....	....	....	83,939	17,238	2,518 17
....	....	....	....	....	....	6,168	1,786	185 04
....	....	....	....	....	....	18,877	2,209	566 31
....	....	....	....	....	....	38,833	6,062	1,164 99
....	....	....	....	....	....	490,176	102,049	14,705 28
....	....	....	....	....	....	6,607	1,197	198 21
....	....	....	....	....	....	220	24	6 60
....	....	....	....	....	....	46,853	8,114	1,405 59
....	....	....	....	....	....	2,274	228	68 22
....	....	....	....	....	....	425,560	80,812	12,766 80
26,844	6,142	536 88	....	....	....	1,162,465	229,094	34,605 51

11—ii—14½

No. 1.—General Statement

Articles Imported.	Countries.	Total Imports.		Entered		
		Quantity.	Value.	General Tariff.		
				Quantity.	Value.	Duty.
DUTIABLE GOODS—*Con.*		Lb.	$	Lb.	$	$ cts.
Provisions—*Con.*						
Lard.....................	Unit'd Kingdom	4,803	648	....	....	....
	Germany......	6,232	881	4,552	624	91 04
	United States..	724,781	77,393	694,527	74,772	13,890 54
	Total......	735,816	78,922	699,079	75,396	13,981 58
Lard compound and similar sub-stances, cottolene and animal stearine of all kinds, n.o.p.	Unit'd Kingdom	446,785	40,411	315,076	27,477	6,301 52
	France.........	28,031	5,865	28,031	5,865	560 62
	Germany......	1,120	118	1,120	118	22 40
	United States..	1,896,026	170,639	1,933,657	172,712	38,673 14
	Total.......	2,371,962	217,033	2,277,884	206,172	45,557 68
Meats, viz.—						
Bacon and hams, shoulders and sides, cured.	Unit'd Kingdom	13,227	2,875	6,521	1,356	130 42
	Australia.......	895	156	895	156	17 90
	Hong Kong.....	3,726	800	3,726	800	74 52
	China..........	468	89	468	89	9 36
	Italy...........	62	12	62	12	1 24
	United States...	1,478,872	238,891	1,493,708	239,551	29,874 16
	Total.......	1,497,250	242,823	1,505,380	241,964	30,107 60
Beef, fresh, chilled or frozen..	Australia.......	8,713	707	318,921	22,488	9,567 63
	New Zealand...	412,489	26,545	60,348	5,034	1,810 44
	United States...	156,305	26,800	156,305	26,800	4,689 15
	Total.......	577,507	54,052	535,574	54,322	16,067 22
Beef, salted, in barrels........	Unit'd Kingdom	5,861	517	5,761	509	115 22
	Newfoundland..	1,570	175	1,570	175	31 40
	Norway........	200	12	200	12	4 00
	United States...	1,497,350	118,548	1,005,010	78,944	20,100 20
	Total.......	1,504,981	119,252	1,012,541	79,640	20,250 82
Canned meats and canned poultry and game.	Unit'd Kingdom	1,022,382	174,147	57,284	9,304	2,558 60
	Australia.......	61,668	8,075	22,260	2,481	682 27
	Hong Kong.....	2,511	501	2,511	501	137 78
	Newfoundland..	20	8	20	8	2 20
	New Zealand...	16,421	2,468	....	....	....
	Argentina.......	28,800	3,686	....	....	....
	Belgium........	180	44	180	44	12 10
	China..........	1,106	205	1,106	205	56 38
	France.........	17,764	4,227	1,871	553	152 08
	Germany......	5,177	748	1,870	326	89 65
	Japan..........	8,552	978	611	59	16 23
	Miquelon and St. Pierre.....	42	27	....	....	....
	Sweden........	100	27	100	27	7 43
	United States...	307,358	60,038	283,884	46,610	12,818 26
	Uruguay........	8,211	1,415	8,211	1,415	389 12
	Total.......	1,480,292	256,594	379,908	61,533	16,922 10
Extracts of meats and fluid beef, not medicated, and soups of all kinds.	Unit'd Kingdom	....	182,229	....	3,430	943 25
	B. W. Indies....	....	3	....	3	0 83
	Hong Kong....	....	47	....	47	12 93
	Argentina.......	....	5,765	....	757	208 18
	Belgium........	....	169	....	....	....
	France.........	....	4,291	....	1,035	284 63
	Germany......	....	1,682	....	3,342	919 05
	Japan..........	....	223	....	....	....
	Sweden........	....	17	....	17	4 68
	Switzerland.....	....	3,415	....	....	....
	United States...	....	270,709	....	269,250	74,044 78
	Total.......	....	468,550	....	277,881	76,418 33

OF IMPORTS—*Continued.*

FOR HOME CONSUMPTION.

Preferential Tariff.			Treaty Rates.			Total.		
Quantity.	Value.	Duty.	Quantity.	Value.	Duty.	Quantity.	Value.	DutyColl'd.
Lb.	$	$ cts.	Lb.	$	$ cts.	Lb.	$	$ cts.
4,803	648	72 05	....	....	....	4,803	648	72 05
....	....	....	....	....	....	4,552	624	91 04
....	....	....	....	....	....	694,527	74,772	13,890 54
4,803	648	72 05	....	....	....	703,882	76,044	14,053 63
255,483	23,814	3,832 26	....	....	....	570,559	51,291	10,133 78
....	....	....	....	....	....	28,031	5,865	560 62
....	....	....	....	....	....	1,120	118	22 40
....	....	....	....	....	....	1,933,657	172,712	38,673 14
255,483	23,814	3,832 26	....	....	....	2,533,367	229,986	49,389 94
6,706	1,519	100 59	....	....	....	13,227	2,875	231 01
....	....	....	....	....	....	895	156	17 90
....	....	....	....	....	....	3,726	800	74 52
....	....	....	....	....	....	468	89	9 36
....	....	....	....	....	....	62	12	1 24
....	....	....	....	....	....	1,493,708	239,551	29,874 16
6,706	1,519	100 59	....	....	....	1,512,086	243,483	30,208 19
....	....	....	....	....	....	318,921	22,488	9,567 63
235,721	16,508	4,714 42	....	....	....	296,069	21,542	6,524 86
....	....	....	....	....	....	156,305	26,800	4,689 15
235,721	16,508	4,714 42	....	....	....	771,295	70,830	20,781 64
100	8	1 50	....	....	....	5,861	517	116 72
....	....	....	....	....	....	1,570	175	31 40
....	....	....	....	....	....	200	12	4 00
....	....	....	....	....	....	1,005,010	78,944	20,100 20
100	8	1 50	....	....	....	1,012,641	79,648	20,252 32
148,158	39,068	6,837 06	804,898	125,228	31,307 00	1,010,340	173,600	40,702 66
....	....	....	64,450	7,662	1,915 50	86,710	10,143	2,597 77
....	....	....	....	....	....	2,511	501	137 78
....	....	....	....	....	....	20	8	2 20
16,151	2,366	414 05	....	....	....	16,151	2,366	414 05
....	....	....	28,800	3,686	921 50	28,800	3,686	921 50
....	....	....	112	3	0 75	292	47	12 85
....	....	....	....	....	....	1,106	205	56 38
....	....	....	16,096	3,854	963 50	17,967	4,407	1,115 58
....	....	....	....	....	....	1,870	326	89 65
....	....	....	7,941	919	229 75	8,552	978	245 98
....	....	....	42	27	6 75	42	27	6 75
....	....	....	....	....	....	100	27	7 43
....	....	....	....	....	....	283,884	46,610	12,818 26
....	....	....	....	....	....	8,211	1,415	389 12
164,309	41,434	7,251 11	922,339	141,379	35,344 75	1,466,556	244,346	59,517 96
....	152,288	26,650 65	....	26,886	6,721 50	....	182,604	34,315 40
....	....	....	....	....	....	....	3	0 83
....	....	....	....	....	....	....	47	12 93
....	....	....	....	5,008	1,252 00	....	5,765	1,460 18
....	....	....	....	184	46 00	....	184	46 00
....	....	....	....	3,103	775 75	....	4,138	1,060 38
....	....	....	....	....	....	....	3,342	919 05
....	....	....	....	223	55 75	....	223	55 75
....	....	....	....	....	....	....	17	4 68
....	....	....	....	6,631	1,657 75	....	6,631	1,657 75
....	....	....	....	....	....	....	269,250	74,044 78
....	152,288	26,650 65	....	42,035	10,508 75	....	472,204	113,577 73

6 GEORGE V, A. 1916

No. 1.—General Statement

Articles Imported.	Countries.	Total Imports.		Entered		
				General Tariff.		
		Quantity.	Value.	Quantity.	Value.	Duty.
DUTIABLE GOODS—*Con.*		Lb.	$	Lb.	$	$ cts.
Provisions—*Con.*						
Meats—*Con.*						
Mutton and lamb, fresh, chilled or frozen.	Australia.......	485,037	39,106	491,250	34,030	14,737 50
	New Zealand...	34	4	34	4	1 02
	United States...	2,983,005	338,508	2,955,592	335,933	88,667 76
	Total......	3,468,076	377,618	3,446,876	369,967	103,406 28
Pork, barrelled, in brine......	Unit'd Kingdom	6,850	693	6,850	693	137 00
	Newfoundland..	3,200	388	3,200	388	64 00
	Hong Kong.....	367	85	367	85	7 34
	Norway........	100	10	100	10	2 00
	United States...	8,430,052	818,226	8,465,088	817,128	169,301 76
	Total......	8,440,569	819,402	8,475,605	818,304	169,512 10
Pork, fresh, chilled or frozen.	United States...	114,683	14,282	23,900	3,107	717 00
Poultry and game, n.o.p......	Unit'd Kingdom	....	7,052	....	4,903	980 60
	Australia.......	....	1,153	....	2,575	515 00
	Hong Kong.....	....	8,939	....	8,845	1,769 00
	Newfoundland..	....	12	....	12	2 40
	New Zealand...	....	20	....	....	....
	China..........	....	500	....	500	100 00
	Egypt and Soudan.	....	137	....	137	27 40
	Germany.......	....	104	....	104	20 80
	United States...	....	68,210	....	69,494	13,898 80
	Total......	....	86,127	....	86,570	17,314 00
Dried or smoked meats, and meats preserved in any other way than salted or pickled, n.o.p.	Unit'd Kingdom	2,316	500	1,003	166	20 06
	Hong Kong.....	67,624	19,744	67,444	19,701	1,348 88
	Belgium........	6	2	6	2	0 12
	China..........	3,475	708	3,475	708	69 50
	France.........	20	5	20	5	0 40
	Germany.......	170	34	170	34	3 40
	Italy..........	4,667	1,505	1,435	472	28 70
	Sweden........	61	15	61	15	1 22
	United States...	592,211	120,637	646,909	133,979	12,938 18
	Total......	670,550	143,150	720,523	155,082	14,410 46
Other meats, fresh, chilled or frozen.	Unit'd Kingdom	54	3	....	....	....
	Australia.......	32,588	3,046	165,609	13,218	4,968 27
	New Zealand...	55,557	2,316	5,583	566	167 49
	United States...	424,410	63,525	423,981	63,477	12,719 43
	Total......	512,609	68,890	595,173	77,261	17,855 19
Other meats, salted, n.o.p....	Unit'd Kingdom	41,879	3,607	4,000	400	80 00
	Hong Kong.....	2,719	579	2,719	579	54 38
	Newfoundland..	200	23	200	23	4 00
	China..........	6,780	1,672	6,780	1,672	135 60
	France.........	110	42	110	42	2 20
	Italy..........	182	22	182	22	3 64
	United States...	482,366	87,157	447,692	82,960	8,953 84
	Total......	534,236	93,102	461,683	85,698	9,233 66

SESSIONAL PAPER No. 11

OF IMPORTS—*Continued.*

FOR HOME CONSUMPTION.

Preferential Tariff.			Treaty Rates.			Total.		
Quantity.	Value.	Duty.	Quantity.	Value.	Duty.	Quantity.	Value.	DutyColl'd.
Lb.	$	$ cts.	Lb.	$	$ cts.	Lb.	$	$ cts.
4,936	363	98 72				491,250	34,030	14,737 50
						4,970	367	99 74
						2,955,592	335,933	88,667 76
4,936	363	98 72				3,451,812	370,330	103,505 00
						6,850	693	137 00
						3,200	388	64 00
						367	85	7 34
						100	10	2 00
						8,465,088	817,128	169,301 76
						8,475,605	818,304	169,512 10
						23,900	3,107	717 00
	2,261	282 65					7,164	1,263 25
							2,575	515 00
							8,845	1,769 00
							12	2 40
	1,881	235 12					1,881	235 12
							500	100 00
							137	27 40
							104	20 80
							69,494	13,898 80
	4,142	517 77					90,712	17,831 77
1,313	334	19 70				2,316	500	39 76
						67,444	19,701	1,348 88
						6	2	0 12
						3,475	708	69 50
						20	5	0 40
						170	34	3 40
						1,435	472	28 70
						61	15	1 22
						646,909	133,979	12,938 18
1,313	334	19 70				721,836	155,416	14,430 16
54	3	1 08				54	3	1 08
						165,609	13,218	4,968 27
40,543	1,789	810 86				46,126	2,355	978 35
						423,981	63,477	12,719 43
40,597	1,792	811 94				635,770	79,053	18,667 13
37,879	3,207	568 20				41,879	3,607	648 20
						2,719	579	54 38
						200	23	4 00
						6,780	1,672	135 60
						110	42	2 20
						182	22	3 64
						447,692	82,960	8,953 84
37,879	3,207	568 20				499,562	88,905	9,801 86

6 GEORGE V, A. 1916

No. 1.—GENERAL STATEMENT

Articles Imported.	Countries.	Total Imports.		Entered		
		Quantity.	Value.	General Tariff.		
				Quantity.	Value.	Duty.
DUTIABLE GOODS—*Con.*			$		$	$ cts.
Pulleys, belt, of all kinds for power transmission.	Unit'd Kingdom	....	4,500	....	56	15 40
	United States...	....	50,041	....	49,970	13,742 56
	Total......	....	54,541	....	50,026	13,757 96
Regalia and badges............	Unit'd Kingdom	....	19,741	....	820	287 00
	Hong Kong.....	....	17	....	17	5 95
	France..........	....	39	....	39	13 65
	Germany........	....	53	....	53	18 55
	United States...	....	27,222	....	27,217	9,525 95
	Total......	....	47,072	....	28,146	9,851 10
Ribbons of all kinds and materials	Unit'd Kingdom	....	670,890	....	22,658	7,930 30
	Aust.-Hungary..	....	45	....	....	....
	Belgium........	....	982	....	368	128 80
	France..........	....	230,927	....	12,587	4,405 45
	Germany........	....	9,935	....	9,935	3,477 25
	Holland........	....	1,103	....	1,103	386 05
	Japan..........	....	74	....		
	Switzerland.....	....	696,077	....	35,810	12,533 50
	United States...	....	170,660	....	175,867	61,553 45
	Total......	....	1,780,693	....	258,328	90,414 80
Ribbons, undyed, for the manufacture of typewriter ribbons.	Unit'd Kingdom	....	4,111	....	578	86 70
	France..........	....	335	....	335	50 25
	Germany........	....	1,050	....	1,050	157 50
	United States...	....	5,298	....	5,237	785 55
	Total......	....	10,794	....	7,200	1,080 00
Sails for boats and ships..........	Unit'd Kingdom	....	3,134	....	7	1 75
	United States...	....	1,773	....	1,773	443 25
	Total......	....	4,907	....	1,780	445 00
		Cwt.		Cwt.		
Salt, in bulk, n.o.p..............	Italy..........	3,240	420	3,240	420	162 00
	United States..	543,456	85,128	543,456	85,128	27,172 80
	Total......	546,696	85,548	546,696	85,548	27,334 80
Salt, n.o.p., in bags, barrels, and other coverings.	United States..	157,867	67,750	154,246	67,212	11,568 68
Bags, barrels and other coverings used in the importation of salt specified in preceding item.	United States..	....	20,629	....	20,524	5,131 00
Sandpaper, glass, flint and emery paper or emery cloth.	Unit'd Kingdom	....	7,468	....	680	170 00
	Belgium........	....	83	....	83	20 75
	Germany......	....	14	....	14	3 50
	United States..	....	118,630	....	118,605	29,651 25
	Total......	....	126,195	....	119,382	29,845 50

OF IMPORTS—*Continued.*

FOR HOME CONSUMPTION.

Preferential Tariff.			Treaty Rates.			Total.		
Quantity.	Value.	Duty.	Quantity.	Value.	Duty.	Quantity.	Value.	DutyColl'd.
	$ 4,444	$ cts. 666 60		$	$ cts.		$ 4,500	$ cts. 682 00
....	....	....	....	....	....	....	49,970	13,742 56
....	4,444	666 60	....	....	....	....	54,470	14,424 56
....	18,392	4,138 60	....	....	....	....	19,212	4,425 60
....	....	....	....	....	....	....	17	5 95
....	....	....	....	....	....	....	39	13 65
....	....	....	....	....	....	....	53	18 55
....	....	....	....	....	....	....	27,217	9,525 95
....	18,392	4,138 60	....	....	....	....	46,538	13,989 70
....	16,418	3,694 52	....	626,870	156,986 66	....	665,946	168,611 48
....	....	....	....	45	11 25	....	45	11 25
....	....	....	....	614	199 55	....	982	328 35
....	....	....	....	219,752	54,942 13	....	232,339	59,347 58
....	....	....	....	....	....	....	9,935	3,477 25
....	....	....	....	....	....	....	1,103	386 05
....	....	....	....	74	18 50	....	74	18 50
....	....	....	....	629,023	157,255 75	....	664,833	169,789 25
....	....	....	....	....	....	....	175,867	61,553 45
....	16,418	3,694 52	....	1,476,378	369,413 84	....	1,751,124	463,523 16
....	3,533	353 30	....	....	....	....	4,111	440 00
....	....	....	....	....	....	....	335	50 25
....	....	....	....	....	....	....	1,050	157 50
....	....	....	....	....	....	....	5,237	785 55
....	3,533	353 30	....	....	....	....	10,733	1,433 30
....	3,127	469 05	....	....	....	....	3,134	470 80
....	....	....	....	....	....	....	1,773	443 25
....	3,127	469 05	....	....	....	....	4,907	914 05
Cwt.			Cwt.			Cwt. 3,240	420	162 00
....	....	....	....	....	....	543,456	85,128	27,172 80
....	....	....	....	....	....	546,696	85,548	27,334 80
....	....	....	....	....	....	154,246	67,212	11,568 68
....	....	....	....	....	....	....	20,524	5,131 00
....	6,788	1,018 20	....	....	....	....	7,468	1,188 20
....	....	....	....	....	....	....	83	20 75
....	....	....	....	....	....	....	14	3 50
....	....	....	....	....	....	....	118,605	29,651 25
....	6,788	1,018 20	....	....	....	....	126,170	30,863 70

6 GEORGE V, A. 1916

No. 1.—General Statement

Articles Imported.	Countries.	Total Imports.		Entered		
				General Tariff.		
		Quantity.	Value.	Quantity.	Value.	Duty.
DUTIABLE GOODS—*Con.*		Gal.	$	Gal.	$	$ cts.
Sauces and catsups, in bottles.....	Unit'd Kingdom	96,775	127,012	423	301	105 35
	B. India........	168	512	....	....	....
	B. W. Indies....	....	1	....	1	0 35
	Hong Kong....	2,387	1,903	2,387	1,903	666 05
	China...........	4,051	1,591	4,051	1,591	556 85
	France.........	444	499	38	84	29 40
	Germany......	10	13	10	13	4 55
	Italy..........	689	465	689	465	162 75
	Japan...........	110	46	10	4	1 40
	Switzerland.....	....	....	....	....	....
	United States..	74,037	98,111	72,938	98,601	34,510 35
	Total.......	178,671	230,153	80,546	102,963	36,037 05
Sauces and catsups, in bulk.......	Unit'd Kingdom	1,080	425	511	20	7 00
	Hong Kong....	12,507	4,989	12,497	4,986	1,745 10
	China...........	547	83	547	83	29 05
	Italy...........	1,175	314	1,175	314	109 90
	Japan...........	1,529	399	1,490	387	135 45
	United States..	29,371	7,896	26,709	7,341	2,569 35
	Total.......	46,209	14,106	42,569	13,131	4,595 85
Sauces, soy......................	Hong Kong....	22,423	7,888	22,393	7,876	2,756 60
	China...........	9,999	1,859	9,999	1,859	650 65
	Japan...........	56,867	20,022	54,535	19,085	6,679 75
	United States..	230	89	230	89	31 15
	Total.......	89,519	29,858	87,157	28,909	10,118 15
Sausage casings, n.o.p.............	Unit'd Kingdom	....	98,873	....	19,605	3,430 88
	Australia.......	....	5,319	....	5,090	890 75
	Hong Kong....	....	3	....	3	0 53
	New Zealand...	....	11,716	....	....	....
	China...........	....	54	....	....	....
	Germany......	....	597	....	814	142 45
	United States..	....	85,209	....	81,925	14,337 11
	Total.......	....	201,771	....	107,437	18,801 72
Seeds, viz.:—						
Clover and timothy............	Unit'd Kingdom	....	153,486	....	47	4 70
	New Zealand...	....	788	....	....	....
	Holland.......	....	232	....	232	23 20
	Japan...........	....	436	....	436	43 60
	United States..	....	1,520,178	....	1,459,087	145,908 70
	Total.......	....	1,675,120	....	1,459,802	145,980 20
		Bush.		Bush.		
Flax......................	Russia..........	9	13	9	13	0 90
	United States..	212	353	212	353	21 20
	Total.......	221	366	221	366	22 10
Garden, field and other seeds for	Unit'd Kingdom	....	43,946	....	9,296	929 60
agricultural or other purposes,	Hong Kong.....	....	6,878	....	6,878	687 80
n.o.p., sunflower, canary,hemp	New Zealand...	....	6,024	....	....	....
and millet seed, when in pack-	China...........	....	455	....	455	45 50
ages weighing over one pound	Denmark.......	....	4,300	....	4,300	430 00
each.	France.........	....	4,509	....	4,756	475 60
	Germany......	....	326	....	326	32 60
	Holland.......	....	9,238	....	9,238	923 80
	Italy...........	....	1,355	....	1,355	135 50

OF IMPORTS—Continued.

FOR HOME CONSUMPTION.

Preferential Tariff.			Treaty Rates.			Total.		
Quantity.	Value.	Duty.	Quantity.	Value.	Duty.	Quantity.	Value.	DutyColl'd.
Gal.	$	$ cts.	Gal.	$	$ cts.	Gal.	$	$ cts.
95,992	129,608	32,402 00	3	13	4 23	96,418	129,922	32,511 58
33	29	7 25	....	....	....	33	29	7 25
....	....	....	....	....	....	......	1	0 35
....	....	....	....	....	....	2,387	1,903	666 05
....	....	....	....	....	....	4,051	1,591	556 85
....	....	....	786	463	150 51	824	547	179 91
....	....	....	....	....	....	10	13	4 55
....	....	....	....	....	....	689	465	162 75
....	....	....	100	42	13 65	110	46	15 05
....	....	....	5	12	3 90	5	12	3 90
....	....	....	....	....	....	72,938	98,601	34,510 35
96,025	129,637	32,409 25	894	530	· 172 29	177,465	233,130	68,618 59
1,719	507	126 75	....	....	....	1,870	527	133 75
....	....	....	10	3	0 98	12,507	4,989	1,746 08
....	....	....	....	....	....	547	83	29 05
....	....	....	....	....	....	1,175	314	109 90
....	....	....	39	12	3 90	1 529	399	139 35
....	....	....	....	....	....	26,709	7,341	2,569 35
1,719	507	126 75	49	15	4 88	44,337	13,653	4,727 48
....	....	....	30	12	3 90	22,423	7,888	2,760 50
....	....	....	....	....	....	9,999	1,859	650 65
....	....	....	2,157	866	281 49	56,692	19,951	6,961 24
....	....	....	....	....	....	230	89	31 15
....	....	....	2,187	878	285 39	89,344	29,787	10,403 54
....	62,966	9,444 90	....			....	82,571	12,875 78
....			....			....	5,090	890 75
....			....			....	3	0 53
....	4,042	606 30	....			....	4,042	606 30
....			....			....	814	142 45
....			....			....	81,925	14,337 11
....	67,008	10,051 20	....			....	174,445	28,852 92
....	153,439	7,671 95	....			....	153,486	7,676 65
....	788	39 40	....			....	788	39 40
....			....			....	232	23 20
....			....			....	436	43 60
....			....			....	1,459,087	145,908 70
....	154,227	7,711 35	....			....	1,614,029	153,691 55
Bush.			Bush.			Bush.		
....			....			9	13	0 90
....			....			212	353	21 20
....			....			221	· 366	22 10
....	34,670	1,733 50	....			....	43,966	2,663 10
....			....			....	6,878	687 80
....	6,024	301 20	....			....	6,024	301 20
....			....			....	455	45 50
....			....			....	4,300	430 00
....			....			....	4,756	475 60
....			....			....	326	32 60
....			....			....	9,238	923 80
....			....			....	1,355	135 50

·6 GEORGE V, A. 1916

No. 1.—General Statement

Articles Imported.	Countries.	Total Imports.		Entered		
				General Tariff.		
		Quantity.	Value.	Quantity.	Value.	Duty.
DUTIABLE GOODS—*Con.*			$		$	$ cts.
Seeds—*Con.*						
Garden, field and other seeds for	Japan............	....	10,942	....	10,942	1,094 20
agricultural, etc.—*Con.*	Russia...........	....	294	....	294	29 40
	Spain...........	....	226	....	226	22 60
	United States..	....	328,022	....	327,037	32,703 70
	Total......	....	416,515	....	375,103	37,510 30
Garden, field and other seeds for	Unit'd Kingdom	....	12,575	....	173	43 25
agricultural or other purposes,	Hong Kong.....	....	66	....	66	16 50
n.o.p.,sunflower, canary, hemp	France..........	....	182	....	182	45 50
and millet seed, when in pack-	Germany.......	....	105	....	105	26 25
ages weighing one pound each	Holland........	....	393	....	393	98 25
or less.	Italy...........	....	356	....	356	89 00
	Japan...........	....	27	....	27	6 75
	United States..	....	15,366	....	14,629	3,657 25
	Total......	....	29,070	....	·15,931	3,982 75
Garden and field seeds not	Unit'd Kingdom	....	86	....	....	....
specified as free, valued at not	Holland........	....	37	....	37	3 70
less than $5 per pound in pack-	United States..	....	224	....	224	22 40
ages of not less than one oz.						
each.	Total......	....	347	....	261	26 10
		No.		No.		
Ships and other vessels built in any	Norway........	2	25,000	....	....	....
foreign country, if British regis-	United States..	6	212,500	6	212,500	53,125 00
tered since September 1, 1902, on	Total......	8	237,500	6	212,500	53,125 00
application for license to engage						
in the Canadian coasting trade;						
on the fair market value of the						
hull, rigging, machinery, boilers,						
furniture and appurtenances						
thereof, as provided in an Act						
respecting the coasting trade of						
Canada.						
Vessels, dredges, scows, yachts,	Belgium........	....	46,233	....	46,233	11,558 25
boats and other ·water-borne	United States..	....	362,943	....	362,943	90,735 75
craft, built outside of Canada,	Total......	....	409,176	....	409,176	102,294 00
of any material, destined for						
use or service in Canadian						
waters (not to include register-						
ed vessels entitled to engage						
in the coasting trade, nor						
vessels in transit between						
Canada and any place outside						
thereof), n.o.p., on the fair						
market value of the hull, rig-						
ging,machinery,boilers, furni-						
ture and appurtenances there-						
of, on arrival in Canada.						
Ships and vessels, repairs on......	United States..	....	85,770	..:......	85,770	21,442 50
Signs of any material other than	Unit'd Kingdom	....	25,483	....	1,005	301 50
paper, framed or not; letters or	Hong Kong.....	....	26	.....\.....	26	7 80
numerals of any material other	China...........	....	18	....	18	5 40
than paper.	France..........	....	263	....	108	32 40
	Germany.......	.:......	2,881	....	2,881	864 30
	Holland........	....	3	....	3	0 90
	Italy...........	....	241	....	47	14 10
	Japan...........	....	7	....	7	2 10
	Spain...........	....	1	....	1	0 30
	Switzerland.....	....	435	....	435	130 50
	United States..	....	85,275	....	84,949	25,484 70
	Total......	....	114,633	....	89,480	26,844 00

OF IMPORTS—*Continued.*

FOR HOME CONSUMPTION.

	Preferential Tariff.			Treaty Rates.			Total.	
Quantity.	Value.	Duty.	Quantity.	Value.	Duty.	Quantity.	Value.	DutyColl'd.
	$	$ cts.		$	$ cts.		$	$ cts.
....	....	....	....	....	....	....	10,942	1,094 20
....	....	....	....	....	....	....	294	29 40
....	....	....	....	....	....	....	226	22 60
....	....	....	....	....	....	....	327,037	32,703 70
....	40,694	2,034 70	....	....	....	....	415,797	39,545 00
....	12,332	1,849 80	....	....	....	....	12,505	1,893 05
....	....	....	....	....	....	....	66	16 50
....	....	....	....	....	....	....	182	45 50
....	....	....	....	....	....	....	105	26 25
....	....	....	....	....	....	....	393	98 25
....	....	....	....	....	....	....	356	89 00
....	....	....	....	....	....	....	27	6 75
....	....	....	....	....	....	....	14,629	3,657 25
....	12,332	1,849 80	....	....	....	....	28,263	5,832 55
....	86	4 30	....	....	....	....	86	4 30
....	....	....	....	....	....	....	37	3 70
....	....	....	....	....	....	....	224	22 40
....	86	4 30	....	....	....	....	347	30 40
No.			No.			No.		
....	....	....	....	....	....			
....	....	....	....	....	....	6	212,500	53,125 00
....	....	....	....	....	....	6	212,500	53,125 00
....	....	....	....	....	....	....	46,233	11,558 25
....	....	....	....	....	....	....	362,943	90,735 75
....	....	....	....	....	....	....	409,176	102,294 00
....	....	....	....	....	....	....	85,770	21,442 50
....	24,394	4,878 80	....	....	....	....	25,399	5,180 30
....	....	....	....	....	....	....	26	7 80
....	....	....	....	....	....	....	18	5 40
....	....	....	....	....	....	....	108	32 40
....	....	....	....	....	....	....	2,881	864 30
....	....	....	....	....	....	....	3	0 90
....	....	....	....	....	....	....	47	14 10
....	....	....	....	....	....	....	7	2 10
....	....	....	....	....	....	....	1	0 30
....	....	....	....	....	....	....	435	130 50
....	....	....	....	....	....	....	84,949	25,484 70
....	24,394	4,878 80	....	....	....	....	113,874	31,722 80

6 GEORGE V, A. 1916

No. 1.—General Statement

Articles Imported.	Countries.	Total Imports.		Entered		
		Quantity.	Value.	General Tariff.		
				Quantity.	Value.	Duty.
DUTIABLE GOODS—*Con.*			$		$	$ cts.
Silk and manufactures of—						
Fabrics, n.o.p...............	Unit'd Kingdom	....	1,644,499	....	52,902	15,870 60
	B. W. Indies....		13			
	Hong Kong.....		997		997	299 10
	Aust.-Hungary .		102,962		357	107 10
	Belgium.......		296		186	55 80
	China..........		39,872		54,160	16,248 00
	Denmark.......		5		5	1 50
	France.........		863,563		91,310	27,393 00
	Germany.......		61,589		61,589	18,476 70
	Italy..........		37,333		557	167 10
	Japan.........		253,288		16,180	4,854 00
	Switzerland....		1,894,987		8,540	2,562 00
	United States...		387,548		387,460	116,238 00
	Total......	....	5,286,952	....	674,243	202,272 90
Silk fabrics of which silk is the	Unit'd Kingdom	....	48,841	....	39,461	7,892 20
component material of chief	Aust.-Hungary .		3,406		3,406	681 20
value, for the manufacture of	France.........		5,243		4,267	853 40
neckties.	Germany.......		47,573		47,573	9,514 60
	Italy..........		3,041		3,041	608 20
	Switzerland....		153,915		142,915	28,583 00
	United States...		120,335		120,335	24,067 00
	Total......		382,354	....	360,998	72,199 60
Handkerchiefs.................	Unit'd Kingdom	....	28,687	....	607	212 45
	B. W. Indies....		10			
	Hong Kong.....		1,901		1,821	637 35
	China..........		1,025		1,025	358 75
	France.........		177		166	58 10
	Japan.........		41,820		789	276 15
	Switzerland....		439			
	United States...		457		457	159 95
	Total......	....	74,516	....	4,865	1,702 75
Blouses and shirt waists.......	Unit'd Kingdom	....	46,583		60	22 50
	France.........		4,349		2,005	751 88
	Japan.........		425			
	United States...		36,615	....	36,509	13,690 94
	Total......	....	87,972	....	38,574	14,465 32
Clothing...................	Unit'd Kingdom	....	313,369	....	8,175	3,065 63
	Hong Kong.....		450		450	168 75
	Aust.-Hungary .		18			
	Belgium.......		115			
	China..........		339		339	127 13
	Egypt and Soudan......		150		150	56 25
	France.........		27,139		4,720	1,770 00
	Germany.......		5,332		5,332	1,999 50
	Italy..........		814			
	Japan.........		54,626		983	368 63
	Switzerland....		866		35	13 13
	United States...		330,877		331,088	124,158 13
	Total......	....	734,095	....	351,272	131,727 15

SESSIONAL PAPER No. 11

OF IMPORTS—Continued.

FOR HOME CONSUMPTION.

Preferential Tariff.			Treaty Rates.			Total.		
Quantity.	Value.	Duty.	Quantity.	Value.	Duty.	Quantity.	Value.	DutyColl'd.
	$	$ cts.		$	$ cts.		$	$ cts.
....	237,873	41,628 71	....	1,344,775	271,681 65	....	1,635,550	329,180 96
....	....	....	....	....	....	....	....	....
....	....	....	....	56	11 20	....	1,053	310 30
....	....	....	....	102,605	20,526 48	....	102,962	20,633 58
....	....	....	....	110	30 25	....	296	86 05
....	....	....	....			....	54,160	16,248 00
....	....	....	....				5	1 50
....	....	....	....	781,270	156,316 97	....	872,580	183,709 97
....	....	....	....				61,589	18,476 70
....	....	....	....	37,005	10,176 43	....	37,562	10,343 53
....	....	....	....	233,267	46,665 39	....	249,447	51,519 39
....	....	....	....	1,909,139	381,862 68	....	1,917,679	384,424 68
....	....	....	....				387,460	116,238 00
....	237,873	41,628 71	....	4,408,227	887,271 05	....	5,320,343	1,131,172 66
....	9,333	1,633 33	....				48,794	9,525 53
....	....	....	....				3,406	681 20
....	....	....	....				4,267	853 40
....	....	....	....				47,573	9,514 60
....	....	....	....				3,041	608 20
....	....	....	....				142,915	28,583 00
....	....	....	....				120,335	24,067 00
....	9,333	1,633 33	....				370,331	73,832 93
....	24,872	6,218 00	....	3,092	1,004 90	....	28,571	7,435 35
....	....	....	....	21	6 83	....	1,842	644 18
....	....	....	....				1,025	358 75
....	....	....	....	11	3 58		177	61 68
....	....	....	....	40,773	13,251 26	....	41,562	13,527 41
....	....	....	....	439	142 68	....	439	142 68
....	....	....	....				457	159 95
....	24,872	6,218 00	....	44,336	14,409 25	....	74,073	22,330 00
....	45,660	13,698 00	....	891	289 58	....	46,611	14,010 08
....	....	....	....	2,344	764 93		4,349	1,516 81
....	....	....	....	425	138 14	....	425	138 14
....	....	....	....				36,509	13,690 94
....	45,660	13,698 00	....	3,660	1,192 65	....	87,894	29,355 97
....	295,825	88,747 50	....	8,234	2,683 16	....	312,234	94,496 29
....	....	....	....	313	101 72	....	763	270 47
....	....	....	....	18	5 86	....	18	5 86
....	....	....	....	115	40 25	....	115	40 25
....	....	....	....				339	127 13
....	....	....	....				150	56 25
....	....	....	....	22,419	7,289 38	....	27,139	9,059 38
....	....	....	....				5,332	1,999 50
....	....	....	....	814	284 90	....	814	284 90
....	....	....	....	53,443	17,370 31	....	54,426	17,738 94
....	....	....	....	831	270 09	....	866	283 22
....	....	....	....				331,088	124,158 13
....	295,825	88,747 50	....	86,187	28,045 67	....	733,284	248,520 32

6 GEORGE V, A. 1916

No. 1.—General Statement

Articles Imported.	Countries.	Total Imports.		Entered		
				General Tariff.		
		Quantity.	Value.	Quantity.	Value.	Duty.
		Lb.	$	Lb.	$	$ cts.
DUTIABLE GOODS—*Con.*						
Silk and mfrs. of—*Con.*						
Silk, spun, not coloured, n.o.p., silk in the gum not more advanced than single; tram or thrown organzine, not coloured.	Unit'd Kingdom	1,568	2,043	....	....	....
	China..........	51	107	51	107	16 05
	Italy..........	557	1,278	557	1,278	191 70
	United States...	1,417	2,955	1,417	2,955	443 25
	Total........	3,593	6,383	2,025	4,340	651 00
Silk in the gum or spun, imported by the manufacturers of ribbons and shoe laces.	United States...	....	1,522	....	1,522	152 20
Sewing and embroidery silk, silk twist, and silk floss.	Unit'd Kingdom	....	46,764	....	752	188 00
	Hong Kong.....	....	19	....	19	4 75
	France..........	....	61	....	61	15 25
	Germany......	....	173	....	173	43 25
	Japan..........	....	20	....	20	5 00
	Switzerland...:	....	4	....	4	1 00
	United States...	....	71,478	....	71,478	17,869 50
	Total......	....	118,519	....	72,507	18,126 75
Shawls........................	Unit'd Kingdom	....	264	....	119	44 63
	Hong Kong.....	....	164	....	164	61 50
	Aust.-Hungary .	....	122	....	122	45 75
	France..........	....	16	....		
	Germany......	....	274	....	274	102 75
	Italy..........	....	464	....		
	Japan..........	....	24	....	14	5 25
	United States...	....	363	....	363	136 15
	Total......	....	1,691	....	1,056	396 03
		Doz.		Doz.		
Shirts........................	Unit'd Kingdom	169	2,851	1	36	13 50
	Hong Kong.....	8	134	8	134	50 25
	Japan..........	337	4,865	4	91	34 13
	United States...	104	2,303	104	2,303	863 64
	Total......	618	10,153	117	2,564	961 52
Silk and all manufactures of, not otherwise provided for, or of which silk is the component part of chief value, n.o.p.	Unit'd Kingdom	....	91,756	....	3,958	1,484 25
	B. W. Indies....	....	212	....		
	Hong Kong.....	....	288	....	288	108 00
	Aust.-Hungary .	....	105	....		
	Belgium........	....	167	....		
	China..........	....	643	....	643	241 13
	France..........	....	57,632	....	1,111	416 63
	Germany......	....	2,535	....	2,535	950 63
	Italy..........	....	439	....	439	164 63
	Japan..........	....	24,976	....	701	262 88
	Switzerland....	....	416	....	19	6 18
	United States...	....	56,320	....	56,195	21,073 96
	Total......	....	235,489	....	65,889	24,708 29
		Doz. pr.		Doz. pr.		
Socks and stockings...........	Unit'd Kingdom	4,529	17,508	645	2,362	826 70
	Hong Kong.....	1	3	32	193	67 55
	France..........	221	2,377	221	2,377	831 95
	Germany......	15,048	28,654	15,360	29,462	10,311 70
	Japan..........	520	2,758	527	2,800	980 00
	Switzerland....	146	879	146	879	307 65
	United States...	71,016	232,681	77,381	265,393	92,887 55
	Total......	91,481	284,860	94,312	303,466	106,213 10

OF IMPORTS—*Continued.*

FOR HOME CONSUMPTION.

Preferential Tariff.			Treaty Rates.			Total.		
Quantity.	Value.	Duty.	Quantity.	Value.	Duty.	Quantity.	Value.	DutyColl'd.
Lb.	$	$ cts.	Lb.	$	$ cts.	Lb.	$	$ cts.
1,568	2,043	204 30	....	....	....	1,568	2,043	204 30
....	....	....	....	....	....	51	107	16 05
....	....	....	....	....	....	557	1,278	191 70
....	....	....	....	....	....	1,417	2,955	443 25
1,568	2,043	204 30	....	....	....	3,593	6,383	855 30
....						....	1,522	152 20
....	45,895	8,031 72	....			....	46,647	8,219 72
....	....	....					19	4 75
....	....	....					61	15 25
....	....	....					173	43 25
....	....	....					20	5 00
....	....	....					4	1 00
....	....	....					71,478	17,869 50
....	45,895	8,031 72	....			....	118,402	26,158 47
....	80	24 00	....	5	1 63	....	204	70 26
....	....	....					164	61 50
....	....	....					122	45 75
....	....	....	16	5 20			16	5 20
....	....	....					274	102 75
....	....	....	464	162 40			464	162 40
....	....	....	10	3 25			24	8 50
....	....	....					363	136 15
....	80	24 00	....	495	172 48	....	1,631	592 51
Doz. 168	2,815	844 50	Doz.	....	....	Doz. 169	2,851	858 00
....	....	....				8	134	50 25
....	....	....	333	4,774	1,551 57	337	4,865	1,585 70
....	....	....	....	....	....	104	2,303	863 64
168	2,815	844 50	333	4,774	1,551 57	618	10,153	3,357 59
....	78,296	23,488 80	....	9,150	2,989 43	....	91,404	27,962 48
....	....	....	....			....	288	108 00
....	....	....	105	34 25		....	105	34 25
....	....	....	167	58 45		....	167	58 45
....	....	....					643	241 13
....	....	....	56,453	18,359 13			57,564	18,775 76
....	....	....					2,535	950 63
....	....	....					439	164 63
....	....	....	24,471	7,953 99			25,172	8,216 87
....	....	....	397	129 03			416	135 21
....	....	....					56,195	21,073 96
....	78,296	23,488 80	....	90,743	29,524 28	....	234,928	77,721 37
Doz. pr. 3,907	14,928	3,732 00	Doz. pr.			Doz. pr. 4,552	17,290	4,558 70
....	....	....				32	193	67 55
....	....	....				221	2,377	831 95
....	....	....				15,360	29,462	10,311 70
....	....	....				527	2,800	980 00
....	....	....				146	879	307 65
....	....	....				77,381	265,393	92,887 55
3,907	14,928	3,732 00	....	....	....	98,219	318,394	109,945 10

6 GEORGE V, A. 1916

No. 1.—General Statement

Articles Imported.	Countries.	Total Imports.		Entered		
				General Tariff.		
		Quantity.	Value.	Quantity.	Value.	Duty.
		a	$		$	$ cts.
DUTIABLE GOODS—*Con.*			$		$	$ cts.
Silk, and mfrs. of—*Con.*						
Undershirts and drawers......	Unit'd Kingdom	....	3,129	....	1,626	569 10
	Germany., ...	....	37	....	37	12 95
	Japan...........	....	44	....	44	15 40
	Switzerland....	....	402	....	402	140 70
	United States...	....	6,569	....	6,569	2,299 15
	Total......	....	10,181	....	8,678	3,037 30
		Yd.		Yd.		
Velvets, and plush fabrics, n.o.p	Unit'd Kingdom	369,830	307,371	30,922	23,926	7,177 80
	Aust.-Hungary .	294	212	....	....	....
	Belgium........	3,532	4,073	893	1,296	388 80
	France.........	55,687	47,004	5,497	3,705	1,111 50
	Germany.......	31,241	21,468	31,412	21,741	6,522 30
	Italy..........	375	399	....	....	....
	Japan..........	2	8	....	....	....
	United States...	20,363	19,049	18,955	18,175	5,452 50
	Total......	481,324	399,584	87,679	68,843	20,652 90
Slate and manufactures of—						
Mantles.......................	United States...	....	598	....	598	179 40
		Sq. of 100 sq. ft.		Sq. of 100 sq. ft.		
Roofing slate...................	Unit'd Kingdom	1,506	10,153	56	145	42 00
	Belgium........	58	266	58	266	43 50
	United States..	14,830	70,793	14,830	70,793	11,122 50
	Total......	16,394	81,212	14,944	71,204	11,208 00
School writing slates..........	Unit'd Kingdom	....	569	....	58	14 50
	Belgium........	....	9	....	9	2 25
	France..........	....	6	....	6	1 50
	Germany.......	....	886	....	886	221 50
	Holland........	....	17	....	17	4 25
	United States...	....	50,673	....	50,673	12,668 25
	Total......	....	52,160	....	51,649	12,912 25
Slate pencils...................	Unit'd Kingdom	....	20	....	18	4 50
	Belgium........	....	212	....	212	53 00
	France..........	....	13	....	13	3 25
	Germany.......	....	2,001	....	2,001	500 25
	United States...	....	2,861	....	2,861	715 25
	Total......	....	5,107	....	5,105	1,276 25
Slate and manufactures of, n.o.p.	Unit'd Kingdom	....	4,531	....	546	163 80
	Germany.......	....	228	....	228	68 40
	United States...	....	44,244	....	44,244	13,273 20
	Total......	....	49,003	....	45,018	13,505 40
Soap—		Lb.		Lb.		
Common or laundry............	Unit'd Kingdom	301,641	16,411	....	....	....
	Belgium........	10	1	10	1	0 10
	France.........	5,958	72	1,008	59	10 08
	United States...	7,490,206	388,502	7,461,682	387,268	74,616 82
	Total......	7,797 815	404,986	7,462,700	387,328	74,627 00

SESSIONAL PAPER No. 11

OF IMPORTS—*Continued.*

FOR HOME CONSUMPTION.

	Preferential Tariff.			Treaty Rates.			Total.	
Quantity.	Value.	Duty.	Quantity.	Value.	Duty.	Quantity.	Value.	DutyColl'd.
	$	$ cts.		$	$ cts.		$	$ cts.
....	1,503	338 21	....	....	....	....	3,129	907 31
....	....	....	....	....	....	....	37	12 95
....	....	....	....	....	....	....	44	15 40
....	....	....	....	....	....	....	402	140 70
....	....	....	....	....	....	....	6,569	2,299 15
....	1,503	338 21	....	....	....	....	10,181	3,375 51
Yd. 291,051	245,604	42,981 89	Yd. 42,487	35,107	8,669 56	Yd. 364,460	304,637	58,829 25
....	....	....	294	212	55 31	294	212	55 31
....	....	....	2,639	2,777	763 68	3,532	4,073	1,152 48
....	....	....	50,482	43,711	11,311 85	55,979	47,416	12,423 35
....	....	....	....	....	....	31,412	21,741	6,522 30
....	....	....	375	399	109 73	375	399	109 73
....	....	....	2	8	1 60	2	8	1 60
....	....	....	....	....	....	18,955	18,175	5,452 50
291,051	245,604	42,981 89	96,279	82,214	20,911 73	475,009	396,661	84,546 52
....	....	....	....	....	....	....	598	179 40
Sq. of 100 sq. ft. 1,450	10,008	725 00	Sq. of 100 sq. ft.	....	....	Sq. of 100 sq. ft. 1,506	10,153	767 00
....	....	....	....	....	....	58	266	43 50
....	....	....	....	....	....	14,830	70,793	11,122 50
1,450	10,008	725 00	....	....	....	16,394	81,212	11,933 00
....	511	76 65	....	....	....	....	569	91 15
....	....	....	....	....	....	....	9	2 25
....	....	....	....	....	....	....	6	1 50
....	....	....	....	....	....	....	886	221 50
....	....	....	....	....	....	....	17	4 25
....	....	....	....	....	....	....	50,673	12,668 25
....	511	76 65	....	....	....	....	52,160	12,988 90
....	2	0 30	....	....	....	....	20	4 80
....	....	....	....	....	....	....	212	53 00
....	....	....	....	....	....	....	13	3 25
....	....	....	....	....	....	....	2,001	500 25
....	....	....	....	....	....	....	2,861	715 25
....	2	0 30	....	....	....	....	5,107	1,276 55
....	3,985	797 00	....	....	....	....	4,531	960 80
....	....	....	....	....	....	....	228	68 40
....	....	....	....	....	....	....	44,244	13,273 20
....	3,985	797 00	....	....	....	....	49,003	14,302 40
Lb. 301,641	16,411	1,960 77	Lb.	....	....	Lb. 301,641	16,411	1,960 77
....	....	....	....	....	....	10	1	0 10
....	....	....	....	....	....	1,008	59	10 08
....	....	....	....	....	....	7,461,682	387,268	74,616 82
301,641	16,411	1,960 77	....	....	....	7,764,341	403,739	76,587 77

11—ii—15½

6 GEORGE V, A. 1916

No. 1.—General Statemetn

Articles Imported.	Countries.	Total Imports.		Entered		
				General Tariff.		
		Quantity.	Value.	Quantity.	Value.	Duty.
DUTIABLE GOODS—*Con.*		Lb.	$	Lb.	$	$ cts.
Soap—*Con.*						
Castile......................	Unit'd Kingdom	118,447	7,152	120	8	2 40
	France..........	1,704,617	122,424	1,173	84	23 46
	Italy...........	42,574	4,610	28,832	3,317	576 64
	United States...	30,755	3,855	30,791	3,862	615.82
	Total.......	1,896,393	138,041	60,916	7,271	1,218 32
Common soft and liquid........	Unit'd Kingdom	72,469	3,319	125	12	3 90
	France..........	1,914	140	1,914	140	45 50
	Germany.......	1,313	62	1,313	62	20 15
	United States...	196,166	8,069	195,926	8,030	2,609 97
	Total.......	271,862	11,590	199,278	8,244	2,679 52
Harness......................	Unit'd Kingdom	1,852	231	110	12	3 90
	United States...	7,035	632	7,035	632	205 41
	Total.......	8,887	863	7,145	644	209 31
Toilet......................	Unit'd Kingdom	....	71,419	....	1,487	483 28
	Hong Kong.....	....	6	....	6	1 95
	Aust.-Hungary..	....	13	....	13	4 23
	Belgium........	....	26	....	26	8 45
	France..........	....	4,926	....	5,243	1,703 98
	Germany.......	....	1,410	....	1,410	458 25
	Holland........	....	161	....	161	52 33
	Italy...:.......	....	84	....	84	27 30
	Japan..........	....	103	....	103	33 48
	Russia.........	....	48	....	48	15 60
	Sweden........	....	55	....	55	17 88
	United States...	....	369,991	....	372,800	121,163 06
	Total.......	....	448,242	....	381,436	123,969 79
Soap, n.o.p., including pumice, silver and mineral soaps, sapolio and like articles.	Unit'd Kingdom	....	18,964	....	1,636	531 70
	Australia........	....	340	....	340	110 50
	B. W. Indies....	....	45	....	45	14 63
	Hong Kong....	....	13	....	13	4 23
	France..........	....	1,112	....	1,083	351 98
	Germany.......	....	1,240	....	1,240	403 00
	Greece..........	....	60	....	60	19 50
	Japan..........	....	27	....	27	8 78
	Switzerland.....	....	27	....	27	8 78
	United States...	....	65,709	....	65,915	21,422 94
	Total.......	....	87,537	....	70,386	22,876 04
Pearline and other soap powders	Unit'd Kingdom	116,415	4,600	198	35	11 38
	Japan..........	650	26	26	26	8 45
	United States...	2,363,180	93,346	2,404,728	95,458	31,024 36
	Total.......	2,480,245	97,972	2,405,576	95,519	31,044 19
Spices—						
Ginger and spices, n.o.p., unground.	Unit'd Kingdom	743,452	63,685	68,549	9,401	1,175 13
	B. E. Africa....	88,658	7,413	81,244	6,483	810 38
	B. India........	472,354	40,641	14,293	1,562	195 25
	B. E. Indies other.........	17,261	1,739	....	....	....
	B. W. Indies....	369,317	15,340	18,790	875	109 38
	B. Straits Settlements...	595,703	70,012	25,163	2,785	348 13

OF IMPORTS—*Continued.*

FOR HOME CONSUMPTION.

Preferential Tariff.			Treaty Rates.			Total.		
Quantity.	Value.	Duty.	Quantity.	Value.	Duty.	Quantity.	Value.	DutyColl'd.
Lb...	$	$ cts.	Lb.	$	$ cts.	Lb.	$	$ cts.
24,679	1,676	246 79	92,666	5,412	926 66	117,465	7,096	1,175 85
....	....	....	1,718,263	122,035	17,182 63	1,719,436	122,119	17,206 09
....	....	....	14,246	1,356	142 46	43,078	4,673	719 10
....	....	....	....	....	....	30,791	3,862	615 82
24,679	1,676	246 79	1,825,175	128,803	18,251 75	1,910,770	137,750	19,716 86
67,178	3,158	710 61	....	....	....	67,303	3,170	714 51
....	....	....	....	....	....	1,914	140	45 50
....	....	....	....	....	....	1,313	62	20 15
....	....	....	....	....	....	195,926	8,030	2,609 97
67,178	3,158	710 61	....	....	....	266,456	11,402	3,390 13
1,742	219	49 29	....	....	....	1,852	231	53 19
....	....	....	....	....	....	7,035	632	205 41
1,742	219	49 29	....	....	....	8,887	863	258 60
....	68,960	15,516 30	....	....	....	....	70,447	15,999 58
....	....	....	....	....	....	....	6	1 95
....	....	....	....	....	....	....	13	4 23
....	....	....	....	....	....	....	26	8 45
....	....	....	....	....	....	....	5,243	1,703 98
....	....	....	....	....	....	....	1,410	458 25
....	....	....	....	....	....	....	161	52 33
....	....	....	....	....	....	....	84	27 30
....	....	....	....	....	....	....	103	33 48
....	....	....	....	....	....	....	48	15 60
....	....	....	....	....	....	....	55	17 88
....	....	....	....	....	....	....	372,800	121,163 06
....	68,960	15,516 30	....	....	....	....	450,396	139,486 09
....	17,087	3,844 72	....	....	....	....	18,723	4,376 42
....	....	....	....	....	....	....	340	110 50
....	....	....	....	....	....	....	45	14 63
....	....	....	....	....	....	....	13	4 23
....	....	....	....	....	....	....	1,083	351 98
....	....	....	....	....	....	....	1,240	403 00
....	....	....	....	....	....	....	60	19 50
....	....	....	....	....	....	....	27	8 78
....	....	....	....	....	....	....	27	8 78
....	....	....	....	....	....	....	65,915	21,422 94
....	17,087	3,844 72	....	....	....	....	87,473	26,720 76
116,217	4,565	1,027 16	....	....	....	116,415	4,600	1,038 54
....	....	....	....	....	....	650	26	8 45
....	....	....	....	....	....	2,404,728	95,458	31,024 36
116,217	4,565	1,027 16	....	....	....	2,521,793	100,084	32,071 35
607,658	54,002	5,400 20	....	....	....	676,207	63,403	6,575 33
13,304	1,719	171 90	....	....	....	94,548	8,202	982 28
471,716	40,436	4,043 60	....	....	....	486,009	41,998	4,238 85
28,461	2,107	210 70	....	....	....	28,461	2,107	210 70
345,928	14,461	1,446 10	....	....	....	364,718	15,336	1,555 48
570,235	66,167	6,616 70	....	....	....	595,398	68,952	6,964 83

6 GEORGE V, A. 1916

No. 1.—General Statement

Articles Imported.	Countries.	Total Imports.		Entered		
				General Tariff.		
		Quantity.	Value.	Quantity.	Value.	Duty.
DUTIABLE GOODS—*Con.*		Lb.	$	Lb.	$	$ cts.
Spices—*Con.*						
Ginger and spices, n.o.p., un-ground—*Con.*	Hong Kong.....	132,391	4,275	132,391	4,275	534 38
	China..........	254,565	7,826	255,233	7,826	978 25
	Dutch E. Indies	13,699	1,279	13,699	1,279	159 88
	Germany.......	2,604	111	2,604	111	13 88
	Holland........	13,401	1,299	13,401	1,299	162 38
	Italy..........	10,297	905	12,043	1,111	138 88
	Japan..........	45,662	2,646	45,162	2,625	328 13
	Mexico.........	10,310	1,485	10,310	1,485	185 63
	United States...	719,121	77,581	720,678	77,768	9,721 41
	Total......	3,488,795	296,237	1,413,560	118,885	14,861 09
Ginger and spices, n.o.p., ground	Unit'd Kingdom	24,131	6,519	818	187	43 24
	B. India........	1,125	136	560	68	23 60
	Hong Kong.....	677	75	677	75	27 81
	Aust.-Hungary..	441	104	441	104	23 63
	China..........	24	1	24	1	0 82
	France.........	253	117	253	117	19 29
	Japan..........	13	5	13	5	0 89
	Spain..........	9,179	1,090	9,179	1,090	384 37
	Turkey.........	543	60	543	60	22 29
	United States...	109,007	21,974	108,107	21,850	5,428 21
	Total......	145,393	30,081	120,615	23,557	5,974 15
Ginger, preserved..............	Unit'd Kingdom	25,667	4,014	8,344	788	257 95
	B. W. Indies....	34	12	10	8	2 80
	Hong Kong.....	151,756	9,915	151,396	9,900	3,303 10
	China..........	93,426	6,250	93,966	6,179	1,890 60
	Japan..........	2,788	111	2,788	111	35 95
	United States...	2,300	453	2,300	453	152 25
	Total......	275,971	20,755	258,804	17,439	5,642 65
Nutmegs and mace, whole or unground.	Unit'd Kingdom	105,069	13,500	3,959	556	111 20
	B. India........	3,325	426	....	....	....
	B. W. Indies....	76,151	8,122	15	3	0 60
	B. Straits Settlements...	4,646	650	....	....	....
	Germany.......	239	134	239	134	26 80
	Holland........	2,432	673	2,432	673	134 60
	Japan..........	1,500	67	1,500	67	13 40
	United States...	35,308	4,798	25,298	3,739	747 80
	Total......	228,670	28,370	33,443	5,172	1,034 40
Nutmegs and mace, ground.....	Unit'd Kingdom	199	68	....	....	....
	United States...	9,876	3,349	9,876	3,349	1,004 70
	Total......	10,075	3,417	9,876	3,349	1,004 70
Spirits and wines, viz.:—		Gal.		Gal.		
Amyl alcohol or fusil oil, or any substance known as potato spirit or potato oil.	United States..	8	25	8	25	19 80
Ethyl alcohol or the substance known as alcohol, hydrated oxide of ethyl, or spirits of wine.	Unit'd Kingdom	....	....	54	16	129 60
	China..........	48	55	48	55	115 20
	France.........	251	84	251	84	753 00
	Germany.......	9	4	9	4	21 60
	Holland........	4,609	963	4,193	911	11,574 60
	Miquelon and St. Pierre.....	9	10	9	10	27 00
	United States..	32,442	8,120	66	123	162 60
	Total......	37,368	9,236	4,630	1,203	12,783 60

OF IMPORTS—*Continued.*

FOR HOME CONSUMPTION.

Preferential Tariff.			Treaty Rates.			Total.		
Quantity.	Value.	Duty.	Quantity.	Value.	Duty.	Quantity.	Value.	DutyColl'd.
Lb.	$	$ cts.	Lb.	$	$ cts.	Lb.	$	$ cts.
....	....	....	....	....	....	132,391	4,275	534 38
....	....	....	....	....	....	255,233	7,826	978 25
....	....	....	....	....	....	13,609	1,279	159 88
....	....	....	....	....	....	2,604	111	13 88
....	....	....	....	....	....	13,401	1,299	162 38
....	....	....	....	....	....	12,043	1,111	138 88
....	....	....	....	....	....	45,162	2,625	328 13
....	....	....	....	....	....	10,310	1,485	185 63
....	....	....	....	....	....	720,678	77,768	9,721 41
2,037,302	178,892	17,889 20	....	....	....	3,450,862	297,777	32,750 29
23,793	6,509	1,202 14	....	....	....	24,611	6,696	1,245 38
565	68	22 05	....	....	....	1,125	136	45 65
....	....	....	....	....	....	677	75	27 81
....	....	....	....	....	....	441	104	23 63
....	....	....	....	....	....	24	1	0 82
....	....	....	....	....	....	253	117	19 29
....	....	....	....	....	....	13	5	0 89
....	....	....	....	....	....	9,179	1,090	384 37
....	....	....	....	....	....	543	60	22 29
....	....	....	....	....	....	108,107	21,850	5,428 21
24,358	6,577	1,224 19	....	....	....	144,973	30,134	7,198 34
19,601	3,416	780 90	....	....	....	27,945	4,204	1,038 85
24	5	1 25	....	....	....	34	13	4 05
....	....	....	....	....	....	151,396	9,900	3,303 10
....	....	....	....	....	....	93,966	6,179	1,890 60
....	....	....	....	....	....	2,788	111	35 95
....	....	....	....	....	....	2,300	453	152 25
19,625	3,421	782 15	....	....	....	278,429	20,860	6,424 80
95,280	11,691	1,461 46	....	....	....	99,239	12,247	1,572 66
5,033	674	84 25	....	....	....	5,033	674	84 25
76,097	8,295	1,036 88	....	....	....	76,112	8,298	1,037 48
6,326	1,341	167 63	....	....	....	6,326	1,341	167 63
....	....	....	....	....	....	239	134	26 80
....	....	....	....	....	....	2,432	673	134 60
....	....	....	....	....	....	1,500	67	13 40
....	....	....	....	....	....	25,298	3,739	747 80
182,736	22,001	2,750 22	....	....	....	216,179	27,173	3,784 62
1,720	220	44 00	....	....	....	1,720	220	44 00
....	....	....	....	....	....	9,876	3,349	1,004 70
1,720	220	44 00	....	....	....	11,596	3,569	1,048 70
Gal.			Gal.			Gal.		
....	....	....	....	....	....	8	25	19 80
....	....	....	....	....	....	54	16	129 60
....	....	....	....	....	....	48	55	115 20
....	....	....	....	....	....	251	84	753 00
....	....	....	....	....	....	9	4	21 60
....	....	....	....	....	....	4,193	911	11,574 60
....	....	....	....	....	....	9	10	27 00
....	....	....	....	....	....	66	123	162 60
....	....	....	....	....	....	4,630	1,203	12,783 60

6 GEORGE V, A. 1916

No. 1.—General Statement

Articles Imported.	Countries.	Total Imports.		Entered		
				General Tariff.		
		Quantity.	Value.	Quantity.	Value.	Duty.
		Gal.	$	Gal.	$	$ cts.
DUTIABLE GOODS—Con.						
Spirits and wines—Con.						
Methyl alcohol, wood alcohol, wood naphtha, proxylic spirits, or any substance known as wood spirits or methylated spirits.	Unit'd Kingdom	1	4	1	4	3 00
	United States..	33	40	33	40	93 00
	Total......	34	44	34	44	96 00
Absinthe......................	Unit'd Kingdom	....	....	25	57	63 60
	France..........	4,283	7,700	5,974	10,508	15,895 12
	Miquelon and St. Pierre.....	5	8	5	8	15 00
	United States..	290	628	35	75	105 00
	Total......	4,578	8,336	6,039	10,648	16,078 72
Arrack or palm spirits....:.......	Turkey.........	257	361	358	342	887 40
Brandy, including artificial brandy and imitations of brandy, n.o.p.	Unit'd Kingdom	5,762	11,014	6,174	12,597	16,385 02
	Aust.-Hungary..	43	60	1,604	891	3,998 10
	Belgium........	....	....	61	18	146 40
	Denmark.......	....	28	76	299	198 60
	France..........	442,821	869,701	452,534	877,779	1,224,452 59
	Germany.......	2	73	80	101	192 00
	Greece..........	255	511	176	342	513 00
	Holland........	14	96	1	3	3 00
	Italy...........	510	1,257	414	699	1,208 40
	Miquelon and St. Pierre.....	20	34	20	34	58 80
	Russia..........	....	....	484	451	1,174 20
	Spain..........	234	631	298	677	819 60
	Sweden.........	2	12	35	44	105 00
	Turkey.........	8	24	182	581	518 40
	United States..	527	1,635	725	1,997	1,977 00
	Total......	450,198	885,076	462,864	896,513	1,251,750 11
Cordials and liqueurs of all kinds, n.o.p., mescal, pulque, rum shrub, schiedam and other schnapps; tafia, angostura and similar alcoholic bitters or beverages.	Unit'd Kingdom	10,103	26,801	10,600	27,244	27,976 98
	Bermuda.......	2	7	2	7	6 00
	B. W. Indies....	122	739	138	927	378 60
	Hong Kong.....	24,009	36,710	21,146	32,281	56,107 20
	Aust.-Hungary..	....	....	201	456	563 40
	Belgium........	....	....	18	33	43 20
	China..........	39	39	39	39	117 00
	Denmark.......	67	223	26	62	78 00
	France..........	20,536	69,480	18,159	63,916	48,969 07
	Germany.......	1,404	2,885	596	1,677	1,561 29
	Greece..........	856	1,889	241	566	663 60
	Holland........	10,058	17,281	6,627	12,479	17,514 58
	Italy...........	2,839	8,361	2,995	8,516	8,169 46
	Japan..........	28	38	28	38	115 69
	Norway........	768	1,856	653	1,505	1,776 72
	Portugal.......	79	241	7	19	21 00
	Russia..........	....	....	214	528	547 20
	Spain..........	....	....	46	248	123 09
	Sweden.........	1,239	1,884	441	771	1,250 55
	Switzerland.....	....	....	22	80	59 40
	Turkey.........	....	....	7	18	16 80
	United States..	1,952	9,669	2,372	10,441	6,333 34
	Total......	74,101	178,103	64,578	161,851	172,392 17

SESSIONAL PAPER No. 11

OF IMPORTS—*Continued*.

FOR HOME CONSUMPTION.

Preferential Tariff.			Treaty Rates.			Total.		
Quantity.	Value.	Duty.	Quantity.	Value.	Duty.	Quantity.	Value.	DutyColl'd.
Gal.	$	$ cts.	Gal.	$	$ cts.	Gal.	$	$ cts.
....	....	....	....	....	....	1	4	3 00
....	....	....	....	....	....	33	40	93 00
....	....	....	....	....	....	34	44	96 00
....	....	....	....	....	....	25	57	63 60
....	....	....	....	....	....	5,974	10,508	15,895 12
....	....	....	....	....	....	5	8	15 00
....	....	....	....	....	....	35	75	105 00
....	....	....	....	....	....	6,039	10,648	16,078 72
....	....	....	....	....	....	358	342	887 40
....	....	....	....	....	....	6,174	12,597	16,385 02
....	....	....	....	....	....	1,604	891	3,998 10
....	....	....	....	....	....	61	18	146 40
....	....	....	....	....	....	76	299	198 60
....	....	....	....	....	....	452,534	877,779	1,224,452 59
....	....	....	....	....	....	80	101	192 00
....	....	....	....	....	....	176	342	513 00
....	....	....	....	....	....	1	3	3 00
....	....	....	....	....	....	414	699	1,208 40
....	....	....	....	....	....	20	34	58 80
....	....	....	....	....	....	484	451	1,174 20
....	....	....	....	....	....	298	677	819 60
....	....	....	....	....	....	35	44	105 00
....	....	....	....	....	....	182	581	518 40
....	....	....	....	....	....	725	1,997	1,977 00
....	....	....	....	....	....	462,864	896,513	1,251,750 11
....	....	....	....	....	....	10,600	27,244	27,976 98
....	....	....	....	....	....	2	7	6 00
....	....	....	....	....	....	138	927	378 60
....	....	....	....	....	....	21,146	32,281	56,107 20
....	....	....	....	....	....	201	456	563 40
....	....	....	....	....	....	18	33	43 20
....	....	....	....	....	....	39	39	117 00
....	....	....	....	....	....	26	62	78 00
....	....	....	....	....	....	18,159	63,916	48,969 07
....	....	....	....	....	....	596	1,677	1,561 29
....	....	....	....	....	....	241	566	663 60
....	....	....	....	....	....	6,627	12,479	17,514 58
....	....	....	....	....	....	2,995	8,516	8,169 46
....	....	....	....	....	....	28	38	115 69
....	....	....	....	....	....	653	1,505	1,776 72
....	....	....	....	....	....	7	19	21 00
....	....	....	....	....	....	214	528	547 20
....	....	....	....	....	....	46	248	123 09
....	....	....	....	....	....	441	771	1,250 55
....	....	....	....	....	....	22	80	59 40
....	....	....	....	....	....	7	18	16 80
....	....	....	....	....	....	2,372	10,441	6,333 34
....	....	....	....	....	....	64,578	161,851	172,392 17

No. 1.—General Statement

Articles Imported.	Countries.	Total Imports.		Entered		
				General Tariff.		
		Quantity.	Value.	Quantity.	Value.	Duty.
		Gal.	$	Gal.	$	$ cts.
DUTIABLE GOODS—*Con.*						
Spirits and wines—*Con.*						
Gin of all kinds, n.o.p.	Unit'd Kingdom	155,909	209,377	155,363	210,089	417,592 30
	Belgium			201	127	489 60
	France			48	65	115 20
	Holland	937,218	582,594	771,030	492,866	2,072,356 70
	Russia	6	28	6	28	14 40
	United States	1,144	3,897	340	1,141	1,004 40
	Total	1,094,277	795,896	926,988	704,316	2,491,572 60
Rum	Unit'd Kingdom	40,980	28,623	51,907	35,571	145,354 73
	B. Guiana	101,197	28,597	87,206	25,119	241,011 60
	B. W. Indies	23,448	15,503	27,623	18,225	77,010 03
	Dan. W. Indies			74	55	177 60
	France	12,868	19,592	13,632	20,090	37,978 83
	Holland	17	45			
	Miquelon and St. Pierre	26	77	26	77	74 40
	United States	6,234	2,173	5,597	2,030	15,437 40
	Total	184,770	94,610	186,065	101,167	517,044 59
Whiskey	Unit'd Kingdom	1,243,313	2,373,957	1,262,929	2,356,212	3,459,742 11
	B. W. Indies			346	238	942 00
	Hong Kong	90	153	90	153	216 00
	Aust.-Hungary	38	53	38	53	91 20
	France	20	138	163	601	391 20
	Germany	1	5	1	5	2 40
	Holland			3	7	9 00
	Italy			161	137	386 40
	Russia	9	32	126	137	322 20
	Sweden			2	5	6 00
	United States	9,473	28,637	11,191	33,194	29,560 65
	Total	1,252,944	2,402,975	1,275,050	2,390,742	3,491,669 16
All spirituous or alcoholic liquors, n.o.p.	Unit'd Kingdom	221	267			
	Hong Kong	1,710	2,623	1,623	2,468	4,481 40
	China	2,729	3,530	2,793	3,913	7,780 80
	France	140	319	150	336	371 40
	Germany	385	224	385	224	1,043 40
	Greece			85	183	204 00
	Miquelon and St. Pierre	19	20	19	20	45 60
	Russia	36	101	208	522	602 40
	Turkey	123	211	123	211	295 20
	United States	508	2,355	550	2,420	1,526 40
	Total	5,871	9,650	5,936	10,297	16,350 60
Spirits and strong waters of any kind, mixed with any ingredient or ingredients, and being known or designated as anodynes, elixirs, essences, extracts, lotions, tinctures or medicines, or ethereal and spirituous fruit essences, n.o.p.	Unit'd Kingdom	1,680	13,910	1,708	14,069	8,899 50
	Hong Kong	746	1,145	730	1,123	2,461 50
	Belgium	9	128	9	128	60 00
	China	108	69	108	69	315 30
	France	237	3,172	264	3,341	1,713 90
	Germany	58	601	69	706	390 00
	Greece	5	10	4	10	15 00
	Holland	4	51	4	51	24 90
	Italy	2,188	5,954	1,627	4,415	5,690 25
	United States	2,030	24,943	2,043	25,040	12,852 00
	Total	7,065	49,983	6,566	48,952	32,422 35

OF IMPORTS—*Continued.*

FOR HOME CONSUMPTION.

Preferential Tariff.			Treaty Rates.			Total.		
Quantity.	Value.	Duty.	Quantity.	Value.	Duty.	Quantity.	Value.	DutyColl'd.
Gal.	$	$ cts.	Gal.	$	$ cts.	Gal.	$	$ cts.
....	....	....	....	....	....	155,363	210,089	417,592 30
....	....	....	....	....	....	201	127	489 60
....	....	....	....	....	....	48	65	115 20
....	....	....	....	....	....	771,030	492,866	2,072,356 70
....	....	....	....	....	....	6	28	14 40
....	....	....	....	....	....	340	1,141	1,004 40
....	....	....	....	....	....	926,988	704,316	2,491,572 60
....	....	....	....	....	....	51,907	35,571	145,354 73
....	....	....	....	....	....	87,206	25,119	241,011 60
....	....	....	....	....	....	27,623	18,225	77,010 03
....	....	....	....	....	....	74	55	177 60
....	....	....	....	....	....	13,632	20,090	37,978 83
....	....	....	....	....	....	....	....	....
....	....	....	....	....	....	26	77	74 40
....	....	....	....	....	....	5,597	2,030	15,437 40
....	....	....	....	....	....	186,065	101,167	517,044 59
....	....	....	....	....	....	1,262,929	2,356,212	3,459,742 11
....	....	....	....	....	....	346	238	942 00
....	....	....	....	....	....	90	153	216 00
....	....	....	....	....	....	38	53	91 20
....	....	....	....	....	....	163	601	391 20
....	....	....	....	....	....	1	5	2 40
....	....	....	....	....	....	3	7	9 00
....	....	....	....	....	....	161	137	386 40
....	....	....	....	....	....	126	137	322 20
....	....	....	....	....	....	2	5	6 00
....	....	....	....	....	....	11,191	33,194	29,560 65
....	....	....	....	....	....	1,275,050	2,390,742	3,491,669 16
....	....	....	....	....	....	1,623	2,468	4,481 40
....	....	....	....	....	....	2,793	3,913	7,780 80
....	....	....	....	....	....	150	336	371 40
....	....	....	....	....	....	385	224	1,043 40
....	....	....	....	....	....	85	183	204 00
....	....	....	....	....	....	19	20	45 60
....	....	....	....	....	....	208	522	602 40
....	....	....	....	....	....	123	211	295 20
....	....	....	....	....	....	550	2,420	1,526 40
....	....	....	....	....	....	5,936	10,297	16,350 60
....	....	....	....	....	....	1,708	14,069	8,899 50
....	....	....	....	....	....	730	1,123	2,461 50
....	....	....	....	....	....	9	128	60 00
....	....	....	....	....	....	108	69	315 30
....	....	....	....	....	....	264	3,341	1,713 90
....	....	....	....	....	....	69	706	390 00
....	....	....	....	....	....	4	10	15 00
....	....	....	....	....	....	4	51	24 90
....	....	....	....	....	....	1,627	4,415	5,690 25
....	....	....	....	....	....	2,043	25,040	12,852 00
....	....	....	....	....	....	6,566	48,952	32,422 35

6 GEORGE V, A. 1916

No. 1.—GENERAL STATEMENT

Articles Imported.	Countries.	TOTAL IMPORTS.		ENTERED		
				General Tariff.		
		Quantity.	Value.	Quantity.	Value.	Duty.
DUTIABLE GOODS—*Con.*		Gal.	$	Gal.	$	$ cts.
Spirits and wines—*Con.*						
Medicinal, or medicated wines	Unit'd Kingdom	3,000	11,459	2,928	* 11,733	6,506 00
containing not more than 40	Australia......	....	....	85	228	125 40
per cent of proof spirit.	Hong Kong.....	7	11	7	11	5 50
	Aust.-Hungary..	....	....	387	715	414 00
	China..........	2	9	2	9	5 40
	France..........	10,881	22,043	11,573	24,018	12,993 30
	Germany.......	2	10	2	10	5 00
	Holland........	2	5	....	....	....
	Italy...........	....	....	107	222	121 80
	Spain...........	4	15	14	70	36 50
	United States..	606	1,787	595	1,779	1,035 30
	Total.......	14,504	35,339	15,700	38,795	21,248 20
Alcoholic perfumes and per-	Unit'd Kingdom	1,045	9,756	768	9,285	5,137 40
fumed spirits, bay rum,	B. W. Indies...	5	121	7	128	64 70
Cologne and lavender waters,	Hong Kong....	9	59	9	59	31 90
hair, tooth and skin washes,	Aust.-Hungary..	11	111	11	111	55 50
and other toilet preparations	France.........	1,211	17,651	1,275	18,076	9,744 60
containing not more than 4	Germany.......	477	4,853	477	4,920	2,514 80
ounces each.	Holland........	13	230	13	230	115 00
	Japan..........	27	134	27	129	72 30
	Sweden........	5	53	5	53	26 50
	Switzerland.....	....	....	9	42	25 20
	United States...	3,470	28,773	3,484	28,966	16,161 80
	Total.......	6,273	61,741	6,085	61,999	33,949 70
Alcoholic perfumes and perfum-	Unit'd Kingdom	237	3,130	249	3,358	2,028 40
ed spirits, bay rum, Cologne	B. W. Indies....	35	59	35	59	109 40
and lavender waters, hair,	Dan. W. Indies.	124	177	107	153	357 60
tooth and skin washes, and	France..........	4,080	55,307	4,286	57,042	34,032 00
other toilet preparations	Germany.......	71	605	71	605	413 60
containing more than 4 ounces	Holland........	7	54	7	54	38 40
each.	Japan..........	3	16	3	16	15 40
	United States...	913	20,503	917	20,551	10,735 60
	Total.......	5,470	79,851	5,675	81,838	47,730 40
Vermouth, containing not more	Unit'd Kingdom	540	1,166	589	858	458 90
than 40 per cent of proof spirits	France..........	18,503	24,736	20,254	26,799	14,594 20
	Italy...........	20,652	23,341	18,040	20,054	10,867 90
	United States...	735	1,499	544	612	331 00
	Total.......	40,430	50,742	39,427	48,323	26,252 00
Vermouth, containing more than	France..........	....	....	2	8	4 80
40 per cent of proof spirits.						
Nitrous ether, sweet spirits of	Unit'd Kingdom	284	1,341	294	1,369	1,193 10
nitre and aromatic spirits of	Italy...........	....	....	10	33	39 90
ammonia.	United States...	248	1,372	248	1,372	1,068 00
	Total.......	532	2,713	552	2,774	2,301 00
Wines, ginger, containing not	Unit'd Kingdom	4,386	3,624	4,299	3,707	2,029 90
more than 40 per cent of proof	France..........	37	81	28	62	34 50
spirits.						
	Total.......	4,423	3,705	4,327	3,769	2,064 40

SESSIONAL PAPER No. 11

OF IMPORTS—*Continued.*

FOR HOME CONSUMPTION.

Preferential Tariff.			Treaty Rates.			Total.		
Quantity.	Value.	Duty.	Quantity.	Value.	Duty.	Quantity.	Value.	DutyColl'd.
Gal.	$	$ cts.	Gal.	$	$ cts.	Gal.	$	$ cts.
....	....	....	....	....	....	2,928	11,733	6,506 00
....	....	....	....	....	....	85	228	125 40
....	....	....	....	....	....	7	11	5 50
....	....	....	....	....	....	387	715	414 00
....	....	....	....	....	....	2	9	5 40
....	....	....	....	....	....	11,573	24,018	12,903 30
....	....	....	....	....	....	2	10	5 00
....	....	....	....	....	....	....	....	....
....	....	....	....	....	....	107	222	121 80
....	....	....	....	....	....	14	70	36 50
....	....	....	....	....	....	595	1,779	1,035 30
....	....	....	....	....	....	15,700	38,795	21,248 20
....	....	....	....	....	....	768	9,285	5,137 40
....	....	....	....	....	....	7	128	64 70
....	....	....	....	....	....	9	59	31 90
....	....	....	....	....	....	11	111	55 50
....	....	....	....	....	....	1,275	18,076	9,744 60
....	....	....	....	....	....	477	4,920	2,514 80
....	....	....	....	....	....	13	230	115 00
....	....	....	....	....	....	27	129	72 30
....	....	....	....	....	....	5	53	26 50
....	....	....	....	....	....	9	42	25 20
....	....	....	....	....	....	3,484	28,966	16,161 80
....	....	....	....	....	....	6,085	61,999	33,949 70
....	....	....	....	....	....	249	3,358	2,028 40
....	....	....	....	....	....	35	59	109 40
....	....	....	....	....	....	107	153	357 60
....	....	....	....	....	....	4,286	57,042	34,032 00
....	....	....	....	....	....	71	605	413 60
....	....	....	....	....	....	7	54	38 40
....	....	....	....	....	....	3	16	15 40
....	....	....	....	....	....	917	20,551	10,735 60
....	....	....	....	....	....	5,675	81,838	47,730 40
....	....	....	....	....	....	589	858	458 90
....	....	....	....	....	....	20,254	26,799	14,594 20
....	....	....	....	....	....	18,040	20,054	10,867 90
....	....	....	....	....	....	544	612	331 00
....	....	....	....	....	....	39,427	48,323	26,252 00
....	....	....	....	....	....	2	8	4 80
....	....	....	....	....	....	294	1,369	1,193 10
....	....	....	....	....	....	10	33	39 90
....	....	....	....	....	....	248	1,372	1,068 00
....	....	....	....	....	....	552	2,774	2,301 00
....	....	....	....	....	....	4,299	3,707	2,029 90
....	....	....	....	....	....	28	62	34 50
....	....	....	....	....	....	4,327	3,769	2,064 40

6 GEORGE V, A. 1916

No. 1—General Statement

Articles Imported.	Countries.	Total Imports.		Entered		
				General Tariff.		
		Quantity.	Value.	Quantity.	Value.	Duty.
DUTIABLE GOODS—*Con.*		Gal.	$	Gal.	$	$　cts.
Spirits and wines—*Con.* Wines of all kinds, n.o.p., including orange, lemon, strawberry, raspberry, elder and currant wines—						
Containing 20 p.c. or less proof spirits.	Unit'd Kingdom	7,066	4,528	....	....	....
	France..........	127,769	96,300	....	....	....
	French Africa...	2,050	1,021	....	....	....
	Italy..........	213	22	....	....	....
	Miquelon and St. Pierre.....	142	104	....	....	....
	Spain..........	218	291	....	....	....
	Total......	137,458	102,266	....	....	....
Containing over 20 p.c., and not over 23 p.c.	Unit'd Kingdom	753	2,121	....	....	....
	France..........	12,354	16,763	....	....	....
	French Africa...	179	103	....	....	....
	Italy..........	....	....	....	....	....
	Miquelon and St. Pierre.....	33	52	....	....	....
	Spain..........	21,740	9,424	....	....	....
	Total......	35,059	28,463	....	....	....
Containing 26 p.c. or less of proof spirits.	Unit'd Kingdom	3,669	5,573	879	1,733	739 65
	Australia.......	284	585	234	382	173 10
	Hong Kong.....	550	260	550	260	215 50
	Newfoundland..	2	3	2	3	1 40
	Aust.-Hungary..	171	170	171	170	93 75
	Belgium........	390	306	404	336	201 80
	China..........	34	88	34	88	34 90
	France..........	16,241	15,628	1,595	1,688	905 15
	French Africa...	219	111	....	....	....
	Germany.......	2,537	8,215	4,802	12,821	5,046 80
	Greece..........	563	311	605	350	256 25
	Holland........	283	894	192	546	211 80
	Italy..........	22,106	13,981	4,285	2,504	1,822 45
	Japan..........	72	51	40	34	20 20
	Miquelon and St. Pierre.....	49	86	3	2	1 35
	Portugal........	2,242	2,534	2,193	1,833	1,098 15
	Spain...........	144,019	62,181	3,578	1,882	1,459 10
	Switzerland.....	2	5	....	....	....
	Turkey.........	610	597	369	348	196 ·65
	United States..	34,631	17,081	33,894	15,814	13,217 70
	Total......	228,674	128,660	53,830	40,794	25,695 70
Containing over 26 p.c. and not over 27 p.c.	Unit'd Kingdom	533	474	6	10	4 68
	Hong Kong.....	60	32	60	32	26 40
	France..........	633	787	53	54	31 04
	Greece.:........	49	12	49	12	17 32
	Italy..........	1,493	655	18	37	16 14
	Japan..........	2,291	1,789	2,291	1,789	1,178 18
	Miquelon and St. Pierre.....	14	26	....	....	....
	Portugal........	2,039	1,319	2,519	1,533	1,165 22
	Spain..........	15,176	7,268	35	17	14 90
	Turkey.........	....	....	48	30	22 44
	United States..	32	18	74	43	33 62
	Total........	22,320	12,380	5,153	3,557	2,509 94

SESSIONAL PAPER No. 11

OF IMPORTS—*Continued.*

FOR HOME CONSUMPTION.

Preferential Tariff.			Treaty Rates.			Total.		
Quantity.	Value.	Duty.	Quantity.	Value.	Duty.	Quantity.	Value.	DutyColl'd.
Gal.	$	$ cts.	Gal.	$	$ cts.	Gal.	$	$ cts.
....	....	....	3,167	2,125	475 05	3,167	2,125	475 05
....	....	....	140,350	112,402	21,052 50	140,350	112,402	21,052 50
....	....	....	1,502	732	225 30	1,502	732	225 30
....	....	....	126	16	18 90	126	16	18 90
....	....	....	142	104	21 30	142	104	21 30
....	....	....	2,351	1,272	352 65	2,351	1,272	352 65
....	....	....	147,638	116,651	22,145 70	147,638	116,651	22,145 70
....	....	....	776	1,488	155 20	776	1,488	155 20
....	....	....	24,316	26,595	4,863 20	24,316	26,595	4,863 20
....	....	....	179	103	35 80	179	103	35 80
....	....	....	163	70	32 60	163	70	32 60
....	....	....	33	52	6 60	33	52	6 60
....	....	....	31,438	12,707	6,287 60	31,438	12,707	6,287 60
....	....	....	56,905	41,015	11,381 00	56,905	41,015	11,381 00
....	....	....	3,123	3,575	780 75	4,002	5,308	1,520 40
....	....	....	10	17	2 50	244	399	175 60
....	....	....	....	....	....	550	260	215 50
....	....	....	....	....	....	2	3	1 40
....	....	....	....	....	....	171	170	93 75
....	....	....	....	....	....	404	336	201 80
....	....	....	....	....	....	34	88	34 90
....	....	....	12,387	11,880	3,096 75	13,982	13,568	4,001 90
....	....	....	27	25	6 75	27	25	6 75
....	....	....	....	....	....	4,802	12,821	5,046 80
....	....	....	....	....	....	605	350	256 25
....	....	....	....	....	....	192	546	211 80
....	....	....	24,716	16,502	6,179 00	29,001	19,006	8,001 45
....	....	....	....	....	....	40	34	20 20
....	....	....	46	84	11 50	49	86	12 85
....	....	....	....	....	....	2,193	1,833	1,098 15
....	....	....	111,207	46,629	27,801 75	114,785	48,511	29,260 85
....	....	....	2	5	0 50	2	5	0 50
....	....	....	....	....	....	369	348	196 65
....	....	....	....	....	....	33,894	15,814	13,217 70
....	....	....	151,518	78,717	37,879 50	205,348	119,511	63,575 20
....	....	....	115	167	32 20	121	177	36 88
....	....	....	....	....	....	60	32	26 40
....	....	....	387	433	108 36	440	487	139 40
....	....	....	....	....	....	49	12	17 32
....	....	....	1,502	681	420 56	1,520	718	436 70
....	....	....	....	....	....	2,291	1,789	1,178 18
....	....	....	14	26	3 92	14	26	3 92
....	....	....	....	....	....	2,519	1,533	1,165 22
....	....	....	12,001	6,002	3,360 28	12,036	6,019	3,375 18
....	....	....	....	....	....	48	30	22 44
....	....	....	....	....	....	74	43	33 62
....	....	....	14,019	7,309	3,925 32	19,172	10,866	6,435 26

6 GEORGE V, A. 1916

No. 1.—General Statement

Articles Imported.	Countries.	Total Imports.		Entered		
				General Tariff.		
		Quantity.	Value.	Quantity.	Value.	Duty.
DUTIABLE GOODS—*Con.*		Gal.	$	Gal.	$	$ cts.
Spirits and wines—*Con.*						
Wines of all kinds—*Con.*						
Containing over 27 p.c. and not over 28 p.c.	Unit'd Kingdom	567	484	28	110	41 68
	Hong Kong.....	768	318	795	332	346 05
	Azores and Madeira.....	....	....	70	66	41 50
	China..........	105	81	105	81	56 85
	France..........	565	846	116	124	73 16
	Italy..........	2,387	1,487	33	17	15 33
	Japan..........	10,416	8,588	7,959	6,650	4,462 29
	Miquelon and St. Pierre.....	13	18	....	....	....
	Portugal.......	1,761	1,493	2,085	1,932	1,225 95
	Spain..........	8,990	5,891	37	34	21 67
	United States...	106	63	147	89	72 27
	Total......	25,678	19,269	11,375	9,435	6,356 75
Containing over 28 p.c. and not over 29 p.c.	Unit'd Kingdom	258	502	116	273	121 34
	Hong Kong.....	2,132	1,035	2,132	1,035	1,035 38
	China..........	87	48	101	60	52 34
	France..........	1,776	2,665	....	....	....
	Italy..........	1,601	1,202	20	31	16 10
	Japan..........	19,471	16,374	16,571	13,934	9,814 34
	Portugal.......	3,159	2,473	1,699	1,539	1,039 36
	Spain..........	9,501	7,992	147	148	94 38
	Turkey.........	....	....	4	23	8 26
	United States...	299	337	343	379	230 32
	Total......	38,284	32,628	21,133	17,422	12,411 82
Containing over 29 p.c. and not over 30 p.c.	Unit'd Kingdom	1,253	1,925	437	528	320 09
	Hong Kong.....	5,968	2,956	5,947	2,947	3,084 49
	Azores and Madeira.....	90	175	67	146	68 59
	China..........	126	92	126	92	74 22
	France..........	1,070	1,926	10	21	10 00
	Holland.......	1	2	....	....	....
	Italy..........	458	483	177	148	109 89
	Japan..........	31,102	26,080	31,922	26,903	19,882 04
	Miquelon and St. Pierre.....	26	36	....	....	....
	Portugal.......	6,651	6,478	6,563	6,652	4,423 91
	Spain..........	18,743	17,343	633	633	424 11
	United States...	166	172	166	172	113 02
	Total......	65,654	57,668	46,048	38,242	28,510 36
Containing over 30 p.c. and not over 31 p.c.	Unit'd Kingdom	1,626	1,569	319	648	322 00
	Hong Kong.....	9,320	4,745	8,037	4,095	4,443 30
	Azores and Madeira.....	187	329	48	68	– 39 60
	China..........	37	33	37	33	24 70
	France..........	117	153	6	35	12 90
	Greece.........	8	18	8	18	8 60
	Italy..........	153	186	39	37	26 70
	Japan..........	9,023	7,774	8,060	6,976	5,316 80
	Portugal.......	10,823	12,050	10,194	11,492	7,525 20
	Spain..........	16,073	15,770	725	903	560 90
	United States...	3,042	1,671	3,141	1,757	1,783 50
	Total......	50,409	44,298	30,614	26,062	20,064 20

OF IMPORTS—*Continued.*

FOR HOME CONSUMPTION.

Preferential Tariff.			Treaty Rates.			Total.		
Quantity.	Value.	Duty.	Quantity.	Value.	Duty.	Quantity.	Value.	DutyColl'd.
Gal.	$	$ cts.	Gal.	$	$ cts.	Gal.	$	$ cts.
			492	245	152 52	520	355	194 20
						795	332	346 05
						70	66	41 50
						105	81	56 85
			311	499	96 41	427	623	169 57
			1,105	626	342 55	1,138	643	357 88
						7,959	6,650	4,462 29
			13	18	4 03	13	18	4 03
						2,085	1,932	1,225 95
			10,988	7,452	3,406 28	11,025	7,486	3,427 95
						147	89	72 27
			12,909	8,840	4,001 79	24,284	18,275	10,358 54
			365	523	124 10	481	796	245 44
						2,132	1,035	1,035 38
						101	60	52 34
			642	900	218 28	642	900	218 28
			1,444	1,225	490 96	1,464	1,256	507 06
						16,571	13,934	9,814 34
						1,699	1,539	1,039 36
			9,918	9,257	3,372 12	10,065	9,405	3,466 50
						4	23	8 26
						343	379	230 32
			12,369	11,905	4,205 46	33,502	29,327	16,617 28
			602	1,299	222 74	1,039	1,827	542 83
						5,947	2,947	3,084 49
						67	146	68 59
						126	92	74 22
			856	1,478	316 72	866	1,499	326 72
			1	2	0 37	1	2	0 37
			80	96	29 60	257	244	139 49
						31,922	26,903	19,882 04
			26	36	9 62	26	36	9 62
						6,563	6,652	4,423 91
			17,485	16,847	6,469 45	18,118	17,480	6,893 56
						166	172	113 02
			19,050	19,758	7,048 50	65,098	58,000	35,558 86
			703	1,394	281 20	1,022	2,042	603 20
						8,037	4,095	4,443 30
						48	68	39 60
						37	33	24 70
			323	422	129 20	329	457	142 10
						8	18	8 60
			27	41	10 80	66	78	37 50
						8,060	6,976	5,316 80
						10,194	11,492	7,525 20
			16,527	16,202	6,610 80	17,252	17,105	7,171 70
						3,141	1,757	1,783 50
			17,580	18,059	7,032 00	48,194	44,121	27,096 20

6 GEORGE V, A. 1916

No. 1.—GENERAL STATEMENT

Articles Imported.	Countries.	Total Imports.		Entered		
				General Tariff.		
		Quantity.	Value.	Quantity.	Value.	Duty.
		Gal.	$	Gal.	$	$ cts.
DUTIABLE GOODS—*Con.*						
Spirits and wines—*Con.*						
Wines of all kinds—*Con.*						
Containing over 31 p.c. and not over 32 p.c.	Unit'd Kingdom	2,162	4,574	1,410	2,835	1,456 80
	Hong Kong.....	6,119	3,005	5,147	2,545	2,976 71
	Newfoundland..	38	169	26	128	49 58
	China..........	93	43	93	43	52 89
	France.,.......	860	1,005	230	303	189 80
	Italy..........	14	72	77	126	70 91
	Japan..........	103	72	103	72	65 89
	Miquelon and St. Pierre.....	33	74	....	....	....
	Portugal.......	15,003	21,493	12,529	18,748	11,011 87
	Spain..........	13,757	16,519	755	1,032	634 25
	United States..	2,526	1,730	2,490	1,840	1,622 70
	Total......	40,708	48,756	22,860	27,672	18,131 40
Containing over 32 p.c. and not over 33 p.c.	Unit'd Kingdom	2,968	6,146	819	1,914	950 94
	Hong Kong.....	5,870	3,023	5,960	3,069	3,662 30
	Newfoundland..	69	279	69	279	115 44
	China..........	6	3	6	3	3 66
	France.........	181	516	59	160	75 14
	Italy....:.....	270	139	6	24	9 96
	Portugal.......	15,029	19,973	14,208	19,899	12,505 38
	Spain..........	9,097	10,413	892	1,591	887 62
	United States...	2,224	1,409	2,697	1,729	1,759 32
	Total......	35,714	41,901	24,716	28,668	19,969 76
Containing over 33 p.c. and not over 34 p.c.	Unit'd Kingdom	1,813	4,303	504	1,778	780 36
	Hong Kong.....	3,172	1,696	3,112	1,657	2,021 98
	China..........	30	16	30	16	19 50
	France..........	156	281	67	138	74 23
	Germany......	12	20	12	20	11 88
	Holland......	8	33	8	33	13 82
	Japan..........	3	1	3	1	1 77
	Miquelon and St. Pierre.....	....	....	....	....	....
	Portugal.......	13,893	21,540	13,138	23,391	13,454 92
	Spain..........	1,411	2,649	396	727	412 14
	United States...	992	719	1,744	1,368	1,264 96
	Total......	21,490	31,258	19,014	29,129	18,055 56
Containing over 34 p.c. and not over 35 p.c.	Unit'd Kingdom	352	1,024	382	1,111	531 94
	Hong Kong	785	480	764	469	537 98
	Newfoundland..	10	58	10	58	22 60
	China..........	9	7	9	7	6 78
	France..........	97	343	10	47	19 30
	Miquelon and St. Pierre.....	2	5	....	....	....
	Portugal.......	5,915	9,096	6,476	9,793	6,305 42
	Spain..........	620	1,830	509	761	492 98
	United States..	311	238	481	383	365 02
	Total......	8,101	13,081	8,641	12,629	8,282 02
Containing over 35 p.c. and not over 36 p.c.	Unit'd Kingdom	919	2,347	374	1,400	625 70
	Hong Kong.....	357	296	306	252	243 90
	Newfoundland..	8	33	8	33	14 30
	France..........	105	332	95	240	124 25
	Germany......	19	26	19	26	18 25
	Portugal.......	4,555	12,021	3,922	9,541	5,019 40
	Spain..........	10	49	20	57	28 10
	United States...	82	154	213	248	191 55
	Total......	6,055	15,258	4,957	11,797	6,265 45

SESSIONAL PAPER No. 11

OF IMPORTS—*Continued.*

FOR HOME CONSUMPTION.

Preferential Tariff.			Treaty Rates.			Total.		
Quantity.	Value.	Duty.	Quantity.	Value.	Duty.	Quantity.	Value.	DutyColl'd.
Gal.	$	$ cts.	Gal.	$	$ cts.	Gal.	$	$ cts.
....	....	....	765	1,610	328 95	2,175	4,445	1,785 75
....	....	....	....	......	......	5,147	2,545	2,976 71
....	....\....	....	12	41	5 16	38	169	54 74
....	....	....	....	...	......	93	43	52 89
....	....	....	625	831	268 75	855	1,134	458 55
....	....	....	40	25	17 20	117	151	88 11
....	....	....	....	...	......	103	72	65 89
....	....	....	8	28	3 44	8	28	3 44
....	....	....	....	......	......	12,529	18,748	11,011 87
....	...,.....	....	14,067	16,424	6,048 81	14,822	17,456	6,683 06
....	....	....	....	......	......	2,490	1,840	1,622 70
....	....	....	15,517	18,959	6,672 31	38,377	46,631	24,803 71
....	.......●..	....•.....	1,511	2,951	695 06	2,330	4,865	1,646 00
....	....	....	....	......	......	5,960	3,069	3,662 30
....	....	....	....	......	......	69	279	115 44
....	....	....	....	......	......	6	3	3 66
....	....	....	283	529	130 18	342	689	205 32
....	....	....	13	21	5 98	19	45	15 94
....	....	....	....	......	......	14,208	19,899	12,505 38
....	....	....	9,337	9,790	4,295 02	10,229	11,381	5,182 64
....	....	....	....	......	......	2,697	1,729	1,759 32
....	....	....	11,144	13,291	5,126 24	35,860	41,959	25,096 00
....	....	....	1,451	3,279	710 99	1,955	5,057	1,491 35
....	....	....	....	......	......	3,112	1,657	2,021 98
....	....	....	....	......	......	30	16	19 50
....	....	....	224	375	109 76	291	513	183 99
....	....	....	....	......	......	12	20	11 88
....	....	....	....	......	......	8	33	13 82
....	....	....	....	......	......	3	1	1 77
....	....	....	25	46	12 25	25	46	12 25
....	....	....	....	......	......	13,138	23,391	13,454 92
....	....	....	2,330	3,717	1,141 70	2,726	4,444	1,553 84
....	....	....	....	......	......	1,744	1,368	1,264 96
....	....	....	4,030	7,417	1,974 70	23,044	36,546	20,030 26
....	....	....	201	456	104 52	583	1,567	636 46
....	....	....	....	......	......	764	469	537 98
....	....	....	....	......	......	10	58	22 60
....	....	....	....	......	......	9	7	6 78
....	....	....	84	303	43 68	94	350	62 98
....	....	....	2	5	1 04	2	5	1 04
....	....	....	....	......	......	6,476	9,793	6,305 42
....	....	....	780	1,913	405 60	1,289	2,674	898 58
....	....	....	....	......	......	481	383	365 02
....	....	....	1,067	2,677	554 84	9,708	15,306	8,836 86
....	....	....	266	582	146 30	640	1,982	772 00
....	....	....	....	......	......	306	252	243 90
....	....	....	....	......	......	8	33	14 30
....	....	....	10	92	5 50	105	332	129 75
....	....	....	....	......	......	19	26	18 25
....	....	....	....	......	......	3,922	9,541	5,019 40
....	....	....	278	277	152 90	298	334	181 00
....	....	....	....	......	......	213	248	191 55
....	....	....	554	951	304 70	5,511	12,748	6,570 15

11—ii—16½

6 GEORGE V, A. 1916

No. 1.—General Statement

Articles Imported.	Countries.	Total Imports.		Entered		
				General Tariff.		
		Quantity.	Value.	Quantity.	Value.	Duty.
		Gal.	$	Gal.	$	$ cts.
DUTIABLE GOODS—*Con.*						
Spirits and wines—*Con.*						
Wines of all kinds—*Con.*						
Containing over 36 p.c. and not over 37 p.c.	Unit'd Kingdom	434	632	12	44	20 16
	Hong Kong.....	224	165	224	165	179 42
	France..........	259	389	257	380	263 06
	Miquelon and St. Pierre.....	45	70	4	6	4 12
	Portugal........	1,177	3,057	1,309	3,132	1,698 82
	Spain...........	120	143	10	33	15 70
	United States...	2	11	2	11	4 46
	Total......	2,261	4,467	1,818	3,771	2,185 74
Containing over 37 p.c. and not over 38 p.c.	Unit'd Kingdom	70	181	64	180	93 04
	Hong Kong.....	304	239	289	226	244 09
	France..........	81	86	81	86	75 21
	Miquelon and St. Pierre.....	13	20	....	....	....
	Portugal........	277	629	241	693	354 91
	Spain...........	30	131	....	....	....
	United States...	191	187	231	267	221 01
	Total......	966	1,473	906	1,452	988 26
Containing over 38 p.c. and not over 39 p.c.	Unit'd Kingdom	4	23	10	40	18 40
	Hong Kong	342	334	342	334	319 08
	France..........	....	....	10	14	10 60
	Portugal........	441	969	374	891	506 66
	Total......	787	1,326	736	1,279	854 74
Containing over 39 p.c. and not over 40 p.c.	Hong Kong.....	179	140	179	140	161 93
	France..........	185	332	....	....	....
	Miquelon and St. Pierre.....	197	412	2	5	2 84
	Spain...........	586	597	....	....	....
	United States...	4	21	4	21	8 98
	Total......	1,151	1,502	185	166	173 75
Containing more than 40 p.c. of proof spirits, n.o.p.	Unit'd Kingdom	8	46	10	48	25 20
	Hong Kong.....	19,737	31,247	17,691	28,219	48,278 40
	China..........	3,042	4,214	3,198	4,437	8,443 20
	France..........	4	12	4	12	9 60
	Japan..........	153	190	25	23	61 20
	Portugal.......	17	52	....	....	....
	Total......	22,961	35,761	20,928	32,739	56,817 60
		Doz.		Doz.		
Champagne and all other sparkling wines—						
In bottles containing each not more than a quart but more than a pint, old wine measure.	Unit'd Kingdom	611	11,562	54	559	345 90
	Belgium........	....	....	....	....	....
	France..........	5,664	85,282	83	795	512 40
	Germany.......	587	4,073	428	3,092	2,340 00
	Holland........	58	396	16	120	88 80
	Italy..........	177	1,043	63	327	306 00
	Spain..........	....	....	....	....	....
	Switzerland.....	6	65	....	....	....
	United States...	14	184	29	285	181 20
	Total........	7,117	102,605	673	5,178	3,774 30

OF IMPORTS—*Continued.*

FOR HOME CONSUMPTION.

Preferential Tariff.			Treaty Rates.			Total.		
Quantity.	Value.	Duty.	Quantity.	Value.	Duty.	Quantity.	Value.	DutyColl'd.
Gal.	$	$ cts.	Gal.	$	$ cts.	Gal.	$	$ cts.
....	....	....	472	736	273 76	484	780	293 92
....	....	....	....	....	....	224	165	179 42
....	....	....	2	9	1 16	259	389	264 22
....	....	....	41	64	23 78	45	70	27 90
....	....	....	....	....	....	1,309	3,132	1,698 82
....	....	....	110	110	63 80	120	143	79 50
....	....	....	....	....	....	2	11	4 46
....	....	....	625	919	362 50	2,443	4,690	2,548 24
....	....	....	113	234	68 93	177	414	161 97
....	....	....	....	....	....	289	226	244 09
....	....	....	....	....	....	81	86	75 21
....	....	....	13	20	7 93	13	20	7 93
....	....	....	....	....	....	241	693	354 91
....	....	....	....	....	....	231	267	221 01
....	....	....	126	254	76 86	1,032	1,706	1,065 12
....	....	....	....	....	....	10	40	18 40
....	....	....	....	....	....	342	334	319 08
....	....	....	....	....	....	10	14	10 60
....	....	....	....	....	....	374	891	506 66
....	....	....	....	....	....	736	1,279	854 74
....	....	....	....	....	....	179	140	161 93
....	....	....	185	332	123 95	185	332	123 95
....	....	....	195	407	130 65	197	412	133 49
....	....	....	....	....	....	4	21	8 98
....	....	....	380	739	254 60	565	905	428 35
....	....	....	....	....	....	10	48	25 20
....	....	....	....	....	....	17,691	28,219	48,278 40
....	....	....	....	....	....	3,198	4,437	8,443 20
....	....	....	....	....	....	4	12	9 60
....	....	....	....	....	....	25	23	61 20
....	....	....	....	....	....	....	....	....
....	....	....	....	....	....	20,928	32,739	56,817 60
Doz.			Doz.			Doz.		
....	....	....	467	8,550	1,541 10	521	9,109	1,887 00
....	....	....	8	136	26 40	8	136	26 40
....	....	....	6,973	119,484	23,010 90	7,056	120,279	23,523 30
....	....	....	....	....	....	428	3,092	2,340 00
....	....	....	....	....	....	16	120	88 80
....	....	....	61	370	201 30	124	697	507 30
....	....	....	5	57	16 50	5	57	16 50
....	....	....	6	65	19 80	6	65	19 80
....	....	....	....	....	....	29	285	181 20
....	....	....	7,520	128,662	24,816 00	8,193	133,840	28,590 30

6 GEORGE V, A. 1916

No. 1—GENERAL STATEMENT

Articles Imported.	Countries.	TOTAL IMPORTS.		ENTERED		
				General Tariff.		
		Quantity.	Value.	Quantity.	Value.	Duty.
DUTIABLE GOODS—*Con.* Spirits and wines—*Con.* Wines of all kinds—*Con.* Champagne, &c.—*Con.*		Doz.	$	Doz.	$	$ cts.
In bottles containing not more than a pint each, but more than half a pint, old wine measure.	Unit'd Kingdom	404	3,602	25	180	95 25
	Belgium........	....	....	....	....	....
	France.........	14,701	134,672	95	641	349 05
	Germany......	472	2,112	720	2,933	2,067 90
	Holland.......	32	126	20	80	57 00
	Italy..........	210	705	70	237	186 60
	Miquelon and St. Pierre....	7	115	....	....	....
	Spain..........	....	....	....	....	....
	Switzerland.....	9	47	....	....	....
	United States...	52	344	120	615	382 50
	Total.......	15,887	141,723	1,050	4,686	3,138 30
In bottles containing one-half pint each or less.	Unit'd Kingdom	8	21	....	....	....
	France.........	1,337	2,673	....	....	....
	Total......	1,345	2,694	....	....	....
		Gal.		Gal.		
In bottles containing over one quart each.	Unit'd Kingdom	48	239	2	16	7 80
	France.........	62	750	....	....	....
	Total..../..	110	989	2	16	7 80
Sponges of marine production.....	Unit'd Kingdom	....	9,434	....	2,925	511 88
	B. W. Indies..	....	....	....	....	....
	Cuba..........	....	566	....	566	99 05
	France.........	....	370	....	370	64 75
	Germany......	....	4	....	4	0 70
	Greece........	....	310	....	310	54 25
	Russia.........	....	13	....	13	2 28
	United States...	....	62,744	....	62,523	10,942 23
	Total......	....	73,441	....	66,711	11,675 14
		Lb.		Lb.		
Starch, including farina, corn starch, etc.	Unit'd Kingdom	556,168	25,338	7,931	412	118 97
	B. W. Indies....	11,258	487	....	....	....
	B. Straits Settlements......	1,440	95	1,440	95	21 60
	Hong Kong.....	80,370	2,839	80,370	2,839	1,204 55
	Belgium........	32,495	1,090	30,677	965	460 16
	China..........	146	5	146	5	2 19
	France.........	5,842	281	360	18	5 40
	Germany......	77,969	1,748	77,969	1,748	1,169 54
	Holland.......	87,014	2,068	65,014	1,551	975 21
	Japan..........	9,628	891	9,628	891	144 42
	United States...	2,078,735	72,743	2,084,668	73,064	31,271 31
	Total.......	2,941,065	107,585	2,358,203	81,588	35,373 35
Stockinettes for the manufacture of rubber boots and shoes when imported by manufacturers of rubber boots and shoes for use exclusively in the manufacture of such articles in their own factories.	Unit'd Kingdom	....	21,945	....	....	....
	United States...	....	54,714	....	54,714	8,207 10
	Total.......	....	76,659	....	54,714	8,207 10

OF IMPORTS—*Continued.*

FOR HOME CONSUMPTION.

Preferential Tariff.			Treaty Rates.			Total.		
Quantity.	Value.	Duty.	Quantity.	Value.	Duty.	Quantity.	Value.	DutyColl'd.
Doz.	$	$ cts.	Doz.	$	$ cts.	Doz.	$	$ cts.
....	....	....	427	4,373	704 55	452	4,553	799 80
....	....	....	12	116	19 80	12	116	19 80
....	....	....	21,362	215,220	35,247 30	21,457	215,861	35,596 35
....	....	....	....	....	....	720	2,933	2,067 90
....	....	....	....	....	....	20	80	57 00
....	....	....	86	313	141 90	156	550	328 50
....	....	....	2	7	3 30	2	7	3 30
....	....	....	20	65	33 00	20	65	33 00
....	....	....	9	47	14 85	9	47	14 85
....	....	....	....	....	....	120	615	382 50
....	....	....	21,918	220,141	36,164 70	22,968	224,827	39,303 00
....	....	....	16	50	13 12	16	50	13 12
....	....	....	1,075	3,688	881 50	1,075	3,688	881 50
....	....	....	1,091	3,738	894 62	1,091	3,738	894 62
Gal.			Gal.			Gal.		
....	....	....	18	119	27 00	20	135	34 80
....	....	....	86	869	129 00	86	869	129 00
....	....	....	104	988	156 00	106	1,004	163 80
....	5,655	707 11	....	....	....	8,580	1,218 99	
....	562	70 25	....	....	....		562	70 25
....	....	....	....	....	....		566	99 05
....	....	....	....	....	....		370	64 75
....	....	....	....	....	....	4	0 70	
....	....	....	....	....	....		310	54 25
....	....	....	....	....	....		13	2 28
....	....	....	....	....	....	62,523	10,942 23	
....	6,217	777 36	....	....	....	72,928	12,452 50	
Lb.			Lb.			Lb.		
546,956	24,665	5,469 56	....	....	....	554,887	25,077	5,588 53
11,258	487	112 58	....	....	....	11,258	487	112 58
....	....	....	....	....	....	1,440	95	21 60
....	....	....	....	....	....	80,370	2,839	1,204 55
....	....	....	....	....	....	30,677	965	460 16
....	....	....	....	....	....	146	5	2 19
....	....	....	....	....	....	360	18	5 40
....	....	....	....	....	....	77,969	1,748	1,169 54
....	....	....	....	....	....	65,014	1,551	975 21
....	....	....	....	....	....	9,628	891	144 42
....	....	....	....	....	....	2,084,668	73,064	31,271 31
558,214	25,152	5,582 14	....	....	....	2,916,417	106,740	40,955 49
....	21,945	2,194 50	....	....	....		21,945	2,194 50
....	....	....	....	....	....		54,714	8,207 10
....	21,945	2,194 50	....	....	....		76,659	10,401 60

6 GEORGE V, A. 1916

No. 1.—General Statement

Articles Imported.	Countries.	Total Imports.		Entered		
				General Tariff.		
		Quantity.	Value.	Quantity.	Value.	Duty.
DUTIABLE GOODS—*Con.*		Cwt.	$	Cwt.	$	$ cts.
Stone and manufactures of— Building stone other than marble or granite, sawn on more than two sides but not sawn on more than four sides.	United States...	11,571	3,549	11,571	3,549	1,735 65
Building stone-other than marble or granite, planed, turned, cut or further manufactured than sawn on four sides.	United States...	18,163	19,965	18,163	19,965	8,173 35
Flagstone, granite, rough sandstone, and all building stone, not hammered, sawn or chiselled.	Unit'd Kingdom United States...	....	761 73,858	....	335 73,858	50 25 11,078 70
	Total......	....	74,619	....	74,193	11,128 95
Flagstone and all other building stone sawn on not more than two sides.	Unit'd Kingdom United States...	....	1,197 169,515	....	8 169,515	1 60 33,903 00
	Total......	....	170,712	....	169,523	33,904 60
Granite, sawn only.............	Unit'd Kingdom United States...	....	764 3,076	....	 3,076	...... 615 20
	Total......	....	3,840	..,......	3,076	•615 20
Granite, manufactures óf, n.o.p.	Unit'd Kingdom France......... Germany...... Italy.......... United States...	....	177,594 1,300 11 1,785 15,518	....	1,126 1,300 11 1,785 15,518	394 10 455 00 3 85 624 75 5,431 30
	Total......	....	196,208	....	19,740	6,909 00
Grindstones, not mounted and not less than 36 inches in diameter.	Unit'd Kingdom United States...	....	22,353 56,917	....	 56,317	...... 8,447 55
	Total......	....	79,270	....	56,317	8,447 55
Grindstones, n.o.p.............	Unit'd Kingdom Hong Kong..... Japan.......... United States...	....	970 3 3 14,986	....	62 3 3 14,986	15 50 0 75 0 75 3,746 50
	Total......	....	15,962	....	15,054	3,763 50
Paving blocks.................	United States...	....	4,428	....	4,428	885 60
Manufactures of stone, n.o.p....	Unit'd Kingdom Hong Kong..... France.......... Germany...... Holland........ Italy.......... Japan.......... United States...	....• ....•	4,468 56 348 753 70 154 133 23,115	....	933 56 348 753 66 154 133 23,115	279 90 16 80 104 40. 225 90 19 80 46 20 39 90 6,934 50
	Total......	....	29,097	.,.......	25,558	7,667 40

OF IMPORTS—Continued.

FOR HOME CONSUMPTION.

Preferential Tariff.			Treaty Rates.			Total.		
Quantity.	Value.	Duty.	Quantity.	Value.	Duty.	Quantity.	Value.	DutyColl'd.
Cwt.	$	$ cts.	Cwt.	$	$ cts.	Cwt.	$	$ cts.
....	....	....	....	....	....	11,571	3,549	1,735 65
....	....	....	....	....	....	18,163	19,965	8,173 35
....	426	42 60	....	....	....	....	761	92 85
....	....	....	....	....	....	....	73,858	11,078 70
....	426	42 60	....	....	....	....	74,619	11,171 55
....	1,189	178 35	....	....	....	....	1,197	179 95
....	....	....	....	....	....	....	169,515	33,903 00
....	1,189	178 35	....	....	....	....	170,712	34,082 95
....	764	114 60	....	....	....	....	764	114 60
....	....	....	....	....	....	....	3,076	615 20
....	764	114 60	....	....	....	....	3,840	729 80
....	174,829	52,448 70	....	....	....	....	175,955	52,842 80
....	....	....	....	....	....	....	1,300	455 00
....	....	....	....	....	....	....	11	3 85
....	....	....	....	....	....	....	1,785	624 75
....	....	....	....	....	....	....	15,518	5,431 30
....	174,829	52,448 70	....	....	....	....	194,569	59,357 70
....	22,112	2,211 20	....	....	....	....	22,112	2,211 20
....	....	....	....	....	....	....	56,317	8,447 55
....	22,112	2,211 20	....	....	....	....	78,429	10,658 75
....	908	158 91	....	....	....	....	970	174 41
....	....	....	....	....	....	....	3	0 75
....	....	....	....	....	....	....	3	0 75
....	....	....	....	....	....	....	14,986	3,746 50
....	908	158 91	....	....	....	....	15,962	3,922 41
....	....	....	....	....	....	....	4,428	885 60
....	3,540	708 00	....	....	....	....	4,473	987 90
....	....	....	....	....	....	....	56	16 80
....	....	....	....	....	....	....	348	104 40
....	....	....	....	....	....	....	753	225 90
....	....	....	....	....	....	....	66	19 80
....	....	....	....	....	....	....	154	46 20
....	....	....	....	....	....	....	133	39 90
....	....	....	....	....	....	....	23,115	6,934 50
....	3,540	708 00	....	....	....	....	29,098	8,375 40

6 GEORGE V, A. 1916

No. 1.—General Statement

Articles Imported.	Countries.	Total Imports.		Entered		
				General Tariff.		
		Quantity.	Value.	Quantity.	Value.	Duty.
DUTIABLE GOODS—*Con.*		Ton.	$	Ton.	$	$ cts.
Straw..........................	United States...	198	· 2,955	198	2,955	396 00
Straw, carpeting, rugs, mats and matting.	Unit'd Kingdom	....	231	....	25	6 25
	B. India........	....	187	....	....	....
	B. W. Indies....	....	2	....	....	....
	Hong Kong.....	....	1,336	....	1,336	334 00
	Belgium........	....	630	....	....	....
	China..........	....	754	....	754	188 50
	Dutch E. Indies	....	6	....	6	1 50
	France.........	....	50	....	....	....
	Germany.......	....	154	....	154	38 50
	Hawaii.........	....	5	....	5	1 25
	Holland........	....	648	....	418	104 50
	Japan..........	....	35,908	....	11,379	2,844 75
	United States...	....	12,598	....	12,598	3,149 50
	Total......	....	52,509	....	26,675	6,668 75
Straw, manufactures of, n.o.p.....	Unit'd Kingdom	....	824	....	369	64 58
	Hong Kong.....	....	993	....	993	173 78
	Aust.-Hungary..	....	1,348	....	1,348	235 90
	China..........	....	71	....	71	12 43
	France.........	....	651	....	606	106 05
	Germany.......	....	2,862	....	4,219	738 33
	Holland.......	....	7,107	....	7,648	1,338 60
	Japan..........	....	663	....	663	116 03
	United States...	....	1,475	....	1,475	258 13
	Total......	....	15,994	....	17,392	3,043 83
Sugars, syrups and molasses— Sugar, above No. 16 D.S. in colour, and all refined sugars of whatever kinds, grades or standards.		Lb.		Lb.		
	Unit'd Kingdom	3,062,582	87,820	183,388	6,213	3,404 56
	B. W. Indies....	2,247	82	3,334	124	69 90
	Hong Kong.....	2,460,782	83,389	2,405,282	81,821	32,291 95
	Newfoundland..	1,936	85	1,936	85	27 94
	Belgium........	13,579	407	13,579	407	265 69
	China..........	3,233	97	3,233	97	44 46
	Hawaii.........	150	8	150	8	3 11
	United States..	579,950	24,359	348,321	14,355	6,646 28
	Total..........	6,124,459	196,247	2,959,223	103,110	42,753 89
Sugar, n.o.p., not above No. 16 D.S. in colour, sugar drainings, or pumpings drained in transit, melado or concentrated melado, tank bottoms and sugar concrete.	B. Guiana......	98,838,735	2,874,360	550,000	18,200	7,837 50
	B. W. Indies....	184,945,095	4,167,945	45,804	1,007	304 75
	Fiji Islands....	81,774,268	1,996,924	....	....	....
	Hong Kong....	129	3	129	3	0 40
	Brazil..........	6,462,386	220,311	6,572,532	224,442	89,756 73
	Cuba..........	40,008,283	1,138,627	35,494,860	1,009,407	392,389 53
	Dan. W. Indies..	5,453,897	117,509	5,349,461	115,260	75,091 01
	Dutch E. Indies	....	....	2,776,825	71,577	24,319 26
	Dutch Guiana..	7,698,604	202,657	7,854,109	185,135	71,687 64
	Germany...:...	....	....	1,103,078	21,858	6,055 92.
	Guatemala......	1,705,661	35,992	2,158,260	43,828	12,241 86
	Peru..........	51,403,031	1,358,662	54,085,587	1,406,112	395,293 95
	San Domingo...	123,668,104	3,161,954	125,555,033	2,891,238	1,038,662 69
	United States..	55,204,483	1,761,475	41,465,285	1,266,716	540,155 62
	Total......	657,162,676	17,036,419	283,010,963	7,254,783	2,653,796 86

OF IMPORTS—*Continued.*

FOR HOME CONSUMPTION.

Preferential Tariff.			Treaty Rates.			Total.		
Quantity	Value.	Duty.	Quantity	Value.	Duty.	Quantity	Value.	DutyColl'd.
Ton.	$	$ cts.	Ton.	$	$ cts.	Ton.	$	$ cts.
....	....	....	....	....	....	198	2,955	396 00
....	206	36 06	....	....	....		231	42 31
....	187	32 73	....	....	....		187	32 73
....	2	0 35	....	....	....		2	0 35
....	....	....	....	630	141 75		1,336	334 00
....	....	....	....	630	141 75		630	141 75
....	....	....	....				754	188 50
....	....	....	....				6	1 50
....	....	....	....	50	11 25		50	11 25
....	....	....	....				154	38 50
....	....	....	....				5	1 25
....	....	....	....	230	51 75		648	156 25
....	....	....	....	24,529	5,519 08		35,908	8,363 83
....	....	....	....	....	....		12,598	3,149 50
....	395	69 14	....	25,439	5,723 83	....	52,509	12,461 72
....	455	68 25	....	....	....		824	132 83
....	....	....	....	....	....		993	173 78
....	....	....	....	....	....		1,348	235 90
....	....	....	....	....	....		71	12 43
....	....	....	....	....	....		606	106 05
....	....	....	....	....	....		4,219	738 33
....	....	....	....	....	....		7,648	1,338 60
....	....	....	....	....	....		663	116 03
....	....	....	....	....	....		1,475	258 13
....	455	68 25	....	....	....	....	17,847	3,112 08
Lb.			Lb.			Lb.		
2,889,800	82,405	24,856 77	....	....	....	3,073,188	88,618	28,261 33
....	....	....	....	....	....	3,334	124	69 90
....	....	....	....	....	....	2,405,282	81,821	32,291 95
....	....	....	....	....	....	1,936	85	27 94
....	....	....	....	....	....	13,579	407	265 69
....	....	....	....	....	....	3,233	97	44 46
....	....	....	....	....	....	150	8	3 11
....	....	....	....	....	....	348,321	14,355	6,646 28
2,889,800	82,405	24,856 77	....	....	....	5,849,023	185,515	67,610 66
107,546,555	2,931,233	823,769 11	....	....	....	108,096,555	2,949,433	831,606 61
192,315,629	4,279,707	1,140,805 66	....	....	....	192,361,433	4,280,714	1,141,110 41
70,679,974	1,780,368	634,705 27	....	....	....	70,679,974	1,780,368	634,705 27
....	....	....	....	....	....	129	3	0 40
....	....	....	....	....	....	6,572,532	224,442	89,756 73
....	....	....	....	....	....	35,494,860	1,009,407	392,389 53
....	....	....	....	....	....	5,349,461	115,260	75,091 01
....	....	....	....	....	....	2,776,825	71,577	24,319 26
....	....	....	....	....	....	7,854,109	185,135	71,687 64
....	....	....	....	....	....	1,103,078	21,858	6,055 92
....	....	....	....	....	....	2,158,260	43,828	12,241 86
....	....	....	....	....	....	54,085,587	1,406,112	395,293 95
....	....	....	....	....	....	125,555,033	2,891,238	1,038,662 69
....	....	....	....	....	....	41,465,285	1,266,716	540,155 62
370,542,158	8,991,308	2,599,280 04	....	....	....	653,553,121	16,246,091	5,253,076 90

6 GEORGE V, A. 1916

No. 1.—General Statement

Articles Imported.	Countries.	Total Imports.		Entered		
				General Tariff.		
		Quantity.	Value.	Quantity.	Value.	Duty.
DUTIABLE GOODS—*Con.*		Lb.	$	Lb.	$	$ cts.
Sugars, syrups. etc.—*Con.* Raw sugar as described in preceding item, when imported to be refined in Canada by Canadian sugar refiners under provisions of Tariff Item No. 135A. (This item does not include the amount of sugar entered for consumption under Tariff Item 135, on which a refund of duty was subsequently obtained under Item 135A.)	Belgium........ San Domingo... Total......	2,196,900 15,889,816 18,086,716	47,613 302,534 350,147	2,196,900 15,889,816 18,086,716	47,613 302,534 350,147	15,617 51 64,786 00 80,403 51
Syrups and molasses of all kinds, the product of the sugar cane or beet, n.o.p., and all imitations thereof or substitutes therefor.	Unit'd Kingdom Hong Kong..... Dan. W. Indies. Greece......... United States.. Total......	646,483 314 20 2,860 2,716,482 3,366,159	32,653 17 1 30 56,704 89,405	450 314 20 2,860 2,716,552 2,720,196	20 17 1 30 56,707 56,775	2 25 1 57 0 10 14 30 13,582 95 13,601 17
Molasses of cane, testing by polariscope under 35 degrees but not less than 20 degrees.	United States..	Gal. 296,633	24,591	Gal. 296,633	24,591	4,449 55
Molasses, testing over 56 degrees and not more than 75 degrees by the polariscope.	B. W. Indies....	Lb. 19,787	239	Lb.	....	....
Molasses produced in the process of the manufacture of cane sugar from the juice of the cane without any admixture with any other ingredient, when imported direct from the place of production, or its shipping port, in the original package in which it was placed at the point of production and not afterwards subjected to any process of treating or mixing, testing by polariscope not less than 35 degrees nor more than 56 degrees.	B. W. Indies.... Newfoundland.. United States.. Total......	Gal. 15,592 1,257 19,020 35,869	2,337 339 3,765 6,441	Gal. 15,592 1,257 19,020 35,869	2,337 339 3,765 6,441	467 76 37 71 570 60 1,076 07
Sugar cane, shredded.............	Hong Kong..... China.......... United States.. Total......	....	1,180 24 73 1,277	....	1,180 24 73 1,277	206 51 4 20 12 78 223 49
Sugar candy, and confectionery of all kinds, n.o.p., including sweetened gums, candied peel, candied pop corn, candied fruit, candied nuts, flavouring powders, custard powders, jelly powders, sweetmeats, sweetened breads, cakes, pies, puddings and all other confections containing sugar (to August 21st, 1914.)	Unit'd Kingdom Hong Kong..... Aust.-Hungary.. Belgium........ China.......... France......... Germany....... Greece......... Holland........ Italy.......... Japan.......... Turkey......... United States.. Total......	....	155,817 2,117 82 400 441 3,978 962 375 15 258 829 168 102,220 267,662	....	3,428 2,117 82 428 441 3,970 1,004 63 75 327 829 168 102,345 115,277	1,199 80 740 95 28 70 149 80 154 35 1,389 50 351 40 22 05 26 25 114 45 290 15 58 80 35,820 75 40,346 95

SESSIONAL PAPER No. 11

OF IMPORTS.—*Continued.*

FOR HOME CONSUMPTION.

Preferential Tariff.			Treaty Rates.			Total.		
Quantity.	Value.	Duty.	Quantity.	Value.	Duty.	Quantity.	Value.	DutyColl'd.
Lb.	$	$ cts.	Lb.	$	$ cts.	Lb.	$	$ cts.
....	....	....	....	....	....	2,196,900	47,613	15,617 51
....	....	....	....	....	....	15,889,816	302,534	64,786 00
....	....	....	....	....	....	18,086,716	350,147	80,403 51
652,737	32,965	2,284 53	....	....	....	653,187	32,985	2,286 78
....	....	....	....	....	....	314	17	1 57
....	....	....	....	....	....	20	1	0 10
....	....	....	....	....	....	2,860	30	14 30
....	....	....	....	....	....	2,716,552	56,707	13,582 95
652,737	32,965	2,284 53	....	....	....	3,372,933	89,740	15,885 70
Gal.			Gal.			Gal.		
....	....	....	....	....	....	296,633	24,591	4,449 55
Lb.			Lb.			Lb.		
....	....	....	....	....	....	....	....	....
Gal.			Gal.			Gal.		
....	....	....	....	....	....	15,592	2,337	467 76
....	....	....	....	....	....	1,257	339	37 71
....	....	....	....	....	....	19,020	3,765	570 60
....	....	....	....	....	....	35,869	6,441	1,076 07
....	....	....	....	....	....	....	1,180	206 51
....	....	....	....	....	....	....	24	4 20
....	....	....	....	....	....	....	73	12 78
....	....	....	....	....	....	....	1,277	223 49
....	153,319	34,497 11	....	....	....	....	156,747	35,696 91
....	....	....	....	....	....	....	2,117	740 95
....	....	....	....	....	....	....	82	28 70
....	....	....	....	....	....	....	428	149 80
....	....	....	....	....	....	....	441	154 35
....	....	....	....	....	....	....	3,970	1,389 50
....	....	....	....	....	....	....	1,004	351 40
....	....	....	....	....	....	....	63	22 05
....	....	....	....	....	....	....	75	26 25
....	....	....	....	....	....	....	327	114 45
....	....	....	....	....	....	....	829	290 15
....	....	....	....	....	....	....	168	58 80
....	....	....	....	....	....	....	102,345	35,820 75
....	153,319	34,497 11	....	....	....	....	268,596	74,844 06

6 GEORGE V, A. 1916

No. 1.—General Statement

Articles Imported.	Countries.	Total Imports.		Entered		
				General Tariff.		
		Quantity.	Value.	Quantity.	Value.	Duty.
DUTIABLE GOODS—*Con.*		Lb.	$	Lb.	$	$ cts.
Sugars, syrups, etc.—*Con.*						
Sugar candy, and confectionery of all kinds, n.o.p., including sweetened gums, candied peel, candied pop corn, candied fruit, candied nuts, flavouring powders, custard powders, jelly powders, sweetmeats, sweetened breads, cakes, pies, puddings and all other confections containing sugar (from August 21st, 1914.)	Unit'd Kingdom	2,942,959	312,643	49,954	8,713	3,299 32
	B. W. Indies....	19	5	19	5	1 84
	Hong Kong.....	42,189	2,655	42,189	2,655	1,140 19
	Newfoundland..	312	110	312	110	40 06
	Belgium........	11,200	907	8,960	712	294 00
	China..........	4,994	310	4,994	310	133 47
	Holland........			276	9	4 53
	Italy..........	6,075	1,034	5,179	942	355 59
	Germany......			222	13	5 66
	Greece.........	1,277	65	1,277	65	29 14
	Japan..........	18,156	1,942	17,522	1,879	745 26
	France.........	34,523	7,047	32,100	6,695	2,503 80
	Switzerland....	68,936	15,473	68,936	15,473	5,760 23
	Turkey........	2,932	173	2,932	173	75 21
	United States..	1,205,108	116,617	1,205,902	115,720	46,540 16
	Total......	4,338,680	458,981	1,440,783	153,474	60,928 46
Glucose or grape sugar, glucose syrup and corn syrup or any syrups containing any admixture thereof.	Unit'd Kingdom	36,201	1,812			
	France.........	100	3	100	3	0 63
	Japan..........	764	44	764	44	4 78
	United States..	4,389,370	116,672	4,389,370	116,672	27,433 58
	Total......	4,426,435	118,531	4,390,234	116,719	27,438 99
Sugar, maple, and maple syrup.	United States..	37,947	3,983	20,564	2,099	419 80
Surgical trusses, pessaries and suspensory bandages.	Unit'd Kingdom		5,928		382	76 40
	France.........		532		144	28 80
	Germany........		108		108	21 60
	United States..		37,615		37,615	7,523 00
	Total......		44,183		38,249	7,649 80
Tallow........................	Unit'd Kingdom	110,056	13,394	6,803	523	104 60
	United States...	51,307	3,805	51,531	3,840	768 00
	Total......	161,363	17,199	58,334	4,363	872 60
Tape lines of any material.......	Unit'd Kingdom		4,018		704	176 00
	France.........		111		111	27 75
	Germany.......		234		234	58 50
	United States..		3,778		3,778	944 50
	Total......		8,141		4,827	1,206 75
Tape lines, measuring yarn of linen or cotton for the manufcture of.	United States...	1,611	390	1,611	390	39 00
Tea of Ceylon, black...........	Unit'd Kingdom	1,461	441	1,461	441	44 10
	B. India........	25,234	6,703	15,365	4,004	400 40
	China........	56	25	56	25	2 50
	United States...	36,568	8,084	36,568	8,084	808 40
	Total......	63,319	15,253	53,450	12,554	1,255 40
Tea of Ceylon, green...........	B. E. Indies other.........	13,950	2,210	13,950	2,210	221 00
	United States...	14,127	2,641	14,127	2,641	264 10
	Total......	28,077	4,851	28,077	4,851	485 10

OF IMPORTS—*Continued.*

FOR HOME CONSUMPTION.

Preferential Tariff.			Treaty Rates.			Total.		
Quantity.	Value.	Duty.	Quantity.	Value.	Duty.	Quantity.	Value.	DutyColl'd.
Lb.	$	$ cts.	Lb.	$	$ cts.	Lb.	$	$ cts.
2,891,140	302,034	82,413 55	....	....	....	2,941,094	310,747	85,712 87
....	....	....	....	....	....	19	5	1 84
....	....	....	....	....	....	42,189	2,655	1,140 19
....	....	....	....	....	....	312	110	40 06
....	....	....	....	....	....	8,960	712	294 00
....	....	....	....	....	....	4,994	310	133 47
....	....	....	....	....	....	276	9	4 53
....	....	....	....	....	....	5,179	942	355 59
....	....	....	....	....	....	222	13	5 66
....	....	....	....	....	....	1,277	65	29 14
....	....	....	....	....	....	17,522	1,879	745 26
....	....	....	....	....	....	32,109	6,695	2,503 80
....	....	....	....	....	....	68,936	15,473	5,760 23
....	....	....	....	....	....	2,932	173	75 21
....	....	....	....	....	....	1,205,902	115,720	46,540 16
2,891,140	302,034	82,413 55	....	....	....	4,331,923	455,508	143,342 01
36,201	1,812	144 81	....	....	....	36,201	1,812	144 81
....	....	....	....	....	....	100	3	0 63
....	....	....	....	....	....	764	44	4 78
....	....	....	....	....	....	4,389,370	116,672	27,433 58
36,201	1,812	144 81	....	....	....	4,426,435	118,531	27,583 80
....	....	....	....	....	....	20,564	2,099	419 80
....	5,377	672 19	....	169	29 57	....	5,928	778 16
....	....	....	....	388	67 90	....	532	96 70
....	....	....	....	....	....	....	108	21 60
....	....	....	....	....	....	37 615	7,523 00	
....	5,377	672 19	....	557	97 47	....	44,183	8,419 46
98,030	12,153	1,822 95	....	....	....	104,833	12,676	1,927 55
....	....	....	....	....	....	51,531	3,840	768 00
98,030	12,153	1,822 95	....	....	....	156,364	16,516	2,695 55
....	3,314	580 14	....	....	....	4,018	756 14	
....	....	....	....	....	....	111	27 75	
....	....	....	....	....	....	234	58 50	
....	....	....	....	....	....	3,778	944 50	
....	3,314	580 14	....	....	....	....	8,141	1,786 89
....	....	....	....	....	....	1,611	390	39 00
....	....	....	....	....	....	1,461	441	44 10
....	....	....	....	....	....	15,365	4,004	400 40
....	....	....	....	....	....	56	25	2 50
....	....	....	....	....	....	36,568	8,084	808 40
....	....	....	....	....	....	53,450	12,554	1,255 40
....	....	....	....	....	....	13,950	2,210	221 00
....	....	....	....	....	....	14,127	2,641	264 10
....	....	....	....	....	....	28,077	4,851	485 10

6 GEORGE V, A. 1916

No. 1.—General Statement

Articles Imported.	Countries.	Total Imports.		Entered		
		Quantity.	Value.	General Tariff.		
				Quantity.	Value.	Duty.
DUTIABLE GOODS—*Con.* Tea—*Con.*		Lb.	$	Lb.	$	$ cts.
Tea of India, black............	B. India........	2,650	453	2,650	453	45 30
	B. E. Indies other.........	2,640	477	2,640	477	47 70
	United States...	2,088	320	2,088	320	32 00
	.Total.......	7,378	1,250	7,378	1,250	125 00
Tea of India, green............	United States...	800	188	800	188	18 80
Tea of China, black............	China..........	19,725	2,835	19,725	2,835	283 50
	United States...	43,221	6,323	43,221	6,323	632 30
	Total.......	62,946	9,158	62,946	9,158	915 80
Tea of China, green............	Hong Kong....	460	60	460	60	6 00
	United States...	295,110	36,463	297,184	36,639	3,663 90
	Total......	295,570	36,523	297,644	36,699	3,669 90
Tea of Japan, green............	United States...	85,614	15,046	85,614	15,046	1,504 60
Tea of other countries, black....	Unit'd Kingdom	.. 4,749	1,558	4,282	1,253	125 30
	Newfoundland..	70	26	70	26	2 60
	China........	440	42	440	42	4 20
	Holland.......	3,875	775	3,875	775	77 50
	United States...	31,357	6,213	31,357	6,213	621 30
	Total......	40,491	8,614	40,024	8,309	830 90
Tea of other countries, green....	Unit'd Kingdom	315	72	315	72	7 20
	Hong Kong.....	1,955	265	1,955	265	26 50
	Aust.-Hungary..	300	76	300	76	7 60
	United States...	5,738	1,103	5,738	1,103	110 30
	Total......	8,308	1,516	8,308	1,516	151 60
Tinware, japanned or not, and all manufactures of tin, n.o.p.	Unit'd Kingdom	....	116,629	....	2,181	545 25
	Hong Kong.....	....	2	....	2	0 50
	Newfoundland..	....	540	....	13	3 25
	Aust.-Hungary..	....	50	....	50	12 50
	Belgium..	....	238	....	238	59 50
	China..........	....	7	....	7	1 75
	France..........	....	2,006	....	1,886	471 50
	Holland.......	....	44	....	42	10 50
	Germany......	....	5,208	....	5,211	1,302 75
	Italy..........	....	74	....	74	18 50
	Japan..........	....	215	....	215	53 75
	Sweden........	....	20	....	20	5 00
	United States...	....	449,879	....	466,981	116,745 25
	Total......	....	574,912	....	476,920	119,230 00
Tobacco and manufactures of— Cigarettes................	Unit'd Kingdom	35,492	80,802	33,406	77,301	127,842 75
	B. W. Indies....	252	217	77	79	472 25
	Hong Kong.....	7	13	7	13	24 25
	Malta..........	292	507	359	585	1,131 75
	Belgium........	33	112	33	112	127 00
	Cuba..........	571	1,732	590	1,727	2,254 75
	Egypt and Soudan.......	6,728	16,320	7,105	17,147	26,424 75

OF IMPORTS—*Continued.*

FOR HOME CONSUMPTION.

Preferential Tariff.			Treaty Rates.			Total.		
Quantity.	Value.	Duty.	Quantity.	Value.	Duty.	Quantity.	Value.	Duty Coll'd.
Lb.	$	$ cts.	Lb.	$	$ cts.	Lb.	$	$ cts.
....	....	....	....	....	....	2,650	453	45 30
....	....	....	....	....	....	2,640	477	47 70
....	....	....	....	....	....	2,088	320	32 00
....	....	....	....	....	....	7,378	1,250	125 00
....	....	....	....	....	....	800	188	18.80
....	....	....	....	....	....	19,725	2,835	283 50
....	....	....	....	....	....	43,221	6,323	632 30
....	....	....	....	....	....	62,946	9,158	915 80
....	....	....	....	....	....	460	60	6 00
....	....	....	....	....	....	297,184	36,639	3,663 90
....	....	....	....	....	....	297,644	36,699	3,669 90
....	....	....	....	....	....	85,614	15,046	1,504 60
....	....	....	....	....	....	4,282	1,253	125 30
....	....	....	....	....	....	70	26	2 60
....	....	....	....	....	....	440	42	4 20
....	....	....	....	....	....	3,875	775	77 50
....	....	....	....	....	....	31,357	6,213	621 30
....	....	....	....	....	....	40,024	8,309	830 90
....	....	....	....	....	....	315	72	7 20
....	....	....	....	....	....	1,955	265	26 50
....	....	....	....	....	....	300	76	7 60
....	....	....	....	....	....	5,738	1,103	110 30
....	....	....	....	....	....	8,308	1,516	151 60
....	114,896	17,234 40	....	....	....	....	117,077	17,779 65
....	....	....	....	....	....	....	2	0 50
....	....	....	....	....	....	....	13	3 25
....	....	....	....	....	....	....	50	12 50
....	....	....	....	....	....	....	238	59 50
....	....	....	....	....	....	....	7	1 75
....	....	....	....	....	....	....	1,88^	471 50
....	....	....	....	....	....	....	42	10 50
....	....	....	....	....	....	....	5,211	1,302 75
....	....	....	....	....	....	....	74	18 50
....	....	....	....	....	....	....	215	53 75
....	....	....	....	....	....	....	20	5 00
....	....	....	....	....	....	....	466,981	116,745 25
....	114,896	17,234 40	....	....	....	....	591,816	136,464 40
....	....	....	....	....	....	33,406	77,301	127,842 75
....	....	....	....	....	....	77	79	472 25
....	....	....	....	....	....	7	13	24 25
....	....	....	....	....	....	359	585	1,131 75
....	....	....	....	....	....	33	112	127 00
....	....	....	....	....	....	590	1,727	2,254 75
....	....	....	....	....	....	7,105	17,147	26,424 75

6 GEORGE V, A. 1916

No. 1.—General Statement

Articles Imported.	Countries.	Total Imports.		Entered		
				General Tariff.		
		Quantity.	Value.	Quantity.	Value.	Duty.
DUTIABLE GOODS—*Con.*		Lb.	$	Lb.	$	$ cts.
Tobacco and mfrs. of—*Con.*						
Cigarettes—*Con*	France.........	624	787	624	787	2,250 25
	French Africa...	168	120	168	120	534 00
	Germany.......	54	162	54	162	202 50
	Mexico.........	....	....	55	32	178 50
	Russia.........	124	138	46	68	156 00
	Switzerland.....	12	26	12	26	48 50
	Turkey.........	96	157	96	157	375 25
	United States...	1,495	5,126	1,707	5,484	6,733 00
	Total......	45,948	106,219	44,339	103,800	168,755 50
Cigars........................	Unit'd Kingdom	1,091	3,186	1,207	3,662	4,705 50
	B. India.	5	5	36	8	119 00
	B. W. Indies....	391	1,450	430	1,476	1,765 50
	Hong Kong.....	326	857	326	857	1,192 25
	Malta..........	10	22	26	59	100 75
	Belgium...:...	6	4	6	4	19 00
	China..........	51	55	51	55	192 25
	Cuba..........	91,291	377,036	87,188	369,742	375,180 00
	France.........	16	24	16	24	54 00
	Germany.......	269	481	270	484	932 00
	Holland........	733	1,125	497	709	1,746 75
	Japan..........	169	650	244	829	976 75
	Mexico.........	276	630	187	486	717 00
	Philippines.....	1,213	1,361	2,008	2,133	6,984 75
	Switzerland.....	2	5	2	5	7 25
	United States...	6,882	29,521	6,763	28,544	29,309 50
	Total......	102,731	416,412	99,257	409,077	424,002 25
Tobacco, cut................	Unit'd Kingdom	258,972	295,420	274,656	311,156	164,056 30
	B. S. Africa.....	1,000	499	500	251	305 00
	Hong Kong.....	15,095	4,583	15,095	4,583	9,073 80
	Malta..........	125	68	125	68	68 75
	Aust.-Hungary..	336	246	1,086	654	622 30
	China..........	12,993	3,703	12,818	3,641	7,779 55
	Cuba..........	306	94	521	199	320 55
	France.........	1,430	816	1,430	816	863 50
	Germany.......	2,944	1,375	6,156	3,021	3,687 50
	Japan..........	5	1	5	1	2 75
	Miquelon and St. Pierre.....	414	126	414	126	268 20
	Roumania......	696	970	696	970	382 80
	Russia.........	793	799	793	799	461 15
	Turkey........	100	196	100	196	55 00
	United States...	264,603	156,470	261,135	154,722	155,991 85
	Total......	559,812	465,366	575,530	481,203	343,939 00
Snuff.......................	Unit'd Kingdom	1,332	1,150	1,232	1,051	690 20
	France.........	1,430	574	1,430	574	781 00
	Italy..........	....	....	102	53	51 00
	Roumania......	110	20	110	20	55 00
	United States...	3,407	1,204	3,407	1,204	1,859 40
	Total......	6,279	2,948	6,281	2,902	3,436 60
All other manufactures of tobacco, n.o.p.	Unit'd Kingdom	46,782	41,099	47,350	41,778	25,537 90
	Hong Kong.....	135	40	135	40	81 00
	Newfoundland..	180	48	....	....	....
	France.........	330	139	330	139	198 00
	Roumania......	20	3	20	3	10 00
	United States...	84,986	44,964	79,506	43,948	43,237 20
	Total......	132,433	86,293	127,341	85,908	69,064 10

OF IMPORTS—*Continued.*

FOR HOME CONSUMPTION.

Preferential Tariff.			Treaty Rates.			Total.		
Quantity.	Value.	Duty.	Quantity.	Value.	Duty.	Quantity.	Value.	DutyColl'd.
Lb.	$	$ cts.	Lb.	$	$ cts.	Lb.	$	$ cts.
....	....	....	....	....	....	624	787	2,250 25
....	....	....	....	....	....	168	120	534 00
....	....	....	....	....	....	54	162	202 50
....	....	....	....	....	....	55	32	178 50
....	....	....	....	....	....	46	68	156 00
....	....	....	....	....	....	12	26	48 50
....	....	....	....	....	....	96	157	375 25
....	....	....	....	....	....	1,707	5,484	6,733 00
....	....	....	....	....	....	44,339	103,800	168,755 50
....	....	....	....	....	....	1,207	3,662	4,705 50
....	....	....	....	....	....	36	8	119 00
....	....	....	....	....	....	430	1,476	1,765 50
....	....	....	....	....	....	326	857	1,192 25
....	....	....	....	....	....	26	59	100 75
....	....	....	....	....	....	6	4	19 00
....	....	....	....	....	....	51	55	192 25
....	....	....	....	....	....	87,188	369,742	375,180 00
....	....	....	....	....	....	16	24	54 00
....	....	....	....	....	....	270	484	932 00
....	....	....	....	....	....	497	709	1,746 75
....	....	....	....	....	....	244	829	976 75
....	....	....	....	....	....	187	486	717 00
....	....	....	....	....	....	2,008	2,133	6,984 75
....	....	....	....	....	....	2	5	7 25
....	....	....	....	....	....	6,763	28,544	29,309 50
....	....	....	....	....	....	99,257	409,077	424,002 25
....	....	....	....	....	....	274,656	311,156	164,056 30
....	....	....	....	....	....	500	251	305 00
....	....	....	....	....	....	15,095	4,583	9,073 80
....	....	....	....	....	....	125	68	68 75
....	....	....	....	....	....	1,086	654	622 30
....	....	....	....	....	....	12,818	3,641	7,779 55
....	....	....	....	....	....	521	199	320 55
....	....	....	....	....	....	1,430	816	863 50
....	....	....	....	....	....	6,156	3,021	3,687 50
....	....	....	....	....	....	5	1	2 75
....	....	....	....	....	....	414	126	268 20
....	....	....	....	....	....	696	970	382 80
....	....	....	....	....	....	793	799	461 15
....	....	....	....	....	....	100	196	55 00
....	....	....	....	....	....	261,135	154,722	155,991 85
....	....	....	....	....	+	575,530	481,203	343,939 00
....	....	....	....	....	....	1,232	1,051	690 20
....	....	....	....	....	....	1,430	574	781 00
....	....	....	....	....	....	102	53	51 00
....	....	....	....	....	....	110	20	55 00
....	....	....	....	....	....	3,407	1,204	1,859 40
....	....	....	....	....	....	6,281	2,902	3,436 60
....	....	....	....	....	....	47,350	41,778	25,537 90
....	....	....	....	....	....	135	40	81 00
....	....	....	....	....	....	....	....	....
....	....	....	....	....	....	330	139	198 00
....	....	....	....	....	....	20	3	10 00
....	....	....	....	....	....	79,506	43,948	43,237 20
....	....	....	....	....	....	127,341	85,908	69,064 10

11—ii—17½

No. 1.—General Statement

Articles Imported.	Countries.	Total Imports.		Entered		
		Quantity.	Value.	General Tariff.		
				Quantity.	Value.	Duty.
DUTIABLE GOODS—*Con.*			$		$	$ cts.
Tobacco pipes of all kinds, pipe mounts, cigar and cigarette holders and cases for the same, smokers' sets and cases therefor, and tobacco pouches	Unit'd Kingdom	....	201,235	....	10,554	3,693 90
	Hong Kong	....	93	....	93	32 55
	Aust.-Hungary	....	50,885	....	2,385	834 75
	Belgium	....	1,045	....	254	88 90
	China	....	86	....	86	30 10
	France	....	74,237	....	3,935	1,377 25
	Germany	....	9,130	....	9,404	3,291 40
	Holland	....	431	....	....	....
	Italy	....	4,522	....	4,522	1,582 70
	Japan	....	411	....	14	4 90
	Turkey	....	81	....	81	28 35
	United States	....	44,225	....	44,107	15,437 45
	Total	....	386,381	....	75,435	26,402 25
Trawls, trawling spoons, fly hooks, sinkers, swivels and sportsman's fishing bait, and fish hooks, n.o.p.	Unit'd Kingdom	....	24,758	....	744	260 40
	Germany	....	....	....	60	21 00
	Norway	....	67	....	67	23 45
	United States	....	21,974	....	22,014	7,704 90
	Total	....	46,799	....	22,885	8,009 75
Trunks, valises, hat-boxes, carpet bags, and tool bags.	Unit'd Kingdom	....	16,788	....	1,662	498 60
	Hong Kong	....	16	....	2	0 60
	Aust.-Hungary	....	31	....	31	9 30
	Belgium	....	5	....	5	1 50
	Cuba	....	5	....	5	1 50
	France	....	77	....	71	21 30
	Germany	....	185	....	185	55 50
	Japan	....	1,498	....	115	34 50
	United States	....	47,533	....	47,317	14,195 10
	Total	....	66,138	....	49,393	14,817 90
Twine, manufactures of, viz.: hammocks and lawn tennis nets, sportman's fish nets and other articles, n.o.p.	Unit'd Kingdom	....	11,309	....	61	18 30
	Hong Kong	....	2	....	2	0 60
	France	....	11	....	11	3 30
	Germany	....	214	....	214	64 20
	Japan	....	14	....	14	4 20
	United States	....	35,034	....	35,034	10,510 20
	Total	....	46,584	....	35,336	10,600 80
Umbrellas, parasols and sunshades, of all kinds and materials	Unit'd Kingdom	....	55,361	....	596	208 60
	Aust.-Hungary	....	109	....	109	38 15
	Belgium	....	37	....	37	12 95
	France	....	493	....	493	172 55
	Germany	....	2,266	....	2,266	793 10
	Japan	....	2,583	....	2,583	904 05
	United States	....	16,438	....	16,438	5,753 30
	Total	....	77,287	....	22,522	7,882 70
Unenumerated articles	Unit'd Kingdom	....	94,504	....	28,010	4,901 75
	Australia	....	147	....	147	25 73
	B. W. Indies	....	152	....	152	26 60
	Hong Kong	....	2,812	....	2,812	492 10
	Aust.-Hungary	....	7,971	....	7,971	1,394 93
	Belgium	....	679	....	679	118 83
	China	....	33,992	....	33,423	5,849 03
	Denmark	....	35	....	35	6 13
	Dutch E. Indies	....	523	....	523	91 52
	France	....	6,479	....	6,574	1,150 45

OF IMPORTS—*Continued.*

FOR HOME CONSUMPTION.

Preferential Tariff.			Treaty Rates.			Total.		
Quantity.	Value.	Duty.	Quantity.	Value.	Duty.	Quantity.	Value.	DutyColl'd.
	$	$ cts.		$	$ cts.		$	$ cts.
....	160,474	36,107 14	....	34,864	11,330 80	....	205,892	51,131 84
....	....	....	....	....	....	....	93	32 55
....	....	....	....	51,063	16,595 48	....	53,448	17,430 23
....	....	....	....	791	257 07	....	1,045	345 97
....	....	....	....	....	....	....	86	30 10
....	....	....	....	76,624	24,903 10	....	80,559	26,280 35
....	....	....	....	....	....	....	9,404	3,291 40
....	....	....	....	431	140 08	....	431	140 08
....	....	....	....	....	....	....	4,522	1,582 70
....	....	....	....	397	129 03	....	411	133 93
....	....	....	....	....	....	....	81	28 35
....	....	....	....	....	....	....	44,107	15,437 45
....	160,474	36,107 14	....	164,170	53,355 56	....	400,079	115,864 95
....	24,014	5,403 52	....	....	....	....	24,758	5,663 92
....	....	....	....	....	....	....	60	21 00
....	....	....	....	....	....	....	67	23 45
....	....	....	....	....	....	....	22,014	7,704 90
....	24,014	5,403 52	....	....	....	....	46,899	13,413 27
....	15,221	3,044 20	....	....	....	....	16,883	3,542 80
....	....	....	....	14	3 85	....	16	4 45
....	....	....	....	....	....	....	31	9 30
....	....	....	....	....	....	....	5	1 50
....	....	....	....	6	1 65	....	5	1 50
....	....	....	....	....	....	....	77	22 95
....	....	....	....	....	....	....	185	55 50
....	....	....	....	1,387	381 43	....	1,502	415 93
....	....	....	....	....	....	....	47,317	14,195 10
....	15,221	3,044 20	....	1,407	386 93	....	66,021	18,249 03
....	11,235	2,247 00	....	....	....	....	11,296	2,265 30
....	....	....	....	....	....	....	2	0 60
....	....	....	....	....	....	....	11	3 30
....	....	....	....	....	....	....	214	64 20
....	....	....	....	....	....	....	14	4 20
....	....	....	....	....	....	....	35,034	10,510 20
....	11,235	2,247 00	....	....	....	....	46,571	12,847 80
....	55,081	12,393 53	....	....	....	....	55,677	12,602 13
....	....	....	....	....	....	....	109	38 15
....	....	....	....	....	....	....	37	12 95
....	....	....	....	....	....	....	493	172 55
....	....	....	....	....	....	....	2,266	793 10
....	....	....	....	....	....	....	2,583	904 05
....	....	....	....	....	....	....	16,438	5,753 30
....	55,081	12,393 53	....	....	....	....	77,603	20,276 23
....	66,678	10,001 70	....	....	....	....	94,688	14,903 45
....	....	....	....	....	....	....	147	25 73
....	....	....	....	....	....	....	152	26 60
....	....	....	....	....	....	....	2,812	492 10
....	....	....	....	....	....	....	7,971	1,394 93
....	....	....	....	....	....	....	679	118 83
....	....	....	....	....	....	....	33,423	5,849 03
....	....	....	....	....	....	....	35	6 13
....	....	....	....	....	....	....	523	91 52
....	....	....	....	....	....	....	6,574	1,150 45

6 GEORGE V, A. 1916

No. 1.—General Statement

Articles Imported.	Countries.	Total Imports.		Entered		
				General Tariff.		
		Quantity.	Value.	Quantity.	Value.	Duty.
DUTIABLE GOODS—*Con.*			$		$	$ cts.
Unenumerated articles—*Con*	Germany		12,510		12,204	2,135 70
	Greece		813		813	142 28
	Holland		627		627	109 73
	Italy		924		924	161 70
	Japan		2,380		2,380	418 50
	Russia		41			
	Spain		102		102	17 85
	Turkey		1,992		1,992	348 60
	United States		506,535		505,731	88,505 64
	Total		673,218		605,099	105,895 07
		Gal.		Gal.		
Varnish, lacquers, japans, japan dryers, liquid dryers and oil finish, n.o.p.	Unit'd Kingdom	17,702	37,889	139	259	86 07
	Aust.-Hungary	4	16	4	16	4 40
	France	142	354	142	354	108 05
	Germany	89	172	89	172	56 50
	United States	46,830	86,942	46,830	86,942	28,928 87
	Total	64,767	125,373	47,204	87,743	29,183 89
		No.		No.		
Vegetables—						
Melons	Unit'd Kingdom	120	8	120	8	3 60
	China	15	6	15	6	0 45
	Spain	1,457	210	1,457	210	43 71
	United States	2,319,572	223,674	2,313,917	223,334	69,417 51
	Total	2,321,164	223,898	2,315,509	223,558	69,465 27
		Bush.		Bush.		
Potatoes, n.o.p	Unit'd Kingdom	33	31	8	13	1 60
	B. W. Indies	151	222			
	Hong Kong	182	107	182	107	36 40
	Newfoundland	60	40	60	40	12 00
	China	26	21	26	21	5 20
	Japan	163	99	163	99	32 60
	United States	670,493	530,989	668,488	529,882	133,697 60
	Total	671,108	531,509	668,927	530,162	133,785 40
Potatoes, sweet and yams	Unit'd Kingdom	31	33			
	B. W. Indies	12	8	12	8	1 20
	Hong Kong	1,914	2,305	1,914	2,305	191 40
	China	118	92	118	92	11 80
	Japan	600	584	593	560	59 30
	United States	48,320	49,722	48,296	49,683	4,829 60
	Total	50,995	52,744	50,933	52,648	5,093 30
		Lb.		Lb.		
Tomatoes, and cooked corn in cans or other air-tight packages.	Unit'd Kingdom	48	3			
	Hong Kong	696	28	696	28	10 44
	France	9,074	435			
	Italy	429,606	33,277	196,742	15,284	2,951 13
	Spain	482	18			
	United States	97,432	6,924	199,427	9,780	2,991 43
	Total	537,338	40,685	396,865	25,092	5,953 00
		Bush.		Bush.		
Tomatoes, fresh	B. W. Indies	1,166	595			
	United States	297,816	449,613	297,708	449,151	134,745 30
	Total	298,982	450,208	297,708	449,151	134,745 30

OF IMPORTS—*Continued.*

FOR HOME CONSUMPTION.

Preferential Tariff.			Treaty Rates.			Total.		
Quantity.	Value.	Duty.	Quantity.	Value.	Duty.	Quantity.	Value.	DutyColl'd.
	$	$ cts.		$	$ cts.		$	$ cts.
....	....	....	....	....	....	....	12,204	2,135 70
....	....	....	....	....	....	....	813	142 28
....	....	....	....	....	....	....	627	109 73
....	....	....	....	....	....	....	924	161 70
....	....	....	....	....	....	....	2,380	416 50
....	....	....	....	....	....	....	102	17 85
....	....	....	....	....	....	....	1,992	348 60
....	....	....	....	....	....	....	505,731	88,505 64
....	66,678	10,001 70	....	....	....	....	671,777	115,896 77
Gal. 17,532	37,621	Gal. 9,149 57	....			Gal. 17,671	37,880	9,235 64
....	....	....	....			4	16	4 40
....	....	....	....			142	354	108 05
....	....	....	....			89	172	56 50
....	....	....	....			46,830	86,942	28,928 87
17,532	37,621	9,149 57	....	....	....	64,736	125,364	38,333 46
No.			No.			No.		
....	....	....	....	....	....	120	8	3 60
....	....	....	....	....	....	15	6	0 45
....	....	....	....	....	....	1,457	210	43 71
....	....	....	....	....	....	2,313,917	223,334	69,417 51
....	....	....	....	....	....	2,315,509	223,558	69,465 27
Bush. 25	18	3 13	Bush.			Bush. 33	31	4 73
151	222	18 88	....			151	222	18 88
....	....	....	....			182	107	36 40
....	....	....	....			60	40	12 00
....	....	....	....			26	21	5 20
....	....	....	....			163	99	32 60
....	....	....	....			668,488	529,882	133,697 60
176	240	22 01	....	....	....	669,103	530,402	133,807 41
31	33	2 17	....			31	33	2 17
....	....	....	....			12	8	1 20
....	....	....	....			1,914	2,305	191 40
....	....	....	....			118	92	11 80
....	....	....	....			593	560	59 30
....	....	....	....			48,296	49,683	4,829 60
31	33	2 17	....	....	....	50 964	52,681	5,095 47
Lb.			Lb. 2,248	311	28 10	Lb. 2,248	311	28 10
....	....	....	....	....	....	696	28	10 44
....	....	....	11,936	602	149 20	11,936	602	149 20
....	....	....	228,051	19,358	2,850 62	424,793	34,642	5,801 75
....	....	....	482	18	6 02	482	18	6 02
....	....	....	....	....	....	199,427	9,780	2,991 43
....	....	....	242,717	20,289	3,033 94	639,582	45,381	8,986 94
Bush. 1,166	595	119 00	Bush.			Bush. 1,166	595	119 00
....	....	....	....	....	....	297,708	449,151	134,745 30
1,166	595	119 00	....	....	....	298,874	449,746	134,864 30

6 GEORGE V, A. 1916

No. 1.—GENERAL STATEMENT

Articles Imported.	Countries.	TOTAL IMPORTS.		ENTERED		
				General Tariff.		
		Quantity.	Value.	Quantity.	Value.	Duty.
DUTIABLE GOODS—*Con.*		Lb.	$	Lb.	$	$ cts.
Vegetables—*Con.*						
Vegetables and baked beans in cans or other air-tight packages, n.o.p.	Unit'd Kingdom	244,917	16,482	1,013	75	15 20
	Hong Kong.....	219,550	8,844	216,631	8,730	3,249 47
	Belgium........	372,414	25,230	8,660	574	129 90
	China..........	48,843	1,639	48,843	1,639	732 65
	France.........	541,016	55,195	65,992	6,121	989 88
	Holland.......	9,685	738	9,685	738	145 28
	Germany......	2,825	196	3,945	292	59 18
	Greece.........	2,904	154	704	46	10 56
	Italy..........	486,572	36,391	165,291	11,270	2,479 37
	Japan..........	148,162	12,594	12,811	1,828	192 17
	Spain..........	85,242	4,818	5,483	325	82 25
	Sweden........	21	6	21	6	0 31
	Turkey........	15,194	728	13,744	648	206 16
	United States...	1,845,554	136,837	1,774,167	134,143	26,612 75
	Total......	4,022,899	299,852	2,326,990	166,435	34,905 13
Vegetables, n.o.p.............	Unit'd Kingdom	....	125,069	....	117,490	35,247 00
	Australia......	....	15,523	....	15,255	4,576 50
	B. W. Indies....	....	756	....	551	165 30
	Hong Kong.....	....	35,560	....	35,560	10,668 00
	Newfoundland..	....	1	....	1	0 30
	New Zealand...	....	2,930	....	....	....
	Aust.-Hungary..	....	1,284	....	1,284	385 20
	China..........	....	6,407	....	6,407	1,922 10
	Egypt & Soudan	....	2,395	....	2,395	718 50
	France..........	....	1,885	....	1,885	565 50
	Germany......	....	246	....	246	73 80
	Greece.........	....	....	....	600	180 00
	Holland.......	....	425	....	425	127 50
	Italy..........	....	5,352	....	5,146	1,543 80
	Japan..........	....	33,150	....	32,877	9,863 10
	Mexico.........	....	3,583	....	3,583	1,074 90
	Spain.......	....	15,413	....	15,413	4,623 90
	United States...	....	1,160,493	....	1,156,141	346,842 30
	Total......	....	1,410,472	....	1,395,259	418,577 70
		Gal.		Gal.		
Vinegar, of any strength not exceeding strength of proof.	Unit'd Kingdom	139,339	56,575	943	364	141 45
	Hong Kong.....	2,507	686	2,507	686	376 05
	Newfoundland..	2	1	2	1	0 30
	China..........	128	40	128	40	19 20
	France.........	1,998	604	413	70	61 95
	Italy..........	57	23	57	23	8 55
	Japan..........	3,952	996	136	34	20 40
	Spain..........	10	19	....	....	....
	Turkey.........	40	13	....	....	....
	United States...	24,274	3,559	24,303	3,589	3,645 45
	Total......	172,307	62,516	28,489	4,807	4,273 35
Vinegar, above strength of proof..	Unit'd Kingdom	114	155	....	....	....
	Hong Kong....	13	4	13	4	3 87
	Germany......	984	264	984	264	359 41
	United States...	5,004	1,619	5,004	1,619	909 57
	Total......	6,115	2,042	6,001	1,887	1,272 85
		Lb.		Lb.		
Waste or shoddy from cotton, woollen or other fabrics or from yarn or thread, machined, garnetted or prepared for use.	Unit'd Kingdom	1,892,113	114,078	136,183	6,865	858 13
	Germany......	138,596	6,308	138,596	6,308	788 50
	Japan..........	54,000	3,398	54,000	3,398	424 75
	United States...	2,413,363	168,751	2,412,874	168,712	21,089 89
	Total......	4,498,072	292,535	2,741,653	185,283	23,161 27

OF IMPORTS—*Continued.*

FOR HOME CONSUMPTION.

Preferential Tariff.			Treaty Rates.			Total.		
Quantity.	Value.	Duty.	Quantity.	Value.	Duty.	Quantity.	Value.	DutyColl'd.
Lb.	$	$ cts.	Lb.	$	$ cts.	Lb.	$	$ cts.
85,947	5,940	859 47	161,837	10,899	1,890 16	248,797	16,914	2,764 83
			432	20	4 32	217,063	8,750	3,253 79
			575,852	39,601	6,509 47	584,512	40,175	6,639 37
						48,843	1,639	732 65
			565,083	55,542	5,732 85	631,075	61,663	6,722 73
			784	42	9 80	10,469	780	155 08
						3,945	292	59 18
						704	46	10 50
			405,768	38,056	5,760 29	571,059	49,326	8,239 66
			134,871	10,739	1,348 99	147,682	12,567	1,541 16
			80,829	4,604	812 04	86,312	4,929	894 29
						21	6	0 31
						13,744	648	206 16
						1,774,167	134,143	26,612 75
85,947	5,940	859 47	1,925,456	159,503	22,067 92	4,338,393	331,878	57,832 52
	7,319	1,097 85					124,809	36,344 85
							15,255	4,576 50
	205	30 75					756	196 05
							35,560	10,608 00
							1	0 30
	2,930	439 50					2,930	439 50
							1,284	385 20
							6,407	1,922 10
							2,395	718 50
							1,885	565 50
							246	73 80
							600	180 00
							425	127 50
							5,146	1,543 80
							32,877	9,863 10
							3,583	1,074 90
							15,413	4,623 90
							1,156,141	346,842 30
	10,454	1,568 10					1,405,713	420,145 80
Gal.			Gal.			Gal.		
140,593	57,461	14,059 30				141,536	57,825	14,200 75
						2,507	686	376 05
						2	1	0 30
						128	40	19 20
			2,179	630	272 40	2,592	700	334 35
						57	23	8 55
			3,646	937	455 78	3,782	971	476 18
						24,303	3,589	3,645 45
140,593	57,461	14,059 30	5,825	1,567	728 18	174,907	63,835	19,060 83
424	415	409 33				424	415	400 33
						13	4	3 87
						984	264	359 41
						5,004	1,619	909 57
424	415	409 33				6,425	2,302	1,682 18
Lb.			Lb.			Lb.		
1,818,270	103,567	7,767 71				1,954,453	110,432	8,625 84
						138,596	6,308	788 50
						54,000	3,398	424 75
						2,412,874	168,712	21,089 89
1,818,270	103,567	7,767 71				4,559,923	288,850	30,928 98

6 GEORGE V, A. 1916

No. 1.—General Statement

Articles Imported.	Countries.	Total Imports.		Entered General Tariff.		
		Quantity.	Value.	Quantity.	Value.	Duty.
DUTIABLE GOODS—*Con.*			$		$	$ cts.
Watches....................	Unit'd Kingdom	....	23,643	....	1,968	590 40
	Aust.-Hungary..	....	27	....	2	0 60
	France..........	....	1,127	....	202	60 60
	Germany.......	....	3,248	....	3,609	1,082 70
	Switzerland.....	....	21,974	....	3,149	944 70
	United States...	....	23,919	....	23,876	7,162 80
	Total......	....	73,938	....	32,806	9,841 80
Watch cases and parts thereof, finished or unfinished.	Unit'd Kingdom	....	15,295	....	13,063	3,918 90
	France..........	....	470	....	470	141 00
	Germany......	....	968	....	968	290 40
	Japan..........	....	2	....	2	0 60
	Sweden..........	....	41	....	41	12 30
	Switzerland....	....	24,685	....	24,685	7,405 50
	United States...	....	53,563	....	53,563	16,068 90
	Total..........	....	95,024	....	92,792	27,837 60
Watch actions and movements and parts thereof, finished or unfinished, including winding bars and sleeves.	Unit'd Kingdom	....	58,179	....	56,933	7,116 63
	France........	....	4,233	....	4,233	529 13
	Germany......	....	4,499	....	4,499	562 38
	Switzerland....	....	184,282	....	185,028	23,128 50
	United States...	....	456,018	....	456,018	57,002 66
	Total......	....	707,211	....	706,711	88,339 30
		Lb.		Lb.		
Wax, bees...................	Unit'd Kingdom	9,931	4,001	1,951	845	84 50
	Germany.......	10,728	4,343	11,795	4,800	480 00
	Japan..........	267	9	267	9	0 90
	United States...	56,811	19,890	56,811	19,890	1,989 00
	Total......	77,737	28,243	70,824	25,544	2,554 40
Wax, paraffine....................	Unit'd Kingdom	273,268	13,966	1,986	168	42 00
	China..........	666	44	666	44	11 00
	Germany.......	559	50	559	50	12 50
	Japan..........	224	26	224	26	6 50
	United States...	728,705	34,595	728,705	34,595	8,648 75
	Total......	1,003,422	48,681	732,140	34,883	8,720 75
Wax, sealing.....................	Unit'd Kingdom	....	9,913	....	32	8 00
	France..........		91		91	22 75
	United States...	....	3,258	....	3,264	816 00
	Total......	....	13,262	....	3,387	846 75
Wax, vegetable and mineral, n.o.p.	Unit'd Kingdom	20,023	2,447	....	70	7 00
	Germany.......	679	70	679	83	8 30
	Japan..........	1,467	83	1,467	80,962	8,096 20
	United States..	618,537	80,962	618,537		
	Total......	640,706	83,562	620,683	81,115	8,111 50
Wax, and manufactures of, n.o.p...	Unit'd Kingdom	....	3,485	....	69	12 08
	France..........	....	498	....	498	87 15
	Germany......	....	277	....	277	48 48
	United States..	....	46,011	....	46,008	8,052 13
	Total......	....	50,271	....	46,852	8,199 84

OF IMPORTS.—*Continued.*

FOR HOME CONSUMPTION.

	Preferential Tariff.			Treaty Rates.			Total.	
Quantity.	Value.	Duty.	Quantity.	Value.	Duty.	Quantity.	Value.	DutyColl'd.
	$	$ cts.		$	$ cts.		$	$ cts.
....	2,791	558 20	....	18,968	5,216 28	....	23,727	6,364 88
....	....	....	....	25	6 88	....	27	7 48
....	....	....	....	925	254 38	....	1,127	314 98
....	....	....	....	....	....	....	3,609	1,082 70
....	....	....	....	18,825	5,176 96	....	21,974	6,121 66
....	....	....	....	....	....	....	23,876	7,162 80
....	2,791	558 20	....	38,743	10,654 50	....	74,340	21,054 50
....	1,902	380 40	....	....	....	....	14,965	4,299 30
....	....	....	....	....	....	....	470	141 00
....	....	....	....	....	....	....	968	290 40
....	....	....	....	....	....	....	2	0 60
....	....	....	....	....	....	....	41	12 30
....	....	....	....	....	....	....	24,685	7,405 50
....	....	....	....	....	....	....	53,563	16,068 90
....	1,902	380 40	....	....	....	....	94,694	28,218 00
....	434	43 40	....	....	....	....	57,367	7,160 03
....	....	....	....	....	....	....	4,233	529 13
....	....	....	....	....	....	....	4,499	562 38
....	....	....	....	....	....	....	185,028	23,128 50
....	....	....	....	....	....	....	456,018	57,002 66
....	434	43 40	....	....	....	....	707,145	88,382 70
Lb. 7,980	3,156	157 80	Lb.	....	....	Lb. 9,931	4,001	242 30
....	....	....	....	....	....	11,795	4,800	480 00
....	....	....	....	....	....	267	9	0 90
....	....	....	....	....	....	56,811	19,890	1,989 00
7,980	3,156	157 80	....	....	....	78,804	28,700	2,712 20
271,282	13,798	2,070 10	....	....	....	273,268	13,966	2,112-10
....	....	....	....	....	....	666	44	11 00
....	....	....	....	....	....	559	50	12 50
....	....	....	....	....	....	224	26	6 50
....	....	....	....	....	....	728,705	34,595	8,648 75
271,282	13,798	2,070 10	....	....	....	1,003,422	48,681	10,790 85
....	9,881	1,482 15	....	....	....	....	9,913	1,490 15
....	....	....	....	....	....	....	91	22 75
....	....	....	....	....	....	....	3,264	816 00
....	9,881	1,482 15	....	....	....	....	13,268	2,328 90
20,023	2,447	122 35	....	....	....	20,023	2,447	122 35
....	....	....	....	....	....	679	70	7 00
....	....	....	....	....	....	1,467	83	8 30
....	....	....	....	....	....	618,537	80,962	8,096 20
20,023	2,447	122 35	....	....	....	640,706	83,562	8,233 85
....	3,450	517 50	....	....	....	....	3,519	529 58
....	....	....	....	....	....	....	498	87 15
....	....	....	....	....	....	....	277	48 48
....	....	....	....	....	....	....	46,008	8,052 13
....	3,450	517 50	....	....	....	....	50,302	8,717 34

6 GEORGE V, A. 1916

No. 1.—General Statement

Articles Imported.	Countries.	Total Imports.		Entered		
				General Tariff.		
		Quantity.	Value.	Quantity.	Value.	Duty.
DUTIABLE GOODS—*Con.*			$		$	$ cts.
Webbing, elastic, over one inch wide.	Unit'd Kingdom	....	18,535	....	296	59 20
	France..........	....	911	....	911	182 20
	Germany......	....	556	....	556	111 20
	United States..	....	143,186	....	142,818	28,563 60
	Total....	....	163,188	....	144,581	28,916 20
Webbing, non-elastic, when imported by manufacturers of suspenders for use exclusively in the manufacture of such articles in their own factories.	Unit'd Kingdom	....	21	....	....	....
	United States..	....	4,070	....	4,070	814 00
	Total......	....	4,091	....	4,070	814 00
Whips of all kinds, including thongs and lashes.	Unit'd Kingdom	....	4,277	....	142	42 60
	Australia......	....	5	....	5	1 50
	Aust.-Hungary..	....	7	....	7	2 10
	France..........	....	9	....	9	2 70
	Germany......	....	3	....	3	0 90
	United States..	....	21,502	....	21,502	6,450 60
	Total......	....	25,803	....	21,668	6,500 40
Window cornices and cornice poles of all kinds.	Unit'd Kingdom	....	272	....	46	13 80
	United States..	....	5,290	....	5,290	1,587 00
	Total......	....	5,562	....	5,336	1,600 80
Window shade or blind rollers....	Unit'd Kingdom	....	732	....	....	....
	United States...	....	11,687	....	11,687	4,090 45
	Total......	....	12,419	....	11,687	4,090 45
Window shades cut to size or hemmed or mounted on rollers, n.o.p., and window shade cloth in the piece.	Unit'd Kingdom	....	32,066	....	....	....
	Germany......	....	58	....	58	20 30
	United States..	....	3,155	....	3,155	1,104 25
	Total......	....	35,279	....	3,213	1,124 55
Wood and manufactures of— Barrels containing petroleum or its products, or any mixture of which petroleum forms a part, when such contents are chargeable with a specific duty.		No.		No.		
	Unit'd Kingdom	426	432	70	70	17 50
	Russia..........	6	6	6	6	1 50
	United States..	29,609	29,048	27,925	27,364	6,841 00
	Total......	30,041	29,486	28,001	27,440	6,860 00
Barrels, empty..................	Unit'd Kingdom	338	420	239	235	58 75
	B. W. Indies....	421	253	421	253	63 25
	Newfoundland..	3,502	2,023	3,502	2,023	505 75
	Italy..........	2	8	2	8	2 00
	Miquelon and St. Pierre.....	606	362	606	362	90 50
	United States..	41,690	32,512	41,690	32,512	8,128 00
	Total......	46,559	35,578	46,460	35,393	8,848 25
Caskets and coffins and metal parts thereof.	United States..	....	48,924	....	48,924	12,231 00
Curtain stretchers..............	United States..	....	5,679	....	4,708	1,412 40

OF IMPORTS—*Continued.*

FOR HOME CONSUMPTION.

Preferential Tariff.			Treaty Rates.			Total.		
Quantity.	Value.	Duty.	Quantity.	Value.	Duty.	Quantity.	Value.	DutyColl'd.
	$	$ cts.		$	$ cts.		$	$ cts.
....	18,223	2,278 01	....	....	....	....	18,519	2,337 21
....	....	....	....	....	....	....	911	182 20
....	....	....	....	....	....	....	556	111 20
....	....	....	....	....	....	....	142,818	28,563 60
....	18,223	2,278 01	....	....	....	....	162,804	31,194 21
....	21	2 63	....	....	....	....	21	2 63
....	....	....	....	....	....	....	4,070	814 00
....	21	2 63	....	....	....	....	4,091	816 63
....	4,135	827 00	....	....	....	....	4,277	869 60
....	....	....	....	....	....	....	5	1 50
....	....	....	....	....	....	....	7	2 10
....	....	....	....	....	....	....	9	2 70
....	....	....	....	....	....	....	3	0 90
....	....	....	....	....	....	....	21,502	6,450 60
....	4,135	827 00	....	....	....	....	25,803	7,327 40
....	226	45 20	....	....	....	....	272	59 00
....	....	....	....	....	....	....	5,290	1,587 00
....	226	45 20	....	....	....	....	5,562	1,646 00
....	732	164 71	....	....	....	....	732	164 71
....	....	....	....	....	....	....	11,687	4,090 45
....	732	164 71	....	....	....	....	12,419	4,255 16
....	32,338	7,276 14	....	....	....	....	32,338	7,276 14
....	....	....	....	....	....	....	58	20 30
....	....	....	....	....	....	....	3,155	1,104 25
....	32,338	7,276 14	....	....	....	....	35,551	8,400 69
No. 356	362	63 37	No.	....	....	No. 426	432	80 87
....	....	....	....	....	....	6	6	1 50
....	....	....	....	....	....	27,925	27,364	6,841 00
356	362	63 37	....	....	....	28,357	27,802	6,923 37
82	153	26 79	....	....	....	321	388	85 54
....	....	....	....	....	....	421	253	63 25
....	....	....	....	....	....	3,502	2,023	505 75
....	....	....	....	....	....	2	8	2 00
....	....	....	....	....	....	606	362	90 50
....	....	....	....	....	....	41,690	32,512	8,128 00
82	153	26 79	....	....	....	46,542	35,546	8,875 04
....	....	....	....	....	....	....	48,924	12,231 00
....	....	....	....	....	....	....	4,708	1,412 40

6 GEORGE V, A. 1916

No. 1.—General Statement

Articles Imported.	Countries.	Total Imports.		Entered		
				General Tariff.		
		Quantity.	Value.	Quantity.	Value.	Duty.
DUTIABLE GOODS—*Con.*			$	—	$	$ cts.
Wood and mfrs. of—*Con.*						
Doors of wood................	United Kingdom	....	295	....	....	....
	United States...	....	235,944	....	235,944	58,986 00
	Total......	....	236,239	....	235,944	58,986 00
Fishing rods...................	Unit'd Kingdom	....	7,228	....	301	90 30
	Japan..........	....	2	....	2	0 60
	United States..	....	22,374	....	22,388	6,716 40
	Total......	....	29,604	....	22,691	6,807 30
Handles, D. shovel, wholly of	Unit'd Kingdom	....	47	....	....	....
wood and wood handles for	United States..	....	36,009	....	36,009	5,401 35
manufacture of. D. shovel handles.	Total......	....	36,056	....	36,009	5,401 35
Handles of all kinds, ash......	Unit'd Kingdom	.:......	15	....	....	....
	United States...	....	22,434	....	22,434	5,608 50
	Total......	....	22,449	....	22,434	5,608 50
Handles of all kinds, hickory...	Unit'd Kingdom	....	217	....	....	....
	United States...	....	48,663	....	48,649	12,162 25
	Total......	....	48,880	....	48,649	12,162 25
Heading and stave bolts and staves in the rough of poplar.	United States..	....	1,025	....	1,025	205 00
Lasts of wood.................	Unit'd Kingdom	....	133	....	....	....
	United States..	....	65,706	....	65,706	16,426 50
	Total......	....	65,839	....	65,706	16,426 50
Matches of wood..............	Unit'd Kingdom	....	972	....	191	47 75
	Hong Kong.....	....	10	....	10	2 50
	Aust.-Hungary..	....	604	....	594	148 50
	Belgium........	....	2,405	....	1,779	444 75
	France.........	....	189	....	....	....
	Germany......	....	69	....	69	17 25
	Holland........	....	281	....	281	70 25
	Italy...........	....	236	....	71	17 75
	Japan..........	....	2,133	....	1	0 25
	Norway........	....	241	....	....	....
	Sweden........	....	3,140	....	135	33 75
	United States...	....	30,125	....	30,239	7,559 75
	Total......	....	40,405	....	33,370	· 8,342 50
Mouldings, plain, gilded or otherwise further manufactured.	Germany......	....	176	....	176	44 00
	Holland........	....	679	....	679	169 75
	United States...	....	71,836	....	71,890	17,972 50
	Total......	....	72,691	....	72,745	18,186 25
Rakes, hay....................	Unit'dKingdom	No. 6	No. 2	No. 3	1	0 22
	United States...	685	240	685	240	54 02
	Total......	691	242	688	241	54 24

SESSIONAL PAPER No. 11

OF IMPORTS—*Continued.*

FOR HOME CONSUMPTION.

Preferential Tariff.			Treaty Rates.			Total.		
Quantity.	Value.	Duty.	Quantity.	Value.	Duty.	Quantity.	Value.	DutyColl'd.
	$	$ cts.		$	$ cts.		$	$ cts.
....	205	51 63	....	....	....	....	295	51 63
....	....	....	....	....	....	....	235,944	58,986 00
....	295	51 63	....	....	....	....	236,239	59,037 63
....	6,927	1,385 40					7,228	1,475 70
....	....	....					2	0 60
....	....	....					22,388	6,716 40
....	6,927	1,385 40					29;618	8,192 70
....	47	4 70	....				47	4 70
....	....	....					36,009	5,401 35
....	47	4 70	....				36,056	5,406 05
....	15	2 62	....				15	2 62
....	....	....					22,434	5,608 50
....	15	2 62	....				22,449	5,611 12
....	217	37 98	....				217	37 98
....	....	....					48,649	12,162 25
....	217	37 98	....				48,866	12,200 23
....							1,025	205 00
....	133	23 28	....				133	23 28
....	....	....					65,706	16,426 50
....	133	23 28	....				65,839	16,449 78
....	563	98 53	....	230	51 75	....	984	198 03
....							10	2 50
....				10	2 25		604	150 75
....				1,596	359 10		3,375	803 85
....				189	42 53		189	42 53
....							69	17 25
....							281	70 25
....							71	17 75
....				2,132	479 70		2,133	479 95
....				241	54 22		241	54 22
....				3,455	777 62		3,590	811 37
....							30,239	7,559 75
....	563	98 53	....	7,853	1,767 17	....	41,786	10,208 20
....							176	44 00
....							679	169 75
....							71,890	17,972 50
....							72,745	18,186 25
No. 3	1	0 15	No.			No. 6	2	0 37
....	....					685	240	54 02
3	1	0 15	....			691	242	54 39

No. 1.—General Statement

Articles Imported.	Countries.	Total Imports.		Entered		
				General Tariff.		
		Quantity.	Value.	Quantity.	Value.	Duty.
DUTIABLE GOODS—*Con.*		No.	$	No.	$	$ cts.
Wood and mfrs. of—*Con.*						
Refrigerators.................	Unit'd Kingdom	3	35	1	5	1 50
	United States...	1,399	31,442	1,396	31,102	9,330 60
	Total.......	1,402	31,477	1,397	31,107	9,332 10
Show cases of all kinds and metal parts thereof.	Unit'd Kingdom	....	3,996	....	114	39 90
	Germany........	....	33	....	33	11 55
	Switzerland.....	....	18	....	18	6 30
	United States...	....	16,318	....	16,318	5,711 30
	Total.......	....	20,365	....	16,483	5,769 05
Window sash..................	United States...	....	26,543	....	26,543	6,635 75
Woodenware, churns, n.o.p., washboards, pounders and rolling pins.	Unit'd Kingdom	....	319	....	21	4 20
	Belgium........	....	15	....	15	3 00
	Germany........	....	397	....	397	79 40
	Norway.........	....	1	....	1	0 20
	Sweden.........	....	56	....	56	11 20
	United States...	....	20,321	....	20,321	4,064 20
	Total.......	....	21,109	....	20,811	4,162 20
Woodenware pails and tubs.....	Unit'd Kingdom	....	66	....		
	Hong Kong.....	....	6	....	6	1 50
	Japan..........	....	112	....	6	1 50
	United States...	....	22,623	....	22,623	5,655 75
	Total.......	....	22,807	....	22,635	5,658 75
Manufactures of wood, n.o.p.....	Unit'd Kingdom	....	94,950	....	6,360	1,590 00
	B. W. Indies....	....	3	....	3	0 75
	Hong Kong.....	....	1,657	....	1,524	381 00
	Newfoundland..	....	10	....	10	2 50
	Aust.-Hungary..	....	920	....	41	10 25
	Belgium........	....	397	....	302	75 50
	China..........	....	248	....	248	62 00
	France.........	....	14,961	....	1,479	369 75
	Germany.......	....	14,028	....	14,490	3,622 50
	Holland........	....	131	....	129	32 25
	Italy...........	....	214	....	189	47 25
	Japan..........	....	8,310	....	273	68 25
	Norway........	....	4,468	....	1,839	459 75
	Russia.........	....	7,813	....	7,221	1,805 25
	Spain..........	....	28	....		
	Sweden........	....	1,461	....	12	3 00
	Switzerland....	....	29	....	16	4 00
	Turkey.........	....	20	....	20	5 00
	United States...	....	1,188,975	....	1,188,760	297,190 00
	Total.......	....	1,338,623	....	1,222,916	305,729 00
		M ft.		M ft.		
Sawed boards, planks, deals, planed or dressed on one or both sides, when the edges thereof are jointed or tongued and grooved.	Unit'd Kingdom	138	4,685	110	2,708	677 00
	United States...	22,371	325,967	22,371	325,967	81,491 75
	Total.......	22,509	330,652	22,481	328,675	82,168 75

OF IMPORTS—*Continued.*

FOR HOME CONSUMPTION.

Preferential Tariff.			Treaty Rates.			Total.		
Quantity.	Value.	Duty.	Quantity.	Value.	Duty.	Quantity.	Value.	DutyColl'd.
No.	$	$ cts.	No.	$	$ cts.	No.	$	$ cts.
2	30	6 00	....	....	....	3	35	7 50
....	....	....	....	....	....	1,396	31,102	9,330 60
2	30	6 00	....	....	....	1,399	31,137	9,338 10
....	3,882	873 57	....			....	3,996	913 47
....	....	....	....			....	33	11 55
....	....	....	....			....	18	6 30
....	....	....	....			....	16,318	5,711 30
....	3,882	873 57	....			....	20,365	6,642 62
....							26,543	6,635 75
....	298	44 70	....			....	319	48 90
....	....	....	....			....	15	3 00
....	....	....	....			....	397	79 40
....	....	....	....			....	1	0 20
....	....	....	....			....	56	11 20
....	....	....	....			....	20,321	4,064 20
....	298	44 70	....			....	21,109	4,206 90
....	66	11 55	....			....	66	11 55
....	....	....	....			....	6	1 50
....	....	....	....	106	23 85	....	112	25 35
....	....	....	....			....	22,623	5,655 75
....	66	11 55	....	106	23 85	....	22,807	5,694 15
....	81,189	14,208 62	....	7,201	1,620 22	....	94,750	17,418 84
....	....	....	....			....	3	0 75
....	....	....	....	133	29 93	....	1,657	410 93
....	....	....	....			....	10	2 50
....	....	....	....	879	197 77	....	920	208 02
....	....	....	....	190	42 75	....	492	118 25
....	....	....	....			....	248	62 00
....	....	....	....	14,817	3,334 10	....	16,296	3,703 85
....	....	....	....			....	14,490	3,622 50
....	....	....	....	97	21 83	....	226	54 08
....	....	....	....	25	5 63	....	214	52 88
....	....	....	....	7,956	1,790 10	....	8,229	1,858 35
....	....	....	....	2,629	591 52	....	4,468	1,051 27
....	....	....	....	592	133 20	....	7,813	1,938 45
....	....	....	....	180	40 50	....	180	40 50
....	....	....	....	1,771	398 48	....	1,783	401 48
....	....	....	....	13	2 93	....	29	6 93
....	....	....	....	....	....	....	20	5 00
....	....	....	....	....	....	....	1,188,760	297,190 00
....	81,189	14,208 62	....	36,483	8,208 96	....	1,340,588	328,146 58
M ft. 28	1,977	345 98	M ft.			M ft. 138	4,685	1,022 98
....	....	....	....	....	....	22,371	325,967	81,491 75
28	1,977	345 98	....	....	....	22,509	330,652	82,514 73

6 GEORGE V, A. 1916

No. 1.—GENERAL STATEMENT

Articles Imported.	Countries.	TOTAL IMPORTS.		ENTERED		
				General Tariff.		
		Quantity.	Value.	Quantity.	Value.	Duty.
			$		$	$ cts.
DUTIABLE GOODS—*Con.*						
Umbrella, parasol and sunshade	Unit'd Kingdom	....	3,276	....	403	80 60
sticks or handles, n.o.p.	Aust.-Hungary..	....	10	....	10	2 00
	Belgium........	....	14	....	14	2 80
	Germany......	....	902	....	902	180 40
	Japan..........	....	14	....	14	2 80
	United States...	....	6,652	....	6,652	1,330 40
	Total......	....	10,868	....	7,995	1,599 00
Veneers of oak, rosewood, ma-	Unit'd Kingdom	....	43	....		
bogany, Spanish cedar and	United States...	....	148,044	....	148,044	11,103 77
walnut, not over $\frac{3}{32}$ of an inch						
in thickness.	Total......	....	148,087	....	148,044	11,103 77
Veneers of wood, n.o.p. not over	United States...	....	31,679	....	31,679	4,751 85
$\frac{3}{32}$ of an inch in thickness.						
Walking sticks and walking	Unit'd Kingdom	....	15,073	....	106	31 80
canes of all kinds.	B. W. Indies....	....	7	....	7	2 10
	Aust.-Hungary..	....	230	....	230	69 00
	France..........	....	35	....	35	10 50
	Germany......	....	141	....	141	42 30
	Japan..........	....	387	....	329	98 70
	United States...	....	11,428	....	11,407	3,422 10
	Total......	....	27,301	....	12,255	3,676 50
Wood, pulp..................	Unit'd Kingdom	....	620	....	532	133 00
	Aust.-Hungary..	....	786	....	786	196 50
	Norway........	....	1,411	....	24,043	6,010 75
	Sweden........	....	178,800	....	179,829	44,957 25
	Switzerland....	....	5,285	....	5,285	1,321 25
	United States...	....	269,918	....	269,918	67,479 50
	Total......	....	456,820	....	480,393	120,098 25
		Pairs.		Pairs.		
Wool, manufactures of—						
Blankets composed wholly of	Unit'd Kingdom	21,643	74,521	1,405	4,010	1,403 50
pure wool	Aust.-Hungary .	266	774	266	774	270 90
	Belgium........	105	227	105	227	79 45
	France..........	1,232	1,596	1,232	1,596	558,60
	Germany......	678	1,679	678	1,679	587 65
	Sweden........	1	5	1	5	1 75
	Switzerland....	15	29	15	29	10 15
	United States...	3,831	12,303	3,831	12,303	4,306 05
	Total......	27,771	91,134	7,533	20,623	7,218 05
		Yd.		Yd.		
Cassimeres, cloths and doeskins	Unit'd Kingdom	1,596,503	1,399,340	43,030	36,700	12,845 00
	Aust.-Hungary .	248	272	248	272	95 20
	Belgium........	7,134	6,299	7,134	6,299	2,204 65
	China..........	4	8	4	8	2 80
	France..........	58,245	54,636	59,315	55,706	19,497 10
	Germany......	38,957	34,587	40,749	34,670	12,134 50
	Holland........	5,576	4,147	5,576	4,147	1,451 45
	Italy..........	10	20	86	135	47 25
	Switzerland.....	193	226	193	226	79 10
	United States...	143,096	161,585	143,182	161,815	56,635 25
	Total.......	1,849,966	1,661,120	299,517	299,978	104,992 30

OF IMPORTS—*Continued.*

FOR HOME CONSUMPTION.

	Preferential Tariff.			Treaty Rates.			Total.	
Quantity.	Value.	Duty.	Quantity.	Value.	Duty.	Quantity.	Value.	DutyColl'd.
	$	$ cts.		$	$ cts.		$	$ cts.
....	2,873	430 95	....	....	....	....	3,276	511 55
....	....	....	....	....	....	....	10	2 00
....	....	....	....	....	....	....	14	2 80
....	....	....	....	....	....	....	902	180 40
....	....	....	....	....	....	....	14	2 80
....	....	....	....	....	....	....	6,652	1,330 40
....	2,873	430 95	....	....	....	....	10,868	2,029 95
....	43	2 15	....			....	43	2 15
....	....	....				....	148,044	11,103 77
....	43	2 15				....	148,087	11,105 92
....	....	....				....	31,679	4,751 85
....	14,909	2,981 80	....			....	15,015	3,013 60
....	....	....				....	7	2 10
....	....	....				....	230	69 00
....	....	....				....	35	10 50
....	....	....				....	141	42 30
....	....	....				....	329	98 70
....	....	....				....	11,407	3,422 10
....	14,909	2,981 80				....	27,164	6,658 30
....	88	13 20	....			....	620	146 20
....	....	....				....	786	196 50
....	....	....				....	24,043	6,010 75
....	....	....				....	179,829	44,957 25
....	....	....				....	5,285	1,321 25
....	....	....				....	269,918	67,479 50
....	88	13 20	....	....	....	....	480,481	120,111 45
Pairs. 19,911	69,036	15,533 56	Pairs.	....	....	Pairs. 21,316	73,046	16,937 06
....	....	....				266	774	270 90
....	....	....				105	227	79 45
....	....	....				1,232	1,596	558 60
....	....	....				678	1,679	587 65
....	....	....				1	5	1 75
....	....	....				15	29	10 15
....	....	....				3,831	12,303	4,306 05
19,911	69,036	15,533 56	....	....	....	27,444	89,659	22,751 61
Yd. 1,544,845	1,358,185	407,455 50	Yd.			Yd. 1,587,875	1,394,885	420,300 50
....	....	....				248	272	95 20
....	....	....				7,134	6,299	2,204 65
....	....	....				4	8	2 80
....	....	....				-59,315	55,706	19,497 10
....	....	....				40,749	34,670	12,134 50
....	....	....				5,576	4,147	1,451 45
....	....	....				86	135	47 25
....	....	....				193	226	79 10
....	....	....				143,182	161,815	56,635 25
1,544,845	1,358,185	407,455 50	....	....	....	1,844,362	1,658,163	512,447 80

11—ii—18½

6 GEORGE V, A. 1916

No. 1.—General Statement

Articles Imported.	Countries.	Total Imports. Quantity.	Value.	Entered General Tariff. Quantity.	Value.	Duty.
DUTIABLE GOODS—*Con.*		Yd.	$	Yd.	$	$ cts.
Wool, mfrs. of—*Con.*						
Coatings and overcoatings......	Unit'd Kingdom	1,186,983	969,481	33,296	25,485	8,919 75
	Aust.-Hungary .	2,489	2,370	2,489	2,370	829 .50
	Belgium........	5,494	2,413	5,494	2,413	844 55
	France.........	7,747	5,790	7,747	5,790	2,026 50
	Germany......	12,209	11,131	11,960	10,947	3,831 45
	Holland.......	9,642	7,775	9,642	7,775	2,721 25
	United States...	16,136	13,090	16,136	13,090	4,581 50
	Total...	1,240,700	1,012,050	86,764	67,870	23,754 50
Tweeds......................	Unit'd Kingdom	1,604,280	835,476	33,474	12,262	4,291 70
	Aust.-Hungary .	20	27	20	27	9 45
	Belgium.......	230	188	230	188	65 80
	France.........	8,985	2,712	8,985	2,712	949 20
	Germany......	15,541	7,801	18,082	9,532	3,336 20
	Holland.......	12,047	5,119	10,813	4,648	1,626 80
	United States..	104,815	176,147	100,428	169,424	59,298 40
	Total......	1,745,918	1,027,470	172,032	198,793	69,577 55
Felt cloth, n.o.p..............	Unit'd Kingdom	11,776	14,754	151	109	38 15
	Belgium........	2,370	3,869	2,370	3,869	1,354 15
	France.........	11,381	7,904	11,381	7,904	2,766 40
	Germany......	952	460	952	460	161 00
	Holland.......	225	428	225	428	149 80
	United States..	28,648	23,142	28,648	23,142	8,099 70
	Total......	55,352	50,557	43,727	35,912	12,569 20
Flannels, plain, not fancy.......	Unit'd Kingdom	843,237	133,861	40,247	9,770	3,419 50
	France.........	32,364	7,078	32,364	7,078	2,477 30
	Germany......	333	79	333	79	27 65
	United States..	1,361,231	527,586	1,361,231	527,586	184,655 10
	Total......	2,237,165	668,604	1,434,175	544,513	190,579 55
Knitted goods, n.o.p...........	Unit'd Kingdom	....	424,400	....	36,280	12,698 00
	Aust.-Hungary .	....	1,875	....	1,875	656 25
	Belgium.......	....	1,423	....	1,423	498 05
	France.........	....	2,811	....	2,811	983 85
	Germany......	....	21,704	....	21,449	7,507 15
	Holland........	....	331	....	331	115 85
	Japan..........	....	11	....	11	3 85
	Switzerland.....	....	6,816	....	6,803	2,381 05
	United States..	....	52,999	....	52,999	18,549 65
	Total......	....	512,370	....	123,982	43,393 70
		No.		No.		
Bed comforters................	Unit'd Kingdom	103	472	....	....	....
	United States..	162	153	162	153	53 55
	Total	265	625	162	153	53 55
Railway rugs.................	Unit'd Kingdom	....	44,333	....	1,187	415 45
	Belgium.......	....	493	....	493	172 55
	France........	....	245	....	245	85 75
	Germany......	....	354	....	354	123 90
	United States..	....	527	....	527	184 45
	Total......	....	45,952	....	2,806	982 10

OF IMPORTS—*Continued.*

FOR HOME CONSUMPTION.

Preferential Tariff.			Treaty Rates.			Total.		
Quantity.	Value.	Duty.	Quantity.	Value.	Duty.	Quantity.	Value.	DutyColl'd.
Yd.	$	$ cts.	Yd.	$	$ cts.	Yd.	$	$ cts.
1,163,933	951,144	285,343 20	....	....	....	1,197,229	976,629	294,262 95
....	....	....	....	....	....	2,489	2,370	829 50
....	....	....	....	....	....	5,494	2,413	844 55
....	....	....	....	....	....	7,747	5,790	2,026 50
....	....	....	....	....	....	11,960	10,947	3,831 45
....	....	....	....	....	....	9,642	7,775	2,721 25
....	....	....	....	....	....	16,136	13,090	4,581 50
1,163,933	951,144	285,343 20	....	....	....	1,250,697	1,019,014	309,097 70
1,567,939	819,187	245,756 10	....	....	....	1,601,413	831,449	250,047 80
....	....	....	....	....	....	20	27	9 45
....	....	....	....	....	....	230	188	65 80
....	....	....	....	....	....	8,985	2,712	949 20
....	....	....	....	....	....	18,082	9,532	3,336 20
....	....	....	....	....	....	10,813	4,648	1,626 80
....	....	....	....	....	....	100,428	169,424	59,298 40
1,567,939	819,187	245,756 10	....	....	....	1,739,971	1,017,980	315,333 65
11,645	14,667	4,400 10	....	....	....	11,796	14,776	4,438 25
....	....	....	....	....	....	2,370	3,869	1,354 15
....	....	....	....	....	....	11,381	7,904	2,766 40
....	....	....	....	....	....	952	460	161 00
....	....	....	....	....	....	225	428	149 80
....	....	....	....	....	....	28,648	23,142	8,099 70
11,645	14,667	4,400 10	....	....	....	55,372	50,579	16,969 30
783,974	122,082	27,469 32	....	....	....	824,221	131,852	30,888 82
....	....	....	....	....	....	32,364	7,078	2,477 30
....	....	....	....	....	....	333	79	27 65
....	....	....	....	....	....	1,361,231	527,586	184,655 10
783,974	122,082	27,469 32	....	....	....	2,218,149	666,595	218,048 87
....	386,457	86,954 77	....	....	....	....	422,737	99,652 77
....	....	....	....	....	....	....	1,875	656 25
....	....	....	....	....	....	....	1,423	498 05
....	....	....	....	....	....	....	2,811	983 85
....	....	....	....	....	....	....	21,449	7,507 15
....	....	....	....	....	....	....	331	115 85
....	....	....	....	....	....	....	11	3 85
....	....	....	....	....	....	....	6,803	2,381 05
....	....	....	....	....	....	....	52,999	18,549 65
....	386,457	86,954 77	....	....	....	....	510,439	130,348 47
No. 103	472	141 60	No.	....	....	No. 103	472	141 60
....	....	....	....	....	....	162	153	53 55
103	472	141 60	....	....	....	265	625	195 15
....	43,292	12,987 60	....	....	....	....	44,479	13,403 05
....	....	....	....	....	....	....	493	172 55
....	....	....	....	....	....	....	245	85 75
....	....	....	....	....	....	....	354	123 90
....	....	....	....	....	....	....	527	184 45
....	43,292	12,987 60	....	....	....	....	46,098	13,969 70

6 GEORGE V, A. 1916

No. 1.—General Statement

Articles Imported.	Countries.	Total Imports.		Entered		
				General Tariff.		
		Quantity.	Value.	Quantity.	Value.	Duty.
DUTIABLE GOODS—*Con.*			$		$	$ cts.
Wool, mfrs. of—*Con.*						
Shawls..................	Unit'd Kingdom	....	57,756	....	2,224	778 40
	Aust.-Hungary	....	1,403	....	1,403	491 05
	France..........	....	283	....	283	99 05
	Germany......	....	4,132	....	4,132	1,446 20
	Italy..........	....	6	....	6	2 10
	United States..	....	279	....	279	97 65
	Total......	....	63,859	....	8,327	2,914 45
		Doz.		Doz.		
Shirts..................	United Kingdom	2,823	26,753	35	331	115 85
	France..........	6	157	6	157	54 95
	Japan..........	4	48	4	48	16 80
	United States..	620	4,921	620	4,921	1,722 35
	Total......	3,453	31,879	665	5,457	1,909 95
		Doz. pr.		Doz. pr.		
Socks and stockings...........	Unit'd Kingdom	645,585	1,167,888	5,413	10,790	3,776 50
	Hong Kong.....	3	15	3	15	5 25
	Newfoundland..	....	1	....	1	0 35
	Aust.-Hungary	67	272	67	272	95 20
	Belgium........	43	42	201	240	84 00
	France..........	342	608	665	1,073	375 55
	Germany......	8,463	15,308	9,428	16,286	5,700 10
	Holland.......	49	164	49	164	57 40
	Italy..........	3	2	3	2	0 70
	Japan..........	4	9	4	9	3 15
	Switzerland....	80	202	80	202	70 70
	United States..	22,264	47,371	21,898	46,903	16,416 05
	Total......	676,903	1,231,882	37,811	75,957	26,584 95
Undershirts and drawers, n.o.p.	Unit'd Kingdom	....	344,024	....	14,510	5,078 50
	France..........	....	2,443	....	2,443	855 05
	Germany......	....	1,321	....	1,321	462 35
	Switzerland.....	....	7,963	....	7,963	2,787 05
	United States..	....	37,631	....	37,631	13,170 85
	Total......	....	393,382	....	63,868	22,353 80
		Lb.		Lb.		
Yarns, composed wholly or in part of wool, worsted, the hair of the goat or like animal, n.o.p., costing thirty cents per pound or over, when imported on the cop, cone, or tube, or in the hank, by manufacturers of woollen goods, for use exclusively in their own factories.	Unit'd Kingdom	1,832,375	1,150,393	12,195	7,710	1,542 00
	Belgium........	4,998	2,963	4,998	2,963	592 60
	France..........	23,616	14,377	23,616	14,377	2,875 40
	Germany........	141	45	141	45	9 00
	United States...	45,850	29,513	45,896	29,536	5,907 20
	Total......	1,906,980	1,197,291	86,846	54,631	10,926 20
Yarns, woollen and worsted, n.o.p.	Unit'd Kingdom	356,097	221,086	13,634	8,003	2,400 90
	France..........	1,889	2,761	1,889	2,761	828 30
	Germany......	27,143	16,443	27,143	16,443	4,932 90
	Japan..........	4	2	4	2	0 60
	Switzerland....	181	153	181	153	45 90
	United States...	19,207	10,334	19,207	10,334	3,100 20
	Total......	404,521	250,779	62,058	37,696	11,308 80

OF IMPORTS—*Continued.*

FOR HOME CONSUMPTION.

Preferential Tariff.			Treaty Rates.			Total.		
Quantity.	Value.	Duty.	Quantity.	Value.	Duty.	Quantity.	Value.	Duty Coll'd.
	$	$ cts.		$	$ cts.		$	$ cts.
....	55,300	16,590 00	....	....	....	....	57,524	17,368 40
....			....	....	....	....	1,403	491 05
....			....	....	....	....	283	99 05
....			....	....	....	....	4,132	1,446 20
....			....	....	....	....	6	2 10
....			....	....	....	....	279	97 65
....	55,300	16,590 00	....	....	....	....	63,627	19,504 45
Doz. 2,891	27,219	8,165 70	Doz.			Doz. 2,926	27,550	8,281 55
....						6	157	54 95
....						4	48	16 80
....						620	4,921	1,722 35
2,891	27,219	8,165 70	....	....	....	3,556	32,676	10,075 65
Doz. pr. 639,857	1,159,825	289,956 25	Doz. pr.			Doz. pr. 645,270	1,170,615	293,732 75
....			....	....	....	3	15	5 25
....			....	....	....	......	1	0 35
....			....	....	....	67	272	95 20
....			....	....	....	201	240	84 00
....			....	....	....	665	1,073	375 55
....			....	....	....	9,428	16,286	5,700 10
....			....	....	....	49	164	57 40
....			....	....	....	3	2	0 70
....			....	....	....	4	9	3 15
....			....	....	....	80	202	70 70
....			....	....	....	21,898	46,903	16,416 05
639,857	1,159,825	289,956 25	....	....	....	677,668	1,235,782	316,541 20
....	328,280	73,863 45	....	....	....	....	342,790	78,941 95
....			....	....	....	....	2,443	855 05
....			....	....	....	....	1,321	462 35
....			....	....	....	....	7,963	2,787 05
....			....	....	....	....	37,631	13,170 85
....	328,280	73,863 45	....	....	....	....	392,148	96,217 25
Lb. 1,821,815	1,143,826	142,978 64	Lb.			Lb. 1,834,010	1,151,536	144,520 64
....			....	....	....	4,998	2,963	592 60
....			....	....	....	23,616	14,377	2,875 40
....			....	....	....	141	45	9 00
....			....	....	....	45,896	29,536	5,907 20
1,821,815	1,143,826	142,978 64	....	....	....	1,908,661	1,198,457	153,904 84
341,501	211,343	42,268 60	....	....	....	355,135	219,346	44,669 50
....			....	....	....	1,889	2,761	828 30
....			....	....	....	27,143	16,443	4,932 90
....			....	....	....	4	2	0 60
....			....	....	....	181	153	45 90
....			....	....	....	19,207	10,334	3,100 20
341,501	211,343	42,268 60	....	....	....	403,559	249,039	53,577 40

6 GEORGE V, A. 1916

No. 1.—General Statement

Articles Imported.	Countries.	Total Imports.		Entered		
				General Tariff.		
		Quantity.	Value.	Quantity.	Value.	Duty.
			$		$	$ cts.
DUTIABLE GOODS—*Con.*						
Wool, mfrs. of—*Con.*						
All fabrics and manufactures composed wholly or in part of wool, worsted, etc., n.o.p.	Unit'd Kingdom	....	5,803,726	....	413,269	144,644 15
	Hong Kong.....	....	16	....	16	5 60
	Aust.-Hungary..	....	1,362	....	1,362	476 70
	Belgium........	....	26,779	....,.....	26,689	9,341 15
	France........	....	383,290	....	392,561	137,396 35
	Germany.......	....	105,074	....	107,045	37,465 75
	Holland.......	....	25,673	....	25,762	9,016 70
	Japan..........	....	472	....	472	165 20
	Miquelon and St. Pierre.....	....	2	....	2	0 70
	Sweden........	....	1,620	....	1,620	567 00
	Switzerland....	....	7,392	....	7,392	2,587 20
	United States...	....	517,070	....	515,211	180,323 85
	Total......	....	6,872,476	....	1,491,401	521,990 35
		Yd.		Yd.		
Fabrics of wool, or of cotton and wool, commonly described and sold as lustres, mohairs, alpaca and Italian linings.	Unit'd Kingdom	2,683,532	778,687	6,738	2,277	796 95
	Belgium........	420	78	420	78	27 30
	France..........	4,168	1,922	4,168	1,922	672 70
	Germany.......	720	308	720	308	107 80
	United States...	9,143	2,188	6,067	1,736	607 60
	Total.......	2,697,983	783,183	18,113	6,321	2,212 35
		Sq. yd.		Sq. yd.		
Women's and children's dress goods, coat linings, Italian cloths, alpacas, orleans, cashmeres, henriettas, serges, buntings, nun's cloth, bengalines, whip cords, twills, plains or jacquards of similar fabrics, composed wholly or in part of wool, worsted, the hair of the camel, alpaca, goat or like animal, not exceeding in weight six ounces to the square yard, when imported in the gray or unfinished state for the purpose of being dyed or finished in Canada.	Unit'd Kingdom	1,225,808	323,850	1,185	508	127 00
	Belgium........	4,601	1,317	....	....	....
	France..........	4,343	1,802	107	44	11 00
	United States...	1,979	928	1,979	928	232 00
	Total.......	1,236,731	327,897	3,271	1,480	370 00
Clothing, women's and children's outside garments.	Unit'd Kingdom	....	191,567	....	11,417	3,995 95
	Newfoundland..	....	445	....	445	155 75
	Aust.-Hungary..	....	243	....	243	85 05
	France........	....	2,827	....	2,827	989 45
	Germany.......	....	23,407	....	23,407	8,192 45
	Holland.......	....	439	....	419	146 65
	Switzerland....	....	241	....	241	84 35
	United States...	....	349,528	....	349,528	122,334 80
	Total......	....	568,697	....	388,527	135,984 45
Clothing, ready-made, and wearing apparel, composed wholly or in part of wool worsted, etc., n.o.p.	Unit'd Kingdom	....	728,778	....	28,902	10,115 70
	B. India.......	....	82	....	82	28 70
	Hong Kong....	....	74	....	74	25 90
	Newfoundland..	....	58	....	58	20 30
	Aust.-Hungary..	....	398	....	398	139 30
	Belgium........	....	3,734	....	3,734	1,306 90
	France........	....	10,094	....	9,872	3,455 20
	Germany.......	....	20,510	....	22,558	7,895 30
	Holland.......	....	669	....	669	234 15
	Italy..........	....	372	....	198	69 30

OF IMPORTS—*Continued.*

FOR HOME CONSUMPTION.

	Preferential Tariff.			Treaty Rates.			Total.	
Quantity.	Value.	Duty.	Quantity.	Value.	Duty.	Quantity.	Value.	DutyColl'd.
	$	$ cts.		$	$ cts.		$	$ cts.
....	5,473,639	1,642,091 70	....	....	....	....	5,886,908	1,786,735 85
							16	5 60
							1,362	476 70
							26,689	9,341 15
							392,561	137,396 35
							107,045	37,465 75
							25,762	9,016 70
							472	165 20
							2	0 70
							1,620	567 00
							7,392	2,587 20
							515,211	180,323 85
....	5,473,639	1,642,091 70	....	....	....	....	6,965,040	2,164,082 05
Yd. 2,672,501	793,107	178,450 36	Yd.	....	....	Yd. 2,679,239	795,384	179,247 31
						420	78	27 30
						4,168	1,922	672 70
						720	308	107 80
						6,067	1,736	607 60
2,672,501	793,107	178,450 36	....	....	....	2,690,614	799,428	180,662 71
Sq. yd. 1,223,589	323,028	48,454 20	Sq. yd. 1,435	544	122 40	Sq. yd. 1,226,209	324,080	48,703 60
			4,601	1,317	296 32	4,601	1,317	296 32
			4,236	1,758	395 54	4,343	1,802	406 54
						1,979	928	232 00
1,223,589	323,028	48,454 20	10,272	3,619	814 26	1,237,132	328,127	49,638 46
....	180,147	54,044 10	....	....	....	....	191,564	58,040 05
							445	155 75
							243	85 05
							2,827	989 45
							23,407	8,192 45
							419	146 65
							241	84 35
							349,528	122,334 80
....	180,147	54,044 10	....	....	....	....	568,674	190,028 55
....	692,885	207,865 50	....	....	....	....	721,787	217,981 20
							82	28 70
							74	25 90
							58	20 30
							398	139 30
							3,734	1,306 90
							9,872	3,455 20
							22,558	7,895 30
							669	234 15
							198	69 30

6 GEORGE V, A. 1916

No. 1.—General Statement

Articles Imported.	Countries.	Total Imports.		Entered		
				General Tariff.		
		Quantity.	Value.	Quantity.	Value.	Duty.
			$		$	$ cts.
DUTIABLE GOODS—*Con.*						
Wool, mfrs. of—*Con.*						
Clothing, ready-made, and wearing apparel, etc.—*Con.*⁵	Japan		76		76	26 60
	Switzerland		709		709	248 15
	United States		525,458		527,049	184,467 15
	Total		1,291,012		594,379	208,032 65
		Yd.		Yd.		
Carpets, Axminster, including Abusson, Savonerie and Moquette.	Unit'd Kingdom	132,278	136,990	4,541	5,434	1,901 90
	Aust.-Hungary	133	59	133	59	20 65
	Belgium	85	124	85	124	43 40
	Germany	385	307	385	307	107 45
	Switzerland	13	25	13	25	8 75
	United States	584	1,013	584	1,013	354 55
	Total	133,478	138,518	5,741	6,962	2,436 70
Carpets, Brussels, including Wilton and Teprac.	Unit'd Kingdom	145,820	166,246	739	587	205 45
	Aust.-Hungary	650	623	650	623	218 05
	France	305	453	305	453	158 55
	Germany	187	328	187	328	114 80
	Turkey	400	400	400	400	140 00
	United States	969	1,438	969	1,438	503 30
	Total	148,331	169,488	3,250	3,829	1,340 15
Carpets, Tapestry, including drum printed or machine printed, and velvet.	Unit'd Kingdom	388,064	200,806	3,403	1,338	468 30
	France	204	68	204	68	23 80
	French Africa	20	31	20	31	10 85
	Germany	1,625	1,019	1,625	1,019	356 65
	United States	1,578	947	1,578	947	331 45
	Total	391,491	202,871	6,830	3,403	1,191 05
Carpets, Ingrain, 2 and 3 ply all wool or union.	Unit'd Kingdom	19,495	14,821	779	989	346 15
	France	281	226	281	226	79 10
	Germany	2,131	2,481	2,131	2,481	868 35
	United States	338	190	338	190	66 50
	Total	22,245	17,718	3,529	3,886	1,360 10
		Sq. yd.		Sq. yd.		
Whole carpets, including tufted, hand-made or Oriental, Turkish, Persian, Japanese, Indian or Smyrna.	Unit'd Kingdom	257,454	270,281	7,463	29,992	10,497 20
	B. India	60	251	60	251	87 85
	B.E.Indiesother	12	61	12	61	21 35
	Aust.-Hungary	1,849	1,358	1,849	1,358	475 30
	Belgium	3,912	3,533	3,912	3,533	1,236 55
	China	13	22	13	22	7 70
	Egypt & Soudan	250	297	250	297	103 95
	France	1,142	2,412	1,142	2,412	844 20
	Germany	2,296	2,525	2,296	2,525	883 75
	Japan	65	228	65	228	79 80
	Persia	2,607	4,544	2,607	4,544	1,590 40
	Turkey	6,349	21,984	6,349	21,984	7,694 40
	United States	1,958	5,420	1,958	5,420	1,897 00
	Total	277,967	312,916	27,976	72,627	25,419 45

SESSIONAL PAPER No. 11

OF IMPORTS—*Continued.*

FOR HOME CONSUMPTION.

	Preferential Tariff.			Treaty Rates.			Total.	
Quantity.	Value.	Duty.	Quantity.	Value.	Duty.	Quantity.	Value.	DutyColl'd.
	$	$ cts.		$	$ cts.		$	$ cts.
....	....	....	....	....	....	....	76	26 60
....	....	....	....	....	....	....	709	248 15
....	....	....	....	....	....	....	527,049	184,467 15
....	692,885	207,865 50	....	....	....	....	1,287,264	415,898 15
Yd.			Yd.			Yd.		
129,964	134,060	33,515 00	....	....	....	134,505	139,494	35,416 90
						133	59	20 65
						85	124	43 40
						385	307	107 45
						13	25	8 75
						584	1,013	354 55
129,964	134,060	33,515 00	....			135,705	141,022	35,951 70
147,327	. 167,427	41,856 75	....	....	....	148,066	168,014	42,062 20
						650	623	218 05
						305	453	158 55
						187	328	114 80
						400	400	140 00
						969	1,438	503 30
147,327	167,427	41,856 75	....			150,577	171,256	43,196 90
383,958	200,112	50,028 00	....	....	....	387,361	201,450	50,496 30
						204	68	23 80
						20	31	10 85
						1,625	·1,019	356 65
						1,578	947	331 45
383,958	200,112	50,028 00	....			390,788	· 203,515	51,219 05
18,716	13,832	3,458 00	....	....	....	19,495	14,821	3,804 15
						281	226	79 10
						2,131	2,481	868 35
						338	• 190	66 50
18,716	13,832	3,458 00	....			22,245	17,718	4,818 10
Sq. yd.			Sq. yd.			Sq. yd.		
252,804	242,187	60,546 75	....	....	....	260,267	272,179	71,043 95
						60	251	87 85
						12	61	21 35
						1,849	1,358	475 30
						3,912	3,533	1,236 55
						13	22	7 70
						250	297	103 95
						1,142	2,412	844 20
						2,296	2,525	883 75
						65	228	79 80
						2,607	4,544	1,590 40
						6,349	21,984	7,694 40
						1,958	5,420	1,897 00
· 252,804	· 242,187	60,546 75	....			280,780	314,814	85,966 20

6 GEORGE V, A. 1916

No. 1.—GENERAL STATEMENT

Articles Imported.	Countries.	TOTAL IMPORTS.		ENTERED		
				General Tariff.		
		Quantity.	Value.	Quantity.	Value.	Duty.
			$		$	$ cts.
DUTIABLE GOODS—*Con.*						
Wool, mfrs. of—*Con.*						
Mats and rugs, including hearth,	Unit'd Kingdom	....	347,002	....	28,913	10,119 55
sizes 30 sq. ft. and smaller,	B. India.......	....	41	....	41	14 35
wool, n.o.p.	Hong Kong.....	....	22	....	22	7 70
	Aust.-Hungary..	....	387	....	387	135 45
	Belgium........	....	435	....	435	152 25
	Egypt & Soudan	....	786	....	786	275 10
	France.........	....	1,540	....	1,540	539 00
	French Africa...	....	329	....	329	115 15
	Germany......	....	4,224	....	4,224	1,478 40
	Holland.......	....	12	....	12	4 20
	Italy..........	....	2	....	2	0 70
	Japan.........	....	3,143	....	3,143	1,100 05
	Persia........	....	1,463	....	1,463	512 05
	Turkey........	....	3,666	....	9,050	3,167 50
	United States..	....	30,114	....	30,114	10,539 90
	Total......	....	393,166	....	80,461	28,161 35
		Lb.		Lb.		
Felt, pressed, of all kinds not	Unit'd Kingdom	359,569	145,904	9,353	2,792	698 00
filled or covered by or with	Aust.-Hungary..	38,965	9,466	38,965	9,466	2,366 50
any woven fabric.	Belgium........	80	42	80	42	10 50
	Germany......	50,600	20,429	50,600	20,429	5,107 25
	United States..	608,529	120,741	608,229	120,643	30,160 75
	Total......	1,057,743	296,582	707,227	153,372	38,343 00
Wool, viz.:—						
Leicester,Cotswold,Lincolnshire	United States...	1,506	444	1,506	444	45 18
South Down combing wools,						
or wools known as lustre wools						
and other like combing wools,						
* such as are grown in Canada.						
Zinc, manufactures of, n.o.p......	Unit'd Kingdom	....	2,356	....	1,352	338 00
	Belgium.......	....	3,006	....	1,819	454 75
	France........	....	9	....	9	2 25
	Germany......	....	49	....	49	12 25
	United States..	....	26,153	....	26,153	6,538 25
	Total......	....	31,573	....	29,382	7,345 50
Damaged goods, under sections	Unit'd Kingdom	....	2,815	....	833	280 52
49 to 53 of Rev. Stat., cap. 32.	Holland.......	....	68	....	68	7 61
	Italy.........	....		....	68	6 26
	United States..	....	48,163	....	48,163	11,501 83
	Total......	....	51,046	....	49,132	11,796 22
Prepaid postal parcels from	Unit'd Kingdom	....	74,941	....	74,941	21,262 46
Great Britain.						
Special duty on articles shipped	....				....	68,296 47
to Canada at lower than usual						
home trade price.						
Additional duties, post entries,	....			....	....	410,832 60
over collections, etc.						
War tax......................	....				....	2,236,290 16
Total Dutiable Goods....	....	....	318,951,094	....	198,401,802	60903,163 73

OF IMPORTS—*Continued.*

FOR HOME CONSUMPTION.

	Preferential Tariff.			Treaty Rates.			Total.	
Quantity.	Value.	Duty.	Quantity.	Value.	Duty.	Quantity.	Value.	DutyColl'd.
	$	$ cts.		$	$ cts.		$	$ cts.
....	318,034	79,508 50	....	....	....	....	346,947	89,628 05
....	....	....	....	....	....	....	41	14 35
....	....	....	....	....	....	....	22	7 70
....	....	....	....	....	....	....	387	135 45
....	....	....	....	....	....	....	435	152 25
....	....	....	....	....	....	....	786	275 10
....	....	....	..	....	....	....	1,540	539 00
....	....	....	....	....	....	....	329	115 15
....	....	....	....	....	....	....	4,224	1,478 40
....	....	....	....	....	....	....	12	4 20
....	....	....	....	....	....	....	2	0 70
....	....	....	....	....	....	....	3,143	1,100 05
....	....	....	....	....	....	....	1,463	512 05
....	....	....	....	....	....	....	9,050	3,167 50
....	....	....	....	....	....	....	30,114	10,539 90
....	318,034	79,508 50	....	....	....	....	398,495	107,669 85
Lb. 351,166	143,112	21,466 80	Lb.	....	....	Lb. 360,519	145,904	22,164 80
....	....	....	....	....	....	38 965	9,466	2,366 50
....	....	....	....	....	....	80	42	10 50
....	....	....	....	....	....	50,600	20,429	5,107 25
....	....	....	....	....	....	608,229	120,643	30,160 75
351,166	143,112	21,466 80	....			1,058,393	296,484	59,809 80
....	....	....	....	....	....	....	1,506	444	45 18
....	1,004	150 60	....:.	.	....	....	2,356	488 60
....	....	....	....	....	....	....	1,819	454 75
....	....	....	....	....	....	....	9	2 25
....	....	....	....	....	....	....	49	12 25
....	....	....	....	....	....	....	26,153	6,538 25
....	1,004	150 60	....	....	....	.:..........	30,386	7,496 10
....	2,480	80 72	....	....	....	....	3,313	361 24
....	....	....	....	....	....	....	68	7 61
....	....	....	....	....	....	....	68	6 26
....	....	....	....	....	....	....	48,163	11,501 83
....	2,480	80 72	....	....	....	....	51,612	11,876 94
....	....	....	....	....	....	....	74,941	21,262 46
....	....	....	....	....	....	....	....	68,296 47
....	....	....	....	....	....	....	....	410,832 60
....	....	402,182 87	....	....	....	....	....	2,638,473 03
....	69,441,881	15,587,565 52	....	11,948,512	2,715,181 02	....	279,792,195	79,205,910 27

6-GEORGE V, A. 1916

No. 1.—General Statement of Imports—*Continued.*

Articles Imported.	Countries.	Imported.		Entered for Home Consumption.	
		Quantity.	Value.	Quantity.	Value.
Free Goods.		No.	$	No.	$
PRODUCE OF THE MINE.					
Burrstones in blocks, rough or unmanu-factured, not bound up or prepared for binding into mill stones.	Japan...............	2	14	2	14
	United States.....	2	16	2	16
	Total........	4	30	4	30
Chalk, China or Cornwall stone, cliff stone, and felspar, fluorspar, magnesite and mica schist, ground or unground.	United Kingdom.	....	16,324	....-.....	16,324
	Newfoundland...	....	25	....	25
	France............	....	137	....	137
	Germany..........	....	1,187	....	1,187
	Sweden...........	....	2,024	....	2,024
	United States....	....	87,541	....	87,541
	Total........	....	107,238	....	107,238
Clays, viz.:—		Cwt.		Cwt.	
China clay, ground or unground	United Kingdom.	149,944	51,718	149,944	51,718
	United States.....	215,800	79,127	215,800	79,127
	Total........	365,744	130,845	365,744	130,845
Fire clay, ground or unground............	United Kingdom.	....	12,939	....	12,939
	United States....	....	77,784	....	77,784
	Total.:........	....	90,723	....	90,723
Pipe clay, ground or unground..........	United Kingdom..	....	50	....	50
	United States....	....	537	....	537
	Total........	....	587	.	587
Clays, all other, n.o.p................	United Kingdom.	....	1,935	....	1,935
	Germany.........	....	453	....	453
	Japan.............	....	24	....	24
	United States....	....	43,321	....	43,321
	Total........	....	45,733	....	45,733
Coal, anthracite, and anthracite dust......	United Kingdom.	Ton. 27,114	129,712	Ton. 27,114	129,712
	Newfoundland....	25	173	25	173
	United States.....	4,356,268	20,797,654	4,356,268	20,797,654
	Total........	4,383,407	20,927,539	4,383,407	20,927,539
Earths, crude only......................	United Kingdom.	....	79	....	79
	Spain.............	....	68	....	68
	United States....	....	4,159	....	4,159
	Total........	....	4,306	....	4,306
Emery, in bulk, crushed or ground........	United Kingdom.	....	875	....	875
	Germany.........	....	128	....	128
	United States....	....	27,147	....	27,147
	Total........	....	28,150	....	28,150

SESSIONAL PAPER No. 11

No. 1.—General Statement of Imports—*Continued.*

Articles Imported.	Countries.	Imported.		Entered for Home Consumption.	
		Quantity.	Value.	Quantity.	Value.
free goods—the mine—*Con.*		Cwt.	$	Cwt.	$
Flint, and ground flint stones..............	United Kingdom.	22	22	22	22
	Belgium..........	643	904	643	904
	Denmark........	670	479	670	479
	United States.....	88,686	53,299	88,686	53,299
	Total...........	90,021	54,704	90,021	54,704.
Fossils............."	United Kingdom.	....	26	....	26
	Switzerland......	....	75	....	75
	United States....	....	5,165	....	5,165
	Total........	....	5,266	....	5,266
Fuller's earth, in bulk only...............	United Kingdom.	....	5,162	....	5,162
	United States....	....	6,646	....	6,646
	Total........	....	11,808	....	11,808
Gannister................................	United Kingdom.	943	232	943	232
	United States.....	698	209	698	209
	Total........	1,641	441	1,641	441
		Ton.		Ton.	
Gravel and sand...\....................	United Kingdom.	2,949	6,757	2,949	6,757
	Belgium..........	4,000	5,560	4,000	5,560
	Germany........	2,650	4,514	2,650	4,514
	Japan............	22	85	22	85
	United States.....	248,441	199,017	248,441	199,017
	Total........	258,062	215,933	258,062	215,933
Gypsum, crude (sulphate of lime).........	United Kingdom.	9	80	9	80
	United States....	3,308	14,818	3,308	14,818
	Total........	3,317	14,898	3,317	14,898
Pumice and pumice stone, lava and cal-	United Kingdom.	....	47	....	47
careous tufa, not further manufactured	France............	....	26	....	26
than ground.	Italy.............	....	641	....	641
	United States....	....	15,846	....	15,846
	Total........	....	16,560	....	16,560
Minerals, viz:—		Cwt.		Cwt.	
Alumina...........................	United States.'..	250,805	501,807	250,805	501,807
		Lb.		Lb.	
Cinnabar...........................	United Kingdom.	560	341	560	341
	Aust.-Hungary....	200	110	200	110
	Total........	760	451	760	451
		Cwt.		Cwt.	
Cryolite or kryolite..................	Germany........	83	260	83	260
	United States....	10,665	44,423	10,665	44,423
	Total........	10,748	44,683	10,748	44,683

6 GEORGE V, A. 1916

No. 1.—General Statement of Imports—*Continued.*

ARTICLES IMPORTED.	COUNTRIES.	IMPORTED.		ENTERED FOR HOME CONSUMPTION.	
		Quantity.	Value.	Quantity.	Value.
FREE GOODS—THE MINE—*Con.*		Cwt.	$	Cwt.	$
Minerals—*Con.*					
Litharge............................	United Kingdom.	3,855	17,415	3,855	17,415
	Germany.........	1,841	8,640	1,841	8,640
	United States....	4,851	23,865	4,851	23,865
	Total........	10,547	49,920	10,547	49,920
		Gal.		Gal.	
Mineral waters, natural, not in bottles...	France...........	42	10	42	10
	United States....	2,523	541	2,523	541
	Total........	2,565	551	2,565	551
		Lb.		Lb.	
Meerschaum, crude or raw..............	United Kingdom.	45	268	45	268
	Aust.-Hungary....	....	2	....	2
	United States.....	14	85	14	85
	Total........	59	355	59	355
		Cwt.		Cwt.	
Ores of metals, n.o.p..................	United Kingdom.	576	101	576	101
	Spain............	278	266	278	266
	United States.....	765,714	469,578	765,714	469,578
	Total........	766,568	469,945	766,568	469,945
		Ton.		Ton.	
Ore, iron (to Feb. 12th, see dutiable goods)	Newfoundland.,..	374,230	374,230	374,230	374,230
	Norway.........	7,254	24,449	7,254	24,449
	Persia...........	25	509	25	509
	United States.....	669,824	1,727,521	669,824	1,727,521
	Total........	1,051,333	2,126,709	1,051,333	2,126,709
Phosphate rock (fertilizer)........:......	United States....	....	17,122	....	17,122
Diamonds, unset......................	United Kingdom.	....	1,136,174	....	1,136,174
	B. S. Africa.......	....	13,972	....	13,972
	Belgium..........	....	194,242	....	194,242
	France...........	....	48,052	....	48,052
	Germany.........	....	704	....	704
	Holland..........	....	167,699	....	167,699
	Italy.............	....	903	....	903
	United States....	....	31,694	....	31,694
	Total........	....	1,593,440	....	1,593,440
Diamond dust or bort, and black diamonds for borers.	United Kingdom.	....	60,683	....	60,683
	Holland..........	....	558	....	558
	United States....	....	27,942	....	27,942
	Total........	....	89,183	....	89,183
		Cwt.		Cwt.	
Salt, imported from the United Kingdom, or any British Possession; or imported for the use of the sea or gulf fisheries.	United Kingdom.	983,985	237,589	983,985	237,589
	B. W. Indies......	232,107	21,153	232,107	21,153
	Newfoundland....	700	141	700	141
	Italy.............	138,776	10,416	138,776	10,416
	Spain............	379,554	25,646	379,554	25,646
	United States....	245,827	69,905	245,827	69,905
	Total........	1,980,949	364,850	1,980,949	364,850

No. 1.—General Statement of Imports—*Continued.*

ARTICLES IMPORTED.	COUNTRIES.	IMPORTED.		ENTERED FOR HOME CONSUMPTION.	
		Quantity.	Value.	Quantity.	Value.
FREE GOODS—THE MINE—*Con.*		Ton.	$	Ton.	$
Stone, refuse, not sawn, hammered or chiselled, not fit for flagstone, building stone or paving.	Newfoundland....	116,732	75,686	116,732	75,686
	Sweden...........	12	35	12	35
	United States....	272,774	135,955	272,774	135,955
	Total........	389,518	211,676	389,518	211,676
		Cwt.		Cwt.	
Silex or crystallized quartz, ground or unground.	United Kingdom.	403	431	403	431
	Belgium..........	1,501	1,625	1,501	1,625
	United States....	10,920	8,317	10,920	8,317
	Total........	12,824	10,373	12,824	10,373
Talc, ground, bolted or precipitated, not for toilet use.	United Kingdom.	1,612	2,628	1,612	2,628
	Italy.............	100	116	100	116
	United States....	6,563	3,802	6,563	3,802
	Total........	8,275	6,546	8,275	6,546
Whiting, gilders' whiting and Paris white	United Kingdom.	188,815	65,099	188,815	65,099
	Belgium..........	815	376	815	376
	Germany.........	440	139	440	139
	United States....	44,096	21,885	44,096	21,885
	Total........	234,166	87,499	234,166	87,499
The Fisheries.					
Ambergris.............................	United States....	....	222	....	222
Fish offal or refuse.....................	Newfoundland....	....	2,400	....	2,400
	United States....	....	26,436	....	26,436
	Total........	....	28,836	....	28,836
Fur skins, undressed, the produce of marine animals.	Newfoundland....	....	322	....	322
	Argentina........	....	16	....	16
	United States....	....	6,023	....	6,023
	Total........	....	6,361	....	6,361
Pearl, mother of, unmanufactured........	United States....	....	2,804	....	2,804
Squid.................................	Newfoundland....	....	12	....	12
	United States....	....	7,169	....	7,169
	Total........	....	7,181	....	7,181
Tortoise and other shells, unmanufactured.	B. W. Indies......	....	86	....	86
	Germany.........	....	3	....	3
	United States....	....	12,425	....	12,425
	Total........	....	12,514	....	12,514
Turtles...............................	Hong Kong.......	....	3	....	3
	United States....	....	2,647	....	2,647
	Total........	....	2,650	....	2,650

6 GEORGE V, A. 1916

No. 1.—General Statement of Imports—*Continued.*

Articles Imported.	Countries.	Imported.		Entered for Home Consumption.	
		Quantity.	Value.	Quantity.	Value.
FREE GOODS—THE FISHERIES—*Con.*		Lb.	$	Lb.	$
Whale bone, unmanufactured.............	United Kingdom.	152	171	152	171
Seed and breeding oysters, imported for the purpose of being planted in Canadian waters.	Japan............	....	25	....	25
	United States....	....	7,142	....	7,142
	Total........	....	7,167	....	7,167
Live fish and fish eggs for propagating purposes.	United States....	....	665	....	665
Special from Newfoundland.					
Fish—Cod, haddock, ling and pollock, fresh.	Newfoundland....	82,251	2,799	82,251	2,799
		Cwt.		Cwt.	
Fish—Cod, haddock, ling and pollock, dry, salted, or smoked.	Newfoundland....	69,453	345,229	69,453	345,229
Fish—Cod, haddock, ling and pollock, wet, salted.	Newfoundland....	1,037	2,598	1,037	2,598
Fish—Cod, haddock, ling and pollock, pickled.	Newfoundland....	394	1,563	394	1,563
		Lb.		Lb.	
Halibut, fresh.........................	Newfoundland....	147,952	10,405	147,952	10,405
Herring, fresh.........................	Newfoundland....	560,489	13,776	560,489	13,776
Herring, pickled.......................	Newfoundland....	6,701,270	124,656	6,701,270	124,656
Herring, smoked.......................	Newfoundland....	214,080	8,167	214,080	8,167
Sea fish, other, fresh....................	Newfoundland....	18,445	740	18,445	740
Sea fish, other, pickled..................	Newfoundland....	281,910	10,134	281,910	10,134
Lobsters, preserved, in cans.............	Newfoundland....	31,020	8,630	31,020	8,630
		Brl.		Brl.	
Bait—fish, clams or other, fresh or salted.	Newfoundland....	201	1,291	201	1,291
		Lb.		Lb.	
Salmon, fresh.........................	Newfoundland....	174,942	16,101	174,942	16,101
Salmon, smoked.......................	Newfoundland....	1,650	215	1,650	215
Salmon, canned........................	Newfoundland....	16,379	1,753	16,379	1,753
Salmon, pickled........................	Newfoundland....	408,375	20,823	408,375	20,823
Fish oil, viz.:		Gal.		Gal.	
Cod..............................	Newfoundland....	135,244	54,045	135,244	54,045
Seal.............................	Newfoundland....	10,836	4,909	10,836	4,909

SESSIONAL PAPER No. 11

No. 1.—General Statement of Imports—Continued.

ARTICLES IMPORTED.	COUNTRIES.	IMPORTED.		ENTERED FOR HOME CONSUMPTION.	
		Quantity.	Value.	Quantity.	Value.
FREE GOODS—THE FISHERIES—*Con.* Fish oil—*Con.*		Gal.	$	Gal.	$
Other...............................	Newfoundland....	9,382	4,130	9,382	4,130
Other articles, produce of the fisheries, n.o.p.	Newfoundland....	....	577	....	577
THE FOREST.					
Cork-wood, unmanufactured...............	United Kingdom.	....	539	....	539
	France.............	....	1,159	....	1,159
	Portugal...........	....	3,049	....	3,049
	Spain..............	....	4,258	....	4,258
	United States.....	....	12,247	....	12,247
	Total........	....	21,252	....	21,252
		Cords.		Cords.	
Bark, hemlock...........................	United States....	152	968	152	968
Felloes of hickory or oak, not further manufactured than rough sawn or bent to shape.	United States,....	....	41,381	....	41,381
Handle, heading, stave and shingle bolts, n.o.p.	United States....	....	141,006	....	141,006
Hickory billets...........................	United Kingdom.	....	10	....	10
	United States....	....	34,904	....	34,904
	Total........	....	34,914	....	34,914
Hickory and oak spokes, not further manufactured than rough turned and not tenoned, mitred or sized.	United States....	....	185,414	....	185,414
Hub, last, wagon, oar and gun blocks, and all like blocks or sticks, rough hewn or sawn only, and scale board for cheese boxes.	United Kingdom.	....	24	....	24
	United States,...	....	67,868	....	67,868
	Total........	....	67,892	....	67,892
Ivory nuts (vegetable)...................	United States....	....	23,067	....	23,067
Fence posts and railroad ties.............	United Kingdom.	....	10	....	10
	United States....	....	1,255,127	....	1,255,127
	Total........	....	1,255,137	....	1,255,137
Logs, and round unmanufactured timber...	United Kingdom.	....	717	....	717
	Australia.........	....	7,069	....	7,069
	B. Guiana........	....	2,149	....	2,149
	B. W. Indies......	....	957	....	957
	United States....	....	476,211	....	475,061
	Total........	....	487,103	....	485,953
Lumber and timber, planks and boards, when not otherwise manufactured than rough sawn or split or creosoted, vulcanized. or treated by any other preserving process, viz.:—		M.Ft.		M.Ft.	
Cherry, chestnut, gumwood, hickory and whitewood.	Australia.........	37	2,036	37	2,036
	New Zealand.....	1	36	1	36
	Japan.............	6	207	6	207
	United States....	13,619	460,450	13,619	460,450
	Total........	13,663	462,729	13,663	462,729

6 GEORGE V, A. 1916

No. 1.—General Statement of Imports—*Continued.*

Articles Imported.	Countries.	Imported.		Entered for Home Consumption.	
		Quantity.	Value.	Quantity.	Value.
FREE GOODS—THE FOREST—*Con.*		Feet.	$	Feet.	$
Lumber—*Con.*					
Mahogany...........................	United Kingdom.	62,336	8,043	62,336	8,043
	Cuba...............	240	16	240	16
	United States....	1,320,648	144,710	1,320,648	144,710
	Total........	1,383,224	152,769	1,383,224	152,769
		M.Ft.		M.Ft.	
Oak.................................	Japan.............	375	18,101	375	18,101
	United States....	34,079	1,419,823	34,079	1,419,823
	Total........	34,454	1,437,924	34,454	1,437,924
Pitch pine.........................	United States....	95,182	1,608,788	95,182	1,608,788
		Feet.		Feet.	
Red wood...........................	United States....	691,305	20,576	691,305	20,576
Rose wood..........................	Hong Kong.......	1,061	124	1,061	124
	United States....	7,688	2,212	7,688	2,212
	Total........	8,749	2,336	8,749	2,336
Spanish cedar......................	United States....	354,102	38,595	354,102	38,595
Walnut.............................	United States....	384,283	27,561	384,283	27,561
White ash..........................	Japan.............	13,116	656	13,116	656
	United States.....	1,357,144	70,787	1,357,144	70,787
	Total........	1,370,260	71,443	1,370,260	71,443
African teak, amaranth, black heart, ebony, boxwood, cocoboral, dogwood, lignum vitæ, persimmon, red cedar and satin wood.......................	United Kingdom.	....	639	....	639
	Bermuda.........	....	10	....	10
	B. E. Africa......	....	2,092	....	2,092
	B. Guiana........	....	607	....	607
	B. W. Indies.....	....	23	....	23
	Hong Kong.......	....	381	....	381
	Belgium..........	....	16	....	16
	Japan............	....	241	....	241
	Siam.............	....	777	....	777
	United States....	....	16,732	....	16,732
	Total........	....	21,518	....	21,518
Timber, hewn or sawn, squared or sided, or creosoted, etc...................	United Kingdom.	....	435	....	435
	Australia........	....	124	....	124
	United States....	....	543,924	....	543,924
	Total........	....	544,483	....	544,483
		M ft.		M ft.	
Planks, boards and other lumber of wood, sawn, split or cut, and dressed on one side only, but not further manufactured.	Newfoundland....	3	93	3	93
	Alaska...........	3	43	3	43
	United States.....	135,369	2,322,232	135,369	2,322,232
	Total........	135,375	2,322,368	135,375	2,322,368

No. 1.—General Statement of Imports—*Continued.*

Articles Imported.	Countries.	Imported.		Entered for Home Consumption.	
		Quantity.	Value.	Quantity.	Value.
FREE GOODS—THE FOREST—*Con.* Lumber—*Con.*		M.Ft.	$	M.Ft.	$
Pine and spruce clapboards.............	United States.....	49	698	49	698
		M		M	
Laths.................................	United States.....	20,291	46,853	20,291	46,853
Pickets..............................	United States.....	....	8,267	....	8,267
Shingles.............................	Alaska...........	*374	787	374	787
	United States.....	16,232	28,707	16,232	28,707
	Total........	16,606	29,494	16,606	29,494
Staves of oak, sawn, split or cut, not further manufactured, than listed or jointed	United States.....	3,177	122,727	3,177	122,727
Sawdust of wood, of all kinds...........	United Kingdom.	....	25	....	25
	United States.....	....	6,060	....	6,060
	Total........	....	6,085	....	6,085
Treenails.............................	United States.....	2	104	2	104
		Cords		Cords	
Wood for fuel.........................	United States.....	23,145	63,856	23,145	63,856
ANIMALS AND THEIR PRODUCE.		No.		No.	
Animals for improvement of stock, viz.: Horses.............................	United Kingdom.	174	51,884	174	51,884
	Belgium..........	17	12,201	17	12,201
	France...........	26	17,963	26	17,963
	United States.....	227	116,676	241	123,286
	Total........	444	198,724	458	205,334
Cattle...............................	United Kingdom.	47	10,125	47	10,125
	United States.....	284	47,208	284	47,208
	Total........	331	57,333	331	57,333
Sheep................................	United Kingdom.	280	3,924	280	3,924
	United States.....	63	2,184	63	2,184
	Total........	343	6,108	343	6,108
Swine................................	United Kingdom.	3	150	3	150
	United States.....	65	1,814	65	1,814
	Total........	68	1,964	68	1,964
Dogs.................................	United Kingdom.	113	6,911	113	6,911
	Newfoundland....	1	20	1	20
	Belgium..........	4	350	4	350
	Switzerland.......	2	123	2	123
	United States.....	516	20,933	516	20,933
	Total........	636	28,337	636	28,337

6 GEORGE V, A. 1916

No. 1.—General Statement of Imports—*Continued.*

Articles Imported.	Countries.	Imported.		Entered for Home Consumption.	
		Quantity.	Value.	Quantity.	Value.
FREE GOODS— ANIMALS AND THEIR PRODUCE—*Con.*		No.	$	No.	$
Animals for improvement of stock—*Con.* Goats..............................	United States.....	4	110	4	110
Fowls, domestic, pure bred.............	United Kingdom.	492	3,087	492	3,087
	Newfoundland....	3	5	3	5
	France...........	6	42	6	42
	United States.....	75,647	42,236	75,647	42,236
	Total........	76,148	45,370	76,148	45,370
Animals, all other n.o.p.................	Newfoundland....	....	61,803	....	61,803
	Alaska...........	....	4,003	....	4,003
	Argentina........	....	20	....	20
	United States.....	....	87,093	....	87,093
	Total........	....	152,919	....	152,919
Animals brought into Canada temporarily, and for a period not exceeding three months, for the purpose of exhibition or competition for prizes offered by any agricultural or other association, viz.: Horses................................	United States.....	4,639	1,612,375	....	....
Cattle.............................	United States.....	156	86,410	....	....
Swine...............................	United States.....	1	25	....	....
All other, n.o.p.......................	United States....	....	41,013	....	....
Bees...................................	United States....	....	4,775	....	4,775
		Cwt.		Cwt.	
Bones, crude...........................	United Kingdom.	17	303	17	303
	Newfoundland....	4,790	3,878	4,790	3,878
	Aust.-Hungary....	4	131	4	131
	France...........	12	56	12	56
	United States....	8,283	15,419	8,283	15,419
	Total........	13,106	19,787	13,106	19,787
Bone dust, charred bone, and bone ash....	United Kingdom.	40,256	96,901	40,256	96,901
	United States....	56,027	103,762	56,027	103,762
	Total........	96,283	200,663	96,283	200,663
Bone pitch, crude only.................	United States....	....	1,250	....	1,250
		Lb.		Lb.	
Bristles...............................	United Kingdom.	70,790	61,019	70,790	61,019
	France...........	1,134	1,949	1,134	1,949
	Germany.........	5,144	1,515	5,144	1,515
	United States....	61,888	67,557	61,888	67,557
	Total........	138,956	132,040	138,956	132,040
Cat-gut or worm gut unmanufactured, adapted for the manufacture of whip or other cord or of ligatures..	United Kingdom.	....	575	....	575
	Germany.........	....	307	....	307
	Japan............	....	1,042	....	1,042
	United States....	....	2,746	....	2,746
	Total........	....	4,670	....	4,670

SESSIONAL PAPER No. 11

No. 1.—General Statement of Imports—*Continued.*

Articles Imported.	Countries.	Imported.		Entered for Home Consumption.	
		Quantity.	Value.	Quantity.	Value.
FREE GOODS— ANIMALS AND THEIR PRODUCE—*Con.*			**$**		**$**
Fur skins of all kinds, not dressed in any manner, n.o.p.	United Kingdom	....	68,239	....	68,239
	B. W. Indies	....	2,287	....	2,287
	Newfoundland	....	12,536	....	12,536
	Alaksa	....	1,481	....	1,481
	China	....	1,425	....	1,425
	Germany	....	118,601	....	118,601
	Miquelon and St. Pierre	....	99	....	99
	Russia	....	52	....	52
	United States	....	1,124,144	....	1,124,144
	Total	....	1,328,864	....	1,328,864
Fur tails in the raw state	United States	....	615	....	615
		Lb.		Lb.	
Grease and degras for stuffing or dressing leather.	United Kingdom	364,981	10,682	364,981	10,682
	Bermuda	17,280	1,402	17,280	1,402
	Germany	38,775	1,899	38,775	1,899
	United States	1,495,780	80,474	1,495,780	80,474
	Total	1,916,816	94,457	1,916,816	94,457
Grease, rough, the refuse of animal fat, for the manufacture of soap and oils only.	United Kingdom	2,653	198	2,653	198
	Bermuda	25,820	2,095	25,820	2,095
	United States	11,840,628	749,463	11,840,628	749,463
	Total	11,869,101	751,756	11,869,101	751,756
		Cwt.		Cwt.	
Guano and other animal manures	United Kingdom	1	3	1	3
	Newfoundland	7,686	13,452	7,686	13,452
	France	18	24	18	24
	United States	55,877	80,268	55,877	80,268
	Total	63,582	93,747	63,582	93,747
Hair, cleaned or uncleaned, not dyed, curled or otherwise manufactured.	United Kingdom	....	5,746	....	5,746
	Newfoundland	....	2,057	....	2,057
	France	....	2,437	....	2,437
	Germany	....	316	....	316
	United States	....	61,872	....	61,872
	Total	....	72,428	....	72,428
		Lb.		Lb.	
Horse hair, not further manufactured than simply cleaned, and dipped or dyed.	United Kingdom	15,984	17,323	15,984	17,323
	Australia	929	755	929	755
	United States	50,488	41,544	50,488	41,544
	Total	67,401	59,622	67,401	59,622
Hatters' furs, not on the skin	United Kingdom	....	11,616	....	11,616
	Belgium	....	2,891	....	2,891
	Germany	....	184	....	184
	United States	....	91,285	....	91,285
	Total	....	105,976	....	105,976

6 GEORGE V, A. 1916

No. 1.—General Statement of Imports—*Continued.*

ARTICLES IMPORTED.	COUNTRIES.	IMPORTED.		ENTERED FOR HOME CONSUMPTION.	
		Quantity.	Value.	Quantity.	Value.
FREE GOODS— ANIMALS AND THEIR PRODUCE—*Con.*		Lb.	$	Lb.	$
Hides and skins, raw, whether dry salted or pickled.	United Kingdom.	3,636,412	753,856	3,636,412	753,856
	Australia........	853,888	141,935	853,888	141,935
	Bermuda.........	21,198	2,017	21,198	2,017
	B. S. Africa......	980,231	273,753	980,231	273,753
	B. India..........	953,802	221,779	953,802	221,779
	B. W. Indies.....	556,143	76,005	556,143	76,005
	Hong Kong......	16,500	1,440	16,500	1,440
	Newfoundland...	142,996	16,545	142,996	16,545
	New Zealand.....	12,278,142	2,258,875	12,278,142	2,258,875
	Argentina........	9,108,881	2,627,851	9,108,881	2,627,851
	Brazil...........	99,280	30,368	99,280	30,368
	China............	1,616,131	469,299	1,616,131	469,299
	Denmark........	- 54,400	11,036	54,400	11,036
	Egypt and Soudan	65,344	8,604	65,344	8,604
	France...........	2,186,842	508,868	2,186,842	508,868
	French Africa....	26,438	4,811	26,438	4,811
	Germany........	352,068	96,576	352,068	96,576
	Italy............	10,940	2,954	10,940	2,954
	Madagascar......	21,638	4,122	21,638	4,122
	Mexico...........	9,668	2,075	9,668	2,075
	Miquelon and St. Pierre......	5,765	712	5,765	712
	Norway.........	107,352	19,550	107,352	19,550
	Russia...........	76,487	21,203	76,487	21,203
	Sweden..........	226,947	39,453	226,947	39,453
	Switzerland......	8,290	1,400	8,290	1,400
	Turkey..........	49,750	9,629	49,750	9,629
	United States....	25,252,917	5,124,285	25,252,917	5,124,285
	Uruguay.........	26,469	6,023	26,469	6,023
	Venezuela........	365,564	93,191	365,564	93,191
	Total........	59,110,483	12,828,215	59,110,483	12,828,215
Hoofs, horn strips, horn and horn tips, in the rough, not polished or otherwise manufactured than cleaned.	United States....	....	105	....	105
Ivory, unmanufactured...................	United Kingdom.	22	116	22	116
	Germany........	357	1,645	357	1,645
	United States....	187	597	187	597
	Total........	566	2,358	566	2,358
Leeches................................	United Kingdom	....	10	....	10
	United States....	....	347	....	347
	Total........	....	357	....	357
		Oz.		Oz.	
Musk in pods or in grains................	United States....	67	1,006	67	1,006
Pelts, raw..............................	United Kingdom.	....	1,179	....	1,179
	New Zealand....	....	2,843	....	2,843
	United States....	....	10,216	....	10,216
	Total........	....	14,238	....	14,238
Pigeons, homing and messenger, pheasants and quails.	United Kingdom.	....	248	....	248
	Belgium.........	....	11	....	11
	United States....	....	3,420	....	3,420
	Total........	....	3,679	....	3,679

SESSIONAL PAPER No. 11

No. 1.—General Statement of Imports—*Continued.*

ARTICLES IMPORTED.	COUNTRIES.	IMPORTED.		ENTERED FOR HOME CONSUMPTION.	
		Quantity.	Value.	Quantity.	Value.
FREE GOODS— ANIMALS AND THEIR PRODUCE—*Con.*			$		$
Quills in their natural state or unplumed ..	United States....	....	557	....	557
Rennet, raw and prepared................	United Kingdom.	....	5,266	....	5,266
	New Zealand.....	....	5,963	....	5,963
	Aust.-Hungary....	....	348	....	348
	Denmark........	....	5,224	....	5,224
	Germany.........	....	943	....	943
	Holland..........	....	7,538	....	7,538
	Switzerland......	....	457	....	457
	United States....	....	46,825	....	46,825
	Total........	....	72,564	....	72,564
		Lb.		Lb.	
Silk, raw, or as reeled from the cocoon, not being doubled, twisted or advanced in manufacture in any way.	Japan.............	11,604	34,816	11,604	34,816
	Switzerland.......	107	491	107	491
	United States....	82,747	279,173	82,747	279,173
	Total..:.....	94,458	314,480	94,458	314,480
Silk, in the gum, or spun, when imported by manufacturers of silk underwear or of woven labels and spun silk for manufacture of silk thread, for use exclusively for the manufacture of such articles in their own factories.	United Kingdom.	10,833	22,325	10,783	22,192
	Italy.............	441	858	441	858
	Switzerland......	567	1,260	567	1,260
	United States....	25,542	94,926	25,542	94,926
	Total........:	37,383	119,369	37,333	119,236
Silk cocoons and silk waste................	United States....	....	23	....	23
Sausage skins or casings, not cleaned.......	United States....	....	98	....	98
Wool and the hair of the camel, alpaca, goat, and other like animals, not further prepared than washed, n.o.p.	United Kingdom.	3,860,103	1,130,447	3,795,798	1,108,157
	Australia.........	334,820	62,312	215,460	52,284
	B. S. Africa......	93,569	15,100	93,569	15,100
	B. India...:.....	71,266	14,648	71,266	14,648
	Newfoundland....	65	16	65	16
	New Zealand.....	1,186,586	316,340	1,186,586	316,340
	Argentina........	17,670	5,213	17,670	5,213
	France...........	264,582	92,803	264,582	92,803
	Germany.........	21,425	4,556	21,425	4,556
	Italy.............	32,010	4,992	32,010	4,992
	Russia...........	15,200	2,979	15,200	2,979
	United States....	7,503,796	2,106,295	7,460,638	2,094,627
	Uruguay.........	19,717	5,324	19,717	5,324
	Total........	13,420,809	3,761,025	13,193,986	3,717,039
AGRICULTURAL PRODUCTS.					
Bamboo-reed, not further manufactured than cut into suitable lengths for walking sticks or canes, or for sticks for umbrellas, parasols, or sunshades, and bamboos unmanufactured.	Unit'd Kingdom..	....	121	....	121
	Hong Kong......	....	8	....	8
	China............	....	5	....	5
	Japan............	....	1,208	....	1,208
	United States....	....	1,989	....	1,989
	Total........	....	3,331	....	3,331
Bristles, n.o.p............................	United Kingdom.	3,066	1,776	3,066	1,776
	United States....	1,652	102	1,652	102
	Total.......	4,718	1,878	4,718	1,878

6 GEORGE V, A. 1916

No. 1.—General Statement of Imports—*Continued.*

ARTICLES IMPORTED.	COUNTRIES.	IMPORTED.		ENTERED FOR HOME CONSUMPTION.	
		Quantity.	Value.	Quantity.	Value.
FREE GOODS— AGRICULTURAL PRODUCTS—*Con.*			$		$
Broom corn........................	United Kingdom.	....	61	....	61
	United States....	....	285,513	....	285,513
	Total......	....	285,574	....	285,574
Cane and rattans not manufactured and not further manufactured than split, when for use in Canadian manufactures.........	United Kingdom.	....	2,582	....	2,582
	B. Straits Settlements...,	....	421	....	421
	China.............	....	4	....	4
	Holland...........	....	125	....	125
	Japan.............	....	38	....	38
	United States....	....	46,931	....	46,931
	Total......	....	50,101	....	50,101
Cassava root, unground...................	United States....	....	1,312	....	1,312
Citron, lemon and orange rinds, in brine...	United Kingdom.	....	166	....	166
	Hong Kong.......	....	223	....	223
	China.............	....	4	....	4
	Italy.............	....	137	....	137
	United States....	....	83	....	83
	Total......	....	613	....	613
		Lb.		Lb.	
Cocoa beans, not roasted, crushed or ground	United Kingdom.	762,200	102,678	762,200	102,678
	B. Guiana........	15,400	1,649	15,400	1,649
	B. E. Indies, other	115,920	18,742	115,920	18,742
	B. W. Indies......	1,806,853	203,679	1,806,853	203,679
	Total......	2,700,373	326,748	2,700,373	326,748
		No.		No.	
Cocoanuts imported from the place of growth by vessel direct to a Canadian port......	B. Guiana........	453,820	8,913	453,820	8,913
	B. W. Indies......	3,028,219	61,901	3,028,219	61,901
	Total......	3,482,039	70,814	3,482,039	70,814
		Lb.		Lb.	
Cotton wool or raw cotton, not dyed......	United Kingdom.	1,016	183	1,016	183
	United States....	73,031,437	6,533,448	73,031,437	6,533,448
	Total......	73,032,453	6,533,631	73,032,453	6,533,631
Esparto or Spanish grass, and other grasses and pulp of, including fancy grasses dried but not coloured or otherwise manufactured, n.o.p..	United Kingdom.	....	334	....	334
	Hong Kong......	....	4	....	4
	United States....	....	1,192	....	1,192
	Total......	....	1,530	....	1,530
		Cwt.		Cwt.	
Fibre, Mexican, istle, or tampico..........	United Kingdom.	47	588	47	588
	Belgium..........	49	878	49	878
	United States....	864	11,538	864	11,538
	Total......	960	13,004	960	13,004
Fibrilla, flax fibre, and flax tow..........	United Kingdom.	1,418	7,770	1,418	7,770
	Russia............	1,121	6,735	1,121	6,735
	United States....	171	301	171	301
	Total.......	2,710	14,806	2,710	14,806

No. 1.—General Statement of Imports—*Continued*.

Articles Imported.	Countries.	Imported.		Entered for Home Consumption.	
		Quantity.	Value.	Quantity.	Value.
FREE GOODS— AGRICULTURAL PRODCOTS—*Con.*		Cwt.	$	Cwt.	$
Fibre, vegetable, n.o.p..................	United Kingdom.	754	7,691	754	7,691
	Belgium..........	141	1,377	141	1,377
	France...........	9	89	9	89
	Holland.........	114	1,774	114	1,774
	Mexico..........	3	33	3	33
	United States....	7,107	79,418	7,107	79,418
	Total......	8,128	90,382	8,128	90,382
Florist stock, viz.: azaleas, rhododendrons, pot grown lilacs, seedling carnation stock, rose stock, and other stock for grafting, n.o.p.; araucaria, bulbs, corms, tubers, rhizomes, and dormant roots, n.o.p. and rooted carnation cuttings in their first year of introduction....................	United Kingdom.	....	11,369	....	11,369
	Hong Kong......	....	2,741	....	2,741
	Belgium..........	....	16,496	....	16,496
	China...........	....	1,598	....	1,598
	Denmark.........	....	12,408	....	12,408
	France...........	....	17,784	....	17,784
	Germany.........	....	72	....	72
	Guatemala.......	....	46	....	46
	Holland.........	....	165,354	....	165,354
	Italy............	....	10	....	10
	Japan...........	....	21,339	....	21,339
	Mexico..........	....	90	....	90
	Philippines......	....	38	....	38
	United States....	....	36,194	....	36,194
	Total......	....	285,539	....	285,539
Fruit, green, viz.:		Bunches.		Bunches.	
Bananas.............................	B. W. Indies.....	800	452	800	452
	Cuba............	400	237	400	237
	United States....	2,548,726	2,295,692	2,548,726	2,295,692
	Total......	2,549,926	2,296,381	2,549,926	2,296,381
Berries, viz.: wild blueberries, wild strawberries, wild raspberries, and wild edible berries, n.o.p..................	Newfoundland....	....	27	....	27
	United States....	....	18,185	....	18,185
	Total......	....	18,212	....	18,212
Guavas, mangoes, plantains, pomegranates.	Hong Kong......	....	41	....	41
	Spain...........	....	27	....	27
	United States...	....	1,670	....	1,670
	Total..	....	1,738	....	1,738
Lemons and limes......................	United Kingdom.	....	5,737	....	5,737
	B. W. Indies.....	....	140	....	140
	Hong Kong......	....	7	....	7
	Italy............	....	282,765	....	282,765
	United States....	....	429,658	....	429,658
	Total........	....	718,307	....	718,307
Oranges and shaddocks or grape fruit....	United Kingdom.	....	38,646	....	38,646
	B. W. Indies.....	....	17,384	....	17,384
	Hong Kong......	....	7,018	....	7,018
	China...........	....	35	....	35
	Cuba............	....	13,240	....	13,240
	Italy............	....	11,086	....	11,086
	Japan...........	....	72,113	....	72,113
	Mexico..........	....	31,266	....	31,266
	Spain...........	....	20,390	....	20,390
	United States....	....	3,313,428	....	3,313,376
	Total........	....	3,524,606	....	3,524,554

6 GEORGE V, A. 1916

No. 1.—General Statement of Imports—*Continued.*

Articles Imported.	Countries.	Imported.		Entered for Home Consumption.	
		Quantity.	Value.	Quantity.	Value.
FREE GOODS— AGRICULTURAL PRODUCTS—*Con.*			$		$
Fruits—*Con.* Pineapples........................	B. W. Indies......	....	120	....	120
	Cuba............	....	2,421	....	2,421
	United States....	....	302,831	....	302,831
	Total........	....	305,372	....	305,372
		Cwt.		Cwt.	
Foots, being the refuse of the cotton seed or	Cuba............	389	681	389	681
olives after the oil has been pressed out.	United States....	2,629	13,422	2,629	13,422
	Total........	3,018	14,103	3,018	14,103
Hemp, dressed or undressed..............	United Kingdom.	3,057	24,522	3,057	24,522
	New Zealand.....	3,392	17,643	3,392	17,643
	Germany..........	901	5,288	901	5,288
	Italy..........	256	1,598	256	1,598
	Philippines.......	600	3,878	600	3,878
	Russia...........	704	6,159	704	6,159
	United States....	46,460	259,826	46,460	259,826
	Total........	55,370	318,914	55,370	318,914
		Bush.		Bush.	
Indian corn, not for purposes of distillation.	United Kingdom.	15	66	15	66
	Argentina.........	1,097,942	721,461	1,097,942	721,461
	Japan.............	162,090	105,625	162,090	105,625
	United States....	8,101,779	5,907,047	8,101,779	5,907,047
	Total........	9,361,826	6,734,199	9,361,826	6,734,199
		Cwt.		Cwt.	
Jute butts and jute......................	United Kingdom.	525	4,807	525	4,807
	United States....	314	1,929	314	1,929
	Total........	839	6,736	839	6,736
		Lb.		Lb.	
Locust beans and locust bean meal.........	United States....	1,975	81	1,975	81
		Cwt.		Cwt.	
Manila grass........................	United Kingdom.	4,534	24,947	4,534	24,947
	B. E. Africa......	1,974	13,052	1,974	13,052
	B. S. Africa.......	261	1,580	261	1,580
	Dutch E. Indies..	562	3,317	562	3,317
	Germany.........	654	3,761	654	3,761
	German Africa....	17,436	113,305	17,436	113,305
	Mexico...........	11,400	51,981	11,400	51,981
	United States....	246,839	1,671,608	246,839	1,671,608
	Total........	283,660	1,883,551	283,660	1,883,551
Manures, vegetable......................	United States....	65	101	65	101
Osiers or willows, unmanufactured.........	United Kingdom.	....	6,692	....	6,692
	France...........	....	840	....	840
	Germany.........	....	191	....	191
	Holland..........	....	30	....	30
	Japan............	....	3	....	3
	United States....	....	434	....	434
	Total........	....	8,190	....	8,190

No. 1.—GENERAL STATEMENT OF IMPORTS—*Continued.*

ARTICLES IMPORTED.	COUNTRIES.	IMPORTED.		ENTERED FOR HOME CONSUMPTION.	
		Quantity.	Value.	Quantity.	Value.
FREE GOODS— AGRICULTURAL PRODUCTS—*Con.*			$		$
Palm leaf, unmanufactured................	United States....	....	3,926	....	3,926
		Lb.		Lb.	
Rice, uncleaned, unhulled or paddy........	United Kingdom.	672,000	12,410	672,000	12,410
	B. India..........	19,299,924	323,877	19,299,924	323,877
	Hong Kong......	27,834,870	525,884	27,834,870	525,884
	Japan............	11,400,627	332,251	11,400,627	332,251
	Siam............	600,070	11,401	600,070	11,401
	United States....	500	10	500	10
	Total........	59,807,991	1,205,833	59,807,991	1,205,833
Seedling stock for grafting, viz.:— Plum, pear, peach and other fruit trees..	United Kingdom.	....	222	....	222
	France...........	....	1,414	....	1,414
	Holland..........	....	36	....	36
	United States....	....	1,950	....	1,950
	Total........	....	3,622	....	3,622
Seeds, viz.:— Beet and mangold......................	United Kingdom.	210,843	15,209	210,843	15,209
	Denmark........	5,897	895	5,897	895
	France..........	316,636	22,752	316,636	22,752
	Germany........	852	78	852	78
	Holland.........	101,830	7,332	101,830	7,332
	Japan............	56	15	56	15
	Sweden.........	200	11	200	11
	United States....	419,746	44,121	419,746	44,121
	Total........	1,056,060	90,413	1,056,060	90,413
Carrot................................	United Kingdom.	4,636	1,074	4,636	1,074
	Denmark........	326	187	326	187
	France..........	10,613	2,784	10,613	2,784
	Germany........	213	89	213	89
	Holland.........	156	49	156	49
	United States. ...	19,147	5,398	19,147	5,398
	Total........	35,091	9,581	35,091	9,581
Turnip................................	United Kingdom.	1,393,260	107,831	1,393,260	107,831
	Hong Kong......	50	9	50	9
	Denmark........	1,880	213	1,880	213
	France..........	9,468	722	9,468	722
	Germany........	61	9	61	9
	Holland.........	449,598	31,434	449,598	31,434
	Japan............	49	32	49	31
	Sweden.........	600	77	600	77
	United States....	72,347	6,244	72,347	6,244
	Total........	1,927,313	146,571	1,927,313	146,571
Mustard..............................	United Kingdom.	40,248	2,209	40,248	2,209
	France...........	1,190	74	1,190	74
	Holland.........	12,100	766	12,100	766
	Japan............	7	1	7	1
	United States.....	153,536	7,095	153,536	7,095
	Total........	207,081	10,145	207,081	10,145
Beans (seed) from the United Kingdom.	United Kingdom.	17,993	1,513	17,993	1,513

6 GEORGE V, A. 1916

No. 1.—General Statement of Imports—*Continued.*

Articles Imported.	Countries.	Imported.		Entered for Home Consumption.	
		Quantity.	Value.	Quantity.	Value.
FREE GOODS— AGRICULTURAL PRODUCTS—*Con.*		Lb.	$	Lb.	$
Seeds—*Con.* Pease (seed) from the United Kingdom.	United Kingdom.	53,714	4,707	53,714	4,707
Rape, sowing.........................	United Kingdom.	96,443	5,825	96,443	5,825
	Australia.........	3	3	3	3
	Holland.........	114,636	5,686	114,636	5,686
	Japan............	3,937	106	3,937	106
	United States....	235,010	15,181	171,813	11,374
	Total........	450,029	26,801	386,832	22,994
Mushroom spawn...................	United Kingdom.	....	1,214	....	1,214
	France............	....	14	....	14
	United States....	....	2,547	....	2,547
	Total........	....	3,775	....	3,775
Teasels...........................	United Kingdom.	....	5	....	5
	France............	....	202	....	202
	United States....	....	457	....	457
	Total........	....	664	....	664
Tobacco, unmanufactured, for excise pur- poses, under conditions of Inland Revenue Act.	United Kingdom.	171,816	42,905	124,419	30,226
	Belgium..........	32,113	5,154	31,351	5,097
	Cuba............	400,549	165,340	542,487	214,134
	Germany.........	381,518	94,830	521,878	144,027
	Holland.........	368,667	147,855	220,544	98,411
	United States....	16,207,476	4,128,099	17,155,278	4,226,593
	Total........	17,562,139	4,584,183	18,595,957	4,718,488
Trees, n.o.p..........................	France...........	....	69	....	69
	Germany.........	....	283	....	283
	United States....	....	2,122	....	2,122
	Total........	....	2,474	....	2,474
MANUFACTURED AND PARTIALLY MANU- FACTURED ARTICLES.					
Admiralty charts........................	United Kingdom.	....	1,176	....	1,176
	United States....	....	479	....	479
	Total........	....	1,655	....	1,655
Album insides, made of paper............	United States....	....	495	....	495
Artificial abrasives in bulk, crushed or ground, when imported for use in the manufacture of abrasive wheels and polishing composition.	United Kingdom.	....	336	....	336
	Germany.........	....	948	....	948
	United States....	....	10,143	....	10,143
	Total........	....	11,427	....	11,427
Artificial limbs, articles for manufacture of, pressed felt, elastic web and hollow wood blocks.	United Kingdom.	....	4	....	4
	United States....	....	697	....	697
	Total........	....	701	....	701

SESSIONAL PAPER No. 11

No. 1.—General Statement of Imports—*Continued.*

ARTICLES IMPORTED.	COUNTRIES.	IMPORTED.		ENTERED FOR HOME CONSUMPTION.	
		Quantity.	Value.	Quantity.	Value.
FREE GOODS— MANUFACTURED ARTICLES—*Con.*			$		$
Artificial limbs and parts thereof..........	France............	....	329	....	329
	United States....	....	39,093	....	39,093
	Total........	....	39,422	....	39,422
Artificial teeth, not mounted..............	United Kingdom.	....	12,598	....	12,598
	United States....	....	154,488	....	154,488
	Total........	....	167,086	....	167,086
		Cwt.		Cwt.	
Asphaltum or asphalt solid..............	United Kingdom.	3,593	2,154	3,705	2,297
	Belgium..........	17,200	11,468	17,200	11,468
	Germany.........	2,373	1,179	2,373	1,179
	Holland..........	12,120	6,256	12,120	6,256
	Mexico...........	200,786	127,772	200,786	127,772
	United States.....	605,193	486,232	605,193	486,232
	Total........	841,265	635,061	841,377	635,204
Astrachan or Russian hare skins and China	United Kingdom.	....	45,127	....	45,127
goat skins, plates or rugs, wholly or par-	Aust.-Hungary....	....	9,787	....	9,787
tially dressed but not dyed.	China............	....	5,485	....	5,485
	Germany.........	....	1,074	....	1,074
	Turkey...........	....	1,448	....	1,448
	United States ...	....	63,124	....	63,124
	Total........	....	126,045	....	126,045
Bells when imported for use of churches	United Kingdom.	....	13,279	....	13,279
only.	France...........	....	29,456	....	29,456
	Germany.........	....	452	....	452
	United States....	....	16,876	....	16,876
	Total........	....	60,063	....	60,063
		Lb.		Lb.	
Binder twine.............................	United Kingdom.	1,009,890	86,823	1,009,890	86,823
	United States...	27,567,140	2,651,451	27,567,140	2,651,451
	Total........	28,577,030	2,738,274	28,577,030	2,738,274
Binder twine, articles which enter into the	United States....	....	9,947	....	9,947
cost of the manufacture of binder twine or					
twine for harvest binders, when import-					
ed for such use exclusively by manufac-					
turers who manufacture such twine only.					
Blanc fixe and satin white................	United Kingdom.	600,070	6,735	600,070	6,735
	Germany.........	11,936	215	11,936	215
	United States....	3,582,981	37,873	3,582,981	37,873
	Total........	4,194,987	44,823	4,194,987	44,823
Blanketing and lapping and discs or mills	United Kingdom.	....	6,536	....	6,536
for engraving copper rollers, imported by	United States....	....	2,426	....	2,426
cotton manufacturers, calico printers, and					
wall paper manufacturers for use in their	Total........	....	8,962	....	8,962
own factories only.					
Blast furnace slag........................	United Kingdom.	....	9,540	....	9,540
	United States.....	....	2,248	....	2,248
	Total........	....	11,788	....	11,788

6 GEORGE V, A. 1916

No. 1.—GENERAL STATEMENT OF IMPORTS—*Continued.*

ARTICLES IMPORTED.	COUNTRIES.	IMPORTED.		ENTERED FOR HOME CONSUMPTION.	
		Quantity.	Value.	Quantity.	Value.
FREE GOODS— MANUFACTURED ARTICLES—*Con.*			$		$.
Bolting cloth, not made up.............	Italy.................	....	458	....	458
	Switzerland........	....	418	....	418
	United States....	....	20,564	....	20,564
	Total........	....	21,440	....	21,440
Books, viz.: Bibles, prayer books, psalm and hymn books, religious tracts, and Sunday school lesson pictures.	United Kingdom.	....	120,287	....	120,287
	Aust.-Hungary....	....	305	....	305
	Belgium...........	....	17,699	....	17,699
	China.............	....	56	....	56
	France............	....	17,913	....	17,913
	Germany..........	....	2,282	....	2,282
	Italy..............	....	2,819	....	2,819
	Japan.............	....	373	....	373
	Switzerland......	....	2,076	....	2,076
	United States....	....	101,220	....	101,220
	Total........	....	265,030	....	265,030
Books, printed by any government or by any association for the promotion of science or letters and official annual reports of religious or benevolent associations and issued in the proceedings of said associations, to their members and not for the purpose of sale or trade.	United Kingdom.	....	4,708	....	4,708
	Australia.........	....	15	....	15
	New Zealand.....	....	16	....	16
	U. S. of Colombia	....	18	....	18
	United States....	....	6,567	....	6,567
	Total........	....	11,324	....	11,324
Books, embossed and grooved cards for the blind and books for the instruction of the deaf and dumb and blind.	United Kingdom.	....	60	....	60
	France...........	....	6	....	6
	United States....	....	654	....	654
	Total........	....	720	....	720
Maps and charts for the use of schools for the blind.	United States....	....	23	....	23
Books, not printed or reprinted in Canada, which are included and used as text books in the curriculum of any university, college or school in Canada; books especially imported for the bona fide use of incorporated mechanics' institutes, public libraries, libraries of universities, colleges, and schools, or for the library of any incorporated medical, law, literary, scientific or art association or society, and being the property of the organized authorities of such library, and not in any case the property of individuals.	United Kingdom.	....	258,220	....	258,220
	Australia.........	....	604	....	604
	Aust.-Hungary....	....	883	....	883
	Belgium...........	....	2,347	....	2,347
	China.............	....	42	....	42
	France............	....	36,955	....	36,955
	Germany..........	....	2,000	....	2,000
	Holland...........	....	50	....	50
	Switzerland......	....	16	....	16
	United States....	....	333,984	....	333,984
	Total........	....	635,101	....	635,101
Books, bound or unbound, which have been printed and manufactured more than twelve years.	United Kingdom.	....	6,221	....	6,221
	Newfoundland....	....	100	....	100
	Belgium...........	....	40	....	40
	France...........	....	2,202	....	2,202
	French Africa.....	....	4	....	4
	Italy..............	....	185	....	185
	United States.....	....	6,393	....	6,393
	Total........	....	15,145	....	15,145

No. 1.—General Statement of Imports—*Continued.*

Articles Imported.	Countries.	Imported.		Entered for Home Consumption.	
		Quantity.	Value.	Quantity.	Value.
FREE GOODS— MANUFACTURED ARTICLES—*Con.*			$		$
Books on the application of science to in- dustries of all kinds, also books printed in any language other. than the English and French languages, or in any two lan- guages not being English or French, or any three or more languages.	United Kingdom.	....	15,438	....	15,438
	Hong Kong......	....	811	....	811
	Aust.-Hungary....	....	1,735	....	1,735
	Belgium..........	....	153	....	153
	China..............	....	3,014	....	3,014
	Denmark...........	....	20	....	20
	France.............	....	4,151	....	4,151
	Germany..........	....	3,172	....	3,172
	Greece.............	....	120	....	120
	Greenland and Iceland.......	....	8	....	8
	Holland...........	....	50	....	50
	Italy..............	....	1,556	....	1,556
	Japan.............	....	3,011	....	3,011
	Russia............	....	681	....	681
	Sweden............	....	221	....	221
	Switzerland......	....	34	....	34
	United States....	....	137,739	....	137,739
	Total........	....	171,914	....	171,914
Book manuscript and insurance maps......	United Kingdom.	....	136	....	136
	China....:........	....	20	....	20
	France............	....	50	....	50
	Germany..........	....	71	....	71
	United States....	....	80,475	....	80,475
	Total........	....	80,752	....	80,752
Bookbinders' cloth........................	United Kingdom.	....	71,031	....	71,031
	Aust.-Hungary....	....	321	....	321
	Germany..........	....	1,443	....	1,443
	United States:....	....	29,540	....	29,540
	Total........	....	102,335	....	102,335
Brick, fire, of a class or kind not made in Canada.	United Kingdom.	....	48,375	....	48,375
	Belgium..........	....	218	....	218
	Germany..........	....	19	....	19
	Sweden...........	....	2,161	....	2,161
	United States....	....	431,990	....	431,990
	Total........	....	482,763	....	482,763
Buckram, adapted for the manufacture of hat and bonnet shapes,	United Kingdom.	....	12,492	....	12,492
	France............	....	10	....	10
	Germany..........	....	3,994	....	3,994
	United States....	....	44,349	....	44,349
	Total........	....	60,845	....	60,845
Braids or plaits of chip, palm leaf, manila, willow, osier, rattan, straw, Tuscan or grass, suitable for making or ornamenting hats, and plait braids or plaits of glazed cotton thread not over ¼ in. wide, when imported by manufacturers of hats for use only in the manufacture of hat bodies....	United Kingdom.	....	88,824	....	88,824
	Aust.-Hungary....	....	29	....	29
	China.............	....	6,766	....	6,766
	France............	....	1,465	....	1,465
	Germany..........	....	886	....	886
	Italy.............	....	6,822	....	6,822
	Japan.............	....	44,554	....	44,554
	Switzerland......	....	6,825	....	6,825
	United States....	....	136,514	....	136,514
	Total........	....	292,685	....	292,685

6 GEORGE V, A. 1916

No. 1.—General Statement of Imports—*Continued.*

Articles Imported.	Countries.	Imported.		Entered for Home Consumption.	
		Quantity.	Value.	Quantity.	Value.
FREE GOODS— MANUFACTURED ARTICLES—*Con.*			$		$
Bullion or gold fringe.................	United Kingdom.	....	16	....	16
	France............	....	5,828	....	5,828
	United States....	....	1,243	.⁊........	1,243
	Total........	....	7,087	....	7,087
Buttons, shoe, papier mache............	United Kingdom.	....	106	....	106
	Aust. Hungary....	....	49	....	49
	Germany.........	....	571	....	571
	United States....	....	15,295	....	15,295
	Total........	....	16,021	....	16,021
Carbons over three inches in circumference and not exceeding 35 inches.	United Kingdom.	....	307	....	307
	United States....	....	222,987	....	222,987
	Total........	....	223,294	....	223,294
Celluloid, xylonite, or xyolite, in sheets, lumps, blocks, rods, or bars not further manufactured than moulded or pressed.	United Kingdom.	....	34,223	....	34,223
	France...........	....	- 76	....	76
	Germany.........	....	8,271	....	8,271
	United States....	....	72,418	....	72,418
	Total........	....	114,988	....	114,988.
Chronometers and compasses for ships.....	United Kingdom.	....	4,368	....	4,368
	United States....	....	4,317	....	4,317
	Total........	....	8,685	....	8,685
		Gal.		Gal.	
Coal and pine pitch.................	United Kingdom.	93,398	5,267	93,398	5,267
	United States.....	970,871	53,107	970,871	53,107
	Total........	1,064,269	58,374	1,064,269	58,374
Coal and pine tar, crude, in packages of not less than 15 gallons.	United Kingdom.	14,264	1,041	14,264	1,041
	Germany.........	2,236	391	2,236	391
	United States....	2,920,562	122,633	2,920,562	122,633
	Total........	2,937,062	124,065	2,937,062	124,065
		Lb.		Lb.	
Coal tar base or salt (paranitraniline).....	United Kingdom.	2,350	587	2,350	587
	Germany.........	2,800	502	2,800	502
	United States....	15,114	2,905	15,114	2,905
	Total........	20,264	3,994	20,264	3,994
		Ton.		Ton.	
Coke.................................	United Kingdom.	161	844	161	844
	United States.....	506,638	1,444,992	506,638	1,444,992
	Total........	506,799	1,445,836	506,799	1,445,836

SESSIONAL PAPER No. 11

No. 1.—General Statement of Imports—*Continued.*

Articles Imported.	Countries.	Imported.		Entered for Home Consumption.	
		Quantity.	Value.	Quantity.	Value.
FREE GOODS— MANUFACTURED ARTICLES—*Con.*		Cwt.	$	Cwt.	$
Coke, ground, when imported by manufacturers of electric batteries, for use in their own factories in the manufacture of such batteries.	United States.....	11,280	14,420	11,280	14,420
		Lb.		Lb.	
Colours, metallic, viz.: oxide of cobalt, tin and copper, n.o.p.	United Kingdom.	24,691	7,646	24,691	7,646
	Germany.........	10,319	3,450	10,319	3,450
	United States.....	249,022	54,069	249,022	54,069
	Total........	284,032	65,165	284,032	65,165
Colours, dry red lead and orange mineral..	United Kingdom.	416,272	18,883	416,272	18,883
Colours, zinc white.......................	United Kingdom.	861,500	27,293	861,500	27,293
Communion sets of metal, glass or wood...	United Kingdom.	....	751	....	751
	France...........	....	13,239	....	13,239
	Germany.........	....	42	....	42
	Italy.............	....	240	....	240
	United States....	....	8,483	....	8,483
	Total........	....	22,755	....	22,755
Coir and coir yarn.......................	United Kingdom.	56,452	3,626	56,452	3,626
	B. India.........	125,600	5,903	125,600	5,903
	United States....	101,920	3,704	101,920	3,704
	Total........	283,972	13,233	283,972	13,233
Cotton or linen duck, seamless, in circular form, of a class or kind not made in Canada, for use in the manufacture of hose pipe.	United Kingdom.	....	2,790	....	2,790
	United States....	....	71,635	....	71,635
	Total........	....	74,425	....	74,425
Cotton thread, nitrate of thorium and nitrate of cerium, for use in the manufacture of incandescent gas mantles, when imported by manufacturers of such mantles or of stockings for such mantles.	United Kingdom.	....	809	....	809
	Germany.........	....	2,442	....	2,442
	United States....	....	2,276	....	2,276
	Total........	....	5,527	....	5,527
Crucibles, clay, sand or plumbago.........	United Kingdom.	....	13,097	....	13,097
	United States....	....	37,749	....	37,749
	Total........	....	50,846	....	50,846
Crucibles, platinum......................	United Kingdom.	....	3	....	3
	United States....	....	9,493	....	9,493
	Total........	....	9,496	....	9,496
		No.		No.	
Curling stones and handles therefor........	United Kingdom.	1,599	8,928	1,599	8,928

6 GEORGE. V, A. 1916

No. 1.—General Statement of Imports—*Continued.*

Articles Imported.	Countries.	Imported.		Entered for Home Consumption.	
		Quantity.	Value.	Quantity.	Value.
FREE GOODS— MANUFACTURED ARTICLES—*Con.*		Lb.	$	Lb.	$
Drugs, dyes, chemicals and medicines:— Acid, boracic, in packages of not less than 25 pounds.	United Kingdom. Germany......... United States....	107,663 6,720 289,155	7,653 459 19,210	107,663 6,720 272,355	7,653 459 17,866
	Total........	403,538	27,322	386,738	25,978
Acid, hydro-fluo-silicic.................	United States....	1,110,079	32,980	1,110,079	32,980
Acid, oxalic....·....................	United Kingdom. Belgium.......... Germany..·....... Switzerland...... United States....	64,018 34,353 41,904 2,250 131,777	5,644 1,917 2,335 119 13,109	64,018 34,353 41,904 2,250 131,777	5,644 1,917 2,335 119 13,109
	Total........	274,302	23,124	274,302	23,124
Acid, tannic..........................	United Kingdom. Germany......... United States....	632 330 18,551	376 142 6,347	632 330 18,551	376 142 6,347
	Total........	19,513	6,865	19,513	6,865
Alum, in bulk, ground or unground but not calcined.	United Kingdom.	1,947,938	20,196	1,947,938	20,196
Alumina, sulphate of, or alum cake......	United Kingdom.	1,611,863	9,629	1,611,863	9,629
Ammonia, nitrate of....................	United Kingdom. Belgium.......... Germany......... Norway.......... United States....	489,417 1,044,689 49,402 343,800 71,542	27,317 55,267 2,824 19,647 4,443	489,417 1,044,689 49,402 343,800 71,542	27,317 55,267 2,824 19,647 4,443
	Total........	1,998,850	109,498	1,998,850	109,498
Ammonia, sulphate of..................	United Kingdom. Germany......... United States....	533,026 221 419,617	13,540 24 12,415	533,026 221 419,617	13,540 24 12,415
	Total........	952,864	25,979	952,864	25,979
Aniline and coal tar dyes, soluble in water, in bulk or packages of not less than one pound weight including alizarine and artificial alizarine.	United Kingdom. Belgium.......... France.·.......... Germany......... Switzerland....... United States....	256,071 1,750 18,163 487,824 162,068 842,912	48,766 268 1,660 84,789 39,065 339,700	256,071 1,750 18,163 487,824 162,068 842,912	48,766 268 1,660 84,789 39,065 339,700
	Total........	1,768,788	514,248	1,768,788	514,248
Aniline oil, crude......................	United States....	340	103	340	103
Aniline salts..........................	United Kingdom. United States....	58,573 566	10,328 82	58,573 566	10,328 82
	Total........	59,139	10,410	59,139	10,410

SESSIONAL PAPER No. 11

No. 1.—General Statement of Imports—*Continued.*

Articles Imported.	Countries.	Imported.		Entered for Home Consumption.	
		Quantity.	Value.	Quantity.	Value.
FREE GOODS— **MANUFACTURED ARTICLES—***Con.*		Lb.	$	Lb.	$
Drugs, &c.—*Con.*					
Annatto, liquid or solid...............	United Kingdom.	1,589	240	1,589	240
	Denmark........	470	75	470	75
	United States....	64,407	8,145	64,407	8,145
	Total........	66,466	8,460	66,466	8,460
Antimony, or regulus of, not ground, pulverized or otherwise manufactured....	United Kingdom.	1,254,808	133,978	1,254,808	133,978
	Belgium..........	55,940	2,797	55,940	2,797
	United States....	232,270	27,696	232,270	27,696
	Total........	1,543,018	164,471	1,543,018	164,471
Antimony salts, viz.: tartar emetic, chlorine and lactate (antimonine)......	United Kingdom.	22,612	3,374	22,612	3,374
	Germany.........	9,720	2,396	9,720	2,396
	United States....	40,619	8,409	40,619	8,409
	Total........	72,951	14,179	72,951	14,179
Antimony salts for dyeing..............	United Kingdom.	28	2	28	2
Arsenious oxide.......................	United Kingdom.	1,289	47	1,289	47
	United States....	3,944	219	3,944	·219
	Total........	5,233	266	5,233	266
Arsenic, sulphide of...\..................	Germany.........	5,500	293	5,500	293
	United States....	6,381	575	6,381	575
	Total........	11,881	868	11,881	868
Barium, peroxide of, non-alcoholic for use in the manufacture of peroxide of hydrogen when imported by manufacturers of peroxide of hydrogen................	United Kingdom.	50,250	3,199	50,250	3,199
	Belgium..........	8,930	480	8,930	480
	Germany.........	2,380	123	2,380	123
	United States....	16,518	1,771	16,518	1,771
	Total........	78,078	5,573	78,078	5,573
Beans, viz.: Tonquin, crude only.....................	United States....	1,262	1,776	1,262	1,776
Vanilla, crude only.....................	United Kingdom.	765	2,394	765	2,394
	France..........	496	1,118	496	1,118
	United States....	15,866	48,875	15,866	48,875
	Total........	17,127	52,387	17,127	52,387
Binitrotoluol, trinitrotoluol and perchlorate of ammonia, when imported by manufacturers of explosives for use exclusively in the manufacture of such articles in their own factories.	United Kingdom.	111,402	15,911	111,402	15,911
	Belgium..........	6,000	1,013	6,000	1,013
	Germany.........	·120,229	13,257	120,229	13,257
	Sweden..........	25,536	2,886	25,536	2,886
	United States....	173,867	19,345	173,867	19,345
	Total........	437,034	52,412	437,034	52,412
Borax, in bulk of not less than 25 pounds...	United Kingdom.	992,603	38,165	992,603	38,165
	Germany.........	2,240	92	2,240	92
	United States....	1,976,258	84,653	2,041,498	87,811
	Total........	2,971,101	122,910	3,036,341	126,068

6 GEORGE V, A. 1916

No. 1.—General Statement of Imports—*Continued.*

ARTICLES IMPORTED.	COUNTRIES.	IMPORTED.		ENTERED FOR HOME CONSUMPTION.	
		Quantity.	Value.	Quantity.	Value.
FREE GOODS— MANUFACTURED ARTICLES—*Con.*		Lb.	$	Lb.	$
Drugs, etc.—*Con.*					
Brimstone. crude, or in roll or flour, and sulphur in roll or flour.	United Kingdom.	149,711	1,525	149,711	1,525
	New Zealand.....	2,520	34	2,520	34
	Italy............	2,013,370	24,008	2,013,370	24,008
	Japan...........	6,418,463	53,046	6,418,463	53,046
	Spain...........	92,944	1,039	92,944	1,039
	United States....	78,187,401	815,163	78,187,401	815,163
	Total.........	86,864,409	894,815	86,864,409	894,815
Bromides, crude......................	United States....	3,112	890	3,112	890
Bromine	United States....	786	419	786	419
Burgundy pitch........................	Germany.........	18,633	820	18,633	820
	United States.....	117,196	4,652	117,196	4,652
	Total........	135,829	5,472	135,829	5,472
Camwood and sumac and extract thereof	United Kingdom.	50,357	2,057	50,357	2,057
	Aust.-Hungary....	16,550	342	16,550	342
	Italy............	314,705	8,647	314,705	8,647
	United States....	427,085	14,148	427,085	14,148
	Total........	808,697	25,194	808,697	25,194
Carbon bisulphide.................•.....	United States....	10,941	582	10,941	582
Chloride of lime and hypo-chlorite of lime in packages of not less than 25 pounds. (To July 1st, see Dutiable Goods).	United Kingdom.	1,876,044	16,516	1,876,044	16,516
	Belgium.........	55,250	527	55,250	527
	Germany.........	50,433	581	50,433	581
	United States....	3,409,172	28,205	3,409,172	28,205
	Total........	5,390,899	45,829	5,390,899	45,829
Cochineal.............................	United Kingdom.	16	14	16	14
	United States....	1,857	955	1,857	955
	Total........	1,873	969	1,873	969
Cream of tartar in crystals or argols.....	United Kingdom.	59,660	15,387	57,045	14,758
	France..........	879,004	184,432	879,004	184,432
	Germany.........	8,960	1,852	8,960	1,852
	Greece..........	5,000	1,786	5,000	1,786
	United States....	189,206	54,376	189,206	54,376
	Total........	1,141,830	257,833	1,139,215	257,204
Cyanide of potassium, cyanide of sodium, and cyanogen bromide for reducing metals in mining operations.	United Kingdom.	1,038,702	184,009	1,038,702	184,009
	Germany.........	273	124	273	124
	United States....	823,894	147,397	823,894	147,397
	Total........	1,862,869	331,530	1,862,869	331,530
Dragon's blood........................	United States....	546	537	546	537

‾SESSIONAL PAPER No. 11

No. 1.—GENERAL STATEMENT OF IMPORTS—*Continued.*

ARTICLES IMPORTED.	COUNTRIES.	IMPORTED.		ENTERED FOR HOME CONSUMPTION.	
		Quantity.	Value.	Quantity.	Value.
FREE GOODS— **MANUFACTURED ARTICLES—***Con.*		Lb.	$	Lb.	$
Drugs, &c.—*Con.*					
Dyeing or tanning articles in a crude state used in dyeing or tanning, n.o.p.	United Kingdom.	256,479	9,812	256,479	9,812
	B. Guiana........	1,320	8	1,320	8
	France...........	1,390	330	1,390	330
	Germany........	127,190	3,340	127,190	3,340
	United States....	8,957,227	192,756	8,957,227	192,756
	Total........	9,343,606	206,246	9,343,606	206,246
Extract of logwood, fustic, oak, and oak bark and quebracho.	United Kingdom,	991,968	ⵏ 27,126	991,968	27,126
	B. India..........	4,360	255	4,360	255
	France..........	31,684	2,234	31,684	2,234
	United States....	37,191,130	1,036,416	37,191,130	1,036,416
	Total........	38,219,142	1,066,031	38,219,142	1,066,031
Ferment cultures to be used in butter-making.	United States....	....	164	....	164
Glycerine, crude, when imported by manufacturers for use only in their own factories in the manufacture of refined glycerine.	Germany........	161,033	22,459	161,033	22,459
	United States....	161,000	22,820	161,000	22,820
	Total........	322,033	45,279	322,033	45,279
Glycerine, when imported by manufacturers of explosives, for use exclusively for the manufacture of such articles in their own factories.	United Kingdom.	1,602,046	269,721	1,602,046	269,721
	United States....	563,981	123,647	563,981	123,647
	Total........	2,166,027	393,368	2,166,027	393,368
Roots, medicinal, viz.: Alkanet, crude, crushed or ground, aconite, calumba, foliae digitalis, gentian, ginseng, jalap, ipecacuanha, iris, orris root, liquorice, sarsaparilla, squills, taraxacum, rhubarb and valerian, unground.	United Kingdom.	.:......	994	....	994
	Hong Kong......	....	317	....	317
	Alaska..........	....	3	....	3
	France..........	....	2,009	....	2,009
	Italy...........	....	365	....	365
	United States....	....	15,256	....	15,256
	Total........	....	18,944	....	18,944
Gums, viz.:— Amber, arabic, australian, copal, damar, elemy, kaurie, mastic, sandarac, senegal, tragacanth, gedda, barberry, pontianac and lac, crude, seed, button, stick, and shell.	United Kingdom.	....	21,948	....	21,948
	Hong Kong......	....	677	....	677
	New Zealand....	....	2,136	....	2,136
	Aust.-Hungary...	....	603	....	603
	Egypt and Soudan	....	216	....	216
	France..........	....	1	....	1
	Germany........	....	824	....	824
	Switzerland......	....	11	....	11
	Turkey..........	....	6	....	6
	United States....	....	334,045	....	334,045
	Total........	....	360,467	....	360,467
Balata, crude unmanufactured..........	United Kingdom.	10	16	10	16
	United States....	374	288	374	288
	Total........	384	304	384	304
Chicle or Sappato gum, crude..........	B. Honduras......	1,631,440	552,450	1,492,447	497,786
	France..........	32,620	11,744	32,620	11,744
	Mexico..........	2,923,493	989,958	2,665,483	900,144
	Venezuela........	54,818	18,637	54,818	18,637
	United States....	1,261,540	418,128	1,148,024	381,483
	Total........	5,903,911	1,990,917	5,393,392	1,809,794

6 GEORGE V, A. 1916

No. 1.—General Statement of Imports—*Continued.*

Articles Imported.	Countries.	Imported.		Entered for Home Consumption.	
		Quantity.	Value.	Quantity.	Value.
FREE GOODS— MANUFACTURED ARTICLES—*Con.*		Lb.	$	Lb.	$
Drugs, &c.—*Con.* Indigo..............................	Germany.........	1	1	1	·1
	United States....	14,484	2,680	14,484	·2,680
	Total........	·14,485	2,681	14,485	.2,681
Indigo, paste and extract of..............	United Kingdom.	501	578	501	578
	Germany.........	66,060	10,901	66,060	10,901
	United States....	44,844	6,875	44,844	6,875
	Total........	111,405	18,354	111,405	18,354
Iodine, crude..........................	United Kingdom.	2,629	6,593	2,629	6,593
	United States....	5,103	14,807	5,103	14,807
	Total........	7,732	21,400	7,732	21,400
Iron liquor, being solution of acetate or nitrate of iron adapted for dyeing and calico printing......................	United Kingdom.	....	258	....	258
	United States....	....	2,667	....	2,667
	Total........	....	2,925	....	2,925
Kainite, and other crude German potash salts for fertilizers.	United Kingdom.	13,440	88	13,440	88
	Belgium.........	126,112	7,069	126,112	7,069
	United States.....	621,350	6,213	621,350	6,213
	Total........	760,902	13,370	760,902	13,370
Lead, nitrate and acetate of, not ground.	United Kingdom.	153,930	9,189	153,930	9,189
	Belgium	12,241	716	12,241	716
	Germany.........	35,819	2,079	35,819	2,079
	United States....	38,772	3,147	38,772	3,147·
	Total........	240,762	15,131	240,762	15,131
Litmus and all lichens, prepared or not..	United Kingdom.	25	7	25	7
	United States....	124	47	124	47
	Total........	149	54	149	54
Logwood and fustic, ground, and ground oak bark.	United States.·...	28,269	476	28,269	476
Madder and munjeet, or Indian madder, ground or prepared and all extracts of.	United States.·...	....	122	:..........	122
Manganese, oxide of....................	United Kingdom.	523,681	7,196	523,681	,196
	Germany.........	23,232	266	23,232	266
	Holland.........	1,408	36	1,408	36
	Russia...........	88,480	1,508	88,480	1,508
	United States....	2,890,515	39,424	2,890,515	39,424
	Total........	3,527,316	48,430	3,527,316	48,430
Moss, Iceland, and other mosses........	United Kingdom.	366,656	1,300	366,656	1,300
	France...........	16,072	344	16,072	344
	Germany.........	1,624	110	1,624	110
	United States....	962,739	30,648	962,739	30,648
	Total........	1,347,091	32,402	1,347,091	32,402

SESSIONAL PAPER No. 11

No. 1.—General Statement of Imports—*Continued.*

Articles Imported.	Countries.	Imported.		Entered for Home Consumption.	
		Quantity.	Value.	Quantity.	Value.
FREE GOODS— MANUFACTURED ARTICLES—*Con.*		Lb.	$	Lb.	$
Drugs, &c.—*Con.*					
Nitrate compounds adapted for use in the manufacture of explosives..............	United Kingdom. United States....	2,349 60,377	238 6,836	2,349 60,377	238 6,836
	Total........	62,726	7,074	62,726	7,074
Nut galls and extracts thereof..........	United Kingdom. United States....	1,142 19,986	163 2,553	1,142 19,986	163 2,553
	Total........	21,128	2,716	21,128	2,716
Nicotine sulphate......................	United States....	1,596	1,431	1,596	1,431
Persis, or extract of archill and cudbear.	United States....	2,174	325	2,174	325
Phosphorus...........................	United Kingdom. Germany........ United States....	36,302 66 8,025	12,984 31 2,438	36,302 66 8,025	12,984 31 2,438
	Total........	44,393	15,453	44,393	15,453
Potash, caustic, in packages of not less than 25 pounds each..................	Germany........ United States....	11,954 489,440	468 35,983	11,954 489,440	468 35,983
	Total........	501,394	36,451	501,394	36,451
Potash, chlorate of, not further prepared than ground.........................	United Kingdom. United States....	125,130 683,555	7,528 62,667	125,130 683,555	7,528 62,667
	Total........	808,685	70,195	808,685	70,195
Potash, bichromate....................	United Kingdom. United States....	71,823 30,927	5,128 3,480	71,823 30,927	5,128 3,480
	Total........	102,750	8,608	102,750	8,608
Potash, muriate, and sulphate of, crude..	United Kingdom. Germany........ United States....	1,111,187 199,276 6,175,252	23,222 4,123 118,716	1,111,187 199,276 6,175,252	23,222 4,123 118,716
	Total........	7,485,715	146,061	7,485,715	146,061
Potash, red and yellow prussiate of......	United Kingdom, France........... Germany........ United States....	59,712 4,080 2,648 68,320	9,543 411 302 12,095	59,712 4,080 2,648 68,320	9,543 411 302 12,095
	Total........	134,760	22,351	134,760	22,351
Potash and pearl ash in packages of not less than 25 pounds each.	United Kingdom. Germany........ United States....	4,904 50 57,564	471 5 5,750	4,904 50 57,564	471 5 5,750
	Total........	62,518	6,226	62,518	6,226

6 GEORGE V, A. 1916

No. 1.—General Statement of Imports—*Continued.*

Articles Imported.	Countries.	Imported.		Entered for Home Consumption.	
		Quantity.	Value.	Quantity.	Value.
FREE GOODS— MANUFACTURED ARTICLES—*Con.*		Lb.	$	Lb.	$
Drugs, &c.—*Con.* Quicksilver......................	United Kingdom.	42,192	19,335	42,192	19,335
	Hong Kong......	2	1	2	1
	Aust.-Hungary....	15,000	6,500	15,000	6,500
	Italy.............	19,000	8,060	19,000	8,060
	Spain.............	23,180	10,044	23,180	10,044
	United States....	48,163	27,898	48,163	27,898
	Total........	147,537	71,838	147,537	71,838
		Oz.		Oz.	
Quinine, salts of.......................	United Kingdom.	14,390	4,507	14,390	4,507
	Germany........	1,484	443	1,484	443
	United States....	63,627	17,829	63,627	17,829
	Total........	79,501	22,779	79,501	22,779
Radium.............................	United States....	....	1,553	....	1,553
Red liquor, being a crude acetate of aluminum prepared from pyroligneous acid and adapted for dyeing and calico printing.	United States....	....	81	....	81
		Lb.		Lb.	
Saffron, saffron cake, safflower and extracts of.	United Kingdom.	20	180	20	180
	Spain.............	10	97	10	97
	United States....	241	785	241	785
	Total........	271	1,062	271	1,062
Sal ammoniac.........................	United Kingdom.	525,337	25,755	525,337	25,755
	Belgium..........	1,484	51	1,484	51
	France...........	224	28	224	28
	Germany........	235,811	12,884	235,811	12,884
	United States....	185,272	11,644	185,272	11,644
	Total........	948,128	50,362	948,128	50,362
Saltpetre or nitrate of potash............	United Kingdom.	6,800	428	6,800	428
	Hong Kong......	260	9	260	9
	Germany........	99,305	5,157	99,305	5,157
	United States....	2,202,012	137,045	2,173,407	134,637
	Total........	2,308,377	142,639	2,279,772	140,231
Seeds, aromatic, crude, not edible and not advanced in value or condition by grinding or refining or by any other process or manufacture, viz.: Anise, anise-star, caraway, coriander, cardamon, cumin, fenugreek, and fennel.....	United Kingdom.	10,217	1,219	10,217	1,219
	France...........	29,425	1,362	29,425	1,362
	Germany........	2,324	353	2,324	353
	Holland..........	37,959	2,298	37,959	2,298
	Morocco..........	880	89	880	89
	United States....	144,159	11,176	144,159	11,176
	Total........	224,964	16,497	224,964	16,497
Soda ash or barilla......................	United Kingdom.	14,230,783	95,309	14,230,783	95,309
	Germany........	20	2	20	2
	United States....	44,243,482	297,088	44,243,482	297,088
	Total........	58,474,285	392,399	58,474,285	392,399

No. 1.—General Statement of Imports—*Continued.*

Articles Imported.	Countries.	Imported.		Entered for Home Consumption.	
		Quantity.	Value.	Quantity.	Value.
FREE GOODS.— MANUFACTURED ARTICLES—*Con.*		Lb.	$	Lb.	$
Drugs, &c.—*Con.*					
Soda bichromate of....................	United Kingdom.	457,201	21,628	457,201	21,628
	Germany.........	23,550	1,187	23,550	1,187
	United States....	119,597	6,192	119,597	6,192
	Total........	600,348	29,007	600,348	29,007
Soda bisulphite of......................	United Kingdom.	62,276	809	62,276	809
	Germany.........	75,562	1,396	75,562	1,396
	United States....	614,540	10,410	614,540	10,410
	Total........	752,378	12,615	752,378	12,615
Soda caustic, in packages of not less than 25 pounds. (To July 1st, see Dutiable Goods).	United Kingdom.	657,711	11,774	657,711	11,774
	United States....	12,866,876	211,303	12,866,876	211,303
	Total........	13,524,587	223,077	13,524,587	223,077
Soda, chlorate of......................	France...........	275,224	12,013	275,224	12,013
	United States....	49,177	5,490	49,177	5,490
	Total........	324,401	17,503	324,401	17,503
Soda, hyposulphite, when imported by tanners for use in their own factories in the tanning of leather.	United States....	262,648	2,993	262,648	2,993
Soda, nitrate of or cubic nitre..........	United Kingdom.	337,384	8,790	337,384	8,790
	Belgium..........	80,000	1,879	80,000	1,879
	France...........	11,200	389	11,200	389
	Germany.........	101,496	3,836	101,496	3,836
	Norway..........	6,515	286	6,515	286
	United States....	26,022,921	566,219	26,022,921	566,219
	Total........	26,559,516	581,399	26,559,516	581,399
Soda, nitrite of......................	United Kingdom.	9,806	605	9,806	605
	Germany.........	8,120	319	8,120	319
	United States....	416,310	8,579	416,310	8,579
	Total........	434,236	9,503	434,236	9,503
Soda, peroxide of......................	United Kingdom.	260	50	260	50
	United States....	22,892	6,440	22,892	6,440
	Total........	23,152	6,490	23,152	6,490
Soda, sal............................	United Kingdom.	3,144,261	17,044	3,144,261	17,044
	France...........	12,320	73	12,320	73
	Germany.........	2,000	25	2,000	25
	United States....	6,203,372	37,880	6,203,372	37,880
	Total........	9,361,953	55,022	9,361,953	55,022
Soda, silicate of, in crystals or in solution.	United Kingdom.	675,010	6,728	675,010	6,728
	Germany.........	227	36	227	36
	United States....	12,236,640	70,872	12,236,640	70,872
	Total........	12,911,877	77,636	12,911,877	77,636

6 GEORGE V, A. 1916

No. 1.—General Statement of Imports—*Continued.*

Articles Imported.	Countries.	Imported.		Entered for Home Consumption.	
		Quantity.	Value.	Quantity.	Value.
FREE GOODS— MANUFACTURED ARTICLES—*Con.*		Lb.	$	Lb.	$
Drugs, &c.—*Con.* Soda, sulphate of, crude, known as salt cake.	United Kingdom. United States....	8,954,170 28,776,388	40,659 126,604	8,954,170 28,776,388	40,659 126,604
	Total........	37,730,558	167,263	37,730,558	167,263
Soda, arseniate, binarseniate and stannate of.	United Kingdom. United States....	7,910 6,417	310 277	7,910 6,417	310 277
	Total........	14,327	587	14,327	587
Soda, prussiate and sulphite of..........	United Kingdom. France........... United States....	33,994 11,000 166,509	4,391 380 15,361	33,994 11,000 166,509	4,391 380 15,361
	Total........	211,503	20,132	211,503	20,132
Sodium, sulphide of....................	United Kingdom. Belgium.......... Germany......... United States....	4,680 7,444 75,367 1,572,547	85 85 977 29,161	4,680 7,444 75,367 1,572,547	85 85 977 29,161
	Total........	1,660,038	30,308	1,660,038	30,308
Sulphate of iron (copperas)	United Kingdom. Germany......... United States....	78,006 558 660,279	419 7 4,918	78,006 558 660,279	419 7 4,918
	Total........	738,843	5,344	738,843	5,344
Sulphate of copper (blue vitriol)........	United Kingdom. Belgium.......... Germany......... United States....	267,803 4,409 85 1,304,037	11,817 207 11 58,543	267,803 4,409 85 1,304,037	11,817 207 11 58,543
	Total........	1,576,334	70,578	1,576,334	70,578
Tartaric acid crystals..................	United Kingdom. France........... Germany......... United States....	67,381 71,429 44,952 53,376	19,771 16,561 11,045 20,575	67,381 71,429 44,952 53,376	19,771 16,561 11,045 20,575
	Total........	237,138	67,952	237,138	67,952
Terra japonica, gambier or cutch........	United Kingdom. B. E. Indies,other B. Straits Settlements..... United States.....	93,300 4,480 74,194 2,709,733	6,338 164 3,491 85,900	93,300 4,480 74,194 2,709,733	6,338 164 3,491 85,900
	Total........	2,881,707	95,893	2,881,707	95,893
Tin, bichloride of.....................	United States....	200	29	200	29
Tin crystals...........................	United States....	....	7,856	....	7,856

SESSIONAL PAPER No. 11

No. 1.—General Statement of Imports—*Continued.*

Articles Imported.	Countries.	Imported.		Entered for Home Consumption.	
		Quantity.	Value.	Quantity.	Value.
FREE GOODS— **MANUFACTURED ARTICLES—***Con.*		Lb.	$	Lb.	$
Drugs, &c.—*Con.*					
Tumeric...........................	United Kingdom.	3,782	201	3,782	201
	B. India..........	6,720	297	6,720	297
	United States....	34,992	2,009	34,992	2,009
	Total........	45,494	2,507	45,494	2,507
Ultramarine blue, dry or in pulp........	United Kingdom.	115,878	7,218	115,878	7,218
	France...........	4,800	234	4,800	234
	Germany.........	33,217	1,998	33,217	1,998
	Holland..........	3,120	407	3,120	407
	United States...	194,220	12,408	194,220	12,408
	Total........	351,235	22,265	351,235	22,265
Verdigris, or sub-acetate of copper, dry..	France...........	1,386	207	1,386	207
	United States....	2,752	720	2,752	720
	Total........	4,138	927	4,138	927
Zinc dust............................	United Kingdom.	15,960	1,749	15,960	1,749
	Belgium..........	11,000	569	11,000	569
	Germany.........	22,057	1,326	22,057	1,326
	United States....	344,822	34,660	344,822	34,660
	Total........	393,839	38,304	393,839	38,304
Zinc, sulphate and chloride of..........	United Kingdom.	40,922	1,017	40,922	1,017
	Belgium..........	40,264	546	40,264	546
	Germany........	18,000	275	18,000	275
	United States....	261,266	9,147	261,266	9,147
	Total........	360,452	10,985	360,452	10,985
Drugs, crude, such as barks, flowers, roots, beans, berries, balsams, bulbs, fruits insects, grains, gums and gum resins, herbs, leaves, nuts, fruit and stem seeds—which are not edible and which are in a crude state and not advanced in value by refining or grinding or any other process of manufacture, n.o.p.	United Kingdom.		9,324		9,324
	B. S. Africa......		2,577		2,577
	B. W. Indies.....		1,631		1,631
	Hong Kong......		4,162		4,162
	Newfoundland....		1		1
	Aust.-Hungary....		1,061		1,061
	China............		465		465
	France...........		536		536
	French Africa....		663		663
	Germany.........		1,637		1,637
	Holland..........		28		28
	Italy............		706		706
	Turkey..........		17		17
	United States....		69,827		69,827
	Total........		92,635		92,635
Fashion plates, tailors', milliners' and mantle makers', when imported in single copies in sheet form with magazines, etc.	United Kingdom.		1,083		1,083
	France..........		43		43
	United States....		17,504		17,504
	Total........		18,630		18,630
Felt, adhesive, for sheating vessels.......	United Kingdom.		1,409		1,409

No. 1.—General Statement of Imports—*Continued.*

ARTICLES IMPORTED.	COUNTRIES.	IMPORTED.		ENTERED FOR HOME CONSUMPTION.	
		Quantity.	Value.	Quantity.	Value.
FREE GOODS— MANUFACTURED ARTICLES—*Con.*			$		$
Fertilizers, unmanufactured, n.o.p.........	United Kingdom.	....	19	....	19
	United States....	....	733	....	733
	Total........	....	752	....	752
Fillets of cotton and rubber, not exceeding seven inches wide when imported by manufacturers of card clothing, for use exclusively in the manufacture of card clothing in their own factories.	United States....	....	22	....	22
Fisheries, for the use of, viz.: Fish hooks for deep sea or lake fishing not smaller in size than No. 2·0, not including hooks commonly used for sportsman's purposes.	United Kingdom.	....	16,623	....	16,623
	Norway..........	....	4,481	....	4,481
	United States....	....	885	....	885
	Total........	....	21,989	....	21,989
Bank, cod, pollock and mackerel fish lines; and mackerel, herring, salmon, seal, seine, mullet, net and trawl twine in hanks or coils, barked or not, in variety of sizes and threads, including gilling thread in balls, and head ropes for fishing nets, manila rope not exceeding 1½ inches in circumference for holding traps in the lobster fishery; barked marline, and net norsels of cotton, hemp or flax, and fishing nets or seines, when used exclusively for the fisheries, and not including lines or nets commonly used for sportsman's purposes.	United Kingdom.	....	674,766	....	674,766
	Newfoundland....	....	609	....	609
	Alaska..........	....	100	....	100
	Aust.-Hungary...	....	460	....	460
	Germany.........	....	1,496	....	1,496
	Japan...........	....	5,089	....	5,089
	United States....	....	663,642	....	663,642
	Total........	....	1,346,162	....	1,346,162
Fuse heads of metal, foil and cardboard, when imported by manufacturers of electric fuses, for use in their own factories in the manufacture of such fuses.	United States....	....	14	....	14
Glass, cut to size for manufacture of dry plates for photographic purposes when imported by the manufacturers of such dry plates for use exclusively in the manufacture thereof in their own factories. ·	United Kingdom.	....	18,094	....	18,094
	Belgium.........	....	2,222	....	2,222
	United States....	....	1,418	....	1,418
	Total........	....	21,734	....	21,734
Glass plates or discs, rough cut or unwrought, for use in the manufacture of optical instruments, when imported by manufacturers of such optical instruments	United Kingdom.	....	234	....	234
	France..........	....	38	....	38
	Germany.........	....	238	....	238
	United States....	....	4,235	....	4,235
	Total........	....	4,745	....	4,745
Glove fasteners, metal, shoe eyelets, corset eyelets, shoe eyelet hooks, shoe lace wire fasteners.	United Kingdom.	....	9,922	....	9,922
	Aust.-Hungary....	....	4,425	....	4,425
	Belgium.........	....	232	....	232
	France..........	....	2,333	....	2,333
	Germany.........	....	9,410	....	9,410
	Spain...........	....	5,051	....	5,051
	United States....	....	169,520	....	169,520
	Total........	....	200,893	....	200,893
Globes, geographical, topographical and astronomical.	United Kingdom.	....	387	....	387
	France..........	....	855	....	855
	United States....	....	3,325	....	3,325
	Total........	....	4,567	....	4,567

SESSIONAL PAPER No. 11

No. 1.—GENERAL STATEMENT OF IMPORTS—*Continued.*

ARTICLES IMPORTED.	COUNTRIES.	IMPORTED.		ENTERED FOR HOME CONSUMPTION.	
		Quantity.	Value.	Quantity.	Value.
FREE GOODS— **MANUFACTURED ARTICLES—***Con.*			$		$
Gold beaters' moulds and gold beaters' skins.	United Kingdom.	....	98	....	98
	France...........	....	7	....	7
	United States....	....	2,254	....	2,254
	Total........	....	2,359	....	2,359
Gold and silver sweepings................	Newfoundland....	....	50	....	50
	United States...	....	3,600	....	3,600
	Total........	....	3,650	....	3,650
Hatters' bands (not cords), bindings and hat sweats; hatters' tips and sides when cut to shape, and cashmere when cut to shape for under brims and hat covers, for use exclusively in the manufacture of these articles in their own factories.	United Kingdom.	....	33,425	....	33,425
	B. W. Indies......	....	198	....	198
	Aust.-Hungary....	....	115	....	115
	Belgium..........	....	893	....	893
	France...........	....	1,346	....	1,346
	Germany.........	....	2,698	....	2,698
	Italy.............	....	12	....	12
	United States.....	....	82,395	....	82,395
	Total........	....	121,082	....	121,082
Hatters' plush of silk or cotton...........	United Kingdom.	....	7,764	....	7,764
	Belgium..........	....	244	....	244
	France...........	....	6,795	....	6,795
	Germany.........	....	59,903	....	61,213
	Holland..........	....	617	....	617
	United States.....	....	15,418	....	15,418
	Total........	....	90,741	....	92,051
Hemp paper, made on four cylinder machines and calendered to between ·006 and ·008 thickness, adapted for the manufacture of shot shells; and felt board sized and hydraulic pressed and covered with paper or uncovered, adapted for the manufacture of gun wads.	United Kingdom.	....	360	....	360
	United States.....	....	26,671	....	26,671
	Total........	....	27,031	....	27,031
Hoods, unfinished, composed of "Leghorn," "Manila," palm leaf, grass, willow or chip, not bleached or blocked.	United Kingdom.	....	74	....	74
	B. W. Indies......	....	4,335	....	3,941
	Total........	....	4,409	....	4,015
Iron sand or globules or iron shot, and dry putty adapted for polishing glass or granite or for sawing stone.	United Kingdom.	....	3,775	....	3,775
	United States.....	....	9,274	....	9,274
	Total........	....	13,049	....	13,049
Ivories, piano key.....................	United Kingdom.	....	29,228	....	29,228
	France...........	....	1,730	....	1,730
	Germany.........	....	39,154	....	39,154
	United States.....	....	10,587	....	10,587
	Total........	....	80,699	....	80,699
		Cwt.		Cwt.	
Junk, old.............................	B. Guiana........	90	90	90	90
	Newfoundland....	136	219	136	219
	France...........	2	9	2	9
	Miquelon and St. Pierre..........	370	610	370	610
	United States.....	8,073	17,420	8,073	17,420
	Total........	8,671	18,348	8,671	18,348

6 GEORGE V, A. 1916

No. 1.—General Statement of Imports—*Continued.*

Articles Imported.	Countries.	Imported.		Entered for Home Consumption.	
		Quantity.	Value.	Quantity.	Value.
FREE GOODS— MANUFACTURED ARTICLES—*Con.*		Yd.	$	Yd.	$
Jute cloth as taken from the loom, not coloured, cropped, mangled, pressed, calendered, nor finished in any way.	United Kingdom.	4,469,668	333,950	4,469,668	333,950
	B. India..........	11,169,521	533,494	11,169,521	533,494
	Germany........	1,782	115	1,782	115
	United States.....	1,810,611	95,466	1,810,611	95,466
	Total........	17,451,582	963,025	17,451,582	963,025
		Lb.		Lb.	
Jute or hemp yarn, plain, dyed or coloured for weaving purposes, for insulating wire, and for the manufacture of hammocks or twines.	United Kingdom.	1,732,700	161,167	1,732,700	161,167
	New Zealand.....	46,566	2,605	46,566	2,605
	Belgium..........	41,420	3,948	41,420	3,948
	Italy.............	75,371	11,613	75,371	11,613
	United States.....	276,038	25,793	276,038	25,793
	Total........	2,172,095	205,126	2,172,095	205,126
		Yd.		Yd.	
Jute canvas, as taken from the loom, not coloured, cropped, mangled, pressed, calendered, nor finished in any way.	United Kingdom.	2,899,030	276,490	2,899,030	276,490
	B. India..........	3,470,039	190,622	3,470,039	190,622
	United States.....	14,810	899	14,810	·899
	Total........	6,383,879	468,011	6,383,879	468,011
		Lb.		Lb.	
Kelp, sea grass and sea weed in their natural state or cleaned only, n.o.p.	United Kingdom.	200	9	200	9
	Hong Kong......	1,437	310	1,437	310
	China............	316	50	316	50
	France...........	2,290	159	2,290	159
	Japan............	14,251	815	14,251	815
	United States.....	16,341	909	16,341	909
	Total........	34,835	2,252	34,835	2,252
Lamp black, bone black, ivory black and carbon black.	United Kingdom.	28,782	5,966	28,782	5,966
	France...........	155	20	155	20
	Germany........	6,710	70	6,710	70
	Holland..........	82,253	3,921	82,253	3,921
	Sweden..........	3,600	93	3,600	93
	United States.....	1,629,257	70,400	1,629,257	70,400
	Total........	1,750,757	80,470	1,750,757	80,470
Lenses and shutters for manufacturing cameras.	United Kingdom.	....	3,453	....	3,453
	Germany.........	....	386	....	386
	United States.....	....	28,815	....	28,815
	Total........	....	32,654	....	32,654
Life boats and life-saving apparatus, specially imported by societies to encourage the saving of human life.	United Kingdom.	....	200	....	200
	United States.....	....	2,914	....	2,914
	Total........	....	3,114	....	3,114
Life saving appliances, miners' rescue and automatic resuscitation apparatus for artificial breathing.	United Kingdom.	....	5,366	....	5,366
	France..........	....	2,340	....	2,340
	United States.....	....	13,095	....	13,095
	Total........	....	20,801	....	20,801

SESSIONAL PAPER No. 11

No. 1.—General Statement of Imports—*Continued.*

Articles Imported.	Countries.	Imported.		Entered for Home Consumption.	
		Quantity.	Value.	Quantity.	Value.
FREE GOODS— MANUFACTURED ARTICLES—*Con.*		Gal.	$	Gal.	$
Lime juice, crude only.....................	United Kingdom.	200	69	200	69
	B. W. Indies......	66,403	20,594	66,403	20,594
	Total.........	66,603	20,663	66,603	20,663
Lastings, mohair cloth, or other manufac-	Germany........:	....	472	....	472
tures of cloth, woven or made in patterns	United States.....	....	4,471	....	4,471
of such size, shape or form or cut in any					
such manner as to be fit only for covering	Total.........	....	4,943	....	4,943
buttons, when imported by manufac-					
turers of buttons.					
Medals of gold, silver or copper, and other	United Kingdom.	....	4,369	....	4,369
metallic articles, actually bestowed as	France............	....	61	....	61
trophies or prizes and received and	United States.....	....	5,261	....	5,196
accepted as honorary distinctions, and					
cups or other metallic prizes won in bona	Total.........	....	9,691	....	9,626
fide competitions.					
Mexican saddle trees and stirrups of wood.	United States....	....	12,997	....	12,997
Aluminum leaf or foil......................	United Kingdom.	....	1,322	....	1,322
	Germany.........	....	2,582	....	2,582
	United States....	....	1,882	....	1,882
	Total.........	....	5,786	....	5,786
Metals, viz.— Aluminium in ingots, blocks, bars, rods,		Lb.		Lb.	
	United Kingdom.	966,940	244,905	966,940	244,905
strips, sheets or plates.	Germany.........	56,019	12,402	56,019	12,402
	United States....	2,272,264	402,845	2,272,264	402,845
	Total.........	3,295,223	660,152	3,295,223	660,152
Aluminium tubing in lengths of not less	United Kingdom.	9,592	4,151	9,592	4,151
than 6 feet, not bent, etc.	United States....	5,507	2,438	5,507	2,438
	Total.........	15,099	6,589	15,099	6,589
Anchors for vessels......................		Cwt.		Cwt.	
	United Kingdom.	5,488	16,091	5,488	16,091
	France...........	46	85	46	85
	United States ...	2,786	14,248	2,786	14,248
	Total.........	8,320	30,424	8,320	30,424
Bismuth, metallic, in its natural state....		Lb.		Lb.	
	United Kingdom.	1,127	2,059	1,127	2,059
	United States....	788	1,496	788	1,496
	Total.........	1,915	3,555	1,915	3,555
Brass caps adapted for use in the manufac-	United States....	....	5,948	....	5,948
ture of electric batteries.					
Brass cups, being rough blanks, for the	United Kingdom.	....	6,595	....	6,595
manufacture of paper shells or cartridges,	United States....	....	162,237	....	162,237
when imported by manufacturers of					
brass and paper shells and cartridges, for	Total.........	....	168,832	....	168,832
use exclusively in the manufacture of such					
articles in their own factories.					

- 6 GEORGE V, A. 1916

No. 1.—General Statement of Imports—*Continued.*

Articles Imported.	Countries.	Imported.		Entered for Home Consumption.	
		Quantity.	Value.	Quantity.	Value.
FREE GOODS— MANUFACTURED ARTICLES—*Con.*		Cwt.	$	Cwt.	$
Metals—*Con.* Brass, old and scrap....................	United Kingdom.	370	4,045	370	4,045
	Miquelon and St. Pierre..........	10	60	10	60
	United States....	12,081	128,379	12,081	128,379
	Total........	12,461	132,484	12,461	132,484
Brass in blocks, ingots or pigs............	United States....	8,929	102,067	8,929	102,067
		Lb.		Lb.	
Brass tubing not polished, bent or otherwise manufactured in lengths not less than 6 feet.	United Kingdom.	165,425	29,555	165,425	29,555
	Germany.........	31,682	6,144	31,682	6,144
	United States....	1,417,911	276,818	1,417,911	276,818
	Total........	1,615,018	312,517	1,615,018	312,517
		Cwt.		Cwt.	
Brass in bars or rods, not less than 6 feet in length, and brass in strips, sheets or plates, not polished, etc., for use in Canadian manufacture. (To July 1st. See Dutiable Goods.)	United Kingdom.	42	728	42	728
	Germany.........	49	807	49	807
	United States....	5,349	91,965	5,349	91,965
	Total........	5,440	93,500	5,440	93,500
Britannia metal, in pigs, blocks, or bars..	United States....	368	13,056	368	13,056
Canada plates; Russia iron; terne plates and rolled sheets of iron or steel coated with zinc, spelter or other metal, of all widths or thicknesses, n.o.p.	United Kingdom.	114,654	269,178	114,654	269,178
Chain coil, coil chain links including repair links and chain shackles of iron or steel 1¼ inches in diameter and over.	United Kingdom.	5,417	20,178	5,417	20,178
Chain, malleable sprocket or link belting imported by manufacturers of agricultural implements for use in the manufacture of such implements in their own factories.	United Kingdom.	....	1,069	....	1,069
	United States....	....	78,650	....	78,650
	Total........	....	79,719	....	79,719
Copper, old and scrap....................	United Kingdom.	1	18	1	18
	Newfoundland....	134	1,036	134	1,036
	Miquelon and St. Pierre..........	8	40	8	40
	United States....	880	10,625	880	10,625
	Total........	1,023	11,719	1,023	11,719
Copper, in blocks, pigs or ingots.........	United Kingdom.	1	10	1	10
	United States....	44,225	585,600	44,225	585,600
	Total........	44,226	585,610	44,226	585,610
Copper, in bars and rods in coil or otherwise, in lengths of not less than 6 feet, unmanufactured.	United States....	144,782	2,056,510	144,782	2,056,510
Copper, in strips, sheets or plates, not polished, planished or coated, etc.	United Kingdom.	90	1,735	90	1,735
	United States.....	33,486	551,155	33,486	551,155
	Total..........	33,576	552,890	33,576	552,890

No. 1.—General Statement of Imports—*Continued.*

Articles Imported.	Countries.	Imported.		Entered for Home Consumption.	
		Quantity.	Value.	Quantity.	Value.
FREE GOODS— MANUFACTURED ARTICLES—*Con.*		Lb.	$	Lb.	$
Metals—*Con.* Copper, tubing in lengths of not less than 6 feet, and not polished, bent or otherwise manufactured.	United Kingdom. France............ Germany......... United States.....	55,955 2,247 63,508 500,616	11,024 433 15,665 110,369	55,955 2,247 63,508 500,616	11,024 433 15,665 110,369
	Total........	622,326	137,491	622,326	137,491
Copper, rollers adapted for use in calico printing.	United Kingdom. Germany......... United States....	....	1,270 146 1,895	....	1,270 146 1,895
	Total........	....	3,311	....	3,311
Cream separators and steel bowls for.....	United Kingdom. Newfoundland.... New Zealand.... Belgium.......... France............ Germany......... Sweden.......... United States....	....	41,016 55 187 39,619 154 7,785 27,927 291,959	....	41,016 55 187 39,619 154 7,785 27,927 291,959
	Total........	....	408,702	....	408,702
Cream separators—materials which enter into the construction and form part of, when imported by manufacturers of cream separators to be used in the manufacture thereof, and articles of metal for use in the manufacture of cream separator parts.	United Kingdom. Denmark........ Russia............ United States.... Total........	....	942 528 3,039 193,062 197,571	....	942 528 3,039 193,607 198,116
		Ton.		Ton.	
Ferromanganese and spiegeleisen containing more than 15 per cent manganese....	United Kingdom. France............ United States...	6,153 1 11,354	224,673 149 251,644	6,153 1 11,354	224,673 149 251,644
	Total........	17,508	476,466	17,508	476,466
Gas buoys:— The following articles and materials when imported by manufacturers of automatic gas buoys and automatic gas beacons, for use in the manufacture of such buoys and beacons for the Government of Canada or for export, viz.: Iron or steel tubes over 16 inches in diameter; flanged and dished steel heads made from boiler plate over 5 feet in diameter; hardened steel balls, not less than 3 inches in diameter; acetylene gas lanterns and parts thereof and tobin bronze in bars or rods.	Germany......... Sweden.......... United States... Total........	.... Cwt.	6,690 295 19,525 26,510	.... Cwt.	6,690 295 19,525 26,510
Iron or steel rods over 5-16 inch for manufacture of chains. (To July 1st. See Dutiable Goods.)	United States....	933	1,041	933	1,041

11—ii—21½

6 GEORGE V, A. 1916

No. 1.—GENERAL STATEMENT OF IMPORTS—*Continued*.

ARTICLES IMPORTED.	COUNTRIES.	IMPORTED.		ENTERED FOR HOME CONSUMPTION.	
		Quantity.	Value.	Quantity.	Value.
FREE GOODS— MANUFACTURED ARTICLES—*Con.*		Cwt.	$	Cwt.	$
Metals—*Con.* Iron or steel, rolled round wire rods, in the coil, not over ¼ inch in diameter, when imported by wire manufacturers for use in making wire in the coil in their own factories. (To July 1st. See Dutiable Goods.)	United Kingdom. Belgium.......... Germany......... United States....	3,334 13,887 65,652 617,085	3,597 15,034 74,304 712,479	3,334 13,887 65,652 617,085	3,597 15,034 74,304 712,479
	Total........	699,958	805,414	699,958	805,414
Boiler plate of iron or steel not less than 30 inches in width and not less than ¼ inch in thickness, for use exclusively in the manufacture of boilers.	United Kingdom. Belgium.......... Germany......... United States....	2,231 34 25 102,374	3,484 43 53 143,335	2,231 34 25 102,374	3,484 43 53 143,335
	Total........	104,664	146,915	104,664	146,915
Rolled iron or steel, and cast steel in bars, band, hoop, scroll or strip, sheet or plate of any size, thickness or width, galvanized or coated with any material, or not, and steel blanks for the manufacture of milling cutters when of greater value than 3½ cents per pound.	United Kingdom.	40,341	326,813	40,341	326,813
Rolled iron or steel sheets in strips, polished or not, 14 gauge and thinner, n.o.p.	United Kingdom.	145,200	318,939	145,200	318,939
Rolled iron or steel hoop, band, scroll or strip, No. 14 gauge and thinner, galvanized, or coated with other metal or not, n.o.p.	United Kingdom.	8,382	18,961	8,382	18,961
Sheets, flat, of galvanized iron..........	United Kingdom.	403,704	1,197,223	403,704	1,197,223
Metallic elements and tungstic acid when imported by manufacturers for use only in their own factories in the manufacture of metal filaments for electric lamps.	United Kingdom. Germany......... Italy........... Sweden.......... United States....	....	678 4,063 21 1,553 25,793	....	678 4,063 21 1,553 25,793
	Total........	....	32,108	....	32,108
Iron tubing, brass covered, not over 3 inches in diameter, and brass trimmings, not polished, lacquered or otherwise manufactured when imported by manufacturers of iron or brass bedsteads for use exclusively in the manufacture of such articles in their own factories.	United Kingdom. United States....	....	14,295 101,243	....	14,295 101,243
	Total........	....	115,538	....	115,538
Iron tubing, brass covered, not over 2 inches in diameter, in the rough, when imported by manufacturers for use only in their own factories in the manufacture of towel bars, bathtub rails and clothes carriers.	United Kingdom. United States....	....	38 186	....	38 186
	Total........	....	224	....	224

No. 1.—General Statement of Imports—*Continued.*

Articles Imported.	Countries.	Imported.		Entered for Home Consumption.	
		Quantity.	Value.	Quantity.	Value.
Free Goods— **Manufactured articles—**Con.			$		$
Metals—*Con.*					
Iron tubing, lacquered or brass covered, not over 2 inches in diameter, brass cased rods and brass trimmings, when imported by manufacturers of carriage rails for use exclusively in the manufacture of such articles in their own factories.	United Kingdom.	....	1,078	....	1,078
	United States....	....	860	....	860
	Total........	....	1,938	....	1,938
Iron tubing, lacquered or brass covered for manufacturing extension rods for windows.	United Kingdom.	....	69	....	69
	United States....	....	3,810	....	3,810
	Total........	....	3,879	....	3,879
		Cwt.		Cwt.	
Iron or steel beams, sheets, plates, angles, knees, masts or parts thereof, and cable chains for wooden, iron, steel or composite ships or vessels.	United Kingdom.	29,124	45,590	29,124	45,590
	Belgium..........	150	159	150	159
	Germany..........	459	565	459	565
	United States....	280,969	370,088	280,969	370,088
	Total........	310,702	416,402	310,702	416,402
Iron or steel bands, strips or sheets, No. 14 gauge or thinner, coated, polished or not, and rolled iron or steel sections, not being ordinary square, flat, or round bars, when imported by manufacturers of saddlery and hames, for use exclusively in the manufacture of such articles in their own factories.	United States....	....	14,676	....	14,676
Locomotive and car wheel tires of steel in the rough.	United Kingdom.	35,404	106,638	35,404	106,638
	Belgium..........	3,474	7,105	3,474	7,105
	Germany..........	39,653	77,218	39,653	77,218
	United States....	44,506	123,668	44,506	123,668
	Total........	123,037	314,629	123,037	314,629
Manufactured articles of iron or steel or brass which at the time of their importation are of a class or kind not manufactured in Canada, imported for use in the construction or equipment of ships or vessels.	United Kingdom.	....	36,323	....	36,323
	Belgium..........	....	494	....	494
	France...........	....	8,978	....	8,978
	United States....	....	51,515	....	51,515
	Total........	....	97,310	....	97,310
Scrap iron and scrap steel, old, and fit only to be remanufactured, being part of or recovered from any vessel wrecked in waters subject to the jurisdiction of Canada.	United States....	9,604	2,190	9,604	2,190
Skelp iron or steel sheared or rolled in grooves, not over 4¼ inches wide, for the manufacture of rolled iron tubes not over 1½ inches in diameter.	United States....	7,447	9,988	7,447	9,988
		Lb.	$	Lb.	$
Lead, tea...........................	United Kingdom.	1,199,646	77,368	1,199,646	77,368
	United States....	162,695	11,799	162,695	11,799
	Total........	1,362,341	89,167	1,362,341	89,167

6 GEORGE V, A. 1916

No. 1.—General Statement of Imports—*Continued.*

Articles Imported.	Countries.	Imported.		Entered for Home Consumption.	
		Quantity.	Value.	Quantity.	Value.
FREE GOODS— **MANUFACTURED ARTICLES—***Con.*			$		$
Metals—*Con.* Machinery, viz.:					
Articles of metal as follows, when for use exclusively in mining or metallurgical operations, viz.: coal cutting machines, except percussion coal cutters; coal heading machines; coal augers; rotary coal drills; core drills; miners' safety lamps and parts thereof, also accessories for cleaning, filling and testing such lamps; electric or magnetic machines for separating or concentrating iron ores; furnaces for the smelting of copper, zinc, and nickel ores; converting apparatus for metallurgical processes in metals ; copper plates, plated or not; machinery for extraction of precious metals by the chlorination or cyanide processes; amalgam safes; automatic ore samplers; automatic feeders; retorts; mercury pumps; pyrometers ; bullion furnaces; amalgam cleaners ; blast furnace blowing engines; and integral parts of all machinery mentioned in this item; blowers of iron or steel for use in the smelting of ores, or in the reduction, separation or refining of metals; rotary kilns, revolving roasters and furnaces of metal designed for roasting ore, mineral, rock or clay; furnace slag trucks and slag pots of a class or kind not made in Canda; buddles, vanners, and slime tables adapted for use in gold mining.	United Kingdom. Germany. Switzerland. United States. Total	....	10,707 7,246 703 431,847 450,503	....	10,707 6,508 703 447,597 465,515
Diamond drills and parts of, not to include motive power.	United States.	....	41,117	....	41,117
Appliances of iron or steel, of a class or kind not made in Canada, and elevators and machinery of floating dredges, when for use exclusively in alluvial gold mining.	United Kingdom. Alaska. United States. Total	....	267 1,000 182,388 183,655	....	267 1,000 182,388 183,655
Well-drilling, and apparatus of a class or kind not made in Canada, for drilling for water, natural gas or oil, and for prospecting for minerals, not to include motive power.	United States.	....	214,379	....	214,379
Briquette making machines	United Kingdom. United States. Total	....	1,615 1,291 2,906	....	1,615 1,291 2,906
		No.		No.	
Newspaper printing presses, of not less value by retail than $1,500 each, of a class or kind not made in Canada.	United Kingdom. United States. Total	4 53 57	8,484 334,534 343,018	4 53 57	8,484 334,534 343,018
Machinery and tools not manufactured in Canada up to the required standard necessary for any factory to be established in Canada for the manufacture of rifles for the Government of Canada.	United Kingdom. United States. Total	....	3,579 268,139 271,718	....	3,579 268,139 271,718

No. 1.—General Statement of Imports—*Continued*.

Articles Imported.	Countries.	Imported.		Entered for Home Consumption.	
		Quantity.	Value.	Quantity.	Value.
FREE GOODS— MANUFACTURED ARTICLES—*Con.*			$		$
Metals—*Con.*					
All materials or parts on the rough, unfinished, and screws, nuts, bands and springs, and steel for rough unfinished parts, to be used in rifles to be manufactured at any such factory for the Government of Canada.	United Kingdom.	....	822	....	822
	Germany.........	....	9,792	....	9,792
	United States....	....	331,033	....	331,033
	Total........	....	341,647	....	341,647
Machines, typecasting and typesetting, and parts thereof, adapted for use in printing offices.	United Kingdom.	....	237	....	237
	United States....	....	478,941	....	478,941
	Total........	....	479,178	....	479,178
Machinery of every kind and structural iron and steel, for use in the construction and equipment of factories for the manufacture of sugar from beet root..	Germany.........	....	608	....	608
	United States....	....	2,075	....	2,075
	Total........	....	2,683	....	2,683
Machinery of a class or kind not made in Canada, and parts thereof, for the manufacture of twine, cordage, or linen or for the preparation of flax fibre.....	United Kingdom.	....	6,183	....	6,183
	France.........	....	2,896	....	2,896
	United States...	....	29,605	....	29,605
	Total........	....	38,684	....	38,684
Machines, traction ditching (not being ploughs), adapted for tile drainage on farms, valued by retail at not more than $3,000 each, and parts therof for repairs.	United States....	31	78,768	31	78,768
		Cwt.		Cwt.	
Mould boards or shares, or plough plates, land sides, and other plates for agricultural implements, when cut to shape from rolled plates of steel, but not moulded, punched, polished, or otherwise manufactured	United States....	50,681	135,425	50,681	135,425
Material to be used in Canada for the construction of bridges and tunnels crossing the boundary between Canada and the United States, when similar materials are admitted free under similar circumstances into the United States, under regulations prescribed hy the Minister of Customs.	United States....	....	20,097	....	20,097
Metal tips, studs, and eyes for the manufacture of corset clasps and corset wires.	United States...	....	5,504	....	5,504
		Lbs.		Lbs.	
Nickel, nickel silver, and German silver, in bars and rods, and also in strips, sheets or plates.	United Kingdom.	85	117	85	117
	United States....	584,546	139,523	584,546	139,523
	Total........	584,631	139,640	584,631	139,640
Nickel, nickel silver, and German silver, in ingots or blocks, n.o.p.	United States....	90,396	32,397	90,396	32,397
Platinum retorts, pans, condensers, tubing and pipe, and preparations of platinum, when imported by manufacturers of sulphuric acid for use exclusively in the manufacture or concentration of sulphuric acid in their own factories.	United States....	....	59	....	59
Platinum wire and platinum in bars, strips, sheets or plates......................	United Kingdom.	....	5,721	....	5,721
	United States....	....	49,732	....	49,732
	Total........	....	55,453	....	55,453

No. 1.—General Statement of Imports—*Continued.*

Articles Imported.	Countries.	Imported.		Entered for Home Consumption.	
		Quantity.	Value.	Quantity.	Value.
FREE GOODS— MANUFACTURED ARTICLES—*Con.*			$		$
Metals—*Con.* Ribs of brass, iron or steel, runners, rings, caps, notches, ferrules, mounts, and sticks or canes in the rough, or not further manufactured than cut into lengths, suitable for umbrella, parasol or sunshade or walking sticks, when imported by manufacturers of such articles for use exclusively in their own factories.	United Kingdom.	....	17,952	....	17,831
	Australia.........	....	183	....	183
	Aust.-Hungary....	....	1,972	....	1,972
	France............	....	191	....	191
	Germany.........	....	10,032	....	10,032
	Japan............	....	373	....	373
	United States....	....	67,861	....	67,861
	Total........	....	98,564	....	98,443
Sewing machine attachments............	United Kingdom.	....	7	....	7
	Germany.........	....	90	....	90
	United States....	....	26,353	....	26,353
	Total........	....	26,450	....	26,450
Steel balls adapted for use on bearings on machinery and vehicles................	United Kingdom.	....	4,317	....	4,317
		Cwt.		Cwt.	
Steel rolled for saws and straw cutters not tempered or ground nor further manufactured than cut to shape, without indented edges.	United Kingdom.	818	7,590	818	7,590
	United States....	16,106	116,709	16,106	116,709
	Total........	16,924	124,299	16,924	124,299
Steel wire Bessemer soft drawn spring of Nos. 10, 12 and 13 gauge, respectively, and homo steel spring wire of Nos. 11 and 12 gauge, respectively, when imported by manufacturers of wire mattresses to be used exclusively in their own factories in the manufacture of such articles.	United States....	10,511	25,338	10,511	25,338
Steel, crucible sheet, 11 to 16 gauge, 2½ to 18 inches wide for the manufacture of mower and reaper knives when imported by manufacturers thereof for use exclusively in the manufacture of such articles in their own factories.	United Kingdom.	132	1,395	132	1,395
	United States....	6,644	23,073	6,644	23,073
	Total........	6,776	24,468	6,776	24,468
Steel of No. 20 gauge and thinner, but not thinner than No. 30 gauge, for the manufacture of corset steels, clock springs and shoe shanks, imported by manufacturers of such articles for exclusive use in the manufacture of such articles in their own factories.	United Kingdom.	650	2,318	650	2,318
	United States....	214	1,760	214	1,760
	Total........	864	4,078	864	4,078
Steel wire flat, of 16 gauge or thinner imported by the manufacturers of crinoline or corset wires and dress stays, for use exclusively in the manufacture of such articles in their own factories.	United States....	6,237	48,003	6,237	48,003
Steel of No. 12 gauge and thinner, but not thinner than No. 30 gauge, for the manufacture of buckle clasps, bed fasts, furniture casters and ice creepers, imported by the manufacturers of such articles, for use exclusively in the manufacture of such articles in their own factories.	United States....	1,551	4,351	1,551	4,351

No. 1.—General Statement of Imports—*Continued.*

Articles Imported.	Countries.	Imported.		Entered for Home Consumption.	
		Quantity.	Value.	Quantity.	Value.
FREE GOODS— **MANUFACTURED ARTICLES—***Con.*		Cwt.	$	Cwt.	$
Metals—*Con.* Steel No. 24 and 17 gauge, in sheets 63 inches long, and from 18 to 32 inches wide when imported by the manufacturers of tubular bow sockets for use exclusively in the manufacture of such articles in their own factories.	United States....	1,620	3,951	1,620	3,951
Steel springs for the manufacture of surgical trusses when imported by manufacturers of surgical trusses for use exclusively in the manufacture thereof in their own factories.	United States....	Lb. 388	187	Lb. 388	187
Stereotypes, electrotypes and celluloids of newspaper columns in any language other than English and French and of books, and bases and matrices and copper shells for the same, whether composed wholly or in part of metal or celluloid.	United Kingdom. United States.... Total........	Sq. in. 630 671,915 672,545	26 11,529 11,555	Sq. in. 630 671,915 672,545	26 11,529 11,555
Rolled iron and rolled steel nail rods, under half an inch in diameter, for the manufacture of horse shoe nails.	Sweden.......... United States.... Total........	Cwt. 24,283 7,405 31,688	57,352 14,745 72,097	Cwt. 24,283 7,405 31,688	57,352 14,745 72,097
Tagging metal, plain, japanned or coated, in coils, not over 1½ inches wide, when imported by the manufacturers of shoe and corset laces for use exclusively in the manufacture of such articles in their own factories.	United Kingdom. France.......... United States.... Total........	1 1 119 121	24 26 1,503 1,553	1 1 119 121	24 26 1,503 1,553
Tin in blocks, pigs and bars..............	United Kingdom. B. Straits Settlements.......... Hong Kong...... Alaska.......... Germany........ United States.... Total........	12,173 1,876 892 20 112 14,329 29,402	402,594 65,589 32,031 980 3,922 498,684 1,003,800	12,173 1,876 892 20 112 14,329 29,402	402,594 65,589 32,031 980 3,922 498,684 1,003,800
Tin plates and sheets....................	United Kingdom. France.......... United States.... Total........	136,935 61 848,107 985,103	450,950 365 2,580,909 3,032,224	136,935 61 848,107 985,103	450,950 365 2,580,909 3,032,224
Tin foil..............................	United Kingdom. France.......... Germany........ Holland......... United States.... Total........	Lb. 9,154 680 4,398 720 1,111,430 1,126,382	3,181 84 2,007 364 149,632 155,268	Lb. 9,154 680 4,398 720 1,111,430 1,126,382	3,181 84 2,007 364 149,632 155,268
Steel seamless tubing valued at not less than 3½ cents per pound.	United Kingdom.	Cwt. 550	4,842	Cwt. 550	4,842

6. GEORGE V, A. 1916

No. 1.—General Statement of Imports—*Continued.*

ARTICLES IMPORTED.	COUNTRIES.	IMPORTED.		ENTERED FOR HOME CONSUMPTION.	
		Quantity.	Value.	Quantity.	Value.
FREE GOODS— MANUFACTURED ARTICLES—*Con.*			$		$
Metals—*Con.* Steel or iron tubes rolled, not joined or welded, not more than 1½ inches in diameter, n.o.p.	United Kingdom. France. United States.....	....	6,482 18 31,382	....	6,482 18 31,382
	Total........	....	37,882	....	37,882
Seamless steel or wrought iron boiler tubes, including flues and corrugated tubes for marine boilers.	United Kingdom. Belgium........ Germany........ Holland........ United States....	....	52,688 4,414 19,815 15 280,060	....	52,688 4,414 19,815 15 280,060
	Total........	....	356,992	....	356,992
		Cwt.		Cwt.	
Barbed fence wire of iron or steel.........	United Kingdom. United States.....	15 325,375	41 627,162	15 325,375	41 627,162
	Total........	325,390	627,203	325,390	627,203
		Lb.		Lb.	
Wire, crucible cast steel valued at not less than 6 cents per pound.	United Kingdom.	23,402	2,765	23,402	2,765
Wire of brass, zinc, iron or steel, screwed or twisted, or flattened or corrugated, for use in connection with nailing machines for the manufacture of boots and shoes, when imported by the manufacturers of boots and shoes, to be used exclusively for such purposes in their own factories.	United States....	116,894	40,721	116,894	40,721
		Cwt.	.	Cwt.	
Wire, curved or not, galvanized iron or steel Nos. 9, 12 and 13 gauge, with variations not exceeding 4-1000 of an inch, but not for use in telegraph or telephone lines.	United Kingdom. Newfoundland.... Belgium.......... Germany........ United States...	225 4 677 11,981 745,371	756 8 1,604 22,817 1,281,757	225 4 677 11,981 745,371	756 8 1,604 22,817 1,281,757
	Total........	758,258	1,306,942	758,258	1,306,942
Wire rope for use exclusively for rigging of ships and vessels.	United Kingdom. United States....	685 63	3,787 565	685 63	3,787 565
	Total........	748	4,352	748	4,352
Wire, steel, valued at not less than 2¾ cents per pound when imported by manufacturers of rope for use exclusively in the manufacture of rope.	United Kingdom. United States....	55,306 229	216,306 1,891	55,306 229	216,306 1,891
	Total........	55,535	218,197	55,535	218,197
Yellow metal in bars, bolts and sheets, for use in the construction or repairs of vessels.	United Kingdom. United States....	259 241	3,111 3,262	259 241	3,111 3,262
	Total........	500	6,373	500	6,373
Zinc in blocks, pigs, bars, rods, sheets and plates.	United Kingdom. Newfoundland.... Belgium.......... France.......... Germany........ United States....	715 3 6,920 12 5,426 17,164	4,432 6 36,616 120 28,714 129,731	715 3 6,920 12 5,426 17,164	4,432 6 36,616 120 28,714 129,731
	Total.......	30,240	199,619	30,240	199,619

No. 1.—General Statement of Imports—*Continued.*

Articles Imported.	Countries.	Imported.		Entered for Home Consumption.	
		Quantity.	Value.	Quantity.	Value.
FREE GOODS— **MANUFACTURED ARTICLES—***Con.*		Cwt.	$	Cwt.	$
Metals—*Con.*					
Zinc spelter.............................	United Kingdom.	4,246	20,157	4,246	20,15
	Belgium..........	14,478	72,043	14,478	72,043
	Germany.........	8,209	39,751	8,209	39,751
	Holland..........	560	2,688	560	2,688
	United States....	101,626	577,170	101,626	577,170
	Total........	129,119	711,809	129,119	711,809
		Gal.		Gal.	
Molasses not testing more than 56 degrees by the polariscope the produce of any British country entitled to the benefits of the British Preferential Tariff when produced from sugar cane and imported direct by ship, from the country of production, or from any British country, in *t*he original package in which it was placed at the point of production and not afterwards subjected to any process of treating or mixing.	United Kingdom.	2,205	331	2,205	331
	B. W. Indies......	7,312,464	1,283,915	7,312,464	1,283,915
	Total........	7,314,669	1,284,246	7,314,669	1,284,246
Newspapers, and quarterly, monthly and semi-monthly magazines, and weekly literary papers, unbound.	United Kingdom.	....	82,137	....	82,137
	France............	....	3,757	....	3,757
	Japan............	....	224	....	224
	United States....	....	1,339,730	....	1,339,730
	Total........	....	1,425,848	....	1,425,848
Noils, being the short wool that falls from the combs in worsted factories; and worsted tops, n.o.p.	United Kingdom.	....	1,033,504	....	1,033,504
	Belgium..........	....	1,005	....	1,005
	United States....	....	278,376	....	278,376
	Total........	....	1,312,885	....	1,312,885
		Cwt.		Cwt.	
Oakum of jute or hemp.................	United Kingdom.	4,615	21,532	4,615	21,532
	Japan............	8	41	8	41
	United States....	7,235	27,057	7,235	27,057
	Total........	11,858	48,630	11,858	48,630
Oil cake, linseed and linseed oil cake meal, cotton seed cake and meal, palm nut cake and meal.	United Kingdom.	5,851	10,554	5,851	10,554
	China............	2,800	3,218	2,800	3,218
	Japan............	7,110	8,675	7,110	8,675
	United States....	239,613	309,192	239,613	309,192
	Total........	255,374	331,639	255,374	331,639
Soya beans and soya bean cake, for use in the manufacture of cattle foods and of fertilizers, when imported by manufacturers of such cattle food and fertilizers.	Japan............	2,206	2,930	2,206	2,930
Oils, viz.:—		Gal.		Gal.	
Carbolic or heavy oil.................	United Kingdom.	187,490	32,784	187,490	32,784
	Germany.........	7,186	2,516	7,186	2,516
	United States....	541,863	62,148	541,863	62,148
	Total........	736,539	97,448	736,539	97,448

6 GEORGE V, A. 1916

No. 1.—General Statement of Imports—*Continued*.

Articles Imported.	Countries.	Imported.		Entered for Home Consumption.	
		Quantity.	Value.	Quantity.	Value.
.FREE GOODS— MANUFACTURED ARTICLES—*Con.*		Gal.	$	Gal.	$
Oils—*Con.* Cocoanut, palm and palm kernel not edible, peanut and soya bean, for manufacture of soap.	United Kingdom.	145,268	127,559	145,268	127,559
	Australia.........	8,866	8,260	8,866	8,260
	B. India.........	5,550	5,174	5,550	5,174
	China...........	8,541	3,254	8,541	3,254
	France..........	11,488	10,819	11,488	10,819
	Germany........	16,223	13,779	16,223	13,779
	Holland.........	9,610	7,813	9,610	7,813
	Japan...........	27,515	15,289	27,515	15,289
	United States....	178,736	161,338	178,736	161,338
	Total........	411,797	353,285	411,797	353,285
Cotton seed, refined, edible, and peanut, for canning fish.	United States....	32,000	20,309	32,000	20,309
Cotton seed, crude, for the manufacture of refined cotton seed oil.	United States....	2,938,492	1,327,386	2,938,492	1,327,386
Gasoline, under ·725 specific gravity at 60 degrees temperature.	United States....	26,504,649	2,828,383	26,504,649	2,828,383
		Lb.		Lb.	
Palm bleached and Shea butter....'......	United Kindgom.	72,462	15,658	72,462	15,658
	United States.....	629	74	629	74
	Total........	73,091	15,732	73,091	15,732
Asphaltum oil.........................	United States.....	....	35,802	....	35,802
		Gal.		Gal.	
Olive, for manufacturing soap or tobacco or for canning fish.	United States.....	2,022	1,712	2,022	1,712
Petroleum, crude, fuel and gas oils (8235 specific gravity or heavier) at 60 degrees temperature.	United Kingdom.	1,996	276	1,996	276
	Peru..............	3,355,940	86,521	3,355,940	86,521
	United States.....	193,490,351	5,166,730	192,845,351	5,143,700
	Total........	196,848,287	5,253,527	196,203,287	5,230,497
Rosin oil and Chinawood oil...........	United Kingdom.	....	7,337	....	7,337
	China............	....	19,546	....	19,546
	United States.....	....	114,106	....	114,106
	Total........	....	140,989	....	140,989
Paper, matrix, not being tissue paper, for use in printing.	United Kingdom.	....	1,365	....	1,365
	France..........	....	330	....	330
	United States....	....	11,843	....	11,843
	Total........	....	13,538	....	13,538
Paper tubes and cones of all sizes adapted for winding yarn thereon.	United Kingdom.	....	1,525	....	1,525
	United States....	....	14,066	....	14,066
	Total........	....	15,591	....	15,591
Paper and materials of paper, gutta percha and rubber for the manufacture of music rolls for piano players.	United States.....	....	4,062	....	4,062

No. 1.—General Statement of Imports—*Continued.*

ARTICLES IMPORTED.	COUNTRIES.	IMPORTED.		ENTERED FOR HOME CONSUMPTION.	
		Quantity.	Value.	Quantity.	Value.
FREE GOODS— MANUFACTURED ARTICLES—*Con.*			$		$
Paper, photographic, plain basic, baryta coated, adapted for use exclusively in the manufacture of albumenized of sensitized paper.	United Kingdom.	....	149	....	149
	Belgium.........	....	145	....	145
	France...........	....	1,421	....	1,421
	Germany.......	....	3,438	....	3,438
	United States.....	....	43,404	....	43,404
	Total........	....	48,557	....	48,557
Paper decalcomania, not printed, when imported by manufacturers of decalcomania transfers, to be used in their own factories in the manufacture of such transfers.	United Kingdom.	....	808	....	808
	Germany.........	....	146	....	146
	United States.....	....	2,273	....	2,273
	Total........	....	3,227	....	3,227
Philosophical and scientific apparatus, utensils, instruments and preparations, including boxes and bottles containing the same, maps, photographic reproductions, casts as models, etchings, lithographic prints or charts, when specially imported in good faith for use and by order of any society or institution, incorporated or established solely for religious, philosophical, educational, scientific or literary purposes, or for the encouragement of the fine arts or for the use or by order of any college, academy, school or seminary of learning in Canada, and not for sale.	United Kingdom.	....	39,268	....	39,268
	Australia.........	....	56	....	56
	Alaska..........	....	25	....	25
	Aust. Hungary....	....	92	....	92
	Belgium..........	....	551	....	551
	Denmark.........	....	169	....	169
	France..........	....	4,737	....	4,737
	Germany.........	....	8,721	....	8,721
	Holland..........	....	59	....	59
	Italy............	....	590	....	590
	Sweden..........	....	357	....	357
	Switzerland......	....	216	....	216
	Turkey..........	....	21	....	21
	United States.....	....	172,028	....	172,028
	Total........	....	226,890	....	226,890
Piano and organ parts:—key pins, damper springs, jack springs, rail springs, regulating screws; spoons, bridle wires, damper wires, back check wires, dowel wires, German center pins, brass pins, rail hooks brass brackets, plates, damper rod nuts, damper sockets and screws, shell, brass capstan screws, brass flange plates and screws, brass flanges, brass whitened spring wire, hammer wires, felt, butt felt, damper felt, hammer rail cloth, back check felt, catch felt, thin damper felt, whip cloth, bushing cloth, hammer felt, back hammer felt, bridle leather and buckskin when imported by manufacturers of piano keys, actions, hammers, base dampers and organ keys, for use exclusively in the manufacture of such articles in their own factories.	United Kingdom.	....	7,163	....	7,163
	Germany.........	....	6,067	....	6,067
	United States.....	....	46,533	....	46,533
	Total........	....	59,763	....	59,763
Prunella cloth of wool....................	United Kingdom.	....	42,997	....	42,997
		Cwt.		Cwt.	
Rags of cotton, jute, hemp, and wool; paper waste clippings, and waste of all kinds, n.o.p., except metallic; broken glass or glass cullet.	United Kingdom.	97,440	141,791	97,440	141,791
	Newfoundland....	7	6	7	6
	Belgium.........	856	3,043	856	3,043
	France...........	675	2,319	675	2,319
	Germany........	3,656	16,627	3,656	16,627
	Holland..........	2,105	6,243	2,105	6,243
	Portugal..........	8,311	16,128	8,311	16,128
	Spain............	6,146	9,208	6,146	9,208
	United States.....	421,726	1,049,104	421,726	1,049,104
	Total........	540,922	1,244,469	540,922	1,244,469

6 GEORGE V, A. 1916

No. 1.—General Statement of Imports—*Continued.*

Articles Imported.	Countries.	Imported.		Entered for Home Consumption.	
		Quantity.	Value.	Quantity.	Value.
FREE GOODS— MANUFACTURED ARTICLES—*Con.*		Cwt.	$	Cwt.	$
Resin or rosin in packages of not less than 100 lbs.	United Kingdom.	11,373	27,848	11,373	27,848
	France............	10	28	10	28
	Germany.........	1	15	1	15
	United States....	240,557	416,710	240,557	416,710
	Total.........	251,941	444,601	251,941	444,601
		Lb.		Lb.	
Rubber and gutta percha, crude caoutchouc or India rubber unmanufactured.	United Kingdom.	1,912,743	1,048,211	1,458,192	814,591
	B. India.........	114,111	73,195	114,111	73,195
	B. E. Indies, other	290,637	155,092	202,837	107,669
	B. Oceania, other.	11,860	7,709	11,860	7,709
	B. Straits Settlements..........	1,422,513	718,401	987,378	503,197
	Belgium..........	61,677	26,867	61,677	26,867
	France............	2,265	1,101	2,265	1,101
	Germany.........	36,200	15,139	36,200	15,139
	Kongo Free State.	35,486	12,952	35,486	12,952
	United States....	3,594,470	2,041,605	3,594,470	2,041,605
	Total.........	7,481,962	4,100,272	6,504,476	3,604,025
Rubber, recovered, and rubber substitute and hard rubber in sheets but not further manufactured, also hard rubber in strips or rods but not further manufactured, when imported for use in Canadian manufactures.	United Kingdom.	30,309	3,672	30,309	3,672
	B.E. Indies, other	11,393	2,021	11,393	2,021
	France...........	1,296	128	1,296	128
	Germany.........	1,431	197	1,431	197
	United States....	5,737,087	775,426	5,737,087	775,426
	Total.........	5,781,516	781,444	5,781,516	781,444
Rubber powdered and rubber or gutta percha waste or junk.	United Kingdom.	100	25	100	25
	Newfoundland....	14,766	495	14,766	495
	Miquelon and St. Pierre..........	600	24	600	24
	United States....	642,885	83,407	642,885	83,407
	Total.........	658,351	83,951	658,351	83,951
Rubber thread not covered...............	United States.....	24,032	35,855	24,032	35,855
Soap, whale oil...........,...............	United Kingdom.	4,245	99	4,245	99
	United States....	131,089	5,184	131,089	5,184
	Total.........	135,334	5,283	135,334	5,283
		Gal.		Gal.	
Spirits, amyl alcohol or refined fusil oil, when imported by the Department of Inland Revenue or by a person licensed by the Minister of Inland Revenue to be denatured for use in the manufacture of metal varnishes or lacquers.	United States....	42	135	42	135
Spirits, ethyl alcohol, when imported by the Department of Inland Revenue or by a person licensed by the Minister of Inland Revenue to be denatured for use in the arts and industries, and for fuel, light and power.	United States....	7,464	3,544	7,464	3,544
Spurs and stilts adapted for use in the manufacture of earthenware.	United States....	....	288	....	288

No. 1.—General Statement of Imports—*Continued.*

Articles Imported.	Countries.	Imported.		Entered for Home Consumption.	
		Quantity.	Value.	Quantity.	Value.
FREE GOODS— **MANUFACTURED ARTICLES—***Con.*		.	$		$
Square or round reeds and raw hide centres, textile leather or rubber heads, thumbs and tips, and steel, iron or nickel caps for whip ends, imported by whip manufacturers for use exclusively in the manufacture of whips in their own factories.	United States....	....	25,281	....	25,281
Scientific apparatus, glassware and other for laboratory work, also apparatus for sterilizing purposes, not including washing or laundry machines, all for use in public hospitals.	United Kingdom.	....	2,738	....	2,738
	United States....	....	15,586	....	15,586
	Total........	....	18,324	....	18,324
Surgical and dental instruments of metal and surgical needles, and surgical operating tables for use in hospitals, X-ray apparatus and parts thereof, and microscopes valued at not less than $50 each by retail.	United Kingdom.	....	30,032	....	30,032
	Aust.-Hungary...	....	1,411	....	1,411
	France..........	....	3,016	....	3,016
	Germany........	....	13,018	....	13,018
	Holland.........	....	202	....	202
	Switzerland.....	....	277	....	277
	United States....	....	345,385	....	345,385
	Total........	....	393,341	....	393,341
Turpentine, raw or crude................	United States....	Lb. 59,473	1,956	Lb. 59,473	1,956
Turpentine, spirits of....................	United Kingdom.	Gal. 884	582	Gal. 884	582
	United States....	904,553	458,561	904,553	458,561
	Total........	905,437	459,143	905,437	459,143
Twine or yarn of paper imported by manufacturers for the purpose of being woven into fabrics.	United States....	....	291	....	291
Twine or yarn of paper for use in the manufacture of furniture.	United States....	....	275	....	275
Typewriters, type tablets with movable figures, and musical instruments, when imported by and for use of schools for the blind.	United Kingdom.	....	12	....	12
	United States....	....	28	....	28
	Total........	....	40	....	40
Wool waste in the white, garnetted, for the manufacture of woolen goods.	United Kingdom.	.Lb. 30,519	10,076	Lb. 30,519	10,076
	United States.....	73,270	20,454	73,270	20,454
	Total........	103,789	30,530	103,789	30,530
Yarn. cotton, No. 40 and finer............	United Kingdom.	1,548,000	691,740	1,536,059	687,063
	France..........	128	116	128	116
	Germany........	400	244	400	244
	Switzerland......	762	529	762	529
	United States....	353,364	155,581	353,364	155,581
	Total........	1,902,654	848,210	1,890,713	843,473
Yarn, cotton, polished or glazed, when imported by manufacturers of shoe laces for use exclusively for the manufacture of such articles in their own factories.	United Kingdom.	2,325	730	2,325	730
	France..........	10	7	10	7
	Germany........	5,225	1,361	5,225	1,361
	United States....	59,598	21,290	59,598	21,290
	Total........	67,158	23,388	67,158	23,388

6 GEORGE V, A. 1916

No. 1.—General Statement of Imports—*Continued.*

ARTICLES IMPORTED.	COUNTRIES.	IMPORTED.		ENTERED FOR HOME CONSUMPTION.	
		Quantity.	Value.	Quantity.	Value.
FREE GOODS— MANUFACTURED ARTICLES—*Con.*		Lb.	$	Lb.	$
Yarn, linen, for the manufacture of towels, damask or seamless linen, fire hose duck, when imported by the manufacturers of such articles for use exclusively in the manufacture of such articles in their own factories.	United Kingdom.	332,059	96,092	332,059	96,092
	Italy.............	5,788	1,352	5,788	1,352
	United States....	15,546	6,043	15,546	6,043
	Total........	353,393	103,487	353,393	103,487
Yarn, mohair..................	United Kingdom.	5,556	3,316	5,556	3,316
	Germany.........	88	73	88	73
	United States....	228	· 183	228	183
	Total........	5,872	3,572	5,872	3,572
Yarn, wool or worsted, when genapped, dyed or finished and imported by manufacturers of braid, cords, tassels, buttons and fringes for use exclusively in the manufacture of such articles in their own factories.	United Kingdom.	16,986	8,331	16,986	8,331
	United States....	191	172	191	172
	Total........	17,177	8,503	17,177	8,503
Yarns, thread and filaments of artificial and imitation silk, produced from a form cellulose obtained by chemical processes from cotton or wool when imported by manufacturers of knitted, woven or braided fabrics, for use only in their own factories in the manufacture of such knitted, woven or braided fabrics.	United Kingdom.	37,661	49,682	37,661	49,682
	Belgium..........	36,248	46,603	36,248	46,603
	France...........	1,315	1,603	1,315	1,603
	Germany........	1,045	1,546	1,045	1,546
	Holland..........	143	202	143	202
	United States....	51,736	90,653	51,736	90,653
	Total........	128,148	190,289	128,148	190,289
MISCELLANEOUS ARTICLES.					
Anatomical preparations and skeletons or parts thereof.	United Kingdom.	....	49	....	49
	France...........	....	250	....	250
	Germany.........	....	1,213	....	1,213
	United States....	....	968	....	968
	Total........	....	2,480	....	2,480
*Apparel, wearing, and other personal and household effects, not merchandise, of British subjects dying abroad, but domiciled in Canada; books, pictures, family plate or furniture, personal effects and heirlooms left by bequest.	United Kingdom.	....	19,147	....	19,147
	Australia.........	....	100	....	100
	Bermuda.........	....	100	....	100
	B. S. Africa......	....	85	....	85
	B. India.........	....	250	....	250
	Newfoundland....	....	30	....	30
	Belgium..........	....	30	....	30
	Denmark.........	....	95	....	95
	Dutch E. Indies..	....	100	....	100
	France...........	....	1,340	....	1,340
	Germany.........	....	591	....	591
	Hawaii...........	....	50	....	50
	Italy.............	....	566	....	566
	Japan............	....	15	....	15
	Norway..........	....	40	....	40
	United States....	....	16,568	....	16,568
	Total........	....	39,107	....	39,107
Articles and other goods, the growth, produce or manufacture of Canada, returned within five years after having been exported.	United Kingdom.	....	126,005	....	126,005
	Australia.........	....	2,086	....	2,086
	Bermuda.........	....	189	....	189
	B. India.........	....	100	....	100
	B. W. Indies.....	....	9,223	·	9,223
	Br. Straits Settlements.....	....	330	....	330
	Hong Kong......	....	25	....	25

SESSIONAL PAPER No. 11

No. 1.—General Statement of Imports—*Continued.*

Articles Imported.	Countries.	Imported.		Entered for Home Consumption.	
		Quantity.	Value.	Quantity.	Value.
FREE GOODS— MISCELLANEOUS ARTICLES—*Con.*			$		$
Articles Canadian, returned, etc.—*Con.*	Newfoundland....	....	11,156	....	11,156
	Alaska...........	....	6,191	....	6,191
	Aust.-Hungary....	....	55	....	55
	France...........	....	580	....	580
	Germany.........	....	3,700	....	3,700
	Hawaii...........	....	700	....	700
	Italy.............	....	651	....	651
	Miquelon and St. Pierre......	....	110	....	110
	Sweden..........	....	62	....	62
	Switzerland......	....	247	....	247
	United States....	....	557,242	....	557,242
	Total........	....	718,652	....	718,652
Articles brought into Canada temporarily and for a period not exceeding three months for the purpose of exhibition or of competition for prizes offered by any agricultural or other association.	United Kingdom.	....	98,249	....	....
	B. Guiana.......	....	185	....	....
	B. W. Indies.....	....	839	....	....
	United States....	....	316,389	....	....
	Total........	....	415,662	....	....
Articles for the use of the Governor General	United Kingdom.	....	7,712	....	7,712
	Holland..........	....	35	....	35
	United States....	....	2,127	....	2,127
	Total........	....	9,874	....	9,874
Articles for the personal or official use of Consuls General who are natives or citizens of the Country they represent, and who are not engaged in any other business or profession.	United Kingdom.	....	871	....	871
	Alaska...........	....	10	....	10
	Belgium..........	....	10	....	10
	Denmark.........	....	20	....	20
	France...........	....	85	....	101
	Germany.........	....	105	....	105
	Italy.............	....	808	....	808
	Japan............	....	57	....	57
	Spain............	....	3	....	3
	Switzerland......	....	14	....	14
	United States....	....	5,766	....	5,766
	Total........	....	7,749	....	7,765
Articles for the use of the Army and Navy, viz.: Arms, military stores, munitions of war, and other articles the property of the Imperial Government and to remain the property of such Government; articles consigned direct to officers and men of His Majesty's Imperial Navy, for their own personal use or consumption, on board their own ships.	United Kingdom.	....	465,740	....	465,448
	Bermuda.........	....	16,500	....	16,500
	Newfoundland....	....	1,445	....	1,445
	United States....	....	2,721,610	....	2,727,305
	Total........	....	3,205,295	....	3,210,698
Articles ex-warehoused for ship's stores....	United Kingdom.	....	....	....	31,577
	Australia........	....	....	....	2,923
	Bermuda.........	....	....	....	9
	B. Guiana.......	....	....	....	3
	B. India.........	....	....	....	10
	B. W. Indies.....	....	....	....	227
	Malta...........	....	....	....	13
	Newfoundland....	....	....	....	23
	New Zealand.....	....	....	....	4,780
	Belgium..........	....	....	....	1,151
	China...........	....	....	....	343
	Cuba............	....	....	....	505

6 GEORGE V, A. 1916

No. 1.—General Statement of Imports—*Continued.*

Articles Imported.	Countries.	Imported.		Entered for Home Consumption.	
		Quantity.	Value.	Quantity.	Value.
FREE GOODS— MISCELLANEOUS ATRICLES—*Con.*			$		$
Articles ex-warehoused for ship's stores— *Con.*	Egypt and Soudan	....	....	....	10
	France	....	....	....	1,802
	Germany	....	....	....	22
	Hawaii	....	....	....	43
	Holland	....	....	....	182
	Italy	....	....	....	26
	Japan	....	....	....	150
	Norway	....	....	....	25
	Philippines	....	....	....	51
	Portugal	....	....	....	36
	Spain	....	....	....	104
	United States	....	....	....	923,158
	Total	....	....	....	967,173
Articles for the Anglo-American Telegraph Company.	United States	....	16	....	16
Articles presented from abroad in recognition of the saving of human life.	United States	....	1,739	....	1,739
Bacteriological products or serum for sub-cutaneous injection.	United Kingdom	....	6,600	....	6,600
	France	....	4,253	....	4,253
	Germany	....	49	....	49
	Italy	....	678	....	678
	United States	....	95,988	....	95,988
	Total	....	107,568	....	107,568
Barrels or packages of Canadian manufacture which have been exported filled with Canadian products, when returned, or exported empty and returned filled with foreign products.	United Kingdom	....	22,702	....	22,702
	B. W. Indies	....	18	....	18
	Newfoundland	....	8,360	....	8,360
	Miquelon and St. Pierre	....	342	....	342
	United States	....	181,803	....	181,803
	Total	....	213,225	....	213,225
Bird skins and skins of animals not native to Canada, and fish skins for taxidermic purposes, not further manufactured than prepared for preservation.	Newfoundland	....	50	....	50
	United States	....	673	....	673
	Total	....	723	....	723
Botanical, entomological and mineralogical specimens.	United Kingdom	....	287	....	287
	Australia	....	172	....	172
	B. India	....	54	....	54
	Newfoundland	....	8	....	8
	France	....	230	....	230
	Holland	....	14	....	14
	Turkey	....	2	....	2
	United States	....	1,509	....	1,509
	Total	....	2,276	....	2,276
Cabinets of coins, collections of medals and collections of postage stamps.	United Kingdom	....	487	....	487
	Belgium	....	95	....	95
	United States	....	1,995	....	1,995
	Total	....	2,577	....	2,577
Collections of antiquities when imported for or by public museums, public libraries, universities, colleges or schools, and which are to be placed in such institutions.	United Kingdom	....	5,038	....	5,038
	Newfoundland	....	40	....	40
	United States	....	816	....	816
	Total	....	5,894	....	5,894

No. 1.—General Statement of Imports—*Continued.*

Articles Imported.	Countries.	Imported.		Entered for Home Consumption.	
		Quantity.	Value.	Quantity.	Value.
FREE GOODS— MISCELLANEOUS ARTICLES—*Con.*			$		$
Clothing and books, donations of, for charitable purposes.	United Kingdom	....	4,993	....	4,993
	Bermuda	....	10	....	10
	B. S. Africa	....	3	....	3
	B. India	....	25	....	25
	B. W. Indies	....	15	....	15
	Hong Kong	....	5	....	5
	Newfoundland	....	123	....	123
	China	....	15	....	15
	Denmark	....	10	....	10
	France	....	849	....	849
	Germany	....	70	....	70
	Greece	....	2	....	2
	Holland	....	10	....	10
	Italy	....	3	....	3
	Switzerland	....	25	....	25
	United States	....	59,890	....	59,890
	Total	....	66,048	....	66,048
Casual donations from abroad sent by friends, and not being advertising matter, tobacco, articles containing spirits or merchandise for sale—when the duty otherwise payable thereon does not exceed fifty cents in any one case—under regulations by the Minister of Customs.	United Kingdom	....	65	....	65
	United States	....	349	....	349
	Total	....	414	....	414
		Lb.		Lb.	
Coffee, green, imported direct from the country of growth and production or purchased in bond in the United Kingdom. (To August 22nd, See Dutiable Goods).	United Kingdom	591,160	92,837	591,160	92,837
	Aden	83,920	14,531	83,920	14,531
	B. W. Indies	505,496	64,799	505,496	64,799
	Brazil	3,508,892	395,429	3,508,892	395,429
	Costa Rica	91,621	15,026	91,621	15,026
	Dutch E. Indies	126,416	21,126	126,416	21,126
	Guatemala	274,715	45,545	274,715	45,545
	Hawaii	43,562	7,370	43,562	7,370
	Mexico	424,014	64,561	424,014	64,561
	Salvador	45,813	6,789	45,813	6,789
	Turkey	25,167	4,255	25,167	4,255
	U.S. of Colombia	763,316	114,407	763,316	114,407
	Venezuela	352,702	46,762	352,702	46,762
	Total	6,836,794	893,437	6,836,794	893,437
Ice	Alaska	....	2,411	....	2,411
	United States	....	15,150	....	15,150
	Total	....	17,561	....	17,561
Models of inventions and other improvements in the Arts, but no article shall be deemed a model which can be fitted for use.	United Kingdom	....	6,289	....	6,289
	France	....	139	....	139
	Germany	....	10	....	10
	United States	....	27,738	....	27,738
	Total	....	34,176	....	34,176
Paintings in oil or water colours, and pastels, valued at not less than twenty dollars each: paintings and sculptures by artists domiciled in Canada but residing temporarily abroad for purposes of study, under regulations by the Minister of Customs.	United Kingdom	....	173,401	....	173,401
	Belgium	....	13,018	....	13,018
	France	....	16,967	....	16,967
	Germany	....	807	....	807
	Holland	....	3,789	....	3,789
	Italy	....	29,471	....	29,471
	Norway	....	400	....	400
	Switzerland	....	1,938	....	1,938
	United States	....	213,190	....	213,190
	Total	....	452,981	....	452,981

6 GEORGE V, A. 1916

No. 1.—General Statement of Imports—*Continued.*

Articles Imported.	Countries.	Imported.		Entered for Home Consumption.	
		Quantity.	Value.	Quantity.	Value.
FREE GOODS— MISCELLANEOUS ARTICLES—*Con.*			$		$
Passover bread.........................	United States....	....	52,951	....	52,951
Photographs, press, for use only as news-paper pictures.	United States....	....	125	....	125
Settler's effects.........................	United Kingdom.	....	2,467,701	....	2,467,101
	Australia.........	....	1,435	....	1,435
	Bermuda.........	....	1,540	....	1,540
	B. E. Africa.....	....	25	....	25
	B. S. Africa......	....	397	....	397
	B. India.........	....	3,189	....	3,189
	B. W. Indies.....	....	2,820	....	2,820
	Gibraltar........	....	150	....	150
	Hong Kong......	....	660	....	660
	Newfoundland...	....	8,794	....	8,794
	New Zealand....	....	715	....	715
	Alaska..........	....	490	....	490
	Aust.-Hungary....	....	765	....	765
	Belgium.........	....	23,667	....	23,667
	China...........	....	2,180	....	2,180
	Cuba............	....	1,650	....	1,650
	Denmark.........	....	2,370	....	2,370
	France..........	....	88,001	....	88,001
	Germany.........	....	13,237	....	13,237
	Greece..........	....	50	....	50
	Greenland and Iceland....	....	200	....	200
	Hawaii..........	....	1,275	....—...	1,275
	Holland.........	....	17,680	....	17,680
	Italy............	....	1,150	....	1,150
	Japan...........	....	5,955	....	5,955
	Miquelon and St. Pierre......	....	25	....	25
	Norway.........	....	25	....	25
	Peru............	....	175	....	175
	Philippines.......	....	60	....	60
	Roumania....:...	.	185	....	185
	Russia..........	....	585	....	585
	Servia..........	....	140	....	140
	Sweden.........	....	40	....	40
	Switzerland......	....	2,550	....	2,550
	Turkey.........	..—.....	1,000	....	1,000
	United States....	....	5,213,211	....	5,213,211
	Total........	....	7,864,092	....	7,864,092
Specimens, models and wall diagrams for illustrations of natural history for universities and public museums..............	United Kingdom.	....	852	....	852
	United States....	....	6,232	....	6,232
	Total........	....	7,084	....	7,084
Menageries, horses, cattle, carriages and harness of	Australia........	....	845	....	845
	New Zealand....	....	100	....	100
	United States....	....	1,067,351	......—..	1,696
	Total........	....	1,068,296	....	2,641
Vaccine and ivory vaccine points..........	United Kingdom.	....	133	....	133
	France..........	....	387	....	387
	United States....	....	12,951	....	12,951
	Total........	....	13,471	....	13,471

SESSIONAL PAPER No. 11

No. 1.—General Statement of Imports—*Continued*.

Articles Imported.	Countries.	Imported.		Entered for Home Consumption.	
		Quantity.	Value.	Quantity.	Value.
FREE GOODS— MISCELLANEOUS ARTICLES—*Con.*			$		$
Works of Art in bronze cast from models made in Canada and designed by sculptors domiciled therein.	Belgium.........	....	3,949	....	3,949
	France..........	....	14,513	....	14,513
	United States...	....	3,638	....	3,638
	Total........	....	22,100	....	22,100
		Lb.		Lb.	
Tea of Ceylon, black, imported direct or purchased in bond in the United Kingdom	United Kingdom.	8,766,329	1,810,747	8,766,329	1,810,747
	B. E. Indies, other	6,516,078	1,188,687	6,516,078	1,188,687
	Total........	15,282,407	2,999,434	15,282,407	2,999,434
Tea of Ceylon, green, imported direct or purchased in bond in the United Kingdom	United Kingdom.	128,651	27,433	128,651	27,433
	B. E. Indies, other	1,290,407	257,711	1,290,407	257,711
	Total........	1,419,058	285,144	1,419,058	285,144
Tea of China, black, imported direct or purchased in bond in the United Kingdom.	United Kingdom.	351,358	67,323	351,358	67,323
	Hong Kong.......	272,798	39,190	272,798	39,190
	China............	1,382,798	163,003	1,382,798	163,003
	Total........	2,006,954	269,516	2,006,954	269,516
Tea of China, green, imported direct or purchased in bond in the United Kingdom..	United Kingdom.	56,605	9,220	56,605	9,220
	Hong Kong.......	5,196	720	5,196	720
	China............	1,058,686	133,629	1,058,686	133,629
	Total........	1,120,487	143,569	1,120,487	143,569
Tea of India, black, imported direct or purchased in bond in the United Kingdom..	United Kingdom.	3,926,985	770,143	3,926,985	770,143
	B. India..........	11,341,249	1,926,616	11,341,249	1,926,616
	Total........	15,268,234	2,696,759	15,268,234	2,696,759
Tea of India, green, imported direct or purchased in bond in the United Kingdom..	United Kingdom.	248,038	47,261	248,038	47,261
	B. India..........	43,111	7,535	43,111	7,535
	Total........	291,149	54,796	291,149	54,796
Tea, of Japan, green, imported direct or purchased in bond in the United Kingdom..	United Kingdom.	1,200	351	1,200	351
	Japan............	4,236,771	718,823	4,236,771	718,823
	Total........	4,237,971	719,174	4,237,971	719,174
Tea, of other countries, black, imported direct or purchased in bond in the United Kingdom.............................	United Kingdom.	78,583	15,124	78,583	15,124
	B. W. Indies......	25	6	25	6
	Dutch E. Indies..	325,204	55,949	325,204	55,949
	Japan............	209,836	34,111	209,836	34,111
	Total........	613,648	105,190	613,648	105,190
Tea of other countries, green, imported direct or purchased in bond in the United Kingdom.	Dutch E. Indies..	6,552	1,097	6,552	1,097
Coins, British and Canadian and foreign gold coins.	United Kingdom.	....	2,612	....	2,612
	Newfoundland....	....	2,360	....	2,360
	United States....	....	117,050,052	....	117,050,052
	Total........	....	117,055,024	....	117,055,024

6 GEORGE V, A. 1916

No. 1.—General Statement of Imports—*Continued.*

Articles Imported.	Countries.	Imported.		Entered for Home Consumption.	
		Quantity.	Value.	Quantity.	Value.
FREE GOODS— MICSELLANEOUS ARTICLES—*Con.*			$		$
Gold bullion in bars, blocks, ingots, drops, sheets or plates, unmanufactured.	United Kingdom	....	7	....	7
	Alaska	....	3,549	....	3,549
	United States	....	14,424,816	....	14,424,816
	Total	....	14,428,372	....	14,428,372
Silver bullion in bars blocks, ingots, drops sheets or plates, unmanufactured.	United Kingdom	....	43	....	43
	United States	....	509,553	....	509,553
	Total	....	509,596	....	509,596
Rifles and cartridges for home guard	United States	....	67,942	....	67,942
Other free articles	United Kingdom	....	149,989	....	149,989
	B. India	....	124	....	124
	France	....	1,958	....	1,958
	Germany	....	951	....	951
	United States	....	22,051	....	22,051
	Total	....	175,073	....	175,073
	Total, free goods	....	310,493,800	....	307,647,109

No. 1.—GENERAL STATEMENT OF IMPORTS—*Concluded*—RECAPITULATION.

Totals	Provinces	Imported Value	General Tariff Value	General Tariff Duty	Preferential Tariff Value	Preferential Tariff Duty	Treaty Rates Value	Treaty Rates Duty	Total Value	Total Duty
Dutiable goods	Ontario	125,407,933	96,124,149	26,841,935 44	23,938,317	5,212,307 19	5,278,663	1,164,518 25	125,341,129	33,218,760 88
	Quebec	117,304,436	48,479,013	15,884,316 99	25,784,901	5,953,125 83	4,586,874	1,081,622 33	78,850,788	22,919,065 15
	Nova Scotia	9,287,039	4,893,895	2,016,992 25	4,123,372	882,977 95	136,828	30,035 00	9,154,095	2,930,005 20
	New Brunswick	6,258,839	4,417,506	1,799,567 93	1,403,751	315,381 68	205,160	47,821 07	6,026,417	2,162,770 68
	Manitoba	22,620,945	16,160,936	4,994,105 74	5,695,594	1,226,714 12	856,513	192,769 36	22,713,043	6,413,589 22
	B. Columbia	24,689,700	16,949,294	5,635,095 03	6,678,332	1,595,236 84	626,733	142,767 94	24,254,359	7,373,099 81
	P. E. Island	432,254	255,978	121,250 50	168,517	37,350 65	7,384	1,624 54	431,879	160,225 69
	Alberta	7,727,442	6,299,699	2,161,678 56	1,246,542	276,766 97	215,150	46,493 24	7,761,391	2,484,938 77
	Saskatchewan	4,562,563	4,164,542	1,265,050 06	388,372	84,490 91	29,935	6,804 40	4,582,849	1,356,345 37
	Yukon	585,002	581,849	160,782 60	14,183	3,213 38	5,272	724 89	601,304	164,720 87
	Territories			1,126 17						1,126 17
Prepaid postal packages		74,941	74,941	21,262 46					74,941	21,262 46
Totals		318,951,094	198,401,802	60,903,163 73	69,441,881	15,587,565 52	11,948,512	2,715,181 02	279,792,195	79,205,910 27
Free goods	Ontario	220,357,075							219,352,756	
	Quebec	51,660,580							51,137,848	
	Nova Scotia	7,040,747							7,103,210	
	New Brunswick	6,724,530							6,710,291	
	Manitoba	7,236,702							6,735,475	
	B. Columbia	11,533,380							10,722,476	
	P. E. Island	501,588							498,588	
	Alberta	2,225,853							2,191,665	
	Saskatchewan	2,987,854							2,959,319	
	Yukon	235,491							235,491	
		310,493,800							307,647,109	
Grand totals	Ontario	345,765,008	96,124,149	26,841,935 44	23,938,317	5,212,307 19	5,278,663	1,164,518 25	344,693,885	33,218,760 88
	Quebec	168,965,016	48,479,013	15,884,316 99	25,784,901	5,953,125 83	4,586,874	1,081,622 33	129,988,636	22,919,065 15
	Nova Scotia	16,327,786	4,893,895	2,016,992 25	4,123,372	882,977 95	136,828	30,035 00	16,237,305	2,930,005 20
	New Brunswick	12,983,369	4,417,506	1,799,567 93	1,403,751	315,381 68	205,160	47,821 07	12,736,708	2,162,770 68
	Manitoba	29,847,647	16,160,936	4,994,105 74	5,695,594	1,226,714 12	856,513	192,769 36	29,448,518	6,413,589 22
	B. Columbia	36,223,080	16,949,294	5,635,095 03	6,678,332	1,595,236 84	626,733	142,767 94	34,976,835	7,373,099 81
	P. E. Island	933,842	255,978	121,250 50	168,517	37,350 65	7,384	1,624 54	930,467	160,225 69
	Alberta	9,953,295	6,299,699	2,161,678 56	1,246,542	276,766 97	215,150	46,493 24	9,953,046	2,484,938 77
	Saskatchewan	7,550,417	4,164,542	1,265,050 06	388,372	84,490 91	29,935	6,804 40	7,542,168	1,356,345 37
	Yukon	820,493	581,849	160,782 60	14,183	3,213 38	5,272	724 89	836,795	164,720 87
	Territories			1,126 17						1,126 17
Prepaid postal packages		74,941	74,941	21,262 46					74,941	21,262 46
Grand total		629,444,894	198,401,802	60,903,163 73	69,441,881	15,587,565 52	11,948,512	2,715,181 02	587,439,304	79,205,910 27

6 GEORGE V, A. 1916

No. 2.—Abstract by Countries

Number.	Countries.	IMPORTS.			General Tariff.	
		Dutiable.	Free.	Total.		
		Value.	Value.	Value.	Value.	Duty.
		$	$	$	$	$ cts.
1	United Kingdom	67,867,733	22,490,554	90,358,287	6,788,775	5,453,340 38
2	Aden	3,437	14,531	17,968	3,437	535 95
3	Bermuda	51	23,863	23,914	51	20 30
4	British East Africa	7,558	15,169	22,727	6,628	839 38
5	" South Africa	7,668	307,467	315,135	301	312 50
6	" India	829,265	3,307,137	4,136,402	68,955	8,405 30
7	" Straits Settlements	206,370	788,232	994,602	6,241	1,405 82
8	" East Indies, other	62,647	1,622,417	1,685,064	17,016	4,082 07
9	" Guiana	2,909,514	13,601	2,923,115	43,868	248,984 67
10	" Honduras		552,450	552,450		
11	" West Indies	4,267,015	1,772,580	6,039,595	54,075	87,804 51
12	" Oceania: Australia and Tasmania	157,484	227,990	385,474	183,641	50,960 56
13	" Oceania: New Zealand	1,298,969	2,607,493	3,906,462	87,571	14,261 27
14	" Oceania: All other	1,715	7,709	9,424	1,715	91 50
15	Fiji Islands	1,996,924		1,996,924		
16	Gibraltar		150	150		
17	Hong Kong	651,959	616,801	1,268,760	603,057	291,346 67
18	Malta	821		821	858	1,350 85
19	Newfoundland	14,767	1,230,913	1,245,680	14,183	3,486 54
	Total British Empire	80,283,897	35,599,057	115,882,954	7,880,372	6,167,228 27
20	Alaska	109,053	21,073	130,126	20,768	3,851 86
21	Argentina	10,226	3,354,561	3,364,787	1,532	283 18
22	Austria-Hungary	581,670	31,501	613,171	349,762	96,742 62
23	Azores and Madeira Islands	2,089		2,089	1,865	645,44
24	Belgium	1,204,517	651,050	1,855,567	1,050,777	224,621 24
25	Brazil	728,180	425,797	1,153,977	723,754	235,694 59
26	Bulgaria	1,725		1,725	1,725	269 50
27	Cen.Am. States: Costa Rica	2,407	15,026	17,433	453	95 60
28	" " Guatemala	38,722	45,591	84,313	46,558	12,812 43
29	" " Salvador	9,650	6,789	16,439	3,600	856 08
30	Chili	190		190	190	9 20
31	China	311,868	813,113	1,124,981	228,927	79,177 50
32	Cuba	1,520,619	183,585	1,704,204	1,384,407	770,799 00
33	Denmark	10,403	33,729	44,132	10,398	2,106 14
34	Danish West Indies	117,687		117,687	115,469	75,626 31
35	Dutch East Indies	47,000	81,589	128,589	116,153	40,184 18
36	" Guiana	203,898		203,898	186,376	72,217 62
37	Ecuador	1,155		1,155	1,155	404 25
38	Egypt and Soudan	20,845	8,820	29,665	21,652	27,825 98
39	France	6,995,425	1,256,185	8,251,610	3,539,598	2,099,784 48
40	French Africa	3,216	5,478	8,694	1,899	876 17
41	Germany	3,760,566	1,149,289	4,909,855	3,887,906	1,089,038 74
42	German Africa		113,305	113,305		
43	Greece	414,173	1,958	416,131	415,953	60,827 80
44	Greenland, Iceland, etc		208	208		
45	Hawaii	22,106	9,395	31,501	23,217	9,366 92
46	Holland	1,335,815	589,013	1,924,828	1,206,806	2,271,650 17
47	Italy	1,090,291	417,257	1,507,548	734,251	198,853 73
48	Japan	1,331,297	1,481,323	2,812,620	660,811	198,633 45
49	Kongo Free State		12,952	12,952		
50	Korea	75		75	75	22 50
51	Madagascar	138	4,122	4,260	203	53 30
52	Mexico	58,497	1,267,736	1,326,233	52,055	12,291 12
53	Miquelon and St. Pierre Islands	40,264	2,022	42,286	1,260	732 41
54	Morocco		89	89		
55	Norway	319,931	68,878	388,809	112,045	31,135 84
56	Peru	1,359,940	86,696	1,446,636	1,407,350	395,404 70

DUTIABLE AND FREE.

				ENTERED FOR CONSUMPTION.				
Preferential Tariff.		Treaty Rates.		Total Dutiable.	Total Free.	Grand Total.		Number.
Value.	Duty.	Value.	Duty.	Value.	Value.	Value.	Duty.	
$	$ cts.	$	$ cts.	$	$	$	$ cts.	
58,170,806	12,299,501 61	3,051,676	694,692 19	68,011,257	22,149,524	90,160,781	18,447,534 18	1
				3,437	14,531	17,968	535 95	2
				51	23,872	23,923	20 30	3
1,719	171 90			8,347	15,169	23,516	1,011 28	4
7,119	714 10			7,420	307,467	314,887	1,026 60	5
757,745	66,167 91			826,700	3,307,147	4,133,847	74,573 21	6
196,447	44,605 34			202,688	573,028	775,716	46,011 16	7
45,975	13,930 18			62,991	1,574,994	1,637,985	18,012 25	8
2,936,246	824,595 16	1	0 23	2,980,115	13,419	2,993,534	1,073,580 06	9
					497,786	497,786		10
4,336,684	1,150,311 78	5	1 13	4,390,764	1,771,574	6,162,338	1,238,117 42	11
		7,679	1,918 00	191,320	220,885	412,205	52,878 56	12
1,208,772	150,679 40			1,296,343	2,612,273	3,908,616	164,940 67	13
				1,715	7,709	9,424	91 50	14
1,780,368	634,705 27			1,780,368		1,780,368	634,705 27	15
					150	150		16
		28,717	7,904 90	631,774	616,801	1,248,575	299,251 57	17
		78	22 85	936	13	949	1,373 70	18
		41	5 16	14,224	1,230,936	1,245,160	3,491 70	19
69,441,881	15,185,382 65	3,088,197	704,544 46	80,410,450	34,937,278	115,347,728	22,057,155 38	
				20,768	21,073	41,841	3,851 86	20
		8,694	2,173 50	10,226	3,354,561	3,364,787	2,456 68	21
		260,919	67,624 90	610,681	31,501	642,182	164,367 52	22
				1,865		1,865	645 44	23
		173,042	41,498 22	1,223,819	652,144	1,875,963	266,119 46	24
				723,754	425,797	1,149,551	235,694 59	25
				1,725		1,725	269 50	26
				453	15,026	15,479	95 60	27
				46,558	45,591	92,149	12,812 43	28
				3,600	6,789	10,389	856 08	29
				190		190	9 20	30
				228,927	813,456	1,042,383	79,177 50	31
		217	49 63	1,384,407	232,884	1,617,291	770,799 00	32
				10,615	33,729	44,344	2,155 77	33
				115,469		115,469	75,626 31	34
				116,153	81,589	197,742	40,184 18	35
				180,376		186,376	72,217 62	36
				1,155		1,155	404 25	37
				21,652	8,830	30,482	27,825 98	38
		3,651,585	800,495 98	7,191,183	1,258,003	8,449,186	2,900,280 46	39
		984	295 75	2,883	5,478	8,361	1,171 92	40
				3,887,906	1,199,080	5,086,986	1,089,038 74	41
					113,305	113,305		42
				415,953	1,958	417,911	60,827 80	43
					208	208		44
		22,699	5,641 68	23,217	9,438	32,655	9,366 92	45
		321,265	80,327 60	1,229,505	539,751	1,769,256	2,277,291 85	46
		641,181	161,831 70	1,055,516	417,283	1,472,799	279,181 33	47
				1,301,992	1,481,473	2,783,465	360,465 15	48
					12,952	12,952		49
				75		75	22 50	50
				203	4,122	4,325	53 30	51
				52,055	1,177,922	1,229,977	12,291 12	52
		962	254 97	2,222	2,022	4,244	987 38	53
					89	89		54
		204,699	75,969 52	316,744	68,903	385,647	107,105 36	55
				1,407,350	86,696	1,494,046	395,404 70	56

6 GEORGE V, A. 1916

No. 2.—Abstract by Countries

Number.	Countries.	Imports.			General Tariff.	
		Dutiable.	Free.	Total.		
		Value.	Value.	Value.	Value.	Duty.
		$	$	$	$	$ cts.
57	Persia	6,015	509	6,524	6,015	2,104 05
58	Philippines	1,399	3,976	5,375	2,177	6,995 35
59	Portugal	200,072	19,177	219,249	196,395	87,207 21
60	Roumania	4,379	185	4,564	6,960	1,694 13
61	Russia	61,013	42,941	103,954	61,868	22,075 72
62	San Domingo	3,464,512	....	3,464,512	3,193,796	1,103,452 42
63	Servia	....	140	140	....	....
64	Siam	494	12,178	12,672	494	148,75
65	Spain	902,908	76,097	979,005	477,561	81,864 42
66	Sweden	412,153	134,547	546,700	347,979	86,731 20
67	Switzerland	3,943,913	58,869	4,002,782	833,960	195,230 79
68	Turkey	279,119	16,378	295,497	306,849	57,941 05
69	Uruguay	1,415	11,347	12,762	1,434	391 62
70	U. S. of Colombia	67,963	114,425	182,388	67,657	14,590 68
71	United States	207,614,812	262,107,254	469,722,066	168,658,299	42,335,574 74
72	Venezuela	53,392	158,590	211,982	51,036	11,620 05
	Total other countries	238,667,197	274,894,743	513,561,940	190,521,430	52,020,516 23
	Duty on articles lower than home trade price	....	....	....	....	68,296 47
	Additional duties	....	....	....	....	410,832 60
	War tax	....	....	....	....	2,236,290 16
	Grand total	318,951,094	310,493,800	629,444,894	198,401,802	60,903,163 73

SESSIONAL PAPER No. 11

DUTIABLE AND FREE—*Conclu*ded.

Preferential Tariff.		Treaty Rates.		Total Dutiable.	Total Free.	Grand Total.		Number.
Value.	Duty.	Value.	Duty.	Value.	Value.	Value.	Duty.	
$	$ cts.	$	$ cts.	$	$	$	$ cts.	
				6,015	509	6,524	2,104 05	57
				2,177	4,027	6,204	6,995 35	58
				196,395	19,213	215,608	87,207 21	59
				6,960	185	7,145	1,694 13	60
		646	148 05	62,514	42,941	105,455	22,223 77	61
				3,193,796		-3,193,796	1,103,452 42	62
					140	140		63
				494	12,178	12,672	148 75	64
		423,686	107,748 29	901,247	76,201	977,448	189,612 71	65
		63,309	15,909 04	411,288	134,547	545,835	102,640 24	66
		3,086,427	650,667 73	3,920,387	58,869	3,979,256	845,898 52	67
				306,849	16,378	323,227	57,941 05	68
				1,434	11,347	12,781	391 62	69
				67,657	114,425	182,082	14,590 68	70
				168,658,299	259,958,628	428,616,927	42,335,574 74	71
				51,036	158,590	209,626	11,620 05	72
		8,860,315	2,010,636 56	199,381,745	272,709,831	472,091,576	54,031,152 79	
							68,296 47	
							410,832 60	
	402,182 87						2,638,473 03	
69,441,881	15,587,565 52	11,948,512	2,715,181 02	279,792,195	307,647,109	587,439,304	79,205,910 27	

Entered for Consumption.

6 GEORGE V, A. 1916

No. 3.—GENERAL STATEMENT by Countries of the Total Quantities and Values of Merchandise exported from the Dominion of Canada, distinguishing Canadian Produce and Manufactures from those of Other Countries, during the twelve months ended March 31, 1915.

Articles Exported.	Countries.	GOODS, THE PRODUCE OF CANADA.		GOODS, NOT THE PRODUCE OF CANADA.		TOTAL EXPORTS.	
		Quantity.	Value.	Quantity.	Value.	Quantity.	Value.
THE MINE.		Cwt.	$	Cwt.	$	Cwt.	$
Arsenic................	United States..	32,655	120,242	....	....	32,655	120,242
		Ton.		Ton.		Ton.	
Asbestos.............	Unit'd Kingdom	14,726	513,877	....	....	14,726	513,877
	Aust.-Hungary..	1,514	37,024			1,514	37,024
	Belgium........	1,645	42,780			1,645	42,780
	France.........	1,475	55,259			1,475	55,259
	Germany.......	2,391	74,494			2,391	74,494
	Holland........	460	16,440			460	16,440
	Italy..........	952	39,254			952	39,254
	Japan..........	294	10,606			294	10,606
	United States..	51,447	1,437,653			51,447	1,437,653
	Total......	74,904	2,227,387	....	....	74,904	2,227,387
Asbestos sand........	Unit'd Kingdom	967	12,223	....	....	967	12,223
	B. W. Indies....	30	75			30	75
	Aust.-Hungary..	20	100			20	100
	France.........	22	160			22	160
	Germany.......	114	597			114	597
	Holland........	28	168			28	168
	Japan..........	18	90			18	90
	United States..	18,729	98,314			18,729	98,314
	Total......	19,928	111,727	....	....	19,928	111,727
Coal................	Unit'd Kingdom	28,663	96,834	15	106	28,678	96,940
	Australia......	32,840	125,313			32,840	125,313
	B. S. Africa.....	2,693	8,092			2,693	8,092
	B. E. Indies, other........	1,468	4,404			1,468	4,404
	B. W. Indies....	401	1,365	20	180	421	1,545
	Gibraltar......	657	1,974			657	1,974
	Newfoundland..	169,560	510,962	471	3,604	170,031	514,566
	Alaska.........	52,374	243,231			52,374	243,231
	Argentina......	1,149	3,447			1,149	3,447
	Belgium........	401	1,504			401	1,504
	Brazil.........	1,053	3,159			1,053	3,159
	China..........	1,614	5,994			1,614	5,994
	Cuba...........	486	1,461			486	1,461
	Denmark.......	163	611			163	611
	France.........	4,459	13,932			4,459	13,932
	Hawaii........	7,509	26,262			7,509	26,262
	Holland........	92	276			92	276
	Italy..........	653	2,099			653	2,099
	Mexico........	451	1,579			451	1,579
	Miquelon and St. Pierre....	12,028	36,495			12,028	36,495
	Norway.......	672	2,662			672	2,662
	Panama........	1,031	3,891			1,031	3,891
	Philippines.....	1,502	5,257			1,502	5,257
	Portugal.......	211	633			211	633
	Russia.........	765	2,678			765	2,678
	Spain..........	243	911			243	911
	Sweden........	115	345			115	345
	United States..	1,189,234	3,360,887	88,136	165,274	1,277,370	3,526,161
	Total......	1,512,487	4,466,258	88,642	169,164	1,601,129	4,635,422
Chromite (chromic iron).	United States..	79	878	....	....	79	878

No. 3.—General Statement of Exports—Continued.

Articles Exported.	Countries.	Goods, the Produce of Canada.		Goods, not the Produce of Canada.		Total Exports.	
		Quantity.	Value.	Quantity.	Value.	Quantity.	Value.
THE MINE—Con.		Ton	$	Ton.	$	Ton.	$
Felspar................	Unit'd Kingdom	22	176	....	....	22	176
	United States..	13,627	56,492	....	....	13,627	56,492
	Total.......	13,649	56,668	....	....	13,649	56,668
Gold-bearing quartz, dust, nuggets, etc.	Unit'd Kingdom	....	105,324	....	....	....	105,324
	Germany.........	....	6,831	....	....	....	6,831
	United States..	....	15,294,355	....	2,509	....	15,296,864
	Total.......	....	15,406,510	....	2,509	....	15,409,019
Gypsum or plaster—crude.	United States..	322,680	378,648	....	....	322,680	378,648
Metals, viz—		Lb.		Lb.		Lb.	
Copper, fine, contained in ore, matte, regulus, etc.	Unit'd Kingdom	11,062,501	853,900	....	....	11,062,501	853,900
	United States..	51,614,537	5,319,457	....	....	51,614,537	5,319,457
	Total.......	62,677,038	6,173,357	....	....	62,677,038	6,173,357
Copper, black or coarse, cement copper and copper in pigs.	United States..	9,861,780	1,371,889	....	....	9,861,780	1,371,889
Lead, metallic, contained in ore, etc.	United States..	723,100	12,534	....	....	723,100	12,534
Lead, pig............	China..........	1,007,317	38,016	....	....	1,007,317	38,016
	Japan..........	1,514,982	58,787	....	....	1,514,982	58,787
	United States...	12,203	483	....	....	12,203	483
	Total.......	2,534,502	97,286	....	....	2,534,502	97,286
Nickel, fine, contained in ore, matte or speiss.	Unit'd Kingdom	10,838,477	1,601,251	....	....	10,838,477	1,601,251
	Germany......	179,454	22,866	....	....	179,454	22,866
	United States..	34,394,086	3,439,539	....	....	34,394,086	3,439,539
	Total.......	45,412,017	5,063,656	....	....	45,412,017	5,063,656
Platinum, contained in concentrates or other forms.	United States..	Oz. 46	2,171	Oz. 98	4,656	Oz. 144	6,827
Silver, metallic, contained in ore, concentrates, etc.	Unit'd Kingdom	16,533,652	8,848,064	....	....	16,533,652	8,848,064
	Hong Kong.....	384,774	213,254	....	....	384,774	213,254
	China..........	100,890	50,193	....	....	100,890	50,193
	Germany......	229,261	130,145	....	....	229,261	130,145
	United States..	8,106,728	4,274,734	....	....	8,106,728	4,274,734
	Total.......	25,355,305	13,516,390	....	....	25,355,305	13,516,390
Mica.................		Lb.		Lb.		Lb.	
	Unit'd Kingdom	126,397	31,856	....	....	126,397	31,856
	B. India........	3,774	612	....	....	3,774	612
	France.........	2,360	400	....	....	2,360	400
	Germany......	2,000	650	....	....	2,000	650
	Holland........	1,000	200	....	....	1,000	200
	United States..	717,221	184,082	377	59	717,598	184,141
	Total.......	852,752	217,800	377	59	853,129	217,859

6 GEORGE V, A. 1916

No. 3.—General Statement of Exports—*Continued.*

Articles Exported.	Countries.	Goods, the Produce of Canada.		Goods, not the Produce of Canada.		Total Exports.	
		Quantity.	Value.	Quantity.	Value.	Quantity.	Value.
THE MINE—*Con.*		Cwt.	$	Cwt.	$	Cwt.	$
Mineral pigment, iron	Unit'd Kingdom	9,825	5,940	....	....	9,825	5,940
oxides, ochres, etc.	Newfoundland..	1	2	....	....	1	2
	Belgium........	505	168	....	....	505	168
	Germany.......	5,690	2,231	....	....	5,690	2,231
	Holland........	4,765	1,981	....	....	4,765	1,981
	United States..	11,981	10,422	....	....	11,981	10,422
	Total......	32,767	20,744	....	....	32,767	20,744
		Gal.		Gal.		Gal.	
Mineral water, natural,	Unit'd Kingdom	800	40	....	....	800	40
not in bottles.	United States...	181	42	....	....	181	42
	Total......	981	82	....	....	981	82
Oil—							
Mineral, coal and	Newfoundland..	....	....	9,000	600	9,000	600
kerosene—crude.	United States..	17,120	1,177	192,780	3,616	209,900	4,793
	Total......	17,120	1,177	201,780	4,216	218,900	5,393
Refined...........	Newfoundland..	1,213	228	152,245	11,526	153,458	11,754
	Miquelon and St. Pierre....	43	7	9,919	932	9,962	939
	Total......	1,256	235	162,164	12,458	163,420	12,693
Ores—		Ton.		Ton.		Ton.	
Antimony..........	Unit'd Kingdom	332	18,285	....	....	332	18,285
	United States..	5	1,484	....	....	5	1,484
	Total......	337	19,769			337	19,769
Corundum..........	Unit'd Kingdom	142	14,970	....	....	142	14,970
	Germany.......	74	7,365	....	....	74	7,365
	United States..	717	60,023	....	....	717	60,023
	Total......	933	82,358	....	....	933	82,358
Iron................	United States..	130,496	345,119	....	....	130,496	345,119
Manganese..........	United States..	90	1,950	....	....	90	1,950
Other.............	Unit'd Kingdom	112	113,249	....	....	112	113,249
	France.........	10	21,700	....	....	10	21,700
	Germany.......	54	42,361	....	....	54	42,361
	Holland........	39	68,142	....	....	39	68,142
	United States..	12,549	400,421	....	....	12,549	400,421
	Total......	12,764	645,873	....	....	12,764	645,873
Phosphates..........	United States..	60	180	....	....	60	180
		Cwt.		Cwt.		Cwt.	
Plumbago, crude ore,	Germany.......	556	2,630	....	....	556	2,630
and concentrates.	United States..	9,388	21,490	....	....	9,388	21,490
	Total......	9,944	24,120	....	....	9,944	24,120
		Ton.		Ton.		Ton.	
Pyrites..............	United States..	95,901	393,085	....	....	95,901	393,085

SESSIONAL PAPER No. 11

No. 3.—General Statement of Exports—*Continued.*

Articles Exported.	Countries.	Goods, the Produce of Canada.		Goods, not the Produce of Canada.		Total Exports.	
		Quantity.	Value.	Quantity.	Value.	Quantity.	Value.
THE MINE—*Con.*		Cwt.	$	Cwt.	$	Cwt.	$
Salt................	Unit'dKingdom	15	15	....	....	15	15
	B. W. Indies....	300	112	....	....	300	112
	Newfoundland..	5,104	3,516	38,493	16,943	43,597	20,459
	Belgium........	2	8	....	....	2	8
	France.........	10	6	....	....	10	6
	Miquelon and St. Pierre.....	8	5	....	....	8	5
	United States..	4,080	1,847	16,941	6,703	21,021	8,550
	Total......	9,519	5,509	55,434	23,646	64,953	29,155
		Ton.		Ton.		Ton.	
Sand and gravel.......	United States.	959,039	808,012	....	....	959,039	808,012
Stone— Ornamental, granite, marble, etc., un-wrought.	United States..	95	399	13	420	108	819
Building, freestone, limestone, etc., un-wrought..........	United States..	62,600	45,950	....	....	62,600	45,950
Crushed.............	United States..	28,995	20,080	....	....	28,995	20,080
For manufacture of grindstones, rough.	United States..	54	294			54	294
Other articles of the mine.	Unit'dKingdom	....	3,933	....	....	....	3,933
	Australia......	....	590	....	....	....	590
	Newfoundland..	....	2,048	....	....	....	2,048
	New Zealand...	....	130	....	....	....	130
	Belgium........	....	1,208	....	....	....	1,208
	France.........	....	400	....	....	....	400
	Germany......	....	106	....	....	....	106
	Mexico........	....	349	....	....	....	349
	Miquelon and St. Pierre.....	....	12	....	....	....	12
	United States..	....	93,876	....	108,420	....	202,296
	Total......	....	102,652	....	108,420	....	211,072
THE FISHERIES.		Lb.		Lb.		Lb.	
Codfish, including had-dock, ling, and pol-lock—Fresh.	Unit'd Kingdom	300	9	....	....	300	9
	B. W. Indies,...	200	11	....	....	200	11
	United States..	3,402,657	110,984	13,525	632	3,416,182	111,616
	Total......	3,403,157	111,004	13,525	632	3,416,682	111,636
		Cwt.		Cwt.		Cwt.	
Dry salted.........	Unit'd Kingdom	12,411	54,134	....	....	12,411	54,134
	Bermuda.......	3,057	21,152	....	....	3,057	21,152
	B. S. Africa....	21	133	....	....	21	133
	B. Guiana......	10,239	53,547	187	1,048	10,426	54,595
	B. Honduras....	12	91	....	....	12	91
	B. W. Indies....	103,493	674,807	3,652	22,063	107,145	696,870
	Hong Kong.....	120	150	....	....	120	150
	Newfoundland..	5,826	29,138	....	....	5,826	29,138
	Belgium........	303	1,338	....	....	303	1,338
	Brazil..........	66,798	487,494	133	517	66,931	488,011
	Costa Rica.....	3,299	23,149	....	....	3,299	23,149
	Cuba..........	72,050	502,724	4,283	21,451	76,333	524,175
	Dan. W. Indies.	443	3,583	....	....	443	3,583
	Dutch Guiana..	6,995	35,145	101	495	7,096	35,640
	Ecuador.......	80	570	....	....	80	570
	FrenchW. Indies	45	300	....	....	45	300

6 GEORGE V, A. 1916

No. 3.—General Statement of Exports—*Continued.*

Articles Exported.	Countries.	Goods, the Produce or Canada.		Goods, not the Produce of Canada.		Total Exports.	
		Quantity.	Value.	Quantity.	Value.	Quantity.	Value.
THE FISHERIES—*Con.*		Cwt.	$	Cwt.	$	Cwt.	$
Codfish, dry salted—*Con.*	Hawaii.........	1,629	11,223	....	....	1,629	11,223
	Hayti..........	90	710	....	....	90	710
	Italy..........	52,055	346,595	112	750	52,167	347,345
	Miquelon and St. Pierre.....	1	4	....	....	1	4
	Nicaragua.....	8	55	....	....	8	55
	Panama........	9,216	64,814	505	3,047	9,721	67,861
	Porto Rico....	63,820	429,046	....	....	63,820	429,046
	Portugal.......	2,919	20,242	....	....	2,919	20,242
	U. S. of Colombia..........	610	4,524	....	....	610	4,524
	United States..	244,334	1,357,079	311	1,521	244,645	1,358,600
	Uruguay.......	19	135	....	....	19	135
	Venezuela......	10	80	....	....	10	80.
	Total.......	659,903	4,121,962	9,284	50,892	669,187	4,172,854
Wet salted..........	Unit'd Kingdom	14,360	54,000	....	....	14,360	54,000
	Newfoundland..	4,562	29,686	....	....	4,562	29,686
	United States..	48,295	185,290	2,527	8,057	50,822	193,347
	Total.......	67,217	268,976	2,527	8,057	69,744	277,033
Pickled.............	United States..	34,386	128,910	....	....	34,386	128,910
		Lb.		Lb.		Lb.	
Tongues and sounds..	Bermuda......	690	45			690	45
	B. W. Indies....	310	16	....	....	310	16
	United States..	137,723	30,725	9,735	568	147,458	31,293
	Total.......	138,723	30,786	9,735	568	148,458	31,354
Mackerel—Fresh..............	United States..	3,229,558	156,487	....	....	3,229,558	156,487
		Brl.		Brl.		Brl.	
" Pickled....	Bermuda......	89	1,082	30	268	119	1,350
	B. Guiana......	591	5,524	1	13	592	5,537
	B. W. Indies....	6,092	58,409	197	1,661	6,289	60,070
	Costa Rica,....	16	167	4	37	20	204
	Dan. W.Indies..	11	109	2	17	13	126
	Dutch Guiana..	1	10	....	....	1	10
	Panama........	949	10,817	28	254	977	11,071
	Porto Rico.....	327	2,984	....	....	327	2,984
	U. S. of Colombia.	9	139	10	90	19	229
	United States..	19,691	219,967	163	718	19,854	220,685
	Total.......	27,776	299,208	435	3,058	28,211	302,266
Halibut—Fresh..............	Unit'd Kingdom	Lb. 194,000	14,300	Lb.	....	Lb. 194,000	14,300
	Newfoundland..	4,489	449	....	....	4,489	449
	Miquelon and St. Pierre.....	150	15	....	....	150	15
	United States...	7,071,875	437,148	473,475	23,678	7,545,350	460,826
	Total.......	7,270,514	451,912	473,475	23,678	7,743,989	475,590
Pickled.............	United States..	Brl. 163	2,296	Brl.	....	Brl. 163	2,296

SESSIONAL PAPER No. 11

No. 3.—General Statement of Exports—*Continued.*

Articles Exported.	Countries.	Goods, the Produce of Canada.		Goods, not the Produce of Canada.		Total Exports.	
		Quantity.	Value.	Quantity.	Value.	Quantity.	Value.
THE FISHERIES—*Con.*		Lb.	$	Lb.	$	Lb.	$
Herring—							
Fresh or frozen......	Australia......	250	15	....	....	250	15
	Alaska.........	990,000	13,625	....	....	990,000	13,625
	United States...	29,735,473	492,896	130,000	1,300	29,865,473	494,196
	Total.......	30,725,723	506,536	130,000	1,300	30,855,723	507,836
		Brl.		Brl.		Brl.	
Pickled............	Unit'd Kingdom	30,651	30,656	20	240	30,671	30,896
	Australia......	4	56	....	....	4	56
	Bermuda......	18	91	....	....	18	91
	B. Guiana......	1,258	5,408	159	929	1,417	6,337
	B. W. Indies....	31,910	139,780	99	541	32,009	140,321
	Hong Kong.....	66,362	140,787	....	....	66,362	140,787
	Newfoundland..	36	124			36	124
	Belgium........	261	1,381			261	1,381
	China..........	54,135	116,888			54,135	116,888
	Cuba..........	50	200			50	200
	Dan. W. Indies..	184	905	....	....	184	905
	Japan..........	96,659	201,388	....	....	96,659	201,388
	Korea.........	625	1,250	....	....	625	1,250
	Miquelon and St. Pierre.....	6	32			6	32
	Panama.......	60	269			60	269
	Porto Rico.....	3,326	14,892			3,326	14,892
	U.S. of Colombia..........	3	14	....	....	3	14
	United States..	45,508	167,131	4,686	17,985	50,194	185,116
	Total.......	331,056	821,252	4,964	19,695	336,020	840,947
		Lb.		Lb.		Lb.	
Canned............	Unit'd Kingdom	59,046	8,500	....	....	59,046	8,500
	Bermuda......	9,168	929	1,900	131	11,068	1,060
	B. W. Indies....	50	9	....	....	50	9
	New Zealand...	1,245	80	....	....	1,245	80
	France..........	550,000	43,800	....	....	550,000	43,800
	Miquelon and St. Pierre.....	20	3	....	....	20	3
	United States..	405	17	....	....	405	17
	Total.......	619,934	53,338	1,900	131	621,834	53,469
Smoked............	Unit'd Kingdom	4,950	256	....	....	4,950	256
	Bermuda......	8,685	477	....	....	8,685	477
	B. Guiana.....	8,325	307	....	....	8,325	307
	B. W. Indies....	227,966	7,427	....	....	227,966	7,427
	Newfoundland..	6,125	256	....	....	6,125	256
	Cuba..........	61,750	1,635	....	....	61,750	1,635
	Dutch Guiana..	44,200	1,692	....	....	44,200	1,692
	Miquelon and St. Pierre.....	900	26	....	....	900	26
	Panama.......	18,493	764	....	....	18,493	764
	Porto Rico.....	973	44	....	....	973	44
	United States..	3,811,052	129,079	....	....	3,811,052	129,079
	Total.......	4,193,419	141,963	....	....	4,193,419	141,963
Smelts...............	United States..	7,073,036	427,873	....	....	7,073,036	427,873
Sea fish, other—							
Fresh..............	Unit'd Kingdom	1,800	36	....	....	1,800	36
	B. W. Indies....	1,600	69	....	....	1,600	69
	United States..	1,615,684	81,579	....	....	1,615,684	81,579
	Total.......	1,619,084	81,684	....	....	1,619,084	81,684

6 GEORGE V, A. 1916

No. 3.—GENERAL STATEMENT OF EXPORTS—*Continued.*

Articles Exported.	Countries.	GOODS, THE PRODUCE OF CANADA.		GOODS, NOT THE PRODUCE OF CANADA.		TOTAL EXPORTS.	
		Quantity.	Value.	Quantity.	Value.	Quantity.	Value.
THE FISHERIES—*Con.*		Brl.	$	Brl.	$	Brl.	$
Sea fish, other—*Con.*							
Pickled...............	Unit'd Kingdom	261	979	....	....	261	979
	B. Guiana......	43	181	....	....	43	181
	B. W. Indies....	8,991	44,545	....	....	8,991	44,545
	Costa Rica.....	3	13	....	....	3	13
	Dan. W. Indies.	16	87	....	....	16	· 87
	Denmark......	30	600	....	....	30	600
	Dutch Guiana..	163	870	....	....	163	870
	Panama........	24	127	....	....	24	127
	United States..	2,336	20,656	5	51	2,341	20,707
	Total.....	11,867	68,058	5	51	11,872	68,109
		Lb.		Lb.		Lb.	
Preserved..........	Unit'd Kingdom	115,150	22,968	......	....	115,150	22,968
	Bermuda.......	10,599	712	900	55	11,499	767
	B. W. Indies....	2,216	146	....	....	2,216	146
	Hong Kong.....	195	21	....	....	195	21
	Newfoundland..	31,507	2,205	....	....	31,507	2,205
	Alaska..........	460	33	....	....	460	33
	France..........	50	3	....	....	50	3
	Japan..........	500	45	480	100	980	145
	Miquelon and St. Pierre.....	75	6	....	....	75	6
	United States..	1,566,140	92,145	18,700	2,148	1,584,840	94,293
	Total.......	1,726,892	118,284	20,080	2,303	1,746,972	120,587
Oysters—		Brl.		Brl.		Brl.	
Fresh..............	Unit'd Kingdom	14	194	....	....	14	194
	Bermuda.......	1	6	....	....	1	6
	Newfoundland..	10	59	....	....	10	59
	Miquelon and St. Pierre.....	21	127	....	....	21	127
	United States..	577	6,471	....	....	577	6,471
	Total.......	623	6,875	....	....	623	6,857
		Lb.				Lb.	
Preserved in cans ...	United States..	170	40	....	....	170	40
Lobsters—							
Fresh..............	United States..	5,500,586	849,368	....	....	5,500,586	849,368
Canned..............	Unit'd Kingdom	2,796,102	1,123,691	19,056	-5,955	2,815,158	1,129,646
	Australia.......	18,585	7,530	....	....	18,585	7,530
	Bermuda.......	264	87	....	....	264	87
	B. Guiana..;...	3,035	1,201	....	....	3,035	1,201
	B. W. Indies....	1,450	512	....	....	1,450	512
	Newfoundland..	....	....	1,920	680	1,920	680
	New Zealand...	2,450	815	....	....	2,450	815
	Argentina......	7,876	2,988	....	....	7,876	2,988
	Belgium.......	228,874	93,675	....	....	228,874	93,675
	Cuba...........	360	132	....	....	360	132
	Denmark......	78,875	31,397	....	....	78,875	31,397
	Dutch Guiana..	7	3	....	....	7	3
	France.........	1,396,909	556,317	....	....	1,396,909	556,317
	Germany.......	415,384	173,455	....	....	415,384	173,455
	Holland........	86,040	36,756	....	....	86,040	36,756
	Miquelon and St. Pierre.....	48	23	....	....	48	23
	Norway........	54,546	22,887	....	....	54,546	22,887
	Sweden........	156,318	68,994	....	....	156,318	68,994
	United States...	2,268,838	892,442	....	....	2,268,838	892,442
	Uruguay........	2,780	877	....	....	2,780	877
	Total.......	7,518,741	3,013,782	20,976	6,635	7,539,717	3,020,417

No. 3.—General Statement of Exports—*Continued.*

Articles Exported.	Countries.	Goods, the Produce of Canada.		Goods, not the Produce of Canada.		Total Exports.	
		Quantity.	Value.	Quantity.	Value.	Quantity.	Value.
THE FISHERIES—*Con.*		Brl.	$	Brl.	$	Brl.	$
Bait—fish.............	Newfoundland..	200	425	....	....	200	425
	United States..	34	34	....	....	34	34
	Total......	234	459	....	....	234	459
Clams...............	Unit'd Kingdom	250	1,750	....	....	250	1,750
	Newfoundland..	2	16	....	....	2	16
	Miquelon and St. Pierre.....	36	226			36	226
	United States..	28,860	65,282	....	....	28,860	65,282
	Total......	29,148	67,274	....	....	29,148	67,274
Salmon—		Lb.		Lb.		Lb.	
Fresh..............	Unit'd Kingdom	854,429	92,023	....	....	854,429	92,023
	Australia.......	13,618	1,390	....	....	13,618	1,390
	Bermuda.......	560	56	....	....	560	56
	B. Straits Settelments...	3,427	300	....	....	3,427	300
	Hong Kong.....	605	70	....	....	605	70
	New Zealand...	100	10	....	....	100	10
	France..........	4,926	739	....	....	4,926	739
	Miquelon and St. Pierre.....	3,300	396	....	....	3,300	396
	United States...	4,688,580	292,559	150	15	4,688,730	292,574
	Total......	5,569,545	387,543	150	15	5,569,695	387,558
Smoked.............	Unit'd Kingdom	100	10	....	....	100	10
	Australia.......	100	10	....	....	100	10
	Bermuda.......	30	8	....	....	30	8
	Miquelon and St. Pierre.....	78	14	....	....	78	14
	United States..	1,852	271	....	....	1,852	271
	Total......	2,160	313	....	....	2,160	313
Canned.............	Unit'd Kingdom	25,385,101	4,018,304	....	....	25,385,101	4,018,304
	Australia.......	2,577,494	386,022	....	....	2,577,494	386,022
	Bermuda.......	11,760	1,608	....	....	11,760	1,608
	B. S. Africa.....	13,536	1,006	....	....	13,536	1,006
	B. India........	220,848	13,040	....	....	220,848	13,040
	B. W. Indies....	42,676	5,143	....	....	42,676	5,143
	B. Oceania, other........	55,680	8,008	....	....	55,680	8,008
	B. Straits Settlements...	2,192,784	144,691	....	....	2,192,784	144,691
	Fiji Islands.....	675,056	51,812	....	....	675,056	51,812
	Hong Kong.....	40,320	3,978	....	....	40,320	3,978
	Newfoundland..	1,152	153	....	....	1,152	153
	New Zealand...	1,398,236	172,004	....	....	1,398,236	172,004
	Belgium........	20,000	2,000	....	....	20,000	2,000
	China..........	1,572	89	....	....	1,572	89
	Dutch E. Indies	303,168	16,267	....	....	303,168	16,267
	France..........	1,188,816	88,603	....	....	1,188,816	88,603
	French Oceania.	19,200	1,488	....	....	19,200	1,488
	German Oceania	28,800	4,800	....	....	28,800	4,800
	Miquelon and St. Pierre.....	1,248	130	....	....	1,248	130
	Russia..........	1,220	81	....	....	1,220	81
	Siam...........	201,696	12,280	....	....	201,696	12,280
	United States..	274,745	17,216	....	....	274,745	17,216
	Total......	34,655,108	4,948,723	....	....	34,655,108	4,948,723

6 GEORGE V, A. 1916

No. 3.—General Statement of Exports—*Continued.*

Articles Exported.	Countries.	Goods, the Produce of Canada.		Goods, not the Produce of Canada.		Total Exports.	
		Quantity.	Value.	Quantity.	Value.	Quantity.	Value.
THE FISHERIES—*Con.*		Brl.	$	Brl.	$	Brl.	$
Salmon—Con.							
Pickled............	Unit'd Kingdom	43	471	....	....	43	471
	Bermuda.......	15	158	....	....	15	158
	B. Guiana......	164	1,905	22	270	186	2,175
	B. W. Indies....	659	8,040	13	183	672	8,223
	Hong Kong.....	11,958	36,859	....	....	11,958	36,859
	Newfoundland..	36	468	....	....	36	468
	Belgium........	5	21	....	....	5	21
	Costa Rica.....	3	35	....	....	3	35
	Denmark.......	1,065	23,088	....	....	1,065	23,088
	Dan. W. Indies.	15	135	....	....	15	135
	Dutch Guiana..	167	2,031	....	....	167	2,031
	French Guiana.	15	172	....	....	15	172
	Germany.......	1,127	23,364	....	....	1,127	23,364
	Japan..........	17,066	43,588	....	....	17,066	43,588
	Panama........	221	2,823	....	....	221	2,823
	Sweden........	7	84	....	....	7	84
	United States..	8,126	163,196	71	840	8,197	164,036
	Total......	40,692	306,438	106	1,293	40,798	307,731
		Lb.		Lb.		Lb.	
Dog..............	Japan..........	783,520	9,029	....	....	783,520	9,029
	United States..	5,528,710	44,638	....	....	5,528,710	44,638
	Total......	6,312,230	53,667	....	....	6,312,230	53,667
Salmon or lake trout...	United States..	1,360,875	76,947	....	....	1,360,875	76,947
Fish, all other—							
Fresh..............	United States..	....	1,735,943	....	....	....	1,735,943
		Brl.		Brl.		Brl.	
Pickled............	B. W. Indies....	16	160	....	....	16	160
	Newfoundland..	27	117	....	....	27	117
	Dan. W. Indies.	2	11	....	....	2	11
	United States..	4,396	18,770	....	....	4,396	18,770
	Total......	4,441	19,058	....	....	4,441	19,058
Fish oil—		Gal.		Gal.		Gal.	
Cod..............	Unit'd Kingdom	4,248	1,275	4,000	1,500	8,248	2,775
	B. Guiana......	80	32	....	....	80	32
	B. W. Indies....	905	306	....	....	905	306
	Newfoundland..	8,976	1,707	....	....	8,976	1,707
	United States..	581,928	185,478	28,570	9,440	610,498	194,918
	Total......	596,137	188,798	32,570	10,940	628,707	199,738
Seal..............	Unit'd Kingdom	3,120	312	....	....	3,120	312
	United States..	6,566	2,114	1,335	375	7,901	2,489
	Total......	9,686	2,426	1,335	375	11,021	2,801
Whale..............	Unit'd Kingdom	25,633	8,934	....	....	25,633	8,934
	Norway........	135,720	64,737	....	....	135,720	64,737
	United States..	172,870	70,717	....	....	172,870	70,717
	Total......	334,223	144,388	....	....	334,223	144,388
Other..............	Unit'd Kingdom	35,795	8,572	....	....	35,795	8,572
	China..........	100	80	....	....	100	80
	United States..	14,741	4,342	145	57	14,886	4,399
	Total......	50,636	12,994	145	57	50,781	13,051

SESSIONAL PAPER No. 11

No. 3.—General Statement of Exports—*Continued.*

Articles Exported.	Countries.	Goods, the Produce of Canada.		Goods, not the Produce of Canada.		Total Exports.	
		Quantity.	Value.	Quantity.	Value.	Quantity.	Value.
THE FISHERIES—*Con.*			$		$		$
Furs, or skins, the pro-	Unit'd Kingdom	....	7,528	....	....	....	7,528
duce of fish or marine	Newfoundland..	....	4	....	....	....	4
animals.	United States..	....	5,042	....	189	....	5,231
	Total......	....	12,574	....	189	....	12,763
Other articles of the	Hong Kong.....	....	16,351	....	....	....	16,351
fisheries.	Newfoundland..	....	10	....	....	....	10
	Japan.........	....	1,817	....	44	....	1,861
	United States..	....	50,769	....	1,756	....	52,525
	Total......	....	68,947	....	1,800	....	70,747
THE FOREST.		Brl.		Brl.		Brl.	
Ashes:—							
Pot and pearl........	Unit'd Kingdom	436	22,081	....	....	436	22,081
	France.........	15	553	....	....	15	553
	Miquelon apd						
	St. Pierre.....	1	4	....	......	1	4
	United States..	1	47	116	3,487	117	3,534
	Total......	453	22,685	116	3,487	569	26,172
All other......'......	United States..	....	34,359	....	....	....	34,359
		Cords.		Cords.		Cords.	
Bark for tanning.......	United States..	5,675	42,370	....	....	5,675	42,370
Firewood....	Miquelon and						
	St. Pierre.....	163	519	....	....	163	519
	United States..	23,133	80,257	....	....	23,133	80,257
	Total.......	23,296	80,776	....	....	23,296	80,776
		No.		No.		No.	
Knees and futtocks....	Miquelon and						
	St. Pierre.....	20	33	....	....	20	33
	United States..	11,344	15,844	....	....	11,344	15,844
	Total......	11,364	15,877	....	....	11,364	15,877
		Cords.		Cords.		Cords.	
Lathwood............	United States..	12	42	....	....	12	42
Logs—							
Cedar capable of	United States..	....	471,165	....	....	....	471,165
being made into							
shingle bolts.							
Elm................	Unit'd Kingdom	....	8,132	....	....	.	8,132
	United States...	....	5,626	....	....		5,626
	Total......	....	13,758	....	....		13,758
Hemlock............	United States..	....	63,822	....	....	....	63,822
Oak................	United States..	....	238	....	....		238
Pine................	United States..	....	100,715	....	....	....	100,715

6 GEORGE V, A. 1916

No. 3.—General Statement of Exports—*Continued.*

Articles Exported.	Countries.	Goods, the Produce of Canada.		Goods, not the Produce of Canada.		Total Exports.	
		Quantity.	Value.	Quantity.	Value.	Quantity.	Value.
THE FOREST—*Con.*			$		$		$.
Logs—*Con.*							
Spruce...............	Newfoundland..	....	471	....	....	....	471
	United States..	....	490,738	....	....	....	490,738
	Total......	....	491,209	....	....	....	491,209
Tamarac...........	United States..	....	278	....	....	....	278
All other...........	Unit'd Kingdom	....	17,953	....	....	....	17,953
	United States..	....	99,795	....	....	....	99,795
	Total......	....	117,748	....	....	....	117,748
Lumber—							
Battens..............	Unit'd Kingdom	....	4,379	....	....	....	4,379
		M. Ft.		M. Ft.		M. Ft.	
Basswood...........	Unit'd Kingdom	197	7,195	....	....	197	7,195
	France..........	160	6,344	....	....	160	6,344
	United States..	926	24,514	....	....	926	24,514
	Total......	1,283	38,053	....	....	1,283	38,053
		St. hund.		St. hund.		St. hund.	
Deals, pine.........	Unit'd Kingdom	13,318	1,073,420	....	....	13,318	1,073,420
	B. S. Africa.....	107	10,000	....	....	107	10,000
	Belgium........	37	4,017	.........·.	....	37	4,017
	Holland........	64	5,350	....	....	64	5,350
	United States..	873	55,951	....	....	873	55,951
	Total......	14,399	1,148,738	....	....	14,399	1,148,738
Deals, spruce and other.	Unit'd Kingdom	126,417	5,829,977	....	....	126,417	5,829,977
	B. S. Africa.....	739	36,472	....	....	739	36,472
	Spain..........	356	19,583	....	....	356	19,583
	United States..	10,988	507,388	....	....	10,988	507,388
	Total......	138,500	6,393,420	....	....	138,500	6,393,420
Deal ends..........	Unit'd Kingdom	5,767	241,310	....	....	5,767	241,310
	B. S. Africa.....	514	17,498	....	....	514	17,498
	United States..	301	11,041	....	....	301	·11,041
	Total......	6,582	269,849	....	....	6,582	269,849
		M. Ft.		M. Ft.		M. Ft.	
Hickory.............	United States..	8	355	8	545	16	900
		M.		M.		M.	
Laths..............;	Unit'd Kingdom	777	2,104	....	....	777	2,104
	Australia.......	4,222	6,395	....	....	4,222	6,395
	Bermuda.......	~ 381	1,201	....	....	381	1,201
	B. W. Indies....	191	689	....	....	191	689
	New Zealand...	1,046	2,323	....	....	1,046	2,323
	United States..	629,357	1,785,507	....	....	629,357	1,785,507
	Total......	635,974	1,798,219	....	....	635,974	1,798,219
Pickets.............	Unit'd Kingdom	....	25,153	....	....	....	25,153
	Australia.......	....	5,724	....	....	....	5,724
	B. Oceania, other........	....	80	....	....	....	80
	New Zealand...	....	65	....	....	....	65
	United States..	....	83,100	....	....	....	83,100
	Total......	....	114,122	....	....	....	⁻ 114,122

No. 3.—General Statement of Exports—*Continued.*

Articles Exported.	Countries.	Goods, the Produce of Canada.		Goods, not the Produce of Canada.		Total Exports.	
		Quantity.	Value.	Quantity.	Value.	Quantity.	Value.
THE FOREST—*Con.*		M. Ft.	$	M. Ft.	$	M. Ft.	$
Lumber—*Con.*							
Planks and boards...	Unit'd Kingdom	68,348	1,580,251	....	....	68,348	1,580,251
	Australia.......	8,313	93,305	....	....	8,313	93,305
	Bermuda,......	221	4,137	....	....	221	4,137
	B. S. Africa....	9,997	137,643	....	....	9,997	137,643
	B. Guiana.....	1,782	37,342	....	....	1,782	37,342
	B. India........	345	3,705	6	200	351	3,905
	B. W. Indies....	8,144	165,913	....	....	8,144	165,913
	Fiji Islands.....	861	18,264	....	....	861	18,264
	Hong Kong.....	202	3,102	....	....	202	3,102
	Newfoundland..	181	3,921	1	73	182	3,994
	New Zealand...	872	10,888	....	....	872	10,888
	Alaska..........	5	334	23	644	28	978
	Argentina,.....	19,236	423,445	....	....	19,236	423,445
	Azores and Madeira......	348	6,244	....	....	348	6,244
	Belgium........	217	4,171	....	....	217	4,171
	Canary Islands.	502	13,301	....	....	502	13,301
	Chili...........	988	10,192	....	....	988	10,192
	China..........	152	1,982	....	....	152	1,982
	Cuba...........	17,169	303,097	....	....	17,169	303,097
	Dan. W. Indies.	15	439	....	....	15	439
	France.........	274	7,360	....	....	274	7,360
	French Guiana..	45	1,432	....	....	45	1,432
	French W.Indies	736	21,562	....	....	736	21,562
	Hayti..........	75	2,218	....	....	75	2,218
	Japan..........	1,650	29,046	....	....	1,650	29,046
	Miquelon and St. Pierre.....	343	6,817	....	....	343	6,817
	Peru...........	54	597	....	....	54	597
	Philippines.....	61	549	....	....	61	549
	Porto Rico.....	846	13,904	....	....	846	13,904
	United States..	831,319	15,978,499	424	16,933	831,743	15,995,432
	Uruguay........	2,119	37,785	....	....	2,119	37,785
	Total......	975,420	18,921,445	454	17,850	975,874	18,939,295
Scantling...........	Unit'd Kingdom	25,817	381,730	....	....	25,817	381,730
	B. Guiana.....	5	148	....	....	5	148
	Newfoundland..	2	34	....	....	2	34
	Argentina......	704	12,161	....	....	704	12,161
	Miquelon and St. Pierre....	8	148	....	....	8	148
	United States.	50,029	802,338	....	....	50,029	802,338
	Total......	76,565	1,196,559	....	....	76,565	1,196,559
		M.		M.		M.	
Shingles............	Unit'd Kingdom	782	2,475	....	....	782	2,475
	Australia.......	1	3	....	....	1	3
	Bermuda.......	6	24	....	....	6	24
	B. S. Africa....	45	83	....	....	45	83
	B. W. Indies....	18,019	23,831	....	....	18,019	23,831
	Newfoundland..	816	2,115	....	....	816	2,115
	New Zealand...	5,645	12,534	....	....	5,645	12,534
	Miquelon and St. Pierre....	510	1,330	....	....	510	1,330
	Porto Rico.....	80	210	....	....	80	210
	United States..	1,333,165	2,945,159	....	....	1,333,165	2,945,159
	Total......	1,359,069	2,987,764	....	....	1,359,069	2,987,764
Shooks.............	Unit'd Kingdom	....	85,618	....	50	....	85,668
	Australia......	....	3,895	....	....	....	3,895
	Bermuda......	....	23,328	....	....	....	23,328
	B. W. Indies....	....	2,475	....	....	....	2,475
	Fiji Islands....	....	18,425	....	....	....	18,425

6 GEORGE V, A. 1916

No. 3.—General Statement of Exports—*Continued.*

Articles Exported.	Countries.	Goods, the Produce of Canada.		Goods, not the Produce of Canada.		Total Exports.	
		Quantity.	Value.	Quantity.	Value.	Quantity.	Value.
THE FOREST—*Con.*			$		$		$
Lumber—*Con.*							
Shooks—*Con.*	Newfoundland..	....	711	....	....	....	711
	New Zealand...	....	2,215	....	....	....	2,215
	China..........	....	50	....	....	....	50
	Miquelon and St. Pierre.....	....	130	....	....	....	130
	United States..	....	21,550	....	2,300	....	23,850
	Total......	....	158,397	....	2,350	....	160,747
Staves and headings.	United Kingdom	....	18,106	....	252	....	18,358
	Australia......	....	883	....	....	....	883
	B. Guiana......	....	12	....	....	....	12
	B. W. Indies....	....	9,601	....	....	....	9,601
	Newfoundland..	....	2,498	....	....	....	2,498
	Hawaii........	....	607	....	....	....	607
	Miquelon and St. Pierre...	....	367	....	....	....	367
	United States..	....	45,688	....	963	....	46,651
	Total......	....	77,762	....	- 1,215	....	78,977
All other, n.o.p......	Unit'd Kingdom	....	89,662	....	....	....	89,662
	Newfoundland..	....	....	....	13	....	13
	United States..	....	18,801	....	181	....	18,982
	Total......	....	108,463	....	194	....	108,657
Match blocks..........	Unit'd Kingdom	....	923	....	....	....	923
	United States..	....	4,267	....	....	....	4,267
	Total......	....	5,190	....	....	....	5,190
		No.		No.		No.	
Masts and spars........	B. Guiana......	12	575	....	....	12	575
	B. W. Indies....	56	664	....	....	56	664
	Newfoundland..	6	135	1	190	7	325
	Miquelon and St. Pierre.....	31	507	2	193	33	700
	United States..	63	535	12	300	75	835
	Total......	168	2,416	15	683	183	3,099
Piling................	China..........	....	77	....	....	....	77
	Japan..........	....	1,570	....	....	....	1,570
	United States..	....	170,111	....	....	....	170,111
	Total......	....	171,758	....	....	....	171,758
Poles, hop, hoop, telegraph, and other.	Bermuda.......	....	42	....	....	....	42
	B. W. Indies....	....	1,500	....	....	....	1,500
	United States..	....	160,611	....	404	....	161,015
	Total......	....	162,153	....	404	....	162,557
Posts, sleepers, and railroad ties.	Unit'd Kingdom	....	4,542	....	....	....	4,542
	B. S. Africa.....	....	337	....	....	....	337
	B. India........	....	93,670	....	....	....	93,670
	Newfoundland..	....	131	....	....	....	131
	China..........	....	2	....	....	....	2
	France.........	....	5	....	....	....	5
	Japan..........	....	363	....	....	....	363
	United States..	....	148,812	....	77	....	148,889
	Total:......	....	247,862	....	77	....	247,939

SESSIONAL PAPER No. 11

No. 3.—General Statement of Exports—*Continued.*

Articles Exported.	Countries.	Goods, the Produce of Canada		Goods, not the Produce of Canada		Total Exports.	
		Quantity.	Value.	Quantity.	Value.	Quantity.	Value.
THE FOREST—*Con.*		Cords.	$	_Cords.	$	Cords.	$
Shingle bolts of pine or cedar.	Japan..........	25	75	....	....	25	75
	United States..	7,744	24,705	....	....	7,744	24,705
	Total......	7,769	24,780	....	....	7,769	24,780
Timber, square—							
Ash..............	Unit'd Kingdom	....	1,086	....	....	....	1,086
Birch.............	Unit'd Kingdom	....	113,874	....	....	....	113,874
	France..........	....	4,055	....	....	....	4,055
	Germany.......	....	725	....	....	....	725
	United States..	....	732	....	....	....	732
	Total......	....	119,386	....	....	....	119,386
Elm..............	Unit'd Kingdom	....	95,965	....	163,770	....	259,735
	France..........	....	2,420	....	....	....	2,420
	United States..	....	603	....	....	....	603
	Total......	....	98,988	....	163,770	....	262,758
Maple..... .°......	United States..	....	10				10
Oak...............	Unit'd Kingdom	....	71,578	....	143,389	....	214,967
	United States..	....	1,673	....	....	....	1,673
	Total......	....	73,251	....	143,389	....	216,640
Pine, red..........	United States..	....	....	....	940	....	940
Pine, white........	Unit'd Kingdom	....	236,656	....	151,004	....	387,660
	Cuba...........	....	564	....	....	....	564
	Total......	....	237,220	....	151,004	....	388,224
All other..........	Unit'd Kingdom	....	75	....	....	....	75
	Bermuda.......	....	11	....	....	....	11
	United States..	....	2,928	....	188	....	3,116
	Total......	....	3,014	....	188	....	3,202
Wood, blocks and other for pulp.	United States..	1,010,914	6,817,311	....	....	1,010,914	6,817,311
Other articles of the forest.	Unit'd Kingdom	....	303	....	....	....	303
	United States..	....	13,388	....	2	....	13,390
	Total......	....	13,691	....	2	....	13,693
ANIMALS AND THEIR PRODUCE.		No.		No.		No.	
Animals—							
Horses, one year old or less.	United States..	16	1,272	....	....	16	1,272
Horses, over one year old.	Unit'd Kingdom	7,736	1,382,345	11,539	1,195,920	19,275	2,578,265
	Bermuda.......	7	1,300	....	....	7	1,300
	Newfoundland..	114	14,708	....	....	114	14,708
	Alaska.........	6	1,590	....	....	6	1,590
	France..........	19	1,900	1,025	102,500	1,044	104,400
	Mexico.........	3	600	....	....	3	600
	United States..	2,513	438,652	2,236	637,001	4,749	1,075,653
	Total......	10,398	1,841,095	14,800	1,935,421	25,198	3,776,516

6 GEORGE V, A. 1916

No. 3.—General Statement of Exports—*Continued.*

Articles Exported.	Countries.	Goods, the Produce of Canada.		Goods, not the Produce of Canada.		Total Exports.	
		Quantity.	Value.	Quantity.	Value.	Quantity.	Value.
ANIMALS, ETC.—*Con.*		No.	$	No	$	No.	$
Animals—*Con.*							
Cattle, one year old or less............	Bermuda.......	2	25	....	....	2	25
	Miquelon and St. Pierre.....	32	124	....	....	32	124
	United States..	34,048	415,889	1	200	34,049	416,089
	Total......	34,082	416,038	1	200	34,083	416,238
Cattle, over one year	Bermuda.......	149	9,746	....	....	149	9,746
	Newfoundland..	1,736	91,746	1	50	1,737	91,796
	Miquelon and St. Pierre.....	332	13,304	....	....	332	13,304
	United States..	149,604	8,736,700	19	4,800	149,623	8,741,500
	Total......	151,821	8,851,496	20	4,850	151,841	8,856,346
Swine..............	Newfoundland..	186	1,079	....	....	186	1,079
	Miquelon and St. Pierre.....	94	1,489	....	....	94	1,489
	United States..	243,031	3,114,437	1	50	243,032	3,114,487
	Total......	243,311	3,117,005	1	50	243,312	3,117,055
Sheep, one year old or less.	United States..	35,293	211,714	....	....	35,293	211,714
Sheep, over one year old.	B. Guiana......	25	202	....	....	25	202
	Newfoundland..	894	5,042	....	....	894	5,042
	Miquelon and St. Pierre.....	271	1,334	....	....	271	1,334
	United States..	6,349	68,320	460	9,380	6,809	77,700
	Total......	7,539	74,898	460	9,380	7,999	84,278
Poultry..............	Unit'd Kingdom	....	20	....	....	....	20
	Australia......	....	435	....	....	....	435
	Bermuda.......	....	10	....	....	....	10
	B. W. Indies....	....	28	....	....	....	28
	Figi Islands.....	....	16	....	....	....	16
	Newfoundland..	....	288	....	....	....	288
	Miquelon and St. Pierre.....	....	338	....	....	....	338
	United States..	....	334,319	....	2,632	....	336,951
	Total......	....	335,454	....	2,632	....	338,086
Other..............	Unit'd Kingdom	....	10,740	....	....	....	10,740
	Australia......	....	30	....	....	....	30
	Hong Kong.....	....	50	....	....	....	50
	Newfoundland..	....	305	....	....	....	305
	Alaska.........	....	40	....	....	....	40
	Norway........	....	5,000	....	....	....	5,000
	United States..	....	65,855	....	11,157	....	77,012
	Total......	....	82,020	....	11,157	....	93,177
		Cwt.		Cwt.		Cwt.	
Bones..............	Unit'd Kingdom	....	....	455	500	455	500
	Japan..........	270	752	....	....	270	752
	Norway........	1,460	1,465	....	....	1,460	1,465
	United States..	71,060	93,448	1,740	1,926	72,800	95,374
	Total......	72,790	95,665	2,195	2,426	74,985	98,091

No. 3.—GENERAL STATEMENT OF EXPORTS—Continued.

Articles Exported.	Countries.	GOODS, THE PRODUCE OF CANADA.		GOODS, NOT THE PRODUCE OF CANADA.		TOTAL EXPORTS.	
		Quantity.	Value.	Quantity.	Value.	Quantity.	Value.
ANIMALS, ETC.—Con.		Lb.	$	Lb.	$	Lb.	$
Butter...............	Unit'd Kingdom	585,605	150,612	7,950	2,385	593,555	152,997
	Bermuda.......	84,112	24,568	6,272	1,634	90,384	26,202
	B. Guiana......	13,402	3,861	....	....	13,402	3,861
	B. Honduras....	2,740	956	....	....	2,740	956
	B. W. Indies....	132,988	41,710	....	....	132,988	41,710
	Newfoundland..	437,861	121,548	560	146	438,421	121,694
	Alaska..........	68	21	....	....	68	21
	Belgium........	420	126	....	....	420	126
	Costa Rica.....	1,440	499	....	....	1,440	499
	Cuba...........	528	194	....	....	528	194
	Dan. W. Indies.	6,124	1,719	....	....	6,124	1,719
	Japan...........	56	20	....	....	56	20
	Mexico.........	960	340	....	....	960	340
	Miquelon and St. Pierre.....	69,978	17,368	2,280	598	72,258	17,966
	Nicaragua.....	1,200	422	....	....	1,200	422
	Panama........	14,020	4,888	....	....	14,020	4,888
	U. S. of Colombia...........	6,240	2,232	....	....	6,240	2,232
	United States..	1,367,171	268,541	28,349	4,900	1,395,520	273,441
	Total......	2,724,913	639,625	45,411	9,663	2,770,324	649,288
Casein	United States..	230,045	13,923	....	....	230,045	13,923
Cheese.............	Unit'd Kingdom	135,900,614	18,936,704	....	....	135,900,614	18,936,704
	Australia......	1,350	213	....	....	1,350	213
	Bermuda......	166,612	26,478	....	....	166,612	26,478
	B. S. Africa....	401,295	73,009	....	....	401,295	73,009
	B. Guiana......	84,806	14,765	....	....	84,806	14,765
	B. W. Indies...	124,637	21,283	....	....	124,637	21,283
	Hong Kong....	11,175	2,830	....	....	11,175	2,830
	Malta..........	22,370	3,050	....	....	22,370	3,050
	Newfoundland..	495,998	68,522	....	....	495,998	68,522
	Alaska.........	36	9	....	....	36	9
	Aust.-Hungary..	16,560	2,131	....	....	16,560	2,131
	Belgium........	70,700	15,000	....	....	70,700	15,000
	China..........	4,867	1,569	....	....	4,867	1,569
	Cuba...........	360	73	....	....	360	73
	Dan. W. Indies.	24,474	4,009	....	....	24,474	4,009
	Japan...........	9,951	2,007	....	....	9,951	2,007
	Miquelon and St. Pierre.....	3,350	682	....	....	3,350	682
	Spain..........	8,697	1,706	....	....	8,697	1,706
	United States..	253,809	39,461	179,223	34,102	433,032	73,563
	Total......	137,601,661	19,213,501	179,223	34,102	137,780,884	19,247,603
Cream, fresh.........	United States..	Gal. 1,895,575	1,836,006	Gal.	....	Gal. 1,895,575	1,836,006
Milk, fresh............	United States..	477,692	68,205	....	....	477,692	68,205
Cream and milk, condensed, canned or preserved.	Unit'd Kingdom	Lb. 208,073	12,075	Lb.	....	Lb. 208,073	12,075
	Bermuda.......	4,170	336	....	....	4,170	336
	B. S. Africa....	4,600	225	....	....	4,600	225
	B. Guiana......	480	40	....	....	480	40
	B. W. Indies....	143,594	12,384	....	....	143,594	12,384
	B. Straits Settlements...	12,250	510	....	....	12,250	510
	Hong Kong.....	123,100	8,792	....	....	123,100	8,792
	Newfoundland..	183,760	16,171	....	....	183,760	16,171

6 GEORGE V, A. 1916

No. 3.—General Statement of Exports—*Continued.*

Articles Exported.	Countries.	Goods, the Produce of Canada.		Goods, not the Produce of Canada.		Total Exports.	
		Quantity.	Value.	Quantity.	Value.	Quantity.	Value.
ANIMALS, ETC.—*Con.*		Lb.	$	Lb.	$	Lb.	$
Cream and milk, condensed—*Con.*	Alaska.........	520	60	....	....	520	60
	Belgium.......	52,880	4,488			52,880	4,488
	China..........	398,065	31,212			398,065	31,212
	Holland........	2,250	100			2,250	100
	Japan..........	1,746,800	148,784			1,746,800	148,784
	Miquelon and St. Pierre.....	1,663	188			1,663	188
	Philippines......	18,430	746			18,430	746
	United States..	15,455,340	945,189			15,455,340	945,189
	Total......	18,355,975	1,181,300	....	....	18,355,975	1,181,300
		Doz.		Doz.		Doz.	
Eggs.................	Unit'd Kingdom	3,100,247	850,808	588,330	165,988	3,688,577	1,016,796
	Bermuda.......	5,180	1,666			5,180	1,666
	Newfoundland..	38,060	11,464			38,060	11,464
	Alaska..........	1,530	654			1,530	654
	Miquelon and St. Pierre.....	11,313	2,777	....	....	11,313	2,777
	United States..	436,569	98,271	528,800	74,890	965,369	173,161
	Total......	3,592,899	965,640	1,117,130	240,878	4,710,029	1,206,518
Furs:.							
Dressed............	Unit'd Kingdom	....	6,300	....	3,029	....	9,329
	France..........		4,056		4,805		8,861
	Germany.......				714		714
	United States..		19,506		4,449		23,955
	Total......	....	29,862	....	12,997	....	42,859
Undressed..........	Unit'd Kingdom	....	1,297,702		706	....	1,298,408
	Newfoundland..		2,198		1,600		3,798
	Alaska..........		670				670
	Aust.-Hungary..		....		78		78
	Belgium........		3,170				3,170
	France..........		7,524		1,300		8,824
	Germany.......		94,530		759		95,289
	Russia..........		40				40
	Sweden........		240				240
	United States..		1,320,887		81,530		1,402,417
	Total......	....	2,726,961	....	85,973	....	2,812,934
		Lb.		Lb.		Lb.	
Grease and grease scraps.	Unit'd Kingdom	83,623	3,889		....	83,623	3,889
	Australia.......	336	42			336	42
	Newfoundland..	1,456	78			1,456	78
	New Zealand...	274	24			274	24
	Cuba..........	37,748	1,887			37,748	1,887
	France..........	18,892	772			18,892	772
	United States..	2,268,909	71,255	78,678	3,071	2,347,587	74,326
	Total.........	2,411,238	77,947	78,678	3,071	2,489,916	81,018
Glue stock............	Unit'd Kingdom	....	341	....	....	....	341
	United States..	....	41,009				41,009
	Total......	....	41,350	....	....	....	41,350
Hair.................	Unit'd Kingdom	....	6,210		8,200	....	14,410
	Germany.......		920				920
	United States..		276,061		8,747		284,808
	Total......	....	283,191	....	16,947	....	300,138

SESSIONAL PAPER No. 11

No. 3.—GENERAL STATEMENT OF EXPORTS—*Continued.*

Articles Exported.	Countries.	GOODS, THE PRODUCE OF CANADA.		GOODS, NOT THE PRODUCE OF CANADA.		TOTAL EXPORTS.	
		Quantity.	Value.	Quantity.	Value.	Quantity.	Value.
ANIMALS, ETC.—*Con.*			$		$		$
Hides and skins, other than fur.	Unit'd Kingdom	....	7,634	....	....	....	7,634
	Newfoundland..	....	2,758	....	....	....	2,758
	Alaska..........	....	3,171	....	....	....	3,171
	France..........	....	498	....	....	....	498
	United States..	....	7,420,149	....	36,571	....	7,456,720
	Total.:.....	....	7,434,210	....	36,571	....	7,470,781
Horns and hoofs......	Japan..........	....	1,943	....	....	....	1,943
	United States..	....	14,243	....	81	....	14,324
	Total......	....	16,186	....	81	....	16,267
		Lb.		Lb.		Lb.	
Honey...............	Unit'd Kingdom	101	14	....	....	101	14
	Newfoundland..	100	16	....	....	100	16
	United States..	6,728	762	675	48	7,403	810
	Total......	6,929	792	675	48	7,604	840
Lard...........	Unit'd Kingdom	1,807,146	213,207	....	....	1,807,146	213,207
	B. W. Indies....	517	60	....	....	517	60
	Newfoundland..	6,835	832	2,146	206	8,981	1,038
	Alaska..........	50	9	102	17	152	26
	Belgium........	62,510	6,585	....	....	62,510	6,585
	Holland........	11,314	1,056	....	....	11,314	1,056
	Miquelon and St. Pierre.....	5,635	661	....	....	5,635	661
	United States..	795,029	83,523	1,450	178	796,479	83,701
	Total......	2,689,036	305,933	3,698	401	2,692,734	306,334
Meats:— Bacon...............	Unit'd Kingdom	72,036,025	11,080,424	....	....	72,036,025	11,080,424
	Bermuda.......	3,230	586	....	....	3,230	586
	B. W. Indies....	219	46	....	....	219	46
	Newfoundland..	31,935	4,779	....	....	31,935	4,779
	Belgium........	117,500	17,625	....	....	117,500	17,625
	Cuba..........	461	99	....	....	461	99
	France.........	5,274	845	....	....	5,274	845
	Miquelon and St. Pierre.....	540	87	....	....	540	87
	United States..	4,606,235	707,334	2,410	361	4,608,645	707,695
	Total......	76,801,419	11,811,825	2,410	361	76,803,829	11,812,186
Beef...............	Unit'd Kingdom	1,330,282	179,998	200	16	1,330,482	180,014
	Bermuda.......	14,818	1,954	....	....	14,818	1,954
	B. W. Indies....	1,600	152	8,400	665	10,000	817
	Newfoundland..	428,864	42,951	171,625	13,774	600,489	56,725
	Alaska..........	3,449	818	....	....	3,449	818
	Belgium........	800	80	1,000	81	1,800	161
	Germany.......	769	174	....	....	769	174
	Miquelon and St. Pierre.....	10,977	1,217	....	....	10,977	1,217
	United States..	17,036,698	1,761,145	660,219	58,405	17,696,917	1,819,550
	Total......	18,828,257	1,988,489	841,444	72,941	19,669,701	2,061,430
Hams...............	Unit'd Kingdom	9,198,208	1,376,151	....	....	9,198,208	1,376,151
	Bermuda.......	2,560	482	....	....	2,560	482
	B. W. Indies....	952	105	....	....	952	105
	Hong Kong.....	308	52	....	....	308	52
	Newfoundland..	9,710	1,742	1,536	213	11,246	1,955
	Cuba..........	1,093	220	....	....	1,093	220

6 GEORGE V, A. 1916

No. 3.—General Statement of Exports—*Continued.*

Articles Exported.	Countries.	Goods, the Produce of Canada.		Goods, not the Produce of Canada.		Total Exports.	
		Quantity.	Value.	Quantity.	Value.	Quantity.	Value.
ANIMALS, ETC.—*Con.*		Lb.	$	Lb.	$	Lb.	$
Meats—*Con.*							
Hams—*Con.*	France............	149	29	....	....	149	29
	Miquelon and St. Pierre.....	1,815	326	....	....	1,815	326
	United States..	8,744,079	1,273,810	6,040	934	8,750,119	1,274,744
	Total......	17,958,874	2,652,917	7,576	1,147	17,966,450	2,654,064
Mutton..............	Bermuda.......	4,402	573	....	....	4,402	573
	B. W. Indies....	1,454	265	....	....	1,454	265
	Newfoundland..	26,322	2,785	....	....	26,322	2,785
	Alaska..........	386	160	....	....	386	160
	Miquelon and St. Pierre.....	3,378	393	....	....	3,378	393
	United States..	1,029,021	119,911	....	....	1,029,021	119,911
	Total......	1,064,963	124,087	....	....	1,064,963	124,087
Pork..............	Unit'd Kingdom	5,849,254	781,643	....	....	5,849,254	781,643
	Bermuda.......	1,791	217	....	....	1,791	217
	B. W. Indies....	65,937	3,799	200	17	66,137	3,816
	Newfoundland..	128,088	13,419	120,457	10,897	248,545	24,316
	Alaska..........	292	109	....	....	292	109
	Belgium........	5,400	450	....	....	5,400	450
	Dan. W. Indies.	....	....	200	18	200	18
	France..........	30,666	5,458	....	....	30,666	5,458
	Miquelon and St. Pierre.....	28,457	3,157	....	....	28,457	3,157
	United States..	15,178,341	1,791,592	....	....	15,178,341	1,791,592
	Total......	21,288,226	2,599,844	120,857	10,932	21,409,083	2,610,776
Poultry, dressed or undressed.........	Unit'd Kingdom	....	64,791	....	....	....	64,791
	Bermuda.......	....	169	....	....	....	169
	B. W. Indies....	....	8	....	....	....	8
	Newfoundland..	....	8,807	....	....	....	8,807
	Miquelon and St. Pierre.....	....	603	....	....	....	603
	United States..	....	138,614	....	....	....	138,614
	Total......	....	212,992	....	....	....	212,992
Game, dressed or undressed.	Miquelon and St. Pierre.....	....	197	....	....	....	197
	United States..	....	2,143	....	....	....	2,143
	Total......	....	2,340	....	....	....	2,340
Tongues.............	Unit'd Kingdom	12,272	2,369	....	....	12,272	2,369
	Switzerland.....	1,300	260	....	....	1,300	260
	United States..	178,897	22,074	....	....	178,897	22,074
	Total......	192,469	24,703	....	....	192,469	24,703
Canned..............	Unit'd Kingdom	6,039,495	1,627,964	....	....	6,039,495	1,627,964
	Bermuda.......	14,171	1,138	....	....	14,171	1,138
	B. W. Indies....	900	87	....	....	900	87
	Hong Kong.....	60	6	460	45	520	51
	Newfoundland..	22,000	1,295	....	....	22,000	1,295
	Belgium........	284,320	28,432	....	....	284,320	28,432
	Cuba...........	56,615	7,349	....	....	56,615	7,349
	France..........	3,204,594	633,903	....	....	3,204,594	633,903
	Miquelon and St. Pierre.....	432	81	40	8	472	89
	United States..	260,075	39,826	8,207	1,301	268,282	41,127
	Total......	9,882,662	2,340,081	8,707	1,354	9,891,369	2,341,435

SESSIONAL PAPER No. 11

No. 3.—General Statement of Exports—*Continued.*

Articles Exported.	Countries.	Goods, the Produce of Canada.		Goods, not the Produce of Canada.		Total Exports.	
		Quantity.	Value.	Quantity.	Value.	Quantity.	Value.
ANIMALS, ETC.—*Con.*		Lb.	$	Lb.	$	Lb.	$
Meats—*Con.*							
All other, n.o.p......	Unit'd Kingdom	1,011,256	96,862	....	....	1,011,256	96,862
	Bermuda......	120	6	....	....	120	6
	B. Guiana.....	17,628	967	....	....	17,628	967
	B. W. Indies....	106,240	4,869	....	....	106,240	4,869
	Newfoundland..	27,512	2,684	....	....	27,512	2,684
	Cuba..........	44,900	2,253	....	....	44,900	2,253
	France.........	904	82	....	....	904	82
	French Guiana..	12,000	770	....	....	12,000	770
	French W.Indies	7,000	412	....	....	7,000	412
	Germany......	17,589	.1,111	....	....	17,589	1,111
	Miquelon and						
	St. Pierre.....	90	22	....	....	90	22
	Sweden........	50,500	2,000	....	....	50,500	2,000
	United States..	3,107,698	198,625	31,465	3,943	3,139,163	202,568
	Total......	4,403,437	310,663	31,465	3,943	4,434,902	314,606
		Gal.		Gal.		Gal.	
Oil, Neats foot and	United Kingdom	35,488	40,146	....	....	35,488	40,146
other animal, n.o.p.	Newfoundland..	2,885	2,493	206	273	3,091	2,766
	Belgium........	225	197	....	....	225	197
	Denmark......	14,591	17,822	....	....	14,591	17,822
	Germany......	32,504	28,999	....	....	32,504	28,999
	Holland.......	57,625	58,565	....	....	57,625	58,565
	Norway........	20,595	23,880	....	....	20,595	23,880
	United States..	64,213	67,536	....	....	64,213	67,536
	Total......	228,126	239,638	206	273	228,332	239,911
Sausage casings........	Unit'd Kingdom	....	91,121			....	91,121
	Australia......	....	24,903			....	24,903
	B. S. Africa.....	....	4,459			....	4,459
	Newfoundland..	....	1,400			....	1,400
	New Zealand...	....	4,476			....	4,476
	Aust.-Hungary..	....	304			....	304
	Germany......	....	18,724			....	18,724
	Holland........	....	1,596			....	1,596
	Norway........	....	154			....	154
	United States..	....	294,450		12,276	....	306,726
	Total......	....	441,587		12,276	....	453,863
Sheep pelts...........	United States..	....	265,332	....	7,356	....	272,688
Tails.................	United States..	....	14,192	....	....		14,192
		Lb.		Lb.		Lb.	
Tallow...............	Unit'd Kingdom	10,000	700	....	....	10,000	700
	Newfoundland..	9,056	543	....	....	9,056	543
	Belgium........	2,236	196	....	....	2,236	196
	Cuba..........	72,170	3,609	....	....	72,170	3,609
	United States..	946,410	59,794	....	....	946,410	59,794
	Total......	1,039,872	64,842	....	....	1,039,872	64,842
Wool.................	Unit'd Kingdom	560	125	12,348	1,852	12,908	1,977
	Newfoundland..	1,937	543	....	....	1,937	543
	Belgium........	350	70			350	70
	United States..	5,657,123	1,359,003	124,840	36,452	5,781,963	1,395,455
	Total......	5,659,970	1,359,741	137,188	38,304	5,797,158	1,398,045

6 GEORGE V, A. 1916

No. 3.—General Statement of Exports—*Continued.*

Articles Exported.	Countries.	Goods, the Produce of Canada.		Goods, not the Produce of Canada.		Total Exports.	
		Quantity.	Value.	Quantity.	Value.	Quantity.	Value.
ANIMALS, ETC.—*Con.*			$		$		$
Other articles of the animals.	Unit'd Kingdom	....	1,803	....	39	....	1,842
	Australia..........	....	50	....	....	....	50
	Bermuda......	....	35	....	....	....	35
	Newfoundland..	....	461	....	....	....	461
	China..........	....	....	....	730	....	730
	Cuba..........	....	275	....	....	....	275
	Germany......	....	365	....	5,608	....	5,973
	Mexico.........	....	45	....	....	....	45
	Miquelon and St. Pierre....	....	69	....	794	....	863
	United States..	....	73,078	....	2,353	....	75,431
	Total......	....	76,181	....	9,524	....	85,705
AGRICULTURAL PRODUCTS.							
Balsam..............	Unit'd Kingdom	....	2,878	....	....	....	2,878
	Newfoundland..	....	15	....	....	....	15
	France........	....	58	....	....	....	58
	Germany......	....	477	....	....	....	477
	United States..	....	20,526	....	950	....	21,476
	Total......	....	23,954	....	950	....	24,904
		Gal.		Gal.		Gal.	
Cider..............	Unit'd Kingdom	85,362	15,169	....	....	85,362	15,169
	B. W. Indies....	29	6	....	....	29	6
	Newfoundland..	30	7	....	....	30	7
	Miquelon and St. Pierre.....	40	5	....	....	40	5
	United States..	3,275	528	215	72	3,490	600
	Total......	88,736	15,715	215	72	88,951	15,787
		Cwt.		Cwt.		Cwt.	
Flax..............	Unit'd Kingdom	1,110	7,022	....	....	1,110	7,022
	United States..	5,619	27,208	....	....	5,619	27,208
	Total......	6,729	34,230	....	....	6,729	34,230
		Lb.		Lb.		Lb.	
Fruits:— Apples, dried........	Unit'd Kingdom	2,307,481	138,048	....	....	2,307,481	138,048
	Bermuda......	2,140	132	....	....	2,140	132
	Newfoundland..	53,325	4,700	....	....	53,325	4,700
	Belgium........	41,700	2,973	....	....	41,700	2,973
	Denmark.......	173,150	9,346	....	....	173,150	9,346
	France.........	60,000	3,432	....	....	60,000	3,432
	Germany......	45,550	4,275	....	....	45,550	4,275
	Holland........	1,546,344	98,908	....	....	1,546,344	98,908
	Miquelon and St. Pierre....	200	17	....	....	200	17
	Sweden.........	87,350	4,433	....	....	87,350	4,433
	United States..	170,810	9,796	....	....	170,810	9,796
	Total......	4,488,050	276,060	....	....	4,488,050	276,060
		Brl.		Brl.		Brl.	
Apples, green or ripe..	Unit'd Kingdom	1,041,913	2,460,413	....	....	1,041,913	2,460,413
	Australia.......	7,880	32,558	668	2,084	8,548	34,642
	Bermuda......	2,169	4,407	....	....	2,169	4,407
	B. S. Africa....	5,220	15,539	....	....	5,220	15,539
	B. Guiana.....	484	1,001	....	....	484	1,001
	B. W. Indies...	923	1,955	....	....	923	1,955
	Fiji Islands.....	65	234	85	324	150	558
	Hong Kong.....	70	150	....	....	70	150

No. 3.—General Statement of Exports—*Continued.*

Articles Exported.	Countries.	Goods, the Produce of Canada.		Goods, not the Produce of Canada.		Total Exports.	
		Quantity.	Value.	Quantity.	Value.	Quantity.	Value.
AGRICULTURAL PRO- DUCTS—*Con.*		Brl.	$.	Brl.	$	Brl.	$
Fruits—*Con.*							
Apples, green or ripe— *Con.*	Newfoundland..	18,036	40,384	....	....	18,036	40,384
	New Zealand...	4,740	21,054	133	400	4,873	21,454
	Alaska..........	....	....	1	14	1	14
	Argentina......	1,095	3,284	....	....	1,095	3,284
	Belgium........	972	1,215	....	....	972	1,215
	China...........	214	855	....	....	214	855
	Cuba..........	1,618	3,950	....	....	1,618	3,950
	Denmark......	902	2,206	....	....	902	2,206
	Holland........	500	1,025	....	....	500	1,025
	Miquelon and St. Pierre....	624	1,227	7	26	631	1,253
	Sweden........	2,381	4,213	....	....	2,381	4,213
	United States..	27,530	61,445	594	1,429	28,124	62,874
	Total......	1,117,336	2,657,115	1,488	4,277	1,118,824	2,661,392
Berries of all kinds...	Bermuda......	....	2	....	6	....	8
	B. Guiana.....	....	7	....	....	....	7
	Newfoundland..	....	50	....	....	....	50
	Alaska........	....	66	....	....	....	66
	Miquelon and St. Pierre.....	....	8	....	....	....	8
	United States..	....	106,412	....	3,036	....	109,448
	Total......	....	106,545	....	3,042	....	109,587
Canned or preserved.	Unit'd Kingdom	....	433,146	....	662	....	433,808
	Bermuda......	....	1,733	....	28	....	1,761
	B. S. Africa....	....	74	....	....	....	74
	B. India......	....	45	....	....	....	45
	B. W. Indies....	....	29	....	61	....	90
	Fiji Islands....	....	3	....	....	....	3
	Hong Kong....	....	10	....	....	....	10
	Newfoundland..	....	699	....	76	....	775
	New Zealand..	....	8,428	....	....	....	8,428
	Alaska........	....	100	....	64	....	164
	Argentina.....	....	4	....	....	....	4
	China........	....	326	....	....	....	326
	France........	....	65	....	....	....	65
	Holland......	....	329	....	....	....	329
	Japan........	....	183	....	....	....	183
	Miquelon and St. Pierre....	....	80	....	....	....	80
	United States..	....	31,243	....	2,375	....	33,618
	Total......	....	476,497	....	3,266	....	479,763
All other, n.o.p......	Unit'd Kingdom	....	41,962	....	498	....	42,460
	Bermuda......	....	80	....	717	....	797
	B. S. Africa....	....	87	....	....	....	87
	B. Guiana.....	....	41	....	....	....	41
	B. W. Indies....	....	18	....	73	....	91
	Hong Kong....	....	....	....	110	....	110
	Newfoundland..	....	4,143	....	5,843	....	9,986
	New Zealand...	....	210	....	....	....	210
	Alaska........	....	15	....	55	....	70
	China........	....	10	....	....	....	10
	France........	....	2,215	....	....	....	2,215
	Holland......	....	18,949	....	4	....	18,953
	Japan........	....	....	....	339	....	339
	Mexico........	....	50	....	....	....	50
	Miquelon and St. Pierre....	....	109	....	1,073	....	1,182
	United States..	....	12,915	....	150,701	....	163,616
	Total......	....	80,804	....	159,413	....	240,217

6 GEORGE V, A. 1916

No. 3.—General Statement of Exports—*Continued.*

Articles Exported.	Countries.	Goods, the Produce of Canada.		Goods, not the Produce of Canada.		Total Exports.	
		Quantity.	Value.	Quantity.	Value.	Quantity.	Value.
AGRICULTURAL PRODUCTS—*Con.*		Bush.	$	Bush.	$	Bush.	$
Grain and products of, viz.:—							
Barley..............	Unit'd Kingdom	4,388,577	2,520,084	861,587	507,444	5,250,164	3,027,528
	Bermuda.......	14	17	....	....	14	17
	B. W. Indies....	81	71	....	....	81	71
	Newfoundland..	1	2	....	....	1	2
	Belgium........	126,815	71,755	41,520	22,855	168,335	94,610
	Germany......	180,387	107,399	....	....	180,387	107,399
	Holland........	514,670	359,579	111,500	59,575	626,170	419,154
	United States..	366,101	203,118	....	....	366,101	203,118
	Total......	5,576,646	3,262,025	1,014,607	589,874	6,591,253	3,851,899
Beans..............	Unit'd Kingdom	530	1,030	....	....	530	1,030
	Bermuda.......	188	523	70	111	258	634
	B. W. Indies....	68	159	....	....	68	159
	Newfoundland..	1,130	2,581	1,855	2,725	2,985	5,306
	Belgium........	11,272	27,943	....	....	11,272	27,943
	Cuba...........	800	2,560	....	....	800	2,560
	Dan. W. Indies.	11	32	....	....	11	32
	France.........	1,466	3,812	....	....	1,466	3,812
	Holland........	632	2,000	....	....	632	2,000
	Miquelon and St. Pierre.....	38	95	27	39	65	134
	United States...	12,526	32,773	2,310	4,547	14,836	37,320
	Total..........	28,661	73,508	4,262	7,422	32,923	80,930
Buckwheat........	Unit'd Kingdom	225,309	176,845	....	....	225,309	176,845
	Denmark.......	2,509	1,975	....	....	2,509	1,975
	United States..	115,531	93,696	....	....	115,531	93,696
	Total..........	343,349	272,516	....	....	343,349	272,516
Indian corn........	Unit'd Kingdom	139,511	106,848	....	....	139,511	106,848
	Bermuda.......	5,640	3,541	....	....	5,640	3,541
	B. W. Indies....	3,376	1,911	....	....	3,376	1,911
	Newfoundland..	1,041	1,186	....	....	1,041	1,186
	France.........	157,515	91,162	....	....	157,515	91,162
	Miquelon and St. Pierre.....	512	497	....	....	512	497
	United States..	69,068	50,945	34,030	21,954	103,098	72,899
	Total......	376,663	256,090	34,030	21,954	410,693	278,044
Oats..............	Unit'd Kingdom	8,537,236	4,067,540	1,819,621	820,352	10,356,857	4,887,892
	Australia......	29	19	....	....	29	19
	Bermuda.......	93,783	44,570	....	....	93,783	44,570
	B. Guiana......	38,113	22,456	....	....	38,113	22,456
	B. W. Indies....	369,905	209,214	....	....	369,905	209,214
	Newfoundland..	416,168	221,299	....	....	416,168	221,299
	Alaska.........	1,225	783	....	....	1,225	783
	Belgium........	110,261	51,295	188,051	88,099	298,312	139,394
	Cuba...........	203,889	95,695	....	....	203,889	95,695
	France.........	4,072,653	2,666,608	86,000	47,299	4,158,653	2,713,907
	Holland........	61,605	25,534	520,475	223,650	582,080	249,184
	Miquelon and St. Pierre.....	2,116	931	....	....	2,116	931
	Philippines.....	35,634	18,717	....	....	35,634	18,717
	United States..	3,825,549	1,536,465	2,060	618	3,827,609	1,537,083
	Total......	17,768,166	8,961,126	2,616,207	1,180,018	20,384,373	10,141,144

No. 3.—General Statement of Exports—*Continued.*

Articles Exported.	Countries.	Goods, the Produce of Canada.		Goods, not the Produce of Canada.		Total Exports.	
		Quantity.	Value.	Quantity.	Value.	Quantity.	Value.
AGRICULTURAL PRODUCTS—*Con.*		Bush.	$	Bush.	$	Bush.	$
Grain—*Con.*							
Pease, whole........	Unit'd Kingdom	25,587	66,013	....	....	25,587	66,013
	Bermuda.......	4	12	....	....	4	12
	B. S. Africa.....	100	250	....	....	100	250
	B. W. Indies....	4,470	9,763	....	....	4,470	9,763
	Newfoundland..	7,646	17,187	222	339	7,868	17,526
	Belgium........	480	720	....	....	480	720
	Denmark......	1,000	1,700	....	....	1,000	1,700
	Dan. W. Indies.	14	33	....	....	14	33
	France.........	8,796	19,089	....	....	8,796	19,089
	Miquelon and St. Pierre....	33	73	....	....	33	73
	United States..	213,224	417,331	30	49	213,254	417,380
	Total......	261,354	532,171	252	388	261,606	532,559
Pease, split.........	Bermuda......	18	47	....	....	18	47
	B. S. Africa...,	700	1,445	....	....	700	1,445
	B. Guiana......	11,624	29,784	....	....	11,624	29,784
	B. W. Indies....	13,066	30,837	....	....	13,066	30,837
	Newfoundland..	2,061	5,620	199	147	2,260	5,767
	Miquelon and St. Pierre....	252	421	2	3	254	424
	Panama..... ...	18	40	....	....	18	40
	United States..	13,885	39,483	....	....	13,885	39,483
	Total......	41,624	107,677	201	150	41,825	107,827
Rye................	Unit'd Kingdom	87,282	93,291	17,142	11,999	104,424	105,290
	Denmark......	12,747	11,796	79,899	71,902	92,646	83,698
	Holland........	10,197	8,367	261,531	193,790	271,728	202,157
	Norway........	7,141	7,313	....	....	7,141	7,313
	United States..	146,055	138,855	....	....	146,055	138,855
	Total......	263,422	259,622	358,572	277,691	621,994	537,313
Wheat..............	Unit'd Kingdom	64,301,202	66,363,044	20,909,254	20,695,937	85,210,456	87,058,981
	Australia.......	6	10	....	....	6	10
	Bermuda.......	17	18	....	....	17	18
	B. S. Africa.....	160,902	161,683	59,143	59,143	220,045	220,826
	B. W. Indies....	5	6	....	....	5	6
	Gibraltar.......	167,626	167,626	1,226,011	1,226,011	1,393,637	1,393,637
	Hong Kong....	350	500	....	....	350	500
	Malta..........	....	....	40,000	39,200	40,000	39,200
	Newfoundland..	36	21	....	....	36	21
	New Zealand...	406,812	574,254	....	....	406,812	574,254
	Aust.-Hungary..	128,270	126,902	58,697	58,065	186,967	184,967
	Belgium........	984,520	965,570	978,160	919,731	1,962,680	1,885,301
	Denmark......	40,000	40,000	116,494	116,494	156,494	156,494
	France.........	838,521	900,123	3,868,113	3,830,894	4,706,634	4,731,017
	Germany.......	366,974	351,765	645,996	626,218	1,012,970	977,983
	Holland........	245,118	237,668	3,235,662	3,149,127	3,480,780	3,386,795
	Italy..........	....	....	1,362,220	1,311,769	1,362,220	1,311,769
	Japan..........	5,000	4,853	....	....	5,000	4,853
	Portugal.......	....	....	775,829	763,279	775,829	763,279
	Spain..........	176,000	176,000	246,500	246,500	422,500	422,500
	United States..	4,092,026	4,223,505	....	....	4,092,026	4,223,505
	Total......	71,913,385	74,293,548	33,522,079	33,042,368	105,435,464	107,335,916
Bran.....:..........		Cwt.		Cwt.		Cwt.	
	Unit'd Kingdom	77,986	53,042	....	....	77,986	53,042
	Bermuda......	26,077	32,203	....	....	26,077	32,203
	B. Guiana.....	159	229	....	....	159	229
	B. W. Indies....	24,860	34,001	....	....	24,860	34,001
	Newfoundland..	31,132	41,994	....	....	31,132	41,994
	Alaska.........	45	73	220	407	265	480
	Cuba..........	26	65	....	....	26	65

6 GEORGE V, A. 1916

No. 3.—General Statement of Exports—*Continued.*

Articles Exported.	Countries.	Goods, the Produce of Canada.		Goods, not the Produce of Canada.		Total Exports.	
		Quantity.	Value.	Quantity.	Value.	Quantity.	Value.
AGRICULTURAL PRODUCTS—*Con.*		Cwt.	$	Cwt.	$	Cwt.	$
Bran—*Con*	Denmark	559	509			559	509
	France	400	410			400	410
	Germany	1,232	1,117			1,232	1,117
	Holland	4,148	3,859			4,148	3,859
	Miquelon and St. Pierre	137	170			137	170
	Porto Rico	15	33			15	33
	United States	871,358	778,626			871,358	778,626
	Total	1,038,134	946,331	220	407	1,038,354	946,738
		Brl.		Brl.		Brl.	
Flour of wheat	Unit'd Kingdom	3,137,146	15,901,713			3,137,146	15,901,713
	Australia	170	709			170	709
	Bermuda	8,351	43,543			8,351	43,543
	B. E. Africa	1,524	7,634			1,524	7,634
	B. S. Africa	317,807	1,573,395			317,807	1,573,395
	B. W. Africa	2,333	11,237			2,333	11,237
	B. Guiana	85,723	392,780			85,723	392,780
	B. W. Indies	499,932	2,340,259			499,932	2,340,259
	Fiji Islands	2,428	12,948			2,428	12,948
	Gibraltar	8,059	40,703			8,059	40,703
	Hong Kong	59,627	217,698			59,627	217,698
	Malta	3,690	17,804	1,090	3,564	4,780	21,368
	Newfoundland	245,340	1,374,529			245,340	1,374,529
	New Zealand	3,849	21,684			3,849	21,684
	Alaska	25	136			25	136
	Argentina	900	3,368			900	3,368
	Aust.-Hungary	3,495	13,169			3,495	13,169
	Belgium	26,257	132,820			26,257	132,820
	Brazil	643	2,851			643	2,851
	Canary Islands	3,311	15,420			3,311	15,420
	China	2,351	10,722			2,351	10,722
	Cuba	1,941	9,071			1,941	9,071
	Denmark	61,400	270,434			61,400	270,434
	Dan. W. Indies	485	2,436			485	2,436
	Dutch W. Indies	1,200	5,772			1,200	5,772
	Dutch Guiana	42	249			42	249
	Ecuador	800	3,622			800	3,622
	Egypt and Soudan	3,668	17,016			3,668	17,016
	France	77,331	412,198			77,331	412,198
	French Africa	50	345			50	345
	French W.Indies	2,204	10,175			2,204	10,175
	Germany	3,709	15,046			3,709	15,046
	Greece	16,107	82,124			16,107	82,124
	Greenland and Iceland	376	1,518			376	1,518
	Hayti	291	1,367			291	1,367
	Holland	86,351	406,342			86,351	406,342
	Honduras	48	200			48	200
	Japan	7,495	27,762			7,495	27,762
	Liberia	14	63			14	63
	Mexico	100	450			100	450
	Miquelon and St. Pierre	1,027	5,976			1,027	5,976
	Norway	188,066	808,941			188,066	808,941
	Panama	2,125	10,273			2,125	10,273
	Porto Rico	50	232			50	232
	Portuguese Africa	13,718	70,155			13,718	70,155
	Russia	5,689	26,356			5,689	26,356
	San Domingo	600	2,559			600	2,559
	Sweden	4,849	21,312			4,849	21,312
	Turkey	350	1,630			350	1,630
	United States	52,429	232,967	35	162	52,464	233,129
	Venezuela	6,861	29,233			6,861	29,233
	Total	4,952,337	24,610,946	1,125	3,726	4,953,462	24,614,672

SESSIONAL PAPER No. 11

No. 3.—General Statement of Exports—*Continued.*

Articles Exported.	Countries.	Goods, the Produce of Canada.		Goods, not the Produce of Canada.		Total Exports.	
		Quantity.	Value.	Quantity.	Value.	Quantity.	Value.
AGRICULTURAL PRODUCTS—*Con.*		Brl.	$	Brl.	$	Brl.	$
Indian meal...........	Bermuda......	48	226	....	....	48	226
	B. W. Indies....	6	20	....	....	6	20
	Newfoundland..	2,126	7,880	....	....	2,126	7,880
	Belgium.......	1	3	....	....	1	3
	Miquelon and St. Pierre.....	373	1,395	....	....	373	1,395
	United States..	6	25	....	....	6	25
	Total......	2,560	9,549	....	....	2,560	9,549
Oatmeal..............	Unit'd Kingdom	57,505	275,786	....	....	57,505	275,786
	Bermuda......	12	56	....	....	12	56
	B. W. Africa....	425	2,060	....	....	425	2,060
	B. Guiana.....	20	100	....	....	20	100
	B. W. Indies....	75	232	....	....	75	232
	Newfoundland..	442	2,290	....	....	442	2,290
	Aust.-Hungary..	370	1,314	....	....	370	1,314
	Canary Islands.	211	1,120	....	....	211	1,120
	Miquelon and St. Pierre.....	2	19	....	....	2	19
	Russia.........	233	939	....	....	233	939
	United States..	1,025	3,928	....	....	1,025	3,928
	Total......	60,320	287,844	....	....	60,320	287,844
Meal, all other, n.o.p...	Bermuda......	27	88	....	....	27	88
	B. Guiana.....	5	23	....	....	5	23
	B. W. Indies....	34	165	....	....	34	165
	Newfoundland..	265	967	....	....	265	967
	Miquelon and St. Pierre.....	11	36	....	....	11	36
	United States..	90	337	....	....	90	337
	Total......	432	1,616	....	....	432	1,616
Cereal foods, prepared, of all kinds.	Unit'd Kingdom	....	1,474,907	....	....	....	1,474,907
	Australia......	....	42,824	....	....	....	42,824
	Bermuda......	....	24,617	....	42	....	24,659
	B. S. Africa....	....	114,061	....	....	....	114,061
	B. W. Africa....	....	255	....	....	....	255
	B. Guiana.....	....	3,559	....	....	....	3,559
	B. W. Indies....	....	24,144	....	....	....	24,144
	Hong Kong.....	....	53	....	3	....	56
	Newfoundland..	....	23,820	....	71	....	23,891
	New Zealand...	....	6,743	....	....	....	6,743
	Belgium.......	....	11,545	....	....	....	11,545
	Cuba..........	....	71,252	....	....	....	71,252
	Denmark......	....	27,287	....	....	....	27,287
	Dutch W. Indies	....	57	....	....	....	57
	France........	....	6,084	....	....	....	6,084
	Germany......	....	130	....	....	....	130
	Holland.......	....	38,938	....	....	....	38,938
	Italy.........	....	101	....	....	....	101
	Miquelon and St. Pierre.....	....	146	....	3	....	149
	Norway.......	....	45,786	....	....	....	45,786
	Porto Rico.....	....	576	....	....	....	576
	Portugal......	....	73	....	....	....	73
	Russia........	....	2,042	....	....	....	2,042
	Spain.........	....	283	....	....	....	283
	Sweden........	....	26,560	....	....	....	26,560
	United States..	....	24,559	....	3,613	....	28,172
	Total......	....	1,970,402	....	3,732	....	1,974,134

6 GEORGE V, A. 1916

No. 3.—General Statement of Exports—*Continued.*

Articles Exported.	Countries.	Goods, the Produce of Canada.		Goods, not the Produce of Canada.		Total Exports.	
		Quantity.	Value.	Quantity.	Value.	Quantity.	Value.
AGRICULTURAL PRODUCTS—*Con.*		Ton.	$	Ton.	$	Ton.	$
Hay	Unit'd Kingdom	6,411	88,813	47	376	6,458	89,189
	Bermuda	1,331	19,659	....	....	1,331	19,659
	B. Guiana	152	2,756	....	....	152	2,756
	B. W. Indies	925	13,483	....	....	925	13,483
	Newfoundland	5,622	78,467	....	....	5,622	78,467
	Alaska	11	606	12	818	23	1,424
	Cuba	830	7,644	....	....	830	7,644
	France	56,380	1,387,439	....	....	56,380	1,387,439
	Miquelon and St. Pierre	207	3,609	....	....	207	3,609
	Porto Rico	42	354	....	....	42	354
	United States	59,964	629,728	13	250	59,977	629,978
	Total	131,875	2,232,558	72	1,444	131,947	2,234,002
		Cwt.		Cwt.		Cwt.	
Hemp	United States	....	....	460	2,090	460	2,090
		Lb.		Lb.		Lb.	
Hops	Unit'd Kingdom	167,935	35,430	....	....	167,935	35,430
	Newfoundland	1,080	220	....	....	1,080	220
	United States	1,211	242	1,200	276	2,411	518
	Total	170,226	35,892	1,200	276	171,426	36,168
		Bush.		Bush.		Bush.	
Malt	Newfoundland	2,881	2,605	2,000	2,069	4,881	4,674
	United States	1,600	1,536	....	....	1,600	1,536
	Total	4,481	4,141	2,000	2,069	6,481	6,210
		Lb.		Lb.		Lb.	
Maple sugar	Unit'd Kingdom	80,029	6,670	....	....	80,029	6,670
	Australia	35	6	....	....	35	6
	Bermuda	400	40	....	....	400	40
	B. S. Africa	42	5	....	....	42	5
	Newfoundland	120	12	....	....	120	12
	Belgium	100	20	....	....	100	20
	France	100	20	....	....	100	20
	United States	1,381,590	124,704	....	....	1,381,590	124,704
	Total	1,462,416	131,477	....	....	1,462,416	131,477
		Gal.		Gal.		Gal.	
Maple syrup	Unit'd Kingdom	2,216	2,389	....	....	2,216	2,389
	Bermuda	65	64	....	....	65	64
	B.S. Africa	5	7	....	....	5	7
	Newfoundland	206	220	....	....	206	220
	Belgium	75	63	....	....	75	63
	United States	3,598	3,944	....	....	3,598	3,944
	Total	6,165	6,687	....	....	6,165	6,687
		Lb.		Lb.		Lb.	
Nuts	Unit'd Kingdom	1,605	471	26,440	745	28,045	1,216
	Bermuda	354	42	2,653	303	3,007	345
	B. W. Indies	....	....	195	20	195	20
	Newfoundland	825	23	14,090	454	14,915	477
	Miquelon and St. Pierre	2,940	87	200	20	3,140	107
	United States	31,227	1,623	97,735	5,770	128,962	7,393
	Total	36,951	2,246	141,313	7,312	178,264	9,558

No. 3.—General Statement of Exports—*Continued.*

Articles Exported.	Countries.	Goods, the Produce of Canada.		Goods, not the Produce of Canada.		Total Exports.	
		Quantity.	Value.	Quantity.	Value.	Quantity.	Value.
AGRICULTURAL PRODUCTS—*Con.*		Bush.	$	Bush.	$	Bush.	$
Seeds:—							
Clover............	Unit'd Kingdom	18,485	152,848	....	....	18,485	152,848
	Australia.......	227	2,500			227	2,500
	New Zealand...	2,307	23,145			2,307	23,145
	Belgium........	83	760			83	760
	Denmark.......	2,258	21,208			2,258	21,208
	France.........	- 55	560			55	560
	Germany.......	1,670	6,814			1,670	6,814
	United States..	19,650	167,370	1,207	9,745	20,857	177,115
	Total......	44,735	375,205	1,207	9,745	45,942	384,950
Flax................	Unit'd Kingdom	675,318	928,346	58,983	88,475	734,301	1,016,821
	Belgium........	6,582	9,215	....	....	6,582	9,215
	France.........	10	15			10	15
	Holland........	1,366	1,864			1,366	1,864
	United States..	7,006,249	9,420,263			7,006,249	9,420,263
	Total......	7,689,525	10,359,703	58,983	88,475	7,748,508	10,448,178
Grass..............	Unit'd Kingdom	5,499	6,461	....	....	5,499	6,461
	Australia.......	436	494	140	156	576	650
	Newfoundland..	....	....	25	204	25	204
	New Zealand...	868	2,746	70	78	938	2,824
	Denmark.......	117	349	....	....	117	349
	France.........	428	400			428	400
	Germany.......	2,518	4,510			2,518	4,510
	Holland........	800	560			800	560
	United States..	63,140	53,598			63,140	53,598
	Total......	73,806	69,118	235	438	74,041	69,556
Other..............	United Kingdom	....	73	....	65	....	138
	Bermuda.......				367		367
	Newfoundland..		697		43		740
	China..........		9				9
	Germany.......		325				325
	United States..		4,651		79,583		84,234
	Total......	....	5,755	....	80,058	....	85,813
		Ton		Ton.		Ton	
Straw..............	Unit'd Kingdom	24	194	....	....	24	194
	Bermuda.......	43	315			43	315
	Newfoundland..	65	497			65	497
	France.........	5	28			5	28
	Miquelon and St. Pierre.....	9	82			9	82
	United States..	4,816	28,502			4,816	28,502
	Total......	4,962	29,618	....	....	4,962	29,618
		Lb.		Lb.		Lb.	
Tobacco, leaf..........	Unit'd Kingdom	1,419	624	....	....	1,419	624
	Cuba..........	....	....	11,849	14,840	11,849	14,840
	Holland........	6,302	2,684	....	....	6,302	2,684
	United States..	28,724	18,336	128,008	77,850	156,732	96,186
	Total......	36,445	21,644	139,857	92,690	176,302	114,334

6 GEORGE V, A. 1916

No. 3.—General Statement of Exports—*Continued.*

Articles Exported.	Countries.	Goods, the Produce of Canada. Quantity.	Value.	Goods, not the Produce of Canada. Quantity.	Value.	Total Exports. Quantity.	Value.
AGRICULTURAL PRODUCTS—*Con.*			$		$		$
Trees, shrubs and plants.	Unit'd Kingdom	....	18	....	2,200	....	2,218
	Bermuda	....	50	....	....	....	50
	Newfoundland	....	1,653	....	602	....	2,255
	New Zealand	....	15	....	....	....	15
	Miquelon and St. Pierre	....	54	....	....	....	54
	United States	....	20,748	....	989	....	21,737
	Total	....	22,538	....	3,791	....	26,329
Vegetables:—							
Canned or preserved.	Unit'd Kingdom	....	262,918	....	....	....	262,918
	Bermuda	....	4,406	....	5	....	4,411
	B. S. Africa	....	5,854	....	....	....	5,854
	B. Guiana	....	178	....	....	....	178
	B. W. Indies	....	1,394	....	....	....	1,394
	Newfoundland	....	2,582	....	....	....	2,582
	New Zealand	....	275	....	....	....	275
	Alaska	....	52	....	....	....	52
	Argentina	....	100	....	....	....	100
	Belgium	....	9,930	....	....	....	9,930
	France	....	30	....	....	....	30
	Japan	....	....	....	27	....	27
	Miquelon and St. Pierre	....	66	....	7	....	73
	United States	....	11,627	....	1,033	....	12,660
	Total	....	299,412	....	1,072	....	300,484
		Bush.		Bush.		Bush.	
Potatoes	Unit'd Kingdom	102,090	71,447	....	....	102,090	71,447
	Bermuda	25,986	17,834	....	....	25,986	17,834
	B. Guiana	79,067	53,994	....	....	79,067	53,994
	B. W. Indies	51,084	34,901	....	....	51,084	34,901
	Fiji Islands	240	168	....	....	240	168
	Newfoundland	112,137	47,081	20	40	112,157	47,121
	Alaska	42	66	2	8	44	74
	Belgium	95,964	47,982	....	....	95,964	47,982
	China	100	100	....	....	100	100
	Cuba	617,698	382,179	....	....	617,698	382,179
	Miquelon and St. Pierre	17,745	5,933	....	....	17,745	5,933
	Panama	495	333	....	....	495	333
	United States	89,610	34,765	50	70	89,660	34,835
	Total	1,192,258	696,783	72	118	1,192,330	696,901
Turnips	Bermuda	110	54	....	....	110	54
	B. W. Indies	32	14	....	....	32	14
	Newfoundland	9,469	1,827	....	....	9,469	1,827
	Alaska	13	16	....	....	13	16
	Miquelon and St. Pierre	2,074	379	....	....	2,074	379
	United States	2,138,701	284,171	....	....	2,138,701	284,171
	Total	2,150,399	286,461	....	....	2,150,399	286,461
Other	Unit'd Kingdom	....	73,970	....	....	....	73,970
	Bermuda	....	129	....	....	....	129
	B. Guiana	....	1,014	....	....	....	1,014
	B. W. Indies	....	633	....	....	....	633
	Fiji Islands	....	157	....	....	....	157
	Hong Kong	....	....	....	63	....	63
	Newfoundland	....	9,757	....	1,147	....	10,904
	Alaska	....	36	....	9	....	45

No. 3.—GENERAL STATEMENT OF EXPORTS—*Continued.*

Articles Exported.	Countries.	GOODS, THE PRODUCE OF CANADA.		GOODS, NOT THE PRODUCE OF CANADA.		TOTAL EXPORTS.	
		Quantity.	Value.	Quantity.	Value.	Quantity.	Value.
AGRICULTURAL PRODUCTS—*Con.*			$		$		$
Vegetables—*Con.*							
Other—*Con*	Cuba..........	....	57	....	....	....	57
	Miquelon and St. Pierre.....	....	2,750	....	2,390	....	5,140
	United States..	....	129,124	....	6,754	....	135,878
	Total......	....	217,627	....	10,363	....	227,990
Other articles of agriculture.	Unit'd Kingdom	....	5,007	....	....	....	5,007
	B. W. Indies....	....	60	....	....	....	60
	Newfoundland..	....	788	....	39	....	827
	New Zealand...	....	4	....	....	....	4
	Germany......	....	1,515	....	....	....	1,515
	Holland.......	....	2,287	....	....	....	2,287
	United States..	....	423,633	....	5,284	....	428,917
MANUFACTURES.	Total......	....	433,294	....	5,323	....	438,617
Agricultural Implements and machines—		No.		No.		No.	
Mowing machines.	Unit'd Kingdom	1,258	42,885	....	....	1,258	42,885
	Australia.......	467	16,123	....	....	467	16,123
	B. S. Africa.....	65	2,519	....	....	65	2,519
	Newfoundland..	50	2,036	....	....	50	2,036
	New Zealand...	485	14,314	....	....	485	14,314
	Aust.-Hungary .	40	1,359	....	....	40	1,359
	Belgium........	155	5,449	....	....	155	5,449
	Chili..........	8	342	....	....	8	342
	Denmark......	40	1,535	....	....	40	1,535
	France.........	1,805	58,335	....	....	1,805	58,335
	Germany......	1,871	68,353	....	....	1,871	68,353
	Holland.......	847	34,423	....	....	847	34,423
	Italy..........	20	703	....	....	20	703
	Russia.........	323	9,561	....	....	323	9,561
	Spain..........	75	2,577	....	....	75	2,577
	United States..	3	195	....	....	3	195
	Total......	7,512	260,709	....	....	7,512	260,709
Cultivators........	Unit'd Kingdom	183	4,641	....	....	183	4,641
	Australia.......	2,952	89,497	....	....	2,952	89,497
	B. S. Africa.....	835	4,374	....	....	835	4,374
	Newfoundland..	4	25	....	....	4	25
	New Zealand...	302	7,744	....	....	302	7,744
	Argentina......	3	90	.:	....	3	90
	Chili..........	4	164	....	....	4	164
	Cuba..........	60	261	....	....	60	261
	Denmark......	2	52	....	....	2	52
	France.........	752	18,507	....	....	752	18,507
	French Africa...	19	344	....	....	19	344
	Germany......	15	278	....	....	15	278
	Spain..........	490	11,807	....	....	490	11,807
	United States..	210	6,023	....	....	210	6,023
	Total......	5,831	143,807	....	....	5,831	143,807
Reapers..........	Unit'd Kingdom	4	220	....	....	4	220
	B. S. Africa.....	18	1,127	....	....	18	1,127
	France.........	49	2,582	....	....	49	2,582
	Germany......	278	19,530	....	....	278	19,530
	Holland.......	5	300	....	....	5	300
	Russia.........	393	16,017	.:	....	393	16,017
	Spain..........	150	8,244	....	....	150	8,244
	Sweden........	3	170	....	....	3	170
	United States..	2	111	....	....	2	111
	Total......	·902	48,301	....	....	902	48,301

No. 3.—General Statement of Exports—*Continued.*

Articles Exported.	Countries.	Goods, the Produce of Canada. Quantity.	Value.	Goods, not the Produce of Canada. Quantity.	Value.	Total Exports. Quantity.	Value.
		No.	$	No.	$	No.	$
MANUFACTURES—*Con.*							
Agricultural implements—*Con.*							
Drills............	Unit'd Kingdom	748	36,642	....	....	748	36,642
	Australia......	1,771	130,334	....	....	1,771	130,334
	B. S. Africa.....	26	1,524	....	....	26	1,524
	Newfoundland..	2	89	....	....	2	89
	New Zealand...	733	51,539	....	....	733	51,539
	Argentina......	9	614	....	....	9	614
	Denmark......	10	660	....	....	10	660
	French Africa...	10	644	....	....	10	644
	Italy..........	25	1,121	....	....	25	1,121
	Norway.......	7	403	....	....	7	403
	Roumania.....	50	3,120	....	....	50	3,120
	Russia........	560	30,864	....	....	560	30,864
	Spain.........	6	60	....	....	6	60
	United States..	39	2,704	4	1,862	43	4,566
	Total......	3,996	260,318	4	1,862	4,000	262,180
Harvesters and binders.	Unit'd Kingdom	1,442	146,059	....	....	1,442	146,059
	Australia......	1,660	179,495	....	....	1,660	179,495
	B. S. Africa.....	310	20,861	....	....	310	20,861
	New Zealand...	270	28,485	....	....	270	28,485
	Aust.-Hungary.	78	8,305	....	....	78	8,305
	Belgium........	198	17,698	....	....	198	17,698
	Chili..........	8	864	....	....	8	864
	Denmark......	244	23,212	....	....	244	23,212
	France........	499	53,751	....	....	499	53,751
	French Africa...	4	390	....	....	4	390
	Germany......	1,035	104,484	....	....	1,035	104,484
	Holland........	418	42,607	....	....	418	42,607
	Italy..........	63	6,495	....	....	63	6,495
	Norway.......	4	360	....	....	4	360
	Russia........	281	31,651	....	....	281	31,651
	Spain.........	170	17,400	....	....	170	17,400
	Sweden........	56	6,429	....	....	56	6,429
	United States..	59	7,312	2	3,540	61	10,852
	Total......	6,799	695,858	2	3,540	6,801	699,398
Ploughs............	Unit'd Kingdom	502	9,766	....	....	502	9,766
	Australia......	4,418	93,864	....	....	4,418	93,864
	B. S. Africa.....	5,278	137,343	....	....	5,278	137,343
	B. India.......	67	779	....	....	67	779
	B. W. Indies...	12	87	....	....	12	87
	Newfoundland..	101	613	....	....	101	613
	New Zealand...	732	12,243	....	....	732	12,243
	Argentina......	1,441	54,180	....	....	1,441	54,180
	Brazil.........	45	876	....	....	45	876
	Chili..........	1	40	....	....	1	40
	Cuba..........	44	1,558	....	....	44	1,558
	France........	4	163	....	....	4	163
	French Africa...	1	455	....	....	1	455
	Germany......	12	2,911	....	....	12	2,911
	Greece........	4	282	....	....	4	282
	Norway.......	138	1,145	....	....	138	1,145
	United States..	532	15,987	65	7,450	597	23,437
	Uruguay.......	241	7,009	....	....	241	7,009
	Total......	13,573	339,301	65	7,450	13,638	346,751
Harrows............	Unit'd Kingdom	380	4,738	....	....	380	4,738
	Australia......	2,448	13,121	....	....	2,448	13,121
	B. S. Africa.....	1,442	26,478	....	....	1,442	26,478
	B. India.......	17	327	....	....	17	327
	B. E. Indies, other........	24	963	....	....	24	963
	B. Straits Settlements......	25	444	....	....	25	444

SESSIONAL PAPER No. 11

No. 3.—General Statement of Exports—*Continued.*

Articles Exported.	Countries.	Goods, the Produce of Canada.		Goods, not the Produce of Canada.		Total Exports.	
		Quantity.	Value.	Quantity.	Value.	Quantity.	Value.
MANUFACTURES—*Con.*		No.	$	No.	$	No.	$
Agricultural imple-ments—*Con.*							
Harrows—*Con.*	Newfoundland..	42	734	....	....	42	734
	New Zealand...	857	20,728	....	....	857	20,728
	Argentina......	85	2,780	....	....	85	2,780
	Aust.-Hungary .	2	40	....	....	2	40
	Chili...........	12	240	....	....	12	240
	Cuba...........	1	87	....	....	1	87
	French Africa...	12	114	....	....	12	114
	Italy...........	6	132	....	....	6	132
	Russia.........	119	2,172	....	....	119	2,172
	United States..	584	18,993	29	2,479	613	21,472
	Uruguay........	108	600	....	....	108	600
	Total......	6,164	92,691	29	2,479	6,193	95,170
Hay rakes..........	Unit'd Kingdom	317	6,427	....	....	317	6,427
	Australia......	535	10,975	....	....	535	10,975
	B. S. Africa....	59	1,499	....	....	59	1,499
	Newfoundland..	46	941	....	....	46	941
	New Zealand...	311	6,269	....	....	311	6,269
	Aust.-Hungary..	30	579	....	....	30	579
	Denmark......	6	113	....	....	6	113
	France........	24	726	....	....	24	726
	Germany......	60	1,158	....	....	60	1,158
	Holland.......	52	1,877	....	....	52	1,877
	Italy..........	10	427	....	....	10	427
	Russia.........	312	5,162	....	....	312	5,162
	Spain...,.....	48	866	....	....	48	866
	Sweden........	48	887	....	....	48	887
	United States..	197	9,867	....	....	197	9,867
	Total......	2,055	47,773	....	....	2,055	47,773
Seeders..............	Newfoundland..	1	11	....	....	1	11
	United States..	10	659	....	....	10	659
	Total......	11	670	....	....	11	670
Threshing machines.	Australia......	1,758	545,382	2	2,245	1,760	547,627
	United States..	285	321,611	6	7,579	291	329,190
	Total......	2,043	866,993	8	9,824	2,051	876,817
All other. ·..........	Unit'd Kingdom	....	49,982	....	....	....	49,982
	Australia......	....	17,380	....	12	....	17,392
	Bermuda......	....	20	....	....	....	20
	B. S. Africa....	....	6,133	....	....	....	6,133
	B. W. Indies....	....	60	....	....	....	60
	Newfoundland..	....	2,450	....	....	....	2,450
	New Zealand...	....	10,282	....	....	....	10,282
	Argentina......	....	9,827	....	....	....	9,827
	Belgium........	....	700	....	....	....	700
	Brazil.........	....	15	....	....	....	15
	Denmark......	....	5,833	....	....	....	5,833
	France........	....	38,172	....	....	....	38,172
	Germany......	....	20,680	....	....	....	20,680
	Greece........	....	107	....	....	....	107
	Holland.......	....	8,135	....	....	....	8,135
	Norway.......	....	8,475	....	....	....	8,475
	Russia.........	....	285	....	....	....	285
	Spain.........	....	546	....	....	....	546
	Sweden....,...	....	5,233	....	....	....	5,233
	Turkey........	....	175	....	....	....	175
	United States..	....	78,232	....	11,927	....	90,159
	Uruguay.......	....	800	....	....	....	800
	Venezuela......	....	254	....	....	....	254
	Total......	....	263,776	....	11,939	....	275,715

6 GEORGE V, A. 1916

No. 3.—General Statement of Exports—*Continued.*

Articles Exported.	Countries.	Goods, the Produce of Canada.		Goods, not the Produce of Canada.		Total Exports.	
		Quantity.	Value.	Quantity.	Value.	Quantity.	Value.
MANUFACTURES—*Con.*			$		$		$
Agricultural imple- ments—*Con.*							
Parts of.............	Unit'd Kingdom	....	53,524	....	....	....	53,524
	Australia.......	....	288,814	....	....	....	288,814
	B. E. Africa....	....	19	....	....	....	19
	B. S. Africa....	....	67,499	....	....	....	67,499
	B. India.......	....	172	....	....	....	172
	B. W. Indies....	....	31	....	....	....	31
	B. Straits Set- tlements.....	....	214	....	....	....	214
	Fiji Islands.....	....	178	....	....	....	178
	New Zealand...	....	24,938	....	....	....	24,938
	Argentina......	....	22,274	....	....	....	22,274
	Aust.-Hungary..	....	132	....	....	....	132
	Belgium........	....	3,033	....	....	....	3,033
	Chili..........	....	2,964	....	....	....	2,964
	Cuba..........	....	65	....	....	....	65
	Denmark......	....	1,664	....	....	....	1,664
	France........	....	82,172	....	....	....	82,172
	French Africa...	....	1,243	....	....	....	1,243
	Germany......	....	10,819	....	....	....	10,819
	Greece........	....	250	....	....	....	250
	Holland.......	....	1,779	....	....	....	1,779
	Italy..........	....	1,082	....	....	....	1,082
	Norway........	....	1,223	....	....	....	1,223
	Portugal.......	....	22	....	....	....	22
	Portugese Africa	....	289	....	....	....	289
	Roumania.....	....	30	....	....	....	30
	Russia........	....	28,961	....	....	....	28,961
	Spain.........	....	2,647	....	....	....	2,647
	Sweden........	....	367	....	....	....	367
	Turkey........	....	7	....	....	....	7
	United States..	....	51,891	....	20,164	....	72,055
	Uruguay.......	....	589	....	....	....	589
	Total......	....	648,892	....	20,164	....	669,056
Asbestos, mnfrs. of....	Unit'd Kingdom	....	37,169	....	....	....	37,169
	Australia.......	....	16	....	....	....	16
	Bermuda.......	....	44	....	....	....	44
	B. S. Africa....	....	1,737	....	....	....	1,737
	B. Honduras....	....	3,392	....	....	....	3,392
	B. India.......	....	17,535	....	....	....	17,535
	B. W. Indies....	....	207	....	....	....	207
	Newfoundland..	....	250	....	....	....	250
	Brazil.........	....	1,170	....	....	....	1,170
	China.........	....	100	....	....	....	100
	Dutch E. Indies	....	1,194	....	....	....	1,194
	Guatemala......	....	486	....	....	....	486
	Mexico........	....	1,531	....	....	....	1,531
	Miquelon and St. Pierre....	....	34	....	....	....	34
	Peru..........	....	210	....	....	....	210
	United States..	....	13,254	....	964	....	14,218
	Total......	....	78,329	....	964	....	79,293
		Lb.		Lb.		Lb.	
Baking powders.......	Bermuda.......	30	3	....	....	30	3
	Newfoundland..	84,672	13,076	....	....	84,672	13,076
	Miquelon and St. Pierre.....	75	17	....	....	75	17
	United States..	....	....	1,380	194	1,380	194
	Total......	84,777	13,096	1,380	194	86,157	13,290

No. 3.—General Statement of Exports—*Continued*.

Articles Exported.	Countries.	Goods, the Produce of Canada.		Goods, not the Produce of Canada.		Total Exports.	
		Quantity.	Value.	Quantity.	Value.	Quantity.	Value.
MANUFACTURES—*Con.*		Lb.	$	Lb.	$	Lb.	$
Binder twine.........	Unit'd Kingdom	1,550,610	105,611	....	....	1,550,610	105,611
	B. S. Africa....	957,950	74,790	....	....	957,950	74,790
	Aust.-Hungary..	56,330	5,304	....	....	56,330	5,304
	Denmark......	276,000	18,724	....	....	276,000	18,724
	United States..	9,440,818	872,592	35,850	3,050	9,476,668	875,642
	Total.......	12,281,708	1,077,021	35,850	3,050	12,317,558	1,080,071
Books, pamphlets,	Unit'd Kingdom	....	133,971	....	68,532	....	202,503
maps, etc.	Australia......	....	8,065	....	433	....	8,498
	Bermuda......	....	629	....	2	....	631
	B. S. Africa....	....	1,285	....	5	....	1,290
	B. W. Africa...	....	45	....	....	....	45
	B. Guiana.....	....	132	....	....	....	132
	B. Honduras...	....	66	....	....	....	66
	B. India.......	....	851	....	15	....	866
	B. E. Indies, other........	....	45	....	....	....	45
	B. W. Indies...	....	4,761	....	95	....	4,856
	B. Straits Settlements.....	....	408	....	....	....	408
	Fiji Islands....	....	18	....	....	....	18
	Hong Kong....	....	16	....	....	....	16
	Newfoundland..	....	15,178	....	779	....	15,957
	New Zealand...	....	1,102	....	55	....	1,157
	Alaska........	....	180	....	125	....	305
	Argentina.....	....	151	....	....	....	151
	Aust.-Hungary.	....	70	....	....	....	70
	Belgium......	....	426	....	....	....	426
	Chili........	....	30	....	....	....	30
	China.......	....	1,221	....	....	....	1,221
	Costa Rica....	....	49	....	....	....	49
	Cuba........	....	9,450	....	....	....	9,450
	Denmark......	....	....	....	20	....	20
	Dutch Guiana..	....	75	....	....	....	75
	France........	....	2,260	....	3,475	....	5,735
	Germany......	....	233	....	236	....	469
	Hawaii.......	....	6	....	....	....	6
	Honduras.....	....	8	....	....	....	8
	Japan........	....	599	....	....	....	599
	Mexico.......	....	234	....	....	....	234
	Miquelon and St. Pierre....	....	36	....	....	....	36
	Norway......	....	5	....	....	....	5
	Philippines....	....	405	....	....	....	405
	Porto Rico....	....	3	....	....	....	3
	Siam........	....	15	....	....	....	15
	Switzerland....	....	83	....	....	....	83
	United States..	....	237,915	....	159,969	....	397,884
	Total......	....	420,026	....	233,741	....	653,767
		Cwt.		Cwt.		Cwt.	
Biscuits and bread.....	Unit'd Kingdom	578	4,430	10	148	588	4,578
	Bermuda......	660	4,960	....	....	660	4,960
	B. Guiana.....	68	753	....	....	68	753
	B. W. Indies....	382	4,142	....	....	382	4,142
	Newfoundland..	137	2,323	....	....	137	2,323
	Alaska........	25	382	5	64	30	446
	Belgium.......	782	6,392	....	....	782	6,392
	Miquelon and St. Pierre.....	30	265	....	....	30	265
	United States..	370	2,805	14	203	384	3,008
	Total.......	3,032	26,452	29	415	3,061	26,867

6 GEORGE V, A. 1916

No. 3.—GENERAL STATEMENT OF EXPORTS—*Continued.*

Articles Exported.	Countries.	GOODS, THE PRODUCE OF CANADA.		GOODS, NOT THE PRODUCE OF CANADA.		TOTAL EXPORTS.	
		Quantity.	Value.	Quantity.	Value.	Quantity.	Value.
MANUFACTURES—*Con.*		M.	$	M.	$	M.	$
Bricks.................	Newfoundland..	51	478	....	....	51	478
	United States..	1,431	11,542	22	224	1,453	11,766
	Total.......	1,482	12,020	22	224	1,504	12,244
Brooms and whisks....	Unit'd Kingdom	....	1,271	....	....	....	1,271
	Australia......	....	217	....	....	....	217
	Bermuda.......	....	938	....	....	....	938
	B. S. Africa....	....	961	....	....	....	961
	B. Guiana......	....	4,364	....	....	....	4,364
	B. W. Indies....	....	6,306	....	....	....	6,306
	Newfoundland..	....	9	....	3	....	12
	New Zealand...	....	102	....	....	....	102
	Dutch Guiana..	....	115	....	....	....	115
	Miquelon and St. Pierre.....	....	150	....	....	....	150
	Peru...........	....	38	....	....	....	38
	Total......	....	14,471	....	3	....	14,474
Brushes of all kinds....	Unit'd Kingdom	....	587	....	73	....	660
	Australia......	....	1,437	....	....	....	1,437
	Bermuda.......	....	15	....	....	....	15
	B. Guiana......	....	180	....	....	....	180
	B. W. Indies....	....	971	....	....	....	971
	Newfoundland..	....	4,775	....	132	....	4,907
	New Zealand...	....	1,121	....	....	....	1,121
	France.........	....	12	....	....	....	12
	Japan..........	....	10	....	30	....	40
	Miquelon and St. Pierre.....	....	37	....	....	....	37
	Panama........	....	66	....	....	....	66
	United States..	....	358	....	1,100	....	1,458
	Total......	....	9,569	....	1,335	....	10,904
Buttons...............	Unit'd Kingdom	....	5	....	92	....	97
	Newfoundland..	....	50	....	....	....	50
	Germany......	....	....	....	432	....	432
	Japan..........	....	....	....	218	....	218
	United States..	....	339	....	2,029	....	2,368
	Total......	....	394	....	2,771	....	3,165
		Lb.		Lb.		Lb.	
Candles...............	Bermuda......	30	4	....	....	30	4
	Newfoundland..	288	40	395	52	683	92
	United States..	334	45	984	155	1,318	200
	Total......	652	89	1,379	207	2,031	296
Cartridges, gun, rifle and pistol.	Unit'd Kingdom	....	116,014	....	370	....	116,384
	B. S. Africa....	....	150	....	....	....	150
	B. India........	....	913	....	....	....	913
	Newfoundland..	....	1,399	....	....	....	1,399
	New Zealand...	....	810	....	....	....	810
	Cuba...........	....	171	....	....	....	171
	Russia.........	....	3,962	....	....	....	3,962
	United States..	....	97,718	....	1,535	....	99,253
	Total......	....	221,137	....	1,905	....	223,042
Charcoal.............	Newfoundland..	....	1,887	....	....	....	1,887
	United States..	....	1,991	....	....	....	1,991
	Total......	....	3,878	....	....	....	3,878

SESSIONAL PAPER No. 11

No. 3.—General Statement of Exports—*Continued.*

Articles Exported.	Countries.	Goods, the Produce of Canada.		Goods, not the Produce of Canada.		Total Exports.	
		Quantity.	Value.	Quantity.	Value.	Quantity.	Value.
MANUFACTURES—*Con.*			$		$		$
Cement...............	Unit'd Kingdom	....	....	....	2	....	2
	B. S. Africa....	....	265	....	....	....	265
	B. W. Indies...	....	5	....	....	....	5
	Newfoundland..	....	350	....	1,018	....	1,368
	Miquelon and St. Pierre.....	....	....	....	167	....	167
	United States..	....	445	....	109	....	554
	Total......	....	1,065	....	1,296	....	2,361
Cinders...............	United States..	....	885	....	....	....	885
Clay, manufactures of.	Unit'd Kingdom	....	77	....	....	....	77
	United States..	....	17,319	....	985	....	18,304
	Total......	....	17,396	....	985	....	18,381
Clothing and wearing apparel.	Unit'd Kingdom	....	6,288,694	....	28,175	....	6,316,869
	Australia......	....	119,821	....	....	....	119,821
	Bermuda......	....	512	....	....	....	512
	B. S. Africa....	....	2,669	....	203	....	2,872
	B. Guiana.....	....	9	....	....	....	9
	B. W. Indies....	....	6,850	....	....	....	6,850
	Hong Kong....	....	57	....	420	....	477
	Newfoundland..	....	29,089	....	2,667	....	31,756
	New Zealand...	....	41,362	....	50	....	41,412
	Alaska.........	....	3,986	....	451	....	4,437
	Argentina......	....	655	....	....	....	655
	Aust.-Hungary..	....	205	....	....	....	205
	Belgium.......	....	422,677	....	....	....	422,677
	China.........	....	562	....	....	....	562
	Dutch W. Indies	....	358	....	....	....	358
	France........	....	303,509	....	1,397	....	304,906
	Germany......	....	1,426	....	1,307	....	2,733
	Holland.......	....	....	....	22	....	22
	Italy..........	....	135	....	1,342	....	1,477
	Japan.........	....	32	....	23	....	55
	Miquelon and St. Pierre.....	....	715	....	....	....	715
	Norway.......	....	286	....	....	....	286
	Russia........	....	27	....	....	....	27
	Switzerland....	....	....	....	15	....	15
	United States..	....	120,752	....	103,879	....	224,631
	Total......	....	7,344,388	....	139,951	....	7,484,339
		Ton.		Ton.		Ton.	
Coke.................	United States..	52,874	240,818	....	....	52,874	240,818
Confectionery........	Unit'd Kingdom	....	28,538	....	1,694	....	30,232
	Australia......	....	147	....	....	....	147
	Bermuda......	....	134	....	....	....	134
	B. India......	....	22	....	....	....	22
	B. W. Indies...	....	169	....	....	....	169
	Newfoundland..	....	37,963	....	367	....	38,330
	New Zealand...	....	3,282	....	....	....	3,282
	Alaska........	....	17	....	....	....	17
	Belgium.......	....	600	....	....	....	600
	China.........	....	83	....	....	....	83
	Holland.......	....	....	....	200	....	200
	Italy..........	....	3	....	....	....	3
	Japan.........	....	309	....	....	....	309
	Miquelon and St. Pierre.....	....	1,131	....	....	....	1,131
	United States...	....	10,304	....	3,899	....	14,203
	Total......	....	82,702	....	6,160	....	88,862

No. 3.—General Statement of Exports—*Continued.*

Articles Exported.	Countries.	Goods, the Produce of Canada.		Goods, not the Produce of Canada.		Total Exports.	
		Quantity.	Value.	Quantity.	Value.	Quantity.	Value.
MANUFACTURES—*Con.*			$		$		$
Cordage, ropes, and twine.	Unit'd Kingdom	....	1,220	....	3,187	....	4,407
	Bermuda.......	....	236	....	....	....	236
	B. Guiana.....	....	1,758	....	....	....	1,758
	B. W. Indies.....	....	22,831	....	....	....	22,831
	Newfoundland..	....	4,509	....	2,379	....	6,888
	New Zealand...	....	96	....	....	....	96
	Alaska..........	....	....	....	1,255	....	1,255
	Cuba..........	....	....	....	51	....	51
	United States..	....	16,530	....	14,205	....	30,735
	Total......	....	47,180	....	21,077	....	68,257
		Yd.		Yd.		Yd.	
Corton fabrics........	Unit'd Kingdom	813,894	158,649	24,665	3,241	838,559	161,890
	Australia......	26,004	11,482	....	....	26,004	11,482
	B. S. Africa....	28,074	7,336	....	....	28,074	7,336
	B. E. Indies, other........	1,031	239	....	....	1,031	239
	B. W. Indies....	411	113	....	....	411	113
	Newfoundland..	71,971	16,487	151	67	72,122	16,554
	New Zealand...	93,827	33,588	....	....	93,827	33,588
	Brazil.........	10,790	2,692	....	....	10,790	2,692
	Chili.........	2,196	905	....	....	2,196	905
	China.........	27,446	8,648	....	....	27,446	8,648
	Costa Rica....	411	342	....	....	411	342
	Ecuador.......	2,096	1,735	....	....	2,096	1,735
	France.........	43,980	13,184	....	....	43,980	13,184
	Germany......	67,479	15,567	....	....	67,479	15,567
	Japan.........	5,406	3,776	1,140	89	6,546	3,865
	Mexico........	418	384	....	....	418	384
	Miquelon and St. Pierre.....	958	356	....	....	958	356
	Nicaragua......	1,055	350	....	....	1,055	350
	San Domingo...	1,118	174	....	....	1,118	174
	U.S.ofColombia	3,548	733	....	....	3,548	733
	United States..	14,442	3,972	78,331	9,360	92,773	13,332
	Venezuela......	6,409	2,116	....	....	6,409	2,116
	Total......	1,222,964	282,828	104,287	12,757	1,327,251	295,585
Cottons, other........	Unit'd Kingdom	....	33,275	....	23,596	....	56,871
	Australia......	....	3,642	....	....	....	3,642
	Bermuda......	....	110	....	....	....	110
	B. S. Africa....	....	420	....	....	....	420
	B. W. Indies....	....	155	....	....	....	155
	Malta.........	....	....	....	6	....	6
	Newfoundland..	....	3,254	....	47	....	3,301
	New Zealand...	....	378	....	....	....	378
	Argentina......	....	40	....	....	....	40
	Aust.-Hungary .	....	21,000	....	100	....	21,100
	Belgium.......	....	....	....	100	....	100
	France........	....	12,081	....	75	....	12,156
	Germany......	....	6,140	....	61,190	....	67,330
	Miquelon and St. Pierre....	....	1,049	....	....	....	1,049
	Russia........	....	....	....	60,250	....	60,250
	Switzerland....	....	....	....	574	....	574
	United States..	....	69,799	....	309,515	....	379,314
	Total......	....	151,343	....	455,453	....	606,796
		Lb.		Lb.		Lb.	
Cotton waste.........	Unit'd Kingdom	231,625	12,403	....	....	231,625	12,403
	Bermuda.......	268	38	....	....	268	38
	Newfoundland..	5,540	163	....	....	5,540	163
	United States..	1,369,448	60,132	195,758	9,180	1,565,206	69,312
	Total......	1,606,881	72,736	195,758	9,180	1,802,639	81,916

SESSIONAL PAPER No. 11

No. 3.—General Statement of Exports—*Continued.*

Articles Exported.	Countries.	Goods, the Produce of Canada.		Goods, not the Produce of Canada.		Total Exports.	
		Quantity.	Value.	Quantity.	Value.	Quantity.	Value.
MANUFACTURES—*Con.*			$		$		$
Cream separators......	Unit'd Kingdom	....	2,250	....	130	....	2,380
	B. S. Africa.....	....	2,002	....	......	....	2,002
	Newfoundland..	....	207	....	15	....	222
	Germany.......	....	......	....	190	....	190
	United States..	....	45,360	....	16,054	....	61,414
	Total......	....	49,819	....	16,389	....	66,208
Drugs, Chemicals and Medicines, viz.—		Lb.		Lb.		Lb.	
Acetate of lime......	Unit'd Kingdom	7,667,068	130,519	....	....	7,667,068	130,519
	Belgium........	491,087	9,041	....	....	491,087	9,041
	Germany.......	376,139	5,606	....	....	376,139	5,606
	Holland........	695,867	13,289	....	....	695,867	13,289
	United States..	5,908,846	111,136	....	....	5,908,846	111,136
	Total......	15,139,007	269,591	....	....	15,139,007	269,591
Acid, sulphuric......	Newfoundland..	....	....	360	9	360	9
	Miquelon and St. Pierre.....	290	27	....	....	290	27
	United States..	6,409,545	41,308	....	....	6,409,545	41,308
	Total......	6,409,835	41,335	360	9	6,410,195	41,344
Calcium carbide....	Australia.......	3,308,300	99,210	....	....	3,308,300	99,210
	B. S. Africa.....	6,576,670	198,054	....	....	6,576,670	198,054
	B. Guiana......	20,000	605	....	....	20,000	605
	B. W. Indies....	99,460	2,997	....	....	99,460	2,997
	Newfoundland..	11,632	365	....	....	11,632	365
	New Zealand...	896,400	27,192	....	....	896,400	27,192
	Argentina......	647,340	19,719	....	....	647,340	19,719
	Brazil..........	364,900	10,937	....	....	364,900	10,937
	Chili..........	748,960	22,476	....	....	748,960	22,476
	U. S. of Colombia..........	4,000	120	....	....	4,000	120
	United States..	23,531,577	731,416	....	....	23,531,577	731,416
	Uruguay.......	50,600	1,518	....	....	50,600	1,518
	Venezuela......	82,880	2,509	....	....	82,880	2,509
	Total......	36,342,719	1,117,118	....	....	36,342,719	1,117,118
Gum chicle.........	Unit'd Kingdom	10,000	4,750	10,000	5,000	20,000	9,750
	Australia......	5,823	3,278	....	....	5,823	3,278
	United States..	1,882,049	913,776	323,093	125,972	2,205,142	1,039,748
	Total......	1,897,872	921,804	333,093	130,972	2,230,965	1,052,776
Lye................	Newfoundland..	....	1,670	....	....	....	1,670
	United States..	....	109,148	....	....	....	109,148
	Total......	....	110,818	....	....	....	110,818
Phosphorus.........	Unit'd Kingdom	558,050	84,458	....	....	558,050	84,458
Senega root.........	Unit'd Kingdom	4,540	2,510	....	....	4,540	2,510
	Australia......	2,107	1,054	....	....	2,107	1,054
	Germany.......	14,150	8,205	....	....	14,150	8,205
	Japan..........	4,829	2,373	....	....	4,829	2,373
	United States..	348,217	157,177	....	....	348,217	157,177
	Total......	373,843	171,319	....	....	373,843	171,319

No. 3.—General Statement of Exports—*Continued.*

Articles Exported.	Countries.	Goods, the Produce of Canada.		Goods, not the Produce of Canada.		Total Exports.	
		Quantity.	Value.	Quantity.	Value.	Quantity.	Value.
			$		$		$
MANUFACTURES—*Con.*							
Drugs, etc.—*Con.*							
All other, n.o.p......	Unit'd Kingdom	....	241,190	....	23,533	....	264,723
	Australia......	....	5,825	....	....	....	5,825
	Bermuda.......	....	1,187	....	24	....	1,211
	B. S. Africa....	....	12,910	....	....	....	12,910
	B. W. Africa....	....	96	....	....	....	96
	B. Guiana......	....	649	....	....	....	649
	B. Honduras...	....	5	....	....	....	5
	B. India.......	....	24,957	....	....	....	24,957
	B. W. Indies....	....	6,309	....	135	....	6,444
	Hong Kong.....	....	48	....	....	....	48
	Newfoundland.	....	71,800	....	4,810	....	76,610
	New Zealand...	....	489	....	....	....	489
	Alaska.........	....	6	....	....	....	6
	Argentina.....	....	512	....	....	....	512
	Belgium.......	....	1,198	....	2,271	....	3,469
	Chili.........	....	560	....	....	....	560
	China.........	....	153	....	....	....	153
	Costa Rica.....	....	95	....	....	....	95
	Cuba.........	....	355	....	....	....	355
	Dutch W. Indies.......	....	5	....	....	....	5
	Dutch Guiana..	....	84	....	....	....	84
	Ecuador.......	....	302	....	....	....	302
	France.......	....	2,669	....	57,891	....	60,560
	Germany......	....	687	....	1,104	....	1,791
	Guatemala....	....	80	....	....	....	80
	Hawaii........	....	....	....	100	....	100
	Holland.......	....	....	....	48	....	48
	Honduras......	....	76	....	....	....	76
	Japan.........	....	180	....	53,629	....	53,809
	Miquelon and St. Pierre.....	....	341	....	303	....	644
	Nicaragua.....	....	20	....	....	....	20
	Panama.......	....	710	....	....	....	710
	Russia........	....	40	....	....	....	40
	San Domingo...	....	48	....	....	....	48
	Siam.........	....	788	....	....	....	788
	U. S. of Colombia.........	....	179	....	....	....	179
	United States..	....	382,402	....	214,684	....	597,086
	Venezuela......	....	834	....	....	....	834
	Total......	....	757,789	....	358,532	....	1,116,321
Dye stuffs.............	Newfoundland..	....	3,125	....	47	....	3,172
	United States..	....	21,609	....	45,972	....	67,581
	Total......	....	24,734	....	46,019	....	70,753
Earthenware and all manufactures of.....	Unit'd Kingdom	....	1,976	....	576	....	2,552
	Australia......	....	114	....	....	....	114
	Bermuda......	....	75	....	....	....	75
	Newfoundland..	....	185	....	7	....	192
	Alaska.........	....	272	....	....	....	272
	Aust.-Hungary..	....	....	....	16	....	16
	Belgium.......	....	25	....	....	....	25
	China.........	....	38	....	....	....	38
	Cuba.........	....	449	....	....	....	449
	Hawaii........	....	25	....	....	....	25
	Miquelon and St. Pierre.....	....	39	....	34	....	73
	Panama.......	....	27	....	....	....	27
	United States..	....	3,873	....	6,542	....	10,415
	Total......	....	7,098	....	7,175	....	14,273

SESSIONAL PAPER No. 11

No. 3.—General Statement of Exports—Continued.

Articles Exported.	Countries.	Goods, the Produce of Canada.		Goods, not the Produce of Canada.		Total Exports.	
		Quantity.	Value.	Quantity.	Value.	Quantity.	Value.
MANUFACTURES—*Con.*			$		$		$
Electrical apparatus....	Unit'd Kingdom	....	17,012	....	13,227	....	30,239
	Australia......	....	1,282	....	1,345	....	2,627
	B. S. Africa.....	....	5,184	....	....	....	5,184
	B. W. Indies....	....	1,341	....	....	....	1,341
	Fiji Islands....	....	37	....	....	....	37
	Newfoundland..	....	15,792	....	486	....	16,278
	New Zealand...	....	593	....	....	....	593
	Alaska.........	....	10	....	264	....	274
	Aust.-Hungary..	....	5	....	....	....	5
	Belgium......	....	....	....	30	....	30
	Denmark......	....	90	....	....	....	90
	France.........	....	903	....	76	....	979
	Germany......	....	2,749	....	597	....	3,346
	Greece.........	....	2,659	....	....	....	2,659
	Holland.......	....	....	....	436	....	436
	Mexico........	....	619	....	....	....	619
	Miquelon and St. Pierre....	....	179	....	71	....	250
	United States..	....	49,417	....	208,049	....	257,466
	Uruguay.......	....	18	....	....	....	18
	Total......	....	97,890	....	224,581	....	322,471
Electrotypes and stereotypes.	Unit'd Kingdom	....	66	....	151	....	217
	Australia.....	....	72	....	....	....	72
	B. India......	....	2	....	....	....	2
	New Zealand...	....	4	....	....	....	4
	Russia.........	....	63	....	....	....	63
	United States..	....	6,080	....	7,118	....	13,198
	Total......	....	6,287	....	7,269	....	13,556
		Brl.		Brl.		Brl.	
Extract of hemlock bark.	Unit'd Kingdom	2,371	28,512	....	....	2,371	28,512
	B. S. Africa.....	55	660	....	....	55	660
	Newfoundland..	61	732	....	....	61	732
	France.........	55	660	....	....	55	660
	United States..	8	248	....	....	8	248
	Total......	2,550	30,812	....	....	2,550	30,812
Explosives and fulminates, n.o.p.	Unit'd Kingdom	....	51,543	....	....	....	51,543
	Newfoundland..	....	44,440	....	165	....	44,605
	Alaska.:.......	....	110	....	....	....	110
	Japan..........	....	8,048	....	....	....	8,048
	Mexico........	....	1,960	....	....	....	1,960
	Miquelon and St. Pierre.....	....	1,184	....	....	....	1,184
	United States..	....	158,293	....	17,870	....	176,163
	Total......	....	265,578	....	18,035	....	283,613
Felt, manufactures of..	Unit'd Kingdom	....	556	....	700	....	1,256
	Bermuda......	....	....	....	30	....	30
	B. S. Africa....	....	422	....	....	....	422
	B. W. Indies....	....	88	....	....	....	88
	Newfoundland..	....	2,179	....	160	....	2,339
	United States..	....	3,682	....	1,455	....	5,137
	Total......	....	6,927	....	2,345	....	9,272
Fertilizers............	Unit'd Kingdom	....	877	....	7,000	....	7,877
	B. Guiana.....	....	1,875	....	....	....	1,875
	B. W. Indies....	....	136,934	....	....	....	136,934
	Newfoundland..	....	1,483	....	....	....	1,483
	Germany......	....	5,279	....	....	....	5,279

6 GEORGE V, A. 1916

No. 3.—General Statement of Exports—*Continued.*

Articles Exported.	Countries.	Goods, the Produce of Canada.		Goods, not the Produce of Canada.		Total Exports.	
		Quantity.	Value.	Quantity.	Value.	Quantity.	Value.
MANUFACTURES—*Con.*			$		$		$
Fertilizers—*Con.*	Hawaii		20,668				20,668
	Japan		90				90
	Porto Rico		120				120
	United States		1,996,591		255		1,996,846
	Total		2,163,917		7,255		2,171,172
Films for photograph-ers' use and for mov-ing pictures.	Unit'd Kingdom		1,415		2,235		3,650
	Newfoundland				200		200
	Alaska		3,900		680		4,580
	France				808		808
	Germany		210				210
	Unit'd States		25,719		53,022		78,741
	Total		31,244		56,945		88,189
Fur, manufactures of	Unit'd Kingdom		17,097		2,789		19,886
	Australia		1,017				1,017
	Bermuda		50				50
	Newfoundland		2,657		500		3,157
	Aust.-Hungary				80		80
	Belgium		200				200
	China		250				250
	United States		8,537		4,851		13,388
	Total		29,808		8,220		38,028
		No.		No.		No.	
Gasoline engines	Unit'd Kingdom	37	7,218	4	1,353	41	8,571
	Newfoundland	774	94,019	47	4,543	821	98,562
	New Zealand	8	1,125			8	1,125
	Miquelon and St. Pierre	9	930			9	930
	U. S. of Colombia	1	643			1	643
	United States	65	12,672	396	86,801	461	99,473
	Total	894	116,607	447	92,697	1,341	209,304
Gasoline launches	Newfoundland	1	100			1	100
	Alaska	2	2,300			2	2,300
	United States	8	4,067	10	7,543	18	11,610
	Total	11	6,467	10	7,543	21	14,010
Glass and glassware, n.o.p.	Unit'd Kingdom		14,016		1,216		15,232
	Australia		20,640				20,640
	B. Guiana		68				68
	B. W. Indies		185				185
	B. Straits Settlements		500				500
	Newfoundland		3,103		268		3,371
	New Zealand		1,632				1,632
	Aust.-Hungary		10		3		13
	Belgium		5				5
	China		20				20
	Germany		14		17		31
	Hawaii		15		600		615
	Miquelon and St. Pierre		13				13
	United States		15,332		20,237		35,569
	Total		55,553		22,341		77,894

No. 3.—General Statement of Exports—*Continued.*

Articles Exported.	Countries.	Goods, the Produce of Canada.		Goods, not the Produce of Canada.		Total Exports.	
		Quantity.	Value.	Quantity.	Value.	Quantity.	Value.
MANUFACTURES—*Con.*			$		$		↳
Grindstones, manu-factured.	B. W. Indies....	....	8	....	....	....	8
	Newfoundland..	....	320	....	....	....	320
	Alaska.........	....	....	....	41	↳	41
	Panama.......	....	46	....	....	....	46
	United States..	....	45,515	....	1,817	....	47,332
	Total......	....	45,889	....	1,858	....	47,747
Guns, rifles and fire-arms of all kinds.	Unit'd Kingdom	....	153,224	....	8,039	....	161,263
	Australia......	....	226	....	....	....	226
	B. S. Africa....	....	30	....	....	....	30
	B. India.......	....	3,545	....	60	....	3,605
	B. W. Indies....	....	88	....	....	....	88
	Newfoundland..	....	20,324	....	8	....	20,332
	New Zealand...	....	1,388	....	....	....	1,388
	Alaska........	....	35	....	50	....	85
	Belgium.......	....	....	....	668	....	668
	China........	....	50	....	....	....	50
	Russia........	....	93	....	....	....	93
	United States..	....	32,321	....	12,648	....	44,969
	Total......	....	211,324	....	21,473	....	232,797
Gypsum or plaster, ground.	Unit'd Kingdom	....	216	....	....	....	216
	Australia......	....	1,955	....	....	....	1,955
	Newfoundland..	....	223	....	....	....	223
	New Zealand...	....	5,439	....	....	....	5,439
	Miquelon and St. Pierre....	....	6	....	....	....	6
	United States..	....	24,039	....	....	....	24,039
	Total......	....	31,878	....	....	....	31,878
Hats and caps........	Unit'd Kingdom	....	917	....	4,515	....	5,432
	Australia......	....	55	....	....	....	55
	B. S. Africa....	....	72	....	....	....	72
	B. W. Indies....	....	20	....	....	....	20
	Hong Kong....	....	8	....	....	....	8
	Newfoundland..	....	12,904	....	....	....	12,904
	Aust.-Hungary..	....	55	....	13	....	68
	China........	....	180	....	....	....	180
	Greece........	....	3	....	....	....	3
	Italy..........	....	21	....	2,770	....	2,791
	Japan........	....	21	....	....	....	21
	United States..	....	1,947	....	8,217	....	10,164
	Total......	....	16,203	....	15,515	....	31,718
Household effects, n.o.p.	Unit'd Kingdom	....	356,918	....	54,612	....	411,530
	Australia......	....	13,343	....	750	....	14,093
	Bermuda......	....	3,701	....	....	....	3,701
	B. S. Africa....	....	3,212	....	....	....	3,212
	B. W. Africa....	....	35	....	....	....	35
	B. Guiana.....	....	930	....	....	....	930
	B. India......	....	1,700	....	....	....	1,700
	B. W. Indies....	....	3,960	....	....	....	3,960
	Hong Kong....	....	1,962	....	....	....	1,962
	Newfoundland..	....	26,744	....	1,010	....	27,754
	New Zealand...	....	8,647	....	....	....	8,647
	Alaska........	....	7,615	....	132	....	7,747
	Aust.-Hungary..	....	341	....	....	....	341
	Belgium.......	....	1,475	....	500	....	1,975
	Chili..........	....	5,900	....	....	....	5,900
	China........	....	9,101	....	....	....	9,101
	Cuba.........	....	1,370	....	....	....	1,370

No. 3.—General Statement of Exports—*Continued.*

Articles Exported.	Countries.	Goods, the Produce of Canada.		Goods, not the Produce of Canada.		Total Exports.	
		Quantity.	Value.	Quantity.	Value.	Quantity.	Value.
MANUFACTURES—*Con.*			$		$		· $
Household effects, n.o.p.—*Con.*	Denmark......	....	100	....	25	....	125
	France.........	....	10,307	....	60	....	10,367
	Germany......	....	4,450	....	....	....	4,450
	Greece........	....	16	....	....	....	16
	Greenland and Iceland......	....	150	....	....	....	150
	Hawaii........	....	834	....	....	....	834
	Holland.......	....	900	....	99	....	999
	Italy..........	....	1,378	....	....	....	1,378
	Japan.........	....	3,537	....	....	....	3,537
	Korea.........	....	462	....	....	....	462
	Miquelon and St. Pierre.....	....	248	....	....	....	248
	Norway........	....	500	....	....	....	500
	Sweden........	....	......	....	500	..:..	500
	Switzerland....	....	75	....	....	....	75
	United States..	....	3,211,798	....	290,057	....	3,501,855
	Total......	....	3,681,709	....	347,745	....	4,029,454
Ice.........,........	Alaska........	....	275	....	....	....	275
	United States..	....	7,240	....	....	....	7,240
	Total......	....	7,515	....	....	....	7,515
India - rubber, manufactures of, viz:—							
Belting.....	Unit'd Kingdom	....	484	....	398	....	882
	Newfoundland..	....	1,566	....	....	....	1,566
	Alaska.........	....	....	....	384	....	384
	Brazil.........	....	156	....	....	....	156
	United States..	....	68	....	554	....	622
	Total......	....	2,274	....	1,336	....	3,610
Hose..............	Unit'd Kingdom	....	292	....	77	....	369
	Bermuda.......	....	8	....	....	....	8
	B. S. Africa.....	....	632	....	....	....	632
	B. W. Indies....	....	8	....	....	....	8
	Newfoundland..	....	2,765	....	....	....	2,765
	New Zealand...	....	3,062	....	....,...	,	3,062
	Alaska.........	....	....	....	96	....	96
	Miquelon and St. Pierre.....	....	8	·	....	....	8
	United States..	....	9,701	....	2,599	....	12,300
	Total......	....	16,476	....	2,772	....	19,248
Boots and shoes.....	Unit'd Kingdom	....	59,032	....	15	....	59,047
	Australia......	....	37,975	....	....	....	37,975
	Bermuda.......	....	620	....	....	....	620
	B. Guiana.....	....	763	....	....	....	763
	B. W. Indies....	....	585	....	....	....	585
	B.Oceania,other	....	156	....	....	....	156
	Fiji Islands.....	....	279	....	....	....	279
	Newfoundland..	....	62,469	....	....	....	62,469
	New Zealand...	....	23,572	....	....	....	23,572
	Alaska.........	....	....	....	45	....	45
	Dutch W. Indies	....	87	....	....	....	87
	France.........	....	33	....	....	....	33
	Miquelon and St. Pierre.....	....	....	....	35	....	35
	Norway........	....	2,088	....	....	....	2,088
	United States..	....	9,445	....	1,113	....	10,558
	Total......	....	197,104	....	1,208	....	198,312

No. 3.—General Statement of Exports—*Continued.*

Articles Exported.	Countries.	Goods, the Produce of Canada.		Goods, not the Produce of Canada.		Total Exports.	
		Quantity.	Value.	Quantity.	Value.	Quantity.	Value.
MANUFACTURES—*Con.*			$		$		$
India-rubber, etc,-*Con.*							
Mats and matting....	Newfoundland..	....	34	....	....	....	34
Clothing.............	Unit'd Kingdom	....	472	....	1,106	....	1,578
	Bermuda......	....	25	....	....	....	25
	Newfoundland..	....	208	....	28	....	236
	United States..	....	25	....	26	....	51
	Total......	....	730	....	1,160	....	1,890
		Lb.		Lb.		Lb.	
Waste...............	United States..	4,221,476	276,128	14,134	2,314	4,235,610	278,442
All other, n.o.p......	Unit'd Kingdom	....	122,563	....	1,691	....	124,254
	Australia......	....	2,323	....	....	....	2,323
	Bermuda......	....	214	....	....	....	214
	B. S. Africa....:	....	2,952	....	....	....	2,952
	B. W. Indies...	....	2,000	....	....	....	2,000
	Newfoundland..	....	4,416	....	531	....	4,947
	New Zealand..	....	7,145	....	....	....	7,145
	Belgium.......	....	....	....	34	....	34
	Brazil...........	....	49	....	....	....	49
	France........	....	588	....	....	....	588
	Germany......	....	300	....	2,204	....	2,504
	Nicaragua.....	....	18	....	....	....	18
	United States..	....	87,591	....	1,287,808	....	1,375,399
	Total......	....	230,159	....	1,292,268	....	1,522,427
Iron and steel and man-							
ufactures of, viz.:—		No.		No.		No.	
Stoves..............	Unit'd Kingdom	38	1,488	....	....	38	1,488
	Australia......	1	42	....	....	1	42
	B. S. Africa....	12	720	....	....	12	720
	B. W. Indies....	7	116	....	....	7	116
	Hong Kong....	2	381	....	....	2	381
	Newfoundland..	955	12,419	24	236	979	12,655
	New Zealand...	11	215	....	....	11	215
	China..........	5	69	....	....	5	69
	Japan..........	2	121	....	....	2	121
	Miquelon and						
	St. Pierre.....	41	481	....	....	41	481
	United States..	3,151	8,656	2,332	6,799	5,483	15,455
	Total......	4,225	24,708	2,356	7,035	6,581	31,743
Gas buoys and parts	Unit'd Kingdom	....	1,850	....	....	....	1,850
of.	Aden..........	....	62	....	....	....	62
	Australia......	....	2,000	....	....	....	2,000
	Bermuda......	....	10	....	....	....	10
	Newfoundland..	....	9,409	....	....	....	9,409
	Brazil.........	....	1,025	....	....	....	1,025
	Japan.........	....	3,839	....	....	....	3,839
	Panama.......	....	150	....	....	....	150
	U.S. of Colom-						
	bia..........	....	35	....	....	....	35
	United States..	....	1,700	....	607	....	2,307
	Total......	....	20,080	....	607	....	20,687
Castings, n.o.p......:	Unit'd Kingdom	....	127,522	....	25	....	127,547
	Newfoundland..	....	2,945	....	3,224	....	6,169
	Cuba..........	....	87	....	....	....	87
	Germany......	....	5	....	....	....	5
	Miquelon and						
	St. Pierre....	....	230	....	....	....	230
	United States..	....	17,356	....	14,784	....	32,140
	Total......	....	148,145	....	18,033	....	166,178

6 GEORGE V, A. 1916

No. 3.—General Statement of Exports—*Continued.*

Articles Exported.	Countries.	Goods, the Produce of Canada.		Goods, not the Produce of Canada.		Total Exports.	
		Quantity.	Value.	Quantity.	Value.	Quantity.	Value.
MANUFACTURES—*Con.*		Ton.	$	Ton.	$	Ton.	$
Iron and steel—*Con.*							
Pig iron............	Australia.......	563	7,184	....	....	563	7,184
	Newfoundland..	1,250	15,347	....	....	1,250	15,347
	United States..	8,664	104,444	1,115	12,452	9,779	116,896
	Total......	10,477	126,975	1,115	12,452	11,592	139,427
Ferro silicon and ferro compounds.	Unit'd Kingdom	39	1,900	....	....	39	1,900
	Australia.......	85	7,132	....	....	85	7,132
	Japan...........	146	11,819	....	....	146	11,819
	United States..	6,631	377,637	....	....	6,631	377,637
	Total......	6,901	398,488			6,901	398,488
		Cwt.		Cwt.		Cwt.	
Wire and wire nails..	Unit'd Kingdom	266,919	543,451	4	11	266,923	543,462
	Australia.......	73,818	116,245	....	....	73,818	116,245
	Bermuda.......	86	223	....	....	86	223
	B. Guiana......	3,429	6,830	....	....	3,429	6,830
	B. India........	1,068	1,562	....	....	1,068	1,562
	B. W. Indies....	5,668	12,370	....	....	5,668	12,370
	Newfoundland..	10,098	19,367	9	37	10,107	19,404
	New Zealand...	35,737	60,315	....	....	35,737	60,315
	Cuba...........	1,237	3,984	....	....	1,237	3,984
	France..........	41,676	92,231	....	....	41,676	92,231
	Miquelon and St. Pierre.....	3	11	....	....	3	11
	Portugal.......	2,290	4,046	....	....	2,290	4,046
	United States..	4,880	9,684	22,342	11,316	27,222	21,000
	Total......	446,909	870,319	22,355	11,364	469,264	881,683
Machinery, viz.—							
Linotype machines and parts of.	Australia.......	....	1,674	....	....	....	1,674
	B. S. Africa....	....	78	....	....	....	78
	Newfoundland.	....	83	....	....	....	83
	United States..	....	4,200	....	29,759	....	33,959
	Total......	....	6,035	....	29,759	....	35,794
Machinery, n.o.p.....	Unit'd Kingdom	....	39,742	....	23,124	....	62,866
	Australia.......	....	8,613	....	1,294	....	9,907
	B. E. Africa....	....	800	....	....	....	800
	B. S. Africa....	....	4,163	....	....	....	4,163
	B. Honduras...	....	14	....	....	....	14
	B. India........	....	....	....	300	....	300
	B. W. Indies....	....	400	....	....	....	400
	Fiji Islands....	....	197	....	....	....	197
	Hong Kong....	....	29	....	163	....	192
	Malta..........	....	1,938	....	....	....	1,938
	Newfoundland.	....	20,136	....	959	....	21,095
	New Zealand...	....	5,375	....	107	....	5,482
	Alaska.........	....	460	....	2,013	....	2,473
	Argentina......	....	21,170	....	....	....	21,170
	Belgium........	....	200	....	....	....	200
	Brazil..........	....	94	....	....	....	94
	Chili...........	....	53	....	....	....	53
	China..........	....	....	....	556	....	556
	Cuba...........	....	250	....	....	....	250
	Denmark.......	....	336	....	....	....	336
	Egypt and Soudan.	....	116	....	....	....	116
	France..........	....	8,766	....	56	....	8,822
	Germany.......	....	234	....	1,412	....	1,646
	Guatemala.....	....	160	....	....	....	160
	Hawaii.........	....	30	....	....	....	30
	Japan..........	....	....	....	963	....	963
	Miquelon and St. Pierre.....	....	381	....	....	....	381

SESSIONAL PAPER No. 11

No. 3.—GENERAL STATEMENT OF EXPORTS—*Continued.*

Articles Exported.	Countries.	GOODS, THE PRODUCE OF CANADA.		GOODS, NOT THE PRODUCE OF CANADA.		TOTAL EXPORTS.	
		Quantity.	Value.	Quantity.	Value.	Quantity.	Value.
MANUFACTURES—*Con.*							
Iron and steel—*Con.*			$		$		$
Machinery, n.o.p.— *Con.*	Norway.......	....	30	....	....	....	30
	Portugal.......	....	190	....	....	....	190
	Russia.........	....	11,401	. ...	....	....	11,401
	United States..	....	188,432	....	493,143	....	681,575
	Venezuela......	....	70	....	....	....	70
	Total.......	....	313,780	....	524,090	....	837,870
		No.		No.		No.	
Sewing machines....	Unit'd Kingdom	163	4,988	1	200	164	5,188
	B. Guiana......	1	30	....	....	1	30
	Newfoundland..	338	3,700	2	36	340	3,736
	Aust.-Hungary .	2	175	....	....	2	175
	United States..	2,522	24,351	340	13,854	2,862	38,205
	Total.......	3,026	33,244	343	14,090	3,369	47,334
Washing machines, domestic and wringers.........	Unit'd Kingdom	....	15,735	....	66	....	15,801
	Australia......	....	1,594	....	....	....	1,594
	Bermuda.......	....	61	....	....	....	61
	B. S. Africa....	....	141	....	....	....	141
	B. W. Indies....	....	15	....	....	....	15
	Newfoundland..	....	450	....	....	....	450
	New Zealand...	....	7,905	....	....	....	7,905
	Argentina......	....	11	....	....	....	11
	Denmark.......	....	545	....	....	....	545
	France.........	....	109	....	....	....	109
	Germany......	....	2,974	....	....	....	2,974
	Miquelon and St. Pierre.....	....	3	....	....	....	3
	Norway........	....	6	....	....	....	6
	Russia.........	....	547	....	....	....	547
	Sweden........	....	489	....	....	....	489
	United States..	....	667	....	1,198	....	1,865
	Total......	....	31,252	....	1,264	....	32,516
Typewriters........	Unit'd Kingdom	1,857	119,825	4	268	1,861	120,093
	Bermuda.......	1	35	....	....	1	35
	B. India........	1	80	....	....	1	80
	Hong Kong....	4	260	....	....	4	260
	Newfoundland..	13	1,140	11	610	24	1,750
	Belgium........	17	1,285	....	....	17	1,285
	France.........	283	20,781	....	....	283	20,781
	Germany......	114	7,320	....	....	114	7,320
	Holland.......	228	14,042	....	....	228	14,042
	United States..	156	8,443	1,205	55,933	1,361	64,376
	Total......	2,674	173,211	1,220	56,811	3,894	230,022
		Cwt.		Cwt.		Cwt.	
Scrap iron or steel.....	Unit'd Kingdom	17,206	6,864	....	....	17,206	6,864
	Hong Kong....	3,347	2,058	....	....	3,347	2,058
	Belgium........	3,364	1,408	....	....	3,364	1,408
	China..........	638	488	....	....	638	488
	Germany......	1,650	756	....	....	1,650	756
	Holland........	1,442	824	....	....	1,442	824
	United States..	831,208	522,548	9,083	4,750	840,291	527,298
	Total.......	858,855	534,946	9,083	4,750	867,938	539,696

6 GEORGE V, A. 1916

No. 3.—General Statement of Exports—*Continued.*

Articles Exported.	Countries.	Goods, the Produce of Canada.		Goods, not the Produce of Canada.		Total Exports.	
		Quantity.	Value.	Quantity.	Value.	Quantity.	Value.
MANUFACTURES—*Con.*			$		$		$
Iron and steel—*Con.*							
Hardware, viz:—							
Tools, hand or machine.	Unit'd Kingdom	....	51,948	....	2,415	....	54,363
	Australia......		5,226				5,226
	Bermuda......		20				20
	B. S. Africa....		4,411				4,411
	B. W. Indies....		9				9
	Newfoundland..		9,440		52		9,492
	New Zealand...		2,899				2,899
	Alaska..........		53				53
	Argentina....		59				59
	Brazil..........		23				23
	Denmark.....		551				551
	Germany......		527		395		922
	Mexico........		20				20
	Miquelon and St. Pierre....		25				25
	Norway.....		500				500
	Portuguese Africa..		15				15
	Russia........		51				51
	Spain..........		20				20
	Sweden........		5,659				5,659
	United States...		38,201		48,441		86,642
	Uruguay.......		59				59
	Venezuela......		63				63
	Total......		119,779		51,303		171,082
Hardware, n.o.p....	Unit'd Kingdom	....	89,375	....	4,720	....	94,095
	Australia......		9,785				9,785
	Bermuda....		267		317		584
	B. S. Africa....		7,079				7,079
	B. Guiana.....		121				121
	B. India.......		802				802
	B. W. Indies....		697				697
	Fiji Islands....		611				611
	Newfoundland..		14,954		620		15,574
	New Zealand...		7,651		158		7,809
	Alaska.........		57		291		348
	Argentina......		896				896
	Aust.-Hungary.				155		155
	Azores and Madeira.....		8				8
	Belgium......		873				873
	Brazil.........		156				156
	Chili..........		62				62
	China.........		432				432
	Cuba.........		572				572
	Denmark:		5,632		1,789		7,421
	France........		2,974		25		2,999
	Germany......		732		160		892
	Holland......		2,302				2,302
	Italy.........		413		70		483
	Japan.........		81				81
	Miquelon and St. Pierre....		502		169		671
	Norway......		201		75		276
	Russia........		95				95
	Spain........		348				348
	Switzerland....		1,191				1,191
	United States..		101,066		76,610		177,676
	Total......		249,935		85,159		335,094
All other, n.o.p......	Unit'd Kingdom	....	4,442,511	....	36,196	....	4,478,707
	Australia......		664,101		5,041		669,142
	Bermuda.....		732				732
	B. S. Africa.....		947,049		55		947,104
	B. Guiana.....		1,676				1,676

SESSIONAL PAPER No. 11

No. 3.—General Statement of Exports—*Continued.*

Articles Exported.	Countries.	Goods, the Produce of Canada.		Goods, not the Produce of Canada.		Total Exports.	
		Quantity.	Value.	Quantity.	Value.	Quantity.	Value.
MANUFACTURES—*Con.*			$		$		$
Iron and steel—*Con.*							
All other n.o.p.—*Con.*	B. India........	....	24,649	....	....	....	24,649
	B. W. Indies....	....	6,206	....	2,445	....	8,651
	B. Straits						
	Settlements...	....	433	....	....	....	433
	Fiji Islands.....	....	453	....	....	....	453
	Hong Kong....	....	307	....	105	....	412
	Malta..........	....	521	....	....	....	521
	Newfoundland..	....	53,862	....	4,481	....	58,343
	New Zealand...	....	130,848	....	....	....	130,848
	Alaska.........	....	3,090	....	1,207	....	4,297
	Argentina......	....	9,188	....	....	....	9,188
	Belgium.......	....	250	....	....	....	250
	Brazil.........	....	20,948	....	....	....	20,948
	Chili..........	....	2,704	....	....	....	2,704
	Cuba..........	....	232	....	....	....	232
	Dutch W. Indies	....	32	....	....	....	32
	France.........	....	175,876	....	19	....	175,895
	French Africa...	....	612	....	....	....	612
	Germany......	....	1,277	....	202	....	1,479
	Guatemala.....	....	165	....	....	....	165
	Holland.......	....	2,055	....	....	....	2,055
	Italy..........	....	91	....	....	....	91
	Japan.........	....	2,034	....	....	....	2,034
	Miquelon and						
	St. Pierre.....	....	1,935	....	381	....	2,316
	Nicaragua.....	....	24	....	....	....	24
	Norway.......	....	658	....	....	....	658
	Russia........	....	940	....	....	....	940
	Turkey.......	....	58	....	....	....	58
	U.S. of Colom-						
	bia..........	....	979	....	....	....	979
	United States.	....	614,977	....	305,607	....	920,584
	Venezuela......	....	56	....	....	....	56
	Total......	....	7,111,529	....	355,739	....	7,467,268
Jewellery of all kinds, n.o.p.	Unit'd Kingdom	....	13,811	....	115,893	....	129,704
	Australia......	....	2,182	....	....	....	2,182
	Bermuda......	....	2,617	....	60	....	2,677
	B. E. Africa....	....	13	....	....	....	13
	B. Guiana.....	....	273	....	....	....	273
	B. India......	....	100	....	....	....	100
	B. W. Indies...	....	1,360	....	....	....	1,360
	Hong Kong....	....	10	....	....	....	10
	Newfoundland..	....	18,113	....	30	....	18,143
	New Zealand...	....	366	....	....	....	366
	Alaska.........	....	10	....	....	....	10
	Argentina......	....	725	....	....	....	725
	Belgium.......	....	500	....	3,057	....	3,557
	China.........	....	810	....	....	....	810
	Cuba.........	....	1,646	....	....	....	1,646
	France.........	....	204	....	623	....	827
	Germany.....	....	300	....	1,976	....	2,276
	Greece........	....	30	....	....	....	30
	Mexico........	....	123	....	....	....	123
	Norway.......	....	212	....	....	....	212
	Panama.......	....	1,776	....	105	....	1,881
	Siam..........	....	16	....	....	....	16
	Sweden.......	....	150	....	....	....	150
	Switzerland....	....	480	....	2,132	....	2,612
	Turkey.......	....	22	....	....	....	22
	United States..	....	34,493	....	279,531	....	314,024
	Venezuela......	....	372	....	....	....	372
	Total......	....	80,714	....	403,407	....	484,121

No. 3.—General Statement of Exports—*Continued.*

Articles Exported.	Countries.	Goods, the Produce of Canada.		Goods, not the Produce of Canada.		Total Exports.	
		Quantity.	Value.	Quantity.	Value.	Quantity.	Value.
MANUFACTURES—*Con.*			$		$		$
Jewellers' sweepings...	Unit'd Kingdom	....	29,661	....	75	....	29,736
	B. W. Indies....	....	228	....	....	....	228
	Newfoundland..	....	5	....	....	....	5
	Switzerland.....	....	....	....	201	....	201
	United States..	....	140,826	....	18,054	....	158,880
	Total......	....	170,720	....	18,330	....	189,050
		Cwt.		Cwt.		Cwt.	
Junk, except metallic and rubber.	Unit'd Kingdom	167	408	....	....	167	408
	Hong Kong.....	1,083	1,004	....	....	1,083	1,004
	United States..	77,258	159,809	465	1,476	77,723	161,285
	Total......	78,508	161,221	465	1,476	78,973	162,697
Lamps and lanterns....	Unit'd Kingdom	....	5,211	....	129	....	5,340
	Australia......	....	59	....	....	....	59
	B. Guiana......	....	14	....	....	....	14
	B.. India......	....	5	....	....	....	5
	B. W. Indies....	....	93	....	....	....	93
	Newfoundland..	....	1,100	....	119	....	1,219
	New Zealand...	....	481	....	....	....	481
	Belgium.......	....	100	....	....	....	100
	Ecuador.......	....	130	....	....	....	130
	France.........	....	....	....	70	....	70
	Holland.......	....	....	....	1,906	....	1,906
	Miquelon and St. Pierre.....	....	20	....	4	....	24
	United States..	....	7,081	....	6,007	....	13,088
	Total......	....	14,294	....	8,235	....	22,529
Leather—		Lb.		Lb.		Lb.	
Sole	Unit'd Kingdom	7,544,817	2,294,902	....	....	7,544,817	2,294,902
	B. W. Indies....	1,321	409	....	....	1,321	409
	Newfoundland..	98,607	29,853	....	....	98,607	29,853
	New Zealand...	148,849	57,845	....	....	148,849	57,845
	Belgium.......	31,241	11,054	....	....	31,241	11,054
	France.........	832	217	....	....	832	217
	Miquelon and St. Pierre.....	235	97	....	....	235	97
	United States..	5,932,825	1,701,704	4,834	2,128	5,937,659	1,703,832
	Total......	13,758,727	4,096,081	4,834	2,128	13,763,561	4,098,209
Upper..............	Unit'd Kingdom	896,389	531,927	....	....	896,389	531,927
	Newfoundland..	4,842	2,026	400	249	5,242	2,275
	France.........	82,400	65,332	....	....	82,400	65,332
	United States..	1,195,390	851,625	14,687	12,419	1,210,077	864,044
	Total......	2,179,021	1,450,910	15,087	12,668	2,194,108	1,463,578
All other, n.o.p......	Unit'd Kingdom	418,275	124,796	470	327	418,745	125,123
	Bermuda.......	....	....	185	94	185	94
	B. W. Indies....	542	132	....	....	542	132
	Newfoundland..	53,339	15,192	....	....	53,339	15,192
	New Zealand...	110	45	....	....	110	45
	Germany.......	6,231	1,600	....	....	6,231	1,600
	United States..	2,535,302	872,725	18,457	7,597	2,553,759	880,322
	Total......	3,013,799	1,014,490	19,112	8,018	3,032,911	1,022,508

No. 3.—General Statement of Exports—*Continued*.

Articles Exported.	Countries.	Goods, the Produce of Canada.		Goods, not the Produce of Canada.		Total Exports.	
		Quantity.	Value.	Quantity.	Value.	Quantity.	Value.
MANUFACTURES—*Con.*			$		$		$
Leather—*Con.*							
Boots and shoes.....	Unit'd Kingdom	....	32,725	...:.....	2,861	....	35,586
	Australia......	....	6	....	348	....	354
	Bermuda......	....	176	....	....	....	176
	B. S. Africa.....	....	125	....	....	....	125
	Hong Kong....	....	19	...:.....	....	....	19
	Newfoundland..	....	8,233	....	....	....	8,233
	New Zealand...	....	1,028	....	....	....	1,028
	Alaska..,......	....	....	....	30	....	30
	Aust.-Hungary..	...:.....	5	....	....	....	5
	Belgium......	....	250	....	....	....	250
	France........	....	33,359	....	....	....	33,359
	Italy.........	....	213	....	....	....	213
	Miquelon and						
	St. Pierre.....	....	7,697	....	....	....	7,697
	Turkey........	....	60	....	....	....	60
	United States..	....	104,188	....	45,563	....	149,751
	Total......:	....	188,084	....	48,802	....	236,886
Harness and saddlery.	Unit'd Kingdom	....	1,651,562	....	833	....	1,652,395
	Australia......	....	....	....	40	....	40
	Bermuda......•	....	135	....	....	....	135
	B. S. Africa....	....	20	....	....	....	20
	B. W. Indies....	....	65	....	....	....	65
	Newfoundland...	....	577	....	50	....	627
	Brazil..........	....	36	....	....	....	36
	France.........	....	1,153,685	....	....	....	1,153,685
	Russia.........	....	1,052,356	....	....	....	1,052,356
	United States..	....	123,523	....	5,167	....	128,690
	Total......	....	3,981,959	....	6,090	....	3,988,049
Other manufactures of	Unit'd Kingdom	....	33,768	...:.....	6,097	....	39,865
	Australia......	....	160	....	....	....	160
	Bermuda......	....	3	....	....	....	3
	B. S. Africa..,..	....	123	....	....	....	123
	B. W. Indies....	....	50	....	....	....	50
	Newfoundland..	....	488	....	6	....	494
	New Zealand...	....	29	....	....	....	29
	Aust.-Hungary..	....	100	....	....	....	100
	China..........	....	260	....	...:.....	....	260
	France.........	....	313	....	589	....	902
	Germany......	....	....	....	1,197	....	1,197
	Holland......	....	....	....	28	....	28
	Japan........	....	....	....	226	....	226
	Miquelon and						
	St. Pierre.....	....	21	....	....	...:	21
	Switzerland....	....	5	....	....	....	5
	United States..	....	40,445	....	11,722	....	52,167
	Total......	....	75,765	....	19,865	....	95,630
Lime...............	Newfoundland..	....	133	...:....	....	....	133
	Alaska........	....	50	...:....	....	....	50
	Hawaii........	....	5,730	.:......	....	....	5,730
	Miquelon and						
	St. Pierre.....	....	22	....	....	....	22
	United States..	....	11,202	....	....	....	11,202
	Total......	....	17,137	....	....	....	17,137

6 GEORGE V, A. 1916

No. 3.—General Statement of Exports—*Continued*.

Articles Exported.	Countries.	Goods, the Produce of Canada.		Goods, not the Produce of Canada.		Total Exports.	
		Quantity.	Value.	Quantity.	Value.	Quantity.	Value.
MANUFACTURES—*Con.*		Gal.	$	Gal.	$	Gal.	$
Liquors—							
Ale and beer.........	Unit'd Kingdom	36	16	935	997	971	1,013
	Australia........	31	27	....	....	31	27
	B. W. Indies....	368	126	....	....	368	126
	Newfoundland..	3,824	1,520	....	....	3,824	1,520
	New Zealand...	1,999	999	....	....	1,999	999
	Alaska..........	....	....	42	74	42	74
	China...........	6	6	....	....	6	6
	United States..	4,951	1,707	9,463	7,122	14,414	8,829
	Total.......	11,215	4,401	10,440	8,193	21,655	12,594
Brandy.............	Alaska..........	....	....	48	338	48	338
	United States..	3	28	676	2,596	679	2,624
	Total.......	3	28	724	2,934	727	2,962
Gin................	Unit'd Kingdom	....	....	74	183	74	183
	B. W. Indies...	90	53	....	....	90	53
	Hong Kong.....	....	....	6	14	6	14
	Newfoundland..	....	....	35	18	35	18
	Alaska..........	14	19	70	136	84	155
	United States..	43	61	11,743	8,986	11,786	9,047
	Total.......	147	133	11,928	9,337	12,075	9,470
Rum...............	Newfoundland..	....	....	149	52	149	52
	Alaska.........	....	....	72	120	72	120
	Miquelon and St. Pierre.....	....	....	5,644	1,723	5,644	1,723
	United States..	....	....	88	165	88	165
	Total.......	....	....	5,953	2,060	5,953	2,060
Whiskey............	Unit'd Kingdom	7,385	22,142	2	6	7,387	22,148
	Australia.......	1,672	5,208	....	....	1,672	5,208
	Bermuda........	313	641	....	....	313	641
	B. E. Africa....	79	238	....	....	79	238
	B. S. Africa.....	798	2,445	....	....	798	2,445
	B. Guiana......	15	48	....	....	15	48
	B. Honduras...	1,166	3,792	....	....	1,166	3,792
	B. India........	155	476	....	....	155	476
	B. W. Indies...	1,016	3,234	22	71	1,038	3,305
	Hong Kong.....	548	1,665	10	33	558	1,698
	Newfoundland..	3	8	74	588	77	596
	New Zealand...	1,246	3,762	....	....	1,246	3,762
	Alaska..........	37	167	254	851	291	1,018
	Argentina......	2,671	7,800	....	....	2,671	7,800
	Brazil.........	527	1,690	....	....	527	1,690
	Chili..........	1,831	6,090	....	....	1,831	6,090
	China..........	468	1,427	....	....	468	1,427
	Costa Rica....	2,748	8,667	....	....	2,748	8,667
	Cuba..........	1,054	3,462	....	....	1,054	3,462
	Dutch W.Indies	102	328	....	....	102	328
	Dutch Guiana..	30	96	....	....	30	96
	Ecuador.......	467	1,502	....	....	467	1,502
	Egypt..........	2,933	9,352	....	....	2,933	9,352
	France.........	1,036	3,325	....	....	1,036	3,325
	Germany.......	1,005	2,140	....	....	1,005	2,140
	Guatemala.....	6,528	21,947	....	....	6,528	21,947
	Hawaii.........	1,550	4,991	....	....	1,550	4,991
	Honduras......	1,497	5,077	....	....	1,497	5,077
	Italy..........	292	950	....	....	292	950
	Japan..........	123	309	....	....	123	309
	Mexico.........	2,277	7,323	....	....	2,277	7,323
	Miquelon and St. Pierre.....	....	....	370	406	370	406

No. 3.—General Statement of Exports—*Continued.*

Articles Exported.	Countries.	Goods, the Produce of Canada.		Goods, not the Produce of Canada.		Total Exports.	
		Quantity.	Value.	Quantity.	Value.	Quantity.	Value.
MANUFACTURES—*Con.*		Gal.	$	Gal.	$	Gal.	$
Liquors—*Con.*							
Whiskey—*Con.*	Nicaragua	225	729	....	....	225	729
	Panama	3,301	10,812	....	....	3,301	10,812
	Peru	364	1,166	....	....	364	1,166
	Philippines	1,678	5,351	....	....	1,678	5,351
	Portuguese Africa	15	48	....	....	15	48
	Salvador	458	1,463	....	....	458	1,463
	Sweden	288	636	....	....	288	636
	Turkey	145	475	....	....	145	475
	U. S. of Colombia	51	163	....	....	51	163
	United States	234,535	709,036	1,541	3,798	236,076	712,834
	Uruguay	22	68	....	....	22	68
	Venezuela	213	683	....	....	213	683
	Total	282,867	860,932	2,273	5,753	285,140	866,685
Wines	Unit'd Kingdom	568	392	1,164	872	1,732	1,264
	Bermuda	7	8	18	180	25	188
	B. Guiana	120	60	97	107	217	167
	B. W. Indies	613	488	....	....	613	488
	Newfoundland	150	158	52	527	202	685
	Alaska	....	....	50	656	50	656
	China	....	....	59	55	59	55
	Dan. W. Indies	80	38	....	....	80	38
	France	....	....	16	189	16	189
	Mexico	183	159	....	....	183	159
	United States	1,058	1,995	4,762	46,716	5,820	48,711
	Total	2,779	3,298	6,218	49,302	8,997	52,600
Wood alcohol	Unit'd Kingdom	125,405	74,828	....	....	125,405	74,828
	Newfoundland	116	77	....	....	116	77
	New Zealand	5,663	4,095	....	....	5,663	4,095
	France	144,123	91,475	....	....	144,123	91,475
	United States	221,831	58,568	5	3	221,836	58,571
	Uruguay	3,200	2,240	....	....	3,200	2,240
	Total	500,338	231,283	5	3	500,343	231,286
Other spirits, n.o.p.	United Kingdom	....	....	104	303	104	303
	B. W. Indies	29	20	....	....	29	20
	Newfoundland	4	40	55	291	59	331
	Alaska	....	....	29	80	29	80
	United States	949	1,478	712	1,264	1,661	2,742
	Total	982	1,538	900	1,938	1,882	3,476
Metals, viz.:—		Cwt.		Cwt.		Cwt.	
Aluminum in bars, blocks, etc	Unit'd Kingdom	51,755	810,227	....	....	51,755	810,227
	B. India	268	4,032	....	....	268	4,032
	Belgium	5,177	77,712	....	....	5,177	77,712
	Japan	7,651	123,676	....	....	7,651	123,676
	Russia	2,240	39,044	....	....	2,240	39,044
	United States	73,350	1,264,109	435	10,643	73,785	1,274,752
	Total	140,441	2,318,800	435	10,643	140,876	2,329,443
Aluminum, manufactures of.	Unit'd Kingdom	....	448,127	....	....	....	448,127
	United States	....	4,581	....	2,024	....	6,605
	Total	....	452,708	....	2,024	....	454,732

6 GEORGE V, A. 1916

No. 3.—General Statement of Exports—*Continued.*

Articles Exported.	Countries.	Goods, the Produce of Canada.		Goods, not the Produce of Canada.		Total Exports.	
		Quantity.	Value.	Quantity.	Value.	Quantity.	Value.
· MANUFACTURES—*Con.*		Cwt.	$	Cwt.	$	Cwt.	$
Metals—*Con.*							
Brass, old and scrap.	Unit'd Kingdom	5,041	54,282	....	....	5,041	54,282
	United States..	22,301	204,249	294	2,508	22,595	206,757
⎰⎱	Total.......	27,342	258,531	294	2,508	27,636	261,039
Copper, old and scrap	Unit'd Kingdom	3,655	45,258	....	....	3,655	45,258
	Germany......	516	5,999	....	....	516	5,999
	United States..	16,948	189,793	....	....	16,948	189,793
	Total.......	21 119	241,050	....	....	21,119	241,050
Metallic shingles and laths and corrugated roofing.	Unit'd Kingdom	....	54,308	....	....	....	54,308
	Australia......	....	238	....	....	....	238
	B. S. Africa....	....	9,003	....	....	....	9,003
	B. India........	....	203	....	....	....	203
	B. E. Indies other........	....	4,626	....	....	....	4,626
	B. W. Indies....	....	986	....	....	....	986
	Fiji islands......	....	70	....	....	....	70
	Newfoundland..	....	523	....	45	....	568
	New Zealand...	....	1,148	....	....	....	1,148
	Argentina......	....	2,507	....	....	....	2,507
	Belgium.......	....	640	....	....	....	640
	Dutch E. Indies	....	281	....	....	....	281
	Ecuador.......	....	330	....	....	....	330
	Holland........	....	3,280	....	....	....	3,280
	Japan..........	....	3,911	....	....	....	3,911
	Miquelon and St. Pierre....	....	200	....	....	....	200
	Peru...........	....	110	....	....	....	110
	Russia.........	....	3,592	....	....	....	3,592
	Siam..........	....	83	....	....	....	83
	Turkey........	....	60	....	....	....	60
	U. S. of Colombia.....	....	760	....	....	....	760
	United States..	....	1,489	....	1,250	....	2,739
	Total.......	....	88,348	....	1,295	....	89,643
Metals n.o.p............	Unit'd Kingdom	....	157,350	....	11,545	....	168,895
	Australia......	....	1,916	....	....	....	1,916
	Bermuda......	....	115	....	....	....	115
	B. S. Africa....	....	251	....	....	....	251
	B. India........	....	84	....	....	....	84
	B. W. Indies...	....	311	....	56	....	367
	Newfoundland..	....	8,552	....	185	....	8,737
	New Zealand...	....	705	....	....	....	705
	Aust.-Hungary..	....	1,140	....	....	....	1,140
	Belgium.......	....	....	....	308	....	308
	Chili..........	....	23	....	....	....	23
	Cuba..........	....	225	....	....	....	225
	Denmark......	....	654	....	....	....	654
	France........	....	7,367	....	....	....	7,367
	Germany......	....	1,865	....	1,227	....	3,092
	Holland.......	....	12	....	....	....	12
	Italy.........	....	536	....	149	....	685
	Mexico........	....	212	....	....	....	212
	Miquelon and St. Pierre....	....	84	....	50	....	134
	Panama.......	....	31	....	....	....	31
	Porto Rico.....	....	225	....	....	....	225
	Russia........	....	1,867	....	....	....	1,867
	Switzerland....	....	500	....	....	....	500
	United States..	....	218,686	....	107,795	....	326,481
	Venezuela......	....	195	....	....	....	195
	Total.......	....	402,906	....	121,315	....	524,221

No. 3.—General Statement of Exports—*Continued.*

Articles Exported.	Countries.	Goods, the Produce of Canada.		Goods, not the Produce of Canada.		Total Exports.	
		Quantity.	Value.	Quantity.	Value.	Quantity.	Value.
MANUFACTURES—*Con.*			$		$		$
Mineral and aerated waters in bottles.	Unit'd Kingdom	....	130	....	10	....	140
	Bermuda......	....	497	....	....	....	497
	B. W. Indies....	....	66	....	....	....	66
	Newfoundland..	....	328	....	12	....	340
	United States..	....	784	....	34	....	818
	Total......	....	1,805	....	56	....	1,861
		Gal.		Gal.		Gal.	
Molasses..............	Newfoundland..	....	....	108,654	29,643	108,654	29,643
	Miquelon and St. Pierre.....	....	....	3,443	1,122	3,443	1,122
	United States..	....	....	89,997	20,623	89,997	20,623
	Total......	....	....	202,094	51,388	202,094	51,388
Musical instruments, viz.:—		No.		No.		No.	
Organs.............	Unit'd Kingdom	699	39,484	....	....	699	39,484
	Australia.......	100	5,760	....	....	100	5,760
	B. S. Africa.....	95	5,210	....	....	95	5,210
	B. W. Indies....	2	285	....	....	2	285
	Newfoundland..	15	1,041	1	20	16	1,061
	New Zealand...	105	7,134	22	350	127	7,484
	Belgium........	2	150	....	....	2	150
	Germany......	18	990	....	....	18	990
	Holland........	24	1,185	....	....	24	1,185
	Turkey........	1	150	....	....	1	150
	United States..	32	1,810	4	222	36	2,032
	Total......	1,093	63,199	27	592	1,120	63,791
Pianos...............	Unit'd Kingdom	41	14,828	6	1,826	47	16,654
	Australia.......	30	6,544	....	....	30	6,544
	Bermuda......	1	300	....	....	1	300
	B. W. Indies....	1	285	....	....	1	285
	Newfoundland..	6	1,216	....	....	6	1,216
	New Zealand...	1	150	....	....	1	150
	Alaska.........	....	....	1	250	1	250
	China..........	1	415	....	....	1	415
	France.........	1	230	....	....	1	230
	Japan.........	1	250	....	....	1	250
	United States..	156	37,329	37	12,682	193	50,011
	Total......	239	61,547	44	14,758	283	76,305
Other, and parts of..	Unit'd Kingdom	....	66,771	....	775	....	67,546
	Australia......	....	6,323	....	....	....	6,323
	Bermuda......	....	50	....	....	....	50
	Newfoundland..	....	1,985	....	123	....	2,108
	New Zealand...	....	416	....	....	....	416
	Alaska.........	....	....	....	500	....	500
	Aust.-Hungary.	....	810	....	....	....	810
	Belgium........	....	2,116	....	....	....	2,116
	China.........	....	83	....	....	....	83
	Denmark......	....	632	....	....	....	632
	France........	....	493	....	....	....	493
	Germany......	....	1,891	....	600	....	2,491
	Italy..........	....	50	....	....	....	50
	Miquelon and St. Pierre....	....	....	....	60	....	60
	United States..	....	19,209	....	29,930	....	49,139
	Total......	....	100,829	....	31,988	....	132,817

6 GEORGE V, A. 1916

No. 3.—General Statement of Exports—*Continued.*

Articles Exported.	Countries.	Goods, the Produce of Canada.		Goods, not the Produce of Canada.		Total Exports.	
		Quantity.	Value.	Quantity.	Value.	Quantity.	Value.
MANUFACTURES—*Con.*		Cwt.	$	Cwt.	$	Cwt.	$
Oakum...............	Newfoundland..	. 10	50	25	168	35	218
Oilcake..............	Unit'd Kingdom	158,720	221,482	....	....	158,720	221,482
	B. Guiana......	1,619	2,386	....	....	1,619	2,386
	B. W. Indies....	11,545	17,510	....	....	11,545	17,510
	Newfoundland..	562	1,099	....	....	562	1,099
	Belgium........	46,919	62,261	....	....	46,919	62,261
	France.:.......	3,440	4,413	....	....	3,440	4,413
	Holland........	31,281	46,845	....	....	31,281	46,845
	United States..	25,248	36,334	....	....	25,248	36,334
	Total.......	279,334	392.330	....	....	279,334	392,330
		Sq. yd.		Sq. yd.		Sq. yd.	
Oilcloths, all kinds....	Unit'd Kingdom	1,005	353	400	120	1,405	473
	B. W. Indies....	8,546	960	....	....	8,546	960
	Newfoundland..	49,707	6,914	....	....	49,707	6,914
	Miquelon and St. Pierre.....	737	167	....	....	737	167
	United States..	47	23	....	....	47	23
	Total.......	60,042	8,417	400	120	60,442	8,537
Oils:—		Gal.		Gal.		Gal.	
Creosote............	United States...	632,563	45,392	....	....	632,563	45,392
Gasoline and naphtha	Newfoundland..	27,969	7,437	132,179	29,340	160,148	36,777
	Miquelon and St. Pierre.....	9,373	2,691	4,265	821	13,638	3,512
	United States..	507	191	202	49	709	240
	Total.......	37,849	10,319	136,646	30,210	174,495	40,529
Oils, n.o.p.......:...	Unit'd Kingdom	4,121	1,608	40	15	4,161	1,623
	Australia.......	44,800	13,134	13,424	1,337	58,224	14,471
	Bermuda.......	....	....	2,696	198	2,696	198
	B. Guiana......	186	113	8,319	712	8,505	825
	B. W. Indies....	3,570	1,004	8,576	1,911	12,146	2,915
	Fiji Islands.....	.84	20	....	....	84	20
	Newfoundland..	19,542	7,978	9,312	1,360	28,854	9,338
	New Zealand...	450	120	7,647	757	8,097	877
	Holland........	2,686	4,030	....	....	2,686	4,030
	Miquelon and St. Pierre.....	474	215	1,789	716	2,263	931
	United States..	348,719	72,158	271,411	104,212	620,130	176,370
	Total.......	424,632	100,380	323,214	111,218	747,846	211,598
		Roll.		Roll.		Roll.	
Paper, viz:— Wall...............	Unit'd Kingdom	....	....	333	51	333	51
	Australia.......	119,142	10,049	1,048	216	120,190	10,265
	B. S. Africa.....	8,253	720	....	....	8,253	720
	B. Guiana.....	2,250	2,111	....	....	2,250	2,111
	B. W. Indies....	5,136	83	....	....	5,136	83
	Newfoundland..	365,272	14,130	1,400	317	366,672	14,447
	New Zealand...	203,612	19,702	5,944	1,502	209,556	21,204
	Argentina....,	2,856	191	....	....	2,856	191
	Panama........	45,230	3,810	....	....	45,230	3,810
	Peru...........	7,208	634	....	....	7,208	634
	United States..	24,936	2,486	16,465	1,561	41,401	4,047
	Total.......	783,895	53,916	25,190	3,647	809,085	57,563

SESSIONAL PAPER No. 11

No. 3.—General Statement of Exports—*Continued.*

Articles Exported.	Countries.	Goods, the Produce of Canada.		Goods, not the Produce of Canada.		Total Exports.	
		Quantity.	Value.	Quantity.	Value.	Quantity.	Value.
MANUFACTURES—*Con.* Paper—*Con.*		Roll.	$	Roll.	$	Roll.	$
Felt..............	Unit'd Kingdom	8,715	22,725	....	....	8,715	22,725
	Newfoundland..	42,594	42,228	48	84	42,642	42,312
	France.........	2,000	5,000	....	....	2,000	5,000
	United States..	25,484	15,113	829	2,026	26,313	17,139
	Total......	78,793	85,066	877	2,110	79,670	87,176
		Lb.		Lb.		Lb.	
Wrapping...........	Unit'd Kingdom	102,260	2,792	....	....	102,260	2,792
	Australia.......	3,813,694	112,232	....	....	3,813,694	112,232
	Bermuda.......	33,074	1,193	....	....	33,074	1,193
	B. S. Africa....	176,000	5,280	....	....	176,000	5,280
	B. Guiana......	3,570	110	....	....	3,570	110
	B. W. Indies...	85,636	3,014	....	....	85,636	3,014
	Newfoundland..	54,739	2,462	....	....	54,739	2,462
	New Zealand...	60,000	1,800	....	....	60,000	1,800
	France.........	8,220	294	....	....	8,220	294
	Miquelon and St. Pierre.....	1,900	72	....	....	1,900	72
	United States..	9,200,553	279,111	783	90	9,201,336	279,201
	Total......	13,539,646	408,360	783	90	13,540,429	408,450
		Cwt.		Cwt.		Cwt.	
Printing............	Unit'd Kingdom	89,252	180,598	....	....	89,252	180,598
	Australia.......	388,014	745,946	....	....	388,014	745,946
	Bermuda.......	104	154	....	....	104	154
	B. S. Africa....	185,420	366,682	....	....	185,420	366,682
	B. Guiana......	369	923	....	....	369	923
	B. Honduras...	29	54	....	....	29	54
	B. India........	6,871	12,672	....	....	6,871	12,672
	B. W. Indies...	2,750	5,241	....	....	2,750	5,241
	New Zealand...	255,493	509,907	....	....	255,493	509,907
	Argentina......	6,760	13,221	....	....	6,760	13,221
	Brazil.........	4,448	8,494	....	....	4,448	8,494
	Chili..........	926	1,693	....	....	926	1,693
	China.........	252	502	....	....	252	502
	Costa Rica.....	1,650	3,026	....	....	1,650	3,026
	Cuba..........	19,794	37,460	....	....	19,794	37,460
	Dutch W. Indies	42	76	....	....	42	76
	Dutch Guiana..	27	51	....	....	27	51
	Ecuador.......	245	455	....	....	245	455
	Guatemala.....	2,284	4,457	....	....	2,284	4,457
	Honduras......	127	226	....	....	127	226
	Mexico.........	1,307	2,441	....	....	1,307	2,441
	Panama........	4,826	9,163	....	....	4,826	9,163
	Peru..........	5,441	10,386	....	....	5,441	10,386
	Philippines.....	5,278	10,549	....	....	5,278	10,549
	Porto Rico.....	2,579	5,209	....	....	2,579	5,209
	Salvador.......	415	752	....	....	415	752
	U. S. of Colombia...........	6,913	13,489	....	....	6,913	13,489
	United States..	6,289,530	12,126,982	....	....	6,289,530	12,126,982
	Uruguay.......	699	1,122	....	....	699	1,122
	Venezuela......	10,202	19,731	....	....	10,202	19,731
	Total......	7,292,047	14,091,662	....	....	7,292,047	14,091,662
Paper, n.o.p..........	Unit'd Kingdom	....	386,923	....	1,032	....	387,955
	Australia.......	....	892	....	....	....	892
	Bermuda.......	....	1,209	....	....	....	1,209
	B. S. Africa....	....	953	....	....	....	953
	B. Guiana......	....	791	....	52	....	843
	B. W. Indies....	....	1,508	....	....	....	1,508
	Newfoundland..	....	13,517	....	207	....	13,724
	New Zealand....	....	696	....	....	....	696

No. 3.—General Statement of Exports—*Continued.*

Articles Exported.	Countries.	Goods, the Produce of Canada.		Goods, not the Produce of Canada.		Total Exports.	
		Quantity.	Value.	Quantity.	Value.	Quantity.	Value.
			$		$		$
MANUFACTURES—*Con.*							
Paper—*Con.*							
Paper, n.o.p.—*Con.*	Alaska		11				11
	Argentina		39				39
	China		544				544
	France		1,500				1,500
	Italy		180				180
	Japan		451				451
	Mexico		8				8
	Miquelon and St. Pierre		85				85
	Switzerland		234				234
	United States		429,793		14,588		444,381
	Total		839,334		15,879		855,213
Paints and varnishes of all kinds.	Unit'd Kingdom		70,287		3,530		73,817
	Australia		2,353				2,353
	Bermuda		1,029				1,029
	B. S. Africa		3,399				3,399
	B. Guiana		6,319				6,319
	B. India		122				122
	B. W. Indies		13,097		30		13,127
	Hong Kong		175				175
	Newfoundland		42,880		1,008		43,888
	New Zealand		1,912				1,912
	Belgium		200				200
	Cuba		2,061				2,061
	Denmark		673				673
	Germany				34		34
	Miquelon and St. Pierre		1,991		8		1,999
	Norway		1,470				1,470
	Sweden		781				781
	United States		20,705		17,359		38,064
	Total		169,454		21,969		191,423
Paintings	Unit'd Kingdom		13,924		123,088		137,012
	Newfoundland		34				34
	Belgium		30				30
	France		500		3,852		4,352
	Germany		1,000				1,000
	Holland				1,771		1,771
	United States		50,858		93,747		144,605
	Total		66,346		222,458		288,804
Photographs	Unit'd Kingdom		1,117		207		1,324
	B. W. Indies		17				17
	Aust.-Hungary		36				36
	Belgium		100				100
	France		200		26		226
	Italy		24				24
	United States		8,643		3,322		11,965
	Total		10,137		3,555		13,692
Philosophical and scientific apparatus and instruments.	Unit'd Kingdom		14,633		16,105		30,738
	Australia		83				83
	B. S. Africa		359				359
	B. India		910				910
	B. W. Indies		50				50
	Newfoundland		496		838		1,334
	Alaska		85		310		395
	Aust.-Hungary				6		6

SESSIONAL PAPER No. 11

No. 3.—GENERAL STATEMENT OF EXPORTS—*Continued.*

Articles Exported.	Countries.	GOODS, THE PRODUCE OF CANADA.		GOODS, NOT THE PRODUCE OF CANADA.		TOTAL EXPORTS.	
		Quantity.	Value.	Quantity.	Value.	Quantity.	Value.
MANUFACTURES—*Con.*			$		$		$
Philosophical and scientific apparatus and instruments—*Con.*	France	....	453	....	222	....	675
	Germany	....	....	....	1,064	....	1,064
	Italy	....	60	....	....	....	60
	Japan	....	72	....	....	....	72
	Switzerland	....	692	....	1,262	....	1,954
	United States	....	28,732	....	86,723	....	115,455
	Total	....	46,625	....	106,530	....	153,155
Plumbago, mfrs. of	Unit'd Kingdom	....	8,378	....	80	....	8,458
	Germany	....	1,800	....	1,957	....	3,757
	United States	....	51,960	....	486	....	52,446
	Total	....	62,138	....	2,523	....	64,661
		Cwt.		Cwt.		Cwt.	
Rags	Unit'd Kingdom	52,018	388,611	....	....	52,018	388,611
	Australia	62	140	....	....	62	140
	Newfoundland	98	157	....	....	98	157
	Belgium	2,638	5,032	....	....	2,638	5,032
	China	397	343	....	....	397	343
	France	489	5,152	....	....	489	5,152
	Germany	35	365	....	....	35	365
	United States	604,185	680,969	240	369	604,425	681,338
	Total	659,922	1,080,769	240	369	660,162	1,081,138
Sails, awnings, tents and tarpaulins	Unit'd Kingdom	....	616	....	....	....	616
	Newfoundland	....	20	....	....	....	20
	United States	....	1,266	....	13,813	....	15,079
	Total	....	1,902	....	13,813	....	15,715
		No. Ton.		No. Ton.		No. Ton.	
Ships sold to other countries	B. W. Indies	3— 716	44,000	....	....	3— 716	44,000
	Newfoundland	4— 350	13,400	....	....	4— 350	13,400
	Japan	....	....	1— 2,535	16,000	1— 2,535	16,000
	United States	8—13,237	391,500	1— 2,442	600,000	9—15,679	991,500
	Total	15—14,303	448,900	2— 4,977	616,000	17—19,280	1,064,900
Silk and manufactures of	Unit'd Kingdom	....	4,675	....	15,484	....	20,159
	Australia	....	17,173	....	....	....	17,173
	Bermuda	....	195	....	....	....	195
	B. India	....	10	....	....	....	10
	B. W. Indies	....	233	....	43	....	276
	Hong Kong	....	....	....	235	....	235
	Newfoundland	....	1,702	....	75	....	1,777
	Argentina	....	....	....	4,083	....	4,083
	Aust.-Hungary	....	14	....	....	....	14
	Belgium	....	1,500	....	....	....	1,500
	France	....	....	....	2,830	....	2,830
	Germany	....	....	....	200	....	200
	Italy	....	....	....	771	....	771
	Japan	....	140	....	1,428	....	1,568
	Switzerland	....	260	....	366	....	626
	United States	....	5,031	....	15,534	....	20,565
	Total	....	30,933	....	41,049	....	71,982

No. 3.—GENERAL STATEMENT OF EXPORTS—*Continued.*

Articles Exported.	Countries.	Goods, the Produce of Canada.		Goods, not the Produce of Canada.		Total Exports.	
		Quantity.	Value.	Quantity.	Value.	Quantity.	Value.
MANUFACTURES—*Con.*		Lb.	$	Lb.	$	Lb.	$
Soap...............	Unit'd Kingdom	151,080	13,927	48,837	2,202	199,917	16,129
	Australia.......	95	15	....	....	95	15
	Bermuda.......	510	36	....	....	510	36
	B. W. Indies....	375,624	16,568	....	....	375,624	16,568
	Newfoundland..	41,935	2,324	925	49	42,860	2,373
	New Zealand...	8,950	734	....	....	8,950	734
	Japan..........	250	15	....	....	250	15
	Miquelon and St. Pierre....	40	7	....	....	40	7
	United States..	5,853	492	4,783	528	10,636	1,020
	Total........	584,337	34,118	54,545	2,779	638,882	36,897
Starch...............	Unit'd Kingdom	58,340	1,555	....	....	58,340	1,555
	Bermuda.......	80	6	....	....	80	6
	Newfoundland..	12,068	650	800	64	12,868	714
	New Zealand...	20	4	....	....	20	4
	United States..	5,650	224	125	6	5,775	230
	Total.......	76,158	2,439	925	70	77,083	2,509
Stationery.............	Unit'd Kingdom	....	15,262	....	1,971	....	17,233
	Australia......	....	1,646	....	....	....	1,646
	Bermuda......	....	149	....	147	....	296
	B. S. Africa....	....	149	....	....	....	149
	B. Guiana.....	....	800	....	....	....	800
	B. Honduras...	....	618	....	....	....	618
	B. India.......	....	361	....	....	....	361
	B. W. Indies...	....	3,764	....	....	....	3,764
	B. Straits Settlements...	....	10	....	....	....	10
	Newfoundland..	....	10,583	....	57	....	10,640
	New Zealand...	....	3,652	....	....	....	3,652
	Alaska.........	....	48	....	20	....	68
	Argentina......	....	323	....	....	....	323
	Belgium.......	....	36	....	....	....	36
	China.........	....	431	....	....	....	431
	Cuba..........	....	5,540	....	....	....	5,540
	France........	....	311	....	....	....	311
	Germany......	....	500	....	....	....	500
	Italy..........	....	624	....	....	....	624
	Japan.........	....	545	....	....	....	545
	Mexico........	....	55	....	....	....	55
	Miquelon and St. Pierre.....	....	12	....	....	....	12
	Porto Rico.....	....	860	....	....	....	860
	San Domingo...	....	1,157	....	....	....	1,157
	Switzerland....	....	1,547	....	....	....	1,547
	U. S. of Colombia....	....	11	....	....	....	11
	United States..	....	14,786	....	5,759	....	20,545
	Total.......	....	63,780	....	7,954	....	71,734
Stone, ornamental, viz: Granite, marble, etc., dressed.	Bermuda......	....	105	....	....	....	105
	B. W. Indies....	....	14	....	....	....	14
	Italy..........	....	....	....	1,437	....	1,437
	United States..	....	1,343	....	630	....	1,973
	Total.......	....	1,462	....	2,067	....	3,529
Stone, building, dressed	United States..	....	370	....	....	....	370

SESSIONAL PAPER No. 11

No. 3.—General Statement of Exports—*Continued.*

Articles Exported.	Countries.	Goods, the Produce of Canada.		Goods, not the Produce of Canada.		Total Exports.	
		Quantity.	Value.	Quantity.	Value.	Quantity.	Value.
MANUFACTURES—*Con.*		Lb.	$	Lb.	$	Lb.	$
Sugar, of all kinds,n.o.p	Unit'd Kingdom	....	....	4,485,980	224,299	4,485,980	224,299
	B. W. Indies....	....	....	2,000	·87	2,000	87
	Newfoundland..	2,780	172	201,962	10,974	204,742	11,146
	Belgium........	500	15	....	....	500	15
	United States..	9,270	453	85,433	3,411	94,703	3,864
	Total......	12,550	640	4,775,375	238,771	4,787,925	239,411
		Gal.		Gal.		Gal.	
Sugar house syrup.....	Unit'd Kingdom	76,718	11,582	11,932	1,790	. 88,650	13,372
	United States..	58,190	5,193	....	....	58,190	5,193
	Total......	134,908	16,775	11,932	1,790	146,840	18,565
Tar..............	Unit'd Kingdom	....	15	....	....	....	15
	B. Guiana......	....	50	....	....	....	50
	B. W. Indies....	....	18	....	....	....	18
	Newfoundland..	....	5,590	....	6	....	5,596
	United States..	., ...	36,063	..:........	345	....	36,408
	Total..:....	....	41,736	....	351	....	42,087
Tin, manufactures of..	Unit'd Kingdom	....	79,733	....	595	....	80,328
	Australia,.....	....	354	....	....	....	354
	B. S. Africa.....	....	12	....	....	....	12
	B. W. Indies....	....	597	....	....	....	597
	Newfoundland..	....	5,134	....	314	....	5,448
	New Zealand...	....	368	....	....	....	368
	Japan..........	....	3	....	....	....	3
	Miquelon and St. Pierre.....	....	13	......:	26	....	39
	United States..	....	12,656	....	98,163	....	110,819
	Total.......	....	98,870	....	99,098	....	197,968
Tobacco:—		M.		M.		M.	
Cigars..............	Unit'd Kingdom	1	25	1	18	2	43
	Bermuda.......	5	300	....	....	5	300
	B. W. Indies....	2	50	....	....	2	50
	Newfoundland..	3	158	....	....	3	158
	New Zealand...	5	196	....	....	5	196
	United States..	2	33	1	· 25	3	58
	Total,.....	18	762	2	43	20	805
Cigarettes...........	Unit'd Kingdom	118	1,351	1	5	119	1,356
	Bermuda.......	60	335	10	56	70 ·	391
	Chili...........	....	....	4	36	4	36
	United States..	7	68	207	1,138	214	1,206
	Total,......	185	1,754	222	1,235	407	2,989
		Lb.		Lb.		Lb.	
Stems and cuttings..	Belgium........	54,326	5,225	....	....	54,326	,5,225
	Canary Islands.	....	....	3,121	328	3,121	328
	Germany......	12,465	1,064	....	....	12,465	1,064
	Holland........	158,154	15,106	....	....	158,154	15,106
	United States..	69,018	6,120	2,865	·220	71,883	6,340
	Total.......	293,963	27,515	5,986	548	299,949	28,063

6 GEORGE V, A. 1916

No. 3.—General Statement of Exports—*Continued.*

Articles Exported.	Countries.	Goods, the Produce of Canada.		Goods, not the Produce of Canada.		Total Exports.	
		Quantity.	Value.	Quantity.	Value.	Quantity.	Value.
MANUFACTURES—*Con.*							
Tobacco—*Con.*		Lb.	$	Lb.	$	Lb.	$
All other, n.o.p......	Unit'd Kingdom	4,391	4,185	4,981	4,712	9,372	8,897
	Bermuda........	966	242	....	....	966	242
	Newfoundland..	592	279	1,306	389	1,898	668.
	Miquelon and						
	St. Pierre....	....	....	450	125	450	125
	United States..	7,344	3,602	5,563	5,536	12,907	9,138
	Total......	13,293	8,308	12,300	10,762	25,593	19,070
		Cwt.		Cwt.		Cwt.	
Tow........'.	United States..	1,356	1,947	....	....	1,356	1,947
Trunks and valises.....	Unit'd Kingdom	....	345	....	199	....	544
	Bermuda........	....	1,620	....	....	....	1,620
	B. Guiana......	....	232	....	....	....	232
	B. W. Indies ...	....	9,163	....	....	....	9,163
	Newfoundland..	....	1,417	....	60	....	1,477
	New Zealand...	....	566	....	....	....	566
	Germany......	....	110	....	80	....	190
	United States..	....	2,910	....	1,460	....	4,370
	Total......	....	16,363	....	1,799	....	18,162
Vehicles, viz.:—		No.		No.		No.	
Automobiles.........	Unit'd Kingdom	23	76,050	22	71,031	45	147,081
	Aden...........	14	6,056	....	....	14	6,056
	Australia......	2,310	1,101,284	....	....	2,310	1,101,284
	B. E. Africa...	100	45,329	....	....	100	45,329
	B. S. Africa....	830	373,741	....	....	830	373,741
	B. W. Africa....	58	21,128	....	....	58	21,128
	B. Guiana......	3	2,148	....	....	3	2,148
	B. Honduras....	1	462	....	....	1	462
	B. India........	449	198,067	....	....	449	198,067
	B. E. Indies, other.........	27	12,402	....	....	27	12,402
	B. W. Indies....	57	25,527	....	....	57	25,527
	B. Straits Settlements...	153	88,295	....	....	153	88,295
	Fiji Islands.....	15	7,094	....	....	15	7,094
	Hong Kong.....	3	1,030	....	....	3	1,030
	Newfoundland..	12	5,162	1	2,500	13	7,662
	New Zealand...	981	479,178	....	....	981	479,178
	Alaska.........	1	1,500	....	....	1	1,500
	Belgium........	3	3,105	....	....	3	3,105
	China..........	6	5,985	....	....	6	5,985
	Cuba..........	3	7,700	....	....	3	7,700
	Dutch E. Indies	19	7,506	....	....	19	7,506
	France.........	29	29,615	8	28,935	37	58,550
	Germany......	1	2,840	....	....	1	2,840
	Greece.........	1	2,014	....	....	1	2,014
	Holland........	3	2,876	....	....	3	2,876
	Portuguese Africa........	20	9,080	....	....	20	9,080
	Siam..........	7	2,810	....	....	7	2,810
	Sweden........	24	23,423	....	....	24	23,423
	Switzerland....	6	6,210	....	....	6	6,210
	Turkey.........	3	1,194	....	....	3	1,194
	United States..	76	97,013	310	541,944	386	638,957
	Total......	5,238	2,645,824	341	644,410	5,579	3,290,234
Automobile, parts of.	Unit'd Kingdom	....	130,001	....	9,999	....	140,000
	Aden...........	....	2,896	....	....	....	2,896
	Australia......	....	120,468	....	3,829	....	124,297
	B. E. Africa....	....	5,805	....	....	....	5,805
	B. S. Africa....	....	40,695	....	....	....	40,695
	B. W. Africa....	....	6,071	....	....	....	6,071

No. 3.—General Statement of Exports—*Continued.*

Articles Exported.	Countries.	Goods, the Produce of Canada.		Goods, not the Produce of Canada.		Total Exports.	
		Quantity.	Value.	Quantity.	Value.	Quantity.	Value.
MANUFACTURES—*Con.*			$		$		$
Vehicles—*Con.*							
Automobile, parts of—*Con.*	B. Guiana.....	....	596	....	....	....	596
	B. India......	....	7,954	....	....	....	7,954
	B.E.Indies, other	....	1,226	....	....	....	1,226
	B. W. Indies....	....	4,378	....	....	....	4,378
	B. Straits Settlements...	....	9,550	....	....	....	9,550
	Fiji Islands.....	....	321	....	....	....	321
	Hong Kong.....	....	17	....	....	....	17
	Newfoundland..	....	1,163	....	....	....	1,163
	New Zealand...	....	38,513	....	300	....	38,813
	Argentina......	....	135	....	....	....	135
	Belgium.......	....	1,275	....	....	....	1,275
	Dutch E. Indies	....	589	....	....	....	589
	France........	....	864	....	41	....	905
	Germany......	....	....	....	111	....	111
	Hawaii........	....	200	....	....	....	200
	Portuguese Africa....	....	24	....	....	....	24
	Siam.........	....	330	....	....	....	330
	United States..	....	35,558	....	184,422	....	219,980
	Total......	....	408,629	....	198,702	....	607,331
		No.		No.		No.	
Carriages..........	Unit'd Kingdom	1	96	....	....	1	96
	Bermuda......	2	175	....	....	2	175
	B. S. Africa....	12	940	....	....	12	940
	B. W. Indies....	11	1,071	....	....	11	1,071
	Newfoundland..	7	435	....	....	7	435
	United States..	26	1,721	12	1,656	38	3,377
	Total......	59	4,438	12	1,656	71	6,094
Carriages, parts of...	Unit'd Kingdom	....	14,808	....	250	....	15,058
	Australia......	....	12,071	....	....	....	12,071
	Bermuda......	....	57	....	....	....	57
	B. S. Africa....	....	3,958	....	....	....	3,958
	B. India.......	....	25	....	....	....	25
	B. W. Indies....	....	245	....	....	....	245
	Newfoundland..	....	1,006	....	213	....	1,219
	New Zealand...	....	9,257	....	....	....	9,257
	Argentina......	....	854	....	....	....	854
	French Africa...	....	23	....	....	....	23
	United States..	....	1,223	....	926	....	2,149
	Total......	....	43,527	....	1,389	....	44,916
Carts..............	Unit'd Kingdom	4	240	....	....	4	240
	B. W. Indies....	1	102	....	....	1	102
	Argentina......	586	15,152	....	....	586	15,152
	United States..	7	275	....	....	7	275
	Total......	598	15,769	....	....	598	15,769
Wagons..............	Unit'd Kingdom	2,053	309,595	....	....	2,053	309,595
	Newfoundland..	11	435	....	....	11	435
	Miquelon and St. Pierre....	....	....	1	20	1	20
	United States..	78	3,144	28	3,051	106	6,195
	Total......	2,142	313,174	29	3,071	2,171	316,245
Bicycles..........	Unit'd Kingdom	21	2,405	5	940	26	3,345
	Newfoundland..	3	91	2	186	5	277
	Dutch E. Indies	2	90	....	....	2	90
	Japan.......	1	75	....	....	1	75
	United States..	91	7,987	118	17,026	209	25,013
	Total......	118	10,648	125	18,152	243	28,800

6 GEORGE V, A. 1916

No. 3.—General Statement of Exports—*Continued.*

Articles Exported.	Countries.	Goods, the Produce of Canada.		Goods, not the Produce of Canada.		Total Exports.	
		Quantity.	Value.	Quantity.	Value.	Quantity.	Value.
MANUFACTURES—*Con.*			$		$		$
Vehicles—*Con.*							
Bicycles, parts of....	Unit'd Kingdom	....	78	....	220	....	298
	Australia......	....	2,741	....	....	....	2,741
	United States..	....	407	....	1,940	....	2,347
	Total......	....	3,226	....	2,160	....	5,386
Other vehicles.......	Unit'd Kingdom	....	15,009	....	....	....	15,009
	Australia.......	....	116	....	7,812	....	7,928
	B. S. Africa.....	....	2,311	....	....	....	2,311
	Newfoundland..	....	326	....	20	....	346
	New Zealand..	....	565	....	....	....	565
	Argentina......	....	400	....	....	....	400
	France.........	....	20,713	....	....	....	20,713
	United States..	....	13,095	....	127,748	....	140,843
	Total......	....	52,535	....	135,580	....	188,115
		Gal.		Gal.		Gal.	
Vinegar..............	Newfoundland..	20	5	27	6	47	11
Wood, viz:—		No.		No.		No.	
Barrels, empty......	Unit'd Kingdom	69	439	1,233	3,056	1,302	3,495
	B. Guiana......	573	898	....	....	573	898
	B. W. Indies....	3,183	4,693	1,520	2,242	4,703	6,935
	Newfoundland..	2,781	2,035	....	....	2,781	2,035
	Aust.-Hungary	....	....	68	50	68	50
	Belgium........	....	....	54	216	54	216
	France..........	....	....	46	175	46	175
	Germany......	....	....	930	703	930	703
	United States..	7,724	8,848	11,385	17,635	19,109	26,483
	Total......	14,330	16,913	15,236	24,077	29,566	40,990
Household furniture.	Unit'd Kingdom	....	30,076	....	1,569	....	31,645
	Australia......	....	57,837	....	950	....	58,787
	Bermuda......	....	3,468	....	....	....	3,468
	B. S. Africa....	....	45,603	....	392	....	45,995
	B. Guiana.....	....	2,130	....	6	....	2,136
	B. India.......	....	382	....	....	....	382
	B. W. Indies...	....	10,858	....	....	....	10,858
	Newfoundland..	....	34,720	....	15	....	34,735
	New Zealand..	....	26,378	....	39	....	26,417
	Argentina.....	....	285	....	....	....	285
	Azores and Madeira......	....	27	....	....	....	27
	Belgium......	....	750	....	....	....	750
	China.........	....	338	....	....	....	338
	Cuba.........	....	788	....	....	....	788
	Dutch Guiana..	....	32	....	....	....	32
	France........	....	140	....	200	....	340
	Mexico........	....	69	....	....	....	69
	Miquelon and St. Pierre....	....	9	....	....	....	9
	United States..	....	85,789	....	21,456	....	107,245
	Total......	....	299,679	....	24,627	....	324,306
Doors, sashes, and blinds.	Unit'd Kingdom	....	4,975	....	....	....	4,975
	Australia......	....	145	....	...	....	145
	Bermuda.....	....	990	....	....	....	990
	B. S. Africa....	....	205	....	....	....	205
	B. W. Indies....	....	215	....	....	....	215
	Newfoundland..	....	506	....	....	....	506

SESSIONAL PAPER No. 11

No. 3.—General Statement of Exports—*Continued.*

Articles Exported.	Countries.	Goods, the Produce of Canada.		Goods, not the Produce of Canada.		Total Exports.	
		Quantity.	Value.	Quantity.	Value.	Quantity.	Value.
MANUFACTURES—*Con.*			$		$		$
Wood—*Con.*							
Doors, sashes and blinds—*Con.*	New Zealand...	....	4,754	....	....	....	4,754
	China..........	....	153	....	....	....	153
	United States..	....	497	....	213	....	710
	Total......	....	12,440	....	213	....	12,653
Matches..........	B. W. Indies...	....	198	....	....	....	198
	Newfoundland..	....	26	....	....	....	26
	Miquelon and St. Pierre.....	....	246	....	....	....	246
	United States..	....	....	....	207	....	207
	Total......	....	470	....	207	....	677
Match splints........	Unit'd Kingdom	....	12,893	....	....	....	12,893
Mouldings, trimmings, and other house furnishings.	Unit'd Kingdom	....	35	....	....		35
	Bermuda......	....	453	....	....	....	453
	B. Guiana......	....	5	....	....	....	5
	B. W. Indies....	....	19	....	....	....	19
	Newfoundland..	....	1,079	....	....	....	1,079
	New Zealand...	....	72	....	....	....	.72
	United States..	....	3,068	....	1,714	....	4,782
	Total......	....	4,731	....	1,714	....	6,445
Pails, tubs, churns, and other hollow woodenware.	Unit'd Kingdom	....	516	....	190	....	706
	Australia......	....	6	....	....	....	6
	B. S. Africa....	....	566	....	....	....	566
	B. W. Indies....	....	62	....	....	....	62
	Newfoundland..	....	792	....	....	....	792
	New Zealand...	....	1,452	....	....	....	1,452
	Holland........	....	125	....	....	....	125
	Miquelon and St. Pierre.....	....	13	....	....	....	13
	United States..	....	514	....	398	....	912
	Total......	....	4,046	....	588	....	4,634
Spool wood and spools.	Unit'd Kingdom	....	87,479	....	....	....	87,479
	Miquelon and St. Pierre.....	....	61	....	....	....	61
	United States..	....	10,707	....	3,901	....	14,608
	Total......	....	98,247	....	3,901	....	102,148
		Cwt.		Cwt.		Cwt.	
Wood pulp, chemically prepared....	Unit'd Kingdom	450	800	....	....	450	800
	Australia......	698	2,094	....	....	698	2,094
	France....,....	448	825	....	....	448	825
	Japan..........	.133,071	252,707	....	....	133,071	252,707
	United States..	2,289,661	4,550,196	....	....	2,289,661	4,550,196
	Total......	2,424,328	4,806,622	....	....	2,424,328	4,806,622
Wood pulp, mechanically ground......	Unit'd Kingdom	2,195,036	1,495,521	....	....	2,195,036	1,495,521
	France........	113,400	70,400	....	....	113,400	70,400
	United States..	3,855,266	2,893,618	....	....	3,855,266	2,893,618
	Total......	6,163,702	4,459,539	....	....	6,163,702	4,459,539

6 GEORGE V, A. 1916

No. 3.—General Statement of Exports—*Continued.*

Articles Exported.	Countries.	Goods, the Produce of Canada.		Goods, not the Produce of Canada.		Total Exports.	
		Quantity.	Value.	Quantity.	Value.	Quantity.	Value.
MANUFACTURES—*Con.*			$		$		$
Wood—*Con.*							
Wood, other manufactures of.........	Unit'd Kingdom	....	192,091	....	11,356	....	203,447
	Australia......	....	7,757	....	....	....	7,757
	Bermuda......	....	251	....	....	....	251
	B. S. Africa....	....	11,133	....	....	....	11,133
	B. Guiana.....	....	679	....	....	.	679
	B. India........	....	14	....	....	....	14
	B. W. Indies....	....	3,686	....	100	....	3,786
	Newfoundalnd..	....	18,323	....	728	....	19,051
	New Zealand...	....	16,716	....	....	....	16,716
	Argentina......	....	791	....	....	....	791
	Belgium........	....	1,217	....	....	....	1,217
	Cuba..........	....	40	....	....	....	40
	Denmark......	....	684	....	....	....	684
	France.........	....	5,495	....	....	....	5,495
	French W.Indies	....	30	....	....	....	30
	Germany......	....	2,885	....	30	....	2,915
	Holland.......	....	....	....	768	....	768
	Japan.........	....	812	....	....	....	812
	Miquelon and St. Pierre...	....	348	....	....	....	348
	Russia.........	....	54	....	....	....	54
	United States..	....	97,366	....	63,574	....	160,940
	Total......	....	360,372	....	76,556	....	436,928
Woollens..............	Unit'd Kingdom	....	113,629	....	54,535	....	168,164
	Australia......	....	196	....	....	....	196
	Bermuda......	....	103	....	....	....	103
	B. Guiana.....	....	10	....	....	....	10
	Newfoundland..	....	15,893	....	1,522	....	17,415
	New Zealand...	....	2,282	....	503	....	2,785
	Alaska........	....	53	....	246	....	299
	Aust.-Hungary .	....	25	....	440	....	465
	Belgium........	....	350	....	....	....	350
	China.........	....	291	....	....	....	291
	France.........	....	1,099,927	....	4,003	....	1,103,930
	Germany......	....	1,290	....	943	....	2,233
	Miquelon and St. Pierre.....	....	127	....	....	....	127
	Switzerland.....	....	40	....	....	....	40
	Turkey........	....	....	....	1,982	....	1,982
	United States..	....	67,455	....	22,775	....	90,230
	Total......	....	1,301,671	....	86,949	....	1,388,620
Other articles of manufacture.	Unit'd Kingdom	....	383,927	....	87,956	....	471,883
	Australia......	....	7,738	....	2,200	....	9,938
	Bermuda......	....	3,366	....	75	....	3,441
	B. S. Africa....	....	1,810	....	....	....	1,810
	B. Guiana.....	....	282	....	....	....	282
	B. India.......	....	720	....	....	....	720
	B. W. Indies....	....	2,259	....	35	....	2,294
	B. Straits Settlements.....	....	....	....	101	....	101
	Fiji Islands....	....	1,050	....	....	....	1,050
	Hong Kong....	....	79	....	24	....	103
	Newfoundland..	....	21,297	....	3,659	....	24,956
	New Zealand...	....	4,528	....	....	....	4,528
	Alaska........	....	2,372	....	3,723	....	6,095
	Argentina.....	....	1,001	....	999	....	2,000
	Aust.-Hungary .	....	....	....	128	....	128
	Belgium.......	....	8,927	....	700	....	9,627
	Brazil.........	....	133	....	....	....	133
	Chili..........	....	....	....	9	....	9
	China.........	....	3,094	....	811	....	3,905
	Costa Rica.....	....	3	....	....	....	3

SESSIONAL PAPER No. 11

No. 3.—General Statement of Exports—*Continued.*

Articles Exported.	Countries.	Goods, the Produce of Canada.		Goods, not the Produce of Canada.		Total Exports.	
		Quantity.	Value.	Quantity.	Value.	Quantity.	Value.
MANUFACTURES—*Con.*			$		$		$
Other articles of manu-facture—*Con.*	Cuba.........	....	9	....	3,000	....	3,009
	Denmark......	....	7,672	....	....	....	7,672
	France........	....	45,656	....	3,590	....	49,246
	Germany......	......•.....	1,832	....	1,752	....	3,584
	Holland.......	....	27,890	....	....	....	27,890
	Honduras.....	....	....	....	20	......•.	20
	Italy..........	....	119,115	....	50	....	119,165
	Japan.........	....	788	....	254	....	1,042
	Miquelon and St. Pierre.....	....	566	....	....	....	566
	Norway.......	....	328	....	....	....	328
	Porto Rico.....	....	6	....	....	....	6
	Servia........	....	8	....	....	....	8
	Spain.........	......•....	3	....	....	....	3
	Sweden.......	....	391	....	....	....	391
	Switzerland....	....	276	....	42	......•.	318
	Turkey........	....	148	....	....	....	148
	U. S. of Colombia..........	.	6	....	....	.	6
	United States..	....	371,109	....	976,499	....	1,347,608
	Total......	....	1,018,389	....	1,085,627	....	2,104,016
MISCELLANEOUS ARTICLES.							
Contractors' outfits....	Newfoundland..	....	15,904	....	....	....	15,904
	Alaska........	....	3,736	....	....	....	3,736
	United States..	....	167,191	....	220,345	....	387,536
	Total......	....	186,831	....	220,345	....	407,176
		Lb.		Lb.		Lb.	
Coffee...............	Unit'd Kingdom	6,000	1,440	200	64	6,200	1,504
	Bermuda.......	70	12	....	....	70	12
	Newfoundland.	5,876	1,614	244	58	6,120	1,672
	Belgium........	5,050	1,010	....	....	5,050	1,010
	Miquelon and St. Pierre.....	....	....	517	134	517	134
	United States..	90,401	17,041	36,873	5,769	127,274	22,810
	Total......	107,397	21,117	37,834	6,025	145,231	27,142
Dried fruits, n.o.p.....	Unit'd Kingdom	....	....	26,224	1,639	26,224	1,639
	Bermuda.......	......•....	....	19,537	1,437	19,537	1,437
	B. W. Indies....	....	....	52	5	52	5
	Newfoundland..	175	24	11,880	519	12,055	543
	Miquelon and St. Pierre.....	....	....	2,920	249	2,920	249
	Spain.........	....	....	2,605	179	2,605	179
	United States..	3,154	81	147,750	11,050	150,904	11,131
	Total......	3,329	105	210,968	15,078	214,297	15,183
Menageries, etc........	United States..	....	7,480	....	1,998,132	....	2,005,612
Rice..................	Bermuda.......	....	......•...	1,120	47	1,120	47
	B. W. Indies....	....	....	4,386	121	4,386	121
	Newfoundland..	....	....	6,832	145	6,832	145
	Belgium........	92,600	1,720	....	....	92,600	1,720
	Cuba....•.....	198,000	6,582	....	....	198,000	6,582
	Miquelon and St. Pierre.....	1,972	42	334	12	2,306	54
	United States..	1,915,108	76,154	624,230	23,401	2,539,338	99,555
	Total......	2,207,680	84,498	636,902	23,726	2,844,582	⁻108,234

No. 3.—GENERAL STATEMENT OF EXPORTS—*Concluded.*

Articles Exported.	Countries.	GOODS, THE PRODUCE OF CANADA.		GOODS, NOT THE PRODUCE OF CANADA.		TOTAL EXPORTS.	
		Quantity.	Value.	Quantity.	Value.	Quantity.	Value.
MISCELLANEOUS—*Con.*		Lb.	$	Lb.	$	Lb.	$
Rice meal.............	United States..	4,310,910	109,242	....	....	4,310,910	109,242
Tea.................	Unit'd Kingdom	....	....	68,732	9,972	68,732	9,972
	Bermuda.......	....	....	17,188	4,217	17,188	4,217
	B. W. Indies....	....	....	3,277	857	3,277	857
	Newfoundland..	....	....	111,094	24,324	111,094	24,324
	Alaska.........	....	....	330	127	330	127
	Miquelon and St. Pierre.....	....	....	6,024	1,513	6,024	1,513
	United States..	....	....	3,556,026	1,030,678	3,556,026	1,030,678
	Total......	....	....	3,762,671	1,071,688	3,762,671	1,071,688
Other miscellaneous articles.............	Unit'd Kingdom	....	178,210	....	....	....	178,210
	Newfoundland..	....	35	....	....	....	35
	Japan...........	....	300	....	....	....	300
	United States..	....	75,984	....	47,067	....	123,051
	Total......	....	254,529	....	47,067	....	301,596
Coin:— Gold...............	Unit'd Kingdom	....	45			....	45
	Hong Kong.....	....	40	....	....	....	40
	Newfoundland..	....	....	....	285,841	....	285,841
	Alaska.........	....	....	....	10,000	....	10,000
	United States..	....	15	....	27,939,032	....	27,939,047
	Total......	....	100	....	28,234,873	....	28,234,973
Silver.............	Unit'd Kingdom	....	....	....	1,100	....	1,100
	Newfoundland..	....	....	....	2,872	....	2,872
	United States..	....	467	....	1,117,955	....	1,118,422
	Total......	....	467	....	1,121,927	....	1,122,394
Copper.............	United States..	....	100	....	8,901	....	9,001
Grand Total Exports...	....	....	409,419,503	....	81,389,374	....	490,808,877

SESSIONAL PAPER No. 11

No. 4—ABSTRACT of the total value of Exports by Countries.

Countries to which Exported.	Canadian.	Foreign.	Total.
	$	$	$
United Kingdom	186,668,554	25,089,164	211,757,718
Aden	9,014		9,014
Australia	5,522,594	30,092	5,552,686
Bermuda	357,712	10,551	368,263
British E. Africa	59,838		59,838
" S. Africa	4,585,791	59,798	4,645,589
" W. Africa	40,927		40,927
" Guiana	675,660	3,137	678,797
" Honduras	9,450		9,450
" India	415,105	575	415,680
" East Indies, other	23,905		23,905
" West Indies	4,333,095	33,697	4,366,792
" Oceania, other	8,244		8,244
" Straits Settlements	245,355	101	245,456
Fiji Islands	112,355	324	112,679
Gibraltar	210,303	1,226,011	1,436,314
Hong Kong	653,838	1,215	655,053
Malta	23,313	42,770	66,083
Newfoundland	3,976,160	216,303	4,192,463
New Zealand	2,619,556	4,299	2,623,855
Total British Empire	210,550,769	26,718,037	237,268,806
Alaska	297,282	16,595	313,877
Argentina	634,387	5,082	639,469
Austria-Hungary	220,654	59,134	279,788
Azores and Madeira	6,279		6,279
Belgium	2,220,709	1,038,650	3,259,359
Brazil	541,998	517	542,515
Canary Islands	29,841	328	30,169
Chili	55,302	45	55,347
China	294,251	2,152	296,403
Costa Rica	36,045	37	36,082
Cuba	1,482,649	39,342	1,521,991
Denmark	529,690	190,230	719,920
Danish West Indies	13,536	35	13,571
Dutch East Indies	25,927		25,927
Dutch West Indies	6,715		6,715
Dutch Guiana	40,453	495	40,948
Ecuador	8,646		8,646
Egypt and Soudan	26,484		26,484
France	10,499,680	4,096,025	14,595,705
French Africa	4,170		4,170
French Guiana	2,374		2,374
French Oceania	1,488		1,488
French West Indies	32,479		32,479
Germany	1,447,391	714,619	2,162,010
German Oceania	4,800		4,800
Greece	87,485		87,485
Greenland, Iceland, etc	1,668		1,668
Guatemala	27,295		27,295
Hawaii	70,591	700	71,291
Hayti	4,295		4,295
Holland	1,623,405	3,631,424	5,254,829
Honduras	5,587	20	5,607
Italy	521,802	1,319,108	1,840,910
Japan	963,631	73,370	1,037,001
Korea	1,712		1,712
Liberia	63		63
Mexico	18,551		18,551
Miquelon and St. Pierre	141,097	14,235	155,332
Nicaragua	1,618		1,618
Norway	1,000,715	75	1,000,790
Panama	125,630	3,406	129,036
Peru	13,141		13,141
Philippines	41,574		41,574

No. 4—Abstract of the total value of Exports by Countries—*Concluded.*

Countries to which Exported.	Canadian.	Foreign.	Total.
	$	$	$
Porto Rico..	468,698	....	468,698
Portugal...	25,206	763,279	788,485
Portuguese Africa......................................	79,611	....	79,611
Roumania...	3,150	....	3,150
Russia...	1,270,941	60,250	1,331,191
Salvador...	2,215	....	2,215
San Domingo..	3,938	....	3,938
Servia...	8	....	8
Siam...	16,322	....	16,322
Spain..	243,001	246,679	489,680
Sweden...	172,796	500	173,296
Switzerland..	11,853	4,592	16,445
Turkey...	3,979	1,982	5,961
U. S. of Colombia......................................	24,027	90	24,117
United States..	173,320,216	13,022,640	186,342,856
Uruguay..	52,820	....	52,820
Venezuela..	56,196	....	56,196
Total other countries................	198,868,067	25,305,636	224,173,703

	Canadian	Foreign			
United Kingdom........coin	45	1,100			
Hong Kong............. "	40				
Newfoundland........... "	....	288,713			
Alaska................. "	....	10,000			
United States........... "	582	29,065,888			
Total coin................ 667	29,365,701		667	29,365,701	29,366,368
Grand total exports................			409,419,503	- 81,389,374	490,808,877

STATEMENT No. 5.

No. 5.—STATEMENT of Vessels, British, Canadian and Foreign, entered Inwards,

		BRITISH.					CANADIAN.				
				Quantity of Freight.					Quantity of Freight.		
Number.	Ports and Outports.	Number of Vessels.	Tons Register.	Tons Weight.	Tons Measurement.	Crew, Number.	Number of Vessels.	Tons Register.	Tons Weight.	Tons Measurement.	Crew, Number.
1	Albert, N.B.										
2	Alert Bay, B.C.										
3	Amherst, N.S.	1	209	400		6	2	440	775		11
4	Annapolis Royal, N.S.	2	517	931	1,116	12	6	811	1,421	1,701	21
5	Anyox, B.C.						5	3,755	3,326		66
6	Arichat, N.S.	1	65	1		5	64	1,527	1,013		385
7	Baddeck, N.S.						5	1,285	16		110
8	Baie Verte, N.B.										
9	Barrington Passage, N.S.										
10	Barton, N.S.						19	2,025	271	9	103
11	Bathurst, N.B.	3	727	842		20	1	196	197		5
12	Bear River, N.S.						5	576	706		30
13	Belliveau's Cove, N.S.	3	593	128		18	1	99	1	4	6
14	Bridgetown, N.S.						2	273	513	615	10
15	Bridgewater, N.S.	1	174	292		6	2	198	388		12
16	Buctouche, N.B.										
17	Campbellton, N.B.	1	174	370		6					
18	Campo Bello, N.B.						35	5,141	168		294
19	Canning, N.S.						2	393			12
20	Canso, N.S.	3	497	845		17	8	1,045	1,664		57
21	Caraquet, N.B.						165	2,539	2,600		693
22	Charlottetown, P.E.I.	9	4,571	3,751		89	43	53,939	3,333	895	2,303
23	Chatham, N.B.	2	546	887		17	1	97	97		6
24	Chemainus, B.C.						2	142	9		18
25	Chester, N.S.	1	199	425		6	31	404	162		99
26	Cheticamp, N.S.						1	93	53		6
27	Chicoutimi, Que.	4	7,334	3,688		100					
28	Church Point, N.S.						1	92	180		5
29	Clarks Harbour, N.S.						8	566	230		44
30	Clementsport, N.S.						9	1,306	57	71	53
31	Dalhousie, N.B.						1	97	187		5
32	Digby, N.S.						8	1,016	1,002		45
33	Dorchester, N.B.	2	445		550,281	13	2	496	500		13
34	Fredericton, N.B.						6	1,737	3,061		32
35	Freeport, N.S.										
36	Gaspe, Que.						2	394	829		13
37	Georgetown, P.E.I.	2	90	3		11	1	39	1		6
38	Glace Bay, N.S.						197	10,557			549
39	Halifax, N.S.	375	1,136,783	231,316		31,451	146	102,466	28,095		4,510
40	Hantsport, N.S.						3	687	1,456		17
41	Hillsboro, N.B.										
42	Indian Head, N.B.						2	26	13		4
43	Isaacs Harbour, N.S.										
44	Joggins Mines, N.S.										
45	Kentville, N.S.						1	74			3
46	Kingsport, N.S.	2	520	12		5	2	272	210		10
47	Ladner, B.C.										
48	Ladysmith, B.C.										
49	La Have, N.S.	4	894	1,654		26	78	6,760	5,924		992
50	Lévis, Que.	9	21,115	682		309					
51	Liverpool, N.S.	6	1,024	523	725	73	12	1,295	2,349		62
52	Lockport, N.S.	5	709	415		89	57	2,399	3,788		497
53	Lords Cove, N.B.						27	255	97		61
54	Louisburg, N.S.	25	25,393	31,136		679	10	4,048	2,147		109
55	Lower East Pubnico, N.S.		174			6	41	2,130			502
56	Lunenburg, N.S.	13	2,966	5,268		101	255	20,669	17,784		3,659
57	Magdalen Islands, Que.										
58	Mahone Bay, N.S.						20	1,845	1,859		320
59	Maitland, N.S.						4	433	6		19

SESSIONAL PAPER No. 11

from Sea, at each Port and Outport, during the Fiscal Year ended March 31, 1915.

						IN BALLAST.								
FOREIGN.					BRITISH.			CANADIAN.			FOREIGN.			
Number of Vessels.	Tons Register.	Quantity of Freight. Tons Weight.	Tons Measurement.	Crew, Number.	Number of Vessels.	Tons Register.	Crew, Number.	Number of Vessels.	Tons Register.	Crew, Number.	Number of Vessels.	Tons Register.	Crew, Number.	Number.
2	282	145		74	1	221	17	5	2,391	82	1	315	6	1
1	173	318		5							32	2,547	225	2
											1	590	12	3
								5	637	20	3	588	14	4
2	2,841	3,271		12				1	635	45	5	106	20	5
11	868	304		97	5	423	46	9	101	29	17	1,553	5,341	6
1	1,052	50		30				28	3,966	313	33	8,155	419	7
1	876		18,370	19										8
1	266	406		5				11	456	48	48	2,141	611	9
					18	1,911	99							10
4	1,981	2,753		36							1	751	8	11
								3	351	17				12
								3	334	17				13
								1	74	3				14
					11	4,513	71	17	5,234	114	24	13,448	190	15
1	204	589		7										16
1	439	640		6	1	1,526	25				10	13,284	213	17
31	518	87		88				104	16,553	947	478	12,514	1,776	18
														19
9	1,063	614		54	40	7,059	590	63	5.941	1,172	225	17,245	4,022	20
														21
12	6,488	10,562		94	3	134	15	5	1,140	54	1	270	18	22
2	405	787		13	33	12,120	909				7	9,594	146	23
								15	3,895	151	5	293	53	24
								5	60	15	3	876	32	25
											3	2,735	52	2b
					5	8,489	115				1	1,547	18	27
								2	238	11				28
								13	415	56	28	942	207	29
								10	1,261	55				30
					3	4,878	69				9	10,546	143	31
1	253	493		6				7	1,179	39	6	670	17	32
2	1,576	2,468	574,700	41				1	98	5	1	230	5	33
9	2,050	3,772		52										34
					3	204	16							35
2	833	1,210		14				1	1,176	19	1	1,029	16	36
1	398	724		7				2	125	10				37
											4	181	27	38
134	185,417	77,993		5,293	43	84,335	1,607	223	10,827	1,763	149	69,599	2,774	39
2	654	1,156		14				4	3,231	22	14	4,949	164	40
								5	4,350	19	28	17,530	408	41
								13	214	35	114	1,151	239	42
1	74	90		8							12	728	185	43
					1	336	8	8	1,078	35	11	2,730	55	44
														45
1	685			15	3	2,251	73							46
								36	10					47
								50	5,367	296	66	27,588	664	48
2	370	588		12	1	392	7	11	941	70	10	1,075	146	49
1	2,036	100		28										50
217	15,029	13,181	1,766	3,426	5	3,116	51	21	2,195	108	5	1,665	35	51
65	4,727	2,575		1,172							8	103	19	52
18	158	68		36				325	14,398	1,410	158	1,544	318	53
205	40,660	68,219		2,740	98	124,290	2,458	46	28,342	829	72	81,225	1,556	54
18	816			218				2	160	26	21	1,423	349	55
2	485	698		27	1	475	8	27	2,454	302	21	1,827	337	56
					9	777	181				37	5,203	811	57
								2	288	11	2	697	12	58
								3	344	14	4	1,120	21	59

11—ii—27½

6 GEORGE V, A. 1916

No. 5.—STATEMENT of Vessels, British, Canadian and Foreign, entered Inwards,

WITH CARGOES.

Number.	Ports and Outports.	BRITISH.					CANADIAN.				
		Number of Vessels.	Tons Register.	Tons Weight.	Tons Measurement.	Crew, Number.	Number of Vessels.	Tons Register.	Tons Weight.	Tons Measurement.	Crew, Number.
60	Meteghan, N.S.						2	247	29		11
61	Moncton, N.B.	1	2,416	5,100		29	7	1,513	3,250		44
62	Montreal, Que.	285	1,311,523	442,741	188,237	37,788	26	70,395	8,052	2,141	3,905
63	Murray Harbour, P.E.I						3	66	49		14
64	Nanaimo, B.C.	1	3,058	600		39	5	447	176		37
65	Newcastle, N.B.										
66	New Campbellton, N.S										
67	Newport, B.C.	2	6,627	6,647		83	1	570	1		18
68	New Westminster, B.C						13	1,521	2,081		85
69	North East Harbour, N. S.						4	86	73		23
70	North Head, N.B.						124	18,801	2,149		1,167
71	North Sydney, N.S.	263	174,401	5,646		10,113	8	2,467	4,313		125
72	Parrsboro..N.S.										
73	Paspebiac, Que.										
74	Percé, Que.	5	3,002			86					
75	Pictou, N.S.	2	4,269	11,100		57	3	416	861		18
76	Port Clyde, N.S.										
77	Port Hood, N.S.										
78	Port la Tour, N.S.										
79	Port Mulgrave, N.S.						3	395	576		19
80	Port Simpson, B.C.	1	221			18	29	33,946			1,653
81	Port Wade, N.S.						5	460	5	8	25
82	Port Williams, N.S.						3	869			20
83	Powell River, B.C.						4	565	751		41
84	Prince Rupert, B.C.	107	95,898	3,568		5,686	77	3,481	1,312	51	1,265
85	Pugwash, N.S.										
86	Quebec, Que.	259	1,257,648	48,663	23,694	43,278					
87	Rimouski, Que.										
88	River Hebert, N.S.										
89	St. Andrews, N.B.						65	4,461	2,704		257
90	St. George, N.B.						1	1	1		1
91	St. John, N.B.	171	522,303	100,700	59660	12,092	84	25,564	24,992	605	1,108
92	St. Martins, N.B.						2	1,130	4		8
93	St. Stephen, N.B.	1	168			5					
94	Sackville, N.B.						5	497	307		25
95	Salmon River, N.S.	11	231	508		62					
96	Sandy Point, N.S.	4	632	1,149		26	8	616	908	25	61
97	Shediac, N.B.										
98	Shelburne, N.S.						19	1,812	1,274		142
99	Sherbrooke, N.S.										
100	Shippegan, N.B.										
101	Sidney, B.C.						8	876	913		15
102	Souris, P.E.I.	2	349	534		10	29	1,615	1,096		302
103	Steveston, B.C.						30	4,716	971		618
104	Stickeen, B.C.						4	1,197	232		63
105	Summerside, P.E.I.	2	470	839		12	1	191	426		5
106	Sydney, N.S.	10	16,058	25,165		270	31	30,577	49,620		796
107	Three Rivers, Que.	7	17,612	25,239		222					
108	Truro, N.S.										
109	Tusket, N.S.										
110	Union Bay, B.C.						2	207	55		7
111	Vancouver, B.C.	238	561,153	308,326	110,730	19,380	469	647,080	32,859	122	27,440
112	Victoria, B.C.	371	516,237	25,986	6,537	27,828	161	169,172	18,902	160	6,916
113	Westport, N.S.						7	968	982		40
114	Weymouth, N.S.						7	979	306	120	41
115	White Rock, B.C.						4	60	1,001		8
116	Windsor, N.S.	3	855	1,077		19	19	7,601	4,358		95
117	Wolfville, N.S.	1	297			7	2	411			10
118	Yarmouth, N.S.	10	3,165	5,105		74	293	154,034	22,382		14,048
	Total	2232	5,704,312	1,302,322	940,980	190,249	2861	1,424,647	274,259	6,527	76,253

from Sea, at each Port and Outport, during the Fiscal Year ended March 31, 1915.

					IN BALLAST.									
FOREIGN.					BRITISH.			CANADIAN.			FOREIGN.			
Number of Vessels.	Tons Register.	Quantity of Freight.		Crew Number.	Number of Vessels.	Tons Register.	Crew Number.	Number of Vessels.	Tons Register.	Crew Number.	Number of Vessels.	Tons Register.	Crew Number.	Number.
		Tons Weight.	Tons Measurement.											
								5	526	26				60
1	613	1,360		6	6	13,120	183	4	2,576	39	17	10,891	184	61
38	90,981	58,655	13,324	2,311	186	487,887	6,518				17	39,398	552	62
								7	210	5				63
15	8,698	3,354		245	10	26,328	328	95	9,256	686	203	158,238	3,043	64
					3	4,516	56				18	16,468	286	65
					1	1,826	26	4	169	16				66
3	7,032	8,565		115				15	10,019	255	21	19,070	196	67
11	2,852	1,788		198				13	5,036	183	4	2,409	38	68
22	1,477	175		378							9	659	150	69
1	194	447		6				61	5,450	335	19	358	47	70
10	19,033	49,343		258	380	72,070	3,039	100	19,689	1,100	241	47,968	5,330	71
					23	30,473	557	53	12,825	353	52	17,361	683	72
2	615	852		12							3	3,902	63	73
2	1,169			26	1	2,210	28							74
1	683	1,000		17	5	7,566	108				2	2,630	42	75
								1	281	7	2	958	15	76
1	91	8		18										77
								17	223	79	18	1,669	366	78
1	96	25		8	5	643	67	5	503	104	22	2,535	419	79
											7	55	32	80
					1	161	7	2	468	12	1	11	3	81
														82
65	34,863	17,596	725	1,574	1	4,419	33	3	345	29	5	1,361	73	83
84	82,511	2,359	267	5,727	9	995	309	8	135	54	70	32,786	2,597	84
								1	2,263	25	2	3,258	43	85
19	65,968	4,361	1,964	2,162	17	66,056	1,609				4	3,131	70	86
					9	19,465	240	12	10,890	186	7	8,681	122	87
								3	274	12	1	155	4	88
231	11,190	6,584		1,040				273	16,667	1,251	768	44,739	4,047	89
2	321	577		7				13	968	47	124	8,744	444	90
213	343,405	64,652	9,300	12,716	45	115,764	1,726	120	14,446	576	354	47,688	1,474	91
1	430	1		4	1	209	6	24	7,459	106	50	10,578	370	92
53	5,855	11,882	15	168				215	19,801	1,407	79	1,596	311	93
2	343	550		9							1	163	4	94
											2	33	5	95
110	8,302	4,735		2,054	1	197	6	2	491	12	128	10,767	2,424	96
1	214	917		5										97
47	3,918	1,017		925				9	1,445	86	34	2,961	648	98
								1	357	6				99
2	478	966		16				79	1,097	336				100
7	148	70		5				48	1,132	166	20	789	57	101
					6	301	63	29	1,275	292	26	2,168	476	102
2	786	49		60	1	156	15	119	3,374	416	27	756	91	103
32	412	127		108				1	379	19	8	72	25	104
6	3,049	5,573		43				1	856	38				105
96	176,239	455,569		2,531	95	167,191	2,505	51	37,709	1,021	45	83,875	1,427	106
					16	38,880	587							107
								4	420	20	1	388	7	108
2	164	250		36				1	14	2	6	482	92	109
1	598	6		30	17	55,741	846	18	5,358	139	33	32,671	490	110
428	433,835	293,573	29,072	16,172	100	94,175	7,207	240	98,320	4,371	128	57,354	1,657	111
607	678,088	54,866	16,887	31,041	-67	231,528	7,722	163	26,568	1,478	299	389,282	15,649	112
								7	1,179	59	30	438	73	113
1	363	489		5	1	194	6	10	1,508	53	13	4,177	78	114
5	38	875		10				59	450	118	50	297	109	115
7	2,893	3,363		47	3	933	21	55	63,841	276	69	59,578	566	116
3	907			17										117
53	8,598	2,665		1,466				22	3,340	338	97	6,472	1,164	118
2948	2,271,127	1,250,105	666,390	95,225	1294	1,760,454	40,183	3031	510,077	24,311	4,816	1,462,327	62,730	

6 GEORGE V, A. 1916

No. 6.—STATEMENT of Vessels, British, Canadian and Foreign
Fiscal Year ended
ABSTRACT BY

Number	Countries whence Arrived.	BRITISH.					CANADIAN.				
		Number of Vessels.	Tons Register.	Quantity of Freight. Tons Weight.	Tons Measurement.	Crew, Number.	Number of Vessels.	Tons Register.	Quantity of Freight. Tons Weight.	Tons Measurement.	Crew, Number.
1	United Kingdom.......	775	3,633,918	601,984	243,336	105,532	211	80,380	11,020	2,745	4,640
2	Australia.............	30	163,192	13,087	34,987	5,209					
3	Bermuda.............										
4	B. South.Africa.......										
5	B. West Africa........	1	2,788	100		39					
6	B. Guiana...........	1	1,980	3,730		24					
7	B. West Indies........	108	187,976	135,815	7,082	5,566	38	6,485	11,065		235
8	Fiji Islands...........	7	19,277	32,030	16,395	261					
9	Gibraltar............										
10	Malta...............										
11	Newfoundland........	377	271,557	17,820		13,786	130	55,700	60,365		2,254
12	Argentina............	7	16,552	25,156		209					
13	Aust.-Hungary........										
14	Belgium.............	29	121,111	36,179	42,965	2,071					
15	Brazil...............										
16	Canary Islands........										
17	Chili...............	3	8,479	7,343		109					
18	China...............	15	79,072	22,031	40,294	4,666					
19	Cuba................	1	2,802	5,650		34					
20	Denmark............	1	2,895	653	4	36					
21	Danish West Indies....										
22	Ecuador.............										
23	Egypt...............										
24	France..............	13	75,663	4,568	2,786	2,358	1	1,595	928		23
25	French Africa........										
26	French West Indies....										
27	Germany............										
28	Greece..............	1	1,686	3,247		24					
29	Guatemala...........	1	2,308	4,500		44					
30	Hayti										
31	Holland.............	11	45,464	9,230		992					
32	Iceland.............										
33	Italy...............	2	4,443	6,675		59					
34	Japan...............	4	18,530	6,369	159	341					
35	Mexico.............										
36	Norway.............	1	1,090	1,892		18					
37	Peru...............	6	14,613	26,276		188					
38	Philippines..........										
39	Porto Rico...........										
40	Portugal............	1	1,926	2,248		34					
41	Russia.............										
42	San Domingo.........	6	4,705	11,048		134					
43	St. Pierre...........	1	65	1		5	1	126	5		6
44	Sea Fisheries........	112	9,052	3,835		2,566	932	46,714	27,188		10,766
45	Spain...............	8	16,599	18,253		248	3	297	525		20
46	Spanish Africa........										
47	Sweden.............										
48	United States.........	709	994,178	298,102	552,972	45,663	1,545	1,233,350	163,163	3,782	53,309
49	Uruguay.............	1	2,391	4,500		33					
50	Sea................										
	Total.............	2232	5,704,312	1,302,322	940,980	190,249	2861	1424,647	274,259	6,527	76,253

entered Inwards, *from Sea*, in the Dominion of Canada, during the March 31, 1915.

COUNTRIES.

| | | | | | IN BALLAST. | | | | | | | | | |
| | FOREIGN. | | | | BRITISH. | | | CANADIAN. | | | FOREIGN. | | | |
Number of Vessels.	Tons Register.	Quantity of Freight. Tons Weight.	Tons Measurement.	Crew, Number.	Number of Vessels.	Tons Register.	Crew, Number.	Number of Vessels.	Tons Register.	Crew, Number.	Number of Vessels.	Tons Register.	Crew, Number.	Number.
13	23,952	23,027	....	427	211	553,695	7,805	19	26,298	378	72	102,027	1,573	1
...	...	...	...	...	1	2,465	30	1	1,863	17	1	1,289	13	2
1	214	917	...	5	2	4,259	56	...	...	...	...	...	...	3
...	...	...	...	...	1	2,820	40	...	...	...	3	6,440	74	4
...	...	...	...	...	1	2,534	29	...	...	...	...	...	...	5
3	4,179	8,316	...	80	...	...	...	...	...	...	...	...	...	6
34	27,961	33,266	213	681	24	45,665	603	...	...	...	11	13,318	191	7
...	...	...	...	...	...	...	...	...	...	...	...	...	...	8
...	...	...	...	...	4	10,271	129	...	...	...	...	...	...	9
...	...	...	...	...	1	2,737	29	...	...	...	...	...	...	10
83	170,963	473,460	...	2,292	419	82,826	3,657	174	57,617	2,611	24	17,872	426	11
...	...	...	...	...	11	28,175	329	...	...	...	3	5,153	62	12
2	7,347	1,794	124	74	...	...	...	...	...	...	...	...	...	13
1	5,489	10	...	150	...	...	...	...	...	...	...	...	...	14
...	...	...	...	...	7	17,417	219	...	...	...	4	4,935	65	15
...	...	...	...	...	2	5,092	70	...	...	...	...	...	...	16
...	...	...	...	...	5	16,539	202	...	...	...	3	3,882	47	17
30	111,980	3,286	6,162	2,353	11	63,260	3,824	...	...	...	...	...	...	18
4	4,294	11,255	...	83	...	...	...	1	349	8	...	...	...	19
2	6,096	670	185	68	3	4,094	72	...	...	...	6	4,806	89	20
1	1,178	2,425	...	22	...	...	...	...	...	...	...	...	...	21
...	...	...	...	...	...	...	...	...	...	...	1	3,084	43	22
...	...	...	...	...	3	7,440	82	...	...	...	1	1,920	28	23
8	25,571	2,485	812	1,613	16	38,466	505	1	1,159	26	26	11,398	653	24
...	...	...	...	...	3	8,136	83	...	...	...	...	...	...	25
...	...	...	...	...	...	...	...	...	...	...	1	469	10	26
9	36,854	3,044	2,659	1,059	1	2,110	25	...	...	...	2	3,674	54	27
...	...	...	...	...	...	...	...	...	...	...	...	...	...	28
...	...	...	...	...	...	...	...	...	...	...	...	...	...	29
1	878	1,930	...	19	...	...	...	...	...	...	...	...	...	30
20	85,141	5,573	3,594	2,272	2	6,043	65	...	...	...	7	16,402	203	31
...	...	...	...	...	...	...	...	...	...	...	1	189	7	32
3	7,320	1,866	...	165	31	79,831	928	...	...	...	10	20,450	243	33
42	154,316	9,801	21,570	3,796	2	3,564	51	...	...	...	1	2,487	30	34
7	10,509	19,200	...	178	...	...	...	...	...	...	...	...	...	35
7	15,969	3,961	439	371	...	...	...	...	...	...	12	10,049	203	36
2	6,461	11,409	...	67	...	...	...	...	...	...	2	3,254	38	37
1	3,833	53	702	86	...	...	...	...	...	...	...	...	...	38
...	...	...	...	...	...	...	...	1	293	6	...	...	...	39
1	2,758	1,353	87	32	12	25,110	316	1	256	7	3	4,330	60	40
11	52,856	62	...	1,831	...	...	...	...	...	...	...	...	...	41
9	6,924	14,988	...	161	...	...	...	...	...	...	...	...	...	42
16	3,425	391	...	354	18	1,315	92	13	1,108	68	68	10,068	1,555	43
648	43,025	17,863	...	11,151	90	11,377	1,489	523	20,037	4,426	694	54,941	12,355	44
6	4,233	1,753	1,319	70	7	13,812	180	...	...	...	2	4,234	71	45
...	...	...	...	...	1	392	7	...	...	...	...	...	...	46
3	4,595	3,600	...	76	...	...	...	...	...	...	2	4,423	56	47
1,980	1,442,806	592,347	628,524	65,689	385	692,933	18,833	2295	400,736	16,723	3,848	1,144,067	44,071	48
...	...	...	...	...	3	8,003	87	1	99	19	...	...	...	49
...	...	...	...	...	17	20,073	346	1	272	22	8	7,166	510	50
2948	2,271127	1,250105	666,390	95,225	1294	1,760454	40,183	3031	510,077	24,311	4,816	1,462327	62,730	

6 GEORGE V, A. 1916

No. 6.—STATEMENT of Vessels, British, Canadian and Foreign, entered Inwards

RECAPITU

	Number. of vessels.	Tons Register.	QUANTITY OF FREIGHT.		Crew Number.
——			Tons Weight.	Tons Measurement.	
With Cargo—					
British............................	2,232	5,704,312	1,302,322	940,980	190,249
Canadian..........................	2,861	1,424,647	274,259	6,527	76,253
Foreign...........................	2,948	2,271,127	1,250,105	666,390	95,225
Total......................	8,041	9,400,086	2,826,686	1,613,897	361,727

SESSIONAL PAPER No. 11

from Sea, by Ports and Outports, &c.—*Concluded.*

LATION.

	Number of Vessels.	Tons Register.	QUANTITY OF FREIGHT.		Crew Number.
			Tons Weight.	Tons Measure-ment.	
In Ballast—					
British............................	1,294	1,760,454	....	....	40,183
Canadian..........................	3,031	510,077	....	....	24,311
Foreign...........................	4,816	1,462,327	....	....	62,730
Total......................	9,141	3,732,858	....	....	127,224
Grand total................	17,182	13,132,944	2,826,686	1,613,897	488,951

No. 7.—STATEMENT of Vessels, British, Canadian and Foreign, entered Outwards

Number	Ports and Outports	WITH CARGOES.									
		BRITISH.					CANADIAN.				
		Number of Vessels.	Tons Register.	Quantity of Freight.		Crew, Number.	Number of Vessels.	Tons Register.	Quantity of Freight.		Crew, Number.
				Tons Weight.	Tons Measurement.				Tons Weight.	Tons Measurement.	
1	Albert, N.B.........						1	98		210	3
2	Alert Bay, B.C.......	2	442	552		35					
3	Amherst, N.S........						1	274	400		7
4	Annapolis Royal, N.S..	2	410	1,050	1,050	14	3	558	1,454	1,510	19
5	Anyox, B.C...........						20	13,029	10,146		325
6	Arichat, N.S.........						1	96	5		20
7	Baddeck, N.S........						56	4,288	60		679
8	Barrington, N.S......										
9	Barton, N.S.........						29	3,211	2	5,687	163
10	Bathurst, N.B.......	11	2,058			75	3	441			16
11	Bear River, N.S.....	1	161		394	6	20	3,587		4,967	110
12	Belliveau's Cove, N.S..	3	595	9	1,850	18	2	271	2	474	12
13	Bridgetown, N.S......						1	149	270	300	6
14	Bridgewater, N.S.....	27	9,965		23,386	191	35	8,391		19,453	206
15	Buctouche, N.B.......										
16	Campbellton, N.B....	9	10,059		6,838	141	3	443		260	20
17	Campo Bello, N.B....						7	137	75		16
18	Canning, N.S.........						2	847			15
19	Canso, N.S...........	4	806	662	90	28	13	1,583	1,377	188	66
20	Caraquet, N.B........						2	180	360		11
21	Cardigan, P.E.I.......	1	76	110		6					
22	Charlottetown, P.E.I..	14	728	806		64	62	75,376	6,519	750	3,025
23	Chatham, N.B........	40	75,881		263,650	964					
24	Chemainus, B.C.......	1	2,829		4,850	33	16	7,055	479	17,286	191
25	Chester, N.S.........	5	1,112	1,953		34					
26	Cheticamp, N.S.......										
27	Chicoutimi, Que......	17	33,843	76,442		429					
28	Church Point, N.S....	1	195		556	7	9	999		2,166	48
29	Clark's Harbour, N.S.						9	572	76		44
30	Clementsport, N.S....						17	2,228	5,388	6,735	97
31	Dalhousie, N.B.......	16	19,128		41,709	305	2	296		488	12
32	Digby, N.S...........						16	1,670	383	3,823	80
33	Dorchester, N.B......	1	249		773	7	4	490		1,375	20
34	Fredericton, N.B.....										
35	Gaspé, Que...........	7	7,910	700	6,100	200	13	5,247	1,600	4,110	137
36	Georgetown, P.E.I.....	9	606	611		44					
37	Glace Bay, N.S.......						108	6,524			441
38	Halifax, N.S.........	355	1,079,119	243,366	169,054	32,616	522	123,420	46,537	9,272	8,304
39	Hantsport, N.S.......						4	756	1,425		22
40	Hillsboro, N.B.......						10	6,249	9,579		49
41	Indian Island, N.B....						2	26	13		4
42	Isaac's Harbour, N.S..						5	514	157	150	28
43	Joggins Mines, N.S...	1	209	375		6	19	2,625	4,650		91
44	Kentville, N.S........						3	674			16
45	Kingsport, N.S.......	3	2,251			72	3	865			18
46	Ladner, B.C..........						7	36	38		11
47	Ladysmith, B.C.......	1	37	32		11	22	2,891	4,725		85
48	La Have, N.S.........	7	1,714	2,868		45	11	1,490	2,616		65
49	Liverpool, N.S.......	47	7,511	400	13,348	296	1	219		500	7
50	Lockeport, N.S.......	4	555	175		76	53	1,856	714		482
51	Lords Cove, N.S......						146	1,169	1,735		291
52	Louisburg, N.S	98	101,646	216,344		2,276	54	29,434	49,755		909
53	Lower East Pubnico, N.S.						18	1,329			252
54	Lunenburg, N.S.......	7	2,010	3,512		45	27	3,592	6,318		176
55	Magdalen Islands, Que.										
56	Mahone Bay, N.S.....	3	558	983		20	5	496	875		32
57	Maitland, N.S........	1	209		585	6	15	2,012		5,295	78
58	Meteghan River, N.S..						9	1,026		1,916	48
59	Moncton, N.B.........	6	13,312	10,500	16,928	186	8	2,938	900	5,234	56
60	Montague, P.E.I.......	3	154	165		12	1	70	112		6
61	Montreal, Que.........	472	1,823,333	2,177,695	219,014	45,111	37	79,896	20,776	101	4,121

SESSIONAL PAPER No. 11

for Sea, at each Port and Outport, during the Fiscal Year ended March 31, 1915:

					IN BALLAST									
		FOREIGN			BRITISH			CANADIAN			FOREIGN			
Number of Vessels	Tons Register	Quantity of Freight — Tons Weight	Tons Measurement	Crew, Number	Number of Vessels	Tons Register	Crew, Number	Number of Vessels	Tons Register	Crew, Number	Number of Vessels	Tons Register	Crew, Number	Number
1	360		650	7										1
14	1,474	1,056		127	1	222	17				23	6,928	303	2
											1	703	10	3
														4
1	1,452	2,000		7				6	6,140	45	8	5,716	42	5
11	868	408		95	2	131	28	80	1,742	484	17	1,553	341	6
40	15,225	56		637				12	24,428	245				7
								11	456	48	49	2,407	616	8
														9
15	8,383			132										10
														11
														12
1	134	400	325	4										13
36	20,860		43,453	295										14
1	204		759	7										15
31	32,196		21,395	490										16
14	221		481	31				150	26,132	1,467	14	231	36	17
														18
27	3,442	2,529	187	368	42	7,343	642	62	5,379	1,174	209	15,872	3,741	19
								166	2,269	679				20
														21
10	13,996		61,594	194				4	68	20	2	1,269	25	22
														23
7	2,943	665	5,754	89				3	343	33				24
5	1,477	2,584		30				24	274	75	1	77	19	25
5	4,171	8,314		85										26
10	12,542	29,383		203										27
														28
18	305	306		57				12	409	56	10	637	150	29
														30
18	19,177		49,670	323										31
11	793	46	1,168	45							4	112	12	32
2	677		975	10							1	788	20	33
								6	1,737	32	9	2,050	52	34
15	16,030		15,300	297										35
														36
4	181			27				1	39	6				37
238	220,542	90,163	57,386	7,837	13	24,678	428	98	4,565	288				38
9	2,999	5,125		51				4	149	33	21	23,848	378	39
31	19,390	44,502		448				2	18	19	6	1,986	126	40
90	752	993		192				5	25	10	2	10	4	41
1	74	70		8							12	728	185	42
13	3,485	5,350		68										43
														44
														45
								4	248	25				46
48	23,695	16,836		476				19	1,150	139	17	517	90	47
1	26	3		6				83	6,552	1,314	8	519	129	48
225	18,907	12,272	8,200	3,359										49
73	4,751	2,647		1,196										50
120	1,195	2,108		242				159	12,561	1,045	26	199	52	51
237	96,821	223,655		3,609	9	6,408	227	7	891	175	34	21,799	642	52
17	760			212				24	684	229	20	1,339	347	53
1	91	10		20	3	553	35	298	20,600	4,271	20	1,672	330	54
16	1,699	480		93										55
2	697	1,219		12				12	964	197				56
3	944	550	1,189	16										57
														58
17	12,728	10,880	14,455	203							1	388	4	59
					1	175	6							60
34	109,376	181,130	1,050	2,582	3	6,744	108				5	11,696	147	61

6 GEORGE V, A. 1916

No. 7.—STATEMENT of Vessels, British, Canadian and Foreign entered Outwards,

		WITH CARGOES.									
		BRITISH.					CANADIAN.				
		Number of Vessels.	Tons Register.	Quantity of Freight.		Crew, Number.	Number of Vessels.	Tons Register.	Quantity of Freight.		Crew, Number.
Number.	Ports and Outports.			Tons Weight.	Tons Measurement.				Tons Weight.	Tons Measurement.	
62	Murray Harbour, P.E.I										
63	Nanaimo, B.C	35	45,693	17,203		1,202	102	11,031	11,332	978	947
64	Newcastle, N.B	12	8,465	4,530	14,000	125	5	822		2,050	29
65	Newport. B.C	1	3,488	60		39	12	9,506	11,060		255
66	New Westminster, B. C						25	4,304	10,317		193
67	North East Harbour. N.S						1	66	45		3
68	North Head, N.B						41	3,861	458		236
69	North Sydney, N.S	377	239,713	38,537		11,420	46	10,082	20,772		510
70	Parrsboro, N.S	25	33,670	65,934		621	89	21,513	35,089		591
71	Paspebiac, Que	9	8,035		12,002	127	5	933	168	1,863	31
72	Percé, Que	1	2,210			28	1	92			5
73	Pictou, N.S	17	37,019	36,150		369					
74	Port Clyde, N.S	1	249		380	6	2	380	575	155	12
75	Port Hood, N.S										
76	Port La Tour, N.S										
77	Port Mulgrave, N.S						2	181	100		10
78	Port Simpson, B.C	3	663			54	30	33,120			1,605
79	Port Wade, N.S						9	996	1,710	1,881	49
80	Port Williams, N.S						2	668			17
81	Powell River, B.C	4	15,770	4,607		159					
82	Prince Rupert, B.C						32	33,959	455	4	649
83	Pugwash , N.S	1	2,263	4,300		25					
84	Quebec, Que	126	586,394	57,276	4,922	22,590					
85	Rimouski, Que	8	17,074	19,346		207	12	10,890	19,866		186
86	River Hebert, N.S	2	418	800		12	8	1,040	1,525		34
87	St. Andrews, N.B						100	1,328	1,018		201
88	St. George, N.B						10	1,135	1,156	1,296	38
89	St. John, N.B	148	430,819	323,090	184,626	9,164	98	27,991	8,477	24,539	1,000
90	St. Martins. N.B						17	7,634		19,085	73
91	St. Stephen, N.B						4	137	15	35	9
92	Sackville, N.B	1	296		1,300	7	4	398	700		20
93	Salmon River, N.S	1	71		174	5					
94	Sandy Cove, N.S						1	42	50		2
95	Sandy Point, N.S	1	82	100		7	8	1,284	313	1,685	44
96	Shediac, N.B										
97	Sheet Harbour, N.S						3	128	165	236	14
98	Shelburne, N.S						19	3,565	26	4,963	129
99	Sherbrooke, N.S						6	1,408	300	432	34
100	Shippegan, N.B						2	98			6
101	Sidney, B.C						2	98	110		3
102	Sorel, Que	1	1,972		4,500	27	1	99	160		5
103	Souris, P. E. I	4	315	218	63	23	5	548	258	319	32
104	Steveston, B.C						111	3,328	2,484		368
105	Stickeen, B.C						3	758	611		11
106	Summerside, P.E.I						15	13,140	1,288		528
107	Sydney, N.S	331	171,272	330,510		3,367	118	60,591	96,523		1,902
108	Three Rivers, Que	15	36,671	19,820		561					
109	Truro, N.S						6	993	1,250		29
110	Tusket, N.S						1	95	100		4
111	Union Bay, B.C	32	117,168	38,987		1,790	7	2,636	2,113		69
112	Vancouver, B.C	346	570,778	79,903	95,934	29,846	211	237,275	43,114	515	9,924
113	Victoria B.C	82	183,018	3,589	270	6,995	251	453,400	13,939	3	18,732
114	Westport, N.S						5	200	162		14
115	Weymouth, N.S	7	1,870	2,248	1,046	42	17	1,898	175	4,408	89
116	White Rock, B.C						53	332	1,620		99
117	Windsor, N.S	11	3,413	2,725	3,584	76	71	74,295	114,000	4,636	327
118	Yarmouth, N.S	204	166,508	20,084		14,581	14	620	428		214
	Total	2985	5,884,748	3,809352	1,092,976	186854	3023	1,440,521	583,548	161,333	60,222

for Sea, at each Port and Outport, during the Fiscal Year ended March 31, 1915.

| | | | | | IN BALLAST. | | | | | | | | | |
| FOREIGN. | | | | | BRITISH. | | | CANADIAN. | | | FOREIGN. | | | |
Number of Vessels	Tons Register	Quantity of Freight — Tons Weight	Tons Measurement	Crew, Number	Number of Vessels	Tons Register	Crew, Number	Number of Vessels	Tons Register	Crew, Number	Number of Vessels	Tons Register	Crew, Number	Number
206	192,132	196,113	1,860	3,974				9	253	53	71	12,866	618	62
24	16,205		34,300	266				51	4,367	382				63
														64
15	17,207	19,665		141	1	3,139	39	6	2,740	77	9	7,252	138	65
12	5,929	4,114		227				16	2,398	186	6	831	68	66
22	1,477	175		369				4	86	21	10	750	179	67
12	210	365		27				141	22,154	1,252	4	126	15	68
25	22,030	28,170		467	54	9,833	820	36	9,894	913	261	56,195	6,048	69
27	10,893	18,155		187							26	7,808	509	70
13	10,145	295	17,820	192										71
8	3,830			77							2	982	27	72
3	3,908	8,000		70										73
2	850	1,496		14										74
1	91	8		18										75
								17	223	79	18	1,669	366	76
1	127	200		6	5	643	67	8	703	146	19	1,657	378	77
		20									7	55	32	78
4		40	20	10										79
											11	2,673	99	80
68	33,906	26,641	62	1,608										81
43	35,783	201	6	1,895	50	4,213	1,218	102	17,468	2,123	105	72,190	5,492	82
7	9,697	21,440		138										83
8	8,377	6,349		377	13	5,095	386				4	4,660	67	84
6	7,830	9,385		103	1	2,391	30							85
3	617	975		14										86
505	12,300	9,654		1,530				152	19,966	1,203	470	41,282	3,493	87
62	7,695	10,123	4,918	212				3	133	9	68	2,129	276	88
552	399,006	19,018	138,744	14,277	11	24,387	407	36	470	94	35	10,149	291	89
26	9,714	5	25,313	110							29	2,291	294	90
59	6,660		240	163				187	20,169	1,373	65	1,543	251	91
2	357			10										92
2	33	58		5	10	160	57							93
2	30	22		4										94
111	8,659	1,888	560	2,053				3	32	10	125	9,605	2,396	95
1	917	2,000		14										96
1	99			23										97
48	4,850	987	1,525	922				14	569	113	35	3,274	685	98
														99
								79	1,102	336				100
								30	834	115	28	1,103	60	101
														102
29	1,560	1,033		156	4	176	53	57	2,483	580	26	2,168	476	103
14	209	20		60	27	4,086	751	16	574	72	1	14	5	104
								6	824	56	22	261	71	105
														106
61	59,459	140,080		1,123	4	8,216	141	17	15,362	317	90	175,113	2,843	107
					8	19,821	246							108
														109
3	286	400		40				2	28	4	5	360	88	110
29	32,566	43,535	1,749	307				15	3,215	163	10	513	72	111
350	317,822	72,220	39,661	13,482	78	173,539	4,721	272	226,652	10,151	202	173,528	4,526	112
282	315,378	5,940	643	16,429	98	279,624	10,784	329	155,030	6,811	566	710,403	28,814	113
22	270	76		50										114
13	5,880	5,234	6,248	100				1	10	4				115
40	326	715		89				21	328	41	14	91	28	116
90	69,338	113,055	15,918	587										117
69	11,276	7,528		906				106	3,876	1,122	76	4,428	914	118
4356	2,322017	1,421579	573,097	87,022	438	531,577	21,211	2988	629,766	39,945	2,940	1,411013	67,420	

No. 8.—STATEMENT of Vessels, British, Canadian and Foreign entered Outwards,

.ABSTRACT BY

		WITH CARGOES.									
		BRITISH.					CANADIAN.				
	Countries to which Departed.	Number of Vessels.	Tons Register.	Quantity of Freight.		Crew, Number.	Number of Vessels.	Tons Register.	Quantity of Freight.		Crew, Number.
Number.				Tons Weight.	Tons Measurement.				Tons Weight.	Tons Measurement.	
1	United Kingdom.......	871	3,457,371	2,579,556	546,328	93,522	132	92,146	26,880	15,340	4,742
2	Australia..............	50	223,350	73,687	144,178	5,218	1	398	1,046	....	10
3	British South Africa...	19	53,929	88,165	29,089	807	1	1,862	2,050	....	19
4	British Guiana........	28	74,543	89,820	620	2,547	...	....	....	....	.....
5	British West Indies....	18	6,530	1,660	6,877	149	20	3,655	2,267	4,287	118
6	British Oceania, other.	5	14,015	4,600	4,850	164	...	....	....	....	.....
7	Fiji Islands............	...	....	....	....	....	...	....	....	....	.....
8	Malta.................	...	....	....	....	....	...	....	....	....	.....
9	Newfoundland........	756	310,455	129,811	....	480	15,613	306	139,900	139,434	62	5,414
10	Gibraltar.............	8	18,496	45,925	....	219	...	....	....	....	.....
11	Argentina.............	2	3,874	4,217	....	48	...	....	....	....	.....
12	Azores and Madeira...	3	776	....	2,448	20	1	268	470	....	6
13	Belgium..............	5	17,216	29,106	2,000	312	...	....	....	....	.....
14	Brazil.................	8	5,300	9,066	....	91	...	....	....	....	.....
15	Chili.................	...	....	....	....	....	...	....	....	....	.....
16	China................	15	77,009	20,965	19,086	4,468	...	....	....	....	.....
17	Canary Islands........	1	392	....	1,045	7	...	....	....	....	.....
18	Cuba..................	13	5,392	2,522	4,126	150	10	3,252	....	1,794	68
19	Danish West Indies...	...	....	....	....	....	...	....	....	....	.....
20	Denmark..............	.	....	....	....	....	...	....	....	....	.....
21	France................	69	208,586	289,845	7,533	3,603	4	5,566	9,174	....	117
22	Egypt.................	...	....	....	....	....	...	....	....	....	.....
23	Greenland, Iceland, etc	...	....	....	....	....	...	....	....	....	.....
24	Germany.............	2	5,412	13,412	....	56	...	....	....	....	.....
25	Holland...............	11	27,101	57,256	....	345	...	....	....	....	.....
26	Hayti.................	...	....	....	....	....	...	....	....	....	.....
27	Italy.................	11	27,752	65,169	....	326	...	....	....	....	.....
28	Japan................	3	11,489	2,200	....	197	...	....	....	....	.....
29	Norway...............	...	....	....	....	....	...	....	....	....	.....
30	Peru..................	1	2,948	70	....	32	...	....	....	....	.....
31	Porto Rico...:........	2	348	610	....	11	15	2,062	2,291	2,523	89
32	Portugal..............	6	12,224	22,495	700	163	...	....	....	....	.....
33	Portuguese Africa.....	...	....	....	....	....	...	....	....	....	.....
34	Russia................	1	5,809	4	....	95	...	....	....	....	.....
35	San Domingo..........	...	....	....	....	....	...	....	....	....	.....
36	Spain.................	3	8,004	10152	....	91	...	....	....	....	.....
37	Sweden...............	...	....	....	....	....	...	....	....	....	.....
38	St. Pierre.............	29	2,081	3,051	158	149	26	2,426	3,443	943	144
39	Sea Fisheries.........	30	3,280	1,915	....	791	491	22,866	936	....	5,186
40	United States........	994	1,278,228	364,073	323,458	56,117	2016	1,166,120	395,557	136,384	44,309
41	Uruguay..............	...	....	....	....	....	...	....	....	....	.....
42	Sea..................	21	22,838	....	....	1,543	...	....	....	....	.....
	Total.............	2985	5,834,748	3809352	1,092976	186854	3023	1,440521	583,548	161,333	60,222

SESSIONAL PAPER No. 11

for Sea, in the Dominion of Canada, during the Fiscal Year ended March 31, 1915.

COUNTRIES.

					IN BALLAST.									
FOREIGN.					BRITISH.			CANADIAN.			FOREIGN.			
Number of Vessels.	Tons Register.	Quantity of Freight.		Crew, Number.	Number of Vessels.	Tons Register.	Crew, Number.	Number of Vessels.	Tons Register.	Crew, Number.	Number of Vessels.	Tons Register.	Crew, Number.	Number.
		Tons Weight.	Tons Measurement.											
171	215,172	230,357	257,446	3,308	13	31,756	410	100	6,519	342	5	7,047	90	1
6	10,241	8,430	7,405	116	8	43,225	1,257							2
7	9,157	4,330	12,348	107							2	3,155	38	3
														4
25	18,811	30,400		528	1	1,011	52	1	147	6				5
2	5,302	2,640		58										6
1	621		1,790	10										7
1	2,821	5,065		34										8
42	33,169	47,132		665	37	12,684	754	79	45,734	1,424	87	157,710	2,138	9
2	3,902	7,949		47										10
8	9,933	1,622	12,792	136										11
														12
														13
6	7,995	5,462	7,650	101										14
1	776		2,050	12										15
13	45,050	4,115	1,220	918	14	74,205	4,433				16	60,650	1,317	16
														17
17	11,449	9,680	10,050	231	1	259	7							18
														19
3	8,299	6,931		85							1	3,458	33	20
12	32,811	37,660	284	1,191							2	322	73	21
1	2,659			37										22
1	718	2,000		15										23
4	16,881	18,471	68	352										24
17	52,259	68'752	681	1,152										25
											1	684	17	26
														27
6	20,973	3,024	1,726	481							24	94,624	2,604	28
5	4,401	5,580		94							1	622	23	29
														30
2	732		2,032	15										31
1	2,758	5,131	17	32							1	25	3	32
1	1,395	1,733		16										33
4	12,326	5,208	3,122	287	1	291	17							34
											1	656	16	35
3	3,682	1,000	2,040	157										36
2	1,452	1,500		32										37
38	5,748	6,418		550				2	387	23	17	3,474	337	38
782	49,858	20,205		12,321	190	21,301	3,553	1,169	52,957	12,516	930	80,266	18,332	39
3,163	1,720,565	879,129	247,756	63,392	173	396,845	10,728	1637	524,022	25,634	1,852	998,320	42,399	40
2	2,289	1,655	2,620	21										41
7	7,812			521										42
4356	2,322,017	1,421,579	573,097	87,022	438	581,577	21,211	2988	629,766	39,945	2,940	1,411013	67,420	...

6 GEORGE V, A. 1916

No. 8.—STATEMENT of Vessels, British, Canadian and Foreign, entered
Year ended

RECAPITU

	Number of Vessels.	Tons Register.	Quantity of Freight.		Crew Number.
			Tons Weight.	Tons Measurement.	
With Cargoes.					
British.........	2,985	5,884,748	3,809,352	1,092,976	186,854
Canadian.......	3,023	1,440,521	583,548	161,333	60,222
Foreign........	4,356	2,322,017	1,421,579	573,097	87,022
Total..........	10,364	9,647,286	5,814,479	1,827,406	334,098

Outwards, *for Sea*, in the Dominion of Canada during the Fiscal
March 31, 1915.

LATION.

	Number of Vessels.	Tons Register.	Quantity of Freight.		Crew, Number.
			Tons Weight.	Tons Measurement.	
In Ballast—					
British..........	438	581,577	....	....	21,211
Canadian........	2,988	629,766	....	....	39,945
Foreign..........	2.940	1,411,013	....	....	67,420
Total..........	6,366	2,622,356	....	....	128,576
Grand total.....	16,730	12,269,642	5,814,479	1,827,406	462,674

6 GEORGE V, A. 1916

No. 9.—Summary Statement of Sea-going Vessels entered and cleared at each Port during the Twelve Months ended March 31, 1915.

RECAPITULATION BY PORTS AND OUTPORTS.

Ports and Outports	Vessels Arrived						Vessels Departed					
	British		Foreign		Total		British		Foreign		Total	
	No.	Tons	No.	Tons	No.	Tons	No.	Tons	No.	Tons	No.	Tons
Albert, N.B.			1	315	1	315	1	98	1	360	2	458
Alert Bay, B.C.	6	2,612	34	2,829	40	5,441	3	664	37	8,402	40	9,066
Amherst, N.S.	3	649	2	763	5	1,412	1	274	1	703	2	977
Annapolis Royal, N.S.	13	1,965	3	588	16	2,553	5	968			5	968
Anyox, B.C.	6	4,390	7	2,947	13	7,337	26	19,169	9	7,168	35	26,337
Arichat, N.S.	79	2,116	28	2,421	107	4,537	83	1,969	28	2,421	111	4,390
Baddeck, N.S.	33	5,251	34	9,207	67	14,458	68	28,716	40	15,225	108	43,941
Baie Verte, N.B.			1	876	1	876						
Barrington, N.S.	11	456	49	2,407	60	2,863	11	456	49	2,407	60	2,863
Barton, N.S.	37	3,936			37	3,936	29	3,211			29	3,211
Bathurst, N.B.	4	923	5	2,732	9	3,655	14	2,499	15	8,383	29	10,882
Bear River, N.S.	8	927			8	927	21	3,748			21	3,748
Belliveaus Cove, N.S.	7	1,026			7	1,026	5	866			5	866
Bridgetown, N.S.	3	347			3	347	1	149	1	134	2	283
Bridgewater, N.S.	31	10,119	24	13,448	55	23,567	62	18,356	36	20,860	98	39,216
Buctouche, N.B.			1	204	1	204			1	204	1	204
Campbellton, N.B.	2	1,700	11	13,790	13	15,423	12	10,502	31	32,196	43	42,698
Campo Bello, N.B.	139	21,694	509	13,032	648	34,726	157	26,269	28	452	185	26,721
Canning, N.S.	2	393			2	393	2	847			2	847
Canso, N.S.	114	14,542	234	18,308	348	32,850	121	15,111	236	19,314	357	34,425
Caraquet, N.B.	165	2,539			165	2,539	168	2,449			168	2,449
Charlottetown, P.E.I.	60	59,784	13	6,758	73	66,542	80	76,172	2	1,269	82	77,441
Chatham, N.B.	36	72,763	9	9,999	45	82,762	40	75,881	10	13,996	50	89,877
Chemainus, B.C.	17	4,037	5	293	22	4,330	20	10,227	7	2,943	27	13,170
Chester, N.S.	37	663	3	876	40	1,539	29	1,386	6	1,554	35	2,940
Cheticamp, N.S.	1	93	3	2,735	4	2,828			5	4,171	5	4,171
Chicoutimi, Que.	9	15,823	1	1,547	10	17,370	17	33,843	10	12,542	27	46,385
Church Point, N.S.	3	330			3	330	10	1,194			10	1,194
Clark's Harbour, N.S.	21	981	28	942	49	1,923	21	981	28	942	49	1,923
Clementsport, N.S.	19	2,567			19	2,567	17	2,328			17	2,328
Dalhousie, N.S.	4	4,975	9	10,546	13	15,521	18	19,424	18	19,177	36	38,601
Digby, N.S.	15	2,195	7	923	22	3,118	16	1,670	15	905	31	2,575
Dorchester, N.B.	5	1,039	3	1,806	8	2,845	5	739	3	1,465	8	2,204
Fredericton, N.B.	6	1,737	9	2,050	15	3,787	6	1,737	9	2,050	15	3,787
Freeport, N.S.	3	204			3	204						

Port												
Gaspe, Que.	3	1,570	3	1,862	6	3,432	20	13,157	15	16,030	35	29,187
Georgetown, P.E.I.	5	254	1	398	6	652	10	645			10	645
Glace Bay, N.S.	197	10,557	4	181	201	10,738	206	11,089		181	210	11,270
Halifax, N.S.	787	1,334,411	283	255,016	1,070	1,589,427	894	1,227,366	259	244,390	1,153	1,471,756
Hantsport, N.S.	4	3,918	16	5,603		9,521	6	774	15	774	21	5,759
Hbo, N.S.	7	4,350	28	17,530	1,070	21,880	10	6,249	31	19,390	41	25,639
Isaac's Harbour, N.S.	5	240	114	1,151	33	9,521	7	51	92	762	99	813
Joggins	15		13	802	129	1,391	5	514	13	802	18	1,316
Kentville, N.S.	9	1,414	11	2,730	13	802	20	2,834	13	3,485	33	6,319
Kingsport, N.S.	1	74	1		20	4,144		674			3	674
Baer, B.C.	7	3,043		635	1	74	3	3,116			6	3,116
Ladysmith, B.C.	7	36			8	3,728	6	284			11	284
La Have, N.S.	50	5,367	66	27,588	116	32,955	11	4,078	65	24,212	107	28,290
Levis, Que.	94	8,987	12	1,445	106	10,432	42	9,756	9	545	110	10,301
Liverpool, N.S.	9	21,115	1	2,036	10	23,151	101					26,637
Lockeport, N.S.	44	7,630	222	16,694	266	24,324	48	7,730	225	18,907	273	7,162
Lords Cove, N.B.	62	3,108	73	4,830	135	7,938	57	41	73	4,751	130	15,124
Louisburg, N.S.	353	14,653	176	1,702	528	16,355	305	13,730	146	1,394	451	256,999
Lower East Pubnico, N.S.	179	182,073	277	121,885	456	303,958	168	138,379	271	118,620	439	4,112
Lunenburg, N.S.	44	2,464	39	2,239	83	4,703	42	2,013	37	2,099	79	28,518
Magdalen Islands, Que.	296	26,564	23	2,312	319	28,876	335	26,755	21	1,763	356	1,699
Mahone Bay, N.S.	9	777	37	5,203	46	5,980			16	1,699	16	2,715
Md, N.S.	22	2,133	2	697	24	2,830	20	2,018	2	697	22	3,165
Meteghan River, N.S.	7	777	4	1,120	11	1,897	16	2,221	3	944	19	1,026
Moncton, N.B.	7	773			7	773	9	1,026			9	29,366
Montague, B.E.I.	18	19,625	18	11,504	36	31,129	14	16,250	18	13,116	32	399
Montreal, Que.	497	1,869,805	55	130,379	552	2,000,184	512	1,909,973	39	121,072	551	2,031,045
Murray Harbour, P.E.I.	111	276	10	276	10	276	9	253			5	253
Nanaimo, B.C.	111	39,089	218	166,936	329	206,025	188	61,091	277	204,998	465	266,089
Newcastle, N.B.	18	4,516	18	16,468	21	20,984	17	253	24	16,205	41	25,492
Newport, B.C.	18	17,216	24	26,102	42	43,318	20	18,873	24	24,450	44	43,332
New Campbellton, N.S.	5	1,995			41	11,818						13,462
New Westminster, B.C.	26	6,557	15	5,261	41	1,818	41	6,702	18	6,760	59	13,462
North East Harbour, N.S.	4	86	31	2,136	35	2,222	5	152	32	2,227	37	2,379
North Head, N.	185	24,251	20	552	205	24,803	182	26,015	16	336	198	26,351
North Sydney, N.S.	751	268,627	251	67,001	1,002	335,628	513	269,522	286	78,225	799	347,747
Parrsboro, N.S.	76	43,298	52	17,361	128	60,659	114	55,183	53	18,701	167	73,884
Paspebiac, Que.	6	5,212	5	4,517	8	6,381	14	8,968	13	10,145	27	19,113
Percé, Que.	10	12,251	13	1,169	13	15,564	2	2,302	10	4,812	12	7,114
Pou, N.S.	1	281	3	3,313	3	1,239	17	37,019	3	3,908	20	40,927
Port Clyde, N.S.			3	958	3	91	3	629	2	850	5	1,479
Port Hood, N.S.	17	223	2	91	91	1,892	1	223	1	91	1	91
Port La Tour, N.S.	13	1,541	18	1,669	35	4,172	17	1,527	18	1,669	35	1,892
Port Mulgrave, N.S.	30	34,167	23	2,631	36	34,222	15	33,783	20	1,784	40	3,311
Port Simpson, B.C.	8	1,089	7	55	37	1,100	33	996	7	55	40	33,838
Port Wade, N.S.	3	869	3	11	9	869	9	668	4	40	13	1,036
Prb Ms, N.S.					2	869	2	668			2	668
Powell River, B.C.	201	5,329	70	36,224	78	41,553	184	15,770	79	36,579	83	52,349
Prince Rupert, B.C.	201	100,509	154	115,297	355	215,806	184	55,640	148	107,973	332	163,613
Pugwash, N.S.	1	2,263	2	3,258	3	5,521	1	2,263	7	9,697	8	11,960

No. 9.—Summary Statement of Sea-going Vessels entered and cleared at each Port during the Twelve Months ended March 31, 1915.—Concluded.

RECAPITULATION BY PORTS AND OUTPORTS—Concluded.

| Ports and Outports. | VESSELS ARRIVED. | | | | | | VESSELS DEPARTED. | | | | | |
| | British. | | Foreign. | | Total. | | British. | | Foreign. | | Total. | |
	No.	Tons.	No.	Tons.	No.	Tons.	No.	Tons.	No.	Tons.	No.	Tons.
..., Que.	276	1,323,704	23	69,099	299	1,392,803	139	591,489	12	13,037	151	604,526
Rimouski, Que.	21	30,355	7	8,681	28	39,036	21	30,355	6	7,830	27	38,185
River Hebert, N.S.	3	274	1	155	4	429	10	1,458	3	617	13	2,075
St. ..., N.B.	338	21,128	999	55,929	1,337	77,057	252	21,294	975	53,582	1,227	74,876
St. ..., N.B.	14	969	126	9,065	140	10,034	13	1,288	130	9,824	143	11,092
St. John, N.B.	420	678,077	567	391,093	987	1,069,170	293	483,667	587	409,155	880	892,822
St. ..., N.B.	27	8,798	51	11,008	78	19,806	17	7,634	55	12,005	72	19,639
St. Stephen, N.B.	216	19,969	132	7,451	348	27,420	191	20,306	124	8,203	315	28,509
Sackville, N.B.	5	497	3	506	8	1,003	5	694	2	357	7	1,051
Salmon River, N.S.	11	231	2	434	13	264	11	231	2	33	13	264
Sandy Cove, N.S.	15	1,936	238	19,069	253	21,005	12	1,388	236	18,264	248	19,662
Sandy Point, N.S.			1	214	1	214		42	2	917	4	917
Shediac, N.B.									1	99	1	227
Sheet Harbour, N.S.	28	3,257	81	6,879	109	10,136	33	4,134	83	8,124	116	12,258
..., N.S.	1	357			1	357	6	1,408			6	1,408
Shippegan, N.B.	79	1,097	2	478	81	1,575	80	1,200			80	1,200
Sidney, B.C.	56	2,008	27	937	83	2,945	32	932	28	1,103	60	2,035
Sorel, Que.							2	2,071			2	2,071
Souris, P.E.I.	66	3,540	26	2,168	92	5,708	70	3,522	26	2,168	96	5,690
Steveston, B.C.	150	8,246	29	1,542	179	9,788	154	7,988	30	1,574	184	9,562
Stickeen, B.C.	5	1,576	40	484	45	2,060	9	1,582	36	470	45	2,052
Summerside, P.E.I.	4	1,517	6	3,049	10	4,566	15	13,140			15	13,140
Sydney, N.S.	187	251,535	141	260,114	328	511,649	470	255,441	151	234,572	621	490,013
Three Rivers, Que.	23	56,492			23	56,492	23	56,492			23	56,492
Truro, N.S.		420	1	388	5	808	6	993			11	993
Tusket, N.S.		14	8	646	9	660	3	123	8	646		769
Union Bay, B.C.	37	61,306	34	33,299	71	94,575	54	123,019	39	33,079	93	156,098
Vancouver, B.C.	1,047	1,400,728	556	491,189	1,603	1,891,917	907	1,208,244	552	491,350	1,459	1,699,594
..., B.C.	762	943,505	906	1,067,370	1,668	2,010,875	760	1,071,072	848	1,025,781	1,608	2,096,853
Westport, N.S.	14	2,147	30	438	44	2,585	5	200	22	270	27	470
Weymouth, N.S.	18	2,681	14	4,540	32	7,221	5	3,478	13	5,880	38	9,338
... Rok, B.C.	63	510	55	335	118	845	74	3,660	54	417	128	1,077
Windsor, N.S.	80	73,230	76	62,471	156	135,701	82	77,708	90	69,338	172	147,046
Wolfville, N.S.	3	708			6	1,615						
Yarmouth, N.S.	325	100,539	150	15,070	475	175,609	324	171,004	145	15,704	469	186,708
	9,418	9,399,490	7,704	3,733,454	17,182	13,132,944	9,434	8,536,612	7,296	3,733,030	16,730	12,269,642

No. 10.—Statement of Nationalities of Sea-going Vessels entered and cleared during the Twelve Months ended March 31, 1915.

ABSTRACT BY NATIONALITIES.

	Arrived.		Departed.		
Under the Flag of	No.	Tons.	Under the Flag of	No.	Tons.
United Kingdom	9,418	9,399,490	United Kingdom	9,434	8,536,612
Argentina	1	1,933	Agtina	1	1,933
Austria-Hungary	7	20,933	Austria-Hungary	6	18,622
Belgium	2	11,599	Belgium	10	21,998
Cuba	1	1,139	China	1	3,179
Denmark	65	90,056	Denmark	53	73,333
France	173	62,192	Fran œ	179	61,484
G.	28	92,331	Germany	28	91,274
G.	2	5,533	Greece	2	5,533
Holland	18	67,452	Holland	8	26,543
Italy	11	19,085	Italy	8	12,800
Japan	120	454,401	Japan	120	453,320
Mo.	1	1,193	Mexico	1	1,193
Norway	437	569,278	y.	469	703,968
Pan rna	1	199	Portugal	1	25
Russia	28	73,534	Russia	31	87,152
Spain	5	11,636	Spain	5	11,636
Sweden	9	15,259	Sweden	15	23,093
Uruguay	1	289	Uruguay	1	299
United States	6,854	2,135,412	U nd States	6,357	2,135,645
Total	17,182	13,132,944	Total	16,730	12,269,642

DESCRIPTION OF VESSELS.

	Arrived.						
	Steamers.		Sailing Vessels.		Total.		
	No.	Tons.	No.	Tons.	No.	Tons.	
British	6,268	9,026,906	3,150	372,584	9,418	9,399,490	
Foreign	5,076	3,297,925	2,688	435,529	7,764	3,733,454	
Total	11,344	12,324,831	5,838	808,113	17,182	13,132,944	

	Departed.					
	Steamers.		Sailing Vessels.		Total.	
	No.	Tons.	No.	Tons.	No.	Tons.
British	6,072	8,223,811	3,362	312,801	9,434	8,536,612
Foreign	4,617	3,321,706	2,679	411,324	7,296	3,733,030
Total	10,689	11,545,517	6,041	724,125	16,730	12,269,642

No. 11.—SUMMARY STATEMENT of Sea-going Vessels entered Inwards and Outwards in the Dominion of Canada during the Fiscal Year ended March 31, 1915.

NATIONALITIES.	SEA-GOING VESSELS, INWARDS.					SEA-GOING VESSELS, OUTWARDS.					TOTAL SEA-GOING VESSELS, INWARDS AND OUTWARDS.				
	Number of Vessels.	Tons Register.	Quantity of Freight.		Crew Number.	Number of Vessels.	Tons Register.	Quantity of Freight.		Crew Number.	Numb'r of Vessels.	Tons Register.	Quantity of Freight.		Crew Number.
			Tons Weight.	Tons Measurement.				Tons Weight.	Tons Measurement.				Tons Weight.	Tons Measurement.	
British.........	3,536	7,464,766	1,302,322	940,980	230,432	3,423	6,466,325	3,809,352	1,002,976	208,065	6,949	13,931,091	5,111,674	2,033,956	438,497
Canadian........	5,892	1,934,724	274,259	6,527	100,564	6,011	2,070,287	583,548	161,333	100,167	11,903	4,005,011	857,807	167,860	200,731
Foreign	7,764	3,733,454	1,250,105	666,390	157,955	7,296	3,733,030	1,421,579	573,097	154,412	15,060	7,466,484	2,671,684	1,239,487	312,397
Total.........	17,182	13,132,944	2,826,686	1,613897	488,951	16,730	12,269,642	5,814,479	1,827,406	462,674	33,912	25,402,586	8,641,165	3,441,303	951,625

No. 12.—SUMMARY STATEMENT of Vessels arrived and departed (exclusive of Coasting Vessels) during the Fiscal Year ended March 31, 1915.

	SEA-GOING VESSELS, INWARDS AND OUTWARDS.			VESSELS OF THE INLAND WATERS BETWEEN CANADA AND THE UNITED STATES.			TOTAL SHIPPING (EXCLUSIVE OF COASTING VESSELS) INWARDS AND OUTWARDS.		
	Number of Vessels.	Tons Register.	Crew Number.	Number of Vessels.	Tons Register.	Crew Number.	Number of Vessels.	Tons Register.	Crew Number.
British	6,949	13,931,091	438,497				6,949	13,931,091	438,497
Canadian	11,903	4,005,011	200,731	17,456	13,499,740	430,285	29,359	17,504,751	631,016
Foreign	15,060	7,466,484	312,397	33,575	14,701,827	444,086	48,635	22,108,311	756,483
Total	33,912	25,402,586	951,625	51,031	28,201,567	874,371	84,943	53,604,153	1,825,996

6 GEORGE V, A. 1916

TRADE WITH EACH COUNTRY

No. 13.—STATEMENT of the Number and Tonnage of Sailing and Steam Vessels
Canada from Foreign Countries, distinguishing the Nationality of the
March 31,

Ports and Outports and Countries whence arrived.	British.		United States.		Norwegian.		Austrian.		Belgian.	
	Vessels.	Tons Register.	Vessels.	Tons Register.	Vessels.	Tons Register.	Vessels.	Tons Register.	Vessels.	Tons Register.
Albert, N.B.—										
United States............Sail	....	....	1	315	....	....	....	....	....	....
Alert Bay, B.C.—										
United States.........Steam.	6	2,612	34	2,829	....	....	....	....	....	....
Amherst, N.S.—										
Great Britain......... Sail.	..	....	...	....	...	....	....	....	....	....
British W. Indies..... "	1	209	...	....	...	....	....	....	....	....
United States......... "	2	440	1	173	...	....	....	....	....	....
Total...............	3	649	1	173	....	....	....	....	....	....
Annapolis Royal, N.S.—										
United States......... Sail.	13	1,965	3	588	....	....	....	....	....	....
Anyox, B.C.—										
United States.........Steam.	6	4,390	7	2,947	....	....	....	....	....	....
Arichat, N.S.—										
Newfoundland........ Sail.	4	350	...	....	...	....	....	....	....	....
Saint-Pierre........... "	1	65	...	....	...	....	....	....	....	....
United States......... "	2	195	8	917	...	....	....	....	....	....
Sea Fisheries........ "	72	1,506	20	1,504	...	....	....	....	....	....
Total.................	79	2,116	28	2,421	....	....	....	....	....	....
Baddeck, N.S.—										
Newfoundland........Steam.	9	2,457	...	....	1	1,052	....	....	....	....
Newfoundland........ Sail.	...	1,682	...	....	7	6,532	....	....	....	....
United States........Steam.	1	1,682	...	....	7	6,532	....	....	....	....
Sea Fisheries........ Sail.	23	1,112	25	1,566	...	....	....	....	....	....
Total.................	33	5,251	25	1,566	8	7,584	....	....	....	....
Baie Verte, N.B.—										
United States.........Steam.	....	....	...	....	1	876	....	....	....	....
Barrington, N.S.—										
United States......... Sail.	2	361	17	1,081	....	....	....	....	....	....
Sea Fisheries......... "	9	95	32	1,326	....	....	....	....	....	....
Total.................	11	456	49	2,407	....	....	....	....	....	....
Barton, N.S.—										
United States......... Sail.	37	3,936	.	....	...	....	....	....	....	....
Bathurst, N.B.—										
British W. Indies..... Sail.	1	212	...	....	...	....	....	....	....	....
United States........Steam.	...	....	...	....	1	446	....	....	....	....
United States......... Sail.	3	711	4	2,286	...	....	....	....	....	....
Total.................	4	923	4	2,286	1	446	....	....	....	....
Bear River, N.S.—										
United States......... Sail.	8	927	...	....	...	....	....	....	....	....

SESSIONAL ·PAPER No. 11

AND NATIONALITY OF VESSELS.

entered Inwards *from Sea* at each of the undermentioned Ports and Outports in Vessels employed in the trade with each Country, during the Fiscal Year ended 1915.

or VESSELS.

Danish.		French.		German.		Italian.		Russian.		Other Nationalities.			Total.	
Vessels.	Tons Register.	Vessels.	Tons Register.	Vessels.	Tons Register.	Vessels.	Tons Register.	Vessels.	Tons Register.	Names.	Vessels.	Tons Register.	Vessels.	Tons Register.
....	......	....	......	....	......	....	......	....	......	....	....	....	1	315
....	......	....	......	....	......	....	......	....	......	....	....	....	40	5,441
....	......	....	......	....	......	...	......	1	590	....	....	....	1	590
....	......	....	......	....	......	....	......	....	......	....	....	....	1	209
....	......	....	......	....	......	....	......	....	......	....	....	....	3	613
....	......	....	......	....	......	....	......	1	590	....	....	....	5	1,412
....	......	....	......	....	......	....	......	....	......	....	....	....	16	2,553
....	......	....	......	...	.J.....	....	......	....	......	....	....	....	13	7,337
....	......	....	......	....	......	....	......	....	......	....	....	....	4	350
....	......	....	......	....	......	....	......	....	......	....	....	....	1	65
....	......	....	......	....	......	....	......	....	......	....	....	....	10	1,112
....	......	....	......	....	......	....	......	....	......	....	....	....	92	3,010
....	......	....	......	....	......	....	......	....	......	....	....	....	107	4,537
....	......	1	57	....	......	....	......	....	......	....	....	....	10	3,509
....	......	....	......	....	......	....	......	....	......	....	....	....	1	57
....	......	....	......	....	......	....	......	....	......	....	....	....	8	8,214
....	......	....	......	....	......	....	......	....	......	....	....	....	48	2,678
....	......	1	57	....	......	....	......	....	......	....	....	....	67	14,458
....	......	....	......	....	......	....	......	....	......	....	....	....	1	876
....	......	....	......	....	......	....	......	....	......	....	....	....	19	1,442
....	......	....	......	....	......	....	......	....	......	....	....	....	41	1,421
....	......	....	......	....	......	....	......	....	......	....	....	....	60	2,863
....	......	....	......	....	......	....	......	....	......	....	....	../....	37	3,936
....	......	....	......	....	......	....	......	....	......	....	....	....	1	212
....	......	....	......	....	......	....	......	....	......	....	....	....	1	446
....	......	....	......	....	......	....	......	....	......	....	....	....	7	2,997
....	......	....	......	....	......	....	......	....	......	....	....	....	9	3,655
....	......	....	......	....	......	....	......	....	......	....	....	....	8	927

6 GEORGE V, A. 1916

No. 13.—STATEMENT of the Number and Tonnage of Sailing

Ports and Outports and Countries whence arrived.		British. Vessels.	British. Tons Register.	United States. Vessels.	United States. Tons Register.	Norwegian. Vessels.	Norwegian. Tons Register.	Austrian. Vessels.	Austrian. Tons Register.	Belgian. Vessels.	Belgian. Tons Register.
Belliveau's Cove, N.S.—											
British W. Indies.....	Sail.	3	593								
United States........	"	4	433								
Total.................		7	1,026								
Bridgetown, N.S.—											
United States........	Sail.	3	347								
Bridgewater, N.S.—											
British W. Indies.....	Sail.			1	1,438	1	1,345				
Argentina.............	"										
Porto Rico...........	"	1	293								
United States........	"	30	9,826	20	7,560						
Total.................		31	10,119	21	8,998	1	1,345				
Buctouche, N.B.—											
Great Britain.........	Sail.					1	204				
Campbellton, N.B.—											
Great Britain.........	Steam.					2	2,494				
Newfoundland........	"	1	1,526								
Germany.............	"					1	1,165				
United States........	Sail.	1	174	1	439						
Total.................		2	1,700	1	439	3	3,659				
Campo Bello, N.B.—											
United States........	Steam.	139	21,694	509	13,032						
Canning, N.S.—											
United States........	Sail.	2	393								
Canso, N.S.—											
Great Britain.........	Steam.	1	136								
British W. Indies.....	Sail.	3	393								
Newfoundland........	"	20	1,932								
United States........	Steam.			4	265						
United States........	Sail.	6	965	51	4,650						
Sea Fisheries........	Steam.	37	6,663	30	1,229						
Sea Fisheries........	Sail.	47	4,453	149	12,164						
Total.................		114	14,542	234	18,308						
Caraquet, N.B.—											
United States........	Sail.	2	281								
Sea Fisheries........	Steam.	2	22								
Sea Fisheries........	Sail.	161	2,236								
Total.................		165	2,539								
Charlottetown, P.E.I.—											
Great Britain.........	Steam.	1	2,431								
British West Indies...	"	1	588			1	446				
British West Indies...	Sail.	4	827								
Newfoundland........	Steam.	2	1,713								
Newfoundland........	Sail.	5	246								
Saint Pierre..........	"	4	284								
United States........	Steam.	30	51,436	2	1,269						
United States........	Sail.	10	2,203	10	5,043						
Sea Fisheries........	"	3	56								
Total.................		60	59,784	12	6,312	1	446				

and Steam Vessels entered Inwards *from Sea, &c.—Continued.*

of Vessels.

Danish.		French.		German.		Italian.		Russian.		Other Nationalities.			Total.	
Vessels.	Tons Register.	Vessels.	Tons Register.	Vessels.	Tons Register.	Vessels.	Tons Register.	Vessels.	Tons Register.	Names.	Vessels.	Tons Register.	Vessels.	Tons Register.
....	......	...	......	....	......	....	......	....	......	....	....	......	3	593
....	......	...	......	....	......	....	......	....	......	....	....	......	4	433
....	......	...	......	....	......	....	......	....	......	....	....	......	7	1,026
....	......	...	......	....	......	....	......	....	......	....	....	......	3	347
....	......	...	......	....	......	....	......	....	......	Argentinian.	1	1,933	2	2,783
....	......	...	......	....	......	....	......	....	......	....	....	......	1	1,933
....	......	...	......	....	......	1	1,172	....	......	....	....	......	1	293
....	......	...	......	....	......	....	......	....	......	....	....	......	51	18,558
....	......	...	......	....	......	1	1,172	....	......	....	1	1,933	55	23,567
....	......	...	......	....	......	....	......	....	......	....	....	......	1	204
6	8,620	...	......	1	1,005	....	......	....	......	....	....	......	8	11,114
....	......	...	......	....	......	....	......	....	......	....	....	......	2	2,531
....	......	...	......	....	......	....	......	....	......	....	....	......	1	1,165
....	......	...	......	....	......	....	......	....	......	....	....	......	2	613
6	8,620	...	......	1	1,005	....	......	....	......	....	....	......	13	15,423
....	......	...	......	....	......	....	......	....	......	....	....	......	648	34,726
....	......	...	......	....	......	....	......	....	......	....	....	......	2	393
....	......	...	......	....	......	....	......	....	......	....	....	......	1	136
....	......	...	......	....	......	....	......	....	......	....	....	......	3	393
....	......	...	......	....	......	....	......	....	......	....	....	......	20	1,932
....	......	...	......	....	......	....	......	....	......	....	....	......	4	265
....	......	...	......	....	......	....	......	....	......	....	....	......	57	5,615
....	......	...	......	....	......	....	......	....	......	....	....	......	67	7,892
....	......	...	......	....	......	....	......	....	......	....	....	......	196	16,617
....	......	...	......	....	......	....	......	....	......	....	....	......	348	32,850
....	......	...	......	....	......	....	......	....	......	....	....	......	2	281
....	......	...	......	....	......	....	......	....	......	....	....	......	2	22
....	......	...	......	....	......	....	......	....	......	....	....	......	161	2,236
....	......	...	......	....	......	....	......	....	......	....	....	......	165	2,539
....	......	...	......	....	......	....	......	....	......	....	....	......	1	2,431
....	......	...	......	....	......	....	......	....	......	....	....	......	2	1,034
....	......	...	......	....	......	....	......	....	......	....	....	......	4	827
....	......	...	......	....	......	....	......	....	......	....	....	......	2	1,713
....	......	...	......	....	......	....	......	....	......	....	....	......	5	246
....	......	...	......	....	......	....	......	....	......	....	....	......	4	284
....	......	...	......	....	......	....	......	....	......	....	....	......	32	52,705
....	......	...	......	....	......	....	......	....	......	....	....	......	20	7,246
....	......	...	......	....	......	....	......	....	......	....	....	......	3	56
....	......	...	......	....	......	....	......	....	......	....	....	......	73	66,542

No. 13.—STATEMENT of the Number and Tonnage of Sailing

Ports and Outports and Countries whence arrived.	British.		United States.		Norwegian.		Austrian.		Belgian.	
	Vessels.	Tons Register.	Vessels.	Tons Register.	Vessels.	Tons Register.	Vessels.	Tons Register.	Vessels.	Tons Register.
Chatham, N.B—										
Great Britain........Steam.	9	18,057	....	....	2	3,300	....	......	....	......
Great Britain........ Sail.	....	....	....	....	....	....	....	......	....	......
British West Indies... "	1	266	....	....	....	....	....	......	....	......
Newfoundland........Steam.	1	1,945	....	....	....	....	....	......	....	......
Norway............. Sail	....	....	....	....	1	1,036	....	......	....	......
Spain............. "	....	....	....	....	....	....	....	......	....	......
United States........Steam.	22	51,850	....	....	....	....	....	......	....	......
United States........ Sail.	3	645	....	....	....	....	....	......	....	......
Total..................	36	72,763	....	....	3	4,336	....	......	....	......
Chemainus, B.C—.										
United States........Steam.	16	3,876	5	293	....	....	....	......	....	......
United States........ Sail.	1	161	....	....	....	....	....	......	....	......
Total..................	17	4,037	5	293	....	....	....	......	....	......
Chester, N.S.—										
United States........ Sail.	1	199	2	799	....	....	....	......	....	......
Sea Fisheries........Steam.	2	21	....	....	....	....	....	......	....	......
Sea Fisheries........ Sail.	34	443	1	77	....	....	....	......	....	......
Total..................	37	663	3	876	....	....	....	......	....	......
Cheticamp, N.S.—										
Newfoundland........Steam.	....	....	....	....	1	689	....	......	....	......
Newfoundland........ Sail.	1	93	....	....	....	....	....	......	....	......
United States........Steam.	....	....	....	....	1	747	....	......	....	......
Total..................	1	93	....	....	2	1,436	....	......	....	......
Chicoutimi, Que.—										
Great Britain........Steam.	7	13,698	....	....	....	....	....	......	....	......
British West Indies...Sail.	1	198	....	....	....	....	....	......	....	......
Newfoundland........Steam.	1	1,927	....	....	....	....	....	......	....	......
Total..................	9	15,823	....	....	....	....	....	......	....	......
Church Point, N.S.—										
United States........ Sail.	3	330	....	....	....	....	....	......	....	......
Clarke's Harbour, N.S.—										
United States........Steam.	9	572	....	....	....	....	....	......	....	......
United States........ Sail.	3	312	18	305	....	....	....	......	....	......
Sea Fisheries........ "	9	97	10	637	....	....	....	......	....	......
Total..................	21	981	28	942	....	....	....	......	....	......
Clementsport, N.S.—										
United States........ Sail.	19	2,567	....	....	....	....	....	......	....	......
Dalhousie, N.B.—										
Great Britain........Steam.	2	2,973	....	....	....	....	....	......	....	......
Great Britain........ Sail.	....	....	....	....	1	998	....	......	....	......
British West Indies...Steam.	1	1,905	....	....	....	....	....	......	....	......
France............. Sail.	....	....	....	....	2	3,225	....	......	....	......
Italy............. "	....	....	....	....	....	....	....	......	....	......
Norway............. "	....	....	....	....	1	566	....	......	....	......
United States........ "	1	97	....	....	....	....	....	......	....	......
Brazil............. "	....	....	....	....	....	....	....	......	....	......
British S. Africa...... "	....	....	....	....	....	....	....	......	....	......
Total..............	4	4,975	....	....	4	4,789	....	......	....	......

and Steam Vessels entered Inwards *from Sea, &c.—Continued.*

or VESSELS.

	Danish.		French.		German.		Italian.		Russian.		Other Nationalities.			Total.	
	Vessels.	Tons Register.	Vessels.	Tons Register.	Vessels.	Tons Register.	Vessels.	Tons Register.	Vessels.	Tons Register.	Names.	Vessels.	Tons Register.	Vessels.	Tons Register.
	2	2,696	....	......	....	......	....	......	....	......	....	....	......	13	24,053
	....	......	....	......	....	......	....	......	1	313	....	....	......	1	313
	....	......	....	......	....	......	....	......	....	......	....	....	......	1	266
	....	......	....	......	....	......	....	......	....	......	....	....	......	1	1,945
	....	......	....	......	....	......	....	......	....	......	....	....	......	1	1,036
	....	......	....	......	1	2,249	....	......	2	405	....	....	......	2	405
	....	......	....	......	....	......	....	......	....	......	....	....	......	23	54,099
	....	......	....	......	....	......	....	......	....	......	....	....	......	3	645
	2	2,696	....	......	1	2,249	....	......	3	718	....	....	......	45	82,762
	....	......	....	......	....	......	....	......	....	......	....	....	......	21	4,169
	....	......	....	......	....	......	....	......	....	......	....	....	......	1	161
	....	......	....	......	....	......	....	......	....	......	....	....	......	22	4,330
	....	......	....	......	....	......	....	......	....	......	....	....	......	3	998
	....	......	....	......	....	......	....	......	....	......	....	....	......	2	21
	....	......	....	......	....	......	....	......	....	......	....	....	......	35	520
	....	......	....	......	....	......	....	......	....	......	....	....	......	40	1,539
	....	......	....	......	....	......	....	......	....	......	Dutch......	1	1,299	2	1,988
	....	......	....	......	....	......	....	......	....	......	....	....	......	1	93
	....	......	....	......	....	......	....	......	....	......	....	....	......	1	747
	....	......	....	......	....	......	....	......	....	......	....	1	1,299	4	2,828
	1	1,547	....	......	....	......	....	......	....	......	....	....	......	8	15,245
	....	......	....	......	....	......	....	......	....	......	....	....	......	1	198
	....	......	....	......	....	......	....	......	....	......	....	....	......	1	1,927
	1	1,547	....	......	....	......	....	......	....	......	....	....	......	10	17,370
	....	......	....	......	....	......	....	......	....	......	....	....	......	3	330
	....	......	....	......	....	......	....	......	....	......	....	....	......	9	572
	....	......	....	......	....	......	....	......	....	......	....	....	......	21	617
	....	......	....	......	....	......	....	......	....	......	....	....	......	19	734
	....	......	....	......	....	......	....	......	....	......	....	....	......	49	1,923
	....	......	....	......	....	......	....	......	....	......	....	....	......	19	2,567
	....	......	....	......	....	......	....	......	....	......	....	....	......	2	2,973
	....	......	....	......	....	......	....	......	....	......	....	....	......	1	998
	....	......	....	......	....	......	....	......	....	......	....	....	......	1	1,905
	....	......	....	......	....	......	....	......	1	968	....	....	......	3	4,193
	....	......	....	......	....	......	2	2,227	....	......	....	....	......	2	2,227
	....	......	....	......	....	......	....	......	....	......	....	....	......	1	566
	....	......	....	......	....	......	....	......	....	......	....	....	......	1	97
	....	......	....	......	....	......	1	1,280	....	......	....	....	......	1	1,280
	....	......	....	......	....	......	....	......	1	1,282	....	....	......	1	1,282
	....	......	....	......	....	......	3	3,507	2	2,250	....	....	......	13	15,521

6 GEORGE V, A. 1916

No. 13.—Statement of the Number and Tonnage of Sailing

	British.		United States.		Norwegian.		Austrian.		Belgian.	
Ports and Outports and Countries whence arrived.	Vessels.	Tons Register.	Vessels.	Tons Register.	Vessels.	Tons Register.	Vessels.	Tons Register.	Vessels.	Tons Register.
Digby, N.S.—										
United States.......... Sail.	15	2,195	7	923	....	....	....	....	....	....
Dorchester, N.B.—										
United States........Steam.	....	....	....	....	2	1,576	....	....	....	....
United States........ Sail.	5	1,039	1	230	....	....	....	....	....	....
Total..................	5	1,039	1	230	2	1,576	....	....	....	....
Fredericton, N.B.—										
United States........ Sail.	6	1,737	9	2,050	....	....	....	....	....	....
Freeport, N.S.—										
United States........ Sail.	3	204	....	....	....	....	....	....	....	....
Gaspé, Que.—										
Great Britain......... Sail.	....	....	....	....	1	1,029	....	....	....	....
British W. Indies..... "	1	148	....	....	....	....	....	....	....	....
United States........Steam.	1	1,176	1	573	....	....	....	....	....	....
United States........Sail.	1	246	1	260	....	....	....	....	....	....
Total..................	3	1,570	2	833	1	1,029	....	....	....	....
Georgetown, P.E.I.—										
Newfoundland........ Sail.	3	145	....	....	....	....	....	....	....	....
Saint Pierre.......... "	1	70	....	....	....	....	....	....	....	....
United States........ "	....	....	1	398	....	....	....	....	....	....
Sea Fisheries......... "	1	39	....	....	....	....	....	....	....	....
Total..................	5	254	1	398	....	....	....	....	....	....
Glace Bay, N.S.—										
Great Britain.........Steam.	18	1,973	....	....	....	....	....	....	....	....
British W. Indies..... "	179	8,584	....	....	....	....	....	....	....	....
Saint Pierre.......... Sail.	....	....	....	....	....	....	....	....	....	....
Sea Fisheries,........ "	....	....	1	43	....	....	....	....	....	....
Total..................	197	10,557	1	43	....	....	....	....	....	....
Halifax, N.S.—										
Great Britain.........Steam.	156	643,425	....	....	7	12,214	....	....	....	....
Great Britain........ Sail.	....	....	....	....	1	1,207	....	....	....	....
British W. Indies....Steam.	26	72,784	....	....	20	14,705	....	....	....	....
British W. Indies..... Sail.	21	4,934	1	155	2	1,888	....	....	....	....
Newfoundland.......Steam.	56	82,570	....	....	1	1,178	....	....	....	....
Newfoundland........ Sail.	56	6,965	1	50	....	....	....	....	....	....
Belgium.............Steam.	1	5,552	....	....	....	....	....	....	....	....
Brazil...............Sail.	....	....	....	....	1	1,748	....	....	....	....
Cuba................Steam.	....	....	....	....	2	2,396	....	....	....	....
France.............. "	1	2,488	....	....	....	....	....	....	....	....
Germany............ "	....	....	....	....	....	....	....	....	....	....
Holland............. "	9	39,836	....	....	....	....	....	....	....	....
Italy................ "	1	1,930	....	....	....	....	....	....	....	....
Norway............. "	....	....	1	308	5	12,387	....	....	....	....
Norway............. Sail	....	....	....	....	2	1,580	....	....	....	....
San Domingo.......Steam.	....	....	....	....	7	5,569	....	....	....	....
Portugal............ "	1	2,752	....	....	....	....	....	....	....	....
Portugal............ Sail.	1	256	....	....	....	....	....	....	....	....
Russia..............Steam.	....	....	....	....	....	....	....	....	....	....
Saint Pierre......... "	....	....	....	....	....	....	....	....	....	....
Saint Pierre.......... Sail.	1	69	....	....	....	....	....	....	....	....
Spain................Steam.	5	9,727	....	....	....	....	....	....	....	....
Sweden.............. "	....	....	....	....	1	3,332	....	....	....	....
United States........ "	149	412,668	10	6,347	21	25,667	....	....	....	....
United States........ Sail.	75	18,148	58	22,539	....	....	....	....	....	....

and Steam Vessels entered Inwards *from Sea, &c.—Continued.*

or VESSELS.

Danish		French		German		Italian		Russian		Other Nationalities			Total	
Vessels.	Tons Register.	Vessels.	Tons Register.	Vessels.	Tons Register.	Vessels.	Tons Register.	Vessels.	Tons Register.	Names.	Vessels.	Tons Register.	Vessels.	Tons Register.
....	.....	....	.....	....	.....	....	.....	....	.....	.....	....	.....	22	3,118
....	.....	....	.....	....	.....	....	.....	....	.....	.....	....	.....	2	1,576
....	.....	....	.....	....	.....	....	.....	....	.....	.....	....	.....	6	1,269
....	.....	....	.....	....	.....	....	.....	....	.....	.....	....	.....	8	2,845
....	.....	....	.....	....	.....	....	.....	....	.....	.....	....	.....	15	3,787
....	.....	....	.....	....	.....	....	.....	....	.....	.....	....	.....	3	204
....	.....	....	.....	....	.....	....	.....	....	.....	.....	....	.....	1	1,029
....	.....	....	.....	....	.....	....	.....	....	.....	.....	....	.....	1	148
....	.....	....	.....	....	.....	....	.....	....	.....	.....	....	.....	2	1,749
....	.....	....	.....	....	.....	....	.....	....	.....	.....	....	.....	2	506
....	.....	....	.....	....	.....	....	.....	....	.....	.....	....	.....	6	3,432
....	.....	....	.....	....	.....	....	.....	....	.....	.....	....	.....	3	145
....	.....	....	.....	....	.....	....	.....	....	.....	.....	....	.....	1	70
....	.....	....	.....	....	.....	....	.....	....	.....	.....	....	.....	1	398
....	.....	....	.....	....	.....	....	.....	....	.....	.....	....	.....	1	39
....	.....	....	.....	....	.....	....	.....	....	.....	.....	....	.....	6	652
....	.....	....	.....	....	.....	....	.....	....	.....	.....	....	.....	18	1,973
....	.....	....	.....	....	.....	....	.....	....	.....	.....	....	.....	179	8,584
....	.....	3	138	....	.....	....	.....	....	.....	.....	....	.....	3	138
....	.....	....	.....	....	.....	....	.....	....	.....	.....	....	.....	1	43
....	.....	3	138	....	.....	....	.....	....	.....	.....	....	.....	201	10,738
....	.....	....	.....	....	.....	....	.....	....	.....	.....	....	.....	163	655,639
....	.....	....	.....	....	.....	....	.....	....	.....	.....	....	.....	1	1,297
....	.....	....	.....	....	.....	....	.....	....	.....	.....	....	.....	46	87,489
....	.....	....	.....	....	.....	1	1,151	....	.....	Panamanian	1	199	26	8,327
....	.....	....	.....	....	.....	....	.....	....	.....	.....	....	.....	57	83,748
....	.....	....	.....	....	.....	....	.....	....	.....	.....	....	.....	57	7,015
....	.....	....	.....	....	.....	....	.....	....	.....	.....	....	.....	1	5,552
....	.....	....	.....	....	.....	....	.....	....	.....	.....	....	.....	1	1,748
....	.....	....	.....	....	.....	....	.....	....	.....	.....	....	.....	2	2,396
....	.....	3	7,799	....	.....	....	.....	....	.....	.....	....	.....	4	10,287
....	.....	....	.....	5	20,801	....	.....	....	.....	.....	....	—...	5	20,801
2	2,930	....	.....	....	.....	1	5,846	....	.....	Dutch	2	10,586	11	50,422
....	.....	....	.....	....	.....	....	.....	....	.....	.....	....	.....	4	10,706
....	.....	....	.....	....	.....	....	.....	....	.....	.....	....	.....	6	12,695
....	.....	....	.....	....	.....	....	.....	....	.....	.....	....	.....	2	1,580
....	.....	....	.....	....	.....	....	.....	....	.....	.....	....	.....	7	5,569
....	.....	....	.....	....	.....	....	.....	....	.....	.....	....	.....	1	2,752
....	.....	....	.....	....	.....	....	.....	11	52,856	.....	....	.....	1	256
....	.....	17	3,519	....	.....	....	.....	....	.....	.....	....	.....	11	52,856
....	.....	....	.....	....	.....	....	.....	....	.....	.....	....	.....	17	3,519
....	.....	....	.....	....	.....	....	.....	....	.....	.....	....	.....	1	69
....	.....	....	.....	....	.....	....	.....	....	.....	Spanish	1	2,351	6	12,078
....	.....	....	.....	....	.....	....	.....	....	.....	Swedish	2	2,796	3	6,128
2	3,599	....	.....	....	.....	....	.....	....	.....	Swedish	1	1,799	183	450,080
....	.....	....	.....	....	.....	1	1,020	1	591	Spanish	1	2,306	136	44,604

6 GEORGE V, A. 1916

No. 13.—STATEMENT of the Number and Tonnage of Sailing

Ports and Outports and Countries whence arrived.	British.		United States.		Norwegian.		Austrian.		Belgian.	
	Vessels.	Tons. Register.	Vessels.	Tons Register.	Vessels.	Tons Register.	Vessels.	Tons Register.	Vessels.	Tons Register.
Halifax, N.S.—*Con.*										
Denmark............Steam.	1	106	....	....	1	580	....	....	....	....
Sea.................."	18	20,345	2	470	....	....	....	....	....	....
Uruguay,...........Sail.	1	99	....	....	....	....	....	....	....	....
Argentina..........Steam.	1	2,193	....	....	....	....	....	....	....	....
Argentina..........Sail.	....	....	....	....	1	899	....	....	....	....
Austria............Steam.	....	....	....	....	....	....	1	4,526	....	....
British S. Africa......Sail.	....	....	....	....	1	1,597	....	....	....	....
Sea Fisheries........."	207	7,564	76	5,172	....	....	....	....	....	....
French West Indies..."	....	....	....	....	1	469	....	....	....	....
Total.................	787	1,334,411	149	35,041	74	87,506	1	4,526	....	
Hantsport, N. S.—										
United States.........Steam	.	....	6	1,986	....	....				
United States.........Sail.	7	3,918	10	3,617	....	....				
Total...................	7	3,918	16	5,603	....					
Hillsboro, N.B.—										
United States.........Steam	....	....	....	....	22	15,162				
United States.........Sail.	5	4,350	6	2,368	....					
Total.................	5	4,350	6	2,368	22	15,162	....			
Indian Island, N.B.—										
United States.........Steam.	15	240	114	1,151	....	....				
Isaacs Harbour, N.S.—										
United States.........Sail.	....	....	8	405	....					
Sea fisheries........."	....	....	5	397	....					
Total................	....	....	13	802	....					
Joggins Mines, N.S.—										
United States.........Sail.	9	1,414	11	2,730	....					
Kentville, N.S.—										
United States.........Sail.	1	74	....		....					
Kingsport, N.S.—										
United States.........Steam.	3	2,251	....	....	1	685				
United States.........Sail.	4	792	....	....	....					
Total................	7	3,043	....	....	1	685	....			
Ladner, B.C.—										
United States.........Steam.	7	36	....							
Ladysmith, B.C.—										
United States.........Steam.	37	3,000	42	22,639	....	....				
United States.........Sail.	13	2,367	24	4,949	....	....				
Total................	50	5,367	66	27,588	....					
LaHave, N.S.—										
Newfoundland........Sail.	4	681	....	....	....					
Spanish Africa........"	1	392	....		....					
United States........."	20	2,386	3	900	....					
Sea fisheries........Steam.	....	....	1	28	....					
Sea fisheries.........Sail.	69	5,528	8	517	....					
Total.................	94	8,987	12	1,445	....	....	....	....	....	

and Steam Vessels entered Inwards *from Sea, &c.—Continued.*

OF VESSELS.

Danish.		French.		German.		Italian.		Russian.		Other Nationalities.			Total.	
Vessels.	Tons Register.	Vessels.	Tons Register.	Vessels.	Tons Register.	Vessels.	Tons Register.	Vessels.	Tons Register.	Names.	Vessels.	Tons Register.	Vessels.	Tons Register.
1	1,098	....	......	....	......						....	....	3	1,784
....	......	6	6,696	....	......						....	....	26	27,511
....	......	....	......	....	......	....	......	....	......		....	....	1	99
....	......	....	......	....	......	....	......	....	......		....	....	1	2,193
....	......	....	......	....	......	....	......	....	......		....	....	1	899
....	......	....	......	....	......	..:	......	....	......		....	....	1	4,526
....	......	....	......	....	......	....	......	....	......		....	....	1	1,597
....	......	....	......	....	......	....	......	....	......		....	....	283	12,736
....	......	....	......	....	......	....	......	....	......		....	....	1	469
5	7,627	26	18,014	5	20,801	3	8,017	12	53,447	....	8	20,037	1,070	1,589,427
....	......	....		....							....	....	6	1,986
....	......	....		....							....	....	17	7,535
....	......	....		....		....					....	....	23	9,521
....	......	....		....		....		....			\....	....	22	15,162
....	......	....		....		....		....			....	....	11	6,718
....	......	....		....		....		....			....	....	33	21,880
....	......	....		....		....		....			....	..:....	129	1,391
....	......	....		....		....		....			....	....	8	405
....	......	....		....		....		....			....	....	5	397
....	......	....		....		....		....			....	....	13	802
....,	......	....		....		....		....			....	....	20	4,144
....	......	....		....		....		....			....	....	1	74
....	......	....		....		....		....			....	....	4	2,936
....	......	....		....		....		....			....	....	4	792
....	......	....		....		....		....			....	....	8	3,728
....	......	....		....				....			....	....	7	36
....	......	....		....		....		....			....	....	79	25,639
....	......	....		....		....		....			....	....	37	7,316
....	......	....		....		....		....			....	....	116	32,955
....	......	....		....		....		....			....	....	4	681
....	......	....		....		....		....			....	....	1	392
....	......	....		....		....		....			....	....	23	3,286
....	......	....		....		....		....			....	....	1	28
....	......	....		....		....		....			....	....	77	6,045
....	......	....	....'.	....		....		....			....	....	106	10,432

6 GEORGE V, A. 1916

No. 13.—Statement of the Number and Tonnage of Sailing

Ports and Outports and Countries whence arrived.	British.		United States.		Norwegian.		Austrian.		Belgian.	
	Vessels.	Tons Register.	Vessels.	Tons Register.	Vessels.	Tons Register.	Vessels.	Tons Register.	Vessels.	Tons Register.
Levis, Que.—										
Great Britain........Steam.	7	17,601	....	....	....		....		....	
United States........ "	2	3,514	....	....	1	2,036	....		....	
Total..............	9	21,115	....	....	1	2,036	....		....	
Liverpool, N.S.—										
Newfoundland........Sail.	....	....	1	/5	....					
Portugal.............Steam.	1	1,927	....	....	....					
United States......... "	....		33	1,335	1	683	....			
United States........Sail.	42	5,593	44	5,464	....					
Sea fisheries........Steam.	....		60	2,771	....					
Sea fisheries........Sail.	1	110	83	6,366	....					
Total..............	44	7,630	221	16,011	1	683	....			
Lockeport, N.S.—										
Newfoundland........Sail.	1	38	....							
United States........ "	7	687	8	103	....					
Sea fisheries........Steam.	5	709	....							
Sea fisheries........Sail.	49	1,674	65	4,727	....					
Total..............	62	3,108	73	4,830	....					
Lord's Cove, N.B.—										
United States........Steam.	352	14,653	176	1,702	....					
Louisburg, N.S.—										
Great Britain........Steam.	6	18,499	....	....	7	9,659				
British W. Indies..... "	3	6,951	....		....					
Newfoundland........ "	45	27,716	....		4	6,378				
Newfoundland........ Sail.	38	3,534	3	171	....					
Mexico..............Steam.	....	....	....		1	2,584				
Denmark........, ... "	1	2,230	....		....					
Argentina............ "	5	10,459	....		....					
France.............. "	....		....		1	2,009				
Germany............ "	....		....		2	4,850				
Holland............. "	....		....		....					
Italy................ "	3	8,039	....		....					
Norway............. "	....		....		2	1,600				
Malta............... "	1	2,737	....		....					
Portugal............ "	1	2,224	....		....					
Saint Pierre......... "	....		....		....					
Saint Pierre........ Sail.	4	312	....		....					
Spain...............Steam.	4	7,722	....		....					
Sweden............. "	....		....		....					
United States........ "	51	73,379	....		35	60,512				
United States........Sail.	6	905	12	1,066	....					
B. South Africa.....Steam.	1	2,820	....		....					
San Domingo........ "	1	867	....		....					
Gibraltar............ "	3	8,021	....		....					
French Africa........ "	2	5,309	....		....					
Sea fisheries........ "	....		....		1	432				
Sea fisheries........Sail.	4	349	189	9,644	....					
Total..............	179	182,073	204	10,881	53	88,524	....			
Lower East Pubnico, N.S.—										
British W. Indies.....Sail....	1	174	....		....					
United States........Steam.	1	67	....		....					
United States........Sail....	6	377	18	1,135	....					
Sea Fisheries......... "	36	1,846	21	1,104	....					
Total..............	44	2,464	39	2,239	....					

and Steam Vessels entered Inwards *from Sea, &c.—Continued.*

or VESSELS.

Danish.		French.		German.		Italian.		Russian.		Other Nationalities.			Total.	
Vessels.	Tons Register.	Vessels.	Tons Register.	Vessels.	Tons Register.	Vessels.	Tons Register.	Vessels.	Tons Register.	Names.	Vessels.	Tons Register.	Vessels.	Tons Register.
....	......	....	......	....	......	....	......	....	......		....	......	7	17,601
....	......	....	......	....	......	....	......	....	......		....	......	3	5,550
....	......	....	......	....	......	....	......	....	......		....	......	10	23,151
....	......													
....	......	....	......	....	......	....	......	....	......		....	......	1	75
....	......	....	......	....	......	....	......	....	......		....	......	1	1,927
....	......	....	......	....	......	....	......	....	......		....	......	34	2,018
....	......	....	......	....	......	....	......	....	......		....	......	86	11,057
....	......	....	......	....	......	....	......	....	......		....	......	60	2,771
....	......	....	......	....	......	....	......	....	......		....	......	84	6,476
....	......	....	......	....	......	....	......	....	......		....	......	266	24,324
....	......	....	......	....	......	....	......	....	......		....	......	1	38
....	......	....	......	....	......	....	......	....	......		....	......	15	790
....	......	....	......	....	......	....	......	....	......		....	......	5	709
....	......	....	......	....	......	....	......	....	......		....	......	114	6,401
....	......	....	......	....	......	....	......	....	......		....	......	135	7,938
....	......	....	......	....	......	....	......	....	......		....	......	528	16,355
4	7,289	....	......	....	......	....	......	....	......		....	......	17	35,447
1	1,338	....	......	....	......	....	......	....	......		....	......	4	8,289
....	......	....	......	....	......	....	......	....	......		....	......	49	34,094
1	1,660	....	......	....	......	....	......	....	......		....	......	41	3,705
....	......	....	......	....	......	....	......	....	......		....	......	1	1,660
....	......	....	......	....	......	....	......	....	......		....	......	1	2,584
....	......	....	......	....	......	....	......	....	......		....	......	1	2,230
....	......	....	......	....	......	....	......	....	......		....	......	5	10,459
....	......	....	......	....	......	....	......	....	......		....	......	1	2,509
....	......	....	......	....	......	....	......	....	......	Dutch......	1	2,266	3	7,116
....	......	....	......	....	......	....	......	....	......		....	......	3	8,039
....	......	....	......	....	......	....	......	....	......		....	......	2	1,600
....	......	....	......	....	......	....	......	....	......		....	......	1	2,737
....	......	....	......	....	......	....	......	....	......		....	......	1	2,224
....	......	1	94	....	......	....	......	....	......		....	......	1	94
....	......	4	288	....	......	....	......	....	......		....	......	8	600
....	......	....	......	....	......	....	......	....	......		....	......	4	7,722
....	......	....	......	....	......	....	......	....	......	Swedish....	1	1,799	1	1,799
4	4,751	....	......	1	1,005	....	......	....	......	Swedish....	1	1,963	92	141,610
....	......	....	......	....	......	....	......	....	......		....	......	18	1,971
....	......	....	......	....	......	....	......	....	......		....	......	1	2,820
....	......	....	......	....	......	....	......	....	......		....	......	1	867
....	......	....	......	....	......	....	......	....	......		....	......	3	8,021
....	......	....	......	....	......	....	......	....	......		....	......	2	5,309
....	......	....	......	....	......	....	......	....	......		....	......	1	432
....	......	1	27	....	......	....	......	....	......		....	......	194	10,020
10	15,038	6	409	1	1,005	....	......	....	......		3	6,028	456	303,958
....	......	....	......	....	......	....	......	....	......		....	......	1	174
....	......	....	......	....	......	....	......	....	......		....	......	1	67
....	......	....	......	....	......	....	......	....	......		....	......	24	1,512
....	......	....	......	....	......	....	......	....	......		....	......	57	2,950
....	......	....	......	....	......	....	......	....	......		....	......	83	4,703

6 GEORGE V, A. 1916

No. 13.—STATEMENT of the Number and Tonnage of Sailing

Ports and Outports and Countries whence arrived.	British.		United States.		Norwegian.		Austrian.		Belgian.	
	Vessels.	Tons Register.	Vessels.	Tons Register.	Vessels.	Tons Register.	Vessels.	Tons Register.	Vessels.	Tons Register.
Lunenburg, N.S.—										
British W. Indies.....Sail....	20	2,860								
Newfoundland......... " ..	11	1,083	1	155						
Spain............... " ...	3	297								
United States......... " ...	26	4,629	1	394						
Sea Fisheries........Steam.	21	279	1	78						
Sea Fisheries........Sail...	215	17,416	20	1,685						
Total................	296	26,564	23	2,312						
Magdalen Islands, Que.—										
Newfoundland.......Sail....	9	777	1	78						
France............. "										
Saint Pierre.......... "			8	1,002						
United States......... "										
Total.............	9	777	9	1,080						
Mahone Bay, N.S.—										
Newfoundland.......Sail....	2	198								
United States......... " ...	6	674	2	697						
Sea Fisheries......... "	14	1,261								
Total.............	22	2,133	2	697						
Maitland, N.S.—										
United States....... ...Sail....	7	777	4	1,120						
Meteghan River, N.S.—										
United States........Sail....	7	773								
Moncton, N.B.—										
Great Britain.........Steam.	6	12,943								
British W. Indies.....Sail....	3	680								
Norway.............Steam.					2	2,427				
Spain................ "										
Sweden.............. "					1	1,091				
United States......... "	2	4,848								
United States....... ...Sail....	7	1,154	13	4,531						
Total................	18	19,625	13	4,531	3	3,518				
Montreal, Que.—										
Great Britain.........Steam.	322	1,426,188			3	6,592				
British W. Indies..... "	17	39,795			1	1,520				
Newfoundland....... "	21	23,231			1	689				
Belgium............ "	13	56,101								
Brazil.............. "	3	7,659								
San Domingo........ "	4	3,044			1	699				
France............. "	14	51,801								
Germany............ "	1	2,110								
Holland............ "	4	11,671								2	11,599
Italy............... "	20	54,259			2	5,234				
Norway............ "	1	1,090								
Danish West Indies... "					1	1,178				
Portugal............ "	7	15,518					1	2,758		
Denmark............ "	1	1,994								
Mexico............. "					2	2,203				
Spain.............. "	3	6,852								
Greece............. "	1	1,686								
United States........ "	45	117,999	3	1,839	6	6,566	1	3,033		
Austria............. "							1	2,821		
Chili.............. "	2	4,676								
Argentina........... "	9	22,061					1	2,321		

and Steam Vessels entered Inwards *from Sea, &c.—Continued.*

or VESSELS.

	Danish.		French.		German.		Italian.		Russian.		Other Nationalities.			Total.	
Vessels.	Tons Register.	Vessels.	Tons Register.	Vessels.	Tons Register.	Vessels.	Tons Register.	Vessels.	Tons Register.	Names.	Vessels.	Tons Register.	Vessels.	Tons Register.
....	....	....	....	....	....	....	....	....	....	....	....	....	20	2,860
....	.*..	....	....	....	....	....	....	....	....	....	....	....	12	1,238
....	......	....	....	....	....	....	....	....	....	....	....	....	3	297
....	......	....	....	....	....	....	....	....	....	....	....	....	27	5,023
....	......	....	....	....	....	....	....	....	....	....	....	....	22	357
....	......	....	....	....	....	....	....	....	....	....	....	....	235	19,101
....	....	..	....	....	....	....	....	....	....	....	...	....	319	28,876
...	....	.19	2,913	....	....	....	....	....	....	....	....	••••	10	855
....	....	9	1,210	....	....	....	....	....	....	....	....	••••	19	2,913
....	....	....	....	....	....	....	....	....	....	....	....	....	9	1,210
....	....	....	....	....	....	....	....	....	....	....	....	....	8	1,002
....	......	28	4,123	....	....	....	....	....	....	....	...	....	46	5,080
...	....	....	....	....	....	....	....	....	....	....	....	....	2	198
....	....	....	....	....	....	....	....	....	....	....	....	....	8	1,371
....	....	....	....	....	....	....	....	....	....	....	....	....	14	1,261
....	....	....	....	....	....	....	....	....	....	....	....	....	24	2,830
....	....	....	....	....	....	....	....	....	....	....	....	....	11	1,897
...	....	....	....	....	....	....	....	....	....	....	...	....	7	773
'	....	....	....	....	....	....	....	....	....	....	....	'	6	12,943
....	....	....	....	....	....	....	....	....	....	....	....	....	3	680
....	....	....	....	....	....	....	....	....	....	....	....	....	2	2,427
....	....	....	....	....	....	....	....	....	....	Spanish....	1	1,883	1	1,883
....	....	....	....	....	....	....	....	....	....	....	....	....	1	1,091
1	1, 72	....	....	....	....	....	....	....	....	....	....	....	3	6,420
....	....	....	....	....	....	....	....	....	....	....	....	....	20	5,685
1	1,572	....	....	....	....	....	....	....	....	....	1	1,883	36	31,129
...	....	.2	2,214	....	....	....	....	....	....	....	....	....	325	1,432,780
....	....	....	....	....	....	....	....	....	....	....	....	....	20	43,529
....	....	....	....	....	....	....	....	....	....	....	....	....	22	23,920
....	....	....	....	....	....	....	....	....	....	....	....	....	13	56,101
....	....	....	....	....	....	....	....	....	....	....	....	....	3	7,659
....	....	2	6,756	....	....	....	....	....	....	Greccian...	1	2,184	5	3,743
....	....	....	....	3	12,877	....	....	....	....	....	....	....	17	61,041
....	....	....	....	6	19,698	....	....	....	....	Dutch......	2	8,048	4	14,987
....	....	....	....	....	....	....	....	....	....	Greccian...	1	3,049	14	51,016
....	....	....	....	....	....	....	....	....	....	......	....	....	23	62,542
....	....	....	....	....	....	....	....	....	....	....	....	....	1	1,090
1	2,526	....	....	....	....	....	....	....	....	....	....	....	1	1,178
....	....	....	....	....	....	....	....	....	....	....	....	....	9	20,802
1	1,660	....	....	....	....	....	....	....	....	....	....	....	1	1,994
....	....	....	....	....	....	....	....	....	....	....	....	....	3	3,868
1	1,400	1	4,080	1	4,463	....	....	....	....	Dutch.....	1	1,857	3	6,852
....	....	....	....	....	....	....	....	....	....	Swedish...	3	5,971	1	1,686
....	....	....	....	....	....	....	....	....	....	....	....	....	62	147,268
....	....	....	....	....	....	....	....	....	....	....	....	....	1	2,821
....	....	....	..-..	....	....	....	....	....	••••	....	....	....	2	4,676
....	....	....	....	....	....	....	....	....	....	....	....	....	10	24,382

6 GEORGE V, A. 1916

No. 13.—STATEMENT of the Number and Tonnage of Sailing

Ports and Outports and Countries whence arrived.	British.		United States.		Norwegian.		Austrian.		Belgian.	
	Vessels.	Tons Register.	Vessels.	Tons Register.	Vessels.	Tons Register.	Vessels.	Tons Register.	Vessels.	Tons Register.
Montreal—*Con.*										
Uruguay............Steam.	1	3,069	....	......	....	......	....	......	....	......
British Guiana....... "	1	1,980	....	......	1	1,987	....	......	....	......
British West Africa... "	2	5,322	....	......	....	......	....	......	....	......
Egypt............... "	3	7,440	....	......	....	......	....	......	....	......
Bermuda.......... "	2	4,259	....	......	....	......	....	......	....	......
Total................	497	1,869,305	3	1,839	18	26,673	4	10,993	2	11,599
Murray Harbour, P.E.I.—										
Sea Fisheries........Sail....	10	276	....	......	....	......	....	......	....	......
Nanaimo, B.C.—										
United States.......Steam.	108	32,735	135	88,354	10	28,535	....	......	....	......
United States........Sail.	1	89	70	41,719	....	......	....	......	....	......
Chili................Steam.	2	6,265	....	......	....	......	....	......	....	......
Ecuador............. "	....	......	....	......	....	......	....	......	....	......
Total...............	111	39,089	205	130,073	10	28,535	....	......	....	......
Newcastle, N.B.—										
Great Britain........Steam.	1	1,947	....	......	2	2,946	....	......	....	......
Great Britain........Sail.	....	......	....	......	2	1,789	....	......	....	......
British W. Indies..... "	1	296	....	......	....	......	....	......	....	......
Spain................Steam.	1	2,273	....	......	....	......	....	......	....	......
United States........Sail.	....	......	2	689	....	......	....	......	....	......
Denmark............ "	....	......	....	......	....	......	....	......	....	......
Total................	3	4,516	2	689	4	4,735	....	......	....	......
Newport, B.C.—										
United States........Steam.	18	17,216	23	22,923	1	3,179	....	......	....	......
New Campbellton, N.S.—										
United States........Steam.	1	1,826	....	......	....	......	....	......	....	......
Sea Fisheries........Sail.	4	169	....	......	....	......	....	......	....	......
Total................	5	1,995	....	......	....	......	....	......	....	......
New Westminster, B.C.—										
United States........Steam.	24	6,159	15	5,261	....	......	....	......	....	......
United States........Sail.	2	398	....	......	....	......	....	......	....	......
Total................	26	6,557	15	5,261	....	......	....	......	....	......
North East Harbour, N.S.—										
United States........Sail.	....	......	8	633	....	......	....	......	....	......
Sea Fisheries........Steam.	2	66	2	18	....	......	....	......	....	......
Sea Fisheries........Sail.	2	20	21	1,485	....	......	....	......	....	......
Total................	4	86	31	2,136	....	......	....	......	....	......
North Head, N.B.—										
United States........Steam.	180	23,850	18	341	....	......	....	......	....	......
United States........Sail.	5	401	2	211	....	......	....	......	....	......
Total................	185	24,251	20	552	....	......	....	......	....	......
North Sydney, N.S.—										
Great Britain........Steam.	11	10,922	....	......	4	4,572	....	......	....	......
British W. Indies..... "	6	13,035	....	......	....	......	....	......	....	......
Newfoundland........ "	313	201,265	....	......	18	22,016	....	......	....	......
Newfoundland........Sail.	354	25,449	....	......	....	......	....	......	....	......
France...............Steam.	....	......	....	......	....	......	....	......	....	......
Italy................ "	2	1,290	....	......	....	......	....	......	....	......

and Steam Vessels entered Inwards *from Sea, &c.—Continued.*

OF VESSELS.

	Danish		French		German		Italian		Russian		Other Nationalities			Total	
	Vessels	Tons Register	Vessels	Tons Register	Vessels	Tons Register	Vessels	Tons Register	Vessels	Tons Register	Names	Vessels	Tons Register	Vessels	Tons Register
	....	......	....	......	....	......	....	......	....	......	....	....	......	1	3,069
	2	2,192	....	......	....	......	....	......	....	......	....	....	......	4	6,159
	....	......	....	......	....	......	....	......	....	......	....	....	......	2	5,322
	....	......	....	......	....	......	....	......	....	......	....	....	......	3	7,440
	....	......	....	......	....	......	....	......	....	......	....	....	......	2	4,259
	7	9,992	3	10,836	10	37,038			....	......	....	8	21,409	552	2,000,184
	....	......	....	......	....	......	....	......	....	......	....	....	......	10	276
	1	2,625	....	......	....	......	....	......	1	2,619	....	....	......	255	154,868
	....	......	....	......	....	......	....	......	....	......	....	....	......	71	41,808
	....	......	....	......	....	......	....	......	....	......	....	....	......	2	6,265
	....	......	....	......	1	3,084	....	......	....	......	....	....	......	1	3,084
	1	2,625	....	......	1	3,084	....	......	1	2,619	....	....	......	329	206,025
	7	9,905	....	......	....	......	....	......	....	......	....	....	......	10	14,798
	1	246	....	......	....	......	....	......	1	349	....	....	......	4	2,384
	....	......	....	......	....	......	....	......	....	......	....	....	......	1	296
	....	......	....	......	....	......	....	......	....	......	....	....	......	1	2,273
	....	......	....	......	....	......	....	......	....	......	....	....	......	2	689
	3	544	....	......	....	......	....	......	....	......	....	....	......	3	544
	11	10,695	....	......	....	......	....	......	1	349	....	....	......	21	20,984
	....	......	....	......	....	......	....	......	....	......	....	....	......	42	43,318
	....	......	....	......	....	......	....	......	....	......	....	....	......	1	1,826
	....	......	....	......	....	......	....	......	....	......	....	....	......	4	169
	....	......	....	......	....	......	....	......	....	......	....	....	......	5	1,995
	....	......	....	......	....	......	....	......	....	......	....	....	......	39	11,420
	....	......	....	......	....	......	....	......	....	......	....	....	......	2	398
	....	......	....	......	....	......	....	......	....	......	....	....	......	41	11,818
	....	......	....	......	....	......	....	......	....	......	....	....	......	8	633
	....	......	....	......	....	......	....	......	....	......	....	....	......	4	84
	....	......	....	......	....	......	....	......	....	......	....	....	......	23	1,505
	....	......	....	......	....	......	....	......	....	......	....	....	......	35	2,222
	....	......	....	......	....	......	....	......	....	......	....	....	......	198	24,191
	....	......	....	......	....	......	....	......	....	......	....	....	......	7	612
	....	......	....	......	....	......	....	......	....	......	....	....	......	205	24,803
	....	......	....	......	....	......	....	......	....	......	....	....	......	15	15,494
	....	......	....	......	....	......	....	......	....	......	....	....	......	6	13,035
	....	......	....	......	....	......	....	......	....	......	....	....	......	331	223,281
	....	......	....	......	....	......	....	......	....	......	....	....	......	354	25,449
	....	......	2	344	....	......	....	......	....	......	....	....	......	2	344
	....	......	....	......	....	......	1	3,049	....	......	....	....	......	3	4,339

6 GEÓRGE V, A. 1916

No. 13.—Statement of the Number and Tonnage of Sailing

Ports and Outports and Countries whence arrived.	British.		United States.		Norwegian.		Austrian.		Belgian.	
	Vessels.	Tons Register.	Vessels.	Tons Register.	Vessels.	Tons Register.	Vessels.	Tons Register.	Vessels.	Tons Register.
North Sydney, N.S.—*Con.*										
Norway..............Steam.	....	....	....	....	3	2,510	....	....	....	....
Portugal..............Sail.	1	144	....	....	....	....	....	....	....	....
Saint Pierre..........Steam.	....	....	....	....	....	....	....	....	....	....
Saint Pierre..........Sail.	15	1,145	....	....	....	....	....	....	....	....
United States........Steam.	5	8,167	....	....	6	8,963	....	....	....	....
United States........Sail.	11	1,197	12	1,004	....	....	....	....	....	....
Argentina...........Steam.	1	3,140	....	....	....	....	....	....	....	....
Sea Fisheries....... "	7	1,116	....	....	....	....	....	....	....	....
Sea Fisheries........Sail.	25	1,757	112	8,711	....	....	....	....	....	....
Total....:	751	268,627	124	9,715	31	38,061	....	....	....	....
Parrsboro, N.S.—										
Great Britain........Steam.	2	3,905	....	....	....	....	....	....	....	....
Spain................ "	1	1,723	....	....	....	....	....	....	....	....
United States........ "	26	29,443	26	7,708	1	850	....	....	....	....
United States........Sail.	47	8,527	24	6,844	....	....	....	....	....	....
Total..................	76	43·298	50	14,552	1	850	....	....	....	....
Paspebiac, Que.—										
Great Britain........Steam.	....	....	....	....	....	....	....	....	....	....
United States........ "	..	....	....	....	2	2,548	....	....	....	....
United States........Sail.	....	....	2	615	....	....	....	....	....	....
Total..................	....	....	2	615	2	2,548	....	....	....	....
Percé, Que.—										
Great Britain........Steam.	1	2,210	....	....	....	....	....	....	....	....
Newfoundland.......Sail.	1	31	....	....	....	....	....	....	....	....
Spain.............. "	....	....	....	....	....	....	....	....	....	....
United States........Steam.	4	2,971	....	....	1	912	....	....	....	....
Total..................	6	5,212	....	....	1	912	....	....	....	....
Pictou, N.S.—										
Great Britain, ...Steam.	....	....	....	....	2	2,630	....	....	....	....
Newfoundland....... "	2	2,569	....	....	....	....	....	....	....	....
Spain................ "	1	2,114	....	....	....	....	....	....	....	....
United States........: "	4	7,152	....	....	1	683	....	....	....	....
United States........Sail.	3	416	....	....	....	....	....	....	....	....
Total..................	10	12,251	....	....	3	3,313	....	....	....	....
Port Clyde, N.S.—										
United States........Sail.	1	281	2	958	....	....	....	....	....	....
Port Hood, N.S.—										
Sea Fisheries........Sail.	....	....	1	91	....	....	....	....	....	....
Port La Tour, N.S.—										
Sea Fisheries......... Sail.	17	223	18	1,669	....	....	....	....	....	....
Port Mulgrave, N.S.—										
Newfoundland........ Sail.	1	99	....	....	....	....	....	....	....	....
United States........Steam.	....	....	4	279	1	747	....	....	....	....
United States........ Sail.	2	296	9	778	....	....	....	....	....	....
Sea Fisheries........Steam.	5	643	2	194	...	....	....	....	....	....
Sea Fisheries........ Sail.	5	503	7	633	....	....	....	....	....	....
Total.................	13	1,541	22	1,884	1	747	....	....	....	....

and Steam Vessels entered Inwards *from Sea, &c.—Continued.*

or VESSELS.

	Danish.		French.		German.		Italian.		Russian.		Other Nationalities.			Total.	
	Vessels.	Tons Register.	Vessels.	Tons Register.	Vessels.	Tons Register.	Vessels.	Tons Register.	Vessels.	Tons Register.	Names.	Vessels.	Tons Register.	Vessels.	Tons Register.
	....	......	....	....	....	....	....	......	....	......	....	....	....	3	2,510
	....	......	....	....	....	....	....	......	....	......	....	....	....	1	144
	....	......	39	7,462	....	....	....	......	....	......	....	....	....	39	7,462
	....	......	10	574	....	....	....	......	....	......	....	....	....	25	1,719
	....	......	....	....	....	....	....	......	....	......	....	....	....	11	17,130
	....	......	....	....	....	....	....	......	....	......	....	....	...:....	23	2,201
	....	......	....	....	....	....	....	......	....	......	....	....	....	1	3,140
	....	......	41	7,665	....	....	....	......	....	......	....	....	....	48	8,781
	....	......	3	131	....	....	....	......	....	......	....	....	....	140	10,599
	....	......	95	16,176	....	....	1	3,049	....	......	....	....	....	1,002	335,628
	....	......	....	....	....	....	....	......	....	......	....	....	....	2	3,905
	....	......	....	....	....	....	....	......	....	......	....	....	....	1	1,723
	....	......	....	....	....	....	....	..:...	....	......	Spanish.....	1	1,959	54	39,660
	....	......	....	....	....	....	....	......	....	......	....	....	....	71	15,371
	....	......	....	....	....	....	....	......	....	......	....	1	1,959	128	60,659
	1	1,354	....	....	....	....	....	......	....	......	....	....	....	1	1,354
	....	......	....	....	....	....	....	......	....	......	....	....	....	2	2,548
	....	......	....	....	....	....	....	......	....	......	....	....	....	2	615
	1	1,354	....	....	....	....	....	......	....	......	....	....	....	5	4,517
	....	......	....	....	....	....	....	......	....	......	....	....	....	1	2,210
	....	......	....	....	....	....	....	......	....	......	....	....	....	1	31
	1	257	....	....	....	....	....	......	....	......	....	....	....	1	257
	....	......	....	....	....	....	....	......	....	......	....	....	....	5	3,883
	1	257	....	....	....	....	....	......	....	......	....	....	....	8	6,381
	....	......	....	....	....	....	....	......	....	......	....	....	....	2	2,630
	....	......	....	....	....	....	....	......	....	......	....	....	....	2	2,569
	....	......	....	....	....	....	....	......	....	......	....	....	....	1	2,114
	....	......	....	....	....	....	....	.:...	....	......	....	....	....	5	7,835
	....	......	....	....	....	....	....	......	....	......	....	....	....	3	416
	....	......	....	....	....	....	....	......	....	......	....	....	....	13	15,564
	....	......	....	....	....	....	....	......	....	......	....	....	....	3	1,239
	....	......	....	....	....	....	....	......	....	......	....	....	....	1	91
	....	......	....	....	....	....	....	......	....	......	....	....	....	35	1,892
	....	......	....	....	....	....	....	......	....	......	....	....	....	1	99
	....	......	....	....	....	....	....	......	....	......	....	....	....	5	1,026
	....	......	....	....	....	....	....	......	....	......	....	....	....	11	1,074
	....	......	....	....	....	....	....	......	....	......	....	....	....	7	837
	....	......	....	....	....	....	....	......	....	......	....	....	....	12	1,136
	....	......	....	....	....	....	....	......	....	......	....	....	....	36	4,172

6 GEORGE V, A. 1916

No. 13.—STATEMENT of the Number and Tonnage of Sailing

										NATIONALITY
Ports and Outports and Countries whence arrived.	British.		United States.		Norwegian.		Austrian.		Belgian.	
	Vessels.	Tons Register.	Vessels.	Tons Register.	Vessels.	Tons Register.	Vessels.	Tons Register.	Vessels.	Tons Register.
Port Simpson, B.C.— United States........Steam.	30	34,167	7	55	....	....	....	....	....	....
Port Wade, N.S.— United States........ Sail.	8	1,089	1	11	....	....	....	....	....	....
Port Williams, N.S.— United States........ Sail.	3	869	....	....						
Powell River, B.C.— United States........Steam.	8	5,329	70	36,224	....	....				
Prince Rupert, B.C.— United States........Steam. Sea Fisheries......... "	82 119	92,757 7,752	154 ...	115,297	....	....				
Total.................	201	100,509	154	115,297						
Pugwash, N.S.— Great Britain........Steam.	1	2,263	....	....						
Quebec, Que.— Great Britain........Steam. British W. Indies..... " Newfoundland........ " Newfoundland........ Sail. Belgium.............Steam. France.............. " Holland............. " Italy................ " Spain............... " United States........ " United States........ Sail. Argentina...........Steam.	218 3 22 10 6 8 .... 1 .... 6 2	1,183,763 7,824 9,372 1,010 26,145 45,691 2,716 42,435 4,748	... ... 1 ... ... 2 ...	.... 96 181	1 1 1 1	1,520 862 648 	 1	 3,093	••••	
Total.................	276	1,323,704	3	277	3	3,030	1	3,093		
Rimouski, Que.— Great Britain,........Steam. Great Britain......... Sail. Brazil.............. " France.............. " Norway............. " Portugal............ "	21	30,355	....	.... 	1 1 1 1 1 	2,136 1,464 884 1,464 929 	.... 	.... 		
Total.................	21	30,355	....	....	5	6,877	....	....	....	....
River Hebert, N.S.— United States........ Sail.	3	274	1	155	....	....				
St. Andrews, N.B.— United States........Steam. United States........ Sail.	320 18	19,470 1,658	990 9	53,629 2,300	....	.... 	....	....	....	
Total.................	338	21,128	999	55,929	....					
St. George, N.B.— United States........Steam. United States........ Sail.	2 12	172 797	57 69	2,502 6,563	....	.... 			....	
Total.................	14	969	126	9,065	....	....	....	....		

SESSIONAL PAPER No. 11

and Steam Vessels entered Inwards *from Sea, &c.—Continued.*

or VESSELS.

Danish.		French.		German.		Italian.		Russian.		Other Nationalities.			Total.	
Vessels.	Tons Register.	Vessels.	Tons Register.	Vessels.	Tons Register.	Vessels.	Tons Register.	Vessels.	Tons Register.	Names.	Vessels.	Tons Register.	Vessels.	Tons Register.
....	......	....	......	....	......	....	......	....	......	....	....	....	37	34,222
....	......	....	......	....	......	....	......	....	......	....	....	....	9	1,100
....	......	....	......	....	......	....	......	....	......	....	....	....	3	869
....	......	....	......	....	......	....	......	....	......	....	....	....	78	41,553
....	......	....	......	....	......	....	......	....	......	....	....	....	236	208,054
....	......	....	......	....	......	....	......	....	......	....	....	....	119	7,752
....	......	....	......	....	......	....	......	....	......	....	....	....	355	215,806
1	1,354	....	......	....	......	....	......	....	......	....	....	....	2	3,617
....	......	....	......	....	......	....	......	....	......	Dutch......	2	7,647	220	1,191,410
....	......	....	......	....	......	....	......	....	......	....	....	....	4	9,344
....	......	....	......	....	......	....	......	....	......	....	....	....	23	10,234
....	......	....	......	....	......	....	......	....	......	....	....	....	11	1,106
....	......	3	11,016	....	......	....	......	....	......	Dutch.....	1	5,489	7	31,634
....	......	....	......	....	......	....	......	....	......	....	....	....	11	56,707
....	......	....	......	2	9,374	....	......	....	......	Dutch.....	7	27,773	9	37,147
....	......	....	......	....	......	....	......	....	......	....	....	....	1	2,716
....	......	....	......	....	......	....	......	....	......	....	....	....	1	3,093
1	1,400	....	......	....	......	....	......	....	......	....	....	....	8	44,483
....	......	....	......	....	......	....	......	....	......	....	....	....	2	181
....	......	....	......	....	......	....	......	....	......	....	....	....	2	4,748
1	1,400	3	11,016	2	9,374	....	......	....	......	....	10	40,909	299	1,392,803
....	......	....	......	....	......	....	......	....	......	....	....	....	22	32,491
....	......	....	......	....	......	....	......	....	......	....	....	....	1	1,464
....	......	....	......	....	......	....	......	....	......	....	....	....	1	884
....	......	....	......	....	......	....	......	....	......	....	....	....	1	1,464
....	......	....	......	....	......	....	......	....	......	....	....	....	1	929
....	......	....	......	1	851	....	......	1	953	....	....	....	2	1,804
....	......	....	......	1	851	....	......	1	953	....	....	....	28	39,036
....	......	....	......	....	......	....	......	....	......	....	....	....	4	429
....	......	....	......	....	......	....	......	....	......	....	....	....	1,310	73,099
....	......	....	......	....	......	....	......	....	......	....	....	....	27	3,958
....	......	....	......	....	......	....	......	....	......	....	....	....	1,337	77,057
....	......	....	......	....	......	....	......	....	......	....	....	....	59	2,674
....	......	....	......	....	......	....	......	....	......	....	....	....	81	7,360
....	......	....	......	....	......	....	......	....	......	....	....	....	140	10,034

6 GEORGE V, A. 1916

No. 13.—STATEMENT of the Number and Tonnage of Sailing

	British.		United States.		Norwegian.		Austrian.		Belgian.	
Ports and Outports and Countries whence arrived.	Vessels.	Tons Register.	Vessels.	Tons Register.	Vessels.	Tons Register.	Vessels.	Tons Register.	Vessels.	Tons Register.
St. John, N.B.—										
Great Britain.........Steam.	148	532,733	....	....	3	4,912	....	...	...	......
Great Britain......... Sail.										
British, W. Indies....Steam.	30	79,942	...	....						
British W. Indies..... Sail.	11	2,903	...		5	4,806				
Brazil...............Steam.	2	4,412								
Brazil............... Sail.					1	1,023				
Cuba................Steam.					1	1,021				
Cuba................ Sail.'	1	349	..							
France..............Steam.	1	2,210	...							
Italy................ Sail.										
United States.......Steam.	18	29,912	144	315,268	13	13,821				
United States........ Sail.	164	24,240	385	35,528	3	2,970				
San Domingo........Steam.	....				1	656				
Iceland.............. Sail.			...							
Hayti...............Steam.					1	878				
Sea Fisheries........ Sail.	45	1,376	...	....						
Total................	420	678,077	529	350,796	28	30.087	....		....	
St. Martins, N.B.—										
United States.........Steam	....	....	27	2,133	....					
United States......... Sail.	27	8,798	24	8,875	....					
Total..................	27	8,798	51	11,008	....					
St. Stephen, N.B.—										
British W. Indies..... Sail.	1	168	...	....	....					
United States.....:...Steam.	214	19,757	108	2,264	....					
United States........ Sail.	1	44	24	5,187	....					
Total................	216	19,969	132	7,451	....					
Sackville, N.S.—										
United States........ Sail.	5	497	3	506	....					
Salmon River, N.S.—										
United States......... Sail.	1	71	2	33	....					
Sea fisheries.........Steam.	10	160	...		....					
Total.................	11	231	2	33	....					
Sandy Point, N.S.—										
Newfoundland........,Sail.	3	260	2	169	....					
United States........Sail.	9	·1,527	129	10,790	....					
Sea fisheries..........Steam.	1	40	....		....					
Sea fisheries......... Sail.	2	109	107	8,110	....					
Total.................	15	1,936	238	19,069	....					
Shediac, N.B.—										
British S. Africa.......Sail.	....	....	1	214	....					
Shelburne, N.S.—										
British W. Indies..... Sail.	1	147	...							
Newfoundland........ "	....		2	248						
United States........Steam.	....		2	94						
United States........ Sail.	14	2,590	29	2,636						
Sea fisheries.........Steam.	5	191	...							
Sea fisheries......... Sail.	8	329	48	3,901						
Total................	28	3,257	81	6,879	....					

and Steam Vessels entered Inwards *from Sea*, &c.—*Continued.*

or VESSELS.

s.	Tons Register.	Vessels.	Tons Register.	Vessels.	Tons Register.	Vessels.	Tons Register.	Vessels.	Tons Register.	Names.	Vessels.	Tons Register.	Vessels.	Tons Register.
		Danish.		French.		German.		Italian.		Russian.			Other Nationalities.		Total.
2	2,508	....	....	....	....	....	....	....	....	1	1,412	....	....	....	154	541,565
1	271	....	....	....	....	....	....	....	....	....	....	Swedish....	1	931	2	1,202
....	....	....	....	....	....	....	....	....	....	....	....	....	....	....	30	79,942
....	....	....	....	....	....	....	....	....	....	....	....	....	....	....	16	7,709
....	....	....	....	....	....	....	....	....	....	....	....	....	....	....	2	4,412
....	....	....	....	....	....	....	....	....	....	....	....	....	....	....	1	1,023
1	877	....	....	....	....	....	....	....	....	....	....	....	....	....	2	1,898
....	....	....	....	....	....	....	....	....	....	....	....	....	....	....	1	249
....	....	....	....	....	....	....	....	....	....	....	....	....	....	....	1	2,210
....	....	....	....	....	....	....	....	1	596	....	....	....	....	....	1	596
....	....	....	....	....	....	....	....	....	....	....	....	Spanish..:..	1	3,137	176	362,138
....	....	....	....	....	....	....	....	....	....	....	....	Uruguayan..	1	289	553	63,027
....	....	....	....	....	....	....	....	....	....	....	....	....	....	....	1	656
1	189	....	....	....	....	....	....	....	....	....	....	....	....	....	1	189
....	....	....	....	....	....	....	....	....	....	....	....	....	....	....	1	878
....	....	....	....	....	....	....	....	....	....	....	....	....	....	....	45	1,376
5	3,845	....	....	....	....	1	596	1	1,412		....	....	3	4,357	987	1,069,170
....	....	....	....	....	....	....	....	....	....	....	....	....	....	....	27	2,133
....	....	....	....	....	....	....	....	....	....	....	....	....	....	....	51	17,673
....	....	....	....	....	....	....	....	....	....	....	....	....	....	....	78	19,806
....	....	....	....	....	....	....	....	....	....	....	....	....	....	....	1	168
....	....	....	....	....	....	....	....	....	....	....	....	....	....	....	322	22,021
....	....	....	....	....	....	....	....	....	....	....	....	....	....	....	25	5,231
....	....	....	....	....	....	....	....	....	....	....	....	....	....	....	348	27,420
....	....	....	....	....	....	....	....	....	....	....	....	....	....	....	8	1,003
....	....	....	....	....	....	....	....	....	....	....	....	....	....	....	3	104
....	....	....	....	....	....	....	....	....	....	....	....	....	....	....	10	160
....	....	....	....	....	....	....	....	....	....	....	....	....	....	....	13	264
....	....	....	....	....	....	....	....	....	....	....	....	....	....	....	5	429
....	....	....	....	....	....	....	....	....	....	....	....	....	....	....	138	12,317
....	....	....	....	....	....	....	....	....	....	....	....	....	....	....	1	40
....	....	....	....	....	....	....	....	....	....	....	....	....	....	....	109	8,219
....	....	....	....	....	....	....	....	....	....	....	....	....	....	....	253	21,005
....	....	....	....	....	....	....	....	....	....	....	....	....	....	....	1	214
....	....	....	....	....	....	....	....	....	....	....	....	....	....	....	1	147
....	....	....	....	....	....	....	....	....	....	....	....	....	....	....	2	248
....	....	....	....	....	....	....	....	....	....	....	....	....	....	....	2	94
....	....	....	....	....	....	....	....	....	....	....	....	....	....	....	43	5,226
....	....	....	....	....	....	....	....	....	....	....	....	....	....	....	5	191
....	....	....	....	....	....	....	....	....	....	....	....	....	....	....	56	4,230
....	....	....	....	....	....	....	....	....	....	....	....	....	....	....	109	10,136

6 GEORGE V, A. 1916

No. 13.—STATEMENT of the Number and Tonnage of Sailing

Ports and Outports and Countries whence arrived.	British. Vessels	British. Tons Register.	United States. Vessels	United States. Tons Register.	Norwegian. Vessels	Norwegian. Tons Register.	Austrian. Vessels	Austrian. Tons Register.	Belgian. Vessels	Belgian. Tons Register.
Sherbrooke, N.S.—										
United States......... Sail.	1	357								
Shippegan, N.B.—										
Spain................. Sail.										
Sea fisheries......... Steam.	16	180								
Sea fisheries......... Sail.	63	917								
Total.................	79	1,097								
Sidney, B.C.—										
United States........ Steam.	49	1,248	17	443						
United States......... Sail.	7	760	10	494						
Total.................	56	2,008	27	937						
Souris, P.E.I.—										
British W. Indies..... Sail.	2	349								
Newfoundland........Steam.	1	44								
Newfoundland........ Sail.	1	38								
Saint Pierre............ "	2	213								
United States......... "	1	190								
Sea fisheries.......... "	59	2,706	26	2,168						
Total.................	66	3,540	26	2,168						
Steveston, B.C.—										
Great Britain.........Steam.	1	156								
United States......... "	123	4,160	29	1,542						
Sea fisheries.......... "	26	3,930								
Total.................	150	8,246	29	1,542						
Stickeen, B.C.—										
United States........ Steam.	5	1,576	40	484						
Summerside, P.E.I.—										
British W. Indies..... Sail.	1	199								
Newfoundland.......Steam.	1	856								
United States........ Sail.	2	462	6	3,049						
Total.................	4	1,517	6	3,049						
Sydney, N.S.—										
Great Britain........:..Steam.	24	71,403	1	337	9	17,650				
British West Indies... "	1	690			3	3,165	1	2,321		
Newfoundland........ "	78	65,562			65	152,568				
Newfoundland........ Sail.	23	2,018								
Brazil................Steam.	2	5,346								
France.............. "	2	4,234								
British S. Africa...... "					1	3,561				
Holland.............. "					3	7,349				
Italy................ "	6	16,040			1	2,712				
Egypt............... "					1	1,920				
Portugal.............. "	2	4,471								
Mexico.............. "					2	2,208				
Saint Pierre........... "										
Saint Pierre.......... Sail.	5	456								
United States........Steam.	27	47,856			27	52,645				
United States........ Sail.	3	514	2	680						
Argentina.............Steam.	4	10,355								
Canary Islands....... "	2	5,092								
San Domingo......... "	1	794								
Gibraltar............. "	1	2,250								
Uruguay.............. "	3	7,325								

and Steam Vessels entered Inwards *from Sea, &c.—Continued.*

OF VESSELS.

Danish.		French.		German.		Italian.		Russian.		Other Nationalities.			Total.	
Vessels.	Tons Register.	Vessels.	Tons Register.	Vessels.	Tons Register.	Vessels.	Tons Register.	Vessels.	Tons Register.	Names.	Vessels.	Tons Register.	Vessels.	Tons Register.
....	......	....	......	....	......	....	......	...	......	....	....	....	1	357
...	......	...	......	....		....	......	2	478	....	....	....	2	478
...	......	...	......	....	......	...	......	...	......	....	....	....	16	180
...	......	...	......	...	......	...	......	...	......	....	....	....	63	917
....	......	....	......	....	......	....	......	2	478	....	....	....	81	1,575
...	......	...	......	....	......	....	......	...	......	....	....	....	66	1,691
...	......	...	......	....	......	...	......	...	......	....	....	....	17	1,254
....	......	....	......	....	......	....	......	...	......	....	....	....	83	2,945
...	......	...	......	...	......	...	......	...	......	....	....	....	2	342
...	......	...	......	...	......	...	......	...	......	....	....	....	1	44
...	......	...	......	...	......	...	......	...	......	....	....	....	1	38
...	......	...	......	...	......	...	......	...	......	....	....	....	2	218
...	......	...	......	...	......	...	......	...	......	....	....	....	1	190
..	......	...	......	...	......	...	......	...	......	....	....	....	85	4,874
....	......	...	......	...	......	....	......	...	......	......▸.....	....	....	92	5,708
...	......	...	......	...	......	...	......	...	......	......⸱.....	....	..▸.....	1	156
...	......	...	......	...	......	...	......	...	......	....	....	....	152	5,702
...	......	...	......	...	......	...	......	...	......	....	....	....	26	3,930
....	......	...	......	...	......	...	......	...	......	....	....	....	179	9,788
....	......	...	......	....	......	...	......	...	......	....	....	....	45	2,060
...	......	...	......	...	......	...	......	...	......	....	....	......⸱.	1	199
...	......	...	......	...	......	...	......	...	......	....	....	....	1	856
...	......	...	......	...	......	...	......	...	......	....	....	....	8	3,511
....	......	...	......	...	......	...	......	...	......	....	....	....	10	4,566
2	2,724	...	......	...	..⸱.	...	......	...	......	....	....	....	36	92,114
3	3,068	...	......	...	......	...	......	...	......	....	....	....	8	9,244
....	......	...	......	...	......	.⸱.	......	...	......	....	....	....	143	218,130
...	......	...	......	...	......	...	......	...	......	....	....	....	23	2,018
...	......	...	......	...	......	...	......	...	......	....	....	....	2	5,346
...	......	...	......	...	......	...	......	...	......	....	....	....	2	4,234
...	......	...	......	...	......	...	......	...	......	....	....	....	1	3,561
1	1,249	...	......	...	......	...	......	...	......	....	.⸱.	....	3	7,349
...	......	...	......	...	......	...	......	...	......	....	...	....	8	20,001
...	......	...	......	...	......	...	......	...	......	....	...	....	1	1,920
...	......	...	......	...	......	...	......	...	......	....	...	....	2	4,471
...	......	1	208	...	......	...	......	...	......	....	...	....	2	2,208
..	......	...	......	...	..⸱.	...	......	...	......	....	...	....	1	208
2	2,947	...	......	⸱..	......	...	......	...	......	Cuban......	1	1,139	5	456
...	......	...	......	...	..▸..	...	......	...	......	....	...	....	57	104,587
...⸱	......	...	......	...	......	...	......	...	......	....	...	....	5	1,194
...	......	...	......	...	......	...	......	...	......	....	...	....	4	10,355
...	......	...	......	...	......	...	......	...	......	....	...	....	2	5,092
...	......	...	......	...	......	...	......	...	......	....	...	....	1	794
...	......	...	......	...	......	...	......	...	......	....	...	....	1	2,250
...	......	...	......	...	......	...	......	...	......	....	...	....	3	7,325

6 GEORGE V, A. 1916

No. 13.—STATEMENT of the Number and Tonnage of Sailing

Ports and Outports and Countries whence arrived.	British.		United States.		Norwegian.		Austrian.		Belgian.	
	Vessels.	Tons Register.	Vessels.	Tons Register.	Vessels.	Tons Register.	Vessels.	Tons Register.	Vessels.	Tons Register.
Sydney, N.S.—*Con.*										
French Africa........Steam.	1	2,827	....	....	....	....	....	....	....	....
Guatemala........... "	1	2,308	....	....	....	....	....	....	....	....
Denmark............ "	1	1,994	....	....	....	....	....	....	....	....
Sea Fisheries........ "	....	....								
Sea Fisheries........ Sail.	....	....	8	448	....	....	....	....	....	....
Total..............	187	251,535	11	1,465	112	243,778	1	2,321	....	....
Three Rivers, Que.—										
Great Britain........Steam.	20	48,873	....	....	....	....				
United States........ "	3	7,619	....	....	....	....				
Total..............	23	56,492	....	....	....	....				
Truro, N.S.—										
United States.......Sail.	4	420	1	388	....	....				
Tusket, N.S.—										
United States........ Sail.	1	14	1	122	....	....				
Sea Fisheries........ "	....	....	7	524	....	....				
Total..............	1	14	8	646	....	....				
Union Bay, B.C.—										
Great Britain........Steam.	1	4,278	....	....	....	....				
United States........ "	26	41,427	20	18,602	3	9,001				
United States........ Sail.	6	1,295	10	3,179	....	....				
Chili................Steam.	3	10,938	....	....	....	....				
Japan............... "	1	3,368	....	....	....	....				
Total..............	37	61,306	30	21,781	3	9,001				
Vancouver, B.C.—										
Great Britain........Steam.	20	91,991	....	....	....	....				
China................ "	13	71,166	....	....	....	....				
Japan............... "	4	18,530	....	....	....	....				
Belgium............. "	9	33,313	....	....	....	....				
Fiji Islands......... "	7	19,277	....	....	....	....				
Cuba................ "	1	2,802	....	....	....	....				
Australia............ "	17	87,857	....	....	....	....				
Germany............ "	....	....	....	....	....	....				
Norway............. "	....	....	....	....	....	....				
Chili................ "	....	....	1	621	....	....				
United States........ "	894	1,051,919	502	375,227	2	7,687				
United States........ Sail.	....	....	....	....	....	....				
Denmark............Steam.	1	2,895	....	....	....	....				
Peru................ "	5	12,842	1	3,863	2	4,397				
Peru................ Sail.	1	1,771	....	....	....	....				
Mexico..............Steam.	....	....	....	....	1	2,773				
Philippines.......... "	....	....	....	....	....	....				
Sea Fisheries........ "	75	6,385	18	2,187	....	....				
Total..............	1047	1,400,728	522	381,898	5	14,847	....	....	....	....
Victoria, B.C.—										
Great Britain........Steam.	32	141,595	....	....	....	....	....	....	....	....
Great Britain........ Sail.	1	1,389	....	....	....	....	....	....	....	....
Australia............Steam.	14	77,800	....	....	....	....	....	....	....	....
Australia............ Sail.	1	1,863	1	1,289	....	....	....	....	....	....
Chili................Steam.	1	3,139	....	....	....	....	....	....	....	....
Chili................ Sail.	....	....	....	....	1	1,395	....	....	....	....
France..............Steam.	....	....	....	....	....	....	....	....	....	....
China...............Steam.	13	71,166	....	....	....	....	....	....	....	....

and Steam Vessels entered Inwards *from Sea, &c.—Continued.*

OF VESSELS.

Danish.		French.		German.		Italian.		Russian.		Other Nationalities.			Total.	
Vessels.	Tons Register.	Vessels.	Tons Register.	Vessels.	Tons Register.	Vessels.	Tons Register.	Vessels.	Tons Register.	Names.	Vessels.	Tons Register.	Vessels.	Tons Register.
....	....	....	....	....	....	....	....	....	....		....	....	1	2,827
....	....	....	....	....	....	....	....	....	....		....	....	1	2,308
....	....	....	....	....	....	....	....	....	....		....	....	1	1,994
....	....	7	1,215	....	....	....	....	....	....		....	....	7	1,215
....	....	....	....	....	....	....	....	....	....		....	....	8	448
8	9,988	8	1,423	....	....	....	....	....	....		1	1,139	328	511,649
....	....	....	....	....	....	....	....	....	....		....	....	20	48,873
....	....	....	....	....	....	....	....	....	....		....	....	3	7,619
....	....	....	....	....	....	....	....	....	....		....	....	23	56,492
....	....	....	....	....	....	....	....	....	....		....	....	5	808
....	....	....	....	....	....	....	....	....	....		....	....	2	136
....	....	....	....	....	....	....	....	....	....		....	....	7	524
....	....	....	....	....	....	....	....	....	....		....	....	9	660
....	....	....	....	....	....	....	....	....	....		....	....	1	4,278
....	....	....	....	....	....	....	....	....	....		....	....	49	69,030
....	....	....	....	....	....	....	....	....	....		....	....	16	4,474
....	....	....	....	....	....	....	....	....	....		....	....	3	10,938
....	....	....	....	....	....	....	....	....	....	Dutch.....	1	2,487	2	5,855
....	....	....	....	....	....	....	....	....	....		1	2,487	71	94,575
....	....	....	....	....	....	....	....	....	....		....	....	20	91,991
....	....	....	....	....	....	....	....	....	....	Japanese....	4	15,325	17	86,491
....	....	....	....	....	....	....	....	2	5,885	Japanese....	12	40,278	18	64,693
....	....	....	....	....	....	....	....	....	....		....	....	9	33,313
....	....	....	....	....	....	....	....	....	....		....	....	7	19,277
....	....	....	....	....	....	....	....	....	....		....	....	1	2,802
....	....	....	....	....	....	....	....	....	....		....	....	17	87,857
1	2,675	....	....	1	3,176	....	....	....	....		....	....	1	3,176
....	....	....	....	....	....	....	....	....	....		....	....	1	2,675
....	....	....	....	....	....	....	....	....	....		....	....	1	621
....	....	....	....	1	2,527	....	....	1	3,368	Japanese....	3	9,816	1,402	1,448,017
2	6,096	....	....	....	....	....	....	....	....		....	....	1	2,527
....	....	....	....	....	....	....	....	....	....		....	....	3	8,991
....	....	....	....	....	....	....	....	....	....		....	....	8	21,092
....	....	....	....	....	....	....	....	1	1,465		....	....	2	3,236
....	....	....	....	....	....	....	....	....	....		....	....	1	2,773
....	....	....	....	....	....	....	....	....	....	Japanese....	1	3,833	1	3,833
....	....	....	....	....	....	....	....	....	....		....	....	93	8,552
3	8,771	....	....	2	5,703	....	....	4	10,718		20	69,252	1,603	1,891,917
....	....	....	....	....	....	....	....	....	....		....	....	32	141,595
....	....	....	....	....	....	....	....	....	....		....	....	1	1,389
....	....	....	....	....	....	....	....	....	....		....	....	14	77,800
....	....	....	....	....	....	....	....	....	....		....	....	2	3,152
....	....	....	....	....	....	....	....	....	....		....	....	1	3,139
....	....	....	....	3	9,317	....	....	1	1,866	Japanese....	23	87,338	2	3,261
....	....	....	....	....	....	....	....	....	....		....	....	39	167,821
....	....	....	....	....	....	....	....	....	....		....	....	....	....

6 GEORGE V, A. 1916

No. 13.—STATEMENT of the Number and Tonnage of Sailing

									NATIONALITY	
Ports and Outports and Countries whence arrived.	British.		United States.		Norwegian.		Austrian.		Belgian.	
	Vessels.	Tons Register.	Vessels.	Tons Register.	Vessels.	Tons Register.	Vessels.	Tons Register.	Vessels.	Tons Register.
Victoria, B.C.—*Con.*										
Japan.................Steam.	1	196	....	....	3	8,796	....	....	....	....
United States........ "	614	636,071	774	646,024	3	8,796	....	....	....	....
United States........ Sail.	54	9,276	21	9,666	....	....	....	....	....	....
Sea Fisheries........Steam.	31	1,010	....	....	....	....	....	....	....	....
Total................	762	943,505	796	656,979	4	10,191	....	....	....	....
Westport, N.S.—										
United States........ Sail.	14	2,147	30	438	....	....	....	....	....	....
Weymouth, N.S.—										
British West Indies... Sail.	1	194	....	....	....	....	....	....	....	....
United States........Steam.	....	....	....	....	1	689	....	....	....	....
United States........ Sail.	17	2,487	13	3,851	....	....	....	....	....	....
Total................	18	2,681	13	3,851	1	689	....	....	....	....
White Rock, B.C..										
United States........Steam.	63	510	55	335	....	....	....	....	....	....
Windsor, N.S.—										
United States........Steam.	5	45	....	....	20	14,040	....	....	....	....
United States........ Sail.	75	73,185	56	48,431	....	....	....	....	....	....
Total................	80	73,230	56	48,431	20	14,040	....	....	....	....
Wolfville, N.S.—										
United States........ Sail.	3	708	3	907	....	....	....	....	....	....
Yarmouth, N.S.—										
British West Indies... Sail.	4	862	....	....	....	....	....	....	....	....
Italy................. "	....	....	....	....	....	....	....	....	....	....
United States........Steam.	174	148,533	2	3,998	....	....	....	....	....	....
United States........ Sail.	48	7,281	31	1,527	1	1,345	....	....	....	....
Sea Fisheries........Steam.	2	22	....	....	....	....	....	....	....	....
Sea Fisheries........ Sail.	97	3,841	115	7,322	....	....	....	....	....	....
Total................	325	160,539	148	12,847	1	1,345	....	....	....	....

and Steam Vessels entered Inwards *from Sea, &c.—Concluded.*

or VESSELS.

Danish.		French.		German.		Italian.		Russian.		Other Nationalities.			Total.	
Vessels.	Tons Register.	Vessels.	Tons Register.	Vessels.	Tons Register.	Vessels.	Tons Register.	Vessels.	Tons Register.	Names.	Vessels.	Tons Register.	Vessels.	Tons Register.
....	......	...	......	...	......	...	......	...	......	Japanese....	28	108,153	29	108,349
1	2,675	...	......	...	......	...	......	...	......	Japanese....	40	189,658	}1,442	1,484,417
....	......	...	......	...	......	...	......	...	......	Mexican.....	1	1,193	}75	18,942
....	......	...	......	...	......	...	......	...	......	....	....	....	31	1,010
1	2,675	...	......	3	9,317	...	......	1	1,866	....	101	386,342	1,668	2,010,875
....	......	...	......	...	......	...	......	...	......	....	....	....	44	2,585
....	......	...	......	...	......	...	......	...	......		....	....	1	194
....	......	...	......	...	......	...	......	...	......		....	....	1	689
....	......	...	......	...	......	...	......	...	......		....	....	30	6,338
....	......	...	......	...	......	...	......	...	......		....	....	32	7,221
....	......	...	......	...	......	...	......	...	......		....	....	118	845
....	......	...	......	...	......	...	......	...	......		....	....	25	14,085
....	......	...	......	...	......	...	......	...	......		....	....	131	121,616
....	......	...	......	...	......	...	......	...	......		....	....	156	135,701
....	......	...	......	...	......	...	......	...	......		....	....	6	1,615
....	......	...	......	...	......	...	......	...	......		....	....	4	862
....	......	...	......	...	......	1	878	...	......		....	....	1	878
....	......	...	......	...	......	...	......	...	......		....	....	176	152,531
....	......	...	......	...	......	...	......	...	......		....	....	80	10,153
....	......	...	......	...	......	...	......	...	......		....	....	2	22
....	......	...	......	...	......	...	......	...	......		....	....	212	11,163
....	......	...	......	...	......	1	878	...	......		....	....	475	175,609

11—11—30½

No. 14.—SUMMARY STATEMENT of the Nationality,. of Sea-going Vessels entered
March 31,

		NATIONALITY								
	Countries from which Arrived.	British.		United States.		Norweigan.		Austrian.		Belgian.
Number.		Vessels.	Tons. Register.	Vessels.	Tons. Register.	Vessels.	Tons. Register.	Vessels.	Tons. Register.	Vessels.	Tons. Register.
1	United Kingdom........	1,216	4,294,291	1	337	49	75,886				
2	Australia...............	32	167,520	1	1,289						
3	British Guiana.........	1	1,980			1	1,987				
4	British West Africa.....	2	5,322								
5	British West Indies.....	170	240,126	2	1,593	34	29,395	1	2,321		
6	British South Africa.....	1	2,820	1	214	2	5,158				
7	Bermuda...............	2	4,259								
8	Gibraltar..............	4	10,271								
9	Fiji Islands...........	7	19,277								
10	Malta.................	1	2,737								
11	Newfoundland.........	1,100	467,700	12	1,042	92	185,432				
12	Argentina.............	18	44,727			1	899	1	2,321		
13	Aust.-Hungary.........							2	7,347		
14	Belgium...............	29	121,111								
15	Brazil.................	7	17,417			3	3,655				
16	Canary Islands.........	2	5,092								
17	Chili.................	8	25,018	1	621	1	1,395				
18	China.................	26	142,332								
19	Cuba.................	2	3,151			3	3,417				
20	Denmark.............	4	6,989			2	3,164				
21	Danish West Indies....					1	1,178				
22	Ecuador..............										
23	Egypt................	3	7,440			1	1,920				
24	France...............	31	116,883			3	4,689				
25	French West Indies.....					1	469				
26	French Africa..........	3	8,136								
27	Germany..............	1	2,110			2	3,674				
28	Greece...............	1	1,686								
29	Guatemala............	1	2,308								
30	Hayti................					1	878				
31	Holland..............	13	51,507			5	12,199			2	11,599
32	Greenland, Iceland, etc.										
33	Italy.................	33	84,274			3	7,946				
34	Japan................	6	22,094								
35	Mexico...............					5	7,189				
36	Norway..............	1	1,090	1	308	17	23,035				
37	Peru.................	6	14,613	1	3,863	2	4,387				
38	Portugal.............	14	27,292					1	2,758		
39	Porto Rico...........	1	293								
40	Philippines...........										
41	Russia...............										
42	San Domingo.........	6	4,705			9	6,924				
43	Spanish Africa.........	1	392								
44	St. Pierre.............	33	2,614								
45	Sea Fisheries..........	1,657	87,180	1,289	88,496	1	432				
46	Spain................	18	30,708					1	3,093		
47	Sweden..............					2	4,423				
48	Uruguay.............	5	10,493								
49	United States..........	4,934	3,321,187	5,543	2,037,179	196	279,547	1	3,093		
50	Sea..................	18	20,345	2	470						
	Total..........	9,418	9,399,490	6,854	2,135,412	437	669,278	7	20,933	2	11,599

Inwards, *from Sea*, from each Country, during the Fiscal Year ended 1915.

OF VESSELS.

Danish.		French.		German.		Italian.		Russian.		Other Nationalities.				Total.		
Vessels.	Tons. Register.	Vessels.	Tons. Register.	Vessels.	Tons. Register.	Vessels.	Tons. Register.	Vessels.	Tons. Register.	Name. of Flag.	Vessels.	Tons. Register.	Vessels.	Tons. Register.	Number.
28	38,514	....	....	....	....	....	....	4	2,664	Dutch.....	2	7,647	1,301	4,420,270	1
										Swedish...	1	931			
													33	168,809	2
2	2,192	....	....	....	....	....	....	....	....				4	6,159	3
													2	5,322	4
6	6,620	....	....	....	....	1	1,151	....	....	Panamanian	1	199	215	281,405	5
....	....	....	....	....	....	....	....	1	1,282				5	9,474	6
....	....	....	....	....	....	....	....	....	....				2	4,259	7
....	....	....	....	....	....	....	....	....	....				4	10,271	8
....	....	....	....	....	....	....	....	....	....				7	19,277	9
....	....	....	....	....	....	....	....	....	....				1	2,737	10
....	....	1	57	1	1,005	....	....	....	....	Dutch.....	1	1,299	1,207	656,535	11
....	....	....	....	....	....	....	....	....	....	Argentinian.	1	1,933	21	49,880	12
....	....	....	....	....	....	....	....	....	....				2	7,347	13
....	....	....	....	....	....	....	....	....	....	Dutch.....	1	5,489	30	126,600	14
....	....	....	....	....	....	1	1,280	....	....				11	22,352	15
....	....	....	....	....	....	....	....	....	....				2	5,092	16
....	....	....	....	....	....	1	1,866	....	....				11	28,900	17
1	877	....	....	3	9,317	....	....	....	....	Japanese..	27	102,663	56	254,312	18
6	7,738	....	....	....	....	....	....	....	....				6	7,445	19
....	....	....	....	....	....	....	....	....	....				12	17,891	20
....	....	....	....	1	3,084	....	....	....	....				1	1,178	21
....	....	....	....	....	....	....	....	....	....				1	3,084	22
....	....	....	....	....	....	....	....	....	....				4	9,360	23
....	....	29	28,828	....	....	....	....	1	968	Grecian.....	1	2,484	65	153,852	24
....	....	....	....	....	....	....	....	....	....				1	469	25
....	....	....	....	....	....	....	....	....	....				3	8,136	26
....	....	....	....	9	36,854	....	....	....	....				12	42,638	27
....	....	....	....	....	....	....	....	....	....				1	1,686	28
....	....	....	....	....	....	....	....	....	....				1	2,308	29
....	....	....	....	....	....	....	....	....	....				1	878	30
1	189	....	....	8	29,072	....	....	....	....	Dutch......	12	48,673	40	153,050	31
....	....	....	....	....	....	....	....	....	....				1	189	32
3	4,179	....	....	....	....	6	12,596	....	....	Grecian....	1	3,049	46	112,044	33
....	....	....	....	....	....	....	....	2	5,885	Dutch....	1	2,487	49	178,897	34
										Japanese...	40	148,431			
2	3,320	....	....	....	....	....	....	....	....				7	10,509	35
1	2,675	....	....	....	....	....	....	....	....				20	27,108	36
....	....	....	....	....	....	....	....	1	1,465				10	24,328	37
1	2,526	....	....	1	851	....	....	1	953				18	34,380	38
....	....	....	....	....	....	....	....	....	....				1	293	39
....	....	....	....	....	....	....	....	....	....	Japanese..	1	3,833	1	3,833	40
....	....	....	....	....	....	....	....	11	52,856				11	52,856	41
....	....	....	....	....	....	....	....	....	....				15	11,629	42
....	....	....	....	....	....	....	....	....	....				1	392	43
....	....	84	13,493	....	....	....	....	....	....				117	16,107	44
....	....	52	9,038	....	....	....	....	....	....				2,999	185,146	45
1	257	....	....	....	....	....	....	4	883	Spanish.....	2	4,234	26	39,175	46
....	....	....	....	....	....	....	....	....	....	Swedish....	3	4,595	5	9,018	47
....	....	....	....	....	....	....	....	....	....				5	10,493	48
										Cuban.....	1	1,139			
										Dutch.....	1	1,857			
										Mexican...	1	1,193			
13	20,969	1	4,080	5	12,148	2	2,192	3	6,578	Japanese...	52	199,474	10,762	5,908,060	49
										Spanish....	3	7,402			
										Swedish...	5	9,733			
										Uruguayan	1	289			
....	....	6	6,696	....	....	....	....	....	....				26	27,511	50
65	90,056	173	62,192	28	92,331	11	19,085	28	73,534	....	159	559,034	17,182	13,132,944	

6 GEORGE V, A. 1916

TRADE WITH EACH COUNTRY

No. 15.—STATEMENT of the Number and Tonnage of Sailing and Steam Vessels in Canada, for foreign countries, distinguishing the Nationality the Fiscal Year ended

										NATIONALITY
Ports and Outports and Countries for which Departed.	British.		United States.		Norwegian.		Austrian.		Belgian.	
	Vessels.	Tons Register.	Vessels.	Tons Register.	Vessels.	Tons Register.	Vessels.	Tons Register.	Vessels.	Tons Register.
Albert, N.B.—										
United States.........Sail....	1	98	1	360	....	....	....	....	....	....
Alert Bay, B.C.—										
United States.........Steam.	3	664	34	8,334	....	....	....	....	....	....
Sea Fisheries......... "	....	....	3	68	....	....	....	....	....	....
Total.................	3	664	37	8,402	....	....	....	....	....	....
Amherst, N.S.—										
Great Britain......... Sail.	....	....	....	....						
United States........ "	1	274	....	....						
Total............./.....	1	274	....	....						
Annapolis Royal, N.S.—										
British W. Indies.....Sail.	2	448	....	....						
Cuba................ "	1	249	....	....						
United States........ "	2	271	....	....						
Total...............	5	968	....	....						
Anyox, B.C.—										
United States.........Steam.	26	19,169	9	7,168	....	....	....	....	....	....
Arichat, N.S.—										
United States......... Sail.	....	....	3	134	....	....				
Sea Fisheries......... "	83	1,969	25	2,287	....	....				
Total.................	83	1,969	28	2,421	....	....				
Baddeck, N.S.—										
Newfoundland........Steam.	18	24,916								
Saint Pierre.......... "	1	46	....	....						
United States........ "	1	1,682	....	....	13	13,508				
Sea Fisheries......... Sail.	48	2,072	26	1,660	....	....				
Total.................	68	28,716	26	1,660	13	13,508				
Barrington, N.S.—										
United States......... Sail.	....	....	1	266	....					
Sea Fisheries......... "	11	456	48	2,141	....	....				
Total.................	11	456	49	2,407	....	....				
Barton, N.S.—										
United States......... Sail.	29	3,211	....	....						
Bathurst, N.B.—										
Cuba................Steam.	....	....	....	....	3	2,405	....			
Cuba................Sail....	....	....	1	440	....	....				
United States........Steam.	....	....	....	....	.. 1	446	....	....		
United States........Sail....	14	2,499	10	5,092	....	....				
Total.................	14	2,499	11	5,532	4	2,851	....	....	....	....

SESSIONAL PAPER No. 11

AND NATIONALITY OF VESSELS.

entered outwards, *for Sea,* at each of the undermentioned Ports and Outports of the Vessels employed in the trade with each country, during March 31, 1915.

OF VESSELS.

Danish.		French.		German.		Italian.		Russian.		Other Nationalities.			Total.	
Vessels.	Tons Register.	Vessels.	Tons Register.	Vessels.	Tons Register.	Vessels.	Tons Register.	Vessels.	Tons Register.	Names.	Vessels.	Tons Register.	Vessels.	Tons Register.
....	......	....	......	....	......	....	......	....	......		....	....	2	458
....	......	....	......	....	......	....	......	....	......		....	....	37	8,998
....	......	....	......	....	......	....	......	....	......		....	....	3	68
....		....	......	....	......	....	......	....	......		....	....	40	9,066
1	703	....	......	....	......	....	......	....	......		....	....	1	703
....	......	....	......	....	......	....	......	....,	......		....	....	1	274
1	703	....	......	....	......	....	......	....	......		....	....	2	977
....	......	....	......	....	......	....	......	....	......		....	....	2	448
....	......	....	......	....	......	....	......	....	......		....	....	1	249
....	......	....	......	....	......	....	......	....	......		....	....	2	271
....	......	....	......	....	......	....	......	....	......		....	....	5	968
....	......	....	......	....	......	....	......	....	......		....	....	35	26,337
....	......	....	......	....	......	....	......	....	......		....	....	3	134
....	......	....	......	....	......	....	......	....	......		....	....	108	4,256
....	......	....	......	....	......	....	......	....	......		....	....	111	4,390
....	......	....	......	....	......	....	......	....	......		....	....	18	24,916
....	......	....	......	....	......	....	......	....	......		....	....	1	46
....	......	....	......	....	......	....	......	....	......		....	....	14	15,190
....	......	1	57	....	......	....	......	....	......		....	....	75	3,789
....	......	1	57	....	......	....	......	....	......		....	....	108	43,941
....	......	....	......	....	......	....	......	....	......		....	....	1	266
....	......	....	......	....	......	....	......	....	......		....	....	59	2,597
....	......	....	......	....	......	....	......	....	......		....	....	60	2,863
....	......	....	......	....	......	....	......	....	......		....	....	29	3,211
....	......	....	......	....	......	....	......	....	......		....	....	3	2,405
....	......	....	......	....	......	....	......	....	......		....	....	1	440
....	......	....	......	....	......	....	......	....	......		....	....	1	446
....	......	....	......	....	......	....	......	....	......		....	....	24	7,591
....	......	....	......	....	......	....	......	....	......		....	....	29	10,882

6 GEORGE V, A. 1916

No. 15.—STATEMENT of the Number and Tonnage of Sailing

Ports and Outports and Countries for which Departed.	British.		United States.		Norwegian.		Austrian.		Belgian.	
	Vessels.	Tons Register.	Vessels.	Tons Register.	Vessels.	Tons Register.	Vessels.	Tons Register.	Vessels.	Tons Register.
Bear River, N.S.—										
British W. Indies.....Sail...	1	161	....	....	....	....	....	....	....	....
Cuba................... " ...	2	669	....	....	....	....	....	....	....	....
United States......... " ...	18	2,918	....	....	....	....	....	....	....	....
Total....................	21	3,748	....	....	....	....	....	....	....	....
Belliveau's Cove, N.S.—										
British W. Indies.....Sail...	4	743	....	....	....	....	....	....	....	....
United States......... " ...	1	123	....	....	....	....	....	....	....	....
Grand Total............	5	866	....	....	....	....	....	....	....	....
Bridgetown, N.S.—										
United States.........Sail...	1	149	1	134	....	....	....	....	....	....
Bridgewater, N.S.—										
British W. Indies.....Sail...	1	249	....	....	....	....	....	....	....	....
Argentina............ " ...	....	....	....	....	1	1,597	....	....	....	....
Cuba.............:.. " ...	2	683	3	1,264	1	874	....	....	....	....
Azores and Madeira... " ...	3	776	....	....	....	....	....	....	....	....
Brazil............... " ...	....	....	1	1,488	1	1,344	....	....	....	....
Porto Rico........... " ...	2	586	2	732	....	....	....	....	....	....
United States........ " ...	54	16,062	25	10,455	....	....	....	....	....	....
Total.................	62	18,356	31	13,939	3	3,815	....	....	....	....
Buctouche, N.B.—										
Great Britain.........Sail...	....	....	....	....	1	204	....	....	....	....
Campbellton, N.B.—										
Great Britain.........Steam.	5	9,228	....	....	4	5,670	....	....	7	10,142
Great Britain.........Sail...	....	....	....	....	1	566	....	....	1	257
British W. Indies..... " ...	3	461	....	....	....	....	....	....	....	....
Australia........... " ...	....	....	....	....	1	1,954	....	....	....	....
Argentina........... " ...	....	....	....	....	2	2,269	....	....	....	....
Uruguay............. " ...	....	....	....	....	....	....	....	....	....	....
United States.........Steam.	....	....	....	....	4	2,710	....	....	....	....
United States.........Sail...	4	813	4	1,920	....	....	....	....	....	....
Total.................	12	10,502	4	1,920	12	13,169	....	....	8	10,399
Campo Bello, N.B.—										
United States.........Steam.	157	26,269	28	452	....	....	....	....	....	....
Canning, N.S—										
Cuba....,..........Sail...	2	847	....	....	....	....	....	....	....	....
Canso, N.S.—										
British W. Indies.....Sail...	1	97	....	....	....	....	....	....	....	....
Newfoundland........ " ...	1	109	1	89	....	....	....	....	....	....
United States.........Steam.	1	67	4	235	....	....	....	....	....	....
United States........Sail...	15	2,183	24	3,262	....	....	....	....	....	....
Sea Fisheries.........Steam.	41	7,206	31	1,286	....	....	....	....	....	....
Sea Fisheries.........Sail...	62	5,449	176	14,442	....	....	....	....	....	....
Total....................	121	15,111	236	19,314	....	....	....	....	....	....
Caraquet, N.B.—										
United States.........Sail...	2	180	....	....	....	....	....	....	....	....
Sea Fisheries.........Steam.	2	22	....	....	....	....	....	....	....	....
Sea Fisheries.........Sail...	164	2,247	....	....	....	....	....	....	....	....
Total....................	168	2,449	....	....	....	....	....	....	....	....

and Steam Vessels entered Outwards *for Sea, &c.—Continued.*

or VESSELS.

Danish.		French.		German.		Italian.		Russian.		Other Nationalities.			Total.	
Vessels.	Tons Register.	Vessels.	Tons Register.	Vessels.	Tons Register.	Vessels.	Tons Register.	Vessels.	Tons Register.	Names.	Vessels.	Tons Register.	Vessels.	Tons Register.
....	......	....	......	....	......	....	......	....	......		....	......	1	161
....	......	....	......	....	......	....	......	....	......		....	......	2	669
....	......	....	......	....	......	....	......	....	......		....	......	18	2,918
....	......	....	......	....	......	....	......	....	......		....	......	21	3,748
....	......	....	......	....	......	....	......	....	......		....	......	4	743
....	......	....	......	....	......	....	......	....	......		....	......	1	123
....	......	....	......	....	......	....	......	....	......		....	......	5	866
....	......	....	......	....	......	....	......	....	......		....	......	2	283
....	......	....	......	....	......	....	......	....	......		....	......	1	249
....	......	....	......	....	......	....	......	....	......	Argentinean	1	1,933	2	3,530
....	......	....	......	....	......	....	......	....	......		....	......	6	2,821
....	......	....	......	....	......	....	......	....	......		....	......	3	776
....	......	....	......	....	......	1	1,173	....	......		....	......	3	4,005
....	......	....	......	....	......	....	......	....	......		....	......	4	1,318
....	......	....	......	....	......	....	......	....	......		....	......	79	26,517
....	......	....	......	....	......	1	1,173	....	......		1	1,933	98	39,216
....	......	....	......	....	......	....	......	....	......		....	......	1	204
....	......	....	......	....	......	....	......	....	......		....	......	16	25,040
....	......	....	......	....	......	....	......	2	1,265		....	......	4	2,088
....	......	....	......	....	......	....	......	....	......		....	......	3	461
....	......	....	......	....	......	....	......	1	1,282		....	......	2	3,236
....	......	....	......	....	......	2	2,164	....	......		....	......	4	4,433
....	......	....	......	....	......	1	992	....	......		....	......	1	992
....	......	....	......	1	1,005	....	......	....	......		....	......	5	3,715
....	......	....	......	....	......	....	......	....	......		....	......	8	2,733
....	......	....	......	1	1,005	3	3,156	3	2,547		....	......	43	42,698
....	......	....	......	....	......	....	......	....	......		....	......	185	26,721
....	......	....	......	....	......	....	......	....	......		....	......	2	847
....	......	....	......	....	......	....	......	....	......		....	......	1	97
....	......	....	......	....	......	....	......	....	......		....	......	2	198
....	......	....	......	....	......	....	......	....	......		....	......	5	302
....	......	....	......	....	......	....	......	....	......		....	......	39	5,445
....	......	....	......	....	......	....	......	....	......		....	......	72	8,492
....	......	....	......	....	......	....	......	....	......		....	......	238	19,891
....	......	....	......	....	......	....	......	....	......		....	......	357	34,425
....	......	....	......	....	......	....	......	....	......		....	......	2	180
....	......	....	......	....	......	....	......	....	......		....	......	2	22
....	......	....	......	....	......	....	......	....	......		....	......	164	2,247
....	......	....	......	....	......	....	......	....	......		....	......	168	2,449

6 GEORGE V, A. 1916

No. 15.—STATEMENT of the Number and Tonnage of Sailing

Ports and Outports and Countries for which Departed.	British.		United States.		Norwegian.		Austrian.		Belgian.	
	Vessels.	Tons Register.	Vessels.	Tons Register.	Vessels.	Tons Register.	Vessels.	Tons Register.	Vessels.	Tons Register.
Cardigan, P.E.I.—										
Newfoundland, ... Sail....	1	76	....	....			....	....	....	....
Charlottetown, P.E.I.—										
Newfoundland........Steam.	25	22,635	....	....	....	....	....	....	....	....
Newfoundland........ Sail.	15	786	....	....	....	....	....	....	....	....
France...............Steam.	1	857	....	....	....	....	....	....	....	....
Saint Pierre.......... Sail.	5	390	..	....	....	....	....	....	....	....
United States........Steam.	30	51,436	2	1,269	....	....	....	....	....	....
Sea Fisheries......... Sail.	4	68	....	....	....	....	....	....	....	....
Total..................	80	76,172	2	1,269	....	....	....	....	....	....
Chatham, N.B.—										
Great Britain.........Steam.	8	15,491	....	....	4	6,227	....	....	....	....
Great Britain......... Sail.	1	165	....	....	1	1,036	....	....	....	....
Newfoundland........ "	1	84	....	....	.*.	....	....	....	....	....
United States........Steam.	25	59,007	....	....	....	....	....	....	....	....
United States........ Sail.	5	1,134	....	....	....	....	....	....	....	....
Total..................	40	75,881	....	....	5	7,263	....	....	....	....
Chemainus, B..C.										
United States........Steam.	19	7,398	5	301	....	....	....	....		
B. Oceania, other.....Steam.	1	2,829	....	....	....	....				
B. South Africa....... Sail.	....	....	.: .	....	....	....				
Chili................ "	..	....	1	776	....	....				
Total..................	20	10,227	6	1,077	....	....				
Chester, N.S.—										
United States........ Sail.	5	1,112	5	1,477	....	....				
Sea Fisheries.........Steam.	11	123	1	77	....	....				
Sea Fisheries......... Sail.	13	151	....	....	....	....				
Total..................	29	1,386	6	1,554		....	....	....	....	....
Cheticamp, N.S.—										
United States........Steam.	....	....	....	....	4	2,872	....	....	....	....
Chicoutimi, Que.—										
Great Britain.........Steam.	16	33,153	....	....	1	1,850	....	....	....	....
France .... "	....	....	....	....	..	....				
United States,....... "	1	690	....	....	3	3,307	....	....	....	....
Total..................	17	33,843	....	....	4	5,157	....	....	....	....
Church Point, N.S.—										
United States........ Sail.	10	1,194	....	....						
Clarks Harbour, N.S.—										
United States........Steam.	9	572	....	....	....	....				
United States........ Sail.	....	....	18	305	....	....				
Sea Fisheries......... "	12	409	10	637	....	....				
Total..................	21	981	28	942	....	....	....	....	....	....
Clementsport, N.S.—										
United States........Sail.	17	2,228	....	....	....	....	....	....	....	....

and Steam Vessels entered Outwards *for Sea, &c.—Continued.*

OF VESSELS.

Danish.		French.		German.		Italian.		Russian.		Other Nationalities.			Total.	
Vessels.	Tons Register.	Vessels.	Tons Register.	Vessels.	Tons Register.	Vessels.	Tons Register.	Vessels.	Tons Register.	Names.	Vessels.	Tons Register.	Vessels.	Tons Register.
....	......	....	......	....	......	....	......	....	......	....	....	......	1	76
....	......	....	......	....	......	....	......	....	......	....	....	......	25	22,635
....	......	....	......	....	.....	....	......	....	......	....	....	......	15	786
....	......	....	......	....	......	....	......	....	......	....	....	......	1	857
....	......	....	......	....	......	....	......	....	......	....	....	......	5	390
....	......	....	......	....	......	....	......	....	......	....	....	......	32	52,705
....	......	....	......	....	......	....	......	....	......	....	....	......	4	68
....	......	....	......	....	......	....	......	....	......	....	....	......	82	77,441
3	4,271	....	......	1	2,249	....	......	....	......	....	....	......	16	28,238
....	......	....	......	..	......	....	......	1	213	....	....	......	3	1,414
....	......	....	......	....	......	....	......	....	......	....	....	......	1	84
....	......	....	......	....	......	....	......	....	......	....	....	......	25	59,007
....	......	....	......	....	......	....	......	....	......	....	....	......	5	1,134
3	4,271	....	......	1	2,249	....	......	1	213	....	....	......	50	89,877
....	......	....	......	....	......	....	......	....	......	....	....	......	24	7,699
....	......	....	......	....	......	....	......	....	......	....	....	......	1	2,829
....	......	....	......	....	......	....	......	1	1,866	....	....	......	1	1,866
....	......	....	......	....	......	....	......	....	......	....	....	......	1	776
....	......	....	......	....	......	....	......	1	1,866	....	....	......	27	13,170
....	......	....	......	..	......	....	......	....	......	....	....	......	10	2,589
....	......	....	......	..	—	....	......	....	......	....	....	......	12	200
....	......	....	......	....	......	....	......	....	......	....	....	......	13	151
....	......	....	......	....	......	....	......	....	......	....	....	......	35	2,940
....	......	....	......	....	......	....	......	....	......	Dutch......	1	1,299	5	4,171
1	846	....	......	....	......	....	......	....	......	....	....	......	18	35,849
1	1,547	....	......	....	......	....	......	....	......	....	....	......	1	1,547
4	4,992	....	......	....	......	....	......	....	......	....	....	......	8	8,989
6	7,385	....	......	....	......	....	......	....	......	....	....	......	27	46,385
....	......	....	......	....	......	....	......	....	......	....	....	......	10	1,194
....	......	....	......	....	......	....	......	....	......	....	....	......	9	572
....	......	....	......	....	......	....	......	....	......	....	....	......	18	305
....	......	....	......	....	......	....	......	....	......	....	....	......	22	1,046
....	......	....	......	....	......	....	......	....	......	....	....	......	49	1,923
....	......	....	......	..	......	....	......	....	......	....	....	......	17	2,228

6 GEORGE V, A. 1916

No. 15.—Statement of the Number and Tonnage of Sailing

Ports and Outports and Countries for which Departed.	British.		United States.		Norwegian.		Austrian.		Belgian.	
	Vessels.	Tons Register.	Vessels.	Tons Register.	Vessels.	Tons Register.	Vessels.	Tons Register.	Vessels.	Tons Register.
Dalhousie, N.B.—										
Great Britain........Steam.	5	9,550								
British W. Indies..... Sail.	1	199								
Saint Pierre.......... "	1	56								
United States.......Steam.	7	8,483	13	13,226						
United States........ Sail.	4	1,136	3	1,620						
Australia............ "										
Total...............	18	19,424	16	14,846						
Digby, N.S.—										
United States........ Sail.	16	1,670	15	905						
Dorchester, N.B.—										
United States.......Steam.					1	788				
United States........ Sail.	5	739	2	677						
Total...............	5	739	2	677	1	788				
Fredericton, N.B.—										
United States........ Sail.	6	1,737	9	2,050						
Gaspé, Que.—										
Great Britain........Steam.			1	1,572	1	2,136				
Great Britain........ Sail.					1	1,029		—		
British W. Indies..... "	2	347								
United States.......Steam.	11	11,725	10	9,539	1	878				
United States........ Sail.	7	1,085								
Total...............	20	13,157	11	11,111	3	4,043				
Georgetown, P.E.I.—										
Newfoundland,....... Sail.	8	542								
Saint Pierre.......... "	1	64								
Sea Fisheries........ "	1	39								
Total...............	10	645								
Glace Bay, N.S.—										
Great Britain........Steam.	18	1,973								
Great Britain........ Sail.	188	9,116								
Saint Pierre.......... "										
Sea Fisheries........ "			1	43						
Total...............	206	11,089	1	43						
Halifax, N.S.—										
Great Britain........Steam.	138	597,945			11	10,860				
Great Britain........ Sail.	8	3,287			6	5,551				
British W. Indies.....Steam.					24	17,850				
British W. Indies ... Sail.	5	1,287								
Newfoundland.......Steam.	52	73,286			3	4,218				
Newfoundland........ Sail.	48	4,085	2	227						
Denmark............Steam.					1	3,578				
Brazil............... Sail.	6	1,340								
Cuba...............Steam.					3	2,773				
Cuba.......\....... Sail.	1	249								
France.............Steam.	1	2,572								
British Guiana....... "	26	74,096								
British Guiana........ Sail.	2	447								
Holland.............Steam.			1	2,086	3	5,515				
British South Africa.. "	1	2,199								
Norway.............. "					1	765				
Uruguay............. Sail.					1	1,297				
Portugal........... "										

and Steam Vessels entered Outwards *for Sea, &c.—Continued.*

OF VESSELS.

Danish.		French.		German.		Italian.		Russian.		Other Nationalities.			Total.	
Vessels.	Tons Register.	Vessels.	Tons Register.	Vessels.	Tons Register.	Vessels.	Tons Register.	Vessels.	Tons Register.	Names.	Vessels.	Tons Register.	Vessels.	Tons Register.
										Greecian....	1	3,049	6	12,599
													1	199
													1	56
													20	21,709
													7	2,756
								1	1,282				1	1,282
								1	1,282		1	3,049	36	38,601
													31	2,575
													1	788
													7	1,416
													8	2,204
													15	3,787
													2	3,708
													1	1,029
													2	347
1	876												23	23,018
													7	1,085
1	876												35	29,187
													8	542
													1	64
													1	39
													10	645
													18	1,973
													188	9,116
		3	138										3	138
													1	43
		3	138										210	11,270
2	2,631									Swedish....	2	3,170	153	614,606
				1	1,151	1	590						16	10,579
													24	17,850
													5	1,287
													55	77,504
													50	4,312
1	2,199												2	5,777
													6	1,340
													3	2,773
													1	249
													1	2,572
													26	74,096
													2	447
													4	7,601
													1	2,199
													1	765
													1	1,297
										Portuguese..	1	25	1	25

No. 15.—Statement of the Number and Tonnage of Sailing

Ports and Outports and Countries for which Departed.	British. Vessels.	British. Tons Register.	United States. Vessels.	United States. Tons Register.	Norwegian. Vessels.	Norwegian. Tons Register.	Austrian. Vessels.	Austrian. Tons Register.	Belgian. Vessels.	Belgian. Tons Register.
Halifax, N.S.—*Con.*										
Russia...............Steam.	1	291								
Saint Pierre........ "										
Saint Pierre......... Sail.	4	364								
Spain...............Steam.										
Sweden............. "					1	686				
United States........ "	165	417,745	6	1,058	16	29,085	1	4,536		
United States.......Sail.	47	7,351	48	15,334						
Sea..................Steam.	21	22,838								
Argentina............ "					1	1,145				
Hayti............... "					1	684				
Danish West Indies... Sail.	1	259								
Egypt...............Steam.			1	2,659						
Sea Fisheries........ "	2	359								
Sea Fisheries........ Sail.	365	17,366	70	4,662						
Total...............	894	1,227,366	128	26,026	72	84,007	1	4,536		
Hantsport, N.S.—										
United States........Steam	2	18	6	1,986						
United States........ Sail.	4	756	9	2,999						
Total...............	6	774	15	4,985						
Hillsboro, N.B.—										
United States.......Steam.					24	16,656				
United States........ Sail.	10	6,249	7	2,734						
Total...............	10	6,249	7	2,734	24	16,656				
Indian Island, N.B.—										
United States.......Steam.	7	51	92	762						
Isaacs Harbour, N.S.—										
Newfoundland........ Sail.			1	74						
United States........ "	5	514								
Sea Fisheries......... "			12	728						
Total...............	5	514	13	802						
Joggins Mines, N.S.—										
United States....... Sail.	20	2,834	13	3,485						
Kentville, N.S.—										
Cuba................ Sail.	2	600								
United States......... "	1	74								
Total...............	3	674								
Kingsport, N.S.—										
Cuba...............Steam.	3	2,251								
Cuba................ Sail.	3	865								
Total...............	6	3,116								
Ladner, B.C.—										
United States........Steam.	11	284								
Ladysmith, B.C.—										
United States........Steam.	30	2,256	39	18,784						
United States........ Sail.	11	1,785	26	5,428						
Sea Fisheries........Steam.	1	37								
Total...............	42	4,078	65	24,212						

and Steam Vessels entered Outwards *for Sea, &c.—Continued.*

OF VESSELS.

	Danish.		French.		German.		Italian.		Russian.		Other Nationalities.			Total.	
	Vessels.	Tons Register.	Vessels.	Tons Register.	Vessels.	Tons Register.	Vessels.	Tons Register.	Vessels.	Tons Register.	Names.	Vessels.	Tons Register.	Vessels.	Tons Register.
	....	......	....	......	....	......	....	......	....	......	....	....	....	1	291
	....	......	15	3,252	....	......	....	......	....	......	....	....	....	15	3,252
	....	......	....	......	....	......	....	......	....	......	....	....	....	4	364
	....	......	....	......	....	......	....	......	....	......	Spanish....	1	2,306	1	2,306
	....	......	....	......	....	......	....	......	....	......	....	....	....	1	686
											Swedish...	3	3,470		
	1	1,098	2	6,683	5	23,701	1	5,846	11	52,856	Dutch.....	2	10,586		
											Spanish...	1	2,351	214	559,015
	....	......	7	7,812	....	......	....	......	....	......	....	....	....	95	22,685
	....	......	....	......	....	......	....	......	....	......	....	....	....	28	30,650
	....	......	....	......	....	......	....	......	....	......	....	....	....	1	1,145
	....	......	....	......	....	......	....	......	....	......	....	....	....	1	684
	....	......	....	......	....	......	....	......	....	......	....	....	....	1	259
	....	......	1	94	....	......	....	......	....	......	....	....	....	1	2,659
	....	......	....	......	....	......	....	......	....	......	....	....	....	3	453
	....	......	....	......	....	......	....	......	....	......	....	....	....	435	22,028
	4	5,928	25	17,841	5	23,701	2	6,997	12	53,446	....	10	21,908	1,153	1,471,756
	....	......	....	......	....	......	....	......	....	......	....	....	....	8	2,004
	....	......	....	......	....	......	....	......	....	......	....	....	....	13	3,755
	....	......	....	......	....	......	....	......	....	......	....	....	....	21	5,759
	....	......	....	......	....	......	....	......	....	......	....	....	....	24	16,656
	....	......	....	......	....	......	....	......	....	......	....	....	....	17	8,983
	....	......	....	......	....	......	....	......	....	......	....	....	....	41	25,639
	....	......	....	......	....	......	....	......	....	......	....	....	....	99	813
	....	......	....	......	....	......	....	......	....	......	....	....	....	1	74
	....	......	....	......	....	......	....	......	....	......	....	....	....	5	514
	....	......	....	......	....	......	....	......	....	......	....	....	....	12	728
	....	......	....	......	....	......	....	......	....	......	....	....	....	18	1,316
	....	......	....	......	....	......	....	......	....	......	....	....	....	33	6,319
	....	......	....	......	....	......	....	......	....	......	....	....	....	2	600
	....	......	....	......	....	......	....	......	....	......	....	....	....	1	74
	....	......	....	......	....	......	....	......	....	......	....	....	....	3	674
	....	......	....	......	....	......	....	......	....	......	....	....	....	3	2,251
	....	......	....	......	....	......	....	......	....	......	....	....	....	3	865
	....	......	....	......	....	......	....	......	....	......	....	....	....	6	3,116
	....	......	....	......	....	......	....	......	....	......	....	....	....	11	284
	....	......	....	......	....	......	....	......	....	......	....	....	....	69	21,040
	....	......	....	......	....	......	....	......	....	......	....	....	....	37	7,213
	....	......	....	......	....	......	....	......	....	......	....	....	....	1	37
	....	......	....	......	....	......	....	......	....	......	....	....	....	107	28,290

6 GEORGE V, A. 1916

No. 15.—STATEMENT of the Number and Tonnage of Sailing

					NATIONALITY					
Ports and Outports and Countries for which Departed.	British.		United States.		Norwegian.		Austrian.		Belgian.	
	Vessels.	Tons Register.	Vessels.	Tons Register.	Vessels.	Tons Register.	Vessels.	Tons Register.	Vessels.	Tons Register.
La Have, N.S.—										
Newfoundland........ Sail.	6	705								
United States.........Steam.	1	248								
United States......... Sail.	16	2,744								
Sea Fisheries.........Steam.			1	28						
Sea Fisheries......... Sail.	78	6,059	8	517						
Total..................	101	9,756	9	545						
Liverpool, N.S.—										
British W. Indies..... Sail.	5	1,196								
Newfoundland........ "	1	109	2	199						
Cuba................ "	1	249								
Portugal............. "	1	249								
United States.........Steam.			15	412						
United States......... Sail.	39	5,818	24	6,225						
Sea Fisheries.........Steam.			77	3,675						
Sea Fisheries......... Sail.	1	109	107	8,396						
Total..................	48	7,730	225	18,907						
Lockeport, N.S.—										
Newfoundland........ Sail.	1	38								
United States.........Steam.	3	96								
United States......... Sail.			7	97						
Sea Fisheries.........Steam.	4	555								
Sea Fisheries......... Sail.	49	1,722	66	4,654						
Total..................	57	2,411	73	4,751						
Lord's Cove, N.B.—										
United States.........Steam.	305	13,730	145	1,311						
United States....... Sail.			1	83						
Total..................	305	13,730	146	1,394						
Louisburg, N.S.—										
Great Britain.........Steam.	12	23,945			17	17,936				
British W. Indies..... Sail.					1	961				
Newfoundland........Steam.	49	27,453								
Newfoundland........ Sail.	41	4,207	6	475						
France...............Steam.	2	4,258								
Holland............. "	1	2,534								
Italy................ "	1	2,737								
Norway............. "					3	2,988				
Saint Pierre........... Sail.	2	191								
Spain................Steam.					1	688				
United States........ "	46	71,609			33	70,490				
United States......... Sail.	1	84	3	258						
Greenland,Iceland,etc.Steam.					1	718				
Sea Fisheries.........Steam.	3	562								
Sea Fisheries......... Sail.	10	799	192	9,791						
Total..................	168	138,379	201	10,524	56	93,781				
Lower East Pubnico, N.S.—										
United States......... Sail.	6	356	5	219						
Sea Fisheries......... "	36	1,657	32	1,880						
Total..................	42	2,013	37	2,099						

SESSIONAL PAPER No. 11

and Steam Vessels entered Outwards *for Sea, &c.—Continued.*

OF VESSELS.

Danish.		French.		German.		Italian.		Russian.		Other Nationalities.			Total.	
Vessels.	Tons Register.	Vessels.	Tons Register.	Vessels.	Tons Register.	Vessels.	Tons Register.	Vessels.	Tons Register.	Names.	Vessels.	Tons Register.	Vessels.	Tons Register.
...	......	...	......	...	......	...	......	...	......		...	......	6	705
...	......	...	......	...	......	...	......	...	......		...	......	1	248
...	......	...	......	...	......	...	......	...	......		...	......	16	2,744
...	......	...	......	...	......	...	......	...	......		...	......	1	28
...	......	...	......	...	......	...	......	...	......		...	......	86	6,576
...	......	...	......	...	......	...	......	...	......		...	......	110	10,301
...	......	...	......	...	......	...	......	...	......		...	......	5	1,196
...	......	...	......	...	......	...	......	...	......		...	......	3	308
...	......	...	......	...	......	...	......	...	......		...	......	1	249
...	......	...	......	...	......	...	......	...	......		...	......	1	249
...	......	...	......	...	......	...	......	...	......		...	......	15	412
...	......	...	......	...	......	...	......	...	......		...	......	63	12,043
...	......	...	......	...	......	...	......	...	......		...	......	77	3,675
...	......	...	......	...	......	...	......	...	......		...	......	108	8,505
...	......	...	......	...	......	...	......	...	......		...	......	273	26,637
.	......	...	......	...	......	...	......	...	......		...	......	1	38
...	......	...	......	...	......	...	......	...	......		...	......	3	96
...	......	...	......	...	......	...	......	...	......		...	......	7	97
...	......	...	......	...	......	...	......	...	......		...	......	4	555
...	......	...	......	...	......	...	......	...	......		...	......	115	6,376
...	......	...	......	...	......	...	......	...	......		...	......	130	7,162
...	......	...	......	...	......	...	......	...	......		...	......	450	15,041
...	......	...	......	...	......	...	......	...	......		...	......	1	83
...	......	...	......	...	......	...	......	...	......		...	......	451	15,124
3	3,188	...	......	1	1,904	...	......	...	......	Swedish....	1	1,963	34	48,936
...	......	...	......	...	......	...	......	...	......		...	......	1	961
...	......	...	......	1	1,005	...	......	...	......		...	......	50	28,458
...	......	...	......	...	......	...	......	...	......		...	......	47	4,682
...	......	...	......	...	......	...	......	...	......		...	......	2	4,258
...	......	...	......	...	......	...	......	...	......		...	......	1	2,534
...	......	...	......	...	......	...	......	...	......		...	......	1	2,737
...	......	3	189	...	......	...	......	...	......		...	......	3	2,988
...	......	...	......	...	......	...	......	...	......		...	......	5	380
...	......	...	......	...	......	...	......	...	......		...	......	1	688
3	3,773	...	......	...	......	...	......	...	......	Dutch......	1	2,266	83	148,138
...	......	...	......	...	......	...	......	...	......		...	......	4	342
...	......	...	......	...	......	...	......	...	......		...	......	1	718
...	......	1	27	...	......	...	......	...	......		...	......	3	562
...	......	...	......	...	......	...	......	...	......		...	......	203	10,017
6	6,961	4	216	2	2,909	...	......	...	......		2	4,229	439	256,999
...	......	...	......	...	......	...	......	...	......		...	......	11	575
...	......	...	......	...	......	...	......	...	......		...	......	68	3,537
...	......	...	......	...	......	...	......	...	......		...	......	79	4,112

6 GEORGE V, A. 1916

No. 15.—STATEMENT of the Number and Tonnage of Sailing

Ports and Outports and Countries for which Departed.		NATIONALITY								
		British.		United States.		Norwegian.		Austrian.		Belgian.
		Vessels.	Tons Register.	Vessels.	Tons Register.	Vessels.	Tons Register.	Vessels.	Tons Register.	Vessels.	Tons Register.
Lunenburg, N.S.—											
British W. Indies.....	Sail.	2	266	....	....	....	....	....	....	....	....
Newfoundland........	"	22	2,827	....	....	....	....	....	....	....	....
Porto Rico..........	"	14	1,650	....	....	....	....	....	....	....	....
United States........	"	16	2,975	....	....	....	....	....	....	....	....
Azores and Madeira..	"	1	268	....	....	....	....	....	....	....	....
Sea Fisheries........	Steam.	47	719	1	78	...		....	....	....	....
Sea Fisheries.........	Sail.	233	18,050	20	1,685	....	....	....	....	....	....
Total...................		335	26,755	21	1,763	....	....	....	....	....	....
Magdalen Islands, Que.—											
United States.........	Sail.	....	....	16	1,699	....	....	....	....	....	....∴..
Mahone Bay, N.S.—											
British W. Indies.....	Sail.	1	100	....	....	....	....	....	....	....	....
United States........	"	7	954	2	697	....	....	....	....	....	....
Sea Fisheries........	"	12	964	....	....	....	....	....	....	....	....
Total.................		20	2,018	2	697	....	....	....	....	....	....
Maitland, N.S.—											
United States........	Sail.	16	2,221	3	944	....	....	....	....	....	....
Meteghan River, N.S.—											
Porto Rico..........	Sail.	1	174	....	....	....	....	....	....	....	....
United States........	"	8	852	....	....	....	....	....	....	....	....
Total.................		9	1,026	....	....	....	....	....	....	....	....
Moncton, N.B.—											
Great Britain........	Steam.	7	15,567	....	....	2	2,427	....	....	....	....
Great Britain........	Sail.	...	......	....	....	1	1,036	....	....	....	....
United States........	"	7	683	11	2,883	....	....	....	....	....	....
Total.................		14	16,250	11	2,883	3	3,463	....	....	....	....
Montague, P.E.I.—											
Newfoundland........	Sail.	4	329	....	....	....	....	....	....	....	..:.
Saint Pierre..........	"	1	70	....	....	....	....	....	....	....	....
Total.................		5	399	....	....	....	....	....	....	....	....
Montreal, Que.— ·											
Great Britain........	Steam.	395	1,624,769	....	....	4	9,437	1	2,321	....	....
Denmark............	"	...	......	....	....	1	2,522	....	....	....	....
Newfoundland.......	"	27	23,110	....	....	1	4,131	....	....	....	....
Belgium.............	"	5	17,216	....	....	....	....	....	....	....	....
Brazil..............	"	1	1,980	....	....	....	....	....	....	....	....
Gibraltar............	"	6	14,412	....	....	1	1,951	....	....	....	....
France.............	"	38	115,600	....	....	....	....	1	3,093	....	....
Germany...........	"	2	5,412	....	....	....	....	....	....	1	6,110
Holland............	"	9	22,655	....	....	1	2,340	....	....	1	5,489
Italy.................	"	8	19,904	....	....	....	....	....	....	....	....
Malta...............	"	...	......	....	....	....	....	1	2,821	....	....
Portugal............	"	3	6,803	....	....	....	....	1	2,758	....	....
Australia.....:......	"	7	27,062	....	....	....	....	....	....	....	....
British S. Africa.....	"	8	23,340	....	....	....	....	....	....	....	....
Spain...............	"	2	5,272	....	....	....	....	....	....	....	....
United States.........	"	1	2,438	2	1,994	1	3,087	....	....	....	....
Total................		512	1,909,973	2	1,994	9	23,468	4	10,993	2	11,599

and Steam Vessels entered Outwards *for Sea, &c.—Continued.*

OF VESSELS.

	Danish.		French.		German.		Italian.		Russian.		Other Nationalities.			Total.	
Vessels.	Tons Register.	Vessels.	Tons Register.	Vessels.	Tons Register.	Vessels.	Tons Register.	Vessels.	Tons Register.	Names.	Vessels.	Tons Register.	Vessels.	Tons Register.
....	......	....	......	....	......	....	......	....	......	....	....	....	2	266
....	......	....	......	....	......	....	......	....	......	....	....	....	22	2,827
....	......	....	......	....	......	....	......	....	......	....	....	....	14	1,650
....	......	....	......	....	......	....	......	....	......	....	....	....	16	2,975
....	......	....	......	....	......	....	......	....	......	....	....	....	1	268
....	......	....	......	....	......	....	......	....	......	....	....	....	48	797
....	......	....	......	....	......	....	......	....	......	....	....	....	253	19,735
....	......	....	......	....	......	....	......	....	......	....	....	....	356	28,518
....	......	....	......	....	......	....	......	....	......	....	....	....	16	1,699
....	......	....	......	....	......	....	......	....	......	....	....	....	1	100
....	......	....	......	....	......	....	......	....	......	....	....	....	9	1,651
....	......	....	......	....	......	....	......	....	......	....	....	....	12	964
....	......	....	......	....	......	....	......	....	......	....	....	....	22	2,715
....	......	....	......	....	......	....	......	....	......	....	....	....	19	3,165
....	......	....	......	....	......	....	......	....	......	....	....	....	1	174
....	......	....	......	....	......	....	......	....	......	....	....	....	8	852
....	......	....	......	....	......	....	......	....	......	....	....	....	9	1,026
1	1,572	....	......	....	......	....	......	....	......	Spanish....	{1	1,883	13	24,764
....	......	....	......	....	......	....	......	....	......	Swedish....	{2	3,315	1	1,036
....	......	....	......	....	......	....	......	....	......	....	....	....	18	3,566
1	1,572	....	......	....	......	....	......	....	......	....	3	5,198	32	· 29,366
....	......	....	......	....	......	....	......	....	......	....	....	....	4	329
....	......	....	......	....	......	....	......	....	......	....	....	....	1	70
....	......	....	......	....	......	....	......	....	......	....	....	....	5	399
....	......	....	......	1	4,463	....	......	....	......	Swedish....	2	3,355	403	1,644,345
....	......	....	......	....	......	....	......	....	......	....	....	....	1	2,522
....	......	....	......	....	......	....	......	....	......	....	....	....	28	27,241
....	......	....	......	....	......	....	......	....	......	....	....	....:.	5	17,216
....	......	....	......	....	......	....	......	....	......	....	....	....	1	1,980
1	2,526	4	15,094	....	......	....	......	....	......	....	....	....	7	16,363
....	......	....	......	2	7,595	....	......	....	......	....	....	....	44	136,313
....	......	....	......	6	21,968	....	......	....	......	....	....	....	5	19,117
....	......	....	......	....	......	....	......	....	......	Swedish...{	1	2,616	21	64,973
....	......	....	......	....	......	....	......	....	......	Dutch.....{	3	9,905		
....	......	....	......	....	......	....	......	....	......	....	....	....	8	19,901
....	......	....	......	....	......	....	......	....	......	....	....	....	1	2,821
....	......	....	......	....	......	....	......	....	......	....	....	....	4	9,561
....	......	....	......	....	......	....	......	....	......	....	....	....	7	27,062
....	......	....	......	....	......	....	......	....	......	....	....	....	8	23,340
....	......	....	......	....	......	....	......	....	......	....	....	....	2	5,272
....	......	....	......	1	3,012	....	......	....	......	Grecian....	1	2,484	6	13,015
1	2,526	4	15,094	10	37,038	....	......	....	......	....	7	18,360	551	2,031,045

6 GEORGE V, A. 1916

No. 15.—STATEMENT of the Number and Tonnage of Sailing

										NATIONALITY
Ports and Outports and Countries for which Departed.	British.		United States.		Norwegian.		Austrian.		Belgian.	
	Vessels.	Tons Register.	Vessels.	Tons Register.	Vessels.	Tons Register.	Vessels.	Tons Register.	Vessels.	Tons Register.
Murray Harbour, P.E.I.—										
Sea Fisheries..........Sail.	9	253	....	....	....	....	....	....	....	....
Nanaimo, B.C.—										
United States.........Steam.	159	49,497	164	108,263	11	31,017	....	....	....	....
United States......... Sail.	6	1,062	81	41,505	....	....	....	....	....	....
British Oceania, other.Steam.	2	5,643	....	....	1	2,889	....	....	....	....
Japan................ "	1	2,840	....	....	....	....	....	....	....	....
China............... "	....	....	....	....	1	2,789	....	....	....	....
Sea Fisheries......... "	20	2,049	13	1,577	....	....	....	....	....	....
Total.................	188	61,091	258	151,345	13	36,695	....	....	....	....
Newcastle, N.B.—										
Great Britain........Steam.	2	4,220	....	....	2	2,948	....	....	....	....
Great Britain......... Sail.	....	....	....	....	2	1,789	....	....	....	....
United States........Steam.	1	1,863	....	....	....	....	....	....	....	....
United States......... Sail.	14	3,204	7	2,758	....	....	....	....	....	....
Total.................	17	9,287	7	2,758	4	4,737	....	....	....	....
Newport, B.C.—										
Australia.............Steam.	1	3,139	....	....	....	....	....	....	....	....
Japan................ "	....	....	....	....	....	....	....	....	....	....
United States......... "	19	15,734	23	21,280	....	....	....	....	....	....
Total.................	20	18,873	23	21,280	....	....	....	....	....	....
New Westminster, B.C.—										
United States........Steam.	37	5,713	16	5,273	....	....	....	....	....	....
United States......... Sail.	3	591	1	198	....	....	....	....	....	....
Australia............ "	1	398	....	....	....	....	....	....	....	....
British S. Africa.... "	....	....	1	1,289	....	....	....	....	....	....
Total.................	41	6,702	18	6,760	....	....	....	....	....	....
North East Harbour, N.S.—										
United States........Steam.	....	....	1	26	....	....	....	....	....	....
United States......... Sail.	1	66	....	....	....	....	....	....	....	....
Sea Fisheries........Steam.	2	66	....	....	....	....	....	....	....	....
Sea Fisheries......... Sail.	2	20	31	2,201	....	....	....	....	....	....
Total.................	5	152	32	2,227	....	....	....	....	....	....
North Head, N.B.—										
United States........Steam.	176	25,705	16	336	....	....	....	....	....	....
United States......... Sail.	6	310	....	....	....	....	....	....	....	....
Total.................	182	26,015	16	336	....	....	....	....	....	....
North Sydney, N.S.—										
Great Britain........Steam.	19	38,193	....	....	3	5,006	....	....	....	....
British W. Indies....... "	1	2,689	....	....	....	....	....	....	....	....
Newfoundland.......Steam.	340	205,007	....	....	23	26,471	....	....	....	....
Newfoundland.......Sail...	104	7,943	12	1,144	....	....	....	....	....	....
France..............Steam.	1	2,193	....	....	....	....	....	....	....	....
Norway..............Steam.	....	....	....	....	1	622	....	....	....	....
Saint Pierre.........Steam.	1	341	....	....	....	....	....	....	....	....
Saint Pierre..........Sail...	1	99	....	....	....	....	....	....	....	....
Spain................Steam.	1	2,732	....	....	....	....	....	....	....	....
United States........Steam.	4	6,315	....	....	10	10,302	....	....	....	....
United States........Sail...	1	79	1	52	....	....	....	....	....	....
Denmark.............Steam.	....	....	....	....	1	3,458	....	....	....	....
Sea Fisheries........Steam.	8	1,385	....	....	....	....	....	....	....	....
Sea Fisheries........Sail...	32	2,546	121	9,127	....	....	....	....	....	....
Total.................	513	269,522	134	10,323	38	45,859	....	....	....	....

and Steam Vessels entered Outwards *for Sea, &c.—Continued.*

OF VESSELS.

Danish.		French.		German.		Italian.		Russian.		Other Nationalities.			Total.	
Vessels.	Tons Register.	Vessels.	Tons Register.	Vessels.	Tons Register.	Vessels.	Tons Register.	Vessels.	Tons Register.	Names.	Vessels.	Tons Register.	Vessels.	Tons Register.
....	......	...	......	....	......	....	......	....	......	....	....	......	9	253
2	5,420	...	......	1	3,084	...	......	2	5,746	Japanese....	1	2,708	340	205,735
....	......	...	......	...	......	...	......	...	......	....	...	....	87	42,567
....	......	...	......	...	......	...	......	...	......	....	...	....	3	8,532
....	......	...	......	...	......	...	......	...	......	....	...	....	1	2,840
....	......	...	......	...	......	...	......	...	......	....	...	....	1	2,789
....	......	...	......	...	......	...	......	...	......	....	...	....	33	3,626
2	5,420	...	......	1	3,084	...	......	2	5,746	....	1	2,708	465	266,089
5	6,973	...	......	...	......	...	......	...	......	....	...	....	9	14,141
6	1,182	...	......	...	......	...	......	2	555	....	...	....	10	3,526
....	......	...	......	...	......	...	......	...	......	....	...	....	1	1,863
....	......	...	......	...	......	...	......	...	......	....	...	....	21	5,962
11	8,155	...	......	...	......	...	......	2	555	....	...	....	41	25,492
....	......	...	......	...	......	...	......	...	......	Chinese....	1	3,179	1	3,139
....	......	...	......	...	......	...	......	...	......	....	...	....	1	3,179
....	......	...	......	...	......	...	......	...	......	....	...	....	42	37,014
....	......	...	......	...	......	...	......	...	......	....	.1	3,179	44	43,332
....	......	...	......	...	......	...	......	...	......	....	...	....	53	10,986
....	......	...	......	...	......	...	......	...	......	....	...	....	4	789
....	......	...	......	...	......	...	......	...	......	....	...	....	1	398
....	......	...	......	...	......	...	......	...	......	....	...	....	1	1,289
..	......	...	......	...	......	...	......	...	......	....	...	....	59	13,462
....	......	...	......	...	......	...	......	...	......	....	...	....	1	26
....	......	...	......	...	......	...	......	...	......	....	...	....	1	66
....	......	...	......	...	......	...	......	...	......	....	...	....	2	66
....	......	...	......	...	......	...	......	...	......	....	...	....	33	2,221
....	......	...	......	...	......	...	......	...	......	....	...	....	37	2,379
....	......	...	......	...	......	...	......	...	......	....	...	....	192	26,041
....	......	...	......	...	......	...	......	...	......	....	...	....	6	310
....	......	...	......	...	......	...	......	...	......	....	...	....	198	26,351
1	1,338	...	......	...	......	...	......	...	......	....	...	....	23	44,537
....	......	...	......	...	......	...	......	...	......	....	...	....	1	2,689
....	......	...	......	...	......	...	......	...	......	....	...	....	363	231,478
....	......	...	......	...	......	...	......	...	......	....	...	....	116	9,087
....	......	...	......	...	......	...	......	...	......	....	...	....	1	2,193
....	......	...	......	...	......	...	......	...	......	....	...	....	1	622
....	......	19	4,123	...	......	...	......	...	......	....	...	....	20	4,464
....	......	3	318	...	......	...	......	...	......	....	...	....	4	417
....	......	...	......	...	......	...	......	...	......	....	...	....	1	2,732
....	......	...	......	...	......	...	......	...	......	....	...	....	14	16,617
....	......	...	......	...	......	...	......	...	......	....	...	....	2	131
....	......	...	......	...	......	...	......	...	......	....	...	....	1	3,408
....	......	86	15,960	...	......	...	......	...	......	....	...	....	94	17,345
....	......	5	304	...	......	...	......	...	......	....	...	....	158	11,977
1	1,338	113	20,705	...	......	...	......	...	......	....	...	....	799	347,747

6 GEORGE V, A. 1916

No. 15.—STATEMENT of the Number and Tonnage of Sailing

Ports and Outports and Countries for which Departed.	British.		United States.		Norwegian.		Austrian.		Belgian.	
	Vessels.	Tons Register.	Vessels.	Tons Register.	Vessels.	Tons Register.	Vessels.	Tons Register.	Vessels.	Tons Register.
Parrsboro, N.S—										
Great Britain........Steam.	10	20,650	....	....	1	850	....	....	....	....
Great Britain........Sail...	1	349	....	....	....	....	....	....	....	....
United States........Steam.	21	17,318	26	7,808	....	....	....	....	....	....
United States........Sail...	82	16,866	25	8,084	....	....	....	....	....	....
Total..................	114	55,183	51	15,892	1	850	....			
Paspebiac, Que.—										
Great Britain........Steam.	3	6,651	....	....	3	4,585	....	....	....	....
Great Britain........Sail...	....	....	....	....	....	....	....	....	....	....
British W. Indies.....Sail...	2	298	....	....	....	....	....	....	....	....
United States........Steam.	....	....	....	....	3	1,831	....	....	....	....
United States........Sail...	9	2,019	4	978	....	....	....	....	....	....
Total..................	14	8,968	4	978	6	6,416	....			
Percé, Que.—										
Great Britain........Steam.	1	2,210	....	....	1	1,338	....	....	....	....
Newfoundland......Sail...	....	....	1	84	....	....	....	....	....	....
United States........Steam.	....	....	....	....	2	1,772	....	....	....	....
United States........Sail...	1	92	6	1,618	....	....	....	....	....	....
Total..................	2	2,302	7	1,702	3	3,110	....			
Pictou. N.S.—										
Great Britain........Steam.	6	10,958	....	....	3	3,908	....			
United States........Steam.	11	26,061	....	....	....	....	....			
Total..................	17	37,019	....	....	3	3,908	....			
Port Clyde, N.S.—										
Newfoundland,........Sail...	1	249	....	....	....					
United States......... " ...	2	380	2	850	....					
Total..................	3	629	2	850	....					
Port Hood, N.S.—										
Sea Fisheries-........Sail...	....	....	1	91	....					
Port La Tour, N.S.—										
Sea Fisheries.........Sail...	17	223	18	1,669	....					
Port Mulgrave, N.S.—										
Newfoundland, ...Sail...	2	181	....	....	....					
United States........Sail...	....	....	1	127	....					
Sea Fisheries........Steam.	6	656	4	342	....					
Sea Fisheries........Sail...	7	690	15	1,315	....					
Total..................	15	1,527	20	1,784	....					
Port Simpson, B.C.—										
United States........Steam.	33	33,783	7	55	....					
Port Wade, N.S.—										
United States.........Sail...	9	996	4	40	....					
Port Williams, N.S.—										
British W. Indies.....Sail...	1	397	....	....	....					
Cuba.................Sail...	1	271	....	....	....					
Total..................	2	668	....	....	....					

and Steam Vessels entered Outwards *for Sea, &c.—Continued.*

OF VESSELS.

Danish.		French.		German.		Italian.		Russian.		Other Nationalities.			Total.	
Vessels.	Tons Register.	Vessels.	Tons Register.	Vessels.	Tons Register.	Vessels.	Tons Register.	Vessels.	Tons Register.	Names.	Vessels.	Tons Register.	Vessels.	Tons Register.
...	......	...	......	...	......	...	......	...	......	Spanish.....	1	1,959	12	23,459
...	......	...	......	...	......	...	......	...	......	....	...	......	1	349
...	......	...	......	...	......	...	......	...	......		...	......	47	25,126
...	......	...	......	...	......	...	......	...	......		...	......	107	, 24,950
...	......	...	......	...	......	...	......	...	......	....	1	1,959	167	73,884
1	1,354	...	......	...	......	...	......	...	......		...	......	7	12,590
...	......	...	......	...	......	...	......	1	392	....	...	......	1	392
...	......	...	......	1	1,005	...	......	...	......		...	......	2	298
...	......	...	......			...	......	...	......		...	......	4	2,836
...	......	...	......	...	......	...	......	...	......		...	......	13	2,997
1	1,354	...	......	1	1,005	...	......	1	392	....	...	......	27	19,113
...	......	...	......	...	......	...	......	...	......	....	...	......	2	3,548
...	......	...	......	...	......	...	......	...	......		...	......	1	84
...	......	...	......	...	......	...	......	...	......		...	......	2	1,772
...	......	...	......	...	......	...	......	...	......		...	......	7	1,710
...	......	...	......	...	......	...	......	...	......	....	...	......	12	7,114
...	......	...	......	...	......	...	......	...	......	....	...	......	9	14,866
...	......	...	......	...	......	...	......	...	......		...	......	11	26,061
...	......	...	......	...	......	...	......	...	......	....	...	......	20	40,927
...	......	...	......	...	......	...	......	...	......	....	...	......	1	249
...	......	...	......	...	......	...	......	...	......		...	......	4	1,230
...	......	...	......	...	......	...	......	...	......	....	...	......	5	1,479
...	......	...	......	...	......	...	......	...	......	....	...	......	1	91
...	......	...	......	...	......	...	......	...	......	....	...	......	35	1,892
...	......	...	......	...	......	...	......	...	......		...	......	2	181
...	......	...	......	...	......	...	......	...	......		...	......	1	127
...	......	...	......	...	......	...	......	...	......		...	......	10	998
...	......	...	......	...	......	...	......	...	......		...	......	22	2,005
...	......	...	......	...	......	...	......	...	......	....	...	......	35	3,311
...	......	...	......	...	......	...	......	...	......	....	...	......	40	33,838
...	......	...	......	...	......	...	......	...	......	....	...	......	13	1,036
...	......	...	......	...	......	...	......	...	......	....	...	......	1	397
...	......	...	......	...	......	...	......	...	......		...	......	1	271
...	......	...	......	...	......	...	......	...	......	....	...	......	2	· 668

6 GEORGE V, A. 1916

No. 15.—STATEMENT of the Number and Tonnage of Sailing

	British.		United States.		Norwegian.		Austrian.		Belgian.	
Ports and Outports and Countries for which Departed.	Vessels.	Tons Register.	Vessels.	Tons Register.	Vessels.	Tons Register.	Vessels.	Tons Register.	Vessels.	Tons Register.
Powell River, B.C.—										
Australia............Steam.	4	15,770	....		....		....		....	
United States........ "	....	....	79	36,579	....		....		....	
Total..........	4	15,770	79	36,579	....		....		....	
Prince Rupert, B.C.—										
United States......Steam.	59	46,571	148	107,973	....		....		....	
Sea Fisheries......Steam.	125	9,069	....		....		....		....	
Total.............	184	55,640	148	107,973	....		....		....	
Pugwash, N.S.—										
Great Britain.......Steam.	1	2,263	....		1	1,166	....		....	
Quebec, Que.—										
Great Britain........Steam.	104	571,781	....		....		....		....	
Newfoundland....... "	19	7,389	....		....		....		....	
Newfoundland........Sail...	9	654	3	258	....		....		....	
France...........Steam.	....		....		....		....		....	
Norway............. "	....		....		1	648	....		....	
United States......... "	2	2,408	....		2	2,097	1	3,093	....	
United States.......Sail....	3	422	1	233	1	99	....		....	
Australia..........Steam.	2	8,835	....		....		....		....	
Total.............	139	591,489	4	491	4	2,844	1	3,093	....	
Rimouski, Que.—										
Great Britain.......Steam.	8	17,528	....		1	2,136	....		....	
Great Britain......Sail...	....		....		4	4,741	....		....	
United States.......Steam.	12	10,890	....		....		....		....	
Argentina........... "	1	1,937	....		....		....		....	
Total.............	21	30,355	....		5	6,877	....		....	
River Hebert, N.S.—										
United States.......Sail....	10	1,458	3	617	....		....		....	
St. Andrew's, N.B.—										
United States........Steam.	239	20,167	974	53,455	....		....		....	
United States........Sail.	13	1,127	1	127	....		....		....	
Total..............	252	21,294	975	53,582	....		....		....	
St. George, N.B.—.										
United States........Steam.	....		59	2,084	....		....		....	
United States........Sail.	12	1,258	71	7,740	....		....		....	
Sea Fisheries........ "	1	10	....		....		....		....	
Total..............	13	1,268	130	9,824	....		....		....	
St. John, N.B.—										
Great Britain.......Steam.	68	264,636	....		10	12,855	....		....	
Great Britain........Sail.	1	316	....		10	8,434	....		....	
British West Indies...Steam.	1	1,011	....		....		....		....	
British West Indies..Sail.	3	498	....		....		....		....	
Cuba............. "	3	928	....		....		....		....	
France.............Steam.	22	69,408	....		....		....		....	
Spain............. "	....		....		1	688	....		....	
United States......... "	39	103,192	159	335,721	3	2,980	....		....	
United States........Sail.	118	13,389	393	34,597	1	825	....		....	
Australia...........Steam.	5	18,553	....		1	2,726	....		....	
Australia.......... "	5	18,553	....		1	2,726	....		....	
British S. Africa..... "	4	10,967	....		....		....		....	
San Domingo......... "	....		....		1	656	....		....	
Canary Islands.......Sail.	1	392	....		....		....		....	
Sea Fisheries........ "	28	377	....		....		....		....	
Total..............	293	483,667	552	370,318	27	29,164	....		....	

SESSIONAL PAPER No. 11

and Steam Vessels entered Outwards *for Sea, &c.—Continued.*

OF VESSELS.

Danish.		French.		German.		Italian.		Russian.		Other Nationalities.			Total.	
Vessels.	Tons Register.	Vessels.	Tons Register.	Vessels.	Tons Register.	Vessels.	Tons Register.	Vessels.	Tons Register.	Names.	Vessels.	Tons Register.	Vessels.	Tons Register.
....	......	....	......	....	......	....	......	....	......		....	......	4	15,770
....	......	....	......	....	......	....	......	....	......		....	......	79	36,579
....	......	....	......	....	......	....	......	....	......		....	......	83	52,349
....	......	....	......	....	......	....	......	....	......		....	......	207	154,544
....	......	....	......	....	......	....	......	....	......		....	......	125	9,069
....	......	....	......	....	......	....	......	....	......		....	......	332	163,613
4	5,409	....	......	1	1,904	....	......	....	......	Swedish....	1	1,218	8	11,960
1	1,572	....	......	....	......	....	......	....	......		....	......	105	573,353
....	......	....	......	....	......	....	......	....	......		....	......	19	7,389
....	......	....	......	....	......	....	......	....	......		....	......	12	912
1	1,660	1	3,377	....	......	....	......	....	......		....	......	2	5,037
....	......	....	......	....	......	....	......	....	......		....	......	1	648
....	......	....	......	....	......	....	......	....	......		....	......	5	7,598
....	......	....	......	....	......	....	......	....	......		....	......	5	754
....	......	....	......	....	......	....	......	....	......		....	......	2	8,835
2	3,232	1	3,377	....	......	....	......	....	......		....	......	151	604,526
....	......	....	......	....	......	....	......	....	......		....	......	9	19,664
....	......	....	......	....	......	....	......	1	953		....	......	5	5,694
....	......	....	......	....	......	....	......	....	......		....	......	12	10,890
....	......	....	......	....	......	....	......	....	......		....	......	1	1,937
....	......	....	......	....	......	....	......	1	953		....	......	27	38,185
....	......	....	......	....	......	....	......	....	......		....	......	13	2,075
....	......	....	......	....	......	....	......	....	......		....	......	1,213	73,622
....	......	....	......	....	......	....	......	....	......		....	......	14	1,254
....	......	....	......	....	......	....	......	....	......		....	......	1,227	74,876
....	......	....	......	....	......	....	......	....	......		....	......	59	2,084
....	......	....	......	....	......	....	......	....	......		....	......	83	8,998
....	......	....	......	....	......	....	......	....	......		....	......	1	10
....	......	....	......	....	......	....	......	....	......		....	......	143	11,092
1	1,203	....	......	....	......	....	......	1	1,412	Spanish....	1	3,137	82	284,461
....	......	....	......	....	......	....	......	....	......	Swedish...	1	1,218	13	9,980
....	......	....	......	....	......	....	......	....	......	Swedish...	1	931	1	1,011
....	......	....	......	....	......	....	......	....	......	Uruguayan	1	299	3	498
....	......	....	......	....	......	....	......	....	......		....	......	3	928
....	......	....	......	....	......	....	......	....	......		....	......	22	69,408
....	......	....	......	....	......	....	......	....	......		....	......	1	688
1	877	....	......	....	......	....	......	....	......		....	......	202	442,770
....	......	....	......	....	......	1	596	....	......		....	......	513	49,407
....	......	....	......	....	......	....	......	....	......		....	......	6	21,279
....	......	....	......	....	......	....	......	....	......		....	......	4	10,967
....	......	....	......	....	......	....	......	....	......		....	......	1	656
....	......	....	......	....	......	....	......	....	......		....	......	1	392
....	......	....	......	....	......	....	......	....	......		....	......	28	377
2	2,080	....	......	....	......	1	596	1	1,412	....	4	5,585	880	892,822

6 GEORGE V, A. 1916

No. 15.—STATEMENT of the Number and Tonnage of Sailing.

Ports and Outports and Countries for which Departed.	British.		United States.		Norwegian.		Austrian.		Belgian.	
	Vessels.	Tons Register.	Vessels.	Tons Register.	Vessels.	Tons Register.	Vessels.	Tons Register.	Vessels.	Tons Register.
St. Martin's, N.B.—										
United States........Steam.	....	....	29	2,291	....	....	....	....	....	....
United States........Sail.	17	7,634	26	9,714	....	....	....	....	....	....
Total................	17	7,634	55	12,005	....	....	....	....	....	....
St. Stephen. N.B.—										
United States........Steam.	190	19,683	102	1,961	....	....	....	....	....	....
United States........Sail.	1	623	22	6,242	....	....	....	....	....	....
Total................	191	20,306	124	8,203	....	....	....	....	....	....
Sackville, N.B.—										
United States......... Sail..	5	694	2	357	....	....	....	....	....	....
Salmon River, N.S.—										
United States........Sail.	1	71	2	33	....	....	....	....	....	....
Sea Fisheries......... "	10	160	....	....	....	....	....	....	....	....
Total................	11	231	2	33..	....	....	....	....	....	....
Sandy Cove, N.S.—										
United States........Sail.	1	42	2	30	..	....	....	....	....	....
Sandy Point, N.S.—										
Newfoundland........Sail.	....	....	5	473	....	....	....	....	....	....
United States......... "	9	1,366	14	1,364	....	....	....	....	....	....
Sea Fisheries......... "	3	32	217	16,427	....	....	....	....	....	....
Total................	12	1,398	236	18,264	....	....	....	....	....	....
Shediac, N.B.—										
Great Britain........Sail.	....	....	...	....	1	917	....	....	....	....
Sheet Harbour, N.S.—										
United States........Sail.	1	98	....	....	....	....	....	....	....	....
Sea Fisheries......... "	2	30	1	99	....	....	....	....	....	....
Total................	3	128	1	99	....	....	....	....	....	....
Shelburne, N.S.—										
British W. Indies.....Sail.	3	702	..	....	....	....	....	....	....	....
Newfoundland........ "	3	414	2	231	....	....	....	....	....	....
United States........Steam.	....	....	2	326	....	....	....	....	....	....
United States........Sail.	13	2,569	8	1,605	....	....	....	....	....	....
Sea Fisheries........Steam.	5	191	..	....	....	....	....	....	....	....
Sea Fisheries........Sail.	9	258	71	5,962	....	....	....	....	....	....
Total................	33	4,134	83	8,124	....	....	....	....	....	....
Sherbrooke, N.S.—										
United States........Sail.	6	1,408	...	....	....	....	....	....	....	....
Shippegan, N.B.—										
United States........Sail.	1	98	....	....	....	....	....	....	....	....
Sea Fisheries........Steam.	16	180	....	....	....	....	....	....	....	....
Sea Fisheries........Sail.	63	922	....	....	....	....	....	....	....	....
Total................	80	1,200	....	....	....	....	....	....	....	....
Sidney, B.C.—										
United States........Steam.	30	760	17	443	....	....	....	....	....	....
United States........Sail.	2	172	11	660	....	....	....	....	....	....
Total................	32	932	28	1,103	....	....	....	....	....	....

and Steam Vessels entered Outwards *for Sea, &c.—Continued.*

OF VESSELS.

Danish.		French.		German.		Italian.		Russian.		Other Nationalities.			Total.	
Vessels.	Tons Register.	Vessels.	Tons Register.	Vessels.	Tons Register.	Vessels.	Tons Register.	Vessels.	Tons Register.	Names.	Vessels.	Tons Register.	Vessels.	Tons Register.
....	......	...	....	....	....	....	....	....	....	....	....	....	29	2,291
....	......	...	....	....	....	....	....	....	....	....	....	....	43	17,348
....	......	...	....	....	....	....	....	....	....	....	....	....	72	19,639
....	......	...	....	....	....	....	....	....	....	....	....	....	292	21,644
....	......	...	....	....	....	....	....	....	....	....	....	....	23	6,865
....	......	...	....	....	....	....	....	....	....	....	....	....	315	28,509
....	......	...	....	....	....	....	....	....	....	....	....	....	7	1,051
....	......	...	....	....	....	....	....	....	....	....	....	....	3	104
....	......	...	....	....	....	....	....	....	....	....	....	....	10	160
....	......	...	....	....	....	....	....	....	....	....	....	....	13	264
....	......	...	....	....	....	....	....	....	....	....	....	....	3	72
....	......	...	....	....	....	....	....	....	....	....	....	....	5	473
....	......	...	....	....	....	....	....	....	....	....	....	....	23	2,730
....	......	...	....	....	....	....	....	....	....	....	....	....	220	16,459
....	......	...	....	....	....	....	....	....	....	....	....	....	248	19,662
....	......	...	....	....	....	....	....	....	....	....	....	....	1	917
....	......	...	....	....	....	....	....	....	....	....	....	....	1	98
....	......	...	....	....	....	....	....	....	....	....	....	....	3	129
....	......	...	....	....	....	....	....	....	....	....	....	....	4	227
....	......	...	....	....	....	....	....	....	....	....	....	....	3	702
....	......	...	....	....	....	....	....	....	....	....	....	....	5	645
....	......	...	....	....	....	....	....	....	....	....	....	....	2	326
....	......	...	....	....	....	....	....	....	....	....	....	....	21	4,174
....	......	...	....	....	....	....	....	....	....	....	....	....	5	191
....	......	...	....	....	....	....	....	....	....	....	....	....	80	6,220
....	......	...	....	....	....	....	....	....	....	....	....	....	116	12,258
....	......	...	....	....	....	....	....	....	....	....	....	....	6	1,408
....	......	...	....	....	....	....	....	....	....	....	....	....	1	98
....	......	...	....	....	....	....	....	....	....	....	....	....	16	180
....	......	...	....	....	....	....	....	....	....	....	....	....	63	922
....	......	...	....	....	....	....	....	....	....	....	....	....	80	1,200
....	......	...	....	....	....	....	....	....	....	....	....	....	47	1,203
....	......	...	....	....	....	....	....	....	....	....	....	....	13	832
....	......	...	....	....	....	....	....	....	....	....	....	....	60	2,035

6 GEORGE V, A. 1916

No. 15.—Statement of the Number and Tonnage of Sailing

Ports and Outports and Countries for which Departed	British.		United States.		Norwegian.		Austrian.		Belgian.	
	Vessels.	Tons Register.	Vessels.	Tons Register.	Vessels.	Tons Register.	Vessels.	Tons Register.	Vessels.	Tons Register.
Sorel, Que.—										
Great Britain.........Steam.	1	1,972								
Newfoundland........ Sail.	1	99								
, Total..................	2	2,071								
Souris, P.E.I.—										
Newfoundland........ Sail.	2	92								
Saint Pierre........... "	7	771								
Sea Fisheries......... "	61	2,659	26	2,168						
Total..................	70	3,522	26	2,168						
Steveston, B.C.—										
United States.........Steam.	127	3,902	30	1,574						
Sea Fisheries......... "	27	4,086								
Total..................	154	7,988	30	1,574						
Stickeen, B.C.—										
United States.........Steam.	6	1,579	35	469						
United States......... Sail.	3	3	1	1						
Total..................	9	1,582	36	470						
Summerside, P.E.I.—										
Newfoundland........Steam.	15	13,140								
Sydney, N.S.—										
Great Britain.........Steam.	29	63,427			7	9,070				
Newfoundland....... "	85	68,814			65	151,679				
Newfoundland........ Sail.	276	19,480			1	121				
Brazil..............Steam.	1	1,980								
Cuba................ "	1	588			3	2,405				
France.............. "	6	14,671			2	2,988				
Holland............. "	1	1,912			1	2,340				
Italy................. "	2	5,111								
Portugal............. "	1	1,931								
Saint Pierre........... "										
Saint Pierre.......... Sail.	33	2,502								
Sweden.............Steam.					1	766				
United States........ "	19	35,343	1	337	22	51,187				
United States........ Sail.			2	91						
British S. Africa.....Steam.	6	17,423								
Australia............ "	4	15,837								
Argentina........... "	1	1,937								
Gibraltar............ "	2	4,084			1	1,951				
Sea Fisheries........ "	1	285								
Sea Fisheries........ Sail.	2	116	13	616						
Total................	470	255,441	16	1,044	103	222,507				
Three Rivers, Que.—										
Great Britain........Steam.	22	53,785								
United States........ "	1	2,707								
Total..................	23	56,492								
Truro, N.S.—										
United States........ Sail.	6	993								

and Steam Vessels entered Outwards *for Sea, &c.—Continued.*

OF VESSELS.

Danish.		French.		German.		Italian.		Russian.		Other Nationalities.			Total.	
Vessels.	Tons Register.	Vessels.	Tons Register.	Vessels.	Tons Register.	Vessels.	Tons Register.	Vessels.	Tons Register.	Names.	Vessels.	Tons Register.	Vessels.	Tons Register.
....	......	....	......	....	....	....	....	....	....		....	....	1	1,972
....	......	....	......	....	....	....	....	...	....		....	....	1	99
....	......	....	......	....	....	....	....	....	....		....	....	2	2,071
....	......	....	......	....	....	....	....	....	....		....	....	2	92
....	......	....	......	....	....	....	....	....	....		....	....	7	771
....	......	....	......	....	....	....	....	....	....		....	....	87	4,827
....	......	....	......	....	....	....	....	....	....		....	....	96	5,690
....	......	....	......	....	....	....	....	....	....		....	....	157	5,476
....	......	....	......	....	....	....	....	....	....		....	....	27	4,086
....	......	....	......	....	....	....	....	....	....		....	....	184	9,562
....	......	....	......	....	....	....	....	....	....		....	....	41	2,048
....	......	....	......	....	....	....	....	....	....		....	....	4	4
....	......	....	......	....	....	....	....	....	....		....	....	45	2,052
....	......	....	......	....	....	....	....	....	....		....	....	15	13,140
....	......	....	......	....	....	....	....	....	....	Swedish....	1	1,837	37	74,334
....	......	....	......	....	....	....	....	....	....		....	....	150	220,493
....	......	....	......	....	....	....	....	....	....		....	....	277	19,601
....	......	....	......	....	....	....	....	....	....		....	....	1	1,980
1	2,526	2	322	....	....	....	....	....	....		....	....	4	2,993
....	......	....	......	....	....	....	....	....	....		....	....	11	20,507
....	......	....	......	....	....	....	....	....	....		....	....	2	4,252
....	......	....	......	....	....	....	....	....	....		....	....	2	5,111
....	......	....	......	....	....	....	....	....	....		....	....	1	1,931
....	......	4	654	....	....	....	....	....	....		....	....	4	654
....	......	8	548	....	....	....	....	....	....		....	....	41	3,050
2	2,602	....	......	....	....	....	....	....	....		....	.....✓.	1	766
....	......	....	......	....	....	....	....	....	....		....	....	44	89,469
....	......	....	......	....	....	....	....	....	....		....	....	2	91
....	......	....	......	....	....	....	....	....	....		....	....	6	17,423
....	......	....	......	....	....	....	....	....	....		....	....	4	15,837
....	......	....	......	....	....	....	....	....	....		....	....	1	1,937
....	......	14	2,532	....	....	....	....	....	....		....	....	3	6,035
....	......	....	......	....	....	....	....	....	....		....	....	15	2,817
....	......	....	......	....	....	....	....	....	....		....	....	15	732
3	5,128	28	4,056	....	....	....	....	....	....		1	1,837	621	490,013
....	......	....	......	....	....	....	....	....	....		....	....	22	53,785
....	......	....	......	....	....	....	....	....	....		....	....	1	2,707
....	......	....	......	....	....	....	....	....	....		....	....	23	56,492
....	......	....	......	....	....	....	....	....	....		....	....	6	993

No. 15.—STATEMENT of the Number and Tonnage of Sailing

Ports and Outports and Countries for which Departed.	British.		United States.		Norwegian.		Austrian.		Belgian.	
	Vessels.	Tons Register.	Vessels.	Tons Register.	Vessels.	Tons Register.	Vessels.	Tons Register.	Vessels.	Tons Register.
Tusket, N.S.—										
Newfoundland .... Sail.	1	14	....	....	....	....	....	....	....	....
United States .... "	2	109	1	122	....					
Sea Fisheries .... "	....	....	7	524	....					
Total	3	123	8	646	....	....	....	....	....	....
Union Bay, B.C.—										
Portugal .... Steam.	1	3,241	....	....	....					
Russia .... : ..... "	....	....	1	1,947	....					
United States .... "	45	102,194	18	11,778	3	8,738				
United States .... Sail.	3	588	16	8,203	....					
Japan .... Steam.	2	8,649	....	....	....					
China .... "	1	2,804	....							
British Oceania, other "	2	5,543	....		1	2,413	....			
Total	54	123,019	35	21,928	4	11,151	....	....	....	....
Vancouver, B.C.—										
Great Britain .... Steam.	27	116,647	1	3,065	....					
Australia .... "	22	102,042	....	....	1	2,413				
Australia .... Sail.	....	....	1	584	....					
China .... Steam.	14	74,205	....		1	2,788				
Japan .... "										
Peru .... "	1	2,948	....							
Germany .... "										
Russia .... "										
Fiji Islands .... "	....		1	621	....					
British S. Africa ...... "	....		....		1	1,789				
British S. Africa ... ... Sail.	....		2	2,095	1	1,465				
United States .... Steam.	840	910,319	476	353,231	4	13,058				
United States .... Sail.	1	1,771	....							
Sea Fisheries .... Steam.	2	312	31	4,458	....					
Total	907	1,208,244	512	364,054	8	21,513	....	....	....	....
Victoria, B.C.—										
Great Britain .... Steam.	12	68,017	....							
Australia .... "	13	75,337	....							
British S. Africa ...... Sail.	1	1,862	2	1,942	....					
China .... Steam.	14	74,205	....							
Japan .... "	....		....							
Portuguese Africa ..... Sail.	....				1	1,395				
Russia .... Steam.	1	5,809	....							
United States .... Steam.	631	831,330	724	613,957	2	6,023				
United States ... : ... Sail.	76	14,142	14	5,841	....					
Sea Fisheries .... Steam.	12	370	....							
Total	760	1,071,072	740	621,740	3	7,418	....		....	
Westport, N.S.—										
United States .... Sail.	5	200	22	270	....					
Weymouth, N.S.—										
British W. Indies ..... Sail.	1	194	....							
Cuba .... "	1	195	2	931	....					
Argentina .... "	....		....		1	825				
United States .... : ... Steam.	....		....		1	689				
United States .... Sail.	22	3,079	9	3,435	....					
Sea Fisheries .... "	1	10	....							
Total	25	3,478	11	4,366	2	1,514	....		....	

SESSIONAL PAPER No. 11

and Steam Vessels entered Outwards *for Sea, &c.—Continued.*

OF VESSELS.

Danish.		French.		German.		Italian.		Russian.		Other Nationalities.			Total.	
Vessels.	Tons Register.	Vessels.	Tons Register.	Vessels.	Tons Register.	Vessels.	Tons Register.	Vessels.	Tons Register.	Names.	Vessels.	Tons Register.	Vessels.	Tons Register.
													1	14
													3	231
													7	524
													11	769
													1	3,241
													1	1,947
													66	122,710
													19	8,791
													2	8,649
													1	2,804
													3	7,956
													93	156,098
				1	2,527								20	122,239
													23	104,475
													1	584
										Japanese....	3	9,104	18	86,097
				1	3,359					Japanese....	3	10,632	4	13,991
													1	2,948
				1	3,176								1	3,176
								3	10,379				3	10,379
													1	621
													1	1,789
													3	3,560
4	10,995			1	3,176			2	6,495	Japanese....	13	45,940	1,340	1,343,214
													1	1,771
													33	4,770
4	10,995			4	12,238			5	16,874		19	65,676	1,459	1,699,594
													12	68,017
													13	75,337
						1	1,866						4	5,670
										Japanese....	24	91,019	38	165,224
										Japanese....	25	98,427	25	98,427
													1	1,395
													1	5,809
										Mexican....	1	1,193		
				2	6,141					Dutch.....	1	2,487	1,412	1,656,621
										Japanese....	51	195,490		
													90	19,983
													12	370
				2	6,141			1	1,866		102	388,616	1,608	2,096,853
													27	470
													1	194
													3	1,126
													1	825
													1	689
													31	6,514
													1	10
													38	9,358

6 GEORGE V, A. 1916

No. 15.—STATEMENT of the Number and Tonnage of Sailing

Ports and Outports and Countries for which Departed.	British.		United States.		Norwegian.		Austrian.		Belgian.	
	Vessels.	Tons Register.	Vessels.	Tons Register.	Vessels.	Tons Register.	Vessels.	Tons Register.	Vessels.	Tons Register.
White Rock, B.C.—										
United States........Steam.	74	660	54	417	....	....	....	....	....	....
Windsor, N.S.—										
United States........Steam.	3	27	....	....	26	18,287	....	....	....	....
United States........ Sail.	79	77,681	64	51,051	....	....	....	....	....	....
Total................	82	77,708	64	51,051	26	18,287	....	....	....	....
Yarmouth, N.S.—										
Brazil................ Sail.	....	....	....	....	3	3,990	....	....	....	....
Cuba................ "	....	....	1	357	....	....	....	....	....	....
France..............Steam.	2	4,593	....	....	....	....	....	....	....	....
United States........ "	179	160,164	2	3,998	....	....	....	....	....	....
United States........ Sail.	27	1,967	10	642	....	....	....	....	....	....
Sea Fisheries........Steam.	2	22	....	....	....	....	....	....	....	....
Sea Fisheries......... Sail.	114	4,258	128	5,839	....	....	....	....	....	....
Total................	324	171,004	141	10,836	3	3,990	....	....	....	....

and Steam Vessels entered Outwards *for Sea, &c.—Concluded.*

OF VESSELS.

Danish.		French.		German.		Italian.		Russian.		Other Nationalities.			Total.	
Vessels.	Tons Register.	Vessels.	Tons Register.	Vessels.	Tons Register.	Vessels.	Tons Register.	Vessels.	Tons Register.	Names.	Vessels.	Tons Register.	Vessels.	Tons Register.
....	......	....	......	....	......	....	......	....	....	....	....	....	128	1,077
....	......	....	......	....	......	....	......	....	....	....	....	....	29	18,314
....	......	....	......	....	......	....	......	....	....	....	....	....	143	128,732
....	......	....	......	....	......	....	......	....	....	....	....	....	172	147,046
....	......	....	......	....	......	....	......	....	....	....	....	....	3	3,990
....	......	....	......	....	......	....	......	....	....	....	....	....	1	357
....	......	....	......	....	......	....	......	....	....	....	....	....	2	4,593
....	......	....	......	....	......	....	......	....	....	....	....	....	181	164,162
....	......	....	......	....	......	1	878	....	....	....	....	....	38	3,487
....	......	....	......	....	......	....	......	....	....	....	....	....	2	22
....	......	....	......	....	......	....	......	....	....	....	....	....	242	10,097
....	......	....	......	....	......	1	878	....	....	....	....	....	469	186,708

No. 16.—SUMMARY STATEMENT of the Nationality of Sea-going Vessels entered

Number	COUNTRIES TO WHICH DEPARTED.	British.		United States.		Norwegian.		Austrian.		Belgian.	
		Vessels.	Tons Register.	Vessels.	Tons Register.	Vessels.	Tons Register.	Vessels.	Tons Register.	Vessels.	Tons Register.
1	United Kingdom	1,116	3,587,792	2	4,637	104	125,708	1	2,321	8	10,399
2	Australia	59	266,973	1	584	3	7,093				
3	British South Africa	20	55,791	5	5,326	2	3,254				
4	British Guiana	28	74,543								
5	British West Indies	40	11,343			25	18,811				
6	British Oceania, other	5	14,015			2	5,302				
7	Fiji Islands			1	621						
8	Malta							1	2,821		
9	Newfoundland	1,178	508,773	35	3,254	93	186,620				
10	Gibraltar	8	18,496			2	3,902				
11	Argentina	2	3,874			5	5,836				
12	Azores and Madeira	4	1,044								
13	Belgium	5	17,216								
14	Brazil	8	5,300	1	1,488	4	5,334				
15	Chili			1	776						
16	China	29	151,214			2	5,577				
17	Canary Islands	1	392								
18	Cuba	23	8,644	7	2,992	10	8,457				
19	Danish West Indies	1	259								
20	Denmark					3	9,558				
21	France	73	214,152			2	2,988	1	3,093		
22	Egypt			1	2,659						
23	Greenland, Iceland, etc					1	718				
24	Germany	2	5,412							1	6,110
25	Holland	11	27,101	1	2,086	5	10,195			1	5,489
26	Hayti					1	684				
27	Italy	11	27,752								
28	Japan	3	11,489								
29	Norway					6	5,023				
30	Peru	1	2,948								
31	Porto Rico	17	2,410	2	732						
32	Portugal	6	12,224					1	2,758		
33	Portuguese Africa					1	1,395				
34	Russia	2	6,100	1	1,947						
35	San Domingo					1	656				
36	Spain	3	8,004			2	1,376				
37	Sweden					2	1,452				
38	St. Pierre	57	4,894								
39	Sea Fisheries	1,880	100,404	1,604	111,150						
40	United States	4,820	3,365,215	4,695	1,997,393	192	292,732	2	7,629		
41	Uruguay					1	1,297				
42	Sea	21	22,838								
	Total	9,434	8,536,612	6,357	2,135,645	469	703,968	6	18,622	10	21,998

SESSIONAL PAPER No. 11

Outwards, *for Sea*, for each Country, during the Fiscal year ended March 31, 1915.

or VESSELS.

| Danish | | French | | German | | Italian | | Russian | | Other Nationalities | | | Total | | |
Vessels.	Tons Register.	Vessels.	Tons Register.	Vessels.	Tons Register.	Vessels.	Tons Register.	Vessels.	Tons Register.		Vessels.	Tons Register.	Vessels.	Tons Register.	Number.
30	32,242	....	......	5	13,047	1	1,151	9	5,380	Swedish... Grecian... Spanish... Uruguayan	11 1 3 1	17,007 3,049 6,979 299	1,292	3,810,011	1
..	......	....	......	....	......	....	...	2	2,564				65	277,214	2
..	......	....	......	....	......	....	...	2	3,732	..	....	......	29	68,103	3
..	......	....	......	....	......	....	...	..	......				28	74,543	4
..	......	....	......	....	...	..	...	..	......				65	30,154	5
..	......	....	......	....	...	..	...	..	......				7	19,317	6
..	......	....	......	....	...	..	...	..	......				1	621	7
..	......	....	......	1	1,005	..	...	..	......				1	2,821	8
..	......	....	......	....	......	....	...	..	......			.....	1,307	699,652	9
..	......	....	......	2	2,164	..	...	..	......	Argentinean	1	1,933	10	22,398	10
..	......	....	......	....	......	....	...	..	......			.....	10	13,807	11
..	......	....	......	....	......	....	...	..	......				4	1,044	12
..	......	....	......	....	......	1	1,173	..	...				5	17,216	13
..	......	....	......	....	......	....	...	..	......			.....	14	13,295	14
..	......	....	......	....	......	....	...	..	......				1	776	15
..	......	....	......	....	......	....	...	..	......	Japanese...	27	100,123	58	256,914	16
..	......	....	......	....	......	....	...	..	......				1	392	17
..	......	....	......	....	......	....	...	..	......			.....	40	20,093	18
..	......	....	......	....	......	....	...	..	......				1	259	19
1	2,199	..	......	....	......	....	...	..	......				4	11,757	20
4	8,259	7	18,793	....	......	....	...	..	......				87	247,285	21
..	......	....	......	....	......	....	...	..	......				1	2,659	22
..	......	....	......	....	......	....	...	..	......				1	718	23
..	......	....	......	3	10,771	..	...	..	......	Swedish...	1	2,616	6	22,293	24
..	......	....	......	6	21,968	..	...	..	......	Dutch.....	3	9,905	28	79,360	25
..	......	....	......	....	......	....	...	..	......				1	684	26
..	......	....	......	1	3,359	..	...	..	......	Japanese...	28	109,059	11	27,752	27
..	......	....	......	....	......	....	...	..	......	Chinese....	1	3,179	33	127,086	28
..	......	....	......	....	......	....	...	..	......				6	5,023	29
..	......	....	......	....	......	....	...	..	......				1	2,948	30
..	......	....	......	....	......	....	...	..	......				19	3,142	31
..	......	....	......	....	......	....	...	..	......	Portuguese..	1	25	8	15,007	32
..	......	....	......	....	......	....	...	..	......				1	1,395	33
..	......	....	......	....	......	....	...	3	10,379				6	18,426	34
..	......	....	......	....	......	....	...	..	......				1	656	35
..	......	....	......	....	......	....	...	..	......	Spanish....	1	2,306	6	11,686	36
..	......	....	......	....	......	....	...	..	......			.....	2	1,452	37
..	......	55	9,222	....	......	....	...	..	......				112	14,116	38
..	......	108	18,974	....	......	....	...	..	......				3,592	230,528	39
18	30,633	2	6,683	12	41,124	3	7,320	15	65,097	Dutch.... Grecian.... Japanese... Mexican... Spanish... Swedish...	5 1 65 1 1 3	16,638 2,484 244,138 1,193 2,351 3,470	9,835	6,084,100	40
..	......	....	......	....	......	1	992	..	...				2	2,289	41
..	......	7	7,812	....	......	....	...	..	......			......	28	30,650	42
53	73,333	179	61,484	28	91,274	8	12,800	31	87,152	....			155	526,754	16,730	12,269,642

No. 17.—STATEMENT showing the Description, Number and Tonnage of Canadian and United States Vessels trading on the Rivers and Lakes between Canada and the United States (exclusive of Ferriage) which arrived at each Port and Outport during the Fiscal Year ended March 31, 1915.

VESSELS ARRIVED.

Number	Ports and Outports	CANADIAN Steam			CANADIAN Sail			UNITED STATES Steam			UNITED STATES Sail		
		No. of Vessels	Tons Register	No. of Crew	No. of Vessels	Tons Register	No. of Crew	No. of Vessels	Tons Register	No. of Crew	No. of Vessels	Tons Register	No. of Crew
1	...e, Ont.	64	5,234	275	10	524	33	731	224,710	9,704	19	8,231	67
2	Aoltsville, Ont.							4	308	23			
3	Bath, Ont.	65	33,686	2,733	4	698	20						
4	Belleville, Ont.	57	31,737	1,133	48	9,361	228						
5	Blind River, Ont.	7	913	72				60	19,043	719	8	3,893	57
6	Bowmanville, Ont.	1	1,199	28	9	2,152	53						
7	Bridgeburg, Ont.							178	5,223	699	252	98,789	522
8	Brighton, Ont.	63	32,287	2,804	13	7,629	56	841	105,269	9,303	19	6,537	116
9	...le, Ont.	131	187,873	8,863	1	517	6	22	12,380	331	3	2,661	18
10	...Mines, Ont.	5	1,130	37				22	38,941	425	1	550	7
11	Byng Inlet, Ont.	39	68,918	732				154	14,249	1,017			
12	Cardinal, Ont.	31	5,084	310	4	752	28	7	445	36	3	948	21
13	...am, Ont.	107	32,138	1,487				4	4,525	78	4	591	15
14	Chicoutimi, Que.	23	25,134	415				4	110	15			
15	Chippawa, Ont.												
16	Cobourg, Ont.	364	1,064,749	15,005	5	1,129	30	17	408	60	2	1,420	16
17	...rn Island, Ont.	20	1,270	135				65	111,971	2,577	20	11,147	137
18	Collingwood, Ont.	2	785	41				263	11,506	830	14	4,242	28
19	Cornwall, Ont.	6	870	75				1,549	250,017	18,819	17	1,862	9
20	...t, Ont.							33	12,033	424	17	568	36
21	Cutler, Ont.	2	216	11	4	802	8	23	11,437	761			
22	Dawson, Y.T.							105	280,741	2,358			
23	Depot Harbour, Ont.	22	30,391	408	6	792	24	2	157	9			
24	Deseronto, Ont.	60	31,340	2,635				28	13,485	920	17	5,164	17
25	Ellis Bay, Que.	1	493	20	4	802	4						
26	Forty Mile, Y.T.	1	489	30									
27	Fort Frances, Ont.	53	7,579	636				413	1,028,214	10,685	8	11,664	63
28	Fort William, Ont.	148	375,282	6,113	23	5,413	118	1,875	30,055	5,396	1	15	2
29	...e, Ont.	834	33,805	2,490									
30	Georgeville, Que.												
31	...n, Ont.	3	665	11				32	17,755	1,322			
32	Gore Bay, Ont.	2	114	12				10	9,490	806	5	2,322	18
33	Hamilton, Ont.	67	29,183	2,362				5	1,589	78			

No.	Port															
34	Iroquois, Ont.	41	11,541	640					160	14,799	1,135	2	684	12
35	Kenora, Ont.	10	18,128	199					16	285	89			
36	Key Har'our, Ont.								9	15,622			2,811	15
37	Kincardine, Ont.								22	8,243	988	3	1,386	18
38	Kingston, Ont.	719	348,500	16,378	263	65,184	1,215	184	37,103	2,947	11	352	25
39	... Ont.	4	128	22				4	976	34	1	499	7
40	Leamington, Ont.	1	306	10				117	10,895	885			
41	Levis, Que.	3	2,566	51				6	5,416	111	43	4,293	66
42	Lime Current, Ont.	32	24,460	662	1	305	6	99	83,081	3,515	27	13,936	161
43	Magog, Que.	3	665	11									
44	Meaford, Ont.							3	2,576	48	3	873	21
45	... Harbour, Ont.							7	9,801	119	1	1,862	9
46	Midland, Ont.	32	46,067	587	13	4,028	78	77	179,950	1,570	2	1,456	14
47	Montreal, Que.	326	339,240	5,836	61	33,871	373	286	313,915	5,179	91	26,734	333
48	Morrisburg, Ont.							413	28,948	2,213	2	543	10
49	Murray Bay, Que.			88	1	970	5						
50	Napanee, Ont.	12	856	88	19	2,941	87						
51	Niagara, Ont.	683	573,999	27,386				9	9,125	410	6	595	11
52	Ottawa, Ont.		381	29	1	149	2	29	26,305	1,819	1	738	7
53	Owen Sound, Ont.	37	22,043	625				4	2,463	52	1	388	7
54	Parry Sound, Ont.											538	
55	Penetanguishene, Ont.	2	474	23									
56	Picton, Ont.	110	48,345	2,272	36	10,659	252	78	17,394	646	10	10,770	60
57	Point Edward, Ont.	67	120,541	2,077	24	6,454	99						
58	Port Arthur, Ont.	732	1,537,803	35,647				11	104				
59	Port Burwell, Ont.	5	97	23				117	1,580	2,407	14	7,826	53
60	Port Colborne, Ont.	127	23,506	1,636	39	30,562	238	7	333,059	55	2	630	6
61	Port Dalhousie, Ont.	14	2,014	132				7	549	66			
62	Port Dover, Ont.	50	1,350	203				7	226				
63	Port Hope, Ont.												
64	Port McNicoll, Ont.	6	1,548	76	6	1,700	34	29	86,381	633	1	439	7
65	Port Stanley, Ont.							411	595,539	14,361			
66	Prescott, Ont.	66	52,485	3,310	11	3,954	70	87	64,678	3,576	5	2,465	30
67	... Ont.	38	38,019	558	2	1,796	13	17	17,275	312	537	54,809	1,074
68	Rainy River, Ont.	621	479,615	23,618									
69	Rimouski, Que.	56	2,127	268									
70	Rockport, Ont.	12	10,890	180				4	97	13	7	266	28
71	Rondeau, Ont.	61	21,377	2,023	1	499	7	155	143,963	3,284			
72	Rykerts, B.C.	1	24	4									
73	St. John's, Que.	2	86	10	22	2,511	46	73	4,855	597	558	58,054	1,027
74	Sandwich, Ont.	4	58	13				522	192,308	4,822	17	4,318	66
75	Sarnia, Ont.	252	74,721	1,995	43	20,369	208	1,455	539,705	45,635	18	8,701	70
76	Sault Ste. M, Ont.	697	300,792	3,030	4	962	30	585	381,322	9,708	62	39,246	405
77	Smith's Falls, Ont.	54	4,322	8,410									
78	Sorel, Que.	2	914	335	1	348	5					28,522	540
79	Southampton, Ont.			15				40	484	133	269		
80	... B.C.	5	1,576	82				55	11,322	425			
81	... Ont.	25	3,547	191	1	312	6	38	59,924	755	13	6,365	88
82	Harold, Ont.	3	3,697	58									
83	Three Rivers, Que.	8	1,256	83	5	588	10				269	27,704	538

No. 17.—STATEMENT showing the Description, Number and Tonnage of Canadian and United States Vessels trading on the Rivers and Lakes, etc.—*Concluded.*

VESSELS ARRIVED.

Number.	Ports and Outports.	CANADIAN.						UNITED STATES.					
		Steam.			Sail.			Steam.			Sail.		
		Number of Vessels.	Tons Register.	Number of Crew.	Number of Vessels.	Tons Register.	Number of Crew.	Number of Vessels.	Tons Register.	Number of Crew.	Number of Vessels.	Tons Register.	Number of Crew.
85	Toronto, Ont.	976	795,900	46,300	10	4,096	47	81	75,208	2,798	2	450	7
86	Valleyfield, Que.	6	1,581	50									
87	M..e, Ont.	57	29,812	838				172	107,529	5,331	47	16,606	310
88	Wallaceburg, Ont.	28	2,166	140	1	230	4	460	167,887	15,469	12	3,366	80
89	Welland, Ont.							17	28,139	307	6	10,540	46
90	W. Dock, Ont.	74	10,533	551	16	801	71	1,277	333,803	12,834	1	216	10
91	Whitby, Ont..Y.T.	4	684	48	1	326	6	6	2,422	198	9	2,446	9
92	W.. Horse, Y.T.	1	489	24				3	725	29	1	677	6
93	Wiarton, Ont.	138	138,134	2,522	2	275	2	281	221,003	5,002	5	1,650	18
94	W.., Ont.		132	19	3	531	9						
95	W.. Island, Ont.	8						13	302	46	3	79	6
	Total	8,398	7,104,254	236,161	718	224,992	3,531	13,893	6,340,243	218,230	2,459	504,437	5,856

No. 17.—SUMMARY STATEMENT of Canadian and United States Vessels trading on *Inland* Waters, which arrived at Canadian ports during the Fiscal Year ended March 31, 1915.

RECAPITULATION.

	Number of Vessels.	Tons Register.	Number of Crew.
Canadian—Steam	8,398	7,104,254	236,161
Sail	718	224,992	3,531
United States—Steam	13,893	6,340,243	218,230
Sail	2,459	504,437	5,856
Total	25,468	14,173,926	463,778

DESCRIPTION OF VESSELS.

Description.	Number of Vessels.	Tons Register.
Steam—Screw	18,892	11,097,066
Paddle	3,282	2,309,954
Stern wheel	117	37,477
Sail—Schooners	701	263,420
Sloops	26	615
Barges	2,450	465,394
Total	25,468	14,173,926

No. 18.—STATEMENT showing the Description, Number and Tonnage of Canadian and United States Vessels trading on the Rivers, and Lakes between Canada and the United States (exclusive of Ferriage) which Departed from each Port and Outport during the Fiscal Year ended March 31, 1915.

VESSELS DEPARTED.

Number.	Ports and Outports.	CANADIAN						UNITED STATES					
		Steam.			Sail.			Steam.			Sail.		
		Number of Vessels.	Tons Register.	Number of Crew.	Number of Vessels.	Tons Register.	Number of Crew.	Number of Vessels.	Tons Register.	Number of Crew.	Number of Vessels.	Tons Register.	Number of Crew.
1	▉g, Ont.	48	5,207	270	8	420	19	698	207,926	920	19	8,938	73
2	▉ale, Ont.							2	184	12			
3	Bath, Ont.	18	9,110	767	4	698	20						
4	Belleville, Ont.	41	23,330	536	47	9,551	230						
5	Blind ▉r, Ont.	8	509	55	1	517	6	60	19,043	719	8	3,893	57
6	Bowmanville, Ont.				8	1,826	47						
7	▉g, Ont.	54	33,869	2,829				178	5,223	699	252	98,789	522
8	Brighton, Ont.	114	183,862	8,704	12	6,860	65	842	101,201	9,225	20	7,153	120
9	Brockville, Ont.	6		62				22	12,380	331	3	2,661	18
10	Bruce ▉s, Ont.	26	45,479	491				22	38,990	425	1	550	7
11	Bying ▉, Ont.	31	5,084	310				154	1,104	1,017			
12	Cardinal, ▉.	108	32,130	1,287	1	188	7	7	608	44			
13	▉, Ont.							1	14,249	22	4	907	28
14	Chicoutimi, Que.							4	110	15	2	336	8
15	▉, Ont.	357	1,042,967	14,535	11	2,395	66	17	408	60			
16	▉, Ont.	18	976	101				63	101,637	3,200			
17	▉n, Island, Ont.	24	21,836	653				256	10,613	801			
18	▉d, Ont.	2	60	18				1,549	250,017	18,819	2	1,420	16
19	Cornwall, Ont.							33	12,033	424			
20	Courtright, Ont.	35	4,982	259	4	802	8	26	12,934	818	18	11,147	137
21	Cutler, Ont.	2	492	35				103	274,630	2,316	1	6,041	36
22	Dawson, Y.T.	18	25,908	337				2	157	9	17	1,862	9
23	▉t, Ont.				15	2,184	66						36
24	Deseronto, Ont.	1	50	141							18	1,568	
25	Ellis Bay, Que.	8	7,227	26									
26	Forty ▉e, Y.T.	1	489	636				28	13,361	848	18	5,429	18
27	F▉t Frances, Ont.	53	7,579		4	802	4						

No.	Port													
28	Fort William, Ont.	62	119,525	2,142	23			496	1,101,969	11,208	8	11,664	63
29	Gananoque, Ont.	778	8,245	1,304		169	5,405	1,824	29,905	5,297	1	15	2
30	... Que.	20	24,928	306				33	18,019	1,333		2,322	18
31	Goderich, Ont.	1	36	9				10	9,490	806	5		
32	Gore Bay, Ont.	2	2,917	39				5	1,589	78		342	6
33	Hamilton, Ont.							160	14,758	1,532	1		
34	Iroquois, Ont.	19	4,754	275				9	15,622	175	2	2,811	15
35	Kenora, Ont.	5	11,013	103				22	8,243	988	11	1,386	18
36	Key Harbour, Ont.							292	320,162	2,997		712	22
37	Kincardine, Ont.	786	425,445	12,490	334	1,012	53,841	5	1,020	38			
38	Kingston, Ont.	2	76	9				117	11,188	864	129	13,397	266
39	Kingsville, Ont.	1	306	10							27	13,936	161
40	Leamington, Ont.	3	3,156	54	1	2	120	99	83,081	3,515			
41	Lévis, Que.	6	1,765	76									
42	Isle Current, Ont.	3	665	11									
43	Magog, Que.										3	873	21
44	Meaford, Ont.							3	2,576	48	1	1,862	9
45	... Harbour, Ont.	33	47,873	589	14	84	4,340	7	9,801	119	2	1,456	14
46	Midland, Ont.	328	310,251	5,851	60	367	33,640	73	171,926	1,500	105	27,887	368
47	Montreal, Que.							278	303,926	5,040	1	201	4
48	..., Ont.					42	6,842	412	28,921	2,375			
49	Murray Bay, Que.	11	788	81	7	69	2,369						
50	Napanee, Ont.	493	357,464	17,942	15								
51	Niagara, Ont.	19	2,443	185				10	10,769	433	137	13,632	180
52	Ottawa, Ont.	34	6,847	345		6	305	30	26,310	1,815	1	738	7
53	Owen Sound, Ont.					208	9,136	4	2,463	52	1	538	7
54	Parry Sound, Ont.	2	474	23	1	15	498						
55	Penetanguishene, Ont.	20	7,183	447	30								
56	Picton, Ont.	39	100,453	1,078	4			71	17,240	642	12	12,924	72
57	Point Edward, Ont.	400	641,069	13,491									
58	Port Arthur, Ont.	6	137	29		205	26,062	12	1,614	109	13	10,979	49
59	Port Burwell, Ont.	303	477,851	5,276	34			121	343,515	2,484	1	630	6
60	Port ..., Ont.	23	11,066	276				10	2,137	99			
61	Port Dalhousie, Ont.	50	1,350	203				7	226	64			
62	Port ..., Ont.				6	34	1,700				2	2,355	15
63	Port Hope, Ont.	14	19,286	231				29	86,382	634	4	1,972	24
64	Port ..., Ont.							416	596,822	14,580	422	42,808	844
65	Port Stanley, Ont.	79	52,142	3,518	12	59	5,459	205	127,288	4,347			
66	Prescott, Ont.	53	51,839	945	7	60	4,239	4	5,037	60			
67	..., Que.	677	594,194	27,694									
68	..., Ont.	69	2,737	319				16	539	53	7	194	20
69	Rainy River, Ont.	12	10,890	186				154	740,825	3,221	1	474	5
70	Rimouski, Que.	12	1,691	100									
71	Rockport, Ont.	7	565	45									
72	Rondeau, Ont.		86	10									
73	Rykerts, B.C.	4		44									
74	Sandwich, Ont.		1,995		45	224	23,026	522	191,589	4,869	17	4,318	66
75	Sarnia, Ont.	231	62,935	2,613	3	18	922	1,499	547,289	46,380	20	15,297	99
76	Sault Ste. Marie, Ont.	653	236,286	7,123				585	381,320	9,708	62	39,246	405
77	Smith's Falls, Ont.	34	417	216									
78	Sorel, Que.	2		15							260	27,285	520

No. 18.—STATEMENT showing the Description, Number and Tonnage of Canadian and United States Vessels trading on the Rivers and Lakes, etc.—*Concluded.*

VESSELS DEPARTED.

Number	Ports and Outports	CANADIAN						UNITED STATES					
		Steam			Sail			Steam			Sail		
		Number of Vessels	Tons Register	Number of Crew	Number of Vessels	Tons Register	Number of Crew	Number of Vessels	Tons Register	Number of Crew	Number of Vessels	Tons Register	Number of Crew
79	Southampton, Ont.	6	1,579	84	1	348	5						
80	Stickeen, B.C.	2	58	13	3	4	13						
81	St. John's, Que.	38	1,368	151	29	3,133	82	35	469	128		1	3
82	...n, Ont.												
83	Thorold, Ont.	8	6,356	144				74	4,975	608	1,167	116,720	2,272
84	Three Rivers, Que.	8	1,256	88	5	588	10	55	11,322	425	13	6,365	88
85	Toronto, Ont.	978	757,945	46,349	20	8,434	111	38	61,301	763	263	26,717	526
86	Valleyfield, Que.	6	1,581	50	2	460	8	82	24,276	2,100			
87	Walkerville, Ont.	12	8,148	168	2	487	6	172	117,682	6,402	47	15,966	365
88	...g, Ont.	35	3,168	190				465	167,298	15,543	12	3,209	71
89	Welland, Ont.				16	801	64	22	37,308	415	7	12,394	57
90	West ..., Ont.	72	10,563	552	1	326	6	1,276	332,731	12,526	1	216	10
91	Whitby, Ont.	5	1,883	76				3	1,580	107	6	1,777	6
92	... Horse, Y.T.								37	6			
93	Wiarton, Ont.				4	920	16						
94	Windsor, Ont.	86	59,240	1,421	6	750	21	281	220,063	4,993	5	1,650	19
95	Wolfe Island, Ont.	10	156	22				11	296	36	3	89	6
	All	7,540	5,944,096	187,139	800	226,398	3,454	14,052	7,269,707	212,239	3,171	587,440	7,761

No. 18.—SUMMARY STATEMENT of Canadian and United States Vessels, trading on Inland Waters, which *departed* from Canadian Ports during the Fiscal Year ended March 31, 1915.

RECAPITULATION.

—	Number of Vessels.	Tons Register.	Number of Crew.
Canadian—Steam..	7,540	5,944,096	187,139
Sail..	800	226,398	3,454
United States—Steam..	14,052	7,269,707	212,239
Sail..	3,171	587,440	7,761
Total....................................	25,563	14,027,641	410,593

DESCRIPTION OF VESSELS.

Description.	Number of Vessels.	Tons Register.
Steam—Screw...	18,484	11,022,164
Paddle...	2,990	2,153,628
Sternwheel...	118	38,011
Sail—Schooners...	809	279,708
Sloops...	29	578
Barges...	3,133	533,552
Total...	25,563	14,027,641

No. 19.—STATEMENT showing the Description, Number and Tonnage of Canadian and United States Vessels, trading on the Rivers and Lakes between Canada and the United States (exclusive of Ferriage), which Arrived and Departed during the Fiscal Year ended March 31, 1915.

	CANADIAN.			UNITED STATES.			TOTAL.		
	Number of Vessels.	Tons Register.	Number of Crew.	Number of Vessels.	Tons Register.	Number of Crew.	Number of Vessels.	Tons Register.	Number of Crew.
Arrived............	9,116	7,329,246	239,692	16,352	6,844,680	224,086	25,468	14,173,926	463,778
Departed..........	8,340	6,170,494	190,593	17,223	7,857,147	220,000	25,563	14,027,641	410,593
Total........	17,456	13,499,740	430,285	33,575	14,701,827	444,086	51,031	28,201,567	874,371

No. 20.—STATEMENT of Vessels, British and Foreign, employed in the Coasting Trade of the Dominion of Canada, which arrived at, or departed from, the undermentioned Ports and Outports, during the Fiscal Year ended March 31, 1915.

STEAMERS.

Ports and Outports.	VESSELS ARRIVED.						VESSELS DEPARTED.					
	BRITISH.			FOREIGN.			BRITISH.			FOREIGN.		
	Number of Vessels.	Tons Register.	Crew Number.	Number of Vessels.	Tons Register.	Crew Number.	Number of Vessels.	Tons Register.	Crew Number.	Number of Vessels.	Tons Register.	Crew Number.
....rt, N.B.	41	1,892	246				9	416	70			
...., P.E.I.	1	48	6				1	48	6			
Alert Bay, B.C.	634	387,556	22,062				633	384,537	22,075			
Amherst, N.S.	1	46	6				1	46	6			
Amherstburg, Ont.	81	17,064	807				20	2,224	109			
Annapolis Royal, N.S.	115	6,250	804				116	6,280	806			
...th, N.S.	58	4,561	451				58	4,561	451			
Anyox, B.C.	215	181,150	9,348				203	171,329	9,294			
...rt, N.S.	985	90,592	8,412				980	88,983	8,377			
...ville, Ont.	10	2,270	170				10	2,270	170			
...ck, N.S.	281	67,412	3,346	18	11,723	371	265	59,351	3,071	34	19,776	637
Baie ...rte, N.B.	630	35,151	5,355	1	876	19	630	35,151	5,355			
Barrington Passage, N.S.	1	24	3	15	252	53	1	24	3	15	252	53
Barton, N.S.	408	63,738	5,966				52	724	112			
Bath, Ont.	16	922	110				17	1,034	118			
Bathurst, N.B.	47	3,208	324	4	2,851	71	47	3,208	334	4	2,851	71
Bear River, N.S.	200	113,806	7,798				14	1,054	87			
Belleville, Ont.	5	57	11				5	57	11			
Belliveau's Cove, N.S.	187	79,033	4,081				44	21,772	888			
Blind River, Ont.	1	1,199	28				1	1,199	28			
Bowmanville, Ont.	38	2,128	228				39	2,184	234			
Bridgetown, N.S.	67	3,367	431	2	883	15	67	3,367	431	2	883	15
Bridgewater, N.S.	70	41,989	3,397				67	34,570	2,877			
Brighton, Ont.	349	316,515	15,370				160	186,830	8,717			
...le, Ont.	361	103,550	4,924				114	36,142	1,472			
Bruce Mines, Ont.	34	7,303	422				45	30,362	640			
Buctouche, N.B.	33	16,610	607				30	9,485	569			
Byng Inlet, Ont.												
Campbellton, N.B.	154	25,854	1,465	5	3,487	66	134	20,944	1,221			
...po Bello, N.B.										15	155	30
...ng, N.S.	31	2,209	247				30	2,137	239			

Port												
Canso, N.S.	1,559	196,126	14,961				1,559	197,052	14,806	1	26	4
...., N.B.	8	269	40				8	269	40			
Carcross, Y.T.	70	8,174	832				71	8,229	86			
...., P.E.I.	32	3,008	438				34	3,284	466			
...., Que.	72	31,219	1,499	1	912	19	71	31,098	1,494	1	912	19
...., B.E.I.	624	251,313	13,721				619	245,983	13,372			
Chatham, Ont.	35	8,501	270				36	7,614	268			
Chemainus, B.C.	52	12,486	617				12	996	73			
...., N.S.	211	22,292	2,141				210	22,238	2,137			
...., Que.	41	1,400	223				44	1,479	243			
...., N.S.	79	7,359	866	2	1,463	34	79	6,286	867			
Church Point, N.S.	127	140,595	6,153	8	10,177	170	134	137,902	6,311	5	5,867	97
Clark's Harbour, N.S.	1	24	3				1	24	3			
...., N.S.	410	22,798	3,313				410	22,798	3,313			
...., Ont.	8	462	49				8	462	49			
Cockburn Island, Ont.	49	27,800	1,884				3	4,755	13			
...., Ont.	153	35,890	2,487				34	79,529	261			
Cornwall, Ont.	140	78,764	2,960				137	4,089	2,627			
Courtwright, Ont.	255	212,018	12,380				6	122,782	79			
Crapaud, P.E.I.	88	120,823	1,695				91	12,226	1,736			
Cutler, Ont.	60	12,660	530				58	42,815	512			
Dalhousie, N.B.	319	45,903	2,404	14	16,275	286	297	486	2,242			
Dawson, Y.T.	13	13,659	255				3	49,837	42			
Dep ... Harbour, Ont.	D9	50,326	2,289				108	39,207	2,272			
Deseronto, Ont.	20	24,617	295				26	931	483			
Digby, N.S.	133	66,371	5,172				10	303,364	73			
Dorchester, N.B.	499	302,866	18,932				498	23	18,025	2	1,474	37
Dunnville, Ont.	2	46	7					50,804	4			
Ellis Bay, Que.	82	58,122	1,632				74	49,084	1,497			
Esquimaux Point, Que.	53	49,084	1,627				53	6,389	1,627			
Forty-Mile, Y.T.	16	6,389	255				16	1,850,855	259			
Fort William, Ont.	881	1,663,449	31,313				986	1,384	34,786			
Freeport, N.S.	47	1,695	189				42	8,154	146			
Gananoque, Ont.	364	99,543	7,235				44	57,704	610			
Gaspe, Que.	84	57,704	2,700				84	20,038	2,700			
...., P.E.I.	202	20,136	2,807				201	1,973	2,799			
Glace Bay, N.S.	18	1,973	184				18	72,366	184			
...., Ont.	107	105,848	1,629				80	55,362	743			
Gore Bay, Ont.	414	121,008	6,608				270	4,425	2,703			
...., N.S.	44	4,425	392				44	39,916	392			
Guysborough, N.S.	353	40,694	3,181				353	486,599	3,083			
Halifax, N.S.	1,453	432,629	20,360	5	4,705	122	1,456	305,282	23,136	9	5,742	158
Hamilton, Ont.	686	308,540	21,136				607	1,530	17,539	1	331	21
Hantsport, N.S.	32	1,475	194				34	5	207			
Indian ..., N.B.	4	316	42	1			1	316	42			
Inverness, N.S.	247	19,122	1,042				247	19,122	1,042	22	383	44
Iona, N.S.	14	7,798	544	1	331	21	14	7,798	544			
Iroquois, Ont.	143	29,071	1,633	2	1,494	33	144	29,089	1,635			
Isaac's Harbour, N.S.												

No. 20.—STATEMENT of Vessels, British and Foreign, employed in the Coasting Trade, etc.—*Continued.*

STEAMERS—*Continued.*

Ports and Outports.	VESSELS ARRIVED.						VESSELS DEPARTED.					
	BRITISH.			FOREIGN.			BRITISH.			FOREIGN.		
	Number of Vessels.	Tons Register.	Crew Number.	Number of Vessels.	Tons Register.	Crew Number.	Number of Vessels.	Tons Register.	Crew Number.	Number of Vessels.	Tons Register.	Crew Number.
Joggins Mines, N.S.	49	2,279	305				47	2,185	283			
...lo, B.C.	378	80,247	7,452				378	80,735	7,457			
Kenora, Ont.	22	6,310	356				19	4,396	275			
Kentville, N.S.	89	4,346	623				90	4,398	630			
Key Harbour, Ont.	1	1,375	20				6	8,490	116			
Kincardine, Ont.	27	1,396	149				27	1,396	149			
Kingsport, N.S.	7	362	46				7	362	46			
Kingston, Ont.	931	909,019	21,496				633	290,418	12,461			
...ille, ...	166	39,282	1,804				167	39,089	1,803	1	685	15
Ladner, B.C.	178	16,831	1,366				177	16,688	1,355			
Ladysmith, B.C.	856	79,715	7,900				866	78,770	8,039			
La...d, N.S.	144	7,433	875	30	70,907	814	153	7,046	942	36	79,407	960
...s, Que.	8	16,123	229				18	33,506	483			
Little Current, Ont.	261	119,412	4,657	6	127	32	59	36,374	1,394	12	872	64
Liverpool, N.S.	190	9,107	929				199	11,322	986			
Lockeport, N.S.	38	1,589	171				41	1,689	189			
Lord's Cove, N.B	91	4,560	527	2	27	4	88	4,602	529	8	143	17
Louisburg, N.S.	387	187,498	4,728	16	27,031	422,401	401	166,993	4,749	17	30,973	434
...er East Pubnico, N.S.	136	11,304	1,254				131	10,827	1,202			
Lunenburg, N.S.	126	7,721	614				134	7,992	740			
Mabou, N.S.	23	1,797	259				23	1,797	259			
Magdalen Islands, Que.	60	21,411	1,341				64	28,480	1,306			
...ine ...y, N.S.	46	2,776	329				48	2,860	351			
Maitland, N.S.	1	36	5					36	5			
...e, N.S.	97	7,716	1,019				95	7,387	1,001			
Meaford, Ont.	101	4,981	707				102	5,151	717			
...an River, N.S.	145	72,224	3,118				145	72,224	3,118			
Michipicoten Harbour, Ont.	1	24	3				1	24	3			
...in, N.S.	56	47,069	1,277				58	48,944	1,327			
Midland, Ont.	53	2,693	371				53	2,693	371			
...n, N.B.	160	195,504	2,604				176	198,247	2,839			
Montague Bridge, P.E.I	97	6,839	571				93	6,669	550			
Montreal, Que.	104	9,904	1,396				103	9,854	1,392			
	5,035	2,450,683	97,188	79	220,767	2,576	5,014	2,504,485	96,571	81	227,016	2,625
Morrisburg, Ont.	7	3,765	255				7	3,765	255			
Murray ...ur, P.E.I.	37	3,557	509				37	3,557	509			

Port											
Nanaimo, B.C.	2,296	659,829	27,980	4	6,111		2,249	653,584	44,247	4	59	9
Napanee, Ont.	16	451	58	1	1,826		17	596	73	74	108,992	1,802
..., B.C.	1,301	397,353	22,087				1,301	397,353	22,087			
Newcastle, N.B.	4	6,777	98			95	5	595	55			
New Campbellton, N.S.	5	595	55			26	695	46,290	4,450			
New Westminster, B.C.	695	42,928	4,398	2	46		512	203,662	9,542			
Newport, B. O.	519	203,532	9,615	70	112,498	1,854	866	775,603	36,268			
Niagara, Ont.	687	569,544	27,468				88	5,300	760			
North East Harbour, N.S.	62	3,745	750				71	4,080	292			
...th Head, J.B.	387	124,186	272				348	115,576	4,362			
...th Sydney, N.S.	208	-23,117	4,740	36	47,731	3,303	212	22,445	2,296	43	56,381	3,444
Ottawa, Ont.	405	193,531	2,287				317	89,772	4,740			
...en Sound, Ont.	216	66,237	8,730				202	65,293	2,170			
Parrsboro', N.S.	109	31,165	2,234	5	4,873	95	98	23,075	1,760			
Parry Sound, Ont.	71	34,523	2,162				71	28,778	1,701			
Paspebiac, Que.	119	2,143	1,721				6	1,885	110			
Penetanguishene, Ont.	690	74,991	124	3	3,110	59	119	72,483	1,885			
Percé, Que.	476	189,312	3,201				272	53,365	3,194			
Picton, Ont.	215	159,456	13,768				485	168,111	4,385	2	2,470	46
Pictou, N.S.	108	272,125	10,894	2	2,470	46	257	242,886	11,142			
Point Edward, Ont.	96	63,533	8,057				110	63,569	8,381			
Port Alberni, B.C.	78	248,365	3,566				84	200,987	3,574			
Port Arthur, ...	93	2,988	1,851	322	614,454	6,876	72	2,847	4,052	336	641,169	7,127
Port Burwell, Ont.	870	5,260	467				95	5,349	452			
Port ...le, N.S.	638	1,050,683	793				667	770,953	809			
Port ...ie, Ont.	2	355,288	15,928				537	301,430	11,214			
...rt Dalhousie, Ont.	62	157	13,893				2	157	12,200			
Port Dover, Ont.	248	3,157	2				62	3,157	16			
Port George, N.S.	48	17,430	46				226	17,006	434			
Port Hood, N.S.	106	29,552	434				48	29,552	2,300			
Port Hope, N.S.	40	6,396	2,316				106	6,396	2,078			
Port La...ur, N.S.	1,173	4,277	2,078				39	4,158	931			
Port Morien, N.S.	242	108,816	931				1,172	109,688	366			
Port Mulgrave, N.S.	334	525,753	377				223	489,819	10,042	3	878	42
Port ...ill, Ont.	92	195,100	10,026				330	191,629	11,008			
Port Simpson, B.C.	34	16,365	11,433				86	9,099	10,915			
Port ...ly, Ont.	1,127	1,570	11,110				35	1,613	587			
Powell River, B.C.	321	361,971	677				1,116	359,706	244			
Prescott, Ont.	1,295	320,822	238				203	264,425	25,896	4	48	42
Prince R... ...t, B.C.	765	511,269	26,131	5	60	50	1,353	608,936	14,833			
Pugwash, N.S.	266	1,286,501	17,887	37	7,046	107	1,048	2,061,826	33,680			
Quebec, Que.	108	273,059	29,892		65,339	1,175	212	152,076	71,495	49	109,078	2,332
Rainy River, Ont.	33	26,812	50,025				108	26,812	7,822			
River Hébert, N.S.	34	1,484	12,046				33	1,484	1,620			
Rivière du Loup, Que.	67	35,610	1,620				34	35,610	191			
Rockport, Ont.	3	16,134	191		40	6	75	26,941	1,840			
Rondeau, Ont.	346	179	1,840	3			3	179	2,095			
St. ...as, N.B.	46	18,574	1,123				367	18,599	16	7	153	24
St. ...e, N.B.		2,859	16				46	2,944	1,546			
			1,522						362			
			357									

No. 20.—STATEMENT of Vessels, British and Foreign, employed in the Coasting Trade, etc.—Continued.

STEAMERS—Continued.

Ports and Outports	Vessels Arrived						Vessels Departed					
	British			Foreign			British			Foreign		
	Number of Vessels	Tons Register	Crew Number	Number of Vessels	Tons Register	Crew Number	Number of Vessels	Tons Register	Crew Number	Number of Vessels	Tons Register	Crew Number
St. John, N.B.	1,318	476,231	24,284	3	4,641	74	1,403	724,606	33,274	2	4,849	56
St. John's, Que.	3	144	15				4	146	17			
St. Martins, N.B.	7	297	38				8	297	37			
St. Peter's, N.S.	106	11,164	1,174				101	10,386	1,111			
St. Stephen, N.B.	105	1,488	290				108	2,261	264			
St. Thomas, Ont.	92	16,365	677				86	9,099	587			
Sackville, N.B.	1	31	5				1	31	5			
Sandy Point, N.S.	36	1,270	264				35	1,240	264			
Sandwich, Ont.	1	48	7				2	1,692	28			
Sandy Cove, N.S.	39	1,247	137				36	1,147	144			
Sarnia, Ont.	362	569,028	15,318				371	544,844	16,092			
Sault Ste. Marie, Ont.	3,505	2,308,330	79,891				1,146	833,852	25,738			
Shediac, N.B.	228	126,823	7,129	2	2,811	45,227	227	125,944	6,980	2	2,811	45
Sheet Harbour, N.S.	171	32,364	2,314				191	34,932	2,568	2	44	4
Shelburne, N.S.	18	767	87						92			
Sherbrooke, N.S.	52	5,243	513				52	5,243	513			
Shippegan, N.B.	26	440	108				27	451	105			
Sidney, B.C.	395	58,181	5,331				415	60,765	5,413			
Smith's Falls, Ont.	132	23,973	1,981				131	23,684	1,944			
Sorel, Que.	774	909,947	36,294	3	5,231	75	773	904,647	36,208	3	5,231	75
Souris, P.E.I.	130	45,018	2,947				123	42,591	2,554			
Steveston, B.C.	379	28,251	2,740				430	32,568	3,373			
Stewart, B.C.	19	30,875	1,311	1	254	18	19	30,875	1,311			
Summerside, P.E.I.	283	169,744	8,946				270	157,235	8,468			
Sydney, N.S.	905	903,187	19,356	144	303,096	4,316	906	832,073	19,439	150	326,466	4,329
Thessalon, Ont.	369	129,089	7,017	11	25,371	303	231	68,119		11	25,371	303
Tilbury, Ont.	25	20,652	449				18	15,988	330			
Three Rivers, Que.	484	722,381	20,282				484	722,381	20,282			
Toronto, Ont.	1,727	966,815	46,635				1,620	828,169	43,999			
Truro, N.S.	31	2,209	258				31	2,209	258			
Union Bay, B.C.	938	253,115	16,382				934	252,457	16,448			
Valleyfield, Que.	6	1,581	50				6	1,581	50			
Vancouver, B.C.	7,733	3,070,311	175,799				8,049	3,213,570	169,574			
Victoria, B.C.	3,182	2,348,747	106,983				3,220	2,209,079	106,940			
Walkerville, Ont.	73	55,036	1,026				96	45,998	1,259			
Wallaceburg, Ont.	57	17,891	455				53	15,889	389			

Welland, Ont.	32	41,572	588				32	10,673	8	141	
West Dock, Ont.	190	44,802	2,058				190	44,802	190	2,061	
Westport, N.S.	279	19,075	2,678				282	19,278	282	2,698	
Weymouth, N.S.	409	10,820	1,409				408	11,013	408	1,276	
Whitby, Ont.	1	1,199	28				1	1,199	1	28	
Whte Horse, Y.T.	91	46,023	2,036				91	46,024	91	2,029	
Whte Rock, B.C.	5	273	34				6	215	6	31	
Wiarton, Ont.	176	32,193	1,899	3	725	29	178	35,632	178	1,888	1 / 37 / 6
...or, N.S.	57	2,387	339	7	4,966	122	56	2,381	56	320	2 / 1,437 / 31
Windsor, Ont.	289	124,685	2,500				202	153,119	202	3,253	
Wolfe ...ld, Ont.	1	35	5				1	35	1	5	
Wolfville, N.S.	38	1,805	267				38	1,805	38	267	
Yarmouth, N.S.	339	33,663	3,013				464	41,898	464	4,337	
Total	68,505	32,856,755	1,436,800	880	1,587,007	23,826	63,029	30,083,292	1,332,671	961	1,663,222 / 25,018

SAILING VESSELS.

Albert, N.B.	14	1,074	47	1	360	7	2	130	6		
Alberton, P.E.I.	62	3,588	234				62	3,510	228		
Alert Bay, B.C.	4	3,738	28				4	4,048	23	5	
Amherst, N.S.	63	1,799	135				67	2,232	153		
Amherstburg, Ont.	1	230	4				3	329	12		
Annapolis Royal, N.S.	72	2,879	212		173		83	424	253	1	173
...h, N.S.	137	4,923	423				137	4,923	423		
...fox, B.C.	9	10,165	56		588	14	4	4,464	26	3	588 / 14
Arichat, N.S.	385	17,079	1,212				394	17,333	1,205		
...k, N.S.	225	9,659	946	49	2,735	540	204	8,629	881	75	3,789 / 565
Barrington Passage, N.S.	46	2,617	163	2	119	21	46	2,617	163	2	119 / 21
Bass..., N.S.	21	906	65				28	1,614	94		
Bath, Ont.	5	507	15				3	507	15		
Bathurst, N.B.	82	6,282	350	26	7,910	141	82	6,262	350	26	7,910 / 141
Bc... River, N.S.	18	2,685	83	1	276	5	10	1,118	42		5
Belleville, Ont.	3	1,041	17				·1	196	5		
Belliveau's ... N.S.	56	2,093	143				58	2,447	158		
Blind River, Ont.	6	2,482	48								
Bowmanville, Ont.											
Bridgetown, N.S.	7	474	23	2	233	9	2	524	11		
Bridgewater, N.S.	56	10,927	297	10	5,600	80	9	672	31	1	337 / 6
Bruce ..., Ont.	1	517	5				24	2,031	112		
Buctouche, N.B.	50	2,662	181				1	1,034	10		
Byng Inlet, Ont.	1	500	5				59	2,949	185		
...	40	4,435	184	13	12,448	178	37	500	163		
Campbellton, N.B.	1	53	4				1	4,000	5		
Campo Bello, N.B.							1	39	2		
Canning, N.S.	23	1,850	69				22	1,501	66		
Canso, N.S.	558	28,046	2,267	11	2,306	66	585	28,181	2,387	9	1,410 / 52
Caraquet, N.B.	220	4,259	882	2	266	14	220	4,259	882	1	181 / 7

No. 20.—STATEMENT of Vessels, British and Foreign, employed in the Coasting Trade, &c.—Continued.

SAILING VESSELS—Continued.

Ports and Outports.	VESSELS ARRIVED.						VESSELS DEPARTED.					
	BRITISH.			FOREIGN.			BRITISH.			FOREIGN.		
	Number of Vessels.	Tons Register.	Crew Number.	Number of Vessels.	Tons Register.	Crew Number.	Number of Vessels.	Tons Register.	Crew Number.	Number of Vessels.	Tons Register.	Crew Number.
Cardigan, P.E.I.	33	2,170	133				31	1,955	121			
...r, Que.	6	429	31				7	550	36			
Charlottetown, P.E.I.	736	50,729	2,431	5	900	30	744	53,649	2,501	4	801	25
Chatham, N.B.	199	11,530	740				182	9,194	648			
Chatham, Ont.	15	1,618	55	1	489	5	20	2,723	83			
Chemainus, B.C.	4	1,512	12				4	1,512	12			
Chester, N.S.	200	9,999	676				198	8,660	734			
Cheticamp, N.S.	49	1,424	299				52	1,518	200			
Chicoutimi, Que.	10	836	40				11	902	39			
Church Point, N.S.	16	1,428	69				10	573	37			
Clarenceville, Que.	1	5	5				1	5	2			
Clark's Harbour, N.S.	58	3,012	195	16	498	55	58	3,012	190	16	498	55
Clementsport, N.S.	2	103	6				6	673	25			
Cobourg, Ont.	1	195										
...rn Island, Ont.	5	1,134	31				5	1,134	31			
Courtright, Ont.	5	1,269	22				8	1,951	34			
Crapaud, P.E.I.	35	2,778	118				36	2,823	121			
C... r, Ont.	1	531	5				1	531	5			
Dalhousie, N.B.	31	2,999	129	4	3,475	39	26	2,281	108	9	10,546	145
Dawson, Y.	59	15,254	118				62	15,800	124			
Deseronto, Ont.	10	1,045	39				4	182	16			
Digby, N.S.	173	7,184	712	1	447	7	164	6,726	649			
Dorchester, N.B.	6	684	26				5	862	24			
Ellis Bay, Que.	11	164	33				12	857	53			
Esquimaux Point, Que.	71	3,107	291				71	3,107	291			
Forty-Mile, Y.T.	10	5,550	10				70	5,550	10			
Freeport, N.S.	66	1,221	271				66	2,278	278			
Gananoque, Ont.	12	1,238	35				14	401	38			
Gaspé, Que.	88	17,986	691				68	11,274	501	4	181	27
Georgetown, P.E.I.	96	5,883	355				91	5,516	322			
G..., N.S.	179	8,584	365				188	9,116	383			
Grand Narrows, N.S.	3	129	8				3	129				
Guysborough, N.S.	44	2,180	122				41	1,889	112			
Halifax, N.S.	2,580	134,965	11,977	14	7,712	121	2,455	138,928	8,984	33	16,765	268
Hantsport, N.S.	10	2,194	77	9	3,349	55	13	4,497	51	10	4,037	57
H...h, N.B.	29	2,708	84	1	366	6	23	535	54			

Port												
Isaac's Harbour, N.S.	45	3,797	200	1	315		44	3,519	190			
Joggins Mines, N.S.	26	2,947	89				19	1,518	89			
...ville, N.S.	33	1,242	79				34	1,299	79			
Kincardine, Ont.	5	695	23				5	695	23			
...t, N.S.	28	2,961	88				28	2,882	91			
Kingston, Ont.	189	89,585	1,100				343	110,556	1,985			
...	1	188	7									
Ladysmith, B.C.	423	375,729	2,072				423	375,729	2,072			
La Have, N.S.	103	10,865	674				119	12,874	752	3	780	35
Little Current, Ont.	1	2,137	32					517	4	8	114	24
Liverpool, N.S.	161	10,326	629	10	4,020	65	157	8,847	616			
Lockeport, N.S.	48	3,254	224	8	117	25	53	3,877	255			
Londonderry, N.S.	29	1,899	87				29	1,899	87			
Lords Cove, N.B.	7	379	19				6	349	16	2	177	14
Louisburg, N.S.	189	43,212	863	3	71	10	184	40,897	809	2	47	6
Lower East Pubnico, N.S.	67	2,019	203				81	1,737	129			
Lunenburg, N.S.	383	23,567	1,962	2	171	39	383	25,174	1,891	38	4,796	783
Magdalen Islands, Que.	144	8,643	1,334				141	6,297	1,209			
Mahone Bay, N.S.	65	5,018	190				82	3,248	500			
Maitland, N.S.	56	4,631	64				46	866	150			
Margaree, N.S.	21	296	19				22	192	70			
Margaretsville, N.S.	6		296				4	1,733	12			
Meteghan River, N.S.	45	2,015	145				42	340	133			
...in, N.S.	15	340	45				15	1,687	45			
...ind, Ont.	5	2,171	26				4	7,006	19			
...an, N.B.	81	5,070	255				92	4,338	310			
Montague Bridge, P.E.I.	79	4,920	278				72	490,646	251			
Montreal, Que.	1,958	494,897	8,846				1,954	2,688	8,847	1	819	8
Murray Harbour, P.E.I.	66	2,588	159				66	715	159			
Napanee, Ont.		143	4				5	362,800	20			
Nelson, B.C.	731	362,800	1,462				731	4,607	1,462			
Newcastle, N.B.	100	9,701	407	4	1,255	28	71	668	258			
New Campbellton, N.S.	20	668	55	4	169	55	20	71,316	65			
Newport, B.C.	93	71,714	385				92	4,118	381			
New Glasgow, N.S.	120	4,219	315				118	37,800	313			
New Westminster, B.C.	101	38,198	218	2	113	24	100	510	211			
N...eth East Harbour, N.S.	13	605	39				12	2,054	32			
...rth ..., N.B.	28	1,697	92				30	41,432	107			
...rth Sydney, N.S.	354	21,993	1,630	4	363	25	640	47,387	2,960	14	1,374	110
Ottawa, Ont.	218	37,907	785	10	954	20	288	42,685	919	3	260	6
...en Sound, Ont.	731	57,781	2,431	2	1,476	14	726	7,671	2,247	2	1,476	-14
Parrsboro', N.S.	119	9,895	569	14	1,973	75	110	517	499	9	1,906	59
Paspebiac, Que.	23	822	10				1	1,784	4			
Penetanguishene, Ont.	11	1,836	120				23	2,772	118			
Percé, Que.	590	4,327	94	13	1,782	215	7	37,432	57	10	1,058	184
Picton, Ont.	134	36,511	1,843				594	35,710	1,865			
Pictou, N.S.	8	31,019	562				158	1,051	685			
Point Edward, Ont.		1,051	11				4	343	11	43	19,558	300
Port Arthur, Ont.	64	1,088	39				74	61,383	19	1	492	8
Port Clyde, N.S.		365,265	322	43	19,558	300			400			
Port Colborne, Ont.												

6 GEORGE V, A. 1916

No. 20.—STATEMENT of Vessels, British and Foreign, employed in the Coasting Trade, &c.—Concluded.

SAILING VESSELS—Concluded.

Ports and Outports.	VESSELS ARRIVED. British. Number of Vessels	Tons Register	Crew Number	Foreign. Number of Vessels	Tons Register	Crew Number	VESSELS DEPARTED. British. Number of Vessels	Tons Register	Crew Number	Foreign. Number of Vessels	Tons Register	Crew Number
Port Credit, Ont.	4	120	12				4	120	12			
Port Dalhousie, Ont.	5	1,891	33				4	1,156	15			
Port George, N.S.	3	78	11				3	78	11			
Port ___, N.S.	21	718	81				17	691	81			
Port La ___, N.S.	22	1,136	78	1	26	3	22	1,136	78	1	26	3
Port ___, N.S.	45	3,064	221	2	424	12	44	2,659	165	2	393	14
Port ___, N.S.	19	847	88	4	51	10	22	1,145	124	1	22	2
Port Williams, N.S.	39	2,102	109				39	2,132	107			
Pugwash, N.S.	60	2,543	160				65	2,566	177			
Quebec, Que.	150	15,509	620				354	26,285	1,059	12	1,240	30
___, N.B.	80	2,890	236	1	9	3	88	4,082	255	1	159	5
River Hebert, N.S.	22	2,204	74				14	943	45			
Rockport, Ont.	1	27	4				1	27	4			
St. Andrew's, N.B.	51	2,878	157	2	462	9	61	4,025	216			
St. ___, N.B.	19	625	41				22	530	48	5	1,559	27
St. John, N.B.	870	37,451	2,481				866	47,064	2,496			
St. Johns, Que.	3	25	6				6	55	12			
St. ___, N.B.	40	3,522	129				52	4,345	178	4	943	19
St. Stephen, N.B.	61	2,969	181				59	2,930	180			
Sackville, N.B.	14	1,763	62				20	447	88			
Salmon River, N.S.	4	543	21	3	44	7	6	135	21	3	44	7
Sandy Point, N.S.	26	2,357	126	1	373	7	4	3,140	14	3	137	11
Sandwich, Ont.	1	135	4				32	280	168			
Sandy Cove, N.S.	27	648	58				2	4	4			
Sarnia, Ont.	60	20,809	292				27	24,639	68			
Sault Ste. Marie, Ont.	17	9,521	94				73	5,722	358	1	917	15
Sheediac, N.B.	69	3,110	203				19	3,392	107			
Sheet Harbour, N.S.	29	1,581	118				73	1,329	216			
___, N.S.	53	4,599	244	4	2,024	24	26	3,055	87			
___, N.S.	129	2,435	93	1	353	7	50	1,508	225	1	353	7
Shippegan, N.B.	99	3,324	524	2	478	16	19	1,585	70	2	478	16
Sidney, B.C.	129	37,422	209				132	37,044	535			
Sorel, Que.	4	1,707	17				98	2,119	207			

SESSIONAL PAPER No. 11

Port												
Souris, P.E.I.	105	8,145	397				109	8,659	417			
Southampton, Ont.	1	348	5									
..e, P.E.I.	305	21,318	1,051	11			309	22,463	1,080	2	320	10
Sydney, N.S.	594	42,046	2,517		725	66	316	25,193	1,244	5	2,615	877
..an, Ont.	1	500	4					500	4			
Three Rivers, Que.	8	1,578	32				13	1,578	32			
..ith, P.E.I.	14	469	35					414	32			
Toronto, Ont.	300	26,622	854				296	22,746	812			
Truro, N.S.	153	10,235	458				151	10,026	454			
Tusket, N.S.	6	308	26				5	213	22			
Union Bay, B.C.	24	22,096	116				25	23,231	121			
Vancouver, B.C.	537	480,632	2,654				535	479,433	2,651			
..ia, B.C.	38	34,566	183				38	35,539	189			
..le, Ont.	28	5,682	103				27	5,281	110			
Wallace, N.S.	63	5,253	212				64	5,150	213			
Wallaceburg, Ont.	25	3,509	114				28	3,744	118			
..rd, Ont.	1	284	5				1	284	5			
..t, N.S.	78	2,817	306				75	3,054	329			
Weymouth, N.S.	125	5,591	360	7	81	17	124	5,035	389	10	140	34
Whitby, Ont.	34	5,982	34	5	959	20	1	57	2	7	409	24
..te dist., Y.T.	4	1,158	16	1			31	5,404	31			
Wiarton, Ont.	260	31,191	780		677	6	3	984	16			
Windsor, N.S.	57	13,110	228	20	8,629	111	264	29,994	762	10	4,864	60
Windsor, Ont.	1	150	5				55	12,465	219			
Wolfe Isl and, Ont.	40	2,086	118				46	150	5			
..lville, N.S.	273	13,412	1,280				257	3,468	147			
..h, N.S.				2	54	7		12,696	1,181	1	34	4
Total	19,914	3,509,585	78,221	355	97,205	2,605	20,204	3,208,071	76,213	401	94,815	4,104

˙6 GEORGE V, A. 1916

No. 20.—STATEMENT of Vessels, British and Foreign, employed in the Coasting Trade, &c.—*Continued.*

RECAPITULATION.

—	STEAMERS.			SAILING VESSELS.			TOTAL.		
	Number of Vessels	Tonnage	Crew Number	Number of Vessels	Tonnage	Crew Number	Number of Vessels	Tonnage	Crew Number
Arrived.									
British.....	68,505	32,856,755	1,436,800	19,914	3,509,585	78,221	88,419	36,366,340	1,515,021
Foreign....	880	1,587,007	23,826	355	97,205	2,605	1,235	1,684,212	26,431
Total....	69,385	34,443,762	1,460,626	20,269	3,606,790	80,826	89,654	38,050,552	1,541,452
Departed.									
British.....	63,029	30,083,292	1,332,671	20,204	3,208,071	76,213	83,233	33,291,363	1,408,884
Foreign....	961	1,663,222	25,018	401	94,845	4,104	1,362	1,758,067	29,122
Total....	63,990	31,746,514	1,357,689	20,605	3,302,916	80,317	84,595	35,049,430	1,438,006

SESSIONAL PAPER No. 11

No. 20.—STATEMENT of Vessels, British and Foreign, employed in the Coasting Trade, &c.—*Concluded.*

DESCRIPTIONS OF VESSELS

	ARRIVED.		DEPARTED.		TOTAL.	
—	Number of Vessels.	Tonnage.	Number of Vessels.	Tonnage.	Number of Vessels.	Tonnage.
Steamers.						
Screw..........................	61,948	29,183,992	57,398	26,860,653	119,346	56,044,645
Paddle.........................	6,128	4,747,128	5,283	4,371,624	11,411	9,118,752
Sternwheel....................	1,309	512,642	1,309	514,237	2,618	1,026,879
Total Steamers.............	69,385	34,443,762	63,990	31,746,514	133,375	66,190,276
Sailing Vessels.						
Ships..........................	4	6,115	3	5,098	7	11,213
Barques.......................	22	16,084	21	16,597	43	32,681
Barquentines.................	4	1,255	1	257	5	1,512
Brigantines...................	14	1,961	30	4,840	44	6,801
Schooners....................	15,428	1,016,794	14,705	947,523	30,133	1,964,317
Sloops.........................	426	42,709	414	42,028	840	84,737
Barges, canal boats, etc........	4,371	2,521,872	5,431	2,286,573	9,802	4,808,445
Total Sailing...............	20,269	3,606,790	20,605	3,302,916	40,874	6,909,706
Grand Total..............	89,654	38,050,552	84,595	35,049,430	174,249	73,099,982

No. 21.—STATEMENT showing the Description, Number and Tonnage of Vessels built and registered, also the Number, Tonnage and Value of Vessels sold to other Countries at each Port and Outport in the Dominion of Canada, during the Fiscal Year ended March 31, 1915.

Ports and Outports.	BUILT.						REGISTERED.						SHIPS SOLD TO OTHER COUNTRIES.		
	Steam. No.	Steam. Tonnage.	Sail. No.	Sail. Tonnage.	Total. No.	Total. Tonnage.	Steam. No.	Steam. Tonnage.	Sail. No.	Sail. Tonnage.	Total. No.	Total. Tonnage.	No.	Tonnage.	Value.
Amherstburg, Ont.								10	2	22	3	32	1	3	250
Annapolis Royal, N.S.			2	22	2	22	1		1	70	1	70	1	318	10,000
Arichat, N.S.	1	16	2	32	3	48	1	16	2	32	3	48			
Barrington Passage, N.S.	1	15	1	20	2	35	2	127	9	573	11	700			
Canso, N.S.			1	40	1	40			1	40	1	40			
...p, N.S.	4	5,975	1	389	5	6,364	1	28	1	389	3	417			
...d, Ont.	1	34			1	34	1	34			1	34			
...ll, Ont.								3			1	3			
Dawson, Y.T.	1	6	1		1	6	1	6			1	6			
Economy, N.S.	2	64			2	64	2	64			2	64			
...n, Ont.	4	74	1	23	5	97	10	15	6	808	7	823	2	2,467	600,300
...t, N.S.								279			10	279			
Kenora, Ont.	2	106	1	1,580	3	1,686	1	1,036	2	687	3	1,723			
Kin...n, Ont.	1	78	1	293	2	371	1	10	1	10	2	20			
...l, N.S.			1	24	1	24		24	1	24	1	24			
Lockeport, N.S.	10	148	15	1,578	25	1,726	18	336	19	2,204	37	2,540	7	1,067	57,400
Lunenburg, N.S.		59			7	59	7		1	517	8	6,544			
...nd, Ont.	35	10,922	22	5,780	57	16,702	35	6,833	22	5,573	57	12,406			
...de, Que.	8	290	1	310	9	600	31	670	1	310	32	980			
New Westminster, B.C.	2	51	8	2,144	10	2,195	11	2,843	9	2,943	20	5,786			
Ottawa, Ont.			1	16	1	16			1	15	1	15			
Paspebiac, Que.			4	207	4	245		26			2	26			
Peterboro, Ont.	2	38	2		2	6,625	2	6,625			2	6,625			
Port Arthur, Ont.	2	6,625			2	24	2	31			2	31			
Port Burwell, Ont.	1	24	1		1	21	1	19			1	19			
Port ...y, N.S.	1	21			1	35	1	35			1	35			
Port Stanley, Ont.	1	35					4	385	1	145	5	530			
Prince ...rt, Sask.	3	43			3	48	2	52	2	1,299	4	1,351			
Prince Rupert, B.C.															

...e, Que	5	1,218	6	600	11	1,818	8	3,103	8	888	16	3,991	2	314	8,500
St. Catharines, Ont	1	52	....	....	1	52	4	298	1	529	5	827	....	....	....
Shelburne, N.S	1	22	2	215	3	237	1	22	2	215	3	237	....	....	....
Sorel, Que	4	937	4	2,296	8	3,233	2	937	4	2,296	8	3,233	....	....	....
Sydney, N.S	3	162	1	11	4	173	4	162	1	11	4	173	....	....	....
...r, B.C	23	345	2	531	25	876	1	1,799	54	1,308	54	3,107	6	10,125	380,500
Victoria, B.C	17	1,307	4	370	21	1,677	8	12	2		2	12	....	....	....
...h, N.S	1	35	1	198	2	233	1	35	2	198	....	233	....	....	....
Windsor, N.S	....	....	....	....	....	....	....	....	....	....	....	....	1	400	4,000
Winnipeg, Man	2	254	2	....	2	254	4	524	8	1,795	8	2,319	....	....	....
Yarmouth, N.S	2	72	1	9	3	81	1	72	3	9	3	81	1	2,350	90,000
	143	29,033	81	16,688	224	45,721	112	32,474	327	22,910	327	55,384	21	17,044	1,150,950

INDEX TO IMPORTS.

INDEX TO IMPORTS—*Continued.*

INDEX TO IMPORTS—*Continued.*

INDEX TO IMPORTS—*Continued.*

INDEX TO IMPORTS—*Continued.*

INDEX TO IMPORTS—*Continued.*

INDEX TO IMPORTS—*Continued.*

INDEX TO IMPORTS—*Continued.*

INDEX TO IMPORTS—*Continued.*

6 GEORGE V, A. 1916

Index to Imports—*Continued.*

SESSIONAL PAPER No. 11

INDEX TO IMPORTS—*Continued.*

6 GEORGE V, A. 1916

INDEX TO IMPORTS—*Continued.*

INDEX TO IMPORTS—*Continued.*

INDEX TO IMPORTS—*Continued.*

INDEX TO IMPORTS—*Continued.*

Articles.	Summary Statement. Page, part 1	General Statement. Page, part 2	Articles.	Summary Statement. Page, part 1	General Statement. Page, part 2
L			**L**		
Lace, white, etc., cotton.............	94	50	Lenos, cotton........................	94	54
" " "linen..............	102	92	Lenses, eye-glass....................	130	188
Laces, boot, shoe and stay..........	84	12	" and shutters for manufacture		
" and lace collars, net, etc......	100	78	of cameras............Free	163	320
" shoe and corset, tagging metal			" silvered for automobile lamps	130	190
for......................Free	167	329	Letters for signs....................	138	220
" shoe, cotton yarn for...... "	170	335	Life boats and life-saving apparatus.		
Lacquers, n.o.p......................	146	262	Free	163	320
" spirit.....................	130	196	Life-saving appliances for miners "	163	320
Lactate (antimonine)............Free	160	309	Ligatures, catgut for............. "	156	294
Lag screws..........................	116	144	Lignum vitæ..................... "	156	292
Lager beer	82	2	Lilacs, pot grown................ "	158	299
Lamb, fresh........................	134	214	Limbs, artificial................ "	158	302
" skins........................	122	162	Lime........................... "	122	166
Lampblack....................Free	163	320	" chloride of..............Free	160	310
Lamp chimneys, glass..............	106	110	" juice...................... "	122	166
" shade blanks, celluloid.......	88	30	" " crude................Free	163	321
" springs......................	126	174	" sulphate of, crude......... "	154	287
Lampwick cotton....................	94	50	Limes........................... "	158	299
Lamps............................	126	174	"	104	104
Landsides.....................Free	166	327	Linen bags or sacks................	102	92
Lanterns	126	174	" blouses and shirtwaists.......	104	96
" acetylene gas, for gas buoys.			" clothing................... "	104	96
Free	164	323	" damask, etc.................	102	92
" magic and slides............	124	168	" duck for hose pipe.........Free	160	307
Lard and lard compound............	134	212	" machinery, not made in Can-		
" oil...........................	128	184	ada...................Free	166	327
Lashes, whip.......................	148	268	" shirts......................	104	96
Last blocks, rough..............Free	155	291	" tape......................	104	96
Lasting, mohair, for buttons..... "	163	321	" thread....................	104	96
Lasts of wood......................	150	270	" yarn for manfr. of towels..Free	170	336
Laths.......... •................Free	156	293	Lines for fisheries................ "	162	318
Launches, pleasure..................	122	160	Ling............................	100	82
Laundry blueing....................	82	6	" from Newfoundland.........Free	155	290
" soap.....................	138	226	Linings, carpet.....................	88	30
" tubs........................	82	4	" chimney................ "	86	24
Lava, or other tips................	124	172	Link, belting.................Free	164	322
Lavatories.........................	82	4	Links, chain.......................	110	130
Lavender waters, alcoholic..........	140	236	Linoleum..........................	128	188
Lawn mowers......................	110	124	Linseed oil........................	128	184
" tennis nets........	146	260	" oil cake and meal.......Free	168	331
Lawns, cotton......................	94	54	Lint, etc., antiseptic................	82	4
Lead and manufactures of...........	122	160	Liqueurs..........................	140	232
" manufactures of, n.o.p........	122	160	Liquid paint, n.o.p.................	130	194
" nitrate and acetate of.....Free	161	312	" soap.....................	138	228
" pencils......................	132	202	Liquorice..........................	96	62
" red, dry......................	130	194	" root, unground....... Free	161	311
" " ....Free	160	307	Liquors, alcoholic, n.o.p............	140	234
" tea......................... "	165	325	Litharge.....................Free	154	288
" white, dry..............	130	194	Lithographed advertising matter....	84	10
" " ground in oil.............	130	194	Lithographic presses and type making		
Leather board, leatheroid and manu-			accessories for....................	114	138
factures..................	130	198	Lithographic stones, not engraved....	124	166
" dressing...................	82	6	Litmus and lichens.............Free	161	312
" grease and degras for dress-			Loaders, hay.......................	110	124
ing................. .....Free	157	295	Loading tools......................	108	118
" and manufactures of........	122	162	Lobsters..........................	102	86
" manufactures of, n.o.p......	122	166	" from Newfoundland....Free	155	290
" and skins, all other, n.o.p....	122	164	Lock joint pipe.....................	118	148
Leaves, artificial for hats............	100	76	Locks............................	112	134
" crude drugs.......... .....Free	162	317	Locomotive wheel tires, steel, rough.		
Leeches........................... "	157	296	Free	165	325
Leghorn hoods, unfinished........ "	163	319	Locomotives for railways............	112	130
Lemon rinds in brine............. "	157	298	Locust beans and meal.........Free	158	300
Lemons.......................... "	158	299	Logs............................ "	155	291

6 GEORGE V, A. 1916

INDEX TO IMPORTS—*Continued.*

INDEX TO IMPORTS—Continued.

6 GEORGE V, A. 1916

INDEX TO IMPORTS—*Continued.*

INDEX TO IMPORTS—Continued.

6 GEORGE V, A. 1916

INDEX TO IMPORTS—Continued.

INDEX TO IMPORTS—*Continued.*

INDEX TO IMPORTS—Continued.

INDEX TO IMPORTS—Continued.

6 GEORGE V, A. 1916

INDEX TO IMPORTS—*Continued.*

Articles.	Sum-mary State-ment.	Gen-eral State-ment.	Articles.	Sum-mary State-ment.	Gen-eral State-ment.
	Page, part 1	Page, part 2		Page, part 1	Page, part 2
S			**S**		
Shoe eyelets and hooks..........Free	163	318	Skins of animals, oirds and fish.Free	171	338
" laces...........................	84	12	" Astrachan and Russian... "	158	303
" lace wire fasteners........Free	163	318	" calf, kid, goat, lamb, sheep...	122	162
" makers' ink....................	82	6	" chamois, dressed..............	122	162
" shanks, steel for...........Free	167	328	" fur, dressed, n.o.p.............	106	106
" tacks.........................	112	130	" " not dressed...........Free	156	295
Shoes, horse, mule and ox...........	112	134	" for morocco leather, tanned...	122	164
" leather......................	122	164	" gold beaters..............Free	163	319
" rubber.......................	108	116	" raw......................... "	157	296
" except rubber and leather.....	84	12	" n.o.p.........................	122	164
Shot, iron, for polishing glass, etc.Free	163	319	Skin washes, alcoholic...............	140	236
" lead...........................	122	160	Slabs, iron or steel.................	112	134
Shoulders, (pork)...................	134	212	Slag, blast furnace............Free	159	303
Shovel handles, wood...............	150	270	Slate and manufactures of...........	138	226
Shovels and blanks.................	110	126	Sledges...........................	120	156
" steam and electric..........	114	136	Sleds, children's..................	88	30
" steel for mfr. of............	120	154	Sleeves, watch....................	148	266
Show cards........................	84	10	Sleighs..........................	88	28
Show cases and metal parts.........	150	272	Slides for magic lanterns.............	124	168
Shrubs..... . .	132	208	Slippers, leather.................	122	164
Shutters for mfr. of cameras.....Free	163	320	" not leather.................	84	12
Side lights	126	174	Slugs, printing...................	126	176
Sides (bacon;...	134	212	Smelting machinery............Free	165	326
Sickles.... .	110	126	Smoked fish......................	102	86
Siennas....	130	194	" meats......................	134	214
Signs...... ......,...........	138	220	Smokers' sets....................	146	260
Silex.......... . ...Free	154	289	Smoothing irons..................	116	144
Silk and manufactures of............	138	222	Smyrna carpets..................	152	282
" for the manufacture of neckties..	138	222	Snaths..........................	110	126
" cocoons and waste..........Free	157	297	Snuff............................	146	258
" in the gum or spun..............	138	224	Soap............................	138	226
" for the manufacture of ribbons and shoe laces................	138	224	" grease for.................Free	157	295
" in the gum or spun for manufactures.....................Free	157	297	" n.o.p.......................	138	228
" hats, etc......................	108	120	" olive oil for...............Free	168	332
" and all manufactures of, n.o.p....	138	224	" palm oil and kernel for mfr. of soap............. "	168	332
" oiled.........................	128	188	" powders.................... "	138	228
" raw.......................Free	157	297	" whale oil.................Free	169	334
" twist and floss..................	138	224	Sockets, electric..................	98	72
Silver anodes.......................	124	170	Socks and stockings, cotton..........	94	52
" bullion...............Free	172	342	" " silk............	138	224
" coin, foreign...............	106	116	" " wool...........	150	278
" German, etc., mfrs. of.........	126	174	Soda, arseniate, binarseniate and stannate of............Free	182	316
" " bars, rods, etc.....Free	166	327	" ash......................	161	314
" " in ingots and blocks "	166	327	" bicarbonate of..............	96	66
" leaf...........................	106	114	" bichromate of...........Free	161	315
" manufactures ot, n.o.p........:	106	114	" bisulphite of............... "	161	315
" soap.........................	138	228	" caustic.................... "	162	315
" sweepings.................Free	163	319	" "	96	66
Silvered glass......................	106	112	" chlorate of.............Free	162	315
Silverware, cases for.................	100	76	" hyposulphite for tanning leather.................Free	162	315
" sterling..................	106	114	" nitrate of.................. "	162	315
Sinkers and swivels, fishing..........	146	260	" nitrite of.................. "	162	315
Sinks..............................	82	4	" peroxide of................ "	162	316
Sizing cream and enamel..............	86	24	" prussiate of................ "	162	315
Skates and parts of..................	116	146	" sal........................ "	162	315
Skeins, cart or wagon................	110	128	" silicate of.................. "	162	315
Skeletons and parts of..........Free	170	336	" sulphate of, crude.......... "	162	316
Skelp iron or steel, for manuf. of iron or steel pipe..................	118	146	" sulphite of................. "	162	316
Skelp iron or steel, n.o.p........,....	116	144	Sodium, hyposulphite...............	98	66
" " for the manufacture of tubes..............Free	165	325	" sulphide of............Free	162	316
Skiffs..............................	82	6	Soft soap....:....................	138	228
			Sole leather......................	122	162

SESSIONAL PAPER No. 11

INDEX TO IMPORTS—*Continued.*

INDEX TO IMPORTS—*Continued.*

SESSIONAL PAPER No. 11

INDEX TO IMPORTS—Continued.

INDEX TO IMPORTS—*Continued.*

SESSIONAL PAPER No. 11

INDEX TO IMPORTS—*Continued.*

INDEX TO IMPORTS—*Concluded.*

INDEX TO EXPORTS

INDEX TO EXPORTS—*Continued.*

INDEX TO EXPORTS—Continued.

INDEX TO EXPORTS—*Continued.*

SESSIONAL PAPER No. 11

INDEX TO EXPORTS—*Continued.*

INDEX TO EXPORTS—*Concluded.*